Combined Statement
Of Receipts, Outlays, and Balances

Of the United States Government

Fiscal Year 2007

ISBN 978-0-16-079797-2

DEPARTMENT OF THE TREASURY
FINANCIAL MANAGEMENT SERVICE
WASHINGTON, D.C. 20227

December 6, 2007

To: Citizens of the United States of America

In accordance with the provisions of Section 114(a) of the Act of
September 12, 1950 (31 U.S.C. 3513(a)), I am transmitting herewith the
Combined Statement of Receipts, Outlays, and Balances of the United
States Government for the fiscal year ended September 30, 2007.

This statement presents budget results and the cash-related assets and
liabilities of the Federal Government with supporting details.

The financial results for the year include total receipts of $2,567.7 billion,
an increase of $161.0 billion over 2006 receipts; total outlays of $2,730.5
billion, an increase of $75.6 billion over 2006 outlays; and a $162.8 billion
deficit, a decrease of $85.4 billion under the 2006 deficit.

The budget figures presented in this statement represent agency reporting
for fiscal year 2007 and adjustments to those year-end figures as reported
through October 22, 2007. Revisions may be necessary once agencies
have fully reconciled their data.

Sincerely,

Kenneth R. Papaj

Kenneth R. Papaj

Enclosure

Contents

*Note: *Accounts With Negative Balances At Fiscal Year End* will be discontinued after this issue.

Preface

Treasury Profile

On September 2, 1789, an act of Congress created the Department of the Treasury. Many subsequent acts influenced the development of the Department. Those acts delegated new duties and established the numerous bureaus and divisions that now compose the Department. Today, the Treasury's mission can be categorized into four basic functions: formulating and recommending economic, financial, tax and fiscal policies; serving as financial manager and financial agent for the U.S. Government; enforcing the law; and manufacturing coins and currency.

Financial Management Service

The Financial Management Service (FMS), which is a bureau of the Department of the Treasury, performs a critical role in fulfilling the Treasury's mission as the Government's financial manager. For example, FMS makes Federal payments and collections. It also maintains the Government's central accounting and reporting systems. In addition, FMS administers the Government's cash management programs, credit and debt collection activities, and various other financial services.

In its role as Federal financial agent, FMS publishes the "Combined Statement of Receipts, Outlays, and Balances of the United States Government." This statement includes data maintained in the central accounts, which are provided by Federal entities, disbursing officers and the Federal Reserve Banks.

The last page of this statement contains an order form for the publication. An electronic version of the report can be found on FMS' website at **www.fms.treas.gov/annualreport/.**

Legislative Requirement

The Constitution of the United States, Article 1, Section 9, clause 7, outlines requirements for a report on the receipts and outlays of the Government. It provides, in part, that "No Money shall be drawn from the Treasury, but in Consequence of Appropriations made by law; and a regular Statement and Account of the Receipts and Expenditures of all public Money shall be published from time to time." (Emphasis added.)

31 U.S.C. 3513(a) provides in part, "The Secretary of the Treasury shall prepare reports that will inform the President, Congress, and the public on the financial operations of the United States Government."

This statement is recognized as the official publication of receipts and outlays. Several major Government bodies rely on data found in this report. The Congressional Budget Office uses it to serve the needs of Congress; the Office of Management and Budget uses the data to review the President's Budget programs; the General Accounting Office uses it to perform audit activities; the various departments and agencies of the Government use it to reconcile their accounts; and the public uses it to review the operations of their Government. The budget figures presented in this statement represent agency reporting for fiscal 2007 and adjustments to those year-end figures as reported through October 22, 2007. Revisions may be necessary once agencies have fully reconciled their data. Any changes will be published in other reports prepared by FMS that contain related information. These include: the "Daily Treasury Statement," the "Monthly Treasury Statement of Receipts and Outlays of the United States Government" and the "Treasury Bulletin".

Description Of Accounts Relating To Cash Operations

The classes of accounts maintained in connection with the cash operation of the Federal Government, exclusive of public debt operations, include: (1) The accounts of fiscal officers or agents, collectively, who receive money for deposit in the U.S. Treasury or for the authorized disposition or who make expenditures by drawing checks on the Treasury of the United States or by effecting payments in some other manner; (2) the accounts of administrative agencies which classify receipt and outlay transactions according to the individual receipt, appropriation, or fund account; and (3) the accounts of the Treasury of the United States which office is responsible for the receipt and custody of money deposited by fiscal officers or agents, for the payment of checks drawn on the Treasury, and the payment of public debt securities redeemed. A set of central accounts is maintained in the Department of Treasury for the purpose of consolidating financial data reported periodically from these three sources in order to present the results of cash operations in central financial reports, for the Government as a whole, and as a means of internal control.

The central accounts relating to cash operations disclose monthly and fiscal year information on: (1) the Government's receipts by principle sources, and its outlays according to the different appropriations and other funds involved; and (2) the cash transactions, classified by types, together with certain directly related assets and liabilities which underlie such receipts and outlays. Accounting for receipts is on the basis of collections, accounting for outlays is on the basis of checks issued and cash payment made (cash basis). However, the interest on the public debt, public issues, is on the accrual basis while the interest on special issues is on the cash basis. The structure of the accounts provides for reconciliation, on a firm accounting basis, between the published reports of receipts and outlays for the Government as a whole and changes in the Treasury cash balances by means of such factors as checks outstanding, deposits in transit, and cash held outside the Treasury. Within the central accounts, receipt and outlay accounts are classified as described in the following paragraphs.

Budget Receipt and Outlay Accounts

General fund receipt accounts – General fund receipt accounts are credited with all receipts, which are not earmarked by law for a specific purpose. General fund receipts consist principally of internal revenue collections, which include income taxes, excise taxes, estate, gift, and employment taxes. The remainder consists of customs duties and a large number of miscellaneous receipts, including fees for permits and licenses, fines penalties, and forfeitures; interest and dividends; rentals; royalties; and sale of Government property.

Special fund receipt accounts – Special fund receipt accounts are credited with receipts from specific sources which are earmarked by law for a specific purpose but which are not generated from a cycle of operations. The Congress may appropriate these receipts on an annual basis or for an indefinite period of time. Examples of special fund receipts are those arising from rents and royalties under the Mineral Leasing Act, the revenue from visitors to Yellowstone National Park, the proceeds of the sale of certain timber and reserve lands, and other receipts authorized to be credited to the reclamation fund.

General fund expenditure accounts – General fund expenditure accounts are established to record amounts appropriated by Congress to be expended for the general support of the Government. Such accounts are classified according to the limitations that are established by the Congress with respect to the period of availability for obligation of the appropriation, as 1-year, multiple-year, or "no-year"(without a time limit), and with respect to the agency authorized to enter into obligations and approve outlays.

Special fund expenditure accounts – Special fund expenditure accounts are established to record appropriated amounts of special fund receipts to be expended for special programs in accordance with specific provisions of law. These accounts are generally available without time limit, but may also be subject to time limitations as in the case of general fund accounts.

Revolving fund accounts – These are funds authorized by specific provisions of law to finance a continuing cycle of operations in which outlays generate receipts, and the receipts are available for outlay without further action by Congress. They are classified as (a) public enterprise funds where receipts come primarily from sources outside the Government and (b) intragovernmental funds where receipts come primarily from other appropriations or funds. These accounts are usually designated as "no-year" accounts, i.e. they are without limitation as to period of availability for outlay. Examples of public enterprise revolving funds are the Tennessee Valley Authority and the Commodity Credit Corporation. Examples of intergovernmental revolving funds are the General Supply Fund administered by the General services Administration and the Government Printing Office Revolving Fund.

Consolidated working fund accounts – These accounts are established to receive (and subsequently disburse) advance payment from the agencies or bureaus pursuant to Section 601 of the Economy Act (31 U.S.C. 1535) or other provisions of law. Consolidated working funds may be credited with advances from more than one appropriation for the procurement of goods and services to be furnished by the performing agency with the use of its own facilities within the same fiscal year. Outlays recorded in these accounts are stated net of advances credited and are classified under the agencies administering the accounts. The accounts are subject to the fiscal year limitations of the appropriations or funds from which advanced.

Management fund accounts – These are working fund accounts authorized by law to facilitate accounting for and administration of intragovernmental activities (other than a continuing cycle of operations), which are financed by two or more appropriations. This classification is also often applied to the consolidated working funds for interagency activities described above.

Trust fund accounts – These are accounts maintained to record the receipt and outlay of monies held in trust by the Government for use in carrying out specific purposes or programs in accordance with the terms of a trust agreement or statute. The receipts of many trust funds, especially the major ones, not needed for current payments, are invested in public debt and Government Agency securities. Generally, trust fund accounts consist of separate receipt and outlay accounts, but when the trust corpus is established to perform a business-type operation, the fund is called a "trust revolving fund" and a combined receipt and outlay account is used. Some of the major trust fund accounts are the Federal Old Age and Survivors Insurance Trust Fund, Unemployment Trust Fund, Civil Service Retirement and Disability Trust Fund, The National Service Life Insurance Trust Fund, and the Highway Trust Fund.

Transfer appropriation accounts – These accounts are established to receive (and subsequently disburse) allocations which are treated as non-expenditure transactions at the time the allocation is made including certain transfers under Section 601 of the Economy Act (31 U.S.C. 1535), and similar provisions of law.

Explanation Of Transactions And Basis Of Figures

As indicated in the "Table Of Contents," the **Combined Statement of Receipts, Outlays, and Balances of the United States Government** consists of Part One – Fiscal Year Summary Statement; Part Two – Details of Receipts; and Part Three – Details of Appropriations, Outlays, and Balances.

Part One: Fiscal Year Summary

Part One consists of a summary statement representing the Federal Government's General Ledger Account Balances.

Part Two: Details of Receipts

Part Two of this report contains the detail of internal revenue, customs, and miscellaneous receipts. Internal revenue and customs receipts are included in this report on the basis of reports of collections, which means they are reported as of the time that the cash received is placed under accounting control. Other receipts of the Government are reported on a collections received basis. Revolving fund and management fund receipts, reimbursements, and refunds of monies previously expended are not included in the receipt tables but are deducted from gross outlays.

Part Three: Details of Appropriations, Outlays, and Balances

Part Three of this report contains the detailed tabulations of outlays accounts, by organizational unit showing the various transactions that relate to such accounts which affect the budget surplus or deficit of the Government. The accounts are arranged according to general, special, revolving, management and trust funds; showing the titles, period of availability, and account symbols. Following are explanations of the column headings in the tabulations.

1. **Balances beginning of fiscal year** – The amounts shown in the first money column represent ending balances as of the close of the preceding fiscal year. An analysis of the totals of these balances, expressed in terms of Fund Resources and Fund Equities, is presented on the basis of reports of the administrative agencies, submitted on Treasury FMS Form 2108, Year-End Closing Statement, in accordance with the Treasury Financial Manual.

    A. Fund Resources include:
    a. Undisbursed balances (by fiscal year account).
    b. Investments in Federal securities – The amounts represent investment holding (as par value) of Government accounts in public debt or agency securities.
    c. Unfunded contract authority – These amounts represent unused authority.
    d. Funds held outside the Treasury – These amounts represent cash held outside Treasury, including cashier funds.
    e. Borrowing authority – Borrowing authority may be classified as either "definite" or "indefinite." Definite authority to borrow is stated by law as a specific aggregate sum that cumulative borrowings cannot exceed. Indefinite borrowing authority is categorized as either (1) unlimited borrowing authority – whereby the law allows the agency to borrow as needed or (2) authority set by legislative ceiling – whereby the law allows the agency to borrow as needed but sets a specific dollar limit on the amount outstanding at any one time. For accounts with definite borrowing authority, these amounts represent unused authority. For accounts with indefinite borrowing authority, these amounts represent those unpaid obligations covered by borrowing authority at the beginning of the fiscal year.
    f. Accounts receivable – These amounts represent receivables which, when collected will be credited directly to the appropriation or fund, and are reported as deductions to unpaid obligations. Such amounts consist of reimbursements earned and refunds receivable, i.e. amounts earned (both billed and unbilled) for accomplished delivery or performance as of September 30, overpayment refund receivables, travel advances and other advances which did not liquidate specific oObligations, e.g. advances to General Service Administration Supply Fund are included.
    g. Unfilled customer orders – These amounts consist of undelivered customer orders to the extent that they represent valid obligations recorded by the ordering agency for those appropriations using an authority to obligate anticipated reimbursements. The amount shown for an annual appropriation covers only those orders for which valid obligations where incurred under such annual accounts or orders for common-use items to be delivered from stock in accordance with 32 Comp. Gen. 436.

    B. Fund Equities include:
    a. Unobligated balances – Amounts reported in this column represent unobligated balances of no-year and multiple-year accounts for which authority to obligate has not expired and fiscal year accounts for which authority to obligate has expired.
    b. Accounts payable – These amounts represent liabilities for goods and services received as of September 30, representing valid obligations supported by documentary evidence.
    c. Undelivered orders – These amounts represent orders for goods and services remaining undelivered as of September 30, representing valid obligations supported by documentary evidence, for which the liability has not yet accrued.

2. **Appropriations and other obligational authority**

    A. Appropriations – Article I, Section 9, of the Constitution of the United States provides in part that "No Money shall be drawn from the Treasury, but in Consequence of Appropriations made by Law . . . " The appropriations included in this report are the amounts which Congress authorized to be established for the fiscal amounts which agencies may obligate during the time period specified in the respective appropriation acts. In some instances, the Congress reappropriates part or all of the unobligated balances of prior-year appropriations that would otherwise expire. In other instances, the Congress authorizes the transfer of obligational authority of particular appropriation accounts and is explained by applicable footnotes. The appropriations are classified to show the amounts appropriated from an organizational standpoint, and are shown in the second money column.

    B. Contract authorities – contract authorities represent a grant of authority by the Congress to incur obligations prior to the enactment of appropriations. Contract authority does not, in itself, permit the spending of money. It must be allowed by an appropriation to permit payment of the obligations that are incurred thereunder. New contract authority granted during the fiscal year is shown in the second money column. Appropriations enacted for the fiscal year to liquidate such authority are included in this column as current year appropriations with a corresponding decrease to unfunded contract authority.

Explanation Of Transactions And Basis Of Figures

C. Authority to borrow from the Treasury and the public – In some instances, the Congress grants authority to Government corporations or agencies to make outlays from funds to be borrowed from the Secretary of the Treasury or from the public. In the case of borrowing from the Treasury, the Secretary is directed to use proceeds from the sale of public debt securities. Legislation is generally specific with respect to the amount of money that can be advanced by the Treasury to each corporation or agency and often requires that borrowing transaction be accomplished by the issuance of formal notes of the agency. A few agencies of the Government are authorized by law to issue their own securities to the public. Before issuing these securities, the agencies are required to secure approval from, or consult with the Secretary of the Treasury with respect to terms of the borrowing and timing thereof. Such borrowings and repayment of borrowings from the Treasury or the public represent financing transactions and therefore, do not affect the budget surplus or deficit. (Note: The Federal Financing Bank, created by Public Law 93-224 (87 Stat. 937) dated December 29, 1973, for the purpose of consolidating the market financing of other Federal agencies, such as the U.S. Postal Service, the Export-Import Bank of the United States, the Tennessee Valley Authority and others, similarly does not affect the budget surplus or deficit.) Increases and rescissions in borrowing authority during the fiscal year are shown in the second money column.

3. **Transfers, borrowings, and investments (net)**

A. Transfers shown in the third money column are, in the majority of cases, for the benefit of advancing appropriation accounts. Outlays from such transfer appropriation accounts are associated with the account to which the funds were originally made available.

B. Other transactions shown in this column include the following:
   a. Borrowings – representing the net amount of actual borrowings made during the fiscal year.
   b. Investments – representing the net par value of purchases and sale of public debt and government agency securities.
   c. Funds held outside the Treasury – representing cash held outside the Treasury and net cash advances to government cashiers.

4. **Outlays (net)** – The outlays shown in the fourth money column are reported generally on the basis of checks issued by Government disbursing officers net of collections. Certain modifications of this basis are described as follows:

A. Interest on public issues of the public debt is on an accrual basis; interest on special issues is on a cash basis.

B. Where payment is made in cash rather than by check, the cash payment is the outlay.

C. Certain outlays of an intragovernmental nature do not require the issuance of checks; for example, charges made against appropriations representing a part of employees' salaries which are withheld for individual income taxes and for savings bond allotments.

Outlays are stated net of collections representing reimbursements as authorized by law, refunds of monies previously expended, and receipts of revolving and management funds. In this connection, public debt or agency securities which are acquired in lieu of other properties, or donated, are considered as "constructive" receipt of cash and therefore, the par amounts of such securities are included as receipts (reductions of outlays) of the acquiring agency.

5. **Balances withdrawn and other transactions** – The fifth money column includes net transactions for several types of activities as follows:

A. Unobligated balances withdrawn – Represents amounts for obligations that are no longer valid and have been canceled.

B. Unexpended balances withdrawn – Represents reductions of appropriations pursuant to 2 U.S.C. 102(a) which provides that the unexpended balances of appropriations which are subject to disbursement by the Secretary of the Senate of the Clerk of the House of Representatives shall be withdrawn as of September 30, of the second fiscal year following the year for which provided.

C. Unobligated balances canceled – Represents the unobligated balances canceled pursuant to 31 U.S.C. 1552(a) which provides that "On September 30th of the 5th fiscal year after the period of availability for obligations of a fixed appropriation account ends, the account shall be closed and any remaining balance (whether obligated or unobligated) in the account shall be cancelled and thereafter shall not be available for obligation or expenditure for any purpose.

D. Capital transfers – Represents nonexpenditure transfers from revolving funds on account of repayment of investment or distribution of earnings.

E. Adjustments to borrowing authority - represents a reduction in borrowing authority when fund resources other than borrowings were used or are available to liquidate or cover unpaid obligations.

F. Changes in receivables, payables, undelivered orders, unfilled customer orders, and unobligated balances.

6. **Balances end of fiscal year** – These year-end balances represent the column 1 (opening) balances as adjusted by the transactions in columns 2, 3, 4, and 5. As such, these figures become the opening balances for the succeeding fiscal period unless otherwise footnoted (i.e. September 30, 2007 closing balances will be the corresponding opening balances for fiscal year 2008). The closing balances of accounts with borrowing authority represent either (1) definite borrowing authority – unused borrowing authority at the close of the fiscal year or (2) indefinite borrowing authority – the amount equal to those unpaid obligations covered by borrowing authority at the close of the fiscal year.

Off-Budget Federal Entities – Pursuant to the Balanced Budget and Emergency Deficit Control Act of 1985 (public Law 99-177), those entities that were formerly off-budget are now included in the budget totals. This same legislation shifted Social Security (the Federal Old-Age Survivors Insurance Trust Fund and the Federal Disability Insurance Trust Fund) off-budget. The budgetary presentation shows federal receipts, outlays, and surpluses or deficits including Social Security, and also shows separately the on-budget and off-budget components.

Part One

Fiscal Year 2007 Summary

FINANCIAL HIGHLIGHTS

This report shows only those financial highlights of the U.S. Government directly related to the cash operations of the Department of the Treasury and the rest of the Federal Government.

Total Receipts, Outlays and Surplus (+) or Deficit (-)

(In billions of dollars)

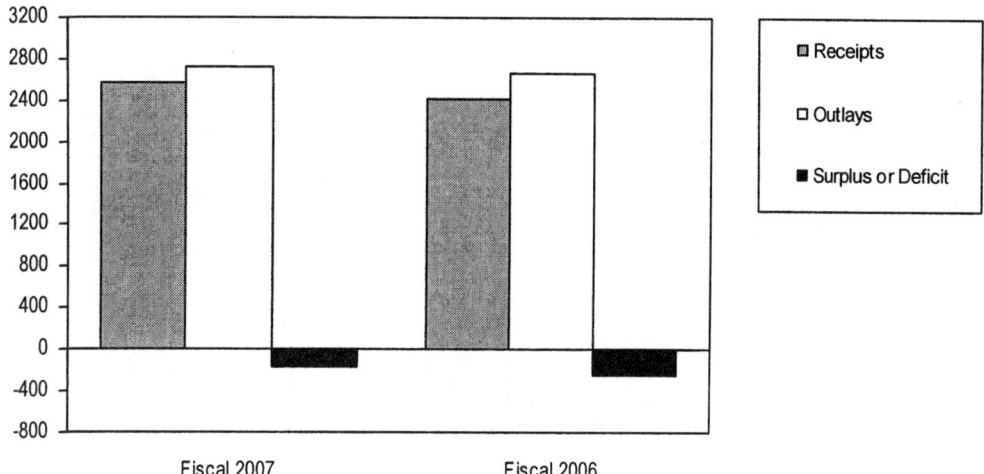

	Fiscal 2007	Fiscal 2006	Percent change
Total receipts	2,567.7	2,406.7	6.7
Total outlays	2,730.5	2,654.9	2.8
Total surplus (+) or deficit (-)	-162.8	-248.2	34.4

RECEIPTS BY SOURCE

Total receipts increased by $161.0 billion from fiscal 2006, totaling $2,567.7 billion in fiscal 2007. The graph below shows receipts by source.

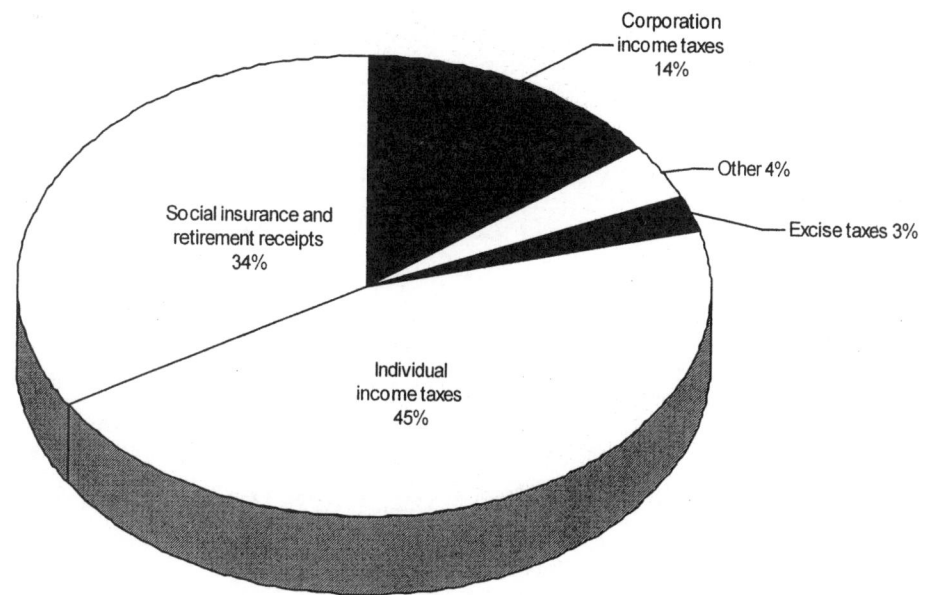

The text below describes major changes in the amount of receipts by source category. The table that follows shows the amount of receipts for fiscal 2007 and 2006 by source category. It also includes the amount and percentage change from fiscal 2006.

- **Individual income taxes** were $1,163.5 billion in fiscal 2007. This was an increase of $119.6 billion, or 11.5 percent.

- **Corporation income taxes** were $370.2 billion in fiscal 2007. This was an increase of $16.3 billion, or 4.6 percent.

- **Social insurance taxes and contributions** were $869.6 billion in fiscal 2007. This was an increase of $31.8 billion, or 3.8 percent.

    — **Employment and general retirement contributions** totaled $824.3 billion, a change of $34.2 billion, or 4.3 percent from the prior year.
    — **Unemployment insurance** receipts were $41.1 billion in fiscal 2007. Receipts decreased by $2.3 billion from fiscal 2006, which amounts to 5.4 percent.
    — **Other retirement contributions** totaled $4.3 billion in fiscal 2007, a decrease of 2.3 percent from fiscal 2006.

- **Excise taxes** were $65.1 billion in fiscal 2007. This was a decrease of $8.9 billion, or 12.0 percent.

- **Other** receipts, including estate and gift taxes, customs duties and miscellaneous receipts increased from $97.1 billion in fiscal 2006 to $99.3 billion in fiscal 2007. The major components are shown below.

    — **Estate and gift tax** receipts were $26.0 billion, a $1.8 billion decrease from fiscal 2006 to fiscal 2007.
    — **Customs duties** were $26.0 billion, a $1.2 billion increase from fiscal 2006 to fiscal 2007.
    — **Miscellaneous** receipts were $47.2 billion, a $2.8 billion increase from fiscal 2006 to fiscal 2007.

RECEIPTS BY SOURCE CATEGORY

IN MILLIONS OF DOLLARS

	Fiscal 2007	Fiscal 2006	Amount change from 2006	Percent change
Income taxes:				
Individual income taxes..	1,163,472	1,043,908	119,564	11.5
Corporate income taxes..	370,243	353,915	16,328	4.6
Total income taxes..	1,533,714	1,397,823	135,891	9.7
Social insurance and retirement receipts:				
Employment and general retirement..	824,257	790,042	34,216	4.3
Unemployment insurance	41,091	43,420	-2,329	-5.4
Other retirement..	4,258	4,358	-100	-2.3
Total social insurance and retirement receipts	869,607	837,820	31,787	3.8
Excise taxes	65,069	73,962	-8,893	-12.0
Other:				
Estate and gift taxes..	26,044	27,877	-1,833	-6.6
Customs duties..	26,010	24,810	1,200	4.8
Miscellaneous receipts...	47,228	44,384	2,844	6.4
Total other	99,282	97,071	2,211	2.3
Total receipts...	2,567,673	2,406,675	160,997	6.7

Details may not add to totals due to rounding.

OUTLAYS BY FUNCTION

Outlays occur when the Government pays its obligations whether with cash, check or electronic funds transfer. Total outlays were $2,730.5 billion in fiscal 2007, an increase of $75.6 billion or 2.8 percent over the amount from fiscal 2006. The text below shows how outlays were divided in fiscal 2007. The seven largest categories of outlays are detailed below and correspond directly to the Government's functional classification system.

The functional classification system groups Government activities-budget authority and outlays, loan guarantees and tax expenditures-into categories that reflect the national need addressed by each transaction. The system identifies 17 broad categories that address national needs. This provides a coherent and comprehensive basis for analyzing and understanding the budget. Two additional categories-interest and undistributed offsetting receipts-do not address specific national needs but are included to cover the entire budget. Under the functional classification system, each outlay is assigned to a classification that best defines its most important purpose, even though the outlay may serve more than one purpose.

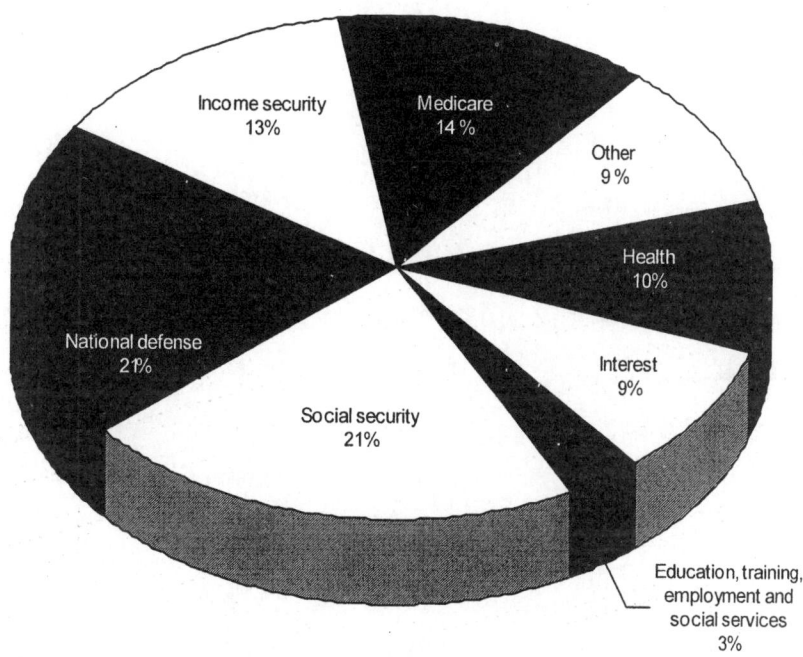

The table that follows shows fiscal 2007 and 2006 outlays for each functional classification. It also shows the amount and percentage change in outlay levels between these two fiscal years. Changes in outlays for the largest functional classifications are discussed briefly below.

- **National defense**—This function includes those activities directly related to the defense and security of the United States. This amount encompasses Government spending for conventional forces, strategic forces, atomic energy defense activities and other defense related activities. National defense outlays for fiscal 2007 increased by $38.2 billion, to $560.1 billion.

- **Education, training, employment and social services**—These programs assist citizens in developing and learning skills to expand their potential opportunities and job placement possibilities. Outlays for this function were $89.7 billion for fiscal 2007, a decrease of 24.2 percent or $28.6 billion from fiscal 2006 outlays.

- **Health**—The Federal Government helps meet the nation's health care needs by financing and providing health care services, aiding disease prevention, and supporting research and training. Outlays for this function were $266.3 billion in fiscal 2007. This represents an increase of $13.6 billion over the prior fiscal year.

- **Medicare**—Through Medicare, the Federal Government contributes to the health and well being of aged and disabled Americans. Outlays for this function were $375.4 billion in fiscal 2007. That is an increase of 13.8 percent or $45.5 billion over fiscal 2006 outlays.

- **Income security**—Income security benefits are paid to the aged, the disabled, and the unemployed and low-income families. Included within this classification are programs such as general retirement and disability, public assistance and unemployment compensation. Outlays for these benefits were $367.4 billion in fiscal 2007, an increase of 4.2 percent or $14.9 billion over the fiscal 2006 level.

- **Social security**—Through social security, the Federal Government contributes to the income security of aged and disabled Americans. This function's outlays were $586.2 billion for fiscal 2007. That represents an increase of 6.9 percent or $37.6 billion over fiscal 2006 outlays.

- **Interest**—This function includes interest paid by the Federal Government offset by interest collections from the public and interest received by Government trust funds. Net interest outlays are very sensitive to both interest rates and the amount of debt outstanding. Net interest outlays increased in fiscal 2007 to $237.9 billion. This is a 5.0 percent increase from the prior fiscal year.

OUTLAYS BY FUNCTION

IN MILLIONS OF DOLLARS

	Fiscal 2007	Fiscal 2006	Amount change from 2006	Percent change
National defense	560,078	521,840 r	38,238	7.3
International affairs	28,528	29,549 r	-1,021	-3.5
General science, space, and technology	20,958	23,616 r	-2,658	-11.3
Energy	-915	751 r	-1,666	-221.9
Natural resources and environment	31,693	33,055 r	-1,362	-4.1
Agriculture	19,634	25,970 r	-6,336	-24.4
Commerce and housing credit	380	6,030 r	-5,650	-93.7
Transportation	72,962	70,244 r	2,718	3.9
Community and regional development	28,641	54,531 r	-25,890	-47.5
Education, training, employment and social services	89,677	118,253 r	-28,576	-24.2
Health	266,297	252,666 r	13,631	5.4
Medicare	375,408	329,868 r	45,540	13.8
Income security	367,364	352,506 r	14,858	4.2
Social security	586,180	548,549 r	37,631	6.9
Veterans benefits and services	72,846	69,842 r	3,004	4.3
Administration of justice	37,311	41,016 r	-3,705	-9.0
General Government	17,764	18,234 r	-470	-2.6
Net interest	237,931	226,603 r	11,328	5.0
Undistributed offsetting receipts	-82,237	-68,250 r	-13,987	20.5
Total outlays	2,730,499	2,654,873 r	75,626	2.8

Details may not add to totals due to rounding.
r = revised

United States Summary General Ledger Account Balances

Item	Balance September 30, 2007	Balance September 30, 2006	Net Change
Asset Accounts			
Cash And Monetary Assets:			
U.S. Treasury Operating Cash:[1]			
1009　U.S. Treasury Operating Cash - Tax And Loan Note Accounts	69,698,410,328.24	46,676,384,511.29	23,022,025,816.95
1010　U.S. Treasury Operating Cash - Federal Reserve Account	5,538,743,963.00	5,450,713,036.19	88,030,926.81
Balance	75,237,154,291.24	52,127,097,547.48	23,110,056,743.76
Special Drawing Rights:			
1420　Total Holdings Of Special Drawing Rights	9,300,549,950.56	8,654,509,743.98	646,040,206.58
1425　SDR Certificates Issued To Federal Reserve Banks	-2,200,000,000.00	-2,200,000,000.00	0.00
Balance	7,100,549,950.56	6,454,509,743.98	646,040,206.58
Reserve Position On The U.S. Quota In The IMF:			
U.S. Subscription To The International Monetary Fund:			
1410　Investment In The International Monetary Fund, Direct Quota Payments	46,524,922,766.08	46,524,922,766.08	0.00
1411　Investment In The International Fund, Maintenance Of Value Adjustments	11,303,549,925.77	8,321,349,757.25	2,982,200,168.52
1416　Due International Monetary Fund For Subscriptions And Drawings (Letter Of Credit)	-52,101,081,863.17	-47,909,934,073.71	-4,191,147,789.46
1418　Receivable/Payable (-) For Interim Maintenance Of Value Adjustments	-1,110,984,789.72	-180,341,096.77	-930,643,692.95
1422　Dollar Deposits With The International Monetary Fund	-152,585,131.91	-134,844,323.77	-17,740,808.14
Balance	4,463,820,907.05	6,621,153,029.08	-2,157,332,122.03
Other Cash And Monetary Assets:			
1011　Other U.S. Treasury Monetary Assets	79,890.00	79,890.00	0.00
1015　General Depositaries - Deferred Accounts	8,574,811.24	7,888,824.78	685,986.46
1040　Mutilated Paper Currency Held By The Bureau Of Engraving And Printing	6,876,407.06	9,067,702.56	-2,191,295.50
1210　Cash - Accountability Of Disbursing And Collecting Officers	3,339,466,320.62	3,173,672,479.65	165,793,840.97
1211　RFC Accountability	4,659,083.42	-683,885.85	5,342,969.27
1212　Undeposited Collections And Unconfirmed Deposits (Agencies Reporting Transactions On FMS-224 - Revised)	-23,338,693.82	-23,358,131.37　r	19,437.55
1213　Change In Non-Federal Securities (Market Value)	1,142,677,954.73	1,586,943,691.36	-444,265,736.63
1214　Funds Held Outside Of Treasury (Budgetary)	1,451,839,645.65	874,277,009.00	577,562,636.65
1217　Transit Account - Transfers Of Cash – U.S. Disbursing Officers	39,889,748.66	232,684.23	39,657,064.43
1218　Offset Of Change In Non-Federal Securities	-1,142,677,954.73	-1,586,943,691.36	444,265,736.63
1219　Accountability For Investment In The Exchange Stabilization Fund	21,963,232,702.07	19,812,047,111.97	2,151,185,590.10
1220　Revaluation Of Investments In Exchange Stabilization Fund	-1,762,310,097.36	0.00	-1,762,310,097.36
1225　Cash Accountability For USDO - Charleston	102,519,122.24	0.00	102,519,122.24
1226　Cash Accountability For USDO - Bangkok	36,136,261.47	0.00	36,136,261.47
1227　Cash Accountability For The Bureau Of Engrave And Printing	53,401.00	97,497.50	-44,096.50
Total Other Cash And Monetary Assets	25,167,678,602.25	23,853,321,182.47　r	1,314,357,419.78
Total Cash And Monetary Assets	111,969,203,751.10	89,056,081,503.01　r	22,913,122,248.09
1216　Investments In Non-Federal Securities, NRRIT, RRB	30,779,883,576.00	28,211,293,138.17	2,568,590,437.83
Guaranteed Loan Financing			
1452　Net Activity, Guaranteed Loan Financing	-48,042,561,934.98	-56,677,996,538.81　r	8,635,434,603.83
Direct Loan Financing			
1454　Net Activity, Direct Loan Financing	168,548,723,894.58	160,304,791,127.95　r	8,243,932,766.63
Miscellaneous Asset Accounts:			
1012　U.S. Treasury Miscellaneous Assets	20,685,324.88	20,685,324.88	0.00
1016　Federal Reserve Banks, Deferred Items	159,556,607.33	143,898,670.47	15,657,936.86
1053　U.S. Treasury - Owned Gold	11,041,058,821.09	11,041,058,821.09	0.00
1054　Gold Certificate Fund, Board Of Governors Of The Federal Reserve System[2]	-11,036,836,601.10	-11,036,836,601.10	0.00
1423　U.S. Currency With The International Monetary Fund	152,585,131.91	134,844,323.77	17,740,808.14
1670　Receivable For Forged, Or Incorrect Payment Of All U.S. Government Checks	8,713,631.11	10,788,861.81	-2,075,230.70
1840　Deposits In Transit To The Treasury Account	-2,006,665,162.60	-366,565,108.86　r	-1,640,100,053.74
1869　Deposit In Suspense, Electronic Funds Transfer	3,591,854.39	3,591,384.17	470.22
1870　E-Commerce Collections	1,316,936.73	1,049,760.66	267,176.07
1875　Undistributed Disbursing Transactions (Agencies Reporting On Statement Of Transactions, FMS-224 - Revised)	89,225,549.98	84,200,916.04	5,024,633.94
Total Miscellaneous Asset Accounts	-1,566,767,906.28	36,716,352.93　r	-1,603,484,259.21
Total Asset Accounts	261,688,481,380.42	220,930,885,583.25　r	40,757,595,797.17

United States Summary General Ledger Account Balances

Excess Of Liabilities			
Budget And Off-Budget Financing:			
3010 Accumulated Excess Of Liabilities	4,679,733,581,006.66	4,432,202,257,852.47 r	247,531,323,154.19
3040 Total Receipts (On Budget/Off Budget)	-2,567,672,504,535.67	-2,406,675,323,260.68	-160,997,181,274.99
3045 Total Outlays (On Budget/Off Budget)	2,730,498,786,036.79	2,654,872,649,376.87 r	75,626,136,659.92
Total Budget And Off-Budget Financing	4,842,559,862,507.78	4,680,399,583,968.66 r	162,160,278,539.12
Transactions Not Applied To Current Year's Surplus Or Deficit:			
3080 Seigniorage - Transactions Not Applied To Current Fiscal Year Budget Surplus Or Deficit	782,000,000.00	666,000,000.00	116,000,000.00
3088 Special Reclass & Write-Off Of Aged BCA Balances	53,337.43	2,962.00	50,375.43
Total Transactions Not Applied To Current Year Surplus Or Deficit	782,053,337.43	666,002,962.00	116,050,375.43
Total Excess Of Liabilities (+) Or Assets (-)	4,841,777,809,170.35	4,679,733,581,006.66 r	162,044,228,163.69
Total Assets And Excess Of Liabilities	5,103,466,290,550.77	4,900,664,466,589.91	202,801,823,960.86
Liability Accounts			
Borrowing From The Public:			
Treasury Securities, Issued Under General Financing Authorities:			
8410 Debt Held By The Public	5,049,305,165,315.60	4,843,120,613,601.25	206,184,551,714.35
8412 Intragovernmental Holdings	3,958,347,869,336.00	3,663,853,163,022.80	294,494,706,313.20
Total Treasury Securities Outstanding	9,007,653,034,651.60	8,506,973,776,624.05	500,679,258,027.55
Plus Premium On Treasury Securities:			
8040 Deferred Interest (Premium) On Public Debt Subscriptions, U.S. Securities	4,144,938,739.37	4,261,666,055.82	-116,727,316.45
Less Discount On Treasury Securities:			
8322 Deferred Interest (Discount) On Government Account Series	86,223,329,293.33	85,636,588,231.61	586,741,061.72
Total Treasury Securities Net Of Premium And Discount	8,925,574,644,097.64	8,425,598,854,448.26	499,975,789,649.38
Agency Securities, Issued Under Special Financing Authorities			
8420 Principal Of Outstanding Agency Securities	22,959,078,483.56	23,391,839,066.41	-432,760,582.85
Total Federal Securities	8,948,533,722,581.20	8,448,990,693,514.67	499,543,029,066.53
Deduct:			
Federal Securities Held As Investments Of Government Accounts			
8440 Investment Of Certain Deposits Funds	-1,169,000.00	-1,169,000.00	0.00
8442 Investment Of Government Accounts In Public Debt Securities	3,958,410,871,371.76	3,663,766,343,819.70	294,644,527,552.06
8444 Investment Of Government Accounts In Agency Securities	7,164,000.00	8,164,000.00	-1,000,000.00
Total Federal Securities Held As Investments Of Government Accounts	3,958,416,866,371.76	3,663,773,338,819.70	294,643,527,552.06
Less Discount On Federal Securities:			
8321 Discount On Federal Securities Held As Investment In Government Accounts	42,795,930,123.68	41,370,445,968.11	1,425,484,155.57
Net Federal Securities Held As Investments Of Government Accounts Less Discount	3,915,620,936,248.08	3,622,402,892,851.59	293,218,043,396.49
Total Borrowing From The Public	5,032,912,786,333.12	4,826,587,800,663.08	206,324,985,670.04
Accrued Interest Payable To The Public:			
8720 Accrued Interest Payable On Exchanges Of Deferred Public			
Debt Subscriptions, United States Treasury Securities	44,389,817,290.38	41,122,272,351.64	3,267,544,938.74
Allocations Of Special Drawing Rights:			
8240 Allocations Of Special Drawing Rights	7,626,853,374.50	7,233,519,106.10	393,334,268.40
Deposit Funds:			
8220 Deposit Funds Unexpended	10,419,202,803.37	14,359,989,081.90	-3,940,786,278.53
Miscellaneous Liability Accounts:			
8010 Corporate Securities And Interest Checks Outstanding	0.00	4,812.50	-4,812.50
8015 Disbursing Officers Checks Outstanding - Unfunded Accounts Of Four-Digit Symbols	7,825,879,137.62	10,307,602,554.72	-2,481,723,417.10
8017 Transit Account - Adjustment Of U.S. Treasury Check Payments With Federal Reserve Banks	-2,140,338.67	-10,229.13	-2,130,109.54
8033 Postal Money Orders Outstanding	723,746,918.13	743,594,206.87	-19,847,288.74
8021 Transit Account – U.S. Treasury Checks	-224,919,200.99	-157,620,979.29	-67,298,221.70
8047 Unamortized Premium (Discount) On Public Debt Securities	-8,889,975.89	-15,194,342.04	6,304,366.15
8056 Transfer Of Unprocessed U.S. Treasury Checks - Unclassified	-220,241,605.21	-348,799,714.56	128,558,109.35
8060 Transit Account Unclassified Charges (EFT)	-5,000.00	0.00	-5,000.00
8063 Transit Account - Checks On U.S. Treasury Cashed - Unclassified	-485,934,961.93	-514,802,316.40	28,867,354.47
8073 Transfer Of U.S. Treasury Check Data	-1,257,808,757.91	-628,752,729.26	-629,056,028.65
8075 Adjustment Of U.S. Treasury Check Data	-915.68	-596.79	-318.89

United States Summary General Ledger Account Balances

8118	Cash-Link ACH Transfers	-490,050,444.07	-434,526,044.56	-55,524,399.51
8131	Cash-Link ACH Receiver Book Entry	149.80	-40.20	190.00
8133	Cash-Link ACH Receiver Pad	-30,651.49	-100,662.43	70,010.94
8183	Check Claims (Suspense)	53,408,687.80	62,401,989.34	-8,993,301.54
8255	Tennessee Valley Auth Alternative Financing Transactions	2,209,911,269.70	2,352,307,675.23	-142,396,405.53
8869	Transit Account - Statement Of Accountability (Department Of Defense - Air Force)	243,091.08	243,091.08	0.00
8871	Transit Account - Statement Of Accountability (Department Of Defense - Army)	-5,481,305.86	-5,481,305.86	0.00
8877	Transit Account - Payments By One Disbursing Officer For Account Of Another Disbursing Officer, Division Of Disbursement And U.S. Disbursing Officers - Not Yet Classified	-55,347.03	-55,347.03	0.00
8999	Capital Transfer Account	0.00	75,365.00	-75,365.00
	Total Miscellaneous Liability Accounts	8,117,630,749.40	11,360,885,387.19	-3,243,254,637.79
	Total Liability Accounts	5,103,466,290,550.77	4,900,664,466,589.91	202,801,823,960.86

[1] Major sources of information used to determine Treasury's operating cash include Federal Reserve Banks, the Treasury Regional Finance Centers, the Internal Revenue Service Centers, the Bureau of Public Debt and various electronic systems. Deposits are reflected as received and withdrawals are reflected as processed.

[2] The difference between Gold and Gold Certificates represents 100,000 fine troy ounces of unmonetized gold held by the U.S. Mint as assurance that Gold Certificates are fully backed by Reserve Gold.

r Revised

Part Two

Detail Of Receipts

Table A – Receipts By Source Categories

Classification	Receipt Symbol	Receipt Offset Against Outlays
Budget Receipts		
Individual Income Taxes		
Withheld Individual Income And FICA Taxes	0101	928,550,651,788.49
Federal Tax Withheld From Payments To Nonresident Aliens (Suspense), Health And Human Services	75 F0109	-1,711,466.26
Individual Income Tax, Other	0110	437,608,984,148.69
Refunding Internal Revenue Collections (Indefinite)	20 X0903	-202,778,830,629.58
Unidentified Cash Collections, Federal Tax Deposits, Internal Revenue Service, Kansas City, Missouri	20 F3820.009	1,070,751.89
Unidentified Cash Collections, Federal Tax Deposits, Internal Revenue Service, Austin, Texas	20 F3820.017	228,796.88
Unidentified Cash Collections, Federal Tax Deposits, Internal Revenue Service, Cincinnati, Ohio	20 F3820.018	-994,256.81
Unidentified Cash Collections, Federal Tax Deposits, Internal Revenue Service, Philadelphia, Pennsylvania	20 F3820.028	-6,660,354.18
Unidentified Cash Collections, Federal Tax Deposits, Internal Revenue Service, Ogden, Utah	20 F3820.029	38,250,449.73
Presidential Election Campaign Fund	5081.001	49,779,182.00
Private Collection Agent Program, Internal Revenue Service, Department Of The Treasury	5510.001	10,757,233.23
Total, Individual Income Taxes		1,163,471,525,644.08
Corporation Income Taxes		
Corporation Income And Excess Profits Taxes	0111	395,531,833,523.35
Refunding Internal Revenue Collections (Indefinite)	20 X0903	-25,291,790,736.36
Transfer From The General Fund Of Amounts Equivalent To Corporate Environmental Tax, Hazardous Substance Superfund	8145.015	2,601,882.00
Total, Corporation Income Taxes		370,242,644,668.99
Total, Income Taxes		1,533,714,170,313.07
Social Insurance And Retirement Receipts		
Employment And General Retirement		
Federal Old-Age And Survivors Insurance:		
Federal Old-Age And Survivors Insurance Trust Fund	20 X8006	-1,897,400,000.00
Transfers From General Fund Of Amounts Equal To FICA Taxes, Federal Old-Age And Survivors Insurance Trust Fund	8006.001	513,673,412,651.93
Transfers From General Fund Of Amounts Equal To SECA Taxes, Federal Old-Age And Survivors Insurance Trust Fund	8006.011	31,123,718,734.64
Total, Federal Old-Age And Survivors Insurance		542,899,731,386.57
Federal Disability Insurance:		
Federal Disability Insurance Trust Fund	20 X8007	-322,200,000.00
Transfers From General Fund Of Amounts Equal To FICA Taxes, Federal Disability Insurance Trust Fund	8007.001	87,227,050,145.60
Transfers From General Fund Of Amounts Equal To SECA Taxes, Federal Disability Insurance Trust Fund	8007.011	5,283,202,098.33
Total, Federal Disability Insurance		92,188,052,243.93
Federal Hospital Insurance:		
Transfers From General Fund Of Amounts Equal To FICA Taxes, Federal Hospital Insurance Trust Fund	8005.001	171,022,293,125.69
Receipts From Railroad Retirement Account, Federal Hospital Insurance Trust Fund	8005.010	454,700,000.00
Transfers From General Fund Of Amounts Equal To SECA Taxes, Federal Hospital Insurance Trust Fund	8005.011	13,431,416,744.51
Total, Federal Hospital Insurance		184,908,409,870.20
Railroad Retirement:		
Social Security Equivalent Benefit Account, Railroad Retirement Board	60 X8010	-1,066,007.88
Taxes, Social Security Equivalent Benefit Account, Railroad Retirement Board	8010.002	2,408,064,890.40
Receipts Transferred To Federal Hospital Insurance Trust Fund, Social Security Equivalent Benefit Account, Railroad Retirement Board	8010.021	-454,700,000.00
Railroad Retirement Account	60 X8011	-1,027,768.72
Railroad Retirement Taxes, Railroad Retirement Account	8011.002	2,309,832,589.94
Total, Railroad Retirement		4,261,103,703.74
Total, Employment And General Retirement		824,257,297,204.44
Unemployment Insurance		
Unemployment Trust Fund	20 X8042	-125,091,677.66
Transfers From General Fund Of Amounts Equal To FUTA Taxes, Unemployment Trust Fund	8042.001	7,416,738,310.47
State Accounts, Deposits By States, Unemployment Trust Fund	8042.003	33,709,269,676.61
Deposits By Railroad Retirement Board, Unemployment Trust Fund	8042.005	90,368,602.42
Total Unemployment Insurance		41,091,284,911.84

Table A – Receipts By Source Categories

Classification	Receipt Symbol	Receipt Offset Against Outlays
Budget Receipts		
Other Retirement		
Federal Employees' Retirement--Employee Share:		
Deductions From Employees Salaries, Judicial Survivors Annuities Fund............	8110.001	5,085,568.27
Deductions From Employees Salaries, Tax Court Judges Survivors Annuity Fund..........	8115.001	338,549.64
Judicial Officers Annuities Deducted From Employees Salaries..........	8122.001	351,313.23
Deductions From Employees Salaries, Civil Service Retirement And Disability Fund..........	8135.001	3,588,837,880.24
Voluntary Contributions, Donations, Service Credit Payments, Etc., Civil Service Retirement And Disability Fund..........	8135.003	565,031,728.63
Deductions From Employees' Salaries, Foreign Service Retirement And Disability Fund, State..........	8186.001	22,912,664.19
Voluntary Contributions, Donations, Service Credit Payments, Etc., Foreign Service Retirement And Disability Fund, Suspense..........	8186.003	871,488.97
Deductions From Employees Salaries..........	8212.001	576,603.56
Employee Contributions, United States Court Of Appeals For Veterans Claims	8290.001	37,881.96
Fines And Gifts, Naval Home..........	8522.001	23,127,857.68
Total, Federal Employees' Retirement--Employee Share..........		4,207,171,536.37
Non-Federal Employees Retirement:		
Contributions From Employing Non-Federal Agencies, Civil Service Retirement And Disability Fund..........	8135.021	51,242,810.56
Total, Non-Federal Employees Retirement..........		51,242,810.56
Total, Other Retirement..........		4,258,414,346.93
Total, Social Insurance And Retirement Receipts..........		869,606,996,463.21
Excise Taxes		
Excise Taxes..........	0152	15,374,130,442.39
Refunding Internal Revenue Collections (Indefinite)..........	20 X0903	-6,241,354,345.10
Recovery From Highway Trust Fund For Refunds Of Taxes	3092	1,040,135,668.00
Recovery From Airport And Airway Trust Fund For Refunds Of Taxes..........	3094	67,229,332.00
Recovery From Treasury-Managed Trust Funds Other Than Highway And Airport For Refunds Of Taxes	3095	2,063,000.00
Land And Water Conservation Fund, Motorboat Fuels Tax, National Park Service..........	5005.003	1,000,000.00
Federal Aid To Wildlife Restoration Fund 1975..........	5029.003	321,562,458.69
Aviation User Fees, Overflight Fees, Federal Aviation Administration..........	5422.001	48,507,501.51
Deposits, Internal Revenue Collections For Puerto Rico..........	5737.001	461,630,408.77
Highway Trust Fund..........	20 X8102	-1,508,138,668.00
Deposits, Highway Account, (Highway Trust Fund)..........	8102.001	35,705,454,725.83
Deposits, Mass Transit Account (Highway Trust Fund)..........	8102.011	5,164,494,269.00
Airport And Airway Trust Fund..........	20 X8103	-67,229,332.00
Deposits, Airport And Airway Trust Fund	8103.001	11,534,814,612.00
Transfer From General Fund, Black Lung Benefits Revenue Act Taxes, Black Lung Disability Trust Fund	8144.001	639,197,000.00
Transfers From The General Fund For The Sport Fish Restoration Account, Aquatic Resources Trust Fund	8147.002	580,750,000.00
Leaking Underground Storage Tank Fund..........	20 X8153	-2,063,000.00
Transfers From General Fund Of Amounts Equal To Certain Taxes, Leaking Underground Storage Tank Trust Fund	8153.001	228,257,000.00
Excise Taxes For Tobacco Assessments, Tobacco Trust Fund, Commodity Credit Corporation..........	8161.001	933,790,655.31
Transfer From General Fund Of Amounts Equivalent To Certain Taxes, Vaccine Injury Compensation Trust Fund	8175.001	241,254,250.00
Transfers From General Fund Of Amount Equal To Certain Taxes, Oil Spill Liability Trust Fund	8185.001	452,372,000.00
Transfer From General Fund, Inland Waterways Revenue Act Taxes, Inland Waterways Trust Fund..........	8861.001	91,097,000.00
Total, Excise Taxes		65,068,954,978.40
Estate And Gift Taxes		
Estate And Gift Taxes..........	0153	26,977,952,522.53
Refunding Internal Revenue Collections (Indefinite)..........	20 X0903	-933,988,865.43
Total, Estate And Gift Taxes		26,043,963,657.10
Customs Duties		
Duties On Imports..........	0310	18,268,353,168.88
Refunds And Drawbacks, United States Customs Service (Indefinite)..........	70 X0505	-1,537,980,178.42
Import Duties On Arms And Ammunition..........	5137.002	21,180,766.00
30 % Of Customs Duties, Funds For Strengthening Markets, Income, And Supply (Section 32)..........	5209.001	7,886,597,959.89
Wool Manufacturers Trust Fund, United States Customs And Border Protection, Department Of Homeland Security..........	5533.001	17,392,129.86
Pima Cotton Trust Fund, United States Customs And Border Protection, Department Of Homeland Security	5544.001	16,000,000.00
Transfers From General Fund Of Amounts Equal To Certain Customs Duties, Reforestation Trust Fund, Forest Service	8046.001	30,004,200.00
Custom Duties, Aquatic Resources Trust Fund, Sport Fish Restoration	8147.005	46,885,841.87
Transfers From General Fund Of Amounts Equal To Certain Taxes, Harbor Maintenance Trust Fund..........	8863.001	1,261,731,132.50
Total, Customs Duties		26,010,165,020.58

Table A – Receipts By Source Categories

Classification	Receipt Symbol	Receipt Offset Against Outlays
Budget Receipts		
Miscellaneous Receipts		
Miscellaneous Taxes		
National Indian Gaming Commission, Gaming Activity Fees, Interior....................	5141.003	12,832,739.40
Deposits, Duties And Taxes, Puerto Rico, USCS, Department Of Homeland Security....................	5687.001	93,354,952.48
Total, Miscellaneous Taxes....................		106,187,691.88
Exercise Of Warrants		
Proceeds For Exercise Of Warrants, Air Transportation Stabilization Board (ATSB)	0401	23,733,593.53
Total, Exercise Of Warrants....................		23,733,593.53
Deposit Of Earnings, Federal Reserve System		
Deposit Of Earnings, Federal Reserve System....................	0650	32,042,737,949.78
Total, Deposit Of Earnings, Federal Reserve System....................		32,042,737,949.78
Defense Cooperation		
Contributions From Japan, Host Nation Support For U.S. Relocation Activities....................	8337.003	12,700,897.92
Contributions From South Korea, Host Nation Support For U.S. Relocation Activities....................	8337.004	21,304,488.00
Total, Defense Cooperation....................		34,005,385.92
Fees For Permits And Regulatory And Judicial Services		
Immigration, Passport, And Consular Fees....................	0830	1,067,103,733.23
Breached Bond Penalties, Immigration And Customs Enforcement, Department Of Homeland Security....................	0834	8,000,000.00
Registration And Filing Fees....................	0850	2,975,266.95
Registration And Filing Fees, Commodity Futures Trading Commission....................	0850.140	287,615.05
Registration Fees, Drug Enforcement Administration....................	0854	15,000,000.00
Filing Fees, The Judiciary....................	0864	53,758,185.39
Fees For Legal And Judicial Services, Not Otherwise Classified....................	0869	55,593,100.77
Fees For Legal And Judicial Services, Not Otherwise Classified, Court Of Appeals For Veterans Affairs....................	0869.042	88,459.50
Miscellaneous Fees For Regulatory And Judicial Services, Not Otherwise Classified....................	0891	7,391,875.71
Hazardous Waste Permits, PMN, And Other Services, Environmental Protection Agency....................	0895	1,233,065.17
Users Fees For IRS Ruling And Determination....................	2411	38,130,299.40
Coal Mining Reclamation Fees, Office Of Surface Mining Reclamation And Enforcement....................	5015.006	304,711,037.16
Registry Fees, Appraisal Subcommittee....................	5026.001	2,985,771.00
Deposits, Perishable Agricultural Commodities Act Fund....................	5070.001	7,228,944.81
Filing Fees, The Judiciary....................	5100.001	189,316,611.54
Registry Administration Account, The Judiciary....................	5101.001	10,931,220.03
Licenses Under Federal Power Act From Public Lands And National Forests, Payment To States....................	5105	3,094,042.35
Fees For Fishermen's Contingency Fund....................	5120.001	999,599.66
Earnings On Investments, Fishermen's Contingency Fund....................	5120.002	32,758.37
Earnings On Investments, Foreign Fishing Observer Fund....................	5122.002	41,441.86
Licenses Under Federal Power Act, Improvement Of Navigable Waters, Maintenance And Operation Of Dams, Etc.	5125	13,153,812.28
Migratory Birds Hunting Stamps....................	5137.001	22,542,541.20
Agricultural Quarantine Inspection User Fee Account, Animal And Plant Health Inspection Service....................	5161	-11,920.99
Agricultural Quarantine Inspection User Fee Account, Animal And Plant Health Inspection Service....................	5161.001	472,248,627.96
Fees From Jukebox And Cable Television, Copyright Office....................	5175.001	233,740,063.87
Universal Service Fund, Federal Communications Commission....................	5183.001	7,513,166,543.51
Assessment, Decontamination, Decommissioning Services, Energy....................	5231.001	213,170,839.56
Interstate Land Sales Fund, Housing And Urban Development....................	5270.001	665,454.90
Permit Title Registration Fee, Limited Access System Administration Fund, National Oceanic And Atmospheric Administration....................	5284.001	6,911,354.84
Enrolled Agent Fees Increase, Internal Revenue Service, Miscellaneous Retained Fees, Treasury....................	5432.004	7,109,105.85
Total, Fees For Permits And Regulatory And Judicial Services....................		10,251,599,450.93
Fines, Penalties, And Forfeitures		
Fines, Penalties, And Forfeitures, Agricultural Laws....................	1010	3,835,039.25
Fines, Penalties, And Forfeitures, Immigration And Labor Laws....................	1030	76,893,935.28
Fines, Penalties, And Forfeitures, Customs, Commerce And Antitrust Laws....................	1040	120,931,561.34
Fines, Penalties, And Forfeitures, Narcotic, Prohibition And Alcohol Laws....................	1050	6,997,747.47
Forfeitures Of Unclaimed Money And Property....................	1060	13,505,324.91
Fines, Penalties, And Forfeitures, Mine Safety And Health Administration....................	1080	30,306,856.40
Fines, Penalties, And Forfeitures, Not Otherwise Classified....................	1099	583,384,599.56
Fines, Penalties, And Forfeitures, Corporation For National Services....................	1099.055	6,103.99
Fines, Penalties, And Forfeitures, Not Otherwise Classified, District Of Columbia....................	1099.070	227,844.37
Fines, Penalties, And Forfeitures, Not Otherwise Classified, Commodity Futures Trading Commission....................	1099.140	12,143,639.24

Table A – Receipts By Source Categories

Classification	Receipt Symbol	Receipt Offset Against Outlays
Budget Receipts		
Fines, Penalties, And Forfeitures: Continued		
Fines, Penalties, And Forfeitures, Not Otherwise Classified, Federal Election Commission	1099.160	4,529,300.96
Fines, Penalties, And Forfeitures, Crime Victims Fund	5041.001	1,017,977,474.59
Forfeited Cash And Proceeds From The Sale Of Forfeited Property	5042.001	1,477,916,002.25
Deposits, Civil Penalties, Office Of Surface Mining Reclamation And Enforcement	5063.001	160,064.90
Fines, Penalties, And Forfeitures, Migratory Bird, North American Wetlands Conservation Fund, United States Fish And Wildlife Service	5241	4,582,501.00
Antidumping And Countervailing Duties, Continued Dumping And Subsidy Offset, United States Customs Service	5688.001	388,138,966.93
Forfeited Cash And Proceeds From The Sale Of Forfeited Properties, Treasury Forfeiture Fund	5697.001	413,992,482.95
Federal Hospital Insurance Trust Fund Civil Penalties And Damages	8005.049	211,114,362.46
Receipts, Relief And Rehabilitation, Longshoremen's And Harbor Workers' Compensation Act, As Amended, Department Of Labor	8130.001	127,997,284.99
Receipts, Relief And Rehabilitation, Workmen's Compensation Act, Within The District Of Columbia, Department Of Labor	8134.001	10,808,652.00
Fines And Penalties, Hazardous Substance Superfund	8145.003	1,062,750.24
Fines And Penalties, Oil Spill Liability Trust Fund	8185.003	6,856,307.02
Fines And Gifts, Soldiers' Home	8522.003	23,656,743.67
Proceeds Of Sales Of Unclaimed, Abandoned, And Seized Goods, USCS, Department Of Homeland Security	8789.001	4,221,444.95
Total, Fines, Penalties, And Forfeitures		4,541,246,990.72
Restitutions, Reparations, And Recoveries Under Military Occupation		
Recoveries Under Military Occupation	1125	3,350.00
Total, Restitutions, Reparations, And Recoveries Under Military Occupation		3,350.00
Gifts And Contributions		
Contributions To "Conscience Fund"	1210	3,594,405.25
Gifts To The United States, Not Otherwise Classified	1299	9,729,105.62
Gifts To The United States To Reduce Debt Held By The Public, Bureau Of The Public Debt	5080.001	2,374,862.42
Unclaimed Checkpoint Money, Transportation Security Administration, Department Of Homeland Security	5390.001	254,310.14
Gifts And Donations, White House Commission On The National Moment Of Remembrance	5484.001	154,703.41
Gifts, Abraham Lincoln Bicentennial Commission	5490.001	77,329.00
Gifts, Federal Supplementary Medical Insurance Trust Fund	8004.042	20,061.40
Gifts, Federal Hospital Insurance Trust Fund	8005.042	20,061.38
Gifts, Federal Old-Age And Survivors Insurance Trust Fund	8006.042	578,467.85
Contributions To Library Of Congress Gift Fund	8031.001	4,178,669.92
Contributions, Library Of Congress Trust Fund	8032.001	10,252,075.50
Gifts, Donations And Bequests For Forest And Rangeland Research, Forest Service	8034.001	55,831.11
Donations To National Park Service	8037.001	27,227,456.93
Gifts And Donations, National Endowment For The Arts	8040.001	1,643,943.16
Gifts And Donations, National Endowment For The Humanities	8050.001	293,043.47
Grants And Donations, Institute Of Museum Services, National Endowment For The Humanities	8080.001	1,370,683.00
Gifts And Donations, Federal Judicial Center	8123.001	102,699.79
Donations, National Archives Gift Fund, National Archives And Records Administration	8127.001	1,724,223.32
Department Of Veterans Affairs Cemetery Gift Fund, Department Of Veterans Affairs	8129.001	128,377.63
Gifts And Donations, Open World Leadership Center Trust Fund	8148.001	200,200.00
Contributions, Educational And Cultural Exchange, United States Information Agency	8167.002	-372,588.00
Deposits, General Post Fund, National Homes, Department Of Veterans Affairs	8180.001	28,000,382.86
Gifts And Donations, Christopher Columbus Fellowship Foundation	8187.003	25,000.00
Unconditional Gifts Of Real, Personal, Or Other Property, General Services Administration	8198.001	3,726,000.00
Gifts And Bequests, Department Of Agriculture	8203.001	828,072.18
Gifts And Donations, African Development Foundation	8239.001	4,216,406.06
Gifts And Donations, Departmental Management, Department Of Homeland Security	8244.001	282.61
Contributions To National Institutes Of Health Unconditional Gift Fund	8248.001	12,831,932.38
Gifts And Donations, Centers For Disease Control	8250.001	5,353,813.03
Contributions To National Institutes Of Health Conditional Gift Fund	8253.001	34,342,716.57
Contributions, Department Of Education	8258.001	389,164.48
Gifts And Donations, Commission For The Preservation Of American Heritage Abroad	8268.001	464,391.79
Gifts And Donations, Israeli Arab Scholarship Program	8271.001	-16,500.00
Trust Fund, The Barry Goldwater Scholarship And Excellence In Education Fund	8281.003	108.00
Donations, Advisory Council On Historic Preservation	8298.001	273,820.03
Gifts, Crime Victims Fund	8306.001	2,925.00
Gifts And Donations, National Institute For Literacy, Department Of Education	8324.001	1,955.00
Gifts And Donations, Bureau Of Indian Affairs	8361.001	3,449,961.12
Gifts And Bequests, Take Pride In America, Department Of The Interior	8369.001	102,579.21
Gifts And Bequests, Departmental Management	8501.001	1,201,587.58
Contributions To The Administration On Aging Gift Fund	8510.001	6,721.99
Contributions To The Indian Health Service Gift Fund	8511.001	471,826.00
Contributions To The Agency For Healthcare Research And Quality Gift Fund	8512.001	15.09
Contributions, American Battle Monuments Commission	8569.001	892,318.76
Deposits, Department Of The Navy General Gift Fund	8716.001	1,385,681.51
Contributions To United States Naval Academy General Gift Fund	8733.001	5,878,737.76
Department Of State Unconditional Gift Fund	8821.001	8,025,073.14
Conditional Gift Fund, General, Department Of State	8822.001	1,865,393.93
Gifts And Donations, Agency For International Development	8824.001	14,467,995.99
Deposits, Patients' Benefit Fund, National Fund, National Institutes Of Health	8888.001	1,623.00

Table A – Receipts By Source Categories

Classification	Receipt Symbol	Receipt Offset Against Outlays
Budget Receipts		
Deposits, Department Of The Army General Gift Fund	8927.001	5,805,721.51
Deposits, Department Of The Air Force General Gift Fund	8928.001	1,845,531.55
Donations To National Science Foundation	8960.001	41,280,961.11
Total, Gifts And Contributions		240,730,121.54
Refunds And Recoveries		
Refund Of Moneys Erroneously Received And Covered (Indefinite)	20 X1807	-28,107,718.36
Recoveries, Oil Spill Liability Trust Fund	8185.004	16,117,287.37
Total, Refunds And Recoveries		-11,990,430.99
Total, Miscellaneous Receipts		47,228,254,103.31
Total, Budget Receipts		2,567,672,504,535.67
Proprietary Receipts From The Public		
Interest		
Interest On Foreign Loans And Deffered Foreign Collections:		
Interest On Quota In International Monetary Fund (Article V, Section 9), Treasury	1463.001	107,183,214.25
Interest Received On Loans And Credits To Foreign Nations, Treasury	1464	83,435,083.20
Interest On Loans, Foreign Assistance Act Of 1961, Agency For International Development	1466	3,007.88
Total, Interest On Foreign Loans And Deferred Foreign Collections		190,621,305.33
Interest On Deposits In Tax And Loan Accounts:		
Interest Received From Tax And Loan Depositaries, Treasury	1484	1,173,927,186.87
Total, Interest On Deposits In Tax And Loan Accounts		1,173,927,186.87
Other Interest (Domestic--Civil):		
General Fund Proprietary Interest, Not Otherwise Classified	1435	165,040,803.88
General Fund Proprietary Interest, Not Otherwise Classified, Corporation For National And Community Service	1435.055	14,478.38
Interest Payments From States, Cash Management Improvement, Treasury	1450	51,556,060.24
Interest Received From Credit Reform Financing Accounts, Executive Office Of The President	1499	9,642,566,567.25
Miscellaneous Interest, Reclamation Fund, Interior	5000.021	14,128,489.84
Interest On Late Payment Of Coal Mining Reclamation Fees, Office Of Surface Mining Reclamation And Enforcement	5015.007	90,558.71
Other, Office Of Surface Mining Reclamation And Enforcement	5015.008	78,286.81
Interest On Investment In GSES, Tribal Special Fund, Office Of The Special Trustee For American Indians	5265.003	21,021,684.19
Other Proprietary Receipts, Federal Supplementary Medical Insurance Trust Fund	8004.029	11,928,928.71
Other Proprietary Receipts, Federal Hospital Insurance Trust Fund	8005.029	4,376,031.59
Interest Income, Cash Management Improvement Act, Federal Disability Trust Fund	8007.014	358,555.00
Interest On Investment In GSES, Tribal Trust Fund, Office Of The Special Trustee For American Indians	8030.003	4,784,085.93
Income From Donated Securities, Library Of Congress Trust Fund	8032.021	2,454,035.97
Interest On Unemployment Insurance Loans To States, Federal Unemployment Trust Fund	8042.004	4,481,785.88
Interest Income, Cash Management Improvement Act, Unemployment Trust Fund	8042.014	4,096,040.00
Interest Income, Cash Management Improvement Act, Highway Account (Highway Trust Fund)	8102.014	2,385,724.00
Interest Income, Cash Management Improvement Act, Mass Transit Account (Highway Trust Fund)	8102.015	8.00
Interest Income, Cash Management Improvement Act, Airport And Airway Trust Fund	8103.014	64,456.00
Interest And Dividends On Private Sector Holdings, National Railroad Retirement Investment Trust	8118.003	475,429,047.61
Interest Earned On Non-Federal Securities, National Archives And Records Administration	8127.003	850,033.53
Miscellaneous Interest, Black Lung Disability Trust Fund	8144.004	316,992.23
Total, Other Interest (Domestic--Civil)		10,406,022,653.75
Total, Interest		11,770,571,145.95
Dividends And Other Earnings		
Gains And Losses On Private Sector Holdings, National Railroad Retirement Investment Trust	8118.001	3,451,695,095.29
Realized Gains On Non-Federal Securities, National Archives Gift Fund	8127.004	397,382.74
Total, Dividends And Other Earnings		3,452,092,478.03

Table A – Receipts By Source Categories

Classification	Receipt Symbol	Receipt Offset Against Outlays
Proprietary Receipts From the Public		
Royalties And Rents		
Rent And Bonuses From Land Leases For Resource Exploration And Extraction, Agriculture And Interior (31 USC 3513)	1811	186,800,228.26
Rent Of Equipment And Other Personal Property, Army, Navy, Air Force	1840	90,284.50
Royalties On Natural Resources, Not Otherwise Classified, Interior	2039	376,084,752.26
Receipts From Grazing Fees, Federal Share, Interior	2484	4,706,317.76
Royalties On Natural Resources, Reclamation Fund, Interior	5000.024	1,461,998,358.98
Receipts From Mineral Leasing, Public And Acquired Military Lands (Act February 25, 1920 And December 17, 1981, As Amended)	5003.002	1,883,010,482.30
Recreation Fees For Collection Costs, Department Of Agriculture	5010.001	-3,401.04
Receipts From Grazing, Etc., Public Lands Outside Grazing Districts, Bureau Of Land Management	5016	696,856.81
Receipts From Grazing, Etc., Public Lands Within Grazing Districts, Bureau Of Land Management	5032	-17,539.93
Receipts From Grazing, Etc., Public Lands Within Grazing Districts, Miscellaneous, Bureau Of Land Management	5044	755,833.11
Receipts From Oil And Gas Leases, National Petroleum Reserve In Alaska, Bureau Of Land Management	5045	11,093,200.10
Rents And Charges For Quarters, National Park Service	5049.001	18,331,113.03
Rents And Charges For Quarters, United States Fish And Wildlife Service	5050.001	2,832,119.06
Rents And Charges For Quarters, Bureau Of Indian Affairs	5051.001	5,181,131.13
Rents And Charges For Quarters, Geological Survey	5055.001	98,255.02
Hydraulic Mining In California, Water Storage And Use Of Facilities, Debris Reservoirs	5066.002	226,583.84
Rents And Charges For Quarters, Indian Health Services	5071.001	7,956,215.97
Receipts From Leases Of Lands Acquired For Flood Control, Navigation, And Allied Purposes	5090	10,653,060.43
Grazing Fees For Range Improvements, Taylor Grazing Act, As Amended	5132	9,173,414.10
Rental Payments, Park Buildings Lease And Maintenance Fund, National Park Service	5163.001	3,869,023.32
Disposal Of Department Of Defense Real Property For Navy	5188.017	3,131,857.75
Disposal Of Department Of Defense Real Property For Army	5188.021	1,125,913.89
Disposal Of Department Of Defense Real Property For Air Force	5188.057	1,120,442.41
Lease Of Department Of Defense Real Property For Navy	5189.017	9,133,607.10
Lease Of Department Of Defense Real Property For Army	5189.021	1,908,338.19
Lease Of Department Of Defense Real Property For Air Force	5189.057	6,138,503.77
Lease Of Department Of Defense Real Property For Defense Agencies	5189.097	1,120,628.49
Receipts For Construction Of Administrative Improvements - Taos, New Mexico, Land Conveyance, Forest Service	5212.003	18,000.00
Royalties From Character Merchandising, Forest Service	5214.001	73,566.97
Forfeitures And Recoveries, Forest Service Lands	5215.001	21,289,168.58
Operation And Maintenance Of Quarters, Forest Service	5219.001	7,745,882.13
OCS Receipts, Ultra Deepwater And Unconventional Natural Gas And Other Petroleum Research Fund	5523.001	50,000,000.00
Rent From Mineral Leases, Permit Processing Fund, Bureau Of Land Management	5573.001	21,949,562.69
Geothermal Lease Revenues, County Share	5574.001	4,360,025.63
Geothermal Lease Revenues, Department Of Interior Share	5575.001	4,359,936.41
Leases From Naval Petroleum Reserve Numbered 2 Lands	5576.001	2,081,099.50
Payments To Counties, National Grasslands	5896.003	7,838,000.00
National Grasslands Receipts, Forest Service	5896.005	1,802,583.27
Receipts From National Grasslands, Bureau Of Land Management	5896.011	1,246,606.33
Royalties, Federal Aviation Administration, Department Of Transportation	8108.001	11,877.23
Total, Royalties And Rents		4,129,991,889.35
Sale Of Products		
Sale Of Timber And Other Natural Land Products:		
National Forests Fund, Agriculture	2221	32,365,261.47
Sale Of Timber, Wildlife And Other Natural Land Products, Not Otherwise Classified, Interior	2229	7,159.65
National Forest Fund Receipts	5008.001	29,537,469.02
National Wildlife Refuge Fund, United States Fish And Wildlife Service	5091.001	12,376,554.23
Proceeds From Sales, Water Resource Development Projects, United States Fish And Wildlife Service	5092.001	86,745.83
Forest Ecosystems Health And Recovery-Disposal Of Salvage Timber, Bureau Of Land Management	5165.001	7,274,219.84
National Forests Fund, Payments To States	5201.001	-20,390,847.15
Timber Roads, Purchaser Elections, Forest Service	5202.001	6,800,000.00
Timber Salvage Sales, Forest Service	5204.001	43,558,304.36
Deposits, Brush Disposal	5206.001	10,514,081.02
National Forest Lands Under Special Acts	5208.001	1,069,000.00
National Forests Fund, Payment To Minnesota (Cook, Lake, And Saint Louis Counties)	5213.001	2,101,500.00
Timber Sales Pipeline Restoration Fund, Bureau Of Land Management	5249.001	10,921,620.84
Timber Sales Pipeline Restoration Fund, Forest Service	5264.001	6,999,708.36
MNP Rental Fee Account, Forest Service	5277.001	789,882.66
Reserve Account, Department Of Defense, Forest Products Program	5285.001	523,031.52
Miscellaneous Collections, Valles Caldera Fund, Forest Service	5363.001	2,484,952.57
Stewardship Contracting Product Sales, Funds Retained, Bureau Of Land Management	5506.001	107,673.68
Stewardship Contracting Product Slaws, Funds Retained, Department Of Agriculture, Forest Service	5540.001	1,260,594.04
Oregon And California Land-Grant Fund(See 2229 For General Account: 5136 And 5885 For Special Accounts)	5882	2,750,410.96
Funds Reserved, Oregon And California Grant Lands, Bureau Of Land Management	5884.001	11,720,026.61
Coos Bay Wagon Road Grant Fund(By Years) (See 2229 For General Account; And 5898 For Special Account)	5897	116,560.24
Funds Reserved, Coos Bay Wagon Road Grant Lands, Bureau Of Land Management	5898.001	530,063.44
Total, Sale Of Timber And Other Natural Land Products		163,503,973.19

Table A – Receipts By Source Categories

Classification	Receipt Symbol	Receipt Offset Against Outlays
Proprietary Receipts From the Public		
Sale Of Minerals And Mineral Products:		
Sale Of Minerals And Mineral Products, Energy	2230	6,160,552.23
National Forest Fund Receipts	5008.001	9,290,090.33
National Forest Fund, Payments To States	5243.001	15,471,470.12
Receipts From Leases Of Lands Acquired For Flood Control Navigation And Allied Purposes	5248.001	3,939,663.26
Sale Of Natural Gas And Oil Shale, 1N3, Bureau Of Land Management, Department Of Interior	5294.001	18,930,694.86
Total, Sale Of Minerals And Mineral Products		53,792,470.80
Sale Of Power And Other Utilities:		
Sale And Transmission Of Electric Energy, Falcon Dam, Energy	2245	1,800,000.00
Sale And Transmission Of Electric Energy, Southwestern Power Administration	2247	98,578,199.34
Sale And Transmission Of Electric Energy, Southeastern Power Administration	2248	125,426,600.34
Sale Of Power And Other Utilities, Not Otherwise Classified, Energy	2249	14,598,836.00
Sale Of Electric Energy, Bonneville Power Administration, Reclamation Fund, Interior	5000.026	32,116,311.35
Sale Of Power And Other Utilities, Reclamation Fund, Energy	5000.027	143,823,446.95
Falcon And Amistad Operating And Maintenance Fund, Department Of Energy	5178.001	3,087,979.00
Sale Of Northeast Home Heating Oil Reserve, Department Of Energy	5369.003	2,965,872.00
Proceeds From Uranium Sales, Department Of Energy	5530.001	43,057,413.17
Power Revenues, Indian Irrigation Projects	5648.001	67,596,601.43
Deposits From Sale And Transmission Of Electric Energy, Southeastern Power Administration	5653	35,969,359.00
Revenues, Colorado River Dam Fund, Boulder Canyon Project, Bureau Of Reclamation	5656.001	80,939,174.92
Total, Sale Of Power And Other Utilities		649,959,793.50
Other:		
Revenue, Central Valley Project Restoration Fund, Bureau Of Reclamation	5173.003	40,082,078.32
Debt Collection Fund	5445.003	58,440,919.04
Total, Other		98,522,997.36
Total, Sale Of Products		965,779,234.85
Fees And Other Charges For Services And Special Benefits:		
Medicare Premiums And Other Charges (Trust Funds):		
Premiums Collected For The Aged, Federal Supplementary Medical Insurance Trust Fund	8004.005	38,552,445,877.85
Premiums Collected For The Disabled, Federal Supplementary Medical Insurance Trust Fund	8004.007	7,190,410,726.01
Premiums Collected, Medicare Prescription Drug Account, FSMI	8004.035	1,628,079,772.26
Basic Premiums, Medicare Advantage, FSMI	8004.040	66,556,615.11
Premiums Collected For Uninsured Individuals Not Otherwise Eligible, Federal Hospital Insurance Trust Fund	8005.009	2,760,624,492.90
Basic Premiums, Medicare Advantage, FHI	8005.040	75,053,204.35
Total, Medicare Premium And Other Charges (Trust Funds)		50,273,170,688.48
Nuclear Waste Disposal Revenues:		
Fees For Disposal Of Spent Nuclear Fuel, Nuclear Waste Disposal Fund, Department Of Energy	5227.001	754,202,210.78
Total, Nuclear Waste Disposal Revenues		754,202,210.78
Veterans Life Insurance (Trust Funds):		
Premium And Other Receipts, National Service Life Insurance Fund	8132.001	139,424,086.41
Total, Veterans Life Insurance (Trust Funds)		139,424,086.41
Other:		
Hardrock Mining Claim Maintenance Fee, Interior	2032	21,960,770.00
Sale Of Publications And Reproductions, Not Otherwise Classified	2259	81,424.25
SSI, Attorney Fees	2417	3,728,822.73
SSI Administrative Fee Receipts Account, Social Security Administration	2418	127,074,285.77
Fees And Other Charges For Program Administrative Services, Interior	2419.001	262,728.34
Fees And Other Charges For Other Services, Department Of Commerce	2419.002	104,767.48
Fees And Other Charges For Communication And Transportation Service, Not Otherwise Classified	2429	22,638,205.48
Deposits For Survivor Annuity Benefits, Army, Navy, Air Force, Defense	2462	27,923,856.85
Contributions From Military Personnel, Veterans Administration Educational Assistance Act Of 1984	2473	202,991,077.30
Special Recreation Use Fees, Army, Corps Of Engineers, Civil	5007	42,953,325.81
Service Charges, Deposits And Forfeitures, Bureau Of Land Management	5017.001	26,387,607.37
Deposits For Road Maintenance And Reconstruction, Bureau Of Land Management	5018.001	2,083,646.92

Table A – Receipts By Source Categories

Classification	Receipt Symbol	Receipt Offset Against Outlays
Proprietary Receipts From the Public		
Sale Of Products: Continued		
Other: Continued		
Rents And Charges For Quarters, Bureau Of Land Management	5048.001	521,726.71
Delaware Water Gap Route 209 Commercial Operation Fees, National Park Service	5076.001	61,098.05
Sale Of Hunting And Fishing Permits, Military Reservations	5095.001	3,042,871.91
Recreation, Entrance And Use Fees, National Park Service	5107	56,697.87
Recreational Fee Demonstration Program, National Park Service	5110.001	165,649,118.65
Revenues, Indian Arts And Crafts Board	5130.001	40,066.95
Cooperative Research And Development Agreements, National Institutes Of Health	5145.001	21,667,998.95
Cooperative Research And Development Agreements, Centers For Disease Control	5146.001	3,495,974.75
Cooperative Research And Development Agreements, Food And Drug Administration	5148.001	3,918,245.70
Transportation Systems Fund, National Park Service	5164.001	11,637,268.30
Concessioner Improvement Accounts Deposit, National Park Service	5169.001	12,994,966.00
Receipts, Range Betterment Fund	5207	2,617,537.94
Deposits, Operation And Maintenance, Indian Irrigation Systems	5240.001	25,968,311.01
Alaska Resupply Program, Bureau Of Indian Affairs	5242.001	1,483,514.66
Filming And Special Use Fee Program, National Park Service	5247.001	1,347,099.88
Recreation Fee Enhancement Program, U.S. Fish And Wildlife Service	5252.001	4,409,528.26
National Park Passport Program, National Park Service	5262.001	3,192,059.01
Recreation Fee Demonstration Program, Forest Service	5268.001	61,042,072.24
Concessions Fees And Volunteer Services, Agriculture Research Service	5279.003	76,793.00
Fees For Training And Planning, Emergency Preparedness Grant, Pipeline And Hazardous Materials Safety Administration	5282.001	14,674,126.47
Medical Care Collections Fund, First Party Collections, Department Of Veterans Affairs	5287.003	150,963,829.54
Medical Care Collections Fund, Third Party Collections, Department Of Veterans Affairs	5287.004	1,261,345,593.44
Parking Fee, Medical Care Collections Fund, Department Of Veterans Affairs	5287.006	3,136,585.64
Compensated Work Therapy, Medical Care Collections Fund, Department Of Veterans Affairs	5287.007	43,295,657.05
Medical Care Collections Fund, Long-Term Care Co-Payments, Department Of Veterans Affairs	5287.009	3,699,341.66
Deposits For Administration Of Rights-Of-Way And Other Land Uses Fund, Forest Service	5361.001	971,973.15
Registration Service Fees, Pesticide Registration Fund, Environmental Protection Agency	5374.001	13,167,269.00
Fees For Glacier Bay National Park, National Park Service	5412.001	1,385,889.25
Recreational Fee Demonstration Program, Bureau Of Land Management	5413.001	14,550,199.93
Fees For Services, Environmental Dispute Resolution Fund	5415.001	2,729,914.57
State Supplemental Fees, Social Security Administration	5419.001	119,199,481.23
Park Concessions Franchise Fees, National Park Service	5431.001	47,704,419.57
New Installment Agreements, Internal Revenue Service, Miscellaneous Retained Fees, Treasury	5432.001	101,717,697.00
Restructured Installment Agreements, Internal Revenue Service, Miscellaneous Retained Fees, Treasury	5432.003	20,411,494.00
General Fees, Internal Revenue Service	5432.005	38,119,986.28
Burdensharing Contribution, Defense (Kuwait)	5441.001	215,342,608.00
Burdensharing Contribution, Defense (Japan)	5441.003	164,217,633.98
Burdensharing Contribution, Defense (South Korea)	5441.004	599,646,672.66
User Fees, Fund For Non-Federal Use Of Disposal Facilities, Corps Of Engineers	5493.001	558,576.78
Administration Fees, Special Benefits For Certain World War Ii Veterans, Social Security Administration	5555.001	210,314.98
Deposits For Educational Expenses, Children Of Employees, Yellowstone National Park	5663.001	365,000.00
Fees From Visitors To Grand Teton And Yellowstone National Parks, 25% Fund	5666.001	11,467.10
User Fees, Small Airports, USCS, Department Of Homeland Security	5694	6,690,246.48
Payments From States, Medicare Prescription Drug Accounts, FSMI	8004.036	6,977,455,272.56
Attorney Fees, Federal Old-Age And Survivors Insurance Trust Fund	8006.031	441,988.14
Non-Attorney Fees, Federal Disability Insurance Trust Fund	8007.028	-130,000.00
Attorney Fees, Federal Disability Insurance Trust Fund	8007.031	18,203,157.81
Deposits Of Fees, Inspection And Grading Of Farm Products, Agricultural Marketing Service	8015.001	138,097,068.91
Forest Service Cooperative Fund	8028.001	69,576,105.68
Advances From State Cooperating Agencies And Foreign Governments, Federal Highway Administration	8054.001	8,046,385.60
Contributions And Deposits, Bureau Of Land Management	8069.001	25,056,864.72
Deposits, Reclamation Trust Funds	8070.001	1,579,696.21
Contributions, Indian Health Facilities, Indian Health Services	8073.001	29,478,886.42
Fees For Services, Appalachian Regional Commission	8090.003	3,838,861.80
Deductions From Military Pay	8133.001	232,573.00
Deposits Of Fees, Inspection Of Farm Products, Food Safety And Inspection Service	8137.001	8,456,556.36
Deposits, Service Fees, Library Of Congress	8208.001	268,892.51
Deposits Of Miscellaneous Contributed Funds, Agricultural Research Service	8214.001	19,000,269.69
Deposits, Contributed Funds, United States Fish And Wildlife Service	8216.001	2,213,367.34
Deposits Of Miscellaneous Contributed Funds, National Agricultural Statistics Service	8218.001	434,561.08
Deposits Of Miscellaneous Contributed Funds, Animal And Plant Health Inspection Service	8226.001	17,126,887.69
Deposits Of Miscellaneous Contributed Funds, Economic Research Service	8227.001	-55,798.63
Deposits Of Miscellaneous Contributed Funds, Foreign Agricultural Service	8232.001	26,477.95
Contributions For Highway Research Program	8264.001	441,566.00
Contributions From States, Etc., Cooperative Work, Forest Highways, Federal Highway Administration	8265.001	17,010,648.00
Technical Assistance, United States Dollars Advanced From Foreign Governments, Federal Highway Administration, Department Of Transportation	8502.001	934,859.23
Gifts And Bequests, Maritime Administration	8503.001	640,042.56
Fees Paid By Residents, Soldiers' Home	8522.005	11,254,979.98
Land Sales, Armed Forces Retirement Home	8522.006	1,088,168.25
Deposits, General Gift Fund, USCG, Department Of Homeland Security	8533.001	1,394,336.45
Contributed Funds, Geological Survey, Interior	8562.001	2,710,950.79
Contributions And Advances, Rivers And Harbors, Corps Of Engineers	8862.001	396,298,198.36
Total, Other		11,376,751,270.36

Table A – Receipts By Source Categories

Classification	Receipt Symbol	Receipt Offset Against Outlays
Proprietary Receipts From the Public		
Sale Of Products:		
Total, Fees And Other Charges For Services And Benefits		62,543,548,256.03
Sale Of Government Property		
Sale Of Land And Other Real Property:		
Sale Of Public Domain, Reclamation Fund, Interior	5000.029	15,190,844.92
Land And Water Conservation Fund, Surplus Property Sales, National Park Service	5005.002	2,069,000.00
Proceeds From Sale Of Property, Judiciary Automation Fund	5114.001	65,276,005.97
Receipts From Sale Of Public Lands, Clark County, Nevada, Bureau Of Land Management	5128	-19,711,500.00
Receipts From Clark County, Nevada Land Sales, 15% Fund, Bureau Of Land Management	5129.001	7,713,450.00
Sale Of Public Land And Materials, 5% Fund To States	5133	3,310,849.99
Moneys Due Oklahoma From Royalties, Oil And Gas, South Half Of Red River, Act, March 4, 1923, As Amended	5134	16,753.89
Deposits, Department Of Defense Overseas Military Facility Investment Recovery Account For Air Force	5193.057	222,718.18
Land Acquisition Proceeds For Exchanges, Acquisition Of Lands To Complete Land Exchanges, Forest Service	5216.001	22,791,972.11
Facility Realignment And Enhancement Receipts, Acquisition Of Lands To Complete Land Exchanges, Forest Service	5216.004	3,741,935.60
Land Sales, South Nevada Public Land Management	5232.001	35,472,366.09
Other Receipts, Surplus Real And Related Personal Property, General Services Administration	5254.002	3,406,407.48
Transfers Of Surplus Real And Related Personal Property Receipts, General Services Administration	5254.003	-2,069,000.00
Federal Land Disposal Account, Bureau Of Land Management	5260.001	6,689,466.62
Medical Care Collections Fund, Asset Sales, Department Of Veterans Affairs	5287.005	5,762.21
Sale Of Public Land And Materials	5881	1,424,252.01
Total, Sale Of Land And Other Real Property		145,551,285.07
Military Assistance Program Sales (Trust Funds):		
Deposits, Advances, Foreign Military Sales, Executive	8242.001	15,833,018,688.79
Total, Military Assistance Program Sales (Trust Funds)		15,833,018,688.79
Other		
Sale Of Certain Material In National Defense Stockpile, Defense	2236	201,183,991.91
Defense Vessel Transfer Receipt Account	2644	1,345,390.02
Sale Of Scrap And Salvage Materials, Defense	2651	2,465,285.16
Total, Other		204,994,667.09
Total, Sale Of Government Property		16,183,564,640.95
Realization Upon Loans And Investments		
Negative Subsidies And Downward Reestimates (Credit Reform):		
Agricultural Credit Insurance, Negative Subsidies	2701.001	1,356,750.00
Agricultural Credit Insurance, Downward Reestimates Of The Subsidy	2701.003	52,909,079.00
Rural Electrification And Telephone Loans, Negative Subsidies	2702.001	49,947,766.40
Rural Electrification And Telephone Loans, Downward Reestimates Of Subsidies	2702.003	188,708,479.00
Rural Water And Waste Disposal, Negative Subsidies	2703.001	60,925.82
Rural Water And Waste Disposal, Downward Reestimates Of Subsidies	2703.003	100,001,558.00
Rural Community Facility, Negative Subsidies	2705.001	727,618.22
Rural Community And Facility, Downward Reestimates Of Subsidies	2705.003	12,280,259.00
Rural Housing Insurance, Negative Subsidies	2706.001	5,496.61
Rural Business And Industry, Downward Reestimates Of Subsidies	2707.003	33,433,636.00
P.L. 480, Downward Re-Estimates Of Subsidies	2708.003	66,452,913.00
Rural Development Loan Fund, Downward Reestimates Of Subsidies	2710.003	8,710,037.00
Rural Telephone Bank, Negative Subsidies	2711.001	430,459.42
Rural Telephone Bank, Downward Reestimates Of Subsidies	2711.004	87,316,964.00
Agricultural Credit Insurance Fund Guaranteed Loan, Downward Re-Estimate Of The Subsidy, Consolidated Farm Service Agency	2712.003	34,744,786.00
Rural Economic Development Loans, Downward Reestimates Of Subsidies	2713.003	3,664,958.00
Fisheries Finance, National Oceanic Atmospheric Administration, Negative Subsidies	2717.001	4,384,454.28
Fisheries Finance, Downward Re-Estimates Of Subsidies	2717.003	15,019,188.54
Federal Family Education Loan Program, Downward Re-Estimate Of Subsidies	2718.003	3,714,626,317.00
FHA-General And Special Risk Insurance, Negative Subsidies	2719.001	1,012,636,079.43
FHA-General And Special Risk Insurance, Re-Estimates	2719.003	1,746,453,648.27
Disaster Loan Program, Downward Reestimates Of Subsidies	2721.003	11,194,715.00
Business Loan Program, Downward Reestimates Of Subsidies	2722.003	762,528,124.00
Foreign Military Financing, Downward Reestimate Of Subsidies	2724.003	26,275,046.71
Export-Import Bank Guaranteed Loans Negative Subsidies	2727.001	62,195,595.15
Export Import Bank Guaranteed Loans, Downward Reestimates	2727.003	1,612,023,000.00
Maritime (Title XI Loan Program, Downward Re-Estimates Of Subsidies, Maritime Administration, Department	2728.003	37,802,000.00
Indian Loan Guarantee, Downward Reestimates, Bureau Of Indian Affairs	2729.003	6,158,808.00
Micro Enterprise & Small Enterprise Development Account, Downward Reestimates, Agency For International Development	2730.003	3,230,332.00

Table A – Receipts By Source Categories

Classification	Receipt Symbol	Receipt Offset Against Outlays
Proprietary Receipts From the Public		
Realization Upon Loans And Investments: Continued		
Negative Subsidies And Downward Reestimates (Credit Reform): Continued		
Guaranty And Indemnity Direct Loan Finance, Department Of Veterans Affairs, Downward Reestimates Of Subsidies	2733.003	961,292,000.00
Spectrum Auction Direct Loan Downward Reestimates Of Subsidies, Federal Communications Commission	2736.003	2,628,233.00
Minority Business Resource Center Guaranteed Loans, Downward Reestimates Of Subsidies	2739.003	115,227.00
Disaster Assistance, Downward Reestimates Of Subsidies, Federal Emergency Management Agency, Department Of Homeland Security	2740.003	286,291.00
Indian Housing Loan Guarantee Receipt Account, Downward Reestimates Of Subsidies	2743.003	679,779.00
Urban And Environmental Credit Program, Downward Reestimates Of Subsidies, Agency For International Development	2744.003	20,596,903.00
Health Education Assistance Loan Program, Negative Subsidy	2745.003	33,901,499.14
Distance Learning And Telemedicine Program, Negative Subsidies, Rural Utilities Service	2746.001	26,322.48
Distance Learning And Telemedicine Program, Downward Reestimates, Rural Utilities Service	2746.003	511,725.00
Indian Direct Loan, Downward Reestimates Of Subsidies, Bureau Of Indian Affairs	2747.003	1,193,728.00
Overseas Private Investment Corporation Loans, Negative Subsidies	2749.001	38,311,763.84
Overseas Private Investment Corporation Direct Loan, Financing Account, Downward Reestimates	2749.003	283,474,838.00
Native American Veterans Housing Loans, Negative Subsidies, Department Of Veterans Affairs	2751.001	664,054.95
Development Credit Authority Program Account, Downward Reestimates Of Loan Guarantees, Agency For International Development	2752.003	1,446,597.00
Downward Reestimates Of Subsidies, Abatement, Control And Compliance Loans, Environmental Protection Agency	2753.003	28,896.00
Apple Loan Program, Downward Reestimates Of Subsidies	2754.003	8,905.00
Veterans Housing Benefit Loan Program, Negative Subsidies, Department Of Veterans Affairs	2755.001	88,659,575.81
Farm Storage Facility Loans, Negative Subsidies	2756.001	453,674.05
Commodity Credit Corporation Export Guarantee Financing, Downward Reestimates Of Subsidies	2757.003	390,722,095.00
Emergency Steel Guaranteed Loans, Downward Reestimates Of Subsidies, Department Of Commerce	2759.003	32,947,651.08
Downward Reestimates, Railroad Rehabilitation And Improvement Program, Federal Railroad Administration	2760.003	5,038,528.00
Family Housing Improvement Fund, Downward Reestimates Of Subsidies, Defense	2761.003	9,279,699.79
Title VI Indian Loan Guaranteed Receipt Account, Downward Reestimates Of Subsidies	2762.003	7,210,177.00
Community Development Financial Institutions Fund, Downward Re-Estimates Of Subsidies	2763.003	397,315.00
Vocational Rehabilitation And Employment Direct Loan Financing, Department Of Veterans Affairs, Downward Reestimaters Of Subsidies	2767.003	-528,000.00
Downward Re-Estimates, Emergency Oil And Gas Guaranteed Loans	2769.003	64,068.00
Air Transportation Stabilization Guaranteed Loan, Downward Reestimates Of Subsidies	2771.003	104,855,269.74
Community Development Loan Guarantees, Downward Reestimates Of Subsidies	2773.003	5,145,676.00
Debt Restructuring, Downward Reestimates Of Subsidies	2775.003	6,976,089.36
Federal Direct Loan Program, Downward Reestimates Of Subsidies, Department Of Education	2781.003	984,537,652.00
GNMA Guarantees Of Mortgage-Backed Securities, Guaranteed Loans, Negative Subsidies	5301.001	192,748,579.64
		12,828,953,806.73
Total, Negative Subsidies And Downward Reestimates (Credit Reform)		
Other:		
Repayment Of Loans And Credits To Foreign Nations, Treasury	2869	142,396.05
Repayments On Miscellaneous Recoverable Costs, Not Otherwise Classified, Energy	2889	24,054,294.00
Repayments Of Loans, Capital Contributions, Higher Educational Activities, Department Of Education	2915	34,871,351.65
Receipts Of Rent, Leases And Lease Payments For Government-Owned Real Property, General Services Administration	5254.001	146,983.80
Proceeds From Non-Federal Securities Not Immediately Reinvested, National Archives Gift Fund	8127.005	12,653,961.97
		71,868,987.47
Total, Other		
		12,900,822,794.20
Total, Realization Upon Loans And Investments		
Recoveries And Refunds		
Recoveries For Government Property Lost Or Damaged, Not Otherwise Classified Army, Navy, Air Force	3019	14,064,415.79
Recoveries Under The Foreign Military Sales Program, Army, Navy, Air Force, Defense	3041	89,301,689.46
Recovery Of Beneficiary Overpayments From The Supplemental Security Income Program, Health And Human Services	3096	2,756,948,235.61
Miscellaneous Recoveries And Refunds, Not Otherwise Classified, Transportation, Treasury	3099	176,545.00
Federal Share Of Child Support Collections, HHS, ACF	3107	1,022,990,559.00
Natural Resource Damage Assessment And Restoration Fund, U.S. Fish And Wildlife Service, Interior	5198.001	64,096,167.67
Receipts, Transportation Audit Contracts And Contract Administration, General Services Administration	5250	10,200,000.00
Medical Care Collections Fund, Department Of Veterans Affairs	5287.001	760,616,314.94
Medical Care Collections Enhanced-Use Lease Proceeds, Department Of Veterans Affairs	5287.010	1,686,165.40
Medicare Refunds, Federal Supplementary Medical Insurance Trust Fund	8004.045	3,416,454,777.00
Medicare Refunds, Federal Hospital Insurance Trust Fund	8005.053	4,674,402,414.00
Tax Refund, Offset Collections, Federal Old-Age Survivors Insurance Trust Fund	8006.009	9,857,199.96
Non-Attorney Fees, Federal Old Age Survivors Insurance Trust Fund	8006.028	253,000.00
Other Proprietary Receipts, Federal Old-Age And Survivors Insurance Trust Fund	8006.029	64,113.25
Tax Refund, Offset Collections, Federal Disability Insurance Trust Fund	8007.009	41,288,751.66
Other Proprietary Receipts, Federal Disability Insurance Trust Fund	8007.029	1,057,373.55
Recoveries, Hazardous Substance Superfund	8145.004	234,049,915.54
		13,097,507,637.83
Total, Recoveries And Refunds		
Miscellaneous Receipt Accounts:		
Net Gains On Transactions In Foreign Currencies, Treasury Securities, Treasury	1682	12,125,728.05
Sale Of Lands, Etc., Account Of Military Post Construction Fund	2621	442.62
General Fund Proprietary Receipts, Defense Military, Not Otherwise Classified	3210	660,130,956.28

Table A – Receipts By Source Categories

Classification	Receipt Symbol	Receipt Offset Against Outlays
Proprietary Receipts From the Public		
General Fund Proprietary Receipts, Not Otherwise Classified, All Other	3220	1,542,297,209.72
General Fund Proprietary Receipts, Not Otherwise Classified, All Other, Botanic Garden	3220.002	2,560.00
General Fund Proprietary Receipts, Not Otherwise Classified, All Other, National Transportation Safety Board	3220.003	483.54
General Fund Proprietary Receipts, Not Otherwise Classified, All Other, Occupational Safety And Health Review Commission	3220.021	1,206.25
General Fund Proprietary Receipts, Not Otherwise Classified, All Other, National Mediation Board	3220.024	163.80
General Fund Proprietary Receipts, Not Otherwise Classified, All Other, National Capitol Planning Commission	3220.025	121.00
General Fund Proprietary Receipts, Not Otherwise Classified, All Other, Office Of Government Ethics	3220.048	765.02
General Fund Proprietary Receipts, Not Otherwise Classified, All Other, Corporation For National And Community Service	3220.055	1,279,984.92
General Fund Proprietary Receipts, Not Otherwise Classified, All Other, Chemical Safety And Hazard Investigation Board	3220.064	1,204.20
General Fund Proprietary Receipts, Not Otherwise Classified, All Other, Denali Commission	3220.067	5,755.90
General Fund Proprietary Receipts, Not Otherwise Classified, All Other, Broadcasting Board Of Governors	3220.068	375,086.10
General Fund Proprietary Receipts, Not Otherwise Classified, All Other, District Of Columbia	3220.069	1,680.25
General Fund Proprietary Receipts, Not Otherwise Classified, All Other, Millennium Challenge Corporation	3220.077	1,624,761.67
General Fund Proprietary Receipts, Not Otherwise Classified, All Other, Commodity Futures Trading Commission	3220.140	12,377.56
General Fund Proprietary Receipts, Not Otherwise Classified, All Other, Federal Election Commission	3220.160	215,674.17
Other, Reclamation Fund, Interior	5000.028	181,347,990.28
Rents And Charges For Quarters, Office Of Youth Programs, Bureau Of Reclamation	5053.001	43,114.63
Receipts From Operations Of North Platte Project (Gering And Fort Laramie, Goshen, And Pathfinder Irrigation Districts), Bureau Of Reclamation	5058.001	362.00
Recreation Enhancement Fee Program, Bureau Of Reclamation	5109.001	389,561.82
State Cost Sharing, Lahontan Valley And Pyramid Lake Fish And Wildlife Fund	5157.004	522,750.00
Proceeds From The Transfer Or Disposition Of Commissary Facilities	5195.001	9,784,927.23
National Forests Fund, Roads And Trails For States	5203.001	16,439,638.23
Return Of Principal From Private Sector Investments, Tribal Special Fund, Office Of The Special Trustee For American Indians	5265.004	148,666,293.89
Miscellaneous Sales Of Assets, Tribal Special Fund, Office Of The Special Trustee For American Indians	5265.005	6,128.68
Fees Collected For Use Of National Science Center Facilities	5286.001	10,270.00
Charges, User Fees And Natural Resource Utilization, Land Between The Lakes, Forest Service	5360.001	3,837,950.05
Lease Of Land And Buildings, National Cemetery Administration Facilities Operation Fund, Department Of Veterans Affairs	5392.001	40,200.00
Hardwood Technology Transfer And Applied Research Fund, Forest Service	5462.001	104,800.00
Return Of Principal From Private Sector Investments, Tribal Trust Fund, Office Of The Special Trustee For American Indians	8030.004	28,780,021.25
Miscellaneous Sales Of Assets, Tribal Trust Fund, Office Of The Special Trustee For The American Indians	8030.005	2,966,500.00
Total, Miscellaneous Receipt Accounts		2,611,016,669.11
Receipt Clearing Accounts		
Proceeds Of Sales, Personal Property (Suspense), The Judiciary	10 F3845	1,650.00
Proceeds Of Sales, Personal Property (Suspense), Peace Corps	11 F3845	5,181.76
Proceeds Of Sales, Personal Property (Suspense), State	19 F3845	6,304,502.09
Proceeds Of Sales, Personal Property (Suspense), Army	21 F3845	59,914.79
Proceeds Of Sales, Personal Property (Suspense), Department Of Veterans Affairs	36 F3845	-4,862.73
Proceeds Of Sales, Personal Property (Suspense), Agency For International Development	72 F3845	-3,080,373.68
Proceeds Of Sales, Personal Property (Suspense), Departmental Management	75 F3845	91,841.44
Proceeds Of Sales, Personal Property, Defense	97 F3845	71,758.22
Proceeds Of Sales, Personal Property, General Administration	13 F3845.001	-294.45
Proceeds Of Sales, Personal Property, Justice Management Division	15 F3845.001	717.64
Proceeds Of Sales, Personal Property	70 F3845.001	22,983.40
Proceeds Of Sales, Personal Property, Federal Bureau Of Investigation	15 F3845.002	839,485.63
Proceeds Of Sales, Personal Property, Bureau Of The Census	13 F3845.004	-194.23
Proceeds Of Sales, Personal Property, Treasury Inspector General For Tax Administration	20 F3845.004	76,193.88
Proceeds Of Sales, Personal Property	70 F3845.005	2,656,640.67
Proceeds Of Sales, Personal Property, Bureau Of Reclamation	14 F3845.006	-16,180.80
Proceeds Of Sales, Personal Property, ATF, Department Of Justice	15 F3845.007	-30,198.29
Proceeds Of Sales, Personal Property	70 F3845.007	58,400,461.09
Proceeds Of Sales, Personal Property, Geological Survey	14 F3845.008	32,386.00
Proceeds Of Sales, Personal Property, Internal Revenue Service	20 F3845.009	2,655,349.07
Proceeds Of Sales, Personal Property, Soil Conservation Service	12 F3845.010	-5,152,265.80
Proceeds Of Sales, Personal Property, Bureau Of Alcohol, Tobacco, And Firearms	20 F3845.010	55.19
Proceeds Of Sales, Personal Property, Drug Enforcement Administration	15 F3845.011	129,640.03
Proceeds Of Sales, Personal Property, International Trade Administration	13 F3845.012	-9,357.84
Proceeds Of Sales, Personal Property, Agricultural Research Service	12 F3845.014	-461,415.92
Proceeds Of Sales, Personal Property, National Oceanic And Atmospheric Administration	13 F3845.014	-173,921.77
Proceeds Of Sales, Personal Property, Animal And Plant Health Inspection Service	12 F3845.016	468,733.95
Proceeds Of Sales, Personal Property, United States Fish And Wildlife Service	14 F3845.016	139,106.48
Proceeds Of Sales, Personal Property, Office Of Surface Mining Reclamation And Enforcement	14 F3845.018	70,030.07
Proceeds Of Sales, Personal Property, United States Marshals Service	15 F3845.018	-121,737.88
Proceeds Of Sales, Personal Property, Minerals Management Service	14 F3845.019	-23,912.00
Proceeds Of Sales, Personal Property, Foreign Agricultural Service	12 F3845.029	94,134.71
Proceeds Of Sales, Personal Property (Suspense), Peace Corps	11 F3845.044	332,846.25
Budget Clearing Account (Suspense), Capitol Police	02 F3875	21,807.71
Budget Clearing Account (Suspense), Library Of Congress	03 F3875	41,749.79
Budget Clearing Account (Suspense), Government Printing Office	04 F3875	761.17
Budget Clearing Account (Suspense), Justice	15 F3875	9,212,886.98
Budget Clearing Account (Suspense), Labor	16 F3875	23,123.78
Budget Clearing Account (Suspense), State	19 F3875	11,624,833.28
Budget Clearing Account (Suspense), United States Tax Court	23 F3875	420,540.52
Budget Clearing Account (Suspense), Federal Communications Commission	27 F3875	868,663.38
Budget Clearing Account (Suspense), Centers For Disease Control	28 F3875	-559,968.52

Table A – Receipts By Source Categories

Classification	Receipt Symbol	Receipt Offset Against Outlays
Proprietary Receipts From the Public		
Receipt Clearing Accounts: Continued		
Budget Clearing Account (Suspense), Federal Trade Commission	29 F3875	-10,226,295.68
Budget Clearing Account (Suspense), Nuclear Regulatory Commission	31 F3875	-1,491,824.68
Budget Clearing Account (Suspense), International Trade Commission	34 F3875	175,000.00
Budget Clearing Account (Suspense), Department Of Veterans Affairs	36 F3875	-36,571,046.87
Budget Clearing Account (Suspense), Denver, CO	47 F3875	-13,431,523.21
Budget Clearing Account (Suspense), Securities And Exchange Commission	50 F3875	368,598.43
Budget Clearing Account (Suspense), Railroad Retirement Board	60 F3875	-990.85
Budget Clearing Account (Suspense), Tennessee Valley Authority	64 F3875	34,025.37
Budget Clearing Account (Suspense), Environmental Protection Agency	68 F3875	-8,798,225.84
Budget Clearing Account (Suspense), Agency For International Development	72 F3875	-484,467.95
Budget Clearing Account (Suspense), National Aeronautics And Space Administration	80 F3875	-289,910.46
Budget Clearing Account (Suspense), Export-Import Bank Of The United States	83 F3875	11,424,931.86
Budget Clearing Account (Suspense), Energy	89 F3875	-13,652,226.73
Budget Clearing Account (Suspense), Education	91 F3875	2,405,818.90
Budget Clearing Account (Suspense), Corps Of Engineers	96 F3875	287,331.57
Budget Clearing Account (Suspense)	97 F3875	-65,663.50
Budget Clearing Account (Suspense), House Restaurant Fund	00 F3875.001	775,916.19
Budget Clearing Account (Suspense), Supreme Court	10 F3875.001	3,240.80
Budget Clearing Account (Suspense), White House Office	11 F3875.001	-298,840.43
Budget Clearing Account (Suspense), General Administration	13 F3875.001	4,315.29
Budget Clearing Account (Suspense), Office Of The Secretary	14 F3875.001	-1,454,168.98
Budget Clearing Account (Suspense), General Legal Activities	15 F3875.001	-19,705,757.88
Budget Clearing Account (Suspense), Navy	17 F3875.001	-10,248,455.73
Budget Clearing Account (Suspense), Office Of Finance	19 F3875.001	-6,500.42
Budget Clearing Account (Suspense), Office Of The Secretary	20 F3875.001	35,985.59
Budget Clearing Account (Suspense), Army	21 F3875.001	-396,993,940.33
Budget Clearing Account (Suspense), Washington, DC	24 F3875.001	7,065,444.21
Budget Clearing Account (Suspense), Smithsonian Institution	33 F3875.001	-13,046.64
Budget Clearing Account (Suspense), Air Force	57 F3875.001	1,954,744.34
Budget Clearing Account (Suspense), Office Of The Secretary	69 F3875.001	-25,900.80
Budget Clearing Account (Suspense)	70 F3875.001	-23,726.35
Budget Clearing Account (Suspense), Centers For Disease Control	75 F3875.001	-46,445,773.47
Budget Clearing Account (Suspense), Cash Control And Reconciliation Division	86 F3875.001	5,568,758.71
Budget Clearing Account (Suspense), Defense	97 F3875.001	39,675,466.05
Budget Clearing Account (Suspense), United States Courts	10 F3875.002	3,994,995.56
Budget Clearing Account (Suspense), Office Of Administration	11 F3875.002	6.00
Budget Clearing Account (Suspense), Office Of Inspector General	14 F3875.002	27,301.73
Budget Clearing Account (Suspense), Navy	17 F3875.002	4,148,022.52
Budget Clearing Account (Suspense), Army	21 F3875.002	-529,919,361.95
Budget Clearing Account (Suspense)	57 F3875.002	-5,389,839.11
Budget Clearing Account (Suspense), Offset Program, Defense	97 F3875.002	207,411.59
Budget Clearing Account (Suspense), Office Of Management And Budget	11 F3875.003	-64.98
Budget Clearing Account (Suspense), For Capps Only, Office Of Finance	19 F3875.003	-296,570.09
Budget Clearing Account (Suspense)	70 F3875.003	-294,705.00
Budget Clearing Account (Suspense), Centers For Disease Control	75 F3875.003	-9,560,085.08
Budget Clearing Account (Suspense), House Restaurant Fund	00 F3875.004	-66,950.01
Budget Clearing Account (Suspense), Bureau Of The Census	13 F3875.004	-263,758.81
Budget Clearing Account (Suspense), Office Of Justice Programs	15 F3875.004	9,701.32
Budget Clearing Account (Suspense), Navy (Special)	17 F3875.004	12,440,509.16
Budget Clearing Account (Suspense)	70 F3875.004	-157,071.15
Budget Clearing Account (Suspense), Federal Highway Administration	69 F3875.005	976.55
Budget Clearing Account (Suspense)	70 F3875.005	-81,403,087.62
Budget Clearing Account (Suspense), Centers For Medicare And Medicaid Services	75 F3875.005	36,517,320.22
Budget Clearing Account (Suspense), Bureau Of Reclamation	14 F3875.006	-230,853.09
Budget Clearing Account (Suspense), Justice Employee Data Service	15 F3875.006	519,228.30
Budget Clearing Account (Suspense), National Highway Traffic Safety Administration	69 F3875.006	-82.78
Budget Clearing Account (Suspense)	70 F3875.006	-5,745,506.34
Budget Clearing Account (Suspense), Centers For Disease Control	75 F3875.006	-72,430,135.46
Budget Clearing Account (Suspense), ATF, Department Of Justice	15 F3875.007	-1,590,249.36
Budget Clearing Account (Suspense), Federal Railroad Administration	69 F3875.007	250.96
Budget Clearing Account (Suspense)	70 F3875.007	-1,929,924.54
Budget Clearing Account (Suspense), Program Support Center (DPM)	75 F3875.007	3,793,922.83
Budget Clearing Account (Suspense), House Of Representatives, Sergeant At Arms	00 F3875.008	16,760.40
Budget Clearing Account (Suspense), Geological Survey	14 F3875.008	985.00
Budget Clearing Account (Suspense), Centers For Disease Control	75 F3875.008	2,460,052.65
Budget Clearing Account (Suspense), Office Of The Inspector General	12 F3875.009	-51.00
Budget Clearing Account (Suspense), Internal Revenue Service	20 F3875.009	-2,292,495.43
Budget Clearing Account (Suspense), Centers For Disease Control	75 F3875.009	140,020.92
Budget Clearing Account (Suspense), Soil Conservation Service	12 F3875.010	-307,114.93
Budget Clearing Account (Suspense), National Park Service	14 F3875.010	-22,733.75
Budget Clearing Account (Suspense), Federal Prison System	15 F3875.010	-2,522,447.41
Budget Clearing Account (Suspense), International Boundary And Water Commission, United States And Mexico	19 F3875.010	133,774.74
Budget Clearing Account (Suspense), Bureau Of Alcohol, Tobacco, And Firearms	20 F3875.010	-1.50
Budget Clearing Account (Suspense), Forest Service	12 F3875.011	-8,512,655.17
Budget Clearing Account (Suspense), Bureau Of Land Management	14 F3875.011	76,295.03
Budget Clearing Account (Suspense), Drug Enforcement Administration	15 F3875.011	46.86

Table A – Receipts By Source Categories

Classification	Receipt Symbol	Receipt Offset Against Outlays
Proprietary Receipts From the Public		
Budget Clearing Account (Suspense), Urban Mass Transportation Administration	69 F3875.011	-27,478.98
Budget Clearing Account (Suspense)	70 F3875.011	24,298,557.72
Budget Clearing Account (Suspense), International Trade Administration	13 F3875.012	-18,889.08
Budget Clearing Account (Suspense)	70 F3875.012	704.54
Budget Clearing Account (Suspense), Federal Aviation Administration	69 F3875.013	-18,362,976.28
Budget Clearing Account (Suspense), Agricultural Research Service	12 F3875.014	14,950.61
Budget Clearing Account (Suspense), National Oceanic And Atmospheric Administration	13 F3875.014	516,767.08
Budget Clearing Account (Suspense), Pipeline And Hazardous Materials Safety Administration	69 F3875.014	-973,863.59
Budget Clearing Account (Suspense), Cooperative State Research, Education, And Extension Service	12 F3875.015	-1,001.10
Budget Clearing Account (Suspense), Bureau Of Transportation Statistics	69 F3875.015	-452.86
Budget Clearing Account (Suspense), Animal And Plant Health Inspection Service	12 F3875.016	-326,301.60
Budget Clearing Account (Suspense), United States Fish And Wildlife Service	14 F3875.016	32,552.10
Budget Clearing Account (Suspense), Holocaust Memorial Council	95 F3875.016	-456,054.01
Budget Clearing Account (Suspense), Financial Management Service	20 F3875.017	-16,665,735.08
Budget Clearing Account (Suspense), Maritime Administration	69 F3875.017	-35,344.89
Budget Clearing Account (Suspense), National Agricultural Statistical Service	12 F3875.018	-7,538.13
Budget Clearing Account (Suspense), United States Marshals Service	15 F3875.018	1,957,360.77
Budget Clearing Account (Suspense), Financial Management Service	20 F3875.018	-909,954.02
Budget Clearing Account (Suspense), Council Of Economic Advisors	11 F3875.019	-36,390.19
Budget Clearing Account (Suspense)	70 F3875.019	-198,277.97
Budget Clearing Account (Suspense), National Security Council	11 F3875.020	4,310.64
Budget Clearing Account (Suspense), Farmers Home Administration	12 F3875.020	378,543.37
Budget Clearing Account (Suspense), Bureau Of Indian Affairs	14 F3875.020	1,173,119.02
Budget Clearing Account (Suspense)	70 F3875.020	-11,753.24
Budget Clearing Account (Suspense)	70 F3875.023	-83,417.95
Budget Clearing Account (Suspense), Federal Grain Inspection Service	12 F3875.024	-12,447.64
Budget Clearing Account (Suspense), Agricultural Marketing Service	12 F3875.025	-686,999.04
Budget Clearing Account (Suspense), Federal Motor Carrier Safety Administration	69 F3875.026	-54,126.96
Budget Clearing Account (Suspense), Foreign Agricultural Service	12 F3875.029	326,756.68
Budget Clearing Account (Suspense), Research And Innovative Technology Administration	69 F3875.030	-51,508.28
Budget Clearing Account (Suspense), Bangkok, Thailand	19 F3875.031	221,472.52
Budget Clearing Account (Suspense), Food And Nutrition Service	12 F3875.035	-2,367,849.08
Budget Clearing Account (Suspense), Food Safety And Inspection Service	12 F3875.037	-1,950.19
Budget Clearing Account (Suspense), Central Voucher Payment Center	12 F3875.040	-245,072.43
Budget Clearing Account (Suspense), Peace Corps	11 F3875.044	142,363.80
Budget Clearing Account (Suspense), Manila, Philippines	19 F3875.050	5,779.55
Budget Clearing Account (Suspense), Management Service Center	13 F3875.060	-30,746.91
Budget Clearing Account (Suspense), Riyadh, Saudi Arabia	19 F3875.060	1,285.06
Budget Clearing Account (Suspense), Charleston, SC	19 F3875.061	96,149.08
Budget Clearing Account (Suspense), Bangkok, Thailand	19 F3875.068	49,364.18
Budget Clearing Account (Suspense), Broadcasting Board Of Governors	95 F3875.068	-285,526.51
Budget Clearing Account (Suspense), Charleston, SC	19 F3875.069	-2,633,139.47
Budget Clearing Account (Suspense), District Of Columbia	95 F3875.070	-113.37
Budget Clearing Account (Suspense), FCAS	20 F3875.085	227,973.76
Budget Clearing Account (Suspense)	20 F3875.099	7,388.10
Unavailable Check Cancellations And Overpayments (Suspense), Architect Of The Capitol	01 F3880	4.00
Unavailable Check Cancellations And Overpayments (Suspense), Labor	16 F3880	2,911.74
Unavailable Check Cancellations And Overpayments (Suspense), Navy	17 F3880	-1,613,536.96
Unavailable Check Cancellations And Overpayments (Suspense), Postal Service	18 F3880	0.26
Unavailable Check Cancellations And Overpayments (Suspense), State	19 F3880	-102,825.00
Unavailable Check Cancellations And Overpayments (Suspense), Army	21 F3880	-14,735,105.96
Unavailable Check Cancellations And Overpayments (Suspense), Centers For Disease Control	28 F3880	-49,728.25
Unavailable Check Cancellations And Overpayments (Suspense), Veterans Administration	36 F3880	-8,127.00
Unavailable Check Cancellations And Overpayments (Suspense), Securities And Exchange Commission	50 F3880	598,824.21
Unavailable Check Cancellations And Overpayments (Suspense), Air Force	57 F3880	-179,453.46
Unavailable Check Cancellations And Overpayments (Suspense), Railroad Retirement Board	60 F3880	86.60
Unavailable Check Cancellations And Overpayments (Suspense), Environmental Protection Agency	68 F3880	-60.50
Unavailable Check Cancellations And Overpayments (Suspense), Agency For International Development	72 F3880	-4,547.58
Unavailable Check Cancellations And Overpayments (Suspense), Small Business Administration	73 F3880	-5.50
Unavailable Check Cancellations And Overpayments (Suspense), Export-Import Bank Of The United States	83 F3880	22.00
Unavailable Check Cancellations And Overpayments (Suspense), Corps Of Engineers	96 F3880	167,642.96
Unavailable Check Cancellations And Overpayments (Suspense), Secretary Of Defense	97 F3880	-4,250,538.76
Unavailable Check Cancellations And Overpayments (Suspense), White House Office	11 F3880.001	-99,547.03
Unavailable Check Cancellations And Overpayments (Suspense), Office Of Finance	19 F3880.001	-1,173.00
Unavailable Check Cancellations And Overpayments (Suspense), Smithsonian Institution	33 F3880.001	125.00
Unavailable Check Cancellations And Overpayments (Suspense), Department Of Veterans Affairs	36 F3880.001	1,295.00
Unavailable Check Cancellations And Overpayments (Suspense)	70 F3880.001	5.50
Unavailable Check Cancellations And Overpayments (Suspense), Centers For Disease Control	75 F3880.001	-2,278,616.28
Unavailable Check Cancellations And Overpayments (Suspense), Cash Control And Reconciliation Division	86 F3880.001	8,262.69
Unavailable Check Cancellations And Overpayments (Suspense), United States Courts	10 F3880.002	399.06
Unavailable Check Cancellations And Overpayments (Suspense), Federal Bureau Of Investigation	15 F3880.002	345,591.22
Unavailable Check Cancellations And Overpayments (Suspense), Department Of Veterans Affairs	36 F3880.002	-50,494.02
Unavailable Check Cancellations And Overpayments (Suspense), Centers For Disease Control	75 F3880.003	-800,740.98
Unavailable Check Cancellations And Overpayments (Suspense), House Of Representatives	00 F3880.004	1,777.72
Unavailable Check Cancellations And Overpayments (Suspense), Bureau Of The Census	13 F3880.004	11.00
Unavailable Check Cancellations And Overpayments (Suspense), National Institute Of Standards And Technology	13 F3880.006	5.50
Unavailable Check Cancellations And Overpayments (Suspense), National Highway Traffic Safety Administration	69 F3880.006	-30.00

Table A – Receipts By Source Categories

Classification	Receipt Symbol	Receipt Offset Against Outlays
Proprietary Receipts From the Public		
Receipt Clearing Accounts: Continued		
Unavailable Check Cancellations And Overpayments (Suspense)	70 F3880.006	-10,196.92
Unavailable Check Cancellations And Overpayments (Suspense), Centers For Disease Control	75 F3880.006	11.00
Unavailable Check Cancellations And Overpayments (Suspense), Federal Railroad Administration	69 F3880.007	-436.58
Unavailable Check Cancellations And Overpayments (Suspense)	70 F3880.007	-1,292.50
Unavailable Check Cancellations And Overpayments (Suspense), Internal Revenue Service	20 F3880.009	-35,889.45
Unavailable Check Cancellations And Overpayments (Suspense), Insurance Accounting Division	86 F3880.009	-124.93
Unavailable Check Cancellations And Overpayments (Suspense), Patent And Trademark Office	13 F3880.010	5.50
Unavailable Check Cancellations And Overpayments (Suspense), Bureau Of Land Management	14 F3880.011	-5.50
Unavailable Check Cancellations And Overpayments (Suspense)	70 F3880.011	609,733.30
Unavailable Check Cancellations And Overpayments (Suspense), Department Of Veterans Affairs	36 F3880.012	-1,133.00
Unavailable Check Cancellations And Overpayments (Suspense), Bureau Of Engraving And Printing	20 F3880.013	-27.50
Unavailable Check Cancellations And Overpayments (Suspense), Compensation Group, Office Of Personnel Management	24 F3880.013	-99.00
Unavailable Check Cancellations And Overpayments (Suspense), Federal Aviation Administration	69 F3880.013	-9,665,933.55
Unavailable Check Cancellations And Overpayments (Suspense), National Oceanic And Atmospheric Administration	13 F3880.014	-120,887.24
Unavailable Check Cancellations And Overpayments (Suspense) Bureau Of Transportation Statistics	69 F3880.015	6,099.53
Unavailable Check Cancellations And Overpayments (Suspense), National Transportation Safety Board	95 F3880.016	3,589.57
Unavailable Check Cancellations And Overpayments (Suspense), United States Marshals Service	15 F3880.018	1,223.62
Unavailable Check Cancellations And Overpayments (Suspense), Financial Management Service	20 F3880.018	12,150.85
Unavailable Check Cancellations And Overpayments (Suspense), Farmers Home Administration	12 F3880.020	-137,048.98
Unavailable Check Cancellations And Overpayments (Suspense), BIA, Trust Activities	14 F3880.021	-2,981.64
Unavailable Check Cancellations And Overpayments (Suspense), Paris, France	19 F3880.021	127,248.13
Unavailable Check Cancellations And Overpayments (Suspense), Office Of Motor Carriers	69 F3880.026	6,420.45
Unavailable Check Cancellations And Overpayments (Suspense), Bangkok, Thailand	19 F3880.031	-74,734.16
Unavailable Check Cancellations And Overpayments (Suspense), Central Voucher Payment Center	12 F3880.040	-5.50
Unavailable Check Cancellations And Overpayments (Suspense), Peace Corps	11 F3880.044	659.96
Unavailable Check Cancellations And Overpayments (Suspense), Riyadh, Saudi Arabia	19 F3880.060	105,636.00
Unavailable Check Cancellations And Overpayments (Suspense), Charleston, SC	19 F3880.061	-665,762.60
Unavailable Check Cancellations And Overpayments (Suspense), Bangkok, Thailand	19 F3880.068	207,272.22
Unavailable Check Cancellations And Overpayments (Suspense), Charleston, SC	19 F3880.069	1,097,508.76
Unavailable Check Cancellations And Overpayments (Suspense), Department Of Veterans Affairs	36 F3880.090	9,850.84
Debt Collection Collections	20 F3887.001	6,201,940.20
Foreign Currency Payments (Kansas City Financial Center)	20 F3891	149,676.45
Total, Receipt Clearing Accounts		-1,104,118,185.41
Total, Proprietary Receipts From The Public		126,550,776,560.89
Intrabudgetary Receipts Deducted By Agency		
Intrafund Transactions		
Interest From The Federal Financing Bank:		
Interest On Loans To Federal Financing Bank, Treasury	1418	736,538,396.42
Total, Interest From The Federal Financing Bank		736,538,396.42
Interest On Government Capital In Enterprises:		
Interest On Loans To The Helium Fund, Department Of Interior	1337	150,000,000.00
Interest On Loans From The Presidio Trust	1338	2,999,086.70
Interest On Loans To The Secretary Of Transportation, Ocean Freight Differential, Maritime Administration	1350	4,877,156.20
Interest On Loans And Federal Investment, Bonneville Power Administration Fund, Department Of Energy	1351	326,321,627.86
Interest On Loans To The Secretary Of Transportation, Railroad Rehabilitation And Improvement Fund, Federal Railroad Administration	1361	973,173.86
Interest On Loans For College Housing And Academic Facilities Loans, Department Of Education	1363	6,084,540.26
Interest On Loans To Commodity Credit Corporation	1401	719,422,527.23
Interest On Investment, Economic Development Revolving Fund	1410	480,881.18
Interest On Loans To Tennessee Valley Authority	1417	6,416,230.58
Interest On Loans, Higher Education Facilities Loan Fund	1422	624,685.66
Interest On Investments, Colorado River Projects	1424	5,391,047.68
Interest On Advances To Colorado River Dam Fund, Boulder Canyon Project	1427	11,212,068.05
Interest On Advances To Small Business Administration	1428	7,153,911.29
Interest On Loans To National Flood Insurance Fund, Federal Emergency Management Agency	1433	717,480,947.91
Total, Interest On Government Capital In Enterprises		1,959,437,884.46
Interest Received By Retirement And Health Benefits Funds:		
Earnings On Investments, DC Federal Pension Fund	5511.002	191,083,112.72
Total, Interest Received By Retirement And Health Benefits Funds		191,083,112.72

Table A – Receipts By Source Categories

Classification	Receipt Symbol	Receipt Offset Against Outlays
Intrabudgetary Receipts Deducted By Agency		
General Fund Payments To Retirement And Health Benefits Funds		
Employees Health Benefits Fund:		
Postal Service Contributions For Benefits For Current Retirees, Office Of Personnel Management	5391.003	5,400,000,000.00
Total, Employees Health Benefits Fund		5,400,000,000.00
DOD Retiree Health Care Fund:		
Earnings On Investments, DOD Medicare-Eligible Retiree Health Care Fund	5472.002	4,045,178,588.86
Federal Contributions, DOD Medicare-Eligible Retiree Health Care Fund	5472.003	15,608,000,000.00
Total, DOD Retiree Health Care Fund		19,653,178,588.86
Miscellaneous Federal Retirement Funds:		
Federal Contribution, DC Federal Pension Fund	5511.001	345,400,000.00
Total, Miscellaneous Federal Retirement Funds		345,400,000.00
Payments To Railroad Retirement:		
Receipts From Federal Old-Age And Survivors Insurance (OASI) Trust Fund, Social Security Equivalent Benefit Account, Railroad Retirement Board	8010.031	3,574,558,000.00
Receipts From Disability Insurance (DI) Trust Fund, Social Security Equivalent Benefit Account, Railroad Retirement Board	8010.032	445,219,000.00
Payment From The National Railroad Retirement Investment Trust, Rail Industry Pension Fund, Railroad Retirement Board	8011.016	1,391,000,000.00
Total, Payments To Railroad Retirement		5,410,777,000.00
Other:		
Recoveries From Federal Agencies For Settlement Of Claims For Contract Disputes	3101	145,200,549.00
Recoveries From Federal Agencies Resulting From Reductions In The Civilian Salaries Of Military Retirees, Federal Funds	3102.001	67.00
Recoveries From Federal Agencies Resulting From Reductions In The Civilian Salaries Of Military Retirees, Trust Funds	3102.003	317.90
Reimbursements From Federal Agencies For Payments Made As A Result Of Discriminatory Conduct	3112	21,476,176.14
Collections Of Receivables From Cancelled Accounts	3200	223,440,600.08
Collections Of Receivables From Cancelled Accounts, National Endowment For The Arts	3200.001	42,698.97
Earnings On Investments, Office Of Surface Mining Reclamation And Enforcement	5015.009	105,818,192.04
Earnings On Investments, Federal Aid To 1975 Wildlife Restoration Fund	5029.002	18,000,896.36
Earnings On Investments, Assets Forfeiture Fund	5042.002	111,439,511.81
Earnings On Investments, United States Trustee System Fund	5073.002	10,283,535.05
Earnings On Investments, Oliver Wendell Holmes Devise Fund	5075.002	3,337.11
Advances And Reimbursements, Judiciary Automation Fund	5114.003	198,952,381.00
Payment From The General Fund, Cooperative Endangered Species Conservation Fund	5143	46,199,560.00
Interest On Investments, Panama Canal Commission Compensation Fund	5155.002	5,799,380.57
Interest On Principal, Utah Reclamation Mitigation And Conservation Account	5174.002	9,875,178.40
Contributions From Project Beneficiaries (WAPA), Utah Reclamation Mitigation And Conservation Account	5174.005	6,633,000.00
Earnings On Investments, Copyright Office	5175.002	54,773,810.76
Earnings On Federal Securities, Universal Service Fund, FCC	5183.002	248,407,878.95
Earnings On Investments, Natural Resource Damage Assessment And Restoration Fund, U.S. Fish And Wildlife Service, Interior	5198.002	11,663,186.73
Federal Payment To The Native American Institutions Endowment Fund	5205.001	40,687.38
Earnings On Investments, Native American Institutions Endowment Fund	5205.002	3,160,964.58
Earnings On Investments, Nuclear Waste Disposal Fund, Department Of Energy	5227.002	795,121,866.15
Earnings On Investment, Department Of Energy	5231.002	196,052,707.78
General Fund Payment - Defense, Department Of Energy	5231.004	452,000,000.00
Earnings On Investment, Southern Nevada Public Land Management	5232.002	111,414,425.91
Earnings On Investments, Operation And Maintenance, Indian Irrigation Systems	5240.002	1,532,803.67
Earnings On Investment, Tribal Special Fund, Office Of The Special Trustee For American Indians	5265.002	3,170,188.46
Payments From Compensation And Pension, Medical CRE Collections Fund, Department Of Veterans Affairs	5287.008	1,903,740.10
Interest On Investments, Environmental Improvement And Restoration Fund, National Oceanic And Atmospheric Administration	5362.002	8,649,695.90
Vietnam Debt Repayment Fund, Vietnam Education Foundation	5365.001	6,357,767.80
Receipts, Acquisition Workforce Training Fund, General Services Administration	5381.001	9,622,129.57
Earnings On Investments, Postal Service Contributions For Retiree Health, Office Of Personnel Management	5391.002	32,725,065.79
Transfer From Postal Service Fund 2006 Escrow Amounts, Retiree Health Benefits Fund, Office Of Personnel Management	5391.005	2,958,400,000.00
Interest On Investments, Environmental Dispute Resolution Fund	5415.002	47,760.65
Interest Earned, Environmental Improvement And Restoration Fund, Minerals Management Service	5425.002	37,656,648.80
Underpayment And Fraud Collection, Internal Revenue Service	5433.001	13,198,576.83
Earnings On Investments, Lincoln County Land Act, Bureau Of Land Management	5469.002	2,205,043.78
Earnings On Investments, San Gabriel Basin Restoration Fund	5483.002	743,242.32
Employing Agency Contributions, Foreign Service National Defined Contributions Retirement Fund, State	5497.001	507,636.82
Earnings On Investments, Senate Preservation Fund, Library Of Congress	5509.002	25,693.08
Earnings On Investments, Pajarito Plateau Homesteaders Compensation Fund	5520.002	216,264.89
Earnings On Investments, Power Revenues, Indian Irrigation Projects	5648.002	2,266,334.12
Earnings On Investments, Treasury Forfeiture Fund	5697.002	37,470,565.58
Receipts From Civil Service Retirement And Disability Fund, Suspense	8186.005	812,660.43

Table A – Receipts By Source Categories

Classification	Receipt Symbol	Receipt Offset Against Outlays
Intrabudgetary Receipts Deducted By Agency		
General Fund Payments To Retirement And Health Benefits Funds: Continued		
Other: Continued		
Total, Other		5,893,339,728.26
General Fund Payments To Retirement And Health Benefits Funds		
Clearing Accounts:		
Undistributed Intragovernmental Payments, Library Of Congress...	03 F3885	532,939.48
Undistributed Intergovernmental Payments, Congressional Budget Office...	08 F3885	2,683.32
Undistributed Intragovernmental Payments, Navy...	17 F3885	1,156,721.23
Undistributed Intragovernmental Payments, Army...	21 F3885	3,904,962.67
Undistributed Intragovernmental Payments, Department Of Veterans Affairs	36 F3885	-801,124.42
Undistributed Intragovernmental Payments, General Services Administration..	47 F3885	-831,380.83
Undistributed Intragovernmental Payments, Air Force	57 F3885	9,261,978.40
Undistributed Intragovernmental Payments, Environmental Protection Agency	68 F3885	6,633.45
Undistributed Intragovernmental Payments, Agency For International Development	72 F3885	49,966,355.51
Undistributed Intragovernmental Payments, National Aeronautics And Space Administration....................	80 F3885	-857,768.79
Undistributed Intragovernmental Payments, Department Of Energy	89 F3885	-16,237,077.02
Undistributed Intragovernmental Payments, Department Of Education	91 F3885	1,399,896.65
Undistributed Intragovernmental Payments, Corps Of Engineers...	96 F3885	333,285.01
Undistributed Intragovernmental Payments, Defense	97 F3885	-7,253,859.96
Undistributed Intragovernmental Payments, Office Of The Secretary	14 F3885.001	-340,357.79
Undistributed Intragovernmental Payments, Legal Activities	15 F3885.001	675,931,383.67
Undistributed Intragovernmental Payments, Departmental Management, Department Of Labor	16 F3885.001	268,947.92
Undistributed Intragovernmental Payments, Office Of Finance, State..	19 F3885.001	1,936,345.23
Undistributed Intragovernmental Payments, Treasury...	20 F3885.001	308,263.93
Undistributed Intergovernmental Payments, Office Of The Secretary	69 F3885.001	5,823,490.85
Undistributed Intergovernmental Payments	70 F3885.001	-813,970.24
Undistributed Intergovernmental Payments, Office Of The Secretary, Department Of Housing and Urban Development..	86 F3885.001	4,367,820.84
Undistributed Intragovernmental Payments, For Capps Only, Office Of Finance, State	19 F3885.003	-2,931,782.42
Undistributed Intragovernmental Payments	70 F3885.003	-1,379,992.21
Undistributed Intragovernmental Payments, Health Resources And Services Administration	75 F3885.003	-35,062,040.52
Undistributed Intragovernmental Payments, Office Of Justice Programs, Department Of Justice................	15 F3885.004	390,147.44
Undistributed Intragovernmental Payments, Federal Highway Administration...	69 F3885.005	-10,022,817.17
Undistributed Intragovernmental Payments	70 F3885.005	879,125.32
Undistributed Intragovernmental Payments, Farm Service Agency..	12 F3885.006	39,975.00
Undistributed Intragovernmental Payments, Bureau Of Reclamation...	14 F3885.006	0.30
Undistributed Intragovernmental Payments, National Highway Traffic Safety Administration.....................	69 F3885.006	1,525,676.39
Undistributed Intragovernmental Payments	70 F3885.006	8,925,956.86
Undistributed Intragovernmental Payments, National Technical Information Service, Department Of Commerce.......................................	13 F3885.007	-7,330,007.45
Undistributed Intragovernmental Payments, Navy (OPAC-Difference)..	17 F3885.007	3,789,508.50
Undistributed Intragovernmental Payments, Army (OPAC-Difference)..	21 F3885.007	2,207,126.96
Undistributed Intragovernmental Payments, Air Force (OPAC-Difference)...	57 F3885.007	-14,787,574.12
Undistributed Intergovernmental Payments, Federal Railroad Administration	69 F3885.007	-23,777.66
Undistributed Intragovernmental Payments, Defense (OPAC-Difference)...	97 F3885.007	16,131,530.16
Undistributed Intragovernmental Payments, Office Of Risk Management, Farm Service Agency................	12 F3885.008	-4,448.57
Undistributed Intragovernmental Payments, U.S. Geological Survey..	14 F3885.008	-646,656.94
Undistributed Intragovernmental Payments, Office Of Inspector General...	20 F3885.008	-255,049.00
Undistributed Intragovernmental Payments	70 F3885.008	-414,863.74
Undistributed Intragovernmental Payments, National Institutes Of Health...	75 F3885.008	97,398,309.65
Undistributed Intragovernmental Payments, Office Of The Inspector General	12 F3885.009	-76,662.61
Undistributed Intergovernmental Payments, Internal Revenue Service	20 F3885.009	-6,143,968.05
Undistributed Intragovernmental Payments, Centers For Disease Control...	75 F3885.009	-362,414.47
Undistributed Intragovernmental Payments, Natural Resources Conservation Service..............................	12 F3885.010	-722,060.02
Undistributed Intragovernmental Payments, Patent And Trademark Office, Department Of Commerce	13 F3885.010	-4,497,599.87
Undistributed Intragovernmental Payments, National Park Service	14 F3885.010	-1,413,715.46
Undistributed Intragovernmental Payments	70 F3885.010	-16,693.00
Undistributed Intragovernmental Payments, Forest Service, Department Of Agriculture...........................	12 F3885.011	46,186,328.90
Undistributed Intragovernmental Payments, Bureau Of Land Management..	14 F3885.011	41,439,460.35
Undistributed Intragovernmental Payments, Drug Enforcement Administration	15 F3885.011	-1,053.03
Undistributed Intergovernmental Payments, Internal Revenue Service	20 F3885.011	66,973,632.20
Undistributed Intragovernmental Payments, Federal Transit Administration...	69 F3885.011	5,727,582.26
Undistributed Intragovernmental Payments	70 F3885.011	-32,422.25
Undistributed Intergovernmental Payments, Federal Aviation Administration...	69 F3885.013	-6,118,017.54
Undistributed Intragovernmental Payments, Agricultural Research Service	12 F3885.014	67,134.06
Undistributed Intergovernmental Payments, National Oceanic Atmospheric Administration, Department Of Commerce...........	13 F3885.014	3,531,241.01
Undistributed Intergovernmental Payments, Pipeline And Hazardous Materials Safety Administration.......	69 F3885.014	8,849,866.53
Undistributed Intergovernmental Payments, Cooperative State Research, Education And Extension Service	12 F3885.015	-523,792.59
Undistributed Intergovernmental Payments, Bureau Of Transportation Statistics	69 F3885.015	-1,546.10
Undistributed Intragovernmental Payments, Animal And Plant Health Inspection Service	12 F3885.016	7,873,170.58
Undistributed Intragovernmental Payments, United States Fish And Wildlife Service.................................	14 F3885.016	-188.42
Undistributed Intragovernmental Payments, Office Of Administration, Executive Office Of The President...	11 F3885.017	2,321,197.87
Undistributed Intragovernmental Payments, Economic Research Service	12 F3885.017	-27,074.30

Table A – Receipts By Source Categories

Classification	Receipt Symbol	Receipt Offset Against Outlays
Intrabudgetary Receipts Deducted By Agency		
Undistributed Intragovernmental Payments, Maritime Administration	69 F3885.017	18,133,622.44
Undistributed Intragovernmental Payments, National Agricultural Statistics Service	12 F3885.018	-246,076.08
Undistributed Intragovernmental Payments	70 F3885.019	-334,346.56
Undistributed Intragovernmental Payments, Rural Housing Service	12 F3885.020	1,721,846.83
Undistributed Intragovernmental Payments, Bureau Of Indian Affairs	14 F3885.020	-363,834.03
Undistributed Intragovernmental Payments	70 F3885.020	10,462.00
Undistributed Intragovernmental Payments	70 F3885.023	-5,394,247.06
Undistributed Intragovernmental Payments, Grain Inspection, Packers And Stockyards Administration	12 F3885.024	-4,703.71
Undistributed Intragovernmental Payments, Agricultural Marketing Service	12 F3885.025	-1,050,914.76
Undistributed Intragovernmental Payments, Office Of Special Trustee For American Indians	14 F3885.025	-220,588.38
Undistributed Intergovernmental Payments, Office Of Motor Carriers	69 F3885.026	2,001,360.84
Undistributed Intragovernmental Payments, Foreign Agricultural Service	12 F3885.029	-181,332.88
Undistributed Intergovernmental Payments, Office Of The Secretary	69 F3885.030	56,677.10
Undistributed Intragovernmental Payments, Food And Nutrition Service	12 F3885.035	-900,188.60
Undistributed Intragovernmental Payments, Food Safety And Inspection Service	12 F3885.037	-1,684,163.73
Undistributed Intragovernmental Payments, National Finance Center, Department Of Agriculture	12 F3885.040	22,696,843.05
Undistributed Intragovernmental Payments, Millennium Challenge Corporation	95 F3885.077	1,401,242.57
Total, Clearing Accounts		985,168,580.98
Total, Intrafund Transactions		40,574,923,291.70
Interfund Transactions		
Contributions To Insurance Programs:		
Federal Contributions, Federal Supplementary Medical Insurance Trust Fund	8004.001	137,821,877,211.35
Miscellaneous Federal Payments, Federal Supplementary Medical Insurance Trust Fund	8004.006	766,765.47
Federal Contributions, Transitional Assistance Account, Federal Supplementary Medical Insurance	8004.039	9,814,846.92
Federal Contributions For Administrative Costs, Medicare Prescription Drug Account, FSMI	8004.046	1,016,785,585.26
Federal Contributions For Benefits, Medicare Prescription Drug Account, FSMI	8004.047	40,332,585,206.66
Payments From The General Fund, Federal Hospital Insurance Trust Fund	8005.006	643,625,281.47
Federal Hospital Trust Fund, Transfer From General Fund (OASI) Taxes	8005.035	10,593,000,000.00
Payments From The General Fund For Health Care Fraud And Abuse Control Account, Fraud And Abuse Control Program, Federal Hospital Insurance Trust Fund	8005.044	118,218,000.00
Miscellaneous Federal Payments, Federal Old-Age And Survivors Insurance Trust Fund	8006.006	17,845,258,402.78
Federal Payments For Pension Reform Administrative Expenses, Federal Old-Age And Survivors Insurance Trust Fund	8006.043	1,124,891.00
Miscellaneous Federal Payments, Federal Disability Insurance Trust Fund	8007.006	1,478,986,254.33
Income Tax Credits, Social Security Equivalent Benefit Account, Railroad Retirement Board	8010.012	131,000,000.00
Federal Payments To Railroad Retirement Trust Funds, Railroad Retirement Account	8011.007	329,000,000.00
Federal Employees Compensation Account Deposits By Federal Agencies, Unemployment Trust Fund	8042.010	756,025,077.00
Federal Contribution, Department Of Defense Military Retirement Fund	8097.003	26,048,000,000.00
Employing Agency Contributions, Department Of Defense, Education Benefits Fund	8098.001	540,495,108.19
Federal Payment To The Judicial Survivors Annuities Fund	8110.004	800,000.00
Federal Payment To Judicial Officers Retirement Fund	8122.004	54,000,000.00
Federal Payment To Claims Court, Judges Retirement Fund	8124.001	3,500,000.00
Payments From General And Special Funds, National Service Life Insurance Fund	8132.003	598,794.43
Federal Contribution, Civil Service Retirement And Disability Fund	8135.005	30,995,847,084.00
Receipts Transferred From Foreign Service Retirement And Disability Fund, Civil Service Retirement And Disability Fund	8135.006	113,065.25
Employing Agency Payments For Salaries Of Reemployed Annuitants, (Suspense) Civil Service Retirement And Disability	8135.007	37,940,273.21
Employing Agency Contributions, Defense	8165.001	75,266,679.61
Federal Contribution, Foreign Service Retirement And Disability Fund	8186.008	241,400,000.00
Federal Payments To D.C. Judicial Retirement And Survivors Annuity Fund	8212.003	7,380,000.00
Employing Agency Contributions, Voluntary Separation Incentive Fund	8335.001	67,100,000.00
Foreign Service National Separation Liability Trust Fund, Library Of Congress	8339.001	154,863.78
Foreign Service National Separation Liability Trust Fund, State	8340.001	10,641,118.00
Foreign National Employee Separation Liability Fund, Agency For International Development	8342.001	3,755,278.97
Total, Contributions To Insurance Programs		269,165,059,787.68
Miscellaneous Payments:		
Interest Payments On Advances To The Black Lung Disability Trust Fund	1495	717,213,681.18
Interest On Advances To The Railroad Retirement Account	1497	178,688,183.22
Charges For Services To Trust Funds	2414	41,453.06
Charges For Administrative Expenses Of Social Security Act, As Amended	2416	829,224,726.66
Transfer From Civil Service Fund For Excess Postal Pension, Retiree Health Benefits, Office Of Personnel Management	5391.004	17,100,000,000.00
Federal Hospital Insurance Trust Fund Transfers From The General Fund (Criminal Fines)	8005.046	201,437,182.92
Federal Hospital Insurance Trust Fund Transfers From The General Fund (Civil Monetary Penalties)	8005.047	12,618,811.94
Federal Funds Payments, Tribal Trust Fund, Office Of The Special Trustee For American Indians	8030.001	7,500,000.00
Advances From Other Federal Agencies, Federal Highway Administration	8054.002	129,000.00
General Fund Contributions, Appalachian Regional Commission	8090.001	3,477,550.00
Payments From Wool Research, Development And Promotion Trust Fund	8100.001	2,250,000.00
Receipts, Radiation Exposure Compensation Trust Fund	8116.001	73,650,000.00
Contributions, Department Of Veterans Affairs	8133.002	127,753.00

Table A – Receipts By Source Categories

Classification	Receipt Symbol	Receipt Offset Against Outlays
Intrabudgetary Receipts Deducted By Agency		
Interfund Transactions: Continued		
Miscellaneous Payments: Continued		
Interfund Transactions, Hazardous Substance Superfund	8145.005	1,040,370,865.00
Payment From The General Fund, Open World Leadership Center Trust Fund	8148.003	13,860,000.00
General Fund Payment, Lower Brule Sioux Tribe Terrestrial Wildlife Habitat Restoration Fund	8207.001	1,300,000.00
General Fund Payments, Cheyenne River Sioux Tribe Terrestrial Wildlife Habitat Restoration Trust Fund	8209.001	3,700,000.00
Payment From The General Fund, South Dakota Terrestrial Wildlife Habitat Restoration Trust Fund	8217.001	10,000,000.00
Payments From The General Fund, Corporation For National And Community Service	8267.003	117,720,000.00
Payment To The John C. Stennis Center For Public Service Training And Development	8275.001	1,089,170.40
General Fund Payments, Morris K. Udall Scholarship And Excellence In National Environmental Policy Trust Fund	8615.001	1,983,880.00
Profits From Sale Of Ships, Stores, Navy	8723.001	14,907,139.83
Payments From Federal Funds, Center For Middle Eastern-Western Dialogue Trust Fund, Department Of State	8813.001	-12,206.69
Total, Miscellaneous Payments		20,331,277,190.52
Total, Interfund Transactions		289,496,336,978.20
Total, Intrabudgetary Receipts Deducted By Agency		330,071,260,269.90
Undistributed Off-Setting Receipts		
Employer Share, Employee Retirement:		
Non-DOD Employing Agency Contributions, DOD Medicare-Eligible Retiree Health Care Fund	5472.001	316,812,000.00
Department Of Defense Contributions, DOD Retiree Health Care Fund	5472.005	11,230,630,000.00
Transfers From General Fund Of Amounts Equal To Federal Employer Contributions For FICA Taxes, Federal Hospital Insurance Trust Fund	8005.012	2,826,000,000.00
Postal Service Employer Contributions, Federal Hospital Insurance Trust Fund	8005.013	712,000,000.00
Transfers From General Fund Of Amounts Equal To Federal Employer Contributions For FICA Taxes, Federal Old-Age And Survivors Insurance Trust Fund	8006.012	10,514,000,000.00
Transfers From General Fund Of Amounts Equal To Federal Employer Contributions For FICA Taxes, Federal Disability Insurance Trust	8007.012	1,785,000,000.00
Employing Agency Contributions, Department Of Defense Military Retirement Fund	8097.001	14,364,764,154.87
Federal Contributions (Concurrent Receipt Accruals), Military Retirement Fund	8097.004	2,452,000,000.00
Employing Agency Contributions, Suspense, Civil Service Retirement And Disability Fund	8135.002	14,479,653,124.64
Employer's Contributions From Off-Budget Federal Agencies, Civil Service Retirement And Disability Fund	8135.022	2,882,997,289.00
Employing Agency Contributions, Foreign Service Retirement And Disability Fund, Suspense	8186.004	208,282,058.45
Earnings On Investments, United States Court Of Appeals For Veterans Claims	8290.002	601,126.66
Employing Agency Contributions, United States Court Of Appeals For Veterans Claims	8290.003	1,697,595.20
Total, Employer Share, Employee Retirement		61,774,437,348.82
Interest Received By Trust Funds:		
Earnings On Investments, Federal Supplementary Medical Insurance Trust Fund	8004.002	1,971,865,943.81
Interest Paid To The Federal Hospital Insurance Trust Fund, Federal Supplementary Medical Insurance Trust Fund	8004.023	-2,290,702.00
Interest, Medicare Prescription Drug Account, FSMI	8004.037	16,406,451.58
Earnings On Investments, Federal Hospital Insurance Trust Fund	8005.002	16,109,401,131.58
Interest Payments By Railroad Retirement Board, Federal Hospital Insurance Trust Fund	8005.005	28,636,000.00
Interest Received From Federal Supplementary Medical Insurance Trust Fund, Federal Hospital Insurance Trust Fund	8005.023	2,290,702.00
Earnings On Investments, Federal Old-Age And Survivors Insurance Trust Fund	8006.002	95,068,711,331.72
Earnings On Investments, Federal Disability Insurance Trust Fund	8007.002	10,933,802,343.88
Earnings On Investments, Social Security Equivalent Benefit Account, Railroad Retirement Board	8010.001	29,040,564.79
Interest Transferred To Federal Hospital Insurance Trust Fund, Social Security Equivalent Benefit Account, Railroad Retirement Board	8010.018	-28,636,000.00
Earning On Investments, Railroad Retirement Account	8011.001	18,777,496.76
Earnings On Investments, Inspection And Grading Of Farm Products	8015.002	1,849,853.32
Interest On Bequest Of Gertrude M. Hubbard, Library Of Congress	8022.002	774.25
Earnings On Investments, Japan-United States Friendship Commission Trust Fund	8025.002	2,132,228.30
Earnings On Investment, Tribal Trust Fund, Office Of The Special Trustee For American Indians	8030.002	3,514,824.61
Earnings On Investment, Library Of Congress Trust Fund	8031.002	434,221.51
Earnings On Investments, Library Of Congress Trust Fund	8032.002	2,626,984.33
Earnings On Investments, Land Between The Lakes Trust Fund, Forest Service	8039.002	270,118.02
Interest On U.S. Securities, National Endowment For The Arts	8040.002	103,813.92
Earnings On Investments, Unemployment Trust Fund	8042.002	3,202,870,288.99
Earnings On Investments, Preservation, Birthplace Of Abraham Lincoln	8052.002	3,442.50
Earnings On Investments, Bequest Of Major General Fred C. Ainsworth To Walter Reed General Hospital	8063.002	536.25
Interest On Us Securities, Institute Of Museum And Library Services	8080.002	35,962.79
Earnings On Investments, Department Of Defense Military Retirement Fund	8097.002	10,621,369,524.02
Earnings On Investments, Department Of Defense Education Benefits Fund	8098.002	60,522,696.73
Earnings On Investments, Airport And Airway Trust Fund	8103.002	471,647,864.49
Earnings On Investments, Judicial Survivors Annuities Fund	8110.002	23,137,083.76
Earnings On Investments, Tax Court Judges Survivors Annuity Fund	8115.002	584,078.45
Earnings On Investments In Federal Securities, National Railroad Retirement Investment Trust	8118.002	51,972,528.16
Interest And Profits On Investments, Judicial Officers Annuities Fund	8122.002	8,813,209.06
Interest On Investments, Claims Court Judges Retirement Fund	8124.002	525,024.63
Earnings On Investments, National Archives Gift Fund	8127.002	130,724.13

Table A – Receipts By Source Categories

Classification	Receipt Symbol	Receipt Offset Against Outlays
Undistributed Off-Setting Receipts		
Interest Received By Trust Funds: Continued		
Earnings On Investments, Relief And Rehabilitation, Longshoreman's And Harbor Workers' Compensation Act, As Amended, Department Of Labor	8130.002	2,469,908.34
Earnings On Investments, National Service Life Insurance Fund	8132.002	591,173,536.49
Earnings On Investments, Relief And Rehabilitation, Workmen's Compensation Act, Within The District Of Columbia, Department Of Labor	8134.002	251,790.62
Earnings On Investments, Civil Service Retirement And Disability Fund	8135.004	36,606,306,804.76
Interest Received By The Trust Fund From Federal Financing Bank Obligations, Civil Service Retirement Disability Fund	8135.025	651,238,581.25
Earnings On Investments, Hazardous Substance Superfund	8145.002	138,299,821.02
Earnings On Investments, Aquatic Resources Trust Fund	8147.003	73,512,854.94
Earnings On Investments, Russian Leadership Center Trust Fund	8148.002	771,764.02
Premium And Other Receipts, United States Government Life Insurance Fund	8150.001	3,332.70
Earnings On Investments, United States Government Life Insurance Fund	8150.002	2,175,274.25
Earnings On Investments, Leaking Underground Storage Tank Trust Fund	8153.002	127,561,334.74
Earnings On Investments, National Security Education Trust Fund	8168.002	255,649.46
Earnings On Investments, Vaccine Injury Compensation Trust Fund	8175.002	108,664,186.79
Earnings On Investments, General Post Fund, National Homes	8180.002	2,754,019.49
Earnings On Investments Oil Spill Liability Trust Fund	8185.002	29,777,503.03
Earnings On Investments, Foreign Service Retirement And Disability Fund	8186.002	771,425,018.84
Interest On Investments, Christopher Columbus Fellowship Foundation	8187.002	40,853.98
Earnings On Investments, Lower Brule Sioux Tribe Terrestrial Wildlife Habitat Restoration Trust Fund	8207.002	500,906.49
Earnings On Investments, Cheyenne River Sioux Tribe Terrestrial Wildlife Habitat Restoration Trust Fund	8209.002	1,425,112.18
Interest On Investments	8212.002	6,310,712.35
Earnings On Investments, South Dakota Terrestrial Wildlife Habitat Restoration Trust Fund	8217.002	3,730,976.66
Earnings On Investments, Gifts And Bequests For Disaster Relief, Departmental Management, Department Of Homeland Security	8244.002	1,568,779.41
Earnings On Investments, National Institutes Of Health Unconditional Gift Fund	8248.002	1,392,304.80
Earnings On Investments, National Institutes Of Health Conditional Gift Fund	8253.002	-115,715.65
Earnings On Investments, Public Health Service Conditional Gift Fund	8254.002	87,815.00
Interest On Investments, Corporation For National Community Service	8267.002	19,278,660.05
Interest And Earnings On Investments, Israeli Arab Scholarship Program	8271.002	134,664.79
Interest On Investments, John C. Stennis Center For Public Service Training And Development	8275.002	523,955.87
Earnings On Investments, Eisenhower Exchange Fellowship Program Trust Fund	8276.002	363,698.33
Interest On Investments, The Barry Goldwater Scholarship And Excellence In Education Fund	8281.002	3,745,310.76
Earnings On Investments, James Madison Memorial Fellowship Trust Fund	8282.002	2,236,696.22
Earnings On Investment, Botanic Gardens	8292.002	52,160.25
Earnings On Investments, Harry S. Truman Scholarship Foundation	8296.002	2,831,547.16
Interest On Investments, U.S. Capitol Preservation Commission	8300.002	526,019.05
Earnings On Investments, Voluntary Separation Incentive Fund	8335.002	18,775,350.15
Earnings On Investments, Host Nation Support For U.S. Relocation Activities	8337.002	981,188.68
Earnings On Investments, Armed Forces Retirement Home	8522.002	7,469,531.19
Earnings On Investments, General Gift Fund, USCG, Department Of Homeland Security	8533.002	60,815.57
Earnings On Investments, Gifts And Bequests, Office Of The Secretary	8548.002	120.00
Interest On Investments, Endeavor Teacher Fellowship Trust	8550.002	21,720.18
Interest On Investments, American Battle Monuments Commission	8569.002	202,248.00
Interest On Investments, Morris K. Udall Scholarship And Excellence In National Environmental Policy Trust Fund	8615.002	1,818,728.09
Earnings On Investments, Department Of The Navy General Gift Fund	8716.002	106,380.78
Earnings On Investments, United States Naval Academy General Gift Fund	8733.002	368,546.29
Earnings On Investments, Gifts And Bequests, Treasury	8790.002	43,848.75
Earnings On Investments, Center For Middle Eastern-Western Dialogue Trust Fund, Department Of State	8813.002	769,111.88
Earnings On Investments, Unconditional Gift Fund, General, Department Of State	8821.002	613.11
Earnings On Investments, Conditional Gift Fund, General, State	8822.002	194,937.80
Earnings On Investments, Inland Waterways Trust Fund	8861.002	14,556,559.36
Earnings On Investments, Harbor Maintenance Trust Fund	8863.002	164,875,765.62
Earnings On Investments, Patients' Benefit Fund, National Institutes Of Health	8888.002	35,990.14
Earnings On Investments, Esther Cattell Schmitt Gift Fund	8902.002	32,162.50
Earnings On Investments, Department Of The Army General Gift Fund	8927.002	84,093.80
Earnings On Investments, Department Of The Air Force General Gift Fund	8928.002	34,934.02
Earnings And Investments, Science, Space And Technology Education Trust Fund	8978.002	1,161,386.13
Total, Interest Received By Trust Funds		177,963,420,916.82
Other Interest:		
Interest Received From Outer Continental Shelf Escrow Amounts, Interior	1493	712,717.54
Total, Other Interest		712,717.54
Rents And Royalties On The Outer Continental Shelf:		
Royalties On Outer Continental Shelf Lands, Interior	2020	5,469,613,539.69
Land And Water Conservation Fund, Rent Receipts, Outer Continental Shelf Lands, National Park Service	5005.007	294,201,994.56
Land And Water Conservation Fund, Royalty Receipts, Outer Continental Shelf Lands, National Park Service	5005.008	598,628,033.44
Historic Preservation Fund, Receipts, Outer Continental Shelf Lands	5140	150,000,000.00
Outer Continental Shelf Revenues, Coastal Impact Assistance	5572.001	250,000,000.00
Total, Rents And Royalties On The Outer Continental Shelf		6,762,443,567.69

Table A – Receipts By Source Categories

Classification	Receipt Symbol	Receipt Offset Against Outlays
Undistributed Off-Setting Receipts		
Spectrum Auction Proceeds:		
Auction Receipts, Federal Communications Commission	2474	6,849,883,625.00
Total, Spectrum Auction Proceeds		6,849,883,625.00
Other:		
Spectrum Relocation Activities, Executive Office Of The President	5512.001	6,849,883,625.00
Total, Other		6,849,883,625.00
Total, Undistributed Off-Setting Receipts		260,200,781,800.87
Offsetting Governmental Receipts		
Regulatory Fees		
Registration, Filing, And Permit Fees, Pipeline And Hazardous Man Terials Administration	0855	749,725.00
Fees And Recoveries, Federal Energy Regulatory Commissions, Department Of Energy	0894	43,595,321.63
Marine Safety User Fees U.S. Coast Guard	2421	14,471,890.02
Fees For Bankruptcy Oversight, United States Trustee System Fund	5073.001	120,907,293.00
Immigration User Fees, Department Of Homeland Security	5087.003	586,325,062.11
Immigration Examinations Fee Account	5088.001	2,073,778,794.10
Land Border Inspection Fees	5089.001	28,443,672.88
H-1b Nonimmigrant Petitioner Account	5106.001	268,398,375.20
Breached Bond/detention Fund, Border And Transportation Security, Department Of Homeland Security	5126.001	84,719,105.37
Diversion Control Fee Account	5131.001	204,181,236.46
Pipeline Safety User Fees, Research And Special Programs Administration	5172	60,099,564.79
Federal Housing Enterprises Oversight Fund	5272.001	66,097,270.82
Nuclear Facilities Fees Fund, Nuclear Regulatory Commission	5280.001	669,249,476.05
Environmental Services, Environmental Protection Agency	5295	22,648,442.67
Student And Exchange Visitor Fee, Border And Transportation Security, Department Of Homeland Security	5378.001	57,947,182.88
H1-B And L Fraud Prevention And Detection Account	5389.001	137,216,113.94
Immigration Enforcement Account, Border And Transportation Security, Department Of Homeland Security	5451.001	3,133,412.12
Customs Conveyance, Passenger, And Other Fees, USCS, Department Of Homeland Security	5695.020	353,971,100.27
Customs Merchandise Processing Fee, USCS, Department Of Homeland Security	5695.030	1,450,064,779.46
Mobile Home Inspection And Monitoring Fees, Manufactured Housing Fees Trust Fund	8119.001	6,509,768.00
Total, Regulatory Fees		6,252,507,586.77
Other		
Tonnage Duty Fees	0311	19,660,047.45
Restoration, Rocky Mountain Arsenal, Army	5098.001	7,436,154.28
Defense Cooperation Account	5187.001	13,601.76
Earnings On Investments, Defense Cooperation Account	5187.002	323,172.81
Total, Other		27,432,976.30
Total, Offsetting Governmental Receipts		6,279,940,563.07
Total, Receipts By Source Categories		3,290,775,263,730.40

Part Three

Detail Of Appropriations, Outlays, And Balances

Appropriations, Outlays, and Balances – Continued

Appropriation or Fund Account — Title	Period of Availability	Dept Reg	Tr From	Account Number	Sub No.	Balances, Beginning Of Fiscal Year	Appropriations And Other Obligational Authority[1]	Transfers Borrowings And Investment (Net)[2]	Outlays (Net)	Balances Withdrawn And Other Transactions[3]	Balances, End Of Fiscal Year[4]
Legislative Branch											
Senate											
General Fund Accounts											
Compensation Of Members And Related Administrative Expenses, Senate											
Fund Resources:											
Undisbursed Funds	2007	00		0100		2,549,441.60	22,907,000.00	-------	19,345,335.26	-------	3,561,664.74
	2006					897,775.33		-------	1,705,026.34	897,775.33	844,415.26
	2005										
	Subtotal	00		0100		[5]3,447,216.93	22,907,000.00	-------	21,050,361.60	897,775.33	[5]4,406,080.00
Expense Allowances Of The Vice President, The President Pro Tempore, Majority And Minority Leaders, Majority And Minority Whips, And Chairmen Of The Majority And Minority Conference Committees, Senate											
Fund Resources:											
Undisbursed Funds	2007	00		0107		120,380.55	210,000.00	-------	116,847.45	-------	93,152.55
	2006					79,357.63		-------	22,145.51	79,323.84	98,235.04
	2005								33.79		
	Subtotal	00		0107		[5]199,738.18	210,000.00	-------	139,026.75	79,323.84	[5]191,387.59
Representation Allowances For The Majority And Minority Leaders, Senate											
Fund Resources:											
Undisbursed Funds	2007	00		0108		1,000.00	15,000.00	-------	-------	-------	15,000.00
	2006					7,000.00		-------	-------	-------	1,000.00
	2005									7,000.00	
	Subtotal	00		0108		58,000.00	15,000.00	-------	-------	7,000.00	[5]16,000.00
Salaries, Officers And Employees, Senate											
Fund Resources:											
Undisbursed Funds	2007	00		0110		11,970,153.67	140,730,000.00	-------	127,522,386.59	-------	13,207,613.41
	2006					79,320.17		-------	11,745,404.21	-------	224,749.46
	2005									79,320.17	
	Subtotal	00		0110		[5]12,049,473.84	140,730,000.00	-------	139,267,790.80	79,320.17	[5]13,432,362.87
Contingent Expenses, Senate, Folding Documents											
Fund Resources:											
Undisbursed Funds	No Year	00		0118		[5]1,835.78	-------	-------	-1,835.78	-------	-------
Contingent Expenses, Senate, Miscellaneous Items											
Fund Resources:											
Undisbursed Funds	2007	00		0123		7,329,742.82	19,332,000.00	-------	15,611,713.45	-------	3,720,286.55
	2006					1,496,143.96		-------	1,335,767.01	1,479,438.24	5,993,975.81
	No Year					39,507,284.60		-------	16,705.72		39,507,284.60
	Subtotal	00		0123		[5]48,333,171.38	19,332,000.00	-------	16,964,186.18	1,479,438.24	[5]49,221,546.96
Contingent Expenses, Senate, Secretary Of The Senate											
Fund Resources:											
Undisbursed Funds	2007-2011	00		0126		-------	2,800,000.00	-------	1,061,073.10	-------	2,800,000.00
	2007					-------	1,970,000.00	-------	607,000.00	-------	908,926.90
	2003-2007					3,800,670.79	-------	-2,800,000.00	-------	-------	393,670.79

Appropriations, Outlays, and Balances - Continued

Appropriation or Fund Account — Title	Period of Availability	Reg	Tr From	Account Number	Sub No.	Balances, Beginning Of Fiscal Year	Appropriations And Other Obligational Authority[1]	Transfers Borrowings And Investment (Net)[2]	Outlays (Net)[2]	Balances Withdrawn And Other Transactions[3]	Balances, End Of Fiscal Year[4]
	2006					1,106,280.20	------	------	405,107.67	------	701,172.53
	2005					663,073.32	------	-300,000.00	1,372.10	361,701.22	------
	No Year					4,961,630.09	------	300,000.00	160,422.52	------	5,101,207.57
	Subtotal	00		0126		[5]10,531,654.40	4,770,000.00	-2,800,000.00	2,234,975.39	361,701.22	[5]9,904,977.79
Contingent Expenses, Sergeant At Arms And Doorkeeper Of The Senate Fund Resources: Undisbursed Funds	2007-2011			0127		------	139,200,000.00	------	79,650,499.45	------	59,549,500.55
	2006-2010					61,034,479.01	------	------	31,001,934.99	------	30,032,544.02
	2005-2009					2,432,442.38	------	------	1,368,535.69	------	1,063,906.69
	2004-2008					128,788.05	------	------	36,402.57	------	92,385.48
	2007					------	7,550,000.00	------	------	------	7,550,000.00
	2005-2007					5,512,679.72	------	------	5,400,855.56	------	111,824.16
	2003-2007					6,421,282.44	------	2,800,000.00	1,637,906.06	------	7,583,376.38
	2006					12,500,000.00	------	------	8,694,270.87	------	3,805,729.13
	2004-2006					9,395,132.98	------	------	3,449,186.91	------	5,945,946.07
	2005					16,468,966.20	------	------	13,064,408.39	3,404,557.81	------
	2003-2005					29,095.69	------	------	------	29,095.69	------
	1999					9,901.02	------	------	------	9,901.02	------
	No Year					23,691,294.88	------	-6,037,500.00	3,143,767.06	------	14,510,027.82
	Subtotal	00		0127		[5]137,624,062.37	146,750,000.00	-3,237,500.00	147,447,767.55	3,443,554.52	[5]130,245,240.30
Contingent Expenses, Senate, Expenses Of Inquiries And Investigations Fund Resources: Undisbursed Funds	2007			0128		------	118,592,000.00	------	100,170,362.12	------	18,421,637.88
	2006					15,264,200.46	------	------	10,886,436.06	------	4,377,764.40
	2005					751,280.61	------	------	52,770.00	698,510.61	------
	Subtotal	00		0128		[5]16,015,481.07	118,592,000.00	------	111,109,568.18	698,510.61	[5]2,799,402.28
Contingent Expenses, United States Senate Caucus On International Narcotics Control Fund Resources: Undisbursed Funds	2007			0129		------	520,000.00	------	375,805.46	------	144,194.54
	2006					162,235.80	------	------	28,144.43	------	134,091.37
	2005					79,219.15	------	------	------	79,219.15	------
	Subtotal	00		0129		[5]241,454.95	520,000.00	------	403,949.89	79,219.15	[5]278,285.91
Contingent Expenses, Senator's Official Personnel And Office Expense Account, Senate Fund Resources: Undisbursed Funds	2007			0130		------	365,453,000.00	------	313,605,549.60	------	51,847,450.40
	2006					41,795,359.00	------	------	35,674,201.86	------	6,121,157.14
	2005					180,475.94	------	------	96,247.96	84,227.98	------
	2001					410.94	------	------	------	410.94	------
	1999					4,085.19	------	------	------	4,085.19	------
	Subtotal	00		0130		[5]41,980,331.07	365,453,000.00	------	349,375,999.42	88,724.11	[5]57,968,607.54
Official Mail Costs, Senate Fund Resources: Undisbursed Funds	2007			0132		------	300,000.00	------	122,525.88	------	177,474.12
	2006					184,462.33	------	------	5,879.33	------	178,583.00
	2005					185,516.68	------	------	------	185,516.68	------
	Subtotal	00		0132		[5]369,979.01	300,000.00	------	128,405.21	185,516.68	[5]356,057.12

Footnotes At End Of Chapter

Appropriations, Outlays, and Balances – Continued

Appropriation or Fund Account — Title	Period of Availability	Account Symbol — Dept Reg	Dept Tr From	Account Number	Sub No.	Balances, Beginning Of Fiscal Year	Appropriations And Other Obligational Authority[1]	Transfers Borrowings And Investment (Net)[2]	Outlays (Net)	Balances Withdrawn And Other Transactions[3]	Balances, End Of Fiscal Year[4]
Contingent Expenses, Senate, Senate, Stationery, Revolving Fund											
Fund Resources:											
Undisbursed Funds	No Year	00		0140		[5]387,291.61			46,264.90		[5]341,026.71
Salaries And Expenses, Office Of Senate Legal Counsel											
Fund Resources:											
Undisbursed Funds	2007	00		0171		402,671.45	1,317,000.00		939,413.03		377,586.97
	2006					328,266.39			80,396.59	328,266.39	322,274.86
	2005										
	Subtotal	00		0171		[5]730,937.84	1,317,000.00		1,019,809.62	328,266.39	[5]699,861.83
Expense Allowance For The Secretary Of The Senate, Sergeant At Arms And Doorkeeper Of The Senate And Secretaries For The Majority And For The Minority Of The Senate											
Fund Resources:											
Undisbursed Funds	2007	00		0172		9,049.10	34,000.00		21,516.88		12,483.12
	2006								1,894.61	11,388.10	7,154.49
	2005					11,388.10					
	Subtotal	00		0172		20,437.20	34,000.00		23,411.49	11,388.10	[5]19,637.61
Settlements And Awards Reserve, Contingent Expenses, Senate											
Fund Resources:											
Undisbursed Funds	No Year	00		0184		[5]1,000,000.00					[5]1,000,000.00
Salaries And Expenses, Senate, Office Of The Legislative Counsel Of The Senate											
Fund Resources:											
Undisbursed Funds	2007	00		0185		880,663.05	5,491,000.00		4,958,636.96		532,363.04
	2006					577,123.31			434,563.42	577,123.31	446,099.63
	2005										
	Subtotal	00		0185		[5]1,457,786.36	5,491,000.00		5,393,200.38	577,123.31	[5]978,462.67
Congressional Use Of Foreign Currency, Senate											
Fund Resources:											
Undisbursed Funds	No Year	00		0188	1	[5]12,942,949.50	8,000,000.00		4,713,745.21		[5]16,229,204.29
Public Enterprise Funds											
Contingent Expenses, Senate Computer Center Revolving Fund											
Fund Resources:											
Undisbursed Funds	No Year	00		4046		[5]10,000.00					[5]10,000.00
Senate Health Promotion, Revolving Fund, Senate											
Fund Resources:											
Undisbursed Funds	No Year	00		4051		[5]11,298.00			5,104.00		[5]6,194.00
Senate Office Of Public Records, Revolving Fund, Senate											
Fund Resources:											
Undisbursed Funds	No Year	00		4052		[5]123,177.08			-22,655.60		[5]145,832.68
Senate Gift Shop Revolving Fund, Senate											
Fund Resources:											
Undisbursed Funds	No Year	00		4062		[5]2,060,531.28			-228,895.89		[5]2,289,427.17
Senate Photographic Studio Revolving Fund											
Fund Resources:											
Undisbursed Funds	No Year	00		4086		[5]505,928.73			-32,855.89		[5]538,784.62
Senate Recording Studio Revolving Fund											

Appropriations, Outlays, and Balances - Continued

Appropriation or Fund Account — Title	Account Symbol — Period of Availability	Dept — Reg	Dept — Tr From	Account Number	Sub No.	Balances, Beginning Of Fiscal Year	Appropriations And Other Obligational Authority[1]	Transfers Borrowings And Investment (Net)[2]	Outlays (Net)	Balances Withdrawn And Other Transactions[3]	Balances, End Of Fiscal Year[4]
Fund Resources: Undisbursed Funds	No Year	00		4087		[5]2,132,559.93			-136,500.78		[5]2,269,060.71
Daniel Webster Senate Page Resident Revolving Fund											
Fund Resources: Undisbursed Funds	No Year	00		4101		[5]192,647.33			-17,272.05		[5]209,919.38
Senate Hair Care Revolving Fund											
Fund Resources: Undisbursed Funds	No Year	00		4326		[5]173,401.62			-16,918.31		[5]190,319.93
Total, Senate						[5]292,547,673.90	834,421,000.00	-6,037,500.00	798,866,632.27	8,316,861.67	[5]313,747,679.96
House Of Representatives											
General Fund Accounts											
Compensation Of Members And Related Administrative Expenses, House Of Representatives											
Fund Resources: Undisbursed Funds:	2007	00		0200			95,000,000.00		86,056,369.57		8,943,630.43
	2006					7,774,983.57			7,783,690.79		[6]8,707.22
Fund Equities: Unobligated Balances (Expired):						-7,774,983.57				1,159,939.64	[7]-8,934,923.21
	Subtotal	00		0200		-0-	95,000,000.00		93,840,060.36	1,159,939.64	-0-
Payment To Next Of Kin — Fund Resources: Undisbursed Funds	No Year	00		0215			330,400.00		322,407.43		[5]7,992.57
Salaries And Expenses, House Of Representatives — Fund Resources: Undisbursed Funds:	2007-2009	00		0400			155,938,696.00		145,642,452.01		10,296,243.99
	2007						968,092,732.00	2,071,665.30	908,258,124.03		61,906,273.27
	2006-2007					4,416,408.58		-500,000.00	3,477,418.66		438,989.92
	2005-2007					1,167,520.08		-250,000.00	592,084.76		325,435.32
	2006					43,474,066.54		6,150,190.02	42,450,052.71		7,174,203.85
	2005					13,079,736.38			4,613,709.94	8,466,026.44	
	2004-2005					822,990.44			822,990.44	822,990.44	
	2003-2005					400,010.88			400,010.88	400,010.88	
	Subtotal					47,850,340.75	20,124,702.00	-5,007,855.32	18,625,492.69	9,689,027.76	44,341,694.74
	No Year	00		0400		[5]111,211,073.65	1,144,156,130.00	2,464,000.00	1,123,659,334.80		[5]124,482,841.09
Contingent Expenses, House Of Representatives, Stationery, Revolving Fund — Fund Resources: Undisbursed Funds	No Year	00		0440		[5]5,254,775.73			-173,722.49		[5]5,428,498.22
Congressional Use Of Foreign Currency, House Of Representatives — Fund Resources: Undisbursed Funds	No Year	00		0488	1	[5]26,918,332.19	15,000,000.00		8,456,763.41		[5]33,461,568.78

Footnotes At End Of Chapter

Appropriations, Outlays, and Balances – Continued

Appropriation or Fund Account Title	Period of Availability	Dept Reg	Tr From	Account Number	Sub No.	Balances, Beginning Of Fiscal Year	Appropriations And Other Obligational Authority[1]	Transfers Borrowings And Investment (Net)[2]	Outlays (Net)	Balances Withdrawn And Other Transactions[3]	Balances, End Of Fiscal Year[4]
Public Enterprise Funds											
Contingent Expenses, House Recording Studio, Revolving Fund											
Fund Resources:											
Undisbursed Funds	No Year	00		4004		[5]8,082,718.45			-452,246.01		[5]8,534,964.46
Contingent Expenses, Page Residence Hall And Meal Plan, House Of Representatives											
Fund Resources:											
Undisbursed Funds	No Year	00		4011		[5]1,648,303.44			4,220.68		[5]1,644,082.76
House Services Revolving Fund, House Of Representatives											
Fund Resources:											
Undisbursed Funds	No Year	00		4199		[5]2,061,095.39			-198,817.57		[5]2,259,912.96
Intragovernmental Funds											
Net Expenses Of Equipment Revolving Fund, U.S. House Of Representatives											
Fund Resources:											
Undisbursed Funds	No Year	00		4509		[5]6,619,478.19		-2,464,000.00	-89,483.76		[5]4,244,961.95
Net Expenses Of Telecommunications Revolving Fund, House Of Representatives											
Fund Resources:											
Undisbursed Funds	No Year	00		4515		[5]2,774,936.61			-681,544.24		[5]3,456,480.85
Total, House Of Representatives						[5]164,570,713.65	1,254,486,530.00		1,224,686,972.61	10,848,967.40	[5]183,521,303.64
Joint Items											
General Fund Accounts											
Capitol Guide Service And Special Services Office, U.S. Senate											
Fund Resources:											
Undisbursed Funds	2007	00		0174			8,524,000.00		3,441,660.01		5,082,339.99
	2006					865,946.26			413,807.29		452,138.97
	2005					168,583.12			9,500.00	159,083.12	
	No Year					350,000.00					350,000.00
Subtotal		00		0174		[5]1,384,529.38	8,524,000.00		3,864,967.30	159,083.12	5,884,478.96
Salaries And Contingent Expenses, Senate, Joint Economic Committee											
Fund Resources:											
Undisbursed Funds	2007	00		0181			4,308,000.00		3,192,207.56		1,115,792.44
	2006					1,081,788.73			410,763.01		671,025.72
	2005					457,824.89				457,824.89	
Subtotal		00		0181		[5]1,539,613.62	4,308,000.00		3,602,970.57	457,824.89	[5]1,786,818.16
Contingent Expenses, Senate, Joint Committee On Inaugural Ceremonies											
Fund Resources:											
Undisbursed Funds	2004-2005	00		0186		[5]645,292.00			-69.19	645,361.19	
Statement Of Appropriation											
Fund Resources:											
Undisbursed Funds	2007	00		0199		15,000.00	15,000.00				15,000.00
	2006					15,000.00					15,000.00

Appropriations, Outlays, and Balances - Continued

Appropriation or Fund Account — Title	Period of Availability	Reg	Tr From	Account Number	Sub No.	Balances, Beginning Of Fiscal Year	Appropriations And Other Obligational Authority[1]	Transfers Borrowings And Investment (Net)[2]	Outlays (Net)	Balances Withdrawn And Other Transactions[3]	Balances, End Of Fiscal Year[4]
	Subtotal	00		0199		[5]15,000.00	15,000.00				[5]30,000.00
Contingent Expenses, House Of Representatives, Office Of The Attending Physician Fund Resources: Undisbursed Funds	2007	00		0425			2,519,550.00		560,925.26		1,958,624.74
	2006					120,848.52			48,208.43		72,640.09
	2005					67,042.01			-3,331.25	70,373.26	
	No Year					595,332.85			92,250.83		503,082.02
	Subtotal	00		0425		[5]783,223.38	2,519,550.00		698,053.27	70,373.26	[5]2,534,346.85
Contingent Expenses, House Of Representatives, Joint Committee On Taxation Fund Resources: Undisbursed Funds	2007	00		0460			8,772,901.00		7,780,700.88		992,200.12
	2006					1,224,516.39			204,785.11		1,019,731.28
	2005					43,121.77			-341.95	43,463.72	
Statement Of Appropriations	Subtotal	00		0460		[5]1,267,638.16	8,772,901.00		7,985,144.04	43,463.72	[5]2,011,931.40
Fund Resources: Undisbursed Funds	2007	00		0499		14,850.00	14,850.00				14,850.00
	2006					14,880.00				14,880.00	
	2005										
	Subtotal	00		0499		[5]29,730.00	14,850.00			14,880.00	[5]29,700.00
Total, Joint Items						[5]5,665,026.54	24,154,301.00		16,151,065.99	1,390,986.18	[5]12,277,275.37
Capitol Police											
General Fund Accounts											
General Expenses, Capitol Police, House Of Representatives Fund Resources: Funds Held Outside The Treasury	2001	00		0476		[5]4,000.00					[5]4,000.00
Security Enhancements, Capitol Police Board, U.S. House Of Representatives Fund Resources: Undisbursed Funds	No Year	02		0461		[5]2,303,293.36			279,083.54		[5]2,024,209.82
General Expenses, Capitol Police Fund Resources: Undisbursed Funds	2007-2008	02		0476			38,350,000.00		-38,924.28		38,924.28
	2007					72,989.00			20,631,013.07		17,718,986.93
	2006-2007					24,044,167.05			41,545.77		31,443.23
	2006					781.58			19,705,464.06		4,338,702.99
	2005-2006					3,258,835.55			781.58		1,765,545.33
	2004-2005					0.04			1,493,290.22		0.04
	2004					1,358,072.78			541,543.59		816,529.19
	2003					7,585,827.25			6,840,947.04		744,880.21
	No Year					29,279,974.18	9,158,275.65		8,342,242.15		30,096,007.68

Footnotes At End Of Chapter

Appropriations, Outlays, and Balances – Continued

Appropriation or Fund Account — Title	Period of Availability	Reg	Tr From	Account Number	Sub No.	Balances, Beginning Of Fiscal Year	Appropriations And Other Obligational Authority[1]	Transfers Borrowings And Investment (Net)[2]	Outlays (Net)	Balances Withdrawn And Other Transactions[3]	Balances, End Of Fiscal Year[4]
General Expenses, Capitol Police - Continued											
Fund Resources: - Continued											
Funds Held Outside The Treasury	2003					4,000.00					4,000.00
	2001					-4,000.00					[6]-4,000.00
Fund Equities:											
Unobligated Balances (Expired)										350,137.54	-350,137.54
Accounts Payable										12,463,783.90	-12,463,783.90
Undelivered Orders										4,905,065.49	-4,905,065.49
	Subtotal	02		0476		[5]65,600,647.43	47,508,275.65		57,557,903.20	17,718,986.93	[5]37,832,032.95
Salaries, Capitol Police											
Fund Resources:											
Undisbursed Funds	2007	02		0477		13,244,555.74	218,126,724.35		207,827,611.42		10,299,112.93
	2006					212,616.64			9,229,043.85		4,015,511.89
	2005					156,779.01			185,269.08		27,347.56
	2004					2,936,250.96			156,779.01		
	2003					4,278,671.25			2,936,250.96		
	No Year										4,278,671.25
Fund Equities:											
Unobligated Balances (Expired)										639,851.91	-639,851.91
Unobligated Balances (Unexpired)										4,278,671.25	-4,278,671.25
Accounts Payable										9,631,201.86	-9,631,201.86
Undelivered Orders										28,059.16	-28,059.16
	Subtotal	02		0477		[5]20,828,873.60	218,126,724.35		220,334,954.32	14,577,784.18	[5]4,042,859.45
Special Fund Accounts											
United States Capitol Police Memorial Fund, Capitol Police											
Fund Resources:											
Undisbursed Funds	No Year	02		5083		[5]33,435.00			-31,750.00		[5]65,185.00
Total, Capitol Police						[5]88,770,249.39	265,635,000.00		278,140,191.06	32,296,771.11	[5]43,968,287.22
Office Of Compliance											
General Fund Accounts											
Awards And Settlements, Office Of Compliance											
Fund Resources:											
Undisbursed Funds	No Year	09		1450		55,805.67	4,053,281.06		3,574,761.24		534,325.49
Fund Equities:											
Unobligated Balances (Unexpired)						-500.52				47,037.10	-47,537.62
Accounts Payable						-46,329.68				431,482.72	-477,812.40
Undelivered Orders						-8,975.47					-8,975.47
	Subtotal	09		1450		-0-	4,053,281.06		3,574,761.24	478,519.82	-0-
Salaries And Expenses, Office Of Compliance											
Fund Resources:											
Undisbursed Funds	2007-2008	09		1600			772,200.00		488,852.59		283,347.41
	2007						2,330,365.00		1,910,680.17		419,684.83
	2006-2007					331,872.65			258,391.83		73,480.82

Appropriations, Outlays, and Balances - Continued

Appropriation or Fund Account — Title	Period of Availability	Reg	Tr From	Account Number	Sub No.	Balances, Beginning Of Fiscal Year	Appropriations And Other Obligational Authority[1]	Transfers Borrowings And Investment (Net)[2]	Outlays (Net)	Balances Withdrawn And Other Transactions[3]	Balances, End Of Fiscal Year[4]
	2006					235,156.81			122,401.98		112,754.83
	2005-2006					20,247.51			2,710.12		17,537.39
	2005					112,535.36			3,224.23		109,311.13
	2004-2005					10,798.42					10,798.42
	2004					85,757.35					85,757.35
	2003-2004					2,294.81					2,294.81
	2003					32,509.56					32,509.56
	2002					5,836.42				5,836.42	
Accounts Receivable						1,375.00				1,375.00	
Fund Equities:											
Unobligated Balances (Expired)						-269,311.67				122,264.13	-391,575.80
Unobligated Balances (Unexpired)						-150,519.65				56,153.26	-206,672.91
Accounts Payable						-333,947.61				124,928.20	-458,875.81
Undelivered Orders						-84,604.96				5,747.07	-90,352.03
Subtotal		09		1600		-0-	3,102,565.00		2,786,260.92	316,304.08	-0-
Total, Office Of Compliance							7,155,846.06		6,361,022.16	794,823.90	
Congressional Budget Office											
General Fund Accounts											
Salaries And Expenses, Congressional Budget Office											
Fund Resources:											
Undisbursed Funds	2007						35,203,500.00		32,751,060.57		2,451,739.43
	2006					3,056,850.41		-700.00	2,544,460.89		513,089.52
	2003-2006					8,583.39		700.00			8,583.39
	2005					716,569.77		-700.00	61,527.04		654,342.73
	2004					738,800.33		700.00	-451.01		739,951.34
	2003					433,943.91			81.62		433,862.29
	2002					397,552.12			10.70	397,541.42	
	No Year					27,723.10					27,723.10
Funds Held Outside The Treasury	2007							700.00			700.00
	2006					700.00		-700.00			
	2005					700.00		-700.00			
	2004					700.00		-700.00			
Accounts Receivable						[8]11,332.16				11,332.16	
Fund Equities:											
Unobligated Balances (Expired)						[8]-1,006,257.73				-78,251.03	-928,006.70
Unobligated Balances (Unexpired)						-245.08					-245.08
Accounts Payable						-1,417,384.78				146,324.17	-1,563,708.95
Undelivered Orders						[8]-2,968,167.60				-630,136.53	-2,338,031.07
Subtotal		08		0100		-0-	35,203,500.00		35,356,689.81	-153,189.81	-0-
Total, Congressional Budget Office							35,203,500.00		35,356,689.81	-153,189.81	

Footnotes At End Of Chapter

49

Appropriations, Outlays, and Balances – Continued

Appropriation or Fund Account — Title	Period of Availability	Dept Reg	Tr From	Account Number	Sub No.	Balances, Beginning Of Fiscal Year	Appropriations And Other Obligational Authority[1]	Transfers Borrowings And Investment (Net)[2]	Outlays (Net)	Balances Withdrawn And Other Transactions[3]	Balances, End Of Fiscal Year[4]
Architect Of The Capitol											
General Fund Accounts											
Salaries And Expenses, General Administration, Architect Of The Capitol											
Fund Resources:											
Undisbursed Funds	2005-2009	01		0100		986,566.80			35,724.08		950,842.72
	2004-2008					1,338,125.99		2,519,000.00	497,205.04		3,359,920.95
	2007						78,303,000.00		61,257,498.48		17,045,501.52
	2003-2007					2,029.79		895,645.00			897,674.79
	2006					16,242,598.95			12,884,310.62		3,358,288.33
	2002-2006					51,663.29					51,663.29
	2005					3,438,396.30			845,359.33		2,593,036.97
	2004					2,878,915.67			42,880.97		2,836,034.70
	2003					2,246,797.52			-1,061.19		2,247,858.71
	2002					2,188,368.28				2,188,368.28	
	No Year								-87,680.00		87,680.00
Fund Equities:											
Unobligated Balances (Expired)						-8,807,956.14				-1,035,482.50	-7,772,473.64
Unobligated Balances (Unexpired)						-913,890.25				1,234,067.19	-2,147,957.44
Accounts Payable						-6,468,794.56				-1,693,562.42	-4,775,232.14
Undelivered Orders						-13,182,821.64				5,550,017.12	-18,732,838.76
Subtotal		01		0100		-0-	78,303,000.00	3,414,645.00	75,474,237.33	6,243,407.67	-0-
Capitol Buildings, Architect Of The Capitol											
Fund Resources:											
Undisbursed Funds	2007-2011	01		0105			8,217,000.00		345,426.75		7,871,573.25
	2006-2010					6,748,687.61			1,828,445.80		4,920,241.81
	2004-2008					5,219,036.77		-3,000,000.00	264,971.01		1,954,065.76
	2007						15,669,000.00		13,496,351.76		2,172,648.24
	2003-2007					7,214,413.57		-509,689.00	3,580,831.03		3,123,893.54
	2006					2,040,448.90			1,727,267.63		313,181.27
	2002-2006					818,889.42			385,353.89		433,535.53
	2005					514,450.60			150,211.18		364,239.42
	2004					672,631.01					672,631.01
	2003					119,270.37					119,270.37
	2002					596,431.19			75,677.40	520,753.79	
	No Year					41,863,073.90		-66,132.00	21,863,869.11		19,933,072.79
Fund Equities:											
Unobligated Balances (Expired)						-1,550,282.11				-326,281.22	-1,224,000.89
Unobligated Balances (Unexpired)						-33,661,701.63				-7,007,393.18	-26,654,308.45
Accounts Payable						-4,943,124.07				-1,556,447.25	-3,386,676.82
Undelivered Orders						-25,652,225.53				-15,038,858.70	-10,613,366.83
Subtotal		01		0105		-0-	23,886,000.00	-3,575,821.00	43,718,405.56	-23,408,226.56	-0-
Alterations And Improvements, Buildings And Grounds, To Provide Facilities For The Physically Handicapped, Architect Of The Capitol											
Fund Resources:											
Undisbursed Funds	No Year	01		0106		25,856.60			6,114.34		19,742.26

Appropriations, Outlays, and Balances - Continued

Appropriation or Fund Account — Title	Period of Availability	Reg	Tr From	Account Number	Sub No.	Balances, Beginning Of Fiscal Year	Appropriations And Other Obligational Authority[1]	Transfers Borrowings And Investment (Net)[2]	Outlays (Net)	Balances Withdrawn And Other Transactions[3]	Balances, End Of Fiscal Year[4]
Fund Equities:											
Unobligated Balances (Unexpired)						-25,856.60				-6,114.34	-19,742.26
	Subtotal	01		0106		-0-			6,114.34	-6,114.34	-0-
Capitol Grounds, Architect Of The Capitol											
Fund Resources:											
Undisbursed Funds	2004-2008	01		0108		670,611.09			214,292.25		456,318.84
	2007					776,327.49	7,417,000.00		6,068,860.55		1,348,139.45
	2003-2007					1,794,740.17		469,459.00	531,652.53		714,133.96
	2006					328,070.49			1,034,675.22		760,064.95
	2005-2006					258,776.11			255,782.38		72,288.11
	2005					616,790.42			11,431.16		247,344.95
	2004					445,576.90					616,790.42
	2003					463,191.57				463,191.57	445,576.90
	2002					258,115.13			79,682.30		178,432.83
	No Year										
Fund Equities:											
Unobligated Balances (Expired)						-1,838,547.68				-260,588.22	-1,577,959.46
Unobligated Balances (Unexpired)						-362,271.47				-205,360.15	-156,911.32
Accounts Payable						-1,132,163.34				-485,645.16	-646,518.18
Undelivered Orders						-2,279,216.88				178,484.57	-2,457,701.45
	Subtotal	01		0108		-0-	7,417,000.00	469,459.00	8,196,376.39	-309,917.39	-0-
Senate Office Buildings, Architect Of The Capitol											
Fund Resources:											
Undisbursed Funds	2007-2011	01		0123		10,973,726.69	15,588,000.00		2,809,581.16		12,778,418.84
	2006-2010					4,951,813.03			5,348,144.62		5,625,582.07
	2005-2009					4,633,549.51			1,996,645.09		2,955,167.94
	2004-2008					6,394,569.85			991,528.43		3,642,021.08
	2007					5,063,728.87	50,764,000.00		46,423,118.78		4,340,881.22
	2003-2007					76,502.31			3,772,274.24		2,622,295.61
	2006					1,744,501.52			4,227,427.51		836,301.36
	2002-2006					989,386.26			71,077.63		5,424.68
	2005					594,715.33			193,263.12		1,551,238.40
	2004					988,331.32			-3,399.32		992,785.58
	2003					594,715.33				988,331.32	594,715.33
	2002					11,267,897.16		5,937,500.00	8,879,210.36		8,326,186.80
	No Year										
Fund Equities:											
Unobligated Balances (Expired)						-3,344,890.19				-801,852.46	-2,543,037.73
Unobligated Balances (Unexpired)						-25,466,805.04				-828,678.96	-24,638,126.08
Accounts Payable						-4,887,978.89				222,135.12	-5,110,114.01
Undelivered Orders						-13,979,047.73				-1,999,306.64	-11,979,741.09
	Subtotal	01		0123		-0-	66,352,000.00	5,937,500.00	74,708,871.62	-2,419,371.62	-0-
House Office Buildings, Architect Of The Capitol											
Fund Resources:											
Undisbursed Funds	2007-2011	01		0127		17,922,362.68	20,713,000.00		711,313.07		20,001,686.93
	2006-2010					17,551,523.33			4,143,930.57		13,778,432.11
	2005-2009								9,209,549.91		8,341,973.42

Footnotes At End Of Chapter

Appropriations, Outlays, and Balances – Continued

Title / Period of Availability	Reg	Tr From	Account Number	Sub No.	Balances, Beginning Of Fiscal Year	Appropriations And Other Obligational Authority[1]	Transfers Borrowings And Investment (Net)[2]	Outlays (Net)	Balances Withdrawn And Other Transactions[3]	Balances, End Of Fiscal Year[4]
House Office Buildings, Architect Of The Capitol - Continued										
Fund Resources: - Continued										
Undisbursed Funds - Continued										
2004-2008					12,260,841.82			7,384,955.49		4,875,886.33
2007						39,433,000.00		36,591,749.40		2,841,250.60
2003-2007					4,514,459.38			3,125,877.44		1,388,581.94
2006					3,293,488.09			2,676,709.37		616,778.72
2002-2006					1,218,853.10			573,633.05		645,220.05
2005					774,575.69			213,088.73		561,486.96
2004					316,040.13			-359.31		316,399.44
2003					560,636.81			67,876.71		492,760.10
2002					967,838.39			18,021.00	949,817.39	-0-
No Year					3,272,194.76		-122,382.00	1,844,100.71		1,305,712.05
Fund Equities:										
Unobligated Balances (Expired)					-2,559,037.52				-588,030.64	-1,971,006.88
Unobligated Balances (Unexpired)					-30,796,802.45				8,510,761.49	-39,307,563.94
Accounts Payable					-5,082,985.86				666,577.91	-5,749,563.77
Undelivered Orders					-24,213,988.35				-16,075,954.29	-8,138,034.06
Subtotal	01		0127		-0-	60,146,000.00	-122,382.00	66,560,446.14	-6,536,828.14	-0-
Capitol Power Plant, Architect Of The Capitol										
Fund Resources:										
Undisbursed Funds										
2007-2011	01		0133			51,584,000.00				51,584,000.00
2006-2011					27,492,121.40			6,107,344.98		21,384,776.42
2006-2010					2,967,414.26			1,672,807.83		1,294,606.43
2005-2009					380,534.20			16,670.80		363,863.40
2004-2008					6,011,720.70		481,000.00	3,404,658.07		3,088,062.63
2007						70,506,000.00		54,360,994.40		16,145,005.60
2003-2007					6,783,203.40			4,390,900.25		2,392,303.15
2006					10,225,366.61			7,811,277.26		2,414,089.35
2002-2006					115,360.72			60,729.35		54,631.37
2005					4,646,521.08			426,396.20		4,220,124.88
2004					2,637,214.08			24,486.59		2,612,727.49
2003					336,981.51			173,842.00		163,139.51
2002					6,395,768.23				6,395,768.23	-0-
No Year					81,669.41		-27,183.00	378.00		54,108.41
Accounts Receivable					1,187,297.61				1,187,297.61	-0-
Fund Equities:										
Unobligated Balances (Expired)					-11,121,499.70				-4,188,076.07	-6,933,423.63
Unobligated Balances (Unexpired)					-29,220,582.30				22,925,704.97	-52,146,287.27
Accounts Payable					-14,702,049.66				-6,949,122.72	-7,752,926.94
Undelivered Orders					-14,217,041.55				24,721,759.25	-38,938,800.80
Subtotal	01		0133		-0-	122,090,000.00	453,817.00	78,450,485.73	44,093,331.27	-0-
Structural And Mechanical Care, Library Buildings And Grounds, Architect Of The Capitol										
Fund Resources:										
Undisbursed Funds										
2007-2011	01		0155			5,133,000.00		363,787.87		4,769,212.13
2006-2010					38,407,852.48			21,086,302.89		17,321,549.59
2005-2009					18,385,823.88			6,449,634.03		11,936,189.85
2004-2008					5,994,816.90			1,506,214.02		4,488,602.88

Appropriations, Outlays, and Balances - Continued

Appropriation or Fund Account — Title	Period of Availability	Account Symbol — Dept Reg	Tr From	Account Number	Sub No.	Balances, Beginning Of Fiscal Year	Appropriations And Other Obligational Authority[1]	Transfers Borrowings And Investment (Net)[2]	Outlays (Net)	Balances Withdrawn And Other Transactions[3]	Balances, End Of Fiscal Year[4]
	2007						25,259,000.00		18,225,563.48		7,033,436.52
	2003-2007					127,881.11		1,000,000.00	106,556.37		1,021,324.74
	2006					11,746,819.17			5,746,768.91		6,000,050.26
	2002-2006					14,800.00			12,550.18		2,249.82
	2005					1,749,378.43			1,113,502.75		635,875.68
	2004					878,110.16			56,532.00		821,578.16
	2003					445,854.64			123,694.14		322,160.50
	2002					507,084.06				507,084.06	-0-
	No Year					19,361,615.70			-705,728.27		20,067,343.97
	Subtotal	01		0155							
Fund Equities:											
Unobligated Balances (Expired)						-2,512,733.70				-468,312.27	-2,044,421.43
Unobligated Balances (Unexpired)						-18,915,949.91				388,512.46	-19,304,462.37
Accounts Payable						-3,622,957.76				17,548,638.65	-21,171,596.41
Undelivered Orders						-72,568,395.16				-40,669,301.27	-31,899,093.89
Capitol Visitor Center, Architect Of The Capitol											
Fund Resources:											
Undisbursed Funds						-0-	30,392,000.00	1,000,000.00	54,085,378.37	-22,693,378.37	-0-
	2007						2,277,000.00		1,417,712.87		859,287.13
	2006					1,774,743.66			1,199,002.98		575,740.68
	2004					287,295.00					287,295.00
	No Year					127,066,136.18	41,481,000.00		79,981,307.91		88,565,828.27
	Subtotal	01		0161							
Fund Equities:											
Unobligated Balances (Expired)						-355,428.39				39,616.30	-395,044.69
Unobligated Balances (Unexpired)						-59,170,575.76		3,779,418.92			-62,949,994.68
Accounts Payable						-25,294,255.26				-9,219,647.16	-16,074,608.10
Undelivered Orders						-44,307,915.43				-33,439,411.82	-10,868,503.61
Capitol Police Buildings And Grounds, Architect Of The Capitol											
Fund Resources:											
Undisbursed Funds						-0-	43,758,000.00		82,598,023.76	-38,840,023.76	-0-
	Subtotal	01		0161							
	2007-2011						2,000,000.00				2,000,000.00
	2006-2010					4,950,000.00					4,950,000.00
	2005-2009					460,954.73			45,780.46		415,174.27
	2004-2008					225,802.06			181,130.66		44,671.40
	2007						9,768,000.00		6,063,783.59		3,704,216.41
	2003-2007					20,884,409.05		-1,855,415.00	6,790,214.48		12,238,779.57
	2006					6,023,200.30			3,883,699.03		2,139,501.27
	2005-2006					3,476,023.24			2,787,648.27		688,374.97
	2005					159,396.52			47,310.96		112,085.56
	2004					186,008.47					186,008.47
	2003					185,238.58					185,238.58
	No Year					616,910.36			170,154.93		446,755.43
	Subtotal	01		0171							
Fund Equities:											
Unobligated Balances (Expired)						-2,036,309.30				542,926.87	-2,579,236.17
Unobligated Balances (Unexpired)						-9,989,047.42				-2,217,473.32	-7,771,574.10
Accounts Payable						-1,169,887.76				1,763,026.41	-2,932,914.17
Undelivered Orders						-23,972,698.83				-10,145,617.34	-13,827,081.49
						-0-	11,768,000.00	-1,855,415.00	19,969,722.38	-10,057,137.38	-0-

Footnotes At End Of Chapter

Appropriations, Outlays, and Balances – Continued

Appropriation or Fund Account — Title	Period of Availability	Dept Reg	Tr From	Account Number	Sub No.	Balances, Beginning Of Fiscal Year	Appropriations And Other Obligational Authority[1]	Transfers Borrowings And Investment (Net)[2]	Outlays (Net)	Balances Withdrawn And Other Transactions[3]	Balances, End Of Fiscal Year[4]
Public Enterprise Funds											
Senate Restaurant Fund											
Fund Resources:											
Undisbursed Funds	No Year	00		4022		[5]1,225,827.35	850,000.00		1,342,849.87		[5]732,977.48
House Of Representatives, Gymnasium, Architect Of The Capitol, Revolving Fund											
Fund Resources:											
Undisbursed Funds	No Year	01		4200		37,078.06			-10,871.90		47,949.96
Fund Equities:											
Unobligated Balances (Unexpired)						-28,238.07				1,546.18	-29,784.25
Accounts Payable						-3,215.11				1,144.12	-4,359.23
Undelivered Orders						-5,624.88				8,181.60	-13,806.48
Subtotal		01		4200		-0-			-10,871.90	10,871.90	-0-
Intragovernmental Funds											
Senate Health And Fitness Facility, Architect Of The Capitol											
Fund Resources:											
Undisbursed Funds	No Year	01		4566		309,264.43			-36,566.06		345,830.49
Fund Equities:											
Unobligated Balances (Unexpired)						-309,237.43				-55,501.13	-253,736.30
Accounts Payable						-27.00				25,642.20	-25,642.20
Undelivered Orders						-0-				66,424.99	-66,451.99
Subtotal		01		4566		-0-			-36,566.06	36,566.06	-0-
Judiciary Office Building Development And Operations Fund											
Fund Resources:											
Undisbursed Funds	No Year	10		4518		1,769,763.33		-3,810,957.00	-16,140,497.04		14,099,303.37
Authority To Borrow From The Public							13,419,043.00	-13,419,043.00			
Accounts Receivable						225,852.64				225,852.64	
Fund Equities:											
Unobligated Balances (Unexpired)						-569,442.43				10,164,807.63	-10,734,250.06
Accounts Payable						-1,263,053.11				453,117.15	-1,716,170.26
Undelivered Orders						-163,120.43				1,485,762.62	-1,648,883.05
Subtotal		10		4518		-0-	13,419,043.00	-17,230,000.00	-16,140,497.04	12,329,540.04	-0-
Total, Architect Of The Capitol						[5]1,225,827.35	458,381,043.00	-11,508,197.00	488,922,976.49	-41,557,280.62	[5]732,977.48
Botanic Garden											
General Fund Accounts											
Salaries And Expenses, Botanic Garden											
Fund Resources:											
Undisbursed Funds	2004-2008	09		0200		4,050.10			4,050.00		0.10
	2007						7,655,000.00		5,969,437.50		1,685,562.50
	2003-2007					359.42					359.42

Appropriations, Outlays, and Balances - Continued

| Appropriation or Fund Account | Period of Availability | Account Symbol | | | | Balances, Beginning Of Fiscal Year | Appropriations And Other Obligational Authority[1] | Transfers Borrowings And Investment (Net)[2] | Outlays (Net) | Balances Withdrawn And Other Transactions[3] | Balances, End Of Fiscal Year[4] |
| Title | | Dept | | Account Number | Sub No. | | | | | | |
		Reg	Tr From								
	2006					1,808,867.21	------	------	1,311,957.22	------	496,909.99
	2005					233,535.79	------	------	34,988.68	------	198,547.11
	2004					334,824.75	------	------	3,108.78	------	331,715.97
	2003					183,457.61	------	------	5,000.00	------	178,457.61
	2002					323,777.80	------	------	------	323,777.80	-0-
	No Year					575,734.67	------	315,697.00	------	------	891,431.67
Fund Equities:											
Unobligated Balances (Expired)						-1,217,435.16	------	------	------	-197,570.16	-1,019,865.00
Unobligated Balances (Unexpired)						-484,663.37	------	------	------	315,337.58	-800,000.95
Accounts Payable						-600,792.47	------	------	------	-58,525.00	-542,267.47
Undelivered Orders						-1,161,716.35	------	------	------	259,134.60	-1,420,850.95
						-0-	7,655,000.00	315,697.00	7,328,542.18	642,154.82	-0-
	Subtotal	09		0200							

Trust Fund Accounts

National Garden, Gifts And Donations, Botanic Garden											
Fund Resources:											
Undisbursed Funds	No Year	09		8292		10,000.00	------	1,242,375.17	1,261,365.30	------	43,170.12
Investments In Public Debt Securities						1,392,414.05	52,160.25	-1,242,375.17	------	------	150,038.88
Fund Equities:											
Unobligated Balances (Unexpired)						-514,258.38	------	------	------	-438,657.12	-75,601.26
Accounts Payable						-791,124.06	------	------	------	-752,639.53	-38,484.53
Undelivered Orders						-97,031.61	------	------	------	-17,908.40	-79,123.21
						-0-	52,160.25	315,697.00	1,261,365.30	-1,209,205.05	-0-
	Subtotal	09		8292							
Total, Botanic Garden							7,707,160.25	315,697.00	8,589,907.48	-567,050.23	

Library Of Congress

General Fund Accounts

Salaries And Expenses, Library Of Congress											
Fund Resources:											
Undisbursed Funds	2007	03		0101			350,052,780.00	-40,843.95	[9]284,737,659.66	------	65,274,276.39
	2003-2007					14,839.50	------	------	2,096.85	------	12,742.65
	2006					72,184,609.15	------	40,843.76	57,516,728.58	------	14,708,724.33
	2005					17,902,267.56	------	------	8,719,116.27	------	9,183,151.29
	2004					7,193,043.67	------	------	1,490,451.19	------	5,702,592.48
	2003-2004					88,448.07	------	------	------	------	88,448.07
	2003					4,714,406.85	------	-5,770.19	615,315.88	------	4,093,320.78
	2002					2,560,210.48	------	-17,467.28	32,083.61	------	
Funds Held Outside The Treasury	No Year					139,905,085.71	-18,253,391.00	16,052.35	47,599,561.62	2,510,659.59	74,068,185.44
	2007						------	40,843.95	------	------	40,843.95
	2006					41,243.76	------	-40,843.76	------	------	400.00
	No Year					9,199.19	------	7,185.12	------	------	16,384.31
Accounts Receivable						305,344.19	------	------	------	-119,882.77	425,226.96
Unfilled Customer Orders						54,950.81	------	------	------	22,103.83	32,846.98
Fund Equities:											
Unobligated Balances (Expired)						[8]8,816,864.51	------	------	------	1,389,504.95	-10,206,369.46

Footnotes At End Of Chapter

55

Appropriations, Outlays, and Balances – Continued

Appropriation or Fund Account: Title	Period of Availability	Reg	Tr From	Account Number	Sub No.	Balances, Beginning Of Fiscal Year	Appropriations And Other Obligational Authority[1]	Transfers Borrowings And Investment (Net)[2]	Outlays (Net)	Balances Withdrawn And Other Transactions[3]	Balances, End Of Fiscal Year[4]
Salaries And Expenses, Library Of Congress - Continued											
Fund Equities: - Continued											
Unobligated Balances (Unexpired)						-92,802,947.66				-65,698,606.18	-27,104,341.48
Accounts Payable						-27,839,180.24				-454,422.73	-27,384,757.51
Undelivered Orders						[8.]-115,514,656.53				-6,562,981.35	-108,951,675.18
Subtotal		03		0101		-0-	331,799,389.00		400,713,013.66	-68,913,624.66	-0-
Salaries And Expenses, Copyright Office, Library Of Congress											
Fund Resources:											
Undisbursed Funds	2007	03		0102		1,264,646.65	22,662,000.00		21,575,160.45		1,086,839.55
	2006					601,569.60			1,133,822.10		130,824.55
	2005					84,513.25			252,335.47		349,234.13
	2004					372,752.17			-1,824.95		86,338.20
	2003					137,782.89		-59,253.21	313,498.96		
	2002							-107,592.24	30,190.65		
	No Year					21,822,022.95	-2,700,000.00	166,845.45	3,226,207.54		16,062,660.86
Accounts Receivable						55,035.75				-1,803,237.36	1,858,273.11
Unfilled Customer Orders						29,348.84				4,615.11	24,733.73
Fund Equities:											
Unobligated Balances (Expired)						[8.]-993,580.67				-163,192.05	-830,388.62
Unobligated Balances (Unexpired)						[8.]-7,699,724.47				1,006,837.72	-8,706,562.19
Accounts Payable						-3,427,354.69				-561,208.91	-2,866,145.78
Undelivered Orders						-12,247,012.27				-5,051,204.73	-7,195,807.54
Subtotal		03		0102		-0-	19,962,000.00		26,529,390.22	-6,567,390.22	-0-
Salaries And Expenses, Congressional Research Service, Library Of Congress											
Fund Resources:											
Undisbursed Funds	2007	03		0127		10,794,431.47	100,786,000.00		90,303,182.13		10,482,817.87
	2006					915,723.29			9,405,361.17		1,389,070.30
	2005					269,883.73			539,498.31		376,224.98
	2004					269,952.60			-88.87		269,952.60
	2003-2004					4,954.23					4,954.23
	2003					279,320.74					279,320.74
	2002					256,229.78			-2,544.56	258,774.34	
Accounts Receivable						33,690.20				-6,347.82	40,038.02
Unfilled Customer Orders						25,558.22				5,233.70	20,324.52
Fund Equities:											
Unobligated Balances (Expired)						-866,377.64				91,849.60	-958,227.24
Accounts Payable						-5,349,485.00				-131,559.16	-5,217,925.84
Undelivered Orders						-6,363,929.02				322,621.16	-6,686,550.18
Subtotal		03		0127		-0-	100,786,000.00		100,245,428.18	540,571.82	-0-
Salaries And Expenses, Books For The Blind And Physically Handicapped, Library Of Congress											
Fund Resources:											
Undisbursed Funds	2007	03		0141		18,631,821.19	37,383,000.00		19,938,015.52		17,444,984.48
	2006					2,919,272.14			15,768,564.90		2,863,256.29
	2005					1,724,478.66			1,312,772.10		1,606,500.04
	2004					750,726.42			595,118.64		1,129,360.02
	2003					670,831.71			-56,716.55		807,442.97
	2002								25,079.48	645,752.23	

Appropriations, Outlays, and Balances - Continued

Appropriation or Fund Account — Title	Period of Availability	Dept Reg	Tr From	Account Number	Sub No.	Balances, Beginning Of Fiscal Year	Appropriations And Other Obligational Authority[1]	Transfers Borrowings And Investment (Net)[2]	Outlays (Net)	Balances Withdrawn And Other Transactions[3]	Balances, End Of Fiscal Year[4]
Accounts Receivable	No Year					14,800,594.54	16,231,000.00		12,049,135.02		18,982,459.52
Unfilled Customer Orders						1,979.90				-4,603.03	6,582.93
						976.96				976.96	
Fund Equities:											
Unobligated Balances (Expired)						-2,493,426.33				-160,181.44	-2,333,244.89
Unobligated Balances (Unexpired)						-3,471,415.65				11,785,908.41	-15,257,324.06
Accounts Payable						-6,174,241.54				-2,029,505.88	-4,144,735.66
Undelivered Orders						-27,361,598.00				-6,256,316.36	-21,105,281.64
Subtotal	Subtotal	03		0141		-0-	53,614,000.00		49,631,969.11	3,982,030.89	-0-
Furniture And Furnishings, Library Of Congress											
Fund Resources:											
Undisbursed Funds	2002	03		0146		159,757.12				159,757.12	
Undisbursed Funds	No Year					1,087,424.03	-695,394.00		162,133.12		229,896.91
Fund Equities:											
Unobligated Balances (Expired)						-116,428.60				-116,428.60	-2,244.17
Unobligated Balances (Unexpired)						-693,667.10				-691,422.93	-156,224.00
Accounts Payable						-35,048.00				121,176.00	
Undelivered Orders						-402,037.45				-330,608.71	-71,428.74
Subtotal	Subtotal	03		0146		-0-	-695,394.00		162,133.12	-857,527.12	-0-
Special Fund Accounts											
Oliver Wendell Holmes Devise Fund, Library Of Congress											
Fund Resources:											
Undisbursed Funds	No Year	03		5075		5,648.83	3,337.11		8,416.72		361.47
Unrealized Discount On Investments						-1,461.03		-207.75			-1,253.28
Investments In Public Debt Securities						68,000.00		207.75			68,000.00
Fund Equities:											
Unobligated Balances (Unexpired)						-71,163.25				-12,079.61	-59,083.64
Accounts Payable						-1,024.55				7,000.00	
Undelivered Orders										-5,079.61	-8,024.55
Subtotal	Subtotal	03		5075		-0-	3,337.11		8,416.72	-5,079.61	-0-
Payments To Copyright Owners, Copyright Office, Library Of Congress											
Fund Resources:											
Undisbursed Funds	No Year	03		5175		407,151.43	288,513,874.63	-3,855,258.84	284,790,345.35		275,421.87
Unrealized Discount On Investments						-6,158,201.49		2,490,258.84			-3,667,942.65
Investments In Public Debt Securities						1,125,741,000.00		1,365,000.00			1,127,106,000.00
Fund Equities:											
Unobligated Balances (Unexpired)						-1,119,977,232.20				3,688,627.80	-1,123,665,860.00
Accounts Payable						-12,717.74				34,901.48	-47,619.22
Subtotal	Subtotal	03		5175		-0-	288,513,874.63		284,790,345.35	3,723,529.28	-0-
Public Enterprise Funds											
Cooperative Acquisitions Program Revolving Fund, Library Of Congress											
Fund Resources:											
Undisbursed Funds	No Year	03		4325		4,009,233.23		38,445.00	-260,329.40		4,308,007.63
Funds Held Outside The Treasury	No Year					38,445.00		-38,445.00			

Footnotes At End Of Chapter

Appropriations, Outlays, and Balances – Continued

Appropriation or Fund Account — Title	Period of Availability	Reg	Tr From	Account Number	Sub No.	Balances, Beginning Of Fiscal Year	Appropriations And Other Obligational Authority[1]	Transfers Borrowings And Investment (Net)[2]	Outlays (Net)	Balances Withdrawn And Other Transactions[3]	Balances, End Of Fiscal Year[4]
Cooperative Acquisitions Program Revolving Fund, Library Of Congress - Continued											
Fund Resources: - Continued											
Accounts Receivable						11,526.43				-583.32	12,109.75
Fund Equities:											
Unobligated Balances (Unexpired)						-3,043,452.37				326,185.95	-3,369,638.32
Accounts Payable						-251,372.89				-17,360.93	-234,011.96
Undelivered Orders		03		4325		-764,379.40				-47,912.30	-716,467.10
Subtotal	Subtotal					-0-			-260,329.40	260,329.40	-0-
Duplication Services Associated With Audiovisual Conservation Center, Library Of Congress											
Fund Resources:											
Undisbursed Funds	No Year	03		4339		347,362.93		-740.25	191,087.85		155,534.83
Funds Held Outside The Treasury	No Year							740.25			740.25
Accounts Receivable						-84.54				-84.54	
Fund Equities:											
Unobligated Balances (Unexpired)						-248,612.91				-171,222.58	-77,390.33
Accounts Payable						-40,931.03				-8,785.00	-32,146.03
Undelivered Orders						-57,734.45				-10,995.73	-46,738.72
Subtotal	Subtotal	03		4339		-0-			191,087.85	-191,087.85	-0-
Gift Shop, Decimal Classification, Photo Duplication, And Related Services, Library Of Congress											
Fund Resources:											
Undisbursed Funds	No Year	03		4346		2,968,424.55		15,946.70	139,961.94		2,844,409.31
Funds Held Outside The Treasury	No Year					36,531.38		-15,946.70		-10,828.00	20,584.68
Accounts Receivable						13,104.89					23,932.89
Unfilled Customer Orders						19,538.94				19,538.94	
Fund Equities:											
Unobligated Balances (Unexpired)						-2,026,945.03				-46,795.45	-1,980,149.58
Accounts Payable						-450,022.63				-28,616.27	-421,406.36
Undelivered Orders						-560,632.10				-73,261.16	-487,370.94
Subtotal	Subtotal	03		4346		-0-			139,961.94	-139,961.94	-0-
Intragovernmental Funds											
Fedlink And Federal Research Programs, Library Of Congress											
Fund Resources:											
Undisbursed Funds	No Year	03		4543		36,519,516.25		-5,433.30	-7,336,640.13		43,850,723.08
Funds Held Outside The Treasury	No Year					6,740.62		5,433.30			12,173.92
Accounts Receivable						[8]4,302,852.97				3,488,933.36	813,919.61
Unfilled Customer Orders						[8]9,604,295.69				2,121,849.42	7,482,446.27
Fund Equities:											
Unobligated Balances (Unexpired)						[8]9,836,465.00				-2,336,415.86	-7,500,049.14
Accounts Payable						-17,906,940.19				31,842.30	-17,938,782.49
Undelivered Orders						-22,690,000.34				4,030,430.91	-26,720,431.25
Subtotal	Subtotal	03		4543		-0-			-7,336,640.13	7,336,640.13	-0-

Appropriations, Outlays, and Balances - Continued

Appropriation or Fund Account — Title	Reg	Tr From	Account Number	Sub No.	Period of Availability	Balances, Beginning Of Fiscal Year	Appropriations And Other Obligational Authority[1]	Transfers Borrowings And Investment (Net)[2]	Outlays (Net)	Balances Withdrawn And Other Transactions[3]	Balances, End Of Fiscal Year[4]
Trust Fund Accounts											
Payment Of Interest On Bequest Of Gertrude M. Hubbard, Library Of Congress											
Fund Resources:											
Undisbursed Funds	03		8022		No Year	17,321.95	774.25				18,096.20
Fund Equities:											
Unobligated Balances (Unexpired)	03		8022		Subtotal	-17,321.95	-774.25			774.25	-18,096.20
						-0-	-0-			774.25	-0-
Library Of Congress Gift Fund											
Fund Resources:											
Undisbursed Funds	03		8031		No Year	2,277,933.70	4,612,891.43	634,600.11	5,124,914.44		2,400,510.80
Unrealized Discount On Investments					No Year	-107,728.28		29,409.89			-78,318.39
Funds Held Outside The Treasury					No Year	32,110.00		-31,010.00			1,100.00
Investments In Public Debt Securities						9,837,000.00		-633,000.00			9,204,000.00
Accounts Receivable						76.44				-4.73	81.17
Fund Equities:											
Unobligated Balances (Unexpired)						-9,907,569.41				-1,428,116.73	-8,479,452.68
Accounts Payable						-328,393.46				600,974.32	-929,367.78
Undelivered Orders						-1,803,428.99				315,124.13	-2,118,553.12
	03		8031		Subtotal	-0-	4,612,891.43		5,124,914.44	-512,023.01	-0-
Library Of Congress Trust Fund											
Fund Resources:											
Undisbursed Funds	03		8032		No Year	10,982,460.12	15,333,095.80	5,036,882.47	20,901,939.78		10,450,498.61
Unrealized Discount On Investments					No Year	-664,676.61		29,117.53			-635,559.08
Funds Held Outside The Treasury					No Year	30,000.00		-30,000.00			-0-
Investments In Public Debt Securities						39,825,000.00		-5,036,000.00			34,789,000.00
Accounts Receivable						3,595.05				3,550.68	44.37
Fund Equities:											
Unobligated Balances (Unexpired)						-46,851,432.75				-9,086,841.90	-37,764,590.85
Accounts Payable						-412,776.66				795,544.61	-1,208,321.27
Undelivered Orders						-2,912,169.15				2,718,902.63	-5,631,071.78
	03		8032		Subtotal	-0-	15,333,095.80		20,901,939.78	-5,568,843.98	-0-
Service Fees, Library Of Congress											
Fund Resources:											
Undisbursed Funds	03		8208		No Year	664,622.97	268,892.51	-41.53	483,768.11		449,705.84
Funds Held Outside The Treasury					No Year	149.23		41.53			190.76
Fund Equities:											
Unobligated Balances (Unexpired)						-496,750.44				-132,737.78	-364,012.66
Accounts Payable						-22,083.31				-2,796.89	-19,286.42
Undelivered Orders						-145,938.45				-79,340.93	-66,597.52
	03		8208		Subtotal	-0-	268,892.51		483,768.11	-214,875.60	-0-
Foreign Service National Separation Liability Trust Fund, Library Of Congress											
Fund Resources:											
Undisbursed Funds	03		8339		No Year	771,704.07	154,863.78		56,164.30		870,403.55

Footnotes At End Of Chapter

Appropriations, Outlays, and Balances – Continued

Appropriation or Fund Account — Title	Period of Availability	Reg	Tr From	Account Number	Sub No.	Balances, Beginning Of Fiscal Year	Appropriations And Other Obligational Authority[1]	Transfers Borrowings And Investment (Net)[2]	Outlays (Net)	Balances Withdrawn And Other Transactions[3]	Balances, End Of Fiscal Year[4]
Foreign Service National Separation Liability Trust Fund, Library Of Congress - Continued											
Fund Equities:											
Unobligated Balances (Unexpired)						-771,704.07				89,020.87	-860,724.94
Accounts Payable										9,678.61	-9,678.61
	Subtotal	03		8339		-0-	154,863.78		56,164.30	98,699.48	-0-
Total, Library Of Congress							814,353,724.51		881,381,563.25	-67,027,838.74	
Government Printing Office											
General Fund Accounts											
Salaries And Expenses, Office Of Superintendent Of Documents											
Fund Resources:											
Undisbursed Funds	2007	04		0201			33,095,630.00		23,286,161.82		9,809,468.18
	2006					9,382,490.34			3,948,008.47		5,434,481.87
	2005					3,057,748.20			989,490.60		2,068,257.60
	2004					158,116.04			106,423.00		51,693.04
	2003					420,604.05			139,479.00		281,125.05
Accounts Receivable						[8]195,555.10				58,214.10	137,341.00
Fund Equities:											
Unobligated Balances (Expired)						[8]1,505,828.57				1,348,951.48	-2,854,780.05
Accounts Payable						[8]11,708,685.16				3,218,901.53	-14,927,586.69
Undelivered Orders						-0-				4,626,067.11	-0-
	Subtotal	04		0201		-0-	33,095,630.00		28,469,562.89	4,626,067.11	
Congressional Printing And Binding, Government Printing Office											
Fund Resources:											
Undisbursed Funds	2007	04		0203			87,954,100.00		74,748,107.00		13,205,993.00
	2006					17,267,607.00			17,267,607.00		
	2005					4,927,518.00			1,830,768.00		3,096,750.00
	2004					6,563,739.00			5,373,950.00		1,189,789.00
	2003					1,653,598.00			1,525,816.00		127,782.00
Fund Equities:											
Unobligated Balances (Expired)						[8]30,412,462.00				-12,792,148.00	-17,620,314.00
Undelivered Orders						-0-				-12,792,148.00	-0-
	Subtotal	04		0203		-0-	87,954,100.00		100,746,248.00	-12,792,148.00	
Intragovernmental Funds											
Revolving Fund, Government Printing Office											
Fund Resources:											
Undisbursed Funds	No Year	04		4505	1	185,774,754.81	1,000,000.00	54,016.95	-50,786,441.66		237,615,213.42
Funds Held Outside The Treasury	No Year					59,597.90		-54,016.95			5,580.95
Accounts Receivable						192,019,870.84				-66,105,969.43	258,125,840.27
Unfilled Customer Orders						[8]61,148,376.19				7,460,445.00	53,687,931.19
Fund Equities:											
Unobligated Balances (Unexpired)						[8]26,657,191.03				34,204,520.61	-60,861,711.64
Accounts Payable						-275,832,880.13				46,306,880.07	-322,139,760.20
Undelivered Orders						-136,512,528.58				29,920,565.41	-166,433,093.99

Appropriations, Outlays, and Balances - Continued

Appropriation or Fund Account — Title	Dept Reg	Dept Tr From	Account Number	Sub No.	Period of Availability	Balances, Beginning Of Fiscal Year	Appropriations And Other Obligational Authority[1]	Transfers Borrowings And Investment (Net)[2]	Outlays (Net)	Balances Withdrawn And Other Transactions[3]	Balances, End Of Fiscal Year[4]
Revolving Fund (Printing And Binding), Undistributed Sibac Chargebacks, Government Printing Office	04		4505		Subtotal	-0-	1,000,000.00		-50,786,441.66	51,786,441.66	-0-
Fund Resources:											
Undisbursed Funds	04		4505		No Year				300.00		[6]300.00
Accounts Receivable										-300.00	300.00
Subtotal	04		4505	2		-0-			300.00	-300.00	-0-
Total, Government Printing Office						-0-	122,049,730.00		78,429,669.23	43,620,060.77	
Government Accountability Office											
General Fund Accounts											
Salaries And Expenses, Government Accountability Office											
Fund Resources:											
Undisbursed Funds	05		0107		2007-2008		374,000.00				374,000.00
					2007		480,696,050.00	-2,000.00	[10]433,893,543.18		46,800,506.82
					2006-2007	189,203.37			63,463.18		125,740.19
					2006	47,668,970.33		2,000.00	43,555,032.76		4,115,937.57
					2005	4,345,414.21			2,507,404.17		1,838,010.04
					2004	2,224,189.70			356,769.94		1,867,419.76
					2003	6,012,629.53			1,405,729.72		4,606,899.81
					2002	1,577,741.22			43,927.60	1,533,813.62	
Funds Held Outside The Treasury					No Year	1,898,450.95			-1,997,050.63		3,895,501.58
					2007			2,000.00			2,000.00
					2006	2,000.00		-2,000.00			
Accounts Receivable						1,018,093.00				27,886.58	990,206.42
Fund Equities:											
Unobligated Balances (Expired)						-6,284,668.17				326,980.86	-6,611,649.03
Unobligated Balances (Unexpired)						-2,249,141.11				1,214,151.50	-3,463,292.61
Accounts Payable						-38,943,912.44				-5,007,960.04	-33,935,952.40
Undelivered Orders						-17,458,970.59				3,146,357.56	-20,605,328.15
Subtotal	05		0107			-0-	481,070,050.00		479,828,819.92	1,241,230.08	-0-
Total, Government Accountability Office							481,070,050.00		479,828,819.92	1,241,230.08	
United States Tax Court											
General Fund Accounts											
Salaries And Expenses, United States Tax Court											
Fund Resources:											
Undisbursed Funds	23		0100		2007		47,625,028.00		38,097,282.81		9,527,745.19
					2006	11,794,451.02			3,403,887.77		8,390,563.25
					2005	1,854,952.96			48,815.34		1,806,137.62
					2004	643,934.43					643,934.43
					2003	2,426,675.62			16,865.29		2,409,810.33

Footnotes At End Of Chapter

Appropriations, Outlays, and Balances – Continued

Appropriation or Fund Account	Account Symbol					Balances, Beginning Of Fiscal Year	Appropriations And Other Obligational Authority[1]	Transfers Borrowings And Investment (Net)[2]	Outlays (Net)	Balances Withdrawn And Other Transactions[3]	Balances, End Of Fiscal Year[4]
Title	Period of Availability	Dept Reg	Tr From	Account Number	Sub No.						
Salaries And Expenses, United States Tax Court - Continued											
Fund Resources: - Continued											
Undisbursed Funds - Continued	2002					3,512,869.52				3,512,869.52	
Accounts Receivable						3,750.00					3,750.00
Fund Equities:											
Unobligated Balances (Expired)						-10,808,940.06				-634,743.54	-10,174,196.52
Accounts Payable						-1,843,232.90				-268,164.13	-1,575,068.77
Undelivered Orders						-7,584,460.59				3,448,214.94	-11,032,675.53
	Subtotal	23		0100		-0-	47,625,028.00		41,566,851.21	6,058,176.79	-0-
Special Fund Accounts											
Tax Court Independent Counsel, United States Tax Court											
Fund Resources:											
Undisbursed Funds	No Year	23		5023		409,839.18			-10,470.00		420,309.18
Fund Equities:											
Unobligated Balances (Unexpired)						-409,839.18			-10,470.00	10,470.00	-420,309.18
	Subtotal	23		5023		-0-			-10,470.00	10,470.00	-0-
Trust Fund Accounts											
Tax Court Judges Survivors Annuity Fund											
Fund Resources:											
Undisbursed Funds	No Year	23		8115		120,295.77	922,628.09	-264,026.25	453,843.22		325,054.39
Unrealized Discount On Investments						-7,585.94		-973.75			-8,559.69
Investments In Public Debt Securities						8,561,000.00		265,000.00			8,826,000.00
Fund Equities:											
Unobligated Balances (Unexpired)						-8,673,709.83				468,784.87	-9,142,494.70
Accounts Payable											-0-
	Subtotal	23		8115		-0-	922,628.09		453,843.22	468,784.87	
Total, United States Tax Court	Subtotal	23				-0-	48,547,656.09		42,010,224.43	6,537,431.66	
Other Legislative Branch Agencies											
Legislative Branch Boards And Commissions											
General Fund Accounts											
Salaries And Expenses, Commission On Security And Cooperation In Europe											
Fund Resources:											
Undisbursed Funds	2007-2008	09		0110		378,606.22	2,031,728.00		1,799,314.93		232,413.07
	2006-2007					108,681.15			375,745.90		2,860.32
	No Year								-525.00		109,206.15
Funds Held Outside The Treasury	No Year					450.00					450.00
Fund Equities:											
Unobligated Balances (Expired)						-272,709.52				2,860.32	-2,860.32
Unobligated Balances (Unexpired)										-5,880.84	-266,828.68
Accounts Payable						-215,027.85				-139,787.31	-75,240.54

Appropriations, Outlays, and Balances - Continued

Appropriation or Fund Account — Title	Dept Reg	Tr From	Account Number	Sub No.	Period of Availability	Balances, Beginning Of Fiscal Year	Appropriations And Other Obligational Authority[1]	Transfers Borrowings And Investment (Net)[2]	Outlays (Net)	Balances Withdrawn And Other Transactions[3]	Balances, End Of Fiscal Year[4]
Payment To Open World Leadership Center Trust Fund											
Fund Resources:											
Undisbursed Funds	09		0110		Subtotal	-0-	2,031,728.00		2,174,535.83	-142,807.83	-0-
International Conferences And Contingencies, House And Senate Expenses											
Fund Resources:											
Undisbursed Funds	09		0145		No Year	----	13,860,000.00		13,860,000.00	.	----
Fund Resources:											
Undisbursed Funds	09		0500		No Year	935,674.19	820,000.00		820,018.77		935,655.42
Fund Equities:											
Unobligated Balances (Unexpired)						-350,674.69				-18.77	-350,655.92
Accounts Payable						-584,999.50					-584,999.50
Undisbursed Funds	09		0500		Subtotal	-0-	820,000.00		820,018.77	-18.77	-0-
John C. Stennis Center For Public Service Training And Development											
Fund Resources:											
Undisbursed Funds	09		1200		2007	----	425,700.00		425,700.00		----
National Commission On Terrorist Attacks Upon The United States											
Fund Resources:											
Undisbursed Funds	09		1501		2003-2004	1,469,739.17			-62.75		1,469,801.92
Fund Equities:											
Unobligated Balances (Expired)	09		1501		Subtotal	-1,469,739.17				62.75	-1,469,801.92
	09		1501		Subtotal	-0-			-62.75	62.75	-0-
Salaries And Expenses, Help Commission											
Fund Resources:											
Undisbursed Funds	09		1701		No Year	2,990,630.97			1,734,364.09		1,256,266.88
Fund Equities:											
Unobligated Balances (Unexpired)						-2,769,607.64				-1,710,149.88	-1,059,457.76
Accounts Payable						-31,132.72				-3,130.65	-28,002.07
Undelivered Orders						-189,890.61				-21,083.56	-168,807.05
	09		1701		Subtotal	-0-			1,734,364.09	-1,734,364.09	-0-
Salaries And Expenses, Antitrust Modernization Commission											
Fund Resources:											
Undisbursed Funds	09		1715		No Year	1,683,798.55	418,489.00		1,207,073.59		895,213.96
Fund Equities:											
Unobligated Balances (Unexpired)						-1,428,390.86				-608,587.25	-819,803.61
Accounts Payable						-33,853.74				-33,853.74	----
Undelivered Orders						-221,553.95				-146,143.60	-75,410.35
	09		1715		Subtotal	-0-	418,489.00		1,207,073.59	-788,584.59	-0-
Salaries And Expenses, Medicare Payment Advisory Commission											
Fund Resources:											
Undisbursed Funds	48		1550		2007	3,471,456.61	2,000,000.00		-1,895,967.84		3,895,967.84
					2006	497,471.77			2,156,539.91		1,314,916.70
					2005				166,438.60		331,033.17
					2004	367,352.88					367,352.88
					2003	356,841.81					356,841.81
					2002	544,875.81				544,875.81	
Fund Equities:											
Unobligated Balances (Expired)						-2,515,891.21				1,365,113.27	-3,881,004.48
Accounts Payable						-380,001.11				103,208.55	-483,209.66

Footnotes At End Of Chapter

63

Appropriations, Outlays, and Balances – Continued

Appropriation or Fund Account — Title	Period of Availability	Reg	Tr From	Account Number	Sub No.	Balances, Beginning Of Fiscal Year	Appropriations And Other Obligational Authority[1]	Transfers Borrowings And Investment (Net)[2]	Outlays (Net)	Balances Withdrawn And Other Transactions[3]	Balances, End Of Fiscal Year[4]
Salaries And Expenses, Medicare Payment Advisory Commission - Continued											
Fund Equities: - Continued											
Undelivered Orders						-2,342,106.56				-440,208.30	-1,901,898.26
	Subtotal	48		1550		-0-	2,000,000.00		427,010.67	1,572,989.33	-0-
Expenses, United States-China Security Review Commission											
Fund Resources:											
Undisbursed Funds	2007-2008	48		2973		835,096.44	2,972,761.00		1,797,234.44		1,175,526.56
	2006-2007					60,782.35			792,511.92		42,584.52
	No Year								-25,617.09		86,399.44
Fund Equities:											
Unobligated Balances (Expired)										5,515.66	-5,515.66
Unobligated Balances (Unexpired)						-302,832.98				813,411.69	-1,116,244.67
Accounts Payable						-168,462.83				10,361.73	-178,824.56
Undelivered Orders						-424,582.98				-420,657.35	-3,925.63
	Subtotal	48		2973		-0-	2,972,761.00		2,564,129.27	408,631.73	-0-
Expenses, United States Commission On International Religious Freedom											
Fund Resources:											
Undisbursed Funds	2007-2008	48		2975		173,099.37	3,258,000.00		2,952,668.54		305,331.46
	2006-2007					1,060,120.37			144,351.92		28,747.45
	No Year								324,033.15		736,087.22
Fund Equities:											
Unobligated Balances (Expired)						-955,089.29				34.18	-34.18
Unobligated Balances (Unexpired)						-144,385.39				-338,327.22	-616,762.07
Accounts Payable						-133,745.06				-76,633.92	-67,751.47
Undelivered Orders						-0-				251,873.35	-385,618.41
	Subtotal	48		2975		-0-	3,258,000.00		3,421,053.61	-163,053.61	-0-
Salaries And Expenses, Commission On Online Child Protection											
Fund Resources:											
Undisbursed Funds	No Year	48		2977		547,748.83				547,748.83	
Fund Equities:											
Unobligated Balances (Unexpired)						-547,748.83				-547,748.83	
	Subtotal	48		2977		-0-					-0-
Salaries And Expenses, Dwight D. Eisenhower Memorial Commission											
Fund Resources:											
Undisbursed Funds	No Year	48		2989		1,597,611.27			912,842.45		684,768.82
Fund Equities:											
Unobligated Balances (Unexpired)						-1,355,062.97				-810,503.71	-544,559.26
Accounts Payable						-15.00				-15.00	
Undelivered Orders						-242,533.30				-102,323.74	-140,209.56
	Subtotal	48		2989		-0-			912,842.45	-912,842.45	-0-
Salaries And Expenses, Commission On Affordable Housing And Health Facility Needs For Seniors In The 21st Century											
Fund Resources:											
Undisbursed Funds	2002-2003	48		2991		127,808.23					127,808.23
Fund Equities:											
Unobligated Balances (Expired)						-127,808.23					-127,808.23
	Subtotal	48		2991		-0-					-0-

Appropriations, Outlays, and Balances - Continued

Appropriation or Fund Account — Title	Dept Reg	Tr From	Account Number	Sub No.	Period of Availability	Balances, Beginning Of Fiscal Year	Appropriations And Other Obligational Authority[1]	Transfers Borrowings And Investment (Net)[2]	Outlays (Net)	Balances Withdrawn And Other Transactions[3]	Balances, End Of Fiscal Year[4]
Expenses, Abraham Lincoln Bicentennial Commission											
Fund Resources:											
Undisbursed Funds	48		2995		2001-2002	32,664.43				32,664.43	
					No Year	334,793.58	594,000.00		731,075.42		197,718.16
Accounts Receivable										-100.00	100.00
Fund Equities:											
Unobligated Balances (Expired)						-32,664.43				-32,664.43	
Unobligated Balances (Unexpired)						-292,819.22				-249,619.72	-43,199.50
Accounts Payable						-13,808.40				3,677.97	-17,486.37
Undelivered Orders						-28,165.96				108,966.33	-137,132.29
Subtotal	48		2995			-0-	594,000.00		731,075.42	-137,075.42	-0-
Commission On Review Of Overseas Military Facility Structure Of The United States											
Fund Resources:											
Undisbursed Funds	48		2999		2004-2005	559,273.56					559,273.56
Fund Equities:											
Unobligated Balances (Expired)						-478,945.94				80,327.62	-559,273.56
Undelivered Orders						-80,327.62				-80,327.62	-0-
Subtotal	48		2999			-0-					-0-
Expenses, Congressional-Executive Commission On The People's Republic Of China											
Fund Resources:											
Undisbursed Funds	95		2930		2007-2008	435,744.66			875,324.69		1,017,442.31
					2006-2007	619,977.83			423,557.40		12,187.26
					No Year						619,977.83
Fund Equities:											
Unobligated Balances (Expired)						-966,865.07				1,339.09	-1,339.09
Unobligated Balances (Unexpired)						-57,049.26				409,568.46	-1,376,433.53
Accounts Payable						-31,808.16				-16,645.31	-40,403.95
Undelivered Orders						-0-				199,622.67	-231,430.83
Subtotal	95		2930			-0-	1,892,767.00		1,298,882.09	593,884.91	-0-
Special Fund Accounts											
Senate Preservation Fund, Library Of Congress											
Fund Resources:											
Undisbursed Funds	00		5509		No Year	31,729.29	25,693.08	-24,685.65	1,569.41	25,466.71	31,167.31
Unrealized Discount On Investments						-8,237.16		685.65			-7,551.51
Investments In Public Debt Securities						518,000.00		24,000.00			542,000.00
Fund Equities:											
Unobligated Balances (Unexpired)						-540,149.09					-565,615.80
Accounts Payable						-1,343.04				-1,343.04	
Undelivered Orders						-0-					-0-
Subtotal	00		5509			-0-	25,693.08		1,569.41	24,123.67	-0-
Abraham Lincoln Bicentennial Commission Fund											
Fund Resources:											
Undisbursed Funds	48		5490		No Year	6,198.81	77,329.00		15,695.07		67,832.74

Footnotes At End Of Chapter

Appropriations, Outlays, and Balances – Continued

Appropriation or Fund Account: Title	Period of Availability	Reg	Tr From	Account Number	Sub No.	Balances, Beginning Of Fiscal Year	Appropriations And Other Obligational Authority[1]	Transfers Borrowings And Investment (Net)[2]	Outlays (Net)	Balances Withdrawn And Other Transactions[3]	Balances, End Of Fiscal Year[4]
Abraham Lincoln Bicentennial Commission Fund - Continued											
Fund Equities:											
Unobligated Balances (Unexpired)						-6,198.81				27,079.00	-33,277.81
Accounts Payable										4,803.63	4,803.63
Undelivered Orders										29,751.30	29,751.30
	Subtotal	48		5490		-0-	77,329.00		15,695.07	61,633.93	-0-
Trust Fund Accounts											
Open World Leadership Center Trust Fund											
Fund Resources:											
Undisbursed Funds	No Year	09		8148		1,966,955.55	14,831,964.02	-100,000.00	14,217,762.52		2,481,158.05
Investments In Public Debt Securities						13,097,000.00		100,000.00			13,197,000.00
Accounts Receivable						1,621.33				6.70	1,614.63
Fund Equities:											
Unobligated Balances (Unexpired)						-3,081,631.65				1,922,232.49	-5,003,864.14
Accounts Payable						-1,985,849.16				-178,134.81	-1,807,714.35
Undelivered Orders						-9,998,097.07				-1,129,902.88	-8,868,194.19
	Subtotal	09		8148		-0-	14,831,964.02		14,217,762.52	614,201.50	-0-
John C. Stennis Center For Public Service Training And Development											
Fund Resources:											
Undisbursed Funds	No Year	09		8275		21,812.20	1,613,126.27	-789,000.00	777,870.56		68,067.91
Funds Held Outside The Treasury	No Year					1,000.00					1,000.00
Investments In Public Debt Securities						12,120,000.00		789,000.00			12,909,000.00
Fund Equities:											
Unobligated Balances (Unexpired)						-11,986,519.67				781,467.17	-12,767,986.84
Accounts Payable						-41,644.93				40,032.28	-81,677.21
Undelivered Orders						-114,647.60				13,756.26	-128,403.86
	Subtotal	09		8275		-0-	1,613,126.27		777,870.56	835,255.71	-0-
Capitol Preservation Fund, U.S. Capitol Preservation Commission											
Fund Resources:											
Undisbursed Funds	No Year	09		8300		917.14	526,019.05	-525,615.72			1,320.47
Unrealized Discount On Investments						-222,068.42		17,615.72			-204,452.70
Investments In Public Debt Securities						9,792,000.00		508,000.00			10,300,000.00
Fund Equities:											
Unobligated Balances (Unexpired)						-9,554,657.72				526,019.05	-10,080,676.77
Accounts Payable											
Undelivered Orders						-16,191.00					-16,191.00
	Subtotal	09		8300		-0-	526,019.05			526,019.05	-0-
Total, Legislative Branch Boards And Commissions							45,347,576.42		44,589,520.60	758,055.82	
Total, Other Legislative Branch Agencies							45,347,576.42		44,589,520.60	758,055.82	

Appropriations, Outlays, and Balances - Continued

Appropriation or Fund Account		Account Symbol					Balances, Beginning Of Fiscal Year	Appropriations And Other Obligational Authority[1]	Transfers Borrowings And Investment (Net)[2]	Outlays (Net)	Balances Withdrawn And Other Transactions[3]	Balances, End Of Fiscal Year[4]
Title	Period of Availability	Dept		Account Number	Sub No.							
		Reg	Tr From									
Deductions For Offsetting Receipts												
Proprietary Receipts From The Public							--------	-6,522,445.12	--------	-6,522,445.12	--------	--------
Intrabudgetary Transactions							--------	-70,546,215.81	--------	-70,546,215.81	--------	--------
Total, Offsetting Receipts							--------	-77,068,660.93	--------	-77,068,660.93	--------	--------
Total, Legislative Branch							5552,779,490.83	4,321,444,456.40	-17,230,000.00	4,306,246,594.37	-3,500,170.81	5554,247,523.67

Appropriations, Outlays, and Balances – Continued

Footnotes

1   The amounts in this column, unless otherwise footnoted, represent appropriations, increases and rescissions in borrowing authority or new contract authority. Appropriation accounts with appropriation transfer activity are presented in Table 1 (Appropriations and Appropriation Transfers) at the end of this chapter.

2   The amounts in this column, unless otherwise footnoted, represent transfers - other than appropriation transfers, borrowings (gross), investments (net), unrealized discounts or funds held outside the Treasury.

3   The amounts shown in this column for the "Senate," "The House of Representatives," and "Joint," unless otherwise footnoted, represent unexpended balances withdrawn pursuant to 2 U.S.C. 104 (a). Amounts shown for "Congressional Budget Office," "Architect of the Capitol," "Library of Congress," "Government Printing Office," "General Accounting Office," "Other Legislative Branch Agencies" and "United States Tax Court," unless otherwise footnotes, represent obligated balances canceled for fiscal year 2002 pursuant to 31 U.S.C. 1553, changes in unfilled customer orders, accounts receivable, accounts payable, undelivered orders, unobligated balances.

4   Unobligated balances for no-year or unexpired multiple year accounts are available for obligation; unobligated balances for expired fiscal year accounts are not available for obligation.

5   Pursuant to 31 U.S.C. 3513, only executive agencies are required to report their financial condition.

6   Subject to disposition by the administrative agency.

7   Includes $8,707.22 which is subject to disposition by the administrative agency

8   The opening balances of the following accounts have been adjusted during the current fiscal year and do not agree with last year's closing balances:

Account	Adjustment
08 0100 - Accounts Receivable	$7,130.04
08 0100 - Unobligated Balances (Expired)	2,093.20
08 0100 - Undelivered Orders	-9,223.24
03 06 0101 - Unobligated Balances (Expired)	-2,000.00
03 06 0101 - Undelivered Orders	2,000.00
03 06 0102 - Unobligated Balances (Expired)	-4,194.01
03 X 0102 - Unobligated Balances (Unexpired)	4,194.01
03 X 4543 - Accounts Receivable	52,615.63
03 X 4543 - Unfilled Customer Orders	885,685.50
03 X 4543 - Unobligated Balances (Unexpired)	-938,301.13
04 06 0201 - Accounts Receivable	58,214.10
04 06 0201 - Unobligated Balances (Expired)	2,052,445.50
04 06 0201 - Accounts Payable	58,213.10
04 06 0201 - Undelivered Orders	-2,168,872.70
04 06 0203 - Unobligated Balances (Expired)	17,267,607.00
04 06 0203 - Undelivered Orders	-17,267,607.00
04 X 4505.1 - Unfilled Customer Orders	-1,696,781.05
04 X 4505.1 - Unobligated Balances (Unexpired)	1,696,781.05

9   Includes $4,489.53 which represents payments for obligations of a closed account.

10 Includes $3,612.25 which represents payments for obligations of a closed account.

Appropriations, Outlays, and Balances - Continued

Footnotes

Table 1 - Appropriations And Appropriation Transfers - Legislative Branch

Department Regular	Fiscal Year	Account Symbol	Net Appropriations And Appropriations Transfers	Appropriation Amount	Net Appropriation Transfers	Department Regular Involved	Fiscal Year Involved	Accounts Involved	Amount From or To (-)
00	07	0107	210,000.00	195,000.00	15,000.00	00	07	0108	15,000.00
00	07	0108	15,000.00	30,000.00	-15,000.00	00	07	0107	-15,000.00
00	07	0110	140,730,000.00	148,512,000.00	-7,782,000.00	00	07	0123	-2,032,000.00
						00	07	0127	-5,750,000.00
00	07	0123	19,332,000.00	17,000,000.00	2,332,000.00	00	07	0110	2,032,000.00
						00	07	0128	300,000.00
00	07	0126	1,970,000.00	1,980,000.00	-10,000.00	00	07	0172	-10,000.00
00	0711	0126	2,800,000.00	0.00	2,800,000.00	00	0711	0127	2,800,000.00
00	07	0127	7,550,000.00	0.00	7,550,000.00	00	07	0110	5,750,000.00
						00	07	0128	1,800,000.00
00	0711	0127	139,200,000.00	142,000,000.00	-2,800,000.00	00	0711	0126	-2,800,000.00
00	07	0128	118,592,000.00	120,692,000.00	-2,100,000.00	00	07	0123	-300,000.00
						00	07	0127	-1,800,000.00
00	07	0172	34,000.00	24,000.00	10,000.00	00	07	0126	10,000.00
00	07	0400	968,092,732.00	973,759,399.00	-5,666,667.00	00	07	0400	-5,666,667.00
00	0709	0400	155,938,696.00	150,272,029.00	5,666,667.00	00	0709	0400	5,666,667.00
00	X	4022	850,000.00	0.00	850,000.00	01	07	0123	850,000.00
01	07	0100	78,303,000.00	77,128,000.00	1,175,000.00	01	07	0108	160,000.00
						01	07	0133	973,000.00
						09	07	0200	42,000.00
01	07	0108	7,417,000.00	7,577,000.00	-160,000.00	01	07	0100	-160,000.00
01	07	0123	50,764,000.00	51,614,000.00	-850,000.00	00	X	4022	-850,000.00
01	07	0127	39,433,000.00	39,183,000.00	250,000.00	01	07	0133	250,000.00
01	07	0133	70,506,000.00	71,729,000.00	-1,223,000.00	01	07	0100	-973,000.00
						01	07	0127	-250,000.00
01	07	0155	25,259,000.00	22,559,000.00	2,700,000.00	03	X	0102	2,700,000.00
02	X	0476	9,158,275.65	9,158,275.65	-841,724.35	02	07	0477	-841,724.35
02	07	0476	38,350,000.00	38,500,000.00	-150,000.00	02	07	0477	-150,000.00
02	07	0477	218,126,724.35	218,126,724.35	991,724.35	02	X	0476	841,724.35
						02	07	0476	150,000.00
03	X	0101	-18,253,391.00	-17,659,391.00	-594,000.00	48	X	2995	-594,000.00
03	X	0102	-2,700,000.00	0.00	-2,700,000.00	01	07	0155	-2,700,000.00
09	07	0200	7,655,000.00	7,655,000.00	-42,000.00	01	07	0100	-42,000.00
48	0708	2975	3,258,000.00	3,258,000.00	258,000.00	19	0708	0113	258,000.00
48	X	2995	594,000.00	0.00	594,000.00	03	X	0101	594,000.00
Totals			2,083,185,037.00	2,082,927,037.00	258,000.00				258,000.00

Footnotes At End Of Chapter

Appropriations, Outlays, and Balances – Continued

Title	Period of Availability	Dept Reg	Tr From	Account Number	Sub No.	Balances, Beginning Of Fiscal Year	Appropriations And Other Obligational Authority[1]	Transfers Borrowings And Investment (Net)[2]	Outlays (Net)	Balances Withdrawn And Other Transactions[3]	Balances, End Of Fiscal Year[4]
Judicial Branch											
Supreme Court Of The United States											
General Fund Accounts											
Salaries And Expenses, Supreme Court Of The United States											
Fund Resources:											
Undisbursed Funds	2007	10		0100			60,576,000.00		50,137,752.73	———	10,438,247.27
	2006					10,775,589.27	———	———	5,887,461.82	———	4,888,127.45
	2005					6,872,122.63	———	———	1,363,086.78	———	5,509,035.85
	2004					2,909,027.77	———	———	66,599.10	———	2,842,428.67
	2003-2004					4,908.48	———	———	1,320.00	———	3,588.48
	2003					1,587,536.10	———	———	413,946.09	———	1,173,590.01
	2002					614,428.78	———	———	614,428.78	———	
	No Year					1,732,664.65	2,000,000.00	———	554,485.08	———	3,178,179.57
Fund Equities:											
Unobligated Balances (Expired)						-2,927,637.49				-122,748.74	-2,804,888.75
Unobligated Balances (Unexpired)						-1,732,664.65				-1,472,510.48	-260,154.17
Accounts Payable						-17,927,232.70				2,973,859.15	-20,901,091.85
Undelivered Orders						-1,908,742.84				2,158,319.69	-4,067,062.53
Subtotal		10		0100		-0-	62,576,000.00		59,039,080.38	3,536,919.62	-0-
Care Of The Building And Grounds, Supreme Court											
Fund Resources:											
Undisbursed Funds	No Year	10		0103		84,209,619.40	11,427,000.00	-4,500,000.00	15,284,987.42		75,851,631.98
Transfer To:											
Architect Of The Capitol	No Year	01	10	0103		130,989.31		4,500,000.00	3,007,232.72		1,623,756.59
Accounts Receivable											
Fund Equities:											
Unobligated Balances (Unexpired)						-28,441,766.24				80,472.55	-28,522,238.79
Accounts Payable						-5,984,964.86				104,442.56	-6,089,407.42
Undelivered Orders						-49,913,877.61				-7,050,135.25	-42,863,742.36
Subtotal		10		0103		-0-	11,427,000.00		18,292,220.14	-6,865,220.14	-0-
Total, Supreme Court Of The United States							74,003,000.00		77,331,300.52	-3,328,300.52	
United States Court Of Appeals For The Federal Circuit											
General Fund Accounts											
Salaries And Expenses, United States Court Of Appeals For The Federal Circuit											
Fund Resources:											
Undisbursed Funds	2007	10		0510			25,311,000.00		22,266,625.53	———	3,044,374.47
	2006					4,288,016.39			1,953,715.77	———	2,334,300.62
	2005					251,431.06			53,023.31	———	198,407.75
	2004					683,669.73			19,839.87	———	663,829.86
	2003-2004					583,397.00				———	583,397.00
	2003					855,926.70			202,767.33	———	653,159.37
	2002					287,764.34			15,658.49	272,105.85	

Appropriations, Outlays, and Balances - Continued

Appropriation or Fund Account — Title	Period of Availability	Reg	Tr From	Account Number	Sub No.	Balances, Beginning Of Fiscal Year	Appropriations And Other Obligational Authority[1]	Transfers Borrowings And Investment (Net)[2]	Outlays (Net)	Balances Withdrawn And Other Transactions[3]	Balances, End Of Fiscal Year[4]
Fund Equities:											
Unobligated Balances (Expired)						-1,557,261.64				219,134.98	-1,776,396.62
Accounts Payable						-640,544.49				39,883.89	-680,428.38
Undelivered Orders						-4,752,399.09				268,244.98	-5,020,644.07
Subtotal		10		0510		-0-	25,311,000.00		24,511,630.30	799,369.70	-0-
Total, United States Court Of Appeals For The Federal Circuit							25,311,000.00		24,511,630.30	799,369.70	
United States Court Of International Trade											
General Fund Accounts											
Salaries And Expenses, United States Court Of International Trade											
Fund Resources:											
Undisbursed Funds	2007	10		0400			15,825,000.00		14,772,430.91		1,052,569.09
	2006					1,122,433.16			700,499.39		421,933.77
	2005					957,384.46			164,394.71		792,989.75
	2004					226,189.24			1,291.43		224,897.81
	2003					239,605.90			5,551.27		234,054.63
	2002					382,894.59			10,489.16	372,405.43	-0-
Fund Equities:											
Unobligated Balances (Expired)						-961,431.90				-43,813.54	-917,618.36
Accounts Payable						-380,902.15				27,758.83	-408,660.98
Undelivered Orders						-1,586,173.30				-186,007.59	-1,400,165.71
Subtotal		10		0400		-0-	15,825,000.00		15,654,656.87	170,343.13	-0-
Total, United States Court Of International Trade							15,825,000.00		15,654,656.87	170,343.13	
Courts Of Appeals, District Courts, And Other Judicial Services											
General Fund Accounts											
Salaries And Expenses, Courts Of Appeals, District Courts, And Other Judicial Services											
Fund Resources:											
Undisbursed Funds	2007	10		0920			4,472,281,508.00	6,373,889.00	4,248,320,006.04		230,335,390.96
	2006					57,010,802.28			5,403,620.58		51,607,181.70
	2005					39,874,568.88			5,192,855.33		34,681,713.55
	2004					21,502,240.27			3,455,316.82		18,046,923.45
	2003					6,335,760.53			1,483,599.97		4,852,160.56
	2002					9,727,495.85			9,727,495.85		
	No Year					46,494,017.36	4,034,709.00	-6,373,889.00	16,759,031.02		27,395,806.34
Accounts Receivable						207,243,848.59				151,675,553.43	55,568,295.16
Fund Equities:											
Unobligated Balances (Expired)						-20,233,738.67				17,555,920.90	-37,789,659.57
Unobligated Balances (Unexpired)						-25,496,812.00				-19,116,857.32	-6,379,954.68
Accounts Payable						-145,405,850.42				35,065,498.05	-180,471,348.47

Footnotes At End Of Chapter

Appropriations, Outlays, and Balances – Continued

Appropriation or Fund Account — Title	Period of Availability	Reg	Tr From	Account Number	Sub No.	Balances, Beginning Of Fiscal Year	Appropriations And Other Obligational Authority[1]	Transfers Borrowings And Investment (Net)[2]	Outlays (Net)	Balances Withdrawn And Other Transactions[3]	Balances, End Of Fiscal Year[4]
Salaries And Expenses, Courts Of Appeals, District Courts, And Other Judicial Services - Continued											
Fund Equities: - Continued											
Undelivered Orders						-197,052,332.67				794,176.33	-197,846,509.00
Subtotal		10		0920		-0-	4,476,316,217.00		4,290,341,925.61	185,974,291.39	-0-
Defender Services, Court Of Appeals, District Courts, And Other Judicial Services											
Fund Resources:											
Undisbursed Funds	No Year	10		0923		31,110,209.43	776,506,173.00		771,077,983.15		36,538,399.28
Fund Equities:											
Unobligated Balances (Unexpired)						-9,509,152.02				2,793,155.82	-12,302,307.84
Accounts Payable						-11,962,244.88				1,225,708.79	-13,187,953.67
Undelivered Orders						-9,638,812.53				1,409,325.24	-11,048,137.77
Subtotal		10		0923		-0-	776,506,173.00		771,077,983.15	5,428,189.85	-0-
Fees Of Jurors And Commissioners, Court Of Appeals, District Courts And Other Judicial Services											
Fund Resources:											
Undisbursed Funds	No Year	10		0925		3,969,011.60	60,945,000.00		60,047,993.49		4,866,018.11
Fund Equities:											
Unobligated Balances (Unexpired)						-2,019,334.41				-1,975,574.66	-43,759.75
Accounts Payable						-2,044,734.50				2,627,532.85	-4,672,267.35
Undelivered Orders						95,057.31				245,048.32	-149,991.01
Subtotal		10		0925		-0-	60,945,000.00		60,047,993.49	897,006.51	-0-
Court Security, Court Of Appeals, District Courts, And Other Judicial Services											
Fund Resources:											
Undisbursed Funds	2007	10		0930			374,509,486.00	-310,832,913.00	53,868,672.58		9,807,900.42
	2006					11,467,216.99			10,973,276.75		493,940.24
	2005					111,437.29			71,019.95		40,417.34
	2004					2,897.39					2,897.39
	2003					3,474.25					3,474.25
	2002					1,979.88				1,979.88	
	No Year					11,774,398.72	4,153,514.00	-6,817,456.75	85,997.52		9,024,458.45
Transfer To:											
Justice, United States Marshals Service	2007	15	10	0930	3	59,164,481.68		310,832,913.00	236,676,612.63		74,156,300.37
	2006					883,886.77		-1,000,000.00	44,373,090.01		13,791,391.67
	2005					7,821,509.45			57,153.12		826,733.65
	2004					4,764,488.46		-700,000.00	2,170,918.41		4,950,591.04
	2003					1,914,972.79		-700,000.00	693,580.33		3,370,908.13
	2002							-1,266,344.25	648,628.54		
	No Year					13,651,787.23		10,483,801.00	8,733,090.36		15,402,497.87
Fund Equities:											
Unobligated Balances (Expired)						-3,531,007.64				3,384,866.60	-6,915,874.24
Unobligated Balances (Unexpired)						-12,534,475.35				-3,032,087.38	-9,502,387.97
Accounts Payable						-36,922,263.85				9,230,964.77	-46,153,228.62
Undelivered Orders						-58,574,784.06				10,725,235.93	-69,300,019.99
Subtotal		10		0930		-0-	378,663,000.00		358,352,040.20	20,310,959.80	-0-

Appropriations, Outlays, and Balances - Continued

Appropriation or Fund Account — Title	Period of Availability	Reg	Tr From	Account Number	Sub No.	Balances, Beginning Of Fiscal Year	Appropriations And Other Obligational Authority[1]	Transfers Borrowings And Investment (Net)[2]	Outlays (Net)	Balances Withdrawn And Other Transactions[3]	Balances, End Of Fiscal Year[4]
Furniture And Furnishings, The Judiciary											
Fund Resources:											
Undisbursed Funds	No Year	10		0932		71,091.62					71,091.62
Fund Equities:											
Unobligated Balances (Unexpired)						-71,091.62					-71,091.62
Subtotal		10		0932		-0-					-0-
Special Fund Accounts											
Filing Fees, The Judiciary											
Fund Resources:											
Undisbursed Funds	No Year	10		5100		339,324,289.18	189,316,611.54		204,440,797.08		324,200,103.64
Fund Equities:											
Unobligated Balances (Unexpired)						-134,883,492.10				134,006,707.91	-268,890,200.01
Accounts Payable						-204,440,797.08				-149,130,893.45	-55,309,903.63
Subtotal		10		5100		-0-	189,316,611.54		204,440,797.08	-15,124,185.54	-0-
Registry Administration Account, The Judiciary											
Fund Resources:											
Undisbursed Funds	No Year	10		5101		798,005.79	10,931,220.03		799,005.79		10,930,220.03
Fund Equities:											
Accounts Payable						-798,005.79				10,132,214.24	-10,930,220.03
Subtotal		10		5101		-0-	10,931,220.03		799,005.79	10,132,214.24	-0-
Judicial Information Technology Fund, The Judiciary											
Fund Resources:											
Undisbursed Funds	No Year	10		5114		333,399,870.78	264,228,386.97		324,364,378.84		273,263,878.91
Accounts Receivable						64,322.79				-17,586,279.88	17,650,602.67
Fund Equities:											
Unobligated Balances (Unexpired)						-146,550,667.18				-80,397,355.81	-66,153,311.37
Accounts Payable						-13,415,992.37				4,164,121.50	-17,580,113.87
Undelivered Orders						-173,497,534.02				33,683,522.32	-207,181,056.34
Subtotal		10		5114		-0-	264,228,386.97		324,364,378.84	-60,135,991.87	-0-
Total, Courts Of Appeals, District Courts, And Other Judicial Services							6,156,906,608.54		6,009,424,124.16	147,482,484.38	
Administrative Office Of The United States Courts											
General Fund Accounts											
Salaries And Expenses, Administrative Office Of The United States Courts											
Fund Resources:											
Undisbursed Funds:											
	2007	10		0927			72,377,000.00		88,398,794.27		[5]16,021,794.27
	2006					1,000,000.00			748,052.15		251,947.85
	2005					315,180.57			40,225.34		274,955.23
	2004					402,784.42			-282.59		403,067.01
	2003					154,052.23			895.00		153,157.23
	2002					362,764.01			362,764.01		
	No Year					1,185,223.90			1,069,850.84		115,373.06
Accounts Receivable						10,737,465.32			-16,617,256.06		27,354,721.38

Footnotes At End Of Chapter

Appropriations, Outlays, and Balances – Continued

Title	Reg	Tr From	Account Number	Sub No.	Period of Availability	Balances, Beginning Of Fiscal Year	Appropriations And Other Obligational Authority[1]	Transfers Borrowings And Investment (Net)[2]	Outlays (Net)	Balances Withdrawn And Other Transactions[3]	Balances, End Of Fiscal Year[4]
Salaries And Expenses, Administrative Office Of The United States Courts - Continued											
Fund Equities:											
Unobligated Balances (Expired)						-612,057.28				225,657.57	-837,714.85
Unobligated Balances (Unexpired)						-905,476.96				-872,206.67	-33,270.29
Accounts Payable						-8,820,538.35				18,181.14	-8,838,719.49
Undelivered Orders						-3,819,397.86				-997,675.00	-2,821,722.86
Subtotal	10		0927			-0-	72,377,000.00		90,620,299.02	-18,243,299.02	-0-
Consolidated Working Funds											
Consolidated Working Fund, The Judiciary											
Fund Resources:											
Undisbursed Funds	10		3927		2007	35,261.30			60,020.23		[5]-60,020.23
					2006	411.83			35,261.30		—
					2005						411.83
					2004	558.90			5,455.08		[5]-5,455.08
					2002				558.90		
Accounts Receivable										-68,277.23	68,277.23
Fund Equities:											
Accounts Payable						-45,559.55				-36,890.72	-8,668.83
Undelivered Orders						9,327.52				3,872.44	5,455.08
Subtotal	10		3927			-0-			101,295.51	-101,295.51	-0-
Total, Administrative Office Of The United States Courts							72,377,000.00		90,721,594.53	-18,344,594.53	
Federal Judicial Center											
General Fund Accounts											
Salaries And Expenses, Federal Judicial Center											
Fund Resources:											
Undisbursed Funds	10		0928		2007-2008		1,800,000.00		34,637.89		1,765,362.11
					2007		21,074,000.00		18,778,362.13		2,295,637.87
					2006-2007	1,658,623.58			1,616,865.13		41,758.45
					2006	1,663,049.51			1,551,220.07		111,829.44
					2005-2006	36,671.61			24,604.00		12,067.61
					2005	121,963.43			9,875.51		112,087.92
					2004-2005	35.56			400.20		[5]-364.64
					2004	71,735.48			4,368.65		67,366.83
					2003-2004	2,968.82					2,968.82
					2003	61,626.76			4,269.73		57,357.03
					2002-2003	7,894.67					7,894.67
					2002	18,705.01			-3,552.78	22,257.79	
Fund Equities:											
Unobligated Balances (Expired)						-158,651.35				127,003.88	-285,655.23
Unobligated Balances (Unexpired)						-465,363.90				112,437.31	-577,801.21
Accounts Payable						-694,011.42				-16,813.98	-677,197.44
Undelivered Orders						-2,325,247.76				608,064.47	-2,933,312.23
Subtotal	10		0928			-0-	22,874,000.00		22,021,050.53	852,949.47	-0-

Appropriations, Outlays, and Balances - Continued

Appropriation or Fund Account	Period of Availability	Account Symbol				Balances, Beginning Of Fiscal Year	Appropriations And Other Obligational Authority[1]	Transfers Borrowings And Investment (Net)[2]	Outlays (Net)	Balances Withdrawn And Other Transactions[3]	Balances, End Of Fiscal Year[4]
Title		Dept		Account Number	Sub No.						
		Reg	Tr From								
Total, Federal Judicial Center							22,874,000.00		22,021,050.53	852,949.47	
Judicial Retirement Funds											
General Fund Accounts											
Payment To Judiciary Trust Funds, Judicial Retirement Funds											
Fund Resources:											
Undisbursed Funds	2007	10		0941			58,300,000.00		58,300,000.00		
Trust Fund Accounts											
Judicial Survivors Annuity Fund											
Fund Resources:											
Undisbursed Funds	No Year	10		8110		682,665.34	29,022,652.03	-10,071,849.29	18,347,177.30		1,286,290.78
Unrealized Discount On Investments						-8,564,833.41		574,849.29			-7,989,984.12
Investments In Public Debt Securities						470,271,000.00		9,497,000.00			479,768,000.00
Accounts Receivable						932,142.68				932,142.68	
Fund Equities:											
Unobligated Balances (Unexpired)						-461,682,718.37				8,730,336.04	-470,413,054.41
Accounts Payable						-1,638,256.24				1,012,996.01	-2,651,252.25
Subtotal		10		8110		-0-	29,022,652.03		18,347,177.30	10,675,474.73	-0-
Judicial Officers Retirement Fund											
Fund Resources:											
Undisbursed Funds	No Year	10		8122		731,962.24	63,164,522.29	-31,638,580.38	30,904,096.02		1,353,808.13
Unrealized Discount On Investments						-4,423,921.11		235,580.38			-4,188,340.73
Investments In Public Debt Securities						218,861,000.00		31,403,000.00			250,264,000.00
Accounts Receivable						12,386.38				12,386.38	
Fund Equities:											
Unobligated Balances (Unexpired)						-212,536,583.65				33,527,078.71	-246,063,662.36
Accounts Payable						-2,644,843.86				-1,279,038.82	-1,365,805.04
Subtotal		10		8122		-0-	63,164,522.29		30,904,096.02	32,260,426.27	-0-
Claims Court Judges Retirement Fund											
Fund Resources:											
Undisbursed Funds	No Year	10		8124		162,146.35	4,025,024.63	-1,627,993.76	2,459,254.41		99,922.81
Unrealized Discount On Investments						-307,641.35		33,993.76			-273,647.59
Investments In Public Debt Securities						13,760,000.00		1,594,000.00			15,354,000.00
Fund Equities:											
Unobligated Balances (Unexpired)						-13,421,128.86				1,573,479.75	-14,994,608.61
Accounts Payable						-182,553.24				3,113.37	-185,666.61
Undelivered Orders						-10,822.90				-10,822.90	-0-
Subtotal		10		8124		-0-	4,025,024.63		2,459,254.41	1,565,770.22	-0-
Total, Judicial Retirement Funds							154,512,198.95		110,010,527.73	44,501,671.22	

Footnotes At End Of Chapter

Appropriations, Outlays, and Balances – Continued

Appropriation or Fund Account	Account Symbol					Balances, Beginning Of Fiscal Year	Appropriations And Other Obligational Authority[1]	Transfers Borrowings And Investment (Net)[2]	Outlays (Net)	Balances Withdrawn And Other Transactions[3]	Balances, End Of Fiscal Year[4]
Title	Period of Availability	Dept Reg	Tr From	Account Number	Sub No.						
United States Sentencing Commission											
General Fund Accounts											
Salaries And Expenses, United States Sentencing Commission											
Fund Resources:											
Undisbursed Funds	2007	10		0938		‒‒‒‒‒‒	14,601,000.00		11,416,555.50		3,184,444.50
	2006					2,911,639.03			2,394,653.65		516,985.38
	2005					700,684.70			178,638.35		522,046.35
	2004					513,535.24			-157,108.20		670,643.44
	2003					278,926.07			-200.00		279,126.07
	2002					100,497.65				100,497.65	
	No Year					597,021.80					597,021.80
Fund Equities:											
Unobligated Balances (Expired)						-438,840.85				1,192,574.84	-1,631,415.69
Unobligated Balances (Unexpired)						-588,723.52				8,298.28	-597,021.80
Accounts Payable						-468,377.87				-28,846.59	-439,531.28
Undelivered Orders						-3,606,362.25				-504,063.48	-3,102,298.77
						-0-			13,832,539.30	768,460.70	-0-
	Subtotal	10		0938		-0-	14,601,000.00		13,832,539.30	768,460.70	-0-
Total, United States Sentencing Commission						‒‒‒‒‒‒	14,601,000.00		13,832,539.30	768,460.70	‒‒‒‒‒‒
Deductions For Offsetting Receipts											
Proprietary Receipts From The Public						‒‒‒‒‒‒	-98,001,317.93		-98,001,317.93		
Intrabudgetary Transactions						‒‒‒‒‒‒	-257,252,381.00		-257,252,381.00		
Total, Offsetting Receipts						‒‒‒‒‒‒	-355,253,698.93		-355,253,698.93		
Total, Judicial Branch						‒‒‒‒‒‒	6,181,156,108.56		6,008,253,725.01	172,902,383.55	

Appropriations, Outlays, and Balances - Continued

Footnotes

1. The amounts in this column, unless otherwise footnoted, represent appropriations, increases and rescissions in borrowing authority or new contract authority. Appropriation accounts with appropriation transfer activity are presented in Table 1 (Appropriations and Appropriation Transfers) at the end of this chapter.

2. The amounts in this column, unless otherwise footnoted, represent transfers - other than appropriation transfers, borrowings (gross), investments (net), unrealized discounts or funds held outside the Treasury.

3. The amounts in this column, unless otherwise footnoted, represent obligated balances canceled for fiscal year 2002 pursuant to 31 U.S.C. 1553, changes in unfilled customer orders, accounts receivable, accounts payable, undelivered orders, unobligated balances and adjustments to borrowing and contract authority.

4. Unobligated balances for no-year or unexpired multiple year accounts are available for obligation; unobligated balances for expired fiscal year accounts are not available for obligation.

5. Subject to disposition by the administrative agency.

Appropriations, Outlays, and Balances – Continued

Footnotes

Table 1 - Appropriations And Appropriation Transfers - Judicial Branch

Department Regular	Fiscal Year	Account Symbol	Net Appropriations And Appropriations Transfers	Appropriation Amount	Net Appropriation Transfers	Department Regular Involved	Fiscal Year Involved	Accounts Involved	Amount From or To (-)
10	07	0100	60,576,000.00	59,351,000.00	1,225,000.00	10	07	0920	1,225,000.00
10	X	0103	11,427,000.00	5,628,000.00	5,799,000.00	10	07	0920	5,799,000.00
10	07	0400	15,825,000.00	15,467,720.00	357,280.00	10	07	0920	357,280.00
10	07	0510	25,311,000.00	24,138,970.00	1,172,030.00	10	07	0920	1,172,030.00
10	X	0920	4,034,709.00	0.00	4,034,709.00	10	07	0920	4,257,882.00
						10	X	0923	-223,173.00
10	07	0920	4,472,281,508.00	4,551,313,000.00	-79,031,492.00	10	07	0100	-1,225,000.00
						10	X	0103	-5,799,000.00
						10	07	0400	-357,280.00
						10	X	0510	-1,172,030.00
						10	X	0920	-4,257,882.00
						10	X	0923	-56,798,000.00
						10	X	0925	-240,180.00
						10	07	0927	-1,816,620.00
						10	07	0928	-388,500.00
						10	07	0930	-6,977,000.00
10	X	0923	776,506,173.00	719,485,000.00	57,021,173.00	10	X	0920	223,173.00
						10	07	0920	56,798,000.00
10	X	0925	60,945,000.00	60,704,820.00	240,180.00	10	07	0920	240,180.00
10	07	0927	72,377,000.00	70,560,380.00	1,816,620.00	10	07	0920	1,816,620.00
10	07	0928	21,074,000.00	20,685,500.00	388,500.00	10	07	0920	388,500.00
10	X	0930	4,153,514.00	0.00	4,153,514.00	10	07	0930	4,153,514.00
10	07	0930	374,509,486.00	371,686,000.00	2,823,486.00	10	07	0920	6,977,000.00
						10	X	0930	-4,153,514.00
Totals			5,899,020,390.00	5,899,020,390.00	0.00				0.00

Appropriations, Outlays, and Balances – Continued

Footnotes

This Page Left Blank Intentionally

Appropriations, Outlays, and Balances – Continued

Appropriation or Fund Account — Title	Reg	Tr From	Account Number	Sub No.	Period of Availability	Balances, Beginning Of Fiscal Year	Appropriations And Other Obligational Authority[1]	Transfers Borrowings And Investment (Net)[2]	Outlays (Net)	Balances Withdrawn And Other Transactions[3]	Balances, End Of Fiscal Year[4]
Department Of Agriculture											
Office Of The Secretary											
General Fund Accounts											
Office Of The Secretary, Agriculture											
Fund Resources:											
Undisbursed Funds	12		0115		2007	9,510,337.34	4,914,730.00		3,569,396.50		1,345,333.50
					2006-2007	1,075,973.49			6,648,875.93		2,861,461.41
					2006	272,120.16			42,043.30		1,118,016.79
					2005	343,445.10			91,989.28		180,130.88
					2004	309,184.75			9,872.22		333,572.88
					2003	16,733.81			687.13		308,497.62
					2002	211,338.53			1,403.69	15,330.12	-----
					2001-2002	-334,701.48				211,338.53	
					No Year		10,100,000.00		327,393.95		9,437,904.57
Accounts Receivable						5,778,183.91				2,072,527.31	3,705,656.60
Unfilled Customer Orders						7,445,251.35				3,018,846.28	4,426,405.07
Fund Equities:											
Unobligated Balances (Expired)						-1,131,926.54				649,272.65	-1,781,199.19
Unobligated Balances (Unexpired)						-3,530,310.25				7,716,668.19	-11,246,978.44
Accounts Payable						-882,855.45				-189,578.17	-693,277.28
Undelivered Orders						-19,082,774.72				-9,087,250.31	-9,995,524.41
Subtotal	12		0115			-0-	15,014,730.00		10,607,575.40	4,407,154.60	-0-
Office Of The Assistant Secretary For Administration											
Fund Resources:											
Undisbursed Funds	12		0121		2007		673,240.00		588,666.39		84,573.61
					2006	106,995.04			39,679.18		67,315.86
					2005	18,336.45			10.54		18,325.91
					2004	129,460.14			-0.82		129,460.96
					2003	4,431.16			0.13		4,431.03
					2002	6,666.20				6,666.20	
Fund Equities:											
Unobligated Balances (Expired)						-82,949.25				10,611.86	-93,561.11
Accounts Payable						-18,275.22				3,019.51	-21,294.73
Undelivered Orders						-164,664.52				24,587.01	-189,251.53
Subtotal	12		0121			-0-	673,240.00		628,355.42	44,884.58	-0-
Office Of The Assistant Secretary For Governmental And Public Affairs											
Fund Resources:											
Undisbursed Funds	12		0122		2007		1,887,790.00		1,781,821.63		105,968.37
					2006	182,518.34			87,521.74		94,996.60
					2005	148,964.73			-8,678.68		157,643.41
					2004	441.71			-3.15		444.86
					2003	68,613.29			0.45		68,612.84
					2002	405,414.87				405,414.87	
Accounts Receivable						86,294.89				12,191.45	74,103.44
Unfilled Customer Orders						39,325.75				15,100.70	24,225.05

Appropriations, Outlays, and Balances - Continued

Appropriation or Fund Account — Title	Period of Availability	Dept Reg	Dept Tr From	Account Number	Sub No.	Balances, Beginning Of Fiscal Year	Appropriations And Other Obligational Authority[1]	Transfers Borrowings And Investment (Net)[2]	Outlays (Net)	Balances Withdrawn And Other Transactions[3]	Balances, End Of Fiscal Year[4]
Fund Equities:											
Unobligated Balances (Expired)						-671,876.17				-362,169.85	-309,706.32
Accounts Payable						-54,110.93				9,437.64	-63,548.57
Undelivered Orders						-205,586.48				-52,846.80	-152,739.68
Subtotal		12		0122		-0-	1,887,790.00		1,860,661.99	27,128.01	-0-
Office Of The Under Secretary For Research, Education And Economics											
Fund Resources:											
Undisbursed Funds	2007	12		0124			596,020.00		992,313.58		[5]-396,293.58
	2006					-199,181.06			58,291.40		[5]-257,472.46
	2005					5,300.30			-598.01		5,898.31
	2004					37,771.96			-0.88		37,772.84
	2003					1,251.81			0.14		1,251.67
	2002					25,274.43			5,000.00	20,274.43	
Accounts Receivable						295,672.60				-415,799.81	711,472.41
Unfilled Customer Orders										-65,431.37	65,431.37
Fund Equities:											
Unobligated Balances (Expired)						-79,834.53				-3,453.24	-76,381.29
Accounts Payable						-34,881.20				-7,557.71	-27,323.49
Undelivered Orders						-51,374.31				12,981.47	-64,355.78
Subtotal		12		0124		-0-	596,020.00		1,055,006.23	-458,986.23	-0-
Office Of The Under Secretary For Marketing And Regulatory Programs											
Fund Resources:											
Undisbursed Funds	2007	12		0125			720,760.00		967,944.02		[5]-247,184.02
	2006					28,045.04			51,094.79		[5]-23,049.75
	2005					43,051.47			10.57		[5]-43,062.04
	2004					5,197.66			-0.88		5,198.54
	2003					30,194.93			0.13		30,194.80
	2002					12,168.29				12,168.29	
Accounts Receivable						158,066.08				-295,359.62	453,425.70
Unfilled Customer Orders										-8,640.00	8,640.00
Fund Equities:											
Unobligated Balances (Expired)						-95,421.81				21,917.58	-117,339.39
Accounts Payable						-29,580.61				7,421.07	-37,001.68
Undelivered Orders						-65,618.11				-35,795.95	-29,822.16
Subtotal		12		0125		-0-	720,760.00		1,019,048.63	-298,288.63	-0-
Office Of The Under Secretary For Farm And Foreign Agricultural Services											
Fund Resources:											
Undisbursed Funds	2007	12		0126			632,650.00		754,160.47		[5]-121,510.47
	2006					-105,413.54			-89,271.99		[5]-16,141.55
	2005					20,823.85			10.55		20,813.30
	2004					32,289.90			-0.88		32,290.78
	2003					37,574.06			0.13		37,573.93
	2002					33,057.81			5,000.00	28,057.81	
Accounts Receivable						173,401.35				-42,678.81	216,080.16
Unfilled Customer Orders										-16,000.00	16,000.00
Fund Equities:											
Unobligated Balances (Expired)						-126,823.21				-22,991.07	-103,832.14
Accounts Payable						-26,310.21				5,504.45	-31,814.66

Appropriations, Outlays, and Balances – Continued

Appropriation or Fund Account (Title)	Period of Availability	Tr From	Reg	Account Number	Sub No.	Balances, Beginning Of Fiscal Year	Appropriations And Other Obligational Authority[1]	Transfers Borrowings And Investment (Net)[2]	Outlays (Net)	Balances Withdrawn And Other Transactions[3]	Balances, End Of Fiscal Year[4]
Office Of The Under Secretary For Farm And Foreign Agricultural Services - Continued											
Fund Equities - Continued:											
Undelivered Orders						-38,600.01				10,859.34	-49,459.35
Subtotal			12	0126		-0-	632,650.00		669,898.28	-37,248.28	-0-
Office Of The Under Secretary For Rural Development											
Fund Resources:											
Undisbursed Funds	2007		12	0127		-257,510.82	632,650.00		1,131,200.68		[5]498,550.68
	2006					43,797.56			86,421.17		[5]343,931.99
	2005					43,047.14			10.56		43,787.00
	2004					74,683.88			-0.87		43,048.01
	2003					24,770.28			0.13		74,683.75
	2002					353,074.76			5,000.00	19,770.28	
Accounts Receivable										-526,948.52	880,023.28
Fund Equities:											
Unobligated Balances (Expired)						-197,348.08				-27,556.27	-169,791.81
Accounts Payable						-45,631.94				-44,375.65	-1,256.29
Undelivered Orders						-38,882.78				-10,871.51	-28,011.27
Subtotal			12	0127		-0-	632,650.00		1,222,631.67	-589,981.67	-0-
Office Of The Assistant Secretary For Natural Resources And Environment											
Fund Resources:											
Undisbursed Funds	2007		12	0128		-171,623.56	741,560.00		854,344.22		[5]112,784.22
	2006					7,422.20			95,868.65		[5]267,492.21
	2005					-55,992.40			904.29		6,517.91
	2004					7,290.28			1,198.95		[5]57,191.35
	2003					5,515.81			0.13		7,290.15
	2002					342,813.87				5,515.81	
Accounts Receivable										-164,356.16	507,170.03
Unfilled Customer Orders										-101,686.77	101,686.77
Fund Equities:											
Unobligated Balances (Expired)						-14,003.90				18,392.68	-32,396.58
Accounts Payable						-52,897.46				-27,927.42	-24,970.04
Undelivered Orders						-68,524.84				59,305.62	-127,830.46
Subtotal			12	0128		-0-	741,560.00		952,316.24	-210,756.24	-0-
Office Of The Under Secretary For Food, Nutrition And Consumer Services											
Fund Resources:											
Undisbursed Funds	2007		12	0129		-139,149.78	597,010.00		623,599.36		[5]26,589.36
	2006					1,322.10			-69,243.57		[5]69,906.21
	2005					16,095.64			908.56		413.54
	2004					8,930.48			-0.87		16,096.51
	2003					5,941.40			0.13		8,930.35
	2002					283,344.22				5,941.40	
Accounts Receivable										107,430.28	175,913.94
Fund Equities:											
Unobligated Balances (Expired)						-136,055.66				-97,568.13	-38,487.53
Accounts Payable						-10,524.47				15,610.98	-26,135.45
Undelivered Orders						-29,903.93				10,331.86	-40,235.79

Appropriations, Outlays, and Balances - Continued

Appropriation or Fund Account Title	Period of Availability	Dept Reg	Tr From	Account Number	Sub No.	Balances, Beginning Of Fiscal Year	Appropriations And Other Obligational Authority[1]	Transfers Borrowings And Investment (Net)[2]	Outlays (Net)	Balances Withdrawn And Other Transactions[3]	Balances, End Of Fiscal Year[4]
Office Of The Assistant Secretary For Civil Rights, Department Of Agriculture											
Fund Resources:											
Undisbursed Funds	Subtotal	12		0129		-0-	597,010.00		555,263.61	41,746.39	-0-
	2007	12		0130			817,790.00		1,020,043.25		[5]202,253.25
	2006					62,261.39			59,034.01		3,227.38
	2005					31,306.67			10.56		31,296.11
	2004					1,021.70			-0.88		1,022.58
	2003					127,125.74					127,125.74
Accounts Receivable						20,263.54				-260,607.80	280,871.34
Unfilled Customer Orders										-21,597.94	21,597.94
Fund Equities:											
Unobligated Balances (Expired)						-88,517.94				25,937.22	-114,455.16
Accounts Payable						-37,671.71				-3,397.08	-34,274.63
Undelivered Orders						-115,789.39				-1,631.34	-114,158.05
	Subtotal	12		0130		-0-	817,790.00		1,079,086.94	-261,296.94	-0-
Office Of The Under Secretary For Food Safety											
Fund Resources:											
Undisbursed Funds	2007	12		3701			599,980.00		545,474.49		54,505.51
	2006					-1,780.10			27,697.11		[5]29,477.21
	2005					34,989.70			10.56		34,979.14
	2004					13,061.37			-0.88		13,062.25
	2003					16,846.61			0.13		16,846.48
	2002					27,608.45			5,000.00	22,608.45	
Accounts Receivable						74,409.46				3,572.97	70,836.49
Fund Equities:											
Unobligated Balances (Expired)						-96,115.52				10,903.01	-107,018.53
Accounts Payable						-19,614.75				-9,318.42	-10,296.33
Undelivered Orders						-49,405.22				-5,967.42	-43,437.80
	Subtotal	12		3701		-0-	599,980.00		578,181.41	21,798.59	-0-
Trust Fund Accounts											
Gifts And Bequests, Department Of Agriculture											
Fund Resources:											
Undisbursed Funds	No Year	12		8203		2,909,015.14	828,072.18		698,223.55		3,038,863.77
Accounts Receivable						92,364.38				92,364.38	
Fund Equities:											
Unobligated Balances (Unexpired)						-2,700,393.90				82,272.79	-2,782,666.69
Accounts Payable						-45,236.82				17,276.47	-62,513.29
Undelivered Orders						-255,748.80				-62,065.01	-193,683.79
	Subtotal	12		8203		-0-	828,072.18		698,223.55	129,848.63	-0-
Total, Office Of The Secretary, Agriculture							23,742,252.18		20,926,249.37	2,816,002.81	

Footnotes At End Of Chapter

Appropriations, Outlays, and Balances – Continued

Appropriation or Fund Account — Title	Account Symbol — Dept — Reg	Tr From	Account Number	Sub No.	Period of Availability	Balances, Beginning Of Fiscal Year	Appropriations And Other Obligational Authority[1]	Transfers Borrowings And Investment (Net)[2]	Outlays (Net)	Balances Withdrawn And Other Transactions[3]	Balances, End Of Fiscal Year[4]
Executive Operations											
General Fund Accounts											
Expenses, Office Of The Chief Information Officer, Agriculture											
Fund Resources:											
Undisbursed Funds	12		0013		2007		16,361,380.00		16,063,428.90		297,951.10
					2006	-8,257,580.94			-8,673,461.94		415,881.00
					2005	-325,616.04			-255,550.61		[5]70,065.43
					2004	450,137.65			774,549.93		[5]324,412.28
					2003	2,244,787.43			1,378,462.85		866,324.58
					2002	-463,004.92			-708,412.91	245,407.99	
Accounts Receivable						36,683,344.81				26,888,437.49	9,794,907.32
Unfilled Customer Orders						26,685,079.58				5,826,605.73	20,858,473.85
Fund Equities:											
Unobligated Balances (Expired)						-22,395,372.07				-19,296,701.49	-3,098,670.58
Accounts Payable						-15,373,378.03				-10,569,950.59	-4,803,427.44
Undelivered Orders						-19,248,397.47				4,688,564.65	-23,936,962.12
Subtotal	12		0013			-0-	16,361,380.00		8,579,016.22	7,782,363.78	-0-
Expenses, Office Of The Chief Financial Officer											
Fund Resources:											
Undisbursed Funds	12		0014		2007		5,850,260.00		7,707,978.67		[5]1,857,718.67
					2006	-1,465,466.79			-1,790,325.92		324,859.13
					2005	-448,308.92			-722,451.44		274,142.52
					2004	333,002.83			-20,980.67		353,983.50
					2003	46,206.53			-65,194.42		111,400.95
					2002	-68,461.61			-231,977.89	163,516.28	
Accounts Receivable						3,965,094.29				-3,927,536.72	7,892,631.01
Unfilled Customer Orders						1,020,072.71				-5,375,293.98	6,395,366.69
Fund Equities:											
Unobligated Balances (Expired)						-799,143.52				4,748,804.82	-5,547,948.34
Accounts Payable						-1,034,897.97				-240,667.76	-794,230.21
Undelivered Orders						-1,548,097.55				5,604,389.03	-7,152,486.58
Subtotal	12		0014			-0-	5,850,260.00		4,877,048.33	973,211.67	-0-
Homeland Security Staff, Agriculture											
Fund Resources:											
Undisbursed Funds	12		0019		2007		930,660.00		1,168,603.97		[5]237,943.97
					2006	32,750.00			-54,211.72		86,961.72
					2005	-58,210.11			-78,488.29		20,278.18
					2004	32,533.94			7,279.00		25,254.94
Accounts Receivable						195,137.57				-445,288.32	640,425.89
Unfilled Customer Orders						158,373.76				16,375.88	141,997.88
Fund Equities:											
Unobligated Balances (Expired)						-66,471.02				90,888.89	-157,359.91
Accounts Payable						-134,638.48				-42,577.37	-92,061.11
Undelivered Orders						-159,475.66				268,077.96	-427,553.62
Subtotal	12		0019			-0-	930,660.00		1,043,182.96	-112,522.96	-0-

Appropriations, Outlays, and Balances - Continued

Appropriation or Fund Account — Title	Period of Availability	Reg	Tr From	Account Number	Sub No.	Balances, Beginning Of Fiscal Year	Appropriations And Other Obligational Authority[1]	Transfers Borrowings And Investment (Net)[2]	Outlays (Net)	Balances Withdrawn And Other Transactions[3]	Balances, End Of Fiscal Year[4]
Expenses, Common Computing Environment											
Fund Resources:											
Undisbursed Funds	No Year	12		0113		44,862,778.45	107,971,000.00		75,387,160.50		77,446,617.95
Accounts Receivable						1,050.40				-5,815,633.93	5,816,684.33
Unfilled Customer Orders						13,278,177.75				7,768,558.95	5,509,618.80
Fund Equities:											
Unobligated Balances (Unexpired)						-27,991,918.54				2,834,839.07	-30,826,757.61
Accounts Payable						-3,028,346.66				19,173,608.77	-22,201,955.43
Undelivered Orders						-27,121,741.40				8,622,466.64	-35,744,208.04
Subtotal		12		0113		-0-	107,971,000.00		75,387,160.50	32,583,839.50	-0-
Chief Economist, Executive Operations											
Fund Resources:											
Undisbursed Funds	2007	12		0123			12,486,610.00		8,146,346.22		4,340,263.78
	2006					4,309,902.83			2,763,741.21		1,546,161.62
	2005					1,911,943.23			1,359,908.28		552,034.95
	2004					683,209.22			275,715.66		407,493.56
	2003					21,380.24			290.44		21,089.80
	2002					289,346.54			-2,507.61	291,854.15	
Accounts Receivable						483,130.27				80,389.07	402,741.20
Unfilled Customer Orders						2,241,084.49				110,168.73	2,130,915.76
Fund Equities:											
Unobligated Balances (Expired)						-572,911.82				136,002.75	-708,914.57
Accounts Payable						-837,011.79				-21,472.25	-815,539.54
Undelivered Orders						-8,530,073.21				-653,826.65	-7,876,246.56
Subtotal		12		0123		-0-	12,486,610.00		12,543,494.20	-56,884.20	-0-
Office Of Budget And Program Analysis, Executive Operations											
Fund Resources:											
Undisbursed Funds	2007	12		0503			8,070,020.00		7,246,834.17		823,185.83
	2006					1,106,681.93			680,630.30		426,051.63
	2005					383,419.00			3,086.86		380,332.14
	2004					362,904.14			791.77		362,112.37
	2003					249,432.79			251.80		249,180.99
	2002					220,026.20			1,370.96	218,655.24	
Fund Equities:											
Unobligated Balances (Expired)						-1,477,191.82				72,794.07	-1,549,985.89
Accounts Payable						-725,364.60				-123,564.25	-601,800.35
Undelivered Orders						-119,907.64				-30,830.92	-89,076.72
Subtotal		12		0503		-0-	8,070,020.00		7,932,965.86	137,054.14	-0-
National Appeals Division, Executive Operations											
Fund Resources:											
Undisbursed Funds	2007	12		0706			14,285,760.00		12,045,323.82		2,240,436.18
	2006					1,915,318.66			1,135,967.53		779,351.13
	2005					588,479.65			-41.12		588,520.77
	2004					81,206.92			52.78		81,154.14
	2003					81,335.37			22,205.51		59,129.86
	2002					197,337.57			79,461.24	117,876.33	
Fund Equities:											
Unobligated Balances (Expired)						-739,627.84				129,178.16	-868,806.00

Footnotes At End Of Chapter

Appropriations, Outlays, and Balances – Continued

Appropriation or Fund Account — Title	Period of Availability	Dept Reg	Dept Tr From	Account Number	Sub No.	Balances, Beginning Of Fiscal Year	Appropriations And Other Obligational Authority[1]	Transfers Borrowings And Investment (Net)[2]	Outlays (Net)	Balances Withdrawn And Other Transactions[3]	Balances, End Of Fiscal Year[4]
National Appeals Division, Executive Operations - Continued											
Fund Equities – Continued:											
Accounts Payable						-722,293.28				109,289.18	-831,582.46
Undelivered Orders						-1,401,757.05				646,446.57	-2,048,203.62
Subtotal		12		0706		-0-	14,285,760.00		13,282,969.76	1,002,790.24	-0-
Intragovernmental Funds											
Working Capital Fund, Department Of Agriculture											
Fund Resources:											
Undisbursed Funds	2006-2007	12		4609		21,830,472.97			18,291,278.10		3,539,194.87
	No Year					145,476,014.15					158,094,053.27
Accounts Receivable						46,182,587.61			-6,286,764.12	-1,359,748.46	47,542,336.07
Unfilled Customer Orders						41,833,820.24				-29,934,385.96	71,768,206.20
Fund Equities:										40.78	-40.78
Unobligated Balances (Expired)						-92,609,583.34				-4,475,221.77	-88,134,361.57
Unobligated Balances (Unexpired)						-112,981,660.28				15,764,878.82	-128,746,539.10
Accounts Payable						-49,731,651.35				14,331,197.61	-64,062,848.96
Undelivered Orders						-0-	6,331,275.00		12,004,513.98	-5,673,238.98	-0-
Subtotal		12		4609			6,331,275.00		135,650,351.81	36,636,613.19	
Total, Executive Operations							172,286,965.00				
Office Of Civil Rights											
General Fund Accounts											
Office Of Civil Rights, Agriculture											
Fund Resources:											
Undisbursed Funds	2007	12		3800		1,345,763.95	20,019,910.00		16,246,157.24		3,773,752.76
	2006					1,319,917.23			685,487.84		660,276.11
	2005					2,274,715.52			245,401.94		1,074,515.29
	2004					4,135,870.10			166,263.98		2,108,451.54
Accounts Receivable						3,930,622.63				4,053,729.89	82,140.21
Unfilled Customer Orders										-1,097,437.25	5,028,059.88
Fund Equities:											
Unobligated Balances (Expired)						-345,929.80				2,501,132.73	-2,847,062.53
Accounts Payable						-5,760,786.89				-4,396,767.31	-1,364,019.58
Undelivered Orders						-6,900,172.74				1,615,940.94	-8,516,113.68
Subtotal		12		3800		-0-	20,019,910.00		17,343,311.00	2,676,599.00	-0-
Total, Office Of Civil Rights							20,019,910.00		17,343,311.00	2,676,599.00	
Departmental Administration											
General Fund Accounts											
Agriculture Buildings And Facilities And Rental Payments, Agriculture											
Fund Resources:											
Undisbursed Funds	No Year	12		0117		28,013,962.95	185,918,660.00		184,763,603.44		29,169,019.51

Appropriations, Outlays, and Balances - Continued

Appropriation or Fund Account — Title	Period of Availability	Account Symbol — Reg	Tr From	Account Number	Sub No.	Balances, Beginning Of Fiscal Year	Appropriations And Other Obligational Authority[1]	Transfers Borrowings And Investment (Net)[2]	Outlays (Net)	Balances Withdrawn And Other Transactions[3]	Balances, End Of Fiscal Year[4]
Accounts Receivable						474,514.96				437,468.17	37,046.79
Unfilled Customer Orders						2,490,419.55				1,031,907.70	1,458,511.85
Fund Equities:											
Unobligated Balances (Unexpired)						-10,137,251.39				-4,364,121.65	-5,773,129.74
Accounts Payable						-17,180,300.92				3,870,907.21	-21,051,208.13
Undelivered Orders						-3,661,345.15				178,895.13	-3,840,240.28
	Subtotal	12		0117		-0-	185,918,660.00		184,763,603.44	1,155,056.56	-0-
Departmental Administration, Agriculture											
Fund Resources:											
Undisbursed Funds											
	2007	12		0120		-7,480,519.05	23,143,970.00		26,017,229.49		[5]-2,873,259.49
	2006					-804,170.56			-1,821,927.33		[5]-5,658,591.72
	2005					-424,385.64			578,293.81		[5]-1,382,464.37
	2004					-1,018,309.40			227,902.95		[5]-652,288.59
	2003					-382,483.43			-113,468.73		[5]-904,840.67
	2002								-632,041.59		
Accounts Receivable						20,315,932.43			249,558.16	2,499,515.86	17,816,416.52
Unfilled Customer Orders						6,835,192.26				-8,613,851.71	15,449,043.97
Fund Equities:											
Unobligated Balances (Expired)						-3,744,901.56				-1,296,750.70	-2,448,150.86
Accounts Payable						-3,050,968.42				3,469,723.88	-6,520,692.30
Undelivered Orders						-10,245,386.58				2,579,785.91	-12,825,172.49
	Subtotal	12		0120		-0-	23,143,970.00		24,255,988.60	-1,112,018.60	-0-
Hazardous Materials Management, Agriculture											
Fund Resources:											
Undisbursed Funds	No Year	12		0500		24,965,908.14	11,887,000.00		10,403,466.03		26,449,442.11
Fund Equities:											
Unobligated Balances (Unexpired)						-958,240.42				1,473,466.63	-2,431,707.05
Accounts Payable						-1,471,509.93				924,607.12	-2,396,117.05
Undelivered Orders						-22,536,157.79				-914,539.78	-21,621,618.01
	Subtotal	12		0500		-0-	11,887,000.00		10,403,466.03	1,483,533.97	-0-
Total, Departmental Administration							220,949,630.00		219,423,058.07	1,526,571.93	
Office Of Communications											
General Fund Accounts											
Office Of Communications, Agriculture											
Fund Resources:											
Undisbursed Funds											
	2007	12		0150		1,196,988.88	9,337,910.00		8,418,839.28		919,070.72
	2006					504,050.35			767,423.90		429,564.98
	2005					195,622.02			72,247.78		431,802.57
	2004					479,273.39			114.37		195,507.65
	2003					216,345.96			2,835.67		476,437.72
	2002								-800.17		
Accounts Receivable						-24,066.95			217,146.13	-88,880.57	64,813.62
Unfilled Customer Orders						144,991.37				22,567.71	122,423.66
Fund Equities:											
Unobligated Balances (Expired)						-792,851.81				477,552.67	-1,270,404.48

Footnotes At End Of Chapter

Appropriations, Outlays, and Balances – Continued

Appropriation or Fund Account — Title	Period of Availability	Reg	Tr From	Account Number	Sub No.	Balances, Beginning Of Fiscal Year	Appropriations And Other Obligational Authority[1]	Transfers Borrowings And Investment (Net)[2]	Outlays (Net)	Balances Withdrawn And Other Transactions[3]	Balances, End Of Fiscal Year[4]
Office Of Communications, Agriculture - Continued											
Fund Equities - Continued:											
Accounts Payable						-634,335.28				-110,960.70	-523,374.58
Undelivered Orders						-1,286,017.93				-440,176.07	-845,841.86
Subtotal		12		0150		-0-	9,337,910.00		9,260,660.83	77,249.17	-0-
Total, Office Of Communications							9,337,910.00		9,260,660.83	77,249.17	
Office Of The Inspector General											
General Fund Accounts											
Office Of The Inspector General, Agriculture											
Fund Resources:											
Undisbursed Funds	2007	12		0900			80,051,640.00		72,214,738.08		7,836,901.92
	2006-2007					445,000.00			445,000.00		
	2006					7,887,988.34			6,340,255.79		1,547,732.55
	2005					2,586,586.47			69,815.54		2,516,770.93
	2004					1,987,363.74			-28,114.31		2,015,478.05
	2003					846,195.74			81.35		846,114.39
	2002					371,579.57			129,198.68	242,380.89	
Accounts Receivable						64,287.00				-72,232.45	136,519.45
Fund Equities:											
Unobligated Balances (Expired)						-3,538,557.49				381,524.36	-3,920,081.85
Unobligated Balances (Unexpired)						-445,000.00				-445,000.00	
Accounts Payable						-3,230,376.64				520,564.42	-3,750,941.06
Undelivered Orders						-6,975,066.73				253,427.65	-7,228,494.38
Subtotal		12		0900		-0-	80,051,640.00		79,170,975.13	880,664.87	-0-
Special Fund Accounts											
Inspector General Assets Forfeiture, Department Of Justice											
Fund Resources:											
Undisbursed Funds	No Year	12		5410		-93,807.71			-31,226.63		[5]62,581.08
Accounts Receivable						2,047,196.52				-117,711.32	2,164,907.84
Unfilled Customer Orders										-537,590.49	537,590.49
Fund Equities:											
Unobligated Balances (Unexpired)						-926,202.25				1,527,955.91	-2,454,158.16
Accounts Payable						-410,835.01				-902,435.74	491,600.73
Undelivered Orders						-616,351.55				61,008.27	-677,359.82
Subtotal		12		5410		-0-			-31,226.63	31,226.63	-0-
Inspector General Assets Forfeiture, Department Of The Treasury											
Fund Resources:											
Undisbursed Funds	No Year	12		5411		1,397,738.67			-2,079,615.25		3,477,353.92
Fund Equities:											
Unobligated Balances (Unexpired)						-1,619,429.15				1,857,924.77	-3,477,353.92
Accounts Payable						221,690.48				221,690.48	
Subtotal		12		5411		-0-			-2,079,615.25	2,079,615.25	-0-

Appropriations, Outlays, and Balances - Continued

Appropriation or Fund Account	Account Symbol					Balances, Beginning Of Fiscal Year	Appropriations And Other Obligational Authority[1]	Transfers Borrowings And Investment (Net)[2]	Outlays (Net)	Balances Withdrawn And Other Transactions[3]	Balances, End Of Fiscal Year[4]
Title	Period of Availability	Dept Reg	Tr From	Account Number	Sub No.						
Total, Office Of The Inspector General						-------	80,051,640.00	-------	77,060,133.25	2,991,506.75	-------
Office Of The General Counsel											
General Fund Accounts											
Office Of The General Counsel, Agriculture											
Fund Resources:											
Undisbursed Funds	2007	12		2300			39,227,490.00	-------	36,449,889.97	-------	2,777,600.03
	2006					3,542,538.96		-------	3,156,999.94	-------	385,539.02
	2005					359,410.23		-------	44,306.09	-------	315,104.14
	2004					529,935.36		-------	1,246.04	-------	528,689.32
	2003					393,871.15		-------	482.18	-------	393,388.97
	2002					295,356.70		-------	42,486.83	252,869.87	-------
Accounts Receivable						58,530.84		-------		-388,684.28	447,215.12
Unfilled Customer Orders						40,756.00		-------		9,725.00	31,031.00
Fund Equities:											
Unobligated Balances (Expired)						-748,809.96		-------		208,233.48	-957,043.44
Accounts Payable						-2,553,398.24		-------		-73,037.10	-2,480,361.14
Undelivered Orders						-1,918,191.04		-------		-477,028.02	-1,441,163.02
Subtotal		12		2300		-0-	39,227,490.00	-------	39,695,411.05	-467,921.05	-0-
Total, Office Of The General Counsel						-------	39,227,490.00	-------	39,695,411.05	-467,921.05	-------
Economic Research Service											
General Fund Accounts											
Economic Research Service											
Fund Resources:											
Undisbursed Funds	2007	12		1701			75,193,000.00	-------	56,568,126.81	-------	18,624,873.19
	2006					18,025,020.13		-------	9,900,896.07	-------	8,124,124.06
	2005					6,622,475.23		-------	3,765,024.32	-------	2,857,450.91
	2004					3,289,779.15		-------	1,235,020.92	-------	2,054,758.23
	2003					1,636,721.45		-------	561,443.80	-------	1,075,277.65
	2002					1,115,170.31		-------	729,828.92	385,341.39	-------
Accounts Receivable						125,769.18		-------		94,093.96	31,675.22
Unfilled Customer Orders						242,555.54		-------		105,172.54	137,383.00
Fund Equities:											
Unobligated Balances (Expired)						-723,056.00		-------		1,637,094.44	-2,360,150.44
Accounts Payable						-5,079,750.76		-------		-254,995.64	-4,824,755.12
Undelivered Orders						-25,254,684.23		-------		465,952.47	-25,720,636.70
Subtotal		12		1701		-0-	75,193,000.00	-------	72,760,340.84	2,432,659.16	-0-

Footnotes At End Of Chapter

Appropriations, Outlays, and Balances – Continued

Appropriation or Fund Account — Title	Period of Availability	Dept Reg	Tr From	Account Number	Sub No.	Balances, Beginning Of Fiscal Year	Appropriations And Other Obligational Authority[1]	Transfers Borrowings And Investment (Net)[2]	Outlays (Net)	Balances Withdrawn And Other Transactions[3]	Balances, End Of Fiscal Year[4]
Trust Fund Accounts											
Miscellaneous Contributed Funds, Economic Research Service											
Fund Resources:											
Undisbursed Funds	No Year	12		8227		49,499.98	-55,798.63		-7,379.11		1,080.46
Fund Equities:											
Unobligated Balances (Unexpired)						-55,798.63				-55,798.63	
Accounts Payable						7,379.11				7,379.11	
Undelivered Orders						-1,080.46				-48,419.52	-1,080.46
Subtotal		12		8227		-0-	-55,798.63		-7,379.11		-0-
Total, Economic Research Service							75,137,201.37		72,752,961.73	2,384,239.64	
National Agricultural Statistics Service											
General Fund Accounts											
National Agricultural Statistics Service											
Fund Resources:											
Undisbursed Funds	2007	12		1801			111,004,222.00		108,051,387.05		2,952,834.95
	2006					4,650,534.18			3,789,953.14		860,581.04
	2005					444,775.73			153,162.35		291,613.38
	2004					1,603,797.38			57,597.30		1,546,200.08
	2003					796,262.04			11,615.72		784,646.32
	2002					146,516.22			-17,467.81		
	No Year					8,436,206.14	36,248,778.00		30,336,962.26		14,348,021.88
Accounts Receivable						4,391,971.78			163,984.03	-1,082,734.67	5,474,706.45
Unfilled Customer Orders						5,630,708.81				5,561,884.85	68,823.96
Fund Equities:											
Unobligated Balances (Expired)						-2,047,794.20				197,524.02	-2,245,318.22
Unobligated Balances (Unexpired)						-1,087,018.32				2,518,116.18	-3,605,134.50
Accounts Payable						-8,122,957.96				-807,854.30	-7,315,103.66
Undelivered Orders						-14,843,001.80				-1,681,130.12	-13,161,871.68
Subtotal		12		1801		-0-	147,253,000.00		142,383,210.01	4,869,789.99	-0-
Trust Fund Accounts											
Miscellaneous Contributed Funds, National Agricultural Statistics Service											
Fund Resources:											
Undisbursed Funds	No Year	12		8218		103,680.01	434,561.08		445,332.65		92,908.44
Fund Equities:											
Unobligated Balances (Unexpired)						-74,822.73				49,228.43	-74,822.73
Accounts Payable						31,142.72				-60,000.00	-18,085.71
Undelivered Orders						-60,000.00					
Subtotal		12		8218		-0-	434,561.08		445,332.65	-10,771.57	-0-
Total, National Agricultural Statistics Service							147,687,561.08		142,828,542.66	4,859,018.42	

Appropriations, Outlays, and Balances - Continued

Appropriation or Fund Account — Title	Period of Availability	Reg	Tr From	Account Number	Sub No.	Balances, Beginning Of Fiscal Year	Appropriations And Other Obligational Authority[1]	Transfers Borrowings And Investment (Net)[2]	Outlays (Net)	Balances Withdrawn And Other Transactions[3]	Balances, End Of Fiscal Year[4]
Agricultural Research Service											
General Fund Accounts											
Salaries And Expenses, Agricultural Research Service											
Fund Resources:											
Undisbursed Funds	2007	12		1400			1,132,031,427.00		897,566,166.97		234,465,260.03
	2006-2007					6,400,694.81			4,245,056.41		2,155,638.40
	2006					214,564,929.31			154,191,806.12		60,373,123.19
	2005					57,215,946.56			33,568,080.27		23,647,866.29
	2004					20,783,743.18			7,734,227.79		13,049,515.39
	2003					12,535,703.09			1,495,719.85		11,039,983.24
	2002-2003					6,594.48					6,594.48
	2002					6,119,331.68			887,334.35	5,231,997.33	
	2001-2002					3,242.26				3,242.26	
	No Year					15,352,806.58			3,011,152.69		12,341,653.89
Accounts Receivable						30,147,425.12				3,314,744.67	26,832,680.45
Unfilled Customer Orders						50,995,844.98				997,876.64	49,997,968.34
Fund Equities:											
Unobligated Balances (Expired)						-18,006,101.73				6,313,868.45	-24,319,970.18
Unobligated Balances (Unexpired)						-12,187,028.69				-10,040,790.29	-2,146,238.40
Accounts Payable						-59,267,504.34				2,852,500.42	-62,120,004.76
Undelivered Orders						-324,665,627.29				20,658,443.07	-345,324,070.36
Subtotal		12		1400		-0-	1,132,031,427.00		1,102,699,544.45	29,331,882.55	-0-
Buildings And Facilities, Agricultural Research Service											
Fund Resources:											
Undisbursed Funds	2006-2007	12		1401		9,161,492.62			264,967.00		8,896,525.62
	No Year					489,285,065.54			190,704,366.37		298,580,699.17
Fund Equities:											
Unobligated Balances (Expired)						-261,815,163.87				1,012,541.11	-1,012,541.11
Unobligated Balances (Unexpired)						-1,974,887.75				-98,874,299.56	-162,940,864.31
Accounts Payable						-234,656,506.54				769,377.14	-2,744,264.89
Undelivered Orders										-93,876,952.06	-140,779,554.48
Subtotal		12		1401		-0-			190,969,333.37	-190,969,333.37	-0-
Special Fund Accounts											
Concessions Fees And Volunteer Services, Agricultural Research Service											
Fund Resources:											
Undisbursed Funds	No Year	12		5279		227,440.15	76,793.00		53,348.66		250,884.49
Fund Equities:											
Unobligated Balances (Unexpired)						-219,462.20				-34,853.28	-184,608.92
Accounts Payable						-2,662.95				-880.38	-1,782.57
Undelivered Orders						-5,315.00				59,178.00	-64,493.00
Subtotal		12		5279		-0-	76,793.00		53,348.66	23,444.34	-0-

Footnotes At End Of Chapter

Appropriations, Outlays, and Balances – Continued

Appropriation or Fund Account — Title	Period of Availability	Dept Reg	Tr From	Account Number	Sub No.	Balances, Beginning Of Fiscal Year	Appropriations And Other Obligational Authority[1]	Transfers Borrowings And Investment (Net)[2]	Outlays (Net)	Balances Withdrawn And Other Transactions[3]	Balances, End Of Fiscal Year[4]
Trust Fund Accounts											
Miscellaneous Contributed Funds, Agricultural Research Service											
Fund Resources:											
Undisbursed Funds	No Year	12		8214		18,654,812.45	19,000,269.69	-------	16,101,240.42	-------	21,553,841.72
Fund Equities:											
Unobligated Balances (Unexpired)						-14,235,017.18				3,566,506.55	-17,801,523.73
Accounts Payable						-725,136.43				15,708.05	-740,844.48
Undelivered Orders						-3,694,658.84				-683,185.33	-3,011,473.51
	Subtotal	12		8214		-0-	19,000,269.69		16,101,240.42	2,899,029.27	-0-
Total, Agricultural Research Service						-------	1,151,108,489.69		1,309,823,466.90	-158,714,977.21	-------
Cooperative State Research, Education, And Extension Service											
General Fund Accounts											
Extension Activities, Cooperative State Research, Education And Extension Service											
Fund Resources:											
Undisbursed Funds	2007-2008	12		0502		-------	5,000,000.00		67,103.76	-------	4,932,896.24
	2007					-------	433,625,000.00		187,673,940.77	-------	245,951,059.23
	2006-2007					4,922,910.77			858,005.36	-------	4,064,905.41
	2006					230,405,562.72			191,351,057.75	-------	39,054,504.97
	2005-2006					4,815,753.52			1,618,872.51	-------	3,196,881.01
	2005					33,446,164.86			25,075,571.38	-------	8,370,593.48
	2004-2005					1,728,976.87			1,551,349.70	-------	177,627.17
	2004					10,349,995.19			7,612,655.23	-------	2,737,339.96
	2003-2004					599,568.27			344,132.53	-------	255,435.74
	2003					6,599,631.60			3,405,311.95	-------	3,194,319.65
	2002-2003					9,146.34			-------	-------	9,146.34
	2002					2,042,833.06			1,238,766.16	804,066.90	-------
	2001-2002					59,318.01			-45,129.24	104,447.25	-------
	No Year					73,475,024.39	16,777,000.00		10,070,896.35	-------	80,181,128.04
Accounts Receivable						-1,091,687.27				-1,494,816.39	403,129.12
Unfilled Customer Orders						38,663,689.04				-6,409,694.82	45,073,383.86
Fund Equities:											
Unobligated Balances (Expired)						-1,031,823.70				1,563,509.13	-2,595,332.83
Accounts Payable						-1,878,460.44				75,000,081.27	-76,878,541.71
Undelivered Orders						-403,116,603.23				-44,988,127.55	-358,128,475.68
	Subtotal	12		0502		-0-	455,402,000.00		430,822,534.21	24,579,465.79	-0-
Outreach For Socially Disadvantaged Farmers, Natural Resources Conservation Service											
Fund Resources:											
Undisbursed Funds	No Year	12		0601		11,440,278.18	5,940,000.00		4,835,683.70	-------	12,544,594.48
Fund Equities:											
Unobligated Balances (Unexpired)						-361,779.73				-28,878.93	-332,900.80
Accounts Payable						-23,659.39				1,892,269.64	-1,915,929.03

Appropriations, Outlays, and Balances - Continued

Appropriation or Fund Account — Title	Period of Availability	Dept Reg	Tr From	Account Number	Sub No.	Balances, Beginning Of Fiscal Year	Appropriations And Other Obligational Authority[1]	Transfers Borrowings And Investment (Net)[2]	Outlays (Net)	Balances Withdrawn And Other Transactions[3]	Balances, End Of Fiscal Year[4]
Undelivered Orders	Subtotal	12		0601		-11,054,839.06				-759,074.41	-10,295,764.65
						-0-	5,940,000.00		4,835,683.70	1,104,316.30	-0-
Research And Education Activities, Cooperative State Research, Education, And Extension Service											
Fund Resources:											
Undisbursed Funds	2007	12		1500			456,468,380.00		208,175,018.16		248,293,361.84
	2006-2007					1,450,149.61			277,368.49		1,172,781.12
	2006					274,855,391.86			149,009,181.24		125,846,210.62
	2005					97,738,203.08			56,099,564.61		41,638,638.47
	2004					32,328,039.52			20,048,922.27		12,279,117.25
	2003					14,391,162.62			7,134,249.58		7,256,913.04
	2002					2,605,508.77			1,910,888.46	694,620.31	
	No Year					511,207,044.94	215,013,620.00		185,587,889.21		540,632,775.73
Accounts Receivable						1,183,903.18				1,568,047.39	-384,144.21
Unfilled Customer Orders						25,762,413.54				-6,122,212.71	31,884,626.25
Fund Equities:											
Unobligated Balances (Expired)						-1,740,553.51				1,981,152.09	-3,721,705.60
Unobligated Balances (Unexpired)						-103,542,525.00				10,272,665.72	-113,815,190.72
Accounts Payable						-2,279,019.84				235,875,861.68	-238,154,881.52
Undelivered Orders						-853,959,718.77				-201,031,216.50	-652,928,502.27
	Subtotal	12		1500		-0-	671,482,000.00		628,243,082.02	43,238,917.98	-0-
Buildings And Facilities, Cooperative State Research, Education, And Extension Service											
Fund Resources:											
Undisbursed Funds	No Year	12		1501		5,499,866.48			652,059.72		4,847,806.76
Fund Equities:											
Unobligated Balances (Unexpired)						-1,035,861.62					-1,035,861.62
Accounts Payable						-875.79					-875.79
Undelivered Orders						-4,463,129.07				-652,059.72	-3,811,069.35
	Subtotal	12		1501		-0-			652,059.72	-652,059.72	-0-
Integrated Activities, Cooperative State Research, Education And Extension Service											
Fund Resources:											
Undisbursed Funds	2007-2008	12		1502			10,636,560.00		682,202.26		9,954,357.74
	2007						46,607,520.00		1,706,950.48		44,900,569.52
	2006-2007					10,082,107.09			7,106,022.36		2,976,084.73
	2006					44,840,377.29			5,978,178.00		38,862,199.29
	2005-2006					4,284,085.21			4,101,297.09		182,788.12
	2005					37,925,305.02			17,920,612.96		20,004,692.06
	2004-2005					658,733.40			845,412.13		[5]-186,678.73
	2004					18,741,887.81			10,630,231.53		8,111,656.28
	2003					9,722,351.45			5,402,777.68		4,319,573.77
	2002					3,583,563.91			2,879,591.93	703,971.98	2,647,387.12
	No Year					2,760,778.72	990,000.00		1,103,391.60		
Fund Equities:											
Unobligated Balances (Expired)						-84,262.91				255,445.21	-339,708.12
Unobligated Balances (Unexpired)						-450,867.00				1,315,162.72	-1,766,029.72
Accounts Payable						-235,708.55				10,660,820.58	-10,896,529.13

Footnotes At End Of Chapter

Appropriations, Outlays, and Balances – Continued

Appropriation or Fund Account — Title	Period of Availability	Reg	Tr From	Account Number	Sub No.	Balances, Beginning Of Fiscal Year	Appropriations And Other Obligational Authority[1]	Transfers Borrowings And Investment (Net)[2]	Outlays (Net)	Balances Withdrawn And Other Transactions[3]	Balances, End Of Fiscal Year[4]
Integrated Activities, Cooperative State Research, Education And Extension Service - Continued											
Fund Equities - Continued:											
Undelivered Orders						-131,828,351.44				-13,057,988.51	-118,770,362.93
Subtotal		12		1502		-0-	58,234,080.00		58,356,668.02	-122,588.02	-0-
Initiative For Future Agriculture And Food Systems, Cooperative Research, Education And Extension Service											
Fund Resources:											
Undisbursed Funds	2006	12		1503		40,331.33			40,331.33		
	2004-2005					10,386.86			10,386.86		
Fund Equities:											
Unobligated Balances (Expired)						-3,434.38				-3,434.38	
Accounts Payable						3,616.06				-5,472.30	9,088.36
Undelivered Orders						-50,899.87			50,718.19	-41,811.51	-9,088.36
Subtotal		12		1503		-0-				-50,718.19	-0-
Special Fund Accounts											
Native American Institutions Endowment Fund											
Fund Resources:											
Undisbursed Funds	No Year	12		5205		8,171,749.95	15,201,651.96	-11,721,852.61	2,276,738.34	11,956,777.09	9,374,810.96
Unrealized Discount On Investments						-744,066.87		52,852.61			-691,214.26
Investments In Public Debt Securities						76,441,000.00		11,669,000.00			88,110,000.00
Fund Equities:											
Unobligated Balances (Unexpired)						-79,373,126.78				11,956,777.09	-91,329,903.87
Accounts Payable						-10,302.66				524,854.77	-535,157.43
Undelivered Orders						-4,485,253.64				443,281.76	-4,928,535.40
Subtotal		12		5205		-0-	15,201,651.96		2,276,738.34	12,924,913.62	
Total, Cooperative State Research, Education And Extension Service							1,206,259,731.96		1,125,237,484.20	81,022,247.76	
Animal And Plant Health Inspection Service											
General Fund Accounts											
Salaries And Expenses, Animal And Plant Health Inspection Service											
Fund Resources:											
Undisbursed Funds	2007	12		1600		64,269,524.86	533,481,925.00		422,632,911.62		110,849,013.38
	2006-2007					129,321,215.73			37,738,968.62		26,530,556.24
	2006					37,251,691.46			102,838,481.86		26,482,733.87
	2005					19,537,086.92			24,326,003.68		12,925,687.78
	2004					22,171,241.53			6,113,994.58		13,423,092.34
	2003					7,995,639.15			3,106,893.22		19,064,348.31
	2002					367,364,356.07			3,941,858.28		
	No Year					18,889,382.62	368,020,150.00	-3,751,484.00	343,989,957.14	4,053,780.87	387,643,064.93
Accounts Receivable										-9,677,639.04	28,567,021.66
Fund Equities:											
Unobligated Balances (Expired)						-32,062,473.40				-790,280.17	-31,272,193.23
Unobligated Balances (Unexpired)						-233,214,082.62				-11,244,730.18	-221,969,352.44
Accounts Payable						-73,515,621.83				-29,433,639.90	-44,081,981.93

Appropriations, Outlays, and Balances - Continued

Appropriation or Fund Account	Period of Availability	Dept Reg	Tr From	Account Number	Sub No.	Balances, Beginning Of Fiscal Year	Appropriations And Other Obligational Authority[1]	Transfers Borrowings And Investment (Net)[2]	Outlays (Net)	Balances Withdrawn And Other Transactions[3]	Balances, End Of Fiscal Year[4]
Title											
Undelivered Orders						-328,007,960.49				154,030.42	-328,161,990.91
	Subtotal	12		1600		-0-	901,502,075.00	-3,751,484.00	944,689,069.00	-46,938,478.00	-0-
Buildings And Facilities, Animal And Plant Health Inspection Service											
Fund Resources:											
Undisbursed Funds	No Year	12		1601		15,906,760.99	4,946,040.00		3,276,562.10		17,576,238.89
Fund Equities:											
Unobligated Balances (Unexpired)						-7,353,376.84				2,269,858.27	-9,623,235.11
Accounts Payable						-203,907.92				-138,903.13	-65,004.79
Undelivered Orders						-8,349,476.23				-461,477.24	-7,887,998.99
	Subtotal	12		1601		-0-	4,946,040.00		3,276,562.10	1,669,477.90	-0-
Special Fund Accounts											
Agricultural Quarantine Inspection User Fee Account, Animal And Plant Health Inspection Service											
Fund Resources:											
Undisbursed Funds	No Year	12		5161		121,705,814.97	472,248,627.96	-286,398,503.00	172,629,242.91		134,926,697.02
Accounts Receivable						200,740.67				197,594.30	3,146.37
Fund Equities:											
Unobligated Balances (Unexpired)						-71,699,966.48				11,706,400.11	-83,406,366.59
Accounts Payable						-7,652,667.38				-1,744,982.79	-5,907,684.59
Undelivered Orders						-42,553,921.78				3,061,870.43	-45,615,792.21
	Subtotal	12		5161		-0-	472,248,627.96	-286,398,503.00	172,629,242.91	13,220,882.05	-0-
Trust Fund Accounts											
Miscellaneous Contributed Funds, Animal And Plant Health Inspection Service											
Fund Resources:											
Undisbursed Funds	No Year	12		8226		13,881,185.78	17,126,887.69		13,980,036.03		17,028,037.44
Fund Equities:											
Unobligated Balances (Unexpired)						-12,529,026.33				2,686,861.79	-15,215,888.12
Accounts Payable						-79,646.73				-40,441.32	-39,205.41
Undelivered Orders						-1,272,512.72				500,431.19	-1,772,943.91
	Subtotal	12		8226		-0-	17,126,887.69		13,980,036.03	3,146,851.66	-0-
Total, Animal And Plant Health Inspection Service							1,395,823,630.65	-290,149,987.00	1,134,574,910.04	-28,901,266.39	
Food Safety And Inspection Service											
General Fund Accounts											
Food Safety And Inspection Service, Department Of Agriculture											
Fund Resources:											
Undisbursed Funds	2007	12		3700		3,953,933.60	882,604,610.00		760,748,636.22		121,855,973.78
	2006-2007								495,976.92		3,457,956.68
	2006					64,944,284.05			54,689,953.60		10,254,330.45
	2005-2006					2,323,981.92			2,310,899.29		13,082.63
	2005					11,968,921.58			5,359,464.77		6,609,456.81

Appropriations, Outlays, and Balances – Continued

Appropriation or Fund Account — Title	Period of Availability	Account Symbol — Dept Reg	Tr From	Account Number	Sub No.	Balances, Beginning Of Fiscal Year	Appropriations And Other Obligational Authority[1]	Transfers Borrowings And Investment (Net)[2]	Outlays (Net)	Balances Withdrawn And Other Transactions[3]	Balances, End Of Fiscal Year[4]
Food Safety And Inspection Service, Department Of Agriculture - Continued											
Fund Resources - Continued											
Undisbursed Funds - Continued											
	2004					11,115,784.83			3,467,820.52		7,647,964.31
	2003-2004					61,168.17					61,168.17
	2003					14,385,608.10			-1,737,456.21		16,123,064.31
	2002					18,096,218.88			1,402,815.68	16,693,403.20	
	No Year					7,208,762.56	8,079,390.00		-8,924,074.48		24,212,227.04
Accounts Receivable						17,364,722.09				-5,826,685.43	23,191,407.52
Fund Equities:											
Unobligated Balances (Expired)						-35,758,282.89				-7,669,955.21	-28,088,327.68
Unobligated Balances (Unexpired)						-3,274,146.65				21,021,981.13	-24,296,127.78
Accounts Payable						-37,070,140.60				4,280,794.81	-41,350,935.41
Undelivered Orders						-75,320,815.64				44,370,425.19	-119,691,240.83
	Subtotal	12		3700		-0-	890,684,000.00		817,814,036.31	72,869,963.69	-0-
Trust Fund Accounts											
Expenses And Refunds, Inspection Of Farm Products, Food Safety And Inspection Service											
Fund Resources:											
Undisbursed Funds	No Year	12		8137		1,504,071.20	8,456,556.36		7,642,793.69		2,317,833.87
Fund Equities:											
Unobligated Balances (Unexpired)						-914,965.53				781,267.36	-1,696,232.89
Accounts Payable						-330,868.46				-67,098.07	-263,770.39
Undelivered Orders						-258,237.21				99,593.38	-357,830.59
	Subtotal	12		8137		-0-	8,456,556.36		7,642,793.69	813,762.67	-0-
Total, Food Safety And Inspection Service							899,140,556.36		825,456,830.00	73,683,726.36	
Grain Inspection, Packers & Stockyards Administration											
General Fund Accounts											
Salaries And Expenses, Grain Inspection, Packers And Stockyards Administration											
Fund Resources:											
Undisbursed Funds	2007	12		2400			37,785,000.00		31,863,433.08		5,921,566.92
	2006					5,892,319.12			5,432,102.26		460,216.86
	2005					1,097,991.77			50,557.70		1,047,434.07
	2004					972,868.45			8,199.45		964,669.00
	2003					2,804,449.92			1,701.27		2,802,748.65
	2002					125,479.82			15,797.18	109,682.64	
	No Year					2,402,822.20			2,396,985.09		5,837.11
Accounts Receivable						83,041.90				82,941.90	100.00
Fund Equities:											
Unobligated Balances (Expired)						-3,269,968.77				1,754,061.65	-5,024,030.42
Unobligated Balances (Unexpired)						-388.27				5,448.84	-5,837.11
Accounts Payable						-4,135,922.36				-2,246,794.08	-1,889,128.28

Appropriations, Outlays, and Balances - Continued

Appropriation or Fund Account — Title	Period of Availability	Dept Reg	Tr From	Account Number	Sub No.	Balances, Beginning Of Fiscal Year	Appropriations And Other Obligational Authority[1]	Transfers Borrowings And Investment (Net)[2]	Outlays (Net)	Balances Withdrawn And Other Transactions[3]	Balances, End Of Fiscal Year[4]
Undelivered Orders						-5,972,693.78				-1,689,116.98	-4,283,576.80
				2400		-0-			39,768,776.03	-1,983,776.03	-0-
	Subtotal	12					37,785,000.00				
Public Enterprise Funds											
Inspection And Weighing Services, Grain Inspection, Packers And Stockyards Administration											
Fund Resources:											
Undisbursed Funds	No Year	12		4050		3,964,507.94					4,232,924.42
Accounts Receivable						4,130,495.44				-1,476,420.22	5,606,915.66
Fund Equities:											
Unobligated Balances (Unexpired)						-5,545,724.96				857,274.96	-6,402,999.92
Accounts Payable						-1,611,293.17				155,299.98	-1,766,593.15
Undelivered Orders						-937,985.25				732,261.76	-1,670,247.01
	Subtotal	12		4050		-0-			-268,416.48	268,416.48	-0-
Total, Grain Inspection, Packers & Stockyards Administration							37,785,000.00		39,500,359.55	-1,715,359.55	
Agricultural Marketing Service											
General Fund Accounts											
Payment To Expenses And Refunds, Inspection And Grading Of Farm Products, Agricultural Marketing Service											
Fund Resources:											
Undisbursed Funds	2007	12		0215			1,750,000.00		1,750,000.00		
Marketing Services, Agricultural Marketing Service											
Fund Resources:											
Undisbursed Funds	2007	12		2500		14,487,918.19	75,036,240.00		57,868,043.41		17,168,196.59
	2006					2,012,079.21			10,946,551.18		3,541,367.01
	2005					1,894,232.66			410,550.53		1,601,528.68
	2004					2,441,186.04			2,505.81		1,891,726.85
	2003					2,281,964.56			150,403.98		2,290,782.06
	2002					38,353,089.50			250,666.85	2,031,297.71	28,797,907.59
Funds Held Outside The Treasury	No Year							-9,894,428.42	-339,246.51		9,894,428.42
Accounts Receivable	No Year					4,351,966.24		9,894,428.42		2,301,408.68	2,050,557.56
Fund Equities:											
Unobligated Balances (Expired)						-7,077,653.34				509,029.16	-7,586,682.50
Unobligated Balances (Unexpired)						-28,480,383.27				-1,025,579.46	-27,454,803.81
Accounts Payable						-3,972,467.38				9,143,871.64	-13,116,339.02
Undelivered Orders						-26,291,932.41				-7,213,262.98	-19,078,669.43
	Subtotal	12		2500		-0-	75,036,240.00		69,289,475.25	5,746,764.75	-0-
Payments To States And Possessions, Agricultural Marketing Service											
Fund Resources:											
Undisbursed Funds	2007	12		2501			1,334,000.00		831,391.41		1,334,000.00
	2006					3,808,530.00			2,975,758.88		2,977,138.59
	2005					3,250,316.62			171,234.20		274,557.74
	2004					225,256.81					54,022.61

Footnotes At End Of Chapter

Appropriations, Outlays, and Balances – Continued

Appropriation or Fund Account — Title	Period of Availability	Account Symbol — Dept Reg	Tr From	Account Number	Sub No.	Balances, Beginning Of Fiscal Year	Appropriations And Other Obligational Authority[1]	Transfers Borrowings And Investment (Net)[2]	Outlays (Net)	Balances Withdrawn And Other Transactions[3]	Balances, End Of Fiscal Year[4]
Payments To States And Possessions, Agricultural Marketing Service - Continued											
Fund Resources - Continued:											
Undisbursed Funds – Continued:											
	2003					77,528.75					37,659.06
	2002					202,998.60			39,869.69	202,998.60	
	No Year					6,928,207.00	6,930,000.00		5,147,590.67		8,710,616.33
Fund Equities:											
Unobligated Balances (Expired)						-281,759.18				-155,944.19	-125,814.99
Unobligated Balances (Unexpired)						-6,928,207.00				1,460,915.73	-8,389,122.73
Accounts Payable						-6,000.00				314,280.13	-320,280.13
Undelivered Orders						-7,276,871.60				-2,724,095.12	-4,552,776.48
	Subtotal	12		2501		-0-	8,264,000.00		9,165,844.85	-901,844.85	-0-
Special Fund Accounts											
Perishable Agricultural Commodities Act Fund, Agricultural Marketing Service											
Fund Resources:											
Undisbursed Funds	No Year	12		5070		19,197,567.80	7,228,944.81	-4,593,574.22	10,193,204.11		11,639,734.28
Funds Held Outside The Treasury	No Year							4,593,574.22			4,593,574.22
Fund Equities:											
Unobligated Balances (Unexpired)						-17,913,424.36				-3,327,645.93	-14,585,778.43
Accounts Payable						-210,178.47				298,917.99	-509,096.46
Undelivered Orders						-1,073,964.97				64,468.64	-1,138,433.61
	Subtotal	12		5070		-0-	7,228,944.81		10,193,204.11	-2,964,259.30	-0-
Funds For Strengthening Markets, Income, And Supply (Section 32)											
Fund Resources:											
Undisbursed Funds	No Year	12		5209		201,612,854.36	1,177,730,655.14		738,551,711.73	80,658,512.90	560,133,284.87
Accounts Receivable						485,240.03					485,240.03
Fund Equities:											
Unobligated Balances (Unexpired)						-146,760,122.95				353,239,877.05	-500,000,000.00
Accounts Payable						-2,598,391.09				-129,720.40	-2,468,670.69
Undelivered Orders						-52,739,580.35				5,410,273.86	-58,149,854.21
	Subtotal	12		5209		-0-	1,177,730,655.14		738,551,711.73	439,178,943.41	-0-
Trust Fund Accounts											
Expenses And Refunds, Inspection And Grading Of Farm Products, Agricultural Marketing Service											
Fund Resources:											
Undisbursed Funds	No Year	12		8015		57,733,354.32	139,946,922.23	-14,030,627.36	136,153,251.44	4,721,082.41	47,496,397.75
Funds Held Outside The Treasury	No Year							14,030,627.36			14,030,627.36
Fund Equities:											
Unobligated Balances (Unexpired)						-39,818,462.83				-3,579,219.51	-44,539,545.24
Accounts Payable						-10,672,656.41				2,651,807.89	-7,093,436.90
Undelivered Orders						-7,242,235.08				3,793,670.79	-9,894,042.97
	Subtotal	12		8015		-0-	139,946,922.23		136,153,251.44	3,793,670.79	-0-

Appropriations, Outlays, and Balances - Continued

Appropriation or Fund Account — Title	Period of Availability	Dept Reg	Tr From	Account Number	Sub No.	Balances, Beginning Of Fiscal Year	Appropriations And Other Obligational Authority[1]	Transfers Borrowings And Investment (Net)[2]	Outlays (Net)	Balances Withdrawn And Other Transactions[3]	Balances, End Of Fiscal Year[4]
Wool Research, Development And Promotion Trust Fund, Agricultural Marketing Service											
Fund Resources:											
Undisbursed Funds	No Year	12		8100		--------	2,250,000.00	--------	2,250,000.00	--------	--------
Total, Agricultural Marketing Service						--------	1,412,206,762.18		967,353,487.38	444,853,274.80	--------
Risk Management Agency											
General Fund Accounts											
Administrative And Operating Expenses, Office Of Risk Management											
Fund Resources:											
Undisbursed Funds	2007	12		2707		17,791,399.08	76,257,520.00		62,567,446.22		13,690,073.78
	2006					1,610,339.91			16,474,336.52		1,317,062.56
	2005					2,177,226.48			463,265.50		1,147,074.41
	2004					894,520.98			735.28		2,176,491.20
	2003					1,912,377.50			-35,446.38		929,967.36
	2002								-379,734.15	2,292,111.65	
Fund Equities:											
Unobligated Balances (Expired)						-3,332,614.87				112,025.65	-3,444,640.52
Accounts Payable						-3,273,669.40				-237,007.76	-3,036,661.64
Undelivered Orders						-17,779,579.68				-5,000,212.53	-12,779,367.15
Subtotal		12		2707		-0-	76,257,520.00		79,090,602.99	-2,833,082.99	-0-
Public Enterprise Funds											
Federal Crop Insurance Corporation Fund, Consolidated Farm Service											
Fund Resources:											
Undisbursed Funds	No Year	12		4085		1,431,023,908.74	4,373,971,924.56	10,409,067.65	3,471,224,968.34	993,071,966.31	2,344,179,932.61
Funds Held Outside The Treasury	No Year					89,571,437.12		-10,409,067.65			79,162,369.47
Fund Equities:											
Unobligated Balances (Unexpired)						-1,265,839,180.23					-2,258,911,146.54
Accounts Payable						-193,490,285.57				-93,701,119.49	-99,789,166.08
Undelivered Orders						-61,265,880.06				3,376,109.40	-64,641,989.46
Subtotal		12		4085		-0-	4,373,971,924.56		3,471,224,968.34	902,746,956.22	-0-
Total, Risk Management Agency							4,450,229,444.56		3,550,315,571.33	899,913,873.23	
Farm Service Agency											
General Fund Accounts											
State Mediation Grants, Consolidated Farm Service Agency											
Fund Resources:											
Undisbursed Funds	2007	12		0170		2,247,892.99	4,207,500.00		2,182,158.97		2,025,341.03
	2006					524,826.41			1,711,991.83		535,901.16
	2005					276,471.07			120,235.55		404,590.86
	2004								-7,862.41		284,333.48

Footnotes At End Of Chapter

Appropriations, Outlays, and Balances – Continued

Appropriation or Fund Account: Title	Period of Availability	Dept Reg	Dept Tr From	Account Number	Sub No.	Balances, Beginning Of Fiscal Year	Appropriations And Other Obligational Authority[1]	Transfers Borrowings And Investment (Net)[2]	Outlays (Net)	Balances Withdrawn And Other Transactions[3]	Balances, End Of Fiscal Year[4]
State Mediation Grants, Consolidated Farm Service Agency - Continued											
Fund Resources - Continued:											
Undisbursed Funds – Continued:											
	2003					393,990.94					393,990.94
	2002					101,249.00				101,249.00	
	No Year					479,962.35			263,833.19		216,129.16
Fund Equities:											
Unobligated Balances (Expired)						-879,512.42				-35,593.60	-843,918.82
Unobligated Balances (Unexpired)						-479,962.35				-366,923.19	-113,039.16
Undelivered Orders						-2,664,917.99				238,410.66	-2,903,328.65
Subtotal		12		0170		-0-	4,207,500.00		4,270,357.13	-62,857.13	-0-
Salaries And Expenses, Farm Service Agency											
Fund Resources:											
Undisbursed Funds	2007-2008	12		0600			59,500,000.00		1,364,461.00		58,135,539.00
	2007					104,493,335.31	320,770,000.00		210,403,121.21		110,366,878.79
	2006					27,782,511.92			79,398,914.54		25,094,420.77
	2005					20,661,636.24			-2,822,667.16		30,605,179.08
	2004					8,309,031.13			782,001.27		19,879,634.97
	2003					13,963,155.22			-23,448.60		8,332,479.73
	2002								879,258.31		
	No Year					111,500,657.29	709,700,000.00	277,265.32	756,162,569.53	13,361,162.23	65,038,087.76
Transfer To:											
Commodity Credit Corporation	2006	12	12	0600	36	89,160.93					89,160.93
	2005					1,791,808.28					1,791,808.28
	2004					120,229.14					120,229.14
	2003					980,456.81			-320.76		980,777.57
	2002					273,987.60		-277,265.32	-3,277.72		
Accounts Receivable						5,649,413.16				-6,044,149.08	11,693,562.24
Unfilled Customer Orders						7,933,248.12				125,449.86	7,807,798.26
Fund Equities:											
Unobligated Balances (Expired)						-51,888,596.56				20,504,738.59	-72,393,335.15
Unobligated Balances (Unexpired)						-77,473,483.56				3,841,497.38	-81,314,980.94
Accounts Payable						-66,834,616.45				-10,840,185.75	-55,994,430.70
Undelivered Orders						-107,351,934.58				22,880,875.15	-130,232,809.73
Subtotal		12		0600		-0-	1,089,970,000.00		1,046,140,611.62	43,829,388.38	-0-
Agricultural Credit Insurance Fund Program Account, Farm Service Agency											
Fund Resources:											
Undisbursed Funds	2007	12		1140		21,014,151.02	564,204,099.00		537,560,504.16		26,643,594.84
	2006					16,969,942.60			11,390,536.76		9,623,614.26
	2005					9,110,135.96			274,711.46		16,695,231.14
	2004					8,930,812.28			18,400.58		9,091,735.38
	2003					6,921,495.90			17,496.56		8,913,315.72
	2002									6,921,495.90	
	No Year					16,230,577.16	308,000.00		8,712,761.26		7,825,815.90
Fund Equities:											
Unobligated Balances (Expired)						-47,408,877.81				8,186,494.55	-55,595,372.36
Unobligated Balances (Unexpired)						-15,750,837.12				-8,537,554.54	-7,213,282.58
Accounts Payable						-2,203,592.22				-253,297.65	-1,950,294.57

Appropriations, Outlays, and Balances - Continued

Appropriation or Fund Account — Title	Reg	Tr From	Account Number	Sub No.	Period of Availability	Balances, Beginning Of Fiscal Year	Appropriations And Other Obligational Authority[1]	Transfers Borrowings And Investment (Net)[2]	Outlays (Net)	Balances Withdrawn And Other Transactions[3]	Balances, End Of Fiscal Year[4]
Undelivered Orders	12		1140		Subtotal	-13,813,807.77				220,549.96	-14,034,357.73
	12					-0-	564,512,099.00		557,974,410.78	6,537,688.22	-0-
Commodity Credit Corporation Export Loans Program Account											
Fund Resources:											
Undisbursed Funds	12		1336		2007		5,260,210.00		5,260,210.00		
	12		1336		No Year	329,336,710.83	143,450,178.00		123,779,361.46		349,007,527.37
Fund Equities:											
Unobligated Balances (Unexpired)	12					-161,481,448.08				21,982,791.89	-183,464,239.97
Accounts Payable	12					-11,938,747.00				-985,018.00	-10,953,729.00
Undelivered Orders	12					-155,916,515.75				-1,326,957.35	-154,589,558.40
	12		1336		Subtotal	-0-	148,710,388.00		129,039,571.46	19,670,816.54	-0-
Tree Assistance Program, Farmer Service Agency											
Fund Resources:											
Undisbursed Funds	12		2701		2004	1,500,000.00					1,500,000.00
Transfer To:											
Commodity Credit Corporation	12	12	2701	36	2004	3,633,283.00		-2,800,000,000.00		2,739,578.00	3,633,283.00
Commodity Credit Corporation	12		2701		No Year	-0-	2,800,000,000.00	2,800,000,000.00		2,800,000,000.00	2,800,000,000.00
Fund Equities:											
Unobligated Balances (Expired)	12		2701		2004	-2,393,705.00				-2,739,578.00	-5,133,283.00
Unobligated Balances (Unexpired)	12		2701		No Year	-2,739,578.00	2,800,000,000.00			2,800,000,000.00	-2,800,000,000.00
Undelivered Orders	12		2701		Subtotal	-0-					-0-
Farm Storage Facility Loans Program Accounts, Farm Service Agency											
Fund Resources:											
Undisbursed Funds	12		3301		No Year	986,122.49	665,000.00		502,469.88		1,148,652.61
Fund Equities:											
Unobligated Balances (Unexpired)	12					-979,162.84				-322,685.91	-656,476.93
Accounts Payable	12					-6,355.44				36,457.89	-42,813.33
Undelivered Orders	12					-604.21				448,758.14	-449,362.35
	12		3301		Subtotal	-0-	665,000.00		502,469.88	162,530.12	-0-
Grassroots Source Water Protection Program, Farm Service Agency											
Fund Resources:											
Undisbursed Funds	12		3304		No Year		100,000.00				
Dairy Indemnity Program, Farm Service Agency											
Fund Resources:											
Undisbursed Funds	12		3314		No Year		3,712,500.00	-100,000.00	3,712,500.00		
Transfer To:											
Commodity Credit Corporation	12	12	3314	36	No Year	233,105.40	100,000.00	100,000.00	181,329.05		151,776.35
Fund Equities:											
Unobligated Balances (Unexpired)	12					-233,105.40				-81,329.05	-151,776.35
	12		3315		Subtotal	-0-			181,329.05	-81,329.05	-0-
Agricultural Conservation Program, Farm Service Agency											
Fund Resources:											
Undisbursed Funds	12		3315		No Year			25,000.00			
Transfer To:											
Commodity Credit Corporation	12	12	3315	36	No Year	98,495.63	-25,000.00	-25,000.00	50,756.65		22,738.98

Footnotes At End Of Chapter

Appropriations, Outlays, and Balances – Continued

Appropriation or Fund Account — Title	Period of Availability	Dept Reg	Dept Tr From	Account Number	Sub No.	Balances, Beginning Of Fiscal Year	Appropriations And Other Obligational Authority[1]	Transfers Borrowings And Investment (Net)[2]	Outlays (Net)	Balances Withdrawn And Other Transactions[3]	Balances, End Of Fiscal Year[4]
Agricultural Conservation Program, Farm Service Agency - Continued											
Fund Equities:											
Unobligated Balances (Unexpired)						-98,495.63				-75,756.65	-22,738.98
	Subtotal	12		3315		-0-	-25,000.00		50,756.65	-75,756.65	-0-
Emergency Conservation Program, Farm Service Agency											
Fund Resources:											
Undisbursed Funds	No Year	12		3316			18,000,000.00	-18,000,000.00			
Transfer To:											
Commodity Credit Corporation	No Year	12	12	3316	36	210,220,883.42	18,000,000.00	18,000,000.00	72,165,818.08		156,055,065.34
Fund Equities:											
Unobligated Balances (Unexpired)						-149,726,915.58				-21,270,191.77	-128,456,723.81
Accounts Payable						-296,070.84				4,497,430.69	-4,793,501.53
Undelivered Orders						-60,197,897.00				-37,393,057.00	-22,804,840.00
	Subtotal	12		3316		-0-	18,000,000.00		72,165,818.08	-54,165,818.08	-0-
Conservation Reserve Program, Farm Service Agency											
Fund Resources:											
Undisbursed Funds	No Year	12		3319		125,000.00					125,000.00
Transfer To:											
Commodity Credit Corporation	No Year	12	12	3319	36	168,322.22			-2,624.44		170,946.66
Fund Equities:											
Unobligated Balances (Unexpired)						-293,322.22				2,624.44	-295,946.66
	Subtotal	12		3319		-0-			-2,624.44	2,624.44	-0-
Public Enterprise Funds											
Agricultural Credit Insurance Fund, Liquidating Account, Consolidated Farm Service Agency											
Fund Resources:											
Undisbursed Funds	No Year	12		4140		26,006,291.81			-388,640,386.89	[6]398,849,196.96	15,797,481.74
Fund Equities:											
Unobligated Balances (Unexpired)						-23,849,196.96				-9,723,717.67	-14,125,479.29
Accounts Payable						-865,688.57				-102,035.76	-763,652.81
Undelivered Orders						-1,291,406.28				-383,056.64	-908,349.64
	Subtotal	12		4140		-0-			-388,640,386.89	388,640,386.89	-0-
Commodity Credit Corporation Fund, Liquidating Account											
Fund Resources:											
Undisbursed Funds	2004	12		4336		245,608.00					245,608.00
Undisbursed Funds	No Year	12		4336		[7]-1,356,620,360.71	21,273,849,107.06	[8]-14,077,199,617.87	9,102,289,510.08		[5]-3,262,260,381.60
Transfer To:											
Agency For International Development	No Year	72	12	4336		1,086,900,217.00		948,545,887.26	1,071,376,584.74		964,069,519.52
Authority To Borrow From The Treasury						[7]7,519,123,988.00	41,185,058,483.07	-28,106,690,901.01		10,080,646,167.26	10,516,845,402.80
Accounts Receivable						[7]1,274,512,798.62				841,203,358.81	433,309,439.81
Unfilled Customer Orders						148,406.00					148,406.00
Fund Equities:											
Unobligated Balances (Expired)						-245,608.00					-245,608.00
Unobligated Balances (Unexpired)						[7]-756,482,791.76				282,364,132.70	-1,038,846,924.46
Accounts Payable						[7]-6,423,130,577.75				-1,616,227,501.94	-4,806,903,075.81
Undelivered Orders						[7]-1,344,451,679.40				1,461,910,706.86	-2,806,362,386.26
	Subtotal	12		4336		-0-	62,458,907,590.13	-41,235,344,631.62	[9]10,173,666,094.82	11,049,896,863.69	-0-

Appropriations, Outlays, and Balances - Continued

Appropriation or Fund Account (Title)	Period of Availability	Dept Reg	Tr From	Account Number	Sub No.	Balances, Beginning Of Fiscal Year	Appropriations And Other Obligational Authority[1]	Transfers Borrowings And Investment (Net)[2]	Outlays (Net)	Balances Withdrawn And Other Transactions[3]	Balances, End Of Fiscal Year[4]
Commodity Credit Corporation Direct Loans, Liquidating Account											
Fund Resources:											
Undisbursed Funds	No Year	12		4338		76,658,559.79			-196,550,333.87	[6]263,839,441.62	9,369,452.04
Fund Equities:											
Unobligated Balances (Unexpired)						-74,107,166.36				-69,133,639.21	-4,973,527.15
Accounts Payable						-2,551,393.43				1,844,531.46	-4,395,924.89
Subtotal		12		4338		-0-			-196,550,333.87	196,550,333.87	-0-
Trust Fund Accounts											
Tobacco Trust Fund, Commodity Credit Corporation											
Fund Resources:											
Undisbursed Funds	No Year	12		8161			933,790,655.31		933,790,655.31		
Total, Farm Service Agency							68,022,550,732.44	-41,235,344,631.62	12,336,301,229.58	14,450,904,871.24	
Natural Resources Conservation Service											
General Fund Accounts											
Conservation Operations, Natural Resources Conservation Service											
Fund Resources:											
Undisbursed Funds	2007-2008	12		1000			763,360,000.00		667,881,056.37		95,478,943.63
	2007						147,000.00		36,197.03		110,802.97
	2006-2007					165,381,056.90			105,381,082.87		59,999,974.03
	2006					328,128.45			251,474.08		76,654.37
	2005-2006					66,480,409.67			32,367,319.34		34,113,090.33
	2005					32,000.00			31,999.79		0.21
	No Year					94,565,082.06	-142,035.37		38,162,532.36		56,260,514.33
Accounts Receivable						14,854,287.58				1,724,717.96	13,129,569.62
Unfilled Customer Orders						556,609.57				-2,448,876.78	3,005,486.35
Fund Equities:											
Unobligated Balances (Expired)						-1,646,718.37				2,528,185.59	-4,174,903.96
Unobligated Balances (Unexpired)						-28,892,195.90				-1,413,716.59	-27,478,479.31
Accounts Payable						-39,517,351.75				2,775,054.82	-42,292,406.57
Undelivered Orders						-272,141,308.21				-83,912,062.21	-188,229,246.00
Subtotal		12		1000		-0-	763,364,964.63		844,111,661.84	-80,746,697.21	-0-
Expenses, Watershed Rehabilitation Program, Natural Resources Conservation Service											
Fund Resources:											
Undisbursed Funds	No Year	12		1002		51,339,543.37	31,309,390.00		22,433,256.38		60,215,676.99
Accounts Receivable										-1,079,145.69	1,079,145.69
Unfilled Customer Orders						894,511.00				894,511.00	
Fund Equities:											
Unobligated Balances (Unexpired)						-3,972,809.39				-1,543,704.95	-2,429,104.44
Accounts Payable						-724,521.11				2,004,210.07	-2,728,731.18
Undelivered Orders						-47,536,723.87				8,600,263.19	-56,136,987.06
Subtotal		12		1002		-0-	31,309,390.00		22,433,256.38	8,876,133.62	-0-

Footnotes At End Of Chapter

Appropriations, Outlays, and Balances – Continued

Appropriation or Fund Account — Title	Period of Availability	Dept Reg	Tr From	Account Number	Sub No.	Balances, Beginning Of Fiscal Year	Appropriations And Other Obligational Authority[1]	Transfers Borrowings And Investment (Net)[2]	Outlays (Net)	Balances Withdrawn And Other Transactions[3]	Balances, End Of Fiscal Year[4]
Farm Security And Rural Investment Programs, Natural Resources Conservation Service											
Fund Resources:											
Undisbursed Funds	2007	12		1004		[7]1,111,850,997.77	1,746,555,859.00		684,661,269.61		1,061,894,589.39
	2006					[7]982,120,241.13			349,683,065.51		762,167,932.26
	2005					567,965,223.24			245,374,865.15		736,745,375.98
	2004					366,919,163.36			126,939,278.34		441,025,944.90
	2003					147,224,744.61			58,894,258.87		308,024,904.49
	2002					29,067,028.14			16,309,468.96		[10]130,915,275.65
Accounts Receivable										20,116,498.57	8,950,529.57
Unfilled Customer Orders										-132,309.40	132,309.40
Fund Equities:											
Unobligated Balances (Expired)						[7]-471,603,012.20				332,396,089.16	-803,999,101.36
Accounts Payable						-33,673,693.61				22,082,675.08	-55,756,368.69
Undelivered Orders						-2,699,870,692.44				-109,769,300.85	-2,590,101,391.59
Subtotal		12		1004		-0-	1,746,555,859.00		1,481,862,206.44	264,693,652.56	-0-
Resource Conservation And Development, Natural Resources Conservation Service											
Fund Resources:											
Undisbursed Funds	No Year	12		1010		11,559,691.82	51,088,000.00		51,621,694.30		11,025,997.52
Accounts Receivable						446,295.47				303,136.31	143,159.16
Unfilled Customer Orders						869,799.49				798,480.10	71,319.39
Fund Equities:											
Unobligated Balances (Unexpired)						-1,307,264.75				229,232.82	-1,536,497.57
Accounts Payable						-2,146,307.73				91,711.97	-2,238,019.70
Undelivered Orders						-9,422,214.30				-1,956,255.50	-7,465,958.80
Subtotal		12		1010		-0-	51,088,000.00		51,621,694.30	-533,694.30	-0-
Watershed Surveys And Planning, Natural Resources Conservation Service											
Fund Resources:											
Undisbursed Funds	2007	12		1066			6,056,170.00		5,123,033.39		933,136.61
	2006					675,088.59			486,777.42		188,311.17
	2005					750,331.41			217,817.87		532,513.54
	2004					950,046.71			44,550.57		905,496.14
	2003					331,646.79			8,115.29		323,531.50
	2002					344,014.11			16,243.96	327,770.15	
Accounts Receivable						142,821.31				142,821.31	
Unfilled Customer Orders										-28,243.68	28,243.68
Fund Equities:											
Unobligated Balances (Expired)						-1,580,500.05				-107,315.64	-1,473,184.41
Accounts Payable						-357,321.27				-60,439.45	-296,881.82
Undelivered Orders						-1,256,127.60				-114,961.19	-1,141,166.41
Subtotal		12		1066		-0-	6,056,170.00		5,896,538.50	159,631.50	-0-
Watershed And Flood Prevention Operations, Natural Resources Conservation Service											
Fund Resources:											
Undisbursed Funds	No Year	12		1072		728,999,227.90	19,566,958.00		321,099,016.01	216,802.17	427,467,169.89
Accounts Receivable						7,266,137.66					7,049,335.49
Unfilled Customer Orders						29,164,565.78				-5,326,972.65	34,491,538.43

Appropriations, Outlays, and Balances - Continued

Appropriation or Fund Account — Title	Period of Availability	Reg	Tr From	Account Number	Sub No.	Balances, Beginning Of Fiscal Year	Appropriations And Other Obligational Authority[1]	Transfers Borrowings And Other Investment (Net)[2]	Outlays (Net)	Balances Withdrawn And Other Transactions[3]	Balances, End Of Fiscal Year[4]
Fund Equities:											
Unobligated Balances (Unexpired)						-322,284,899.21				-140,823,602.88	-181,461,296.33
Accounts Payable						-5,636,884.48				19,161,613.69	-24,798,498.17
Undelivered Orders						-437,508,147.65				-174,759,898.34	-262,748,249.31
Subtotal		12		1072		-0-	19,566,958.00		321,099,016.01	-301,532,058.01	-0-
Wetlands Reserve Program, Natural Resources Conservation Service											
Fund Resources:											
Undisbursed Funds	No Year	12		1080		3,274,248.24			62,702.01		3,211,546.23
Fund Equities:											
Unobligated Balances (Unexpired)						-963,266.05				587,924.19	-1,551,190.24
Accounts Payable						-1,120,852.09				196,971.23	-1,317,823.32
Undelivered Orders						-1,190,130.10				-847,597.43	-342,532.67
Subtotal		12		1080		-0-			62,702.01	-62,702.01	-0-
Healthy Forests Reserve Program, Natural Resources Conservation Service											
Fund Resources:											
Undisbursed Funds	2007	12		1090			2,476,000.00		122,878.88		2,353,121.12
Undisbursed Funds	2006	12		1090		2,394,980.05			78,125.32		2,316,854.73
Fund Equities:											
Unobligated Balances (Expired)						-368.37				298,277.99	-298,646.36
Accounts Payable						-12,598.65				15,950.86	-28,549.51
Undelivered Orders						-2,382,013.03				1,960,766.95	-4,342,779.98
Subtotal		12		1090		-0-	2,476,000.00		201,004.20	2,274,995.80	-0-
Great Plains Conservation Program, Natural Resources Conservation Service											
Fund Resources:											
Undisbursed Funds	No Year	12		2268		546,945.89			-7,335.77		554,281.66
Fund Equities:											
Unobligated Balances (Unexpired)						-574,656.90				-33,062.87	-541,594.03
Accounts Payable						44,348.05				51,035.68	-6,687.63
Undelivered Orders						-16,637.04				-10,637.04	-6,000.00
Subtotal		12		2268		-0-			-7,335.77	7,335.77	-0-
Colorado River Basin Salinity Control Program, Natural Resources Conservation Service											
Fund Resources:											
Undisbursed Funds	No Year	12		3318		369,984.41			43,956.72		326,027.69
Fund Equities:											
Unobligated Balances (Unexpired)						-274,126.41				-5,367.90	-268,758.51
Accounts Payable						-10,899.53				-917.96	-9,981.57
Undelivered Orders						-84,958.47				-37,670.86	-47,287.61
Subtotal		12		3318		-0-			43,956.72	-43,956.72	-0-
Water Bank Program, Natural Resources Conservation Service											
Fund Resources:											
Undisbursed Funds	No Year	12		3320		999,804.98			69,303.00		930,501.98
Fund Equities:											
Unobligated Balances (Unexpired)						-643,102.80				102,078.18	-745,180.98
Accounts Payable						2,140.00				2,140.00	
Undelivered Orders						-358,842.18				-173,521.18	-185,321.00

Footnotes At End Of Chapter

Appropriations, Outlays, and Balances – Continued

Appropriation or Fund Account — Title	Period of Availability	Dept Reg	Tr From	Account Number	Sub No.	Balances, Beginning Of Fiscal Year	Appropriations And Other Obligational Authority[1]	Transfers Borrowings And Investment (Net)[2]	Outlays (Net)	Balances Withdrawn And Other Transactions[3]	Balances, End Of Fiscal Year[4]
	Subtotal	12		3320		-0-			69,303.00	-69,303.00	-0-
Wildlife Habitat Incentives Program, Natural Resources Conservation Service											
Fund Resources:											
Undisbursed Funds	2001	12		3322		3,704,879.50			181,484.47		[1]3,523,395.03
	No Year	12		3322		11,638,949.82			672,136.81		10,966,813.01
Fund Equities:											
Unobligated Balances (Expired)						-2,016,100.10				1,043,630.30	-3,059,730.40
Unobligated Balances (Unexpired)						[7]-4,650,205.06				4,344,399.23	-8,994,604.29
Accounts Payable						3,091.71				3,118.50	-26.79
Undelivered Orders						[7]-8,680,615.87				-6,244,769.31	-2,435,846.56
	Subtotal	12		3322		-0-			853,621.28	-853,621.28	-0-
Forestry Incentives Program, Natural Resources Conservation Service											
Fund Resources:											
Undisbursed Funds	No Year	12		3336		6,056,234.24			43,692.53		6,012,541.71
Fund Equities:											
Unobligated Balances (Unexpired)						-4,806,660.40				1,225,082.05	-6,031,742.45
Accounts Payable						59,990.06				39,094.32	20,895.74
Undelivered Orders						-1,309,563.90				-1,307,868.90	-1,695.00
	Subtotal	12		3336		-0-			43,692.53	-43,692.53	-0-
Trust Fund Accounts											
Miscellaneous Contributed Funds, Natural Resources Conservation Service											
Fund Resources:											
Commodity Credit Corporation	No Year	12		8210		5,388,729.58			1,482,925.76		3,905,803.82
Fund Equities:											
Unobligated Balances (Unexpired)						-2,830,200.19				89,651.59	-2,919,851.78
Accounts Payable						-3,428.69				15,157.00	-18,585.69
Undelivered Orders						-2,555,100.70				-1,587,734.35	-967,366.35
	Subtotal	12		8210		-0-			1,482,925.76	-1,482,925.76	-0-
Total, Natural Resources Conservation Service							2,620,417,341.63		2,729,774,243.20	-109,356,901.57	
Rural Development											
General Fund Accounts											
Rural Community Advancement Program, Rural Economic And Community Development Program											
Fund Resources:											
Undisbursed Funds	1996	12		0400		149,392.46			60,352.46	89,040.00	[12]
	1995					31,608.26			17,224.60		[13]14,383.66
	1994					71,638.14			71,638.14		[12]
	1993					167,856.30				63,140.00	[12]104,716.30
	No Year					2,535,912,478.94	827,237,349.00	-69,545.00	862,732,744.91		2,500,347,538.03
Fund Equities:											
Unobligated Balances (Unexpired)						-145,958,002.89				-3,220,378.74	-142,737,624.15
Accounts Payable						-25,831,308.53				-23,257,738.11	-2,573,570.42

Appropriations, Outlays, and Balances - Continued

Appropriation or Fund Account — Title	Period of Availability	Dept Reg	Tr From	Account Number	Sub No.	Balances, Beginning Of Fiscal Year	Appropriations And Other Obligational Authority[1]	Transfers Borrowings And Investment (Net)[2]	Outlays (Net)	Balances Withdrawn And Other Transactions[3]	Balances, End Of Fiscal Year[4]
Undelivered Orders	Subtotal	12		0400		-2,364,543,662.68	827,237,349.00	-69,545.00	862,881,960.11	-9,388,219.26	-2,355,155,443.42
						-0-				-35,714,156.11	-0-
Salaries And Expenses, Rural Development											
Fund Resources:											
Undisbursed Funds	2007	12		0403			162,135,822.00		80,174,222.23		81,961,599.77
	2006-2007					11,035,530.00			3,982,745.52		7,052,784.48
	2006					77,323,567.52			54,871,681.68		22,451,885.84
	2005					22,361,803.20			7,804,577.89		14,557,225.31
	2004					15,120,901.56			4,927,849.45		10,193,052.11
	2003					14,609,912.52			1,097,530.49		13,512,382.03
	2002					15,791,009.45			936,154.11	14,854,855.34	
	No Year					1,297,892.22	6,471,248.00	1,555,641.23	715,983.22		8,608,798.23
Accounts Receivable						1,219,297.78				322,701.09	896,596.69
Fund Equities:											
Unobligated Balances (Expired)						-33,006,267.78				-3,378,849.98	-29,627,417.80
Unobligated Balances (Unexpired)						-6,932,022.22				-2,136,014.44	-4,796,007.78
Accounts Payable						-27,937,043.40				1,845,881.00	-29,782,924.40
Undelivered Orders						-90,884,580.85				4,143,393.63	-95,027,974.48
	Subtotal	12		0403		-0-	168,607,070.00	1,555,641.23	154,510,744.59	15,651,966.64	-0-
Great Plains Regional Authority, Rural Development											
Fund Resources:											
Undisbursed Funds	2005-2006	12		0404		1,479,072.00					1,479,072.00
	2004					1,491,150.00					1,491,150.00
Fund Equities:											
Unobligated Balances (Expired)						-2,970,222.00					-2,970,222.00
	Subtotal	12		0404		-0-					-0-
Total, Rural Development							995,844,419.00	1,486,096.23	1,017,392,704.70	-20,062,189.47	
Rural Housing Service											
General Fund Accounts											
Rental Assistance Program, Rural Housing And Community Development											
Fund Resources:											
Undisbursed Funds	2007-2008	12		0137			616,020,000.00		91,096,351.45		524,923,648.55
	2006					596,108,875.08			157,785,815.91		438,323,059.17
	2005					390,349,530.61			151,431,967.46		238,917,563.15
	2004					229,382,448.88			131,596,447.59		97,786,001.29
	2003					270,110,758.28			130,943,418.34		139,167,339.94
	2002					181,481,453.96			93,640,008.69	148,086.00	[14]87,693,359.27
	2001					84,803,414.05			47,222,197.37		[15]37,581,216.68
	2000					33,898,103.39			19,121,184.44		[16]14,776,918.95

Footnotes At End Of Chapter

Appropriations, Outlays, and Balances – Continued

Appropriation or Fund Account — Title	Dept Reg	Tr From	Account Number	Sub No.	Period of Availability	Balances, Beginning Of Fiscal Year	Appropriations And Other Obligational Authority[1]	Transfers Borrowings And Investment (Net)[2]	Outlays (Net)	Balances Withdrawn And Other Transactions[3]	Balances, End Of Fiscal Year[4]
Rental Assistance Program, Rural Housing And Community Development - Continued											
Fund Resources - Continued:											
Undisbursed Funds - Continued											
					1999	9,374,766.05			4,759,008.50		[16]4,615,757.55
					1998	7,813,464.93			3,098,538.32		[17]4,714,926.61
					1997	2,779,497.24			1,338,386.78		[18]1,441,110.46
					1996	3,408,162.43			1,351,981.40		[19]2,056,181.03
					1995	369,862.13			-357,798.21		[20]727,660.34
					1994	621,221.48			-193,204.85		[21]814,426.33
					1993	823,809.69			188,064.46		[22]635,745.23
					1992	686,291.97			224,640.95		[22]461,651.02
					No Year	8,240,999.91			53,603,008.87		5,768,343.03
Authority To Borrow From The Treasury						332,764,358.96	51,130,351.99			51,130,351.99	281,634,006.97
Fund Equities:											
Unobligated Balances (Expired)						-364,996.08				-148,636.00	-216,360.08
Unobligated Balances (Unexpired)						-402.09					-402.09
Accounts Payable						-46,850,153.96				-5,401,383.93	-41,448,770.03
Undelivered Orders						-2,105,801,466.91				-265,428,083.54	-1,840,373,383.37
	12		0137		Subtotal	-0-	667,150,351.99		886,850,017.47	-219,699,665.48	-0-
Expenses, Rural Housing Assistance Grants, Rural Housing Service											
Fund Resources:											
Undisbursed Funds											
					1993-1994	1,816,565.70			848,264.00		[23]968,301.70
	12		1953		No Year	52,860,777.50	61,603,028.00	8,266,032.00	51,208,613.54		71,521,223.96
Fund Equities:											
Unobligated Balances (Unexpired)						-15,660,148.17				21,136,808.04	-36,796,956.21
Accounts Payable						-1,142,833.97				720,760.66	-1,863,594.63
Undelivered Orders						-37,874,361.06				-4,045,386.24	-33,828,974.82
	12		1953		Subtotal	-0-	61,603,028.00	8,266,032.00	52,056,877.54	17,812,182.46	-0-
Farm Labor Program Account, Rural Housing Service											
Fund Resources:											
Undisbursed Funds	12		1954		No Year	144,357,730.18	32,137,047.00		25,911,745.47		150,583,031.71
Fund Equities:											
Unobligated Balances (Unexpired)						-4,075,326.14				10,248,136.23	-14,323,462.37
Accounts Payable						-398,845.57				47,625.00	-446,470.57
Undelivered Orders						-139,883,558.47				-4,070,459.70	-135,813,098.77
	12		1954		Subtotal	-0-	32,137,047.00		25,911,745.47	6,225,301.53	-0-
Rental Housing Voucher Program, Rural Housing And Community Development Service											
Fund Resources:											
Undisbursed Funds					2006	990,000.00					990,000.00
	12		2002		No Year	12,089,185.37	14,731,200.00	4,867,463.00	1,894,850.83		29,792,997.54
Transfer To:											
Office Of Federal Housing Enterprise Oversight, Department Of Housing And Urban Development	86	12	2002	3	No Year	5,290,800.00		-5,290,800.00			
Fund Equities:											
Unobligated Balances (Unexpired)						-14,462,868.60				10,878,906.90	-25,341,775.50
Accounts Payable						-1,052,710.30				90,259.78	-1,142,970.08
Undelivered Orders						-2,854,406.47				1,443,845.49	-4,298,251.96

Appropriations, Outlays, and Balances - Continued

Appropriation or Fund Account — Title	Period of Availability	Dept Reg	Tr From	Account Number	Sub No.	Balances, Beginning Of Fiscal Year	Appropriations And Other Obligational Authority[1]	Transfers Borrowings And Investment (Net)[2]	Outlays (Net)	Balances Withdrawn And Other Transactions[3]	Balances, End Of Fiscal Year[4]
Mutual And Self-Help Housing Grants, Rural Housing Service	Subtotal	12		2002		-0-	14,731,200.00	-423,337.00	1,894,850.83	12,413,012.17	-0-
Fund Resources:											
Undisbursed Funds	No Year	12		2006		56,060,124.92	33,660,000.00		34,950,399.03		54,769,725.89
Fund Equities:											
Unobligated Balances (Unexpired)						-1,172,005.51				566,078.26	-1,738,083.77
Accounts Payable						-1,336,815.60				-146,388.65	-1,190,426.95
Undelivered Orders						-53,551,303.81				-1,710,088.64	-51,841,215.17
	Subtotal	12		2006		-0-	33,660,000.00		34,950,399.03	-1,290,399.03	-0-
Rural Community Fire Protection Grants, Rural Housing And Community Development Service											
Fund Resources:											
Undisbursed Funds	No Year	12		2067		56,154.45					56,154.45
Fund Equities:											
Unobligated Balances (Unexpired)						-20,083.50					-20,083.50
Accounts Payable						-3,287.75					-3,287.75
Undelivered Orders						-32,783.20					-32,783.20
	Subtotal	12		2067		-0-					-0-
Rural Housing Insurance Fund Program Account, Rural Housing And Community Development Service											
Fund Resources:											
Undisbursed Funds	2007	12		2081		80,648,254.32	638,096,936.00		566,131,976.23		71,964,959.77
	2006					40,588,626.43			34,681,090.13		45,967,164.19
	2005					30,239,625.83			13,438,050.61		27,150,575.82
	2004					25,033,166.37			8,509,276.19		21,730,349.64
	2003					24,411,039.41			3,482,717.95		21,550,448.42
	2002					4,152,165.71			2,833,847.26	14,992,597.58	[14]6,584,594.57
	2001					2,146,634.76			616,538.66	44,090.07	[15]3,491,536.98
	2000					2,018,748.83			758,304.92	218,109.29	[16]1,170,220.55
	1999					1,727,975.36			953,458.49	792,784.35	[18]272,505.99
	1998					138,251.54			-342.20	11,781.10	[16]1,716,536.46
	1997					5.23			898.74	95,906.58	[16]41,446.22
	1996								5.23		[16]
	1995					866,370.14					[2]866,370.14
	1994					290,459.28					[2]290,459.28
	No Year	12		2081		52,952,729.45	45,540,836.00	-8,468,908.50	53,284,917.22		36,739,739.73
Fund Equities:											
Unobligated Balances (Expired)						-41,443,753.36				-7,762,333.96	-33,681,419.40
Unobligated Balances (Unexpired)						-47,900,188.75				-14,612,799.24	-33,287,389.51
Undelivered Orders						-175,870,110.55				-3,302,011.70	-172,568,098.85
	Subtotal	12		2081		-0-	683,637,772.00	-8,468,908.50	684,690,739.43	-9,521,875.93	-0-
Public Enterprise Funds											
Rural Housing Insurance Fund, Liquidating Account, Rural Housing And Community Development Service											
Fund Resources:											
Undisbursed Funds	No Year	12		4141		88,962,322.98			-1,000,868,226.31	[6]1,057,805,643.98	32,024,905.31

Footnotes At End Of Chapter

Appropriations, Outlays, and Balances – Continued

Appropriation or Fund Account — Title	Dept Reg	Tr From	Account Number	Sub No.	Period of Availability	Balances, Beginning Of Fiscal Year	Appropriations And Other Obligational Authority[1]	Transfers Borrowings And Investment (Net)[2]	Outlays (Net)	Balances Withdrawn And Other Transactions[3]	Balances, End Of Fiscal Year[4]
Rural Housing Insurance Fund, Liquidating Account, Rural Housing And Community Development Service - Continued											
Fund Equities:											
Unobligated Balances (Unexpired)						-59,394,744.98				-59,394,744.98	
Accounts Payable						-124,970.38				264,013.26	-388,983.64
Undelivered Orders						-29,442,607.62				2,193,314.05	-31,635,921.67
Subtotal	12		4141			-0-			-1,000,868,226.31	1,000,868,226.31	-0-
Total, Rural Housing Service						1,492,919,398.99		-626,213.50	685,486,403.46	806,806,782.03	
Rural Business-Cooperative Service											
General Fund Accounts											
Rural Empowerment Zones And Enterprise Communities Grants, Rural Business-Cooperative Service											
Fund Resources:											
Undisbursed Funds	12		0402		No Year	27,232,703.50	11,088,000.00		11,237,008.29		27,083,695.21
Fund Equities:											
Unobligated Balances (Unexpired)						-3,014,219.36				-419,744.39	-2,594,474.97
Accounts Payable						-10,422.85				206,531.55	-216,954.40
Undelivered Orders						-24,208,061.29				64,204.55	-24,272,265.84
Subtotal	12		0402			-0-	11,088,000.00		11,237,008.29	-149,008.29	-0-
Biomass Research And Development, Natural Resource Conservation Service											
Fund Resources:											
Undisbursed Funds	12		1003		No Year	36,554,174.01	14,000,000.00		8,468,864.05		42,085,309.96
Fund Equities:											
Unobligated Balances (Unexpired)						-13,732,271.91				294,203.90	-14,026,475.81
Accounts Payable						-300,000.00					-300,000.00
Undelivered Orders						-22,521,902.10				5,236,932.05	-27,758,834.15
Subtotal	12		1003			-0-	14,000,000.00		8,468,864.05	5,531,135.95	-0-
Rural Cooperative Development Grants, Rural Business-Cooperative Development Service											
Fund Resources:											
Undisbursed Funds	12		1900		2007	7,083,381.00	6,218,000.00		935,550.00		5,282,450.00
					2006	3,577,218.42			4,431,853.15		2,651,527.85
					2005	507,177.05			3,044,097.50		533,120.92
					2004	374,737.91			342,903.82		164,273.23
					2003	2,107.36			201,336.29		173,401.62
					2002					2,107.36	
					No Year	43,152,777.93	20,288,645.75	-2,299.73	22,532,473.78		40,906,650.17
Fund Equities:											
Unobligated Balances (Expired)						-185,119.34				502,622.72	-687,742.06
Unobligated Balances (Unexpired)						-559,823.22				319,678.90	-879,502.12
Accounts Payable						-1,327,704.54				-224,559.12	-1,103,145.42
Undelivered Orders						-52,624,752.57				-5,583,718.38	-47,041,034.19
Subtotal	12		1900			-0-	26,506,645.75	-2,299.73	31,488,214.54	-4,983,868.52	-0-

Appropriations, Outlays, and Balances - Continued

Appropriation or Fund Account (Title)	Reg	Tr From	Account Number	Sub No.	Period of Availability	Balances, Beginning Of Fiscal Year	Appropriations And Other Obligational Authority[1]	Transfers Borrowings And Investment (Net)[2]	Outlays (Net)	Balances Withdrawn And Other Transactions[3]	Balances, End Of Fiscal Year[4]
Rural Business Investment Program Account, Rural Business - Cooperative Service											
Fund Resources:											
Undisbursed Funds	12		1907		No Year	96,124,503.00	-94,495,637.00				1,628,866.00
Transfer To:											
Small Business Administration	73	12	1907		No Year	2,875,497.00			18,782.72		2,856,714.28
Fund Equities:											
Unobligated Balances (Unexpired)						-94,495,637.00	-94,495,637.00			-94,495,637.00	-1,628,866.00
Accounts Payable						-1,628,866.00					-1,628,866.00
Undelivered Orders						-2,875,497.00			18,782.72	-18,782.72	-2,856,714.28
Subtotal	12		1907			-0-	-94,495,637.00		18,782.72	-94,514,419.72	-0-
Renewable Energy Program, Rural Business-Cooperative Service											
Fund Resources:											
Undisbursed Funds	12		1908		2007	21,146,348.39	22,842,622.00		3,966,228.16		18,876,393.84
					2006	18,317,310.06			8,347,728.66		12,798,619.73
					2005	16,233,666.73			1,913,411.17		16,403,898.89
					2004	16,749,316.12			618,586.97		15,615,079.76
					2003				1,569,594.52		15,179,721.60
Fund Equities:											
Unobligated Balances (Expired)						-5,554,566.10				1,935,694.07	-7,490,260.17
Accounts Payable						-171,033.23				65,758.45	-236,791.68
Undelivered Orders						-66,721,041.97				4,425,620.00	-71,146,661.97
Subtotal	12		1908			-0-	22,842,622.00		16,415,549.48	6,427,072.52	-0-
Rural Development Loan Fund Program Account, Rural Business And Cooperative Development Service											
Fund Resources:											
Undisbursed Funds	12		2069		2007	13,140,132.25	28,005,273.00		13,814,167.99		14,191,105.01
					2006	9,949,235.22			5,644,592.31		7,495,539.94
					2005	8,545,260.74			3,942,496.55		6,006,738.67
					2004	5,821,530.71			2,336,306.13		6,208,954.61
					2003	2,570,274.11			2,265,197.54		3,556,333.17
					2002	2,623,296.81			743,545.57	1,029,250.84	[1]797,477.70
					2001	632,557.95			465,178.43	321,400.93	[15]1,836,717.45
					2000	133,955.16			249,722.50	217,150.00	[16]165,685.45
					1999	263,665.02			2,768.23		[24]131,186.93
					1998	117,875.14					[25]263,665.02
					1997	942,429.42			52,570.74		[26]65,304.40
					1996	581.80			1,190.00		[27]941,239.42
					1995						[1]581.80
Fund Equities:											
Unobligated Balances (Expired)						-2,110,614.21				1,915,911.14	-4,026,525.35
Undelivered Orders						-42,630,180.12				-4,996,175.90	-37,634,004.22
Subtotal	12		2069			-0-	28,005,273.00		29,517,735.99	-1,512,462.99	-0-
Rural Economic Development Grants, Rural Business And Cooperative Development Service											
Fund Resources:											
Undisbursed Funds	12		3105		No Year	24,370,284.30	-74,000,000.00		-78,736,043.70		29,106,328.00
Accounts Receivable						69,718,321.09				43,686,658.18	26,031,662.91

Footnotes At End Of Chapter

Appropriations, Outlays, and Balances – Continued

Appropriation or Fund Account: Title	Period of Availability	Reg	Tr From	Account Number	Sub No.	Balances, Beginning Of Fiscal Year	Appropriations And Other Obligational Authority[1]	Transfers Borrowings And Investment (Net)[2]	Outlays (Net)	Balances Withdrawn And Other Transactions[3]	Balances, End Of Fiscal Year[4]
Rural Economic Development Grants, Rural Business And Cooperative Development Service - Continued											
Fund Equities:											
Unobligated Balances (Unexpired)						-81,814,022.48				-39,843,528.95	-41,970,493.53
Accounts Payable						-208,456.91				701,539.10	-909,996.01
Undelivered Orders						-12,066,126.00				191,375.37	-12,257,501.37
Subtotal		12		3105		-0-	-74,000,000.00		-78,736,043.70	4,736,043.70	-0-
Rural Economic Development Loans Program Account, Rural Business And Cooperative Service											
Fund Resources:											
Undisbursed Funds	2007	12		3108			3,361,631.00		3,361,631.00		434,543.65
	2004					434,543.65					331,080.03
	2003					331,080.03				413,160.26 [14]	
	2002					413,160.26					
	No Year					3,612,281.62	5,940,242.00		4,060,843.66		5,491,679.96
Fund Equities:											
Unobligated Balances (Expired)						-937,588.94				-274,320.26	-663,268.68
Unobligated Balances (Unexpired)						-101,120.81				-91,258.80	-9,862.01
Undelivered Orders						-3,752,355.81				1,831,817.14	-5,584,172.95
Subtotal		12		3108		-0-	9,301,873.00		7,422,474.66	1,879,398.34	-0-
Public Enterprise Funds											
Alternative Agricultural Research And Commercialization Revolving Fund, Rural Business And Cooperative Development Service											
Fund Resources:											
Undisbursed Funds	No Year	12		4144		856,970.35			-158,733.61		1,015,703.96
Accounts Receivable						5,581.82					5,581.82
Fund Equities:											
Unobligated Balances (Unexpired)						-695,293.64				155,370.75	-850,664.39
Undelivered Orders						-167,258.53				3,362.86	-170,621.39
Subtotal		12		4144		-0-			-158,733.61	158,733.61	-0-
National Sheep Industry Improvement Center, Department Of Agriculture											
Fund Resources:											
Undisbursed Funds	No Year	12		4202		6,490,030.51			6,148,520.96		341,509.55
Fund Equities:											
Unobligated Balances (Unexpired)						-886,153.45				-544,643.90	-341,509.55
Accounts Payable						-5,489,232.54				-5,489,232.54	
Undelivered Orders						-114,644.52				-114,644.52	-0-
Subtotal		12		4202		-0-			6,148,520.96	-6,148,520.96	-0-
Rural Development Loan Fund, Liquidating Account, Rural Business And Cooperative Development Service											
Fund Resources:											
Undisbursed Funds	No Year	12		4233		455,116.86			-3,869,052.15	[6]3,700,000.00	624,169.01
Fund Equities:											
Unobligated Balances (Unexpired)						-455,116.86				169,052.15	-624,169.01
Subtotal		12		4233		-0-			-3,869,052.15	3,869,052.15	-0-

Appropriations, Outlays, and Balances - Continued

Appropriation or Fund Account — Title	Period of Availability	Dept Reg	Tr From	Account Number	Sub No.	Balances, Beginning Of Fiscal Year	Appropriations And Other Obligational Authority[1]	Transfers Borrowings And Investment (Net)[2]	Outlays (Net)	Balances Withdrawn And Other Transactions[3]	Balances, End Of Fiscal Year[4]
Total, Rural Business-Cooperative Service							-56,751,223.25	-2,299.73	27,953,321.23	-84,706,844.21	
Rural Utilities Service											
General Fund Accounts											
Rural Electrification And Telecommunications Loans Program Account, Rural Utilities Service											
Fund Resources:											
Undisbursed Funds	2007	12		1230			152,949,355.00		149,447,585.34		3,501,769.66
	2006					6,022,887.56			2,469,268.96		3,553,618.60
	2005					3,505,847.02			1,358,151.34		2,147,695.68
	2004					3,559.68					3,559.68
	2003					4,593,594.72			2,645,166.79		1,948,427.93
	2002					2,645,589.45			1,329,869.04	212,348.30	[14]1,103,372.11
	2001					5,443,277.49			677,665.00	121,810.80	[5]4,643,801.69
	2000					1,176,968.58			104,662.26	67,027.70	[6]1,005,278.62
	1999					2,463,149.50			545,163.00	23,825.34	[4]1,894,161.16
	1998					591,362.50			9,551.88	2,501.56	[25]579,309.06
	1997					319,000.68			8,258.95	141,600.73	[8]169,141.00
	1996					2,383,109.04			292,316.61	361,805.66	[27]1,728,986.77
	1995					723,358.91			7,510.07	524,656.34	[13]191,192.50
	1994					1,999,268.58			39,711.00	4,303.61	[2]1,955,253.97
	1993					5,861,638.60			981,110.38	580,464.45	[24]4,300,063.77
	1992					2,380,697.58			76,356.26	715,882.71	[2]1,588,458.61
	No Year					7,092,288.33			77,205.00		7,015,083.33
Fund Equities:											
Unobligated Balances (Expired)						-52,714.57				8,070.75	-60,785.32
Unobligated Balances (Unexpired)						-7,092,288.33				-77,205.00	-7,015,083.33
Undelivered Orders						-40,060,595.32				-9,807,289.83	-30,253,305.49
Subtotal		12		1230		-0-	152,949,355.00		160,069,551.88	-7,120,196.88	-0-
Rural Telephone Bank Program Account, Rural Utilities Service											
Fund Resources:											
Undisbursed Funds	2003	12		1231		2,291,454.51			134,920.25		2,156,534.26
	2002					3,298,230.73			114,813.37	880,556.03	[14]2,302,861.33
	2001					1,860,583.94			39,149.05	18,762.30	[15]1,802,672.59
	2000					1,856,496.91			48,274.01	641,969.71	[16]1,166,253.19
	1999					1,575,750.85			130,237.20	60,295.05	[24]1,385,218.60
	1998					1,260,115.14			49,653.08	73,341.63	[25]1,137,120.43
	1997					446,332.32			51,914.33	156,340.80	[26]238,077.19
	1996					773,368.49			47,237.13	445,357.19	[27]280,774.17
	1995					217,456.76			27,678.96	22,283.32	[13]167,494.48
	1994					60,516.05			2,180.85	15,873.76	[1]242,461.44
	1993					892.53			99.78	39.62	[12]753.13
	1992					290,736.51				76,755.28	[12]213,981.23
Fund Equities:											
Unobligated Balances (Expired)						-758,103.99				-290,614.56	-467,489.43
Undelivered Orders						-13,173,830.75				-2,747,118.14	-10,426,712.61
Subtotal		12		1231		-0-			646,158.01	-646,158.01	-0-

Footnotes At End Of Chapter

Appropriations, Outlays, and Balances – Continued

Appropriation or Fund Account	Account Symbol — Dept		Account Number	Sub No.	Period of Availability	Balances, Beginning Of Fiscal Year	Appropriations And Other Obligational Authority[1]	Transfers Borrowings And Investment (Net)[2]	Outlays (Net)	Balances Withdrawn And Other Transactions[3]	Balances, End Of Fiscal Year[4]
Title	Reg	Tr From									
Distance Learning, Telemedicine, And Broadband Program											
Fund Resources:											
Undisbursed Funds	12		1232		2007-2008		10,467,069.00	175,431.00			10,642,500.00
					2006-2007	10,642,500.00			117,215.44		10,525,284.56
					2005-2006	8,883,789.85			1,062,014.37		7,821,775.48
					2004	11,409,450.12			546,849.10		10,862,601.02
					No Year	163,142,191.88	2,372,329.80	-175,431.00	44,701,517.18		120,637,573.50
Fund Equities:											
Unobligated Balances (Expired)						-964,676.10				12,688,778.94	-13,653,455.04
Unobligated Balances (Unexpired)						-51,266,150.74				-36,098,726.25	-15,167,424.49
Undelivered Orders						-141,847,105.01				-10,178,249.98	-131,668,855.03
	12		1232		Subtotal	-0-	12,839,398.80		46,427,596.09	-33,588,197.29	-0-
High Energy Cost Grants, Rural Utilities Service											
Fund Resources:											
Undisbursed Funds	12		2042		No Year	45,516,164.62	23,938,200.00	-857,583.00	31,549,631.74		37,047,149.88
Fund Equities:											
Unobligated Balances (Unexpired)						-17,514,150.00				3,393,202.17	-20,907,352.17
Undelivered Orders						-28,002,014.62				-11,862,216.91	-16,139,797.71
	12		2042		Subtotal	-0-	23,938,200.00	-857,583.00	31,549,631.74	-8,469,014.74	-0-
Public Enterprise Funds											
Rural Communication Development Fund, Rural Utilities Service											
Fund Resources:											
Undisbursed Funds	12		4142		No Year				-351,789.07	[6]335,000.00	16,789.07
Fund Equities:											
Unobligated Balances (Unexpired)										16,789.07	-16,789.07
	12		4142		Subtotal	-0-			-351,789.07	351,789.07	-0-
Rural Development Insurance Fund, Liquidating Account, Rural Utilities Service											
Fund Resources:											
Undisbursed Funds	12		4155		No Year	22,226,748.12			-250,822,190.52	[6]247,000,000.00	26,048,938.64
Fund Equities:											
Unobligated Balances (Unexpired)						-22,226,748.12				3,822,190.52	-26,048,938.64
	12		4155		Subtotal	-0-			-250,822,190.52	250,822,190.52	-0-
Rural Electrification And Telephone Revolving Fund, Liquidating Account, Rural Utilities Service											
Fund Resources:											
Undisbursed Funds	12		4230		No Year	1,257,945,965.85		[28]-2,473,463,782.18	-2,063,702,811.60		848,184,995.27
Fund Equities:											
Unobligated Balances (Unexpired)						-1,098,902,206.53				-439,874,347.49	-659,027,859.04
Accounts Payable						-69,718,321.09				61,373,560.23	-131,091,881.32
Undelivered Orders						-89,325,438.23				-31,260,183.32	-58,065,254.91
	12		4230		Subtotal	-0-		-2,473,463,782.18	-2,063,702,811.60	-409,760,970.58	-0-
Rural Telephone Bank, Liquidating Account, Rural Utilities Service											
Fund Resources:											
Undisbursed Funds	12		4231		No Year	39,726,690.75					39,726,690.75
Fund Equities:											
Unobligated Balances (Unexpired)						-39,726,690.75					-39,726,690.75
	12		4231		Subtotal	-0-					-0-
Total, Rural Utilities Service							189,726,953.80	-2,474,321,365.18	-2,076,183,853.47	-208,410,557.91	

Appropriations, Outlays, and Balances - Continued

Appropriation or Fund Account — Title	Period of Availability	Dept Reg	Tr From	Account Number	Sub No.	Balances, Beginning Of Fiscal Year	Appropriations And Other Obligational Authority[1]	Transfers Borrowings And Investment (Net)[2]	Outlays (Net)	Balances Withdrawn And Other Transactions[3]	Balances, End Of Fiscal Year[4]
Foreign Agricultural Service											
General Fund Accounts											
Scientific Activities Overseas, Foreign Currency Program, Foreign Agricultural Service											
Fund Resources:											
Undisbursed Funds	No Year	12		1404		318,471.14			226,595.49		91,875.65
Fund Equities:											
Unobligated Balances (Unexpired)						-308,282.14				214,164.84	-522,446.98
Undelivered Orders						-10,189.00				-440,760.33	430,571.33
Subtotal		12		1404		-0-			226,595.49	-226,595.49	-0-
Trade Adjustment Assistance For Farmers, Foreign Agricultural Service											
Fund Resources:											
Undisbursed Funds	2007	12		1406			90,000,000.00		590,569.00		89,409,431.00
	2006					85,968,500.00			100,000.00		85,868,500.00
	2005					67,641,310.88			757,922.79		66,883,388.09
	2004					73,008,726.51			26,400.00		72,982,326.51
	2003					31,353,189.91			216,838.93		31,136,350.98
Fund Equities:											
Unobligated Balances (Expired)						-251,828,140.99				88,718,992.00	-340,547,132.99
Undelivered Orders						-6,143,586.31				-410,722.72	-5,732,863.59
Subtotal		12		1406		-0-	90,000,000.00		1,691,730.72	88,308,269.28	-0-
Expenses, Public Law 480 Title I Ocean Freight Differential Grants											
Fund Resources:											
Undisbursed Funds	No Year	12		2271		32,357,880.55		-8,000,000.00	-2,980,200.22		27,338,080.77
Fund Equities:											
Unobligated Balances (Unexpired)						-16,709,689.72				3,014,170.16	-19,723,859.88
Undelivered Orders						-15,648,190.83				-8,033,969.94	-7,614,220.89
Subtotal		12		2271		-0-		-8,000,000.00	-2,980,200.22	-5,019,799.78	-0-
Public Law 480, Liquidating Account											
Fund Resources:											
Undisbursed Funds	No Year	12		2274		52,334,468.34			-525,401,193.75	502,335,937.14	75,399,724.95
Accounts Receivable						1,468.80				1,468.80	
Fund Equities:											
Unobligated Balances (Unexpired)						-52,335,937.14				23,063,787.81	-75,399,724.95
Subtotal		12		2274		-0-			-525,401,193.75	525,401,193.75	-0-
Public Law 480 Program Account											
Fund Resources:											
Undisbursed Funds	No Year	12		2277		157,815,707.62	16,622,566.00	8,000,000.00	78,614,580.36		103,823,693.26
Fund Equities:											
Unobligated Balances (Unexpired)						-39,467,722.51				-20,994,591.87	-18,473,130.64
Undelivered Orders						-118,347,985.11				-32,997,422.49	-85,350,562.62
Subtotal		12		2277		-0-	16,622,566.00	8,000,000.00	78,614,580.36	-53,992,014.36	-0-
Public Law 480 Title II Grants											
Fund Resources:											
Undisbursed Funds	No Year	12		2278		1,287,523,175.27	1,664,711,000.00		2,550,023,429.50		402,210,745.77

Footnotes At End Of Chapter

Appropriations, Outlays, and Balances – Continued

Title	Reg	Tr From	Account Number	Sub No.	Period of Availability	Balances, Beginning Of Fiscal Year	Appropriations And Other Obligational Authority[1]	Transfers Borrowings And Investment (Net)[2]	Outlays (Net)	Balances Withdrawn And Other Transactions[3]	Balances, End Of Fiscal Year[4]
Public Law 480 Title II Grants - Continued											
Transfer To:											
United States Agency For International Development	72	12	2278		No Year			30,000,000.00			30,000,000.00
Fund Equities:											
Unobligated Balances (Unexpired)						-80,009,560.79				189,906,236.15	-269,915,796.94
Accounts Payable						-1,126,025,673.89				-1,036,916,541.37	-89,109,132.52
Undelivered Orders						-81,487,940.59				-8,302,124.28	-73,185,816.31
Subtotal	12		2278			-0-	1,664,711,000.00	30,000,000.00	2,550,023,429.50	-855,312,429.50	-0-
Ameri Flora '92 Exposition											
Fund Resources:											
Undisbursed Funds	12		2280		No Year	1,030.00					1,030.00
Fund Equities:											
Unobligated Balances (Unexpired)						-1,030.00					-1,030.00
Subtotal	12		2280			-0-					-0-
Foreign Agricultural Service And General Sales Manager											
Fund Resources:											
Undisbursed Funds	12		2900		2007-2008		9,203,000.00		4,015.20		9,198,984.80
					2007		151,393,077.87		159,194,505.79		[5]-7,801,427.92
					2006-2007	12,228,396.84			5,960,977.87		6,267,418.97
					2006	12,062,194.23			17,866,152.79		[5]-5,803,958.56
					2005-2006	9,314,372.26			5,049,610.70		4,264,761.56
					2005	5,719,300.22			-4,754,909.62		10,474,209.84
					2004-2005	3,309,233.74			1,031,019.71		2,278,214.03
					2004	-795,330.00			-827,993.56		32,663.56
					2003-2004	1,767,286.06			106,889.01		1,660,397.05
					2003	1,055,647.58			-808,954.10		1,864,601.68
					2002-2003	1,162,190.69			5,356.37		1,156,834.32
					2002	4,432,582.48			1,643,414.99	2,789,167.49	
					2001-2002	12,676.44				12,676.44	
					No Year	18,824,620.21	3,960,000.00		2,383,619.19	-5,345,824.11	20,401,001.02
Accounts Receivable						38,717,092.47					44,062,916.58
Unfilled Customer Orders										-62,234,786.39	62,234,786.39
Fund Equities:											
Unobligated Balances (Expired)						-16,810,069.67				-363,051.53	-16,447,018.14
Unobligated Balances (Unexpired)						-23,322,901.11				2,942,864.81	-26,265,765.92
Accounts Payable						-12,304,714.63				-395,673.35	-11,909,041.28
Undelivered Orders						-55,372,577.81				40,297,000.17	-95,669,577.98
Subtotal	12		2900			-0-	164,556,077.87		186,853,704.34	-22,297,626.47	-0-
McGovern-Dole International Food For Education And Child Nutrition Program, Foreign Agriculture Service											
Fund Resources:											
Undisbursed Funds	12		2903		No Year	2,010,000.00	99,000,000.00		98,370,512.36		2,639,487.64
Fund Equities:											
Unobligated Balances (Unexpired)						-1,270,000.00				738,440.19	-2,008,440.19
Accounts Payable						-740,000.00				23,222.45	-23,222.45
Undelivered Orders										-132,175.00	-607,825.00
Subtotal	12		2903			-0-	99,000,000.00		98,370,512.36	629,487.64	-0-

Title	Period of Availability	Reg	Tr From	Account Number	Sub No.	Balances, Beginning Of Fiscal Year	Appropriations And Other Obligational Authority[1]	Transfers Borrowings And Investment (Net)[2]	Outlays (Net)	Balances Withdrawn And Other Transactions[3]	Balances, End Of Fiscal Year[4]
Trust Fund Accounts											
Miscellaneous Contributed Funds, Foreign Agricultural Service											
Fund Resources:											
Undisbursed Funds	No Year	12		8232		2,066,845.02	26,477.95		28,491.48		2,064,831.49
Fund Equities:											
Unobligated Balances (Unexpired)						-1,108,103.16				-905,925.39	-202,177.77
Undelivered Orders						-958,741.86				903,911.86	-1,862,653.72
						-0-				-2,013.53	-0-
	Subtotal	12		8232		-0-	26,477.95		28,491.48		-0-
Total, Foreign Agricultural Service							2,034,916,121.82	30,000,000.00	2,387,427,650.28	-322,511,528.46	
Food And Nutrition Service											
General Fund Accounts											
Food Donations Programs For Selected Groups, Food And Nutrition Service											
Fund Resources:											
Undisbursed Funds	2003-2004	12		3503		308,588.63			-176,905.00		485,493.63
	2002-2003					433,297.46			-211.00		433,508.46
	2001-2002					1,655,783.88				1,655,783.88	
Fund Equities:											
Unobligated Balances (Expired)						-1,924,521.33				-1,463,061.88	-461,459.45
Undelivered Orders						-473,148.64				-15,606.00	-457,542.64
	Subtotal	12		3503		-0-			-177,116.00	177,116.00	-0-
Food Stamp Program											
Fund Resources:											
Undisbursed Funds	2007-2008	12		3505			3,000,000,000.00				3,000,000,000.00
	2007						35,071,534,000.00		[2]33,772,711,679.14		1,298,822,320.86
	2006-2007					3,000,000,000.00					3,000,000,000.00
	2006					4,118,781,524.22			850,074,571.58		3,268,706,952.64
	2005-2006					2,050,635,088.78			60,662,014.23		1,989,973,074.55
	2005					352,164,127.37			69,818,689.37		282,345,438.00
	2004					2,115,812,440.16			39,663,561.87		2,076,148,878.29
	2003					800,412,377.89			1,969,693.40		798,442,684.49
	2002					995,414,919.37			2,291,932.12	993,122,987.25	
	No Year					77,497,496.44	78,800,000.00		87,347,967.33		68,949,529.11
Fund Equities:											
Unobligated Balances (Expired)						-8,985,350,223.92				2,327,302,817.82	-11,312,653,041.74
Unobligated Balances (Unexpired)						-3,033,049,110.26				2,531,855.22	-3,035,580,965.48
Accounts Payable						-864,749,765.28				-28,063,949.66	-836,685,815.62
Undelivered Orders						-627,568,874.77				-29,099,819.67	-598,469,055.10
	Subtotal	12		3505		-0-	38,150,334,000.00		34,884,540,109.04	3,265,793,890.96	-0-
Commodity Assistance Program, Food And Nutrition Service											
Fund Resources:											
Undisbursed Funds	2007-2008	12		3507			192,572,340.00		156,625,088.37		35,947,251.63
	2006-2007					32,766,843.57			31,727,042.04		1,039,801.53
	2005-2006					2,037,953.92			1,862,862.98		175,090.94
	2004-2005					195,510.29			-43.10		195,553.39
	2004					1,028,660.75			-1,013.00		1,029,673.75

Footnotes At End Of Chapter

Appropriations, Outlays, and Balances – Continued

Appropriation or Fund Account — Title	Dept Reg	Tr From	Account Number	Sub No.	Period of Availability	Balances, Beginning Of Fiscal Year	Appropriations And Other Obligational Authority[1]	Transfers Borrowings And Investment (Net)[2]	Outlays (Net)	Balances Withdrawn And Other Transactions[3]	Balances, End Of Fiscal Year[4]
Commodity Assistance Program, Food And Nutrition Service - Continued											
Fund Resources: - Continued											
Undisbursed Funds - Continued					2003-2004	820,741.92			-199,407.09		1,020,149.01
					2002-2003	448,355.85			-55,210.46		503,566.31
					2001-2002	674,651.83			21,753.00	652,898.83	115,011.60
					No Year	869,830.00			754,818.40	678,246.00	20,301.00
Unfilled Customer Orders						698,547.00					
Fund Equities:											
Unobligated Balances (Expired)						-1,818,298.58				762,218.85	-2,580,517.43
Unobligated Balances (Unexpired)						-1,132,863.73				-522,852.13	-610,011.60
Accounts Payable						-35,831,325.77				364,384.36	-36,195,710.13
Undelivered Orders						-758,607.05				-98,447.05	-660,160.00
Subtotal	12		3507			-0-	192,572,340.00		190,735,891.14	1,836,448.86	-0-
Nutrition Programs Administration, Food And Nutrition Service											
Fund Resources:											
Undisbursed Funds	12		3508		2007	21,650,931.74	140,518,390.00		118,077,219.16		22,441,170.84
					2006	5,978,124.41			15,777,300.51		5,873,631.23
					2005	2,337,197.03			4,041,430.74		1,936,693.67
					2004	1,540,426.57			612,777.69		1,724,419.34
					2003	1,473,287.14			250,238.62		1,290,187.95
					2002	28,252.53			7,185.17		29,195.43
					No Year				-942.90	1,466,101.97	
Fund Equities:											
Unobligated Balances (Expired)						-3,907,412.05				-820,029.65	-3,087,382.40
Unobligated Balances (Unexpired)						-28,252.53				942.90	-29,195.43
Accounts Payable						-8,006,543.43				-1,007,414.81	-6,999,128.62
Undelivered Orders						-21,066,011.41				2,113,580.60	-23,179,592.01
Subtotal	12		3508			-0-	140,518,390.00		138,765,208.99	1,753,181.01	-0-
Special Supplemental Nutrition Program For Women, Infants And Children (WIC), Food And Nutrition Service											
Fund Resources:											
Undisbursed Funds	12		3510		2007-2008	618,829,245.81	5,204,430,000.00		304,689,959,779.75		514,470,220.25
					2006-2007	18,552,120.56			580,011,781.54		38,817,464.27
					2005-2006	10,350,336.75			9,277,087.88		9,275,032.68
					2004-2005	22,385,629.00			389,553.51		9,960,783.24
					2004	7,310,363.37					22,385,629.00
					2003-2004	201,942.52			156,736.65		7,153,626.72
					2002-2003	6,199,125.27			-225,437.47		201,942.52
					2001-2002	5,653,198.75			-732,956.71		6,424,562.74
					No Year	141,455,903.23			30,090,570.77		111,365,332.46
Fund Equities:											
Unobligated Balances (Expired)						-45,321,079.52				-860,955.25	-44,460,124.27
Unobligated Balances (Unexpired)						-163,060,341.46				-54,948,558.63	-108,111,782.83
Accounts Payable						-618,533,683.72				-54,136,218.92	-564,397,464.80
Undelivered Orders						-4,022,760.56				-937,538.58	-3,085,221.98
Subtotal	12		3510			-0-	5,204,430,000.00		5,308,927,115.92	-104,497,115.92	-0-

Appropriations, Outlays, and Balances - Continued

Title	Dept Reg	Tr From	Account Number	Sub No.	Period of Availability	Balances, Beginning Of Fiscal Year	Appropriations And Other Obligational Authority[1]	Transfers Borrowings And Investment (Net)[2]	Outlays (Net)	Balances Withdrawn And Other Transactions[3]	Balances, End Of Fiscal Year[4]
Child Nutrition Programs, Food And Nutrition Service											
Fund Resources:											
Undisbursed Funds	12		3539		2006-2009	3,507,231.19			1,114,563.79		2,392,667.40
					2007-2008		13,345,596,000.00		[3]11,075,485,643.99		2,270,110,356.01
					2007		4,250,000.00		208,330.00		4,041,670.00
					2006-2007	1,988,821,977.89		-1,501,451.00	1,922,643,015.62		64,677,511.27
					2006	8,316,412.35			6,028,271.21		2,288,141.14
					2005-2006	29,185,827.00			19,931,234.93		9,254,592.07
					2005	2,268,697.83			1,076,248.58		1,192,449.25
					2004-2005	61,776,861.62			1,945,894.30		59,830,967.32
					2004	803,453.65			421,185.67		382,267.98
					2003-2004	8,947,335.99			514,511.93		8,432,824.06
					2003	145,790.98			15,788.16		130,002.82
					2002-2003	18,509,989.66			353,120.75		18,156,868.91
					2001-2002	20,455,363.44			532,244.75	19,923,118.69	-0-
					No Year	33,947,048.34	16,000,000.00	1,501,451.00	14,876,229.06		36,572,270.28
Fund Equities:											
Unobligated Balances (Expired)						-98,616,559.69				33,216,493.19	-131,833,052.88
Unobligated Balances (Unexpired)						-83,039,665.60				169,195,031.70	-252,234,697.30
Accounts Payable						-1,979,022,014.81				99,067,655.94	-2,078,089,670.75
Undelivered Orders						-16,007,749.84				-702,582.26	-15,305,167.58
	12		3539		Subtotal	-0-	13,365,846,000.00		13,045,146,282.74	320,699,717.26	-0-
Total, Food And Nutrition Service							57,053,700,730.00		53,567,937,491.83	3,485,763,238.17	
Forest Service											
General Fund Accounts											
Land Acquisition, Forest Service											
Fund Resources:											
Undisbursed Funds	12		1101		No Year	2,078,841.62					2,078,841.62
Fund Equities:											
Unobligated Balances (Unexpired)						-2,078,744.21					-2,078,744.21
Accounts Payable						-97.41					-97.41
	12		1101		Subtotal	-0-					-0-
Capital Improvement And Maintenance, Forest Service											
Fund Resources:											
Undisbursed Funds	12		1103		No Year	291,474,259.80	447,911,523.56	-5,637,087.00	442,151,380.93		291,597,315.43
Transfer To:											
Department Of Transportation, Federal Highway Administration	69	12	1103	5	No Year	1,473,015.81			1,261.81		1,471,754.00
Accounts Receivable						11,782,102.93				-115,210.85	11,897,313.78
Unfilled Customer Orders						28,834,328.50				2,416,389.26	26,417,939.24
Fund Equities:											
Unobligated Balances (Unexpired)						-98,670,582.07				4,429,608.62	-103,100,190.69
Accounts Payable						-60,697,251.62				-448,211.53	-60,249,040.09
Undelivered Orders						-174,195,873.35				-6,160,781.68	-168,035,091.67
	12		1103		Subtotal	-0-	447,911,523.56	-5,637,087.00	442,152,642.74	121,793.82	-0-

Footnotes At End Of Chapter

Appropriations, Outlays, and Balances – Continued

Title	Period of Availability	Reg	Tr From	Account Number	Sub No.	Balances, Beginning Of Fiscal Year	Appropriations And Other Obligational Authority[1]	Transfers Borrowings And Investment (Net)[2]	Outlays (Net)	Balances Withdrawn And Other Transactions[3]	Balances, End Of Fiscal Year[4]
Forest And Rangeland Research, Forest Service											
Fund Resources:											
Undisbursed Funds	No Year	12		1104		119,443,554.05	303,277,201.00		294,522,551.31		128,198,203.74
Accounts Receivable						3,581,023.73				-2,486,598.24	6,067,621.97
Unfilled Customer Orders						30,822,153.15				4,082,937.24	26,739,215.91
Fund Equities:											
Unobligated Balances (Unexpired)						-35,972,531.21				-11,434,605.59	-24,537,925.62
Accounts Payable						-51,192,397.20				-26,568,195.57	-24,624,201.63
Undelivered Orders						-66,681,802.52				45,161,111.85	-111,842,914.37
Subtotal		12		1104		-0-	303,277,201.00		294,522,551.31	8,754,649.69	-0-
State And Private Forestry, Forest Service											
Fund Resources:											
Undisbursed Funds	2002-2007	12		1105		17,676,029.07			7,667,422.78		10,008,606.29
	2000-2003					500,000.00					500,000.00
	No Year					510,465,358.64	302,051,301.00	-4,089,470.00	352,873,938.13		455,553,251.51
Transfer To:											
Interior, National Park Service	No Year	14	12	1105	10	244,281.36		808,440.00	639,072.28		413,649.08
Interior, Bureau Of Land Management	No Year	14	12	1105	11	150,160.10		121,000.00	174,292.94		96,867.16
Interior, United States Fish And Wildlife Service	No Year	14	12	1105	16	182,879.36		43,000.00	85,784.95		140,094.41
Interior, Bureau Of Indian Affairs	No Year	14	12	1105	20	86,831.29		875,200.00	560,972.83		401,058.46
Navy	No Year	17	12	1105		114,159.16			-2,692.42		116,851.58
Army	No Year	21	12	1105		403,073.29		156,600.00	211,433.51		348,239.78
Air Force	No Year	57	12	1105		239,076.36		39,900.00	86,126.98		192,849.38
Corps Of Engineers	No Year	96	12	1105		71,632.00		45,330.00	59,317.78		57,644.22
Accounts Receivable						8,404,707.46				7,170,456.10	1,234,251.36
Unfilled Customer Orders						13,872,375.26				-330,600.05	14,202,975.31
Fund Equities:											
Unobligated Balances (Expired)						-500,000.00				678,355.81	-1,178,355.81
Unobligated Balances (Unexpired)						-56,846,677.05				-8,980,779.67	-47,865,897.38
Accounts Payable						-63,297,622.26				-41,183,149.87	-22,114,472.39
Undelivered Orders						-431,766,264.04				-19,658,651.08	-412,107,612.96
Subtotal		12		1105		-0-	302,051,301.00	-2,000,000.00	362,355,669.76	-62,304,368.76	-0-
National Forest System, Forest Service											
Fund Resources:											
Undisbursed Funds	2004-2005	12		1106		6,107.25			-293.65		6,400.90
	2003-2004					29,946.95					29,946.95
	2001-2002					43,972.07					43,972.07
						43.28				43.28	
	No Year			1106	11	320,023,095.44	1,447,174,816.00	13,782,886.00	1,395,241,211.41		385,739,586.03
Transfer To:											
Interior, Bureau Of Land Management	No Year	14	12	1106		3,336,177.83		2,745,420.00	2,983,830.65		3,097,767.18
Funds Held Outside The Treasury	No Year					347,506.26					347,506.26
Accounts Receivable						36,818,483.05				2,630,261.21	34,188,221.84
Unfilled Customer Orders						123,480,515.77				-4,249,527.36	127,730,043.13
Fund Equities:											
Unobligated Balances (Expired)						-48,613.20				31,706.72	-80,319.92
Unobligated Balances (Unexpired)						-155,111,119.02				10,735,757.62	-165,846,876.64
Accounts Payable						-116,244,726.03				-10,284,777.95	-105,959,948.08
Undelivered Orders						-212,681,389.65				66,614,910.07	-279,296,299.72

Appropriations, Outlays, and Balances - Continued

Title	Period of Availability	Dept Reg	Tr From	Account Number	Sub No.	Balances, Beginning Of Fiscal Year	Appropriations And Other Obligational Authority[1]	Transfers Borrowings And Investment (Net)[2]	Outlays (Net)	Balances Withdrawn And Other Transactions[3]	Balances, End Of Fiscal Year[4]
Wildland Fire Management, Forest Service											
Subtotal	Subtotal	12		1106		-0-	1,447,174,816.00	16,528,306.00	1,398,224,748.41	65,478,373.59	-0-
Fund Resources:											
Undisbursed Funds	No Year	12		1115		967,847,203.44	2,127,439,419.00	46,728,000.00	2,438,107,694.35	35,818,992.64	703,906,928.09
Accounts Receivable						140,196,961.38					104,377,968.74
Unfilled Customer Orders						29,997,489.76				2,087,866.51	27,909,623.25
Fund Equities:											
Unobligated Balances (Unexpired)						-210,790,376.37				-120,738,001.36	-90,052,375.01
Accounts Payable						-733,103,007.29				-213,495,725.53	-519,607,281.76
Undelivered Orders						-194,148,270.92				32,386,592.39	-226,534,863.31
Subtotal	Subtotal	12		1115		-0-	2,127,439,419.00	46,728,000.00	2,438,107,694.35	-263,940,275.35	-0-
Payments To States, Northern Spotted Owl Guarantee, Forest Service											
Fund Resources:											
Undisbursed Funds	2007-2008	12		1117			314,786,839.00				314,786,839.00
	2007						261,982,755.66		261,982,755.66		
	2006					1,519.52					1,519.52
	2005					0.25					0.25
	2003					5,035.80					5,035.80
	No Year					2,278,974.12			1,039,159.93		1,239,814.19
Fund Equities:											
Unobligated Balances (Expired)						-6,555.57					-6,555.57
Unobligated Balances (Unexpired)						-734,516.71				-137,877.93	-596,638.78
Accounts Payable						-10,977.18				314,870,109.59	-314,881,086.77
Undelivered Orders						-1,533,480.23				-984,552.59	-548,927.64
Subtotal	Subtotal	12		1117		-0-	576,769,594.66		263,021,915.59	313,747,679.07	-0-
Management Of National Forest Lands For Subsistence Uses, Forest Service											
Fund Resources:											
Undisbursed Funds	No Year	12		1119		2,802,757.55	5,035,712.00		5,309,781.70		2,528,687.85
Fund Equities:											
Unobligated Balances (Unexpired)						-1,120,015.92				-813,628.16	-306,387.76
Accounts Payable						-377,587.90				81,354.98	-458,942.88
Undelivered Orders						-1,305,153.73				458,203.48	-1,763,357.21
Subtotal	Subtotal	12		1119		-0-	5,035,712.00		5,309,781.70	-274,069.70	-0-
Emergency Pest Suppression Fund, Forest Service											
Fund Resources:											
Undisbursed Funds	No Year	12		1127		41,548.81			-3,433.24		44,982.05
Fund Equities:											
Unobligated Balances (Unexpired)						-44,751.17				230.88	-44,982.05
Accounts Payable						3,202.05				3,202.05	
Undelivered Orders						0.31				0.31	
Subtotal	Subtotal	12		1127		-0-			-3,433.24	3,433.24	-0-
Federal Infrastructure Improvement, Forest Service											
Fund Resources:											
Undisbursed Funds	No Year	12		1129		1,762,912.94		-1,762,913.00	-1,779.33		1,779.27
Fund Equities:											
Unobligated Balances (Unexpired)						-1,762,912.94				-1,761,133.67	-1,779.27
Subtotal	Subtotal	12		1129		-0-		-1,762,913.00	-1,779.33	-1,761,133.67	-0-

Footnotes At End Of Chapter

Appropriations, Outlays, and Balances – Continued

Appropriation or Fund Account	Account Symbol				Period of Availability	Balances, Beginning Of Fiscal Year	Appropriations And Other Obligational Authority[1]	Transfers Borrowings And Investment (Net)[2]	Outlays (Net)	Balances Withdrawn And Other Transactions[3]	Balances, End Of Fiscal Year[4]
Title	Dept Reg	Tr From	Account Number	Sub No.							
Special Fund Accounts											
Land Acquisition, Forest Service											
Fund Resources:											
Undisbursed Funds	12		5004		2000-2003	97,898.96					97,898.96
Undisbursed Funds					No Year	40,095,514.43	31,936,123.00		55,316,773.23		16,714,864.20
Accounts Receivable						2,663,370.52				-6,064.29	2,669,434.81
Unfilled Customer Orders						1,320,573.57				1,146,608.38	173,966.19
Fund Equities:											
Unobligated Balances (Expired)						-97,898.96					-97,898.96
Unobligated Balances (Unexpired)						-26,175,858.44				-15,740,563.51	-10,435,294.93
Accounts Payable						-1,258,026.55				-231,759.83	-1,026,266.72
Undelivered Orders						-16,645,573.53				-8,548,870.98	-8,096,702.55
Subtotal	12		5004			-0-	31,936,123.00		55,316,773.23	-23,380,650.23	-0-
Recreation Fees For Collection Costs, Forest Service											
Fund Resources:											
Undisbursed Funds	12		5010		No Year	86,882.09	-3,401.04				83,481.05
Accounts Receivable						4,908.59				4,908.59	
Fund Equities:											
Unobligated Balances (Unexpired)						-121,248.77				-22,718.55	-98,530.22
Accounts Payable						6,202.52				-8,846.15	15,048.67
Undelivered Orders						23,255.57				23,255.07	0.50
Subtotal	12		5010			-0-	-3,401.04			-3,401.04	-0-
Fees, Operation And Maintenance Of Recreation Facilities, Forest Service											
Fund Resources:											
Undisbursed Funds	12		5072		No Year	13,449,648.16		-13,449,648.00	0.16		
Fund Equities:											
Unobligated Balances (Unexpired)						-13,449,648.16				-13,449,648.16	
Subtotal	12		5072			-0-		-13,449,648.00	0.16	-13,449,648.16	-0-
Payments To States, National Forests Fund											
Fund Resources:											
Undisbursed Funds	12		5201		No Year	323,611,227.62	-20,390,847.15		157,092,466.95		146,127,913.52
Fund Equities:											
Unobligated Balances (Unexpired)						-299,844,431.66				-184,146,273.71	-115,698,157.95
Accounts Payable						-1,291,024.24				1,332,437.03	-2,623,461.27
Undelivered Orders						-22,475,771.72				5,330,522.58	-27,806,294.30
Subtotal	12		5201			-0-	-20,390,847.15		157,092,466.95	-177,483,314.10	-0-
Timber Roads, Purchaser Elections, Forest Service											
Fund Resources:											
Undisbursed Funds	12		5202		No Year	63,627,665.25	6,800,000.00	-40,000,000.00	1,715,400.86		28,712,264.39
Fund Equities:											
Unobligated Balances (Unexpired)						-61,208,858.51				-34,273,097.20	-26,935,761.31
Accounts Payable						-87,596.74				81,416.50	-169,013.24
Undelivered Orders						-2,331,210.00				-723,720.16	-1,607,489.84
Subtotal	12		5202			-0-	6,800,000.00	-40,000,000.00	1,715,400.86	-34,915,400.86	-0-
Roads And Trails For States, National Forests Fund											
Fund Resources:											
Undisbursed Funds	12		5203		No Year	30,329,634.31	16,439,638.23		15,620,533.34		31,148,739.20

Appropriations, Outlays, and Balances - Continued

Appropriation or Fund Account — Title	Period of Availability	Reg	Tr From	Account Number	Sub No.	Balances, Beginning Of Fiscal Year	Appropriations And Other Obligational Authority[1]	Transfers Borrowings And Investment (Net)[2]	Outlays (Net)	Balances Withdrawn And Other Transactions[3]	Balances, End Of Fiscal Year[4]
Fund Equities:											
Unobligated Balances (Unexpired)						-19,290,004.31				66,556.33	-19,356,560.64
Accounts Payable						-2,562,376.45				-655,212.19	-1,907,164.26
Undelivered Orders						-8,477,253.55				1,407,760.75	-9,885,014.30
	Subtotal	12		5203		-0-	16,439,638.23		15,620,533.34	819,104.89	-0-
Timber Salvage Sales, Forest Service											
Fund Resources:											
Undisbursed Funds	No Year	12		5204		95,105,420.70	43,558,304.36		61,753,006.95		76,910,718.11
Fund Equities:											
Unobligated Balances (Unexpired)						-89,698,558.10				-24,113,105.13	-65,585,452.97
Accounts Payable						-3,306,837.51				1,028,507.82	-4,335,345.33
Undelivered Orders						-2,100,025.09				4,889,894.72	-6,989,919.81
	Subtotal	12		5204		-0-	43,558,304.36		61,753,006.95	-18,194,702.59	-0-
Expenses, Brush Disposal, Forest Service											
Fund Resources:											
Undisbursed Funds	No Year	12		5206		55,381,971.79	10,514,081.02	-13,000,000.00	13,250,874.94		39,645,177.87
Accounts Receivable						-4,746.52					-4,746.52
Fund Equities:											
Unobligated Balances (Unexpired)						-54,109,326.87				-17,311,454.50	-36,797,872.37
Accounts Payable						-655,099.37				282,348.33	-937,447.70
Undelivered Orders						-612,799.03				1,292,312.25	-1,905,111.28
	Subtotal	12		5206		-0-	10,514,081.02	-13,000,000.00	13,250,874.94	-15,736,793.92	-0-
Range Betterment Fund, Forest Service											
Fund Resources:											
Undisbursed Funds	No Year	12		5207		1,984,343.21	2,876,072.00		3,236,522.15		1,623,893.06
Fund Equities:											
Unobligated Balances (Unexpired)						-932,302.32				-53,968.44	-878,333.88
Accounts Payable						-487,966.62				-197,490.45	-290,476.17
Undelivered Orders						-564,074.27				-108,991.26	-455,083.01
	Subtotal	12		5207		-0-	2,876,072.00		3,236,522.15	-360,450.15	-0-
Acquisition Of Lands For National Forests, Special Acts, Forest Service											
Fund Resources:											
Undisbursed Funds	2007	12		5208			1,053,273.00		1,036,794.61		16,478.39
	2006					456,391.75			296,752.00		159,639.75
Fund Equities:											
Unobligated Balances (Expired)						-26,099.75				121,137.98	-147,237.73
Accounts Payable										2,340.41	-2,340.41
Undelivered Orders						-430,292.00				-403,752.00	-26,540.00
	Subtotal	12		5208		-0-	1,053,273.00		1,333,546.61	-280,273.61	-0-
Payment To Minnesota (Cook, Lake, And Saint Louis Counties) From The National Forests Fund											
Fund Resources:											
Undisbursed Funds	No Year	12		5213		2,101,500.00	2,101,500.00		2,101,500.00		2,101,500.00
Fund Equities:											
Unobligated Balances (Unexpired)	Subtotal	12		5213		-2,101,500.00	2,101,500.00		2,101,500.00		-0-

Footnotes At End Of Chapter

124

Appropriations, Outlays, and Balances – Continued

Appropriation or Fund Account – Title	Reg	Tr From	Account Number	Sub No.	Period of Availability	Balances, Beginning Of Fiscal Year	Appropriations And Other Obligational Authority[1]	Transfers Borrowings And Investment (Net)[2]	Outlays (Net)	Balances Withdrawn And Other Transactions[3]	Balances, End Of Fiscal Year[4]
Licensee Programs, Forest Service											
Fund Resources:											
Undisbursed Funds	12		5214		No Year	305,271.59	73,566.97		20,221.22		358,617.34
Accounts Receivable						769.72				769.72	
Fund Equities:											
Unobligated Balances (Unexpired)						-303,145.23				54,848.76	-357,993.99
Undelivered Orders						-2,896.08				-2,272.73	-623.35
Subtotal	12		5214			-0-	73,566.97		20,221.22	53,345.75	-0-
Restoration Of Forest Lands And Improvements, Forest Service											
Fund Resources:											
Undisbursed Funds	12		5215		No Year	20,911,844.60	21,578,668.58	575,000.00	2,485,106.15		40,580,407.03
Accounts Receivable						22,781.26				22,781.26	
Fund Equities:											
Unobligated Balances (Unexpired)						-20,550,993.05				18,555,448.22	-39,106,441.27
Accounts Payable						33,551.32				39,490.88	-5,939.56
Undelivered Orders						-417,184.13				1,050,842.07	-1,468,026.20
Subtotal	12		5215			-0-	21,578,668.58	575,000.00	2,485,106.15	19,668,562.43	-0-
Acquisition Of Lands To Complete Land Exchanges, Forest Service											
Fund Resources:											
Undisbursed Funds	12		5216		No Year	35,274,096.94	26,479,289.11		13,349,443.93		48,403,942.12
Fund Equities:											
Unobligated Balances (Unexpired)						-20,861,775.37				13,899,039.91	-34,760,815.28
Accounts Payable						-842,380.07				289,052.55	-1,131,432.62
Undelivered Orders						-13,569,941.50				-1,058,247.28	-12,511,694.22
Subtotal	12		5216			-0-	26,479,289.11		13,349,443.93	13,129,845.18	-0-
Tongass Timber Supply Fund, Forest Service											
Fund Resources:											
Undisbursed Funds	12		5217		No Year	17,010.50			-227.50		17,238.00
Fund Equities:											
Unobligated Balances (Unexpired)						-490.50				31,077.34	-31,567.84
Accounts Payable						-16,693.41				227.50	-16,920.91
Undelivered Orders						173.41				-31,077.34	31,250.75
Subtotal	12		5217			-0-			-227.50	227.50	-0-
Operation And Maintenance Of Quarters, Forest Service											
Fund Resources:											
Undisbursed Funds	12		5219		No Year	9,973,113.18	7,745,882.13		7,189,194.05		10,529,801.26
Accounts Receivable						58,838.48				58,838.48	
Fund Equities:											
Unobligated Balances (Unexpired)						-9,269,208.32				-1,768,500.26	-7,500,708.06
Accounts Payable						-351,913.24				1,767,447.80	-2,119,361.04
Undelivered Orders						-410,830.10				498,902.06	-909,732.16
Subtotal	12		5219			-0-	7,745,882.13		7,189,194.05	556,688.08	-0-
Resource Management Timber Receipts, Forest Service											
Fund Resources:											
Undisbursed Funds	12		5220		No Year	1,812,347.68					1,812,347.68
Fund Equities:											
Unobligated Balances (Unexpired)						-1,811,982.81				364.61	-1,812,347.42
Accounts Payable						-292.09				-291.83	-0.26
Undelivered Orders						-72.78				-72.78	

Appropriations, Outlays, and Balances - Continued

Appropriation or Fund Account — Title	Dept Reg	Tr From	Account Number	Sub No.	Period of Availability	Balances, Beginning Of Fiscal Year	Appropriations And Other Obligational Authority[1]	Transfers Borrowings And Investment (Net)[2]	Outlays (Net)	Balances Withdrawn And Other Transactions[3]	Balances, End Of Fiscal Year[4]
	12		5220		Subtotal	-0-					-0-
Quinault Special Management Area, Forest Service											
Fund Resources:											
Undisbursed Funds	12		5223		No Year	23,998.86					23,998.86
Fund Equities:											
Unobligated Balances (Unexpired)						-23,998.86					-23,998.86
	12		5223		Subtotal	-0-					-0-
Timber Sales Pipeline Restoration Fund, Forest Service											
Fund Resources:											
Undisbursed Funds	12		5264		No Year	10,170,334.90	6,999,708.36	-39,805.00	5,758,056.91		11,372,181.35
Fund Equities:											
Unobligated Balances (Unexpired)						-7,898,754.38				1,818,361.51	-9,717,135.89
Accounts Payable						-564,306.89				-210,046.96	-354,259.93
Undelivered Orders						-1,707,273.63				-406,488.10	-1,300,785.53
	12		5264		Subtotal	-0-	6,999,708.36	-39,805.00	5,758,056.91	1,201,846.45	-0-
Recreation Fee Demonstration Program, Forest Service											
Fund Resources:											
Undisbursed Funds	12		5268		No Year	132,484,068.71	61,042,072.24	13,449,648.00	57,644,585.62		149,331,203.33
Accounts Receivable						70,498.86				70,498.86	
Fund Equities:											
Unobligated Balances (Unexpired)						-125,020,021.79				14,316,354.05	-139,336,375.84
Accounts Payable						-4,472,337.44				-1,194,229.84	-3,278,107.60
Undelivered Orders						-3,062,208.34				3,654,511.55	-6,716,719.89
	12		5268		Subtotal	-0-	61,042,072.24	13,449,648.00	57,644,585.62	16,847,134.62	-0-
MNP Rental Fee Account, Forest Service											
Fund Resources:											
Undisbursed Funds	12		5277		No Year	1,638,461.85	789,882.66		296,271.67		2,132,072.84
Fund Equities:											
Unobligated Balances (Unexpired)						-1,416,182.94				383,519.05	-1,799,701.99
Accounts Payable						-2,017.65				53,215.49	-55,233.14
Undelivered Orders						-220,261.26				56,876.45	-277,137.71
	12		5277		Subtotal	-0-	789,882.66		296,271.67	493,610.99	-0-
Midewin National Tallgrass Prairie Restoration Fund, Forest Service											
Fund Resources:											
Undisbursed Funds	12		5278		No Year	13,877.60					13,877.60
Fund Equities:											
Unobligated Balances (Unexpired)						-13,877.60					-13,877.60
	12		5278		Subtotal	-0-					-0-
Land Between The Lakes Management Fund, Forest Service											
Fund Resources:											
Undisbursed Funds	12		5360		No Year	2,550,382.13	3,837,950.05		3,118,043.00		3,270,289.18
Fund Equities:											
Unobligated Balances (Unexpired)						-2,227,747.34				49,426.26	-2,277,173.60
Accounts Payable						-138,661.80				151,973.04	-290,634.84
Undelivered Orders						-183,972.99				518,507.75	-702,480.74
	12		5360		Subtotal	-0-	3,837,950.05		3,118,043.00	719,907.05	-0-

Footnotes At End Of Chapter

Appropriations, Outlays, and Balances – Continued

Appropriation or Fund Account	Account Symbol					Balances, Beginning Of Fiscal Year	Appropriations And Other Obligational Authority[1]	Transfers Borrowings And Investment (Net)[2]	Outlays (Net)	Balances Withdrawn And Other Transactions[3]	Balances, End Of Fiscal Year[4]
Title	Period of Availability	Dept Reg	Tr From	Account Number	Sub No.						
Administration Of Rights-Of-Way And Other Land Uses Fund, Forest Service											
Fund Resources:											
Undisbursed Funds	No Year	12		5361		1,459,006.66	971,973.15		-239,265.33		2,670,245.14
Accounts Receivable						13,250.00				13,250.00	
Fund Equities:											
Unobligated Balances (Unexpired)						-1,436,533.37				1,132,843.86	-2,569,377.23
Accounts Payable						-33,243.28				45,669.62	-78,912.90
Undelivered Orders						-2,480.01				19,475.00	-21,955.01
Subtotal		12		5361		-0-	971,973.15		-239,265.33	1,211,238.48	-0-
Valles Caldera Fund, Forest Service											
Fund Resources:											
Undisbursed Funds	No Year	12		5363		2,036,183.84	2,484,952.57		1,850,037.18		2,671,099.23
Fund Equities:											
Unobligated Balances (Unexpired)						-686,547.84				2,476,120.04	-3,162,667.88
Accounts Payable						-1,166,283.92				-1,710,134.77	543,850.85
Undelivered Orders						-183,352.08				-131,069.88	-52,282.20
Subtotal		12		5363		-0-	2,484,952.57		1,850,037.18	634,915.39	-0-
State, Private And International Forestry, Land And Water Conservation Fund, Forest Service											
Fund Resources:											
Undisbursed Funds	No Year	12		5367		85,410,283.93	56,535,802.00		41,120,297.83		100,825,788.10
Fund Equities:											
Unobligated Balances (Unexpired)						-2,615,150.64				-510,433.61	-2,104,717.03
Accounts Payable						-3,393,919.94				-508,297.48	-2,885,622.46
Undelivered Orders						-79,401,213.35				16,434,235.26	-95,835,448.61
Subtotal		12		5367		-0-	56,535,802.00		41,120,297.83	15,415,504.17	-0-
Hardwood Technology Transfer And Applied Research Fund, Forest Service											
Fund Resources:											
Undisbursed Funds	No Year	12		5462		52,975.72	104,800.00				157,775.72
Accounts Receivable						14.75				14.75	
Fund Equities:											
Unobligated Balances (Unexpired)						-52,990.47				104,785.25	-157,775.72
Subtotal		12		5462		-0-	104,800.00			104,800.00	-0-
Stewardship Contracting Product Sales, Department Of Agriculture, Forest Service											
Fund Resources:											
Undisbursed Funds	No Year	12		5540		3,443,273.64	1,260,594.04		746,518.79		3,957,348.89
Fund Equities:											
Unobligated Balances (Unexpired)						-2,648,515.00				-137,701.77	-2,510,813.23
Accounts Payable						-47,136.58				2,568.77	-49,705.35
Undelivered Orders						-747,622.06				649,208.25	-1,396,830.31
Subtotal		12		5540		-0-	1,260,594.04		746,518.79	514,075.25	-0-
Payments To Counties, National Grasslands, Forest Service											
Fund Resources:											
Undisbursed Funds	No Year	12		5896		9,399,542.04	10,538,000.00		12,092,487.35		7,845,054.69

Appropriations, Outlays, and Balances - Continued

Appropriation or Fund Account (Title)	Period of Availability	Dept Reg	Tr From	Account Number	Sub No.	Balances, Beginning Of Fiscal Year	Appropriations And Other Obligational Authority[1]	Transfers Borrowings And Investment (Net)[2]	Outlays (Net)	Balances Withdrawn And Other Transactions[3]	Balances, End Of Fiscal Year[4]
Intragovernmental Funds											
Fund Equities:											
Unobligated Balances (Unexpired)						-9,399,542.04				-1,554,487.35	-7,845,054.69
	Subtotal	12		5896		-0-	10,538,000.00		12,092,487.35	-1,554,487.35	-0-
Working Capital Fund, Forest Service											
Fund Resources:											
Undisbursed Funds	No Year	12		4605		122,987,105.07			-12,698,556.76		135,685,661.83
Accounts Receivable						948,174.59				672,801.94	275,372.65
Fund Equities:											
Unobligated Balances (Unexpired)						-94,116,325.13				3,076,839.30	-97,193,164.43
Accounts Payable						-9,155,327.09				-4,304,946.63	-4,850,380.46
Undelivered Orders						-20,663,627.44				13,253,862.15	-33,917,489.59
	Subtotal	12		4605		-0-			-12,698,556.76	12,698,556.76	-0-
Trust Fund Accounts											
Cooperative Work, Forest Service											
Fund Resources:											
Undisbursed Funds	No Year	12		8028		412,023,302.98	69,576,105.68		143,485,897.56		338,113,511.10
Accounts Receivable						29,064.72					29,064.72
Fund Equities:											
Unobligated Balances (Unexpired)						-349,865,426.11				-73,650,327.50	-276,215,098.61
Accounts Payable						-14,083,831.44				-2,233,510.95	-11,850,320.49
Undelivered Orders						-48,103,110.15				1,974,046.57	-50,077,156.72
	Subtotal	12		8028		-0-	69,576,105.68		143,485,897.56	-73,909,791.88	-0-
Highland Scenic Highway, Forest Service											
Fund Resources:											
Undisbursed Funds	No Year	12		8029		81,825.07					81,825.07
Fund Equities:											
Unobligated Balances (Unexpired)	Subtotal	12		8029		-81,825.07					-81,825.07
	Subtotal	12		8029		-0-					-0-
Donations For Forest And Rangeland Research, Forest Service											
Fund Resources:											
Undisbursed Funds	No Year	12		8034		143,299.23	55,831.11		6,631.69		192,498.65
Accounts Receivable						-86.05				-86.05	
Fund Equities:											
Unobligated Balances (Unexpired)						-140,435.89				45,019.15	-185,455.04
Accounts Payable						-2,777.29				4,108.07	-6,885.36
Undelivered Orders										158.25	-158.25
	Subtotal	12		8034		-0-	55,831.11		6,631.69	49,199.42	-0-
Land Between The Lakes Trust Fund, Forest Service											
Fund Resources:											
Undisbursed Funds	No Year	12		8039		46,596.38	270,118.02	-243,936.99	49,982.33		22,795.08
Unrealized Discount On Investments						-130,148.07		-8,063.01			-138,211.08
Investments In Public Debt Securities						5,414,000.00		252,000.00			5,666,000.00

Footnotes At End Of Chapter

Appropriations, Outlays, and Balances – Continued

Appropriation or Fund Account — Title	Period of Availability	Dept Reg	Tr From	Account Number	Sub No.	Balances, Beginning Of Fiscal Year	Appropriations And Other Obligational Authority[1]	Transfers Borrowings And Investment (Net)[2]	Outlays (Net)	Balances Withdrawn And Other Transactions[3]	Balances, End Of Fiscal Year[4]
Land Between The Lakes Trust Fund, Forest Service - Continued											
Fund Equities:											
Unobligated Balances (Unexpired)						-5,325,482.63				225,101.37	-5,550,584.00
Accounts Payable						-4,965.68				-4,965.68	-0-
	Subtotal	12		8039		-0-	270,118.02		49,982.33	220,135.69	-0-
Reforestation Trust Fund, Forest Service											
Fund Resources:											
Undisbursed Funds	No Year	12		8046		25,003,571.15	30,004,200.00	1,014.50	41,321,200.97		13,687,584.68
Unrealized Discount On Investments						1,014.50		-1,014.50			
Accounts Receivable						410.84				410.84	
Fund Equities:											
Unobligated Balances (Unexpired)						-18,358,490.00				-14,056,015.24	-4,302,474.76
Accounts Payable						-3,066,638.36				-377,938.42	-2,688,699.94
Undelivered Orders						-3,579,868.13				3,116,541.85	-6,696,409.98
	Subtotal	12		8046		-0-	30,004,200.00		41,321,200.97	-11,317,000.97	-0-
Total, Forest Service							5,604,893,707.31	1,391,501.00	5,832,706,343.14	-226,421,134.83	
Deductions For Offsetting Receipts											
Proprietary Receipts From The Public							-1,677,660,549.40		-1,677,660,549.40		
Intrabudgetary Transactions							-81,362,712.05		-81,362,712.05		
Total, Offsetting Receipts							-1,759,023,261.45		-1,759,023,261.45		
Total, Department Of Agriculture							147,540,189,095.32	-43,967,566,899.80	84,436,975,061.67	19,135,647,133.85	
Memorandum											
Financing Accounts											
Public Enterprise Funds											
Rural Business Investment Program Guaranteed Financing Account, Rural Business - Cooperative Service											
Fund Resources:											
Unfilled Customer Orders	No Year	12		4033		1,875,497.00					1,875,497.00
Fund Equities:											
Unobligated Balances (Unexpired)						-1,875,497.00					-1,875,497.00
	Subtotal	12		4033		-0-					-0-
P.L. 480 Direct Loan Financing Account											
Fund Resources:											
Undisbursed Funds	No Year	12		4049		32,035,175.00		18,344,000.00	-126,563,982.61		176,943,157.61
Authority To Borrow From The Treasury						551,339,808.00	18,344,000.00	-18,344,000.00			551,339,808.00
Accounts Receivable						42,747,380.21				-14,532,734.10	57,280,114.31
Fund Equities:											
Unobligated Balances (Unexpired)						-624,543,427.08				84,510,738.68	-709,054,165.76
Accounts Payable						-1,468.80				74,929,978.03	-74,931,446.83
Undelivered Orders						-1,577,467.33				144,907,982.61	-1,577,467.33
	Subtotal	12		4049		-0-	18,344,000.00		-126,563,982.61		-0-

Appropriations, Outlays, and Balances - Continued

Title	Period of Availability	Dept Reg	Tr From	Account Number	Sub No.	Balances, Beginning Of Fiscal Year	Appropriations And Other Obligational Authority[1]	Transfers Borrowings And Investment (Net)[2]	Outlays (Net)	Balances Withdrawn And Other Transactions[3]	Balances, End Of Fiscal Year[4]
Enterprise For The America's Initiative, Financing Account											
Fund Resources:											
Undisbursed Funds	No Year	12		4143		59,294,841.82			46,156,076.71		85,161,153.11
Authority To Borrow From The Treasury						20,739,605.00	72,022,388.00	-72,022,388.00			20,739,605.00
Accounts Receivable										-4,784,422.27	4,784,422.27
Fund Equities:											
Unobligated Balances (Unexpired)						-80,033,569.35				19,241,916.25	-99,275,485.60
Accounts Payable						-877.47				11,408,817.31	-11,409,694.78
Subtotal		12		4143		-0-	72,022,388.00	-72,022,388.00	46,156,076.71	25,866,311.29	-0-
Distance Learning And Telemedicine Direct Loan Financing Account, Rural Utilities Service											
Fund Resources:											
Undisbursed Funds	No Year	12		4146		2,248,723.22		66,527,000.00	66,926,987.94		1,848,735.28
Authority To Borrow From The Treasury						973,861,250.14	292,214,329.83	-121,827,000.00		346,495,166.32	797,753,413.65
Unfilled Customer Orders						20,136,954.53				3,892,304.98	16,244,649.55
Fund Equities:											
Unobligated Balances (Unexpired)						-2,248,723.22				-2,248,723.22	-2,248,723.22
Accounts Payable						-993,998,204.67				-178,151,406.19	-815,846,798.48
Undelivered Orders						-0-				169,987,341.89	-0-
Subtotal		12		4146		-0-	292,214,329.83	-55,300,000.00	66,926,987.94	169,987,341.89	-0-
Farm Storage Facility Direct Loan Financing Account, Farm Service Agency											
Fund Resources:											
Undisbursed Funds	No Year	12		4158		94,722,961.33		122,720,825.16	54,746,501.14		162,697,285.35
Authority To Borrow From The Treasury							189,745,231.00	-187,245,231.00		2,500,000.00	
Accounts Receivable						211,119.00				-578,807.88	789,926.88
Unfilled Customer Orders						604.15				-448,548.98	449,153.13
Fund Equities:											
Unobligated Balances (Unexpired)						-22,609,647.38				21,052,009.07	-43,661,656.45
Accounts Payable						-315,535.09				913,890.74	-1,229,425.83
Undelivered Orders						-72,009,502.01				47,035,781.07	-119,045,283.08
Subtotal		12		4158		-0-	189,745,231.00	-64,524,405.84	54,746,501.14	70,474,324.02	-0-
Rural Economic Development Direct Loans Financing Account, Rural Business And Cooperative Development Service											
Fund Resources:											
Undisbursed Funds	No Year	12		4176		1,448,099.03		6,699,500.00	1,445,924.58		6,701,674.45
Authority To Borrow From The Treasury						13,702,854.16	30,828,629.25	-22,107,000.00		7,098,359.80	15,326,123.61
Unfilled Customer Orders						3,752,355.81				-1,831,817.14	5,584,172.95
Fund Equities:											
Unobligated Balances (Unexpired)										1,476,462.01	-1,476,462.01
Accounts Payable						-18,903,309.00				7,232,200.00	-26,135,509.00
Undelivered Orders						-0-				13,975,204.67	-0-
Subtotal		12		4176		-0-	30,828,629.25	-15,407,500.00	1,445,924.58		-0-

Footnotes At End Of Chapter

Appropriations, Outlays, and Balances – Continued

Appropriation or Fund Account — Title	Period of Availability	Dept Reg	Tr From	Account Number	Sub No.	Balances, Beginning Of Fiscal Year	Appropriations And Other Obligational Authority[1]	Transfers Borrowings And Investment (Net)[2]	Outlays (Net)	Balances Withdrawn And Other Transactions[3]	Balances, End Of Fiscal Year[4]
Agricultural Resource Conservation Demonstration Direct Loan Financing Account, Natural Resources Conservation Service											
Fund Resources:											
Undisbursed Funds	No Year	12		4177		329.31					329.31
Fund Equities:											
Unobligated Balances (Unexpired)						-329.31					-329.31
Subtotal	Subtotal	12		4177		-0-					-0-
Rural Electrification And Telephone Direct Loan Financing Account, Rural Utilities Service											
Fund Resources:											
Undisbursed Funds	No Year	12		4208		235,139,815.74	20,439.00	[3]4,223,158,285.36	4,125,822,877.99	676,404,277.91	332,495,662.11
Authority To Borrow From The Treasury						12,130,030,139.53	6,342,381,673.78	-6,223,696,598.37			11,572,310,937.03
Unfilled Customer Orders						40,060,594.53				9,807,289.04	30,253,305.49
Fund Equities:											
Unobligated Balances (Unexpired)						-229,367,572.27				-87,495,904.14	-141,871,668.13
Accounts Payable						-147,166.50				195,114,522.48	-195,261,688.98
Undelivered Orders						-12,175,715,811.03				-577,789,263.51	-11,597,926,547.52
Subtotal	Subtotal	12		4208		-0-	6,342,402,112.78	-2,000,538,313.01	4,125,822,877.99	216,040,921.78	-0-
Rural Electrification And Telephone Guaranteed Loan Financing Account, Rural Electrification Administration											
Fund Resources:											
Undisbursed Funds	No Year	12		4209		200,385.79			10,762.09	21,976.00	189,623.70
Authority To Borrow From The Treasury							21,976.00				
Fund Equities:											
Unobligated Balances (Unexpired)						-200,385.79				-10,762.09	-189,623.70
Subtotal	Subtotal	12		4209		-0-	21,976.00		10,762.09	11,213.91	-0-
Rural Telephone Bank Direct Loan Financing Account, Rural Utilities Service											
Fund Resources:											
Undisbursed Funds	No Year	12		4210		2,739,341.04		88,101,000.00	90,601,661.61	131,051,209.36	238,679.43
Authority To Borrow From The Treasury						894,983,789.19	115,582,019.59	-168,901,000.00			710,613,599.42
Unfilled Customer Orders						14,931,952.75				2,747,118.14	12,184,834.61
Fund Equities:											
Unobligated Balances (Unexpired)						-2,739,341.04				-2,500,661.61	-238,679.43
Accounts Payable											
Undelivered Orders						-909,915,741.94				-187,117,307.91	-722,798,434.03
Subtotal	Subtotal	12		4210		-0-	115,582,019.59	-80,800,000.00	90,601,661.61	-55,819,642.02	-0-
Apple Loans Direct Loan Financing Account, Farm Service Agency											
Fund Resources:											
Undisbursed Funds	No Year	12		4211		288,119.07		-200,000.00	15,762.12		72,356.95
Authority To Borrow From The Treasury							800,000.00	-800,000.00			
Accounts Receivable										22,301.25	-22,301.25
Fund Equities:											
Unobligated Balances (Unexpired)						-288,119.07				-238,063.37	-50,055.70
Subtotal	Subtotal	12		4211		-0-	800,000.00	-1,000,000.00	15,762.12	-215,762.12	-0-

Appropriations, Outlays, and Balances - Continued

Appropriation or Fund Account: Title	Period of Availability	Dept Reg	Tr From	Account Number	Sub No.	Balances, Beginning Of Fiscal Year	Appropriations And Other Obligational Authority[1]	Transfers Borrowings And Investment (Net)[2]	Outlays (Net)	Balances Withdrawn And Other Transactions[3]	Balances, End Of Fiscal Year[4]
Agricultural Credit Insurance Fund Direct Loan Financing Account, Consolidated Farm Service Agency											
Fund Resources:											
Undisbursed Funds	No Year	12		4212		596,668,770.16		1,015,000,000.00			1,514,935,666.87
Authority To Borrow From The Treasury						186,838,261.25	1,302,330,730.00	-1,139,000,000.00		161,729,507.64	188,439,483.61
Unfilled Customer Orders						13,813,807.77				-220,549.96	14,034,357.73
Fund Equities:											
Unobligated Balances (Unexpired)						-596,668,770.16			96,733,103.29	918,266,896.71	-1,514,935,666.87
Accounts Payable						-72,271.18				7,132.48	-79,403.66
Undelivered Orders						-200,579,797.84				1,814,639.84	-202,394,437.68
Subtotal		12		4212		-0-	1,302,330,730.00	-124,000,000.00	96,733,103.29	1,081,597,626.71	-0-
Agricultural Credit Insurance Fund Guaranteed Loan Financing Account, Consolidated Farm Service Agency											
Fund Resources:											
Undisbursed Funds	No Year	12		4213		460,139,985.41		48,400,000.00	-41,988,329.79		550,528,315.20
Authority To Borrow From The Treasury							48,400,000.00	-48,400,000.00			
Fund Equities:											
Unobligated Balances (Unexpired)						-185,021,384.99				121,699,839.70	-306,721,224.69
Accounts Payable						-275,118,600.42				-31,311,509.91	-243,807,090.51
Subtotal		12		4213		-0-	48,400,000.00		-41,988,329.79	90,388,329.79	-0-
Rural Housing Insurance Fund Direct Loan Financing Account, Community Development Service											
Fund Resources:											
Undisbursed Funds	No Year	12		4215		79,944,779.23		514,931,700.00	479,099,955.67		115,776,523.56
Authority To Borrow From The Treasury						534,412,005.60	1,830,377,199.57	-1,811,879,900.00		57,326,578.23	495,582,726.94
Unfilled Customer Orders						230,853,159.36				12,130,486.70	218,722,672.66
Fund Equities:											
Unobligated Balances (Unexpired)						-79,944,779.23				24,030,872.07	-103,975,651.30
Accounts Payable						-9,141,877.65				2,658,994.61	-11,800,872.26
Undelivered Orders						-756,123,287.31				-41,817,887.71	-714,305,399.60
Subtotal		12		4215		-0-	1,830,377,199.57	-1,296,948,200.00	479,099,955.67	54,329,043.90	-0-
Rural Housing Insurance Fund Guaranteed Loan Financing Account, Rural Housing And Community Development Service											
Fund Resources:											
Undisbursed Funds	No Year	12		4216		590,605,998.07		3,735,500.00	-49,154,728.55		643,496,226.62
Authority To Borrow From The Treasury							3,735,500.00	-3,735,500.00			
Fund Equities:											
Unobligated Balances (Unexpired)						-590,605,998.07				52,890,228.55	-643,496,226.62
Subtotal		12		4216		-0-	3,735,500.00		-49,154,728.55	52,890,228.55	-0-
Rural Development Insurance Fund Guaranteed Loan Financing Account, Rural Utilities Service											
Fund Resources:											
Undisbursed Funds	No Year	12		4218		26,984.89		8,829.00	34,178.42		1,635.47
Authority To Borrow From The Treasury						433,603.73	300,580.86	-29,425.00		99,310.60	605,448.99
Fund Equities:											
Unobligated Balances (Unexpired)						-26,984.89				-25,349.42	-1,635.47

Footnotes At End Of Chapter

Appropriations, Outlays, and Balances – Continued

Appropriation or Fund Account — Title	Period of Availability	Reg	Tr From	Account Number	Sub No.	Balances, Beginning Of Fiscal Year	Appropriations And Other Obligational Authority[1]	Transfers Borrowings And Investment (Net)[2]	Outlays (Net)	Balances Withdrawn And Other Transactions[3]	Balances, End Of Fiscal Year[4]
Rural Development Insurance Fund Guaranteed Loan Financing Account, Rural Utilities Service - Continued											
Fund Equities: - Continued											
Accounts Payable						-433,603.73				171,845.26	-605,448.99
Undelivered Orders						-0-					-0-
	Subtotal	12		4218		-0-	300,580.86	-20,596.00	34,178.42	245,806.44	-0-
Rural Development Loan Fund Direct Loan Financing Account, Rural Business And Cooperative Development Service											
Fund Resources:											
Undisbursed Funds	No Year	12		4219		415,360.76	40,814,510.26	19,323,000.00	13,703,660.28	4,298,817.16	6,034,700.48
Authority To Borrow From The Treasury						51,996,980.97		-48,473,000.00		4,996,175.90	40,039,674.07
Unfilled Customer Orders						42,630,180.12					37,634,004.22
Fund Equities:											
Unobligated Balances (Unexpired)						-708,409.72				-708,409.72	
Accounts Payable											
Undelivered Orders						-94,334,112.13				-10,625,733.36	-83,708,378.77
	Subtotal	12		4219		-0-	40,814,510.26	-29,150,000.00	13,703,660.28	-2,039,150.02	-0-
Emergency Boll Weevil Direct Loan Financing Account, Farm Service Agency											
Fund Resources:											
Undisbursed Funds	No Year	12		4221		4,086,135.00			7,531.00		4,078,604.00
Fund Equities:											
Unobligated Balances (Unexpired)						-4,086,135.00				-7,531.00	-4,078,604.00
	Subtotal	12		4221		-0-			7,531.00	-7,531.00	-0-
Rural Business And Industry Loan, Direct Financing Account, Rural Business Cooperative Service											
Fund Resources:											
Undisbursed Funds						9,187,819.27	31,633.11	-2,867,000.00	-10,254,696.61	163,327.94	16,575,515.88
Authority To Borrow From The Treasury	No Year	12		4223		210,195.55					78,500.72
Fund Equities:											
Unobligated Balances (Unexpired)						-9,187,819.27				7,387,696.61	-16,575,515.88
Accounts Payable						-210,195.55				-131,694.83	-78,500.72
Undelivered Orders						-0-					-0-
	Subtotal	12		4223			31,633.11	-2,867,000.00	-10,254,696.61	7,419,329.72	-0-
Rural Community Facility Loans Direct Financing Account, Rural Housing Service											
Fund Resources:											
Undisbursed Funds						6,675,626.44	581,737,864.55	366,766,000.00	340,462,497.79	162,441,204.04	32,979,128.65
Authority To Borrow From The Treasury	No Year	12		4225		1,157,755,898.94		-560,666,000.00			1,016,386,559.45
Unfilled Customer Orders						40,444,185.57				-3,547,224.31	43,991,409.88
Fund Equities:											
Unobligated Balances (Unexpired)						-6,675,626.44				26,303,502.21	-32,979,128.65
Accounts Payable						-45.00				45.00	
Undelivered Orders						-1,198,200,039.51				-137,822,070.18	-1,060,377,969.33
	Subtotal	12		4225		-0-	581,737,864.55	-193,900,000.00	340,462,497.79	47,375,366.76	-0-
Rural Water And Waste Disposal Loans Direct Financing Account, Rural Utilities Service											
Fund Resources:											
Undisbursed Funds	No Year	12		4226		16,453,844.65		787,163,000.00	760,516,547.50		43,100,297.15

Appropriations, Outlays, and Balances - Continued

Appropriation or Fund Account — Title	Period of Availability	Reg	Tr From	Account Number	Sub No.	Balances, Beginning Of Fiscal Year	Appropriations And Other Obligational Authority[1]	Transfers Borrowings And Investment (Net)[2]	Outlays (Net)	Balances Withdrawn And Other Transactions[3]	Balances, End Of Fiscal Year[4]
Authority To Borrow From The Treasury						2,724,998,742.99	1,513,450,550.99	-1,451,963,000.00	------	43,471,227.78	2,743,015,066.20
Unfilled Customer Orders						224,075,387.28			------	-29,010,707.12	253,086,094.40
Fund Equities:											
Unobligated Balances (Unexpired)						-16,453,844.65				-5,269,380.24	-11,184,464.41
Accounts Payable											
Undelivered Orders						-2,949,074,130.27	-1,513,450,550.99	-664,800,000.00	760,516,547.50	78,942,863.07	-3,028,016,993.34
Subtotal	Subtotal	12		4226		-0-	1,513,450,550.99			88,134,003.49	-0-
Rural Business And Industry Loans Guaranteed Financing Account, Rural Business- Cooperative Service											
Fund Resources:											
Undisbursed Funds	No Year	12		4227		332,205,577.19	33,407,973.00	-87,650,400.00	-3,638,736.63	23,233,373.00	248,193,913.82
Authority To Borrow From The Treasury								-10,174,600.00			
Fund Equities:											
Unobligated Balances (Unexpired)	Subtotal	12		4227		-332,205,577.19	33,407,973.00	-97,825,000.00	-3,638,736.63	-84,011,663.37	-248,193,913.82
Subtotal						-0-				-60,778,290.37	-0-
Rural Community Facility Loans Guaranteed Financing Account, Rural Housing Service											
Fund Resources:											
Undisbursed Funds	No Year	12		4228		32,915,857.41	6,025,350.00	-1,451,960.00	-8,910,336.05	6,119,385.13	40,374,233.46
Authority To Borrow From The Treasury						560,827.69		-214,000.00			252,792.56
Fund Equities:											
Unobligated Balances (Unexpired)	Subtotal	12		4228		-32,915,857.41	6,025,350.00	-1,665,960.00	-8,910,336.05	7,458,376.05	-40,374,233.46
Undelivered Orders						-560,827.69				-308,035.13	-252,792.56
Subtotal						-0-	6,025,350.00			13,269,726.05	-0-
Renewable Energy Guaranteed Loan Financing Account, Rural Business - Cooperative											
Fund Resources:											
Undisbursed Funds	No Year	12		4267		2,200,238.61	25,663.00		-3,846,731.25	25,663.00	6,046,969.86
Fund Equities:											
Unobligated Balances (Unexpired)	Subtotal	12		4267		-2,200,238.61	25,663.00		-3,846,731.25	3,846,731.25	-6,046,969.86
Subtotal						-0-				3,872,394.25	-0-
Multi-Family Housing Revitalization Direct Loan Financing, Rural Housing Service											
Fund Resources:											
Undisbursed Funds	No Year	12		4269		112.25	54,946,399.20	7,940,505.53	7,906,712.37	2,577,348.75	33,905.41
Authority To Borrow From The Treasury						46,793,264.50		-10,149,505.53		-6,055,870.01	89,012,809.42
Unfilled Customer Orders						17,038,267.72					23,094,137.73
Fund Equities:											
Unobligated Balances (Unexpired)						-112.25				33,793.16	-33,905.41
Accounts Payable											
Undelivered Orders						-63,831,532.22				48,275,414.93	-112,106,947.15
Subtotal	Subtotal	12		4269		-0-	54,946,399.20	-2,209,000.00	7,906,712.37	44,830,686.83	-0-
Commodity Credit Corporation Export Guaranteed Financing Account											
Fund Resources:											
Undisbursed Funds	No Year	12		4337		765,632,034.28		-319,852,142.32		-36,316,758.52	1,085,484,176.60
Accounts Receivable						131,227,955.26					167,544,713.78

Footnotes At End Of Chapter

Appropriations, Outlays, and Balances – Continued

Appropriation or Fund Account		Account Symbol								
Title	Period of Availability	Dept		Account Number	Sub No.	Balances, Beginning Of Fiscal Year	Appropriations And Other Obligational Authority[1]	Transfers Borrowings And Investment (Net)[2]	Outlays (Net)	Balances Withdrawn And Other Transactions[3]	Balances, End Of Fiscal Year[4]
		Reg	Tr From								
Commodity Credit Corporation Export Guaranteed Financing Account - Continued											
Fund Equities:											
Unobligated Balances (Unexpired)						-895,651,607.87			-------	350,844,698.84	-1,246,496,306.71
Accounts Payable				4337		-1,208,381.67		-------	-------	5,324,202.00	-6,532,583.67
Subtotal		12				-0-			-319,852,142.32	319,852,142.32	-0-
Total, Financing Accounts							12,477,544,640.99	-4,630,955,974.85	5,519,981,056.69	2,326,607,609.45	

Appropriations, Outlays, and Balances - Continued

Footnotes

1   The amounts in this column, unless otherwise footnoted, represent appropriations, increases and rescissions in borrowing authority or new contract authority. Appropriation accounts with appropriation transfer activity are presented in Table 1 (Appropriations and Appropriation Transfers) at the end of this chapter.

2   The amounts in this column, unless otherwise footnoted, represent transfers - other than appropriation transfers, borrowings (gross), investments (net), unrealized discounts or funds held outside the Treasury.

3   The amounts in this column, unless otherwise footnoted, represent obligated balances canceled for fiscal year 2002 pursuant to 31 U.S.C. 1553, changes in unfilled customer orders, accounts receivable, accounts payable, undelivered orders, unobligated balances and adjustments to borrowing and contract authority.

4   Unobligated balances for no-year or unexpired multiple year accounts are available for obligation; unobligated balances for expired fiscal year accounts are not available for obligation.

5   Subject to disposition by the administrative agency.

6   Represents capital transfer to miscellaneous receipts.

7   The opening balances of the following accounts have been adjusted during the current fiscal year and do not agree with last year's closing balances:

Account	Adjustment
12 x 4336 – Undisbursed Funds	$15,907,160.00
12 x 4336 – Unobligated Balances (Unexpired)	-15,907,160.00
12 x 4336 – Authority to Borrow from the Treasury	-549,089,503.77
12 x 4336 – Accounts Payable	953,298,900.36
12 x 4336 – Accounts Receivable	-415,065,045.23
12 x 4336 – Undelivered Orders	10,855,648.64
12 x 3322 – Unobligated Balances (Unexpired)	108,945.32
12 x 3322 – Undelivered Orders	-108,945.32
12 06 1004 – Undisbursed	-69,345,685.00
12 05 1004 – Undisbursed	53,438,525.00
12 1004 – Unobligated Balances (Expired)	15,907,160.00

8   Includes $13,102,405,214.61 which represents net repayment of borrowing from the U.S. Treasury.

9   Represents Price Support, Supply and Related Programs.

10   Pursuant to P.L. 118 STAT. 2847, the balance for this account has been extended beyond the normal period of availability to liquidate obligations.

11   Pursuant to P.L. 120 STAT. 446, the balance for this account has been extended beyond the normal period of availability to liquidate obligations.

12   Pursuant to P.L. 107 STAT. 1080, the balance for this account has been extended beyond the normal period of availability to liquidate obligations.

13   Pursuant to P.L. 108 STAT. 2468, the balance for this account has been extended beyond the normal period of availability to liquidate obligations.

14   Pursuant to P.L. 115 STAT. 733, the balance for this account has been extended beyond the normal period of availability to liquidate obligations.

15   Pursuant to P.L. 114 STAT. 1549A-29, the balance for this account has been extended beyond the normal period of availability to liquidate obligations.

16   Pursuant to P.L. 113 STAT. 1162, the balance for this account has been extended beyond the normal period of availability to liquidate obligations.

17   Pursuant to P.L. 111 STAT. 2097, 2098, the balance for this account has been extended beyond the normal period of availability to liquidate obligations.

18   Pursuant to P.L. 110 STAT. 1584, the balance for this account has been extended beyond the normal period of availability to liquidate obligations.

19   Pursuant to P.L. 109 STAT. 217,318, the balance for this account has been extended beyond the normal period of availability to liquidate obligations.

20   Pursuant to P.L. 108 STAT. 2454, the balance for this account has been extended beyond the normal period of availability to liquidate obligations.

21   Pursuant to P.L. 107 STAT. 1065, the balance for this account has been extended beyond the normal period of availability to liquidate obligations.

22   Pursuant to P.L. 106 STAT. 893, the balance for this account has been extended beyond the normal period of availability to liquidate obligations.

23   Pursuant to P.L. 106-78, the balance for this account has been extended beyond the normal period of availability to liquidate obligations.

24   Pursuant to P.L. 112 STAT. 2681-26, the balance for this account has been extended beyond the normal period of availability to liquidate obligations.

25   Pursuant to P.L. 111 STAT. 2106, the balance for this account has been extended beyond the normal period of availability to liquidate obligations.

26   Pursuant to P.L. 110 STAT. 1598, the balance for this account has been extended beyond the normal period of availability to liquidate obligations.

27   Pursuant to P.L. 109 STAT. 330, the balance for this account has been extended beyond the normal period of availability to liquidate obligations.

28   Includes $2,011,463,782.18 which represents repayment of borrowing from the Federal Financing Bank in lieu of issuance of agency debt. Also, includes $462,000,000.00 which represents repayment of borrowing from the U.S. Treasury.

29   Includes $907,738.16 which represents payment for obligations of a closed account.

30   Includes $17,778.67 which represents payment for obligations of a closed account.

31   Includes $269,068.76 which represents payment for obligations of a closed account.

32   Includes $2,331,830,278.87 which represents net borrowing from the Federal Financing Bank in lieu of issuance of agency debt. Also, includes $1,891,328,006.49 which represents net borrowing from the U.S. Treasury.

Appropriations, Outlays, and Balances – Continued

Footnotes

Table 1 - Appropriations And Appropriation Transfers - Department Of Agriculture

Department Regular	Fiscal Year	Account Symbol	Net Appropriations And Appropriations Transfers	Appropriation Amount	Net Appropriation Transfers	Department Regular Involved	Fiscal Year Involved	Accounts Involved	Amount From or To (-)
12	07	0115	4,914,730.00	5,096,730.00	-182,000.00	12	X	4609	-182,000.00
12	07	0120	23,143,970.00	23,007,970.00	136,000.00	12	07	0150	136,000.00
12	07	0122	1,887,790.00	3,794,790.00	-1,907,000.00	12	07	0403	-248,000.00
						12	07	0502	-56,000.00
						12	07	0600	-277,000.00
						12	07	1000	-147,000.00
						12	07	1400	-128,000.00
						12	07	1500	-63,000.00
						12	07	1600	-100,000.00
						12	07	2500	-99,000.00
						12	07	2900	-180,000.00
						12	07	3508	-266,000.00
						12	07	3700	-248,000.00
						12	X	4609	-85,000.00
12	07	0123	12,486,610.00	10,486,610.00	2,000,000.00	12	X	4336	2,000,000.00
12	07	0150	9,337,910.00	9,473,910.00	-136,000.00	12	07	0120	-136,000.00
12	07	0215	1,750,000.00	0.00	1,750,000.00	12	X	4336	1,750,000.00
12	X	0400	827,237,349.00	855,537,997.00	-28,300,648.00	12	X	0403	-2,560,648.00
						12	X	2042	-25,740,000.00
12	X	0403	6,471,248.00	1,000,000.00	5,471,248.00	12	X	0400	2,560,648.00
						12	X	2002	1,108,800.00
						12	X	2042	1,801,800.00
12	07	0403	162,135,822.00	161,298,000.00	837,822.00	12	07	0122	248,000.00
						12	07	1230	44,238.00
						12	07	2081	545,584.00
12	07	0502	433,625,000.00	433,569,000.00	56,000.00	12	07	0122	56,000.00
12	0708	0502	5,000,000.00	0.00	5,000,000.00	12	X	4085	5,000,000.00
12	07	0503	8,070,020.00	8,270,020.00	-200,000.00	12	X	4609	-200,000.00
12	X	0600	709,700,000.00	0.00	709,700,000.00	12	07	0600	709,700,000.00
12	07	0600	320,770,000.00	1,030,193,000.00	-709,423,000.00	12	07	0122	277,000.00
						12	X	0600	-709,700,000.00
12	07	0706	14,285,760.00	14,465,760.00	-180,000.00	12	X	4609	-180,000.00
12	X	1000	-142,035.37	0.00	-142,035.37	47	07	0110	-142,035.37
12	07	1000	147,000.00	0.00	147,000.00	12	07	0122	147,000.00
12	X	1003	14,000,000.00	0.00	14,000,000.00	12	X	4336	14,000,000.00
12	07	1004	1,746,555,859.00	0.00	1,746,555,859.00	12	X	4336	1,746,555,859.00
12	X	1103	447,911,523.56	436,400,113.00	11,511,410.56	11	X	5512	21,578,486.00
						12	X	1115	-10,000,000.00
						47	07	0110	-67,075.44
12	X	1104	303,277,201.00	280,487,808.00	22,789,393.00	12	X	1115	22,789,393.00
12	X	1105	302,051,301.00	223,425,304.00	78,625,997.00	12	X	1115	78,625,997.00
12	X	1106	1,447,174,816.00	1,464,728,700.00	-17,553,884.00	12	X	1115	-17,361,409.00
						14	07	5198	24,525.00
						47	07	0110	-217,000.00
12	X	1115	2,127,439,419.00	2,193,603,400.00	-66,163,981.00	12	X	1103	10,000,000.00

Appropriations, Outlays, and Balances - Continued

Footnotes

Table 1 - Appropriations And Appropriation Transfers - Department Of Agriculture

Department Regular	Fiscal Year	Account Symbol	Net Appropriations And Appropriations Transfers	Appropriation Amount	Net Appropriation Transfers	Department Regular Involved	Fiscal Year Involved	Accounts Involved	Amount From or To (-)
						12	X	1104	-22,789,393.00
						12	X	1105	-78,625,997.00
						12	X	1106	17,361,409.00
						12	X	5004	10,000,000.00
						14	X	1125	-2,110,000.00
12	X	1119	5,035,712.00	5,008,952.00	26,760.00	14	X	5198	26,760.00
12	07	1230	152,949,355.00	153,219,393.00	-270,038.00	12	07	0403	-44,238.00
						12	X	4609	-225,800.00
12	07	1400	1,132,031,427.00	1,128,944,427.00	3,087,000.00	11	07	1075	2,959,000.00
						12	07	0122	128,000.00
12	07	1500	456,468,380.00	456,405,380.00	63,000.00	12	07	0122	63,000.00
12	X	1600	368,020,150.00	75,784,600.00	292,235,550.00	12	07	1600	237,063,000.00
						12	X	4336	55,172,550.00
12	07	1600	533,481,925.00	770,444,925.00	-236,963,000.00	12	07	0122	100,000.00
						12	X	1600	-237,063,000.00
12	X	1801	36,248,778.00	0.00	36,248,778.00	12	07	1801	36,248,778.00
12	07	1801	111,004,222.00	147,253,000.00	-36,248,778.00	12	X	1801	-36,248,778.00
12	X	2002	14,731,200.00	15,840,000.00	-1,108,800.00	12	X	0403	-1,108,800.00
12	X	2042	23,938,200.00	0.00	23,938,200.00	12	X	0400	25,740,000.00
						12	X	0403	-1,801,800.00
12	07	2081	638,096,936.00	639,074,900.00	-977,964.00	12	07	0403	-545,584.00
						12	X	4609	-432,380.00
12	07	2500	75,036,240.00	74,937,240.00	99,000.00	12	07	0122	99,000.00
12	07	2707	76,657,520.00	76,657,520.00	-400,000.00	12	X	4609	-400,000.00
12	X	2900	3,960,000.00	0.00	3,960,000.00	12	07	2900	3,960,000.00
12	07	2900	151,393,077.87	156,220,423.00	-4,827,345.13	12	07	0122	180,000.00
						12	X	2900	-3,960,000.00
						12	X	4609	-1,000,000.00
						47	07	0110	-47,345.13
12	0708	2900	9,203,000.00	0.00	9,203,000.00	72	0708	1010	2,100,000.00
						72	0708	1093	7,103,000.00
12	X	3315	-25,000.00	0.00	-25,000.00	12	X	4609	-25,000.00
12	X	3505	78,800,000.00	-11,200,000.00	90,000,000.00	12	07	3505	90,000,000.00
12	07	3505	35,071,534,000.00	35,161,534,000.00	-90,000,000.00	12	X	3505	-90,000,000.00
12	0708	3507	192,572,340.00	177,572,340.00	15,000,000.00	12	X	4336	15,000,000.00
12	07	3508	140,518,390.00	140,252,390.00	266,000.00	12	07	0122	266,000.00
12	0708	3539	13,345,596,000.00	7,614,523,000.00	5,731,073,000.00	12	X	5209	5,731,073,000.00
12	07	3674	0.00	23,098,327,516.06	-23,098,327,516.06	12	X	4336	-23,098,327,516.06
12	X	3700	8,079,390.00	0.00	8,079,390.00	12	X	3700	8,079,390.00
12	07	3700	882,604,610.00	892,136,000.00	-9,531,390.00	12	07	0122	248,000.00
						12	X	3700	-8,079,390.00
						12	X	4609	-1,700,000.00
12	X	4085	4,373,971,924.56	4,379,256,000.00	-5,284,075.44	12	0708	0502	-5,000,000.00
						47	07	0110	-284,075.44
12	X	4336	21,273,849,107.06	10,000,000.00	21,263,849,107.06	12	07	0123	-2,000,000.00
						12	07	0215	-1,750,000.00

Footnotes At End Of Chapter

Appropriations, Outlays, and Balances – Continued

Footnotes

Table 1 - Appropriations And Appropriation Transfers - Department Of Agriculture

Department Regular	Fiscal Year	Account Symbol	Net Appropriations And Appropriations Transfers	Appropriation Amount	Net Appropriation Transfers	Department Regular Involved	Fiscal Year Involved	Accounts Involved	Amount From or To (-)
						12	X	1003	-14,000,000.00
						12	07	1004	-1,746,555,859.00
						12	X	1600	-55,172,550.00
						12	0708	3507	-15,000,000.00
12	X	4609	6,331,275.00	1,891,095.00	4,440,180.00	12	07	3674	23,098,327,516.06
						12	07	0115	182,000.00
						12	07	0122	95,000.00
						12	07	0503	200,000.00
						12	07	0706	180,000.00
						12	07	1230	225,800.00
						12	07	2081	432,380.00
						12	07	2707	400,000.00
						12	07	2900	1,000,000.00
						12	X	3315	25,000.00
						12	07	3700	1,700,000.00
12	X	5004	31,936,123.00	41,936,123.00	-10,000,000.00	12	X	1115	-10,000,000.00
12	X	5209	1,177,730,655.14	6,991,668,059.27	-5,813,937,404.13	12	0708	3539	-5,731,073,000.00
						13	X	5139	-82,817,059.00
						47	07	0110	-47,345.13
12	X	5215	289,500.00	0.00	289,500.00	14	X	5198	289,500.00
Totals			89,300,875,730.82	89,352,526,395.33	-51,650,664.51				-51,650,664.51

Appropriations, Outlays, and Balances – Continued

Footnotes

This Page Left Blank Intentionally

Appropriations, Outlays, and Balances – Continued

Appropriations, Outlays, and Balances – Continued

Appropriation or Fund Account: Title	Period of Availability	Account Symbol — Dept: Reg	Tr From	Account Number	Sub No.	Balances, Beginning Of Fiscal Year	Appropriations And Other Obligational Authority[1]	Transfers Borrowings And Investment (Net)[2]	Outlays (Net)	Balances Withdrawn And Other Transactions[3]	Balances, End Of Fiscal Year[4]
Department Of Commerce											
Departmental Management											
General Fund Accounts											
Salaries And Expenses, Departmental Management											
Fund Resources:											
Undisbursed Funds	2007-2008	13		0120			1,455,000.00				1,455,000.00
	2007						47,120,548.00		42,172,279.72		4,948,268.28
	2006-2007					2,918,000.00			1,767,021.52		1,150,978.48
	2006					6,154,747.95			5,798,712.22		356,035.73
	2005-2006					1,124,913.14			613,028.36		511,884.78
	2005					1,077,408.19			-166,729.55		1,244,137.74
	2004-2005					450,635.54			83,421.47		367,214.07
	2004					904,954.74			-2,196.71		907,151.45
	2003-2004					322,212.95			124,660.78		197,552.17
	2003					653,814.69			39,519.67		614,295.02
	2002-2003					122,454.91			51,728.00		70,726.91
	2002					70,489.35			-51,977.37	122,466.72	-0-
	2001-2002					103,211.83				103,211.83	-0-
	No Year					76,981,068.89			14,339,491.31		62,641,577.58
Accounts Receivable						4,659,285.02				-4,031,972.66	8,691,257.68
Unfilled Customer Orders						6,697,630.33				623,115.52	6,074,514.81
Fund Equities:											
Unobligated Balances (Expired)						-1,956,018.70				2,293,530.09	-4,249,548.79
Unobligated Balances (Unexpired)						-19,922,187.77				-13,961,435.13	-5,960,752.64
Accounts Payable						-9,761,929.41				3,738,657.53	-13,500,586.94
Undelivered Orders						-70,600,691.65				-5,080,985.32	-65,519,706.33
	Subtotal	13		0120		-0-	48,575,548.00		64,768,959.42	-16,193,411.42	-0-
Emergency Oil And Gas Guaranteed Loan Program Account, Departmental Management											
Fund Resources:											
Undisbursed Funds	No Year	13		0121		587,738.07			8,240.31		579,497.76
Fund Equities:											
Unobligated Balances (Unexpired)						-419,133.83				-14,337.26	-404,796.57
Accounts Payable						-4,412.77				-4,412.77	-0-
Undelivered Orders						-164,191.47				10,509.72	-174,701.19
	Subtotal	13		0121		-0-			8,240.31	-8,240.31	-0-
Emergency Steel Guaranteed Loan Program Account, Departmental Management											
Fund Resources:											
Undisbursed Funds	No Year	13		0122		50,636,649.44	440,047.00		910,065.42		50,166,631.02
Fund Equities:											
Unobligated Balances (Unexpired)						-50,137,115.41				-458,363.70	-49,678,751.71
Accounts Payable						-53,214.38				-53,214.38	-0-
Undelivered Orders						-446,319.65				41,559.66	-487,879.31
	Subtotal	13		0122		-0-	440,047.00		910,065.42	-470,018.42	-0-

Appropriations, Outlays, and Balances - Continued

Title	Period of Availability	Dept Reg	Tr From	Account Number	Sub No.	Balances, Beginning Of Fiscal Year	Appropriations And Other Obligational Authority[1]	Transfers Borrowings And Investment (Net)[2]	Outlays (Net)	Balances Withdrawn And Other Transactions[3]	Balances, End Of Fiscal Year[4]
Office Of The Inspector General, Departmental Management											
Fund Resources:											
Undisbursed Funds	2007	13		0126			22,592,319.00		21,827,757.67		764,561.33
	2006					1,512,041.67			953,855.52		558,186.15
	2005					320,480.10			107,993.12		212,486.98
	2004					127,008.82			-16,183.82		143,192.64
	2003					101,535.53			33.00		101,502.53
	2002					22,514.83				22,514.83	
	No Year					14,736.80					14,736.80
Accounts Receivable						2,121.00				1,955.60	165.40
Unfilled Customer Orders						22,112.05					22,112.05
Fund Equities:											
Unobligated Balances (Expired)						-506,822.32				436,589.60	-943,411.92
Accounts Payable						-1,141,386.61				-519,863.34	-621,523.27
Undelivered Orders						-474,341.87				-222,333.18	-252,008.69
Subtotal		13		0126		-0-	22,592,319.00		22,873,455.49	-281,136.49	-0-
National Intellectual Property Law Enforcement Coordination Council, Departmental Management											
Fund Resources:											
Undisbursed Funds	2005-2006	13		0127		819,573.09			509,107.04		310,466.05
Fund Equities:											
Unobligated Balances (Expired)						-109,523.56				-4,573.01	-104,950.55
Accounts Payable						-49,049.53				-50,110.11	1,060.58
Undelivered Orders						-661,000.00				-454,423.92	-206,576.08
Subtotal		13		0127		-0-			509,107.04	-509,107.04	-0-
Special Foreign Currency Program, Department Of Commerce											
Fund Resources:											
Undisbursed Funds	No Year	13		0160		-566.00			-566.00		
Accounts Receivable		13		0160		566.00				566.00	
Subtotal		13		0160		-0-			-566.00	566.00	-0-
Intragovernmental Funds											
Working Capital Fund, Departmental Management											
Fund Resources:											
Undisbursed Funds	No Year	13		4511		34,890,667.53			-2,256,462.53		37,147,130.06
Accounts Receivable						477,351.05				1,292,942.66	-815,591.61
Unfilled Customer Orders						3,374,762.65				3,374,762.65	
Fund Equities:											
Unobligated Balances (Unexpired)						-12,872,067.74				-7,718,648.29	-5,153,419.45
Accounts Payable						-10,739,631.03				3,672,446.42	-14,412,077.45
Undelivered Orders						-15,131,082.46				1,634,959.09	-16,766,041.55
Subtotal		13		4511		-0-			-2,256,462.53	2,256,462.53	-0-
Franchise Fund, Departmental Management											
Fund Resources:											
Undisbursed Funds	No Year	13		4564		3,467,775.34			-167,045.83		3,634,821.17
Accounts Receivable						508,746.65				-2,173.44	510,920.09

Footnotes At End Of Chapter

Appropriations, Outlays, and Balances – Continued

Appropriation or Fund Account — Title	Period of Availability	Dept Reg	Tr From	Account Number	Sub No.	Balances, Beginning Of Fiscal Year	Appropriations And Other Obligational Authority[1]	Transfers Borrowings And Investment (Net)[2]	Outlays (Net)	Balances Withdrawn And Other Transactions[3]	Balances, End Of Fiscal Year[4]
Franchise Fund, Departmental Management - Continued											
Fund Equities:											
Unobligated Balances (Unexpired)						-2,429,388.53				582,359.18	-3,011,747.71
Accounts Payable						-1,145,949.60				18,827.17	-1,164,776.77
Undelivered Orders						-401,183.86				-431,967.08	30,783.22
Subtotal		13		4564		-0-			-167,045.83	167,045.83	-0-
Trust Fund Accounts											
Gifts And Bequests, Departmental Management											
Fund Resources:											
Undisbursed Funds	No Year	13		8501		384,119.56	1,201,587.58		939,284.41		646,422.73
Fund Equities:											
Unobligated Balances (Unexpired)						-332,549.95				198,627.50	-531,177.45
Accounts Payable						-39,512.43				24,881.31	-64,393.74
Undelivered Orders						-12,057.18				38,794.36	-50,851.54
Subtotal		13		8501		-0-	1,201,587.58		939,284.41	262,303.17	-0-
Total, Departmental Management						72,809,501.58			87,585,037.73	-14,775,536.15	
Economic Development Administration											
General Fund Accounts											
Salaries And Expenses, Economic Development Administration											
Fund Resources:											
Undisbursed Funds	2007	13		0125		2,704,586.20	29,882,074.00		26,995,924.83		2,886,149.17
	2006					-120,693.10			2,325,456.89		379,129.31
	2005					838,032.86			-266,332.07		145,638.97
	2004					348,793.58			112,565.48		725,467.38
	2003					65,853.53			10,763.48		338,030.10
	2002									65,853.53	
	No Year					1,290,133.47			-1,759,807.26		3,049,940.73
Accounts Receivable						2,626,228.56				1,844,605.16	781,623.40
Unfilled Customer Orders						28,914.86				2,614.80	26,300.06
Fund Equities:											
Unobligated Balances (Expired)						-1,503,078.41				427,564.89	-1,930,643.30
Unobligated Balances (Unexpired)						-2,523,837.14				-4,684.52	-2,519,152.62
Accounts Payable						-1,394,006.13				145,959.26	-1,539,965.39
Undelivered Orders						-2,360,928.28				-18,410.47	-2,342,517.81
Subtotal		13		0125		-0-	29,882,074.00		27,418,571.35	2,463,502.65	-0-
Economic Development Assistance Programs, Economic Development Administration											
Fund Resources:											
Undisbursed Funds	No Year	13		2050		783,613,344.14	250,741,104.00		241,295,860.11		793,058,588.03
Transfer To:											
Rural Business Cooperative Service, Department Of Agriculture	No Year	12	13	2050	34	4,266,887.84			1,841,050.00		2,425,837.84
Fund Equities:											
Unobligated Balances (Unexpired)						-13,859,383.23				-4,420,795.56	-9,438,587.67

Appropriations, Outlays, and Balances - Continued

Title	Reg	Tr From	Account Number	Sub No.	Period of Availability	Balances, Beginning Of Fiscal Year	Appropriations And Other Obligational Authority[1]	Transfers Borrowings And Investment (Net)[2]	Outlays (Net)	Balances Withdrawn And Other Transactions[3]	Balances, End Of Fiscal Year[4]
Accounts Payable						-275,699,610.00				-15,731,890.00	-259,967,720.00
Undelivered Orders						-498,321,238.75				27,756,879.45	-526,078,118.20
	13		2050		Subtotal	-0-	250,741,104.00		243,136,910.11	7,604,193.89	-0-
Public Enterprise Funds											
Economic Development Revolving Fund, Liquidating Account											
Fund Resources:											
Undisbursed Funds	13		4406		No Year	1,966,011.15				913,655.99	2,458,124.05
Fund Equities:											
Unobligated Balances (Unexpired)						-913,655.99			-1,405,768.89	1,077,654.44	-1,991,310.43
Accounts Payable						-930,972.18				-585,541.54	-345,430.64
Undelivered Orders						-121,382.98					-121,382.98
	13		4406		Subtotal	-0-			-1,405,768.89	1,405,768.89	-0-
Total, Economic Development Administration							280,623,178.00		269,149,712.57	11,473,465.43	
Bureau Of The Census											
General Fund Accounts											
Salaries And Expenses, Bureau Of The Census											
Fund Resources:											
Undisbursed Funds	13		0401		2007	5,864,274.37	216,647,196.00		[6]207,951,357.38		8,695,838.62
					2006	1,230,786.60			5,375,925.66		488,348.71
					2005	747,259.04			348,694.74		882,091.86
					2004	892,697.21			38,639.38		708,619.66
					2003	923,560.83			13,060.40		879,636.81
					2002					923,560.83	
Fund Equities:											
Unobligated Balances (Expired)						-2,424,791.36				-97,980.11	-2,326,811.25
Accounts Payable						-3,934,837.36				429,777.22	-4,364,614.58
Undelivered Orders						-3,298,949.33				1,664,160.50	-4,963,109.83
	13		0401		Subtotal	-0-	216,647,196.00		213,727,677.56	2,919,518.44	-0-
Periodic Censuses And Programs, Bureau Of The Census											
Fund Resources:											
Undisbursed Funds	13		0450		2007-2008	112,742,552.60	696,365,183.00		569,597,542.90		126,767,540.10
					2006-2007	24,870,165.17			103,744,133.07		8,998,419.53
					2005-2006	3,837,393.96			17,956,726.04		6,913,439.13
					2004-2005	1,389,037.03			1,426,069.94		2,411,324.02
					2003	1,461,747.76			24,245.87		1,364,791.16
					2002	18,301,353.48			8,981.10		
					No Year				15,524,543.74	1,452,766.66	2,776,809.74
Fund Equities:											
Unobligated Balances (Expired)						-2,845,367.27				1,180,669.66	-4,026,036.93
Unobligated Balances (Unexpired)						-3,756,030.98				-1,535,671.93	-2,220,359.05
Accounts Payable						-41,443,906.74				-1,759,692.89	-39,684,213.85
Undelivered Orders						-114,556,945.01				-11,255,231.16	-103,301,713.85
	13		0450		Subtotal	-0-	696,365,083.00		708,282,242.66	-11,917,159.66	-0-

Footnotes At End Of Chapter

Appropriations, Outlays, and Balances – Continued

Appropriation or Fund Account — Title	Period of Availability	Reg	Tr From	Account Number	Sub No.	Balances, Beginning Of Fiscal Year	Appropriations And Other Obligational Authority[1]	Transfers Borrowings And Investment (Net)[2]	Outlays (Net)	Balances Withdrawn And Other Transactions[3]	Balances, End Of Fiscal Year[4]
Intragovernmental Funds											
Census Working Capital Fund, Bureau Of The Census, Department Of Commerce	No Year	13		4512							
Fund Resources:											
Undisbursed Funds						237,372,217.53					259,881,813.64
Accounts Receivable						11,516,014.71				547,372.90	10,968,641.81
Unfilled Customer Orders						67,641.86				-5,025,622.98	5,093,264.84
Fund Equities:											
Unobligated Balances (Unexpired)						-125,213,205.71				27,119,946.52	-152,333,152.23
Accounts Payable						-32,779,347.24				2,947,719.77	-35,727,067.01
Undelivered Orders						-90,963,321.15				-3,079,820.10	-87,883,501.05
	Subtotal	13		4512		-0-			-22,509,596.11	22,509,596.11	-0-
Total, Bureau Of The Census							913,012,279.00		899,500,324.11	13,511,954.89	
Economic And Statistical Analysis											
General Fund Accounts											
Salaries And Expenses, Economic And Statistical Analysis				1500							
Fund Resources:											
Undisbursed Funds	2007-2008	13				10,110,830.95	79,750,943.00		70,295,202.70		9,455,740.30
	2006-2007					2,231,740.11			9,127,697.71		983,133.24
	2005-2006					769,686.75			1,703,121.88		528,618.23
	2004-2005					96,324.42			219,431.84		550,254.91
	2003-2004					92,595.10			-11,193.20		107,517.62
	2002-2003					46,835.61			-1,854.28		92,595.10
	2001-2002					30,000.00				30,000.00	
Accounts Receivable										48,689.89	
Unfilled Customer Orders										-166,799.00	166,799.00
Fund Equities:											
Unobligated Balances (Expired)						-302,706.66				43,919.09	-346,625.75
Unobligated Balances (Unexpired)						-1,205,960.44				144,678.19	-1,350,638.63
Accounts Payable						-3,566,678.55				532,846.68	-4,099,525.23
Undelivered Orders						-8,302,667.29				-2,214,798.50	-6,087,868.79
	Subtotal	13		1500		-0-	79,750,943.00		81,332,406.65	-1,581,463.65	-0-
Public Enterprise Funds											
Economics And Statistics Administration Revolving Fund, Economic And Statistical Analysis	No Year	13		4323							
Fund Resources:											
Undisbursed Funds						1,781,627.20			138,817.08		1,642,810.12
Fund Equities:											
Unobligated Balances (Unexpired)						-1,625,477.46				-204,531.80	-1,420,945.66
Accounts Payable						-103,199.13				-23,709.92	-79,489.21
Undelivered Orders						-52,950.61				89,424.64	-142,375.25
	Subtotal	13		4323		-0-			138,817.08	-138,817.08	-0-

Appropriations, Outlays, and Balances - Continued

Appropriation or Fund Account — Title	Period of Availability	Reg	Tr From	Account Number	Sub No.	Balances, Beginning Of Fiscal Year	Appropriations And Other Obligational Authority[1]	Transfers Borrowings And Investment (Net)[2]	Outlays (Net)	Balances Withdrawn And Other Transactions[3]	Balances, End Of Fiscal Year[4]
Total, Economic And Statistical Analysis						-------	79,750,943.00		81,471,223.73	-1,720,280.73	-------
International Trade Administration											
General Fund Accounts											
United States Travel And Tourism Promotion, International Trade Administration											
Fund Resources:											
Undisbursed Funds	2007-2008	13		0124		-------	3,948,912.00		1,214.72	-------	3,947,697.28
	2006-2007					3,948,912.00			1,314,594.51	-------	2,634,317.49
	2005-2006					732,597.89			386,066.88	-------	346,531.01
Fund Equities:											
Unobligated Balances (Expired)						-77,147.31				13,669.28	-90,816.59
Unobligated Balances (Unexpired)						-3,948,912.00				-3,912,544.72	-36,367.28
Accounts Payable										1,191,000.00	-1,191,000.00
Undelivered Orders						-655,450.58				4,954,911.33	-5,610,361.91
Subtotal		13		0124		-0-	3,948,912.00		1,701,876.11	2,247,035.89	-0-
Operations And Administration, International Trade Administration											
Fund Resources:											
Undisbursed Funds	2007-2008	13		1250		68,242,968.39	397,800,865.00		341,552,532.83		56,248,332.17
	2006-2007					-------			51,537,417.99		16,705,550.40
	2002-2007					1,984,479.01		661,726.00	1,448,942.74		661,726.00
	2005-2006					991,401.22			202,743.83		535,536.27
	2004-2005					1,564,941.61			111,741.71		788,657.39
	2003-2004					1,508,025.94			210,566.68		1,453,199.90
	2001-2002					986,356.16		-661,726.00	94,857.40		635,733.26
	No Year					41,253,485.65		-763,388.00	16,016,801.55	128,110.76	26,000,072.10
Accounts Receivable						1,216,145.47		763,388.00		808,244.90	407,900.57
Unfilled Customer Orders						2,996,783.63				-98,820.77	3,095,604.40
Fund Equities:											
Unobligated Balances (Expired)						-3,969,241.82				-1,052,671.86	-2,916,569.96
Unobligated Balances (Unexpired)						-7,042,980.00				-420,401.18	-6,622,578.82
Accounts Payable						-32,291,986.07				-5,566,202.82	-26,725,783.25
Undelivered Orders						-77,440,379.19				-7,172,998.76	-70,267,380.43
Subtotal		13		1250		-0-	397,800,865.00		411,175,604.73	-13,374,739.73	-0-
Special Fund Accounts											
Grants To Manufacturers Of Worsted Wool Fabrics, International Trade Commission											
Fund Resources:											
Undisbursed Funds	No Year	13		5521			5,332,000.00		5,332,000.00		
Total, International Trade Administration							407,081,777.00		418,209,480.84	-11,127,703.84	

Footnotes At End Of Chapter

Appropriations, Outlays, and Balances – Continued

Appropriation or Fund Account — Title	Period of Availability	Dept Reg	Tr From	Account Number	Sub No.	Balances, Beginning Of Fiscal Year	Appropriations And Other Obligational Authority[1]	Transfers Borrowings And Investment (Net)[2]	Outlays (Net)	Balances Withdrawn And Other Transactions[3]	Balances, End Of Fiscal Year[4]
Bureau Of Industry And Security											
General Fund Accounts											
Operations And Administration, Bureau Of Industry And Security, Commerce											
Fund Resources:											
Undisbursed Funds	2004-2005	13		0300		249,405.75			93,553.64		155,852.11
	2003-2004					443,126.62			7,290.00		435,836.62
	No Year					27,963,120.78	75,393,413.00		85,218,378.46		18,138,155.32
Accounts Receivable						1,116,350.89				-186,087.79	1,302,438.68
Unfilled Customer Orders						1,823,748.75				815,724.85	1,008,023.90
Fund Equities:											
Unobligated Balances (Expired)						-397,958.44				149,188.21	-547,146.65
Unobligated Balances (Unexpired)						-8,760,000.34				-4,628,393.84	-4,131,606.50
Accounts Payable						-3,769,267.14				276,945.59	-4,046,212.73
Undelivered Orders						-18,668,526.87				-6,353,186.12	-12,315,340.75
Subtotal		13		0300		-0-	75,393,413.00		85,319,222.10	-9,925,809.10	-0-
Total, Bureau Of Industry And Security							75,393,413.00		85,319,222.10	-9,925,809.10	
Minority Business Development Agency											
General Fund Accounts											
Minority Business Development, Minority Business Development Agency											
Fund Resources:											
Undisbursed Funds	2007	13		0201		8,536,752.98	29,724,825.00		19,893,153.83		9,831,671.17
	2006					179,124.84			7,357,122.13		1,179,630.85
	2005					640,435.60			43,819.43		135,305.41
	2004					323,349.72			190.64		640,244.96
	2003					720,403.20			1,982.79		323,349.72
	2002					69,187.11			300.00		68,887.11
	No Year									718,420.41	
Fund Equities:											
Unobligated Balances (Expired)						-1,532,427.86				741,613.15	-2,274,041.01
Unobligated Balances (Unexpired)						-2,183.25				14,208.81	-16,392.06
Accounts Payable						-3,691,218.46				1,232,481.80	-4,923,700.26
Undelivered Orders						-5,243,423.88				-278,467.99	-4,964,955.89
Subtotal		13		0201		-0-	29,724,825.00		27,296,568.82	2,428,256.18	-0-
Total, Minority Business Development Agency							29,724,825.00		27,296,568.82	2,428,256.18	

Appropriations, Outlays, and Balances - Continued

Title	Period of Availability	Dept Reg	Dept Tr From	Account Number	Sub No.	Balances, Beginning Of Fiscal Year	Appropriations And Other Obligational Authority[1]	Transfers Borrowings And Investment (Net)[2]	Outlays (Net)	Balances Withdrawn And Other Transactions[3]	Balances, End Of Fiscal Year[4]
National Oceanic And Atmospheric Administration											
General Fund Accounts											
Operations, Research And Facilities, National Oceanic And Atmospheric Administration											
Fund Resources:											
Undisbursed Funds	2007-2009	13		1450			18,544,324.00		16,280,619.41		2,263,704.59
	2005-2009					156,585.56			156,359.44		226.12
	2007-2008						2,890,124,958.00		1,694,296,214.04		1,195,828,743.96
	2006-2008					1,670,926.54			732,261.37		938,665.17
	2007						20,607,607.00		17,812,783.69		2,794,823.31
	2006-2007					1,144,967,112.90			684,497,537.07		460,469,575.83
	2005-2007					935,542.69			610,001.00		325,541.69
	2006					3,409,104.97			3,409,104.97		
	2005-2006					419,872,713.39			269,643,513.65		150,229,199.74
	2004-2006					10,864.12					10,864.12
	2005					55,363.55				55,363.55	
	2004-2005					115,999,088.96			55,704,865.67		60,294,223.29
	2004					1,241,557.08			674,354.29		567,202.79
	2003-2004					37,712,962.53			11,733,808.80		25,979,153.73
	2003					11,393,273.29			816,098.25		10,577,175.04
	2002-2003					72,904.63					72,904.63
Funds Held Outside The Treasury	No Year					199,969,852.82	82,091,794.00	-80,155.17	93,995,756.48		187,985,735.17
Accounts Receivable	No Year					410,147.97		80,155.17			490,303.14
Unfilled Customer Orders						104,906,558.10				39,575,529.70	65,331,028.40
Fund Equities:											
Unobligated Balances (Expired)						136,505,076.11				-6,701,066.02	143,206,142.13
Unobligated Balances (Unexpired)						-18,425,749.90				13,531,649.56	-31,957,399.46
Accounts Payable						-179,164,555.26				-17,615,580.99	-161,548,974.27
Undelivered Orders						-221,155,703.26				16,071,694.69	-237,227,397.95
						-1,760,543,626.79				116,087,814.38	-1,876,631,441.17
	Subtotal	13		1450		-0-	3,011,368,683.00		2,850,363,278.13	161,005,404.87	-0-
Expenses, Pacific Coastal Salmon Recovery, National Oceanic And Atmospheric Administration											
Fund Resources:											
Undisbursed Funds	2007	13		1451			66,571,252.00		392,071.96		66,179,180.04
	2006					65,299,712.91			8,821,959.46		56,477,753.45
	2005					75,413,551.93			19,054,869.25		56,358,682.68
	2004					49,806,264.98			19,161,286.59		30,644,978.39
	2003					40,897,123.46			23,440,103.65		17,457,019.81
	2002					8,618,747.53			8,555,199.77	63,547.76	
	No Year					3,011.93			-6,284.99		9,296.92
Fund Equities:											
Unobligated Balances (Expired)						-73,271.65				87,707.59	-160,979.24
Unobligated Balances (Unexpired)						-210.00				9,086.92	-9,296.92
Accounts Payable						-10,432,245.64				1,506,765.86	-11,939,011.50

Footnotes At End Of Chapter

Appropriations, Outlays, and Balances – Continued

Appropriation or Fund Account — Title	Period of Availability	Dept Reg	Tr From	Account Number	Sub No.	Balances, Beginning Of Fiscal Year	Appropriations And Other Obligational Authority[1]	Transfers Borrowings And Investment (Net)[2]	Outlays (Net)	Balances Withdrawn And Other Transactions[3]	Balances, End Of Fiscal Year[4]
Expenses, Pacific Coastal Salmon Recovery, National Oceanic And Atmospheric Administration - Continued											
Fund Equities: - Continued											
Undelivered Orders						-229,532,685.45				-14,515,061.82	-215,017,623.63
	Subtotal	13		1451		-0-	66,571,252.00		79,419,205.69	-12,847,953.69	-0-
Fisheries Finance Program Account, National Oceanic And Atmospheric Administration											
Fund Resources:											
Undisbursed Funds	2007	13		1456			283,051.00				283,051.00
	2006					283,051.00					283,051.00
	2005					775,713.00					775,713.00
	2003					285,134.00					285,134.00
	2002					278,730.85			84.31	278,646.54	
	No Year					5,014,360.47	3,655,866.32		5,005,866.32		3,664,360.47
Fund Equities:											
Unobligated Balances (Expired)						-1,618,026.57				8,922.43	-1,626,949.00
Unobligated Balances (Unexpired)						-3,928,325.97				-1,000,000.00	-2,928,325.97
Undelivered Orders						-1,090,636.78				-354,602.28	-736,034.50
	Subtotal	13		1456		-0-	3,938,917.32		5,005,950.63	-1,067,033.31	-0-
Procurement, Acquisition And Construction, National Oceanic And Atmospheric Administration											
Fund Resources:											
Undisbursed Funds	2007-2009	13		1460			993,329,900.00		426,146,419.04		567,183,480.96
	2005-2009					70,214,263.55			29,281,986.30		40,932,277.25
	2006-2008					502,465,812.13			321,011,207.03		181,454,605.10
	2005-2007					119,274,872.57			61,452,079.61		57,822,792.96
	2004-2006					72,071,750.63			17,795,632.81		54,276,117.82
	2003-2006					12,038,638.26			7,825,437.27		4,213,200.99
	2004					429,541.42			429,541.42		
	No Year					203,055,809.41	91,702,206.00		87,734,333.05		207,023,682.36
Fund Equities:											
Unobligated Balances (Expired)						-292,369.86				2,859,229.56	-3,151,599.42
Unobligated Balances (Unexpired)						-65,429,438.15				-27,842,835.67	-37,586,602.48
Accounts Payable						-83,094,636.91				9,317,668.65	-92,412,305.56
Undelivered Orders						-830,734,243.05			951,676,636.53	149,021,406.93	-979,755,649.98
	Subtotal	13		1460		-0-	1,085,032,106.00		951,676,636.53	133,355,469.47	-0-
Coastal Impact Assistance, National Oceanic And Atmospheric Administration											
Fund Resources:											
Undisbursed Funds	No Year	13		1462		31,125,022.28			16,723,538.13		14,401,484.15
Fund Equities:											
Unobligated Balances (Unexpired)						-213,262.67				379,186.71	-592,449.38
Accounts Payable						-1,486,718.38				-611,580.25	-875,138.13
Undelivered Orders						-29,425,041.23			16,723,538.13	-16,491,144.59	-12,933,896.64
	Subtotal	13		1462		-0-			16,723,538.13	-16,723,538.13	-0-
NOAA Accrual Contribution To The Uniformed Services Retiree Health, Department Of Commerce											
Fund Resources:											
Undisbursed Funds	2007	13		1465			1,820,000.00		1,820,000.00		

Appropriations, Outlays, and Balances - Continued

Appropriation or Fund Account Title	Period of Availability	Reg	Tr From	Account Number	Sub No.	Balances, Beginning Of Fiscal Year	Appropriations And Other Obligational Authority[1]	Transfers Borrowings And Investment (Net)[2]	Outlays (Net)	Balances Withdrawn And Other Transactions[3]	Balances, End Of Fiscal Year[4]
Special Fund Accounts											
Fishermen's Contingency Fund, National Oceanic And Atmospheric Administration											
Fund Resources:											
Undisbursed Funds	No Year	13		5120		837,180.75	1,032,358.03	---	222,535.77		1,647,003.01
Fund Equities:											
Unobligated Balances (Unexpired)						-837,180.75		---		809,822.26	-1,647,003.01
Subtotal	Subtotal	13		5120		-0-	1,032,358.03	---	222,535.77	809,822.26	-0-
Foreign Fishing Observer Fund, National Oceanic And Atmospheric Administration											
Fund Resources:											
Undisbursed Funds	No Year	13		5122		1,681,367.23	41,441.86	---	121,425.00		1,601,384.09
Fund Equities:											
Unobligated Balances (Unexpired)						-1,308,949.58		---		41,441.86	-1,350,391.44
Accounts Payable						-19,318.80				1,681.20	-21,000.00
Undelivered Orders						-353,098.85				-123,106.20	-229,992.65
Subtotal	Subtotal	13		5122		-0-	41,441.86	---	121,425.00	-79,983.14	-0-
Promote And Develop Fishery Products And Research Pertaining To American Fisheries, National Oceanic And Atmospheric Administration											
Fund Resources:											
Undisbursed Funds	No Year	13		5139		6,688,732.11	3,817,059.00	---	5,799,867.92		4,705,923.19
Fund Equities:											
Unobligated Balances (Unexpired)						-187,088.00		---		478,702.51	-665,790.51
Accounts Payable						-31,336.32				122,825.89	-154,162.21
Undelivered Orders						-6,470,307.79				-2,584,337.32	-3,885,970.47
Subtotal	Subtotal	13		5139		-0-	3,817,059.00	---	5,799,867.92	-1,992,808.92	-0-
Marine Mammal Unusual Mortality Event Fund, National Oceanic And Atmospheric Administration											
Fund Resources:											
Undisbursed Funds	No Year	13		5283		800,000.00		---			800,000.00
Fund Equities:											
Unobligated Balances (Unexpired)						-800,000.00		---		-64,656.12	-735,343.88
Undelivered Orders										64,656.12	-64,656.12
Subtotal	Subtotal	13		5283		-0-		---			-0-
Limited Access System Administration Fund, National Oceanic And Atmospheric Administration											
Fund Resources:											
Undisbursed Funds	No Year	13		5284		9,787,960.18	6,911,354.84	---	4,186,992.84		12,512,322.18
Fund Equities:											
Unobligated Balances (Unexpired)						-9,295,188.90		---		1,594,784.09	-10,889,972.99
Accounts Payable						-75,806.15				62,350.58	-138,156.73
Undelivered Orders						-416,965.13				1,067,227.33	-1,484,192.46
Subtotal	Subtotal	13		5284		-0-	6,911,354.84	---	4,186,992.84	2,724,362.00	-0-

Footnotes At End Of Chapter

Appropriations, Outlays, and Balances – Continued

Appropriation or Fund Account — Title	Period of Availability	Dept Reg	Dept Tr From	Account Number	Sub No.	Balances, Beginning Of Fiscal Year	Appropriations And Other Obligational Authority[1]	Transfers Borrowings And Investment (Net)[2]	Outlays (Net)	Balances Withdrawn And Other Transactions[3]	Balances, End Of Fiscal Year[4]
Environmental Improvement And Restoration Fund, National Oceanic And Atmospheric Administration, Department Of Commerce											
Fund Resources:											
Undisbursed Funds	No Year	13		5362		25,010,671.12	8,649,695.90		4,432,734.28		29,227,632.74
Fund Equities:											
Unobligated Balances (Unexpired)						-7,839,598.35				810,097.90	-8,649,696.25
Accounts Payable						-743,359.19				109,137.85	-852,497.04
Undelivered Orders						-16,427,713.58				3,297,725.87	-19,725,439.45
Subtotal		13		5362		-0-	8,649,695.90		4,432,734.28	4,216,961.62	-0-
Public Enterprise Funds											
Coastal Zone Management Fund, National Oceanic And Atmospheric Administration											
Fund Resources:											
Undisbursed Funds	No Year	13		4313		29,083,134.15	-3,000,000.00		-1,659,445.24		27,742,579.39
Fund Equities:											
Unobligated Balances (Unexpired)						-29,059,278.85				-1,328,973.54	-27,730,305.31
Accounts Payable						-12,274.08				-11,581.22	-12,274.08
Undelivered Orders						-11,581.22				-1,340,554.76	-0-
Subtotal		13		4313		-0-	-3,000,000.00		-1,659,445.24	-1,659,445.24	-0-
Damage Assessment And Restoration Revolving Fund, National Oceanic And Atmospheric Administration											
Fund Resources:											
Undisbursed Funds	No Year	13		4316		28,437,896.99	3,788,282.00	14,238,627.09	13,073,232.55		33,391,573.53
Accounts Receivable						19,590.65				-16,563.76	36,154.41
Fund Equities:											
Unobligated Balances (Unexpired)						-20,731,459.42				4,253,979.14	-24,985,438.56
Accounts Payable						-831,176.16				-95,735.03	-735,441.13
Undelivered Orders						-6,894,852.06				811,996.19	-7,706,848.25
Subtotal		13		4316		-0-	3,788,282.00	14,238,627.09	13,073,232.55	4,953,676.54	-0-
Federal Ship Financing Fund, Fishing Vessels, Liquidating Account, National Oceanic And Atmospheric Administration											
Fund Resources:											
Undisbursed Funds	No Year	13		4417		10,882.63			-274,508.83	579,495.64	205,895.82
Fund Equities:											
Accounts Payable						-10,882.63				195,013.19	-205,895.82
Subtotal		13		4417		-0-			-274,508.83	274,508.83	-0-
Total, National Oceanic And Atmospheric Administration						1,077,082,602.25	4,189,971,149.95	14,238,627.09	3,930,911,443.40	273,298,333.64	1,068,773,855.69
U.S. Patent And Trademark Office											
General Fund Accounts											
Salaries And Expenses, Patent And Trademark Office											
Fund Resources:											
Undisbursed Funds	No Year	13		1006		1,550.00	-26,707.08	500.00	8,282,539.48		1,050.00
Funds Held Outside The Treasury	No Year	13						-500.00			

Appropriations, Outlays, and Balances - Continued

Title	Period of Availability	Dept Reg	Tr From	Account Number	Sub No.	Balances, Beginning Of Fiscal Year	Appropriations And Other Obligational Authority[1]	Transfers Borrowings And Investment (Net)[2]	Outlays (Net)	Balances Withdrawn And Other Transactions[3]	Balances, End Of Fiscal Year[4]
Accounts Receivable						-1,043,729.47				-458,855.19	-584,874.28
Fund Equities:											
Unobligated Balances (Unexpired)						-522,214,830.21				34,508,701.08	-556,723,531.29
Accounts Payable						-134,829,815.72				-338,331.46	-134,491,484.26
Undelivered Orders						-418,995,776.85				-42,020,760.99	-376,975,015.86
Subtotal		13		1006		-0-	-26,707.08		8,282,539.48	-8,309,246.56	-0-
Total, U.S. Patent And Trademark Office							-26,707.08		8,282,539.48	-8,309,246.56	
Technology Administration											
General Fund Accounts											
Salaries And Expenses, Technology Administration, Department Of Commerce											
Fund Resources:											
Undisbursed Funds	2007	13		1100		1,915,871.04	2,019,695.00		1,809,038.95		210,656.05
	2006					342,458.89			728,876.78		1,186,994.26
	2005					349,794.05			18,778.29		323,680.60
	2004					351,238.08			6,860.00		342,934.05
	2003					351,238.08					351,238.08
	2002					364,077.94				364,077.94	
Unfilled Customer Orders						7,000.00				-22,274.39	29,274.39
Fund Equities:											
Unobligated Balances (Expired)						-1,296,549.57				-21,554.60	-1,274,994.97
Accounts Payable						-440,289.37				-153,923.83	-286,365.54
Undelivered Orders						-1,593,601.06				-710,184.14	-883,416.92
Subtotal		13		1100		-0-	2,019,695.00		2,563,554.02	-543,859.02	-0-
Total, Technology Administration							2,019,695.00		2,563,554.02	-543,859.02	
National Technical Information Service											
Public Enterprise Funds											
NTIS Revolving Fund, National Technical Information Service											
Fund Resources:											
Undisbursed Funds	No Year	13		4295		21,917,008.51			-4,939,406.24		26,856,414.75
Accounts Receivable						1,788,137.86				453,262.19	1,334,875.67
Unfilled Customer Orders						3,043,917.06				1,281,083.94	1,762,833.12
Fund Equities:											
Unobligated Balances (Unexpired)						-10,137,696.85				-1,222,003.34	-8,915,693.51
Accounts Payable						-9,884,352.90				-16,699.06	-9,867,653.84
Undelivered Orders						-6,727,013.68				4,443,762.51	-11,170,776.19
Subtotal		13		4295		-0-			-4,939,406.24	4,939,406.24	
Total, National Technical Information Service									-4,939,406.24	4,939,406.24	

Footnotes At End Of Chapter

Appropriations, Outlays, and Balances – Continued

Appropriation or Fund Account — Title	Period of Availability	Dept Reg	Tr From	Account Number	Sub No.	Balances, Beginning Of Fiscal Year	Appropriations And Other Obligational Authority[1]	Transfers Borrowings And Investment (Net)[2]	Outlays (Net)	Balances Withdrawn And Other Transactions[3]	Balances, End Of Fiscal Year[4]
National Institute Of Standards And Technology											
General Fund Accounts											
Scientific And Technical Research And Services, National Institute Of Standards And Technology											
Fund Resources:											
Undisbursed Funds	2007	13		0500		1,179,523.25	4,950,000.00		3,580,241.62		1,369,758.38
	2006					596,251.31					583,271.94
	2005					47,762.58			33,015.00		14,747.58
	2002					12,300.06				12,300.06	
	No Year					109,857,594.42	433,071,287.00	5,000,000.00	409,790,569.32		138,138,312.10
Fund Equities:											
Unobligated Balances (Expired)						-15,777.43				6,330.75	-22,108.18
Unobligated Balances (Unexpired)						-4,898,496.64				4,199,323.14	-9,097,819.78
Accounts Payable						-6,338,285.23				4,014,144.27	-10,352,429.50
Undelivered Orders						-99,844,621.01				20,789,111.53	-120,633,732.54
Subtotal		13		0500		-0-	438,021,287.00	5,000,000.00	414,000,077.25	29,021,209.75	-0-
Construction Of Research Facilities, National Institute Of Standards And Technology											
Fund Resources:											
Undisbursed Funds	No Year	13		0515		210,708,590.12	58,685,715.00		59,100,560.47		210,293,744.65
Fund Equities:											
Unobligated Balances (Unexpired)						-9,014,913.13				8,217,597.46	-17,232,510.59
Accounts Payable						-15,500,118.45				10,710,870.31	-26,210,988.76
Undelivered Orders						-186,193,558.54				-19,343,313.24	-166,850,245.30
Subtotal		13		0515		-0-	58,685,715.00		59,100,560.47	-414,845.47	-0-
Industrial Technology Services, National Institute Of Standards And Technology											
Fund Resources:											
Undisbursed Funds	No Year	13		0525		184,357,809.20	176,819,196.00		185,739,056.32		175,437,948.88
Fund Equities:											
Unobligated Balances (Unexpired)						-30,080,136.03				-10,346,210.13	-19,733,925.90
Accounts Payable						-9,779,011.81				-4,616,341.74	-5,162,670.07
Undelivered Orders						-144,498,661.36				6,042,691.55	-150,541,352.91
Subtotal		13		0525		-0-	176,819,196.00		185,739,056.32	-8,919,960.32	-0-
Intragovernmental Funds											
Working Capital Fund, National Institute Of Standards And Technology											
Fund Resources:											
Undisbursed Funds	No Year	13		4650		229,301,058.01	1,300,000.00		-11,820,798.59		242,421,856.60
Accounts Receivable						7,018,503.53				-981,084.28	7,999,587.81
Unfilled Customer Orders						22,135,924.86				-1,823,400.09	23,959,324.95
Fund Equities:											
Unobligated Balances (Unexpired)						-131,598,371.12				9,179,251.83	-140,777,622.95
Accounts Payable						-37,147,160.10				8,439,004.63	-45,586,164.73
Undelivered Orders						-89,709,955.18				-1,692,973.50	-88,016,981.68

Appropriation or Fund Account — Title	Period of Availability	Dept Reg	Dept Tr From	Account Number	Sub No.	Balances, Beginning Of Fiscal Year	Appropriations And Other Obligational Authority[1]	Transfers Borrowings And Investment (Net)[2]	Outlays (Net)	Balances Withdrawn And Other Transactions[3]	Balances, End Of Fiscal Year[4]
Subtotal		13		4650		-0-	1,300,000.00		-11,820,798.59	13,120,798.59	-0-
Total, National Institute Of Standards And Technology						------	674,826,198.00	5,000,000.00	647,018,895.45	32,807,302.55	------

National Telecommunications And Information Administration

General Fund Accounts

Salaries And Expenses, National Telecommunications And Information Administration, Department Of Commerce

Title	Period of Availability	Reg	Tr From	Account Number	Sub No.	Balances, Beginning	Appropriations	Transfers	Outlays (Net)	Withdrawn	End
Fund Resources:											
Undisbursed Funds	2007-2008	13		0550		6,113,390.75	18,061,927.00		12,988,129.02	------	5,073,797.98
	2006-2007					268,345.66			5,019,858.84	------	1,093,531.91
	2005-2006					806,839.14			139,359.22	------	128,986.44
	2004-2005								680,953.35	------	125,885.79
	No Year					21,581,307.59			-8,800,319.49		30,381,627.08
Accounts Receivable										-2,880.00	2,880.00
Unfilled Customer Orders						1,401,075.63				509,388.37	891,687.26
Fund Equities:											
Unobligated Balances (Expired)						-60,055.65				59,829.93	-119,885.58
Unobligated Balances (Unexpired)						-21,976,649.67				2,935,031.72	-24,911,681.39
Accounts Payable						-2,481,321.00				1,411,302.30	-3,892,623.30
Undelivered Orders						-5,652,932.45				3,121,273.74	-8,774,206.19
Subtotal		13		0550		-0-	18,061,927.00		10,027,980.94	8,033,946.06	-0-

Public Telecommunications Facilities, Planning And Construction, National Telecommunications And Information, Commerce

Title	Period of Availability	Reg	Tr From	Account Number	Sub No.	Balances, Beginning	Appropriations	Transfers	Outlays (Net)	Withdrawn	End
Fund Resources:											
Undisbursed Funds	No Year	13		0551		54,377,843.40	21,728,507.00		22,304,596.11	------	53,801,754.29
Fund Equities:											
Unobligated Balances (Unexpired)						-2,383,226.17				919,610.06	-3,302,836.23
Accounts Payable						-21,620,620.38				-4,059,249.22	-17,561,371.16
Undelivered Orders						-30,373,996.85				2,563,550.05	-32,937,546.90
Subtotal		13		0551		-0-	21,728,507.00		22,304,596.11	-576,089.11	-0-

Information Infrastructure Grants, National Telecommunications And Information Administration

Title	Period of Availability	Reg	Tr From	Account Number	Sub No.	Balances, Beginning	Appropriations	Transfers	Outlays (Net)	Withdrawn	End
Fund Resources:											
Undisbursed Funds	No Year	13		0552		14,415,204.08			6,880,853.65	------	7,534,350.43
Fund Equities:											
Unobligated Balances (Unexpired)						-1,785,481.91				34,375.03	-1,819,856.94
Accounts Payable						-6,447,309.08				-3,131,632.11	-3,315,676.97
Undelivered Orders						-6,182,413.09				-3,783,596.57	-2,398,816.52
Subtotal		13		0552		-0-			6,880,853.65	-6,880,853.65	-0-

Footnotes At End Of Chapter

Appropriations, Outlays, and Balances – Continued

Appropriation or Fund Account — Title	Period of Availability	Account Symbol — Dept Reg	Dept Tr From	Account Number	Sub No.	Balances, Beginning Of Fiscal Year	Appropriations And Other Obligational Authority[1]	Transfers Borrowings And Investment (Net)[2]	Outlays (Net)	Balances Withdrawn And Other Transactions[3]	Balances, End Of Fiscal Year[4]
Special Fund Accounts											
Digital Television Transition And Public Safety Fund, National Telecommunications And Information Administration											
Fund Resources:											
Undisbursed Funds	No Year	13		5396					59,983,735.37		104,505,091.63
Authority To Borrow From The Treasury						1,084,163,608.00		164,488,827.00 -164,488,827.00			919,674,781.00
Fund Equities:											
Unobligated Balances (Unexpired)										13,891,297.71	-13,891,297.71
Accounts Payable										3,871,894.96	-3,871,894.96
Undelivered Orders										1,006,416,679.96	-1,006,416,679.96
	Subtotal	13		5396		-0-	1,084,163,608.00		59,983,735.37	1,024,179,872.63	-0-
Total, National Telecommunications And Information Administration							1,123,954,042.00		99,197,166.07	1,024,756,875.93	
Deductions For Offsetting Receipts											
Proprietary Receipts From The Public							-71,388,987.90		-71,388,987.90		
Intrabudgetary Transactions							-1,503,915.18		-1,503,915.18		
Total, Offsetting Receipts							-72,892,903.08		-72,892,903.08		
Total, Department Of Commerce							7,776,247,391.37	19,238,627.09	6,478,672,859.00	1,316,813,159.46	
Memorandum											
Financing Accounts											
Public Enterprise Funds											
Federal Ship Financing Guaranteed Loan Financing Account, National Oceanic And Atmospheric Administration											
Fund Resources:											
Undisbursed Funds	No Year	13		4314		4,483,900.86		-2,840,522.51	-2,542,239.35		4,185,617.70
Authority To Borrow From The Treasury						12,000.00	724,154.12	-736,154.12			
Fund Equities:											
Unobligated Balances (Unexpired)						-4,480,900.86	724,154.12			-295,283.16	-4,185,617.70
Accounts Payable						-15,000.00				-15,000.00	-0-
	Subtotal	13		4314		-0-	724,154.12	-3,576,676.63	-2,542,239.35	-310,283.16	-0-
Fisheries Finance, Direct Loan Financing Account, National Oceanic Atmospheric Administration											
Fund Resources:											
Undisbursed Funds	No Year	13		4324		5,358,799.99	69,484,995.91	62,958,755.01	66,368,429.85	2,113,319.05	1,949,125.15
Authority To Borrow From The Treasury						239,583,298.48		-102,574,607.40			204,380,367.94
Accounts Receivable										183,083.07	-183,083.07
Unfilled Customer Orders						1,090,636.78				354,602.28	736,034.50
Fund Equities:											
Unobligated Balances (Unexpired)						-238,357.57				-17,858.82	-220,498.75

Appropriations, Outlays, and Balances - Continued

Appropriation or Fund Account Title	Account Symbol: Period of Availability	Dept Reg	Tr From	Account Number	Sub No.	Balances, Beginning Of Fiscal Year	Appropriations And Other Obligational Authority[1]	Transfers Borrowings And Investment (Net)[2]	Outlays (Net)	Balances Withdrawn And Other Transactions[3]	Balances, End Of Fiscal Year[4]
Accounts Payable						-------	-------	-------	-------	-------	-------
Undelivered Orders						-245,794,377.68				-39,132,431.91	-206,661,945.77
	Subtotal	13		4324		-0-	69,484,995.91	-39,615,852.39	66,368,429.85	-36,499,286.33	-0-
Emergency Oil And Gas Guaranteed Loan Financing Account, Departmental Management											
Fund Resources:											
Undisbursed Funds	No Year	13		4327		308,669.50					244,601.50
Accounts Receivable						-------			64,068.00	-8,367.84	8,367.84
Fund Equities:											
Unobligated Balances (Unexpired)						-308,669.50				-55,700.16	-252,969.34
	Subtotal	13		4327		-0-			64,068.00	-64,068.00	-0-
Emergency Steel Guaranteed Loan Financing Account, Departmental Management											
Fund Resources:											
Undisbursed Funds	No Year	13		4328		81,791,877.06	4,934,368.00	-857,743.33	32,014,961.13		53,853,540.60
Authority To Borrow From The Treasury						-------	2,373,903.67	-2,373,903.67			
Accounts Receivable						-------				-693,067.12	693,067.12
Fund Equities:											
Unobligated Balances (Unexpired)						-81,699,450.26				-27,347,941.82	-54,351,508.44
Accounts Payable						-66,216.74				110,754.93	-176,971.67
Undelivered Orders						-26,210.06				-8,082.45	-18,127.61
	Subtotal	13		4328		-0-	7,308,271.67	-3,231,647.00	32,014,961.13	-27,938,336.46	-0-
Total, Financing Accounts						-------	77,517,421.70	-46,424,176.02	95,905,219.63	-64,811,973.95	-------

Footnotes At End Of Chapter

Appropriations, Outlays, and Balances – Continued

Footnotes

1 The amounts in this column, unless otherwise footnoted, represent appropriations, increases and rescissions in borrowing authority or new contract authority. Appropriation accounts with appropriation transfer activity are presented in Table 1 (Appropriations and Appropriation Transfers) at the end of this chapter.

2 The amounts in this column, unless otherwise footnoted, represent transfers - other than appropriation transfers, borrowings (gross), investments (net), unrealized discounts or funds held outside the Treasury.

3 The amounts in this column, unless otherwise footnoted, represent obligated balances canceled for fiscal year 2002 pursuant to 31 U.S.C. 1553, changes in unfilled customer orders, accounts receivable, accounts payable, undelivered orders, unobligated balances and adjustments to borrowing and contract authority.

4 Unobligated balances for no-year or unexpired multiple year accounts are available for obligation; unobligated balances for expired fiscal year accounts are not available for obligation.

5 Represents capital transfer to miscellaneous receipts.

6 Includes $1,107.25 which represents payments for obligations of a closed account.

Appropriations, Outlays, and Balances - Continued

Footnotes

Table 1 - Appropriations And Appropriation Transfers - Department Of Commerce

Department Regular	Fiscal Year	Account Symbol	Net Appropriations And Appropriations Transfers	Appropriation Amount	Net Appropriation Transfers	Department Regular Involved	Fiscal Year Involved	Accounts Involved	Amount From or To (-)
13	0708	0120	1,455,000.00	0.00	1,455,000.00	72	0708	1010	600,000.00
						72	0708	1093	855,000.00
13	X	0500	433,071,287.00	434,371,287.00	-1,300,000.00	13	X	4650	-1,300,000.00
13	07	0500	4,950,000.00	0.00	4,950,000.00	95	07	1650	4,950,000.00
13	0708	1250	397,800,865.00	395,705,865.00	2,095,000.00	72	0708	1093	2,095,000.00
13	X	1450	82,091,794.00	0.00	82,091,794.00	13	X	1460	91,794.00
						13	X	4313	3,000,000.00
						13	X	5139	79,000,000.00
13	07	1450	20,607,607.00	20,540,686.00	66,921.00	13	07	1451	66,638.00
						13	07	1456	283.00
13	0708	1450	2,890,124,958.00	2,907,674,958.00	-17,550,000.00	13	0709	1450	-17,550,000.00
13	0709	1450	18,544,324.00	0.00	18,544,324.00	13	0708	1450	17,550,000.00
						13	0709	1460	994,324.00
13	07	1451	66,571,252.00	66,637,890.00	-66,638.00	13	07	1450	-66,638.00
13	07	1456	283,051.00	283,334.00	-283.00	13	07	1450	-283.00
13	X	1460	91,702,206.00	0.00	91,702,206.00	13	X	1450	-91,794.00
						13	0709	1460	91,794,000.00
13	0709	1460	993,329,900.00	1,086,118,224.00	-92,788,324.00	13	0709	1450	-994,324.00
						13	X	1460	-91,794,000.00
13	X	4313	-3,000,000.00	0.00	-3,000,000.00	13	X	1450	-3,000,000.00
13	X	4316	3,788,282.00	0.00	3,788,282.00	14	X	5198	3,788,282.00
13	X	4650	1,300,000.00	0.00	1,300,000.00	13	X	0500	1,300,000.00
13	X	5139	3,817,059.00	0.00	3,817,059.00	12	X	5209	82,817,059.00
						13	X	1450	-79,000,000.00
13	X	5521	5,332,000.00	0.00	5,332,000.00	70	X	5533	5,332,000.00
Totals			5,011,769,585.00	4,911,332,244.00	100,437,341.00				100,437,341.00

Appropriations, Outlays, and Balances – Continued

| Appropriation or Fund Account | Account Symbol | | | | | | | | | | |
Title	Period of Availability	Dept Reg	Dept Tr From	Account Number	Sub No.	Balances, Beginning Of Fiscal Year	Appropriations And Other Obligational Authority[1]	Transfers Borrowings And Investment (Net)[2]	Outlays (Net)	Balances Withdrawn And Other Transactions[3]	Balances, End Of Fiscal Year[4]
Department Of Defense											
Department Of Defense - Military											
Military Personnel											
Department Of The Army											
General Fund Accounts											
Medicare-Eligible Retiree Health Fund Contribution, Army											
Fund Resources:											
Undisbursed Funds	2007	21		1004			2,915,391,000.00		2,915,391,000.00		
Medicare-Eligible Retiree Health Fund Contribution, Reserve Personnel, Army											
Fund Resources:											
Undisbursed Funds	2007	21		1005			742,233,000.00		742,233,000.00		
Medicare-Eligible Retiree Health Fund Contribution, National Guard Personnel, Army											
Fund Resources:											
Undisbursed Funds	2007	21		1006			1,232,152,000.00		1,232,152,000.00		
Military Personnel, Army											
Fund Resources:											
Undisbursed Funds	2007	21		2010		835,539,754.83	41,531,919,800.00	103,580,000.00	40,269,483,082.36		1,366,016,717.64
	2006					103,646,768.63			539,609,604.95		295,930,149.88
	2005					99,773,992.19			76,482,702.70		27,164,065.93
	2004					44,010,458.06			-192,629,385.49		292,403,377.68
	2003					66,554,174.68			-12,384,347.23		56,394,805.29
	2002					-47,879,355.82			772,582.48	65,781,592.20	-1,885,495.04
Accounts Receivable										-45,993,860.78	
Fund Equities:											
Unobligated Balances (Expired)						-2,125,000.00					-2,125,000.00
Accounts Payable						-1,296,427,604.90				532,732,110.74	-1,829,159,715.64
Undelivered Orders						196,906,812.33				401,645,718.07	-204,738,905.74
	Subtotal	21		2010		-0-	41,531,919,800.00	103,580,000.00	40,681,334,239.77	954,165,560.23	
National Guard Personnel, Army											
Fund Resources:											
Undisbursed Funds	2007	21		2060		350,916,960.66	6,743,403,000.00	404,400,000.00	6,555,456,722.97		592,346,277.03
	2006					128,853,422.04			296,506,470.25		54,410,490.41
	2005					99,741,270.22		-17,000,000.00	8,361,551.80		103,491,870.24
	2004					37,543,947.28			1,625,571.75		98,115,698.47
	2003					37,098,356.48			-7,251,349.65		44,795,296.93
	2002								321,370.86	36,776,985.62	4,649,095.83
Accounts Receivable						3,259,198.79				-1,389,897.04	3,312,600.85
Unfilled Customer Orders						1,034,921.57				-2,277,679.28	
Fund Equities:											
Unobligated Balances (Expired)						-215,260,617.47				-24,778,651.46	-190,481,966.01
Accounts Payable						-364,800,949.32				267,238,347.57	-632,039,296.89
Undelivered Orders						-78,386,510.25				213,556.61	-78,600,066.86

Appropriations, Outlays, and Balances - Continued

Appropriation or Fund Account — Title	Dept Reg	Tr From	Account Number	Sub No.	Period of Availability	Balances, Beginning Of Fiscal Year	Appropriations And Other Obligational Authority[1]	Transfers Borrowings And Investment (Net)[2]	Outlays (Net)	Balances Withdrawn And Other Transactions[3]	Balances, End Of Fiscal Year[4]
Reserve Personnel, Army	21		2060		Subtotal	-0-	6,743,403,000.00	387,400,000.00	6,855,020,337.98	275,782,662.02	-0-
Fund Resources:											
Undisbursed Funds	21		2070		2007		3,514,166,000.00		3,318,316,066.87		195,849,933.13
					2006	331,329,589.92			158,601,715.12		172,727,874.80
					2005	20,045,664.09			5,140,561.17		14,905,102.92
					2004	22,948,648.97			1,957,757.31		20,990,891.66
					2003	9,972,725.84			-3,622,223.22		13,594,949.06
					2002	7,402,528.30			210,684.28	7,191,844.02	
Accounts Receivable						3,165,675.54				863,039.47	2,302,636.07
Unfilled Customer Orders						13,301,157.18				5,723,981.56	7,577,175.62
Fund Equities:											
Unobligated Balances (Expired)						-62,183,551.61				99,744,162.10	-161,927,713.71
Accounts Payable						-124,705,069.61				9,022,937.51	-133,728,007.12
Undelivered Orders						-221,277,368.62				-88,984,526.19	-132,292,842.43
	21			2070	Subtotal	-0-	3,514,166,000.00		3,480,604,561.53	33,561,438.47	-0-
Total, Military Personnel, Army							56,679,264,800.00	490,980,000.00	55,906,735,139.28	1,263,509,660.72	

Department Of The Navy

General Fund Accounts

Appropriation or Fund Account — Title	Dept Reg	Tr From	Account Number	Sub No.	Period of Availability	Balances, Beginning Of Fiscal Year	Appropriations And Other Obligational Authority[1]	Transfers Borrowings And Investment (Net)[2]	Outlays (Net)	Balances Withdrawn And Other Transactions[3]	Balances, End Of Fiscal Year[4]
Medicare-Eligible Retiree Health Fund Contribution, Navy											
Fund Resources:											
Undisbursed Funds	17		1000		2007		2,098,369,000.00		2,098,369,000.00		
Medicare-Eligible Retiree Health Fund Contribution, Marine Corps											
Fund Resources:											
Undisbursed Funds	17		1001		2007		1,050,586,000.00		1,050,586,000.00		
Medicare-Eligible Retiree Health Fund Contribution, Reserve Personnel, Navy											
Fund Resources:											
Undisbursed Funds	17		1002		2007		287,140,000.00		287,140,000.00		
Medicare-Eligible Retiree Health Fund Contribution, Reserve Personnel, Marine Corps											
Fund Resources:											
Undisbursed Funds	17		1003		2007		144,647,000.00		144,647,000.00		
Military Personnel, Marine Corps											
Fund Resources:											
Undisbursed Funds	17		1105		2007	373,909,627.74	10,816,117,000.00	164,000.00	10,313,400,087.75		502,880,912.25
					2006	3,200,000.00			175,452,640.04		198,456,987.70
					2005-2006	25,389,965.29			-2,073,000.00		5,273,000.00
					2005	56,968,687.50			-1,679,416.87		27,069,382.16
					2004	63,993,177.23			6,424,137.61		50,544,549.89
					2003	2,904,515.20			444,173.55		63,549,003.68
					2002	2,189,210.13			306,656.54	2,597,858.66	
Accounts Receivable										1,555,855.64	633,354.49
Unfilled Customer Orders										1,746.88	-1,746.88

Footnotes At End Of Chapter

Appropriations, Outlays, and Balances – Continued

Appropriation or Fund Account — Title	Dept Reg	Tr From	Account Number	Sub No.	Period of Availability	Balances, Beginning Of Fiscal Year	Appropriations And Other Obligational Authority[1]	Transfers Borrowings And Investment (Net)[2]	Outlays (Net)	Balances Withdrawn And Other Transactions[3]	Balances, End Of Fiscal Year[4]
Military Personnel, Marine Corps - Continued											
Fund Equities:											
Unobligated Balances (Expired)						-60,007,552.34				67,654,049.78	-127,661,602.12
Accounts Payable						-132,103,602.09				393,692,076.83	-525,795,678.92
Undelivered Orders						-336,444,028.66		164,000.00		-141,495,866.41	-194,948,162.25
Subtotal	17		1105			-0-	10,816,117,000.00	164,000.00	10,492,275,278.62	324,005,721.38	-0-
Reserve Personnel, Marine Corps											
Fund Resources:											
Undisbursed Funds	17		1108		2007	9,670,547.23	564,174,000.00		545,733,906.35		18,440,093.65
					2006	11,482,215.06			-1,063,319.91		10,733,867.14
					2005	10,533,092.41		-6,600,000.00	556,173.24		4,326,041.82
					2004	6,398,336.43			291,153.94		10,241,938.47
					2003	1,032,677.34			-154,668.90		6,553,005.33
					2002	263,722.14			-4,778.15		271,285.00
Accounts Receivable										1,037,455.49	
Unfilled Customer Orders						-27.50				-7,562.86	-27.50
Fund Equities:											
Unobligated Balances (Expired)						-12,483,998.19				12,274,667.19	-24,758,665.38
Accounts Payable						-23,869,995.44				-6,617,228.75	-17,252,766.69
Undelivered Orders						-3,026,569.48				5,528,202.36	-8,554,771.84
Subtotal	17		1108			-0-	564,174,000.00	-6,600,000.00	545,358,466.57	12,215,533.43	-0-
Reserve Personnel, Navy											
Fund Resources:											
Undisbursed Funds	17		1405		2007	153,010,156.09	1,857,974,000.00		1,660,675,938.34		197,298,061.66
					2006	36,908,182.64			93,475,654.19		59,534,501.90
					2005	31,266,111.07		-10,000,000.00	236,572.87		26,671,609.77
					2004	16,674,432.79			-432,139.39		31,698,250.46
					2003	14,663,628.20			-230,519.51		16,904,952.30
					2002	712,407.12			758,558.44	13,905,069.76	614,753.15
Accounts Receivable						-560,748.61				97,653.15	-1,285,069.15
Unfilled Customer Orders										724,320.54	
Fund Equities:											
Unobligated Balances (Expired)						-83,818,793.34				-5,562,091.91	-78,256,701.43
Accounts Payable						-207,819,300.86				63,812,911.85	-271,632,212.71
Undelivered Orders						38,963,924.90				20,512,070.85	18,451,854.05
Subtotal	17		1405			-0-	1,857,974,000.00	-10,000,000.00	1,754,484,064.94	93,489,935.06	-0-
Military Personnel, Navy											
Fund Resources:											
Undisbursed Funds	17		1453		2007	193,769,642.36	24,016,938,000.00		23,208,582,846.22		839,729,153.78
					2006	21,064,615.27			106,091,920.00		87,677,722.36
					2005	14,899,445.59		31,374,000.00	11,011,170.42		10,053,444.85
					2004	19,830,695.43			2,298,022.72		12,601,422.87
					2003	14,900,919.75			-1,401,017.98[5]		21,231,713.41
					2002	24,500,258.01			11,972,168.79	2,928,750.96	23,294,874.06
Accounts Receivable										1,205,383.95	18,286,442.30
Unfilled Customer Orders										-18,286,442.30	
Fund Equities:											
Unobligated Balances (Expired)						-43,168,642.00				1,027,357.97	-44,195,999.97
Accounts Payable						-114,568,173.92				658,290,154.25	-772,858,328.17

Appropriations, Outlays, and Balances - Continued

Title	Period of Availability	Dept Reg	Tr From	Account Number	Sub No.	Balances, Beginning Of Fiscal Year	Appropriations And Other Obligational Authority[1]	Transfers Borrowings And Investment (Net)[2]	Outlays (Net)	Balances Withdrawn And Other Transactions[3]	Balances, End Of Fiscal Year[4]
Undelivered Orders						-131,228,760.49				64,591,685.00	-195,820,445.49
Subtotal		17		1453		-0-	24,016,938,000.00	31,374,000.00	23,338,555,110.17	709,756,889.83	-0-
Total, Military Personnel, Navy							40,835,945,000.00	14,938,000.00	39,711,414,920.30	1,139,468,079.70	
Department Of The Air Force											
General Fund Accounts											
Medicare-Eligible Retiree Health Fund Contribution, Air Force											
Fund Resources:											
Undisbursed Funds	2007	57		1007			2,082,462,000.00		2,082,462,000.00		
Medicare-Eligible Retiree Health Fund Contribution, Reserve Personnel, Air Force											
Fund Resources:											
Undisbursed Funds	2007	57		1008			268,104,000.00		268,104,000.00		
Medicare-Eligible Retiree Health Fund Contribution, National Guard Personnel, Air Force											
Fund Resources:											
Undisbursed Funds	2007	57		1009			409,546,000.00		409,546,000.00		
Military Personnel, Air Force											
Fund Resources:											
Undisbursed Funds	2007	57		3500		486,093,915.80	25,218,561,000.00	407,281,000.00	23,927,786,299.14		1,698,055,700.86
	2006					28,275,809.83			244,910,814.37		241,183,101.43
	2005					57,736,211.82			15,790,125.69		12,485,684.14
	2004					142,654,415.70			1,912,901.52		55,823,310.30
	2003					57,110,382.09			1,574,568.91		141,079,846.79
	2002					-23,856,311.14			-11,815,976.38		-38,486,893.77
Accounts Receivable										68,926,358.47	14,630,582.63
Fund Equities:											
Unobligated Balances (Expired)						-135,759,399.64				-103,351,399.64	-32,408,000.00
Accounts Payable						-613,123,729.46				1,467,066,614.29	-2,080,190,343.75
Undelivered Orders						868,705.00				-1,588,889.00	2,457,594.00
Subtotal		57		3500		-0-	25,218,561,000.00	407,281,000.00	24,180,158,733.25	1,445,683,266.75	-0-
Reserve Personnel, Air Force											
Fund Resources:											
Undisbursed Funds	2007	57		3700		74,884,718.32	1,339,225,000.00		[6]1,233,405,393.36		105,819,606.64
	2006					67,513,367.26			54,354,491.61		20,530,226.71
	2005					13,038,039.58		-48,000,000.00	971,278.39		18,542,088.87
	2004					9,184,588.55			93,003.72		12,945,035.86
	2003					11,981,560.79			-43,563.09		9,228,151.64
	2002					488,275.56			-103,293.83		
Accounts Receivable										12,084,854.62	226,699.00
										261,576.56	
Fund Equities:											
Unobligated Balances (Expired)						-79,957,124.12				-22,877,931.45	-57,079,192.67
Accounts Payable						-92,324,917.52				3,426,109.32	-95,751,026.84
Undelivered Orders						-4,808,508.42				9,653,080.79	-14,461,589.21
Subtotal		57		3700		-0-	1,339,225,000.00	-48,000,000.00	1,288,677,310.16	2,547,689.84	-0-

Footnotes At End Of Chapter

Appropriations, Outlays, and Balances – Continued

Appropriation or Fund Account — Title	Period of Availability	Dept Reg	Tr From	Account Number	Sub No.	Balances, Beginning Of Fiscal Year	Appropriations And Other Obligational Authority[1]	Transfers Borrowings And Investment (Net)[2]	Outlays (Net)	Balances Withdrawn And Other Transactions[3]	Balances, End Of Fiscal Year[4]
National Guard Personnel, Air Force											
Fund Resources:											
Undisbursed Funds	2007	57		3850			2,470,852,000.00	86,300,000.00	[7]2,435,915,331.58		121,236,668.42
	2006					160,067,525.25			65,841,030.77		94,226,494.48
	2005					36,944,771.36			2,011,936.60		34,932,834.76
	2004					31,717,275.38			63,191.93		31,654,083.45
	2003					23,279,741.61			-284,886.89		23,564,628.50
	2002					72,753,945.11			24,330,152.27	48,423,792.84	
Accounts Receivable						405,331.97				-2,463,084.61	2,868,416.58
Unfilled Customer Orders						3,489.20				-33,802.32	37,291.52
Fund Equities:											
Unobligated Balances (Expired)						-205,337,706.35				-41,403,339.69	-163,934,366.66
Accounts Payable						-113,800,774.17				23,503,972.56	-137,304,746.73
Undelivered Orders						-6,033,599.36				1,247,704.96	-7,281,304.32
	Subtotal	57		3850		-0-	2,470,852,000.00	86,300,000.00	2,527,876,756.26	-29,275,243.74	-0-
Total, Military Personnel, Air Force							31,788,750,000.00	445,581,000.00	30,756,824,799.67	1,477,506,200.33	
Defense Agencies											
General Fund Accounts											
Concurrent Receipt Accrual Payments To The Military Retirement Fund, Defense											
Fund Resources:											
Undisbursed Funds	2007	97		0041			2,452,000,000.00		2,452,000,000.00		
Total, Military Personnel, Defense Agencies							2,452,000,000.00		2,452,000,000.00		
Total, Military Personnel							131,755,959,800.00	951,499,000.00	128,826,974,859.25	3,880,483,940.75	
Operation And Maintenance											
Department Of The Army											
General Fund Accounts											
Operation And Maintenance, Army											
Fund Resources:											
Undisbursed Funds	2006-2008	21		2020		198,000,000.00			91,532,266.38		106,467,733.62
	2007						72,169,691,588.00	402,751,000.00	[8]45,398,139,286.98		27,174,303,301.02
	2006-2007							600,000.00	467,291.03		132,708.97
	2006					20,848,003,930.33			[9]16,810,363,903.92		4,037,640,026.41
	2005-2006					484,928.72			420,595.10		64,333.62
	2005					2,600,801,375.38		-6,000,000.00	1,448,408,118.43		1,146,393,256.95
	2004-2005					967,793,205.16			445,565,435.14		522,227,770.02
	2004					2,019,431,178.32			368,594,742.58		1,650,836,435.74
	2003					1,001,432,010.01			126,857,639.56		874,574,370.45
	2002-2003					5,042,575.02			484,291.32		4,558,283.70

Appropriations, Outlays, and Balances - Continued

Title	Period of Availability	Reg	Tr From	Account Number	Sub No.	Balances, Beginning Of Fiscal Year	Appropriations And Other Obligational Authority[1]	Transfers Borrowings And Investment (Net)[2]	Outlays (Net)	Balances Withdrawn And Other Transactions[3]	Balances, End Of Fiscal Year[4]
	2002					317,111,687.03			73,458,148.38	243,653,538.65	
	2000-2002					6,200.00				6,200.00	
	No Year					496,295,279.01	80,180,000.00		27,795,562.96		548,679,716.05
Transfer To:											
Federal Highway Administration	2007	69	21	2020	5			100,000.00	-505.39		100,505.39
	2004					171,107.69			139,537.18		31,570.51
	2003					1,478,239.61			1,407,650.61		70,589.00
	No Year					12,091,280.09			9,712,477.10		2,378,802.99
Fund Equities:											
Accounts Receivable						1,099,986,316.65				-142,019,772.36	1,242,006,089.01
Unfilled Customer Orders						4,987,240,061.86				-1,374,801,126.46	6,362,041,188.32
Fund Equities:											
Unobligated Balances (Expired)						-1,134,972,745.01				570,696,895.67	-1,705,669,640.68
Unobligated Balances (Unexpired)						-384,642,492.47				-134,160,413.66	-250,482,078.81
Accounts Payable						-7,279,413,701.01				-1,757,305,389.43	-5,522,108,311.58
Undelivered Orders						-25,756,340,436.39				10,437,906,214.31	-36,194,246,650.70
Subtotal		21		2020		-0-	72,249,871,588.00	397,451,000.00	64,803,346,441.28	7,843,976,146.72	-0-
Operation And Maintenance, Army National Guard											
Fund Resources:											
Undisbursed Funds	2007	21		2065		42,307,000.00	5,736,680,000.00	122,900,000.00	3,933,079,595.68		1,926,500,404.32
	2006-2007					1,679,598,266.64			12,796,032.10		29,510,967.90
	2006					305,389,020.70			1,373,175,169.16		306,423,097.48
	2005					184,511,708.03		-5,000,000.00	151,643,183.13		148,745,837.57
	2004					96,843,459.91			34,551,095.29		149,960,612.74
	2003					80,527,176.41			12,579,734.36		84,263,725.55
	2002								7,376,208.54	73,150,967.87	
	No Year					518,513.24					518,513.24
Transfer To:											
Federal Highway Administration	No Year	69	21	2065	5	274,839.00			119,930.00		154,909.00
Accounts Receivable						3,423,075.08				195,677.54	3,227,397.54
Unfilled Customer Orders						1,054,200.14				2,514,002.96	-1,459,802.82
Fund Equities:											
Unobligated Balances (Expired)						-284,969,604.00				4,385,454.62	-289,355,058.62
Unobligated Balances (Unexpired)						-9,076,810.16				-8,493,000.00	-583,810.16
Accounts Payable						-1,175,929,550.38				129,755,382.55	-1,305,684,932.93
Undelivered Orders						-924,471,294.61				127,750,566.20	-1,052,221,860.81
Subtotal		21		2065		-0-	5,736,680,000.00	117,900,000.00	5,525,320,948.26	329,259,051.74	-0-
Operation And Maintenance, Army Reserve											
Fund Resources:											
Undisbursed Funds	2007	21		2080		741,462,794.88	2,450,589,000.00		[10]1,499,143,558.44		951,445,441.56
	2006					96,232,532.95			[11]589,916,221.72		151,546,573.16
	2005					69,329,192.02		-10,325,000.00	38,419,591.61		47,487,941.34
	2004					43,126,255.22			10,465,067.08		58,864,124.94
	2003					25,871,822.70			5,882,224.58		37,244,030.64
	2002					93,570.14			-1,038,479.12		93,570.14
	No Year										
Accounts Receivable						21,042,310.12				9,618,317.48	11,423,992.64
Unfilled Customer Orders						9,676,364.12				1,554,930.17	8,121,433.95

Appropriations, Outlays, and Balances – Continued

Appropriation or Fund Account — Title	Period of Availability	Reg	Tr From	Account Number	Sub No.	Balances, Beginning Of Fiscal Year	Appropriations And Other Obligational Authority[1]	Transfers Borrowings And Investment (Net)[2]	Outlays (Net)	Balances Withdrawn And Other Transactions[3]	Balances, End Of Fiscal Year[4]
Operation And Maintenance, Army Reserve - Continued											
Fund Equities:											
Unobligated Balances (Expired)						-127,465,623.49				6,242,092.31	-133,707,715.80
Unobligated Balances (Unexpired)						-93,570.14					-93,570.14
Accounts Payable						-268,968,220.22				-35,819,479.72	-233,148,740.50
Undelivered Orders						-610,307,428.30				288,969,653.63	-899,277,081.93
Subtotal		21		2080		-0-	2,450,589,000.00	-10,325,000.00	2,142,788,184.31	297,475,815.69	-0-
Afghanistan Security Forces Fund, Army											
Fund Resources:											
Undisbursed Funds	2007-2008	21		2091		1,030,075,325.00	7,406,400,000.00		2,359,309,555.00		5,047,090,445.00
	2006-2007					32,165,994.00			1,030,075,323.00		2.00
	2005-2006								32,165,229.00		765.00
Fund Equities:											
Unobligated Balances (Expired)						-765.00				1.00	-766.00
Unobligated Balances (Unexpired)						-1,021,685,853.00				3,765,377,168.00	-4,787,063,021.00
Accounts Payable						829,061,916.00				1,089,089,341.00	-260,027,425.00
Undelivered Orders						-869,616,617.00				-869,616,617.00	-0-
Subtotal		21		2091		-0-	7,406,400,000.00		3,421,550,107.00	3,984,849,893.00	-0-
Iraq Security Forces Fund, Army											
Fund Resources:											
Undisbursed Funds	2007-2008	21		2092		2,997,515,500.57	5,542,300,000.00		872,843,974.87		4,669,456,025.13
	2006-2007					1,846,879,209.54			1,377,759,079.70		1,619,756,420.87
	2005-2006								1,569,491,334.03		277,387,875.51
Fund Equities:											
Unobligated Balances (Expired)						-139.82				56,987,615.40	-56,987,755.22
Unobligated Balances (Unexpired)						-2,273,903,827.47				1,509,160,058.59	-3,783,063,886.06
Accounts Payable						-173,816,611.05				-135,122,347.26	-38,694,263.79
Undelivered Orders						-2,396,674,131.77				291,180,284.67	-2,687,854,416.44
Subtotal		21		2092		-0-	5,542,300,000.00		3,820,094,388.60	1,722,205,611.40	-0-
Joint Improvised Explosive Device Defeat Fund, Army											
Fund Resources:											
Undisbursed Funds	2007-2009	21		2093			4,392,500,000.00		790,110,219.45		3,602,389,780.55
Fund Equities:											
Unobligated Balances (Unexpired)										1,170,922,584.30	-1,170,922,584.30
Accounts Payable										1,125,501,325.93	-1,125,501,325.93
Undelivered Orders										1,305,965,870.32	-1,305,965,870.32
Subtotal		21		2093		-0-	4,392,500,000.00		790,110,219.45	3,602,389,780.55	-0-
Special Fund Accounts											
Restoration, Rocky Mountain Arsenal, Army											
Fund Resources:											
Undisbursed Funds	No Year	21		5098		33,373,884.09	7,436,154.28		2,479,332.90		38,330,705.47
Fund Equities:											
Unobligated Balances (Unexpired)						-11,571,105.67				12,966,817.61	-24,537,923.28
Accounts Payable						-2,128,267.15				-2,589,636.80	461,369.65
Undelivered Orders						-19,674,511.27				-5,420,359.43	-14,254,151.84
Subtotal		21		5098		-0-	7,436,154.28		2,479,332.90	4,956,821.38	-0-

Appropriations, Outlays, and Balances - Continued

Appropriation or Fund Account — Title	Period of Availability	Dept Reg	Tr From	Account Number	Sub No.	Balances, Beginning Of Fiscal Year	Appropriations And Other Obligational Authority[1]	Transfers Borrowings And Investment (Net)[2]	Outlays (Net)	Balances Withdrawn And Other Transactions[3]	Balances, End Of Fiscal Year[4]
Department Of Defense, 50th Anniversary Of World War II, Commemoration Account, Army											
Fund Resources:											
Undisbursed Funds	No Year	21		5194		53,641.57					53,641.57
Fund Equities:											
Unobligated Balances (Unexpired)						-4,386.26					-4,386.26
Accounts Payable						-49,255.31					-49,255.31
Subtotal		21		5194		-0-					-0-
National Science Center, Army											
Fund Resources:											
Undisbursed Funds	No Year	21		5286		70,032.04	10,270.00		-69.45		80,371.49
Fund Equities:											
Unobligated Balances (Unexpired)						-67,177.88				10,270.00	-77,447.88
Accounts Payable						-2,854.16				69.45	-2,923.61
Subtotal		21		5286		-0-	10,270.00		-69.45	10,339.45	-0-
Total, Operation And Maintenance, Army							97,785,787,012.28	505,026,000.00	80,505,689,552.35	17,785,123,459.93	
Department Of The Navy											
General Fund Accounts											
Environmental Restoration, Navy											
Fund Resources:											
Undisbursed Funds	No Year	17		0810		344.00			-1,186,283.74	1,186,283.74	1,186,627.74
Accounts Receivable											-1,186,283.74
Fund Equities:											
Unobligated Balances (Unexpired)						-344.00					-344.00
Subtotal		17		0810		-0-			-1,186,283.74	1,186,283.74	-0-
Operation And Maintenance, Marine Corps											
Fund Resources:											
Undisbursed Funds	2007	17		1106		2,941,730,095.01	7,609,923,000.00		4,485,242,514.17		3,124,680,485.83
	2006					386,930,713.64			2,348,681,485.38		593,048,609.63
	2005					11,954,828.93		-50,800,000.00	198,719,129.33		137,411,584.31
	2004-2005					128,760,789.91			7,914,662.51		4,040,166.42
	2004					87,506,845.89			21,116,931.77		107,643,858.14
	2003					29,335,855.79			10,101,232.10		77,405,613.79
	2002					193,954.26			3,116,592.87		193,208.78
	No Year								745.48	26,219,262.92	
Accounts Receivable						54,452,549.66				-14,102,707.22	68,555,256.88
Unfilled Customer Orders						[12]141,648,296.85				69,538,472.66	72,109,824.19
Fund Equities:											
Unobligated Balances (Expired)						[12]-169,429,015.61				44,884,125.16	-214,313,140.77
Unobligated Balances (Unexpired)						-121,419.73					-121,419.73
Accounts Payable						-196,052,610.50				293,156,296.24	-489,208,906.74
Undelivered Orders						-3,416,910,884.10				64,534,256.63	-3,481,445,140.73
Subtotal		17		1106		-0-	7,609,923,000.00	-50,800,000.00	7,074,893,293.61	484,229,706.39	-0-

Footnotes At End Of Chapter

Appropriations, Outlays, and Balances – Continued

Appropriation or Fund Account Title	Reg	Tr From	Account Number	Sub No.	Period of Availability	Balances, Beginning Of Fiscal Year	Appropriations And Other Obligational Authority[1]	Transfers Borrowings And Investment (Net)[2]	Outlays (Net)	Balances Withdrawn And Other Transactions[3]	Balances, End Of Fiscal Year[4]
Operation And Maintenance, Marine Corps Reserve											
Fund Resources:											
Undisbursed Funds	17		1107		2007	188,534,163.19	269,856,000.00		146,529,714.41		123,326,285.59
					2006	25,168,476.84			112,852,327.57		75,681,835.62
					2005	9,980,533.62		-3,200,000.00	12,235,781.33		9,732,695.51
					2004	6,596,889.52			511,269.08		9,469,264.54
					2003	2,094,914.99			-38,994.18		6,635,883.70
					2002	587,400.59			416,026.28	1,678,888.71	
Accounts Receivable						717,736.81				109,875.65	477,524.94
Unfilled Customer Orders										-670,211.96	1,387,948.77
Fund Equities:											
Unobligated Balances (Expired)						-30,980,383.06				1,406,061.29	-32,386,444.35
Accounts Payable						-8,870,674.95				6,835,194.46	-15,705,869.41
Undelivered Orders						-193,829,057.55				-15,209,932.64	-178,619,124.91
Subtotal	17		1107			-0-	269,856,000.00	-3,200,000.00	272,506,124.49	-5,850,124.49	-0-
Payments To Kahoʻolawe Island Conveyance, Remediation, And Environmental Restoration Fund, Navy											
Fund Resources:											
Undisbursed Funds	17		1236		No Year	238,771.02					238,771.02
Fund Equities:											
Unobligated Balances (Unexpired)						-192,873.70				-0.01	-192,873.69
Accounts Payable						-120.55					-120.55
Undelivered Orders						-45,776.77				0.01	-45,776.78
Subtotal	17		1236			-0-					-0-
Operation And Maintenance, Navy											
Fund Resources:											
Undisbursed Funds	17		1804		2007	29,913,000.00	37,359,120,344.00	46,179,000.00	26,815,741,817.42		10,589,557,526.58
					2006-2007	9,448,863,141.28			10,263,315.07		19,649,684.93
					2006	1,991,556,120.87			7,135,922,748.02		2,312,940,393.26
					2005	27,175,368.68		-170,000,000.00	846,796,594.61		974,759,526.26
					2004-2005	890,892,198.94			16,094,894.55		11,080,474.13
					2004	5,082.77			127,303,302.44		763,588,896.50
					2003-2004	800,143,078.84			5,082.77		
					2003	2,100,532.56			77,551,020.61		722,592,058.23
					2002-2003	411,884,313.21			-21,054.22	393,322,543.50	2,121,586.78
					2002	1,225,953.76			18,561,769.71	1,225,953.76	
					2001-2002	19,407,587.08					76,502,405.95
					No Year	89,429,535.92	57,125,000.00		30,181.13		341,881,342.70
Accounts Receivable						1,414,647,336.03				-252,451,806.78	1,173,420,039.47
Unfilled Customer Orders										241,227,296.56	
Fund Equities:											
Unobligated Balances (Expired)						-825,643,706.06				147,619,270.56	-973,262,976.62
Unobligated Balances (Unexpired)						-43,158,142.24				28,509,732.42	-71,667,874.66
Accounts Payable						-923,202,530.35				274,445,678.19	-1,197,648,208.54
Undelivered Orders						-13,335,238,871.29				1,410,276,003.68	-14,745,514,874.97
Subtotal	17		1804			-0-	37,416,245,344.00	-123,821,000.00	35,048,249,672.11	2,244,174,671.89	-0-
Operation And Maintenance, Navy Reserve											
Fund Resources:											
Undisbursed Funds	17		1806		2007		1,400,511,000.00		935,133,337.43		465,377,662.57

Appropriations, Outlays, and Balances - Continued

Appropriation or Fund Account — Title	Period of Availability	Dept Reg	Dept Tr From	Account Number	Sub No.	Balances, Beginning Of Fiscal Year	Appropriations And Other Obligational Authority[1]	Transfers Borrowings And Investment (Net)[2]	Outlays (Net)	Balances Withdrawn And Other Transactions[3]	Balances, End Of Fiscal Year[4]
	2006-2007					12,755,000.00			1,867,942.32		10,887,057.68
	2006					539,795,503.40			352,711,642.61		187,083,860.79
	2005					113,479,419.07		-14,400,000.00	29,855,256.37		69,224,162.70
	2004					49,466,758.88			[13]5,356,066.85		44,110,692.03
	2003					52,196,943.79			526,347.97		51,670,595.82
	2002					30,148,579.73			354,732.19	29,793,847.54	
Accounts Receivable						2,199,665.18				-764,904.80	2,964,569.98
Unfilled Customer Orders						6,894,029.38				-442,760.79	7,336,790.17
Fund Equities:											
Unobligated Balances (Expired)						-121,988,514.55				43,292,922.95	-165,281,437.50
Unobligated Balances (Unexpired)						-12,755,000.00				-12,755,000.00	
Accounts Payable						-54,298,463.46				3,036,717.35	-57,335,180.81
Undelivered Orders						-617,893,911.42				-1,855,147.99	-616,038,763.43
Subtotal		17		1806		-0-	1,400,511,000.00	-14,400,000.00	1,325,805,325.74	60,305,674.26	-0-

Special Fund Accounts

Kaho'olawe Island Conveyance, Remediation, And Environmental Restoration Fund, Navy

Title	Period of Availability	Dept Reg	Dept Tr From	Account Number	Sub No.	Balances, Beginning Of Fiscal Year	Appropriations And Other Obligational Authority[1]	Transfers Borrowings And Investment (Net)[2]	Outlays (Net)	Balances Withdrawn And Other Transactions[3]	Balances, End Of Fiscal Year[4]
Fund Resources:											
Undisbursed Funds	No Year	17		5185		1,115,385.32			8,168.91		1,107,216.41
Fund Equities:											
Unobligated Balances (Unexpired)						-374,408.06				-333,149.29	-41,258.77
Accounts Payable						-1,019.35					-1,019.35
Undelivered Orders						-739,957.91				324,980.38	-1,064,938.29
Subtotal		17		5185		-0-			8,168.91	-8,168.91	-0-
Total, Operation And Maintenance, Navy							46,696,535,344.00	-192,221,000.00	43,720,276,301.12	2,784,038,042.88	

Department Of The Air Force

General Fund Accounts

Title	Period of Availability	Dept Reg	Dept Tr From	Account Number	Sub No.	Balances, Beginning Of Fiscal Year	Appropriations And Other Obligational Authority[1]	Transfers Borrowings And Investment (Net)[2]	Outlays (Net)	Balances Withdrawn And Other Transactions[3]	Balances, End Of Fiscal Year[4]
Environmental Restoration, Air Force											
Fund Resources:											
Undisbursed Funds	No Year	57		0810		218,250.00					218,250.00
Fund Equities:											
Unobligated Balances (Unexpired)						-218,250.00					-218,250.00
Subtotal		57		0810		-0-					-0-
Operation And Maintenance, Air Force											
Fund Resources:											
Undisbursed Funds	2007	57		3400			40,266,974,835.00	61,051,000.00	[14]27,407,138,095.17		12,920,887,739.83
	2006-2007					37,359,000.00			5,202,644.39		32,156,355.61
	2006					11,792,364,827.24			[15]9,066,762,989.45		2,725,601,837.79
	2005					2,153,609,511.70		-140,000,000.00	1,156,669,047.82		856,940,463.88
	2004-2005					66,441,156.93			25,295,630.21		41,145,526.72
	2004					947,210,207.31			272,589,648.29		674,620,559.02
	2003					957,768,099.85			[16]147,691,921.70		810,076,178.15
	2002-2003					2,616,746.45			269,311.54		2,347,434.91

Footnotes At End Of Chapter

Appropriations, Outlays, and Balances – Continued

Appropriation or Fund Account Title	Period of Availability	Reg	Tr From	Account Number	Sub No.	Balances, Beginning Of Fiscal Year	Appropriations And Other Obligational Authority[1]	Transfers Borrowings And Investment (Net)[2]	Outlays (Net)	Balances Withdrawn And Other Transactions[3]	Balances, End Of Fiscal Year[4]
Operation And Maintenance, Air Force - Continued											
Fund Resources: - Continued											
Undisbursed Funds - Continued											
	2002					398,534,110.12			[1]753,141,547.31	345,645,646.75	
	No Year					3,128,137.79	157,100.00	253,083.94	568,213.57		2,717,024.22
Transfer To:											
Department Of Transportation, Federal Highway Administration											
	2007	69	57	3400	5	2,846,197.70	9,408,000.00		3,608,136.12		5,799,863.88
	2006					756,549.40			2,218,993.01		627,204.69
	2005					421,796.47			208,391.11		548,158.29
	2004					332,715.39			9,713.77		412,082.70
	2003					253,083.94					332,715.39
	2002					253,083.94		-253,083.94			
Accounts Receivable						998,307,608.76				361,589,310.71	636,718,298.05
Unfilled Customer Orders						363,985,472.37				-173,389,842.89	537,375,315.26
Fund Equities:											
Unobligated Balances (Expired)						-925,022,513.81				297,668,035.87	-1,222,690,549.68
Unobligated Balances (Unexpired)						-39,636,255.32				-37,573,087.77	-2,063,167.55
Accounts Payable						-2,137,745,171.52				275,828,700.59	-2,413,573,872.11
Undelivered Orders						-14,623,531,280.77				986,447,888.28	-15,609,979,169.05
	Subtotal	57		3400		-0-	40,267,131,935.00	-69,541,000.00	38,141,374,283.46	2,056,216,651.54	-0-
Operation And Maintenance, Air Force Reserve											
Fund Resources:											
Undisbursed Funds:											
	2007	57		3740			2,723,621,000.00		[8]2,115,212,753.48		608,408,246.52
	2006-2007					998.55					998.55
	2006					461,725,226.68			355,020,982.67		106,704,244.01
	2005					89,842,053.83			28,215,102.07		61,626,951.76
	2004					31,012,115.76			10,301,147.40		20,710,968.36
	2003					28,726,132.96			5,710,858.03		23,015,274.93
	2002					20,265,285.99			561,424.98		
	No Year					193.82				19,703,861.01	193.82
Accounts Receivable						113,690,412.09				60,426,304.65	53,264,107.44
Unfilled Customer Orders						2,056,483.66				1,892,041.58	164,442.08
Fund Equities:											
Unobligated Balances (Expired)						-79,278,580.80				14,192,821.41	-93,471,402.21
Unobligated Balances (Unexpired)						-1,192.37				-998.55	-193.82
Accounts Payable						-104,520,196.42				-26,550,959.58	-77,969,236.84
Undelivered Orders						-563,518,933.75				138,935,660.85	-702,454,594.60
	Subtotal	57		3740		-0-	2,723,621,000.00		2,515,022,268.63	208,598,731.37	-0-
Operation And Maintenance, Air National Guard											
Fund Resources:											
Undisbursed Funds:											
	2007	57		3840			5,246,189,000.00	100,100,000.00	3,950,363,324.30		1,395,925,675.70
	2006					872,461,663.26			736,046,118.51		136,415,544.75
	2005					134,996,990.17			44,117,287.39		90,879,702.78
	2004					57,656,115.59			15,971,101.73		41,685,013.86
	2003					110,708,730.81			8,255,112.04		102,453,618.77
	2002					50,459,101.89			2,881,997.10		-0-
	No Year					14,715.99				47,577,104.79	14,715.99
Accounts Receivable						179,407,309.30				52,246,773.70	127,160,535.60
Unfilled Customer Orders						160,365.97				-2,473,606.58	2,633,972.55

Appropriations, Outlays, and Balances - Continued

Appropriation or Fund Account — Title	Dept Reg	Tr From	Account Number	Sub No.	Period of Availability	Balances, Beginning Of Fiscal Year	Appropriations And Other Obligational Authority[1]	Transfers Borrowings And Investment (Net)[2]	Outlays (Net)	Balances Withdrawn And Other Transactions[3]	Balances, End Of Fiscal Year[4]
Fund Equities:											
Unobligated Balances (Expired)						-176,356,774.02				13,238,848.74	-189,595,622.76
Unobligated Balances (Unexpired)						-14,715.99					-14,715.99
Accounts Payable						-214,330,234.32				50,066,249.52	-264,396,483.84
Undelivered Orders						-1,015,163,268.65				427,998,688.76	-1,443,161,957.41
						-0-					-0-
Total, Operation And Maintenance, Air Force	57		3840		Subtotal	-0-	5,246,189,000.00	100,100,000.00	4,757,634,941.07	588,664,058.93	-0-
							48,236,941,935.00	30,559,000.00	45,414,031,493.16	2,853,469,441.84	
Defense Agencies											
General Fund Accounts											
Operation And Maintenance, Defense-Wide											
Fund Resources:											
Undisbursed Funds	97		0100		2007		24,787,546,000.00	24,306,000.00	[1]16,850,498,074.99		7,961,353,925.01
					2006-2007	911,160,000.00		-687,200,000.00			223,960,000.00
					2006	6,653,540,819.54			5,517,184,043.75		1,136,356,775.79
					2005	1,037,926,286.25		-31,450,000.00	430,876,744.54		575,599,541.71
					2004-2005	36,356,559.15			8,728,358.39		27,628,200.76
					2004	614,721,313.35			78,086,794.75		536,634,518.60
					2003	453,675,833.98			22,359,035.39		431,316,798.59
					2002-2003	23,117,407.68			7,380,537.50		15,736,870.18
					2000-2003	4,936,261.78			3,985,038.83		951,222.95
					2002	210,220,055.13			-6,701,041.54	216,921,096.67	
					2001-2002	924,209.21			46,467.47	877,741.74	
					No Year	1,006,319,279.87		-400,000.00	1,393,557,961.76		548,561,318.11
Accounts Receivable						182,578,886.55				-21,378,028.32	203,956,914.87
Unfilled Customer Orders						454,618,725.87				90,227,068.62	364,391,657.25
Fund Equities:											
Unobligated Balances (Expired)						-797,499,152.11				439,078,881.48	-1,236,578,033.59
Unobligated Balances (Unexpired)						-1,752,693,531.56				-1,216,241,552.90	-536,451,978.66
Accounts Payable						-1,647,211,744.00				336,741,282.71	-1,983,953,026.71
Undelivered Orders						-7,392,691,210.69				876,773,494.17	-8,269,464,704.86
	97		0100		Subtotal	-0-	25,723,746,000.00	-694,744,000.00	24,306,002,015.83	722,999,984.17	-0-
United States Court Of Appeals For The Armed Forces, Defense											
Fund Resources:											
Undisbursed Funds	97		0104		2007		11,673,000.00		9,142,582.05		2,530,417.95
					2006	1,251,227.02			972,843.70		278,383.32
					2005	1,070,910.49			-32,850.38		1,103,760.87
					2004	556,025.00			-34,246.87		590,271.87
					2003	519,084.14			197,341.06		321,743.08
					2002	131,908.95				131,908.95	
Fund Equities:											
Unobligated Balances (Expired)						-518,646.39				-31,598.14	-487,048.25
Accounts Payable						-257,944.09				3,057.08	-261,001.17
Undelivered Orders						-2,752,565.12				1,323,962.55	-4,076,527.67
	97		0104		Subtotal	-0-	11,673,000.00		10,245,669.56	1,427,330.44	-0-

Footnotes At End Of Chapter

Appropriations, Outlays, and Balances – Continued

Title	Account Symbol — Reg	Tr From	Account Number	Sub No.	Period of Availability	Balances, Beginning Of Fiscal Year	Appropriations And Other Obligational Authority[1]	Transfers Borrowings And Investment (Net)[2]	Outlays (Net)	Balances Withdrawn And Other Transactions[3]	Balances, End Of Fiscal Year[4]
Drug Interdiction And Counter-Drug Activities, Defense											
Fund Resources:											
Undisbursed Funds	97		0105		No Year	63,617,000.00	115,615,000.00	-63,617,000.00			115,615,000.00
Fund Equities:											
Unobligated Balances (Unexpired)						-63,617,000.00				51,998,000.00	-115,615,000.00
Subtotal	97		0105			-0-	115,615,000.00	-63,617,000.00		51,998,000.00	-0-
Office Of The Inspector General, Defense											
Fund Resources:											
Undisbursed Funds	97		0107		2007-2009		1,395,000.00		916,422.46		478,577.54
					2006-2008	990,000.00			664,144.30		325,855.70
					2007		214,193,000.00		191,080,499.87		23,112,500.13
					2006-2007	4,310,951.73			3,784,832.88		526,118.85
					2005-2007	1,374,368.63			1,353,968.86		20,399.77
					2006	22,377,469.80			17,863,756.09		4,513,713.71
					2004-2006	62,873.02			27,815.00		35,058.02
					2005	7,549,273.46		-4,300,000.00	390,891.70		2,858,381.76
					2003-2005	2,573.00					2,573.00
					2004	2,868,107.64			-280,429.40		3,148,537.04
					2002-2004	46,273.06					46,273.06
					2003	1,225,748.77			-56,234.88		1,281,983.65
					2001-2003	111,150.78					111,150.78
					2002	1,383,250.44			-101,854.52	1,485,104.96	
					2000-2002	1,126.20				1,126.20	
Accounts Receivable						203.00					203.00
Unfilled Customer Orders						37,956.37				-161,485.84	199,442.21
Fund Equities:											
Unobligated Balances (Expired)						-10,583,625.50				499,120.78	-11,082,746.28
Unobligated Balances (Unexpired)						-4,999,763.46				-4,630,091.22	-369,672.24
Accounts Payable						-8,906,397.84				2,015,449.80	-10,921,847.64
Undelivered Orders						-17,851,539.10				-3,565,037.04	-14,286,502.06
Subtotal	97		0107			-0-	215,588,000.00	-4,300,000.00	215,643,812.36	-4,355,812.36	-0-
Overseas Contingency Operations Transfer Fund, Defense											
Fund Resources:											
Undisbursed Funds	97		0118		No Year	9,972,000.00					9,972,000.00
Fund Equities:											
Unobligated Balances (Unexpired)						-9,972,000.00					-9,972,000.00
Subtotal	97		0118			-0-					-0-
Defense Health Program, Defense											
Fund Resources:											
Undisbursed Funds	97		0130		2007-2009		497,290,000.00		32,560,351.31		464,729,648.69
					2007-2008		1,372,322,000.00		23,470,099.01		1,348,851,900.99
					2006-2008	297,252,043.89		-1,980,000.00	137,820,124.40		157,451,919.49
					2007		22,328,952,000.00	20,737,000.00	17,277,490,227.63		5,072,198,772.37
					2006-2007	518,257,614.88		353,967,000.00	514,112,521.24		358,112,093.64
					2005-2007	124,872,032.43			75,771,527.41		49,100,505.02
					2006	4,411,822,963.60		-351,987,000.00	2,871,114,433.27		1,188,721,530.33
					2005-2006	489,558,559.01			249,652,219.12		239,906,339.89
					2004-2006	48,096,860.17			32,578,816.04		15,518,044.13
					2005	938,225,809.93		-22,862,000.00	346,370,434.54		568,993,375.39

Appropriations, Outlays, and Balances - Continued

Appropriation or Fund Account	Period of Availability	Account Symbol Dept Reg	Account Symbol Dept Tr From	Account Number	Sub No.	Balances, Beginning Of Fiscal Year	Appropriations And Other Obligational Authority[1]	Transfers Borrowings And Investment (Net)[2]	Outlays (Net)	Balances Withdrawn And Other Transactions[3]	Balances, End Of Fiscal Year[4]
	2004-2005					151,856,750.50			71,321,577.42		80,535,173.08
	2003-2005					15,362,248.06			2,038,243.05		13,324,005.01
	2004					785,854,322.66			27,772,374.15		758,081,948.51
	2003-2004					161,194,404.40			28,174,881.98		133,019,522.42
	2002-2004					8,183,554.82			742,541.21		7,441,013.61
	2003					259,439,913.15			11,483,095.82		247,956,817.33
	2002-2003					28,055,167.56			13,704,286.58		14,350,880.98
	2001-2003					5,423,206.37			722,024.97		4,701,181.40
	2002					346,000,642.62			15,029,287.57	330,971,355.05	---
	2001-2002					72,219,308.02			2,264,699.83	69,954,608.19	---
	2000-2002					100,982,414.26			472,455.82	100,509,958.44	---
	No Year					10,067,642.05	2,500,000.00		4,206,758.95		8,360,883.10
Accounts Receivable						199,045,861.91				2,299,364.71	196,746,497.20
Unfilled Customer Orders						91,625,436.60				47,078,271.49	138,703,708.09
Fund Equities:											
Unobligated Balances (Expired)						-1,710,711,800.54			-373,751,813.88		-1,336,959,986.66
Unobligated Balances (Unexpired)						-599,637,481.06				968,951,957.53	-1,568,589,438.59
Accounts Payable						-811,689,950.82				174,120,119.47	-985,810,070.29
Undelivered Orders						-5,941,357,524.47				1,234,088,740.66	-7,175,446,265.13
Subtotal		97		0130		-0-	24,201,064,000.00	-2,125,000.00	21,738,872,981.32	2,460,066,018.68	-0-
Former Soviet Union Threat Reduction, Defense											
Fund Resources:											
Undisbursed Funds	2007-2009	97		0134			370,615,000.00		23,586,247.68		347,028,752.32
	2006-2008					376,821,803.30			151,660,706.41		225,161,096.89
	2005-2007					280,283,252.08			102,734,027.20		177,549,224.88
	2006					44,500,000.00			44,500,000.00		---
	2004-2006					216,776,800.64			121,012,631.42		95,764,169.22
	2003-2005					38,176,158.31			25,030,314.66		13,145,843.65
	2002-2004					24,309,277.04			14,334,643.94		9,974,633.10
	2001-2003					8,473,817.94			-590,588.41		9,064,406.35
	2000-2002					14,657,914.93			161,198.31	14,496,716.62	---
	No Year					37,581,445.73			17,567,617.22		20,013,828.51
Accounts Receivable						494,371.04				786,313.40	-291,942.36
Unfilled Customer Orders						-72,666.47				-72,666.47	---
Fund Equities:											
Unobligated Balances (Expired)						-18,678,334.04			-4,566,041.20		-14,112,292.84
Unobligated Balances (Unexpired)						-71,645,541.95				-13,193,084.04	-58,452,457.91
Accounts Payable						-16,769,309.17				22,352,921.18	-39,122,230.35
Undelivered Orders						-934,908,989.38				-149,185,957.92	-785,723,031.46
Subtotal		97		0134		-0-	370,615,000.00		499,996,798.43	-129,381,798.43	-0-
Iraq Freedom Fund, Defense											
Fund Resources:											
Undisbursed Funds	2007-2008	97		0141			230,673,000.00				230,673,000.00
	2006-2007					30,708,000.00		-30,708,000.00			---
Subtotal		97		0141		30,708,000.00	230,673,000.00	-30,708,000.00		199,965,000.00	230,673,000.00
Fund Equities:											
Unobligated Balances (Unexpired)				0141		-30,708,000.00		-30,708,000.00		199,965,000.00	-230,673,000.00
Subtotal		97		0141		-0-	230,673,000.00	-30,708,000.00		199,965,000.00	-0-

Footnotes At End Of Chapter

Appropriations, Outlays, and Balances – Continued

Appropriation or Fund Account — Title	Period of Availability	Dept Reg	Tr From	Account Number	Sub No.	Balances, Beginning Of Fiscal Year	Appropriations And Other Obligational Authority[1]	Transfers Borrowings And Investment (Net)[2]	Outlays (Net)	Balances Withdrawn And Other Transactions[3]	Balances, End Of Fiscal Year[4]
Foreign Currency Fluctuations, Defense											
Fund Resources:											
Undisbursed Funds	No Year	97		0801		898,598,000.00		-255,041,000.00			643,557,000.00
Fund Equities:											
Unobligated Balances (Unexpired)						-898,598,000.00				-255,041,000.00	-643,557,000.00
Subtotal		97		0801		-0-		-255,041,000.00		-255,041,000.00	-0-
Environmental Restoration, Defense											
Fund Resources:											
Undisbursed Funds	No Year	97		0810		2,658,820.58	6,226,985.00	-180,000.00			8,705,805.58
Fund Equities:											
Unobligated Balances (Unexpired)						-2,658,820.58				6,046,985.00	-8,705,805.58
Subtotal		97		0810		-0-	6,226,985.00	-180,000.00		6,046,985.00	-0-
Environmental Restoration, Formerly Used Defense Sites, Defense											
Fund Resources:											
Undisbursed Funds	No Year	97		0811		9,010,629.12	7,500,000.00	-9,010,000.00	-386,011.50		7,886,640.62
Fund Equities:											
Unobligated Balances (Unexpired)						-9,010,629.12				-1,123,988.50	-7,886,640.62
Subtotal		97		0811		-0-	7,500,000.00	-9,010,000.00	-386,011.50	-1,123,988.50	-0-
Overseas Humanitarian, Disaster, And Civic Aid, Defense											
Fund Resources:											
Undisbursed Funds	2007-2008	97		0819		71,199,534.52	62,947,000.00		2,605,549.75		60,341,450.25
	2006-2007					48,019,379.19			18,813,134.13		52,386,400.39
	2005-2006					8,540,310.78			25,380,309.44		22,639,069.75
	2004-2005					24,707,542.47			1,143,708.57		7,396,602.21
	2004					12,653,390.23			1,291,294.21		23,416,248.26
	2003-2004					4,117,407.47			160,409.89		12,492,980.34
	2002-2003					4,292,317.17			6,095.31		4,111,312.16
	2001-2002					346,948.41			-47,291.94		346,948.41
	No Year					-20,930.78				-6,256.35	-14,674.43
Accounts Receivable										4,339,609.11	
Fund Equities:											
Unobligated Balances (Expired)						-22,568,753.07				2,786,528.77	-25,355,281.84
Unobligated Balances (Unexpired)						-55,519,044.50				-7,000,070.96	-48,518,973.54
Accounts Payable						-26,285,852.48				-1,005,270.77	-25,280,581.71
Undelivered Orders						-69,482,249.41				14,479,250.84	-83,961,500.25
Subtotal		97		0819		-0-	62,947,000.00		49,353,209.36	13,593,790.64	-0-
Defense Emergency Response Fund, Defense											
Fund Resources:											
Undisbursed Funds	2002-2003	97		0833		89,700,000.00					89,700,000.00
	No Year					322,568,064.81			44,237,247.69		278,330,817.12
Accounts Receivable						-449.33				693,650.42	-694,099.75
Fund Equities:											
Unobligated Balances (Expired)						-89,700,000.00					-89,700,000.00
Unobligated Balances (Unexpired)						-122,580,086.81				20,009,691.29	-142,589,778.10
Accounts Payable						-14,084,934.79				-3,852,424.65	-10,232,510.14
Undelivered Orders						-185,902,593.88				-61,088,164.75	-124,814,429.13
Subtotal		97		0833		-0-			44,237,247.69	-44,237,247.69	-0-

Appropriations, Outlays, and Balances - Continued

Appropriation or Fund Account: Title	Period of Availability	Dept Reg	Tr From	Account Number	Sub No.	Balances, Beginning Of Fiscal Year	Appropriations And Other Obligational Authority[1]	Transfers Borrowings And Investment (Net)[2]	Outlays (Net)	Balances Withdrawn And Other Transactions[3]	Balances, End Of Fiscal Year[4]
Support For International Sporting Competitions, Defense											
Fund Resources:											
Undisbursed Funds	No Year	97		0838		26,484,464.16			4,503,801.85		21,980,662.31
Fund Equities:											
Unobligated Balances (Unexpired)						-21,777,069.71				-384,190.17	-21,392,879.54
Accounts Payable						-711.68				-103,553.81	102,842.13
Undelivered Orders						-4,706,682.77				-4,016,057.87	-690,624.90
	Subtotal	97		0838		-0-			4,503,801.85	-4,503,801.85	-0-
Quality Of Life Enhancements, Defense											
Fund Resources:											
Undisbursed Funds	2002-2003	97		0839		1,460.80					1,460.80
	2001-2002					2,900,429.79			349,122.38	2,551,307.41	
Fund Equities:											
Unobligated Balances (Expired)						-2,423,424.38				-2,423,424.38	
Accounts Payable						-403,999.17				-403,999.17	
Undelivered Orders						-74,467.04				-73,006.24	-1,460.80
	Subtotal	97		0839		-0-			349,122.38	-349,122.38	-0-
OPLAN 34A/35 P.O.W. Payments											
Fund Resources:											
Undisbursed Funds	No Year	97		0840		1,021,484.90				1,021,484.90	
Fund Equities:											
Unobligated Balances (Unexpired)						-1,021,324.44				-1,021,324.44	
Accounts Payable						-160.46				-160.46	
	Subtotal	97		0840		-0-					-0-
Special Fund Accounts											
Defense Cooperation Account, Defense											
Fund Resources:											
Undisbursed Funds	No Year	97		5187			336,774.57	-336,774.57			6,405,972.72
Investments In Public Debt Securities						6,069,198.15		336,774.57			
Fund Equities:											
Unobligated Balances (Unexpired)						-6,069,198.15				336,774.57	-6,405,972.72
Accounts Payable											
	Subtotal	97		5187		-0-	336,774.57			336,774.57	-0-
Disposal Of Department Of Defense Real Property											
Fund Resources:											
Undisbursed Funds	No Year	97		5188		16,616,716.86	15,654,840.98		2,386,801.25		29,884,756.59
Fund Equities:											
Unobligated Balances (Unexpired)						-12,793,417.73				16,101,100.19	-28,894,517.92
Accounts Payable						-2,398,840.12				-2,277,500.05	-121,340.07
Undelivered Orders						-1,424,459.01				-555,560.41	-868,898.60
	Subtotal	97		5188		-0-	15,654,840.98		2,386,801.25	13,268,039.73	-0-
Lease Of Department Of Defense Real Property											
Fund Resources:											
Undisbursed Funds	No Year	97		5189		28,165,177.94	22,839,225.95		8,141,697.31		42,862,706.58
Accounts Receivable						-1,201,225.39					-1,201,225.39

Footnotes At End Of Chapter

Appropriations, Outlays, and Balances – Continued

Appropriation or Fund Account — Title	Period of Availability	Dept Reg	Tr From	Account Number	Sub No.	Balances, Beginning Of Fiscal Year	Appropriations And Other Obligational Authority[1]	Transfers Borrowings And Investment (Net)[2]	Outlays (Net)	Balances Withdrawn And Other Transactions[3]	Balances, End Of Fiscal Year[4]
Lease Of Department Of Defense Real Property - Continued											
Fund Equities:											
Unobligated Balances (Unexpired)						-19,834,262.67				15,322,292.02	-35,156,554.69
Accounts Payable						-1,205,071.54				-74,456.84	-1,130,614.70
Undelivered Orders						-5,924,618.34				-550,306.54	-5,374,311.80
Subtotal		97		5189		-0-	22,839,225.95		8,141,697.31	14,697,528.64	-0-
Department Of Defense Overseas Military Facility Investment Recovery Account											
Fund Resources:											
Undisbursed Funds	No Year	97		5193		15,946,161.20			913,111.21		15,033,049.99
Fund Equities:											
Unobligated Balances (Unexpired)						-9,313,842.98				-6,001,000.89	-3,312,842.09
Accounts Payable						-1,291,046.45				99,624.97	-1,390,671.42
Undelivered Orders						-5,341,271.77				4,988,264.71	-10,329,536.48
Subtotal		97		5193		-0-			913,111.21	-913,111.21	-0-
Use Of Proceeds From The Transfer Or Disposition Of Commissary Facilities, Defense											
Fund Resources:											
Undisbursed Funds	No Year	97		5195		20,938.88					20,938.88
Fund Equities:											
Unobligated Balances (Unexpired)						-20,938.88					-20,938.88
Subtotal		97		5195		-0-					-0-
Use Of Proceeds From Cash Equalization Payments From Acquisition Of Facilities											
Fund Resources:											
Undisbursed Funds	No Year	97		5394		17,861,537.00			12,705,772.61		5,155,764.39
Fund Equities:											
Undelivered Orders						-17,861,537.00				-12,705,772.61	-5,155,764.39
Subtotal		97		5394		-0-			12,705,772.61	-12,705,772.61	-0-
Burdensharing Contribution, Defense											
Fund Resources:											
Undisbursed Funds	No Year	97		5441		88,784,367.63	979,206,914.64		888,497,251.42	90,709,663.22	179,494,030.85
Fund Equities:											
Undelivered Orders						-88,784,367.63				90,709,663.22	-179,494,030.85
Subtotal		97		5441		-0-	979,206,914.64		888,497,251.42	90,709,663.22	-0-
Intragovernmental Funds											
Emergency Response Fund, Defense											
Fund Resources:											
Undisbursed Funds	No Year	97		4965		15,087,877.68			-198,272.88	-805.16	15,286,150.56
Fund Equities:											
Unobligated Balances (Unexpired)						-12,068,442.28					-12,067,637.12
Accounts Payable						-1,049,693.18					-1,049,693.18
Undelivered Orders						-1,969,742.22				199,078.04	-2,168,820.26
Subtotal		97		4965		-0-			-198,272.88	198,272.88	-0-
Total, Operation And Maintenance, Defense Agencies							51,963,685,741.14	-1,059,725,000.00	47,781,265,008.20	3,122,695,732.94	
Total, Operation And Maintenance							244,682,950,032.42	-716,361,000.00	217,421,262,354.83	26,545,326,677.59	

Appropriations, Outlays, and Balances - Continued

Appropriation or Fund Account	Account Symbol					Balances, Beginning Of Fiscal Year	Appropriations And Other Obligational Authority[1]	Transfers Borrowings And Investment (Net)[2]	Outlays (Net)	Balances Withdrawn And Other Transactions[3]	Balances, End Of Fiscal Year[4]
Title	Period of Availability	Dept Reg	Tr From	Account Number	Sub No.						
International Reconstruction And Other Assistance											
General Fund Accounts											
Iraq Relief And Reconstruction Fund, Army											
Fund Resources:											
Undisbursed Funds	No Year	21		2089		33,599,440.01					33,599,440.01
Fund Equities:											
Unobligated Balances (Unexpired)						-28,904,916.74				1,934,836.50	-30,839,753.24
Accounts Payable										209,423.41	-209,423.41
Undelivered Orders						-4,694,523.27				-2,144,259.91	-2,550,263.36
Subtotal		21		2089		-0-					-0-
Operating Expenses Of The Coalition Provisional Authority, Army											
Fund Resources:											
Undisbursed Funds	2007-2009	21		2090		22,400,088.51	35,000,000.00				35,000,000.00
	2006-2007					39,475,603.55			18,608,290.63		3,791,797.88
	2004-2005					21,427,340.42			-1,711,167.97		41,186,771.52
	No Year								13,784,286.43		7,643,053.99
Fund Equities:											
Unobligated Balances (Expired)						-920,439.71				6,215.70	-926,655.41
Unobligated Balances (Unexpired)						-32,117,087.83				3,742,459.41	-35,859,547.24
Accounts Payable						-39,256,850.84				1,487,601.74	-40,744,452.58
Undelivered Orders						-11,008,654.10				-917,685.94	-10,090,968.16
Subtotal		21		2090		-0-	35,000,000.00		30,681,409.09	4,318,590.91	-0-
Total, International Reconstruction And Other Assistance							35,000,000.00		30,681,409.09	4,318,590.91	
Procurement											
Department Of The Army											
General Fund Accounts											
Chemical Agents And Munitions Destruction, Army											
Fund Resources:											
Undisbursed Funds	2007-2008	21		0390		115,237,314.78	300,0r5,000.00		116,626,376.96		183,438,623.04
	2006-2008								3,392,466.01		111,844,828.77
	2007						972,328,000.00		641,282,022.94		331,045,977.06
	2006-2007					49,750,471.63			43,407,029.68		6,343,441.95
	2005-2007					61,159,209.02			25,600,713.40		35,558,495.62
	2006					503,938,298.49			471,401,332.54		32,536,965.95
	2005-2006					76,983,307.74			75,234,725.65		1,748,582.09
	2004-2006					36,470,812.05			18,233,875.28		18,236,936.77
	2005					19,589,157.33			3,287,180.88		16,301,976.45
	2004-2005					23,852,719.82			3,412,827.69		20,439,892.13
	2003-2005					4,762,107.62			-109,194.71		4,871,302.33
	2003-2004					29,686,557.65			2,173,973.67		27,512,583.98
	2002-2004					1,100,664.10			-269,030.22		1,369,694.32

Footnotes At End Of Chapter

175

Appropriations, Outlays, and Balances – Continued

Appropriation or Fund Account: Title	Period of Availability	Dept Reg	Dept Tr From	Account Number	Sub No.	Balances, Beginning Of Fiscal Year	Appropriations And Other Obligational Authority[1]	Transfers Borrowings And Investment (Net)[2]	Outlays (Net)	Balances Withdrawn And Other Transactions[3]	Balances, End Of Fiscal Year[4]
Chemical Agents And Munitions Destruction, Army - Continued											
Fund Resources: - Continued											
Undisbursed Funds - Continued	2002-2003					8,739,896.01			1,348,938.48		7,390,957.53
	2001-2003					448,993.20			-92,092.39		541,085.59
	2001-2002					13,630,676.98			52,029.97	13,578,647.01	————
	2000-2002					943,330.15			-236,388.36	1,179,718.51	1,672,627.99
	No Year					1,582,491.05			-90,136.94		
Accounts Receivable						-6,810.97				-6,535.25	-275.72
Unfilled Customer Orders						41,869.32				-4,445,626.20	4,487,495.52
Fund Equities:											
Unobligated Balances (Expired)						-18,225,980.69				24,284,756.88	-42,510,737.57
Unobligated Balances (Unexpired)						-137,886,765.00				11,589,161.77	-149,475,926.77
Accounts Payable						-26,373,207.12				-10,790,306.56	-15,582,900.56
Undelivered Orders						-765,425,113.16				-167,653,486.69	-597,771,626.47
Subtotal				0390	21	-0-	1,272,393,000.00		1,404,656,670.53	-132,263,670.53	-0-
Aircraft Procurement, Army											
Fund Resources:											
Undisbursed Funds:	2007-2009	21		2031		3,004,878,439.89	5,670,658,000.00		720,035,541.27		4,952,172,458.73
	2006-2008					1,235,871,499.01			1,673,091,922.32		1,331,786,517.57
	2005-2007					201,871,320.62		1,550,000.00	932,236,641.38		303,634,857.63
	2004-2006					130,295,376.46			105,445,352.22		96,425,968.40
	2003-2005					39,664,064.41			73,032,168.80		57,263,207.66
	2002-2004					31,324,093.94			11,533,693.05		28,130,371.36
	2001-2003					203,133.45			10,469,394.08		20,854,699.86
	2000-2002					13,301,309.02			187,161.00	7,218,388.98	15,972.45
Accounts Receivable						-698.88				-102,098.48	101,399.60
Unfilled Customer Orders						14,437,190.37			6,082,920.04	-6,704,557.29	21,141,747.66
Fund Equities:											
Unobligated Balances (Expired)						-20,699,574.20				5,107,452.21	-25,807,026.41
Unobligated Balances (Unexpired)						-637,703,634.91				940,434,155.80	-1,578,137,790.71
Accounts Payable						-83,935,436.14				-98,763,091.01	14,827,654.87
Undelivered Orders						-3,929,507,083.04				1,292,902,955.63	-5,222,410,038.67
Subtotal				2031	21	-0-	5,670,658,000.00	1,550,000.00	3,532,114,794.16	2,140,093,205.84	-0-
Missile Procurement, Army											
Fund Resources:											
Undisbursed Funds:	2007-2009	21		2032		1,244,220,457.02	1,617,302,000.00		132,546,487.96		1,484,755,512.04
	2006-2008					647,742,736.49			[20]630,946,697.72		613,273,759.30
	2005-2007					184,217,050.06			[21]411,287,730.25		236,455,006.24
	2004-2006					61,015,769.01			91,842,715.00		92,374,335.06
	2003-2005					23,068,161.20			29,124,522.18		31,891,246.83
	2002-2004					12,600,268.97			5,847,754.14		17,220,407.06
	2001-2003					18,952,625.30			1,527,123.27		11,073,145.70
	2000-2002					142.84			12,907,753.40	6,044,871.90	
Accounts Receivable										-60,664.06	60,806.90
Unfilled Customer Orders						231,179,012.66				97,567,112.74	133,611,899.92
Fund Equities:											
Unobligated Balances (Expired)						-28,750,995.41				-9,539,816.09	-19,211,179.32

Appropriations, Outlays, and Balances - Continued

Appropriation or Fund Account — Title	Period of Availability	Reg	Tr From	Account Number	Sub No.	Balances, Beginning Of Fiscal Year	Appropriations And Other Obligational Authority[1]	Transfers Borrowings And Investment (Net)[2]	Outlays (Net)	Balances Withdrawn And Other Transactions[3]	Balances, End Of Fiscal Year[4]
Unobligated Balances (Unexpired)											
Accounts Payable						-146,813,227.16				154,703,585.86	-301,516,813.02
Undelivered Orders						-94,175,164.77				-20,242,282.85	-73,932,881.92
Subtotal	Subtotal	21		2032		-2,153,256,836.21	1,617,302,000.00		1,316,030,783.92	72,798,408.58	-2,226,055,244.79
Procurement Of Weapons And Tracked Combat Vehicles, Army						-0-				301,271,216.08	-0-
Fund Resources:											
Undisbursed Funds	2007-2009	21		2033		3,692,352,686.06	8,339,683,000.00		[2]743,501,385.15		7,596,181,614.85
	2006-2008					2,133,053,894.66		-27,400,000.00	[3]1,817,612,292.83		1,847,340,393.23
	2005-2007					4,781,249.54			[4]1,664,084,116.02		468,969,778.64
	2004-2007					162,507,130.25			3,733,878.51		1,047,371.03
	2004-2006					86,240,252.16			118,936,838.85		43,570,291.40
	2003-2005					26,437,601.11			58,778,666.52		27,461,585.64
	2002-2004					27,806,438.10			10,544,008.18		15,893,592.93
	2001-2003					20,990,909.59			1,176,137.00		26,630,301.10
	2000-2002					400,946.84			6,398,087.84		313,181.56
Accounts Receivable						44,919,225.08				14,592,821.75	140,683,805.70
Unfilled Customer Orders						-24,761,648.71				87,765.28	
Fund Equities:											
Unobligated Balances (Expired)						-400,352,510.68				-95,764,580.62	-14,693,060.44
Unobligated Balances (Unexpired)						-132,592,796.94				-10,068,588.27	
Accounts Payable										736,842,284.63	-1,137,194,795.31
Undelivered Orders										4,535,991.37	-137,128,788.31
Subtotal	Subtotal	21		2033		-5,641,783,377.06	8,339,683,000.00	-27,400,000.00	4,424,765,410.90	3,237,291,894.96	-8,879,075,272.02
Procurement Of Ammunition, Army						-0-				3,887,517,589.10	-0-
Fund Resources:											
Undisbursed Funds	2007-2009	21		2034		2,479,596,717.62	2,616,821,000.00		234,595,481.99		2,382,225,518.01
	2006-2008					809,668,939.14			[2,5]1,354,474,242.44		1,125,122,475.18
	2005-2007					10,153,742.31			624,313,252.91		185,355,686.23
	2004-2007					105,060,447.13			9,396,163.34		757,578.97
	2004-2006					58,391,444.51			75,682,291.58		29,378,155.55
	2003-2005					25,745,271.20			24,241,671.48		34,149,773.03
	2002-2004					14,127,489.80			10,799,906.44		14,945,364.76
	2001-2003					9,376,599.54			4,382,687.87		9,744,801.93
Transfer To:											
Rural Business-Cooperative Service, Department Of Agriculture	2004-2006	12	21	2034	20	882,050.00			853,026.41	8,523,573.13	882,050.00
Accounts Receivable						24,121,198.97				-24,388,821.89	48,510,020.86
Unfilled Customer Orders						1,816,472,044.19				-46,920,315.55	1,863,392,359.74
Fund Equities:											
Unobligated Balances (Expired)										3,158,778.48	-24,153,332.82
Unobligated Balances (Unexpired)						-20,994,554.34				42,110,861.35	-874,725,626.93
Accounts Payable						-832,614,765.58				-53,784,196.12	-65,886,293.55
Undelivered Orders						-119,650,489.67				349,382,396.14	
Subtotal	Subtotal	21		2034		-4,380,336,134.82	2,616,821,000.00		2,338,738,724.46	278,082,275.54	-4,729,718,530.96
						-0-					-0-

Footnotes At End Of Chapter

Appropriations, Outlays, and Balances – Continued

Title	Period of Availability	Reg	Tr From	Account Number	Sub No.	Balances, Beginning Of Fiscal Year	Appropriations And Other Obligational Authority[1]	Transfers Borrowings And Investment (Net)[2]	Outlays (Net)	Balances Withdrawn And Other Transactions[3]	Balances, End Of Fiscal Year[4]
Other Procurement, Army											
Fund Resources:											
Undisbursed Funds	2007-2009	21		2035		12,528,170,481.87	24,818,117,000.00	19,198,000.00	[2]3,783,404,910.10		21,053,910,089.90
	2006-2008					3,314,828,764.58	-120,200,000.00	7,700,000.00	[2]8,132,946,513.59		4,282,723,968.28
	2005-2007					143,697,899.26			2,593,517,940.25		721,310,824.33
	2004-2007					382,939,897.20			104,267,778.82		39,430,120.44
	2004-2006					174,014,522.76			220,959,404.79		161,980,492.41
	2003-2005					84,120,940.58			68,214,549.13		105,799,973.63
	2002-2004					73,977,529.33			22,603,578.91		61,517,361.67
	2001-2003					78,783,818.88			6,525,303.18		67,452,226.15
	2000-2002								17,152,364.07	61,631,454.81	
	No Year						15,303,043.00				15,303,043.00
Accounts Receivable						6,478,259.64				27,503,869.18	-21,025,609.54
Unfilled Customer Orders						101,320,994.16				-24,028,061.46	125,349,055.62
Fund Equities:											
Unobligated Balances (Expired)						-113,459,376.54				1,960,578.95	-115,419,955.49
Unobligated Balances (Unexpired)						-3,442,653,417.79				4,566,385,145.72	-8,009,038,563.51
Accounts Payable						-2,260,168,888.32				-1,196,253,148.72	-1,063,915,739.60
Undelivered Orders						-11,072,051,425.61				6,353,325,861.68	-17,425,377,287.29
Subtotal		21		2035		-0-	24,713,220,043.00	26,898,000.00	14,949,592,342.84	9,790,525,700.16	-0-
Total, Procurement, Army							44,230,077,043.00	1,048,000.00	27,965,898,726.81	16,265,226,316.19	
Department Of The Navy											
General Fund Accounts											
Coastal Defense Augmentation, Navy											
Fund Resources:											
Undisbursed Funds	No Year	17		0380		56,478,983.40					56,478,983.40
Fund Equities:											
Unobligated Balances (Unexpired)						-1,409,829.63					-1,409,829.63
Accounts Payable						-367.48				51,774,213.24	-51,774,580.72
Undelivered Orders						-55,068,786.29				-51,774,213.24	-3,294,573.05
Subtotal		17		0380		-0-					-0-
Procurement, Marine Corps											
Fund Resources:											
Undisbursed Funds	2007-2009	17		1109		4,637,406,167.69	8,051,796,000.00		1,148,461,434.85		6,903,334,565.15
	2006-2008					2,014,637,968.84		-20,574,000.00	2,343,904,898.57		2,272,927,269.12
	2005-2007					24,436,042.87			1,220,795,329.40		793,842,639.44
	2004-2007					188,546,223.11			19,058,371.57		5,377,671.30
	2004-2006					81,462,742.55			111,085,553.65		77,460,669.46
	2003-2005					13,625,718.48			33,404,815.37		48,057,927.18
	2002-2004					15,117,843.38			1,548,263.68		12,077,454.80
	2001-2003					14,231,763.88			113,834.39		15,004,008.99
	2000-2002								2,293,772.04	11,937,991.84	
Accounts Receivable						-2,193,593.19				-4,919,179.35	2,725,586.16
Unfilled Customer Orders						10,742,471.65				2,546,511.23	8,195,960.42
Fund Equities:											
Unobligated Balances (Expired)						-28,256,310.17				6,918,433.78	-35,174,743.95

Appropriations, Outlays, and Balances - Continued

Appropriation or Fund Account Title	Period of Availability	Dept Reg	Tr From	Account Number	Sub No.	Balances, Beginning Of Fiscal Year	Appropriations And Other Obligational Authority[1]	Transfers Borrowings And Investment (Net)[2]	Outlays (Net)	Balances Withdrawn And Other Transactions[3]	Balances, End Of Fiscal Year[4]
Unobligated Balances (Unexpired)						-2,093,585,434.36				572,286,017.43	-2,665,871,451.79
Accounts Payable						-409,610,510.11				592,268,352.31	-1,001,878,862.42
Undelivered Orders						-4,466,561,094.62				1,969,517,599.24	-6,436,078,693.86
Subtotal		17		1109		-0-	8,051,796,000.00	-20,574,000.00	4,880,666,273.52	3,150,555,726.48	-0-
Aircraft Procurement, Navy Fund Resources: Undisbursed Funds	2007-2009	17		1506			11,922,336,000.00		1,907,415,119.82		10,014,920,880.18
	2006-2008					8,219,409,264.15	-76,700,000.00		3,941,595,660.87		4,201,113,603.28
	2005-2007					3,193,622,836.82			2,148,658,594.01		1,044,964,242.81
	2004-2007					15,262,687.77			9,567,463.74		5,695,224.03
	2004-2006					1,020,152,610.21			571,955,585.02		448,197,025.19
	2003-2005					475,172,676.79			190,895,110.32		284,277,566.47
	2004					-331.62					-331.62
	2002-2004					303,752,956.10			86,530,722.73		217,222,233.37
	2001-2003					198,020,134.91			31,222,485.70		166,797,649.21
	2000-2003					2,272,058.73			64,029.20		2,208,029.53
	2000-2002					155,791,367.22			71,417,358.57	84,374,008.65	
Accounts Receivable						-4,915,893.71				12,890,387.86	-17,806,281.57
Fund Equities: Unobligated Balances (Expired)						-182,135,919.97				27,754,952.60	-209,890,872.57
Unobligated Balances (Unexpired)						-1,998,171,691.60				1,351,331,705.87	-3,349,503,397.47
Accounts Payable						-196,740,620.47				85,138,686.72	-281,879,307.19
Undelivered Orders						-11,201,492,135.33				1,324,824,459.94	-12,526,316,595.27
Subtotal		17		1506		-0-	11,845,636,000.00		8,959,321,798.36	2,886,314,201.64	-0-
Weapons Procurement, Navy Fund Resources: Undisbursed Funds	2007-2009	17		1507			2,836,695,000.00		624,068,095.71		2,212,626,904.29
	2006-2008					2,127,453,121.03			915,418,705.59		1,212,034,415.44
	2005-2007					920,939,142.12			579,722,573.88		341,216,568.24
	2004-2006					334,753,080.67			229,843,086.26		104,909,994.41
	2003-2005					101,678,821.53			55,918,843.89		45,759,977.64
	2002-2004					44,385,449.86			17,585,477.04		26,799,972.82
	2001-2003					36,123,136.65			5,349,998.71		30,773,137.94
	2000-2002					48,206,020.80			20,502,748.44	27,703,272.36	
	No Year						60,692,000.00				60,692,000.00
Accounts Receivable						-1,593,863.52				1,521,087.59	-3,114,951.11
Fund Equities: Unobligated Balances (Expired)						-19,642,801.69				3,257,811.80	-22,900,613.49
Unobligated Balances (Unexpired)						-394,096,228.66				453,841,293.34	-847,937,522.00
Accounts Payable						-150,153,597.43				66,907,650.52	-217,061,247.95
Undelivered Orders						-3,048,052,281.36				-104,253,645.13	-2,943,798,636.23
Subtotal		17		1507		-0-	2,897,387,000.00		2,448,409,529.52	448,977,470.48	-0-
Procurement Of Ammunition, Navy And Marine Corps Fund Resources: Undisbursed Funds	2007-2009	17		1508			1,049,381,000.00		112,808,832.00		936,572,168.00
	2006-2008					1,077,154,754.06			412,274,827.37		664,879,926.69
	2005-2007					503,372,253.48			332,268,139.75		171,104,113.73
	2004-2007					8,324,222.36			7,614,873.60		709,348.76

Footnotes At End Of Chapter

Appropriations, Outlays, and Balances – Continued

Title	Period of Availability	Dept Reg	Dept Tr From	Account Number	Sub No.	Balances, Beginning Of Fiscal Year	Appropriations And Other Obligational Authority[1]	Transfers Borrowings And Investment (Net)[2]	Outlays (Net)	Balances Withdrawn And Other Transactions[3]	Balances, End Of Fiscal Year[4]
Procurement Of Ammunition, Navy And Marine Corps - Continued											
Fund Resources: - Continued											
Undisbursed Funds - Continued											
	2004-2006					84,552,217.33			62,491,758.02		22,060,459.31
	2003-2005					80,441,392.93			52,624,188.96		27,817,203.97
	2002-2004					3,213,075.72			1,047,785.96		2,165,289.76
	2001-2003					8,110,802.69			1,211,959.78		6,898,842.91
	2000-2002					3,991,759.12			4,415.66	3,987,343.46	
Accounts Receivable						24,373,398.78				22,279,465.83	2,093,932.95
Unfilled Customer Orders						-2,355.82				-2,355.82	
Fund Equities:											
Unobligated Balances (Expired)						-33,021,862.63				-20,849,347.63	-12,172,515.00
Unobligated Balances (Unexpired)						-197,088,448.90				-36,288,810.37	-160,799,638.53
Accounts Payable						-10,509,201.65				14,419,190.34	-24,928,391.99
Undelivered Orders						-1,552,912,007.47				83,488,733.09	-1,636,400,740.56
Subtotal		17		1508		-0-	1,049,381,000.00		982,346,781.10	67,034,218.90	-0-
Shipbuilding And Conversion, Navy											
Fund Resources:											
Undisbursed Funds	2007-2011	17		1611			9,719,700,000.00		1,479,897,046.75		8,239,802,953.25
	2006-2010					8,849,481,535.20		88,620,000.00	3,194,571,784.19		5,743,529,751.01
	2001-2010					1,515,705,390.04		1,448,167,909.79	631,937,703.42		816,230,206.37
	2005-2009					6,373,377,323.42	-11,245,000.00	-34,562,000.00	654,305,714.18		826,837,675.86
	2000-2009					448,575,527.57		18,057,000.00	1,384,864,480.40		4,977,267,843.02
	1999-2009					207,231,871.38		31,778,000.00	159,289,677.25		307,342,850.32
	2004-2008					5,188,724,002.64		-8,226,000.00	64,670,672.78		174,339,198.60
	1997-2008					60,837,683.17		-10,333,000.00	1,594,579,200.55		3,594,144,802.09
	1996-2008					10,719,942.23			-14,975,650.17		67,587,333.34
	2007					2,390,162,571.03	512,849,000.00		-90,319.77		477,262.00
	2003-2007					152,044,810.11			222,522,737.50		290,326,262.50
	1998-2007					8,974,601.49		-11,760,000.00	731,230,379.73		1,658,932,191.30
	1995-2007					113,465,049.66		-9,741,000.00	31,785,210.28		108,499,599.83
	2006					1,431,920,909.79		-1,431,920,909.79	-661,795.67		29,104,602.84
	2002-2006					107,641,857.28			109,693,487.50		3,771,562.16
	2005					10,527,480.04			59,667,944.60		47,973,912.68
	2004					120,517,814.49			3,219,957.38		7,307,522.66
	2000-2004					29,563,173.07			120,517,814.49		
	2003					9,000.00			26,644,983.76		2,918,189.31
	2000-2003					21,187,309.60			160,425.26	1,895,219.49	9,000.00
	1994-2003					13,177,325.45			11,282,105.96	149,873.00	21,026,884.34
	2002					953,346.73			803,473.73		
	2001-2002					5,457,996.18			-583.52	5,458,579.70	
	2000-2002					6,333,763.43				6,333,763.43	
	1999-2002					54,085,148.12			9,288,179.67	44,796,968.45	
	1993-2002					51,779,614.26			10,241,288.19	41,538,326.07	
	1990-2002					85,814.91					85,814.91
	No Year										
Accounts Receivable						41,536,687.07				40,922,527.78	614,159.29
Unfilled Customer Orders						3,052,093.48				2,089,540.57	962,552.91

Appropriations, Outlays, and Balances - Continued

Appropriation or Fund Account — Title	Reg	Tr From	Account Number	Period of Availability	Sub No.	Balances, Beginning Of Fiscal Year	Appropriations And Other Obligational Authority[1]	Transfers Borrowings And Investment (Net)[2]	Outlays (Net)	Balances Withdrawn And Other Transactions[3]	Balances, End Of Fiscal Year[4]
Fund Equities:											
Unobligated Balances (Expired)						-608,918,880.20				25,800,615.19	-634,719,495.39
Unobligated Balances (Unexpired)						-8,250,115,581.11				-1,013,957,061.80	-7,236,158,519.31
Accounts Payable						172,052,280.78				147,468,411.98	24,583,868.80
Undelivered Orders						-18,530,147,461.31				513,441,317.70	-19,043,588,779.01
Subtotal	17		1611			-0-	10,221,304,000.00	80,080,000.00	10,485,445,918.44	-184,061,918.44	-0-
Other Procurement, Navy											
Fund Resources:											
Undisbursed Funds	17		1810	2007-2009		4,447,681,799.07	6,030,089,000.00	100,614,000.00	1,541,204,119.34		4,589,498,880.66
				2006-2008		1,631,680,950.37		-33,865,000.00	2,304,746,113.48		2,109,070,685.59
				2005-2007		576,117,166.17			962,528,630.64		669,152,319.73
				2004-2006		280,830,462.34			[30]267,142,103.63		308,975,062.54
				2003-2005		148,732,283.83			[31]102,181,616.61		178,648,845.73
				2002-2004		87,340,171.77			17,955,095.63		130,777,188.20
				2001-2003		37,750,016.90			26,870,806.80		60,469,364.97
				2000-2002					3,637,671.05		
				No Year			900,000.00			34,112,345.85	900,000.00
Accounts Receivable						-49,031,783.08				12,085,456.67	-61,117,239.75
Unfilled Customer Orders										1,369,743.81	-1,369,743.81
Fund Equities:											
Unobligated Balances (Expired)						-89,296,267.12				-9,433,784.53	-79,862,482.59
Unobligated Balances (Unexpired)						-1,473,903,115.72				294,857,073.23	-1,768,760,188.95
Accounts Payable						-101,948,696.65				156,887,771.22	-258,836,467.87
Undelivered Orders						-5,495,952,987.88				381,593,236.57	-5,877,546,224.45
Subtotal	17		1810			-0-	6,030,989,000.00	66,749,000.00	5,226,266,157.18	871,471,842.82	-0-
Total, Procurement, Navy							40,096,493,000.00	126,255,000.00	32,982,456,458.12	7,240,291,541.88	
Department Of The Air Force											
General Fund Accounts											
Aircraft Procurement, Air Force											
Fund Resources:											
Undisbursed Funds	57		3010	2007-2009		10,226,761,803.39	15,827,616,000.00		[32]2,102,788,670.74		13,724,827,329.26
				2006-2008		4,408,783,895.83	-141,100,000.00	33,929,000.00	[33]5,002,686,287.99		5,116,904,515.40
				2005-2007		1,441,059,507.85	-108,000,000.00	-250,000.00	[34]2,648,928,329.69		1,651,605,566.14
				2004-2006		634,712,758.39			727,247,785.18		713,811,722.67
				2003-2005		263,073,068.29			252,126,461.77		382,586,296.62
				2002-2004		172,516,074.00			84,723,495.13		178,349,573.16
				2001-2003		9,627,451.82			19,104,179.13		153,411,894.87
				2000-2003		113,336,264.65			-3,707,089.76		13,334,541.58
				2000-2002		176,433.66			23,834,078.13		
				No Year			40,000,000.00		34,737.60	89,502,186.52	40,141,696.06
Accounts Receivable						11,770,802.45				-1,102,604.35	12,873,406.80
Unfilled Customer Orders						75,672,926.94				-71,983,402.20	147,656,329.14
Fund Equities:											
Unobligated Balances (Expired)						-237,938,189.66				-7,930,250.89	-230,007,938.77
Unobligated Balances (Unexpired)						-5,844,678,074.94				-89,261,736.73	-5,755,416,338.21

Footnotes At End Of Chapter

Appropriations, Outlays, and Balances – Continued

Appropriation or Fund Account — Title	Dept Reg	Tr From	Account Number	Sub No.	Period of Availability	Balances, Beginning Of Fiscal Year	Appropriations And Other Obligational Authority[1]	Transfers Borrowings And Investment (Net)[2]	Outlays (Net)	Balances Withdrawn And Other Transactions[3]	Balances, End Of Fiscal Year[4]
Aircraft Procurement, Air Force - Continued											
Fund Equities: - Continued											
Accounts Payable						-1,559,748,202.65				-1,188,206,036.63	-371,542,166.02
Undelivered Orders						-9,715,126,520.02				6,063,409,908.68	-15,778,536,428.70
Subtotal	57		3010			-0-	15,618,516,000.00	33,679,000.00	10,857,766,935.60	4,794,428,064.40	-0-
Procurement Of Ammunition, Air Force											
Fund Resources:											
Undisbursed Funds	57		3011		2007-2009	985,393,620.45	1,043,614,000.00		47,566,768.42		996,047,231.58
					2006-2008	515,503,760.72		-7,289,000.00	512,924,866.11		465,179,754.34
					2005-2007	111,843,605.59			413,731,277.14		101,772,483.58
					2004-2006	60,350,575.04			62,456,138.50		49,387,467.09
					2003-2005	10,661,712.75			25,322,632.17		35,027,942.87
					2002-2004	7,997,192.16			8,634,012.84		2,027,699.91
					2001-2003	1,892,185.13			376,674.62		7,620,517.54
					2000-2002	1,008,301.46			92,963.43	1,799,221.70	-1,398,960.86
Accounts Receivable										2,407,262.32	
Fund Equities:											
Unobligated Balances (Expired)						-29,349,062.86				-1,230,163.23	-28,118,899.63
Unobligated Balances (Unexpired)						-185,507,377.12				39,293,233.16	-224,800,610.28
Accounts Payable						-136,948,442.78				-53,981,265.86	-82,967,176.92
Undelivered Orders						-1,342,846,070.54				-23,068,621.32	-1,319,777,449.22
Subtotal	57		3011			-0-	1,043,614,000.00	-7,289,000.00	1,071,105,333.23	-34,780,333.23	-0-
Missile Procurement, Air Force											
Fund Resources:											
Undisbursed Funds	57		3020		2007-2009	2,983,414,694.00	4,055,138,000.00		[35]1,676,536,633.33		2,378,601,366.67
					2006-2008	900,830,711.55	-142,000,000.00		[36]1,585,711,481.51		1,255,703,212.49
					2005-2007	619,369,503.19			[37]518,436,292.31		382,394,419.24
					2004-2006	251,993,991.54			[38]319,536,054.59		299,833,448.60
					2003-2005	110,406,314.58			41,834,934.55		210,159,056.99
					2002-2004	47,365,736.20			28,696,880.53		81,709,434.05
					2001-2003	27,034,841.51			1,007,418.00		46,358,318.20
					2000-2002		60,000,000.00		6,483,099.49	20,551,742.02	60,000,000.00
				1	No Year	16,782,400.00					[39]16,782,400.00
	57		3020		1996-1998	20,978,000.00					[40]20,978,000.00
					1995-1997	16,780,000.00					[40]16,780,000.00
					1994-1996	16,780,000.00					[40]16,780,000.00
					1993-1995	23,171,000.00					[40]23,171,000.00
					1992-1994	6,895,619.00			3,351,646.00		[40]3,543,973.00
					1991-1993	1,535,450.89					[40]1,535,450.89
					1990-1992	121,651.80					
Accounts Receivable						121,651.80				41,213.51	80,438.29
Unfilled Customer Orders						1,810,073.80				1,133,055.49	677,018.31
Fund Equities:											
Unobligated Balances (Expired)						-214,576,916.91				8,214,155.04	-222,791,071.95
Unobligated Balances (Unexpired)						-1,325,025,141.60				-546,514,941.68	-778,510,199.92
Accounts Payable						-197,060,528.76				18,742,666.02	-215,803,194.78
Undelivered Orders						-3,308,607,400.79				289,375,669.29	-3,597,983,070.08
Subtotal	57		3020			-0-	3,973,138,000.00		4,181,594,440.31	-208,456,440.31	-0-

Appropriations, Outlays, and Balances - Continued

Appropriation or Fund Account — Title	Account Symbol — Dept Reg	Tr From	Account Number	Sub No.	Period of Availability	Balances, Beginning Of Fiscal Year	Appropriations And Other Obligational Authority[1]	Transfers Borrowings And Investment (Net)[2]	Outlays (Net)	Balances Withdrawn And Other Transactions[3]	Balances, End Of Fiscal Year[4]
Tanker Replacement Transfer Fund, Air Force											
Fund Resources:											
Undisbursed Funds	57		3024		No Year	89,800,000.00					89,800,000.00
Fund Equities:											
Unobligated Balances (Unexpired)						-89,800,000.00					-89,800,000.00
Subtotal	57		3024		Subtotal	-0-	-0-				-0-
Other Procurement, Air Force											
Fund Resources:											
Undisbursed Funds	57		3080		2007-2009		18,899,818,000.00	500,000.00	[4]11,954,919,749.56		6,945,398,250.44
					2006-2008	5,874,112,053.31		4,110,000.00	[42]4,076,893,528.39		1,801,328,524.92
					2005-2007	1,618,004,808.99		250,000.00	[43]1,176,473,206.51		441,781,602.48
					2004-2007	26,309,489.70			15,377,368.70		10,932,121.00
					2004-2006	492,147,018.98			324,282,294.87		167,864,724.11
					2003-2005	130,089,541.66			61,149,074.95		68,940,466.71
					2004	452,920.21			9,200.00		443,720.21
					2002-2004	86,390,475.70			24,206,251.67		62,184,224.03
					2001-2003	47,951,951.27			-88,175,075.92		136,127,027.19
					2000-2002	101,197,352.89			3,161,501.46	98,035,851.43	
					No Year		6,596,381.00				6,596,381.00
Accounts Receivable						33,538,709.00				19,549,309.67	13,989,399.33
Unfilled Customer Orders						108,027,400.31				46,960,435.71	61,066,964.60
Fund Equities:											
Unobligated Balances (Expired)						-196,298,778.75			-72,169,415.94		-124,129,362.81
Unobligated Balances (Unexpired)						-1,689,965,156.59			3,906,685,838.36		-5,596,650,994.95
Accounts Payable						-115,170,184.27			63,417,855.43		-178,588,039.70
Undelivered Orders						-6,516,787,602.41			-2,699,502,593.85		-3,817,285,008.56
Subtotal	57		3080		Subtotal	-0-	18,906,414,381.00	4,860,000.00	17,548,297,100.19	1,362,977,280.81	-0-
Total, Procurement, Air Force							39,541,682,381.00	31,250,000.00	33,658,763,809.33	5,914,168,571.67	
Defense Agencies											
General Fund Accounts											
Procurement, Defense-Wide											
Fund Resources:											
Undisbursed Funds	97		0300		2007-2009		4,096,884,000.00	41,000,000.00	977,373,955.89		3,160,510,044.11
					2006-2008	2,455,204,227.54			1,305,580,425.44		1,149,623,802.10
					2007		8,000,000.00		8,219,679.38		[29]-219,679.38
					2005-2007	1,330,653,721.53			747,302,991.82		583,350,729.71
					2004-2007	20,204,608.12			8,332,395.05		11,872,213.07
					2006	3,332,286.51			3,145,370.28		186,916.23
					2004-2006	518,199,086.30			271,203,634.02		246,995,452.28
					2005	906,487.05			2,567,055.16		[29]-1,660,568.11
					2003-2005	180,956,901.29			69,620,486.89		111,336,414.40
					2004	204,651.24			112,625.33		92,025.91
					2003-2004	9,379,458.18			5,829,432.06		3,550,026.12
					2002-2004	48,828,569.77			10,772,690.88		38,055,878.89
					2003	1,838,932.69			772,473.20		1,066,459.49

Footnotes At End Of Chapter

Appropriations, Outlays, and Balances – Continued

Appropriation or Fund Account: Title	Period of Availability	Reg	Tr From	Account Number	Sub No.	Balances, Beginning Of Fiscal Year	Appropriations And Other Obligational Authority[1]	Transfers Borrowings And Investment (Net)[2]	Outlays (Net)	Balances Withdrawn And Other Transactions[3]	Balances, End Of Fiscal Year[4]
Procurement, Defense-Wide - Continued											
Fund Resources: - Continued											
Undisbursed Funds - Continued											
	2002-2003					7,379,283.41			7,300,537.28		78,746.13
	2001-2003					52,526,869.00			6,761,748.72		45,765,120.28
	2000-2003					320,879.66					320,879.66
	2002					1,267,008.27				1,551,979.36	
	2000-2002					35,195,210.94			-284,971.09	30,846,077.29	
Accounts Receivable						28,148,836.58			4,349,133.65	-10,186,210.66	38,335,047.24
Unfilled Customer Orders						71,669,818.19				-2,574,856.96	74,244,675.15
Fund Equities:											
Unobligated Balances (Expired)						-78,342,018.64				-10,485,892.30	-67,856,126.34
Unobligated Balances (Unexpired)						-906,026,754.45				551,186,922.21	-1,457,213,676.66
Accounts Payable						-143,057,225.05				35,565,407.88	-178,622,632.93
Undelivered Orders						-3,638,790,838.13		41,000,000.00		121,020,909.22	-3,759,811,747.35
	Subtotal	97		0300		-0-	4,104,884,000.00		3,428,959,663.96	716,924,336.04	-0-
National Guard And Reserve Equipment, Defense											
Fund Resources:											
Undisbursed Funds:											
	2007-2009	97		0350		1,157,644,519.20	1,343,835,000.00		15,482,185.44		1,328,352,814.56
	2006-2008					114,992,496.06		6,500,000.00	621,811,528.69		542,332,990.51
	2005-2007					13,303,645.36			78,604,157.14		36,388,338.92
	2004-2007					82,032,095.35			10,802,287.95		2,501,357.41
	2004-2006					8,129,387.03			47,625,156.90		34,406,938.45
	2003-2005					8,727,929.94			6,218,767.86		1,910,619.17
	2002-2004					1,168,157.98			2,515,540.93		6,212,389.01
	2001-2003					1,525,503.25			60,300.87		1,107,857.11
	2000-2002								-74,649.81	1,600,153.06	
Fund Equities:											
Unobligated Balances (Expired)						-3,873,110.72				1,912,593.38	-5,785,704.10
Unobligated Balances (Unexpired)						-454,793,104.70				935,169,228.91	-1,389,962,333.61
Accounts Payable						-42,845,046.06				-40,574,882.18	-2,270,163.88
Undelivered Orders						-886,012,472.69				-330,817,369.14	-555,195,103.55
	Subtotal	97		0350		-0-	1,343,835,000.00	6,500,000.00	783,045,275.97	567,289,724.03	-0-
Defense Production Act Purchases, Defense											
Fund Resources:											
Undisbursed Funds:											
	No Year	97		0360		85,726,397.03	62,930,000.00		37,664,414.33		110,991,982.70
Fund Equities:											
Unobligated Balances (Unexpired)						-35,465,086.49				6,043,327.26	-41,508,413.75
Accounts Payable						-235,360.76				3,099,319.46	-3,334,680.22
Undelivered Orders						-50,025,949.78				16,122,938.95	-66,148,888.73
	Subtotal	97		0360		-0-	62,930,000.00		37,664,414.33	25,265,585.67	-0-
Chemical Agents And Munitions Destruction, Defense											
Fund Resources:											
Undisbursed Funds:											
	No Year	97		0390		1,377,603.08					1,377,603.08
Fund Equities:											
Unobligated Balances (Unexpired)						-708,443.96					-708,443.96
Accounts Payable						-1,491,360.40					-1,491,360.40
Undelivered Orders						822,201.28					822,201.28
	Subtotal	97		0390		-0-					-0-

Appropriations, Outlays, and Balances - Continued

Title	Dept Reg	Dept Tr From	Account Number	Sub No.	Period of Availability	Balances, Beginning Of Fiscal Year	Appropriations And Other Obligational Authority[1]	Transfers Borrowings And Investment (Net)[2]	Outlays (Net)	Balances Withdrawn And Other Transactions[3]	Balances, End Of Fiscal Year[4]
Total, Procurement, Defense Agencies							5,511,649,000.00	47,500,000.00	4,249,669,354.26	1,309,479,645.74	
Total, Procurement							129,379,901,424.00	206,053,000.00	98,856,788,348.52	30,729,166,075.48	
Research, Development, Test, And Evaluation											
Department Of The Army											
General Fund Accounts											
Research, Development, Test, And Evaluation, Army											
Fund Resources:											
Undisbursed Funds	21		2040		2007-2008	6,387,026,629.02	11,324,488,000.00	41,700,000.00	45,240,730,748.50		6,125,457,251.50
					2006-2007	1,343,743,794.48	-21,600,000.00	109,376,000.00	[5]4,889,736,970.31		1,585,065,658.71
					2005-2006	412,735,753.30			[46]946,115,629.75		397,628,164.73
					2004-2005	150,069,118.42			218,348,065.62		194,387,687.68
					2003-2004	115,707,660.85			36,589,038.29		113,480,080.13
					2002-2003	63,394,508.21			14,448,695.40		101,258,965.45
					2001-2002	19,122,356.95			17,711,715.49	45,682,792.72	18,850,063.61
					No Year				272,293.34		
Accounts Receivable						239,296,562.90				85,663,975.96	153,632,586.94
Unfilled Customer Orders						3,724,809,724.09				129,946,387.25	3,594,863,336.84
Fund Equities:											
Unobligated Balances (Expired)						-119,556,453.85				34,395,444.72	-153,951,898.57
Unobligated Balances (Unexpired)						-2,574,062,386.54				-7,892,901.60	-2,566,169,484.94
Accounts Payable						-949,232,689.09				-551,892,962.40	-397,339,726.69
Undelivered Orders						-8,813,054,578.74				354,108,106.65	-9,167,162,685.39
Subtotal	21		2040			-0-	11,302,888,000.00	151,076,000.00	11,363,953,156.70	90,010,843.30	-0-
Total, Research, Development, Test, And Evaluation, Army							11,302,888,000.00	151,076,000.00	11,363,953,156.70	90,010,843.30	
Department Of The Navy											
General Fund Accounts											
Research, Development, Test, And Evaluation, Navy											
Fund Resources:											
Undisbursed Funds	17		1319		2007-2008	8,667,222,188.55	19,600,236,000.00	75,000,000.00	10,621,022,830.75		9,054,213,169.25
					2006-2007	1,315,697,100.25	-35,798,000.00	9,100,000.00	7,073,854,422.11		1,566,669,766.44
					2005-2006	325,139,206.04			902,804,856.16		412,892,244.09
					2004-2005	135,316,434.96			113,571,254.76		211,567,951.28
					2003-2004	106,261,406.48			[4]722,158,611.64		113,157,823.32
					2002-2003	63,146,888.35			12,127,254.93		94,134,151.55
					2001-2002				6,775,812.55	56,371,075.80	
					No Year		72,873,000.00		28,276.20		72,844,723.80
Accounts Receivable						17,926,051.90				-24,305,727.46	42,231,779.36
Unfilled Customer Orders						355,270,249.26			56,946,324.03	56,946,324.03	298,323,925.23

Footnotes At End Of Chapter

Appropriations, Outlays, and Balances – Continued

Appropriation or Fund Account — Title	Dept Reg	Dept Tr From	Account Number	Sub No.	Period of Availability	Balances, Beginning Of Fiscal Year	Appropriations And Other Obligational Authority[1]	Transfers Borrowings And Investment (Net)[2]	Outlays (Net)	Balances Withdrawn And Other Transactions[3]	Balances, End Of Fiscal Year[4]
Research, Development, Test, And Evaluation, Navy - Continued											
Fund Equities:											
Unobligated Balances (Expired)						-167,934,224.59				58,093,514.27	-226,027,738.86
Unobligated Balances (Unexpired)						-1,959,469,467.81				347,540,026.20	-2,307,009,494.01
Accounts Payable						-16,207,232.67				125,544,610.04	-141,751,842.71
Undelivered Orders						-8,842,368,600.72		84,100,000.00		348,877,858.02	-9,191,246,458.74
Subtotal		17		1319		-0-	19,637,311,000.00	84,100,000.00	18,752,343,319.10	969,067,680.90	-0-
Total, Research, Development, Test, And Evaluation, Navy							19,637,311,000.00	84,100,000.00	18,752,343,319.10	969,067,680.90	
Department Of The Air Force											
General Fund Accounts											
Research, Development, Test, And Evaluation, Air Force											
Fund Resources:											
Undisbursed Funds	57		3600		2007-2008	8,600,150,832.98	24,658,745,000.00		[4]14,851,990,037.83		9,806,754,962.17
					2006-2007	1,309,844,787.51	-92,800,000.00	-39,813,000.00	[4]6,904,888,188.10		1,562,649,644.88
					2005-2006	426,230,929.13			907,508,407.04		402,336,380.47
					2004-2005	200,729,916.38			156,734,463.37		269,496,465.76
					2003-2004	281,140,304.25			21,061,168.77		179,668,747.61
					2002-2003	112,539,798.68			53,532,897.45		227,607,406.80
					2001-2002				23,668,748.31	88,871,050.37	
Accounts Receivable						204,335,008.20				10,279,210.02	194,055,798.18
Unfilled Customer Orders						561,376,940.99				-52,585,607.13	613,962,548.12
Fund Equities:											
Unobligated Balances (Expired)						-400,738,305.59				99,244,652.21	-499,982,957.80
Unobligated Balances (Unexpired)						-3,257,855,344.03				117,900,902.68	-3,375,756,246.71
Accounts Payable						-944,346,172.07				149,117,945.67	-1,093,464,117.74
Undelivered Orders						-7,093,408,696.43		-39,813,000.00		1,193,919,935.31	-8,287,328,631.74
Subtotal		57		3600		-0-	24,565,945,000.00	-39,813,000.00	22,919,383,910.87	1,606,748,089.13	-0-
Total, Research, Development, Test, And Evaluation, Air Force							24,565,945,000.00	-39,813,000.00	22,919,383,910.87	1,606,748,089.13	
Defense Agencies											
General Fund Accounts											
Research, Development, Test, And Evaluation, Defense-Wide											
Fund Resources:											
Undisbursed Funds	97		0400		2007-2008	10,394,916,262.93	21,906,675,000.00		10,181,611,115.53		11,725,063,884.47
					2006-2007	2,207,726,223.50	-120,700,000.00	-82,613,000.00	7,834,103,515.33		2,357,499,747.60
					2005-2006	416,266,005.45			1,560,464,609.89		647,261,613.61
					2004-2005	311,391,044.08			208,309,110.77		207,956,894.68
					2003-2004	183,049,989.54			81,848,300.17		229,542,743.91
					2002-2003				42,031,031.95		141,018,957.59
					2002				-1,782.13	1,782.13	
					2001-2002	87,626,542.40			-10,417,483.56	98,044,025.96	
					2000-2002	603,303.32			219.93	603,083.39	
					No Year	63,392,109.01	76,500,000.00		9,788,850.43		130,103,258.58

Appropriations, Outlays, and Balances - Continued

Appropriation or Fund Account — Title	Dept Reg	Tr From	Account Number	Sub No.	Period of Availability	Balances, Beginning Of Fiscal Year	Appropriations And Other Obligational Authority[1]	Transfers Borrowings And Investment (Net)[2]	Outlays (Net)	Balances Withdrawn And Other Transactions[3]	Balances, End Of Fiscal Year[4]
Accounts Receivable						129,064,586.14				-140,317,642.79	269,382,228.93
Unfilled Customer Orders						692,593,854.23				-13,160,971.11	705,754,825.34
Fund Equities:											
Unobligated Balances (Expired)						-397,876,931.66				153,214,689.66	-551,091,621.32
Unobligated Balances (Unexpired)						-3,257,755,365.78				550,385,535.06	-3,808,140,900.84
Accounts Payable						-415,577,986.31				62,063,597.85	-477,641,584.16
Undelivered Orders						-10,415,419,636.85				1,161,290,411.54	-11,576,710,048.39
Subtotal	97		0400			-0-	21,862,475,000.00	-82,613,000.00	19,907,737,488.31	1,872,124,511.69	-0-
Operational Test And Evaluation, Defense											
Fund Resources:											
Undisbursed Funds	97		0460		2007-2008	73,570,985.88	180,204,000.00		105,132,942.98		75,071,057.02
					2006-2007	25,007,487.66			66,322,518.57		7,248,467.31
					2005-2006	8,630,884.48			18,506,607.34		6,500,880.32
					2004-2005	5,169,832.22			2,166,778.59		6,464,105.89
					2003-2004	3,334,687.88			546,540.09		4,623,292.13
					2002-2003	3,810,749.92			195,390.41		3,139,297.47
					2001-2002	433.02			194,316.74	3,616,433.18	
Accounts Receivable										-5,956.44	6,389.46
Fund Equities:											
Unobligated Balances (Expired)						-5,379,620.69				87,811.14	-5,467,431.83
Unobligated Balances (Unexpired)						-9,381,659.83				2,774,490.82	-12,156,150.65
Accounts Payable						-7,107,536.43				358,474.67	-7,466,011.10
Undelivered Orders						-97,656,244.11				-19,692,348.09	-77,963,896.02
Subtotal	97		0460			-0-	180,204,000.00	-82,613,000.00	193,065,094.72	-12,861,094.72	-0-
Total, Research, Development Test, And Evaluation, Defense Agencies							22,042,679,000.00	-82,613,000.00	20,100,802,583.03	1,859,263,416.97	
Total, Research, Development Test, And Evaluation							77,548,823,000.00	112,750,000.00	73,136,482,969.70	4,525,090,030.30	
Military Construction											
Department Of The Army											
General Fund Accounts											
Military Construction, Army											
Fund Resources:											
Undisbursed Funds	21		2050		2007-2011		2,017,321,000.00	65,510,000.00	-234,522,116.01		2,317,353,116.01
					2006-2010	1,999,249,013.29	-43,348,000.00	-3,668,000.00	806,353,240.53		1,145,879,772.76
					2005-2009	1,144,213,968.26			681,380,438.77		462,833,529.49
					2003-2009	13,414,459.00			3,304,197.31		10,110,261.69
					2007-2008		1,255,890,000.00		7,546,405.31		1,248,343,594.69
					2004-2008	570,235,001.27			243,436,850.60		326,798,150.67
					2006-2007	236,559,648.07			103,352,860.04		133,206,788.03
					2003-2007	117,695,608.51			97,399,274.69		20,296,333.82
					2005-2006	397,427,459.37		-119,510,000.00	227,433,522.42		50,483,936.95

Footnotes At End Of Chapter

Appropriations, Outlays, and Balances – Continued

Appropriation or Fund Account — Title	Account Symbol Dept Reg	Tr From	Account Number	Sub No.	Period of Availability	Balances, Beginning Of Fiscal Year	Appropriations And Other Obligational Authority[1]	Transfers Borrowings And Investment (Net)[2]	Outlays (Net)	Balances Withdrawn And Other Transactions[3]	Balances, End Of Fiscal Year[4]
Military Construction, Army - Continued											
Fund Resources: - Continued											
Undisbursed Funds - Continued											
					2002-2006	35,089,219.67			19,729,598.27		15,359,621.40
					2001-2005	3,995,171.15			1,781,845.48		2,213,325.67
					2000-2004	6,951,645.90			2,472,668.59		4,478,977.31
					1999-2003	1,983,151.32			110,521.05		1,872,630.27
					1998-2002	7,304,553.06			665,567.04	6,638,986.02	
					No Year	13,237.17			8,170.97		5,066.20
Transfer To:											
Department Of Transportation, Federal Highway Administration	69	21	2050	5	2006-2010	21,780,000.00			2,855,843.78		18,924,156.22
					2005-2009	9,264,876.00			8,272,913.24		991,962.76
					2004-2008	7,244,645.88			6,830,191.67		414,454.21
					2003-2007	2,365,068.37			1,830,021.60		535,046.77
					2005-2006	568,557.00			424,581.83		143,975.17
					2002-2006	1,989,693.10			972,032.59		1,017,660.51
					2001-2005	1,200,769.99			584,133.88		616,636.11
					2000-2004	904,048.28			332,206.85		571,841.43
					1999-2003						
Accounts Receivable						4,065.51					4,065.51
Unfilled Customer Orders						104,360,862.90				12,410,665.34	91,950,197.56
Fund Equities:						4,728,556,698.34				-1,116,936,671.73	5,845,493,370.07
Unobligated Balances (Expired)						-148,964,972.54				-114,349,885.33	-34,615,087.21
Unobligated Balances (Unexpired)						-2,158,836,816.91				1,458,295,890.59	-3,617,132,707.50
Accounts Payable						-309,838,406.77				-150,106,857.68	-159,731,549.09
Undelivered Orders						-6,781,316,766.19				1,107,102,361.29	-7,888,419,127.48
	21		2050		Subtotal	-0-	3,229,863,000.00	-44,253,541.00	1,982,554,970.50	1,203,054,488.50	-0-
Military Construction, Army National Guard											
Fund Resources:											
Undisbursed Funds	21		2085		2007-2011		473,000,000.00		1,969,923.97		471,030,076.03
					2006-2010	812,448,482.24	-2,129,000.00		284,658,700.14		525,660,782.10
					2005-2009	208,432,339.49			119,646,590.15		88,785,749.34
					2004-2008	73,246,164.80			39,206,716.69		34,039,448.11
					2003-2007	13,916,844.45			5,612,247.43		8,304,597.02
					2006	254,300,000.00			42,788,383.23		211,511,616.77
					2002-2006	13,473,607.81			4,708,172.54		8,765,435.27
					2001-2005	7,571,887.43			3,715,358.41		3,856,529.02
					2000-2004	2,959,913.86			2,895,141.99		64,771.87
					1999-2003	585,286.67			-128,691.04		713,977.71
					1998-2002	348,524.35			-79,442.85	427,967.20	
Fund Equities:											
Unobligated Balances (Expired)						-8,394,683.89				1,327,964.96	-9,722,648.85
Unobligated Balances (Unexpired)						-311,780,768.27				-64,847,686.21	-246,933,082.06
Accounts Payable						-662,458,832.08				83,797,778.89	-746,256,610.97
Undelivered Orders						-404,648,766.86				-54,828,125.50	-349,820,641.36
	21		2085		Subtotal	-0-	470,871,000.00		504,993,100.66	-34,122,100.66	-0-
Military Construction, Army Reserve											
Fund Resources:											
Undisbursed Funds	21		2086		2007-2011		166,000,000.00		6,880,926.86		159,119,073.14

Appropriations, Outlays, and Balances - Continued

Title	Reg	Tr From	Account Number	Sub No.	Period of Availability	Balances, Beginning Of Fiscal Year	Appropriations And Other Obligational Authority[1]	Transfers Borrowings And Investment (Net)[2]	Outlays (Net)	Balances Withdrawn And Other Transactions[3]	Balances, End Of Fiscal Year[4]
					2006-2010	134,800,451.58			74,705,679.88		60,094,771.70
					2005-2009	26,777,021.74			12,889,451.19		13,887,570.55
					2004-2008	14,656,134.61			11,781,945.18		2,874,189.43
					2005-2007	6,448,068.09			5,739,322.19		708,745.90
					2003-2007	4,852,553.85			1,172,819.14		3,679,734.71
					2002-2006	1,100,273.77			516,606.77		583,667.00
					2001-2005	86,782.77			41,043.97		45,738.80
					2000-2004	228,721.85			23,249.39		205,472.46
					1999-2003	88,644.43			11,813.83		76,830.60
					1998-2002	48,295.27			11,037.97	37,257.30	-0-
Subtotal	21		2086			-0-	166,000,000.00		113,773,896.37	52,226,103.63	-0-
Fund Equities:											
Unobligated Balances (Expired)						-175,082.82				279,532.16	-454,614.98
Unobligated Balances (Unexpired)						-68,846,684.95				-14,509,098.16	-54,337,586.79
Accounts Payable						-2,031,170.83				79,731.43	-2,110,902.26
Undelivered Orders						-118,034,009.36				66,338,680.90	-184,372,690.26
Total, Military Construction, Army						-0-	3,866,734,000.00	-44,253,541.00	2,601,321,967.53	1,221,158,491.47	-0-

Department Of The Navy

General Fund Accounts

Military Construction, Navy And Marine Corps

Fund Resources:

Undisbursed Funds

Title	Reg	Tr From	Account Number	Sub No.	Period of Availability	Balances, Beginning Of Fiscal Year	Appropriations And Other Obligational Authority[1]	Transfers Borrowings And Investment (Net)[2]	Outlays (Net)	Balances Withdrawn And Other Transactions[3]	Balances, End Of Fiscal Year[4]
	17		1205		2007-2011	1,520,616,307.59	1,136,421,000.00	7,787,000.00	171,991,719.35		972,216,280.65
					2006-2010	370,474,163.24		-4,500,000.00	539,641,539.26		976,474,768.33
					2005-2009		-8,000,000.00	-1,500,000.00	240,654,852.20		120,319,311.04
					2007-2008		370,990,000.00				370,990,000.00
					2004-2008	258,630,963.63	-19,500,000.00	-42,710,000.00	97,412,771.28		99,008,192.35
					2007				-133,243.70		133,243.70
					2005-2007	109,693,524.80			73,792,500.31		35,901,024.49
					2003-2007	38,848,183.72			-37,433,424.21		76,281,607.93
					2005-2006	98,095,334.39			81,138,345.40		16,956,988.99
					2002-2006	11,906,972.41			6,806,666.51		5,100,305.90
					2001-2005	4,857,549.42			1,521,738.24		3,335,811.18
					2000-2004	8,315,858.51			1,093,983.24		7,221,875.27
					1999-2003	12,289,527.36			9,946,609.46		2,342,917.90
					1998-2002	7,765,660.41			342,210.33	7,423,450.08	-0-
					No Year	584,541.28					584,541.28
Accounts Receivable						13,480,692.55				-91,230,687.98	104,711,380.53
Unfilled Customer Orders						750,727,777.69				-220,854,849.91	971,582,627.60
Fund Equities:											
Unobligated Balances (Expired)						-75,523,508.62				39,330,609.73	-114,854,118.35
Unobligated Balances (Unexpired)						-1,068,274,247.02				195,309,437.56	-1,263,583,684.58
Accounts Payable						-157,527,722.37				94,664,621.10	-252,192,343.47
Undelivered Orders						-1,904,961,578.99				227,569,151.75	-2,132,530,730.74
Subtotal	17		1205			-0-	1,479,911,000.00	-40,923,000.00	1,186,776,267.67	252,211,732.33	-0-

Footnotes At End Of Chapter

Appropriations, Outlays, and Balances – Continued

Appropriation or Fund Account — Title	Period of Availability	Account Symbol — Dept Reg	Account Symbol — Tr From	Account Number	Sub No.	Balances, Beginning Of Fiscal Year	Appropriations And Other Obligational Authority[1]	Transfers Borrowings And Investment (Net)[2]	Outlays (Net)	Balances Withdrawn And Other Transactions[3]	Balances, End Of Fiscal Year[4]
Military Construction, Naval Reserve											
Fund Resources:											
Undisbursed Funds	2007-2011	17		1235			43,000,000.00		4,026,005.50		38,973,994.50
	2006-2010					[12]137,603,135.79			21,860,349.99		115,742,785.80
	2005-2009					17,937,228.85			13,005,753.44		4,931,475.41
	2004-2008					1,526,004.86			212,836.39		1,313,168.47
	2003-2007					4,893,933.74			2,700,468.76		2,193,464.98
	2006					[12]					
Fund Equities:	2002-2006					111,649.98			37,711.30		73,938.68
	2001-2005					247,583.42			107,052.09		140,531.33
	2000-2004					284,685.27					284,685.27
	1999-2003					215,604.53					215,604.53
	1998-2002					15,888.37				15,888.37	-0-
Unobligated Balances (Expired)						[12]371,812.17				38,978.15	-410,790.32
Unobligated Balances (Unexpired)						[12]110,760,694.37				-49,653,519.62	-61,107,174.75
Accounts Payable						-4,073,825.67				-3,018,207.37	-1,055,618.30
Undelivered Orders						-47,629,382.60				53,666,683.00	-101,296,065.60
Subtotal	Subtotal	17		1235		-0-	43,000,000.00		41,950,177.47	1,049,822.53	-0-
Special Fund Accounts											
Ford Island Improvement Account											
Fund Resources:											
Undisbursed Funds	No Year	17		5562		100,000.00					100,000.00
Fund Equities:											
Unobligated Balances (Unexpired)	Subtotal	17		5562		-100,000.00					-100,000.00
Subtotal						-0-					-0-
Total, Military Construction, Navy							1,522,911,000.00	-40,923,000.00	1,228,726,445.14	253,261,554.86	
Department Of The Air Force											
General Fund Accounts											
Military Construction, Air Force											
Fund Resources:											
Undisbursed Funds	2007-2011	57		3300			1,077,849,000.00	37,303,000.00	98,343,997.63		1,016,808,002.37
	2006-2010					1,337,375,714.93		-28,198,000.00	561,598,433.92		747,579,281.01
	2005-2009					407,556,443.88	-2,694,000.00	-249,000.00	226,769,424.93		177,844,018.95
	2007-2008						43,300,000.00				43,300,000.00
	2004-2008					172,378,027.43			95,737,886.78		76,640,140.65
	2006-2007					27,700,000.00		-2,860,000.00	3,735,256.10		21,104,743.90
	2003-2007					74,254,652.32		-568,000.00	45,033,336.97		28,653,315.35
	2005-2006					41,104,012.38		-10,160,000.00	25,017,342.57		5,926,669.81
	2002-2006					9,925,840.98		3,597,000.00	3,826,692.13		9,696,148.85
	2002-2005					496,006.00					496,006.00
	2001-2005					2,249,400.59		2,377,000.00	697,726.05		3,928,674.54
	2000-2004					1,305,503.55			545,091.81		760,411.74
	1999-2003					35,580.48			-518,958.10		554,538.58

Appropriations, Outlays, and Balances - Continued

Appropriation or Fund Account — Title	Period of Availability	Reg	Tr From	Account Number	Sub No.	Balances, Beginning Of Fiscal Year	Appropriations And Other Obligational Authority[1]	Transfers Borrowings And Investment (Net)[2]	Outlays (Net)	Balances Withdrawn And Other Transactions[3]	Balances, End Of Fiscal Year[4]
	1998-2002					1,998,797.89			1,241,712.57	757,085.32	
	No Year					11,109,532.83			1,250,951.45		9,858,581.38
Transfer To:											
Department Of Transportation, Federal Highway Administration	2007-2011	69	57	3300				1,455,000.00			1,455,000.00
Department Of Transportation, Federal Highway Administration	2005-2009	69	57	3300	5			120,000.00			120,000.00
	2003-2007					39,020.00					39,020.00
	2001-2005					26,294.98					26,294.98
	2000-2004					38,347.82					38,347.82
Fund Equities:											
Unobligated Balances (Expired)						-17,384,634.02				4,474,929.56	-21,859,563.58
Unobligated Balances (Unexpired)						-717,722,996.44				-52,398,112.66	-665,324,883.78
Accounts Payable						-30,853,000.05				12,188,205.45	-43,041,205.50
Undelivered Orders						-1,321,632,545.55				92,970,997.52	-1,414,603,543.07
	Subtotal	57		3300		-0-	1,118,455,000.00	2,817,000.00	1,063,278,894.81	57,993,105.19	-0-
Military Construction, Air Force Reserve											
Fund Resources:											
Undisbursed Funds	2007-2011	57		3730			45,000,000.00		376,216.62		44,623,783.38
	2006-2010					94,505,185.09			47,816,602.12		46,688,582.97
	2005-2009					46,997,807.91			35,386,695.15		11,611,112.76
	2004-2008					4,884,155.83			2,629,639.37		2,254,516.46
	2003-2007					2,434,468.00			1,993,436.71		441,031.29
	2002-2006					1,864,549.85			1,385,943.44		478,606.41
	2001-2005					11,396.29					11,396.29
	2000-2004					38,809.44					38,809.44
	1999-2003					2,840.21					2,840.21
	1998-2002					20,000.21			20,000.00	0.21	-0-
Fund Equities:											
Unobligated Balances (Expired)						-8,156.00				17,674.96	-25,830.96
Unobligated Balances (Unexpired)						-31,323,996.98				5,029,965.52	-36,353,962.50
Accounts Payable						-1,693,304.02				-237,118.49	-1,456,185.53
Undelivered Orders						-117,733,755.83				-49,419,055.61	-68,314,700.22
	Subtotal	57		3730		-0-	45,000,000.00		89,608,533.41	-44,608,533.41	-0-
Military Construction, Air National Guard											
Fund Resources:											
Undisbursed Funds	2007-2011	57		3830			126,000,000.00		12,092,515.99		113,907,484.01
	2006-2010					331,583,662.33			176,259,469.48		155,324,192.85
	2005-2009					111,606,586.99			97,849,291.55		13,757,295.44
	2004-2008					28,241,738.22			18,228,324.26		10,013,413.96
	2003-2007					2,628,646.74			1,677,931.75		950,714.99
	2002-2006					2,080,075.11			1,523,374.30		556,700.81
	2001-2005					538,895.70			427,010.66		111,885.04
	2000-2004					272,264.67			100,025.70		172,238.97
	1999-2003					29,813.02			16,620.89		13,192.13
	1998-2002					190,453.88				190,453.88	
Fund Equities:											
Unobligated Balances (Expired)						-573,723.22				-361,437.63	-212,285.59
Unobligated Balances (Unexpired)						-96,263,106.78				-45,224,878.23	-51,038,228.55
Accounts Payable						-5,879,335.60				-5,263,292.97	-616,042.63

Footnotes At End Of Chapter

Appropriations, Outlays, and Balances – Continued

Appropriation or Fund Account Title	Reg	Tr From	Account Number	Sub No.	Period of Availability	Balances, Beginning Of Fiscal Year	Appropriations And Other Obligational Authority[1]	Transfers Borrowings And Investment (Net)[2]	Outlays (Net)	Balances Withdrawn And Other Transactions[3]	Balances, End Of Fiscal Year[4]
Military Construction, Air National Guard - Continued											
Fund Equities: - Continued											
Undelivered Orders						-374,455,971.06				-131,515,409.63	-242,940,561.43
Subtotal	57		3830			-0-	126,000,000.00		308,174,564.58	-182,174,564.58	-0-
Total, Military Construction, Air Force						------	1,289,455,000.00	2,817,000.00	1,461,061,992.80	-168,789,992.80	------
Defense Agencies											
General Fund Accounts											
Chemical Demilitarization Construction, Defense-Wide											
Fund Resources:											
Undisbursed Funds	97		0391		2007-2011	45,401,782.79	131,000,000.00		10,927,527.71	------	120,072,472.29
					2005-2009				22,933,289.81	------	22,468,492.98
Fund Equities:											
Unobligated Balances (Unexpired)						-17,948,077.96			------	16,122,618.29	-34,070,696.25
Accounts Payable						-850.74			------	-944,590.63	943,739.89
Undelivered Orders						-27,452,854.09			------	81,961,154.82	-109,414,008.91
Subtotal	97		0391			-0-	131,000,000.00		33,860,817.52	97,139,182.48	-0-
Military Construction, Defense-Wide											
Fund Resources:											
Undisbursed Funds	97		0500		2007-2011	977,809,518.91	1,125,500,000.00	12,946,000.00	64,878,074.48	------	1,073,567,925.52
					2006-2010	431,163,656.83	-58,229,000.00	-5,956,000.00	405,300,703.98	------	508,323,814.93
					2005-2009	263,859,533.44	-43,000,000.00	-74,000.00	180,954,737.96	------	207,134,918.87
					2004-2008	20,600,000.00	-9,000,000.00	-1,658,000.00	94,501,071.04	------	158,700,462.40
					2006-2007	20,600,000.00					20,600,000.00
					2003-2007	112,112,397.12		-3,325,000.00	40,529,530.32		68,257,866.80
					2002-2006	41,631,297.21		-7,000.00	28,375,344.85		13,248,952.36
					2001-2005	9,518,304.48		-97,000.00	3,164,584.79		6,256,719.69
					2000-2004	3,546,734.62			660,741.64		2,885,992.98
					1999-2003	6,559,433.98			418,223.27		6,141,210.71
					1998-2002	540,886.70			15,663.64	525,223.06	
Transfer To:											
Department Of Transportation, Federal Highway Administration	69		0500	5	2004-2008	18,621,000.00					18,621,000.00
Accounts Receivable						-2,513.62				-10,913.00	8,399.38
Fund Equities:											
Unobligated Balances (Expired)						-31,983,943.71				4,378,208.28	-36,362,151.99
Unobligated Balances (Unexpired)						-958,598,104.46				-194,690,229.37	-763,907,875.09
Accounts Payable						-172,267,802.32				8,732,707.68	-181,000,510.00
Undelivered Orders						-723,110,399.18				379,366,327.38	-1,102,476,726.56
Subtotal	97		0500			-0-	1,015,271,000.00	1,829,000.00	818,798,675.97	198,301,324.03	-0-
Base Realignment And Closure Account, Defense											
Fund Resources:											
Undisbursed Funds	97		0510		2005	6,390.26			3,919.61		2,470.65
					No Year	1,406,844,080.62	252,278,730.00		541,126,089.33		1,117,996,721.29
Accounts Receivable						-15,638,237.66				93,606,486.04	-109,244,723.70
Unfilled Customer Orders						3,151,782.59					3,151,782.59

Appropriations, Outlays, and Balances - Continued

Appropriation or Fund Account (Title)	Reg	Tr From	Account Number	Sub No.	Period of Availability	Balances, Beginning Of Fiscal Year	Appropriations And Other Obligational Authority[1]	Transfers Borrowings And Investment (Net)[2]	Outlays (Net)	Balances Withdrawn And Other Transactions[3]	Balances, End Of Fiscal Year[4]
Fund Equities:											
Unobligated Balances (Expired)						-2,470.65					-2,470.65
Unobligated Balances (Unexpired)						-681,219,092.08				-288,983,867.46	-392,235,224.62
Accounts Payable						-200,592,247.87				-137,939,532.39	-62,652,715.48
Undelivered Orders						-512,550,205.21				44,465,634.87	-557,015,840.08
Subtotal	97		0510			-0-	252,278,730.00		541,130,008.94	-288,851,278.94	-0-
Department Of Defense Base Closure Account 2005											
Fund Resources:											
Undisbursed Funds	97		0512		No Year	1,416,473,997.84	5,626,223,000.00		1,061,980,901.21		5,980,716,096.63
Accounts Receivable										-3,970,330.07	3,970,330.07
Fund Equities:											
Unobligated Balances (Unexpired)						-178,072,310.21				1,145,788,723.23	-1,323,861,033.44
Accounts Payable						-105,093,567.84				203,921,563.09	-309,015,130.93
Undelivered Orders						-1,133,308,119.79				3,218,502,142.54	-4,351,810,262.33
Subtotal	97		0512			-0-	5,626,223,000.00		1,061,980,901.21	4,564,242,098.79	-0-
Foreign Currency Fluctuations, Construction, Defense											
Fund Resources:											
Undisbursed Funds	97		0803		No Year	509,000.00					509,000.00
Fund Equities:											
Unobligated Balances (Unexpired)						-509,000.00					-509,000.00
Subtotal	97		0803			-0-					-0-
North Atlantic Treaty Organization, Security Investment Program, Defense											
Fund Resources:											
Undisbursed Funds	97		0804		No Year	315,991,511.16	204,789,420.00		150,732,705.60		370,048,225.56
Fund Equities:											
Unobligated Balances (Unexpired)						-53,193,231.60				-18,148,425.04	-35,044,806.56
Accounts Payable						-185,055.30				-269,709.49	84,654.19
Undelivered Orders						-262,613,224.26				72,474,848.93	-335,088,073.19
Subtotal	97		0804			-0-	204,789,420.00		150,732,705.60	54,056,714.40	-0-
Total, Military Construction, Defense Agencies							7,229,562,150.00	1,829,000.00	2,606,503,109.24	4,624,888,040.76	
Total, Military Construction							13,908,662,150.00	-80,530,541.00	7,897,613,514.71	5,930,518,094.29	
Family Housing											
Department Of The Army											
General Fund Accounts											
Family Housing, Army											
Fund Resources:											
Undisbursed Funds	97	21	0702		2001-2005	1,824,342.91			1,546,380.33		277,962.58
					2000-2004	1,430,077.77			716,768.76		713,309.01
					1999-2003	827,660.86			571,773.61		255,887.25
					1998-2002	191,132.08			190,158.37	973.71	
Fund Equities:											
Unobligated Balances (Expired)						-1,578,343.69				-896,904.25	-681,439.44
Accounts Payable						-1,068,720.77				-1,032,221.73	-36,499.04

Footnotes At End Of Chapter

Appropriations, Outlays, and Balances – Continued

Appropriation or Fund Account Title	Period of Availability	Reg	Tr From	Account Number	Sub No.	Balances, Beginning Of Fiscal Year	Appropriations And Other Obligational Authority[1]	Transfers Borrowings And Investment (Net)[2]	Outlays (Net)	Balances Withdrawn And Other Transactions[3]	Balances, End Of Fiscal Year[4]
Family Housing, Army - Continued											
Fund Equities: - Continued											
Undelivered Orders				0702		-1,626,149.16				-1,096,928.80	-529,220.36
Subtotal		21				-0-			3,025,081.07	-3,025,081.07	-0-
Family Housing Construction, Army				0720							
Fund Resources:		21									
Undisbursed Funds											
2007-2011	2007-2011					381,701,656.56	579,000,000.00	22,921,000.00	56,287,356.15		545,633,643.85
2006-2010	2006-2010					264,012,723.40		-60,905,000.00	210,633,093.05		110,163,563.51
2005-2009	2005-2009					49,664,506.64		-31,000,000.00	160,435,887.90		72,576,835.50
2004-2008	2004-2008					580,923.19			40,963,700.01		8,700,806.63
2003-2007	2003-2007								300,136.61		280,786.58
2002-2006	2002-2006					10,087,736.81			8,618,496.36		1,469,240.45
Fund Equities:											
Unobligated Balances (Expired)						-140,558.23				456,664.19	-597,222.42
Unobligated Balances (Unexpired)						-163,462,372.16				73,457,391.41	-236,919,763.57
Accounts Payable						-9,581,036.12				1,939,712.63	-11,520,748.75
Undelivered Orders						-532,863,580.09				-43,076,438.31	-489,787,141.78
Subtotal		21		0720		-0-	579,000,000.00	-68,984,000.00	477,238,670.08	32,777,329.92	-0-
Family Housing Operation And Maintenance, Army				0725							
Fund Resources:		21									
Undisbursed Funds											
2007	2007					203,748,597.64	671,311,000.00	55,840,000.00	500,832,193.01		226,318,806.99
2006	2006					40,157,483.53		-15,396,000.00	[50]142,715,272.49		45,637,325.15
2005	2005					32,588,433.30		-4,221,000.00	17,317,063.44		18,619,420.09
2004	2004					17,624,159.03			10,874,637.22		21,713,796.08
2003	2003					12,522,145.82			1,212,315.52		16,411,843.51
2002	2002					212,603.57			1,513,378.19	11,008,767.63	
Accounts Receivable						1,056,200.77				39,936.07	172,667.50
Unfilled Customer Orders										410,844.78	645,355.99
Fund Equities:											
Unobligated Balances (Expired)						-36,818,478.08				-4,098,998.89	-32,719,479.19
Accounts Payable						-53,289,115.88				8,965,039.60	-62,254,155.48
Undelivered Orders						-217,802,029.70				16,743,550.94	-234,545,580.64
Subtotal		21		0725		-0-	671,311,000.00	36,223,000.00	674,464,859.87	33,069,140.13	-0-
Total, Family Housing, Army							1,250,311,000.00	-32,761,000.00	1,154,728,611.02	62,821,388.98	

Department Of The Navy

General Fund Accounts

Appropriation or Fund Account Title	Period of Availability	Reg	Tr From	Account Number	Sub No.	Balances, Beginning Of Fiscal Year	Appropriations And Other Obligational Authority[1]	Transfers Borrowings And Investment (Net)[2]	Outlays (Net)	Balances Withdrawn And Other Transactions[3]	Balances, End Of Fiscal Year[4]
Family Housing, Navy And Marine Corps		17		0703							
Fund Resources:											
Undisbursed Funds											
2001-2005	2001-2005					5,977,881.54			1,088,279.82		4,889,601.72
2000-2004	2000-2004					2,966,418.89			16,629.99		2,949,788.90
1999-2003	1999-2003					1,186,958.15			98,772.94		1,088,185.21
1998-2002	1998-2002					804,326.13			63,006.99	741,319.14	
Fund Equities:											
Unobligated Balances (Expired)						-5,261,679.21				149,820.07	-5,411,499.28
Accounts Payable						-1,181,367.18				792,062.32	-1,973,429.50
Undelivered Orders						-4,492,538.32				-2,949,891.27	-1,542,647.05

Appropriations, Outlays, and Balances - Continued

Title	Reg	Tr From	Account Number	Sub No.	Period of Availability	Balances, Beginning Of Fiscal Year	Appropriations And Other Obligational Authority[1]	Transfers Borrowings And Investment (Net)[2]	Outlays (Net)	Balances Withdrawn And Other Transactions[3]	Balances, End Of Fiscal Year[4]
Family Housing Construction, Navy And Marine Corps											
	17		0703		Subtotal	-0-			1,266,689.74	-1,266,689.74	-0-
Fund Resources:											
Undisbursed Funds	17		0730		2007-2011		130,747,000.00	986,000.00	12,236,835.75		119,496,164.25
					2006-2010	191,489,834.50		-37,896,000.00	39,801,505.13		113,792,329.37
					2005-2009	9,070,092.04			6,087,698.21		2,982,393.83
					2004-2008	59,134,071.39		-3,257,000.00	37,472,462.05		18,404,609.34
					2003-2007	50,602,736.47		-30,624,000.00	9,269,768.71		10,708,967.76
					2002-2006	30,467,638.61			8,839,713.28		21,627,925.33
Fund Equities:											
Unobligated Balances (Expired)						-1,613,712.18				7,440,593.82	-9,054,306.00
Unobligated Balances (Unexpired)						-188,764,277.45				-142,372,717.68	-46,391,559.77
Accounts Payable						-2,622,265.33				9,532,926.32	-12,155,191.65
Undelivered Orders						-147,764,118.05				71,647,214.41	-219,411,332.46
	17		0730		Subtotal	-0-	130,747,000.00	-70,791,000.00	113,707,983.13	-53,751,983.13	-0-
Family Housing Operation And Maintenance, Navy And Marine Corps											
Fund Resources:											
Undisbursed Funds	17		0735		2007		506,638,000.00	2,720,000.00	317,179,167.64		192,178,832.36
					2006-2007	13,405,062.32		-778,000.00	3,403,870.00		9,223,192.32
					2006	238,925,393.05		-4,293,000.00	186,853,079.33		47,779,313.72
					2005	46,927,290.16		-6,712,000.00	18,055,748.41		22,159,541.75
					2004	25,997,961.24			3,227,711.59		22,770,249.65
					2003	15,324,525.48			2,117,654.63		13,206,870.85
					2002	36,848,853.40			561,156.79		36,287,696.61
Accounts Receivable						-12,343,752.42				-813,899.77	-11,529,852.65
Unfilled Customer Orders						2,505,632.11				2,455,237.06	50,395.05
Fund Equities:											
Unobligated Balances (Expired)						-52,757,789.82				-16,720,501.35	-36,037,288.47
Unobligated Balances (Unexpired)						-1,461,401.97				-1,461,401.97	
Accounts Payable						-36,841,099.20				-5,057,785.70	-31,783,313.50
Undelivered Orders						-276,530,674.35				-48,512,733.27	-228,017,941.08
	17		0735		Subtotal	-0-	506,638,000.00	-9,063,000.00	531,398,388.39	-33,823,388.39	-0-
Special Fund Accounts											
Rossmoor Liquidating Trust Settlement Account											
Fund Resources:											
Undisbursed Funds	17		5429		No Year	41,075.54					41,075.54
Fund Equities:											
Unobligated Balances (Unexpired)						-41,075.54					-41,075.54
	17		5429		Subtotal	-0-					-0-
Total, Family Housing, Navy							637,385,000.00	-79,854,000.00	646,373,061.26	-88,842,061.26	

Appropriations, Outlays, and Balances – Continued

		Account Symbol									
Appropriation or Fund Account		**Dept**									
Title	Period of Availability	Reg	Tr From	Account Number	Sub No.	Balances, Beginning Of Fiscal Year	Appropriations And Other Obligational Authority[1]	Transfers Borrowings And Other Investment (Net)[2]	Outlays (Net)	Balances Withdrawn And Other Transactions[3]	Balances, End Of Fiscal Year[4]
Department Of The Air Force											
General Fund Accounts											
Family Housing, Air Force											
Fund Resources:											
Undisbursed Funds	2001-2005	57		0704		6,779,022.94			364,758.37		6,414,264.57
	2000-2004					1,876,976.57			344,791.76		1,532,184.81
	1999-2003					2,027,620.69			381,136.67		1,646,484.02
	1998-2002					1,269,245.58			100,408.27	1,168,837.31	-0-
Fund Equities:											
Unobligated Balances (Expired)						-10,387,296.12				-1,787,259.65	-8,600,036.47
Accounts Payable						-299,554.35				-60,170.79	-239,383.56
Undelivered Orders						-1,266,015.31				-512,501.94	-753,513.37
	Subtotal	57		0704		-0-			1,191,095.07	-1,191,095.07	-0-
Family Housing Construction, Air Force											
Fund Resources:											
Undisbursed Funds	2007-2011	57		0740			1,168,000,000.00	54,399,000.00	40,697,271.85		1,181,701,728.15
	2006-2010					1,327,584,839.49		-68,298,000.00	157,301,777.50		1,101,985,061.99
	2005-2009					673,705,534.52	-18,000,000.00	-104,321,000.00	203,157,576.16		348,226,958.36
	2004-2008					255,794,431.78		-8,030,000.00	113,492,881.06		134,271,550.72
	2003-2007					89,728,130.53		-36,633,000.00	22,259,525.15		30,835,605.38
	2002-2006					40,351,908.18			6,101,443.70		34,250,464.48
Fund Equities:											
Unobligated Balances (Expired)						-4,904,142.29				5,565,300.54	-10,469,442.83
Unobligated Balances (Unexpired)						-1,033,447,908.26				598,501,293.16	-1,631,949,201.42
Accounts Payable						-22,238,802.76				813,938.77	-23,052,741.53
Undelivered Orders						-1,326,573,991.19				-160,774,007.89	-1,165,799,983.30
	Subtotal	57		0740		-0-	1,150,000,000.00	-162,883,000.00	543,010,475.42	444,106,524.58	-0-
Family Housing Operation And Maintenance, Air Force											
Fund Resources:											
Undisbursed Funds	2007	57		0745			750,000,000.00	13,334,000.00	[5]459,852,828.89		303,481,171.11
	2006-2007					44,260,571.28			37,517,789.31		6,742,781.97
	2006					245,987,060.03		-7,000,000.00	185,046,644.08		53,940,415.95
	2005					75,749,739.41		-4,000,000.00	42,964,435.83		28,785,303.58
	2004					33,218,623.22			11,348,207.82		21,870,415.40
	2003					24,139,981.93			2,322,348.88		21,817,633.05
	2002					25,695,650.14			502,954.34	25,192,695.80	
Accounts Receivable						1,063,242.33				-116,811.06	1,180,053.39
Unfilled Customer Orders						350,083.14				-330,030.78	680,113.92
Fund Equities:											
Unobligated Balances (Expired)						-64,216,022.40				-6,446,973.87	-57,769,048.53
Unobligated Balances (Unexpired)						-19,498,947.24				-19,498,947.24	
Accounts Payable						-39,283,538.55				14,190,840.39	-53,474,378.94
Undelivered Orders						-327,466,443.29				-211,982.39	-327,254,460.90
	Subtotal	57		0745		-0-	750,000,000.00	2,334,000.00	739,555,209.15	12,778,790.85	-0-
Total, Family Housing, Air Force						-0-	1,900,000,000.00	-160,549,000.00	1,283,756,779.64	455,694,220.36	-0-

Appropriations, Outlays, and Balances - Continued

Title	Period of Availability	Reg	Tr From	Account Number	Sub No.	Balances, Beginning Of Fiscal Year	Appropriations And Other Obligational Authority[1]	Transfers Borrowings And Investment (Net)[2]	Outlays (Net)	Balances Withdrawn And Other Transactions[3]	Balances, End Of Fiscal Year[4]
Defense Agencies											
General Fund Accounts											
Family Housing, Defense-Wide											
Fund Resources:											
Undisbursed Funds	2002-2006	97		0706		126,826.11					126,826.11
	2000-2004					10,596.03					10,596.03
	1999-2003					13,864.13					13,864.13
	2002					3,901,338.92			34,084.41	3,867,254.51	------
	1998-2002					86,517.40			7,773.95	78,743.45	------
Accounts Receivable						-163,839.03				-163,839.03	------
Fund Equities:											
Unobligated Balances (Expired)						-3,029,129.57				-2,881,400.13	-147,729.44
Accounts Payable						-16,086.98				-16,086.98	------
Undelivered Orders						-930,087.01				-926,530.18	-3,556.83
Subtotal		97		0706		-0-			41,858.36	-41,858.36	-0-
Family Housing Construction, Defense-Wide											
Fund Resources:											
Undisbursed Funds	2007-2011	97		0760			9,000,000.00				9,000,000.00
	2005-2009					14,542.98					14,542.98
	2004-2008					170,280.75			116,006.09		54,274.66
	2003-2007					5,241.44			3,021.91		2,219.53
Fund Equities:											
Unobligated Balances (Unexpired)						-116,045.10				-8,685,790.86	-8,801,835.96
Undelivered Orders						-74,020.07				195,181.14	-269,201.21
Subtotal		97		0760		-0-	9,000,000.00		119,028.00	8,880,972.00	-0-
Family Housing Operation And Maintenance, Defense-Wide											
Fund Resources:											
Undisbursed Funds	2007	97		0765		16,509,275.02	48,671,000.00	600,000.00	39,555,643.57		9,715,356.43
	2006					3,829,689.24		-200,000.00	12,814,110.12		3,495,164.90
	2005					5,398,348.08		-400,000.00	494,320.56		2,935,368.68
	2004					6,522,939.48			222,080.93		5,176,267.15
	2003					2,571,984.29			91,832.71		6,431,106.77
Accounts Receivable										-178,736.43	2,750,720.72
Fund Equities:											
Unobligated Balances (Expired)						-6,861,026.45				2,855,152.64	-9,716,179.09
Accounts Payable						-81,054.31				485,600.37	-566,654.68
Undelivered Orders						-27,890,155.35				-7,669,004.47	-20,221,150.88
Subtotal		97		0765		-0-	48,671,000.00		53,177,987.89	-4,506,987.89	-0-
Department Of Defense Family Housing Improvement Fund											
Fund Resources:											
Undisbursed Funds	No Year	97		0834		307,431,715.04	178,570,109.00	324,399,000.00	288,654,195.87	152,648,865.69	521,746,628.17
Fund Equities:											
Unobligated Balances (Unexpired)						-202,448,701.32				-183,042.64	-355,097,567.01
Accounts Payable						-183,042.64					-183,042.64
Undelivered Orders						-104,799,971.08				61,849,090.08	-166,649,061.16
Subtotal		97		0834		-0-	178,570,109.00	324,399,000.00	288,654,195.87	214,314,913.13	-0-

Footnotes At End Of Chapter

Appropriations, Outlays, and Balances – Continued

Appropriation or Fund Account — Title	Period of Availability	Dept Reg	Tr From	Account Number	Sub No.	Balances, Beginning Of Fiscal Year	Appropriations And Other Obligational Authority[1]	Transfers Borrowings And Investment (Net)[2]	Outlays (Net)	Balances Withdrawn And Other Transactions[3]	Balances, End Of Fiscal Year[4]
Department Of Defense Military Unaccompanied Housing Improvement Fund											
Fund Resources:											
Undisbursed Funds	No Year	97		0836		------		42,710,000.00	42,700,000.00	------	10,000.00
Fund Equities:											
Unobligated Balances (Unexpired)										10,000.00	-10,000.00
	Subtotal	97		0836		-0-		42,710,000.00	42,700,000.00	10,000.00	-0-
Public Enterprise Funds											
Homeowners Assistance Fund, Defense											
Fund Resources:											
Undisbursed Funds	No Year	97		4090		9,875,715.99			1,815,317.04		8,060,398.95
Accounts Receivable						11,791.87					11,791.87
Fund Equities:											
Unobligated Balances (Unexpired)						-9,547,269.19				-1,531,472.06	-8,015,797.13
Accounts Payable						-6,335.35				-7,663.40	1,328.05
Undelivered Orders						-333,903.32				-276,181.58	-57,721.74
	Subtotal	97		4090		-0-			1,815,317.04	-1,815,317.04	-0-
Total, Family Housing, Defense Agencies							236,241,109.00	367,109,000.00	386,508,387.16	216,841,721.84	
Total, Family Housing							4,023,937,109.00	93,945,000.00	3,471,366,839.08	646,515,269.92	
Revolving And Management Funds											
Department Of The Army											
Intragovernmental Funds											
Working Capital Fund, Army Conventional Ammunition											
Fund Resources:											
Undisbursed Funds	No Year	21		4528		18,558,558.32			11,957,909.00		6,600,649.32
Unfilled Customer Orders						3,596,785.89				3,596,785.89	
Fund Equities:											
Unobligated Balances (Unexpired)						-1,499,282.70				4,236,475.64	-5,735,758.34
Accounts Payable						-4,882,394.65				-4,017,503.67	-864,890.98
Undelivered Orders						-15,773,666.86				-15,773,666.86	-0-
	Subtotal	21		4528		-0-			11,957,909.00	-11,957,909.00	
Defense Working Capital Fund, Army											
Fund Resources:											
Undisbursed Funds	No Year	97		4930	1	875,343,188.47	627,790,000.00	-145,700,000.00	-921,650,566.17	11,534,680,782.21	2,279,083,754.64
Unfunded Contract Authority						6,374,038,852.08	[5]10,715,333,056.10				5,554,691,125.97
Accounts Receivable						290,428,234.85				-103,333,636.98	393,761,871.83
Unfilled Customer Orders						3,807,550,928.89				-1,336,140,146.69	5,143,691,075.58
Fund Equities:											
Unobligated Balances (Unexpired)						-1,791,462,591.36				724,854,146.93	-2,516,316,738.29
Accounts Payable						-783,819,463.44				493,499,669.18	-1,277,319,132.62
Undelivered Orders						-8,772,079,149.49				805,512,807.62	-9,577,591,957.11

Appropriations, Outlays, and Balances - Continued

Appropriation or Fund Account — Title	Period of Availability	Dept Reg	Dept Tr From	Account Number	Sub No.	Balances, Beginning Of Fiscal Year	Appropriations And Other Obligational Authority[1]	Transfers Borrowings And Investment (Net)[2]	Outlays (Net)	Balances Withdrawn And Other Transactions[3]	Balances, End Of Fiscal Year[4]
Subtotal		97		4930		-0-	11,343,123,056.10	-145,700,000.00	-921,650,566.17	12,119,073,622.27	-0-
Total, Revolving And Management Funds, Army							11,343,123,056.10	-145,700,000.00	-909,692,657.17	12,107,115,713.27	
Department Of The Navy											
Intragovernmental Funds											
National Defense Sealift Fund, Navy											
Fund Resources:											
Undisbursed Funds	No Year	17		4557		2,387,469,515.46	1,072,752,000.00	-25,641,000.00	1,755,765,590.18		1,678,814,925.28
Accounts Receivable						83,923,469.25				-22,876,744.50	106,800,213.75
Unfilled Customer Orders										-143,979,782.91	143,979,782.91
Fund Equities:											
Unobligated Balances (Unexpired)						-463,201,565.73				635,678,307.47	-1,098,879,873.20
Accounts Payable						-11,262,576.29				-64,535,923.31	53,273,347.02
Undelivered Orders						-1,996,928,842.69				-1,112,940,446.93	-883,988,395.76
Subtotal		17		4557		-0-	1,072,752,000.00	-25,641,000.00	1,755,765,590.18	-708,654,590.18	-0-
Defense Working Capital Fund, Navy											
Fund Resources:											
Undisbursed Funds	No Year	97		4930	2	1,244,508,837.70	115,865,000.00	[5]11,537,160.09	215,509,720.59		1,156,401,277.20
Unfunded Contract Authority						6,039,689,994.85	[5]5,640,908,677.17			6,463,950,772.14	5,216,647,899.88
Accounts Receivable						465,762,267.47				-263,323,026.62	729,085,294.09
Unfilled Customer Orders						6,910,498,580.19				357,666,035.14	6,552,832,545.05
Fund Equities:											
Unobligated Balances (Unexpired)						-2,536,123,778.67				-1,010,956,988.37	-1,525,166,790.30
Accounts Payable						-4,551,565,370.59				-119,084,271.18	-4,432,481,099.41
Undelivered Orders						-7,572,770,530.95				124,548,595.56	-7,697,319,126.51
Subtotal		97		4930		-0-	5,756,773,677.17	11,537,160.09	215,509,720.59	5,552,801,116.67	-0-
Total, Revolving And Management Funds, Navy							6,829,525,677.17	-14,103,839.91	1,971,275,310.77	4,844,146,526.49	
Department Of The Air Force											
Intragovernmental Funds											
Defense Working Capital Fund, Air Force											
Fund Resources:											
Undisbursed Funds	No Year	97		4930	3	1,380,930,936.60	43,882,000.00	-119,600,000.00	-400,271,310.07		1,705,484,246.67
Unfunded Contract Authority						4,354,837,910.75	[5]9,988,202,210.04			9,365,996,797.61	4,977,043,323.18
Accounts Receivable						2,083,564,451.00				251,766,289.28	1,831,798,161.72
Unfilled Customer Orders						3,494,494,287.27				-1,056,970,578.19	4,551,464,865.46
Fund Equities:											
Unobligated Balances (Unexpired)						-663,323,207.37				1,541,137,094.11	-2,204,460,301.48
Accounts Payable						-3,624,983,919.98				-468,179,487.33	-3,156,804,432.65
Undelivered Orders						-7,025,520,458.27				679,005,404.63	-7,704,525,862.90
Subtotal		97		4930		-0-	10,032,084,210.04	-119,600,000.00	-400,271,310.07	10,312,755,520.11	-0-
Total, Revolving And Management Funds, Air Force							10,032,084,210.04	-119,600,000.00	-400,271,310.07	10,312,755,520.11	

Footnotes At End Of Chapter

Appropriations, Outlays, and Balances – Continued

Title	Period of Availability	Dept Reg	Tr From	Account Number	Sub No.	Balances, Beginning Of Fiscal Year	Appropriations And Other Obligational Authority[1]	Transfers Borrowings And Investment (Net)[2]	Outlays (Net)	Balances Withdrawn And Other Transactions[3]	Balances, End Of Fiscal Year[4]
Defense Agencies											
Public Enterprise Funds											
Reserve Mobilization Income Insurance Fund, Defense											
Fund Resources:											
Undisbursed Funds	No Year	97		4179		2,778,052.47			2,778,052.47	--------	--------
Unrealized Discount On Investments						0.01					0.01
Fund Equities:											
Unobligated Balances (Unexpired)						-2,778,052.48				-2,778,052.47	-0.01
Subtotal	Subtotal	97		4179		-0-			2,778,052.47	-2,778,052.47	-0-
Intragovernmental Funds											
National Defense Stockpile Transaction Fund, Defense											
Fund Resources:											
Undisbursed Funds	No Year	97		4555		1,500,053,704.35	-186,000,000.00		-229,012,435.89	-2,128,833.73	1,543,066,140.24
Accounts Receivable						-10,447.91					2,118,385.82
Fund Equities:											
Unobligated Balances (Unexpired)						-1,495,589,431.54				-31,350,903.55	-1,464,238,527.99
Accounts Payable						-58,490.78				232,152.81	-290,643.59
Undelivered Orders						-4,395,334.12				76,260,020.36	-80,655,354.48
Subtotal	Subtotal	97		4555		-0-	-186,000,000.00		-229,012,435.89	43,012,435.89	-0-
Defense Working Capital Fund, Defense Commissary Agency											
Fund Resources:											
Undisbursed Funds	No Year	97		4930	4	310,044,187.80	1,179,423,000.00		1,200,277,305.05		289,189,882.75
Unfunded Contract Authority						184,706,092.57	[5]240,065,040.82			261,722,601.83	163,048,531.56
Accounts Receivable						131,034,972.70				-80,080,250.91	211,115,223.61
Unfilled Customer Orders						2,122,991.14				87,986.15	2,035,004.99
Fund Equities:											
Unobligated Balances (Unexpired)						-6,401,157.23				-184,363,468.82	[5]4177,962,311.59
Accounts Payable						-563,095,755.35				206,619,399.73	-769,715,155.08
Undelivered Orders						-58,411,331.63				15,224,467.79	-73,635,799.42
Subtotal	Subtotal	97		4930		-0-	1,419,488,040.82		1,200,277,305.05	219,210,735.77	-0-
Defense Working Capital Fund, Defense Agencies											
Fund Resources:											
Undisbursed Funds	No Year	97		4930	5	1,463,287,078.88	489,316,000.00	-374,904,000.00	-213,732,482.61	36,103,105,909.44	1,791,431,561.49
Unfunded Contract Authority						8,473,876,075.47	[5]36,590,943,573.65			-187,292,990.39	8,961,713,739.68
Accounts Receivable						2,003,122,114.69				-2,050,434,790.75	2,190,415,105.08
Unfilled Customer Orders						5,071,388,222.34					7,121,823,013.09
Fund Equities:											
Unobligated Balances (Unexpired)						-699,809,555.48				-124,946,074.84	-574,863,480.64
Accounts Payable						-4,433,354,965.07				-233,693,006.48	-4,199,661,958.59
Undelivered Orders						-11,878,508,970.83				3,412,349,009.28	-15,290,857,980.11
Subtotal	Subtotal	97		4930		-0-	37,080,259,573.65	-374,904,000.00	-213,732,482.61	36,919,088,056.26	-0-
Building Maintenance Fund, Defense											
Fund Resources:											
Undisbursed Funds	No Year	97		4931		44,300,196.82			2,790,271.05	8,908,137.08	41,509,925.77
Accounts Receivable						14,226,303.08					5,318,166.00

Appropriations, Outlays, and Balances - Continued

Appropriation or Fund Account — Title	Period of Availability	Reg	Tr From	Account Number	Sub No.	Balances, Beginning Of Fiscal Year	Appropriations And Other Obligational Authority[1]	Transfers Borrowings And Investment (Net)[2]	Outlays (Net)	Balances Withdrawn And Other Transactions[3]	Balances, End Of Fiscal Year[4]
Unfilled Customer Orders						12,196,947.39				-8,387,378.78	20,584,326.17
Fund Equities:											
Unobligated Balances (Unexpired)						-18,900,902.10				4,417,036.54	-23,317,938.64
Accounts Payable						-2,356,833.45				144,800.17	-2,501,633.62
Undelivered Orders						-49,465,711.74				-7,872,866.06	-41,592,845.68
Subtotal		97		4931		-0-			2,790,271.05	-2,790,271.05	-0-
Pentagon Reservation Maintenance Revolving Fund											
Fund Resources:											
Undisbursed Funds	2007-2011	97		4950		434,008,859.82	18,428,000.00		4,538,583.00		13,889,417.00
	No Year								-58,727,141.07		492,736,000.89
Accounts Receivable						992,369.77				-1,651,399.02	2,643,768.79
Unfilled Customer Orders						111,014,254.52				17,439,134.51	93,575,120.01
Fund Equities:											
Unobligated Balances (Unexpired)						-34,962,206.45				24,160,220.15	-59,122,426.60
Accounts Payable						-37,884,795.61				5,177,625.03	-43,062,420.64
Undelivered Orders						-473,168,482.05				27,490,977.40	-500,659,459.45
Subtotal		97		4950		-0-	18,428,000.00		-54,188,558.07	72,616,558.07	-0-
Total, Revolving And Management Funds, Defense Agencies							38,332,175,614.47	-374,904,000.00	708,912,152.00	37,248,359,462.47	
Total, Revolving And Management Funds							66,536,908,557.78	-654,307,839.91	1,370,223,495.53	64,512,377,222.34	
Defense Agencies-Other											
Management Funds											
Consolidated Reporting For DOD Closed Accounts											
Fund Resources:											
Undisbursed Funds	No Year	97		3999			100,757,286.36		100,757,286.36		
Total, Defense Agencies-Other							100,757,286.36		100,757,286.36		
Trust Funds											
Department Of The Army											
Trust Fund Accounts											
Bequest Of Major General Fred C. Ainsworth, Library, Walter Reed General Hospital											
Fund Resources:											
Undisbursed Funds	No Year	21		8063		247.50	536.25		-317.73		1,101.48
Investments In Public Debt Securities						22,000.00					22,000.00
Fund Equities:											
Unobligated Balances (Unexpired)						-22,247.50					-23,101.48
Accounts Payable										853.98	
Subtotal		21		8063		-0-	536.25		-317.73	853.98	-0-

Footnotes At End Of Chapter

Appropriations, Outlays, and Balances – Continued

Title	Period of Availability	Reg	Tr From	Account Number	Sub No.	Balances, Beginning Of Fiscal Year	Appropriations And Other Obligational Authority[1]	Transfers Borrowings And Investment (Net)[2]	Outlays (Net)	Balances Withdrawn And Other Transactions[3]	Balances, End Of Fiscal Year[4]
Department Of The Army General Gift Fund											
Fund Resources:											
Undisbursed Funds	No Year	21		8927		1,050,725.96	5,889,815.31	-58,000.00	5,907,631.99		974,909.28
Investments In Public Debt Securities						3,377,000.00		58,000.00			3,435,000.00
Fund Equities:											
Unobligated Balances (Unexpired)						-4,029,689.34				200,131.28	-4,229,820.62
Accounts Payable						-147,409.72				24,996.84	-172,406.56
Undelivered Orders						-250,626.90				-242,944.80	-7,682.10
	Subtotal	21		8927		-0-	5,889,815.31		5,907,631.99	-17,816.68	-0-
Total, Department Of The Army							5,890,351.56		5,907,314.26	-16,962.70	
Department Of The Navy											
Trust Fund Accounts											
Department Of The Navy General Gift Fund											
Fund Resources:											
Undisbursed Funds	No Year	17		8716		1,758,214.21	1,492,062.29	-57,459.53	1,578,179.37		1,614,637.60
Unrealized Discount On Investments						-23,995.78		23,459.53			-536.25
Investments In Public Debt Securities						2,363,000.00		34,000.00			2,397,000.00
Fund Equities:											
Unobligated Balances (Unexpired)						-2,959,995.27				390,701.52	-3,350,696.79
Accounts Payable						-1,137,223.16				-476,818.60	-660,404.56
	Subtotal	17		8716		-0-	1,492,062.29		1,578,179.37	-86,117.08	-0-
Ships' Stores Profits, Navy											
Fund Resources:											
Undisbursed Funds	No Year	17		8723		1,962,988.17	14,907,139.83		11,659,281.52		5,210,846.48
Fund Equities:											
Unobligated Balances (Unexpired)						-1,962,988.17				3,247,858.31	-5,210,846.48
	Subtotal	17		8723		-0-	14,907,139.83		11,659,281.52	3,247,858.31	-0-
United States Naval Academy General Gift Fund											
Fund Resources:											
Undisbursed Funds	No Year	17		8733		6,195,563.15	6,247,284.05	39,828.44	6,125,658.82		6,357,016.82
Unrealized Discount On Investments						-171.56		171.56			
Investments In Public Debt Securities						7,227,000.00		-40,000.00			7,187,000.00
Fund Equities:											
Unobligated Balances (Unexpired)						-11,649,060.10				718,458.31	-12,367,518.41
Accounts Payable						-1,773,331.49				-596,833.08	-1,176,498.41
	Subtotal	17		8733		-0-	6,247,284.05		6,125,658.82	121,625.23	-0-
Total, Department Of The Navy							22,646,486.17		19,363,119.71	3,283,366.46	

Appropriations, Outlays, and Balances - Continued

Appropriation or Fund Account — Title	Period of Availability	Dept Reg	Dept Tr From	Account Number	Sub No.	Balances, Beginning Of Fiscal Year	Appropriations And Other Obligational Authority[1]	Transfers Borrowings And Investment (Net)[2]	Outlays (Net)	Balances Withdrawn And Other Transactions[3]	Balances, End Of Fiscal Year[4]
Department Of The Air Force											
Trust Fund Accounts											
Air Force Cadet Fund											
Fund Resources:											
Undisbursed Funds	No Year	57		8418		1,227,478.49			-2,888,292.04		4,115,770.53
Fund Equities:											
Accounts Payable						-1,227,478.49				2,888,292.04	-4,115,770.53
Subtotal	Subtotal	57		8418		-0-			-2,888,292.04	2,888,292.04	-0-
Department Of The Air Force General Gift Fund											
Fund Resources:											
Undisbursed Funds	No Year	57		8928		2,716,627.91	1,880,465.57	-101,398.18	1,786,970.51		2,708,724.79
Unrealized Discount On Investments						-2,718.08		1,398.18			-1,319.90
Investments In Public Debt Securities						710,000.00		100,000.00			810,000.00
Fund Equities:											
Unobligated Balances (Unexpired)						-3,174,452.22				96,247.20	-3,270,699.42
Accounts Payable						-77,777.87				-21,090.92	-56,686.95
Undelivered Orders						-171,679.74				18,338.78	-190,018.52
Subtotal	Subtotal	57		8928		-0-	1,880,465.57		1,786,970.51	93,495.06	-0-
Total, Department Of The Air Force		57					1,880,465.57		-1,101,321.53	2,981,787.10	
Defense Agencies											
General Fund Accounts											
General Fund Payment, Surcharge Collections, Sales Of Commissary Stores, Defense											
Fund Resources:											
Undisbursed Funds	2006-2010	97		0766		10,530,000.00					10,530,000.00
Fund Equities:											
Unobligated Balances (Unexpired)						-10,530,000.00					-10,530,000.00
Subtotal	Subtotal	97		0766		-0-					-0-
Trust Fund Accounts											
Surcharge Collections, Sales Of Commissary Stores, Defense Commissary Agency											
Fund Resources:											
Undisbursed Funds	No Year	97		8164		306,812,667.26	41,494,561.78		-10,533,377.04		317,346,044.30
Unfunded Contract Authority											41,494,561.78
Accounts Receivable						-784,586.02				-642,336.94	-142,249.08
Unfilled Customer Orders						27.85				-18.00	45.85
Fund Equities:											
Unobligated Balances (Unexpired)						-13,084,158.14				-13,084,158.14	
Accounts Payable						-21,230,885.39				20,588,982.50	-41,819,867.89
Undelivered Orders						-271,713,065.56				45,165,469.40	-316,878,534.96
Subtotal	Subtotal	97		8164		-0-	41,494,561.78		-10,533,377.04	52,027,938.82	-0-

Appropriations, Outlays, and Balances – Continued

Appropriation or Fund Account — Title	Period of Availability	Dept Reg	Tr From	Account Number	Sub No.	Balances, Beginning Of Fiscal Year	Appropriations And Other Obligational Authority[1]	Transfers Borrowings And Investment (Net)[2]	Outlays (Net)	Balances Withdrawn And Other Transactions[3]	Balances, End Of Fiscal Year[4]
Foreign National Employees Separation Pay Account, Defense											
Fund Resources:											
Undisbursed Funds	No Year	97		8165		559,429,856.72	75,266,679.61		69,094,145.61		565,602,390.72
Accounts Receivable						119,850.79					119,850.79
Fund Equities:											
Unobligated Balances (Unexpired)						-38,253,681.63				87,378.19	-38,341,059.82
Accounts Payable						-563,482,893.53				6,126,032.08	-569,608,925.61
Undelivered Orders						42,186,867.65				-40,876.27	42,227,743.92
Subtotal		97		8165		-0-	75,266,679.61		69,094,145.61	6,172,534.00	-0-
National Security Education Trust Fund											
Fund Resources:											
Undisbursed Funds	No Year	97		8168		-61,076.32	255,649.46	2,213,226.12	604,919.35		1,802,879.91
Unrealized Discount On Investments						-51,296.29		-15,394.47			-66,690.76
Investments In Public Debt Securities						5,960,831.65		-2,197,831.65			3,763,000.00
Fund Equities:											
Unobligated Balances (Unexpired)						-4,844,790.22				103,954.30	-4,948,744.52
Accounts Payable						-1,003,668.82				-453,224.19	-550,444.63
Undelivered Orders						-0-				-349,269.89	-349,269.89
Subtotal		97		8168		-0-	255,649.46		604,919.35		-0-
Voluntary Separation Incentive Fund, Defense											
Fund Resources:											
Undisbursed Funds	No Year	97		8335		2,445,520.19	85,875,350.15	57,542,256.97	141,950,985.71		3,912,141.60
Unrealized Discount On Investments								-2,858,593.75			-2,858,593.75
Investments In Public Debt Securities						614,734,612.25		-54,683,663.22			560,050,949.03
Fund Equities:											
Unobligated Balances (Unexpired)						-604,441,080.64				-55,827,186.79	-548,613,893.85
Accounts Payable											
Undelivered Orders						-12,739,051.80				-248,448.77	-12,490,603.03
Subtotal		97		8335		-0-	85,875,350.15		141,950,985.71	-56,075,635.56	-0-
Host Nation Support For U.S. Relocation Activities, Defense											
Fund Resources:											
Undisbursed Funds	No Year	97		8337		296,713.63	34,986,574.60	-4,215,913.83	30,767,374.40		300,000.00
Investments In Public Debt Securities						17,031,650.03		4,215,913.83			21,247,563.86
Fund Equities:											
Unobligated Balances (Unexpired)						-17,328,363.66				4,219,200.20	-21,547,563.86
Subtotal		97		8337		-0-	34,986,574.60		30,767,374.40	4,219,200.20	-0-
Total, Defense Agencies							237,878,815.60		231,884,048.03	5,994,767.57	
Total, Trust Funds							268,296,118.90		256,053,160.47	12,242,958.43	
Deductions For Offsetting Receipts											
Proprietary Receipts From The Public							-1,114,378,673.03		-1,114,378,673.03		
Intrabudgetary Transactions							-374,558,303.09		-374,558,303.09		
Offsetting Governmental Receipts							-7,772,928.85		-7,772,928.85		
Total, Offsetting Receipts							-1,496,709,904.97		-1,496,709,904.97		

Appropriations, Outlays, and Balances - Continued

Appropriation or Fund Account — Title	Period of Availability	Reg	Tr From	Account Number	Sub No.	Balances, Beginning Of Fiscal Year	Appropriations And Other Obligational Authority[1]	Transfers Borrowings And Investment (Net)[2]	Outlays (Net)	Balances Withdrawn And Other Transactions[3]	Balances, End Of Fiscal Year[4]
Total, Department Of Defense - Military							666,744,485,573.49	-86,952,380.91	529,871,494,332.57	136,786,038,860.01	
Memorandum											
Financing Accounts											
Public Enterprise Funds											
Arms Initiative, Guaranteed Loan Financing Account, Army											
Fund Resources:											
Undisbursed Funds	No Year	21		4275		1,292,396.72		15,301,783.19	16,202,749.09		391,430.82
Authority To Borrow From The Treasury							15,301,783.19	-15,301,783.19			
Fund Equities:											
Unobligated Balances (Unexpired)						-1,292,396.72				-900,965.90	-391,430.82
Subtotal		21		4275		-0-	15,301,783.19		16,202,749.09	-900,965.90	-0-
Department Of Defense Family Housing Improvement Fund, Direct Loan, Financing Account											
Fund Resources:											
Undisbursed Funds	No Year	97		4166		1,221.65		13,064,270.49	13,065,492.14		637,657,934.36
Authority To Borrow From The Treasury						296,676,736.74	355,876,382.03	-14,895,184.41		213,188.25	-213,188.25
Accounts Receivable						[12]276,910,703.00				-53,454,301.00	
Unfilled Customer Orders											130,365,004.00
Fund Equities:											
Undelivered Orders						[12]373,588,661.39				394,221,088.72	-767,809,750.11
Subtotal		97		4166		-0-	355,876,382.03	-1,830,913.92	13,065,492.14	340,979,975.97	-0-
Department Of Defense Family Housing Improvement Fund, Guaranteed Loan, Financing Account											
Fund Resources:											
Undisbursed Funds[55]	No Year	97		4167		30,241,103.79			5,317,265.18		24,923,838.61
Accounts Receivable											
Fund Equities:											
Unobligated Balances (Unexpired)						-30,241,103.73				-5,317,260.29	-24,923,843.44
Undelivered Orders						[12]4,878,257.06				-4,878,261.89	4.83
Subtotal		97		4167		-4,878,257.00			5,317,265.18	-10,195,522.18	-0-
Total, Financing Accounts						-4,878,257.00	371,178,165.22	-1,830,913.92	34,585,506.41	329,883,487.89	

Appropriations, Outlays, and Balances – Continued

Footnotes

1. The amounts in this column, unless otherwise footnoted, represent appropriations, increases and rescissions in borrowing authority or new contract authority. Appropriation accounts with appropriation transfer activity are presented in Table 1 (Appropriations and Appropriation Transfers) at the end of this chapter.

2. The amounts in this column, unless otherwise footnoted, represent transfers - other than appropriation transfers, borrowings (gross), investments (net), unrealized discounts or funds held outside the Treasury.

3. The amounts in this column, unless otherwise footnoted, represent obligated balances canceled for fiscal year 2002 pursuant to 31 U.S.C. 1553, changes in unfilled customer orders, accounts receivable, accounts payable, undelivered orders, unobligated balances and adjustments to borrowing and contract authority.

4. Unobligated balances for no-year or unexpired multiple year accounts are available for obligation; unobligated balances for expired fiscal year accounts are not available for obligation.

5. Includes $5,471.44 which represents payments for obligations of a closed account.

6. Includes $21,831.99 which represents payments for obligations of a closed account.

7. Includes $96,339.52 which represents payments for obligations of a closed account.

8. Includes $1,771,503.80 which represents payments for obligations of a closed account.

9. Includes $50,255.59 which represents payments for obligations of a closed account.

10. Includes $9,783.41 which represents payments for obligations of a closed account.

11. Includes $2,229.08 which represents payments for obligations of a closed account.

12. The opening balances of the following accounts have been adjusted during the current fiscal year and do not agree with last year's closing balances:

Account	Adjustment
17 06 1106 - Unobligated Balances (Expired)	$18,516.53
17 06 1106 - Unfilled Customer Orders	-18,516.53
17 06 1235 - Undisbursed Funds	-70,602,000.00
17 0610 1235 - Unobligated Balances (Expired)	70,602,000.00
17 0610 1235 - Undisbursed Funds	70,602,000.00
17 0610 1235 - Unobligated Balances (Unexpired)	-70,602,000.00
97 X 4166 - Undelivered Orders	-4,387,693.60
97 X 4166 - Accounts Receivable	4,934,930.60
97 X 4166 - Unfilled Customer Orders	-547,237.00
97 X 4167 - Undelivered Orders	16,027,645.94
97 X 4167 - Accounts Receivable	-16,027,645.94

13. Includes $14.69 which represents payments for obligations of a closed account.

14. Includes $1,224,885.97 which represents payments for obligations of a closed account.

15. Includes $1,606,091.29 which represents payments for obligations of a closed account.

16. Includes $156,927.64 which represents payments for obligations of a closed account.

17. Includes $95,946.84 which represents payments for obligations of a closed account.

18. Includes $131,925.47 which represents payments for obligations of a closed account.

19. Includes $335.97 which represents payments for obligations of a closed account.

20. Includes $314,798.15 which represents payments for obligations of a closed account.

21. Includes $114,025.69 which represents payments for obligations of a closed account.

22. Includes $172,520.76 which represents payments for obligations of a closed account.

23. Includes $40,597.69 which represents payments for obligations of a closed account.

24. Includes $6,024.00 which represents payments for obligations of a closed account.

25. Includes $4,866.17 which represents payments for obligations of a closed account.

26. Includes $33,256.77 which represents payments for obligations of a closed account.

27. Includes $3,759,824.00 which represents payments for obligations of a closed account.

28. Includes $883.52 which represents payments for obligations of a closed account.

29. Subject to disposition by the administrative agency.

30. Includes $4,308.45 which represents payments for obligations of a closed account.

31. Includes $74,085.00 which represents payments for obligations of a closed account.

32. Includes $106,764.77 which represents payments for obligations of a closed account.

33. Includes $1,583,423.23 which represents payments for obligations of a closed account.

34. Includes $3,515,814.76 which represents payments for obligations of a closed account.

35. Includes $277,886.00 which represents payments for obligations of a closed account.

36. Includes $1,006,348.33 which represents payments for obligations of a closed account.

37. Includes $1,981,254.67 which represents payments for obligations of a closed account.

38. Includes $779,503.00 which represents payments for obligations of a closed account.

39. Pursuant to 112 Stat. 2320, the balance for this account has been extended beyond the normal period of availability to liquidate obligations.

40. Pursuant to 110 Stat. 3009-112, the balance for this account has been extended beyond the normal period of availability to liquidate obligations.

41. Includes $1,042,971.21 which represents payments for obligations of a closed account.

42. Includes $255,443.03 which represents payments for obligations of a closed account.

43. Includes $12,313.62 which represents payments for obligations of a closed account.

44. Includes $224,686.08 which represents payments for obligations of a closed account.

45. Includes $340,328.98 which represents payments for obligations of a closed account.

Appropriations, Outlays, and Balances - Continued

Footnotes

46   Includes $14,298.80 which represents payments for obligations of a closed account.

47   Includes $378.31 which represents payments for obligations of a closed account.

48   Includes $1,466,318.30 which represents payments for obligations of a closed account.

49   Includes $416,945.22 which represents payments for obligations of a closed account.

50   Includes $124,361.10 which represents payments for obligations of a closed account.

51   Includes $2,434.22 which represents payments for obligations of a closed account.

52   Represents:

Account	New Contract Authority	Appropriations To Liquidate
97 X 4930.1	$10,715,333,056.10	0.00
97 X 4930.2	5,673,308,677.17	32,400,000.00
97 X 4930.3	9,988,202,210.04	0.00
97 X 4930.4	5,761,790,841.74	5,521,725,800.92
97 X 4930.5	36,705,355,573.65	114,412,000.00

53   Includes $100,966,839.91 which represents repayment of borrowing from the Federal Financing Bank in lieu of issuance of agency debt.

54   Covered by contract authority.

55   The opening Undisbursed balance for account 97 X 4167 does not agree with last year's closing balance by $4,878,257.00 due to the year-end closing statement not being processed in Treasury's central accounting system.

Footnotes At End Of Chapter

Appropriations, Outlays, and Balances – Continued

Footnotes

Table 1 - Appropriations And Appropriation Transfers - Department Of Defense

Department Regular	Fiscal Year	Account Symbol	Net Appropriations And Appropriations Transfers	Appropriation Amount	Net Appropriation Transfers	Department Regular Involved	Fiscal Year Involved	Accounts Involved	Amount From or To (-)
17	0711	0730	130,747,000.00	305,000,000.00	-174,253,000.00	97	X	0803	-214,000.00
						97	X	0834	-174,467,000.00
17	07	0735	506,638,000.00	505,472,000.00	1,166,000.00	97	X	0803	1,166,000.00
17	X	0810	0.00	0.00	-301,520,344.00	97	07	1804	-301,520,344.00
17	07	1106	7,609,923,000.00	7,623,464,000.00	-13,541,000.00	17	07	1107	57,000.00
						17	07	1109	200,000.00
						17	0709	1319	-14,342,000.00
						17	0708	1506	46,000.00
						17	0709	1806	300,000.00
						72	07	1021	-8,300,000.00
17	07	1107	269,856,000.00	269,818,000.00	38,000.00	97	X	0105	8,498,000.00
						97	07	1106	-57,000.00
17	07	1108	564,174,000.00	562,848,000.00	1,326,000.00	17	07	0105	95,000.00
						97	07	0100	124,000.00
						97	07	0105	1,202,000.00
17	0709	1109	8,051,796,000.00	8,041,996,000.00	9,800,000.00	17	07	1106	-200,000.00
						17	0708	1319	-34,000,000.00
						17	0709	1810	-16,000,000.00
						17	0709	2035	-75,000,000.00
						21	0709	0143	135,000,000.00
17	0711	1205	1,136,421,000.00	1,130,821,000.00	5,600,000.00	97	X	0803	5,600,000.00
17	X	1319	72,873,000.00	0.00	72,873,000.00	97	X	5512	72,873,000.00
17	0708	1319	19,600,236,000.00	19,128,233,000.00	472,003,000.00	17	07	1106	14,342,000.00
						17	0709	1109	34,000,000.00
						17	0711	1611	344,472,000.00
						17	07	2020	-2,600,000.00
						21	07	0100	2,604,000.00
						97	X	0105	29,600,000.00
						97	07	0105	46,657,000.00
						97	0708	0141	14,120,000.00
17	07	1405	1,857,974,000.00	1,841,976,000.00	15,998,000.00	97	0708	0400	-11,192,000.00
						97	07	1453	3,000,000.00
						97	07	0100	2,760,000.00
						97	07	0105	10,238,000.00
17	07	1453	24,016,938,000.00	24,019,938,000.00	-3,000,000.00	17	07	1405	-3,000,000.00
17	0709	1506	11,922,336,000.00	11,928,736,000.00	-6,400,000.00	17	07	1106	-46,000.00
						17	0711	1611	-845,000.00
						17	07	1804	-4,409,000.00
						57	0709	3020	-1,100,000.00
17	X	1507	60,692,000.00	0.00	60,692,000.00	11	X	5512	60,692,000.00
17	0709	1508	1,049,381,000.00	1,051,945,000.00	-2,554,000.00	17	0709	1810	-2,900,000.00
						97	07	0105	336,000.00
17	0711	1611	9,719,700,000.00	10,023,781,000.00	-304,081,000.00	97	0708	1319	-344,472,000.00
						17	0709	1506	845,000.00

Appropriations, Outlays, and Balances - Continued
Footnotes

Table 1 - Appropriations And Appropriation Transfers - Department Of Defense

Department Regular	Fiscal Year	Account Symbol	Net Appropriations And Appropriations Transfers	Appropriation Amount	Net Appropriation Transfers	Department Regular Involved	Fiscal Year Involved	Accounts Involved	Amount From or To (-)
						17	07	1804	38,000,000.00
						17	0709	1810	1,546,000.00
17	X	1804	57,125,000.00	0.00	57,125,000.00	47	X	4542	57,125,000.00
17	07	1804	37,359,120,344.00	37,056,024,000.00	303,096,344.00	17	X	0810	301,520,344.00
						17	0709	1506	4,409,000.00
						17	0711	1611	-38,000,000.00
						17	0709	1810	-1,704,000.00
						21	0708	2040	-996,000.00
						70	07	0610	-210,293,000.00
						72	X	1037	-6,700,000.00
						97	07	0100	-20,491,000.00
						97	X	0105	20,600,000.00
						97	07	0105	181,010,000.00
						97	0708	0141	3,000,000.00
						97	0709	0143	70,741,000.00
17	07	1806	1,400,511,000.00	1,391,741,000.00	8,770,000.00	17	07	1106	-300,000.00
						97	07	0105	9,070,000.00
17	X	1810	900,000.00	0.00	900,000.00	11	X	5512	900,000.00
17	0709	1810	6,030,089,000.00	5,976,597,000.00	53,492,000.00	17	0709	1109	16,000,000.00
						17	0709	1508	2,900,000.00
						17	0711	1611	-1,546,000.00
						17	07	1804	1,704,000.00
						97	07	0100	7,596,000.00
						97	X	0105	17,850,000.00
						97	07	0105	16,633,000.00
						97	0709	0130	-1,970,000.00
						97	0708	0400	-5,675,000.00
21	07	0390	972,328,000.00	1,042,267,000.00	-69,939,000.00	21	0708	0390	-69,939,000.00
21	0708	0390	300,065,000.00	230,126,000.00	69,939,000.00	21	07	0390	69,939,000.00
21	X	0810	0.00	402,847,828.00	-402,847,828.00	21	07	2020	-402,847,828.00
21	07	2010	41,531,919,800.00	43,013,965,000.00	-1,482,045,200.00	11	X	1022	-7,111,000.00
						11	X	1075	-500,000.00
						19	X	0113	-300,000.00
						21	0709	2035	-511,000,000.00
						21	07	2060	-538,000,000.00
						21	07	2065	-152,000,000.00
						57	07	3500	-155,000,000.00
						72	X	1021	-28,934,200.00
						72	X	1027	-4,000,000.00
						72	X	1037	-13,900,000.00
						97	0708	1037	-70,000,000.00
21	X	2020	80,180,000.00	78,300,000.00	1,880,000.00	11	07	0105	630,000.00
						36	X	5512	1,250,000.00
21	07	2020	72,169,691,588.00	72,713,369,000.00	-543,677,412.00	11	X	0151	-13,250,000.00
						14	X	1039	-2,000,000.00

Footnotes At End Of Chapter

Appropriations, Outlays, and Balances – Continued

Footnotes

Table 1 - Appropriations And Appropriation Transfers - Department Of Defense

Department Regular	Fiscal Year	Account Symbol	Net Appropriations And Appropriations Transfers	Appropriation Amount	Net Appropriation Transfers	Department Regular Involved	Fiscal Year Involved	Accounts Involved	Amount From or To (-)
						17	0708	1319	2,600,000.00
						21	X	0810	402,847,828.00
						21	0709	2031	-127,595,000.00
						21	0709	2035	-995,693,000.00
						21	0708	2040	-7,720,000.00
						21	07	2060	-2,400,000.00
						21	07	2065	-319,000,000.00
						72	X	1021	-150,000.00
						72	X	1037	-1,600,000.00
						97	07	0100	-38,870,000.00
						97	X	0105	38,700,000.00
						97	07	0105	225,792,000.00
						97	0708	0141	40,900,000.00
						97	X	0811	253,760,760.00
21	0709	2031	5,670,658,000.00	5,569,464,000.00	101,194,000.00	21	07	2020	127,595,000.00
						21	0709	2032	-92,400,000.00
						21	0709	2035	57,000,000.00
						21	07	2065	1,499,000.00
						97	0708	0141	7,500,000.00
21	0709	2032	1,617,302,000.00	1,385,303,000.00	231,999,000.00	21	0709	2031	92,400,000.00
						21	0709	2033	85,443,000.00
						21	0709	2034	15,400,000.00
						21	0709	2035	38,756,000.00
21	0709	2033	8,339,683,000.00	8,696,256,000.00	-356,573,000.00	21	0709	2032	-85,443,000.00
						21	0708	2040	-198,010,000.00
						21	0709	2093	-39,000,000.00
						57	07	3400	-2,400,000.00
						97	0708	0400	-31,720,000.00
21	0709	2034	2,616,821,000.00	2,632,221,000.00	-15,400,000.00	21	0709	2032	-15,400,000.00
21	X	2035	15,303,043.00	0.00	15,303,043.00	11	X	5512	15,303,043.00
21	0709	2035	24,818,117,000.00	23,056,909,000.00	1,761,208,000.00	17	0709	1109	75,000,000.00
						21	07	2010	511,000,000.00
						21	07	2020	995,693,000.00
						21	0709	2031	-57,000,000.00
						21	0709	2032	-38,756,000.00
						21	0708	2040	-11,035,000.00
						21	07	2065	2,901,000.00
						21	07	2070	25,000,000.00
						97	07	0100	-474,000.00
						97	X	0105	16,000,000.00
						97	07	0105	26,494,000.00
						97	0708	0141	35,880,000.00
						97	0709	0143	193,459,000.00
						97	0709	0300	-5,500,000.00
						97	0708	0400	-7,454,000.00
21	0708	2040	11,324,488,000.00	11,108,825,000.00	215,663,000.00	17	07	1804	996,000.00
						21	07	2020	7,720,000.00

Appropriations, Outlays, and Balances - Continued

Footnotes

Table 1 - Appropriations And Appropriation Transfers - Department Of Defense

Department Regular	Fiscal Year	Account Symbol	Net Appropriations And Appropriations Transfers	Appropriation Amount	Net Appropriation Transfers	Department Regular Involved	Fiscal Year Involved	Accounts Involved	Amount From or To (-)
						21	0709	2033	198,010,000.00
						21	0709	2035	11,035,000.00
						21	07	2080	678,000.00
						97	0708	0130	-2,746,000.00
						97	0709	0130	-30,000.00
21	07	2060	6,743,403,000.00	6,050,442,000.00	692,961,000.00	21	07	2010	538,000,000.00
						21	07	2020	2,400,000.00
						72	0708	1037	-13,183,000.00
						97	07	0100	6,257,000.00
						97	07	0105	159,487,000.00
21	07	2065	5,736,680,000.00	5,206,751,000.00	529,929,000.00	21	07	2010	152,000,000.00
						21	07	2020	319,000,000.00
						21	0709	2031	-1,499,000.00
						21	0709	2035	-2,901,000.00
						97	07	0105	28,329,000.00
						97	07	0143	35,000,000.00
21	07	2070	3,514,166,000.00	3,599,812,000.00	-86,646,000.00	21	0709	2035	-25,000,000.00
						21	07	2080	-10,000,000.00
						97	07	0100	1,284,000.00
						97	07	0105	3,070,000.00
						97	0709	0350	-55,000,000.00
21	07	2080	2,450,589,000.00	2,437,902,000.00	12,687,000.00	21	0708	2040	-678,000.00
						21	07	2070	10,000,000.00
						97	07	0105	3,365,000.00
21	0709	2090	35,000,000.00	0.00	35,000,000.00	19	0709	0529	35,000,000.00
21	0709	2093	4,392,500,000.00	4,353,500,000.00	39,000,000.00	21	0709	2033	39,000,000.00
57	X	0810	0.00	401,460,835.00	-401,460,835.00	57	07	3400	-401,460,835.00
57	X	3010	40,000,000.00	40,000,000.00	40,000,000.00	11	X	5512	40,000,000.00
57	0709	3010	15,827,616,000.00	15,594,133,000.00	-166,517,000.00	57	07	3400	-89,485,000.00
						57	0708	3600	-5,013,000.00
						57	07	3740	-43,279,000.00
						57	07	3850	-23,400,000.00
						57	07	0105	1,660,000.00
						97	0708	0400	-7,000,000.00
57	0709	3011	1,043,614,000.00	1,056,067,000.00	-12,453,000.00	57	0709	3020	-11,203,000.00
						57	07	3740	-167,000.00
						57	07	3840	-1,083,000.00
57	X	3020	60,000,000.00	0.00	60,000,000.00	11	X	5512	60,000,000.00
57	0709	3020	4,055,138,000.00	4,020,836,000.00	34,302,000.00	17	0709	1506	1,100,000.00
						57	0709	3011	11,203,000.00
						57	0708	3600	21,999,000.00
57	X	3080	6,596,381.00	0.00	6,596,381.00	11	X	5512	6,596,381.00
57	0709	3080	18,899,818,000.00	18,843,371,000.00	56,447,000.00	57	07	3400	31,000,000.00
						57	0708	3600	38,500,000.00
						57	07	3840	-28,811,000.00
						97	07	0100	8,000,000.00

Footnotes At End Of Chapter

Appropriations, Outlays, and Balances – Continued

Footnotes

Table 1 - Appropriations And Appropriation Transfers - Department Of Defense

Department Regular	Fiscal Year	Account Symbol	Net Appropriations And Appropriations Transfers	Appropriation Amount	Net Appropriation Transfers	Department Regular Involved	Fiscal Year Involved	Accounts Involved	Amount From or To (-)
57	0711	3300	1,077,849,000.00	1,083,000,000.00	-5,151,000.00	97	07	0105	7,758,000.00
57	X	3400	157,100.00	0.00	157,100.00	97	X	0803	-5,151,000.00
57	07	3400	40,266,974,835.00	39,591,618,000.00	675,356,835.00	11	X	5512	157,100.00
						11	X	1032	-250,000.00
						19	X	0113	-1,550,000.00
						21	X	2033	2,400,000.00
						57	0709	0810	401,460,835.00
						57	0709	3010	89,485,000.00
						57	0709	3080	-31,000,000.00
						57	0708	3600	-32,000,000.00
						72	X	1021	-8,050,000.00
						72	X	1037	-5,150,000.00
						97	07	0100	1,533,000.00
						97	X	0105	16,300,000.00
						97	07	0105	132,578,000.00
						97	0708	0130	-2,200,000.00
						97	0709	0143	180,800,000.00
						97	0709	0300	-69,000,000.00
57	07	3500	25,218,561,000.00	25,135,081,000.00	83,480,000.00	21	07	2010	155,000,000.00
57	0708	3600	24,658,745,000.00	24,630,499,000.00	28,246,000.00	57	0708	3600	-76,520,000.00
						57	07	3700	5,000,000.00
						57	0709	3010	5,013,000.00
						57	0709	3020	-21,999,000.00
						57	0709	3080	-38,500,000.00
						57	07	3400	32,000,000.00
						57	07	3500	76,520,000.00
						57	07	3740	4,000,000.00
						57	07	3840	29,894,000.00
						97	07	0100	-11,762,000.00
						97	0708	0130	-33,040,000.00
						97	0709	0300	-2,665,000.00
						97	0708	0400	-15,100,000.00
						97	0708	0460	3,885,000.00
57	07	3700	1,339,225,000.00	1,347,411,000.00	-8,186,000.00	57	07	3500	-5,000,000.00
						57	07	3850	-6,600,000.00
						97	07	0100	1,647,000.00
						97	07	0105	1,767,000.00
57	07	3740	2,723,621,000.00	2,682,337,000.00	41,284,000.00	57	0709	3010	43,279,000.00
						57	07	3011	167,000.00
						57	0708	3600	-4,000,000.00
						97	07	0105	1,838,000.00
						57	0709	3011	1,083,000.00
						57	0709	3080	28,811,000.00
						57	0708	3600	-29,894,000.00
57	07	3840	5,246,189,000.00	5,227,931,000.00	18,258,000.00	97	07	0105	18,258,000.00
57	07	3850	2,470,852,000.00	2,369,785,000.00	101,067,000.00	57	0709	3010	23,400,000.00
						57	07	3700	6,600,000.00

Appropriations, Outlays, and Balances - Continued

Footnotes

Table 1 - Appropriations And Appropriation Transfers - Department Of Defense

Department Regular	Fiscal Year	Account Symbol	Net Appropriations And Appropriations Transfers	Appropriation Amount	Net Appropriation Transfers	Department Regular Involved	Fiscal Year Involved	Accounts Involved	Amount From or To (-)
						97	07	0100	1,651,000.00
97	X	0100	936,200,000.00	12,000,000.00	924,200,000.00	97	07	0105	69,416,000.00
						11	X	5512	21,700,000.00
						97	07	0100	905,000,000.00
97	07	0100	24,787,546,000.00	25,450,625,000.00	-663,079,000.00	97	X	0130	-2,500,000.00
						11	07	1032	-20,000,000.00
						17	07	1108	-124,000.00
						17	0708	1319	-2,604,000.00
						17	07	1405	-2,760,000.00
						17	07	1804	20,491,000.00
						17	0709	1810	-7,596,000.00
						21	07	2020	38,870,000.00
						21	0709	2035	474,000.00
						21	07	2060	-6,257,000.00
						21	07	2070	-1,284,000.00
						57	0709	3080	-8,000,000.00
						57	07	3400	-1,533,000.00
						57	0708	3600	11,762,000.00
						57	07	3700	-1,647,000.00
						57	07	3850	-1,651,000.00
						97	X	0100	-905,000,000.00
						97	07	0105	99,116,000.00
						97	0708	0141	46,927,000.00
						97	0709	0300	4,150,000.00
						97	0708	0400	59,493,000.00
97	X	0105	115,615,000.00	254,665,000.00	-139,050,000.00	97	X	0810	14,094,000.00
						17	0708	1319	-29,600,000.00
						17	07	1804	-20,600,000.00
						17	0709	1810	-17,850,000.00
						21	07	2020	-38,700,000.00
						21	0709	2035	-16,000,000.00
						57	07	3400	-16,300,000.00
97	07	0105	0.00	1,073,874,000.00	-1,073,874,000.00	17	07	1106	-8,498,000.00
						17	07	1107	-95,000.00
						17	07	1108	-1,202,000.00
						17	0708	1319	-46,657,000.00
						17	07	1405	-10,238,000.00
						17	0709	1508	-336,000.00
						17	07	1804	-181,010,000.00
						17	07	1806	-9,070,000.00
						17	0709	1810	-16,633,000.00
						21	07	2010	1,300,000.00
						21	07	2020	-225,792,000.00
						21	0709	2035	-26,494,000.00
						21	07	2060	-159,487,000.00
						21	07	2065	-28,329,000.00

Footnotes At End Of Chapter

Appropriations, Outlays, and Balances – Continued

Footnotes

Table 1 - Appropriations And Appropriation Transfers - Department Of Defense

Department Regular	Fiscal Year	Account Symbol	Net Appropriations And Appropriations Transfers	Appropriation Amount	Net Appropriation Transfers	Department Regular Involved	Fiscal Year Involved	Accounts Involved	Amount From or To (-)
						21	07	2070	-3,070,000.00
						21	07	2080	-3,365,000.00
						57	0709	3010	-1,660,000.00
						57	0709	3080	-7,758,000.00
						57	07	3400	-132,578,000.00
						57	07	3700	-1,767,000.00
						57	07	3740	-1,838,000.00
						57	07	3840	-18,258,000.00
						57	07	3850	-69,416,000.00
						97	07	0100	-99,116,000.00
						97	07	0107	-122,000.00
						97	0709	0130	-1,542,000.00
						97	0708	0300	-4,296,000.00
						97	07	0400	-16,547,000.00
97	07	0107	214,193,000.00	214,071,000.00	122,000.00	97	X	0105	122,000.00
97	X	0130	2,500,000.00	0.00	2,500,000.00	97	X	0100	2,500,000.00
97	07	0130	22,328,952,000.00	22,446,153,000.00	-117,201,000.00	36	0708	0165	-35,000,000.00
						72	07	1037	-26,817,000.00
						97	0708	0105	1,542,000.00
						97	0709	0130	-54,636,000.00
						97	0708	0130	-2,290,000.00
97	0708	0130	1,372,322,000.00	1,279,700,000.00	92,622,000.00	21	07	2040	2,746,000.00
						57	0708	3400	2,200,000.00
						57	07	3600	33,040,000.00
						97	0709	0130	54,636,000.00
97	0709	0130	497,290,000.00	493,000,000.00	4,290,000.00	17	0708	1810	1,970,000.00
						21	07	2040	30,000.00
						97	0708	0130	2,290,000.00
97	0708	0141	230,673,000.00	405,600,000.00	-174,927,000.00	17	07	1319	-14,120,000.00
						17	07	1804	-3,000,000.00
						21	0709	2020	-40,900,000.00
						21	0709	2031	-7,500,000.00
						21	07	2035	-35,880,000.00
						97	0709	0100	-46,927,000.00
						97	0709	0300	-26,600,000.00
97	0709	0143	0.00	1,615,000,000.00	-1,615,000,000.00	17	07	1109	-135,000,000.00
						17	0709	1804	-70,741,000.00
						21	0709	2035	-193,459,000.00
						21	07	2065	-35,000,000.00
						57	07	3400	-180,800,000.00
97	0709	0300	4,096,884,000.00	4,017,235,000.00	79,649,000.00	97	0709	0350	-1,000,000,000.00
						21	0709	2035	5,500,000.00
						57	07	3400	69,000,000.00
						57	0708	3600	2,665,000.00
						97	07	0100	-4,150,000.00
						97	07	0105	4,296,000.00
						97	0708	0141	26,600,000.00

Appropriations, Outlays, and Balances - Continued

Footnotes

Table 1 - Appropriations And Appropriation Transfers - Department Of Defense

Department Regular	Fiscal Year	Account Symbol	Net Appropriations And Appropriations Transfers	Appropriation Amount	Net Appropriation Transfers	Department Regular Involved	Fiscal Year Involved	Accounts Involved	Amount From or To (-)
97	0709	0350	1,343,835,000.00	288,835,000.00	1,055,000,000.00	97	0708	0400	-24,262,000.00
						21	07	2070	55,000,000.00
						97	0709	0143	1,000,000,000.00
97	X	0400	76,500,000.00	0.00	76,500,000.00	11	X	5512	76,500,000.00
97	0708	0400	21,906,675,000.00	21,847,218,000.00	59,457,000.00	17	0708	1319	11,192,000.00
						17	0709	1810	5,675,000.00
						21	0709	2033	31,720,000.00
						21	0709	2035	7,454,000.00
						57	0709	3010	7,000,000.00
						57	0708	3600	15,100,000.00
						97	07	0100	-59,493,000.00
						97	07	0105	16,547,000.00
						97	0709	0300	24,262,000.00
97	0708	0460	180,204,000.00	184,089,000.00	-3,885,000.00	57	0708	3600	-3,885,000.00
97	0711	0500	1,125,500,000.00	1,127,000,000.00	-1,500,000.00	97	X	0803	-1,500,000.00
97	07	0765	48,671,000.00	49,000,000.00	-329,000.00	97	X	0803	-329,000.00
97	X	0803	0.00	0.00	0.00	17	0711	0730	-214,000.00
						17	07	0735	-1,166,000.00
						17	0711	1205	-5,600,000.00
						57	0711	3300	5,151,000.00
						97	0711	0500	1,500,000.00
						97	07	0765	329,000.00
	X	0810	6,226,985.00	27,820,985.00	-21,594,000.00	97	07	0100	-14,094,000.00
						97	X	0811	-7,500,000.00
	X	0811	7,500,000.00	253,760,760.00	-246,260,760.00	21	07	2020	-253,760,760.00
						97	X	0810	7,500,000.00
97	X	0834	178,570,109.00	4,103,109.00	174,467,000.00	17	0711	0730	174,467,000.00
97	X	4555	-186,000,000.00	0.00	-186,000,000.00	97	X	5472	-186,000,000.00
97	X	4930	0.00	2,456,276,000.00	-2,456,276,000.00	97	X	4930	-627,790,000.00
						97	X	4930	-115,865,000.00
						97	X	4930	-43,882,000.00
						97	X	4930	-1,179,423,000.00
						97	X	4930	-489,316,000.00
97	X	4930	627,790,000.00	0.00	627,790,000.00	97	X	4930	627,790,000.00
97	X	4930	115,865,000.00	0.00	115,865,000.00	97	X	4930	115,865,000.00
97	X	4930	43,882,000.00	0.00	43,882,000.00	97	X	4930	43,882,000.00
97	X	4930	1,179,423,000.00	0.00	1,179,423,000.00	97	X	4930	1,179,423,000.00
97	X	4930	489,316,000.00	0.00	489,316,000.00	97	X	4930	489,316,000.00
Totals			548,407,414,185.00	548,621,725,861.00	-214,311,676.00				-214,311,676.00

Appropriations, Outlays, and Balances – Continued

Appropriation or Fund Account: Title	Period of Availability	Dept Reg	Dept Tr From	Account Number	Sub No.	Balances, Beginning of Fiscal Year	Appropriations And Other Obligational Authority[1]	Transfers Borrowings And Investment (Net)[2]	Outlays (Net)	Balances Withdrawn And Other Transactions[3]	Balances, End Of Fiscal Year[4]
Department Of Education											
Office Of Elementary And Secondary Education											
General Fund Accounts											
Reading Excellence, Office Of Elementary And Secondary Education, Department Of Education											
Fund Resources:											
Undisbursed Funds	2001-2002	91		0011		8,863,413.82				8,863,413.82	
Fund Equities:											
Unobligated Balances (Expired)						-3,046,371.03				-3,046,371.03	
Accounts Payable						-2.00				-2.00	
Undelivered Orders						-5,817,040.79				-5,817,040.79	
Subtotal		91		0011		-0-					-0-
Indian Education, Office Of Elementary And Secondary Education, Department Of Education											
Fund Resources:											
Undisbursed Funds	2007	91		0101		112,537,907.07	118,690,110.00		7,866,432.76		110,823,677.24
	2006					11,848,941.77			102,419,288.93		10,118,618.14
	2005					6,317,106.79			7,233,538.89		4,615,402.88
	2004					5,320,382.06			444,025.26		5,873,081.53
	2003					5,092,412.87			29,359.64		5,291,022.42
	2002									5,092,412.87	
Fund Equities:											
Unobligated Balances (Expired)						-1,386,669.71				255,491.43	-1,642,161.14
Accounts Payable						-2,795,719.32				-1,397,768.23	-1,397,951.09
Undelivered Orders						-136,934,361.53				-3,252,671.55	-133,681,689.98
Subtotal		91		0101		-0-	118,690,110.00		117,992,645.48	697,464.52	-0-
Impact Aid, Department Of Education											
Fund Resources:											
Undisbursed Funds	2007	91		0102		153,942,574.41	1,223,503,380.00		1,032,580,215.29		190,923,164.71
	2006					25,625,953.86			28,143,141.08		125,799,433.33
	2005-2006					69,088,896.62			1,484,019.36		24,141,934.50
	2005					17,574,237.12			-362,586.36		69,451,482.98
	2004-2005					79,645,262.60			5,655,654.81		11,918,582.31
	2004					16,548,466.99			79,171,008.26		474,254.34
	2003-2004					53,389.46			9,741,145.93		6,807,321.06
	2003					272,104.39			-6,886.52		60,275.98
	2002-2003					505,476.03			86,303.11		185,801.28
	2002					22,569,496.58			-2,357.20	507,833.23	21,197,062.95
	No Year						4,950,000.00		6,322,433.63		
Fund Equities:											
Unobligated Balances (Expired)						-704,378.22				36,915.78	-741,294.00
Unobligated Balances (Unexpired)						-6,105,227.35				-2,629,871.93	-3,475,355.42
Accounts Payable						-474,492.19				-30,376.14	-444,116.05
Undelivered Orders						-378,541,760.30				67,756,787.67	-446,298,547.97
Subtotal		91		0102		-0-	1,228,453,380.00		1,162,812,091.39	65,641,288.61	-0-

Appropriations, Outlays, and Balances - Continued

Appropriation or Fund Account — Title	Period of Availability	Dept Reg	Tr From	Account Number	Sub No.	Balances, Beginning of Fiscal Year	Appropriations And Other Obligational Authority[1]	Transfers Borrowings And Investment (Net)[2]	Outlays (Net)	Balances Withdrawn And Other Transactions[3]	Balances, End Of Fiscal Year[4]
Chicago Litigation Settlement, Department Of Education											
Fund Resources:											
Undisbursed Funds	No Year	91		0220		32,668.90			5,122.00		27,546.90
Fund Equities:											
Undelivered Orders						-32,668.90				-5,122.00	-27,546.90
	Subtotal	91		0220		-0-			5,122.00	-5,122.00	-0-
Education Reform, Department Of Education											
Fund Resources:											
Undisbursed Funds	2001-2002	91		0500		6,527,443.72			905,853.44	5,621,590.28	
Fund Equities:											
Unobligated Balances (Expired)						-1,762,175.49				-1,762,175.49	
Accounts Payable						-160,217.67				-160,217.67	
Undelivered Orders						-4,605,050.56				-4,605,050.56	
	Subtotal	91		0500		-0-			905,853.44	-905,853.44	-0-
Education For The Disadvantaged, Department Of Education											
Fund Resources:											
Undisbursed Funds	2007-2008	91		0900			7,176,431,000.00		215,302,528.12		6,961,128,471.88
	2007						165,861,000.00		1,868,521.37		163,992,478.63
	2006-2007					6,625,918,954.48	7,383,301,000.00		10,999,790,088.67		3,009,429,865.81
	2006					166,802,228.95			71,215,556.11		95,586,672.84
	2005-2006					3,302,069,201.07			2,617,533,503.53		684,535,697.54
	2005					97,234,261.30			39,173,740.33		58,060,520.97
	2004-2005					562,428,742.81			468,864,399.66		93,564,343.15
	2004					51,470,598.25			31,371,585.35		20,099,012.90
	2003-2004					63,073,947.03			10,337,839.01		52,736,108.02
	2003					25,012,986.95			16,229,452.87		8,783,534.08
	2002-2003					29,736,697.47			3,324,016.81		26,412,680.66
	2002					2,301,834.20			274,182.90	2,027,651.30	
	2001-2002					45,255,437.62			11,646,531.35	33,608,906.27	
Fund Equities:											
Unobligated Balances (Expired)						-39,120,247.69				3,712,826.41	-42,833,074.10
Unobligated Balances (Unexpired)						-129,479,462.12				135,897,187.84	-265,376,649.96
Accounts Payable						-39,820,510.46				-15,555,113.93	-24,265,396.53
Undelivered Orders						-10,762,884,669.86				78,969,596.03	-10,841,854,265.89
	Subtotal	91		0900		-0-	14,725,593,000.00		14,486,931,946.08	238,661,053.92	-0-
School Improvement Programs, Department Of Education											
Fund Resources:											
Undisbursed Funds	2007-2008	91		1000			3,625,367,180.00		98,038,172.87		3,527,329,007.13
	2007						195,111,180.00		1,650,044.14		193,461,135.86
	2006-2007					3,527,333,454.76	1,435,000,000.00		3,019,849,923.64		1,942,483,531.12
	2006					192,663,641.85			125,254,356.45		67,409,285.40
	2005-2006					2,119,478,552.93			1,662,065,776.33		457,412,776.60
	2005					75,797,802.50			59,279,811.33		16,517,991.17
	2004-2005					468,272,396.09			386,633,200.28		81,639,195.81
	2004					16,305,134.10			10,834,003.70		5,471,130.40
	2003-2004					149,675,216.70			42,265,516.00		107,409,700.70
	2003					72,854,916.13			35,274,598.56		37,580,317.57
	2002-2003					74,325,208.64			21,590,459.05		52,734,749.59

Footnotes At End Of Chapter

Appropriations, Outlays, and Balances – Continued

		Account Symbol									
		Dept									
Appropriation or Fund Account — Title	Period of Availability	Reg	Tr From	Account Number	Sub No.	Balances, Beginning of Fiscal Year	Appropriations And Other Obligational Authority[1]	Transfers Borrowings And Investment (Net)[2]	Outlays (Net)	Balances Withdrawn And Other Transactions[3]	Balances, End Of Fiscal Year[4]
School Improvement Programs, Department Of Education - Continued											
Fund Resources: - Continued											
Undisbursed Funds - Continued	2002					34,970,612.32			10,326,661.53	24,643,950.79	------
	2001-2002					71,341,118.89			5,921,142.65	65,419,976.24	------
	No Year					10,571,655.65			4,513,749.57		6,057,906.08
Fund Equities:											
Unobligated Balances (Expired)						-55,929,274.05			------	11,181,224.06	-67,110,498.11
Unobligated Balances (Unexpired)						-45,942,811.10				17,502,018.45	-63,444,829.55
Accounts Payable						-321,323,666.61				77,694,619.83	-399,018,286.44
Undelivered Orders						-6,390,393,958.80				-424,460,845.47	-5,965,933,113.33
Subtotal		91		1000		-0-	5,255,478,360.00		5,483,497,416.10	-228,019,056.10	-0-
Total, Office Of Elementary And Secondary Education							21,328,214,850.00		21,252,145,074.49	76,069,775.51	
Office Of Innovation And Improvement											
General Fund Accounts											
Innovation And Improvement, Department Of Education											
Fund Resources:											
Undisbursed Funds	2007	91		0204			837,686,000.00		13,415,748.84		824,270,251.16
	2006-2007					94,050,000.00			13,114,964.36		80,935,035.64
	2006					831,622,419.39			350,992,210.15		480,630,209.24
	2005					552,392,007.89			361,715,002.57		190,677,005.32
	2004-2005					981,549.65			612,146.93		369,402.72
	2004					153,918,703.08			106,007,319.54		47,911,383.54
	No Year					62,912.34			13,726.17		49,186.17
Fund Equities:											
Unobligated Balances (Expired)						-3,595,751.88				3,777,995.84	-7,373,747.72
Unobligated Balances (Unexpired)						-94,050,000.00				-94,050,000.00	-94,050,000.00
Accounts Payable						-27,770,140.70				21,867,216.66	-49,637,357.36
Undelivered Orders						-1,507,611,699.77				60,219,668.94	-1,567,831,368.71
Subtotal		91		0204		-0-	837,686,000.00		845,871,118.56	-8,185,118.56	-0-
Total, Office Of Innovation And Improvement							837,686,000.00		845,871,118.56	-8,185,118.56	
Office Of Safe And Drug-Free Schools											
General Fund Accounts											
Safe Schools And Citizenship Education, Department Of Education											
Fund Resources:											
Undisbursed Funds	2007-2008	91		0203			346,500,000.00		8,087,808.36		338,412,191.64
	2007						388,612,000.00		-58,100,611.47		446,712,611.47
	2006-2007					337,363,917.60			187,150,199.72		150,213,717.88
	2006					435,877,147.31			248,843,874.86		187,033,272.45
	2005-2006					182,875,455.66			148,842,879.63		34,032,576.03
	2005					213,575,178.36			153,065,620.22		60,509,558.14

Appropriations, Outlays, and Balances - Continued

Appropriation or Fund Account — Title	Period of Availability	Reg	Tr From	Account Number	Sub No.	Balances, Beginning of Fiscal Year	Appropriations And Other Obligational Authority[1]	Transfers Borrowings And Investment (Net)[2]	Outlays (Net)	Balances Withdrawn And Other Transactions[3]	Balances, End Of Fiscal Year[4]
	2004-2005					31,902,715.40			24,481,866.92		7,420,848.48
	2004					58,215,885.29			41,965,493.23		16,250,392.06
	No Year					3,000,000.00	3,000,000.00				6,000,000.00
Fund Equities:											
Unobligated Balances (Expired)						-1,186,423.11				2,948,102.87	-4,134,525.98
Unobligated Balances (Unexpired)						-5,000,947.00				4,900,259.00	-9,901,206.00
Accounts Payable						-43,570,234.96				1,863,479.80	-45,433,714.76
Undelivered Orders						-1,213,052,694.55				-25,936,973.14	-1,187,115,721.41
Subtotal		91		0203		-0-	738,112,000.00		754,337,131.47	-16,225,131.47	-0-
Total, Office of Safe And Drug-Free Schools							738,112,000.00		754,337,131.47	-16,225,131.47	

Office Of English Language Acquisition

General Fund Accounts

Bilingual And Immigrant Education, Department Of Education

Appropriation or Fund Account — Title	Period of Availability	Reg	Tr From	Account Number	Sub No.	Balances, Beginning of Fiscal Year	Appropriations And Other Obligational Authority[1]	Transfers Borrowings And Investment (Net)[2]	Outlays (Net)	Balances Withdrawn And Other Transactions[3]	Balances, End Of Fiscal Year[4]
Fund Resources:											
Undisbursed Funds	2007-2008	91		1300		661,313,777.66	669,007,350.00		4,460,226.17		664,547,123.83
	2006-2007					253,552,383.36			432,768,133.97		228,545,643.69
	2005-2006					31,026,833.13			231,187,838.46		22,364,544.90
	2005					33,173,979.27			26,149,989.23		4,876,843.90
	2004-2005					5,880,161.74			30,767,209.39		2,406,769.88
	2004								2,257,135.44		3,623,026.30
	2003-2004					1,785,314.23			367,255.80		1,418,058.43
	2003					4,887,719.56			739,092.08		4,148,627.48
	2002-2003					383,024.79					383,024.79
	2002					6,116,278.88			4,997.48		
Fund Equities:											
Unobligated Balances (Expired)						-8,148,818.05				-1,434,473.77	-6,714,344.28
Unobligated Balances (Unexpired)						-7,006,063.31				2,812,142.94	-9,818,206.25
Accounts Payable						-69,321,668.88				-68,505,654.28	-816,014.60
Undelivered Orders						-913,642,922.38				1,322,175.69	-914,965,098.07
Subtotal		91		1300		-0-	669,007,350.00		728,701,878.02	-59,694,528.02	-0-
Total, Office of English Language Acquisition							669,007,350.00		728,701,878.02	-59,694,528.02	

Office Of Special Education And Rehabilitative Services

General Fund Accounts

Special Education, Department Of Education,

Appropriation or Fund Account — Title	Period of Availability	Reg	Tr From	Account Number	Sub No.	Balances, Beginning of Fiscal Year	Appropriations And Other Obligational Authority[1]	Transfers Borrowings And Investment (Net)[2]	Outlays (Net)	Balances Withdrawn And Other Transactions[3]	Balances, End Of Fiscal Year[4]
Fund Resources:											
Undisbursed Funds	2007-2008	91		0300		5,856,452,410.91	6,175,912,000.00		202,168,771.07		5,973,743,228.93
	2007						202,755,000.00		1,923,176.61		200,831,823.39
	2006-2007						5,424,200,000.00		8,464,033,878.69		2,816,618,532.22
	2006					190,703,863.29			92,702,530.61		98,001,332.68
	2005-2006					2,953,014,410.52			2,728,448,320.91		224,566,089.61

Appropriations, Outlays, and Balances – Continued

Appropriation or Fund Account — Title	Account Symbol — Dept Reg	Dept Tr From	Account Number	Sub No.	Period of Availability	Balances, Beginning of Fiscal Year	Appropriations And Other Obligational Authority[1]	Transfers Borrowings And Investment (Net)[2]	Outlays (Net)	Balances Withdrawn And Other Transactions[3]	Balances, End Of Fiscal Year[4]
Special Education, Department Of Education - Continued											
Fund Resources: - Continued											
Undisbursed Funds - Continued					2005	92,101,722.21			69,787,476.68		22,314,245.53
					2004-2005	220,900,209.39			183,485,162.33		37,415,047.06
					2004	31,312,279.81			21,897,504.61		9,414,775.20
					2003-2004	12,363,194.36			6,138,425.39		6,224,768.97
					2003	6,182,866.77			3,043,533.74		3,139,333.03
					2002-2003	7,737,664.69			573,507.80		7,164,156.89
					2002	5,124,815.07			456,461.88	4,668,353.19	
					2001-2002	11,968,726.27			2,849,082.88	9,119,643.39	
Accounts Receivable						24,650.00					24,650.00
Fund Equities:											
Unobligated Balances (Expired)						-5,185,841.06				-1,428,644.55	-3,757,196.51
Unobligated Balances (Unexpired)						-170,813,334.00				-91,470,281.54	-79,343,052.46
Accounts Payable						-22,103,881.43				1,612,948.69	-23,716,830.12
Undelivered Orders						-9,189,783,756.80				102,857,147.62	-9,292,640,904.42
			0300		Subtotal	-0-	11,802,867,000.00		11,777,507,833.20	25,359,166.80	-0-
Rehabilitation Services And Disability Research, Department Of Education											
Fund Resources:											
Undisbursed Funds	91		0301		2007	1,124,169,688.20	3,242,511,540.00		2,041,213,882.96		1,201,297,657.04
					2006	190,879,718.58			924,570,594.69		199,599,093.51
					2005	41,227,167.49			168,733,218.94		22,146,499.64
					2004	17,845,840.91			26,260,246.53		14,966,920.96
					2003	3,441,444.90			1,361,955.98		16,483,884.93
					2002-2003	25,509,937.95			845,736.02		2,595,708.88
					2002	44,357.27			12,459,986.10	13,049,951.85	
					No Year				18,928.59	25,428.68	
Accounts Receivable						521,656.25				-2,680,723.75	3,202,380.00
Unfilled Customer Orders						2,680,723.75				2,680,723.75	
Fund Equities:											
Unobligated Balances (Expired)						-6,798,778.77				19,838,526.70	-26,637,305.47
Accounts Payable						-205,237,009.82				283,578,949.28	-488,815,959.10
Undelivered Orders						-1,194,284,746.71				-249,445,866.32	-944,838,880.39
	91		0301		Subtotal	-0-	3,242,511,540.00		3,175,464,549.81	67,046,990.19	-0-
American Printing House For The Blind, Special Institutions For Persons With Disabilities, Department Of Education											
Fund Resources:											
Undisbursed Funds	91		0600		2007		17,572,500.00		14,612,004.48		2,960,495.52
					2006	3,747,430.93			3,747,430.93		
Fund Equities:											
Undelivered Orders						-3,747,430.93				-786,935.41	-2,960,495.52
	91		0600		Subtotal	-0-	17,572,500.00		18,359,435.41	-786,935.41	-0-
National Technical Institute For The Deaf, Special Institutions For Persons With Disabilities, Department Of Education											
Fund Resources:											
Undisbursed Funds	91		0601		2006	1,000,000.00	56,140,920.00		56,140,920.00		
					No Year				1,000,000.00		
						914,803.00			695,389.00		219,414.00

Appropriations, Outlays, and Balances - Continued

Appropriation or Fund Account — Title	Period of Availability	Dept Reg	Tr From	Account Number	Sub No.	Balances, Beginning of Fiscal Year	Appropriations And Other Obligational Authority[1]	Transfers Borrowings And Investment (Net)[2]	Outlays (Net)	Balances Withdrawn And Other Transactions[3]	Balances, End Of Fiscal Year[4]
Fund Equities:											
Accounts Payable						-1,000,000.00				-1,000,000.00	
Undelivered Orders						-914,803.00				-695,389.00	-219,414.00
	Subtotal	91		0601		-0-	56,140,920.00		57,836,309.00	-1,695,389.00	-0-
Gallaudet University, Special Institutions For Persons With Disabilities, Department Of Education											
Fund Resources:											
Undisbursed Funds	2007	91		0602			106,998,210.00		106,998,210.00		
	2006					200,000.00			200,000.00		
Fund Equities:											
Unobligated Balances (Expired)						-200,000.00				-200,000.00	
	Subtotal	91		0602		-0-	106,998,210.00		107,198,210.00	-200,000.00	-0-
Total, Office Of Special Education And Rehabilitative Services							15,226,090,170.00		15,136,366,337.42	89,723,832.58	
Office Of Vocational And Adult Education											
General Fund Accounts											
Vocational And Adult Education, Department Of Education											
Fund Resources:											
Undisbursed Funds	2007-2008	91		0400		1,155,378,865.46	1,201,170,583.00		35,993,121.10		1,165,177,461.90
	2006-2007					498,699,046.30	791,000,000.00		1,462,455,399.24		483,923,466.22
	2005-2006					1,068,882.15			359,377,739.25		139,321,307.05
	2005								969,183.18		99,698.97
	2004-2005					214,441,820.63			90,928,534.13		123,513,286.50
	2004					392,418.68			89,957.64		302,461.04
	2003-2004					10,163,958.65			3,464,370.40		6,699,588.25
	2002-2003					7,313,898.47			2,430,907.45		4,882,991.02
	2001-2002					5,680,643.37			-5,858.47	5,686,501.84	
	No Year					222,115.42			115,308.29		106,807.13
Accounts Receivable						24,864.60				-15,454.76	40,319.36
Unfilled Customer Orders						65,063.03				-194,122.60	259,185.63
Fund Equities:											
Unobligated Balances (Expired)						-916,318.36				-108,984.31	-807,334.05
Unobligated Balances (Unexpired)						-130,556,148.36				1,161,357.33	-131,717,505.69
Accounts Payable						-63,351,660.56				14,419,434.80	-77,771,095.36
Undelivered Orders						-1,698,627,449.48				15,403,188.49	-1,714,030,637.97
	Subtotal	91		0400		-0-	1,992,170,583.00		1,955,818,662.21	36,351,920.79	-0-
Trust Fund Accounts											
Gifts And Donations, National Institute For Literacy, Department Of Education											
Fund Resources:											
Undisbursed Funds	No Year	91		8324		17,828.32	1,955.00				19,783.32
Fund Equities:											
Unobligated Balances (Unexpired)						-13,008.65				1,955.00	-14,963.65

Footnotes At End Of Chapter

Appropriations, Outlays, and Balances – Continued

Appropriation or Fund Account — Title	Period of Availability	Reg	Tr From	Account Number	Sub No.	Balances, Beginning of Fiscal Year	Appropriations And Other Obligational Authority[1]	Transfers Borrowings And Investment (Net)[2]	Outlays (Net)	Balances Withdrawn And Other Transactions[3]	Balances, End Of Fiscal Year[4]
Gifts And Donations, National Institute For Literacy, Department Of Education - Continued											
Fund Equities: - Continued											
Accounts Payable						-3,819.67					-3,819.67
Undelivered Orders						-1,000.00					-1,000.00
Subtotal		91		8324		-0-	1,955.00			1,955.00	-0-
Total, Office Of Vocational And Adult Education							1,992,172,538.00		1,955,818,662.21	36,353,875.79	
Office Of Postsecondary Education											
General Fund Accounts											
Higher Education, Department Of Education											
Fund Resources:											
Undisbursed Funds	2007-2008	91		0201			9,699,030.00		5.07		9,699,024.93
	2007					9,699,030.00	1,971,353,370.00		46,110,791.72		1,925,242,578.28
	2006-2007								478,817.69		9,220,212.31
	2006					1,887,444,055.21			1,242,393,688.26		645,050,366.95
	2005-2006					9,154,471.61			7,601,785.27		1,552,686.34
	2005					661,902,590.02			571,348,183.55		90,554,406.47
	2004-2005					1,743,916.55			935,324.32		808,592.23
	2004					109,363,175.69			47,565,906.81		61,797,268.88
	2003-2004					891,762.68			177,327.94		714,434.74
	2003					59,819,240.36			21,305,795.84		38,513,444.52
	2002-2003					1,189,392.72			158,044.81		1,031,347.91
	2002					51,583,639.06			8,659,785.68	42,923,853.38	
	2001-2002					726,002.57			-1,590.00	727,592.57	
	No Year					12,858,165.00			4,284,618.10		8,573,546.90
Fund Equities:											
Unobligated Balances (Expired)						-45,746,061.06				14,352,338.55	-60,098,399.61
Unobligated Balances (Unexpired)						-14,357,699.44				-590,548.41	-13,767,151.03
Accounts Payable						-267,003,579.46				-165,303,333.37	-101,700,246.09
Undelivered Orders						-2,479,268,101.51				137,924,012.22	-2,617,192,113.73
Subtotal		91		0201		-0-	1,981,052,400.00		1,951,018,485.06	30,033,914.94	-0-
Higher Education Facilities Loans And Insurance, Department Of Education											
Fund Resources:											
Undisbursed Funds	No Year	91		0240		129,085.60			-1,492,271.87	51,621,357.47	
Fund Equities:											
Unobligated Balances (Unexpired)						-119,145.60				-119,145.60	
Undelivered Orders						-9,940.00				-9,940.00	
Subtotal		91		0240		-0-			-1,492,271.87	1,492,271.87	-0-
College Housing And Academic Facilities Loans Program, Department Of Education											
Fund Resources:											
Undisbursed Funds	2007	91		0241		73,274.95	608,211.00		358,741.95		249,469.05
	2006					26,858.65			66,644.13		6,630.82
	2005					294,211.63			938.83		25,919.82
	2004										294,211.63

Appropriations, Outlays, and Balances - Continued

Appropriation or Fund Account (Title)	Period of Availability	Dept. Reg	Tr From	Account Number	Sub No.	Balances, Beginning of Fiscal Year	Appropriations And Other Obligational Authority[1]	Transfers Borrowings And Investment (Net)[2]	Outlays (Net)	Balances Withdrawn And Other Transactions[3]	Balances, End Of Fiscal Year[4]
	2003					184,109.78					184,109.78
	2002					78,145.39			1,000.00	77,145.39	
Fund Equities:											
Unobligated Balances (Expired)						-441,540.08				45,443.36	-486,983.44
Accounts Payable						-19,243.59				-8,552.79	-10,690.80
Undelivered Orders						-195,816.73				66,850.13	-262,666.86
Subtotal		91		0241		-0-	608,211.00		427,324.91	180,886.09	-0-
College Housing And Academic Facilities Loans Liquidating Account, Department Of Education											
Fund Resources:											
Undisbursed Funds	No Year	91		0242		613,688.01	1,628,717.62	-8,625,962.11	-6,983,639.01		600,082.53
Fund Equities:											
Unobligated Balances (Unexpired)						-13,688.01					-82.53
Undelivered Orders						-600,000.00				-13,605.48	-600,000.00
Subtotal		91		0242		-0-	1,628,717.62	-8,625,962.11	-6,983,639.01	-13,605.48	-0-
Howard University, Department Of Education											
Fund Resources:											
Undisbursed Funds	2007	91		0603			233,865,720.00		233,865,720.00		3,526,380.00
	No Year	91		0603		10,601,883.00	3,526,380.00		10,601,883.00		
Fund Equities:											
Unobligated Balances (Unexpired)						-10,601,883.00				-7,075,503.00	-3,526,380.00
Subtotal		91		0603		-0-	237,392,100.00		244,467,603.00	-7,075,503.00	-0-
Historically Black College And University Capital Financing, Program Account, Department Of Education											
Fund Resources:											
Undisbursed Funds	2007	91		1901			318,923,424.00		318,831,769.50		91,654.50
	2006					52,440.04			8,938.97		43,501.07
	2005					60,538.75			403.91		60,134.84
	2004					42,357.54					42,357.54
	2003					69,314.40					69,314.40
	2002					102,756.13				102,756.13	
Fund Equities:											
Unobligated Balances (Expired)						-213,396.33				50,928.34	-264,324.67
Accounts Payable						-6,937.81				-2,719.59	-4,218.22
Undelivered Orders						-107,072.72				-68,653.26	-38,419.46
Subtotal		91		1901		-0-	318,923,424.00		318,841,112.38	82,311.62	-0-
Public Enterprise Funds											
College Housing Loans, Department Of Education											
Fund Resources:											
Undisbursed Funds	No Year	91		4250		588,683.59			-25,894,398.86	526,201,296.45[5]	281,786.00
Fund Equities:											
Unobligated Balances (Unexpired)						-472,150.59				-227,323.59	-244,827.00
Undelivered Orders						-116,533.00				-79,574.00	-36,959.00
Subtotal		91		4250		-0-			-25,894,398.86	25,894,398.86	-0-

Footnotes At End Of Chapter

Appropriations, Outlays, and Balances – Continued

Appropriation or Fund Account — Title	Dept Reg	Tr From	Account Number	Sub No.	Period of Availability	Balances, Beginning of Fiscal Year	Appropriations And Other Obligational Authority[1]	Transfers Borrowings And Investment (Net)[2]	Outlays (Net)	Balances Withdrawn And Other Transactions[3]	Balances, End Of Fiscal Year[4]
Total, Office Of Postsecondary Education							2,539,604,852.62	-8,625,962.11	2,480,384,215.61	50,594,674.90	
Office Of Federal Student Aid											
General Fund Accounts											
Student Financial Assistance, Department Of Education											
Fund Resources:											
Undisbursed Funds	91		0200		2007-2008	9,796,229,739.74	15,542,456,000.00		4,111,472,117.38		11,430,983,882.62
					2006-2007	1,421,066,940.33			9,301,032,681.03		495,197,058.71
					2006	153,696,099.76			1,417,633,648.01		3,433,292.32
					2005-2006	24,391,993.12			88,075,931.44		65,620,168.32
					2004-2005	30,346,344.69			6,018,487.99		18,373,505.13
					2003-2004	37,621,961.41			-2,737,968.64		33,084,313.33
					2002-2003	40,488,199.46			4,171,610.54		33,450,350.87
					2001-2002				916,973.52	39,571,225.94	
Fund Equities:											
Unobligated Balances (Expired)						-87,360,431.32				242,337,043.39	-329,697,474.71
Unobligated Balances (Unexpired)						-2,693,382,047.97				-502,494,335.86	-2,190,887,712.11
Accounts Payable						-1,407,483,619.87				-282,809,654.60	-1,124,673,965.27
Undelivered Orders						-7,315,615,179.35				1,119,268,239.86	-8,434,883,419.21
	91		0200		Subtotal	-0-	15,542,456,000.00		14,926,583,481.27	615,872,518.73	-0-
Student Aid Administration, Department Of Education											
Fund Resources:											
Undisbursed Funds	91		0202		2006	37,634,622.61			33,483,295.54		4,151,327.07
					2005	3,249,917.82			318,577.34		2,931,340.48
					2004	3,366,889.68			1,092,502.69		2,274,386.99
					2003	717,406.67			65,321.83		652,084.84
					No Year		717,949,577.00		394,190,730.24		323,758,846.76
Fund Equities:											
Unobligated Balances (Expired)						-852,480.95				-49,094.33	-803,386.62
Unobligated Balances (Unexpired)										258,887.50	-258,887.50
Accounts Payable						-2,855,641.67				47,221,547.24	-50,077,188.91
Undelivered Orders						-41,260,714.16				241,367,808.95	-282,628,523.11
	91		0202		Subtotal	-0-	717,949,577.00		429,150,427.64	288,799,149.36	-0-
Academic Competitiveness Grant Program, Department Of Education											
Fund Resources:											
Undisbursed Funds	91		0205		2007	746,039,824.61	850,000,000.00	743,219,845.69	446,300,928.97		1,146,918,916.72
					2006			-743,219,845.69	2,399,352.39		420,626.53
Fund Equities:											
Unobligated Balances (Expired)						-743,242,966.95				-173,560,251.54	-569,682,715.41
Accounts Payable						-2,796,857.66				-259,858.95	-2,536,998.71
Undelivered Orders										575,119,829.13	-575,119,829.13
	91		0205		Subtotal	-0-	850,000,000.00		448,700,281.36	401,299,718.64	-0-
Federal Family Education Loan, Liquidating Account, Department Of Education											
Fund Resources:											
Undisbursed Funds	91		0230		No Year	294,545,021.79			-661,435,568.06	735,089,437.33	220,891,152.52

Appropriations, Outlays, and Balances - Continued

Appropriation or Fund Account — Title	Dept Reg	Tr From	Account Number	Sub No.	Period of Availability	Balances, Beginning of Fiscal Year	Appropriations And Other Obligational Authority[1]	Transfers Borrowings And Investment (Net)[2]	Outlays (Net)	Balances Withdrawn And Other Transactions[3]	Balances, End Of Fiscal Year[4]
Fund Equities:											
Unobligated Balances (Unexpired)	91					-243,319,174.83			-----	-53,245,412.94	-190,073,761.89
Accounts Payable						-2,436,884.66			-----	2,753,937.87	-5,190,822.53
Undelivered Orders						-48,788,962.30			-----	-23,162,394.20	-25,626,568.10
Subtotal	91		0230		Subtotal	-0-			-661,435,568.06	661,435,568.06	-0-
Federal Family Education Loan Program Account, Department Of Education											
Fund Resources:											
Undisbursed Funds	91		0231		2003	0.60			-----		0.60
					2002	691,235.47			-----	691,235.47	-----
			0231		No Year	2,246,383,786.00	7,405,112,290.00		6,934,811,194.00	[5]802,369,400.00	1,914,315,482.00
Fund Equities:											
Unobligated Balances (Expired)						-353,880.49			-----	-353,879.89	-0.60
Accounts Payable						-46,007.00			-----	-46,007.00	-----
Undelivered Orders						-2,246,675,134.58			-----	-332,359,652.58	-1,914,315,482.00
Subtotal	91		0231		Subtotal	-0-	7,405,112,290.00		6,934,811,194.00	470,301,096.00	-0-
Federal Direct Student Loan Program, Department Of Education											
Fund Resources:											
Undisbursed Funds	91		0243		2007	53,150,323.00	4,966,714,615.00		4,966,714,615.00	-----	22,970,300.00
					2006	12,570,787.00				-----	12,570,787.00
					2005	491,242,859.70			30,180,023.00		96,992,073.83
					No Year				394,250,785.87		
Unfilled Customer Orders						19,664.40					19,664.40
Fund Equities:											
Unobligated Balances (Expired)						-12,570,787.00				22,970,300.00	-35,541,087.00
Unobligated Balances (Unexpired)						-27,814,494.19				-414,481.33	-27,400,012.86
Accounts Payable						-47,528,827.47				-35,697,330.62	-11,831,496.85
Undelivered Orders						-469,069,525.44				-411,289,296.92	-57,780,228.52
Subtotal	91		0243		Subtotal	-0-	4,966,714,615.00		5,391,145,423.87	-424,430,808.87	-0-
Public Enterprise Funds											
Federal Student Loan Reserve Fund, Department Of Education											
Fund Resources:											
Undisbursed Funds	91		4257		No Year	12,556,972.00		-536,646,516.00	-792,831,541.00	[5]266,586,750.00	2,155,247.00
Funds Held Outside The Treasury					No Year	566,140,199.00		536,646,516.00			1,102,786,715.00
Fund Equities:											
Unobligated Balances (Unexpired)						-578,697,171.00				526,244,791.00	-1,104,941,962.00
Accounts Payable										792,831,541.00	-0-
Subtotal	91		4257		Subtotal	-0-			-792,831,541.00	792,831,541.00	-----
Total, Office Of Federal Student Aid							29,482,232,482.00		26,676,123,699.08	2,806,108,782.92	

Appropriations, Outlays, and Balances – Continued

Appropriation or Fund Account — Title	Dept Reg	Tr From	Account Number	Sub No.	Period of Availability	Balances, Beginning of Fiscal Year	Appropriations And Other Obligational Authority[1]	Transfers Borrowings And Investment (Net)[2]	Outlays (Net)	Balances Withdrawn And Other Transactions[3]	Balances, End Of Fiscal Year[4]
Institute Of Education Sciences											
General Fund Accounts											
Institute Of Education Sciences, Department Of Education											
Fund Resources:											
Undisbursed Funds	91		1100		2007-2008		268,844,400.00		10,781,040.59		258,063,359.41
					2007		248,640,102.00		88,481,783.47		160,158,318.53
					2006-2007	258,948,719.52			60,562,267.47		198,386,452.05
					2006	171,806,550.13			128,919,093.31		42,887,456.82
					2005-2006	124,809,740.87			48,075,333.79		76,734,407.08
					2005	107,898,583.84			58,192,498.22		49,706,085.62
					2004-2005	63,676,979.12			27,412,271.92		36,264,707.20
					2004	5,293,467.95			2,765,290.78		2,528,177.17
					2003-2004	15,165,646.48			7,329,406.53		7,836,239.95
					2003	2,358,521.05			169,062.18		2,189,458.87
					2002	8,345,180.24			4,510,517.37	3,834,662.87	
					2001-2002	3,412,686.41			287,887.84	3,124,798.57	
					No Year	4,111.10				4,111.10	
Fund Equities:											
Unobligated Balances (Expired)						-2,325,885.94				1,891,523.65	-4,217,409.59
Unobligated Balances (Unexpired)						-311,234.77				4,288,660.03	-4,599,894.80
Accounts Payable						-31,596,366.83				9,786,508.77	-41,382,875.60
Undelivered Orders						-727,486,699.17				57,067,783.54	-784,554,482.71
Subtotal	91		1100			-0-	517,484,502.00		437,486,453.47	79,998,048.53	-0-
Total, Institute Of Education Sciences							517,484,502.00		437,486,453.47	79,998,048.53	
Departmental Management											
General Fund Accounts											
Office For Civil Rights, Departmental Management, Department Of Education											
Fund Resources:											
Undisbursed Funds	91		0700		2007		91,205,212.00		77,655,051.50		13,550,160.50
					2006	13,234,476.00			10,816,886.30		2,417,589.70
					2005	4,429,523.19			1,756,827.97		2,672,695.22
					2004	3,020,065.45			872,994.49		2,147,070.96
					2003	1,384,127.93			6,945.00		1,377,182.93
					2002	1,135,099.24				1,135,099.24	
Accounts Receivable						19,830.88				-2,000.00	21,830.88
Unfilled Customer Orders						4,169.12				2,000.00	2,169.12
Fund Equities:											
Unobligated Balances (Expired)						-2,169,856.23				-520,236.13	-1,649,620.10
Accounts Payable						-2,686,726.64				219,207.72	-2,905,934.36
Undelivered Orders						-18,370,708.94				-737,564.09	-17,633,144.85
Subtotal	91		0700			-0-	91,205,212.00		91,108,705.26	96,506.74	-0-

Appropriations, Outlays, and Balances - Continued

Appropriation or Fund Account (Title)	Period of Availability	Dept Reg	Tr From	Account Number	Sub No.	Balances, Beginning of Fiscal Year	Appropriations And Other Obligational Authority[1]	Transfers Borrowings And Investment (Net)[2]	Outlays (Net)	Balances Withdrawn And Other Transactions[3]	Balances, End Of Fiscal Year[4]
Program Administration, Departmental Management, Department Of Education											
Fund Resources:											
Undisbursed Funds	2007	91		0800		75,101,129.78	416,486,541.00		329,898,146.73		86,588,394.27
	2006					15,180,633.50			57,803,579.57		17,297,550.21
	2005					10,877,953.80			6,337,161.68		8,843,471.82
	2004					7,519,908.01			1,812,157.43		9,065,796.37
	2003					9,465,871.74			198,665.79		7,321,242.22
	2002					5,551,004.13			367,394.23		
	No Year						2,100,000.00		3,755,133.49	9,098,477.51	3,895,870.64
Accounts Receivable						457,905.95				-286,807.40	744,713.35
Unfilled Customer Orders						478,486.05				-136,448.80	614,934.85
Fund Equities:											
Unobligated Balances (Expired)						-11,911,241.70				-5,816,728.96	-6,094,512.74
Unobligated Balances (Unexpired)						-135,719.53				2,100,000.00	-2,235,719.53
Accounts Payable						-19,352,912.38				1,513,308.74	-20,866,221.12
Undelivered Orders						-93,233,019.35				11,942,500.99	-105,175,520.34
	Subtotal	91		0800		-0-	418,586,541.00		400,172,238.92	18,414,302.08	-0-
Office Of The Inspector General, Departmental Management, Department Of Education											
Fund Resources:											
Undisbursed Funds	2007	91		1400		6,883,732.69	50,266,067.00		41,468,750.40		8,797,316.60
	2006					2,394,154.91			5,013,355.21		1,870,377.48
	2005					1,956,138.59			877,684.97		1,516,469.94
	2004					564,295.54			634,547.60		1,321,590.99
	2003					735,940.25			36,868.85		527,426.69
	2002								59,374.38	676,565.87	
Accounts Receivable						1,000.00				-80,941.57	81,941.57
Unfilled Customer Orders						-1,000.00				-3,326.86	2,326.86
Fund Equities:											
Unobligated Balances (Expired)						-722,686.95				-175,028.64	-547,658.31
Accounts Payable						-1,404,161.83				80,490.31	-1,484,652.14
Undelivered Orders						-10,407,413.20				1,677,726.48	-12,085,139.68
	Subtotal	91		1400		-0-	50,266,067.00		48,090,581.41	2,175,485.59	-0-
Trust Fund Accounts											
Contributions, Department Of Education											
Fund Resources:											
Undisbursed Funds	No Year	91		8258		60,752,751.52	389,164.48		21,677,167.59		39,464,748.41
Fund Equities:											
Unobligated Balances (Unexpired)						-25,484,920.57				-25,207,263.68	-277,656.89
Accounts Payable						-11,132.01				6,656.06	-17,788.07
Undelivered Orders						-35,256,698.94				3,912,604.51	-39,169,303.45
	Subtotal	91		8258		-0-	389,164.48		21,677,167.59	-21,288,003.11	-0-
Total, Departmental Management						-0-	560,446,984.48		561,048,693.18	-601,708.70	-0-

Footnotes At End Of Chapter

Appropriations, Outlays, and Balances – Continued

Appropriation or Fund Account	Account Symbol			Period of Availability	Balances, Beginning of Fiscal Year	Appropriations And Other Obligational Authority[1]	Transfers Borrowings And Investment (Net)[2]	Outlays (Net)	Balances Withdrawn And Other Transactions[3]	Balances, End Of Fiscal Year[4]
Title	Dept		Account Number	Sub No.						
	Reg	Tr From								

Title	Reg	Tr From	Account Number	Sub No.	Period of Availability	Balances, Beginning of Fiscal Year	Appropriations And Other Obligational Authority[1]	Transfers Borrowings And Investment (Net)[2]	Outlays (Net)	Balances Withdrawn And Other Transactions[3]	Balances, End Of Fiscal Year[4]
Hurricane Education Recovery											
General Fund Accounts											
Hurricane Education Recovery, Office Of Elementary And Secondary Education, Department Of Education											
Fund Resources:											
Undisbursed Funds	91		0013		2006	745,350,214.80			414,906,477.44		330,443,737.36
					No Year		30,000,000.00				30,000,000.00
Fund Equities:											
Unobligated Balances (Expired)						-1,571,222.99				61,519.16	-1,632,742.15
Accounts Payable						-425,476.70				2,483,361.35	-2,908,838.05
Undelivered Orders						-743,353,515.11				-387,451,357.95	-355,902,157.16
Total, Hurricane Education Recovery	91		0013		Subtotal	-0-	30,000,000.00		414,906,477.44	-384,906,477.44	30,000,000.00
Deductions For Offsetting Receipts											
Proprietary Receipts From The Public							-4,869,563,294.33		-4,869,563,294.33		
Intrabudgetary Transactions							-1,494,313.12		-1,494,313.12		
Total, Department Of Education							69,049,994,121.65	-8,625,962.11	66,372,132,133.50	2,669,236,026.04	
Memorandum											
Financing Accounts											
Public Enterprise Funds											
Federal Family Education Loan Program, Financing Account, Department Of Education											
Fund Resources:											
Undisbursed Funds	91		4251		No Year	43,541,710,297.33			6,603,268,794.09		36,938,441,503.24
Fund Equities:											
Unobligated Balances (Unexpired)						-40,010,671,635.67				-6,781,639,308.40	-33,229,032,327.27
Accounts Payable						-172,519,279.88				-162,436,963.36	-10,082,316.52
Undelivered Orders						-3,358,519,381.78				340,807,477.67	-3,699,326,859.45
College Housing And Academic Facilities Direct Loan Financing Account, Department Of Education	91		4251		Subtotal	-0-			6,603,268,794.09	-6,603,268,794.09	-0-
Fund Resources:											
Undisbursed Funds	91		4252		No Year	123,294.70		-3,268,321.15	-3,145,026.45	-123,294.70	
Fund Equities:											
Unobligated Balances (Unexpired)	91		4252		Subtotal	-123,294.70		-3,268,321.15	-3,145,026.45	-123,294.70	-0-

Appropriations, Outlays, and Balances - Continued

Appropriation or Fund Account — Title	Account Symbol Period of Availability	Dept Reg	Dept Tr From	Account Number	Sub No.	Balances, Beginning of Fiscal Year	Appropriations And Other Obligational Authority[1]	Transfers Borrowings And Investment (Net)[2]	Outlays (Net)	Balances Withdrawn And Other Transactions[3]	Balances, End Of Fiscal Year[4]
Federal Direct Student Loan Program, Financing Account, Department Of Education											
Fund Resources:											
Undisbursed Funds	No Year	91		4253		8,621,010,444.43		-1,537,044,308.40	1,719,005,895.13		5,364,960,240.90
Authority To Borrow From The Treasury						7,236,825,196.99	19,569,803,927.00	-17,892,417,596.99			8,914,211,527.00
Unfilled Customer Orders						30,180,023.00				30,180,023.00	-0-
Fund Equities:											
Unobligated Balances (Unexpired)						-6,478,898,476.19				-2,916,183,964.32	-3,562,714,511.87
Accounts Payable						-307,815,606.97				199,531,914.66	-507,347,521.63
Undelivered Orders						-9,101,301,581.26				1,107,808,153.14	-10,209,109,734.40
Subtotal		91		4253		-0-	19,569,803,927.00	-19,429,461,905.39	1,719,005,895.13	-1,578,663,873.52	-0-
Historically Black College And University, Capital Financing, Direct Loan Financing Account, Department Of Education											
Fund Resources:											
Undisbursed Funds	No Year	91		4255		1.71		159,305,264.50	-159,885,715.56		319,190,981.77
Authority To Borrow From The Treasury						11,315,589.16	467,000,000.00	-169,869,895.86			308,445,693.30
Fund Equities:											
Unobligated Balances (Unexpired)						-1.71				319,190,980.06	-319,190,981.77
Accounts Payable										297,130,104.14	-308,445,693.30
Undelivered Orders						-11,315,589.16				616,321,084.20	-0-
Subtotal		91		4255		-0-	467,000,000.00	-10,564,631.36	-159,885,715.56		-0-
Total, Financing Accounts							20,036,803,927.00	-19,443,294,857.90	8,159,243,947.21	-7,565,734,878.11	

Footnotes At End Of Chapter

Appropriations, Outlays, and Balances – Continued

Footnotes

1   The amounts in this column, unless otherwise footnoted, represent appropriations, increases and rescissions in borrowing authority or new contract authority. Appropriation accounts with appropriation transfer activity are presented in Table 1 (Appropriations and Appropriation Transfers) at the end of this chapter.

2   The amounts in this column, unless otherwise footnoted, represent transfers - other than appropriation transfers, borrowings (gross), investments (net), unrealized discounts or cash held outside of the Treasury.

3   The amounts in this column, unless otherwise footnoted, represent obligated balances canceled for fiscal year 2002 pursuant to 31 U.S.C. 1553, changes in unfilled customer orders, accounts receivable, accounts payable, undelivered orders, unobligated balances and adjustments to borrowing and contract authority.

4   Unobligated balances for no-year or unexpired multiple year accounts are available for obligation; unobligated balances for expired fiscal year accounts are not available for obligation.

5   Represents capital transfer to miscellaneous receipts.

Appropriations, Outlays, and Balances - Continued

Footnotes

Table 1 - Appropriations And Appropriation Transfers - Department Of Education

Department Regular	Fiscal Year	Account Symbol	Net Appropriations And Appropriations Transfers	Appropriation Amount	Net Appropriation Transfers	Department Regular Involved	Fiscal Year Involved	Accounts Involved	Amount From or To (-)
91	X	0202	717,949,577.00	719,413,637.00	-1,464,060.00	91	07	1400	-1,464,060.00
91	X	0203	3,000,000.00	0.00	3,000,000.00	91	07	0203	3,000,000.00
91	07	0203	388,612,000.00	391,612,000.00	-3,000,000.00	91	X	0203	-3,000,000.00
91	0708	0400	0.00	4,676,760.00	-4,676,760.00	91	0708	0400	-4,676,760.00
91	X	0400	1,201,170,583.00	1,196,493,823.00	4,676,760.00	91	07	0400	4,676,760.00
91	07	0603	3,526,380.00	0.00	3,526,380.00	91	07	0603	3,526,380.00
91	07	0603	233,865,720.00	237,392,100.00	-3,526,380.00	91	X	0603	-3,526,380.00
91	07	1400	50,266,067.00	48,802,007.00	1,464,060.00	91	X	0202	1,464,060.00
Totals			2,598,390,327.00	2,598,390,327.00	0.00				0.00

Appropriations, Outlays, and Balances – Continued

Title	Period of Availability	Reg	Tr From	Account Number	Sub No.	Balances, Beginning Of Fiscal Year	Appropriations And Other Obligational Authority[1]	Transfers Borrowings And Investment (Net)[2]	Outlays (Net)	Balances Withdrawn And Other Transactions[3]	Balances, End Of Fiscal Year[4]
Department Of Energy											
National Nuclear Security Administration											
General Fund Accounts											
Atomic Energy Defense Activities, Department Of Energy											
Fund Resources:											
Undisbursed Funds	2002	89		0240		35,947.86			21,235.07	14,712.79	
	No Year					2,634,434,349.67	6,258,583,000.00		6,278,625,865.50		2,614,391,484.17
Accounts Receivable						337,196,565.34				-15,626,388.30	352,822,953.64
Unfilled Customer Orders						2,903,539,411.09				-59,434,858.24	2,962,974,269.33
Fund Equities:											
Unobligated Balances (Expired)						-9,738.27				-9,738.27	
Unobligated Balances (Unexpired)						-412,251,558.46				-247,119,448.54	-165,132,109.92
Accounts Payable						-1,147,593,002.11				13,934,086.97	-1,161,527,089.08
Undelivered Orders						-4,315,351,975.12				288,177,533.02	-4,603,529,508.14
	Subtotal	89		0240		-0-	6,258,583,000.00		6,278,647,100.57	-20,064,100.57	-0-
Defense Nuclear Nonproliferation, Department Of Energy											
Fund Resources:											
Undisbursed Funds	2004-2005	89		0309		175,326.13			170,107.61		5,218.52
	2003-2005					5,082,852.38			3,142,646.27		1,940,206.11
	2003-2004					17,977.35			4,512.12		13,465.23
	2002-2003					5,179,901.05			32,516.68		5,147,384.37
	2001-2002					5,775.94				5,775.94	
	No Year					1,854,009,181.59	1,812,149,000.00		1,531,319,586.81		2,134,838,594.78
Fund Equities:											
Unobligated Balances (Expired)						-5,222,049.19				-215,040.69	-5,007,008.50
Unobligated Balances (Unexpired)						-457,225,310.33				-28,780,806.47	-428,444,503.86
Accounts Payable						-86,751,120.37				11,600,920.10	-98,352,040.47
Undelivered Orders						-1,315,272,534.55				294,868,781.63	-1,610,141,316.18
	Subtotal	89		0309		-0-	1,812,149,000.00		1,534,669,369.49	277,479,630.51	-0-
Cerro Grande Fire Activities, Department Of Energy											
Fund Resources:											
Undisbursed Funds	No Year	89		0312		13,638,827.10			734,386.12		12,904,440.98
Fund Equities:											
Unobligated Balances (Unexpired)						-20,934.70				39,474.32	-60,409.02
Undelivered Orders						-13,617,892.40				-773,860.44	-12,844,031.96
	Subtotal	89		0312		-0-			734,386.12	-734,386.12	-0-
Office Of The Administrator, Department Of Energy											
Fund Resources:											
Undisbursed Funds	2004	89		0313		-4,765.53			-4,765.53		
	2003					5,149,821.11			341,697.53		4,808,123.58
	No Year					99,808,795.03	369,191,310.00		361,246,961.24		107,753,143.79
Fund Equities:											
Unobligated Balances (Expired)						-2,721,670.03				655,867.22	-3,377,537.25
Unobligated Balances (Unexpired)						-6,539,960.00				8,070,276.45	-14,610,236.45
Accounts Payable						-24,878,025.30				-847,175.83	-24,030,849.47
Undelivered Orders						-70,814,195.28				-271,551.08	-70,542,644.20

Appropriations, Outlays, and Balances - Continued

Appropriation or Fund Account — Title	Period of Availability	Dept Reg	Tr From	Account Number	Sub No.	Balances, Beginning Of Fiscal Year	Appropriations And Other Obligational Authority[1]	Transfers Borrowings And Investment (Net)[2]	Outlays (Net)	Balances Withdrawn And Other Transactions[3]	Balances, End Of Fiscal Year[4]
Naval Reactors, Department Of Energy											
Fund Resources:											
	Subtotal	89		0313		-0-	369,191,310.00		361,583,893.24	7,607,416.76	-0-
Undisbursed Funds	No Year	89		0314		245,764,742.14	781,800,000.00		816,173,941.76		211,390,800.38
Fund Equities:											
Unobligated Balances (Unexpired)						-4,440,998.69				1,758,459.86	-6,199,458.55
Accounts Payable						-139,365,585.18				-24,955,945.42	-114,409,639.76
Undelivered Orders						-101,958,158.27				-11,176,456.20	-90,781,702.07
	Subtotal	89		0314		-0-	781,800,000.00		816,173,941.76	-34,373,941.76	-0-
Special Fund Accounts											
Pajarito Plateau Homesteaders Compensation Fund, Department Of Energy											
Fund Resources:											
Undisbursed Funds	No Year	89		5520		405.04	216,264.89	8,200,000.00	7,694,312.93		722,357.00
Investments In Public Debt Securities						8,200,000.00		-8,200,000.00			
Fund Equities:											
Unobligated Balances (Unexpired)						-3,042,782.49				-2,320,425.49	-722,357.00
Accounts Payable											
Undelivered Orders						-5,157,622.55				-5,157,622.55	-0-
	Subtotal	89		5520		-0-	216,264.89		7,694,312.93	-7,478,048.04	-0-
Total, National Nuclear Security Administration							9,221,939,574.89		8,999,503,004.11	222,436,570.78	
Environmental And Other Defense Activities											
General Fund Accounts											
Defense Environmental Restoration And Waste Management, Department Of Energy											
Fund Resources:											
Undisbursed Funds	No Year	89		0242		4,232,555.49		-5,358,111.97	-1,125,619.92		63.44
Fund Equities:											
Unobligated Balances (Unexpired)						-625,315.31				-625,315.00	-0.31
Accounts Payable						-3,654,488.38				-3,654,443.88	-44.50
Undelivered Orders						47,248.20				47,266.83	-18.63
	Subtotal	89		0242		-0-		-5,358,111.97	-1,125,619.92	-4,232,492.05	-0-
Other Defense Activities, Department Of Energy											
Fund Resources:											
Undisbursed Funds	2004-2005	89		0243		99,498.05			9,854.88		89,643.17
	2002					473,737.24			320.04	473,417.20	
	No Year					362,596,868.09	636,271,020.00		548,689,897.75		450,177,990.34
Fund Equities:											
Unobligated Balances (Expired)						-471,372.95				-381,729.78	-89,643.17
Unobligated Balances (Unexpired)						-52,922,110.77				-10,389,068.46	-42,533,042.31
Accounts Payable						-129,348,189.65				57,988,685.72	-187,336,875.37
Undelivered Orders						-180,428,430.01				39,879,642.65	-220,308,072.66
	Subtotal	89		0243		-0-	636,271,020.00		548,700,072.67	87,570,947.33	-0-

Footnotes At End Of Chapter

Appropriations, Outlays, and Balances – Continued

Appropriation or Fund Account	Account Symbol					Balances, Beginning Of Fiscal Year	Appropriations And Other Obligational Authority[1]	Transfers Borrowings And Investment (Net)[2]	Outlays (Net)	Balances Withdrawn And Other Transactions[3]	Balances, End Of Fiscal Year[4]
Title	Period of Availability	Dept Reg	Tr From	Account Number	Sub No.						
Defense Nuclear Waste Disposal, Department Of Energy											
Fund Resources:											
Undisbursed Funds	No Year	89		0244		57,295,380.79	346,500,000.00		357,390,687.79	--------	46,404,693.00
Fund Equities:											
Unobligated Balances (Unexpired)						-347,066.35				-125,543.32	-221,523.03
Accounts Payable						-6,244,890.33				732,296.32	-6,977,186.65
Undelivered Orders						-50,703,424.11				-11,497,440.79	-39,205,983.32
Subtotal		89		0244		-0-	346,500,000.00		357,390,687.79	-10,890,687.79	-0-
Defense Environmental Services, Department Of Energy											
Fund Resources:											
Undisbursed Funds	No Year	89		0249		2,541,400.90		-1,892,861.87	31,706.83		616,832.20
Fund Equities:											
Unobligated Balances (Unexpired)						-746,905.76				-548,327.69	-198,578.07
Accounts Payable						-1,063,272.43				-771,375.39	-291,697.04
Undelivered Orders						-731,222.71				-604,865.62	-126,357.09
Subtotal		89		0249		-0-		-1,892,861.87	31,706.83	-1,924,568.70	-0-
Defense Site Acceleration Completion, Department Of Energy											
Fund Resources:											
Undisbursed Funds	No Year	89		0251		2,297,855,705.48	5,731,240,000.00	7,250,973.84	5,858,837,796.81		2,177,508,882.51
Fund Equities:											
Unobligated Balances (Unexpired)						-32,769,813.49				70,083,996.97	-102,853,810.46
Accounts Payable						-989,719,360.72				-163,025,911.35	-826,693,449.37
Undelivered Orders						-1,275,366,531.27				-27,404,908.59	-1,247,961,622.68
Subtotal		89		0251		-0-	5,731,240,000.00	7,250,973.84	5,858,837,796.81	-120,346,822.97	-0-
Total, Environmental And Other Defense Activities							6,714,011,020.00		6,763,834,644.18	-49,823,624.18	
Energy Programs											
General Fund Accounts											
Geothermal Loan Guarantee And Interest Assistance Program, Geothermal Resources Development Fund, Department Of Energy											
Fund Resources:											
Undisbursed Funds	No Year	89		0206		46,428.40					46,428.40
Fund Equities:											
Unobligated Balances (Unexpired)						-37,026.92				9,401.48	-46,428.40
Undelivered Orders						-9,401.48				-9,401.48	
Subtotal		89		0206		-0-					-0-
Salaries And Expenses, Federal Energy Regulatory Commission, Department Of Energy											
Fund Resources:											
Undisbursed Funds	No Year	89		0212		28,876,811.98			4,906,215.36		23,970,596.62
Accounts Receivable						5,823.76				-16,816.42	22,640.18
Unfilled Customer Orders						40,479.33				-24,163.01	64,642.34
Fund Equities:											
Unobligated Balances (Unexpired)						-5,748,932.82				-2,319,242.18	-3,429,690.64
Accounts Payable						-19,354,238.83				103,928.00	-19,458,166.83
Undelivered Orders						-3,819,943.42				-2,649,921.75	-1,170,021.67
Subtotal		89		0212		-0-			4,906,215.36	-4,906,215.36	-0-

Appropriations, Outlays, and Balances - Continued

Appropriation or Fund Account — Title	Period of Availability	Account Symbol — Dept — Reg	Account Symbol — Dept — Tr From	Account Number	Sub No.	Balances, Beginning Of Fiscal Year	Appropriations And Other Obligational Authority[1]	Transfers Borrowings And Investment (Net)[2]	Outlays (Net)	Balances Withdrawn And Other Transactions[3]	Balances, End Of Fiscal Year[4]
Fossil Energy Research And Development, Department Of Energy											
Fund Resources:											
Undisbursed Funds	No Year	89		0213		1,160,986,433.33	580,946,060.00	-887,384.15	535,312,045.23		1,205,733,063.95
Fund Equities:											
Unobligated Balances (Unexpired)						-601,350,533.28				-137,375,470.42	-463,975,062.86
Accounts Payable						-168,929,371.69				-12,844,186.58	-156,085,185.11
Undelivered Orders						-390,706,528.36				194,966,287.62	-585,672,815.98
Subtotal		89		0213		-0-	580,946,060.00	-887,384.15	535,312,045.23	44,746,630.62	-0-
Energy Conservation, Department Of Energy											
Fund Resources:											
Undisbursed Funds	No Year	89		0215		4,950,137.30		-5,582,429.53	-777,385.14		145,092.91
Fund Equities:											
Unobligated Balances (Unexpired)						-4,951,323.30				-4,824,132.08	-127,191.22
Accounts Payable						616,917.40				609,431.75	7,485.65
Undelivered Orders						-615,731.40				-590,344.06	-25,387.34
Subtotal		89		0215		-0-		-5,582,429.53	-777,385.14	-4,805,044.39	-0-
Energy Information Administration, Department Of Energy											
Fund Resources:											
Undisbursed Funds	No Year	89		0216		24,962,527.60	90,653,000.00		90,730,511.82		24,885,015.78
Fund Equities:											
Unobligated Balances (Unexpired)						-1,772,539.43				-1,331,445.92	-441,093.51
Accounts Payable						-6,129,050.92				-129,348.05	-5,999,702.87
Undelivered Orders						-17,060,937.25				1,383,282.15	-18,444,219.40
Subtotal		89		0216		-0-	90,653,000.00		90,730,511.82	-77,511.82	-0-
Economic Regulation, Department Of Energy											
Fund Resources:											
Undisbursed Funds	No Year	89		0217		349,648.22			2,439.24		347,208.98
Fund Equities:											
Unobligated Balances (Unexpired)						-263,624.61				1,435.00	-265,059.61
Accounts Payable						-273.63				50,203.37	-50,477.00
Undelivered Orders						-85,749.98				-54,077.61	-31,672.37
Subtotal		89		0217		-0-			2,439.24	-2,439.24	-0-
Strategic Petroleum Reserve, Department Of Energy											
Fund Resources:											
Undisbursed Funds	No Year	89		0218		137,433,256.83	164,441,000.00		192,302,906.51		109,571,350.32
Fund Equities:											
Unobligated Balances (Unexpired)						-18,715,459.07				-4,439,964.90	-14,275,494.17
Accounts Payable						-32,970,323.09				-2,806,442.82	-30,163,880.27
Undelivered Orders						-85,747,474.67				-20,615,498.79	-65,131,975.88
Subtotal		89		0218		-0-	164,441,000.00		192,302,906.51	-27,861,906.51	-0-
Naval Petroleum And Oil Shale Reserves, Department Of Energy											
Fund Resources:											
Undisbursed Funds	No Year	89		0219		22,550,583.86	21,316,000.00		17,983,217.35		25,883,366.51
Fund Equities:											
Unobligated Balances (Unexpired)						-9,026,686.29				4,822,428.31	-13,849,114.60
Accounts Payable						-1,707,321.43				552,244.46	-2,259,565.89
Undelivered Orders						-11,816,576.14				-2,041,890.12	-9,774,686.02
Subtotal		89		0219		-0-	21,316,000.00		17,983,217.35	3,332,782.65	-0-

Footnotes At End Of Chapter

Appropriations, Outlays, and Balances – Continued

Title	Reg	Tr From	Account Number	Sub No.	Period of Availability	Balances, Beginning Of Fiscal Year	Appropriations And Other Obligational Authority[1]	Transfers Borrowings And Investment (Net)[2]	Outlays (Net)	Balances Withdrawn And Other Transactions[3]	Balances, End Of Fiscal Year[4]
Science, Department Of Energy											
Fund Resources:											
Undisbursed Funds	89		0222		No Year	2,251,853,703.52	3,836,613,000.00		3,697,162,427.15		2,391,304,276.37
Fund Equities:											
Unobligated Balances (Unexpired)						-20,060,647.99				-6,027,210.47	-14,033,437.52
Accounts Payable						-1,137,152,029.30				121,832,705.53	-1,258,984,734.83
Undelivered Orders						-1,094,641,026.23				23,645,077.79	-1,118,286,104.02
Subtotal	89		0222			-0-	3,836,613,000.00		3,697,162,427.15	139,450,572.85	-0-
Energy Supply, Department Of Energy											
Fund Resources:											
Undisbursed Funds	89		0224		2007-2008		12,100,000.00				12,100,000.00
					2006-2007	11,538,000.00		400,000.00	20,904.55		11,917,095.45
					2005-2006	15,007,746.20			10,588,208.84		4,419,537.36
					No Year	1,480,488,724.26	2,132,649,000.00	5,582,429.53	1,739,885,217.96		1,878,834,935.83
Accounts Receivable						51,021,772.03				-12,597,827.61	63,619,599.64
Unfilled Customer Orders						403,529,140.10				-66,022,123.06	469,551,263.16
Fund Equities:											
Unobligated Balances (Expired)						-17,000.00				1,095.45	-18,095.45
Unobligated Balances (Unexpired)						-61,014,167.43				103,881,653.35	-164,895,820.78
Accounts Payable						-350,722,525.96				84,045,236.57	-434,767,762.53
Undelivered Orders						-1,549,831,689.20				290,929,063.48	-1,840,760,752.68
Subtotal	89		0224			-0-	2,144,749,000.00	5,982,429.53	1,750,494,331.35	400,237,098.18	-0-
Spr Petroleum Account, Department Of Energy											
Fund Resources:											
Undisbursed Funds	89		0233		No Year	$617,736,218.11			630,111.73		617,106,106.38
Fund Equities:											
Unobligated Balances (Unexpired)						$-591,798,805.26				503,747.53	-592,302,552.79
Accounts Payable						-479,429.95				-18,067.30	-461,362.65
Undelivered Orders						-25,457,982.90				-1,115,791.96	-24,342,190.94
Subtotal	89		0233			-0-			630,111.73	-630,111.73	-0-
Emergency Preparedness, Department Of Energy											
Fund Resources:											
Undisbursed Funds	89		0234		No Year	95,732.96			1,231.00		94,501.96
Fund Equities:											
Unobligated Balances (Unexpired)						-93,676.05				45.00	-93,721.05
Accounts Payable						-1,546.91				-1,081.91	-465.00
Undelivered Orders						-510.00				-194.09	-315.91
Subtotal	89		0234			-0-			1,231.00	-1,231.00	-0-
Clean Coal Technology, Department Of Energy											
Fund Resources:											
Undisbursed Funds	89		0235		No Year	340,139,711.61			-220,559.69		340,360,271.30
Fund Equities:											
Unobligated Balances (Unexpired)						-328,641,548.46				3,184,147.81	-331,825,696.27
Accounts Payable						-9,899,627.69				-1,861,310.71	-8,038,316.98
Undelivered Orders						-1,598,535.46				-1,102,277.41	-496,258.05
Subtotal	89		0235			-0-			-220,559.69	220,559.69	-0-
Non-Defense Site Acceleration Completion, Department Of Energy											
Fund Resources:											
Undisbursed Funds	89		0250		No Year	191,861.72		-331,597.24	-142,937.84		3,202.32

Appropriations, Outlays, and Balances - Continued

Appropriation or Fund Account Title	Period of Availability	Dept Reg	Tr From	Account Number	Sub No.	Balances, Beginning Of Fiscal Year	Appropriations And Other Obligational Authority[1]	Transfers Borrowings And Investment (Net)[2]	Outlays (Net)	Balances Withdrawn And Other Transactions[3]	Balances, End Of Fiscal Year[4]
Fund Equities:											
Accounts Payable						53,892.32					53,892.32
Undelivered Orders						-245,754.04				-242,551.72	-3,202.32
Subtotal		89		0250		-0-		-331,597.24	-142,937.84	-188,659.40	-0-
Non-Defense Environmental Services, Department Of Energy											
Fund Resources:											
Undisbursed Funds	No Year	89		0315		268,427,260.20	349,686,810.00	331,597.24	320,178,706.71		298,266,960.73
Fund Equities:											
Unobligated Balances (Unexpired)						-4,411,424.70				-1,695,942.66	-2,715,482.04
Accounts Payable						-40,852,177.73				-3,905,357.07	-36,946,820.66
Undelivered Orders						-223,163,657.77				35,441,000.26	-258,604,658.03
Subtotal		89		0315		-0-	349,686,810.00	331,597.24	320,178,706.71	29,839,700.53	-0-
Special Fund Accounts											
Payment To States Under Federal Power Act											
Fund Resources:											
Undisbursed Funds	No Year	89		5105		0.21	3,094,042.35		3,094,042.35		0.21
Fund Equities:											
Accounts Payable						-0.21					-0.21
Subtotal		89		5105		-0-	3,094,042.35		3,094,042.35		-0-
Alternative Fuels Production, Department Of Energy											
Fund Resources:											
Undisbursed Funds	No Year	89		5180		9,141,546.04					9,141,546.04
Fund Equities:											
Unobligated Balances (Unexpired)						-7,338.39					-7,338.39
Undelivered Orders						-9,134,207.65					-9,134,207.65
Subtotal		89		5180		-0-					-0-
Nuclear Waste Disposal Fund, Department Of Energy											
Fund Resources:											
Undisbursed Funds	No Year	89		5227		50,905,385.85	1,499,906,448.93	-1,325,728,888.85	210,826,750.91		14,256,195.02
Unrealized Discount On Investments						-2,030,486.56					-2,030,486.56
Unamortized Premium And Discount						-17,760,415,952.94		-1,626,970,335.15			-19,387,386,288.09
Investments In Public Debt Securities						36,482,065,671.00		2,952,699,224.00			39,434,764,895.00
Fund Equities:											
Unobligated Balances (Unexpired)						-18,568,449,227.71				1,371,656,695.76	-19,940,105,923.47
Accounts Payable						-52,781,314.57				-2,701,163.95	-50,080,150.62
Undelivered Orders						-149,294,075.07				-79,875,833.79	-69,418,241.28
Subtotal		89		5227		-0-	1,499,906,448.93		210,826,750.91	1,289,079,698.02	-0-
Uranium Enrichment And Decommissioning Fund, Department Of Energy											
Fund Resources:											
Undisbursed Funds	No Year	89		5231		26,547,109.04	861,223,547.34	-382,797,132.33	503,476,810.52		1,496,713.53
Unrealized Discount On Investments						-30,662,931.23		-12,447,867.67			-43,110,798.90
Investments In Public Debt Securities						4,227,982,000.00		395,245,000.00			4,623,227,000.00
Fund Equities:											
Unobligated Balances (Unexpired)						-4,087,320,733.02				305,029,200.67	-4,392,349,933.69
Accounts Payable						-35,633,485.80				26,690,668.77	-62,324,154.57

Footnotes At End Of Chapter

Appropriations, Outlays, and Balances – Continued

Appropriation or Fund Account — Title	Period of Availability	Dept Reg	Dept Tr From	Account Number	Sub No.	Balances, Beginning Of Fiscal Year	Appropriations And Other Obligational Authority[1]	Transfers Borrowings And Investment (Net)[2]	Outlays (Net)	Balances Withdrawn And Other Transactions[3]	Balances, End Of Fiscal Year[4]
Uranium Enrichment And Decommissioning Fund, Department Of Energy - Continued											
Fund Equities: - Continued											
Undelivered Orders - Continued						-0-				357,746,736.82	-0-
Subtotal	Subtotal	89		5231		-100,911,958.99	861,223,547.34		503,476,810.52	26,026,867.38	-126,938,826.37
Northeast Home Heating Oil Reserve, Department Of Energy											
Fund Resources:											
Undisbursed Funds	No Year	89		5369		7,016,634.44	7,965,872.00		4,813,633.85		10,168,872.59
Fund Equities:											
Unobligated Balances (Unexpired)						-2,151,307.00				-1,043,064.27	-1,108,242.73
Accounts Payable						-2,357.27				-2,357.27	
Undelivered Orders						-4,862,970.17				4,197,659.69	-9,060,629.86
Subtotal	Subtotal	89		5369		-0-	7,965,872.00		4,813,633.85	3,152,238.15	-0-
Ultra-Deepwater And Unconventional Natural Gas And Other Petroleum Research Fund											
Fund Resources:											
Undisbursed Funds	No Year	89		5523			50,000,000.00		1,960,506.08		48,039,493.92
Fund Equities:											
Unobligated Balances (Unexpired)										7,097,640.52	-7,097,640.52
Accounts Payable										432,213.72	-432,213.72
Undelivered Orders										40,509,639.68	-40,509,639.68
Subtotal	Subtotal	89		5523		-0-	50,000,000.00		1,960,506.08	48,039,493.92	-0-
Sales Of Uranium, Energy Programs, Department Of Energy											
Fund Resources:											
Undisbursed Funds	No Year	89		5530		122,390,465.95	43,057,413.17		61,659,825.18		103,788,053.94
Fund Equities:											
Unobligated Balances (Unexpired)						-100,392,326.00				-57,334,912.83	-43,057,413.17
Accounts Payable						-4,201,881.40				4,437,269.93	-8,639,151.33
Undelivered Orders						-17,796,258.55				34,295,230.89	-52,091,489.44
Subtotal	Subtotal	89		5530		-0-	43,057,413.17		61,659,825.18	-18,602,412.01	-0-
Public Enterprise Funds											
Expenses, Isotope Production And Distribution Program Fund, Department Of Energy											
Fund Resources:											
Undisbursed Funds	No Year	89		4180		20,312,864.57			-4,707,552.97		25,020,417.54
Accounts Receivable						28,359.50				-67,403.65	95,763.15
Fund Equities:											
Unobligated Balances (Unexpired)						-9,963,219.99				2,799,747.26	-12,762,967.25
Accounts Payable						-1,887,778.91				-1,882,857.96	-4,920.95
Undelivered Orders						-8,490,225.17				3,858,067.32	-12,348,292.49
Subtotal	Subtotal	89		4180		-0-			-4,707,552.97	4,707,552.97	-0-

Appropriations, Outlays, and Balances - Continued

Title	Period of Availability	Dept Reg	Tr From	Account Number	Sub No.	Balances, Beginning Of Fiscal Year	Appropriations And Other Obligational Authority[1]	Transfers Borrowings And Investment (Net)[2]	Outlays (Net)	Balances Withdrawn And Other Transactions[3]	Balances, End Of Fiscal Year[4]
Trust Fund Accounts											
Advances For Cooperative Work, Departmental Operations, Department Of Energy											
Fund Resources:	No Year	89		8575							
Undisbursed Funds						1,124,547.03			681,957.35		442,589.68
Fund Equities:											
Unobligated Balances (Unexpired)						-67,915.87				-9,166.95	-58,748.92
Accounts Payable						356,699.98				369,121.53	-12,421.55
Undelivered Orders						-1,413,331.14				-1,041,911.93	-371,419.21
						-0-			681,957.35	-681,957.35	-0-
	Subtotal	89		8575					681,957.35	-681,957.35	
Total, Energy Programs							9,653,652,193.79	-487,384.15	7,390,369,234.05	2,262,795,575.59	
Power Marketing Administration											
General Fund Accounts											
Operation And Maintenance, Southeastern Power Administration, Power Marketing Administration, Department Of Energy											
Fund Resources:	No Year	89		0302							
Undisbursed Funds						2,346,033.32	5,602,000.00		6,528,148.38		1,419,884.94
Fund Equities:											
Unobligated Balances (Unexpired)						-473.69				-8.49	-465.20
Accounts Payable						-1,941,613.22				-1,150,162.97	-791,450.25
Undelivered Orders						-403,946.41				224,023.08	-627,969.49
	Subtotal	89		0302		-0-	5,602,000.00		6,528,148.38	-926,148.38	-0-
Operation And Maintenance, Southwestern Power Administration, Power Marketing Administration, Department Of Energy											
Fund Resources:	No Year	89		0303							
Undisbursed Funds						16,226,666.25	38,089,700.00		21,091,286.78		33,225,079.47
Accounts Receivable						120,955.26				-170,370.24	291,325.50
Unfilled Customer Orders						1,995,466.17				552,783.00	1,442,683.17
Fund Equities:											
Unobligated Balances (Unexpired)						-75.00				7,284,256.24	-7,284,331.24
Accounts Payable						-4,193,201.78				1,791,161.62	-5,984,363.40
Undelivered Orders						-14,149,810.90				7,540,582.60	-21,690,393.50
	Subtotal	89		0303		-0-	38,089,700.00		21,091,286.78	16,998,413.22	-0-
Operation And Maintenance, Alaska Power Administration, Power Marketing Administration, Department Of Energy											
Fund Resources:	No Year	89		0304							
Undisbursed Funds						800,413.91			50,444.05		749,969.86
Fund Equities:											
Unobligated Balances (Unexpired)						-300,000.00					-300,000.00
Undelivered Orders						-500,413.91				-50,444.05	-449,969.86
	Subtotal	89		0304		-0-			50,444.05	-50,444.05	-0-

Footnotes At End Of Chapter

Appropriations, Outlays, and Balances – Continued

Special Fund Accounts

Appropriation or Fund Account (Title)	Period of Availability	Reg	Tr From	Account Number	Sub No.	Balances, Beginning Of Fiscal Year	Appropriations And Other Obligational Authority[1]	Transfers Borrowings And Investment (Net)[2]	Outlays (Net)	Balances Withdrawn And Other Transactions[3]	Balances, End Of Fiscal Year[4]
Construction, Rehabilitation, Operation, And Maintenance, Western Area Power Administration, Power Marketing Administration, Department Of Energy											
Fund Resources:											
Undisbursed Funds	No Year	89		5068		285,112,474.04	340,528,280.00		217,037,747.62		408,603,006.42
Accounts Receivable						8,111,815.52				-12,080,847.10	20,192,662.62
Unfilled Customer Orders						8,511,170.45				831,033.57	7,680,136.88
Fund Equities:											
Unobligated Balances (Unexpired)						-83,397,218.85				122,889,333.80	-206,286,552.65
Accounts Payable						-46,039,660.05				3,367,550.86	-49,407,210.91
Undelivered Orders						-172,298,581.11				8,483,461.25	-180,782,042.36
Subtotal		89		5068		-0-	340,528,280.00		217,037,747.62	123,490,532.38	-0-
Emergency Fund, Western Area Power Administration, Power Marketing Administration, Department Of Energy											
Fund Resources:											
Undisbursed Funds	No Year	89		5069		500,000.00	500,000.00		464,703.39		535,296.61
Fund Equities:											
Unobligated Balances (Unexpired)						-500,000.00					-500,000.00
Undelivered Orders										35,296.61	-35,296.61
Subtotal		89		5069		-0-	500,000.00		464,703.39	35,296.61	-0-
Falcon And Amistad Operating And Maintenance Fund, Department Of Energy											
Fund Resources:											
Undisbursed Funds	No Year	89		5178		2,485,549.17	2,665,080.00		3,092,962.41		2,057,666.76
Fund Equities:											
Unobligated Balances (Unexpired)						-200,489.24				7,221.98	-207,711.22
Accounts Payable						-212,159.59				-54,235.60	-157,923.99
Undelivered Orders						-2,072,900.34				-380,868.79	-1,692,031.55
Subtotal		89		5178		-0-	2,665,080.00		3,092,962.41	-427,882.41	-0-
Continuing Fund, Southwestern Power Administration, Power Marketing Administration, Department Of Energy											
Fund Resources:											
Undisbursed Funds	No Year	89		5649		19,884,923.54			11,270,729.54		8,614,194.00
Fund Equities:											
Unobligated Balances (Unexpired)						-300,000.00					-300,000.00
Accounts Payable						-3,299,284.90				-3,299,284.90	
Undelivered Orders						-16,285,638.64				-7,971,444.64	-8,314,194.00
Subtotal		89		5649		-0-			11,270,729.54	-11,270,729.54	-0-
Continuing Fund, Southeastern Power Administration, Power Marketing Administration, Department Of Energy											
Fund Resources:											
Undisbursed Funds	No Year	89		5653		8,914,709.09	35,969,359.00		28,473,556.59		16,410,511.50
Fund Equities:											
Unobligated Balances (Unexpired)						-50,000.00					-50,000.00

Appropriations, Outlays, and Balances - Continued

Appropriation or Fund Account — Title	Dept — Reg	Dept — Tr From	Account Number	Sub No.	Period of Availability	Balances, Beginning Of Fiscal Year	Appropriations And Other Obligational Authority[1]	Transfers Borrowings And Investment (Net)[2]	Outlays (Net)	Balances Withdrawn And Other Transactions[3]	Balances, End Of Fiscal Year[4]
Public Enterprise Funds											
Accounts Payable						-4,515,325.38				3,758,749.89	-8,274,075.27
Undelivered Orders						-4,349,383.71				3,737,052.52	-8,086,436.23
Subtotal	89		5653			-0-	35,969,359.00		28,473,556.59	7,495,802.41	-0-
Bonneville Power Administration Fund, Power Marketing Administration, Department Of Energy											
Fund Resources:											
Undisbursed Funds	89		4045		No Year	1,103,820,036.92	48,627,399.00	[6] 491,912,289.13	-714,686,732.25		1,375,221,879.04
Transfer To:											
Corps Of Engineers	96	89	4045		No Year	10,935,374.27		176,816,251.07	175,725,282.05		12,026,343.29
Unfunded Contract Authority						[5] 871,107,250.93	[7] 692,270,530.50			871,107,250.93	692,270,530.50
Authority To Borrow From The Treasury							315,000,000.00	-315,000,000.00			-0-
Accounts Receivable						383,185,839.10				60,611,901.88	322,573,937.22
Fund Equities:											
Unobligated Balances (Unexpired)						[5] 2,369,048,501.22				47,132,956.23	-47,132,956.23
Accounts Payable										-14,174,334.30	-2,354,874,166.92
Undelivered Orders										85,566.90	-85,566.90
Subtotal	89		4045			-0-	1,055,897,929.50	-630,096,038.06	-538,961,450.20	964,763,341.64	-0-
Colorado River Basins Power Marketing Fund, Western Area Power Administration, Power Marketing Administration, Department Of Energy											
Fund Resources:											
Undisbursed Funds	89		4452		No Year	114,188,865.64			-9,222,192.13		123,411,057.77
Accounts Receivable						2,597,624.93				298,278.20	2,299,346.73
Fund Equities:											
Unobligated Balances (Unexpired)						-87,419,673.89				-3,629,973.92	-83,789,699.97
Accounts Payable						-11,517,232.62				8,220,188.24	-19,737,420.86
Undelivered Orders						-17,849,584.06				4,333,699.61	-22,183,283.67
Subtotal	89		4452			-0-		-9,222,192.13	-9,222,192.13	9,222,192.13	-0-
Total, Power Marketing Administration							1,479,252,348.50	-630,096,038.06	-260,174,063.57	1,109,330,374.01	
Departmental Administration											
General Fund Accounts											
Departmental Administration, Department Of Energy											
Fund Resources:											
Undisbursed Funds	89		0228		2003-2004	143,826.99					143,826.99
					No Year	95,056,118.48	148,942,842.82	-537,670.00	119,016,528.52	6,034.22	124,444,762.78
Fund Equities:											
Unobligated Balances (Expired)						-137,292.77					-143,326.99
Unobligated Balances (Unexpired)						-34,303,348.20				15,513,594.35	-49,816,942.55
Accounts Payable						-10,547,676.09				7,619,489.47	-18,167,165.56
Undelivered Orders						-50,211,628.41				6,249,526.26	-56,461,154.67
Subtotal	89		0228			-0-	148,942,842.82	-537,670.00	119,016,528.52	29,388,644.30	-0-

Footnotes At End Of Chapter

Appropriations, Outlays, and Balances – Continued

Appropriation or Fund Account	Account Symbol				Period of Availability	Balances, Beginning Of Fiscal Year	Appropriations And Other Obligational Authority[1]	Transfers Borrowings And Investment (Net)[2]	Outlays (Net)	Balances Withdrawn And Other Transactions[3]	Balances, End Of Fiscal Year[4]
Title	Dept Reg	Tr From	Account Number	Sub No.							
Expenses, Office Of The Inspector General, Department Of Energy											
Fund Resources:											
Undisbursed Funds	89		0236		No Year	7,123,355.42	41,819,000.00		40,873,636.32		8,068,719.10
Fund Equities:											
Unobligated Balances (Unexpired)						-185,623.91				731,564.45	-917,188.36
Accounts Payable						-3,134,119.69				174,268.75	-3,308,388.44
Undelivered Orders						-3,803,611.82				39,530.48	-3,843,142.30
	Subtotal 89		0236			-0-	41,819,000.00		40,873,636.32	945,363.68	-0-
Intragovernmental Funds											
Working Capital Fund, Departmental Administration, Department Of Energy											
Fund Resources:											
Undisbursed Funds	89		4563		No Year	66,278,509.52			-10,541,383.55		76,819,893.07
Fund Equities:											
Unobligated Balances (Unexpired)						-22,952,764.70				4,557,503.68	-27,510,268.38
Accounts Payable						-12,675,347.81				6,586,382.00	-19,261,729.81
Undelivered Orders						-30,650,397.01				-602,502.13	-30,047,894.88
	Subtotal 89		4563			-0-			-10,541,383.55	10,541,383.55	-0-
Trust Fund Accounts											
Gifts And Donations, Department Of Energy											
Fund Resources:											
Undisbursed Funds	89		8576		No Year	19,402.42					19,402.42
Fund Equities:											
Unobligated Balances (Unexpired)						-18,052.31				1,350.11	-19,402.42
Undelivered Orders						-1,350.11				-1,350.11	-0-
	Subtotal 89		8576			-0-					-0-
Total, Departmental Administration							190,761,842.82	-537,670.00	149,348,781.29	40,875,391.53	
Deductions For Offsetting Receipts											
Proprietary Receipts From The Public							-1,455,318,311.37		-1,455,318,311.37		
Intrabudgetary Transactions							-1,427,162,441.80		-1,427,162,441.80		
Offsetting Governmental Receipts							-43,595,321.63		-43,595,321.63		
Total, Offsetting Receipts							-2,926,076,074.80		-2,926,076,074.80		
Total, Department Of Energy							24,333,540,905.20	-631,121,092.21	20,116,805,525.26	3,585,614,287.73	

Appropriations, Outlays, and Balances - Continued

Footnotes

1. The amounts in this column, unless otherwise footnoted, represent appropriations, increases and rescissions in borrowing authority or new contract authority. Appropriation accounts with appropriation transfer activity are presented in Table 1 (Appropriations and Appropriation Transfers) at the end of this chapter.

2. The amounts in this column, unless otherwise footnoted, represent transfers - other than appropriation transfers, borrowings (gross), investments (net), unrealized discounts or funds held outside the Treasury.

3. The amounts in this column, unless otherwise footnoted, represent obligated balances canceled for fiscal year 2002 pursuant to 31 U.S.C. 1553, changes in unfilled customer orders, accounts receivable, accounts payable, undelivered orders, unobligated balances and adjustments to borrowing and contract authority.

4. Unobligated balances for no-year or unexpired multiple year accounts are available for obligation; unobligated balances for expired fiscal year accounts are not available for obligation.

5. The opening balances of the following accounts have been adjusted during the current fiscal year and do not agree with last year's closing balances:

Account	Adjustment
89 x 0233 - Undisbursed Funds	-$5,034,751.89
89 x 0233 - Unobligated Balances (Unexpired)	5,034,751.89
89 x 4045 - Unfunded Contract Authority	239,554,919.76
89 x 4045 - Accounts Payable	-239,554,920.76

6. Includes $-241,300,000.00 which represents net repayment of borrowing from the U.S. Treasury.

7. Represents new contract authority.

Footnotes At End Of Chapter

Appropriations, Outlays, and Balances – Continued

Footnotes

Table 1 - Appropriations And Appropriation Transfers - Department Of Energy

Department Regular	Fiscal Year	Account Symbol	Net Appropriations And Appropriations Transfers	Appropriation Amount	Net Appropriation Transfers	Department Regular Involved	Fiscal Year Involved	Accounts Involved	Amount From or To (-)
89	X	0213	580,946,060.00	592,621,060.00	-11,675,000.00	89	X	0222	-11,675,000.00
89	X	0222	3,836,613,000.00	3,797,294,000.00	39,319,000.00	89	X	0213	11,675,000.00
						89	X	0224	21,855,000.00
						89	X	0251	599,000.00
						89	X	0309	5,190,000.00
89	X	0224	2,132,649,000.00	2,154,504,000.00	-21,855,000.00	89	X	0222	-21,855,000.00
89	0708	0224	12,100,000.00	0.00	12,100,000.00	72	0708	1093	12,100,000.00
89	X	0228	277,832,000.00	276,832,000.00	1,000,000.00	11	X	5512	1,000,000.00
89	X	0240	6,258,583,000.00	6,275,583,000.00	-17,000,000.00	89	X	0313	-17,000,000.00
89	X	0251	5,731,240,000.00	5,731,839,000.00	-599,000.00	89	X	0222	-599,000.00
89	X	0303	38,089,700.00	29,998,340.00	8,091,360.00	11	X	5512	8,091,360.00
89	X	0309	1,812,149,000.00	1,818,339,000.00	-6,190,000.00	89	X	0222	-5,190,000.00
						89	X	0313	-1,000,000.00
89	X	0313	369,191,310.00	340,291,310.00	28,900,000.00	11	X	5512	10,900,000.00
						89	X	0240	17,000,000.00
						89	X	0309	1,000,000.00
89	X	4045	48,627,399.00	0.00	48,627,399.00	11	X	5512	48,627,399.00
89	X	5068	340,528,280.00	232,326,080.00	106,202,200.00	11	X	5512	108,202,200.00
89	X	5227	-49,417,628.00	0.00	-49,417,628.00	31	X	0200	-45,826,222.00
						48	X	0500	-3,591,406.00
Totals			21,389,131,121.00	21,249,627,790.00	139,503,331.00				139,503,331.00

Appropriations, Outlays, and Balances – Continued

Footnotes

This Page Left Blank Intentionally

Appropriations, Outlays, and Balances – Continued

Appropriation or Fund Account — Title	Period of Availability	Dept Reg	Tr From	Account Number	Sub No.	Balances, Beginning Of Fiscal Year	Appropriations And Other Obligational Authority[1]	Transfers Borrowings And Investment (Net)[2]	Outlays (Net)	Balances Withdrawn And Other Transactions[3]	Balances, End Of Fiscal Year[4]
Department Of Health And Human Services											
Public Health Service											
Food And Drug Administration											
General Fund Accounts											
Salaries And Expenses, Food And Drug Administration											
Fund Resources:											
Undisbursed Funds	2007-2009	75		0600					-79,710.73		79,710.73
	2006-2008					778,083.80			429,612.70		348,471.10
	2007						1,840,319,334.62	96,827,015.38	1,463,117,779.67		474,028,570.33
	2006-2007					15,016,775.46			7,845,953.44		7,170,822.02
	2005-2007					323,519.58			323,519.58		
	2006					350,522,901.43			253,350,617.46		97,172,283.97
	2004-2006					1,598.31			1,598.31		
	2005					55,807,280.93			31,987,598.97		23,819,681.96
	2004					20,979,955.96			6,502,590.58		14,477,365.38
	2003					17,777,822.43			1,022,280.35		16,755,542.08
	2002-2003					48,306.65					48,306.65
	2002					18,225,464.81			1,081,434.94	17,144,029.87	
	No Year					325,596,910.94	-271,075,304.62	-96,827,015.38	-208,086,521.60		165,781,112.54
Funds Held Outside The Treasury	2005					152,500.00					152,500.00
Accounts Receivable						18,899,309.49				6,210,402.88	12,688,906.61
Unfilled Customer Orders						95,529,650.41				9,162,243.13	86,367,407.28
Fund Equities:											
Unobligated Balances (Expired)						-79,087,265.91				-14,082,009.66	-65,005,256.25
Unobligated Balances (Unexpired)						-318,041,196.32				-164,127,384.93	-153,913,811.39
Accounts Payable						-82,096,703.60				18,155,412.29	-100,252,115.69
Undelivered Orders						-440,434,914.37				139,284,582.75	-579,719,497.12
	Subtotal	75		0600		-0-	1,569,244,030.00		1,557,496,753.67	11,747,276.33	-0-
Buildings And Facilities, Food And Drug Administration											
Fund Resources:											
Undisbursed Funds	No Year	75		0603		12,930,755.44	4,950,000.00		6,881,428.57		10,999,326.87
Fund Equities:											
Unobligated Balances (Unexpired)						-7,096,381.81				-5,337,577.08	-1,758,804.73
Accounts Payable						-2,594,612.58				-2,594,612.58	
Undelivered Orders						-3,239,761.05				6,000,761.09	-9,240,522.14
	Subtotal	75		0603		-0-	4,950,000.00		6,881,428.57	-1,931,428.57	-0-
Special Fund Accounts											
Cooperative Research And Development Agreements, Food And Drug Administration											
Fund Resources:											
Undisbursed Funds	No Year	75		5148		3,973,888.61	3,918,245.70		1,922,005.71		5,970,128.60
Fund Equities:											
Unobligated Balances (Unexpired)						-2,991,274.63				1,103,651.94	-4,094,926.57

Appropriations, Outlays, and Balances - Continued

Appropriation or Fund Account — Title	Period of Availability	Account Symbol — Dept Reg	Account Symbol — Tr From	Account Number	Sub No.	Balances, Beginning Of Fiscal Year	Appropriations And Other Obligational Authority[1]	Transfers Borrowings And Investment (Net)[2]	Outlays (Net)	Balances Withdrawn And Other Transactions[3]	Balances, End Of Fiscal Year[4]
Accounts Payable						-60,523.35				-59,436.10	-1,087.25
Undelivered Orders						-922,090.63				952,024.15	-1,874,114.78
Subtotal		75		5148		-0-	3,918,245.70		1,922,005.71	1,996,239.99	-0-
Public Enterprise Funds											
Revolving Fund For Certification And Other Services, Food And Drug Administration											
Fund Resources:											
Undisbursed Funds	No Year	75		4309		4,362,410.25					5,033,093.66
Fund Equities:											
Unobligated Balances (Unexpired)						-2,246,173.36			-670,683.41	-288,973.92	-1,957,199.44
Accounts Payable						-125,321.12				35,171.75	-160,492.87
Undelivered Orders						-1,990,915.77				924,485.58	-2,915,401.35
Subtotal		75		4309		-0-			-670,683.41	670,683.41	-0-
Total, Food And Drug Administration						1,578,112,275.70			1,565,629,504.54	12,482,771.16	
Health Resources And Services Administration											
General Fund Accounts											
Vaccine Injury Compensation, Health Resources And Services Administration											
Fund Resources:											
Undisbursed Funds	No Year	75		0320		4,787,825.13					6,722,308.77
Fund Equities:											
Unobligated Balances (Unexpired)						-4,786,975.06			-1,934,483.64	1,934,483.64	-6,721,458.70
Accounts Payable						-850.07				-850.00	-0.07
Undelivered Orders						-0-				850.00	-850.00
Subtotal		75		0320		-0-			-1,934,483.64	1,934,483.64	-0-
Free Clinics Malpractice Claims Fund, Health Resources And Service Administration											
Fund Resources:											
Undisbursed Funds	No Year	75		0330		4,303,466.09	41,223.00		210,911.48		4,133,777.61
Fund Equities:											
Unobligated Balances (Unexpired)						-3,959,240.61				-351,421.00	-3,607,819.61
Accounts Payable						-3,224.04				13,250.96	-16,475.00
Undelivered Orders						-341,001.44				168,481.56	-509,483.00
Subtotal		75		0330		-0-	41,223.00		210,911.48	-169,688.48	-0-
Health Education Assistance Loans Program Account, Health Resources And Services Administration											
Fund Resources:											
Undisbursed Funds	2007	75		0340		740,096.43	2,898,466.00		1,406,829.57		1,491,636.43
	2006					482,791.03			450,165.36		289,931.07
	2005					540,381.90			103,836.28		378,954.75
	2004					540,381.90					540,381.90
	2003					406,109.83					406,109.83
	2002					49,438.28				49,438.28	

Footnotes At End Of Chapter

Appropriations, Outlays, and Balances – Continued

Title	Period of Availability	Reg	Tr From	Account Number	Sub No.	Balances, Beginning Of Fiscal Year	Appropriations And Other Obligational Authority[1]	Transfers Borrowings And Investment (Net)[2]	Outlays (Net)	Balances Withdrawn And Other Transactions[3]	Balances, End Of Fiscal Year[4]
Health Education Assistance Loans Program Account, Health Resources And Services Administration - Continued											
Fund Equities:											
Unobligated Balances (Expired)						-393,419.27				481,805.60	-875,224.87
Accounts Payable						-77,290.36				36,216.88	-113,507.24
Undelivered Orders						-1,748,107.84				370,174.03	-2,118,281.87
	Subtotal	75		0340		-0-	2,898,466.00		1,960,831.21	937,634.79	-0-
Health Resources And Services, Health Resources And Services Administration											
Fund Resources:											
Undisbursed Funds	2007-2009	75		0350			1,799,493,060.00		429,738,837.89		1,369,754,222.11
	2007-2008								-22,037,328.47		22,037,328.47
	2007					27,457,728.66	4,542,431,767.00		2,134,748,311.84		2,407,683,455.16
	2006-2007					3,956,978,589.80			11,277,855.56		16,179,873.10
	2006					771,680,871.77			3,288,959,533.64		332,566,018.08
	2005					5,558,749.32			439,114,853.69		5,482,672.19
	2004-2005					319,813,353.71			106,298,403.62		213,514,950.09
	2004					3,772,685.42			18,917.88		3,753,767.54
	2003-2004					173,869,629.33			47,956,459.59		125,913,169.74
	2003					4,169,685.34			-77.86		4,169,763.20
	2002-2003					146,213,992.73			46,968,342.99	99,245,649.74	-----
	2002					4,144,358.88			355,510.37	3,788,848.51	-----
	2001-2002					14,218,214.55			9,479,457.32		[5]4,738,757.23
	2001										
	No Year					65,170,299.99	7,181,403.00		-3,098,020.30		75,449,723.29
Accounts Receivable						48,705,951.32				3,132,926.83	45,573,024.49
Unfilled Customer Orders						5,901,176.69				2,763,991.22	3,137,185.47
Fund Equities:											
Unobligated Balances (Expired)						-88,475,607.05				2,191,979.24	-90,667,586.29
Unobligated Balances (Unexpired)						-57,911,409.19				-20,707,221.20	-37,204,187.99
Accounts Payable						-6,674,667.03				410,922,267.18	-417,596,934.21
Undelivered Orders						-5,394,593,604.24				-642,089,346.41	-4,752,504,257.83
	Subtotal	75		0350		-0-	6,349,106,230.00		6,489,857,134.89	-140,750,904.89	-0-
Health Centers Malpractice Claims, Health Resources And Services Administration											
Fund Resources:											
Undisbursed Funds	No Year	75		0365		49,739,810.86	44,554,694.00		40,057,345.80		54,237,159.06
Fund Equities:											
Unobligated Balances (Unexpired)						-47,333,706.35				2,279,044.27	-49,612,750.62
Accounts Payable						-170,339.52				71,778.39	-242,117.91
Undelivered Orders						-2,235,764.99				2,146,525.54	-4,382,290.53
	Subtotal	75		0365		-0-	44,554,694.00		40,057,345.80	4,497,348.20	-0-
Public Enterprise Funds											
Health Professions Graduate Student Loan Insurance Fund, Liquidating Account, Health Resources And Services Administration											
Fund Resources:											
Undisbursed Funds	No Year	75		4305		3,766,133.75	1,000,000.00		-11,010,619.54	[6]11,945,515.08	3,831,238.21

Appropriations, Outlays, and Balances - Continued

Appropriation or Fund Account — Title	Period of Availability	Reg	Tr From	Account Number	Sub No.	Balances, Beginning Of Fiscal Year	Appropriations And Other Obligational Authority[1]	Transfers Borrowings And Investment (Net)[2]	Outlays (Net)	Balances Withdrawn And Other Transactions[3]	Balances, End Of Fiscal Year[4]
Fund Equities:											
Accounts Payable						-5,331.81				484,359.14	-489,690.95
Undelivered Orders						-3,760,801.94				-419,254.68	-3,341,547.26
Subtotal		75		4305		-0-	1,000,000.00		-11,010,619.54	12,010,619.54	-0-
Federal Interest Subsidies For Medical Facilities, Medical Facilities Guarantee And Loan Fund, Health And Human Services											
Fund Resources:											
Undisbursed Funds	No Year	75		4430		553,424.92					553,424.92
Fund Equities:											
Unobligated Balances (Unexpired)						-7,397.23					-7,397.23
Accounts Payable						-422.85					-422.85
Undelivered Orders						-545,604.84					-545,604.84
Subtotal		75		4430		-0-					-0-
Trust Fund Accounts											
Vaccine Injury Compensation Trust Fund											
Fund Resources:											
Undisbursed Funds	No Year	20		8175		13,100,194.45	349,918,436.79	-338,384,342.22	10,689,289.02		13,945,000.00
Transfer To:											
Health And Human Services, Health Resources And Services Administration	No Year	75	20	8175		2,008,771.01		96,000,000.00	91,076,736.96		6,932,034.05
Unrealized Discount On Investments						-15,052,964.65		-3,256,596.63			-18,309,561.28
Investments In Public Debt Securities						2,379,854,000.00		245,640,938.85			2,625,494,938.85
Accounts Receivable						-16,561,552.00				17,957,378.80	-34,518,930.80
Fund Equities:											
Unobligated Balances (Unexpired)						-2,356,049,831.04				220,411,420.26	-2,576,461,251.30
Accounts Payable						-7,298,617.77				9,783,611.75	-17,082,229.52
Subtotal		20		8175		-0-	349,918,436.79		101,766,025.98	248,152,410.81	-0-
Ricky Ray Hemophilia Relief Fund											
Fund Resources:											
Undisbursed Funds	No Year	75		8074		-0.01		-0.01	-0.01		
Unrealized Discount On Investments								0.01			
Fund Equities:											
Accounts Payable						0.01				0.01	
Subtotal		75		8074		-0-			-0.01	0.01	-0-
Total, Health Resources And Services Administration							6,747,519,049.79		6,620,907,146.17	126,611,903.62	
Indian Health Services											
General Fund Accounts											
Indian Health Services, Indian Health Service											
Fund Resources:											
Undisbursed Funds	2007-2008	75		0390			525,099,000.00		409,571,527.59		115,527,472.41
	2007						2,242,313,845.00		2,051,420,994.57		190,892,850.43
	2006-2007					99,077,679.59			71,161,370.98		27,916,308.61
	2006					183,109,603.64			152,247,401.37		30,862,202.27

Footnotes At End Of Chapter

Appropriations, Outlays, and Balances – Continued

Appropriation or Fund Account — Title	Period of Availability	Reg	Tr From	Account Number	Sub No.	Balances, Beginning Of Fiscal Year	Appropriations And Other Obligational Authority[1]	Transfers Borrowings And Investment (Net)[2]	Outlays (Net)	Balances Withdrawn And Other Transactions[3]	Balances, End Of Fiscal Year[4]
Indian Health Services, Indian Health Service - Continued											
Fund Resources: - Continued											
Undisbursed Funds - Continued	2005-2006					24,040,845.18			11,450,140.72	----	12,590,704.46
	2005					33,548,448.95			27,168,752.03	----	6,379,696.92
	2004-2005					7,424,240.47			5,354,090.54	----	2,070,149.93
	2004					14,666,397.85			8,895,094.88	----	5,771,302.97
	2003-2004					6,802,374.91			1,685,969.97	----	5,116,404.94
	2003					12,377,833.30			4,203,013.07	----	8,174,820.23
	2002-2003					4,204,960.54			3,968,844.38	----	236,116.16
	2002					2,085,961.87			1,572,894.01	513,067.86	[7]-311,315.91
	2001-2002					2,958,709.30			3,270,025.21	----	
	2000										
	1999-00										
	No Year					[8]419,346,771.99	201,508,217.00		145,810,787.22	----	475,044,201.77
Accounts Receivable						[8]10,838,178.18				-6,338,910.28	17,177,088.46
Fund Equities:											
Unobligated Balances (Expired)						[8]-24,440,424.65				15,318,859.23	-39,759,283.88
Unobligated Balances (Unexpired)						[8]-175,079,174.85				3,303,074.79	-178,382,249.64
Accounts Payable						-42,559,158.66				9,641,497.64	-52,200,656.30
Undelivered Orders						[8]-578,403,247.61				48,702,566.22	-627,105,813.83
	Subtotal	75		0390		-0-	2,968,921,062.00		2,897,780,906.54	71,140,155.46	-0-
Indian Health Facilities, Indian Health Service											
Fund Resources:											
Undisbursed Funds	No Year	75		0391		482,965,586.14	361,225,637.00		366,164,084.48		478,027,138.66
Accounts Receivable						6,296.67				-1,349,752.57	1,356,049.24
Fund Equities:											
Unobligated Balances (Unexpired)						-247,472,090.26				-1,192,985.10	-246,279,105.16
Accounts Payable						-5,776,465.67				2,151,353.96	-7,927,819.63
Undelivered Orders						-229,723,326.88				-4,547,063.77	-225,176,263.11
	Subtotal	75		0391		-0-	361,225,637.00		366,164,084.48	-4,938,447.48	-0-
Special Fund Accounts											
Operation And Maintenance Of Quarters, Indian Health Services											
Fund Resources:											
Undisbursed Funds	No Year	75		5071		3,918,203.13	7,956,215.97		7,548,281.58		4,326,137.52
Accounts Receivable						6,781,744.97				40,566.46	6,741,178.51
Fund Equities:											
Unobligated Balances (Unexpired)						-2,514,154.06				-1,452,327.65	-1,061,826.41
Accounts Payable						-22,409.72				8,550.57	-30,960.29
Undelivered Orders						-8,163,384.32				1,811,145.01	-9,974,529.33
	Subtotal	75		5071		-0-	7,956,215.97		7,548,281.58	407,934.39	-0-
Consolidated Working Funds											
Consolidated Working Fund, Health And Human Services, Indian Health Services											
Fund Resources:											

Appropriations, Outlays, and Balances - Continued

Appropriation or Fund Account — Title	Period of Availability	Account Symbol — Dept Reg	Tr From	Account Number	Sub No.	Balances, Beginning Of Fiscal Year	Appropriations And Other Obligational Authority[1]	Transfers Borrowings And Investment (Net)[2]	Outlays (Net)	Balances Withdrawn And Other Transactions[3]	Balances, End Of Fiscal Year[4]
Undisbursed Funds	No Year			3921		7,166,245.35			1,500,279.08		5,665,966.27
Fund Equities:											
Unobligated Balances (Unexpired)						-7,103,449.61				-1,500,323.25	-5,603,126.36
Accounts Payable						-62,795.74				44.17	-62,839.91
Subtotal	Subtotal	75		3921		-0-			1,500,279.08	-1,500,279.08	-0-
Total, Indian Health Service							3,338,102,914.97		3,272,993,551.68	65,109,363.29	

Centers For Disease Control And Prevention

General Fund Accounts

Disease Control, Research, And Training, Centers For Disease Control

Appropriation or Fund Account — Title	Period of Availability	Dept Reg	Tr From	Account Number	Sub No.	Balances, Beginning Of Fiscal Year	Appropriations And Other Obligational Authority[1]	Transfers Borrowings And Investment (Net)[2]	Outlays (Net)	Balances Withdrawn And Other Transactions[3]	Balances, End Of Fiscal Year[4]
Fund Resources:											
Undisbursed Funds	2007-2009	75		0943			134,367,656.00		-1,022,174.21		1,022,174.21
	2007-2008								65,965,105.88		68,402,550.12
	2006-2008					-248,679.29			-225,551.43		[7]-23,127.86
	2007						5,054,236,278.00	-31,800.00	[9]1,862,368,952.18		3,191,835,525.82
	2006-2007					68,950,683.11			43,549,182.60		25,401,500.51
	2005-2007					489,531.19			320,491.28		169,039.91
	2006					3,253,196,181.40		31,800.00	2,571,098,514.83		682,129,466.57
	2005-2006					33,881,142.92			16,044,722.50		17,836,420.42
	2004-2006					343,730.86			222,499.39		121,231.47
	2005					519,065,523.62			[10]384,893,362.82		134,172,160.80
	2004-2005					6,657,912.91			621,055.32		6,036,857.59
	2003-2005					161,111.98			7,801.64		153,310.34
	2004					116,657,441.39			45,462,089.41		71,195,351.98
	2003-2004					5,734,389.82			619,228.56		5,115,161.26
	2002-2004					68,508.81					68,508.81
	2003					86,694,737.36			-61,557,283.29		148,252,020.65
	2002-2003					2,153,061.43			122,445.69		2,030,615.74
	2001-2003					97,618.74			4,370.06		93,248.68
	2002					101,803,306.81			11,852,201.90	89,951,104.91	
	2001-2002					4,138,239.11			2,422,164.47	1,716,074.64	
	No Year					1,008,409,490.22	782,287,989.00	31,800.00	535,741,316.58		1,254,956,162.64
Funds Held Outside The Treasury	2007					31,800.00		31,800.00			31,800.00
	2006							-31,800.00			
Accounts Receivable						119,218,988.58				19,743,452.30	99,475,536.28
Unfilled Customer Orders						406,290,338.24				73,297,294.06	332,993,044.18
Fund Equities:											
Unobligated Balances (Expired)						-52,011,302.66				-20,409,134.15	-31,602,168.51
Unobligated Balances (Unexpired)						-464,134,543.23				-48,629,702.13	-415,504,841.10
Accounts Payable						-96,535,368.59				-6,519,870.66	-90,015,497.93
Undelivered Orders						-5,121,113,844.73				383,232,207.85	-5,504,346,052.58
Subtotal	Subtotal	75		0943		-0-	5,970,891,923.00		5,478,510,496.18	492,381,426.82	-0-

Appropriations, Outlays, and Balances – Continued

Title	Reg	Tr From	Account Number	Sub No.	Period of Availability	Balances, Beginning Of Fiscal Year	Appropriations And Other Obligational Authority[1]	Transfers Borrowings And Investment (Net)[2]	Outlays (Net)	Balances Withdrawn And Other Transactions[3]	Balances, End Of Fiscal Year[4]
Toxic Substances And Environmental Public Health, Agency For Toxic Substances And Disease Registry											
Fund Resources:											
Undisbursed Funds	75		0944		2007	28,603,230.94	74,907,505.00		43,038,610.23		31,868,894.77
					2006	8,878,697.54			21,738,194.29		6,865,036.65
					2005	1,950,867.36			7,506,896.03		1,371,801.51
					2004	559,689.38	304,000.00		423,057.31		1,527,810.05
					No Year	1,802,286.74			8,567.45		855,121.93
Accounts Receivable										-757,573.37	2,559,860.11
Unfilled Customer Orders						3,645,342.05				66,219.21	3,579,122.84
Fund Equities:											
Unobligated Balances (Expired)						-914,551.49				167,759.40	-1,082,310.89
Unobligated Balances (Unexpired)						-538,525.93				304,000.00	-842,525.93
Accounts Payable						-2,347,522.70				135,683.74	-2,483,206.44
Undelivered Orders						-41,639,513.89				2,580,090.71	-44,219,604.60
Subtotal	75		0944			-0-	75,211,505.00		72,715,325.31	2,496,179.69	-0-
Special Fund Accounts											
Cooperative Research And Development Agreements, Centers For Disease Control											
Fund Resources:											
Undisbursed Funds	75		5146		No Year	2,682,864.86	3,495,974.75		1,582,089.98		4,596,749.63
Fund Equities:											
Unobligated Balances (Unexpired)						-2,169,862.64				1,326,665.26	-3,496,527.90
Accounts Payable						-75,797.39				-46,383.78	-29,413.61
Undelivered Orders						-437,204.83				633,603.29	-1,070,808.12
Subtotal	75		5146			-0-	3,495,974.75		1,582,089.98	1,913,884.77	-0-
Trust Fund Accounts											
Toxic Substances And Environmental Public Health, Agency For Toxic Substances And Disease Registry											
Fund Resources:											
Undisbursed Funds	75		8252		2003	2,248,324.77			152,563.04		2,095,761.73
					2002	1,583,617.89		-1,370,001.84	213,616.05		
Accounts Receivable						1,031,592.90				261,140.22	770,452.68
Unfilled Customer Orders						597,325.87				615,832.93	-18,507.06
Fund Equities:											
Unobligated Balances (Expired)						-1,694,645.90				-897,732.57	-796,913.33
Accounts Payable						-215,547.09				-135,555.16	-79,991.93
Undelivered Orders						-3,550,668.44				-1,579,866.35	-1,970,802.09
Subtotal	75		8252			-0-		-1,370,001.84	366,179.09	-1,736,180.93	-0-
Total, Centers For Disease Control And Prevention							6,049,599,402.75	-1,370,001.84	5,553,174,090.56	495,055,310.35	

Appropriations, Outlays, and Balances - Continued

Appropriation or Fund Account (Title)	Period of Availability	Dept Reg	Tr From	Account Number	Sub No.	Balances, Beginning Of Fiscal Year	Appropriations And Other Obligational Authority[1]	Transfers Borrowings And Investment (Net)[2]	Outlays (Net)	Balances Withdrawn And Other Transactions[3]	Balances, End Of Fiscal Year[4]
National Institutes Of Health											
General Fund Accounts											
National Library Of Medicine, National Institutes Of Health											
Fund Resources:											
Undisbursed Funds	2007	75		0807		161,236,657.33	317,570,000.00		147,572,796.85		169,997,203.15
	2006					41,144,180.81			120,497,302.06		40,739,355.27
	2005					10,983,832.11			30,713,171.14		10,431,009.67
	2004					5,894,827.26			4,150,225.06		6,833,607.05
	2003					5,629,959.70			681,093.61	5,343,144.59	5,213,733.65
	2002								286,815.11		
	No Year					7,142,384.62	4,000,000.00		3,358,214.94		7,784,169.68
Accounts Receivable						-35,659.16				-430,249.51	394,590.35
Unfilled Customer Orders						13,742,571.77				-5,082,663.21	18,825,234.98
Fund Equities:											
Unobligated Balances (Expired)						-10,221,509.49				-3,224,394.37	-6,997,115.12
Unobligated Balances (Unexpired)										10,419.53	-10,419.53
Accounts Payable						-17,427,434.02				1,513,781.48	-18,941,215.50
Undelivered Orders						-218,089,810.93				16,180,342.72	-234,270,153.65
Subtotal		75		0807		-0-	321,570,000.00		307,259,618.77	14,310,381.23	-0-
John E. Fogarty International Center, National Institutes Of Health											
Fund Resources:											
Undisbursed Funds	2007	75		0819		47,111,665.35	66,371,520.00		19,710,829.05		46,660,690.95
	2006					15,608,045.22			30,928,975.39		16,182,689.96
	2005					3,618,835.31			12,548,506.33		3,059,538.89
	2004					809,619.91			2,230,583.21		1,388,252.10
	2003					707,487.78			354,309.57		455,310.34
	2002					148,239.98			95,615.62		
Accounts Receivable										611,872.16	628,960.72
Unfilled Customer Orders						2,424,069.16				345,285.69	2,078,783.47
Fund Equities:											
Unobligated Balances (Expired)						-926,901.19				196,434.28	-1,123,335.47
Accounts Payable						-666,007.60				59,724.10	-725,731.70
Undelivered Orders						-68,835,053.92				-229,894.66	-68,605,159.26
Subtotal		75		0819		-0-	66,371,520.00		65,868,819.17	502,700.83	-0-
Buildings And Facilities, National Institutes Of Health											
Fund Resources:											
Undisbursed Funds	2007	75		0838			2,500,000.00				2,500,000.00
	2006					4,480,000.00					4,480,000.00
	No Year					416,467,533.63	81,081,000.00		175,305,035.31		322,243,498.32
Funds Held Outside The Treasury	No Year					104,271.35					104,271.35
Accounts Receivable						791,420.05				509,114.27	282,305.78
Unfilled Customer Orders						3,809,626.19				-508,931.19	4,318,557.38
Fund Equities:											
Unobligated Balances (Unexpired)						-77,454,494.73				-5,532,886.25	-71,921,608.48

Appropriations, Outlays, and Balances – Continued

Title	Period of Availability	Reg	Tr From	Account Number	Sub No.	Balances, Beginning Of Fiscal Year	Appropriations And Other Obligational Authority[1]	Transfers Borrowings And Investment (Net)[2]	Outlays (Net)	Balances Withdrawn And Other Transactions[3]	Balances, End Of Fiscal Year[4]
Buildings And Facilities, National Institutes Of Health - Continued											
Fund Equities: - Continued											
Accounts Payable						-4,822,172.10				3,011,496.37	-7,833,668.47
Undelivered Orders						-343,376,184.39				-89,202,828.51	-254,173,355.88
Subtotal	Subtotal	75		0838		-0-	83,581,000.00		175,305,035.31	-91,724,035.31	-0-
National Institute On Aging, National Institutes Of Health											
Fund Resources:											
Undisbursed Funds	2007	75		0843		809,908,177.17	1,045,467,970.00		216,951,372.20		828,516,597.80
	2006					243,597,543.35			557,056,470.42		252,851,706.75
	2005					38,465,279.90			202,527,318.26		41,070,225.09
	2004					20,029,005.59			25,933,848.06		12,531,431.84
	2003					8,403,419.62			8,521,070.82		11,507,934.77
	2002					50,810.51			2,621,595.42	5,781,824.20	
Accounts Receivable						4,101,346.07				420,910.38	-370,099.87
Unfilled Customer Orders										33,905.11	4,067,440.96
Fund Equities:											
Unobligated Balances (Expired)						-10,567,480.41				315,762.43	-10,883,242.84
Accounts Payable						-15,901,887.11				3,384,917.84	-19,286,804.95
Undelivered Orders						-1,098,086,214.69				21,918,974.86	-1,120,005,189.55
Subtotal	Subtotal	75		0843		-0-	1,045,467,970.00		1,013,611,675.18	31,856,294.82	-0-
National Institute Of Child Health And Human Development, National Institutes Of Health											
Fund Resources:											
Undisbursed Funds	2007	75		0844		873,389,376.15	1,252,765,000.00		387,298,326.84		865,466,673.16
	2006					232,478,986.60			631,034,273.00		242,355,103.15
	2005					49,825,058.53			181,469,182.70		51,009,803.90
	2004					18,447,589.25			28,817,457.96		21,007,600.57
	2003					15,610,487.17			5,393,575.53		13,054,013.72
	2002					1,348,908.55			3,155,932.42	12,454,554.75	
Accounts Receivable										-2,477,656.51	3,826,565.06
Unfilled Customer Orders						62,047,177.28				3,821,199.94	58,225,977.34
Fund Equities:											
Unobligated Balances (Expired)						-17,953,340.55				-175,363.14	-17,777,977.41
Accounts Payable						-16,703,661.82				-4,650,702.93	-12,052,958.89
Undelivered Orders						-1,218,490,581.16				6,624,219.44	-1,225,114,800.60
Subtotal	Subtotal	75		0844		-0-	1,252,765,000.00		1,237,168,748.45	15,596,251.55	-0-
Office Of The Director, National Institutes Of Health											
Fund Resources:											
Undisbursed Funds	2007	75		0846		558,463,553.44	1,047,001,000.00		208,405,860.35		838,595,139.65
	2006					151,243,880.33			360,423,351.85		198,040,201.59
	2005					23,406,214.54			115,385,413.84		35,858,466.49
	2004					5,287,950.26			9,683,421.98		13,722,792.56
	2003					3,795,763.55			1,531,825.43		3,756,124.83
	2002					1,878,379.94			572,876.44	3,222,887.11	
Accounts Receivable										195,774.31	1,682,605.63
Unfilled Customer Orders						723,957,653.71				-72,129,860.13	796,087,513.84
Fund Equities:											
Unobligated Balances (Expired)						-6,571,721.28				23,822,523.58	-30,394,244.86
Accounts Payable						-22,699,560.56				-5,182,929.48	-17,516,631.08

Appropriations, Outlays, and Balances - Continued

Appropriation or Fund Account Title	Period of Availability	Dept Reg	Tr From	Account Number	Sub No.	Balances, Beginning Of Fiscal Year	Appropriations And Other Obligational Authority[1]	Transfers Borrowings And Investment (Net)[2]	Outlays (Net)	Balances Withdrawn And Other Transactions[3]	Balances, End Of Fiscal Year[4]
Undelivered Orders	Subtotal	75		0846		-1,438,762,113.93				401,069,854.72	-1,839,831,968.65
						-0-	1,047,001,000.00		696,002,749.89	350,998,250.11	-0-
National Center For Research Resources, National Institutes Of Health											
Fund Resources:											
Undisbursed Funds	2007	75		0848			1,131,633,000.00				924,127,747.18
	2006					904,499,903.55			207,505,252.82		186,915,332.81
	2005					195,763,639.59			717,584,570.74		54,835,162.80
	2004					113,606,333.74			140,928,476.79		75,025,238.50
	2003					49,066,540.43			38,581,095.24		27,066,089.65
	2002					26,832,139.68			22,000,450.78	12,278,942.44	
Accounts Receivable						114,705.40			14,553,197.24	-227,123.26	341,828.66
Unfilled Customer Orders						10,683,556.97				1,281,943.85	9,401,613.12
Fund Equities:											
Unobligated Balances (Expired)						-6,146,590.02				4,823,470.37	-10,970,060.39
Accounts Payable						-1,291,341.86				-263,372.40	-1,027,969.46
Undelivered Orders	Subtotal	75		0848		-1,293,128,887.48				-27,413,904.61	-1,265,714,982.87
						-0-	1,131,633,000.00		1,141,153,043.61	-9,520,043.61	-0-
National Cancer Institute, National Institutes Of Health											
Fund Resources:											
Undisbursed Funds	2007	75		0849		3,408,876,358.52	4,792,624,260.00				3,429,446,414.87
	2006					798,015,060.43			1,363,177,845.13		898,708,254.48
	2005					129,584,798.27			2,510,168,104.04		132,866,289.37
	2004					58,862,759.60			665,148,771.06		53,547,435.62
	2003					25,605,122.37			76,037,362.65		31,624,788.70
	2002					19,493,892.49			27,237,970.90		
	No Year					2,089,580.70			-7,951,416.71	33,556,539.08	19,277,021.13
									216,871.36		
Accounts Receivable						14,236,007.29				-3,175,282.61	5,264,863.31
Unfilled Customer Orders										177,215.51	14,058,791.78
Fund Equities:											
Unobligated Balances (Expired)						-51,282,467.64				-187,199.07	-51,095,268.57
Unobligated Balances (Unexpired)						[8]12,813,842.06				-2,134,716.05	-10,679,126.01
Accounts Payable						-61,961,970.76				-8,206,384.18	-53,755,586.58
Undelivered Orders	Subtotal	75		0849		[8]-4,330,705,299.21			4,634,035,508.43	138,558,578.89	-4,469,263,878.10
						-0-	4,792,624,260.00			158,588,751.57	-0-
National Institute Of General Medical Sciences, National Institutes Of Health											
Fund Resources:											
Undisbursed Funds	2007	75		0851		1,493,629,459.89	1,932,580,300.00				1,505,168,489.83
	2006					206,409,762.16			427,411,810.17		215,903,592.09
	2005					28,207,412.69			1,277,725,867.80		31,164,993.79
	2004					11,218,922.30			175,244,768.37		11,756,575.23
	2003					5,837,259.67			16,450,837.46		4,680,611.28
	2002					784,936.96			6,538,311.02	5,621,269.22	
Accounts Receivable						64,670.05			215,990.45	-170,143.91	234,813.96
Unfilled Customer Orders										-925,587.08	1,710,524.04
Fund Equities:											
Unobligated Balances (Expired)						-15,567,194.24				-1,218,094.95	-14,349,099.29
Accounts Payable						-2,549,325.98				-450,419.33	-2,098,906.65

Footnotes At End Of Chapter

Appropriations, Outlays, and Balances – Continued

Appropriation or Fund Account — Title	Dept Reg	Tr From	Account Number	Sub No.	Period of Availability	Balances, Beginning Of Fiscal Year	Appropriations And Other Obligational Authority[1]	Transfers Borrowings And Investment (Net)[2]	Outlays (Net)	Balances Withdrawn And Other Transactions[3]	Balances, End Of Fiscal Year[4]
National Institute Of General Medical Sciences, National Institutes Of Health - Continued											
Fund Equities: - Continued											
Undelivered Orders						-1,728,035,903.50		----		26,135,690.78	-1,754,171,594.28
	75		0851		Subtotal	-0-	1,932,580,300.00	----	1,903,587,585.27	28,992,714.73	-0-
National Institute Of Environmental Health Sciences, National Institutes Of Health											
Fund Resources:											
Undisbursed Funds	75		0862		2007	459,883,862.04	726,358,676.00	----	246,035,364.70		480,323,311.30
					2006	109,868,253.96		----	347,673,668.29		112,210,193.75
					2005	20,604,928.49		----	92,247,536.35		17,620,717.61
					2004	7,794,233.09		----	10,330,308.49		10,274,620.00
					2003	5,501,227.05		----	2,783,552.96		5,010,680.13
					2002	336.00		----	478,528.59	5,022,698.46	
					No Year	258,623.50		----	336.00		
Accounts Receivable								----		-162,297.40	420,920.90
Unfilled Customer Orders						24,062,174.11		----		3,801,903.21	20,260,270.90
Fund Equities:											
Unobligated Balances (Expired)						-8,968,703.88		----		-703,511.20	-8,265,192.68
Accounts Payable						-16,538,709.69		----		-1,103,083.24	-15,435,626.45
Undelivered Orders						-602,466,224.67		----		19,953,670.79	-622,419,895.46
	75		0862		Subtotal	-0-	726,358,676.00	----	699,549,295.38	26,809,380.62	-0-
National Heart, Lung, And Blood Institute, National Institutes Of Health											
Fund Resources:											
Undisbursed Funds	75		0872		2007	2,257,212,156.07	2,922,391,300.00	----	661,552,399.38		2,260,838,900.62
					2006	615,595,640.17		----	1,602,780,191.68		654,431,964.39
					2005	165,920,872.04		----	481,171,893.03		134,423,747.14
					2004	38,706,053.68		----	80,391,941.65		85,528,930.39
					2003	24,294,362.90		----	16,883,347.19		21,822,706.49
					2002	297,505.54		----	471,795.16	23,822,567.74	
Accounts Receivable								----		1,503,511.68	-1,206,006.14
Unfilled Customer Orders						8,397,864.81		----		-3,076,567.18	11,474,431.99
Fund Equities:											
Unobligated Balances (Expired)						-43,262,821.04		----		12,749,928.76	-56,012,749.80
Accounts Payable						-15,744,195.09		----		-3,628,671.74	-12,115,523.35
Undelivered Orders						-3,051,417,439.08		----		47,768,962.65	-3,099,186,401.73
	75		0872		Subtotal	-0-	2,922,391,300.00	----	2,843,251,568.09	79,139,731.91	-0-
National Institute Of Dental And Craniofacial Research, National Institutes Of Health											
Fund Resources:											
Undisbursed Funds	75		0873		2007	272,286,856.06	389,066,310.00	----	116,408,182.67		272,658,127.33
					2006	75,288,464.67		----	199,104,830.05		73,182,026.01
					2005	14,256,740.60		----	57,442,352.64		17,846,112.03
					2004	8,620,607.74		----	6,725,964.91		7,530,775.69
					2003	4,796,297.16		----	5,100,927.22		3,519,680.52
					2002	62,707.62		----	1,129,096.99	3,667,200.17	
Accounts Receivable								----		60,251.20	2,456.42
Unfilled Customer Orders						513,274.79		----		-186,234.21	699,509.00
Fund Equities:											
Unobligated Balances (Expired)						-9,435,793.81		----		30,085.16	-9,465,878.97

Appropriations, Outlays, and Balances - Continued

Title	Reg	Tr From	Account Number	Sub No.	Period of Availability	Balances, Beginning Of Fiscal Year	Appropriations And Other Obligational Authority[1]	Transfers Borrowings And Investment (Net)[2]	Outlays (Net)	Balances Withdrawn And Other Transactions[3]	Balances, End Of Fiscal Year[4]
Accounts Payable						-3,794,304.31				69,054.88	-3,863,359.19
Undelivered Orders						-362,594,850.52				-485,401.68	-362,109,448.84
	75		0873		Subtotal	-0-	389,066,310.00		385,911,354.48	3,154,955.52	-0-
National Institute Of Diabetes And Digestive And Kidney Diseases, National Institutes Of Health											
Fund Resources:											
Undisbursed Funds	75		0884		2007	1,370,113,490.65	1,852,995,540.00		457,532,894.58		1,395,462,645.42
					2006	385,195,987.59			964,966,672.06		405,146,818.59
					2005	113,759,940.41			265,935,668.51		119,260,319.08
					2004	46,000,175.89			58,097,575.95		55,662,364.46
					2003	33,476,045.67			14,597,555.52		31,402,620.37
					2002				22,105,682.63	11,370,363.04	
Accounts Receivable						687,720.74				1,767,075.53	-1,079,354.79
Unfilled Customer Orders						18,851,574.53				2,748,418.72	16,103,155.81
Fund Equities:											
Unobligated Balances (Expired)						-36,009,881.34				2,138,362.89	-38,148,244.23
Accounts Payable						-16,699,076.46				3,081,868.95	-19,780,945.41
Undelivered Orders						-1,915,375,977.68				48,653,401.62	-1,964,029,379.30
	75		0884		Subtotal	-0-	1,852,995,540.00		1,783,236,049.25	69,759,490.75	-0-
National Institute Of Allergy And Infectious Diseases, National Institutes Of Health											
Fund Resources:											
Undisbursed Funds	75		0885		2007	3,148,140,285.85	4,264,034,050.00		1,137,623,244.28		3,126,410,805.72
					2006	1,165,170,569.31			2,091,757,322.08		1,056,382,963.77
					2005	433,730,402.48			667,548,612.54		497,621,956.77
					2004	339,290,697.80			213,362,107.73		220,368,294.75
					2003	32,448,060.53			178,243,386.30		161,047,311.50
					2002				3,556,309.15	28,891,751.38	
Accounts Receivable						1,782,331.28				1,019,522.57	762,808.71
Unfilled Customer Orders						5,191,010.02				-4,825,326.68	10,016,336.70
Fund Equities:											
Unobligated Balances (Expired)						-48,770,382.44				5,635,919.83	-54,406,302.27
Accounts Payable						-47,260,837.61				-4,760,388.78	-42,500,448.83
Undelivered Orders						-5,029,722,137.22				-54,018,410.40	-4,975,703,726.82
	75		0885		Subtotal	-0-	4,264,034,050.00		4,292,090,982.08	-28,056,932.08	-0-
National Institute Of Neurological Disorders And Stroke, National Institutes Of Health											
Fund Resources:											
Undisbursed Funds	75		0886		2007	1,094,038,871.75	1,532,988,400.00		453,673,071.08		1,079,315,328.92
					2006	244,311,599.50			848,395,163.87		245,643,707.88
					2005	54,301,095.97			189,706,422.49		54,605,177.01
					2004	22,049,000.14			35,255,153.59		19,045,942.38
					2003	16,928,184.40			5,900,691.97		16,148,308.17
					2002				403,801.43	16,524,382.97	
Accounts Receivable						437,519.80				105,889.89	331,629.91
Unfilled Customer Orders						6,665,006.42				153,875.16	6,511,131.26

Footnotes At End Of Chapter

Appropriations, Outlays, and Balances – Continued

Appropriation or Fund Account — Title	Period of Availability	Dept Reg	Dept Tr From	Account Number	Sub No.	Balances, Beginning Of Fiscal Year	Appropriations And Other Obligational Authority[1]	Transfers Borrowings And Investment (Net)[2]	Outlays (Net)	Balances Withdrawn And Other Transactions[3]	Balances, End Of Fiscal Year[4]
National Institute Of Neurological Disorders And Stroke, National Institutes Of Health - Continued											
Fund Equities:											
Unobligated Balances (Expired)						-24,163,919.67				-2,229,990.56	-21,933,929.11
Accounts Payable						-11,358,772.53				-97,590.47	-11,261,182.06
Undelivered Orders						-1,403,208,585.78				-14,802,471.42	-1,388,406,114.36
	Subtotal	75		0886		-0-	1,532,988,400.00		1,533,334,304.43	-345,904.43	-0-
National Eye Institute, National Institutes Of Health											
Fund Resources:											
Undisbursed Funds	2007	75		0887		490,182,721.25	665,986,090.00		167,254,268.94	4,894,492.61	498,731,821.06
	2006					117,353,501.96			368,581,602.69		121,601,118.56
	2005					20,745,188.77			97,632,442.08		19,721,059.88
	2004					8,958,457.51			5,966,614.69		14,778,574.08
	2003					1,778,305.11			4,055,051.49		4,903,406.02
	2002								-3,116,187.50		
Accounts Receivable						1,065,445.58				927,512.52	137,933.06
Unfilled Customer Orders						1,520,218.99				-2,106,662.10	3,626,881.09
Fund Equities:											
Unobligated Balances (Expired)						-9,500,774.53				684,779.81	-10,185,554.34
Accounts Payable						-4,476,458.25				-235,412.39	-4,241,045.86
Undelivered Orders						-627,626,606.39				21,447,587.16	-649,074,193.55
	Subtotal	75		0887		-0-	665,986,090.00		640,373,792.39	25,612,297.61	-0-
National Institute Of Arthritis And Musculoskeletal And Skin Diseases, National Institutes Of Health											
Fund Resources:											
Undisbursed Funds	2007	75		0888		380,602,625.33	507,374,370.00		122,617,947.13	8,763,700.26	384,756,422.87
	2006					101,207,513.57			282,657,837.74		97,944,787.59
	2005					19,556,404.99			76,415,294.84		24,792,218.73
	2004					12,822,699.48			10,541,426.64		9,014,978.35
	2003					10,171,553.68			4,765,912.34		8,056,787.14
	2002								1,407,853.42		
Accounts Receivable						556,704.28				348,246.16	208,458.12
Unfilled Customer Orders						946,757.09				-6,785.57	953,542.66
Fund Equities:											
Unobligated Balances (Expired)						-12,022,554.80				15,322.98	-12,037,877.78
Accounts Payable						-5,274,719.67				-12,388.71	-5,262,330.96
Undelivered Orders						-508,566,983.95				-139,997.23	-508,426,986.72
	Subtotal	75		0888		-0-	507,374,370.00		498,406,272.11	8,968,097.89	-0-
National Institute Of Nursing Research, National Institutes Of Health											
Fund Resources:											
Undisbursed Funds	2007	75		0889		114,064,735.24	137,187,710.00		22,953,191.14	1,955,759.71	114,234,518.86
	2006					38,744,989.00			75,081,721.47		38,983,013.77
	2005					6,190,464.06			33,857,103.99		4,887,885.01
	2004					2,580,006.65			3,523,507.61		2,666,956.45
	2003					1,936,115.57			248,324.59		2,331,682.06
	2002					34,039.11			-19,644.14	-32,001.93	66,041.04
Accounts Receivable						150,523.41				-656,807.95	807,331.36
Unfilled Customer Orders											

Appropriations, Outlays, and Balances - Continued

Appropriation or Fund Account — Title	Period of Availability	Reg	Tr From	Account Number	Sub No.	Balances, Beginning Of Fiscal Year	Appropriations And Other Obligational Authority[1]	Transfers Borrowings And Investment (Net)[2]	Outlays (Net)	Balances Withdrawn And Other Transactions[3]	Balances, End Of Fiscal Year[4]
Fund Equities:											
Unobligated Balances (Expired)						-4,889,487.60				-477,135.18	-4,412,352.42
Accounts Payable						-477,391.77				-34,643.66	-442,748.11
Undelivered Orders						-158,333,993.67				788,334.35	-159,122,328.02
Subtotal	Subtotal	75		0889		-0-	137,187,710.00		135,644,204.66	1,543,505.34	-0-
National Institute On Deafness And Other Communication Disorders, National Institutes Of Health											
Fund Resources:											
Undisbursed Funds	2007	75		0890		281,607,319.11	392,991,680.00		109,745,264.58		283,246,415.42
	2006					63,167,529.15			208,362,897.44		73,244,421.67
	2005					9,676,606.76			53,816,552.10		9,350,977.05
	2004					4,996,575.08			6,261,832.55		3,414,774.21
	2003					3,092,927.82			1,821,655.90		3,174,919.18
	2002					208,178.52			146,657.35	2,946,270.47	
Accounts Receivable										69,583.88	138,594.64
Unfilled Customer Orders						2,079,032.33				9,099.97	2,069,932.36
Fund Equities:											
Unobligated Balances (Expired)						-5,023,350.16				-167,981.62	-4,855,368.54
Accounts Payable						-3,079,690.88				489,552.82	-3,569,243.70
Undelivered Orders						-356,725,127.73				9,490,294.56	-366,215,422.29
Subtotal	Subtotal	75		0890		-0-	392,991,680.00		380,154,859.92	12,836,820.08	-0-
National Human Genome Research Institute, National Institutes Of Health											
Fund Resources:											
Undisbursed Funds	2007	75		0891		272,129,586.08	508,256,410.00		193,783,637.41		314,472,772.59
	2006					50,003,985.17			214,215,798.30		57,913,787.78
	2005					14,631,757.29			42,919,377.33		7,084,607.84
	2004					4,585,314.36			4,770,049.57		9,861,707.72
	2003					5,249,100.69			2,040,219.59		2,545,094.77
	2002					189,437.91			-260,984.38	5,510,085.07	
Accounts Receivable										4,979,779.99	-4,790,342.08
Unfilled Customer Orders						16,633,290.67				-6,993,259.87	23,626,550.54
Fund Equities:											
Unobligated Balances (Expired)						-3,561,496.65				1,906,857.22	-5,468,353.87
Accounts Payable						-8,753,004.45				1,733,354.19	-10,486,358.64
Undelivered Orders						-351,107,971.07				43,651,495.58	-394,759,466.65
Subtotal	Subtotal	75		0891		-0-	508,256,410.00		457,468,097.82	50,788,312.18	-0-
National Institute Of Mental Health, National Institutes Of Health											
Fund Resources:											
Undisbursed Funds	2007	75		0892		1,003,652,829.65	1,402,385,080.00		385,345,263.83		1,017,039,816.17
	2006					225,395,027.29			777,473,732.07		226,179,097.58
	2005					39,987,990.64			186,390,989.13		39,004,038.16
	2004					17,725,496.68			21,253,927.18		18,734,063.46
	2003					10,759,987.56			680,656.42		17,044,840.26
	2002					2,162,910.71			2,763,541.29	7,996,446.27	
Accounts Receivable										2,737,600.88	-574,690.17
Unfilled Customer Orders						[8]8,517,747.75				1,702,292.33	6,815,455.42
Fund Equities:											
Unobligated Balances (Expired)						-18,013,588.00				2,869,225.41	-20,882,813.41

Footnotes At End Of Chapter

Appropriations, Outlays, and Balances – Continued

Appropriation or Fund Account — Title	Period of Availability	Account Symbol — Dept Reg	Account Symbol — Dept Tr From	Account Number	Sub No.	Balances, Beginning Of Fiscal Year	Appropriations And Other Obligational Authority[1]	Transfers Borrowings And Investment (Net)[2]	Outlays (Net)	Balances Withdrawn And Other Transactions[3]	Balances, End Of Fiscal Year[4]
National Institute Of Mental Health, National Institutes Of Health - Continued											
Fund Equities: - Continued											
Accounts Payable						[8]17,124,855.59				-2,656,637.00	-14,468,218.59
Undelivered Orders						[8]1,273,063,546.69				15,828,042.19	-1,288,891,588.88
Subtotal		75		0892		-0-	1,402,385,080.00		1,373,908,109.92	28,476,970.08	-0-
National Institute On Drug Abuse, National Institutes Of Health											
Fund Resources:											
Undisbursed Funds	2007	75		0893			1,001,951,700.00		190,588,321.40		811,363,378.60
	2006					786,221,229.72			525,163,297.40		261,057,932.32
	2005					266,069,015.43			211,931,868.61		54,137,146.82
	2004					44,575,240.33			28,899,276.38		15,675,963.95
	2003					14,034,525.90			3,204,582.55		10,829,943.35
	2002					8,292,246.90			887,514.55	7,404,732.35	
Accounts Receivable						791,461.96				331,954.80	459,507.16
Unfilled Customer Orders						15,842,149.53				2,976,850.36	12,865,299.17
Fund Equities:											
Unobligated Balances (Expired)						-10,549,548.26				4,462,916.47	-15,012,464.73
Accounts Payable						-13,548,370.50				-8,109,426.88	-5,438,943.62
Undelivered Orders						-1,111,727,951.01				34,209,812.01	-1,145,937,763.02
Subtotal		75		0893		-0-	1,001,951,700.00		960,674,860.89	41,276,839.11	-0-
National Institute On Alcohol Abuse And Alcoholism, National Institutes Of Health											
Fund Resources:											
Undisbursed Funds	2007	75		0894			435,584,670.00		116,118,466.65		319,466,203.35
	2006					312,872,705.38			211,137,783.46		101,734,921.92
	2005					96,400,808.31			80,258,708.23		16,142,100.08
	2004					17,267,397.87			12,966,201.83		4,301,196.04
	2003					5,192,541.38			2,099,324.24		3,093,217.14
	2002					1,650,381.54			407,599.60	1,242,781.94	
Accounts Receivable						2,500,219.96				746,235.27	1,753,984.69
Unfilled Customer Orders						[8]1,205,097.56				326,036.47	879,061.09
Fund Equities:											
Unobligated Balances (Expired)						[8]1,524,376.33				2,493,989.55	-4,018,365.88
Accounts Payable						-3,425,027.75				-838,673.46	-2,586,354.29
Undelivered Orders						-432,139,747.92				8,626,216.22	-440,765,964.14
Subtotal		75		0894		-0-	435,584,670.00		422,988,084.01	12,596,585.99	-0-
National Center For Complementary And Alternative Medicine, National Institute Of Health											
Fund Resources:											
Undisbursed Funds	2007	75		0896			121,371,080.00		24,869,403.52		96,501,676.48
	2006					96,180,749.86			56,879,148.83		39,301,601.03
	2005					34,672,401.31			28,704,175.85		5,968,225.46
	2004					13,250,025.46			7,492,868.50		5,757,156.96
	2003					3,621,239.30			1,034,716.54		2,586,522.76
	2002					2,584,598.31			-847,939.27	3,432,537.58	
Accounts Receivable						7,303.04				-18,640.39	25,943.43
Unfilled Customer Orders						22,227.10				16,292.46	5,934.64

Appropriations, Outlays, and Balances - Continued

Appropriation or Fund Account — Title	Period of Availability	Dept Reg	Tr From	Account Number	Sub No.	Balances, Beginning Of Fiscal Year	Appropriations And Other Obligational Authority[1]	Transfers Borrowings And Investment (Net)[2]	Outlays (Net)	Balances Withdrawn And Other Transactions[3]	Balances, End Of Fiscal Year[4]
Fund Equities:											
Unobligated Balances (Expired)						-5,195,727.63				-1,219,980.48	-3,975,747.15
Accounts Payable						-688,213.41				76,474.30	-764,687.71
Undelivered Orders						-144,454,603.34				952,022.56	-145,406,625.90
Subtotal		75		0896		-0-	121,371,080.00		118,132,373.97	3,238,706.03	-0-
National Center On Minority Health And Health Disparities, National Institutes Of Health											
Fund Resources:											
Undisbursed Funds	2007	75		0897			199,107,000.00		31,944,788.27		167,162,211.73
	2006					169,328,515.53			101,010,997.79		68,317,517.74
	2005					62,161,439.43			52,263,313.53		9,898,125.90
	2004					9,713,526.23			6,060,868.49		3,652,667.74
	2003					6,516,809.63			1,181,165.32		5,335,644.31
	2002					3,891,918.18			264,938.48	3,626,979.70	
Accounts Receivable						600,000.00				-73,841.12	73,841.12
Unfilled Customer Orders										-194,004.32	794,004.32
Fund Equities:											
Unobligated Balances (Expired)						-3,070,756.58				-162,859.68	-2,907,896.90
Accounts Payable						-313,287.83				209,956.95	-523,244.78
Undelivered Orders						-248,828,164.59				2,974,706.59	-251,802,871.18
Subtotal		75		0897		-0-	199,107,000.00		192,726,061.88	6,380,938.12	-0-
National Institute Of Biomedical Imaging And Bioengineering, National Institutes Of Health											
Fund Resources:											
Undisbursed Funds	2007	75		0898			296,379,920.00		52,849,184.28		243,530,735.72
	2006					249,618,786.88			178,236,224.57		71,382,562.31
	2005					67,374,670.41			55,705,348.85		11,669,321.56
	2004					10,408,962.39			5,170,384.81		5,238,577.58
	2003					4,314,363.63			1,620,905.39		2,693,458.24
	2002					915,945.55			132,216.08	783,729.47	
Accounts Receivable						2,542.42				-9,695.88	12,238.30
Unfilled Customer Orders						176,392.78				156,148.97	20,243.81
Fund Equities:											
Unobligated Balances (Expired)						-2,468,915.37				2,505,659.08	-4,974,574.45
Accounts Payable						-614,323.38				-213,214.81	-401,108.57
Undelivered Orders						-329,728,425.31				-556,970.81	-329,171,454.50
Subtotal		75		0898		-0-	296,379,920.00		293,714,263.98	2,665,656.02	-0-
Special Fund Accounts											
Cooperative Research And Development Agreements, National Institutes Of Health											
Fund Resources:											
Undisbursed Funds	No Year	75		5145		51,761,839.92	21,667,998.95		19,651,537.14		53,778,301.73
Fund Equities:											
Unobligated Balances (Unexpired)						-30,994,190.34				2,369,704.06	-33,363,894.40

Appropriations, Outlays, and Balances – Continued

Appropriation or Fund Account — Title	Period of Availability	Dept Reg	Tr From	Account Number	Sub No.	Balances, Beginning Of Fiscal Year	Appropriations And Other Obligational Authority[1]	Transfers Borrowings And Investment (Net)[2]	Outlays (Net)	Balances Withdrawn And Other Transactions[3]	Balances, End Of Fiscal Year[4]
Cooperative Research And Development Agreements, National Institutes Of Health - Continued											
Fund Equities: - Continued											
Accounts Payable						-1,690,162.62				718,349.12	-2,408,511.74
Undelivered Orders						-19,077,486.96				-1,071,591.37	-18,005,895.59
	Subtotal	75		5145		-0-	21,667,998.95		19,651,537.14	2,016,461.81	-0-
Management Funds											
Management Fund, National Institutes Of Health											
Fund Resources:											
Undisbursed Funds	2007-2009	75		3966					-77,266,934.28		77,266,934.28
	2007-2008								-203,412,721.51		203,412,721.51
	2006-2008					72,962,432.54			16,671,854.89		56,290,577.65
	2006-2007					179,042,120.39			137,138,831.97		41,903,288.42
	2005-2007					69,496,816.03			33,760,392.95		35,736,423.08
	2005-2006					32,917,202.43			13,964,127.24		18,953,075.19
	2004-2006					16,864,581.54			11,921,415.92		4,943,165.62
	2004-2005					21,972,533.96			5,394,764.92		16,577,769.04
	2003-2005					3,476,876.24			413,661.07		3,063,215.17
	2003-2004					9,843,899.24			1,678,231.31		8,165,667.93
	2002-2004					5,032,071.02			311,645.38		4,720,425.64
	2002-2003					10,734,810.12			456,133.97		10,278,676.15
	2001-2003					2,046,758.46			11,989.50		2,034,768.96
	No Year					603,381.13					603,381.13
Accounts Receivable						92,321.14				-8,025.50	100,346.64
Fund Equities:											
Unobligated Balances (Expired)						-28,274,064.49				5,664,395.13	-33,938,459.62
Unobligated Balances (Unexpired)						-136,740,165.91				11,503,175.66	-148,243,341.57
Accounts Payable						-63,590,552.53				-5,931,928.87	-57,658,623.66
Undelivered Orders						-196,481,021.31				47,728,990.25	-244,210,011.56
	Subtotal	75		3966		-0-			-58,956,606.67	58,956,606.67	-0-
Intragovernmental Funds											
Service And Supply Fund, National Institutes Of Health											
Fund Resources:											
Undisbursed Funds	No Year	75		4554		421,011,555.82			-8,200,440.75		429,211,996.57
Accounts Receivable						3,777,874.32				1,226,502.52	2,551,371.80
Unfilled Customer Orders						129,838,177.08				-88,083,573.90	217,921,750.98
Fund Equities:											
Unobligated Balances (Unexpired)						-123,419,615.46				14,637,962.56	-138,057,578.02
Accounts Payable						-176,626,372.27				-2,711,336.63	-173,915,035.64
Undelivered Orders						-254,581,619.49				83,130,886.20	-337,712,505.69
	Subtotal	75		4554		-0-			-8,200,440.75	8,200,440.75	-0-
Total, National Institutes Of Health							29,051,672,034.95		28,138,051,809.06	913,620,225.89	

Appropriation or Fund Account (Title)	Period of Availability	Dept Reg	Tr From	Account Number	Sub No.	Balances, Beginning Of Fiscal Year	Appropriations And Other Obligational Authority[1]	Transfers Borrowings And Investment (Net)[2]	Outlays (Net)	Balances Withdrawn And Other Transactions[3]	Balances, End Of Fiscal Year[4]
Substance Abuse And Mental Health Services Administration											
General Fund Accounts											
Substance Abuse And Mental Health Services, Substance Abuse And Mental Health Services Administration											
Fund Resources:											
Undisbursed Funds	2007	75		1362		1,929,724,649.91	3,206,108,407.00		1,190,403,866.19		2,015,704,540.81
	2006					504,014,371.98			1,496,797,509.50		432,927,140.41
	2005					118,346,868.30			386,057,876.78		117,956,495.20
	2004					47,492,487.31			79,320,373.05		39,026,495.25
	2003					44,763,979.39			14,646,309.38		32,846,177.93
	No Year								11,238,683.36	33,525,296.03	
	2002					1,097,910.51			862,764.75		235,145.76
Accounts Receivable						2,960,782.05				-6,520,883.21	9,481,665.26
Unfilled Customer Orders						189,029,165.37				2,323,759.80	186,705,405.57
Fund Equities:											
Unobligated Balances (Expired)						-56,827,689.52				-8,181,415.23	-48,646,274.29
Unobligated Balances (Unexpired)						-227,579.90					-227,579.90
Accounts Payable						-2,547,764.86				1,429,419,468.94	-1,431,967,233.80
Undelivered Orders						-2,777,827,180.54				-1,423,785,202.34	-1,354,041,978.20
Subtotal		75		1362		-0-	3,206,108,407.00		3,179,327,383.01	26,781,023.99	-0-
Total, Substance Abuse And Mental Health Services Administration							3,206,108,407.00		3,179,327,383.01	26,781,023.99	
Agency For Health Care Research And Quality											
General Fund Accounts											
Agency For Healthcare Research And Quality, Healthcare Research And Quality											
Fund Resources:											
Undisbursed Funds	2006-2010	75		1700		1,000,000.00					1,000,000.00
	2007					12,483,968.59			58,690,346.34		[7]58,690,346.34
	2006					5,715,858.13			49,456,394.40		[7]36,972,425.81
	2005					8,749,364.44			10,782,848.67		[7]5,066,990.54
	2004					8,736,347.56			8,736,347.56		13,016.88
	2003					6,672,314.98			1,218,155.09		5,454,159.89
	2002					5,851,827.42			690,105.61	5,161,721.81	
	No Year					22,895,624.81			6,666,718.17		16,228,906.64
Accounts Receivable						4,023,406.00				-83,721,033.17	87,744,439.17
Unfilled Customer Orders						346,579,891.93				-65,838,227.27	412,418,119.20
Fund Equities:											
Unobligated Balances (Expired)						-1,514,411.04				-693,277.65	-821,133.39
Unobligated Balances (Unexpired)						-17,341,115.59				-6,738,931.64	-10,602,183.95
Accounts Payable						-1,697,099.13				11,361,626.41	-13,058,725.54

Footnotes At End Of Chapter

Appropriations, Outlays, and Balances – Continued

Appropriation or Fund Account	Account Symbol				Period of Availability	Balances, Beginning Of Fiscal Year	Appropriations And Other Obligational Authority[1]	Transfers Borrowings And Investment (Net)[2]	Outlays (Net)	Balances Withdrawn And Other Transactions[3]	Balances, End Of Fiscal Year[4]
Title	Dept Reg	Tr From	Account Number	Sub No.							
Agency For Healthcare Research And Quality, Healthcare Research And Quality - Continued											
Fund Equities: - Continued											
Undelivered Orders						-393,419,630.54				4,227,205.67	-397,646,836.21
Subtotal	75		1700			-0-			136,240,915.84	-136,240,915.84	-0-
Trust Fund Accounts											
Agency For Healthcare Research And Quality Gift Fund											
Fund Resources:											
Undisbursed Funds	75		8512		No Year	659,143.28	15.09		214,445.42		444,712.95
Fund Equities:											
Unobligated Balances (Unexpired)						-200,569.75					-200,569.75
Accounts Payable										62.50	-62.50
Undelivered Orders						-458,573.53				-214,492.83	-244,080.70
Subtotal	75		8512			-0-	15.09		214,445.42	-214,430.33	-0-
Total, Agency For Health Care Research And Quality							15.09		136,455,361.26	-136,455,361.26	
Total, Public Health Service							49,971,114,100.25	-1,370,001.84	48,466,538,846.28	1,503,205,252.13	
Centers For Medicare And Medicaid Services											
General Fund Accounts											
Payments To Federal Hospital Insurance Trust Fund, Health Care Fraud And Abuse, Treasury											
Fund Resources:											
Undisbursed Funds	20		1806		2007		207,997,686.84		207,997,686.84		
Program Management, Centers For Medicare And Medicaid Services											
Fund Resources:											
Undisbursed Funds	75		0511		2007-2009				122,679.18		[7]-122,679.18
					2007-2008				8,126,043.15		[7]-8,126,043.15
					2007				[1]71,004,562.28		[7]-71,004,562.28
					2006-2007	-5,145,749.24			-2,205,055.78		[7]-2,940,693.46
					2006	-62,859,396.53			[1,2]-53,086,074.08		[7]-9,773,322.45
					2005-2006	-364,442.57			-307,370.96		[7]-57,071.61
					2004-2006	-795,357.48			-795,357.48		
					2005	-13,371,033.15			-12,030,492.47		[7]-1,340,540.68
					2004-2005	-9,883,971.73			-8,193,323.17		[7]-1,690,648.56
					2004	-1,904,987.89			-1,155,610.57		[7]-749,377.32
					2003	6,794,817.99			7,366,353.92		[7]-571,535.93
					2002	2,964,002.27			2,964,002.27		
					No Year	181,913,381.43			-7,125,782.40		189,039,163.83
Accounts Receivable						1,416,542,123.82				-290,041,317.87	1,706,583,441.69
Unfilled Customer Orders						15,402,991.32				-63,042,456.84	78,445,448.16
Fund Equities:											
Unobligated Balances (Expired)						-75,402,481.97				-10,805,818.67	-64,596,663.30
Unobligated Balances (Unexpired)						-115,773,843.97				90,748,338.41	-206,522,182.38
Accounts Payable						-72,727,004.73				5,683,416.15	-78,410,420.88

Appropriations, Outlays, and Balances - Continued

Appropriation or Fund Account — Title	Period of Availability	Dept Reg	Tr From	Account Number	Sub No.	Balances, Beginning Of Fiscal Year	Appropriations And Other Obligational Authority[1]	Transfers Borrowings And Investment (Net)[2]	Outlays (Net)	Balances Withdrawn And Other Transactions[3]	Balances, End Of Fiscal Year[4]
Undelivered Orders	Subtotal			0511		-1,265,389,047.57				262,773,264.93	-1,528,162,312.50
						-0-			4,684,573.89	-4,684,573.89	-0-
Grants To States For Medicaid, Centers For Medicare And Medicaid Services											
Fund Resources:											
Undisbursed Funds	No Year	75		0512		45,668,209,182.12	168,254,781,999.74	-2,805,408,540.00	187,888,141,109.02		23,229,441,532.84
Transfer To:											
Center For Disease Control	No Year	75	75	0512	9	944,197,341.96		2,805,408,540.00	2,735,461,551.40		1,014,144,330.56
Fund Equities:											
Unobligated Balances (Unexpired)						-26,586,131,293.24				-22,672,470,324.15	-3,913,660,969.09
Accounts Payable						-19,200,031,138.94				315,293,213.24	-19,515,324,352.18
Undelivered Orders						-826,244,091.90				-11,643,549.77	-814,600,542.13
	Subtotal	75		0512		-0-	168,254,781,999.74		190,623,602,660.42	-22,368,820,660.68	-0-
Payments For Credits Against Health Care Contributions, Centers For Medicare And Medicaid Services											
Fund Resources:											
Undisbursed Funds	No Year	75		0513			39,243.90		39,243.90		
State Children's Health Insurance Fund, Centers For Medicare And Medicaid Services											
Fund Resources:											
Undisbursed Funds	2007	75		0515		3,163,150,995.86	5,040,000,000.00		2,083,260,369.84		2,956,739,630.16
	2005-2007							137,832,296.00	137,832,296.00		
	2004-2007							146,879,932.00	146,879,932.00		
	2006								2,032,317,339.90		1,130,833,655.96
	2003-2006					5,204,696.00			5,204,696.00		
	2005					1,419,700,612.57			1,101,764,632.99		180,103,683.58
	2002-2005					55,836,288.33			-408,263.77		56,244,552.10
	2004					191,900,187.09		-137,832,296.00	23,170,339.23		21,849,915.86
	2001-2004					71,855,176.87		-146,879,932.00	1.72		71,855,175.15
	2003					0.46			0.46		
	2000-2003					651,944,891.00					651,944,891.00
	2002					829,966.27			829,966.27		
	2000-2002					139,458.20				139,458.20	
	1999-2002					584,642,370.00				584,642,370.00	
	No Year						650,000,000.00		468,835,129.21		181,164,870.79
Fund Equities:											
Unobligated Balances (Expired)						-1,236,726,719.20				-456,756,324.20	-779,970,395.00
Unobligated Balances (Unexpired)										33,982,234.00	-33,982,234.00
Accounts Payable						-284,000,000.00				5,000,000.00	-289,000,000.00
Undelivered Orders						-4,624,477,923.45				-476,694,177.85	-4,147,783,745.60
	Subtotal	75		0515		-0-	5,690,000,000.00		5,999,686,439.85	-309,686,439.85	-0-
State Grants And Demonstration, Centers For Medicare And Medicaid Services											
Fund Resources:											
Undisbursed Funds	2007-2011	75		0516		1,000,000.00	272,000,000.00	10,000,000.00	5,750,113.00		266,249,887.00
	2006-2010								200,000.00		10,800,000.00
	2006-2009					50,000,000.00					50,000,000.00
	2004-2008					1,425,391.00			68,089.00		1,357,302.00

Footnotes At End Of Chapter

Appropriations, Outlays, and Balances – Continued

Appropriation or Fund Account — Title	Period of Availability	Dept Reg	Tr From	Account Number	Sub No.	Balances, Beginning Of Fiscal Year	Appropriations And Other Obligational Authority[1]	Transfers Borrowings And Investment (Net)[2]	Outlays (Net)	Balances Withdrawn And Other Transactions[3]	Balances, End Of Fiscal Year[4]
State Grants And Demonstration, Centers For Medicare And Medicaid Services - Continued											
Fund Resources: - Continued											
Undisbursed Funds - Continued	2007						83,000,000.00		2,505,524.27		80,494,475.73
	2006-2007							12,550,000.00			12,550,000.00
	2004-2007					17,855,418.19			9,421,124.22		8,434,293.97
	2006					149,944,233.34		-22,550,000.00	79,676,075.53		47,718,157.81
	2005					19,015,839.86			-2,344,246.52		21,360,086.38
	2004-2005					2,575,706.87			2,268,385.87		307,321.00
	2003-2004					15,930,613.99			86,920.24		15,843,693.75
	No Year					1,819,036,719.36	342,848,840.00		1,177,640,093.75		984,245,465.61
Fund Equities:											
Unobligated Balances (Expired)						-38,492,986.25				15,680,240.00	-54,173,226.25
Unobligated Balances (Unexpired)						-634,644,550.25				124,680,343.13	-759,324,893.38
Accounts Payable						-876,474,875.02				-713,432,366.92	-163,042,508.10
Undelivered Orders						-527,171,511.09				-4,351,455.57	-522,820,055.52
Subtotal		75		0516		-0-	697,848,840.00		1,275,272,079.36	-577,423,239.36	-0-
Payments To Health Care Trust Funds, Centers For Medicare And Medicaid Services											
Fund Resources:											
Undisbursed Funds	2007	75		0580		27,658,016,789.53	188,508,193,000.00		179,530,851,909.48		8,977,341,090.52
	2006								411,428,940.71	27,246,587,848.82	
Fund Equities:											
Unobligated Balances (Expired)						-27,658,016,789.53				-18,680,675,699.01	-8,977,341,090.52
Subtotal		75		0580		-0-	188,508,193,000.00		179,942,280,850.19	8,565,912,149.81	-0-
Taxation On OASDI Benefits, Hi, Centers For Medicare And Medicaid Services											
Fund Resources:											
Undisbursed Funds	No Year	75		0585			10,593,000,000.00		10,593,000,000.00		
Special Fund Accounts											
Stabilization Fund, Centers For Medicare And Medicaid Services											
Fund Resources:											
Undisbursed Funds	No Year	75		5384						-24,215,831.94	24,215,831.94
Accounts Receivable											24,215,831.94
Fund Equities:											
Unobligated Balances (Unexpired)										24,215,831.94	-24,215,831.94
Subtotal		75		5384		-0-					-0-
Trust Fund Accounts											
Transitional Drug Assistance, Centers For Medicare And Medicaid Services											
Fund Resources:											
Undisbursed Funds	2004-2005	75		8307		58,050,704.05	10,334,120.86	9,780,314.62	9,780,314.62		31,469,042.54
	No Year							-519,273.94	9,814,846.92	26,581,661.51	
Accounts Receivable						-0-					

Appropriations, Outlays, and Balances - Continued

Appropriation or Fund Account — Title	Period of Availability	Reg	Tr From	Account Number	Sub No.	Balances, Beginning Of Fiscal Year	Appropriations And Other Obligational Authority[1]	Transfers Borrowings And Investment (Net)[2]	Outlays (Net)	Balances Withdrawn And Other Transactions[3]	Balances, End Of Fiscal Year[4]
Fund Equities:											
Unobligated Balances (Expired)						-0.83					-0.83
Accounts Payable						-53,007,341.49				-21,580,314.62	-31,427,026.87
Undelivered Orders						-5,043,361.73				-5,001,346.89	-42,014.84
Subtotal	Subtotal	75		8307		-0-	10,334,120.86	9,261,040.68	19,595,161.54		-0-
Medicare Prescription Drug Account, Centers For Medicare And Medicaid Services											
Fund Resources:											
Undisbursed Funds	2007	75		8308			491,642,008.45	401,383,740.84	491,642,008.45		
	2006						111,515,975.97	18,587,394.07	512,899,716.81		
	2004-2005							3,586,918,002.85	18,587,394.07		
	No Year					-15,476,454.30	45,474,845,869.16		49,103,284,112.35		[7]-56,996,694.64
Accounts Receivable						3,080,330,227.20				-1,351,585,506.81	4,431,915,734.01
Fund Equities:											
Unobligated Balances (Expired)						-1,002,840.21				425,459,128.73	-426,461,968.94
Accounts Payable						-3,063,850,932.69				884,490,428.03	-3,948,341,360.72
Undelivered Orders										115,709.71	-115,709.71
Subtotal	Subtotal	75		8308		-0-	46,078,003,853.58	4,006,889,137.76	50,126,413,231.68	-41,520,240.34	-0-
Health Care Fraud And Abuse Control Account, Department Of Health And Human Services											
Fund Resources:											
Undisbursed Funds	2007	75		8393			565,482,925.85	6,396,213.00	[13]553,422,827.43		12,060,098.42
	2006-2007					2,755,187.13		179,461,928.82	1,551,035.45		4,845,177.55
	2006					-1,948,541.03		11,644,913.10	190,590,921.34		[7]-8,373,805.39
	2005					-138,766.31		4,169,121.20	10,009,741.66		[7]-313,369.59
	2004					-702,820.53		1,262,293.72	4,107,868.19		[7]-77,513.30
	2003					-9,063,011.67		9,077,050.20	559,473.19		
	2002							483,684.43	14,038.53		
	2001-2002								483,684.43		
	No Year						158,553,589.53		236,298,055.00		[7]-77,744,465.47
Transfer To:											
Justice	2002	15	75	8393	1	1,630,822.55		-1,633,743.50	-2,920.95		
Office Of The Secretary, Office Of The Inspector General	2002	75	75	8393	1	6,875,535.90		-6,765,535.20	110,000.70		
	2001-2002	75		8393		483,684.43		-483,684.43			
Administration On Aging	2003	75		8393	2	148,500.60			21.39		[7]-21.39
Office Of The Secretary, Office Of The General Counsel	2002	75		8393		440,200.57		-148,689.22	-188.62		
	2002	75	75	8393	11			-440,200.57			
Accounts Receivable						[8]-366,013,865.17				-184,617,133.07	550,630,998.24
Fund Equities:											
Unobligated Balances (Expired)						[8]-23,021,855.21				11,175,059.96	[14]-34,196,915.17
Accounts Payable						-2,520,783.65				2,111,178.80	-4,631,962.45
Undelivered Orders						-340,952,017.95				101,246,203.50	-442,198,221.45
Subtotal	Subtotal	75		8393		-0-	724,036,515.38	203,023,351.55	997,144,557.74	-70,084,690.81	
Subtotal, Centers For Medicare And Medicaid Services							420,764,235,260.30	4,219,173,529.99	439,789,716,485.41	-14,806,307,695.12	

Footnotes At End Of Chapter

Appropriations, Outlays, and Balances – Continued

Appropriation or Fund Account — Title	Period of Availability	Reg	Tr From	Account Number	Sub No.	Balances, Beginning Of Fiscal Year	Appropriations And Other Obligational Authority[1]	Transfers Borrowings And Investment (Net)[2]	Outlays (Net)	Balances Withdrawn And Other Transactions[3]	Balances, End Of Fiscal Year[4]
Federal Hospital Insurance Trust Fund											
Trust Fund Accounts											
Federal Hospital Insurance Trust Fund											
Fund Resources:											
Undisbursed Funds	No Year	20		8005		8,799,442.96					7,726,830.22
Transfer To:											
Department Of Health And Human Services	No Year	75	20	8005		935,208,528.07	223,157,191,031.41	-221,449,403,064.08	1,708,860,580.07		125,379,961.43
Investments In Public Debt Securities						[15]302,186,266,000.00		17,191,104,000.00	204,865,104,279.17		319,377,370,000.00
Accounts Receivable						407,354.00					883,354.00
Unfilled Customer Orders										-476,000.00	
Fund Equities:											
Unobligated Balances (Unexpired)						[8]281,764,265,160.76				8,096,673,280.70	-289,860,938,441.46
Accounts Payable						[8]20,627,604,348.26				8,484,372,177.55	-29,111,976,525.81
Undelivered Orders						-738,811,816.01				-200,366,637.63	-538,445,178.38
Subtotal		20		8005		-0-	223,157,191,031.41	-203,023,351.55	206,573,964,859.24	16,380,202,820.62	-0-
Total, Federal Hospital Insurance Trust Fund						223,157,191,031.41		-203,023,351.55	206,573,964,859.24	16,380,202,820.62	
Federal Supplementary Medical Insurance Trust Fund											
Trust Fund Accounts											
Federal Supplementary Medical Insurance Trust Fund											
Fund Resources:											
Undisbursed Funds	No Year	20		8004		82,265,771.39					145,462,209.35
Transfer To:											
Department Of Health And Human Services	No Year	75	20	8004		135,536,324.47	192,922,825,365.51	-190,466,205,114.41	2,393,423,813.14		[7]247,199,469.72
Investments In Public Debt Securities						[15]533,060,991,000.00		6,187,022,000.00	180,645,768,730.16		39,248,013,000.00
Accounts Receivable										-8,483,565,672.97	8,483,565,672.97
Fund Equities:											
Unobligated Balances (Unexpired)						[8]10,744,842,636.78				12,448,639,511.15	-23,193,482,147.93
Accounts Payable						[8]21,969,325,631.19				2,350,698,473.34	-24,320,024,104.53
Undelivered Orders						-564,624,827.89				-448,289,667.75	-116,335,160.14
Subtotal		20		8004		-0-	192,922,825,365.51	-4,016,150,178.44	183,039,192,543.30	5,867,482,643.77	-0-
Total, Federal Supplementary Medical Insurance Trust Fund						192,922,825,365.51		-4,016,150,178.44	183,039,192,543.30	5,867,482,643.77	
Total, Trust Fund Accounts						416,080,016,396.92		-4,219,173,529.99	389,613,157,402.54	22,247,685,464.39	
Total, Centers For Medicare And Medicaid Services						836,844,251,657.22			829,402,873,887.95	7,441,377,769.27	

Appropriations, Outlays, and Balances - Continued

Appropriation or Fund Account — Title	Period of Availability	Account Symbol — Dept Reg	Tr From	Account Number	Sub No.	Balances, Beginning Of Fiscal Year	Appropriations And Other Obligational Authority[1]	Transfers Borrowings And Investment (Net)[2]	Outlays (Net)	Balances Withdrawn And Other Transactions[3]	Balances, End Of Fiscal Year[4]
Administration For Children And Families											
General Fund Accounts											
Payments To States For Child Support Enforcement And Family Support Programs, Administration For Children And Families											
Fund Resources:											
Undisbursed Funds	No Year	75		1501		806,479,928.84	4,399,104,000.00		4,237,893,200.12		967,690,728.72
Fund Equities:											
Unobligated Balances (Unexpired)						-7,574,047.50				134,637,815.62	-142,211,863.12
Accounts Payable										101,428,261.06	-101,428,261.06
Undelivered Orders						-798,905,881.34				-74,855,276.80	-724,050,604.54
	Subtotal	75		1501		-0-	4,399,104,000.00		4,237,893,200.12	161,210,799.88	-0-
Low Income Home Energy Assistance, Administration For Children And Families											
Fund Resources:											
Undisbursed Funds	2007	75		1502			2,161,170,000.00		1,529,891,154.14		631,278,845.86
	2006					998,474,332.98			931,367,189.55		67,107,143.43
	2005					21,389,445.54			16,269,535.90		5,119,909.64
	2004					14,413,557.44			11,488,580.99		2,924,976.45
	2003					7,220,695.15			3,830,164.28		3,390,530.87
	2002					208,014,470.17			496,962.46	207,517,507.71	
	No Year					39,718,758.28			4,285,036.53		35,433,721.75
Fund Equities:											
Unobligated Balances (Expired)						-200,018,237.59				-200,008,150.05	-10,087.54
Unobligated Balances (Unexpired)						-20,350,004.01					-20,350,004.01
Accounts Payable						-10,190.91				-190.67	-10,000.24
Undelivered Orders						-1,068,852,827.05				-343,967,790.84	-724,885,036.21
	Subtotal	75		1502		-0-	2,161,170,000.00		2,497,628,623.85	-336,458,623.85	-0-
Refugee And Entrant Assistance, Administration For Children And Families											
Fund Resources:											
Undisbursed Funds	2007-2009	75		1503			578,030,093.00		216,277,299.86		361,752,793.14
	2006-2008					324,813,104.98			167,876,604.46		156,936,500.52
	2007						9,817,000.00		378,968.80		9,438,031.20
	2005-2007					127,060,625.67			102,478,276.61		24,582,349.06
	2006					9,571,945.67			7,592,611.47		1,979,334.20
	2004-2006					23,015,949.37			11,143,336.48		11,872,612.89
	2005					1,497,302.91			1,346,812.78		150,490.13
	2003-2005					6,889,299.33			1,350,255.31		5,539,044.02
	2004					835,538.98			-19,741.57		855,280.55
	2002-2004					9,806,055.88			-153,150.06		9,959,205.94
	2003					1,080,919.56			14,616.41		1,066,303.15
	2001-2003					9,100,066.81			219,655.88		8,880,410.93
	2002					78,698.30			-547.34	79,245.64	
	2000-2002					14,619,094.19			118,211.38	14,500,882.81	
Unfilled Customer Orders						910.74					910.74

Footnotes At End Of Chapter

Appropriations, Outlays, and Balances – Continued

Appropriation or Fund Account — Title	Period of Availability	Dept Reg	Tr From	Account Number	Sub No.	Balances, Beginning Of Fiscal Year	Appropriations And Other Obligational Authority[1]	Transfers Borrowings And Investment (Net)[2]	Outlays (Net)	Balances Withdrawn And Other Transactions[3]	Balances, End Of Fiscal Year[4]
Refugee And Entrant Assistance, Administration For Children And Families - Continued											
Fund Equities:											
Unobligated Balances (Expired)						-4,731,202.38			-------	-3,225,091.48	-1,506,110.90
Unobligated Balances (Unexpired)						-17,312,160.60			-------	24,341,932.41	-41,654,093.01
Accounts Payable						-133,385.33			-------	44,877,406.47	-45,010,791.80
Undelivered Orders						-506,192,764.08			-------	-1,350,493.32	-504,842,270.76
Subtotal		75		1503		-0-	587,847,093.00		508,623,210.47	79,223,882.53	-0-
Promoting Safe And Stable Families, Administration For Children And Families											
Fund Resources:											
Undisbursed Funds	2007	75		1512		350,440,401.12	454,100,000.00		143,661,946.28		310,438,053.72
	2006					61,791,026.86			246,070,034.40		104,370,366.72
	2005					7,527,322.39			55,254,251.68		6,536,775.18
	2004					33,890,280.14			-13,888,779.39		21,416,101.78
	2003					8,369,610.95			27,434,041.35		6,456,238.79
	2002								420,514.41	7,949,096.54	
Fund Equities:											
Unobligated Balances (Expired)						-10,112,077.11			-------	-5,125,660.04	-4,986,417.07
Accounts Payable						-14,577,261.01			-------	23,395,952.95	-37,973,213.96
Undelivered Orders						-437,329,303.34			-------	-31,071,398.18	-406,257,905.16
Subtotal		75		1512		-0-	454,100,000.00		458,952,008.73	-4,852,008.73	-0-
Payment To States For The Child Care And Development Block Grant, Administration For Children And Families											
Fund Resources:											
Undisbursed Funds	2007	75		1515		508,168,022.52	2,062,080,900.00	-10,842,688.00	1,619,046,342.28		432,191,869.72
	2006					53,382,096.76			453,865,175.62		54,302,846.90
	2005					8,054,495.36			47,082,663.13		6,299,433.63
	2004					4,874,664.72			4,249,909.55		3,804,585.81
	2003					5,588,343.52			172,699.18		4,701,965.54
	2002								383,256.39	5,205,087.13	
Transfer To:											
Interior, Bureau Of Indian Affairs	2007	14	75	1515	20			10,842,688.00	10,164,859.00		677,829.00
	2005					5,840.00					5,840.00
	2004					583.00					583.00
Unfilled Customer Orders						200,000.00					200,000.00
Fund Equities:											
Unobligated Balances (Expired)						-5,313,535.42			-------	-1,548,477.92	-3,765,057.50
Accounts Payable						-2,987,848.92			-------	150,489,168.37	-153,477,017.29
Undelivered Orders						-571,972,661.54			-------	-227,029,782.73	-344,942,878.81
Subtotal		75		1515		-0-	2,062,080,900.00		2,134,964,905.15	-72,884,005.15	-0-
Contingency Fund For State Welfare Programs, Administration For Children And Families											
Fund Resources:											
Undisbursed Funds	1997-2010	75		1522		1,816,217,618.26			50,977,996.66		1,765,239,621.60
	1997-2006					17,223,201.15			5,215,734.34		12,007,466.81
	1997-2005					4,452,029.55					4,452,029.55
Fund Equities:											
Unobligated Balances (Expired)									-------	10,077,167.00	-10,077,167.00

Appropriations, Outlays, and Balances - Continued

Title	Period of Availability	Reg	Tr From	Account Number	Sub No.	Balances, Beginning Of Fiscal Year	Appropriations And Other Obligational Authority[1]	Transfers Borrowings And Investment (Net)[2]	Outlays (Net)	Balances Withdrawn And Other Transactions[3]	Balances, End Of Fiscal Year[4]
Unobligated Balances (Unexpired)						-1,792,914,897.00				-55,502,501.00	-1,737,412,396.00
Accounts Payable										22,582,688.22	-22,582,688.22
Undelivered Orders						-44,977,951.96				-33,351,085.22	-11,626,866.74
Subtotal		75		1522		-0-			56,193,731.00	-56,193,731.00	-0-
Disabled Voter Services, Administration For Children And Families											
Fund Resources:											
Undisbursed Funds	2003	75		1533		7,067,968.74			2,670,028.41		4,397,940.33
Fund Equities:											
Accounts Payable										365,805.46	-365,805.46
Undelivered Orders						-7,067,968.74				-3,035,833.87	-4,032,134.87
Subtotal		75		1533		-0-			2,670,028.41	-2,670,028.41	-0-
Social Services Block Grant, Administration For Children And Families											
Fund Resources:											
Undisbursed Funds	2007	75		1534		700,391,136.41	1,700,000,000.00		1,447,818,848.63		252,181,151.37
	2006					5,869,041.06			473,571,803.97		226,819,332.44
	2005					285,514.81			5,527,523.18		341,517.88
	2004					371,102.64			27,980.98		257,533.83
	2003					13,612.32			-193,002.40		564,105.04
	2002								2,170.24	11,442.08	
	No Year					141,833,864.90			29,264,860.89		112,569,004.01
Fund Equities:											
Unobligated Balances (Expired)						-0.78				-0.78	
Unobligated Balances (Unexpired)						-16,854,877.13				-16,854,877.13	
Accounts Payable						-0.60				904,318.70	-904,319.30
Undelivered Orders						-831,909,393.63			1,956,020,185.49	-240,081,068.36	-591,828,325.27
Subtotal		75		1534		-0-	1,700,000,000.00			-256,020,185.49	-0-
Children And Family Services Program, Administration For Children And Families											
Fund Resources:											
Undisbursed Funds	2007-2008	75		1536			5,000,000.00				5,000,000.00
	2007						8,983,470,264.00		4,801,755,566.95		4,181,714,697.05
	2006-2007					17,803,759.00			7,102,991.66		10,700,767.34
	2006					4,165,339,302.40			3,713,673,875.47		451,665,426.93
	2005-2006					4,145,808.88			4,118,800.02		27,008.86
	2005					408,048,920.60			255,794,923.18		152,253,997.42
	2004-2005					3,883,113.71			3,349,589.59		533,524.12
	2004					150,249,136.46			49,246,558.38		101,002,578.08
	2003-2004					10,592,570.58					10,592,570.58
	2003					134,917,567.04			25,053,718.55		109,863,848.49
	2002-2003					3,785,344.71					3,785,344.71
	2002					109,214,763.72			9,968,378.43	99,246,385.29	
	2001-2002					512,070.00				512,070.00	
	No Year					3,333,029.28			1,176,620.40		2,156,408.88
Fund Equities:											
Accounts Receivable						12,994,512.59				5,212,215.31	7,782,297.28
Unfilled Customer Orders										-12,324,999.71	12,324,999.71
Unobligated Balances (Expired)						-151,935,950.50				-9,185,207.54	-142,750,742.96
Unobligated Balances (Unexpired)						-9,691,898.17				-2,779,593.09	-6,912,305.08

Footnotes At End Of Chapter

Appropriations, Outlays, and Balances – Continued

| Appropriation or Fund Account | | Account Symbol | | | | Balances, Beginning Of Fiscal Year | Appropriations And Other Obligational Authority[1] | Transfers Borrowings And Investment (Net)[2] | Outlays (Net) | Balances Withdrawn And Other Transactions[3] | Balances, End Of Fiscal Year[4] |
Title	Period of Availability	Dept Reg	Tr From	Account Number	Sub No.						
Children And Family Services Program, Administration For Children And Families - Continued											
Fund Equities: - Continued											
Accounts Payable						-13,381,044.87				599,081,874.06	-612,462,918.93
Undelivered Orders						-4,849,811,005.43				-562,533,502.95	-4,287,277,502.48
	Subtotal	75		1536		-0-	8,988,470,264.00		8,871,241,022.63	117,229,241.37	-0-
Payment To States For Foster Care And Adoption Assistance, Administration For Children And Families											
Fund Resources:											
Undisbursed Funds	2007	75		1545		1,083,344,332.79	6,855,480,598.00		5,907,460,203.37		948,020,394.63
	2006					696,791,139.58			576,660,348.82		506,683,983.97
	2005					430,825,914.73			74,031,583.70		622,759,555.88
	2004					466,124,351.56			-55,397,557.70		486,223,472.43
	2003					557,923,863.09			47,044,815.08		419,079,536.48
	2002								13,672,905.71	544,250,957.38	
Fund Equities:											
Unobligated Balances (Expired)						-2,317,801,159.60				-365,499,897.72	-1,952,301,261.88
Accounts Payable						-21,819,170.74				299,320,935.91	-321,140,106.65
Undelivered Orders						-895,389,271.41				-186,063,696.55	-709,325,574.86
	Subtotal	75		1545		-0-	6,855,480,598.00		6,563,472,298.98	292,008,299.02	-0-
Child Care Entitlement To States, Administration For Children And Families											
Fund Resources:											
Undisbursed Funds	2007	75		1550		654,828,363.71	2,917,000,000.00	-14,793,349.00	2,324,479,296.35		577,727,354.65
	2006-2007							2,889,703.00	2,305,917.42		583,785.58
	2005-2006					64,181,435.88		-2,889,703.00	589,438,699.95		62,499,960.76
	2005					166,336.79			58,519,931.29		5,661,504.59
	2004-2005					8,076,462.95			154,982.03		11,354.76
	2004					28,838.96			4,441,155.19		3,635,307.76
	2003-2004					19,580,265.63			26,780.34		2,058.62
	2003					3,099.74			329,513.16		19,250,752.47
	2002-2003					20,988,889.91			-26.59		3,126.33
	2002								2,286.40	20,986,603.51	
	2001-2002					3,329.18			-322.35	3,651.53	
Transfer To:											
Interior, Bureau Of Indian Affairs	2007	14	75	1550	20	18,905.00		14,793,349.00	14,656,645.00	136,704.00	136,704.00
	2005-2006					8,410.00			18,905.00		
	2004										8,410.00
Fund Equities:											
Unobligated Balances (Expired)						-39,845,953.72				-19,770,056.95	-20,075,896.77
Accounts Payable						-1,003,452.96				175,393,894.68	-176,397,347.64
Undelivered Orders						-727,034,931.07				-253,987,855.96	-473,047,075.11
	Subtotal	75		1550		-0-	2,917,000,000.00		2,994,373,763.19	-77,373,763.19	-0-
Temporary Assistance For Needy Families, Administration For Children And Families											
Fund Resources:											
Undisbursed Funds	2007	75		1552		145,300,045.41	17,058,625,291.00		12,685,706,681.56		4,337,064,525.44
	2006							-35,854,084.00	89,749,726.14		55,550,319.27
	2005-2006					4,512,810,503.76			3,188,724,108.75		1,324,086,395.01

Appropriations, Outlays, and Balances - Continued

Appropriation or Fund Account — Title	Period of Availability	Dept Reg	Dept Tr From	Account Number	Sub No.	Balances, Beginning Of Fiscal Year	Appropriations And Other Obligational Authority[1]	Transfers Borrowings And Investment (Net)[2]	Outlays (Net)	Balances Withdrawn And Other Transactions[3]	Balances, End Of Fiscal Year[4]
	2005					1,055,269,042.17			480,989,853.64		574,279,188.53
	1999-2005					14,112,777.73			5,256,433.78		8,856,343.95
	2004					480,267,484.48			291,298,766.69		188,968,717.79
	1999-2004					9,954,331.60			8,492,516.01		1,461,815.59
	2003					137,769,473.16			63,688,095.48		74,081,377.68
	1999-2003					3,106,006.70			1,584,112.43		1,521,894.27
	2002					82,308,760.97			32,327,342.29	29,998,013.00	[6]19,983,405.68
	2001					11,567,388.95			1,021,638.48		[6]10,545,750.47
	1998-2001					25,511.90					[6]25,511.90
	2000					1,377,556.84			-10,370,766.72	2,755,113.68	[6]8,993,209.88
	1999					13,933,062.12			-2,844,595.97		[6]16,777,658.09
	1998					103,866,226.70			9,220,450.83	296,030.16	[6]94,349,745.71
	1997					448,030.45				350,517.45	[6]97,513.00
Transfer To:											
Interior, Bureau Of Indian Affairs	2007	14	75	1552	20			35,854,084.00	31,405,793.00		4,448,291.00
	2005-2006					66,916.00			66,916.00		-0-
Subtotal		75		1552			17,058,625,291.00		16,876,317,072.39	182,308,218.61	
Fund Equities:											
Unobligated Balances (Expired)						-157,972,814.65				-2,318,548.96	-155,654,265.69
Accounts Payable						-4,565,606.50				999,895,121.13	-1,004,460,727.63
Undelivered Orders						-6,409,644,697.79				-848,668,027.85	-5,560,976,669.94
Children's Research And Technical Assistance, Administration For Children And Families						-0-					
Fund Resources:											
Undisbursed Funds	2007	75		1553		16,370,352.06	21,000,000.00		656,481.60		20,343,518.40
	2006					13,890,074.11			6,327,234.54		10,043,117.52
	2005					11,150,591.34			7,241,718.86		6,648,355.25
	2004					474,964.93			7,912,214.76		3,238,376.58
	2003					318,520.13			2,287.98		472,676.95
	2002								13,132.62		
	No Year					26,972,096.51	36,952,634.00		47,769,605.79	305,387.51	16,155,124.72
Accounts Receivable						957,564.00				-5,450,831.24	6,408,395.24
Unfilled Customer Orders						3,577,812.44				-8,841,277.49	12,419,089.93
Fund Equities:											
Unobligated Balances (Expired)						-3,433,553.12				-920,322.78	-2,513,230.34
Unobligated Balances (Unexpired)						-1,581,781.04				1,402,172.49	-2,983,953.53
Accounts Payable						-365,931.10				1,712,428.51	-2,078,359.61
Undelivered Orders						-68,330,710.26				-177,599.15	-68,153,111.11
Subtotal		75		1553		-0-	57,952,634.00		69,922,676.15	-11,970,042.15	-0-
Total, Administration For Children And Families							47,241,830,780.00		47,228,272,726.56	13,558,053.44	

Footnotes At End Of Chapter

Appropriations, Outlays, and Balances – Continued

Appropriation or Fund Account — Title	Period of Availability	Reg	Tr From	Account Number	Sub No.	Balances, Beginning Of Fiscal Year	Appropriations And Other Obligational Authority[1]	Transfers Borrowings And Investment (Net)[2]	Outlays (Net)	Balances Withdrawn And Other Transactions[3]	Balances, End Of Fiscal Year[4]
Administration On Aging											
General Fund Accounts											
Aging Services Programs, Administration On Aging, Office Of The Secretary											
Fund Resources:											
Undisbursed Funds	2007	75		0142			1,383,006,669.00		895,636,663.76		487,370,005.24
	2005-2007					1,346,707.22			19,770.52		1,326,936.70
	2006					460,344,744.64			420,506,983.92		39,837,760.72
	2004-2006					489,644.93			153.77		489,491.16
	2005					54,670,992.20			37,341,893.57		17,329,098.63
	2004					11,997,247.28			4,510,406.67		7,486,840.61
	2003					8,425,650.75			617,912.91		7,807,737.84
	2002					6,316,477.15			399,742.16	5,916,734.99	
	No Year					24,142.93			24,100.14		42.79
Accounts Receivable						206,396.50				-680,709.95	887,106.45
Unfilled Customer Orders						[8]12,633,969.80				-1,650,936.14	14,284,905.94
Fund Equities:											
Unobligated Balances (Expired)						[8]2,652,259.10				-269,075.77	-2,383,183.33
Unobligated Balances (Unexpired)						[8]135,977.17				-135,934.38	-42.79
Accounts Payable						[8]3,374,364.68				-1,623,387.09	-1,750,977.59
Undelivered Orders						[8]550,293,372.45				22,392,349.92	-572,685,722.37
	Subtotal	75		0142		-0-	1,383,006,669.00		1,359,057,627.42	23,949,041.58	
Total, Administration On Aging							1,383,006,669.00		1,359,057,627.42	23,949,041.58	
Departmental Management											
General Fund Accounts											
General Departmental Management, Departmental Management											
Fund Resources:											
Undisbursed Funds	2007	75		0120			350,445,313.00		175,455,318.63		174,989,994.37
	2006					171,950,009.69			133,348,923.05		38,601,086.64
	2005					89,335,693.91			55,135,713.10		34,199,980.81
	2004					23,917,235.74			8,033,744.86		15,883,490.88
	2003					3,102,787.09			1,796,435.75		1,306,351.34
	2002-2003					571,427.55			40,302.12		531,125.43
	2002					-3,580,371.61			-4,226,908.40	646,536.79	
	2001-2002					10,473.11			3,556.64	6,916.47	
	No Year					2,331,336.29			15,179.56		2,316,156.73
Accounts Receivable						[8]106,171,668.08				10,249,432.16	95,922,235.92
Unfilled Customer Orders						[8]68,200,871.24				-94,135,795.68	162,336,666.92
Fund Equities:											
Unobligated Balances (Expired)						[8]5,231,781.16				10,592,814.26	-15,824,595.42
Unobligated Balances (Unexpired)						[8]-2,310,684.76				-6,372.20	-2,304,312.56
Accounts Payable						[8]-5,985,468.24				5,776,923.14	-11,762,391.38
Undelivered Orders						[8]448,483,196.93				47,712,592.75	-496,195,789.68
	Subtotal	75		0120		-0-	350,445,313.00		369,602,265.31	-19,156,952.31	-0-

Appropriations, Outlays, and Balances - Continued

Appropriation or Fund Account — Title	Dept Reg	Tr From	Account Number	Sub No.	Period of Availability	Balances, Beginning Of Fiscal Year	Appropriations And Other Obligational Authority[1]	Transfers Borrowings And Investment (Net)[2]	Outlays (Net)	Balances Withdrawn And Other Transactions[3]	Balances, End Of Fiscal Year[4]
Policy Research, Departmental Management											
Fund Resources:											
Undisbursed Funds	75		0122		2006	6,065,098.67			-3,656.40		3,656.40
					2005	-75,894.29			3,360,090.87		2,705,007.80
					2004	-2,857,938.49			340,876.31		[7]-416,770.60
					2003	[8]1,163,854.01			1,184,623.66	1,026,854.98	[7]-4,042,562.15
					2002				136,999.03		
					2001						
Accounts Receivable						9,605,357.60					9,605,357.60
Unfilled Customer Orders						2,825,062.91					2,825,062.91
Fund Equities:											
Unobligated Balances (Expired)						[8]-1,584,567.30				-331,545.96	-1,253,021.34
Accounts Payable						[8]31,792.48				55,914.07	-87,706.55
Undelivered Orders						-15,109,180.63				-5,770,156.56	-9,339,024.07
Subtotal	75		0122			-0-			5,018,933.47	-5,018,933.47	-0-
Office Of The National Coordinator For Health Information Technology, Departmental Management											
Fund Resources:											
Undisbursed Funds	75		0130		2007	27,289,933.47	42,401,900.00		11,054,910.87		31,346,989.13
					2006	21,639,945.21			32,097,611.67		[7]-4,807,678.20
Unfilled Customer Orders										-24,551,119.73	46,191,064.94
Fund Equities:											
Unobligated Balances (Expired)						-14,007.49				4,517,053.54	-4,531,061.03
Accounts Payable						-75,036.59				651,956.07	-726,992.66
Undelivered Orders						-48,840,834.60				18,631,487.58	-67,472,322.18
Subtotal	75		0130			-0-	42,401,900.00		43,152,522.54	-750,622.54	-0-
Office For Civil Rights, Departmental Management											
Fund Resources:											
Undisbursed Funds	75		0135		2007	4,021,208.70	31,628,156.00		25,053,170.68		6,574,985.32
					2006	2,351,236.19			2,009,621.47		2,011,587.23
					2005	1,989,749.96			451,192.70		1,900,043.49
					2004	-1,664,079.45			6,592.94		1,983,157.02
					2003	1,291,648.86			65,548.53		1,598,530.92
					2002				221,322.55		
Accounts Receivable										1,070,326.31	10,030.17
Unfilled Customer Orders						343,557.35				-10,030.17	343,557.35
Fund Equities:											
Unobligated Balances (Expired)						-339,869.74				1,375,334.58	-1,715,204.32
Accounts Payable						-1,193,150.77				-457,667.45	-735,483.32
Undelivered Orders						-10,128,460.00				1,842,743.86	-11,971,203.86
Subtotal	75		0135			-0-	31,628,156.00		27,807,448.87	3,820,707.13	-0-
Medicare Appeals, Departmental Management											
Fund Resources:											
Undisbursed Funds	75		0139		2007	29,556,694.26			-22,184,122.89		22,184,122.89
					2006				16,269,162.87		13,287,531.39
Accounts Receivable										-59,726,699.00	59,726,699.00
Fund Equities:											
Unobligated Balances (Expired)						-569,581.71				-172,965.44	-396,616.27

Footnotes At End Of Chapter

Appropriations, Outlays, and Balances – Continued

Appropriation or Fund Account Title	Period of Availability	Reg	Tr From	Account Number	Sub No.	Balances, Beginning Of Fiscal Year	Appropriations And Other Obligational Authority[1]	Transfers Borrowings And Investment (Net)[2]	Outlays (Net)	Balances Withdrawn And Other Transactions[3]	Balances, End Of Fiscal Year[4]
Medicare Appeals, Departmental Management - Continued											
Fund Equities: - Continued											
Accounts Payable						-1,133,347.16				1,344,022.90	-2,477,370.06
Undelivered Orders						[8]-27,853,765.39				64,470,601.56	-92,324,366.95
	Subtotal	75		0139		-0-			-5,914,960.02	5,914,960.02	-0-
Public Health And Social Services Emergency Fund, Office Of The Secretary											
Fund Resources:											
Undisbursed Funds	2007	75		0140		-43,410,473.52	696,325,822.09	7,161,755.17	99,020,161.28		597,305,660.81
	2006							145,498.06	160,917,131.96		[7]-197,165,850.31
	2005-2006										
	2005					558,306,075.90		3,972,521.24	408,235,113.11		154,043,484.03
	2004					181,205,473.26		1,169,927.77	87,777,269.40		94,598,131.63
	2003					86,230,618.46			34,749,403.17		51,481,215.29
	2002					5,770,485.32			4,076,156.41	1,694,328.91	
	No Year					5,888,397,655.18		35,608,144.62	1,245,338,364.14		4,678,667,435.66
Transfer To:											
Social Security Administration	No Year	28	75	0140		291,254.11					291,254.11
Accounts Receivable						1,537,095.39				-10,225,956.98	11,763,052.37
Unfilled Customer Orders						2,222,580,405.78				31,917,531.08	2,190,662,874.70
Fund Equities:											
Unobligated Balances (Expired)						-22,535,042.12				886,001,393.55	-908,536,435.67
Unobligated Balances (Unexpired)						[8]-3,278,788,052.22				-1,193,601,247.76	-2,085,186,804.46
Accounts Payable						-211,116,172.70				23,141,512.72	-234,257,685.42
Undelivered Orders						[8]-5,388,469,322.84				-1,034,657,492.04	-4,353,811,830.80
	Subtotal	75		0140		-0-	696,325,822.09	48,057,846.86	2,040,113,599.47	-1,295,729,930.52	-0-
Total, Departmental Management							1,120,801,191.09	48,057,846.86	2,479,779,809.64	-1,310,920,771.69	
Program Support Center											
General Fund Accounts											
HHS Accrual Contribution To The Uniformed Services Retiree Health Care Fund, Office Of The Assistant Secretary For Health											
Fund Resources:											
Undisbursed Funds	2007	75		0170			36,288,000.00		36,288,000.00		
Retirement Pay And Medical Benefits For Commissioned Officers, Office Of The Assistant Secretary For Health											
Fund Resources:											
Undisbursed Funds	2007	75		0379			370,698,000.00		339,719,870.51		30,978,129.49
	2006					29,221,745.80			24,929,664.57		4,292,081.23
	2005					2,831,600.85			-713.82		2,832,314.67
	2004					2,230,849.97			7,374.06		2,223,475.91
	2003					16,977,517.62					16,977,517.62
	2002					7,007,545.29				7,007,545.29	
Fund Equities:											
Unobligated Balances (Expired)						-26,944,996.25				-4,009,173.86	-22,935,822.39
Accounts Payable						-292.58				-292.58	

Appropriations, Outlays, and Balances - Continued

Title	Period of Availability	Reg	Tr From	Account Number	Sub No.	Balances, Beginning Of Fiscal Year	Appropriations And Other Obligational Authority[1]	Transfers Borrowings And Investment (Net)[2]	Outlays (Net)	Balances Withdrawn And Other Transactions[3]	Balances, End Of Fiscal Year[4]
Undelivered Orders											
Scientific Activities Overseas, Special Foreign Currency Program, Assistant Secretary For Health	Subtotal	75		0379		-31,323,970.70				3,043,725.83	-34,367,696.53
						-0-	370,698,000.00		364,656,195.32	6,041,804.68	-0-
Fund Resources:											
Undisbursed Funds	No Year	75		1102		1,673,705.38			235,303.26		1,438,402.12
Fund Equities:											
Unobligated Balances (Unexpired)						-0.42				-0.42	
Accounts Payable						-1,733.93				184,343.92	-186,077.85
Undelivered Orders						-1,671,971.03				-419,646.76	-1,252,324.27
	Subtotal	75		1102		-0-			235,303.26	-235,303.26	-0-
Public Health Emergency Fund, Public Health Services, Office Of Assistant Secretary For Health											
Fund Resources:											
Undisbursed Funds	No Year	75		1104		56,507.52					56,507.52
Fund Equities:											
Unobligated Balances (Unexpired)						-55,851.44					-55,851.44
Undelivered Orders						-656.08					-656.08
	Subtotal	75		1104		-0-					-0-
Construction And Renovation, Saint Elizabeth's Hospital Substance Abuse And Mental Health Services Administration											
Fund Resources:											
Undisbursed Funds	No Year	75		1312		86.87					86.87
Fund Equities:											
Unobligated Balances (Unexpired)						-86.87					-86.87
	Subtotal	75		1312		-0-					-0-
Intragovernmental Funds											
HHS Service And Supply Fund, Program Support Center											
Fund Resources:											
Undisbursed Funds	No Year	75		4552	1	121,387,255.92			47,660,416.41	-143,940,005.27	73,726,839.51
Accounts Receivable						202,320,841.61					346,260,846.88
Unfilled Customer Orders						15,876,461.02				10,633,960.48	5,242,500.54
Fund Equities:											
Unobligated Balances (Unexpired)						-98,497,946.18				13,602,891.32	-112,100,837.50
Accounts Payable						-15,399,455.63				34,837,158.60	-50,236,614.23
Undelivered Orders						-225,687,156.74				37,205,578.46	-262,892,735.20
	Subtotal	75		4552		-0-			47,660,416.41	-47,660,416.41	-0-
Trust Fund Accounts											
Contributions, Indian Health Facilities, Indian Health Services											
Fund Resources:											
Undisbursed Funds	No Year	75		8073		136,591,177.60	29,478,886.42		29,394,162.44	-17,094,846.48	136,675,901.58
Fund Equities:											
Unobligated Balances (Unexpired)						-29,175,748.69					-12,080,902.21
Accounts Payable										33,917.14	-33,917.14

Footnotes At End Of Chapter

Appropriations, Outlays, and Balances – Continued

Appropriation or Fund Account Title	Period of Availability	Reg (Dept)	Tr From	Account Number	Sub No.	Balances, Beginning Of Fiscal Year	Appropriations And Other Obligational Authority[1]	Transfers Borrowings And Investment (Net)[2]	Outlays (Net)	Balances Withdrawn And Other Transactions[3]	Balances, End Of Fiscal Year[4]
Contributions, Indian Health Facilities, Indian Health Services - Continued											
Fund Equities: - Continued											
Undelivered Orders						-107,415,428.91				17,145,653.32	-124,561,082.23
	Subtotal	75		8073		-0-	29,478,886.42		29,394,162.44	84,723.98	-0-
Food And Drug Administration Unconditional Gift Fund											
Fund Resources:											
Undisbursed Funds	No Year	75		8247		79,500.00			40,500.00		39,000.00
Fund Equities:											
Unobligated Balances (Unexpired)						-79,500.00			40,500.00	-40,500.00	-39,000.00
	Subtotal	75		8247		-0-			40,500.00	-40,500.00	-0-
National Institutes Of Health Unconditional Gift Fund											
Fund Resources:											
Undisbursed Funds	No Year	75		8248		5,123,289.29	14,224,237.18	-11,247,803.55	2,985,124.03		5,114,598.89
Unrealized Discount On Investments						-418,774.01		-396,196.45			-814,970.46
Investments In Public Debt Securities						28,215,000.00		11,644,000.00			39,859,000.00
Fund Equities:											
Unobligated Balances (Unexpired)						-39,188,463.73				9,152,280.40	-48,340,744.13
Accounts Payable						6,014,945.01				34,984,672.89	-28,969,727.88
Undelivered Orders						254,003.44				-32,887,840.14	33,151,843.58
	Subtotal	75		8248		-0-	14,224,237.18		2,985,124.03	11,239,113.15	-0-
Unconditional Gift Fund, Health Resources And Services Administration											
Fund Resources:											
Undisbursed Funds	No Year	75		8249		137,476.68			-4,996.37		142,473.05
Fund Equities:											
Unobligated Balances (Unexpired)						-135,931.68				5,000.00	-140,931.68
Undelivered Orders						-1,545.00				-3.63	-1,541.37
	Subtotal	75		8249		-0-			-4,996.37	4,996.37	-0-
Gifts And Donations, Centers For Disease Control											
Fund Resources:											
Undisbursed Funds	No Year	75		8250		6,311,594.33	5,353,813.03		3,083,740.94		8,581,666.42
Fund Equities:											
Unobligated Balances (Unexpired)						-2,819,778.92				2,216,078.87	-5,035,857.79
Accounts Payable						-42,168.37				72,532.03	-114,700.40
Undelivered Orders						-3,449,647.04				-18,538.81	-3,431,108.23
	Subtotal	75		8250		-0-	5,353,813.03		3,083,740.94	2,270,072.09	-0-
National Institutes Of Health Conditional Gift Fund											
Fund Resources:											
Undisbursed Funds	No Year	75		8253		74,249,686.77	34,227,000.92	-28,464.87	31,126,774.51		77,321,448.31
Unrealized Discount On Investments						120,318.35		-130,866.41			-10,548.06
Investments In Public Debt Securities						179,000.00		259,000.00			438,000.00
Fund Equities:											
Unobligated Balances (Unexpired)						-33,784,212.48				-3,719,414.05	-30,064,798.43
Accounts Payable						-5,966,905.75				-8,010,310.35	2,043,404.60
Undelivered Orders						-34,797,886.89				14,929,619.53	-49,727,506.42
	Subtotal	75		8253		-0-	34,227,000.92	99,668.72	31,126,774.51	3,199,895.13	-0-
Conditional Gift Fund, Health Resources And Services Administration											
Fund Resources:											
Undisbursed Funds	No Year	75		8254		2,143,535.22	87,815.00	-128,668.72	-147,497.30		2,250,178.80
Investments In Public Debt Securities						2,883,000.00		29,000.00			2,912,000.00

Appropriations, Outlays, and Balances - Continued

Appropriation or Fund Account — Title	Period of Availability	Dept Reg	Tr From	Account Number	Sub No.	Balances, Beginning Of Fiscal Year	Appropriations And Other Obligational Authority[1]	Transfers Borrowings And Investment (Net)[2]	Outlays (Net)	Balances Withdrawn And Other Transactions[3]	Balances, End Of Fiscal Year[4]
Fund Equities:											
Unobligated Balances (Unexpired)						-3,506,860.65				197,676.09	-3,704,536.74
Accounts Payable						-1,814.42				-1,814.42	-1,457,642.06
Undelivered Orders						-1,517,860.15				-60,218.09	
	Subtotal	75		8254		-0-	87,815.00	-99,668.72	-147,497.30	135,643.58	-0-
Administration On Aging Gift Fund											
Fund Resources:											
Undisbursed Funds	No Year	75		8510		28,313.86	6,721.99		25,059.99		9,975.86
Fund Equities:											
Unobligated Balances (Unexpired)						-10,413.86				-438.00	-9,975.86
Undelivered Orders						-17,900.00				-17,900.00	
	Subtotal	75		8510		-0-	6,721.99		25,059.99	-18,338.00	-0-
Indian Health Service Gift Fund											
Fund Resources:											
Undisbursed Funds	No Year	75		8511		204,399.65	471,826.00		450,955.15		225,270.50
Fund Equities:											
Unobligated Balances (Unexpired)						-59,311.37				-8,942.75	-50,368.62
Undelivered Orders						-145,088.28				29,813.60	-174,901.88
	Subtotal	75		8511		-0-	471,826.00		450,955.15	20,870.85	-0-
Substance Abuse And Mental Health Administration Gift Fund											
Fund Resources:											
Undisbursed Funds	No Year	75		8513		229,154.85			11,076.07		218,078.78
Fund Equities:											
Unobligated Balances (Unexpired)						-451,622.10				-230,724.80	-220,897.30
Accounts Payable										-4,791.83	4,791.83
Undelivered Orders						222,467.25				224,440.56	-1,973.31
	Subtotal	75		8513		-0-			11,076.07	-11,076.07	-0-
Office Of The Secretary Gift Fund											
Fund Resources:											
Undisbursed Funds	No Year	75		8514		2,566.95					2,566.95
Fund Equities:											
Unobligated Balances (Unexpired)	Subtotal	75		8514		-2,566.95					-2,566.95
Patients' Benefit Fund, National Institutes Of Health											
Fund Resources:											
Undisbursed Funds	No Year	75		8888		139,811.43	37,613.14	-22,495.15	14,560.33		140,369.09
Unrealized Discount On Investments						-29,582.59		23,495.15			-6,087.44
Investments In Public Debt Securities						307,000.00		-1,000.00			306,000.00
Fund Equities:											
Unobligated Balances (Unexpired)						-346,439.10				9,024.13	-355,463.23
Accounts Payable										-56,761.06	-14,028.68
Undelivered Orders						-70,789.74				70,789.74	-70,789.74
	Subtotal	75		8888		-0-	37,613.14		14,560.33	23,052.81	-0-
Patients' Benefit Fund, Health Resources And Services Administration											
Fund Resources:											
Undisbursed Funds	No Year	75		8889		313,514.39			-31,498.30	47,215.25	345,012.69
Fund Equities:											
Unobligated Balances (Unexpired)						-147,431.13					-194,646.38

Footnotes At End Of Chapter

Appropriations, Outlays, and Balances – Continued

Title	Reg	Tr From	Account Number	Sub No.	Period of Availability	Balances, Beginning Of Fiscal Year	Appropriations And Other Obligational Authority[1]	Transfers Borrowings And Investment (Net)[2]	Outlays (Net)	Balances Withdrawn And Other Transactions[3]	Balances, End Of Fiscal Year[4]
Patients' Benefit Fund, Health Resources And Services Administration - Continued											
Fund Equities: - Continued											
Accounts Payable						-10,107.07				-10,107.07	
Undelivered Orders						-155,976.19				-5,609.88	-150,366.31
Subtotal	75		8889			-0-			-31,498.30	31,498.30	-0-
Total, Program Support Center							490,873,913.68		515,787,876.48	-24,913,962.80	
Office Of The Inspector General											
General Fund Accounts											
Office Of The Inspector General, Departmental Management											
Fund Resources:											
Undisbursed Funds	75		0128		2007-2010		3,000,000.00		5,483.37		2,994,516.63
					2007	24,702,020.66	39,807,660.00		57,353,096.90		7,-17,545,436.90
					2006	8,634,565.53			19,388,079.24		7,-5,313,941.42
					2005	4,791,554.00			10,053,918.86		7,-1,419,353.33
					2004	2,612,486.45			738,004.50		4,053,549.50
					2003	8,160,448.69			126,005.33		2,486,481.12
					2002	8					
					2001				4,144.50	156,304.19	
					No Year	24,918,838.04	25,000,000.00		23,921,385.32		25,997,452.72
Accounts Receivable						8,10,755,308.37				-4,793,601.17	15,548,909.54
Unfilled Customer Orders						4,622,698.23				-72,336,170.76	76,958,868.99
Fund Equities:											
Unobligated Balances (Expired)						8,3,278,790.96				8,477,762.24	-11,756,553.20
Unobligated Balances (Unexpired)						-24,918,838.04				-788,962.84	-24,129,875.20
Accounts Payable						8,7,718,368.85				1,356,446.87	-9,074,815.72
Undelivered Orders						-45,281,922.12				24,145,763.45	-69,427,685.57
Subtotal	75		0128			-0-	67,807,660.00		111,590,118.02	-43,782,458.02	-0-
Total, Office Of The Inspector General							67,807,660.00		111,590,118.02	-43,782,458.02	
Deductions For Offsetting Receipts											
Proprietary Receipts From The Public							-66,714,764,365.55		-66,714,764,365.55		
Intrabudgetary Transactions							-190,812,702,746.65		-190,812,702,746.65		
Total, Offsetting Receipts							-257,527,467,112.20		-257,527,467,112.20		
Total, Department Of Health And Human Services							679,592,218,859.04	46,687,845.02	672,036,433,780.15	7,602,472,923.91	

Appropriations, Outlays, and Balances - Continued

Appropriation or Fund Account		Period of Availability	Account Symbol				Balances, Beginning Of Fiscal Year	Appropriations And Other Obligational Authority[1]	Transfers Borrowings And Investment (Net)[2]	Outlays (Net)	Balances Withdrawn And Other Transactions[3]	Balances, End Of Fiscal Year[4]
Title			Dept		Account Number	Sub No.						
			Reg	Tr From								
Memorandum												
Financing Accounts												
Public Enterprise Funds												
Health Professions Graduate Student Loan Guaranteed Loan Financing Account												
Fund Resources:												
Undisbursed Funds		No Year	75		4304		143,296,386.33			36,201,266.08		107,095,120.25
Accounts Receivable							17,577.12			———		17,577.12
Fund Equities:												
Unobligated Balances (Unexpired)							-143,313,963.45			———	-36,201,266.08	-107,112,697.37
Subtotal			75		4304		-0-			36,201,266.08	-36,201,266.08	-0-
Health Care Guaranteed Loan Financing Account, Health Resources And Services Administration												
Fund Resources:												
Undisbursed Funds		No Year	75		4442		2,879,925.15			-1,073,923.45		3,953,848.60
Fund Equities:												
Unobligated Balances (Unexpired)							-2,879,925.15			———	1,073,923.45	-3,953,848.60
Subtotal			75		4442		-0-			-1,073,923.45	1,073,923.45	-0-
Total, Financing Accounts							———			35,127,342.63	-35,127,342.63	———

Appropriations, Outlays, and Balances – Continued

Footnotes

1. The amounts in this column, unless otherwise footnoted, represent appropriations, increases and rescissions in borrowing authority or new contract authority. Appropriation accounts with appropriation transfer activity are presented in Table 1 (Appropriations and Appropriation Transfers) at the end of this chapter.

2. The amounts in this column, unless otherwise footnoted, represent transfers - other than appropriation transfers, borrowings (gross), investments (net), unrealized discounts or funds held outside the Treasury.

3. The amounts in this column, unless otherwise footnoted, represent obligated balances canceled for fiscal year 2002 pursuant to 31 U.S.C. 1553, changes in unfilled customer orders, accounts receivable, accounts payable, undelivered orders, unobligated balances and adjustments to borrowing and contract authority.

4. Unobligated balances for no-year or unexpired multiple year accounts are available for obligation; unobligated balances for expired fiscal year accounts are not available for obligation.

5. Pursuant to 120 Stat 484, the balance for this account has been extended beyond the normal period of availability to liquidate obligations.

6. Represents capital transfer to miscellaneous receipts.

7. Subject to disposition by the administrative agency.

8. The opening balances of the following accounts have been adjusted during the current fiscal year and do not agree with last year's closing balances:

Account	Adjustment
75 X 0390 - Unobligated Balance (Unexpired)	-15,687,652.06
75 X 0390 - Undelivered Orders	-144,258,244.36
75 00 0390 - Undisbursed Funds	246,304.80
75 06 0390 - Unobligated Balance (Expired)	159,341,063.52
75 9900 0390 - Undisbursed Funds	358,528.09
75 X 0849- Unobligated Balance (Unexpired)	-1,770,000.00
75 X 0849 - Undelivered Orders	1,770,000.00
75 05 0892 - Accounts Payable	23,393.18
75 05 0892 - Undelivered Orders	1,549,958.35
75 05 0892 - Unfilled Customer Orders	-1,573,351.53
75 06 0894 - Unobligated Balance (Expired)	-2,681.61
75 06 0894 - Unfilled Customer Orders	2,681.61
75 06 0142 - Unobligated Balance (Expired)	2,012,525.64
75 06 0142 - Unfilled Customer Orders	-960,889.45
75 0406 0142 - Undelivered Orders	-1,051,626.19
75 0507 0142 - Accounts Payable	2,814,352.41
75 0507 0142 - Unobligated Balance (Unexpired)	46,500.50
75 01 0122 - Undisbursed Funds	-46,500.50
75 01 0122 - Accounts Payable	46,500.50
75 02 0122 - Undisbursed Funds	-46,500.50
75 02 0122 - Unobligated Balance (Expired)	58,452.04
75 01 0128 - Undisbursed Funds	-58,452.04
75 01 0128 - Accounts Payable	4,248,408.04
75 02 0128 - Undisbursed Funds	-4,189,956.00
75 02 0128 - Unobligated Balance (Expired)	-17,486,948.54
75 06 0128 - Accounts Receivable	17,486,948.54
75 01 8393 - Accounts Receivable	-14,912,095.07
75 01 8393 - Unobligated Balance (Expired)	14,912,095.07
20 X 8005 - Unobligated Balance (Unexpired)	
20 X 8005 - Accounts Payable	

Account	Adjustment
20 X 8004 - Unobligated Balance (Unexpired)	-15,039,149.19
20 X 8004 - Accounts Payable	15,039,149.19
75 06 0120 - Accounts Receivable	-51,120,495.80
75 06 0120 - Unfilled Customer Orders	51,120,495.80
75 06 0120 - Unobligated Balance (Expired)	1,975,647.84
75 06 0120 -Undelivered Orders	-1,975,647.84
75 06 0139 - Accounts Receivable	-59,359,196.00
75 06 0139 - Undelivered Orders	59,359,196.00
75 0140 - Unobligated Balance (Unexpired)	3,940,492.27
75 0140 - Undelivered Orders	-3,940,492.27

9. Includes $41,248.58 which represents payments for obligations of a closed account.

10. Includes $31,041.99 which represents payments for obligations of a closed account.

11. Includes $11,578,550.36 which represents payments for obligations of a closed account.

12. Includes $3,047,242.00 which represents payments for obligations of a closed account.

13. Includes $161,189.01 which represents payments for obligations of a closed account.

14. Includes $21.39 which is subject to disposition by the administrative agency.

15. "An error in the implementation of CMS' HIGLAS system created a business rule that incorrectly paid hospice benefits from the Part B account of SMI instead of HI for a period beginning in May 2005 to August 2007. The investments reported for HI are overstated and the investments reported for SMI are understated at September 30 for the principal amount of $8,484 million. CMS has reported a payable in HI and a receivable in SMI for the principle amount of $8,484 million to report the hospice benefit expense correctly. The interest impact has not yet been determined. Once the interest impact is determined, the investments will be corrected for both interest and principal in Fiscal Year 2008."

16. Pursuant to 110 Stat 2125, Sec 404(e) the balance for this account has been extended beyond the normal period of availability to liquidate obligations.

Appropriations, Outlays, and Balances - Continued

Footnotes

Table 1 - Appropriations And Appropriation Transfers - Department Of Health And Human Services

Department Regular	Fiscal Year	Account Symbol	Net Appropriations And Appropriations Transfers	Appropriation Amount	Net Appropriation Transfers	Department Regular Involved	Fiscal Year Involved	Accounts Involved	Amount From or To (-)
20	X	8004	-46,088,337,974.44	0.00	-46,088,337,974.44	75	X	8307	-10,334,120.86
						75	X	8308	-45,474,845,869.16
						75	06	8308	-111,515,975.97
						75	07	8308	-491,642,008.45
20	X	8005	-724,036,515.38	0.00	-724,036,515.38	75	X	8393	-158,553,589.53
						75	07	8393	-565,482,925.85
75	X	0140	0.00	100,000,000.00	-100,000,000.00	75	X	0943	-100,000,000.00
75	07	0140	696,325,822.09	60,199,649.00	636,126,173.09	70	07	0712	11,686,948.26
						70	07	0713	30,439,224.83
						75	07	0350	495,000,000.00
						75	07	0846	49,500,000.00
						75	07	0885	49,500,000.00
75	X	0330	41,223.00	0.00	41,223.00	75	07	0350	41,223.00
75	07	0350	4,542,431,767.00	5,082,027,684.00	-539,595,917.00	75	07	0140	-495,000,000.00
						75	X	0330	-41,223.00
						75	X	0365	-44,554,694.00
75	X	0365	44,554,694.00	0.00	44,554,694.00	75	07	0350	44,554,694.00
75	X	0390	201,508,217.00	150,000,000.00	51,508,217.00	75	07	0390	51,508,217.00
75	07	0390	2,242,313,845.00	2,301,122,062.00	-58,808,217.00	75	X	0390	-51,508,217.00
						75	X	0391	-7,300,000.00
75	X	0391	361,225,637.00	353,925,637.00	7,300,000.00	75	07	0390	7,300,000.00
75	X	0600	-271,075,304.62	0.00	-271,075,304.62	75	07	0600	-271,075,304.62
75	07	0600	1,840,319,334.62	1,569,244,030.62	271,075,304.62	75	X	0600	271,075,304.62
75	07	0807	317,570,000.00	316,850,000.00	720,000.00	75	07	0819	62,000.00
						75	07	0889	216,000.00
						75	07	0896	105,000.00
						75	07	0897	337,000.00
75	07	0819	66,371,520.00	66,445,520.00	-74,000.00	75	07	0807	-62,000.00
						75	07	0893	-12,000.00
75	07	0838	2,500,000.00	0.00	2,500,000.00	75	07	0885	2,500,000.00
75	07	0843	1,045,467,970.00	1,047,259,970.00	-1,792,000.00	75	07	0891	-1,792,000.00
75	07	0844	1,252,765,000.00	1,254,707,000.00	-1,942,000.00	75	07	0891	-1,942,000.00
75	07	0846	1,047,001,000.00	1,096,401,000.00	-49,400,000.00	75	07	0140	-49,500,000.00
						75	07	0896	100,000.00
75	07	0848	1,131,633,000.00	1,133,240,000.00	-1,607,000.00	75	07	0862	-1,607,000.00
75	07	0849	4,792,624,260.00	4,797,639,260.00	-5,015,000.00	75	07	0891	-5,015,000.00
75	07	0851	1,932,580,300.00	1,935,808,300.00	-3,228,000.00	75	07	0891	-3,228,000.00
75	07	0862	726,358,676.00	721,118,676.00	5,240,000.00	75	07	0848	1,607,000.00
						75	07	0872	538,000.00
						75	07	0887	1,130,000.00
						75	07	0888	866,000.00
						75	07	0890	600,000.00
						75	07	0898	499,000.00
75	07	0872	2,922,391,300.00	2,922,929,300.00	-538,000.00	75	07	0862	-538,000.00

Footnotes At End Of Chapter

Appropriations, Outlays, and Balances – Continued

Footnotes

Table 1 - Appropriations And Appropriation Transfers - Department Of Health And Human Services

Department Regular	Fiscal Year	Account Symbol	Net Appropriations And Appropriations Transfers	Appropriation Amount	Net Appropriation Transfers	Department Regular Involved	Fiscal Year Involved	Accounts Involved	Amount From or To (-)
75	07	0873	389,066,310.00	389,703,310.00	-637,000.00	75	07	0893	-637,000.00
75	07	0884	1,852,995,540.00	1,855,867,540.00	-2,872,000.00	75	07	0891	-2,872,000.00
75	07	0885	4,264,034,050.00	4,417,208,050.00	-153,174,000.00	72	X	1028	-99,000,000.00
						75	07	0140	-49,500,000.00
						75	07	0838	-2,500,000.00
						75	07	0891	-2,174,000.00
75	07	0886	1,532,998,400.00	1,535,545,400.00	-2,557,000.00	75	07	0891	-2,557,000.00
75	07	0887	665,986,090.00	667,116,090.00	-1,130,000.00	75	07	0862	-1,130,000.00
75	07	0888	507,374,370.00	508,240,370.00	-866,000.00	75	07	0862	-866,000.00
75	07	0889	137,187,710.00	137,403,710.00	-216,000.00	75	07	0807	-216,000.00
75	07	0890	392,991,680.00	393,667,680.00	-676,000.00	75	07	0862	-600,000.00
						75	07	0891	-76,000.00
75	07	0891	508,256,410.00	486,491,410.00	21,765,000.00	75	07	0843	1,792,000.00
						75	07	0844	1,942,000.00
						75	07	0849	5,015,000.00
						75	07	0851	3,228,000.00
						75	07	0884	2,872,000.00
						75	07	0885	2,174,000.00
						75	07	0886	2,557,000.00
						75	07	0890	76,000.00
						75	07	0892	2,109,000.00
75	07	0892	1,402,385,080.00	1,404,494,080.00	-2,109,000.00	75	07	0891	-2,109,000.00
75	07	0893	1,001,951,700.00	1,000,620,700.00	1,331,000.00	75	07	0819	12,000.00
						75	07	0873	637,000.00
						75	07	0894	674,000.00
						75	07	0898	8,000.00
75	07	0894	435,584,670.00	436,258,670.00	-674,000.00	75	07	0893	-674,000.00
75	07	0896	121,371,080.00	121,576,080.00	-205,000.00	75	07	0807	-105,000.00
						75	07	0846	-100,000.00
75	07	0897	199,107,000.00	199,444,000.00	-337,000.00	75	07	0807	-337,000.00
75	07	0898	296,379,920.00	296,886,920.00	-507,000.00	75	07	0862	-499,000.00
						75	07	0893	-8,000.00
75	X	0943	782,287,989.00	679,420,000.00	102,867,989.00	75	X	0140	100,000,000.00
						75	07	0943	2,693,989.00
						75	0708	0943	174,000.00
75	07	0943	5,054,236,278.00	5,055,702,267.00	-1,465,989.00	75	X	0943	-2,693,989.00
						75	0708	0943	1,228,000.00
75	0708	0943	134,367,656.00	135,769,656.00	-1,402,000.00	75	X	0943	-174,000.00
						75	07	0943	-1,228,000.00
75	X	0944	304,000.00	0.00	304,000.00	75	07	0944	304,000.00
75	07	0944	74,907,505.00	75,211,505.00	-304,000.00	75	X	0944	-304,000.00
75	X	8307	10,334,120.86	0.00	10,334,120.86	20	X	8004	10,334,120.86
75	X	8308	45,474,845,869.16	0.00	45,474,845,869.16	20	X	8004	45,474,845,869.16
75	06	8308	111,515,975.97	0.00	111,515,975.97	20	X	8004	111,515,975.97
75	07	8308	491,642,008.45	0.00	491,642,008.45	20	X	8004	491,642,008.45
75	X	8393	158,553,589.53	0.00	158,553,589.53	20	X	8005	158,553,589.53

Appropriations, Outlays, and Balances - Continued

Footnotes

Table 1 - Appropriations And Appropriation Transfers - Department Of Health And Human Services

Department Regular	Fiscal Year	Account Symbol	Net Appropriations And Appropriations Transfers	Appropriation Amount	Net Appropriation Transfers	Department Regular Involved	Fiscal Year Involved	Accounts Involved	Amount From or To (-)
75	07	8393	565,482,925.85	0.00	565,482,925.85	20	X	8005	565,482,925.85
Totals			44,648,671,699.09	44,705,545,526.00	-56,873,826.91				-56,873,826.91

Appropriations, Outlays, and Balances – Continued

Appropriation or Fund Account — Title	Period of Availability	Reg	Tr From	Account Number	Sub No.	Balances, Beginning Of Fiscal Year	Appropriations And Other Obligational Authority[1]	Transfers Borrowings And Investment (Net)[2]	Outlays (Net)	Balances Withdrawn And Other Transactions[3]	Balances, End Of Fiscal Year[4]
Department Of Homeland Security											
Departmental Management And Operations											
General Fund Accounts											
Departmental Operations, Departmental Management											
Fund Resources:											
Undisbursed Funds	2003	70		0100		892,748.35			-256.00		893,004.35
	No Year					30,213,806.42			6,672,008.89		23,541,797.53
Fund Equities:											
Unobligated Balances (Expired)						-125,172.00				1.00	-125,173.00
Unobligated Balances (Unexpired)						-12,084,003.15				2,658,414.63	-14,742,417.78
Accounts Payable						-3,841,952.75				-401,438.37	-3,440,514.38
Undelivered Orders						-15,055,426.87				-8,928,730.15	-6,126,696.72
Subtotal		70		0100		-0-			6,671,752.89	-6,671,752.89	-0-
Counterterrorism Fund, Departmental Management, Department Of Homeland Security											
Fund Resources:											
Undisbursed Funds	No Year	70		0101		39,658,041.95	-16,000,000.00		-113,903.56		23,771,945.51
Fund Equities:											
Unobligated Balances (Unexpired)						-16,043,039.00				-10,491,236.00	-5,551,803.00
Accounts Payable						-15,514,977.67				-7,970,935.15	-7,544,042.52
Undelivered Orders						-8,100,025.28				2,576,074.71	-10,676,099.99
Subtotal		70		0101		-0-	-16,000,000.00		-113,903.56	-15,886,096.44	-0-
Department-Wide Technology Investments, Departmental Management											
Fund Resources:											
Undisbursed Funds	2003-2004	70		0102		4,359,223.78					4,359,223.78
	No Year					22,950,310.48	11,979,761.00		10,280,590.97		24,649,480.51
Fund Equities:											
Unobligated Balances (Expired)						-4,359,223.78					-4,359,223.78
Unobligated Balances (Unexpired)						-3,152,356.73				8,389,953.12	-11,542,309.85
Accounts Payable						-3,692,188.25				-2,490,555.67	-1,201,632.58
Undelivered Orders						-16,105,765.50				-4,200,227.42	-11,905,538.08
Subtotal		70		0102		-0-	11,979,761.00		10,280,590.97	1,699,170.03	-0-
Office Of The Secretary And Executive Management, Departmental Management, Department Of Homeland Security											
Fund Resources:											
Undisbursed Funds	2007	70		0110		32,045,969.25	95,336,500.00		62,203,405.93		33,133,094.07
	2006					12,823,044.90	-1,200,962.00		22,982,739.06		7,862,268.19
	2005					8,992,798.38			5,228,263.67		7,594,781.23
	2004					46,989,811.28			891,731.23		8,101,067.15
	No Year								18,260,239.90		28,729,571.38
Accounts Receivable						671,007.18				655,573.55	15,433.63
Unfilled Customer Orders						419,690.09				47,492.35	372,197.74
Fund Equities:											
Unobligated Balances (Expired)						-7,334,731.94				8,031,840.73	-15,366,572.67
Unobligated Balances (Unexpired)						-26,072,182.16				-20,319,313.52	-5,752,868.64
Accounts Payable						-7,755,957.56				1,840,473.27	-9,596,430.83

Appropriations, Outlays, and Balances - Continued

Appropriation or Fund Account — Title	Account Symbol — Dept Reg	Tr From	Account Number	Sub No.	Period of Availability	Balances, Beginning Of Fiscal Year	Appropriations And Other Obligational Authority[1]	Transfers Borrowings And Investment (Net)[2]	Outlays (Net)	Balances Withdrawn And Other Transactions[3]	Balances, End Of Fiscal Year[4]
Undelivered Orders						-60,779,449.42			109,566,379.79	-5,686,908.17	-55,092,541.25
	70		0110		Subtotal	-0-	94,135,538.00			-15,430,841.79	-0-
Office Of The Under Secretary For Management, Departmental Management, Department Of Homeland Security											
Fund Resources:											
Undisbursed Funds	70		0111		2007	54,407,144.13	141,334,000.00		83,200,425.60		58,133,574.40
					2006	6,769,687.39	-512,855.00		43,772,884.05		10,121,405.08
					2005	1,370,376.66			-2,284,454.19		9,054,141.58
					2004-2005	13,752,539.58			180,376.24		1,190,000.42
					2004	68,203,528.15	8,206,000.00		4,302,259.44		9,450,280.14
					No Year				5,646,973.48		70,762,554.67
Accounts Receivable						346,266.00				-705,124.84	1,051,390.84
Unfilled Customer Orders						5,699,605.13				-9,694,117.27	15,393,722.40
Fund Equities:											
Unobligated Balances (Expired)						-5,305,320.65				5,395,161.11	-10,700,481.76
Unobligated Balances (Unexpired)						-550,946.57				-467,615.04	-83,331.53
Accounts Payable						-15,236,179.05				2,977,612.61	-18,213,791.66
Undelivered Orders						-129,456,700.77				16,702,763.81	-146,159,464.58
	70		0111		Subtotal	-0-	149,027,145.00		134,818,464.62	14,208,680.38	-0-
Office Of The Chief Financial Officer, Departmental Management, Department Of Homeland Security											
Fund Resources:											
Undisbursed Funds	70		0112		2007	6,930,502.61	26,000,000.00		17,082,787.05		8,917,212.95
					2006	250,652.09	-45,080.00		5,921,416.22		964,006.39
					2005				-1,774.34		252,426.43
Fund Equities:											
Unobligated Balances (Expired)						-124,432.95				839,005.37	-963,438.32
Accounts Payable						-1,591,384.87				330,027.70	-1,921,412.57
Undelivered Orders						-5,465,336.88				1,783,458.00	-7,248,794.88
	70		0112		Subtotal	-0-	25,954,920.00		23,002,428.93	2,952,491.07	-0-
Office Of The Chief Information Officer, Departmental Management, Department Of Homeland Security											
Fund Resources:											
Undisbursed Funds	70		0113		2007	42,759,523.39	79,057,022.73		39,943,912.20		39,113,110.53
					2006	7,238,021.84	-461,874.00		32,948,069.68		9,349,579.71
					2005				2,445,458.19		4,792,563.65
					No Year	207,090,033.11	251,492,000.00		164,016,676.76		294,565,356.35
Accounts Receivable						3,057,387.27				-259,397.76	259,397.76
Unfilled Customer Orders										2,010,776.09	1,046,611.18
Fund Equities:											
Unobligated Balances (Expired)						-2,295,065.67				-704,006.46	-1,591,059.21
Unobligated Balances (Unexpired)						-67,636,055.97				18,923,022.24	-86,559,078.21
Accounts Payable						-35,680,970.27				4,933,948.46	-40,614,918.73
Undelivered Orders						-154,532,873.70				65,828,689.33	-220,361,563.03
	70		0113		Subtotal	-0-	330,087,148.73		239,354,116.83	90,733,031.90	-0-

Appropriations, Outlays, and Balances – Continued

Appropriation or Fund Account — Title	Period of Availability	Dept Reg	Tr From	Account Number	Sub No.	Balances, Beginning Of Fiscal Year	Appropriations And Other Obligational Authority[1]	Transfers Borrowings And Investment (Net)[2]	Outlays (Net)	Balances Withdrawn And Other Transactions[3]	Balances, End Of Fiscal Year[4]
Analysis And Operations, Departmental Management And Operations, Department Of Homeland Security											
Fund Resources:											
Undisbursed Funds	2007-2008	70		0115		148,515,427.47	307,663,000.00		112,085,052.54		195,577,947.46
	2006-2007					461,826.49			95,427,228.78		53,088,198.69
Accounts Receivable						905,491.65				-319,683.28	781,509.77
Unfilled Customer Orders										-832,272.28	1,737,763.93
Fund Equities:											
Unobligated Balances (Expired)						-49,962,231.80				1,893,369.40	-1,893,369.40
Unobligated Balances (Unexpired)						-5,374,213.37				-18,187,457.76	-31,774,774.04
Accounts Payable										43,136,534.66	-48,510,748.03
Undelivered Orders						-94,546,300.44				74,460,227.94	-169,006,528.38
	Subtotal	70		0115		-0-	307,663,000.00		207,512,281.32	100,150,718.68	-0-
Office Of The Federal Coordinator For Gulf Coast Rebuilding, Departmental Management And Operations, Department Of Homeland Security											
Fund Resources:											
Undisbursed Funds	2007	70		0116			3,000,000.00		2,062,449.66		937,550.34
Fund Equities:											
Unobligated Balances (Expired)										683,078.53	-683,078.53
Accounts Payable										75,197.84	-75,197.84
Undelivered Orders										179,273.97	-179,273.97
	Subtotal	70		0116		-0-	3,000,000.00		2,062,449.66	937,550.34	-0-
Intragovernmental Funds											
Working Capital Fund Departmental Management, Department Of Homeland Security											
Fund Resources:											
Undisbursed Funds	No Year	70		4640		1,994,738.67			-2,694,739.89		4,689,478.56
Accounts Receivable						11,616,492.11				-19,858,487.92	31,474,980.03
Unfilled Customer Orders						144,735,353.51				-41,755,484.02	186,490,837.53
Fund Equities:											
Unobligated Balances (Unexpired)						-6,780,456.27				1,576,348.99	-8,356,805.26
Accounts Payable						-13,940,211.02				10,084,412.31	-24,024,623.33
Undelivered Orders						-137,625,917.00				52,647,950.53	-190,273,867.53
	Subtotal	70		4640		-0-			-2,694,739.89	2,694,739.89	-0-
Trust Fund Accounts											
Gifts And Donations, Department Management, Department Of Homeland Security											
Fund Resources:											
Undisbursed Funds	No Year	70		8244		17,492,339.62	1,569,062.02	24,639,477.18	40,250,516.78		3,450,362.04
Unrealized Discount On Investments						-379,306.76		324,522.82			-54,783.94
Investments In Public Debt Securities						38,814,000.00		-24,964,000.00			13,850,000.00
Fund Equities:											
Unobligated Balances (Unexpired)						-13,721,667.80				-9,038,780.68	-4,682,887.12
Accounts Payable										1,672.52	-1,672.52
Undelivered Orders						-42,205,365.06				-29,644,346.60	-12,561,018.46

Appropriations, Outlays, and Balances - Continued

Appropriation or Fund Account — Title	Account Symbol Dept — Reg	Dept — Tr From	Account Number	Sub No.	Period of Availability	Balances, Beginning Of Fiscal Year	Appropriations And Other Obligational Authority[1]	Transfers Borrowings And Investment (Net)[2]	Outlays (Net)	Balances Withdrawn And Other Transactions[3]	Balances, End Of Fiscal Year[4]
	70		8244		Subtotal	-0-	1,569,062.02		40,250,516.78	-38,681,454.76	-0-
Total, Departmental Management And Operations							907,416,574.75		770,710,338.34	136,706,236.41	
Office Of The Inspector General											
General Fund Accounts											
Office Of The Inspector General, Department Of Homeland Security											
Fund Resources:											
Undisbursed Funds	70		0200		2007		85,185,000.00		78,583,814.71		6,601,185.29
					2006-2007	2,000,000.00			802,355.66		1,197,644.34
					2006	9,956,006.18			5,747,206.10		4,208,800.08
					2005	3,084,070.51			981,276.39		2,102,794.12
					2004	4,211,544.50			819,094.65		3,392,449.85
					2003	4,522,077.58			7,033.65		4,515,043.93
					2002	16,025,414.72	17,500,000.00		16,613,513.78		16,911,900.94
					No Year	700,485.36				700,485.36	
Accounts Receivable						1,445,151.72				-4,820,456.52	6,265,608.24
Unfilled Customer Orders						5,764,809.67				-2,213,751.17	7,978,560.84
Fund Equities:											
Unobligated Balances (Expired)						-4,038,475.87				32,127.54	-4,070,603.41
Unobligated Balances (Unexpired)						-9,389,937.82				1,338,233.17	-10,728,170.99
Accounts Payable						-4,003,710.01				799,862.59	-4,803,572.60
Undelivered Orders						-30,277,436.54				3,294,204.09	-33,571,640.63
	70		0200		Subtotal	-0-	102,685,000.00		103,554,294.94	-869,294.94	-0-
Total, Office Of The Inspector General							102,685,000.00		103,554,294.94	-869,294.94	
Citizenship And Immigration Services											
General Fund Accounts											
Citizenship And Immigration Services, Immigration Services, Department Of Homeland Security											
Fund Resources:											
Undisbursed Funds	70		0300		2007-2008		8,000,000.00				8,000,000.00
					2007		88,490,000.00		30,500,937.43		57,989,062.57
					2006	70,115,222.67			48,245,334.17		21,869,888.50
					2005	18,748,536.06			15,155,520.37		3,593,015.69
					2004	9,598,360.16			116,783.58		9,481,576.58
					2003	30,651,383.61		-15,465,058.00	923,492.40		14,262,833.21
					2002	33,756,002.23		-18,542,707.00	2,641,015.54	12,572,279.69	
					No Year	2,343,725.21	93,500,000.00		1,684,951.54		94,158,773.67
Accounts Receivable										-437,809.57	437,809.57
Unfilled Customer Orders						8,151,260.73				6,670,778.69	1,480,482.04
Fund Equities:											
Unobligated Balances (Expired)						-49,935,215.88				-38,160,978.31	-11,774,237.57

Footnotes At End Of Chapter

Appropriations, Outlays, and Balances – Continued

Appropriation or Fund Account — Title	Period of Availability	Dept Reg	Tr From	Account Number	Sub No.	Balances, Beginning Of Fiscal Year	Appropriations And Other Obligational Authority[1]	Transfers Borrowings And Investment (Net)[2]	Outlays (Net)	Balances Withdrawn And Other Transactions[3]	Balances, End Of Fiscal Year[4]
Citizenship And Immigration Services, Immigration Services, Department Of Homeland Security - Continued											
Fund Equities: - Continued											
Unobligated Balances (Unexpired)											
Accounts Payable						-2,269,304.00				96,724,053.39	-98,993,357.39
Undelivered Orders						-37,702,727.69				-12,264,731.50	-25,437,996.19
						-83,457,243.10				-8,389,392.42	-75,067,850.68
Subtotal		70		0300		-0-	189,990,000.00	-34,007,765.00	99,268,035.03	56,714,199.97	-0-
Special Fund Accounts											
Immigration Examination Fees, Immigration Services											
Fund Resources:											
Undisbursed Funds	No Year	70		5088		818,508,119.71	2,073,778,794.10		1,647,051,468.75	-1,641,164.77	1,245,235,445.06
Accounts Receivable						2,118,135.90					3,759,300.67
Unfilled Customer Orders						14,730,910.42				7,022,120.30	7,708,790.12
Fund Equities:											
Unobligated Balances (Unexpired)						-334,730,124.38				333,395,589.91	-668,125,714.29
Accounts Payable						-119,405,835.42				19,892,240.70	-139,298,076.12
Undelivered Orders						-381,221,206.23				68,058,539.21	-449,279,745.44
Subtotal		70		5088		-0-	2,073,778,794.10		1,647,051,468.75	426,727,325.35	-0-
Immigration Services, H-1 B Funded											
Fund Resources:											
Undisbursed Funds	No Year	70		5106		12,830,088.66	13,419,918.77		19,406,407.46		6,843,599.97
Fund Equities:											
Unobligated Balances (Unexpired)						-1,676,639.89				479,493.73	-2,156,133.62
Accounts Payable						-1,467,863.04				-404,887.32	-1,062,975.72
Undelivered Orders						-9,685,585.73				-6,061,095.10	-3,624,490.63
Subtotal		70		5106		-0-	13,419,918.77		19,406,407.46	-5,986,488.69	-0-
H-1B And L Fraud Prevention And Detection Account, Citizenship And Immigration Services, Department Of Homeland Security											
Fund Resources:											
Undisbursed Funds	No Year	70		5389		36,727,522.06	45,743,017.48		12,832,422.57		69,638,116.97
Fund Equities:											
Unobligated Balances (Unexpired)						-30,218,888.66				33,139,595.10	-63,358,483.76
Accounts Payable						-1,615,833.39				160,207.91	-1,776,041.30
Undelivered Orders						-4,892,800.01				-389,208.10	-4,503,591.91
Subtotal		70		5389		-0-	45,743,017.48		12,832,422.57	32,910,594.91	-0-
Total, Citizenship And Immigration Services							2,322,931,730.35	-34,007,765.00	1,778,558,333.81	510,365,631.54	
United States Secret Service											
General Fund Accounts											
Salaries And Expenses, United States Secret Service, Department Of Homeland Security											
Fund Resources:											
Undisbursed Funds	2006-2007	70		0400		35,500,564.00	-2,500,000.00		31,000,745.08		1,999,818.92
	2006					160,104,349.67	-450,000.00	157,122.54	115,495,345.51		44,316,126.70
	2005					43,301,854.48			8,343,733.94		34,958,120.54

Appropriations, Outlays, and Balances - Continued

Title	Reg	Tr From	Account Number	Sub No.	Period of Availability	Balances, Beginning Of Fiscal Year	Appropriations And Other Obligational Authority[1]	Transfers Borrowings And Investment (Net)[2]	Outlays (Net)	Balances Withdrawn And Other Transactions[3]	Balances, End Of Fiscal Year[4]
					2004	15,136,381.93			2,208,187.97		12,928,193.96
					2003	23,053,826.76			-6,667,583.24		29,721,410.00
					2002	12,987,202.25			-101,047.00	13,088,249.25	
					No Year	47,559,755.15	209,771,733.49	-14,000,000.00	217,203,747.75		26,127,740.89
					2006	157,122.54		-157,122.54			
Funds Held Outside The Treasury											
Accounts Receivable						8,209,934.96				2,610,267.72	5,599,667.24
Unfilled Customer Orders						12,871,920.67				12,255,363.82	616,556.85
Fund Equities:											
Unobligated Balances (Expired)						-24,998,555.00				9,838,611.59	-34,837,166.59
Unobligated Balances (Unexpired)						-29,439,887.80				-26,762,397.07	-2,677,490.73
Accounts Payable						-84,115,167.81				-45,656,310.48	-38,458,857.33
Undelivered Orders						-220,329,301.80				-140,035,181.35	-80,294,120.45
	70		0400		Subtotal	-0-	206,821,733.49	-14,000,000.00	367,483,130.01	-174,661,396.52	-0-
Acquisition, Construction, Improvements, And Related Expenses, United States Secret Service, Department Of Homeland Security											
Fund Resources:											
Undisbursed Funds	70		0401		No Year	4,215,490.63	3,725,000.00		4,056,239.24		3,884,251.39
Fund Equities:											
Unobligated Balances (Unexpired)						-1,772,501.22				48,663.62	-1,821,164.84
Accounts Payable						-628,174.34				-150,083.19	-478,091.15
Undelivered Orders						-1,814,815.07				-229,819.67	-1,584,995.40
	70		0401		Subtotal	-0-	3,725,000.00		4,056,239.24	-331,239.24	-0-
Protection, Administration, And Training, U.S. Secret Service, Department Of Homeland Security											
Fund Resources:											
Undisbursed Funds	70		0403		2007-2009		18,400,000.00				18,400,000.00
					2007-2008		18,000,000.00				18,000,000.00
					2007		927,357,000.00	12,805,824.17	771,160,897.68		169,001,926.49
					No Year		3,605,800.00		1,500.00		3,604,300.00
Funds Held Outside The Treasury											
Accounts Receivable					2007			1,194,175.83		-778,119.73	1,194,175.83
Unfilled Customer Orders										-1,332,855.22	778,119.73
Fund Equities:											1,332,855.22
Unobligated Balances (Expired)										1,851,379.90	-1,851,379.90
Unobligated Balances (Unexpired)										39,903,349.00	-39,903,349.00
Accounts Payable										58,901,995.55	-58,901,995.55
Undelivered Orders										111,654,652.82	-111,654,652.82
	70		0403		Subtotal	-0-	967,362,800.00	14,000,000.00	771,162,397.68	210,200,402.32	-0-
Investigations And Field Operations, U.S. Secret Service, Department Of Homeland Security											
Fund Resources:											
Undisbursed Funds	70		0404		2007		308,635,000.00		279,059,978.61		29,575,021.39
					No Year		6,000,000.00		4,195,936.82		1,804,063.18
Accounts Receivable										-3,921,678.01	3,921,678.01
Unfilled Customer Orders										-6,959,580.35	6,959,580.35
Fund Equities:											
Unobligated Balances (Expired)										770,408.94	-770,408.94
Accounts Payable										2,907,844.98	-2,907,844.98

Footnotes At End Of Chapter

Appropriations, Outlays, and Balances – Continued

Appropriation or Fund Account: Title	Period of Availability	Reg	Tr From	Account Number	Sub No.	Balances, Beginning Of Fiscal Year	Appropriations And Other Obligational Authority[1]	Transfers Borrowings And Investment (Net)[2]	Outlays (Net)	Balances Withdrawn And Other Transactions[3]	Balances, End Of Fiscal Year[4]
Investigations And Field Operations, U.S. Secret Service, Department Of Homeland Security - Continued											
Fund Equities: - Continued											
Undelivered Orders						-0-				38,582,089.01	-38,582,089.01
Subtotal		70		0404			314,635,000.00		283,255,915.43	31,379,084.57	-0-
Total, United States Secret Service							1,492,544,533.49		1,425,957,682.36	66,586,851.13	
Security, Enforcement, and Investigations											
Office Of The Undersecretary For Border And Transportation Security:											
General Fund Accounts											
Salaries And Expenses, Office Of The Under Secretary For Border And Transportation Security, Department Of Homeland Security											
Fund Resources:											
Undisbursed Funds	2006	70		0520					-175.51		175.51
	2005					718,016.17			9,681.89		708,334.28
	2004					1,700,576.87			-12,867.18		1,713,444.05
Fund Equities:											
Unobligated Balances (Expired)						-899,657.00				-6,451.53	-893,205.47
Accounts Payable						-107,404.73				-49,690.76	-57,713.97
Undelivered Orders						-1,411,531.31				59,503.09	-1,471,034.40
Subtotal		70		0520		-0-			-3,360.80	3,360.80	-0-
Total, Office Of The Undersecretary For Border And Transportation Security									-3,360.80	3,360.80	
Transportation Security Administration:											
General Fund Accounts											
Transportation Security Administration, Border And Transportation Security											
Fund Resources:											
Undisbursed Funds	2003	70		0508		4,962,371.05					4,962,371.05
	2002-2003					2,158,706.89			-903,635.65		3,062,342.54
	No Year					71,817,079.21	69,480,000.00	83,120,000.00	47,953,447.57		176,463,631.64
Accounts Receivable						-1,307,847.15				-2,642,039.50	1,334,192.35
Unfilled Customer Orders						24,070,082.42				10,047,716.51	14,022,365.91
Fund Equities:											
Unobligated Balances (Expired)						-6,807,215.95				-6,063,866.83	-743,349.12
Unobligated Balances (Unexpired)						195,584,601.95				203,048,547.71	-7,463,945.76
Accounts Payable						-86,622,154.86				-26,129,556.45	-60,492,598.41
Undelivered Orders						-203,855,623.56				-72,710,613.36	-131,145,010.20
Subtotal		70		0508		-0-	69,480,000.00	83,120,000.00	47,049,811.92	105,550,188.08	-0-

Appropriations, Outlays, and Balances - Continued

Appropriation or Fund Account — Title	Period of Availability	Reg	Tr From	Account Number	Sub No.	Balances, Beginning Of Fiscal Year	Appropriations And Other Obligational Authority[1]	Transfers Borrowings And Investment (Net)[2]	Outlays (Net)	Balances Withdrawn And Other Transactions[3]	Balances, End Of Fiscal Year[4]
Federal Air Marshals, Transportation Security Administration, Department Of Homeland Security											
Fund Resources:											
Undisbursed Funds	2007-2008	70		0541			5,000,000.00				5,000,000.00
	2007						714,294,000.00		653,048,692.92		61,245,307.08
	2006					67,492,730.95		-386,126.00	54,412,174.70		12,694,430.25
	2005					19,366,929.43			10,645,275.64		8,721,653.79
	No Year					16,858,355.04			6,572,252.27		10,286,102.77
Accounts Receivable						996,045.76				-318,296.81	318,296.81
Unfilled Customer Orders										299,688.88	696,356.88
Fund Equities:											
Unobligated Balances (Expired)						-6,619,222.53				-2,794,532.91	-3,824,689.62
Unobligated Balances (Unexpired)						-7,668,340.73				2,215,181.74	-9,883,522.47
Accounts Payable						-53,181,177.35				-1,779,176.89	-51,402,000.46
Undelivered Orders						-37,245,320.57				-3,393,385.54	-33,851,935.03
	Subtotal	70		0541		-0-	719,294,000.00	-386,126.00	724,678,395.53	-5,770,521.53	-0-
Aviation Security, Transportation Security Administration, Department Of Homeland Security											
Fund Resources:											
Undisbursed Funds	2007-2009	70		0550			80,000,000.00				80,000,000.00
	2007-2008						2,381,398,973.25		1,199,631,856.66		1,181,767,116.59
	2006-2007					1,211,093,605.60	-62,712,000.00	-51,990,187.00	735,821,767.46		360,569,651.14
	2004-2005					474,786.32			317,601.19		157,185.13
	No Year					472,208,711.03	310,000,000.00	-12,660,000.00	191,519,372.41		578,029,338.62
Accounts Receivable						4,097,224.01				3,711,118.86	386,105.15
Unfilled Customer Orders						19,319,567.85				-3,690,160.28	23,009,728.13
Fund Equities:											
Unobligated Balances (Expired)						-102,072.71				12,824,782.30	-12,926,855.01
Unobligated Balances (Unexpired)						-438,079,333.04				156,849,539.45	-594,928,872.49
Accounts Payable						-469,025,303.23				-107,850,937.72	-361,174,365.51
Undelivered Orders						-799,987,185.83				454,901,845.92	-1,254,889,031.75
	Subtotal	70		0550		-0-	2,708,686,973.25	-64,650,187.00	2,127,290,597.72	516,746,188.53	-0-
Surface Transportation Security, Transportation Security Administration, Department Of Homeland Security											
Fund Resources:											
Undisbursed Funds	2007-2008	70		0551			37,200,000.00		26,761,574.83		10,438,425.17
	2006-2007					11,549,026.25		-500,000.00	5,023,751.18		6,025,275.07
	2005-2006					10,518,126.97			5,377,294.24		5,140,832.73
	2004-2005					78,237,113.85			34,066,223.57		44,170,890.28
	No Year					1,486,627.35			793,059.54		693,567.81
Fund Equities:											
Unobligated Balances (Expired)						-3,559,387.90				4,305,072.98	-7,864,460.88
Unobligated Balances (Unexpired)						-7,465,748.58				-4,014,344.25	-3,451,404.33
Accounts Payable						-13,800,620.83				3,522,838.33	-17,323,459.16
Undelivered Orders						-76,965,137.11				-39,135,470.42	-37,829,666.69
	Subtotal	70		0551		-0-	37,200,000.00	-500,000.00	72,021,903.36	-35,321,903.36	-0-

Appropriations, Outlays, and Balances – Continued

Appropriation or Fund Account — Title	Period of Availability	Dept — Reg	Dept — Tr From	Account Number	Sub No.	Balances, Beginning Of Fiscal Year	Appropriations And Other Obligational Authority[1]	Transfers Borrowings And Investment (Net)[2]	Outlays (Net)	Balances Withdrawn And Other Transactions[3]	Balances, End Of Fiscal Year[4]
Intelligence, Transportation Security Administration, Border And Transportation Security, Department Of Homeland Security											
Fund Resources:											
Undisbursed Funds	2005	70		0552		2,636,155.16			193,857.70		2,442,297.46
	2004					663,789.46			50,930.15		612,859.31
Fund Equities:											
Unobligated Balances (Expired)						-1,025,949.81				-20,050.45	-1,005,899.36
Accounts Payable						-769,491.45				-253,055.70	-516,435.75
Undelivered Orders						-1,504,503.36				28,318.30	-1,532,821.66
Subtotal		70		0552		-0-			244,787.85	-244,787.85	-0-
Research And Development, Transportation Security Administration, Border And Transportation Security, Department Of Homeland Security											
Fund Resources:											
Undisbursed Funds	No Year	70		0553		87,963,006.47			49,558,023.78		38,404,982.69
Accounts Receivable						282,069.80				279,002.84	3,066.96
Unfilled Customer Orders						4,795,891.98				339,620.49	4,456,271.49
Fund Equities:											
Unobligated Balances (Unexpired)						-11,418,644.74				-198,258.87	-11,220,385.87
Accounts Payable						-12,329,875.34				-4,240,947.04	-8,088,928.30
Undelivered Orders						-69,292,448.17				-45,737,441.20	-23,555,006.97
Subtotal		70		0553		-0-			49,558,023.78	-49,558,023.78	-0-
Transportation Security Support, Transportation Security Administration, Department Of Homeland Security											
Fund Resources:											
Undisbursed Funds	2007-2008	70		0554		153,422,758.00	525,283,000.00		359,854,195.26		165,428,804.74
	2006-2007					60,431,425.89	-4,000,000.00		101,427,589.69		32,505,168.31
	2005-2006					5,916,028.90		-15,490,000.00	20,790,769.63		39,640,656.26
	2004-2005					4,808,945.20			-2,931,124.70		8,847,153.60
	No Year							-850,000.00	3,153,574.89		805,370.31
Accounts Receivable						1,630,628.46				1,284,042.56	346,585.90
Unfilled Customer Orders						15,703,763.56				10,785,088.85	4,918,674.71
Fund Equities:											
Unobligated Balances (Expired)						-9,541,318.28				-5,401,315.30	-4,140,002.98
Unobligated Balances (Unexpired)						-36,807,373.86				-24,030,835.34	-12,776,538.52
Accounts Payable						-78,932,529.81				-13,217,327.18	-65,715,202.63
Undelivered Orders						-116,632,328.06				53,228,341.64	-169,860,669.70
Subtotal		70		0554		-0-	521,283,000.00	-16,340,000.00	482,295,004.77	22,647,995.23	-0-
Transportation Vetting And Credentialing, Transportation Security Administration, Department Of Homeland Security											
Fund Resources:											
Undisbursed Funds	2007-2008	70		0557		44,528,624.84	43,490,000.00		25,611,258.29		17,878,741.71
	2006-2007					15,727,280.52		-960,000.00	29,091,948.37		14,476,676.47
	No Year								1,682,755.88		14,044,524.64
Unfilled Customer Orders										-1,000,000.00	1,000,000.00
Fund Equities:											
Unobligated Balances (Expired)										1,054,888.85	-1,054,888.85
Unobligated Balances (Unexpired)						-29,021,166.03				-12,999,503.56	-16,021,662.47
Accounts Payable						-10,483,011.09				2,049,926.66	-12,532,937.75
Undelivered Orders						-20,751,728.24				-2,961,274.49	-17,790,453.75

Appropriations, Outlays, and Balances - Continued

Appropriation or Fund Account — Title	Account Symbol — Dept Reg	Account Symbol — Dept Tr From	Account Number	Sub No.	Period of Availability	Balances, Beginning Of Fiscal Year	Appropriations And Other Obligational Authority[1]	Transfers Borrowings And Investment (Net)[2]	Outlays (Net)	Balances Withdrawn And Other Transactions[3]	Balances, End Of Fiscal Year[4]
	70		0557		Subtotal	-0-	43,490,000.00	-960,000.00	56,385,962.54	-13,855,962.54	-0-
Special Fund Accounts											
Aviation Security Capital Fund, Transportation Security Administration, Department Of Homeland Security											
Fund Resources:											
Undisbursed Funds	70		5385		No Year	306,657,497.43					461,598,025.56
Fund Equities:											
Unobligated Balances (Unexpired)						-14,308,907.56			-10,821,970.74		-3,486,936.82
Accounts Payable						-39,475,277.10			38,147,308.19		-77,622,585.29
Undelivered Orders						-252,873,312.77			127,615,190.68		-380,488,503.45
	70		5385		Subtotal	-0-			-154,940,528.13	154,940,528.13	-0-
Unclaimed Checkpoint Money, Transportation Security Administration, Department Of Homeland Security											
Fund Resources:											
Undisbursed Funds	70		5390		No Year	669,812.52	254,310.14	-669,813.00	-126,126.25		380,435.91
Fund Equities:											
Unobligated Balances (Unexpired)						-669,812.52				-289,376.61	-380,435.91
	70		5390		Subtotal	-0-	254,310.14	-669,813.00	-126,126.25	-289,376.61	-0-
Total, Transportation Security Administration							4,099,688,283.39	-386,126.00	3,404,457,833.09	694,844,324.30	
Federal Law Enforcement Training Center:											
General Fund Accounts											
Salaries And Expenses, FLETC, Department Of Homeland Security	70		0509								
Fund Resources:											
Undisbursed Funds					2007-2008		43,498,000.00		20,021,576.70		23,476,423.30
					2007		167,235,000.00		130,729,549.15		36,505,450.85
					2006-2007	34,535,649.20			20,393,665.39		14,141,983.81
					2006	25,874,221.69		-419,661.00	18,829,760.26		6,624,800.43
					2005-2006	10,625,803.54			8,343,041.65		2,282,761.89
					2005	4,735,021.06			1,363,419.86		3,371,601.20
					2004-2005	1,266,113.49			-10,150.56		1,276,264.05
					2003-2005	1,274,272.91			-7,031.63		1,281,304.54
					2004	4,839,439.15			1,266,950.45		3,572,488.70
					2003-2004	452,441.10			321,298.01		131,143.09
					2002-2004	190,845.57			-1,511.62		192,357.19
					2003	3,144,922.28			-106,580.21		3,251,502.49
					2002-2003	14,084.57					14,084.57
					2001-2003	46,152.28					46,152.28
					2002	2,651,419.23				2,651,419.23	
					2000-2002	31,320.84				31,320.84	
					No Year	2,957,421.54	300,000.00		2,316,991.68		940,429.86
Accounts Receivable						11,753,596.58				-4,155,514.69	15,909,111.27
Unfilled Customer Orders						5,596,414.79				-2,543,664.02	8,140,078.81

Appropriations, Outlays, and Balances – Continued

Appropriation or Fund Account — Title	Account Symbol Dept Reg	Tr From	Account Number	Sub No.	Period of Availability	Balances, Beginning Of Fiscal Year	Appropriations And Other Obligational Authority[1]	Transfers Borrowings And Investment (Net)[2]	Outlays (Net)	Balances Withdrawn And Other Transactions[3]	Balances, End Of Fiscal Year[4]
Salaries And Expenses, FLETC, Department Of Homeland Security - Continued											
Fund Equities:											
Unobligated Balances (Expired)						-15,066,219.19				2,173,502.94	-17,239,722.13
Unobligated Balances (Unexpired)						-41,244,788.88				-20,442,398.13	-20,802,390.75
Accounts Payable						-16,002,284.24				12,519,692.21	-28,521,976.45
Undelivered Orders						-37,675,847.51				16,918,001.49	-54,593,849.00
	70		0509		Subtotal	-0-	211,033,000.00	-419,661.00	203,460,979.13	7,152,359.87	-0-
Acquisition, Construction, Improvements And Related Expenses, Border And Transportation Security, FLETC, Department Of Homeland Security											
Fund Resources:											
Undisbursed Funds	70		0510		2006-2007	24,805,874.69			12,946,741.04		11,859,133.65
					2005-2006	105,993.68			76,057.58		29,936.10
					No Year	84,286,588.17	64,246,000.00		90,579,423.66		57,953,164.51
Accounts Receivable						3,080,013.60				-5,495,814.09	8,575,827.69
Unfilled Customer Orders						132,496,651.11				30,944,127.48	101,552,523.63
Fund Equities:											
Unobligated Balances (Expired)						-0.10				49,764.18	-49,764.28
Unobligated Balances (Unexpired)						-33,543,857.21				9,319,294.58	-42,863,151.79
Accounts Payable						-2,871,430.42				14,900,612.87	-17,772,043.29
Undelivered Orders						-208,359,833.52				-89,074,207.30	-119,285,626.22
	70		0510		Subtotal	-0-	64,246,000.00		103,602,222.28	-39,356,222.28	-0-
Trust Fund Accounts											
Gifts And Bequests, FLETC, Department Of Homeland Security											
Fund Resources:											
Undisbursed Funds	70		8360		No Year	382.99			382.99		
Fund Equities:											
Unobligated Balances (Unexpired)						-382.99				-382.99	
	70		8360		Subtotal	-0-			382.99	-382.99	-0-
Total, Federal Law Enforcement Training Center							275,279,000.00	-419,661.00	307,063,584.40	-32,204,245.40	
Immigration And Customs:											
General Fund Accounts											
Immigration And Customs Enforcement, Border And Transportation Security, Department Of Homeland Security											
Fund Resources:											
Undisbursed Funds	70		0504		2003	92,255,111.99		-290,193.03	38,261,254.41		53,703,664.55
					2002-2003	72,728.62					72,728.62
					2002	35,730,094.38			7,655,945.98	28,074,148.40	
					2001-2002	9,160.23				9,160.23	
					No Year	47,600,980.43		-10,492,005.00	-8,392,653.96		45,501,629.39
Funds Held Outside The Treasury					2003	-290,193.03		290,193.03			
Accounts Receivable						234,112.11				234,112.11	
Unfilled Customer Orders						4,191,995.43				1,961,341.02	2,230,654.41

Appropriations, Outlays, and Balances - Continued

Appropriation or Fund Account — Title	Period of Availability	Account Symbol — Dept Reg	Tr From	Account Number	Sub No.	Balances, Beginning Of Fiscal Year	Appropriations And Other Obligational Authority[1]	Transfers Borrowings And Investment (Net)[2]	Outlays (Net)	Balances Withdrawn And Other Transactions[3]	Balances, End Of Fiscal Year[4]
Fund Equities:											
Unobligated Balances (Expired)						-11,929,351.53				3,474,252.44	-15,403,603.97
Unobligated Balances (Unexpired)						-51,118,324.56				-38,261,976.74	-12,856,347.82
Accounts Payable						-22,384,338.96				90,347.45	-22,474,686.41
Undelivered Orders						-94,371,975.11				-43,597,936.34	-50,774,038.77
	Subtotal	70		0504		-0-		-10,492,005.00	37,524,546.43	-48,016,551.43	-0-
Salaries And Expenses, Immigration And Customs Enforcement, Border And Transportation Security, Department Of Homeland Security											
Fund Resources:											
Undisbursed Funds	2007-2008	70		0540			7,569,005.00		1,622.23		7,567,382.77
	2007						3,876,000,000.00		2,911,942,021.16		963,628,568.84
	2006-2007					321,910,675.68		-429,410.00	173,610,548.54		153,300,127.14
	2006					597,399,364.07		5,000,000.00	402,813,540.51		187,969,072.46
	2005-2006					87,627,281.78		-6,616,751.10	55,604,702.15		32,022,579.63
	2005					107,708,619.34			36,982,761.32		70,725,858.02
	2004					20,393,514.80		298,448.04	5,173,920.50		15,518,042.34
	No Year					12,897,294.86	14,559,281.00		10,218,699.27		17,237,876.59
Funds Held Outside The Treasury	2007							429,410.00			429,410.00
	2006					483,248.90		-483,248.90			
	2004					298,448.04		-298,448.04			
Accounts Receivable						27,899,988.71				10,441,044.29	17,458,944.42
Unfilled Customer Orders						153,774,239.92				49,081,530.67	104,692,709.25
Fund Equities:											
Unobligated Balances (Expired)						-42,573,821.30				-4,148,513.66	-38,425,307.64
Unobligated Balances (Unexpired)						-250,985,096.78				-229,048,252.21	-21,936,844.57
Accounts Payable						-306,252,703.50				82,466,096.97	-388,718,800.47
Undelivered Orders						-730,581,054.52				390,888,564.26	-1,121,469,618.78
	Subtotal	70		0540		-0-	3,898,128,286.00	-2,100,000.00	3,596,347,815.68	299,680,470.32	-0-
Federal Protective Service, Immigration And Customs Enforcement, Border And Transportation Security, Department Of Homeland Security											
Fund Resources:											
Undisbursed Funds	2006	70		0542		8,595,127.67			7,128,702.56		1,466,425.11
	No Year					81,759,068.02			-102,548,890.32		184,307,958.34
Accounts Receivable						60,116,002.54				-2,200,653.23	62,316,655.77
Unfilled Customer Orders						237,262,577.07				-6,679,446.52	243,942,023.59
Fund Equities:											
Unobligated Balances (Expired)						-158,419.97					-158,419.97
Unobligated Balances (Unexpired)						-84,749,602.24				139,319,673.51	-224,069,275.75
Accounts Payable						-26,932,945.93				39,990,724.99	-66,923,670.92
Undelivered Orders						-275,891,807.16				-75,010,110.99	-200,881,696.17
	Subtotal	70		0542		-0-			-95,420,187.76	95,420,187.76	-0-
Automation Modernization, Immigration And Customs Enforcement, Border And Transportation Security, Department Of Homeland Security											
Fund Resources:											
Undisbursed Funds	No Year	70		0543		83,502,759.20	15,000,000.00		19,609,578.57		78,893,180.63
Fund Equities:											
Unobligated Balances (Unexpired)						-68,145,776.10				-39,249,790.23	-28,895,985.87
Accounts Payable						-2,128,818.76				5,390,726.31	-7,519,545.07

Footnotes At End Of Chapter

Appropriations, Outlays, and Balances – Continued

Appropriation or Fund Account Title	Period of Availability	Account Symbol Dept Reg	Account Symbol Dept Tr From	Account Number	Sub No.	Balances, Beginning Of Fiscal Year	Appropriations And Other Obligational Authority[1]	Transfers Borrowings And Investment (Net)[2]	Outlays (Net)	Balances Withdrawn And Other Transactions[3]	Balances, End Of Fiscal Year[4]
Automation Modernization, Immigration And Customs Enforcement, Border And Transportation Security, Department Of Homeland Security - Continued											
Fund Equities: - Continued											
Undelivered Orders	Subtotal	70		0543		-13,228,164.34	15,000,000.00		19,609,578.57	29,249,485.35	-42,477,649.69
						-0-				-4,609,578.57	-0-
Construction, Immigration And Customs Enforcement, Border And Transportation Security, Department Of Homeland Security											
Fund Resources:											
Undisbursed Funds	No Year	70		0545		113,087,101.01	56,281,000.00		17,658,042.97		151,710,058.04
Fund Equities:											
Unobligated Balances (Unexpired)						-5,107,817.40				20,573,076.67	-25,680,894.07
Accounts Payable						-11,505,706.48				1,432,433.82	-12,938,140.30
Undelivered Orders						-96,473,577.13				16,617,446.54	-113,091,023.67
	Subtotal	70		0545		-0-	56,281,000.00		17,658,042.97	38,622,957.03	-0-

Special Fund Accounts

Breach Bond/Detention Fund, Border And Transportation Security, Department Of Homeland Security											
Fund Resources:											
Undisbursed Funds	No Year	70		5126		57,077,511.18	84,719,105.37		53,661,082.60		88,135,533.95
Fund Equities:											
Unobligated Balances (Unexpired)						-23,792,481.19				9,246,390.16	-33,038,871.35
Accounts Payable						-14,156,338.88				-1,860,439.11	-12,295,899.77
Undelivered Orders						-19,128,691.11				23,672,071.72	-42,800,762.83
	Subtotal	70		5126		-0-	84,719,105.37		53,661,082.60	31,058,022.77	-0-
Immigration User Fee Account, BICE, Department Of Homeland Security											
Fund Resources:											
Undisbursed Funds	No Year	70		5382		90,516,843.85	101,594,494.24		75,872,204.65		116,239,133.44
Fund Equities:											
Unobligated Balances (Unexpired)						-49,145,438.96				7,315,236.98	-56,460,675.94
Accounts Payable						-9,332,791.56				8,320,992.83	-17,653,784.39
Undelivered Orders						-32,038,613.33				10,086,059.78	-42,124,673.11
	Subtotal	70		5382		-0-	101,594,494.24		75,872,204.65	25,722,289.59	-0-

Trust Fund Accounts

Salaries And Expenses, Violent Crime Reduction Program, Immigration Services, Department Of Homeland Security											
Fund Resources:											
Undisbursed Funds	No Year	70		8597		231,022.33					231,022.33
Fund Equities:											
Unobligated Balances (Unexpired)						-77,930.23					-77,930.23
Undelivered Orders						-153,092.10					-153,092.10
	Subtotal	70		8597		-0-					-0-

Appropriations, Outlays, and Balances - Continued

Appropriation or Fund Account — Title	Period of Availability	Account Symbol — Dept Reg	Account Symbol — Dept Tr From	Account Number	Sub No.	Balances, Beginning Of Fiscal Year	Appropriations And Other Obligational Authority[1]	Transfers Borrowings And Investment (Net)[2]	Outlays (Net)	Balances Withdrawn And Other Transactions[3]	Balances, End Of Fiscal Year[4]
Violent Crime Reduction Program, Immigration Services, Department Of Homeland Security											
Fund Resources:											
Undisbursed Funds	No Year	70		8598		9,794,883.80			2,441,346.29		7,353,537.51
Fund Equities:											
Unobligated Balances (Unexpired)						-348,582.40				2,093,081.15	-2,441,663.55
Accounts Payable						-842,985.07				-742,288.25	-100,696.82
Undelivered Orders						-8,603,316.33				-3,792,139.19	-4,811,177.14
	Subtotal	70		8598		-0-			2,441,346.29	-2,441,346.29	-0-
Total, Immigration And Customs							4,155,722,885.61	-12,592,005.00	3,707,694,429.43	435,436,451.18	
Customs And Border Protection:											
General Fund Accounts											
Customs And Border Protection, United States Customs Service, Department Of Homeland Security											
Fund Resources:											
Undisbursed Funds	2003-2004	70		0503		6,460,105.79			4,494,657.39		1,965,448.40
	2003					21,473,589.49		15,465,058.00	-3,466,371.76		40,405,019.25
	2002-2003					3,276,932.77			34,958.13		3,241,974.64
	2002					17,082,233.75		18,542,707.00	8,000,944.20	27,623,996.55	
	2001-2002					1,457,643.34			6,129.62	1,451,513.72	
	No Year					293,436,543.09			95,767,243.71		197,669,299.38
Accounts Receivable						5,130,217.40				2,353,535.34	2,776,682.06
Unfilled Customer Orders						50,321,845.79				26,349,294.50	23,972,551.29
Fund Equities:											
Unobligated Balances (Expired)						-23,003,163.21				-12,854,815.13	-10,148,348.08
Unobligated Balances (Unexpired)						-44,566,886.92				-18,945,511.47	-25,621,375.45
Accounts Payable						-25,094,201.88				-13,982,096.66	-11,112,105.22
Undelivered Orders						-305,974,859.41				-82,825,713.14	-223,149,146.27
	Subtotal	70		0503		-0-		34,007,765.00	104,837,561.29	-70,829,796.29	-0-
Salaries And Expenses, Customs And Border Protection, Border And Transportation Security, Department Of Homeland Security											
Fund Resources:											
Undisbursed Funds	2007-2008	70		0530			172,692,450.00		21,695,383.62		150,997,066.38
	2007						5,471,160,000.00	-146,795.91	[5]4,353,873,010.10		1,117,140,193.99
	2006-2007					385,615,147.03		2,954,480.00	202,582,964.61		185,986,662.42
	2006					[6]749,638,134.87		-2,559,737.09	637,560,906.07		109,517,491.71
	2005-2006					168,038,860.67			144,154,953.69		23,883,906.98
	2005					116,444,987.49			46,348,920.74		70,096,066.75
	2004-2005					27,200,399.80			14,177,348.83		13,023,050.97
	2004					97,315,515.19			-5,193,690.04		102,509,205.23
	No Year					14,273,760.29	74,349,990.00	286,398,503.00	299,551,151.37		75,471,101.92
Funds Held Outside The Treasury	2007							146,795.91			146,795.91
	2006					118,262.91		-118,262.91			
Accounts Receivable						79,317,481.60				31,462,244.84	47,855,236.76
Unfilled Customer Orders						237,968,395.35				-6,858,332.01	244,826,727.36

Footnotes At End Of Chapter

Appropriations, Outlays, and Balances – Continued

Appropriation or Fund Account — Title	Dept Reg	Tr From	Account Number	Sub No.	Period of Availability	Balances, Beginning Of Fiscal Year	Appropriations And Other Obligational Authority[1]	Transfers Borrowings And Investment (Net)[2]	Outlays (Net)	Balances Withdrawn And Other Transactions[3]	Balances, End Of Fiscal Year[4]
Salaries And Expenses, Customs And Border Protection, Border And Transportation Security, Department Of Homeland Security - Continued											
Fund Equities:											
Unobligated Balances (Expired)	70					[6]-40,519,787.09				16,264,966.60	-56,784,753.69
Unobligated Balances (Unexpired)						-351,429,994.98				-153,425,955.02	-198,004,039.96
Accounts Payable						-580,676,720.12				22,388,552.71	-603,065,272.83
Undelivered Orders						-903,304,443.01				380,294,996.89	-1,283,599,439.90
Subtotal	70		0530			-0-	5,718,202,440.00	286,674,983.00	5,714,750,948.99	290,126,474.01	-0-
Automation Modernization, Customs And Border Protection, Border And Transportation Security, Department Of Homeland Security											
Fund Resources:											
Undisbursed Funds	70		0531		No Year	368,957,634.60	451,440,000.00		474,898,862.75		345,498,771.85
Fund Equities:											
Unobligated Balances (Unexpired)						-83,130,488.23				-13,441,546.85	-69,688,941.38
Accounts Payable						-19,255,520.63				54,524,653.11	-73,780,173.74
Undelivered Orders						-266,571,625.74				-64,541,969.01	-202,029,656.73
Subtotal	70		0531			-0-	451,440,000.00		474,898,862.75	-23,458,862.75	-0-
Construction, Customs And Border Protection, Border And Transportation Security, Department Of Homeland Security											
Fund Resources:											
Undisbursed Funds	70		0532		2006-2007	300,000,000.00			65,310,139.81		234,689,860.19
					2005-2006	49,617,348.22			10,475,176.32		39,142,171.90
					No Year	399,418,852.74			125,635,549.07		506,761,303.67
Fund Equities:											
Unobligated Balances (Expired)						-173,211,402.67				234.95	-234.95
Unobligated Balances (Unexpired)						-6,061,416.14				-94,534,176.18	-78,677,226.49
Accounts Payable										227,916,278.18	-233,977,694.32
Undelivered Orders						-569,763,382.15				-101,825,202.15	-467,938,180.00
Subtotal	70		0532			-0-	232,978,000.00		201,420,865.20	31,557,134.80	-0-
Border Security Fencing, Infrastructure, And Technology, U.S. Customs And Border Protection, Department Of Homeland Security											
Fund Resources:											
Undisbursed Funds	70		0533		No Year		1,187,565,000.00	10,492,005.00	43,339,109.55		1,154,717,895.45
Fund Equities:											
Unobligated Balances (Unexpired)										736,889,371.30	-736,889,371.30
Accounts Payable										203,305,130.98	-203,305,130.98
Undelivered Orders										214,523,393.17	-214,523,393.17
Subtotal	70		0533			-0-	1,187,565,000.00	10,492,005.00	43,339,109.55	1,154,717,895.45	-0-
Air And Marine Interdiction, Operations, Maintenance, And Procurement, Customs And Border Protection, Department Of Homeland Security											
Fund Resources:											
Undisbursed Funds	70		0544		2007-2008	95,000,000.00	75,000,000.00		6,565,652.82		75,000,000.00
					2006-2007	4,800,000.00			4,012,142.14		88,434,347.18
					2006						787,857.86
					No Year	291,084,638.65	597,187,000.00		297,136,734.20		591,134,904.45
Accounts Receivable						-240,125.65				-288,783.76	48,658.11
Unfilled Customer Orders						500,657.72				499,138.53	1,519.19
Fund Equities:											
Unobligated Balances (Expired)						-0.42				189.12	-189.54

Appropriations, Outlays, and Balances - Continued

Appropriation or Fund Account — Title	Period of Availability	Dept Reg	Tr From	Account Number	Sub No.	Balances, Beginning Of Fiscal Year	Appropriations And Other Obligational Authority[1]	Transfers Borrowings And Investment (Net)[2]	Outlays (Net)	Balances Withdrawn And Other Transactions[3]	Balances, End Of Fiscal Year[4]
Unobligated Balances (Unexpired)						-107,561,493.33				182,123,077.96	-289,684,571.29
Accounts Payable						-37,532,541.32				9,814,191.70	-47,346,733.02
Undelivered Orders						-246,051,135.65				172,324,657.29	-418,375,792.94
Subtotal		70		0544		-0-	672,187,000.00		307,714,529.16	364,472,470.84	-0-
Special Fund Accounts											
Customs And Border Protection, Immigration User Fees, Border And Transportation Security											
Fund Resources:											
Undisbursed Funds	No Year	70		5087		192,813,621.86	484,730,567.87		518,425,573.83		159,118,615.90
Fund Equities:											
Unobligated Balances (Unexpired)	No Year	70		5087		-192,813,621.86	484,730,567.87		518,425,573.83		-159,118,615.90
Subtotal		70		5087		-0-					-0-
Customs And Border Protection, Land Border Inspection Fees, Border And Transportation Security											
Fund Resources:											
Undisbursed Funds	No Year	70		5089		6,242,927.51	28,443,672.88		33,161,068.70		1,525,531.69
Fund Equities:											
Unobligated Balances (Unexpired)	No Year	70		5089		-6,227,976.31	28,443,672.88			-4,702,444.62	-1,525,531.69
Undelivered Orders						-14,951.20				-14,951.20	
Subtotal		70		5089		-0-			33,161,068.70	-4,717,395.82	-0-
Student And Exchange Visitor Program, Border And Transportation Security, Department Of Homeland Security											
Fund Resources:											
Undisbursed Funds	No Year	70		5378		51,010,571.05	57,947,182.88		41,688,770.17		67,268,983.76
Fund Equities:											
Unobligated Balances (Unexpired)	No Year	70		5378		-24,957,364.27	57,947,182.88			13,633,874.18	-38,591,238.45
Accounts Payable						-8,584,877.86				-992,285.54	-7,592,592.32
Undelivered Orders						-17,468,328.92				3,616,824.07	-21,085,152.99
Subtotal		70		5378		-0-			41,688,770.17	16,258,412.71	-0-
Immigration Enforcement Account, Border And Transportation Security, Department Of Homeland Security											
Fund Resources:											
Undisbursed Funds	No Year	70		5451		1,092,345.75	3,133,412.12		3,972,320.00		253,437.87
Fund Equities:											
Unobligated Balances (Unexpired)	No Year	70		5451		-1,092,345.75	3,133,412.12			-838,907.88	-253,437.87
Subtotal		70		5451		-0-			3,972,320.00	-838,907.88	-0-
Payments To Wool Manufacturers, United States Customs And Border Protection, Department Of Homeland Security											
Fund Resources:											
Undisbursed Funds	No Year	70		5533			12,060,129.86		12,060,129.86		
Payments To Pima Cotton, United States Customs And Border Protection, Department Of Homeland Security											
Fund Resources:											
Undisbursed Funds	No Year	70		5544			16,000,000.00		16,000,000.00		

Footnotes At End Of Chapter

Appropriations, Outlays, and Balances – Continued

Appropriation or Fund Account — Title	Period of Availability	Dept Reg	Tr From	Account Number	Sub. No.	Balances, Beginning Of Fiscal Year	Appropriations And Other Obligational Authority[1]	Transfers Borrowings And Investment (Net)[2]	Outlays (Net)	Balances Withdrawn And Other Transactions[3]	Balances, End Of Fiscal Year[4]
Customs And Border Protection, Transfer And Expenses Of Operation, Puerto Rico, USCS, Department Of Homeland Security											
Fund Resources:											
Undisbursed Funds	No Year	70		5687		31,814,616.88	93,354,952.48		92,257,511.65		32,912,057.71
Accounts Receivable						197,853.62				133,749.26	64,104.36
Fund Equities:											
Unobligated Balances (Unexpired)						-5,104,050.91				718,570.95	-5,822,621.86
Accounts Payable						-5,036,554.48				-1,015,854.50	-4,020,699.98
Undelivered Orders						-21,871,865.11				1,260,975.12	-23,132,840.23
Subtotal	Subtotal	70		5687		-0-	93,354,952.48		92,257,511.65	1,097,440.83	-0-
Customs And Border Protection, Customs Services At Small Airports, USCS, Department Of Homeland Security											
Fund Resources:											
Undisbursed Funds	No Year	70		5694		8,103,974.66	6,690,246.48		4,379,902.80		10,414,318.34
Accounts Receivable						276,780.23				74,891.93	201,888.30
Unfilled Customer Orders						1,155,898.41				205,597.61	950,300.80
Fund Equities:											
Unobligated Balances (Unexpired)						-8,188,914.06				84,286.46	-8,273,200.52
Accounts Payable						-324,424.96				1,982,222.24	-2,306,647.20
Undelivered Orders						-1,023,314.28				-36,654.56	-986,659.72
Subtotal	Subtotal	70		5694		-0-	6,690,246.48		4,379,902.80	2,310,343.68	-0-
Customs And Border Protection, Customs User Fees Account, USCS, Department Of Homeland Security											
Fund Resources:											
Undisbursed Funds	No Year	70		5695		761,175,315.06	353,971,100.27		385,189,148.55		729,957,266.78
Accounts Receivable						215,067.94				215,042.94	25.00
Fund Equities:											
Unobligated Balances (Unexpired)						-693,120,485.68				-12,823,155.17	-680,297,330.51
Accounts Payable						-34,369,828.24				-15,907,453.13	-18,462,375.11
Undelivered Orders						-33,900,069.08				-2,702,482.92	-31,197,586.16
Subtotal	Subtotal	70		5695		-0-	353,971,100.27		385,189,148.55	-31,218,048.28	-0-
Trust Fund Accounts											
Customs And Border Protection, Violent Crime Reduction Trust Fund, USCS, Department Of Homeland Security											
Fund Resources:											
Undisbursed Funds	No Year	70		8529		6,909,845.71			1,358,508.83		5,551,336.88
Accounts Receivable						9,712.49				9,712.49	
Unfilled Customer Orders						87,471.03					87,471.03
Fund Equities:											
Unobligated Balances (Unexpired)						-255,235.09				-3,342.22	-251,892.87
Accounts Payable						-94,598.08				255,598.13	-350,196.21
Undelivered Orders						-6,657,196.06				-1,620,477.23	-5,036,718.83
Subtotal	Subtotal	70		8529		-0-			1,358,508.83	-1,358,508.83	-0-
Refunds, Transfers And Expenses, Abandoned And Seized Goods, USCS, Department Of Homeland Security											
Fund Resources:											
Undisbursed Funds	No Year	70		8789		1,652,747.26	4,221,444.95		5,523,818.83		350,373.38

Appropriation or Fund Account Title	Period of Availability	Reg	Tr From	Account Number	Sub No.	Balances, Beginning Of Fiscal Year	Appropriations And Other Obligational Authority[1]	Transfers Borrowings And Investment (Net)[2]	Outlays (Net)	Balances Withdrawn And Other Transactions[3]	Balances, End Of Fiscal Year[4]
Fund Equities:											
Unobligated Balances (Unexpired)											-160,859.79
Accounts Payable						-1,603,362.13				160,859.79	-189,513.59
Undelivered Orders						-49,385.13				-1,413,848.54	
	Subtotal	70		8789		-0-	4,221,444.95		5,523,818.83	-49,385.13	-0-
										-1,302,373.88	
Harbor Maintenance Fee Collection, USCS, Department Of Homeland Security											
Fund Resources:											
Undisbursed Funds	No Year	70		8870			3,026,000.00	331,174,753.00	3,026,000.00	1,693,121,272.63	
Total, Customs And Border Protection							9,325,951,149.79	331,174,753.00	7,964,004,630.16	1,693,121,272.63	
Total, Security, Enforcement, And Investigations							17,856,641,318.79	317,776,961.00	15,383,217,116.28	2,791,201,163.51	
United States Coast Guard											
General Fund Accounts											
Retired Pay, USCG											
Fund Resources:											
Undisbursed Funds	2007	70		0602		103,117,553.02	1,063,323,000.00		974,253,469.20		89,069,530.80
	2006					163,415,069.16			93,500,084.81		9,617,468.21
	2005					162,553,209.72			-131,882.05		163,546,951.21
	2004					71,400,612.52			-7,429.57		162,560,639.29
	2003					38,510,860.90			-224,304.75		71,624,917.27
	No Year								1,675.16	8,509,185.74	21,655,742.72
									8,344,257.28		
Fund Equities:											
Unobligated Balances (Expired)						-399,421,536.93				-5,916,853.46	-393,504,683.47
Unobligated Balances (Unexpired)						-139,575,768.39				10,408,955.36	-10,408,955.36
Accounts Payable						-0-				-25,414,157.72	-114,161,610.67
	Subtotal	70		0602			1,063,323,000.00		1,075,735,870.08	-12,412,870.08	-0-
Coast Guard Housing Fund, Department Of Homeland Security											
Fund Resources:											
Undisbursed Funds	No Year	70		0603		6,080,158.62			-6,126,203.48	6,126,203.48	12,206,362.10
Fund Equities:											
Unobligated Balances (Unexpired)						-6,080,158.62		-30,000,000.00		6,126,203.48	-12,206,362.10
								30,000,000.00			
	Subtotal	70		0603		-0-			-6,126,203.48		-0-
Operating Expenses, United States Coast Guard, Department Of Homeland Security											
Fund Resources:											
Undisbursed Funds	2007	70		0610		88,233,000.00	5,663,727,001.00	-5,535,401.62	4,355,639,322.15		1,302,552,277.23
	2006-2007					1,079,146,888.14		5,599,677.00	93,826,262.20		6,414.80
	2006					205,796,211.74	-25,595,532.00	-3,512,284.85	[8]874,024,361.17		176,014,710.12
	2005					72,748,337.49			61,736,223.00		144,059,988.74
	2004					105,788,297.60			10,610,754.69		62,137,582.80
	2003					-5,905.01			4,278,211.77		101,510,085.83
	2002-2003								-5,905.01		

Footnotes At End Of Chapter

Appropriations, Outlays, and Balances – Continued

Appropriation or Fund Account — Title	Period of Availability	Reg	Tr From	Account Number	Sub No.	Balances, Beginning Of Fiscal Year	Appropriations And Other Obligational Authority[1]	Transfers Borrowings And Investment (Net)[2]	Outlays (Net)	Balances Withdrawn And Other Transactions[3]	Balances, End Of Fiscal Year[4]
Operating Expenses, United States Coast Guard, Department Of Homeland Security - Continued											
Fund Resources: - Continued											
Undisbursed Funds - Continued											
	2002					43,080,362.06			-674,341.94	43,754,704.00	[9]-5,598.60
	No Year					-90,300.99			-84,702.39		
Funds Held Outside The Treasury											
	2007							5,535,401.62			5,535,401.62
	2006					6,219,367.15		-6,219,367.15			
Accounts Receivable						90,969,901.10				20,204,349.64	70,765,551.46
Unfilled Customer Orders						58,442,068.59				14,291,060.55	44,151,008.04
Fund Equities:											
Unobligated Balances (Expired)						-209,306,865.54				28,851,117.25	-238,157,982.79
Unobligated Balances (Unexpired)						-88,233,000.00				-88,233,000.00	
Accounts Payable						-517,492,505.08				178,879,985.92	-696,372,491.00
Undelivered Orders						-935,295,857.25				36,901,091.00	-972,196,948.25
Subtotal		70		0610		-0-	5,638,131,469.00	-4,131,975.00	5,399,350,185.64	234,649,308.36	-0-
Environmental Compliance And Restoration, United States Coast Guard, Department Of Homeland Security											
Fund Resources:											
Undisbursed Funds											
	2006-2007	70		0611		267,000.00	10,880,000.00		231,660.00		35,340.00
	No Year					12,647,916.38			11,595,972.44		11,931,943.94
Fund Equities:											
Unobligated Balances (Unexpired)						-3,315,845.19				-280,275.94	-3,035,569.25
Accounts Payable						-226,375.01				142,433.33	-368,808.34
Undelivered Orders						-9,372,696.18				-809,789.83	-8,562,906.35
Subtotal		70		0611		-0-	10,880,000.00		11,827,632.44	-947,632.44	-0-
Reserve Training, United States Coast Guard, Department Of Homeland Security											
Fund Resources:											
Undisbursed Funds											
	2007	70		0612		6,163,969.19	122,448,000.00		120,732,460.60		1,715,539.40
	2006					3,994,848.28			3,419,795.48		2,744,173.71
	2005					3,378,698.54			176,182.68		3,818,665.60
	2004					3,331,032.34			195,978.55		3,182,719.99
	2003					3,144,904.83			24,171.21		3,306,861.13
	2002					38,583.74			22,981.61	3,121,923.22	
Accounts Receivable										-3,560,729.37	3,599,313.11
Fund Equities:											
Unobligated Balances (Expired)						-11,475,771.70				-1,724,324.67	-9,751,447.03
Accounts Payable						475,148.95				311,801.42	-786,950.37
Undelivered Orders						-8,101,116.27				-272,240.73	-7,828,875.54
Subtotal		70		0612		-0-	122,448,000.00		124,571,570.13	-2,123,570.13	-0-
Acquisition, Construction, And Improvements, United States Coast Guard, Department Of Homeland Security											
Fund Resources:											
Undisbursed Funds											
	2007-2011	70		0613		813,699,099.70	1,102,065,000.00		146,341,714.57		955,723,285.43
	2006-2010						-25,616,974.00		357,058,576.75		431,023,548.95
	2007-2009						236,677,508.00		40,261,719.88		196,415,788.12
	2006-2009					77,637,314.49	-63,819,464.00		572,492.46		13,245,358.03
	2005-2009					358,196,636.00	-9,257,070.00		160,038,329.81		188,901,236.19

Appropriations, Outlays, and Balances - Continued

Title	Period of Availability	Reg	Tr From	Account Number	Sub No.	Balances, Beginning Of Fiscal Year	Appropriations And Other Obligational Authority[1]	Transfers Borrowings And Investment (Net)[2]	Outlays (Net)	Balances Withdrawn And Other Transactions[3]	Balances, End Of Fiscal Year[4]
	2006-2008					92,341,635.39	-4,100,000.00		23,596,663.71		64,644,971.68
	2004-2008					123,865,231.57			48,664,233.79		75,200,997.78
	2007						80,396,000.00		74,760,783.85		5,635,216.15
	2005-2007					137,391,318.47			49,610,639.70		87,780,678.77
	2003-2007					5,692,257.66			2,570,917.79		3,121,339.87
	2006					5,426,040.74			1,858,847.31		3,567,193.43
	2004-2006					92,373,686.62			45,089,571.54		47,284,115.08
	2003-2006					22,648,527.64			15,661,759.36		6,986,768.28
	2002-2006					28,475,898.01			17,729,075.46		10,746,822.55
	2005					30,980,577.12			21,777,971.74		9,202,605.38
	2003-2005					29,633,943.20			20,528,020.14		9,105,923.06
	2001-2005					1,394,534.14			493,730.46		900,803.68
	2000-2005					0.87					0.87
	2004					34,507,399.69			32,428,212.84		2,079,186.85
	2003-2004					1,194,326.01			-2,237.36		1,196,563.37
	2002-2004					7,790,631.47			4,067,305.57		3,723,325.90
	2000-2004					717,530.83			342,027.82		375,503.01
	2002-2003					244,883.53					244,883.53
	2001-2003					1,523,277.25			10,463.53		1,512,813.72
	1999-2003					594,498.64			52,753.57		541,745.07
	2001-2002					247,184.78				247,184.78	
	2000-2002					2,320,920.36			62,879.85	2,258,040.51	
	1998-2002					406,008.34			64,950.87	341,057.47	
	No Year					348,131,151.11			51,013,211.99		297,117,939.12
Accounts Receivable						1,032,816.03				-523,023.39	1,555,839.42
Unfilled Customer Orders						39,056,478.28				-2,012,222.32	41,068,700.60
Fund Equities:											
Unobligated Balances (Expired)						-18,704,135.76				5,014,832.63	-23,718,968.39
Unobligated Balances (Unexpired)						-1,035,693,420.53				-211,713,699.49	-823,979,721.04
Accounts Payable						-14,471,899.71				8,777,896.96	-23,249,796.67
Undelivered Orders						-1,188,654,351.94				399,300,315.85	-1,587,954,667.79
Subtotal		70		0613		-0-	1,316,345,000.00		1,114,654,617.00	201,690,383.00	-0-
Alteration Of Bridges, United States Coast Guard, Department Of Homeland Security											
Fund Resources:											
Undisbursed Funds	No Year	70		0614		93,786,134.10	16,000,000.00		962,026.84		108,824,107.26
Fund Equities:											
Unobligated Balances (Unexpired)						-436,544.83				-29,043.61	-407,501.22
Accounts Payable						-89,253.31				-89,253.31	
Undelivered Orders						-93,260,335.96				15,156,270.08	-108,416,606.04
Subtotal		70		0614		-0-	16,000,000.00		962,026.84	15,037,973.16	-0-
Research, Development, Test, And Evaluation, United States Coast Guard, Department Of Homeland Security											
Fund Resources:											
Undisbursed Funds	2006-2007	70		0615		470,000.00					7,486.14
	No Year					11,139,351.52	16,505,000.00		462,513.86	-1,282,888.30	8,434,474.41
Accounts Receivable						285,811.20			19,209,877.11		1,568,699.50
Unfilled Customer Orders						7,167,071.19				565,149.48	6,601,921.71

Footnotes At End Of Chapter

Appropriations, Outlays, and Balances – Continued

Appropriation or Fund Account — Title	Period of Availability	Dept Reg	Tr From	Account Number	Sub No.	Balances, Beginning Of Fiscal Year	Appropriations And Other Obligational Authority[1]	Transfers Borrowings And Investment (Net)[2]	Outlays (Net)	Balances Withdrawn And Other Transactions[3]	Balances, End Of Fiscal Year[4]
Research, Development, Test, And Evaluation, United States Coast Guard, Department Of Homeland Security - Continued											
Fund Equities:											
Unobligated Balances (Expired)						-3,262,094.99				7,486.14	-7,486.14
Unobligated Balances (Unexpired)						-638,733.05				-660,641.29	-2,601,453.70
Accounts Payable						-15,161,405.87				-367,795.77	-270,937.28
Undelivered Orders						-0-				-1,428,701.23	-13,732,704.64
Subtotal		70		0615			16,505,000.00		19,672,390.97	-3,167,390.97	-0-
Medicare-Eligible Retiree Health Fund Contribution, United States Coast Guard, Department Of Homeland Security											
Fund Resources:											
Undisbursed Funds	2007	70		0616			278,704,000.00		278,704,000.00		------
Intragovernmental Funds											
Supply Fund, USCG, Department Of Homeland Security											
Fund Resources:											
Undisbursed Funds	No Year	70		4535		22,571,792.70			-5,169,699.16	39,593.12	27,741,491.86
Accounts Receivable						127,322.30				-104,198.57	87,729.18
Unfilled Customer Orders						385,790.19					489,988.76
Fund Equities:											
Unobligated Balances (Unexpired)						-4,944,686.87				7,856,706.23	-12,801,393.10
Accounts Payable						-11,068,097.91				-6,543,258.04	-4,524,839.87
Undelivered Orders						-7,072,120.41				3,920,856.42	-10,992,976.83
Subtotal		70		4535		-0-			-5,169,699.16	5,169,699.16	-0-
Yard Fund, USCG, Department Of Homeland Security											
Fund Resources:											
Undisbursed Funds	No Year	70		4743		64,535,534.52			-37,303,087.42	-3,779,112.65	101,838,621.94
Accounts Receivable						6,185,577.94				-4,371,459.05	9,964,690.59
Unfilled Customer Orders						29,256,490.06					33,627,949.11
Fund Equities:											
Unobligated Balances (Unexpired)						-64,624,490.98				26,210,820.73	-90,835,311.71
Accounts Payable						-6,716,908.55				2,345,478.17	-9,062,386.72
Undelivered Orders						-28,636,202.99				16,897,360.22	-45,533,563.21
Subtotal		70		4743		-0-			-37,303,087.42	37,303,087.42	-0-
Trust Fund Accounts											
Sport Fish Restoration And Boating Trust Fund											
Fund Resources:											
Undisbursed Funds	No Year	20		8147		31,408,134.38	175,659,318.12	-199,061,272.68		75,341,192.39	8,006,179.82
Unrealized Discount On Investments						-7,728,634.53		1,114,616.72		100,318,125.73	-6,614,017.81
Investments In Public Debt Securities						1,648,781,000.00		197,946,655.96		175,659,318.12	1,846,727,655.96
Fund Equities:											
Unobligated Balances (Unexpired)						-671,649,081.18					-746,990,273.57
Accounts Payable						-1,000,811,418.67					-1,101,129,544.40
Subtotal		20		8147		-0-	175,659,318.12			175,659,318.12	-0-

Appropriations, Outlays, and Balances - Continued

Appropriation or Fund Account — Title	Period of Availability	Dept — Reg	Dept — Tr From	Account Number	Sub No.	Balances, Beginning Of Fiscal Year	Appropriations And Other Obligational Authority[1]	Transfers Borrowings And Investment (Net)[2]	Outlays (Net)	Balances Withdrawn And Other Transactions[3]	Balances, End Of Fiscal Year[4]
Oil Spill Liability Trust Fund											
Fund Resources:											
Undisbursed Funds	No Year	20		8185		6,478,249.16	337,559,450.88	-323,324,275.26	50,424.78		20,663,000.00
Unrealized Discount On Investments						-4,769,357.11		-3,527,454.34			-8,296,811.45
Investments In Public Debt Securities						593,166,000.00		326,874,488.21			920,040,488.21
Fund Equities:											
Unobligated Balances (Unexpired)						-480,817,430.22				338,152,727.35	-818,970,157.57
Accounts Payable						-114,057,461.83				-620,942.64	-113,436,519.19
Subtotal		20		8185		-0-	337,559,450.88	22,758.61	50,424.78	337,531,784.71	-0-
Boat Safety, USCG, Department Of Homeland Security											
Fund Resources:											
Undisbursed Funds	No Year	70		8149		-3,624,927.54	89,500,000.00		73,739,824.25	-27,139,397.00	12,135,248.21
Accounts Receivable						96,068,537.62					123,207,934.62
Fund Equities:											
Unobligated Balances (Unexpired)						-16,737,170.49				4,646,496.72	-21,383,667.21
Accounts Payable						-974.65				938.84	-1,913.49
Undelivered Orders						-75,705,464.94				38,252,137.19	-113,957,602.13
Subtotal		70		8149		-0-	89,500,000.00		73,739,824.25	15,760,175.75	-0-
Oil Spill Liability Trust Fund, USCG, Department Of Homeland Security											
Fund Resources:											
Undisbursed Funds	No Year	70		8312		330,246.77	38,432,383.99		38,513,903.42	-58,873.19	248,727.34
Accounts Receivable										58,873.19	58,873.19
Fund Equities:											
Accounts Payable						-81,519.43				-81,519.43	-307,600.53
Undelivered Orders						-248,727.34				58,873.19	
Subtotal		70		8312		-0-	38,432,383.99		38,513,903.42	-81,519.43	-0-
Trust Fund Share Of Expenses, USCG, Department Of Homeland Security											
Fund Resources:											
Undisbursed Funds	2007	70		8314			44,550,000.00		44,550,000.00		
Oil Spill Recovery, USCG, Department Of Homeland Security											
Fund Resources:											
Undisbursed Funds	No Year	70		8349		1,016,960.75	45,893,323.83		45,893,323.83	-5,106,676.17	1,016,960.75
Accounts Receivable						108,270,969.83					113,377,646.00
Fund Equities:											
Unobligated Balances (Unexpired)						-18,043,144.49				2,213,749.78	-20,256,894.27
Accounts Payable						-69,846.60				-33,939.01	-35,907.59
Undelivered Orders						-91,174,939.49				2,926,865.40	-94,101,804.89
Subtotal		70		8349		-0-	45,893,323.83		45,893,323.83		-0-
Surcharge Collections, Sales Of Commissary Stores, USCG, Department Of Homeland Security											
Fund Resources:											
Undisbursed Funds	No Year	70		8420		68,088.14					68,088.14
Fund Equities:											
Unobligated Balances (Unexpired)						-68,088.14					-68,088.14
Subtotal		70		8420		-0-					-0-
Coast Guard Cadet Fund, USCG, Department Of Homeland Security											
Fund Resources:											
Undisbursed Funds	No Year	70		8428		646,320.05			409,308.18		237,011.87

Footnotes At End Of Chapter

Appropriations, Outlays, and Balances – Continued

Appropriation or Fund Account — Title	Period of Availability	Dept Reg	Tr From	Account Number	Sub No.	Balances, Beginning Of Fiscal Year	Appropriations And Other Obligational Authority[1]	Transfers Borrowings And Investment (Net)[2]	Outlays (Net)	Balances Withdrawn And Other Transactions[3]	Balances, End Of Fiscal Year[4]
Coast Guard Cadet Fund, USCG, Department Of Homeland Security - Continued											
Fund Resources: - Continued											
Accounts Receivable						64,028.91				-276,612.63	340,641.54
Fund Equities:											
Accounts Payable						-710,348.96				-132,695.55	-577,653.41
	Subtotal	70		8428		-0-		409,308.18	409,308.18	-409,308.18	-0-
General Gift Fund, USCG, Department Of Homeland Security											
Fund Resources:											
Undisbursed Funds	No Year	70		8533		428,106.64	1,455,152.02	342.88	1,330,552.90		553,048.64
Unrealized Discount On Investments						-29,063.71		-342.88			-29,406.59
Investments In Public Debt Securities						1,270,000.00					1,270,000.00
Fund Equities:											
Unobligated Balances (Unexpired)						-1,656,752.23				74,850.84	-1,731,603.07
Accounts Payable										5,466.75	-5,466.75
Undelivered Orders						-12,290.70				44,281.53	-56,572.23
	Subtotal	70		8533		-0-	1,455,152.02		1,330,552.90	124,599.12	-0-
Total, United States Coast Guard							9,195,386,097.84	-4,109,216.39	8,181,366,640.40	1,009,910,241.05	
National Protection And Program Directorate											
General Fund Accounts											
Office Of Health Affairs, Departmental Management And Operations, Department Of Homeland Security											
Fund Resources:											
Undisbursed Funds	2007-2008	70		0117			15,287,647.00		26,041.08		15,261,605.92
	2007						4,041,116.00		2,238,971.85		1,802,144.15
	2006-2007							15,961,521.00	141,497.09		15,820,023.91
	2006							515,260.00			515,260.00
	2005-2006							4,276,499.00			4,276,499.00
Fund Equities:											
Unobligated Balances (Expired)										90,737.92	-90,737.92
Unobligated Balances (Unexpired)										10,063,297.37	-10,063,297.37
Accounts Payable										2,483,439.14	-2,483,439.14
Undelivered Orders										25,038,058.55	-25,038,058.55
	Subtotal	70		0117		-0-	19,328,763.00	20,753,280.00	2,406,510.02	37,675,532.98	-0-
United States Visitor And Immigration Status Indicator Technology, Department Of Homeland Security											
Fund Resources:											
Undisbursed Funds	2006-2007	70		0521		404,393,452.13	362,494,000.00		286,077,549.12		480,809,903.01
	No Year							2,100,000.00			2,100,000.00
Unfilled Customer Orders										-1,265,000.00	1,265,000.00
Fund Equities:											
Unobligated Balances (Unexpired)						-198,405,034.18				46,599,114.50	-245,004,148.68
Accounts Payable						-27,959,652.08				-5,520,622.05	-22,439,030.03
Undelivered Orders						-178,028,765.87				38,702,958.43	-216,731,724.30
	Subtotal	70		0521		-0-	362,494,000.00	2,100,000.00	286,077,549.12	78,516,450.88	-0-
Infrastructure Protection And Information Security, Office For Domestic Preparedness,											

Appropriations, Outlays, and Balances - Continued

Appropriation or Fund Account — Title	Period of Availability	Dept Reg	Tr From	Account Number	Sub No.	Balances, Beginning Of Fiscal Year	Appropriations And Other Obligational Authority[1]	Transfers Borrowings And Investment (Net)[2]	Outlays (Net)	Balances Withdrawn And Other Transactions[3]	Balances, End Of Fiscal Year[4]
Department Of Homeland Security											
Fund Resources:											
Undisbursed Funds	2007-2008	70		0565			487,345,353.00		161,902,740.52		325,442,612.48
	2007						77,463,977.27		57,890,368.09		19,573,609.18
	2006-2007					297,604,763.88		-11,023,759.00	229,212,681.96		57,368,322.92
	2006					32,385,163.97	-879,632.00		21,679,509.77		9,826,022.20
	No Year						22,978,000.00		2,140,000.00		20,838,000.00
Unfilled Customer Orders						643,156.00				301,606.42	341,549.58
Fund Equities:											
Unobligated Balances (Expired)						-2,090,643.90				5,721,717.75	-7,812,361.65
Unobligated Balances (Unexpired)						-40,491,827.91				41,233,740.60	-81,725,568.51
Accounts Payable						-28,949,555.89				23,919,762.71	-52,869,318.60
Undelivered Orders						-259,101,056.15				31,881,811.45	-290,982,867.60
Subtotal		70		0565		-0-	586,907,698.27	-11,023,759.00	472,825,300.34	103,058,638.93	-0-
Management And Administration, Preparedness, Department Of Homeland Security											
Fund Resources:											
Undisbursed Funds	2007	70		0566			13,469,097.13		9,403,031.01		4,066,066.12
	2006					3,829,874.45	-88,579.00	-780,396.14	2,801,655.83		159,243.48
Fund Equities:											
Unobligated Balances (Expired)						-202,277.70				1,094,239.66	-1,296,517.36
Accounts Payable						-941,273.84				499,308.78	-441,965.06
Undelivered Orders						-2,686,322.91				199,495.73	-2,486,827.18
Subtotal		70		0566		-0-	13,380,518.13	-780,396.14	12,204,686.84	395,435.15	-0-
Biodefense Countermeasures, Federal Emergency Management Agency, Department Of Homeland Security											
Fund Resources:											
Undisbursed Funds	2005-2013	70		0714		2,385,039,000.00		-1,468,126,069.00			916,912,931.00
	2004-2013					884,749,000.00					884,749,000.00
Transfer To:											
The Department Of Health And Human Services, Office Of The Secretary	2005-2013	75	70	0714				1,468,126,069.00			1,468,126,069.00
Fund Equities:											
Unobligated Balances (Unexpired)						-1,468,126,089.00				-35,525,535.93	-1,432,600,553.07
Undelivered Orders						-1,801,661,911.00				35,525,535.93	-1,837,187,446.93
Subtotal		70		0714		-0-					-0-
Total, National Protection And Program Directorate							982,110,979.40	11,049,124.86	773,514,046.32	219,646,057.94	
Federal Emergency Management Agency											
General Fund Accounts											
Flood Map Modernization Fund, Emergency Preparedness And Response											
Fund Resources:											
Undisbursed Funds	No Year	70		0500		282,363,386.09	198,980,000.00	2,274,391.94	166,698,234.20		316,919,543.83
Accounts Receivable						9,037.04				-109,931.64	118,968.68

Footnotes At End Of Chapter

Appropriations, Outlays, and Balances – Continued

Appropriation or Fund Account — Title	Reg	Tr From	Account Number	Sub No.	Period of Availability	Balances, Beginning Of Fiscal Year	Appropriations And Other Obligational Authority[1]	Transfers Borrowings And Investment (Net)[2]	Outlays (Net)	Balances Withdrawn And Other Transactions[3]	Balances, End Of Fiscal Year[4]
Flood Map Modernization Fund, Emergency Preparedness And Response - Continued											
Fund Resources: - Continued											
Unfilled Customer Orders						1,055,962.96				442,931.64	613,031.32
Fund Equities:											
Unobligated Balances (Unexpired)						-1,277,222.53				1,634,348.27	-2,911,570.80
Accounts Payable						-8,142,291.30				14,832,050.91	-22,974,342.21
Undelivered Orders						-274,008,872.26			166,698,234.20	17,756,758.56	-291,765,630.82
Subtotal	70		0500			-0-	198,980,000.00	2,274,391.94	166,698,234.20	34,556,157.74	-0-
Office Of Domestic Preparedness, Federal Emergency Management Agency, Department Of Homeland Security											
Fund Resources:											
Undisbursed Funds	70		0511		2003-2004	271,284,973.09			191,108,559.00		80,176,414.09
					No Year	109,673,002.60			61,289,346.36		48,383,656.24
Unfilled Customer Orders						4,811.91					4,811.91
Fund Equities:											
Unobligated Balances (Expired)						-62,507.42				153,906.34	-216,413.76
Unobligated Balances (Unexpired)						-12,200,382.18				-1,836,869.93	-10,363,512.25
Accounts Payable						-111,606,564.10				-59,881,461.18	-51,725,102.92
Undelivered Orders						-257,093,333.90			252,397,905.36	-190,833,480.59	-66,259,853.31
Subtotal	70		0511			-0-			252,397,905.36	-252,397,905.36	-0-
State And Local Programs, Federal Emergency Management Agency, Department Of Homeland Security											
Fund Resources:											
Undisbursed Funds	70		0560		2007-2010				-52,019,250.00		52,019,250.00
					2007-2008		35,000,000.00				35,000,000.00
					2007		2,747,970,791.42		125,693,922.84		2,622,276,868.58
					2006-2007	15,000,000.00			976,000.00		14,024,000.00
					2006	2,363,644,187.18			409,142,294.68		[101]1,954,501,892.50
					2005	2,213,135,211.88			1,176,761,943.84		1,036,373,268.04
					2004	831,388,980.67			640,892,338.10		190,496,642.57
					No Year	62,419,500.00			189,056.55		62,230,443.45
Unfilled Customer Orders						1,684,385.00				-919,965,750.00	921,650,135.00
Fund Equities:											
Unobligated Balances (Expired)						-9,613,123.69				-10,896,762.33	1,283,638.64
Unobligated Balances (Unexpired)						-71,419,500.00				2,199,579.30	-73,619,079.30
Accounts Payable						-285,922,916.55				36,330,951.09	-322,253,867.64
Undelivered Orders						-5,120,316,724.49			2,301,636,306.01	1,373,666,467.35	-6,493,983,191.84
Subtotal	70		0560			-0-	2,782,970,791.42		2,301,636,306.01	481,334,485.41	-0-
Firefighter Assistance Grants, Federal Emergency Management Agency, Department Of Homeland Security											
Fund Resources:											
Undisbursed Funds	70		0561		2007-2008	512,009,307.67	662,000,000.00		12,189,218.58		649,810,781.42
					2006-2007	42,622,948.17			307,607,860.35		204,401,447.32
					2005-2006				21,759,160.63		20,863,787.54
					2004-2005	327,041,068.12			155,948,836.64		171,092,231.48
Fund Equities:											
Unobligated Balances (Expired)						-770,856.24				100,070.96	-870,927.20
Unobligated Balances (Unexpired)						-15,275,554.54				459,938,342.16	-475,213,896.70

Appropriations, Outlays, and Balances - Continued

Appropriation or Fund Account — Title	Period of Availability	Reg	Tr From	Account Number	Sub No.	Balances, Beginning Of Fiscal Year	Appropriations And Other Obligational Authority[1]	Transfers Borrowings And Investment (Net)[2]	Outlays (Net)	Balances Withdrawn And Other Transactions[3]	Balances, End Of Fiscal Year[4]
Accounts Payable						-11,719,358.48				-11,311,480.99	-407,877.49
Undelivered Orders						-853,907,554.70				-284,232,008.33	-569,675,546.37
	Subtotal	70		0561		-0-	662,000,000.00		497,505,076.20	164,494,923.80	-0-
Management And Administration, Office Of State And Local Programs, Federal Emergency Management Agency, Department Of Homeland Security											
Fund Resources:											
Undisbursed Funds	2005	70		0562		1,025,674.09					1,025,674.09
Fund Equities:											
Unobligated Balances (Expired)						-881,703.94					-881,703.94
Undelivered Orders						-143,970.15					-143,970.15
	Subtotal	70		0562		-0-					-0-
United States Fire Administration And Training, Federal Emergency Management Agency, Department Of Homeland Security											
Fund Resources:											
Undisbursed Funds	2007	70		0564		14,166,058.62	41,878,208.58		32,000,836.38		9,877,372.20
	2006								9,544,187.23		4,621,871.39
Accounts Receivable						225,000.00				-119,988.40	344,988.40
Unfilled Customer Orders						2,098,605.09				1,388,038.85	710,566.24
Fund Equities:											
Unobligated Balances (Expired)						-2,951,073.95			-560,756.80		-2,390,317.15
Accounts Payable						-352,620.44			1,385,123.87		-1,737,744.31
Undelivered Orders						-13,185,969.32			-1,759,232.55		-11,426,736.77
	Subtotal	70		0564		-0-	41,878,208.58		41,545,023.61	333,184.97	-0-
Management And Administration, Federal Emergency Management Agency, Department Of Homeland Security											
Fund Resources:											
Undisbursed Funds	2007-2008	70		0700			14,000,000.00				14,000,000.00
	2007					53,395,926.99	97,374,713.53		31,553,680.77		65,821,032.76
	2003					34,745,154.51			25,882,944.10		27,512,982.89
	2002-2003					23,804,485.06			10,429,834.95		24,315,319.56
	2002					[6]39,104,183.82			1,319,618.31		
	1999-2001					18,175,597.07			3,883,403.35		16,670,802.65
	No Year							-89,072.67	1,415,721.75		
Accounts Receivable						2,199,691.98				-2,090,744.25	4,290,436.23
Unfilled Customer Orders						5,096,685.04				889,121.68	4,207,563.36
Fund Equities:											
Unobligated Balances (Expired)						[6]-51,463,176.96				-10,200,953.93	-41,262,223.03
Unobligated Balances (Unexpired)						-10,882,197.40				12,004,591.36	-22,886,788.76
Accounts Payable						-4,728,243.78				5,801,991.29	-10,530,235.07
Undelivered Orders						[6]-109,448,106.33				-27,309,215.74	-82,138,890.59
	Subtotal	70		0700		-0-	111,374,713.53	-89,072.67	74,485,203.23	36,800,437.63	-0-
Grant Programs, Emergency Preparedness And Response, Department Of Homeland Security											
Fund Resources:											
Undisbursed Funds	2003-2004	70		0701		9,101,607.37			2,098,444.25		7,003,163.12
	2002-2003					2,830,307.74			23,627.36		2,806,680.38
	2001-2002					6,526,847.72			561,032.00	5,965,815.72	

Appropriations, Outlays, and Balances – Continued

Title	Period of Availability	Reg	Tr From	Account Number	Sub No.	Balances, Beginning Of Fiscal Year	Appropriations And Other Obligational Authority[1]	Transfers Borrowings And Investment (Net)[2]	Outlays (Net)	Balances Withdrawn And Other Transactions[3]	Balances, End Of Fiscal Year[4]
Grant Programs, Emergency Preparedness And Response, Department Of Homeland Security - Continued											
Fund Resources:- Continued											
Undisbursed Funds - Continued	No Year					86,326,273.40			29,396,299.51		56,929,973.89
Fund Equities:											
Unobligated Balances (Expired)						-5,985,986.50				-2,222,603.47	-3,763,383.03
Unobligated Balances (Unexpired)						-4,495,921.76				-2,766,374.60	-1,729,547.16
Accounts Payable						-33,301.76				-33,159.46	-142.30
Undelivered Orders						-94,269,826.21				-33,023,081.31	-61,246,744.90
Subtotal	Subtotal	70		0701		-0-			32,079,403.12	-32,079,403.12	-0-
Disaster Relief, Emergency Preparedness And Response											
Fund Resources:											
Undisbursed Funds	No Year	70		0702		22,450,303,929.79	5,742,500,000.00	-5,337,512.35	9,911,483,593.23		18,275,982,824.21
Unfilled Customer Orders						30,000.00				-30,000.00	30,000.00
Fund Equities:											
Unobligated Balances (Unexpired)						-5,502,734,712.16				-1,111,215,909.09	-4,391,518,803.07
Accounts Payable						-1,837,203,596.41				-1,234,459,632.68	-602,743,963.73
Undelivered Orders						-15,110,365,621.22				-1,828,615,563.81	-13,281,750,057.41
Subtotal	Subtotal	70		0702		-0-	5,742,500,000.00	-5,337,512.35	9,911,483,593.23	-4,174,321,105.58	-0-
Disaster Assistance Direct Loan Program Account, Emergency Preparedness And Response											
Fund Resources:											
Undisbursed Funds	2007	70		0703			1,262,696.00		994,051.84		268,644.16
	2006					251,171,169.44			47,684,593.97		203,486,575.47
	2005					211,099.95					211,099.95
	2004					104,568.41					104,568.41
	2003					816,514.39					816,514.39
	2002					750,248.79					
	No Year					319,013,722.30	327,160,506.96		281,808,377.74		364,365,851.52
Fund Equities:											
Unobligated Balances (Expired)						-78,110,664.90				-498,130.10	-77,612,534.80
Unobligated Balances (Unexpired)						-9,917,051.03				11,709.35	-9,928,760.38
Accounts Payable						-550,947.61				-539,700.81	-11,246.80
Undelivered Orders						-483,488,659.74				-1,787,947.82	-481,700,711.92
Subtotal	Subtotal	70		0703		-0-	328,423,202.96		330,487,023.55	-2,063,820.59	-0-
Emergency Management Planning And Assistance, Emergency Preparedness And Response											
Fund Resources:											
Undisbursed Funds	2003	70		0704		6,938,068.66			6,272,325.48		665,743.18
Fund Equities:											
Undelivered Orders						-6,938,068.66				-6,272,325.48	-665,743.18
Subtotal	Subtotal	70		0704		-0-			6,272,325.48	-6,272,325.48	-0-
Fire Assistance Grants, Emergency Preparedness And Response											
Fund Resources:											
Undisbursed Funds	2003-2004	70		0705		20,747,631.03			3,782,602.27		16,965,028.76
Accounts Receivable						44,435.24				-42,614.51	42,614.51
Unfilled Customer Orders										44,435.24	

Appropriations, Outlays, and Balances - Continued

Appropriation or Fund Account — Title	Period of Availability	Dept Reg	Tr From	Account Number	Sub No.	Balances, Beginning Of Fiscal Year	Appropriations And Other Obligational Authority[1]	Transfers Borrowings And Investment (Net)[2]	Outlays (Net)	Balances Withdrawn And Other Transactions[3]	Balances, End Of Fiscal Year[4]
Fund Equities:											
Unobligated Balances (Expired)						-11,402,862.31				757,615.48	-12,160,477.79
Accounts Payable						-486.94				-43.00	-443.94
Undelivered Orders						-9,388,717.02				-4,541,995.48	-4,846,721.54
	Subtotal	70		0705		-0-			3,782,602.27	-3,782,602.27	-0-
Emergency Food And Shelter, Emergency Preparedness And Response											
Fund Resources:											
Undisbursed Funds	No Year	70		0707		135.00	151,470,000.00		150,150,996.25		1,319,138.75
Fund Equities:											
Unobligated Balances (Unexpired)						-135.00					-135.00
Undelivered Orders										1,319,003.75	-1,319,003.75
	Subtotal	70		0707		-0-	151,470,000.00		150,150,996.25	1,319,003.75	-0-
Office Of The Under Secretary For Emergency Preparedness And Response, Emergency Preparedness And Response, Department Of Homeland Security											
Fund Resources:											
Undisbursed Funds	2005	70		0710		1,247,090.78					1,247,090.78
	2004					587,391.37			-13,549.66		600,941.03
Fund Equities:											
Unobligated Balances (Expired)						-1,450,628.13				69,812.47	-1,520,440.60
Accounts Payable						-3,684.13				-2,280.20	-1,403.93
Undelivered Orders						-380,169.89				-53,982.61	-326,187.28
	Subtotal	70		0710		-0-			-13,549.66	13,549.66	-0-
Preparedness, Mitigation, Response, And Recovery, Emergency Preparedness And Response, Department Of Homeland Security											
Fund Resources:											
Undisbursed Funds	2007	70		0711		114,547,224.74	201,479,079.38		110,184,885.00		91,294,194.38
	2006					2,791,779.87			29,734,874.72		84,812,350.02
	2005-2006					53,899,173.38			1,431,059.61		1,360,720.26
	2005					15,968,577.65		-372,688.22	11,720,441.52		41,806,043.64
	2004					10,000,000.00			3,201,080.71		12,767,496.94
	No Year								4,224,620.32		5,775,379.68
Fund Equities:											
Accounts Receivable						12,124,659.80				-4,656,589.34	16,781,249.14
Unfilled Customer Orders						441,145,538.03				118,955,991.86	322,189,546.17
Unobligated Balances (Expired)						-24,798,996.97				-4,857,390.09	-19,941,606.88
Unobligated Balances (Unexpired)						-6,474,026.00				-1,908,927.62	-4,565,098.38
Accounts Payable						-12,421,912.55				-2,251,471.27	-10,170,441.28
Undelivered Orders						-606,782,017.95				-64,672,184.26	-542,109,833.69
	Subtotal	70		0711		-0-	201,479,079.38	-372,688.22	160,496,961.88	40,609,429.28	-0-
Administrative And Regional Operations, Emergency Preparedness And Response, Department Of Homeland Security											
Fund Resources:											
Undisbursed Funds	2007	70		0712		59,703,170.18	220,895,545.70		169,671,870.48		51,223,675.22
	2006					3,664,803.26	-450,000.00	-1,234,900.31	37,328,443.16		20,689,826.71
	2005-2006								2,118,762.40		1,546,040.86
	2005					19,265,255.62		-39,320.09	1,770,265.09		17,455,670.44
	2004					1,269,431.43		-7,446.53	-4,395,380.86		5,657,365.76

Footnotes At End Of Chapter

Appropriations, Outlays, and Balances – Continued

Appropriation or Fund Account — Title	Period of Availability	Reg	Tr From	Account Number	Sub No.	Balances, Beginning Of Fiscal Year	Appropriations And Other Obligational Authority[1]	Transfers Borrowings And Investment (Net)[2]	Outlays (Net)	Balances Withdrawn And Other Transactions[3]	Balances, End Of Fiscal Year[4]
Administrative And Regional Operations, Emergency Preparedness And Response, Department Of Homeland Security - Continued											
Fund Resources: - Continued											
Undisbursed Funds - Continued	No Year					85,878,950.07			9,248,240.31		76,630,709.76
Accounts Receivable						1,537,966.69				-1,063,243.28	2,601,209.97
Unfilled Customer Orders						19,706,325.42				9,701,069.57	10,005,255.85
Fund Equities:											
Unobligated Balances (Expired)						-8,158,307.78				5,010,512.38	-13,168,820.16
Unobligated Balances (Unexpired)						-84,388,227.49				-42,110,668.25	-42,277,559.24
Accounts Payable						-7,428,422.77				1,409,692.37	-8,838,115.14
Undelivered Orders						-91,050,944.63				30,474,315.40	-121,525,260.03
	Subtotal	70		0712		-0-	220,445,545.70	-1,281,666.93	215,742,200.58	3,421,678.19	-0-
Public Health Programs, Emergency Preparedness And Response, Department Of Homeland Security											
Fund Resources:											
Undisbursed Funds	2007	70		0713			3,445,775.17		3,445,775.17		
	2006					8,884,111.67		-5,661,718.72	3,222,392.95		
	2005-2006					155,367.38		-145,498.06	9,869.32		
	2005					3,839,830.17		-3,560,512.93	279,317.24		
	2004					26,253,798.73		-1,162,481.24	16,064,565.20		9,026,752.29
	No Year					30,181,559.60		-30,181,559.60			
Fund Equities:											
Unobligated Balances (Expired)						-1,223,868.51				2,494,540.45	-3,718,408.96
Unobligated Balances (Unexpired)						-30,054,587.49				-30,054,587.49	
Accounts Payable						-1,420,417.06				-1,420,417.06	
Undelivered Orders						-36,615,794.49				-31,307,451.16	-5,308,343.33
	Subtotal	70		0713		-0-	3,445,775.17	-40,711,770.55	23,021,919.88	-60,287,915.26	-0-
Radiological Emergency Preparedness Program, Federal Emergency Management Agency, Department Of Homeland Security											
Fund Resources:											
Undisbursed Funds	2007-2008	70		0715					-26,940,413.11		[1]26,940,413.11
	2006-2008								-3,204,124.92		3,204,124.92
	2005-2007								-6,594,988.65		6,594,988.65
	2006					95,488.08			-4,781,674.13		4,877,162.21
	No Year					31,974,852.72		1,457,145.12	-8,995,833.17		42,427,831.01
Accounts Receivable						73,609.77				-1,299,305.23	1,372,915.00
Unfilled Customer Orders						13,104,540.01				-1,882,680.30	14,987,220.31
Fund Equities:											
Unobligated Balances (Expired)										190,652.00	-190,652.00
Unobligated Balances (Unexpired)						-27,555,720.93				3,494,337.53	-31,050,058.46
Accounts Payable						-1,061,477.74				725,067.41	-1,786,545.15
Undelivered Orders						-16,631,291.91				50,746,107.69	-67,377,399.60
	Subtotal	70		0715		-0-		1,457,145.12	-50,517,033.98	51,974,179.10	-0-
National Pre-Disaster Mitigation Fund, Emergency Preparedness And Response, Department Of Homeland Security											
Fund Resources:											
Undisbursed Funds	No Year	70		0716		272,489,570.42	100,000,000.00		61,246,213.37		311,243,357.05

Appropriations, Outlays, and Balances - Continued

Appropriation or Fund Account — Title	Period of Availability	Dept Reg	Dept Tr From	Account Number	Sub No.	Balances, Beginning Of Fiscal Year	Appropriations And Other Obligational Authority[1]	Transfers Borrowings And Investment (Net)[2]	Outlays (Net)	Balances Withdrawn And Other Transactions[3]	Balances, End Of Fiscal Year[4]
Fund Equities:											
Unobligated Balances (Unexpired)						-34,337,731.35				29,424,228.60	-63,761,959.95
Accounts Payable						-99,552.17				535,724.31	-635,276.48
Undelivered Orders						-238,052,286.90				8,793,833.72	-246,846,120.62
Subtotal		70		0716		-0-	100,000,000.00		61,246,213.37	38,753,786.63	-0-
National Flood Mitigation Fund, Emergency Preparedness And Response, Department Of Homeland Security											
Fund Resources:											
Undisbursed Funds	2007-2008	70		0717				31,000,000.00	186,206.96		30,813,793.04
	2006-2007					27,623,908.96			2,793,977.13		24,829,931.83
	2005-2006					18,748,562.63			4,988,078.67		13,760,483.96
	2004-2005					16,334,392.24			6,975,188.92		9,359,203.32
Fund Equities:											
Unobligated Balances (Expired)						[6]588,808.81				450,647.40	-1,039,456.21
Unobligated Balances (Unexpired)						-10,465,962.14				963,435.60	-11,429,397.74
Undelivered Orders						[6]-51,652,092.88				14,642,465.32	-66,294,558.20
Subtotal		70		0717		-0-		31,000,000.00	14,943,451.68	16,056,548.32	-0-
Emergency Management Performance Grants, Federal Emergency Management Agency, Department Of Homeland Security											
Fund Resources:											
Undisbursed Funds	2007	70		0718			250,000,000.00		73,288,336.97		176,711,663.03
	2006					111,933,531.11			89,474,259.11		22,459,272.00
	2005					167,434,656.00			5,963,191.04		161,471,464.96
	2004					5,537,960.11			2,731,778.71		2,806,181.40
Fund Equities:											
Unobligated Balances (Expired)						-2,043,427.13				40,018.54	-2,083,445.67
Accounts Payable						-24,454,396.26				6,406,012.79	-30,860,409.05
Undelivered Orders						-258,408,323.83				72,096,402.84	-330,504,726.67
Subtotal		70		0718		-0-	250,000,000.00		171,457,565.83	78,542,434.17	-0-
Cerro Grande Fire Claims, Emergency Preparedness And Response, Department Of Homeland Security											
Fund Resources:											
Undisbursed Funds	No Year	70		0719		9,496,259.03			178,838.88		9,317,420.15
Fund Equities:											
Unobligated Balances (Unexpired)						-301,739.52				8,939,633.63	-9,241,373.15
Accounts Payable						-9,123,580.06				-9,120,214.35	-3,365.71
Undelivered Orders						-70,939.45				1,741.84	-72,681.29
Subtotal		70		0719		-0-			178,838.88	-178,838.88	-0-
Special Fund Accounts											
Radiological Emergency Preparedness Fund, Federal Emergency Management Agency, Department Of Homeland Security											
Fund Resources:											
Undisbursed Funds	No Year	70		5436		2,266,356.95		-1,457,145.12	809,211.83		------
Unfilled Customer Orders						547.59				547.59	------
Fund Equities:											
Unobligated Balances (Unexpired)						-18,882.41				-18,882.41	------

Footnotes At End Of Chapter

Appropriations, Outlays, and Balances – Continued

Appropriation or Fund Account — Title	Period of Availability	Reg	Tr From	Account Number	Sub No.	Balances, Beginning Of Fiscal Year	Appropriations And Other Obligational Authority[1]	Transfers Borrowings And Investment (Net)[2]	Outlays (Net)	Balances Withdrawn And Other Transactions[3]	Balances, End Of Fiscal Year[4]
Radiological Emergency Preparedness Fund, Federal Emergency Management Agency, Department Of Homeland Security - Continued											
Fund Equities: - Continued											
Accounts Payable						-130,453.50				-130,453.50	
Undelivered Orders						-2,117,568.63				-2,117,568.63	-0-
	Subtotal	70		5436		-0-		-1,457,145.12	809,211.83	-2,266,356.95	
Flood Map Modernization Fund, Emergency Preparedness And Response, Department Of Homeland Security											
Fund Resources:											
Undisbursed Funds	No Year	70		5464		2,307,146.97		-2,274,391.94	32,755.03		
Fund Equities:											
Unobligated Balances (Unexpired)						-2,259,971.20				-2,259,971.20	
Accounts Payable						-50,882.26				-50,882.26	
Undelivered Orders						3,706.49				3,706.49	
	Subtotal	70		5464		-0-		-2,274,391.94	32,755.03	-2,307,146.97	-0-
Public Enterprise Funds											
National Flood Insurance Fund, Federal Emergency Management Agency, Department Of Homeland Security											
Fund Resources:											
Undisbursed Funds	2007-2008	70		4236				59,358,000.00	32,231,739.51		27,126,260.49
	2007							38,230,000.00	29,390,601.29		8,839,398.71
	2006-2007					50,711,088.54			27,822,653.36		22,888,435.18
	2006					16,574,229.45			5,988,007.76		10,586,221.69
	No Year					8,455,692.90		[12]521,412,000.00	21,919,653.49		507,948,039.41
Authority To Borrow From The Treasury						4,115,000,000.00		-650,000,000.00			3,465,000,000.00
Fund Equities:											
Unobligated Balances (Expired)						-3,935,391.18				5,713,461.50	-9,648,852.68
Unobligated Balances (Unexpired)						-3,148,920,732.87				-133,742,876.87	-3,015,177,856.00
Accounts Payable						-902,194,756.08				-13,898,152.02	-888,296,604.06
Undelivered Orders						-135,690,130.76				-6,425,088.02	-129,265,042.74
	Subtotal	70		4236		-0-		-31,000,000.00	117,352,655.41	-148,352,655.41	-0-
Total, Federal Emergency Management Agency							10,794,967,316.74	-47,792,710.72	14,483,274,883.24	-3,736,100,277.22	
Science And Technology											
General Fund Accounts											
Research, Development, Operations And Acquisitions, Science And Technology, Department Of Homeland Security											
Fund Resources:											
Undisbursed Funds	2003-2007	70		0800		3,169,293.60					3,169,293.60
	2003-2005					27,693.31					27,693.31
	2003-2004					32,672,391.02			17,687,701.32		14,984,689.70
	2003					144,565.10					144,565.10
	No Year					1,548,587,947.97	713,131,000.00		996,019,108.00		1,265,699,839.97
Accounts Receivable						1,492,451.24				-1,361,545.32	2,853,996.56
Unfilled Customer Orders						32,380,009.93				1,632,280.25	30,747,729.68

Appropriations, Outlays, and Balances - Continued

Appropriation or Fund Account — Title	Period of Availability	Account Symbol — Dept — Reg	Account Symbol — Dept — Tr From	Account Symbol — Account Number	Account Symbol — Sub No.	Balances, Beginning Of Fiscal Year	Appropriations And Other Obligational Authority[1]	Transfers Borrowings And Investment (Net)[2]	Outlays (Net)	Balances Withdrawn And Other Transactions[3]	Balances, End Of Fiscal Year[4]
Fund Equities:											
Unobligated Balances (Expired)						-31,435,354.33				-28,967,554.71	-2,467,799.62
Unobligated Balances (Unexpired)						-404,017,988.07				-116,114,425.79	-287,903,562.28
Accounts Payable						-97,385,422.03				-1,183,728.38	-96,201,693.65
Undelivered Orders						-1,085,635,587.74			1,013,706,809.32	-154,580,835.37	-931,054,752.37
	Subtotal	70		0800		-0-	713,131,000.00			-300,575,809.32	-0-
Management And Administration, Science And Technology, Department Of Homeland Security											
Fund Resources:											
Undisbursed Funds	2007	70		0810		30,815,712.06	135,000,000.00		78,972,267.86		56,027,732.14
	2006					8,229,222.84	-1,215,486.00		21,206,889.79		8,393,336.27
	2005					6,093,800.63			3,883,152.38		4,346,070.46
	2004								129,424.23		5,964,376.40
Accounts Receivable						157,263.09				56,960.92	100,302.17
Unfilled Customer Orders						100,000.00				100,000.00	-0-
Fund Equities:											
Unobligated Balances (Expired)						-3,383,480.35				2,044,375.25	-5,427,855.60
Accounts Payable						-6,555,382.67				2,555,014.42	-9,110,397.09
Undelivered Orders						-35,457,135.60				24,836,429.15	-60,293,564.75
	Subtotal	70		0810		-0-	133,784,514.00		104,191,734.26	29,592,779.74	-0-
Total, Science And Technology							846,915,514.00		1,117,898,543.58	-270,983,029.58	
Domestic Nuclear Detection Office											
General Fund Accounts											
Research, Development, And Operations, Domestic Nuclear Detection Office, Department Of Homeland Security											
Fund Resources:											
Undisbursed Funds	No Year	70		0860			307,500,000.00		87,439,929.73		220,060,070.27
Fund Equities:											
Unobligated Balances (Unexpired)										52,581,599.83	-52,581,599.83
Accounts Payable										2,908,776.13	-2,908,776.13
Undelivered Orders										164,569,694.31	-164,569,694.31
	Subtotal	70		0860		-0-	307,500,000.00		87,439,929.73	220,060,070.27	-0-
Management And Administration, Domestic Nuclear Detection Office, Department Of Homeland Security											
Fund Resources:											
Undisbursed Funds	2007	70		0861			30,468,000.00		16,128,954.13		14,339,045.87
Fund Equities:											
Unobligated Balances (Expired)										736,322.46	-736,322.46
Accounts Payable										675,862.05	-675,862.05
Undelivered Orders										12,926,861.36	-12,926,861.36
	Subtotal	70		0861		-0-	30,468,000.00		16,128,954.13	14,339,045.87	-0-
Systems Acquisition, Domestic Nuclear Detection Office, Department Of Homeland Security											
Fund Resources:											
Undisbursed Funds	2007-2009	70		0862			178,000,000.00		10,127,164.58		167,872,835.42

Footnotes At End Of Chapter

Appropriations, Outlays, and Balances – Continued

Appropriation or Fund Account — Title	Period of Availability	Reg	Tr From	Account Number	Sub No.	Balances, Beginning Of Fiscal Year	Appropriations And Other Obligational Authority[1]	Transfers Borrowings And Investment (Net)[2]	Outlays (Net)	Balances Withdrawn And Other Transactions[3]	Balances, End Of Fiscal Year[4]
Systems Acquisition, Domestic Nuclear Detection Office, Department Of Homeland Security - Continued											
Fund Resources: - Continued											
Undisbursed Funds - Continued											
	No Year						100,000,000.00				100,000,000.00
Fund Equities:											
Unobligated Balances (Unexpired)										164,330,193.54	-164,330,193.54
Undelivered Orders										103,542,641.88	-103,542,641.88
	Subtotal	70		0862		-0-	278,000,000.00			267,872,835.42	-0-
Total, Domestic Nuclear Detection Office							615,968,000.00		10,127,164.58	502,271,951.56	
									113,696,048.44		
Information Anaylsis And Infrastructure Protection											
General Fund Accounts											
Operating Expenses, Information Analysis And Infrastructure Protection (DOD)											
Fund Resources:											
Undisbursed Funds	2003-2004	70		0900		1,545,664.43			-3,583.52		1,549,247.95
	2003					4,369,153.01			12,543.71		4,356,609.30
	2002-2003					11,663,886.61			820,964.14		10,842,922.47
	2002					4,058,997.32				4,058,997.32	
	2001-2002					109,669.17				109,669.17	
	No Year					4,185,072.05			3,609,656.99		575,415.06
Fund Equities:											
Unobligated Balances (Expired)						-20,375,479.70				6,354,283.14	-14,021,196.56
Unobligated Balances (Unexpired)						-11,160.95				19,118.48	-30,279.43
Accounts Payable						485,659.71				-126,927.40	-358,732.31
Undelivered Orders						-5,060,142.23				-2,146,155.75	-2,913,986.48
	Subtotal	70		0900		-0-			4,439,581.32	4,439,581.32	-0-
Management And Administration, Information Analysis And Infrastructure Protection, Department Of Homeland Security											
Fund Resources:											
Undisbursed Funds	2005	70		0910		12,568,763.19			940,539.30		11,628,223.89
	2004					12,564,739.53			6,166,357.28		6,398,382.25
Fund Equities:											
Unobligated Balances (Expired)						-7,984,584.41				1,220,901.76	-9,205,486.17
Accounts Payable						-2,175,980.19				-660,218.06	-1,515,762.13
Undelivered Orders						-14,972,938.12				-7,667,580.28	-7,305,357.84
	Subtotal	70		0910		-0-			7,106,896.58	7,106,896.58	-0-
Assessments And Evaluations, Information Analysis And Infrastructure Protection, Department Of Homeland Security											
Fund Resources:											
Undisbursed Funds	2005-2006	70		0911		203,427,854.64		-4,276,499.00	127,154,253.31		71,997,102.33
	2004-2005					58,663,974.12			13,803,015.49		44,860,958.63
Accounts Receivable						71,298.00				71,298.00	
Unfilled Customer Orders						239,141.07				52,858.72	186,282.35
Fund Equities:											
Unobligated Balances (Expired)						-10,514,174.30				7,093,599.63	-17,607,773.93

Appropriations, Outlays, and Balances - Continued

Appropriation or Fund Account — Title	Period of Availability	Dept Reg	Dept Tr From	Account Number	Sub No.	Balances, Beginning Of Fiscal Year	Appropriations And Other Obligational Authority[1]	Transfers Borrowings And Investment (Net)[2]	Outlays (Net)	Balances Withdrawn And Other Transactions[3]	Balances, End Of Fiscal Year[4]
Accounts Payable						-21,174,927.67				2,082,912.86	-23,257,840.53
Undelivered Orders						-230,713,165.86				-154,534,437.01	-76,178,728.85
Subtotal		70		0911		-0-		-4,276,499.00	140,957,268.80	-145,233,767.80	-0-
Total, Information Analysis And Infrastructure Protection								-4,276,499.00	152,503,746.70	-156,780,245.70	
Deductions For Offsetting Receipts											
Proprietary Receipts From The Public							-32,686,676.01		-32,686,676.01		
Intrabudgetary Transactions							-1,602,253.60		-1,602,253.60		
Offsetting Governmental Receipts							-5,078,129,535.80		-5,078,129,535.80		
Total							-5,112,418,465.41		-5,112,418,465.41		
Total, Department Of Homeland Security							40,005,148,599.95	238,639,894.75	39,171,833,209.00	1,071,955,285.70	
Memorandum											
Financing Accounts											
Public Enterprise Funds											
Disaster Assistance Direct Loan Financing Account, Emergency Preparedness And Response											
Fund Resources:											
Undisbursed Funds	No Year	70		4234		45,887,553.25		44,388,379.46	-161,270,798.92		251,546,731.63
Authority To Borrow From The Treasury						114,868,677.84		45,054,559.60		69,814,118.24	359,962,570.82
Unfilled Customer Orders						481,441,509.73				121,478,938.91	
Fund Equities:											
Unobligated Balances (Unexpired)						-275,727.85				131,283,480.18	-131,559,208.03
Undelivered Orders						-641,922,012.97		-666,180.14		-161,971,918.55	-479,950,094.42
Subtotal		70		4234		-0-		-666,180.14	-161,270,798.92	160,604,618.78	-0-
Total, Financing Accounts								-666,180.14	-161,270,798.92	160,604,618.78	

Footnotes At End Of Chapter

Appropriations, Outlays, and Balances – Continued

Footnotes

1. The amounts in this column, unless otherwise footnoted, represent appropriations, increases and rescissions in borrowing authority or new contract authority. Appropriation accounts with appropriation transfer activity are presented in Table 1 (Appropriations and Appropriation Transfers) at the end of this chapter.

2. The amounts in this column, unless otherwise footnoted, represent transfers - other than appropriation transfers, borrowings (gross), investments (net), unrealized discounts or funds held outside the Treasury.

3. The amounts in this column, unless otherwise footnoted, represent obligated balances canceled for fiscal year 2002 pursuant to 31 U.S.C. 1553, changes in unfilled customer orders, accounts receivable, accounts payable, undelivered orders, unobligated balances and adjustments to borrowing and contract authority.

4. Unobligated balances for no-year or unexpired multiple year accounts are available for obligation; unobligated balances for expired fiscal year accounts are not available for obligation.

5. Includes $254,767.29 which represents payments for obligations of a closed account

6. The opening balances of the following accounts have been adjusted during the current fiscal year and do not agree with last year's closing balances:

Account	Adjustment
70 06 0503 - Undisbursed Balance	$1,138,226.06
70 06 0503 - Unobligated Balance (Expired)	-1,138,226.06
70 9901 0700 - Undisbursed Balance	39,104,183.82
70 9901 0700 - Unobligated Balance (Expired)	-8,277,269.21
70 9901 0700 - Undelivered Orders	-30,826,914.61
70 0506 0717 - Unobligated Balance (Expired)	13,141,920.76
70 0506 0717 - Undelivered Orders	-13,141,920.76

7. Includes $438,344.98 which represents payments for obligations of a closed account.

8. Includes $30,509.52 which represents payments for obligations of a closed account.

9. Subject to disposition by the administrative agency.

10. Includes $9,756,872.00 which is subject to disposition by the administrative agency.

11. Includes $1,000.55 which is subject to disposition by the administrative agency.

12. Includes $650,000,000.00 which represents borrowing from the U.S. Treasury.

Appropriations, Outlays, and Balances - Continued

Footnotes

Table 1 - Appropriations And Appropriation Transfers - Department Of Homeland Security

Department Regular	Fiscal Year	Account Symbol	Net Appropriations And Appropriations Transfers	Appropriation Amount	Net Appropriation Transfers	Department Regular Involved	Fiscal Year Involved	Accounts Involved	Amount From or To (-)
20	X	8147	-525,489,378.69	0.00	-525,489,378.69	14	X	8151	-525,489,378.69
20	X	8185	-167,563,646.54	0.00	-167,563,646.54	14	X	8370	-6,902,924.00
						68	X	8221	-15,733,617.00
						69	0608	8121	-5,000,000.00
						69	0709	8121	-6,850,000.00
						70	X	8312	-38,432,383.99
						70	07	8314	-44,550,000.00
						70	X	8349	-45,893,323.83
						95	X	8056	-4,201,397.72
70	X	0102	11,979,761.00	0.00	11,979,761.00	11	X	5512	11,979,761.00
70	07	0110	95,336,500.00	94,470,000.00	866,500.00	70	X	0508	-300,000.00
						70	07	0566	1,166,500.00
70	07	0111	141,334,000.00	146,334,000.00	-5,000,000.00	70	X	0508	-5,000,000.00
70	X	0113	251,492,000.00	269,492,000.00	-18,000,000.00	70	X	0565	-18,000,000.00
70	07	0113	79,057,022.73	79,521,000.00	-463,977.27	70	07	0565	-463,977.27
70	07	0117	4,041,116.00	0.00	4,041,116.00	70	07	0566	4,041,116.00
70	0708	0117	15,287,647.00	8,000,000.00	7,287,647.00	70	0708	0565	7,287,647.00
70	X	0200	17,500,000.00	0.00	17,500,000.00	70	X	0702	17,500,000.00
70	X	0403	3,605,800.00	2,500,000.00	1,105,800.00	11	X	5512	105,800.00
						70	07	0403	1,000,000.00
70	07	0403	927,357,000.00	961,779,000.00	-34,422,000.00	70	X	0403	-1,000,000.00
						70	0708	0403	-18,000,000.00
						70	0709	0403	-18,400,000.00
						70	07	0404	-3,481,000.00
						70	07	0700	6,459,000.00
70	0708	0403	18,000,000.00	0.00	18,000,000.00	70	07	0403	18,000,000.00
70	0709	0403	18,400,000.00	0.00	18,400,000.00	70	07	0403	18,400,000.00
70	07	0404	308,635,000.00	305,154,000.00	3,481,000.00	70	07	0403	3,481,000.00
						70	07	0110	300,000.00
70	X	0508	69,480,000.00	0.00	69,480,000.00	70	07	0111	5,000,000.00
						70	0708	0550	64,000,000.00
						70	0708	0557	180,000.00
70	07	0509	167,235,000.00	210,733,000.00	-43,498,000.00	70	0708	0509	-43,498,000.00
70	0708	0509	43,498,000.00	0.00	43,498,000.00	70	07	0509	43,498,000.00
70	X	0530	74,349,990.00	0.00	74,349,990.00	11	X	5512	74,349,990.00
70	07	0530	5,471,160,000.00	4,016,095,220.54	1,455,064,779.46	70	X	0544	5,000,000.00
						70	X	5695	1,450,064,779.46
70	0708	0530	172,692,450.00	168,000,000.00	4,692,450.00	11	X	1070	292,450.00
						72	X	1093	4,400,000.00
70	X	0540	14,559,281.00	0.00	14,559,281.00	11	X	5512	3,559,281.00
						70	07	0540	11,000,000.00
70	07	0540	3,876,000,000.00	3,887,000,000.00	-11,000,000.00	70	X	0540	-11,000,000.00
70	0708	0540	7,569,005.00	6,000,000.00	1,569,005.00	11	0708	1070	1,569,005.00
70	X	0544	597,187,000.00	602,187,000.00	-5,000,000.00	70	07	0530	-5,000,000.00

Footnotes At End Of Chapter

Appropriations, Outlays, and Balances – Continued

Footnotes

Table 1 - Appropriations And Appropriation Transfers - Department Of Homeland Security

Department Regular	Fiscal Year	Account Symbol	Net Appropriations And Appropriations Transfers	Appropriation Amount	Net Appropriation Transfers	Department Regular Involved	Fiscal Year Involved	Accounts Involved	Amount From or To (-)
70	0708	0550	2,381,398,973.25	2,449,368,973.25	-67,970,000.00	70	X	0508	-64,000,000.00
						70	0708	0557	-3,970,000.00
70	0708	0557	43,490,000.00	39,700,000.00	3,790,000.00	70	X	0508	-180,000.00
						70	0708	0550	3,970,000.00
70	07	0560	2,747,970,791.42	2,743,000,000.00	4,970,791.42	70	07	0564	4,970,791.42
70	07	0564	41,878,208.58	46,849,000.00	-4,970,791.42	70	07	0560	-4,970,791.42
70	X	0565	22,978,000.00	0.00	22,978,000.00	70	X	0113	18,000,000.00
						70	X	0800	4,978,000.00
70	07	0565	77,463,977.27	77,000,000.00	463,977.27	70	07	0113	463,977.27
70	0708	0565	487,345,353.00	494,633,000.00	-7,287,647.00	70	0708	0117	-7,287,647.00
70	07	0566	13,469,097.13	30,572,000.00	-17,102,902.87	70	07	0110	-1,166,500.00
						70	07	0117	-4,041,116.00
						70	07	0712	-11,895,286.87
70	07	0610	5,663,727,001.00	5,453,402,000.00	210,325,001.00	11	0708	1070	32,001.00
						17	07	1804	210,293,000.00
70	07	0700	97,374,713.53	0.00	97,374,713.53	70	07	0403	-6,459,000.00
						70	07	0711	42,520,920.62
						70	07	0712	61,312,792.91
70	X	0702	5,742,500,000.00	5,610,000,000.00	132,500,000.00	70	X	0200	-17,500,000.00
						73	X	1152	150,000,000.00
70	07	0711	201,479,079.38	244,000,000.00	-42,520,920.62	70	07	0700	-42,520,920.62
70	07	0712	220,895,545.70	282,000,000.00	-61,104,454.30	70	07	0566	11,895,286.87
						70	07	0700	-61,312,792.91
						75	07	0140	-11,686,948.26
70	07	0713	3,445,775.17	33,885,000.00	-30,439,222.83	75	07	0140	-30,439,224.83
70	X	0800	713,131,000.00	718,109,000.00	-4,978,000.00	70	X	0565	-4,978,000.00
70	X	5533	-5,332,000.00	-5,332,000.00	-5,332,000.00	13	X	5521	-5,332,000.00
70	X	5695	0.00	1,450,064,779.46	-1,450,064,775.46	70	07	0530	-1,450,064,779.46
70	X	8149	89,500,000.00	0.00	89,500,000.00	14	X	8151	89,500,000.00
70	X	8312	38,432,383.99	0.00	38,432,383.99	20	X	8185	38,432,383.99
70	07	8314	44,550,000.00	0.00	44,550,000.00	20	07	8185	44,550,000.00
70	X	8349	45,893,323.83	0.00	45,893,323.83	20	X	8185	45,893,323.83
70	X	8870	3,026,000.00	0.00	3,026,000.00	20	X	8863	3,026,000.00
Totals			30,367,320,770.75	30,429,848,973.25	-62,528,202.50				-62,528,202.50

Appropriations, Outlays, and Balances – Continued

Footnotes

This Page Left Blank Intentionally

Appropriations, Outlays, and Balances – Continued

Appropriation or Fund Account — Title	Period of Availability	Dept Reg	Dept Tr From	Account Number	Sub No.	Balances, Beginning Of Fiscal Year	Appropriations And Other Obligational Authority[1]	Transfers Borrowings And Investment (Net)[2]	Outlays (Net)	Balances Withdrawn And Other Transactions[3]	Balances, End Of Fiscal Year[4]
Department Of Housing And Urban Development											
Public And Indian Housing Programs											
General Fund Accounts											
Public Housing Operating Fund, Public And Indian Housing, Housing And Urban Development											
Fund Resources:											
Undisbursed Funds	2007	86		0163		935,707,747.98	3,864,000,000.00		2,772,559,395.61		1,091,440,604.39
	2006					1,131,689.06			935,299,113.64		408,634.34
	2005					440,790.39			292,719.07		838,969.99
	2004					1,129,216.65			-1,493,887.46		1,934,677.85
	2003					62,047.52			-13,808.72		1,143,025.37
	2002-2003								-312,621.09		374,668.61
	No Year					4,040,041.63			-56,310.98		4,096,352.61
Fund Equities:											
Unobligated Balances (Expired)						-1,069,057.81				3,090,480.44	-4,159,538.25
Unobligated Balances (Unexpired)						-1,222,974.28				-1,166,662.02	-56,312.26
Accounts Payable						-145,285,428.21				42,874,744.16	-188,160,172.37
Undelivered Orders						-794,934,072.93				112,926,837.35	-907,860,910.28
Subtotal		86		0163		-0-	3,864,000,000.00		3,706,274,600.07	157,725,399.93	-0-
Drug Elimination Grants For Low-Income Housing, Housing Programs, Housing And Urban Development											
Fund Resources:											
Undisbursed Funds	No Year	86		0197		3,227,715.23			809,234.57		2,418,480.66
Fund Equities:											
Unobligated Balances (Unexpired)						-1.29				650,959.53	-660,960.82
Accounts Payable						-78,502.94				-7,478.53	-71,024.41
Undelivered Orders						-3,149,211.00				-1,452,715.57	-1,696,495.43
Subtotal		86		0197		-0-			809,234.57	-809,234.57	-0-
Revitalization Of Severely Distressed Public Housing, (Hope VI, Public And Indian Housing, Housing And Urban Development											
Fund Resources:											
Undisbursed Funds	2007-2008	86		0218			99,000,000.00		8,030,798.08		99,000,000.00
	2006-2007					96,408,750.00	-8,903.80		20,835,720.56		88,369,048.12
	2005-2006					137,642,476.82			32,731,054.89		116,806,756.26
	2004-2005					121,345,705.95			112,962,076.10		88,614,651.06
	2003-2004					381,885,733.89			89,539,885.55		268,923,657.79
	2002-2003					249,653,970.21			252,393,539.69		570,114,084.66
	No Year					830,494,209.59	-2,525,290.27				575,575,379.63
Fund Equities:											
Unobligated Balances (Expired)						-4,138,796.21				476,212.23	-4,615,008.44
Unobligated Balances (Unexpired)						-59,591,722.46				38,480,114.59	-98,071,837.05
Accounts Payable						-5,224,595.64				-719,704.32	-4,504,891.32
Undelivered Orders						-1,748,475,732.15				-458,263,891.44	-1,290,211,840.71
Subtotal		86		0218		-0-	96,465,805.93		516,493,074.87	-420,027,268.94	-0-

Appropriations, Outlays, and Balances - Continued

Appropriation or Fund Account (Title)	Period of Availability	Dept Reg	Dept Tr From	Account Number	Sub No.	Balances, Beginning Of Fiscal Year	Appropriations And Other Obligational Authority[1]	Transfers Borrowings And Investment (Net)[2]	Outlays (Net)	Balances Withdrawn And Other Transactions[3]	Balances, End Of Fiscal Year[4]
Indian Housing Loan Guarantee Fund Program Account, Public And Indian Housing, Housing And Urban Development											
Fund Resources:											
Undisbursed Funds	No Year	86		0223		6,420,102.26	6,613,842.00	------	6,166,297.00	------	6,867,647.26
Fund Equities:											
Unobligated Balances (Unexpired)						-4,617,304.20	------	------	------	599,098.32	-5,216,402.52
Undelivered Orders						-1,802,798.06	------	------	------	-151,553.32	-1,651,244.74
Subtotal				0223		-0-	6,613,842.00	------	6,166,297.00	447,545.00	-0-
Native Hawaiian Housing Loan Guarantee Fund Program Account, Public And Indian Housing, Housing And Urban Development											
Fund Resources:											
Undisbursed Funds	No Year	86		0233		4,723,047.00	856,350.00	------	------	------	5,579,397.00
Fund Equities:											
Unobligated Balances (Unexpired)						-4,723,047.00	------	------	------	856,350.00	-5,579,397.00
Subtotal				0233		-0-	856,350.00	------	------	856,350.00	-0-
Native Hawaiian Housing Block Grant, Public And Indian Housing, Housing And Urban Development											
Fund Resources:											
Undisbursed Funds	No Year	86		0235		8,726,850.00	8,726,850.00	------	8,377,770.00	------	9,075,930.00
Fund Equities:											
Unobligated Balances (Unexpired)						-8,726,850.00	------	------	------	266,511.00	-8,993,361.00
Undelivered Orders							------	------	------	82,569.00	-82,569.00
Subtotal				0235		-0-	8,726,850.00	------	8,377,770.00	349,080.00	-0-
Tenant-Based Rental Assistance, Public And Indian Housing, Housing And Urban Development											
Fund Resources:											
Undisbursed Funds	2006-2007	86		0302		279,915,641.00		------	174,883,274.00	------	105,032,367.00
Undisbursed Funds	No Year	86				1,724,335,585.00	15,880,766,265.00	------	15,795,775,877.00	------	1,809,325,973.00
Fund Equities:											
Unobligated Balances (Expired)						-723,898,892.00	------	------	------	-373,625,258.00	-350,273,634.00
Unobligated Balances (Unexpired)						-1,599,050.00	------	------	------	-1,259,538.00	-339,512.00
Accounts Payable						-1,278,753,284.00	------	------	------	284,637,218.00	-1,563,390,502.00
Undelivered Orders							------	------	------	354,692.00	-354,692.00
Subtotal				0302		-0-	15,880,766,265.00	------	15,970,659,151.00	-89,892,886.00	-0-
Project-Based Rental Assistance, Public And Indian Housing, Housing And Urban Development											
Fund Resources:											
Undisbursed Funds	No Year	86		0303		2,809,345,802.45	5,975,031,000.00	------	5,706,428,397.91	------	3,077,948,404.54
Fund Equities:											
Unobligated Balances (Unexpired)						-189,352,422.00	------	------	------	194,615,306.82	-383,967,728.82
Accounts Payable						-3,443,213.00	------	------	------	-3,396,072.00	-47,141.00
Undelivered Orders						-2,616,550,167.45	------	------	------	77,383,367.27	-2,693,933,534.72
Subtotal				0303		-0-	5,975,031,000.00	------	5,706,428,397.91	268,602,602.09	-0-
Public Housing Capital Fund, Public And Indian Housing, Housing And Urban Development											
Fund Resources:											
Undisbursed Funds	2007-2010	86		0304			2,428,074,000.00	------	9,823,705.78	------	2,418,250,294.22
Undisbursed Funds	2006-2009					2,343,956,861.38	------	------	697,950,388.45	------	1,646,006,472.93

Footnotes At End Of Chapter

Appropriations, Outlays, and Balances – Continued

Appropriation or Fund Account: Title	Period of Availability	Dept Reg	Tr From	Account Number	Sub No.	Balances, Beginning Of Fiscal Year	Appropriations And Other Obligational Authority[1]	Transfers Borrowings And Investment (Net)[2]	Outlays (Net)	Balances Withdrawn And Other Transactions[3]	Balances, End Of Fiscal Year[4]
Public Housing Capital Fund, Public And Indian Housing, Housing And Urban Development - Continued											
Fund Resources: - Continued											
Undisbursed Funds - Continued											
	2005-2008					1,825,034,565.72			953,092,578.72		871,941,987.00
	2004-2007					992,059,794.54	-197,346.51		463,845,840.40		528,016,607.63
	2003-2006					489,061,707.15			409,682,970.49		79,378,736.66
	2002-2005					68,190,369.92			22,732,175.32		45,458,194.60
	No Year					1,416,495,351.85	-7,387,175.63		514,270,883.48		894,837,292.74
Unfunded Contract Authority						1,581,595,785.21				5,423,339.70	1,576,172,445.51
Fund Equities:											
Unobligated Balances (Expired)						-8,675,771.86				4,202,637.81	-12,878,409.67
Unobligated Balances (Unexpired)						-334,733,540.09				-174,761,639.06	-159,971,901.03
Accounts Payable						-86,726,118.42				-11,093,628.59	-75,632,489.83
Undelivered Orders						-8,286,259,005.40				-474,679,774.64	-7,811,579,230.76
Subtotal		86		0304		-0-	2,420,489,477.86		3,071,398,542.64	-650,909,064.78	-0-
Prevention Of Resident Displacement, Housing Programs, Housing And Urban Development											
Fund Resources:											
Undisbursed Funds	No Year	86		0311		8,254,394.60			3,333,405.77		4,920,988.83
Fund Equities:											
Unobligated Balances (Unexpired)						-7,108,233.75				-4,123,150.41	-2,985,083.34
Accounts Payable										41,333.00	-41,333.00
Undelivered Orders						-1,146,160.85				748,411.64	-1,894,572.49
Subtotal		86		0311		-0-			3,333,405.77	-3,333,405.77	-0-
Native American Housing Block Grants, Public And Indian Housing, Housing And Urban Development											
Fund Resources:											
Undisbursed Funds	No Year	86		0313		1,008,497,988.54	625,062,265.00		582,462,560.51		1,051,097,693.03
Fund Equities:											
Unobligated Balances (Unexpired)						-75,671,030.90				-20,838,239.39	-54,832,791.51
Accounts Payable						-8,759,278.42				-1,762,667.90	-6,996,610.52
Undelivered Orders						-924,067,679.22				65,200,611.78	-989,268,291.00
Subtotal		86		0313		-0-	625,062,265.00		582,462,560.51	42,599,704.49	-0-
Housing Certificate Fund, Public And Indian Housing, Housing And Urban Development											
Fund Resources:											
Undisbursed Funds	No Year	86		0319		3,675,240,171.44	-615,943,964.00		2,714,636,463.24		344,659,744.20
Unfunded Contract Authority						10,740,054,830.09				808,196,797.70	9,931,858,032.39
Fund Equities:											
Unobligated Balances (Unexpired)						-1,329,191,741.36				-862,056,241.64	-467,135,499.72
Accounts Payable						-3,485,488.79				-869,554.00	-2,615,934.79
Undelivered Orders						-13,082,617,771.38				-3,275,851,429.30	-9,806,766,342.08
Subtotal		86		0319		-0-	-615,943,964.00		2,714,636,463.24	-3,330,580,427.24	-0-

Appropriations, Outlays, and Balances - Continued

Title	Reg	Tr From	Account Number	Sub No.	Period of Availability	Balances, Beginning Of Fiscal Year	Appropriations And Other Obligational Authority[1]	Transfers Borrowings And Investment (Net)[2]	Outlays (Net)	Balances Withdrawn And Other Transactions[3]	Balances, End Of Fiscal Year[4]
Public Enterprise Funds											
Low-Rent Public Housing Program, Renewal And Housing Assistance, Housing And Urban Development											
Fund Resources:											
Undisbursed Funds	86		4098		No Year	304,912,175.85		[5]-91,342,964.26	-33,938,238.38	[6]1,129,685.91	246,377,764.06
Authority To Borrow From The Treasury							2,000,000.00	-2,000,000.00			
Fund Equities:											
Accounts Payable						-53,656,544.14				-5,735,614.57	-47,920,929.57
Undelivered Orders						-251,255,631.71				-52,798,797.22	-198,456,834.49
Subtotal	86		4098			-0-	2,000,000.00	-93,342,964.26	-33,938,238.38	-57,404,725.88	-0-
Total, Public And Indian Housing Programs							28,264,067,891.79	-93,342,964.26	32,253,101,259.20	-4,082,376,331.67	
Community Planning And Development											
General Fund Accounts											
Community Development Fund, Community Planning And Development, Housing And Urban Development											
Fund Resources:											
Undisbursed Funds	86		0162		2007-2009		3,770,316,000.00		34,866,722.98		3,735,449,277.02
					2006-2008	4,128,262,647.57			946,653,765.10		3,181,608,882.47
					2005-2007	3,681,512,925.79	-4,782.00		2,510,898,380.23		1,170,609,763.56
					2004-2006	1,086,759,703.07			867,576,893.90		219,182,809.17
					2005	992,000.00			150,000.00		842,000.00
					2003-2005	203,084,486.55			116,594,480.81		86,490,005.74
					2002-2004	93,449,149.39			39,089,483.51		54,359,665.88
					2001-2003	54,387,489.26			12,756,450.98		41,631,038.28
					2000-2002	49,971,391.80			24,783,307.84	25,188,083.96	
					1999-2002	2,352,327.44			1,145.00	2,351,182.44	
					No Year	18,376,939,288.44	-111,522.57		6,313,765,139.12		12,063,062,626.75
Fund Equities:											
Unobligated Balances (Expired)						-29,168,089.83				-6,000,328.37	-23,167,761.46
Unobligated Balances (Unexpired)						-6,235,903,959.90				-5,473,566,295.73	-762,337,664.17
Accounts Payable						-45,513,279.60				21,274,598.87	-66,787,878.47
Undelivered Orders						-21,367,126,079.98				-1,666,183,315.21	-19,700,942,764.77
Subtotal	86		0162			-0-	3,770,199,695.43		10,867,135,769.47	-7,096,936,074.04	-0-
Urban Development Action Grants, Community Planning And Development, Housing And Urban Development											
Fund Resources:											
Undisbursed Funds	86		0170		No Year	6,489,401.34			974,500.00		5,514,901.34
Fund Equities:											
Unobligated Balances (Unexpired)						-2,362,589.77				61,300.00	-2,423,889.77
Undelivered Orders						-4,126,811.57				-1,035,800.00	-3,091,011.57
Subtotal	86		0170			-0-			974,500.00	-974,500.00	-0-

Appropriations, Outlays, and Balances – Continued

Appropriation or Fund Account — Title	Reg	Tr From	Account Number	Sub No.	Period of Availability	Balances, Beginning Of Fiscal Year	Appropriations And Other Obligational Authority[1]	Transfers Borrowings And Investment (Net)[2]	Outlays (Net)	Balances Withdrawn And Other Transactions[3]	Balances, End Of Fiscal Year[4]
Self-Help And Assisted Homeownership Opportunity Program, Community Planning And Development, Housing And Urban Development											
Fund Resources:											
Undisbursed Funds	86		0176		2007-2009		49,390,000.00		1,122,957.00		48,267,043.00
					2006-2008	56,822,474.12			12,162,210.44		44,660,263.68
Fund Equities:											
Unobligated Balances (Unexpired)						-49,500,000.00	49,390,000.00			-1,232,957.00	-48,267,043.00
Accounts Payable										1,093,683.00	-1,093,683.00
Undelivered Orders						-7,322,474.12				36,244,106.56	-43,566,580.68
Subtotal	86		0176			-0-	49,390,000.00		13,285,167.44	36,104,832.56	-0-
Homeless Assistance Grants, Community Planning And Development, Housing And Urban Development											
Fund Resources:											
Undisbursed Funds	86		0192		2007-2009		1,420,810,000.00		5,089,749.25		1,415,720,250.75
					2006-2008	1,299,411,269.78			246,150,403.72		1,053,260,866.06
					2005-2007	988,743,468.09	-7,194,221.59		650,150,354.92		331,398,891.58
					2004-2006	516,126,059.04			177,449,907.40		338,676,151.64
					2003-2005	300,676,133.52			96,839,737.13		203,836,396.39
					2002-2004	199,074,497.15			46,907,801.48		152,166,695.67
					No Year	824,734,205.78	19,797,447.11		163,005,869.30		681,525,783.59
Fund Equities:											
Unobligated Balances (Expired)						-108,455,779.32				46,313,879.54	-154,769,658.86
Unobligated Balances (Unexpired)						-1,545,777,948.69				116,279,634.58	-1,662,057,583.27
Accounts Payable						-11,679,260.28				-2,063,436.50	-9,615,823.78
Undelivered Orders						-2,462,852,645.07				-112,710,675.30	-2,350,141,969.77
Subtotal	86		0192			-0-	1,433,413,225.52		1,385,593,823.20	47,819,402.32	-0-
Community Development Loan Guarantees Program Account, Community Planning And Development, Housing And Urban Development											
Fund Resources:											
Undisbursed Funds	86		0198		2007-2008		2,970,000.00		43,400.00		2,926,600.00
					2007		7,799,627.00		7,799,627.00		
					2006-2007	2,746,392.00			289,044.30		2,457,347.70
					2005-2006	2,998,238.00			405,414.00		2,592,824.00
					2004-2005	3,650,513.50			423,154.00		3,227,359.50
					2003-2004	1,745,044.00			184,644.00		1,560,400.00
					2002-2003	2,208,652.00			134,757.00		2,073,895.00
					2002	877,503.00			129,122.00	748,381.00	
Fund Equities:											
Unobligated Balances (Expired)						-145,402.00				435.80	-145,837.80
Unobligated Balances (Unexpired)						-1,458,292.00				-1,388,345.10	-69,946.90
Undelivered Orders						-12,622,648.50				1,999,993.00	-14,622,641.50
Subtotal	86		0198			-0-	10,769,627.00		9,409,162.30	1,360,464.70	-0-
Home Investment Partnerships Program, Community Planning And Development, Housing And Urban Development											
Fund Resources:											
Undisbursed Funds	86		0205		2007-2009		1,756,260,000.00		13,201,817.89		1,743,058,182.11
					2006-2008	1,742,312,855.30			230,707,495.34		1,511,605,359.96
					2005-2007	1,652,505,511.59	-95,553.23		535,427,965.78		1,116,981,992.58
					2004-2006	1,164,483,904.21			520,122,487.29		644,361,416.92

Appropriations, Outlays, and Balances - Continued

Appropriation or Fund Account — Title	Period of Availability	Dept Reg	Tr From	Account Number	Sub No.	Balances, Beginning Of Fiscal Year	Appropriations And Other Obligational Authority[1]	Transfers Borrowings And Investment (Net)[2]	Outlays (Net)	Balances Withdrawn And Other Transactions[3]	Balances, End Of Fiscal Year[4]
	2003-2005					682,077,465.25			297,108,210.22		384,969,255.03
	2002-2004					302,789,168.43			172,924,084.85		129,865,083.58
	No Year					276,338,842.95			106,705,579.90		169,633,263.05
Fund Equities:											
Unobligated Balances (Expired)						-688,358.74				653,480.86	-1,341,839.60
Unobligated Balances (Unexpired)						-269,402,159.61				50,456,412.26	-319,858,571.87
Accounts Payable						-27,314,807.78				-6,754,796.60	-20,560,011.18
Undelivered Orders						-5,523,102,421.60				-164,388,291.02	-5,358,714,130.58
Subtotal	Subtotal	86		0205		-0-	1,756,164,446.77		1,876,197,641.27	-120,033,194.50	-0-
Youthbuild Programs, Housing Programs, Housing And Urban Development											
Fund Resources: Undisbursed Funds	No Year	86		0219		459,797.55					459,797.55
Fund Equities: Undelivered Orders						-459,797.55					-459,797.55
Subtotal	Subtotal	86		0219		-0-					-0-
Capacity Building For Community Development And Affordable Housing, Housing Programs, Housing And Urban Development											
Fund Resources: Undisbursed Funds	No Year	86		0222		6,640.28			-54,301.41		60,941.69
Fund Equities: Unobligated Balances (Unexpired)						-6,640.28				54,301.41	-54,301.41
Undelivered Orders						-0-					-6,640.28
Subtotal	Subtotal	86		0222		-0-			-54,301.41	54,301.41	-0-
Housing Opportunities For Persons With AIDS, Community Planning And Development, Housing And Urban Development											
Fund Resources: Undisbursed Funds	2007-2009	86		0308			28,462,500.00				28,462,500.00
	2007-2008						257,647,500.00		1,566,326.59		256,081,173.41
	2006-2008					28,462,500.00			2,808,545.03		25,653,954.97
	2006-2007					256,749,171.46	-500.00		87,253,522.17		169,495,149.29
	2005-2006					193,883,910.03			148,943,707.03		44,940,203.00
	2004-2005					41,877,313.75			25,960,493.53		15,916,820.22
	2003-2004					15,209,244.71			8,518,262.72		6,690,981.99
	2002-2003					4,269,639.08			2,190,382.68		2,079,256.40
	No Year					5,225,361.92			547,962.08		4,677,399.84
Fund Equities: Unobligated Balances (Expired)						-915,532.20				253,634.33	-1,169,166.53
Unobligated Balances (Unexpired)						-89,621,945.71				25,049,602.91	-114,671,548.62
Accounts Payable						-4,328,489.74				-1,565,734.64	-2,762,755.10
Undelivered Orders						-450,811,173.30				-15,417,204.43	-435,393,968.87
Subtotal	Subtotal	86		0308		-0-	286,109,500.00		277,789,201.83	8,320,298.17	-0-
Brownfields Redevelopment, Community Planning And Development, Housing And Urban Development											
Fund Resources: Undisbursed Funds	2007-2008	86		0314			9,900,000.00				9,900,000.00
	2006-2007					9,900,000.00	-3,812,870.00				6,087,130.00
	2005-2006					13,808,000.00					13,808,000.00

Footnotes At End Of Chapter

Appropriations, Outlays, and Balances – Continued

Appropriation or Fund Account — Title	Period of Availability	Reg	Tr From	Account Number	Sub No.	Balances, Beginning Of Fiscal Year	Appropriations And Other Obligational Authority[1]	Transfers Borrowings And Investment (Net)[2]	Outlays (Net)	Balances Withdrawn And Other Transactions[3]	Balances, End Of Fiscal Year[4]
Brownfields Redevelopment, Community Planning And Development, Housing And Urban Development - Continued											
Fund Resources: - Continued											
Undisbursed Funds - Continued	2004-2005					22,852,500.00			2,290,787.10		20,561,712.90
	2003-2004					17,753,050.26			739,443.90		17,013,606.36
	2002-2003					14,527,992.10			2,783,892.74		11,744,099.36
	No Year					54,377,301.71			5,349,629.72		49,027,671.99
Fund Equities:											
Unobligated Balances (Expired)						-502,500.00					-502,500.00
Unobligated Balances (Unexpired)						-11,652,312.57				21,012,130.00	-32,664,442.57
Accounts Payable						-72,592.50				-72,592.50	
Undelivered Orders						-120,991,439.00				-26,016,160.96	-94,975,278.04
Subtotal		86		0314		-0-	6,087,130.00		11,163,753.46	-5,076,623.46	-0-
Empowerment Zones Enterprise Communities, Community Planning And Development, Department Of Housing And Urban Development											
Fund Resources:											
Undisbursed Funds	2005	86		0315		9,920,000.00			249,934.11		9,670,065.89
	2004-2005					14,888,348.89			970,948.89		13,917,400.00
	2003-2005					27,177,006.82			4,354,426.49		22,822,580.33
	No Year					42,543,506.16			19,055,701.80		23,487,804.36
Fund Equities:											
Unobligated Balances (Expired)						-5.00					-5.00
Unobligated Balances (Unexpired)						-120,231.00				-10,021.00	-110,210.00
Accounts Payable						-456,554.00				-438,306.00	-18,248.00
Undelivered Orders						-93,952,071.87				-24,182,684.29	-69,769,387.58
Subtotal		86		0315		-0-			24,631,011.29	-24,631,011.29	-0-
Rural Housing And Economic Development, Public And Indian Housing, Housing And Urban Development											
Fund Resources:											
Undisbursed Funds	No Year	86		0324		61,948,079.53	16,630,000.00		19,524,677.66		59,253,401.87
Fund Equities:											
Unobligated Balances (Unexpired)						-19,749,672.76				1,620,223.52	-21,369,896.28
Accounts Payable						-109,940.06				164,993.69	-274,933.75
Undelivered Orders						-42,088,466.71				-4,479,894.87	-37,608,571.84
Subtotal		86		0324		-0-	16,630,000.00		19,524,677.66	-2,694,677.66	-0-
Public Enterprise Funds											
Revolving Fund, Liquidating Programs, Housing And Urban Development											
Fund Resources:											
Undisbursed Funds	No Year	86		4015		2,884,527.68	1,170,000.00		-406,864.98	[5]586,143.82	3,875,248.84
Accounts Receivable						2,389.15				22,117.81	-19,728.66
Fund Equities:											
Unobligated Balances (Unexpired)						-586,143.82				-25,752.24	-560,391.58
Accounts Payable						-109,969.75				2,139.39	-112,109.14
Undelivered Orders						-2,190,803.26				992,216.20	-3,183,019.46
Subtotal		86		4015		-0-	1,170,000.00		-406,864.98	1,576,864.98	-0-

Appropriations, Outlays, and Balances - Continued

Appropriation or Fund Account — Title	Reg	Tr From	Account Number	Sub No.	Period of Availability	Balances, Beginning Of Fiscal Year	Appropriations And Other Obligational Authority[1]	Transfers Borrowings And Investment (Net)[2]	Outlays (Net)	Balances Withdrawn And Other Transactions[3]	Balances, End Of Fiscal Year[4]
Section 8-Community Development Guaranteed Loans, Liquidating Account, Housing And Urban Development											
Fund Resources:											
Undisbursed Funds	86		4097		No Year	-3,871,310.43					[7]-3,862,190.21
Accounts Receivable						3,871,310.43				9,119.72	3,862,190.71
Fund Equities:											
Unobligated Balances (Unexpired)									-9,120.22	0.50	-0.50
	86		4097		Subtotal	-0-			-9,120.22	9,120.22	-0-
Total, Community Planning And Development							7,330,133,624.72		14,485,234,421.31	-7,155,100,796.59	
Housing Programs											
General Fund Accounts											
Rent Supplemental Program, Housing Programs, Housing And Urban Development											
Fund Resources:											
Undisbursed Funds	86		0129		No Year	52,747,327.30	49,524,000.00		47,224,688.20	76,438,604.43	55,046,639.10
Unfunded Contract Authority						478,165,357.08	[8]-42,000,000.00				359,726,752.65
Fund Equities:											
Unobligated Balances (Unexpired)						-71,311,384.50				4,598,880.61	-75,910,265.11
Accounts Payable						-18,489.00				62,702.00	-81,191.00
Undelivered Orders						-459,582,810.88				-120,800,875.24	-338,781,935.64
	86		0129		Subtotal	-0-	7,524,000.00		47,224,688.20	-39,700,688.20	-0-
Homeownership And Rental Housing Assistance, Housing Programs, Housing And Urban Development											
Fund Resources:											
Undisbursed Funds	86		0148		No Year	376,682,039.95	420,612,000.00		511,286,669.51	417,704,123.03	286,007,370.44
Unfunded Contract Authority						5,853,650,118.57	[8]-402,000,000.00				5,033,945,995.54
Fund Equities:											
Unobligated Balances (Unexpired)						-890,617,425.73				-203,458,485.98	-687,158,939.75
Accounts Payable						-518,064.38				-99,932.77	-418,131.61
Undelivered Orders						-5,339,196,668.41				-706,820,373.79	-4,632,376,294.62
	86		0148		Subtotal	-0-	18,612,000.00		511,286,669.51	-492,674,669.51	-0-
FHA-Mutual Mortgage Insurance Program Account											
Fund Resources:											
Undisbursed Funds	86		0183		2007		43,875,810.00	1,350,468,000.00	1,353,503,778.43		40,840,031.57
					2006	35,144,737.16			24,119,000.94		11,025,736.22
					2005	30,792,065.64			5,617,621.81		25,174,443.83
					2004	24,233,923.45			850,772.87		23,383,150.58
					2003	17,931,586.64			4,584.00		17,927,002.64
					2002	17,018,784.70			77,257.34	16,941,527.36	
Fund Equities:											
Unobligated Balances (Expired)						-43,461,470.02				3,974,481.64	-47,435,951.66
Accounts Payable						-1,722,991.89				418,178.26	-2,141,170.15
Undelivered Orders						-79,936,635.68				-11,163,392.65	-68,773,243.03
	86		0183		Subtotal	-0-	43,875,810.00	1,350,468,000.00	1,384,173,015.39	10,170,794.61	-0-

Footnotes At End Of Chapter

Appropriations, Outlays, and Balances – Continued

Appropriation or Fund Account — Title	Period of Availability	Reg	Tr From	Account Number	Sub No.	Balances, Beginning Of Fiscal Year	Appropriations And Other Obligational Authority[1]	Transfers Borrowings And Investment (Net)[2]	Outlays (Net)	Balances Withdrawn And Other Transactions[3]	Balances, End Of Fiscal Year[4]
Homeownership And Opportunity For People Everywhere Grants (Hope Grants), Housing Programs, Housing And Urban Development											
Fund Resources:											
Undisbursed Funds	No Year	86		0196		7,295,818.60	-1,183,672.87		-393,644.77		6,505,790.50
Fund Equities:											
Unobligated Balances (Unexpired)						-497,262.98				-460,032.42	-37,230.56
Undelivered Orders						-6,798,555.62				-329,995.68	-6,468,559.94
Subtotal		86		0196		-0-	-1,183,672.87		-393,644.77	-790,028.10	-0-
FHA, General And Special Risk Program Account, Housing Programs, Housing And Urban Development											
Fund Resources:											
Undisbursed Funds	2007	86		0200		59,845,910.91	68,034,341.00		3,852,640.85		64,181,700.15
	2006					35,255,034.16	-76,216.00		34,307,586.19		25,462,108.72
	2005					31,428,389.36			11,740,946.80		23,514,087.36
	2004					32,004,470.84			668,156.74		30,760,232.62
	2003					61,757,011.64			144,657.40		31,859,813.44
	2002					62,958,940.25			32,898.63	61,724,113.01	
	No Year						78,094,000.00		114,646,315.14		26,406,625.11
Fund Equities:											
Unobligated Balances (Expired)						-125,454,004.30				-47,561,107.55	-77,892,896.75
Unobligated Balances (Unexpired)						-56,298,488.45				-32,341,478.26	-23,957,010.19
Accounts Payable						-1,898,458.90				131,886.44	-2,030,345.34
Undelivered Orders						-99,598,805.51				-1,294,490.39	-98,304,315.12
Subtotal		86		0200		-0-	146,052,125.00		165,393,201.75	-19,341,076.75	-0-
Manufactured Housing Fees Trust Fund, Housing Programs, Housing And Urban Development											
Fund Resources:											
Undisbursed Funds	No Year	86		0234		20,035,937.32	6,360,232.00				26,396,169.32
Fund Equities:											
Unobligated Balances (Unexpired)						-20,035,937.32				6,360,232.00	-26,396,169.32
Subtotal		86		0234		-0-	6,360,232.00			6,360,232.00	-0-
FHA, Mutual Mortgage Insurance Capital Reserve Account, Housing Programs, Housing And Urban Development											
Fund Resources:											
Undisbursed Funds	No Year	86		0236		90,238,180.17		-1,784,974,931.29	-1,724,034,622.76		29,297,871.64
Unrealized Discount On Investments						-360,266,199.57		59,571,931.29			-300,694,268.28
Investments In Public Debt Securities						22,029,700,000.00		374,935,000.00			22,404,635,000.00
Accounts Receivable						198,987,537.48				-62,573,626.14	261,561,163.62
Unfilled Customer Orders						367,462.50				316,009.60	51,452.90
Fund Equities:											
Unobligated Balances (Unexpired)						-21,959,026,980.58				435,824,239.30	-22,394,851,219.88
Accounts Payable											
Subtotal		86		0236		-0-		-1,350,468,000.00	-1,724,034,622.76	373,566,622.76	-0-
Housing For Persons With Disabilities, Housing Programs, Housing And Urban Development											
Fund Resources:											
Undisbursed Funds	2007-2010	86		0237		225,833,886.84	236,214,000.00		11,157,622.22		225,056,377.78
	2006-2009					178,143,308.09			68,752,816.78		157,081,070.06
	2005-2006								36,227,149.71		141,916,158.38

Appropriations, Outlays, and Balances - Continued

Title	Dept Reg	Tr From	Account Number	Sub No.	Period of Availability	Balances, Beginning Of Fiscal Year	Appropriations And Other Obligational Authority[1]	Transfers Borrowings And Investment (Net)[2]	Outlays (Net)	Balances Withdrawn And Other Transactions[3]	Balances, End Of Fiscal Year[4]
					2004-2006	152,626,274.59			54,084,583.15		98,541,691.44
					2003-2006	107,640,872.13			41,134,872.47		66,505,999.66
					2002-2004	53,918,613.74			21,772,653.82		32,145,959.92
					No Year	706,935,586.11			71,376,983.84		635,558,602.27
Fund Equities:											
Unobligated Balances (Expired)						-24,172,923.50				6,610,781.39	-30,783,704.89
Unobligated Balances (Unexpired)						-230,346,052.76				-6,683,863.41	-223,662,189.35
Accounts Payable						-2,453,158.80				-1,312,699.80	-1,140,459.00
Undelivered Orders						-1,168,126,406.44				-66,906,900.17	-1,101,219,506.27
Subtotal	86		0237			-0-	236,214,000.00		304,506,681.99	-68,292,681.99	-0-
Housing For The Elderly, Housing Programs, Housing And Urban Development											
Fund Resources:											
Undisbursed Funds	86		0320		2007-2010		734,184,000.00		26,209,965.98		707,974,034.02
					2006-2009	714,430,907.53			65,635,718.43		648,795,189.10
					2005-2008	692,290,329.98			106,849,133.97		585,441,196.01
					2004-2006	642,913,295.62			264,541,563.96		378,371,731.66
					2003-2006	376,900,321.99			167,659,183.47		209,241,138.52
					2002-2004	285,339,509.87			93,490,994.36		191,848,515.51
					No Year	2,413,083,319.27			253,337,371.65		2,159,745,947.62
Fund Equities:											
Unobligated Balances (Expired)						-79,440,689.86				6,752,869.49	-86,193,559.35
Unobligated Balances (Unexpired)						-834,569,974.50				-10,620,302.68	-823,949,671.82
Accounts Payable						-8,104,148.58				-3,213,892.32	-4,890,256.26
Undelivered Orders						-4,202,842,871.32				-236,458,606.31	-3,966,384,265.01
Subtotal	86		0320			-0-	734,184,000.00		977,723,931.82	-243,539,931.82	-0-

Special Fund Accounts

Title	Dept Reg	Tr From	Account Number	Sub No.	Period of Availability	Balances, Beginning Of Fiscal Year	Appropriations And Other Obligational Authority[1]	Transfers Borrowings And Investment (Net)[2]	Outlays (Net)	Balances Withdrawn And Other Transactions[3]	Balances, End Of Fiscal Year[4]
Interstate Land Sales, Housing Programs, Housing And Urban Development											
Fund Resources:											
Undisbursed Funds	86		5270		No Year		665,454.90		665,454.90		
Manufactured Home Inspection And Monitoring, Housing Programs, Housing And Urban Development											
Fund Resources:											
Undisbursed Funds	86		5271		No Year	22,556.90					22,556.90
Fund Equities:											
Unobligated Balances (Unexpired)						-0.90					-0.90
Undelivered Orders						-22,556.00					-22,556.00
Subtotal	86		5271			-0-					-0-

Public Enterprise Funds

Title	Dept Reg	Tr From	Account Number	Sub No.	Period of Availability	Balances, Beginning Of Fiscal Year	Appropriations And Other Obligational Authority[1]	Transfers Borrowings And Investment (Net)[2]	Outlays (Net)	Balances Withdrawn And Other Transactions[3]	Balances, End Of Fiscal Year[4]
Rental Housing Assistance Fund, Federal Housing Administration, Housing And Urban Development											
Fund Resources:											
Undisbursed Funds	86		4041		No Year	4,414,132.61			-4,018,918.52		8,433,051.13

Footnotes At End Of Chapter

Appropriations, Outlays, and Balances – Continued

Title	Reg	Tr From	Account Number	Sub No.	Period of Availability	Balances, Beginning Of Fiscal Year	Appropriations And Other Obligational Authority[1]	Transfers Borrowings And Investment (Net)[2]	Outlays (Net)	Balances Withdrawn And Other Transactions[3]	Balances, End Of Fiscal Year[4]
Rental Housing Assistance Fund, Federal Housing Administration, Housing And Urban Development – Continued											
Fund Equities:											
Unobligated Balances (Unexpired)						-4,310,032.61			------	4,018,918.52	-8,328,951.13
Accounts Payable						-104,100.00			------		-104,100.00
Subtotal	86		4041		Subtotal	-0-			-4,018,918.52	4,018,918.52	-0-
Homeowner Assistance Fund, Housing Programs, Housing And Urban Development											
Fund Resources:											
Undisbursed Funds	86		4043		No Year	84,451.80					84,451.80
Fund Equities:											
Unobligated Balances (Unexpired)	86		4043			-84,451.80					-84,451.80
Subtotal	86		4043		Subtotal	-0-					-0-
Flexible Subsidy Fund, Housing Programs, Housing And Urban Development											
Fund Resources:											
Undisbursed Funds	86		4044		No Year	42,577,901.96					65,737,626.92
Fund Equities:											
Unobligated Balances (Unexpired)	86		4044			-41,465,256.94				23,159,724.96	-64,624,981.90
Undelivered Orders						-1,112,645.02					-1,112,645.02
Subtotal	86		4044		Subtotal	-0-			-23,159,724.96	23,159,724.96	-0-
College Housing Loans, Housing And Urban Development											
Fund Resources:											
Undisbursed Funds	86		4058		No Year	31,837,904.56			6,276,180.85		25,561,723.71
Unfunded Contract Authority						10,442,848.29					10,442,848.29
Fund Equities:											
Unobligated Balances (Unexpired)						-8,728,239.92				231.00	-8,728,470.92
Accounts Payable						-186,525.00				-186,525.00	
Undelivered Orders						-33,365,987.93				-6,089,886.85	-27,276,101.08
Subtotal	86		4058		Subtotal	-0-			6,276,180.85	-6,276,180.85	-0-
Federal Housing Administration Fund, Housing And Urban Development											
Fund Resources:											
Undisbursed Funds	86		4070		No Year	278,469,807.95			2,862,403.82		275,607,404.13
Accounts Receivable						592,389.53				286,002.63	306,386.90
Fund Equities:											
Unobligated Balances (Unexpired)						-46,461,556.29				17,353,646.41	-63,815,202.70
Accounts Payable						-210,766,465.99				-11,180,943.74	-199,585,522.25
Undelivered Orders						-21,834,175.20				-9,321,109.12	-12,513,066.08
Subtotal	86		4070		Subtotal	-0-			2,862,403.82	-2,862,403.82	-0-
Nehemiah Housing Opportunity Fund, Housing And Urban Development											
Fund Resources:											
Undisbursed Funds	86		4071		No Year	11,216,593.48			-942,113.01		12,158,706.49
Fund Equities:											
Unobligated Balances (Unexpired)						-11,216,593.48				8,040,070.59	-8,040,070.59
Undelivered Orders										-7,097,957.58	-4,118,635.90
Subtotal	86		4071		Subtotal	-0-			-942,113.01	942,113.01	-0-

Appropriations, Outlays, and Balances - Continued

Appropriation or Fund Account — Title	Period of Availability	Dept Reg	Tr From	Account Number	Sub No.	Balances, Beginning Of Fiscal Year	Appropriations And Other Obligational Authority[1]	Transfers Borrowings And Investment (Net)[2]	Outlays (Net)	Balances Withdrawn And Other Transactions[3]	Balances, End Of Fiscal Year[4]
FHA-General And Special Risk Insurance Fund Liquidating Account, Housing And Urban Development											
Fund Resources:											
Undisbursed Funds	No Year	86		4072		712,101,751.42	413,000,000.00	[9]2,149,714.05	167,544,217.57	[6]159,625,021.00	800,082,226.90
Unrealized Discount On Investments						-350,299.70		19,399.96	-------	-------	-330,899.74
Investments In Public Debt Securities						5,664,000.00		-397,000.00	-------	-------	5,267,000.00
Accounts Receivable						6,699,321.62				6,014,917.07	684,404.55
Fund Equities:											
Unobligated Balances (Unexpired)						-159,625,020.57				75,073,167.62	-234,698,188.19
Accounts Payable						-215,833,280.98				36,105,930.14	-251,939,211.12
Undelivered Orders						-348,656,471.79				-29,591,139.39	-319,065,332.40
						-0-					-0-
Subtotal		86		4072		-0-	413,000,000.00	1,772,114.01	167,544,217.57	247,227,896.44	-0-
Housing For The Elderly Or Handicapped Fund, Housing And Urban Development											
Fund Resources:											
Undisbursed Funds	No Year	86		4115		75,704,114.45			-1,346,318,208.53	[6]1,405,267,156.37	16,755,166.61
Fund Equities:											
Unobligated Balances (Unexpired)						-72,539,636.48				-58,615,851.87	-13,923,784.61
Accounts Payable						-43,770.38				-------	-43,770.38
Undelivered Orders						-3,120,707.59				-333,095.97	-2,787,611.62
						-0-					-0-
Subtotal		86		4115		-0-			-1,346,318,208.53	1,346,318,208.53	-0-
Trust Fund Accounts											
Manufactured Housing Fees Trust Fund, Housing Programs, Housing And Urban Development											
Fund Resources:											
Undisbursed Funds	No Year	86		8119		5,038,380.55	6,509,768.00		7,119,899.86		4,428,248.69
Fund Equities:											
Unobligated Balances (Unexpired)						-3,401,265.40				-193,888.50	-3,207,376.90
Accounts Payable						-161,320.00				-161,320.00	-0-
Undelivered Orders						-1,475,795.15				-254,923.36	-1,220,871.79
						-0-				-610,131.86	-0-
Subtotal		86		8119		-0-	6,509,768.00		7,119,899.86	-610,131.86	-0-
Total, Housing Programs							1,611,813,717.03	1,772,114.01	475,909,113.11	1,137,676,717.93	
Government National Mortgage Association											
General Fund Accounts											
Guarantees Of Mortgage-Backed Securities Loan Guarantee, Program Account, Government National Mortgage Association, Housing And Urban Development, 1992											
Fund Resources:											
Undisbursed Funds	2007	86		0186			10,593,000.00		10,593,000.00		

Footnotes At End Of Chapter

Appropriations, Outlays, and Balances – Continued

Appropriation or Fund Account — Title	Period of Availability	Reg	Tr From	Account Number	Sub No.	Balances, Beginning Of Fiscal Year	Appropriations And Other Obligational Authority[1]	Transfers Borrowings And Investment (Net)[2]	Outlays (Net)	Balances Withdrawn And Other Transactions[3]	Balances, End Of Fiscal Year[4]
Public Enterprise Funds											
Management And Liquidating Functions Fund, Government National Mortgage Association, Housing And Urban Development											
Fund Resources:											
Undisbursed Funds	No Year	86		4016		13,802.68					13,802.68
Fund Equities:											
Unobligated Balances (Unexpired)		86		4016		-13,802.68					-13,802.68
	Subtotal	86		4016		-0-					-0-
Guarantees Of Mortgage-Backed Securities Fund, Government National Mortgage Association, Housing And Urban Development											
Fund Resources:											
Undisbursed Funds	No Year	86		4238		54,320.45		-371,033,500.00	-371,043,126.08		63,946.53
Unrealized Discount On Investments						-41,149,076.43		-2,567,500.00			-43,716,576.43
Investments In Public Debt Securities						8,385,015,000.00		373,601,000.00			8,758,616,000.00
Accounts Receivable						56,344,702.96				3,035,284.86	53,309,418.10
Fund Equities:											
Unobligated Balances (Unexpired)						-8,364,958,797.97				361,842,757.80	-8,726,801,555.77
Accounts Payable		86		4238		-35,306,149.01				6,165,083.42	-41,471,232.43
	Subtotal	86		4238		-0-			-371,043,126.08	371,043,126.08	-0-
Total, Government National Mortgage Association							10,593,000.00		-360,450,126.08	371,043,126.08	
Policy Development And Research											
General Fund Accounts											
Research And Technology, Policy Development And Research, Housing And Urban Development											
Fund Resources:											
Undisbursed Funds	2007-2008	86		0108			50,087,000.00		20,787,648.47		29,299,351.53
	2006-2007					35,919,547.92	-598,036.00		9,278,581.05		26,042,930.87
	2005-2006					8,561,479.85			6,044,859.55		2,516,620.30
	2004-2005					3,651,164.93			1,765,470.66		1,885,694.27
	2003-2004					1,577,054.97			535,991.45		1,041,063.52
	2002-2003					822,165.94			139,536.98		682,628.96
	2001-2002					1,073,001.44			119,607.85	953,393.59	
	No Year					149,876.53			-5,956,533.99		6,106,410.52
Fund Equities:											
Unobligated Balances (Expired)						-248,456.78				-65,422.13	-183,034.65
Unobligated Balances (Unexpired)						-27,266,650.05				-23,872,024.49	-3,394,625.56
Accounts Payable						-214,590.67				-123,108.14	-91,482.53
Undelivered Orders						-24,024,594.08				39,880,963.15	-63,905,557.23
	Subtotal	86		0108		-0-	49,488,964.00		32,715,162.02	16,773,801.98	-0-
Total, Policy Development And Research							49,488,964.00		32,715,162.02	16,773,801.98	

Appropriations, Outlays, and Balances - Continued

Appropriation or Fund Account — Title	Period of Availability	Dept Reg	Dept Tr From	Account Number	Sub No.	Balances, Beginning Of Fiscal Year	Appropriations And Other Obligational Authority[1]	Transfers Borrowings And Investment (Net)[2]	Outlays (Net)	Balances Withdrawn And Other Transactions[3]	Balances, End Of Fiscal Year[4]
Fair Housing And Equal Opportunity											
General Fund Accounts											
Fair Housing Activities, Fair Housing And Equal Opportunity, Housing And Urban Development											
Fund Resources:											
Undisbursed Funds	2007-2008	86		0144			45,540,000.00	----	214,279.00	----	45,325,721.00
	2006-2007					41,920,114.50	----	----	25,474,927.07	----	16,445,187.43
	2005-2006					19,053,460.30			15,814,932.80		3,238,527.50
	2004-2005					5,324,163.21			2,467,653.36		2,856,509.85
	2003-2004					2,507,794.13			1,510,384.31		997,409.82
	2002-2003					1,513,877.49			438,889.00		1,074,988.49
	2001-2002					1,775,068.37			678,486.00	1,096,582.37	-0-
Fund Equities:											
Unobligated Balances (Expired)						-3,440,087.24				-107,763.33	-3,332,323.91
Unobligated Balances (Unexpired)						-6,120,622.00				-1,872,544.59	-4,248,077.41
Accounts Payable						-1,096,959.60				-598,386.60	-498,573.00
Undelivered Orders						-61,436,809.16				422,560.61	-61,859,369.77
Subtotal		86		0144		-0-	45,540,000.00		46,599,551.54	-1,059,551.54	----
Total, Fair Housing And Equal Opportunity							45,540,000.00		46,599,551.54	-1,059,551.54	
Office Of Lead Hazard Control And Healthy Homes											
General Fund Accounts											
Lead Hazard Reduction, Office Of Lead Hazard Control, Housing And Urban Development											
Fund Resources:											
Undisbursed Funds	2007-2008	86		0174			150,480,000.00	----	-150,000.00	----	150,630,000.00
	2006-2007					150,258,460.33	-277,845.01		10,023,404.28		139,957,211.04
	2005-2006					154,523,611.13			41,490,811.41		113,032,799.72
	2004-2005					112,254,083.07			55,254,982.84		56,999,100.23
	2003-2004					54,276,698.44			33,180,159.60		21,096,538.84
	2002-2003					8,658,151.81			1,273,679.45		7,384,472.36
	No Year					22,819,761.66			5,834,166.34		16,985,595.32
Fund Equities:											
Unobligated Balances (Expired)						-9,020,347.28				-770,760.13	-8,249,587.15
Unobligated Balances (Unexpired)						-151,478,674.61				-2,098,301.47	-149,380,373.14
Accounts Payable						-3,958,625.69				-1,674,158.77	-2,284,466.92
Undelivered Orders						-338,333,118.86				7,838,171.44	-346,171,290.30
Subtotal		86		0174		-0-	150,202,154.99		146,907,203.92	3,294,951.07	----
Total, Office Of Lead Hazard Control And Healthy Homes							150,202,154.99		146,907,203.92	3,294,951.07	

Footnotes At End Of Chapter

Appropriations, Outlays, and Balances – Continued

Appropriation or Fund Account — Title	Period of Availability	Dept Reg	Tr From	Account Number	Sub No.	Balances, Beginning Of Fiscal Year	Appropriations And Other Obligational Authority[1]	Transfers Borrowings And Investment (Net)[2]	Outlays (Net)	Balances Withdrawn And Other Transactions[3]	Balances, End Of Fiscal Year[4]
Management And Administration											
General Fund Accounts											
Salaries And Expenses, Management And Administration, Housing And Urban Development											
Fund Resources:											
Undisbursed Funds											
	2007	86		0143			1,138,280,476.00		1,038,499,123.37		99,781,352.63
	2006-2007								240,605.00		2,340,395.00
	2006					106,930,116.70		2,581,000.00	78,943,024.47		23,956,092.23
	2005					25,696,101.70		-4,031,000.00	9,144,051.50		16,552,050.20
	2004					23,265,785.88			2,817,639.49		20,448,146.39
	2003-2004					701,638.34			19,498.34		682,140.00
	2003					12,629,607.17			14,571.60		12,615,035.57
	2002					10,768,690.54			935,555.55	9,833,134.99	
	No Year					11,966,492.86			-6,401,011.80		18,367,504.66
Fund Equities:											
Unobligated Balances (Expired)						-44,506,661.89				1,877,161.48	-46,383,823.37
Unobligated Balances (Unexpired)						-9,834,130.00				4,983,454.63	-14,817,584.63
Accounts Payable						-39,591,313.64				1,903,995.89	-41,495,309.53
Undelivered Orders						-98,026,327.66			-5,980,328.51		-92,045,999.15
	Subtotal	86		0143		-0-	1,138,280,476.00	-1,450,000.00	1,124,213,057.52	12,617,418.48	-0-
Office Of Inspector General, Management And Administration, Housing And Urban Development											
Fund Resources:											
Undisbursed Funds											
	2007	86		0189			105,612,503.00		97,372,422.24		8,240,080.76
	2006					11,652,530.62			7,189,510.14		4,463,020.48
	2005					2,729,873.13			1,442,009.15		1,287,863.98
	2004					859,844.95			179,828.42		680,016.53
	2003					684,487.54			10,903.76		673,583.78
	2002					787,391.39			5,390.24	782,001.15	
	No Year					8,571,992.99		7,021,115.00	4,494,322.59		11,098,785.40
Fund Equities:											
Unobligated Balances (Expired)						-2,185,397.03				168,521.64	-2,353,918.67
Unobligated Balances (Unexpired)						-7,740,801.53				2,710,321.65	-10,451,123.18
Accounts Payable						-3,306,969.21				-2,704.86	-3,304,264.35
Undelivered Orders						-12,052,952.85				-1,718,908.12	-10,334,044.73
	Subtotal	86		0189		-0-	112,633,618.00		110,694,386.54	1,939,231.46	-0-
Special Fund Accounts											
Federal Housing Enterprises Oversight Fund, Housing And Urban Development											
Fund Resources:											
Undisbursed Funds											
	No Year	86		5272		22,239,624.43	66,097,270.82		62,954,932.62		25,381,962.63
Fund Equities:											
Unobligated Balances (Unexpired)						-52,729.18				69,225.68	-121,954.86
Accounts Payable						-2,764,397.51				254,880.63	-3,019,278.14
Undelivered Orders						-19,422,497.74				2,818,231.89	-22,240,729.63

Appropriations, Outlays, and Balances - Continued

Appropriation or Fund Account — Title	Period of Availability	Dept Reg	Tr From	Account Number	Sub No.	Balances, Beginning Of Fiscal Year	Appropriations And Other Obligational Authority[1]	Transfers Borrowings And Investment (Net)[2]	Outlays (Net)	Balances Withdrawn And Other Transactions[3]	Balances, End Of Fiscal Year[4]
Intragovernmental Funds											
	Subtotal	86		5272		-0-	66,097,270.82		62,954,932.62	3,142,338.20	-0-
Working Capital Fund, Departmental Management, Department Of Housing And Urban Development		86		4586							
Fund Resources:											
Undisbursed Funds	2007-2008					127,886,576.25	195,355,863.00		81,920,307.43		113,435,555.57
	2006-2007								107,625,579.53		20,260,996.72
	2005-2006					22,891,898.65			19,996,266.99		2,895,631.66
	2004-2005					5,738,403.21			422,233.97		5,316,169.24
	2003-2004					1,953,401.39			90,079.73		1,863,321.66
	No Year					75,814,297.79	51,812,190.00	1,450,000.00	56,347,092.59		72,729,395.20
Accounts Receivable						40,212.61				-154,173.51	194,386.12
Unfilled Customer Orders						10,026,212.59				9,077,039.42	949,173.17
Fund Equities:											
Unobligated Balances (Expired)						-1,825,690.47				2,199,730.26	-4,025,420.73
Unobligated Balances (Unexpired)						-40,827,308.64				-7,208,835.70	-33,618,472.94
Accounts Payable						-25,404,358.54				-10,735,441.29	-14,668,917.25
Undelivered Orders						-176,293,644.84				-10,961,826.42	-165,331,818.42
	Subtotal	86		4586		-0-	247,168,053.00	1,450,000.00	266,401,560.24	-17,783,507.24	-0-
Trust Fund Accounts											
Gifts And Bequests, Department Of Housing And Urban Development											
Fund Resources:											
Undisbursed Funds	No Year	86		8093		75,711.14					75,711.14
Fund Equities:											
Unobligated Balances (Unexpired)						-68,177.55					-68,177.55
Undelivered Orders						-7,533.59					-7,533.59
	Subtotal	86		8093		-0-					-0-
Total, Management And Administration							1,564,179,417.82		1,564,263,936.92	-84,519.10	
Deductions For Offsetting Receipts											
Proprietary Receipts From The Public							-2,997,271,907.65		-2,997,271,907.65		
Intrabudgetary Transactions							-15,430,035.41		-15,430,035.41		
Offsetting Governmental Receipts							-72,607,038.82		-72,607,038.82		
Total, Offsetting Receipts							-3,085,308,981.88		-3,085,308,981.88		
Total, Department Of Housing And Urban Development							35,940,709,788.47	-91,570,850.25	45,558,971,540.06	-9,709,832,601.84	

Footnotes At End Of Chapter

Appropriations, Outlays, and Balances – Continued

Appropriation or Fund Account — Title	Period of Availability	Reg	Tr From	Account Number	Sub No.	Balances, Beginning Of Fiscal Year	Appropriations And Other Obligational Authority[1]	Transfers Borrowings And Investment (Net)[2]	Outlays (Net)	Balances Withdrawn And Other Transactions[3]	Balances, End Of Fiscal Year[4]
Memorandum											
Financing Accounts											
Public Enterprise Funds											
FHA-General And Special Risk Guaranteed Loan, Financing Account, Housing And Urban Development											
Fund Resources:											
Undisbursed Funds	No Year	86		4077		2,924,087,447.08	1,739,274.00	[10]186,572,162.22	1,881,205,872.28		1,231,193,011.02
Authority To Borrow From The Treasury							600,000,000.00	-600,000,000.00			
Accounts Receivable						8,042.47				-41,199,925.91	41,207,968.38
Unfilled Customer Orders						4,900,219.35				4,210,836.88	689,382.47
Fund Equities:											
Unobligated Balances (Unexpired)						-2,713,532,013.78				-1,630,433,899.69	-1,083,098,114.09
Accounts Payable						-29,791,222.56				-9,983,433.37	-19,807,789.19
Undelivered Orders						-185,672,472.56				-15,488,013.97	-170,184,458.59
Subtotal		86		4077		-0-	601,739,274.00	-413,427,837.78	1,881,205,872.28	-1,692,894,436.06	-0-
Community Development Guaranteed Loans, Financing Account, Housing And Urban Development											
Fund Resources:											
Undisbursed Funds	No Year	86		4096		77,937,556.04			-8,727,549.43		86,665,105.47
Unfilled Customer Orders						12,622,648.50				-1,999,993.00	14,622,641.50
Fund Equities:											
Unobligated Balances (Unexpired)						-90,560,204.54				10,727,542.43	-101,287,746.97
Subtotal		86		4096		-0-			-8,727,549.43	8,727,549.43	-0-
Indian Housing Guaranteed Loans, Financing Account, Housing And Urban Development											
Fund Resources:											
Undisbursed Funds	No Year	86		4104		12,641,576.19			-8,316,255.83		20,957,832.02
Unfilled Customer Orders						1,802,798.06				151,553.32	1,651,244.74
Fund Equities:											
Unobligated Balances (Unexpired)						-14,444,374.25				8,164,702.51	-22,609,076.76
Subtotal		86		4104		-0-			-8,316,255.83	8,316,255.83	-0-
FHA-General And Special, Direct Loan, Financing Account											
Fund Resources:											
Undisbursed Funds	No Year	86		4105		216,171.39	100,000.00	-100,000.00	66,678.68		149,492.71
Authority To Borrow From The Treasury											
Fund Equities:											
Unobligated Balances (Unexpired)						-216,171.39				-66,678.68	-149,492.71
Subtotal		86		4105		-0-	100,000.00	-100,000.00	66,678.68	-66,678.68	-0-
FHA-Church Loan, Guaranteed Fund											
Fund Resources:											
Undisbursed Funds	No Year	86		4106		2,718,713.58			-1,029,925.22		3,748,638.80
Unfilled Customer Orders						559,954.00					559,954.00
Fund Equities:											
Unobligated Balances (Unexpired)						-3,278,667.58				1,029,925.22	-4,308,592.80
Subtotal		86		4106		-0-			-1,029,925.22	1,029,925.22	-0-

Appropriations, Outlays, and Balances - Continued

Appropriation or Fund Account — Title	Period of Availability	Dept Reg	Dept Tr From	Account Number	Sub No.	Balances, Beginning Of Fiscal Year	Appropriations And Other Obligational Authority[1]	Transfers Borrowings And Investment (Net)[2]	Outlays (Net)	Balances Withdrawn And Other Transactions[3]	Balances, End Of Fiscal Year[4]
Guarantees Of Mortgage-Backed Securities, Financing Account, Housing And Urban Development											
Fund Resources:											
Undisbursed Funds	No Year	86		4240		1,194,715,544.70			-193,992,487.32		1,388,708,032.02
Accounts Receivable						24,154,785.11				920,981.29	23,233,803.82
Fund Equities:											
Unobligated Balances (Unexpired)						-1,141,843,250.90				183,010,257.44	-1,324,853,508.34
Accounts Payable						-77,027,078.91				10,061,248.59	-87,088,327.50
Subtotal	Subtotal	86		4240		-0-			-193,992,487.32	193,992,487.32	-0-
Mutual Mortgage Insurance, Direct Loan, Financing Loan											
Fund Resources:											
Undisbursed Funds	No Year	86		4242		5,266,395.03		250,000.00	82,276.59		5,434,118.44
Authority To Borrow From The Treasury							1,800,000.00	-1,800,000.00			
Fund Equities:											
Unobligated Balances (Unexpired)						-5,236,260.01				167,723.41	-5,403,983.42
Accounts Payable						-30,135.02				167,723.41	-30,135.02
Subtotal	Subtotal	86		4242		-0-	1,800,000.00	-1,550,000.00	82,276.59	167,723.41	-0-
Title VI Indian Federal Guarantees, Financing Account, Housing And Urban Development											
Fund Resources:											
Undisbursed Funds	No Year	86		4244		17,391,420.41			3,703,900.01		13,687,520.40
Unfilled Customer Orders						527,991.00				-157,837.00	685,828.00
Fund Equities:											
Unobligated Balances (Unexpired)						-17,919,411.41				-3,546,063.01	-14,373,348.40
Subtotal	Subtotal	86		4244		-0-			3,703,900.01	-3,703,900.01	-0-
Native Hawaiian Housing Loan Guarantee Fund, Financing Account, Housing And Urban Development											
Fund Resources:											
Undisbursed Funds	No Year	86		4351		64,260.38			-3,193.72		67,454.10
Fund Equities:											
Unobligated Balances (Unexpired)						-64,260.38				3,193.72	-67,454.10
Subtotal	Subtotal	86		4351		-0-			-3,193.72	3,193.72	-0-
Intragovernmental Funds											
Mutual Mortgage Insurance/Cooperative Management Insurance, Financing Account, Housing And Urban Development											
Fund Resources:											
Undisbursed Funds	No Year	86		4587		5,472,636,213.02		-1,900,000,000.00	-565,252,248.81		4,137,888,461.83
Accounts Receivable						1,551,986.74				-596,697.77	2,148,684.51
Fund Equities:											
Unobligated Balances (Unexpired)						-4,312,995,335.12				-1,324,906,179.08	-2,988,089,156.04
Accounts Payable						-576,161,722.93				-5,197,228.96	-570,964,493.97
Undelivered Orders						-585,031,141.71				-4,047,645.38	-580,983,496.33
Subtotal	Subtotal	86		4587		-0-		-1,900,000,000.00	-565,252,248.81	-1,334,747,751.19	-0-
Total, Financing Accounts							603,639,274.00	-2,315,077,837.78	1,107,737,067.23	-2,819,175,631.01	

Footnotes At End Of Chapter

Appropriations, Outlays, and Balances – Continued

Footnotes

1   The amounts in this column, unless otherwise footnoted, represent appropriations, increases and rescissions in borrowing authority or new contract authority. Appropriation accounts with appropriation transfer activity are presented in Table 1 (Appropriations and Appropriation Transfers) at the end of this chapter.

2   The amounts in this column, unless otherwise footnoted, represent transfers - other than appropriation transfers, borrowings (gross), investments (net), unrealized discounts or funds held outside the Treasury.

3   The amounts in this column, unless otherwise footnoted, represent obligated balances canceled for fiscal year 2002 pursuant to 31 U.S.C. 1553, changes in unfilled customer orders, accounts receivable, accounts payable, undelivered orders, unbigoted balances and adjustments to borrowing and contract authority.

4   Unobligated balances for no-year or unexpired multiple year accounts are available for obligation; unobligated balances for expired fiscal year accounts are not available for obligation.

5   Includes $93,342,964.26 which represents repayment of borrowing from the Federal Financing Bank in lieu of issuance of agency debt. Also, includes $2,000,000.00 which represents net repayment of borrowing from the U.S. Treasury.

6   Represents capital transfer to miscellaneous receipts.

7   Subject to disposition by the administrative agency.

8   Represents appropriations to liquidate.

9   Includes $1,772,114.01 which represents net sale of non-guaranteed Government agency securities.

10 Includes $28,427,837.78 which represents net redemption of non-guaranteed Government agency securities. Also, includes $215,000,000.00 which represents net borrowing from the U.S. Treasury.

Appropriations, Outlays, and Balances - Continued

Footnotes

Table 1 - Appropriations And Appropriation Transfers - Dept Of Housing And Urban Development

Department Regular	Fiscal Year	Account Symbol	Net Appropriations And Appropriations Transfers	Appropriation Amount	Net Appropriation Transfers	Department Regular Involved	Fiscal Year Involved	Accounts Involved	Amount From or To (-)
86	07	0143	1,138,280,476.00	581,108,351.00	557,172,125.00	47	07	0110	-287,025.00
						86	07	0183	347,490,000.00
						86	07	0198	742,500.00
						86	07	0200	209,286,000.00
						86	X	0223	247,500.00
						86	X	0233	34,650.00
						86	X	0313	148,500.00
						86	X	4586	-490,000.00
86	0709	0162	3,770,316,000.00	3,771,900,000.00	-1,584,000.00	86	X	4586	-1,584,000.00
86	07	0183	43,875,810.00	413,424,000.00	-369,548,190.00	86	07	0143	-347,490,000.00
						86	07	0189	-3,960,000.00
						86	X	4586	-18,098,190.00
86	07	0186	10,593,000.00	0.00	10,593,000.00	86	07	5301	10,593,000.00
86	X	0189	7,021,115.00	7,000,000.00	21,115.00	11	X	5512	21,115.00
86	07	0189	105,612,503.00	81,852,503.00	23,760,000.00	86	07	0183	3,960,000.00
						86	07	0200	19,800,000.00
86	0709	0192	1,420,810,000.00	1,421,800,000.00	-990,000.00	86	X	4586	-990,000.00
86	07	0198	7,799,627.00	8,542,127.00	-742,500.00	86	07	0143	-742,500.00
86	07	0200	68,034,341.00	307,812,341.00	-239,778,000.00	86	07	0143	-209,286,000.00
						86	07	0189	-19,800,000.00
						86	X	4586	-10,692,000.00
86	0709	0205	1,756,260,000.00	1,757,250,000.00	-990,000.00	86	X	4586	-990,000.00
86	X	0223	6,613,842.00	6,861,342.00	-247,500.00	86	07	0143	-247,500.00
86	X	0233	856,350.00	891,000.00	-34,650.00	86	07	0143	-34,650.00
86	0710	0237	236,214,000.00	236,610,000.00	-396,000.00	86	X	4586	-396,000.00
86	X	0302	15,880,766,265.00	15,886,666,265.00	-5,900,000.00	86	X	4586	-5,900,000.00
86	X	0303	5,975,031,000.00	5,976,417,000.00	-1,386,000.00	86	X	4586	-1,386,000.00
86	0710	0304	2,428,074,000.00	2,438,964,000.00	-10,890,000.00	86	X	4586	-10,890,000.00
86	0708	0308	257,647,500.00	286,110,000.00	-28,462,500.00	86	X	4586	-28,462,500.00
86	0709	0308	28,462,500.00	0.00	28,462,500.00	86	0709	0308	28,462,500.00
86	X	0313	625,062,265.00	625,210,765.00	-148,500.00	86	0708	0308	-148,500.00
86	0710	0320	734,184,000.00	734,580,000.00	-396,000.00	86	07	0143	-396,000.00
86	X	4586	51,812,190.00	0.00	51,812,190.00	86	07	0143	490,000.00
						86	0709	0162	1,584,000.00
						86	07	0183	18,098,190.00
						86	0709	0192	990,000.00
						86	07	0200	10,692,000.00
						86	0709	0205	990,000.00
						86	0710	0237	396,000.00
						86	X	0302	5,900,000.00
						86	X	0303	1,386,000.00

Appropriations, Outlays, and Balances – Continued

Footnotes

Table 1 - Appropriations And Appropriation Transfers - Dept Of Housing And Urban Development

Department Regular	Fiscal Year	Account Symbol	Net Appropriations And Appropriations Transfers	Appropriation Amount	Net Appropriation Transfers	Department Regular Involved	Fiscal Year Involved	Accounts Involved	Amount From or To (-)
86	07	5301	0.00	10,593,000.00	-10,593,000.00	86 86 86	0710 0710 07	0304 0320 0186	10,890,000.00 396,000.00 -10,593,000.00
Totals			34,553,326,784.00	34,553,592,694.00	-265,910.00				-265,910.00

Appropriations, Outlays, and Balances – Continued

Footnotes

This Page Left Blank Intentionally

Appropriations, Outlays, and Balances – Continued

Appropriation or Fund Account — Title	Period of Availability	Dept Reg	Dept Tr From	Account Number	Sub No.	Balances, Beginning Of Fiscal Year	Appropriations And Other Obligational Authority[1]	Transfers Borrowings And Investment (Net)[2]	Outlays (Net)	Balances Withdrawn And Other Transactions[3]	Balances, End Of Fiscal Year[4]
Department Of The Interior											
Land And Minerals Management											
Bureau Of Land Management											
General Fund Accounts											
Management Of Lands And Resources, Bureau Of Land Management											
Fund Resources:											
Undisbursed Funds	No Year	14		1109		247,175,945.38	866,911,000.00		832,299,061.00		281,787,884.38
Accounts Receivable						13,265,162.70				-6,322,224.57	19,587,387.27
Unfilled Customer Orders						18,595,238.54				-1,562,935.78	20,158,174.32
Fund Equities:											
Unobligated Balances (Unexpired)						-41,176,238.15				3,749,863.37	-44,926,101.52
Accounts Payable						-56,219,902.53				7,291,054.20	-63,510,956.73
Undelivered Orders						-181,640,205.94				31,456,181.78	-213,096,387.72
Subtotal		14		1109		-0-	866,911,000.00		832,299,061.00	34,611,939.00	-0-
Construction, Bureau Of Land Management											
Fund Resources:											
Undisbursed Funds	No Year	14		1110		19,578,083.55	10,674,540.00	491,000.00	10,175,167.27		20,568,456.28
Transfer To:											
Department Of Transportation, Federal Highway Administration	No Year	69	14	1110	5	350,000.00					350,000.00
Fund Equities:											
Unobligated Balances (Unexpired)						-9,664,372.85				5,800,413.37	-15,464,786.22
Accounts Payable						-76,499.22				77,434.29	-153,933.51
Undelivered Orders						-10,187,211.48				4,887,474.93	-5,299,736.55
Subtotal		14		1110		-0-	10,674,540.00	491,000.00	10,175,167.27	990,372.73	-0-
Oregon And California Grant Lands, Bureau Of Land Management											
Fund Resources:											
Undisbursed Funds	No Year	14		1116		34,497,195.91	108,990,606.00		106,634,996.78		36,852,805.13
Transfer To:											
Department Of Transportation, Federal Highway Administration	No Year	69	14	1116	5	-15,070.63					[5]-15,070.63
Fund Equities:											
Unobligated Balances (Unexpired)						-2,198,949.96				1,534,041.68	-3,732,991.64
Accounts Payable						-4,892,937.29				-49,737.27	-4,843,200.02
Undelivered Orders						-27,390,238.03				871,304.81	-28,261,542.84
Subtotal		14		1116		-0-	108,990,606.00		106,634,996.78	2,355,609.22	-0-
Cook Inlet Region, Incorporated Property Account, Bureau Of Land Management											
Fund Resources:											
Undisbursed Funds	No Year	14		1118		2,376,394.44					2,376,394.44
Fund Equities:											
Unobligated Balances (Unexpired)						-2,376,394.44					-2,376,394.44
Subtotal		14		1118		-0-					-0-
Fire Protection, Bureau Of Land Management											
Fund Resources:											
Undisbursed Funds	No Year	14		1119		1,186,576.17					1,186,576.17

Appropriations, Outlays, and Balances - Continued

Appropriation or Fund Account (Title)	Period of Availability	Dept Reg	Tr From	Account Number	Sub No.	Balances, Beginning Of Fiscal Year	Appropriations And Other Obligational Authority[1]	Transfers Borrowings And Investment (Net)[2]	Outlays (Net)	Balances Withdrawn And Other Transactions[3]	Balances, End Of Fiscal Year[4]
Fund Equities:											
Accounts Payable						-455,002.37					-455,002.37
Undelivered Orders						-731,573.80					-731,573.80
Subtotal		14		1119		-0-					-0-
Emergency Department Of The Interior Firefighting Fund, Bureau Of Land Management											
Fund Resources:											
Undisbursed Funds	No Year	14		1120							
Transfer To:											
Bureau Of Indian Affairs	No Year	14	14	1120	20	12,538.10			12,538.10		12,538.10
Fund Equities:											
Accounts Payable						-12,538.10			12,538.10	-12,538.10	
Subtotal		14		1120		-0-			12,538.10	-12,538.10	-0-
Wildland Fire Management, Bureau Of Land Management											
Fund Resources:											
Undisbursed Funds	No Year	14		1125		307,393,285.89	900,637,003.00	-429,366,494.75	560,999,933.84		217,663,860.30
Transfer To:											
Interior, Office Of The Secretary	No Year	14	14	1125	1	4,246,335.06		4,774,000.00	5,735,254.97		3,285,080.09
Interior, National Park Service	No Year	14	14	1125	10	33,805,477.15		122,726,288.00	121,606,994.96		34,924,770.19
Interior, United States Fish & Wildlife Service	No Year	14	14	1125	16	26,520,045.27		95,610,735.00	95,034,501.81		27,096,278.46
Interior, Bureau Of Indian Affairs	No Year	14	14	1125	20	46,194,787.57		177,255,471.75	172,499,839.49		50,950,419.83
Accounts Receivable						5,601,096.47				863,676.76	4,737,419.71
Unfilled Customer Orders						3,549,711.12				1,507,267.95	2,042,443.17
Fund Equities:											
Unobligated Balances (Unexpired)						-153,277,041.51				-98,450,322.98	-54,826,718.53
Accounts Payable						-49,085,275.51				4,047,671.71	-53,132,947.22
Undelivered Orders						-224,948,421.51				7,792,184.49	-232,740,606.00
Subtotal		14		1125		-0-	900,637,003.00	-29,000,000.00	955,876,525.07	-84,239,522.07	-0-
Calista Corporation Property Account, Bureau Of Land Management											
Fund Resources:											
Undisbursed Funds	No Year	14		1140		4,731.03					4,731.03
Fund Equities:											
Unobligated Balances (Unexpired)						-4,731.03					-4,731.03
Subtotal		14		1140		-0-					-0-
Special Fund Accounts											
Payments To States From Grazing Receipts, Etc., Public Lands Outside Grazing Districts, Bureau Of Land Management											
Fund Resources:											
Undisbursed Funds	No Year	14		5016			1,026,751.41		1,026,751.41		
Service Charges, Deposits And Forfeitures, Bureau Of Land Management											
Fund Resources:											
Undisbursed Funds	No Year	14		5017		29,203,349.95	26,387,607.37		22,029,763.30		33,561,194.02
Fund Equities:											
Unobligated Balances (Unexpired)						-25,713,609.22				3,574,108.80	-29,287,718.02
Accounts Payable						-617,578.62				100,849.00	-718,427.62
Undelivered Orders						-2,872,162.11				682,886.27	-3,555,048.38

Footnotes At End Of Chapter

Appropriations, Outlays, and Balances – Continued

Appropriation or Fund Account — Title	Period of Availability	Reg	Tr From	Account Number	Sub No.	Balances, Beginning Of Fiscal Year	Appropriations And Other Obligational Authority[1]	Transfers Borrowings And Investment (Net)[2]	Outlays (Net)	Balances Withdrawn And Other Transactions[3]	Balances, End Of Fiscal Year[4]
Service Charges, Deposits And Forfeitures, Bureau Of Land Management - Continued	Subtotal	14		5017		-0-	26,387,607.37		22,029,763.30	4,357,844.07	-0-
Expenses, Road Maintenance Deposits, Bureau Of Land Management											
Fund Resources:											
Undisbursed Funds	No Year	14		5018		2,491,510.42	2,083,646.92		2,127,468.69		2,447,688.65
Fund Equities:											
Unobligated Balances (Unexpired)						-2,355,276.91				-58,410.83	-2,296,866.08
Accounts Payable						-74,863.98				-15,282.54	-59,581.44
Undelivered Orders						-61,369.53				29,871.60	-91,241.13
Subtotal	Subtotal	14		5018		-0-	2,083,646.92		2,127,468.69	-43,821.77	-0-
Payments To States From Grazing Receipts, Etc., Public Lands Within Grazing Districts, Bureau Of Land Management											
Fund Resources:											
Undisbursed Funds	No Year	14		5032			1,516,565.28		1,516,565.28		
Land Acquisition, Bureau Of Land Management											
Fund Resources:											
Undisbursed Funds	No Year	14		5033		21,529,689.53	8,634,266.00	3,000,000.00	13,717,455.41		19,446,500.12
Unfilled Customer Orders						755,138.00				755,138.00	
Fund Equities:											
Unobligated Balances (Unexpired)						-13,549,461.78				430,097.22	-13,979,559.00
Accounts Payable						-95,371.41				-16,395.16	-78,976.25
Undelivered Orders						-8,639,994.34				-3,252,029.47	-5,387,964.87
Subtotal	Subtotal	14		5033		-0-	8,634,266.00	3,000,000.00	13,717,455.41	-2,083,189.41	-0-
Payments To States From Grazing Receipts, Etc., Public Lands Within Grazing Districts, Miscellaneous, Bureau Of Land Management											
Fund Resources:											
Undisbursed Funds	No Year	14		5044			20,192.94		20,192.94		
Payments To Alaska From Oil And Gas Leases, National Petroleum Reserve, Bureau Of Land Management											
Fund Resources:											
Undisbursed Funds	No Year	14		5045			12,772,299.00		12,772,299.00		
Operation And Maintenance Of Quarters, Bureau Of Land Management											
Fund Resources:											
Undisbursed Funds	No Year	14		5048		772,820.37	521,726.71		454,037.11	71,860.01	840,509.97
Fund Equities:											
Unobligated Balances (Unexpired)						-706,639.53				-1,907.39	-778,499.54
Accounts Payable						-5,430.65					-3,523.26
Undelivered Orders						-60,750.19				-2,263.02	-58,487.17
Subtotal	Subtotal	14		5048		-0-	521,726.71		454,037.11	67,689.60	-0-
Fee Collection Support, Public Lands, Bureau Of Land Management											
Fund Resources:											
Undisbursed Funds	No Year	14		5056		47,815.20	1,185.00		1,185.00		46,630.20
Fund Equities:											
Unobligated Balances (Unexpired)						-46,906.20				-276.00	-46,630.20
Undelivered Orders						-909.00				-909.00	
Subtotal	Subtotal	14		5056		-0-	1,185.00		1,185.00	-1,185.00	-0-

Appropriations, Outlays, and Balances - Continued

Appropriation or Fund Account — Title	Period of Availability	Dept Reg	Dept Tr From	Account Number	Sub No.	Balances, Beginning Of Fiscal Year	Appropriations And Other Obligational Authority[1]	Transfers Borrowings And Investment (Net)[2]	Outlays (Net)	Balances Withdrawn And Other Transactions[3]	Balances, End Of Fiscal Year[4]
Payments To State And County From Clark County, Nevada Land Sales, Bureau Of Land Management											
Fund Resources:											
Undisbursed Funds	No Year	14		5129		-----	7,713,450.00	-----	7,713,450.00	-----	-----
Range Improvements, Bureau Of Land Management											
Fund Resources:											
Undisbursed Funds	No Year	14		5132		7,984,309.98	10,000,000.00	-----	9,108,461.64	-----	8,875,848.34
Fund Equities:											
Unobligated Balances (Unexpired)						-4,405,539.46				1,620,630.68	-6,026,170.14
Accounts Payable						-197,227.07				-26,288.66	-170,938.41
Undelivered Orders						-3,381,543.45				-702,803.66	-2,678,739.79
Subtotal		14		5132		-0-	10,000,000.00		9,108,461.64	891,538.36	-0-
Payments To States (Proceeds Of Sales), Bureau Of Land Management											
Fund Resources:											
Undisbursed Funds	No Year	14		5133		-----	3,310,849.99	-----	3,310,849.99	-----	-----
Payment To Oklahoma (Royalties), Bureau Of Land Management											
Fund Resources:											
Undisbursed Funds	No Year	14		5134		-----	19,533.28	-----	19,533.28	-----	-----
Forest Ecosystems Health And Recovery, Bureau Of Land Management											
Fund Resources:											
Undisbursed Funds	No Year	14		5165		12,714,341.82	7,274,219.84	-----	5,448,891.03	-----	14,539,670.63
Fund Equities:											
Unobligated Balances (Unexpired)						-11,244,565.97				1,469,346.92	-12,713,912.89
Accounts Payable						-293,177.42				-60,987.80	-232,189.62
Undelivered Orders						-1,176,598.43				416,969.69	-1,593,568.12
Subtotal		14		5165		-0-	7,274,219.84		5,448,891.03	1,825,328.81	-0-
Southern Nevada Public Land Management, Bureau Of Land Management											
Fund Resources:											
Undisbursed Funds	No Year	14		5232		672,643.16	146,886,792.00	21,019,977.82	167,540,092.77		1,039,320.21
Transfer To:											
Forest Service, Department Of Agriculture	No Year	12	14	5232	11	34,347,942.99		64,710,336.33	49,647,174.31		49,411,105.01
Southern Nevada Public Land Management, Bureau Of Reclamation	No Year	14	14	5232	6			1,237,160.00	56,256.72		1,180,903.28
Department Of The Interior, National Park Service	No Year	14	14	5232	10	1,461,785.94		32,780,428.59	1,696,475.71		32,545,738.82
Department Of The Interior, U.S. Fish And Wildlife Service	No Year	14	14	5232	16	1,196,882.00		30,532,487.41	3,989,386.89		27,739,982.52
Federal Highway Administration	No Year	69	14	5232	5	8,995,000.00		5,733,000.00			14,728,000.00
Unrealized Discount On Investments						-46,818,676.72		-2,967,390.15			-49,786,066.87
Investments In Public Debt Securities						2,296,438,000.00		-153,046,000.00			2,143,392,000.00
Fund Equities:											
Unobligated Balances (Unexpired)						[6]-1,368,231,391.76				-457,640,758.86	-910,590,632.90
Accounts Payable						-27,300,925.51				7,833,687.12	-35,134,612.63
Undelivered Orders						[8]-900,761,260.10				373,764,477.34	-1,274,525,737.44
Subtotal		14		5232		-0-	146,886,792.00		222,929,386.40	-76,042,594.40	-0-
Timber Sales Pipeline Restoration Fund, Bureau Of Land Management											
Fund Resources:											
Undisbursed Funds	No Year	14		5249		24,792,866.47	10,921,620.84	39,805.00	8,147,360.29	-----	27,606,932.02
Fund Equities:											
Unobligated Balances (Unexpired)						-23,182,370.87				2,678,616.82	-25,860,987.69
Accounts Payable						-185,548.70				93,582.81	-279,131.51

Footnotes At End Of Chapter

Appropriations, Outlays, and Balances – Continued

Appropriation or Fund Account	Account Symbol					Balances, Beginning Of Fiscal Year	Appropriations And Other Obligational Authority[1]	Transfers Borrowings And Investment (Net)[2]	Outlays (Net)	Balances Withdrawn And Other Transactions[3]	Balances, End Of Fiscal Year[4]
Title	Period of Availability	Dept Reg	Tr From	Account Number	Sub No.						
Timber Sales Pipeline Restoration Fund, Bureau Of Land Management - Continued											
Fund Equities: - Continued											
Undelivered Orders						-1,424,946.90				41,865.92	-1,466,812.82
	Subtotal	14		5249		-0-	10,921,620.84	39,805.00	8,147,360.29	2,814,065.55	-0-
Federal Land Disposal Account, Bureau Of Land Management											
Fund Resources:											
Undisbursed Funds	No Year	14		5260		86,158,818.98	6,689,466.62	-7,850,000.00	5,954,766.83		79,043,518.77
Transfer To:											
Forest Service, Department Of Agriculture	No Year	12	14	5260	11	1.00		3,500,000.00	645,534.94		2,854,466.06
Department Of The Interior, National Park Service	No Year	14	14	5260	10	1.00		2,600,000.00	2,075,000.00		525,001.00
Department Of The Interior, U.S. Fish And Wildlife Service	No Year	14	14	5260	16	1.00		1,750,000.00			1,750,001.00
Fund Equities:											
Unobligated Balances (Unexpired)						-85,851,031.56				-1,884,810.41	-83,996,221.15
Accounts Payable						-30,273.53				-12,864.45	-17,409.08
Undelivered Orders						-277,516.89				-88,160.29	-189,356.60
	Subtotal	14		5260		-0-	6,689,466.62		8,675,301.77	-1,985,835.15	-0-
Use Of Receipts From Mineral Leasing Activities On Certain Naval Oil Shale Reserves, Bureau Of Land Management											
Fund Resources:											
Undisbursed Funds	No Year	14		5294		6,674,190.46			201,995.23		6,472,195.23
Fund Equities:											
Unobligated Balances (Unexpired)						-6,505,502.40				-229,805.41	-6,275,696.99
Accounts Payable						-639.90				1,642.00	-2,281.90
Undelivered Orders						-168,048.16				26,168.18	-194,216.34
	Subtotal	14		5294		-0-			201,995.23	-201,995.23	-0-
Recreation Enhancement Fee Program, Bureau Of Land Management											
Fund Resources:											
Undisbursed Funds	No Year	14		5413		13,063,743.89	14,550,199.93		14,030,049.37		13,603,894.45
Fund Equities:											
Unobligated Balances (Unexpired)						-10,508,196.11				174,424.13	-10,682,620.24
Accounts Payable						-428,027.34				-93,864.53	-334,162.81
Undelivered Orders						-2,147,520.44				439,590.96	-2,587,111.40
	Subtotal	14		5413		-0-	14,550,199.93		14,030,049.37	520,150.56	-0-
Land Sale Deschutes County, Oregon, Bureau Of Land Management											
Fund Resources:											
Undisbursed Funds	No Year	14		5465		205,000.00					205,000.00
Fund Equities:											
Unobligated Balances (Unexpired)						-205,000.00					-205,000.00
	Subtotal	14		5465		-0-					-0-
Lincoln County Land Act, Bureau Of Land Management											
Fund Resources:											
Undisbursed Funds	No Year	14		5469		54,576.74	2,205,043.78	-1,916,639.82	335,231.72	2,104,298.92	7,748.98
Unrealized Discount On Investments						-989,554.11		-68,360.18			-1,057,914.29
Investments In Public Debt Securities						44,793,000.00		1,985,000.00			46,778,000.00
Fund Equities:											
Unobligated Balances (Unexpired)						-43,545,644.34				2,104,298.92	-45,649,943.26
Accounts Payable						-2,408.78				5,149.22	-7,558.00
Undelivered Orders						-309,969.51				-239,636.08	-70,333.43

Appropriations, Outlays, and Balances - Continued

Appropriation or Fund Account — Title	Dept Reg	Dept Tr From	Account Number	Sub No.	Period of Availability	Balances, Beginning Of Fiscal Year	Appropriations And Other Obligational Authority[1]	Transfers Borrowings And Investment (Net)[2]	Outlays (Net)	Balances Withdrawn And Other Transactions[3]	Balances, End Of Fiscal Year[4]
Title II Projects On Federal Lands, Bureau Of Land Management											
Fund Resources:											
Undisbursed Funds	14		5469		Subtotal	-0-	2,205,043.78		335,231.72	1,869,812.06	-0-
Fund Equities:											
Undisbursed Funds	14		5485		No Year	10,475,651.74	8,252,883.58		7,421,485.20		11,307,050.12
Fund Equities:											
Unobligated Balances (Unexpired)						-4,831,624.76				-1,114,129.62	-3,717,495.14
Accounts Payable						-73,647.46				-31,111.09	-42,536.37
Undelivered Orders						-5,570,379.52				1,976,639.09	-7,547,018.61
	14		5485		Subtotal	-0-	8,252,883.58		7,421,485.20	831,398.38	-0-
Stewardship Contracting Product Sales, Bureau Of Land Management											
Fund Resources:											
Undisbursed Funds	14		5506		No Year	25,745.41	107,673.68		25,000.00		108,419.09
Fund Equities:											
Unobligated Balances (Unexpired)	14		5506		Subtotal	-25,745.41	107,673.68		25,000.00	82,673.68	-108,419.09
						-0-				82,673.68	-0-
Permit Processing Fund, Bureau Of Land Management											
Fund Resources:											
Undisbursed Funds	14		5573		No Year	15,360,968.76	21,949,562.69	-2,612,000.00	14,069,808.56		20,628,722.89
Transfer To:											
U.S. Forest Service, Department Of Agriculture	12	14	5573	11	No Year	791,507.50		1,172,000.00	737,725.00		1,225,782.50
U.S. Fish And Wildlife Service, Department Of The Interior	14	14	5573	16	No Year	1,631,813.28		1,440,000.00	1,053,883.82		2,017,929.46
Corps Of Engineers	96	14	5573		No Year	418,390.39			187,591.89		230,798.50
Fund Equities:											
Unobligated Balances (Unexpired)						-13,328,161.87				1,300,869.24	-14,629,031.11
Accounts Payable						-474,862.69				-45,675.06	-429,187.63
Undelivered Orders						-4,399,655.37				4,645,359.24	-9,045,014.61
	14		5573		Subtotal	-0-	21,949,562.69		16,049,009.27	5,900,553.42	-0-
Geothermal Steam Implementation Fund											
Fund Resources:											
Undisbursed Funds	14		5575		No Year	2,409,861.86	4,359,936.41		2,412,755.48		4,357,042.79
Fund Equities:											
Unobligated Balances (Unexpired)						-1,975,153.24				1,238,259.33	-3,213,412.57
Accounts Payable						-32,096.84				162,660.29	-194,757.13
Undelivered Orders						-402,611.78				546,261.31	-948,873.09
	14		5575		Subtotal	-0-	4,359,936.41		2,412,755.48	1,947,180.93	-0-
Naval Petroleum Reserve Numbered 2 Lease Revenue Account											
Fund Resources:											
Undisbursed Funds	14		5576		No Year	113,440.27	2,081,099.50		427,299.84		1,767,239.93
Fund Equities:											
Unobligated Balances (Unexpired)						-75,574.19				1,676,917.95	-1,752,492.14
Accounts Payable						-15,689.34				-8,318.55	-7,370.79
Undelivered Orders						-22,176.74				-14,799.74	-7,377.00
	14		5576		Subtotal	-0-	2,081,099.50		427,299.84	1,653,799.66	-0-
Payment From Proceeds, Sale Of Water, Mineral Leasing Act Of 1920, Sec. 40(D), Bureau Of Land Management											
Fund Resources:											
Undisbursed Funds	14		5662		No Year	49,461.81					49,461.81

Footnotes At End Of Chapter

Appropriations, Outlays, and Balances – Continued

Appropriation or Fund Account — Title	Dept Reg	Tr From	Account Number	Sub No.	Period of Availability	Balances, Beginning Of Fiscal Year	Appropriations And Other Obligational Authority[1]	Transfers Borrowings And Investment (Net)[2]	Outlays (Net)	Balances Withdrawn And Other Transactions[3]	Balances, End Of Fiscal Year[4]
Payment From Proceeds, Sale Of Water, Mineral Leasing Act Of 1920, Sec. 40(D), Bureau Of Land Management - Continued											
Fund Equities:											
Unobligated Balances (Unexpired)	14		5662		Subtotal	-49,461.81					-49,461.81
						-0-					-0-
Payments To Counties, Oregon And California Grant Lands, Bureau Of Land Management											
Fund Resources:											
Undisbursed Funds	14		5884		No Year		107,927,931.40		107,927,931.40		
Payments To Counties, National Grasslands, Bureau Of Land Management											
Fund Resources:											
Undisbursed Funds	14		5896		No Year		980,432.46		980,432.46		
Payments To Coos And Douglas Counties, Oregon, From Receipts, Coos Bay Wagon Road Grant Lands, Bureau Of Land Management											
Fund Resources:											
Undisbursed Funds	14		5898		No Year		924,336.93		924,336.93		
Public Enterprise Funds											
Helium Fund, Bureau Of Land Management											
Fund Resources:											
Undisbursed Funds	14		4053		No Year	21,023,410.23			981,298.97		20,042,111.26
Accounts Receivable						6,396,673.70				411,309.55	5,985,364.15
Fund Equities:											
Unobligated Balances (Unexpired)						-21,851,338.51				-3,515,205.90	-18,336,132.61
Accounts Payable						-1,089,154.65				222,948.15	-1,312,102.80
Undelivered Orders						-4,479,590.77				1,899,649.23	-6,379,240.00
Fund Resources: Undisbursed Funds	14		4053		Subtotal	-0-			981,298.97	-981,298.97	-0-
Intragovernmental Funds											
Working Capital Fund, Bureau Of Land Management											
Fund Resources:											
Undisbursed Funds	14		4525		No Year	65,800,917.46		-1,125.00	-1,906,733.85	-523,462.69	67,706,526.31
Funds Held Outside The Treasury						52,863.85		1,125.00		133,000.56	53,988.85
Accounts Receivable										-250.00	250.00
Fund Equities:											
Unobligated Balances (Unexpired)						-53,040,125.26				-523,462.69	-52,516,662.57
Accounts Payable						-169,138.79				133,000.56	-302,139.35
Undelivered Orders						-12,644,517.26				2,297,445.98	-14,941,963.24
Fund Resources: Undisbursed Funds	14		4525		Subtotal	-0-			-1,906,733.85	1,906,733.85	-0-
Trust Fund Accounts											
Land And Resources Management Trust Fund, Bureau Of Land Management											
Fund Resources:											
Undisbursed Funds	14		8069		No Year	29,387,980.32	25,056,864.72		23,294,756.53		31,150,088.51

Appropriations, Outlays, and Balances - Continued

Appropriation or Fund Account — Title	Dept Reg	Dept Tr From	Account Number	Sub No.	Period of Availability	Balances, Beginning Of Fiscal Year	Appropriations And Other Obligational Authority[1]	Transfers Borrowings And Investment (Net)[2]	Outlays (Net)	Balances Withdrawn And Other Transactions[3]	Balances, End Of Fiscal Year[4]
Fund Equities:											
Unobligated Balances (Unexpired)						-16,923,144.79				7,902,174.84	-24,825,319.63
Accounts Payable						-244,362.82				-11,692.78	-232,670.04
Undelivered Orders						-12,220,472.71				-6,128,373.87	-6,092,098.84
			8069		Subtotal	-0-	25,056,864.72		23,294,756.53	1,762,108.19	-0-
Trustee Funds, Alaska Townsites, Bureau Of Land Management											
Fund Resources:											
Undisbursed Funds	14		8565		No Year	419.93					419.93
Fund Equities:											
Unobligated Balances (Unexpired)						-419.93					-419.93
	14		8565		Subtotal	-0-					-0-
Total, Bureau Of Land Management							2,321,388,102.28	-25,469,195.00	2,397,122,089.31	-101,203,182.03	
Minerals Management Service											
General Fund Accounts											
Leasing And Royalty Management, Minerals Management Service											
Fund Resources:											
Undisbursed Funds	14		1917		2007-2008		2,955,863.00		2,901,420.69		54,442.31
					2007		149,656,562.00		139,741,441.51		9,915,120.49
					2006-2007	11,554,680.11			4,419,399.57		7,135,280.54
					2006	7,854,219.61			6,207,419.01		1,646,800.60
					2005-2006	83,058.76					83,058.76
					2005	1,652,205.08			524,384.60		1,127,820.48
					2004-2005	60,057.68					60,057.68
					2004	1,071,245.63			53,955.59		1,017,290.04
					2003	161,930.44			-2,704.05		164,634.49
					2002	490,829.86			54,591.83	436,238.03	
					No Year	119,999,240.61			-25,002,679.00		145,001,919.61
Accounts Receivable						464,187.84				322,715.73	141,472.11
Unfilled Customer Orders						1,198,086.16				-255,495.44	1,453,581.60
Fund Equities:											
Unobligated Balances (Expired)						-2,319,864.89				661,239.51	-2,981,104.40
Unobligated Balances (Unexpired)						-38,116,165.79				11,544,830.23	-49,660,996.02
Accounts Payable						-27,066,139.24				1,945,707.79	-29,011,847.03
Undelivered Orders						-77,087,571.86				9,059,959.40	-86,147,531.26
	14		1917		Subtotal	-0-	152,612,425.00		128,897,229.75	23,715,195.25	-0-
Special Fund Accounts											
Payments To States From Receipts Under Mineral Leasing, Public And Acquired Military Lands, Minerals Management Service											
Fund Resources:											
Undisbursed Funds	14		5003		No Year		1,883,010,482.30		1,883,010,482.30		

Footnotes At End Of Chapter

Appropriations, Outlays, and Balances – Continued

Appropriation or Fund Account — Title	Period of Availability	Dept Reg	Tr From	Account Number	Sub No.	Balances, Beginning Of Fiscal Year	Appropriations And Other Obligational Authority[1]	Transfers Borrowings And Investment (Net)[2]	Outlays (Net)	Balances Withdrawn And Other Transactions[3]	Balances, End Of Fiscal Year[4]
Payments To States, National Forest Fund, Minerals Management Service											
Fund Resources:											
Undisbursed Funds	No Year	14		5243			15,471,470.12		15,471,470.12		
Payments To States, Flood Control Act Of 1954, Mineral Management Service											
Fund Resources:											
Undisbursed Funds	No Year	14		5248			3,939,663.26		3,939,663.26		
Environmental Improvement And Restoration Fund, Minerals Management Service											
Fund Resources:											
Undisbursed Funds	No Year	14		5425		105.20	37,656,648.80	-37,655,929.06			824.94
Unrealized Discount On Investments						-10,629,387.82		-1,103,070.94			-11,732,458.76
Investments In Public Debt Securities						1,050,525,000.00		38,759,000.00			1,089,284,000.00
Fund Equities:											
Unobligated Balances (Unexpired)						-1,039,895,717.38					-1,077,552,366.18
Subtotal		14		5425		-0-	37,656,648.80			37,656,648.80	-0-
Coastal Impact Assistance, Minerals Management Service											
Fund Resources:											
Undisbursed Funds	No Year	14		5572			250,000,000.00		950,781.95		249,049,218.05
Fund Equities:											
Unobligated Balances (Unexpired)										248,933,492.18	-248,933,492.18
Accounts Payable										97,560.30	-97,560.30
Undelivered Orders										18,165.57	-18,165.57
Subtotal		14		5572		-0-	250,000,000.00		950,781.95	249,049,218.05	-0-
Geothermal Lease Revenues, Payment To Counties											
Fund Resources:											
Undisbursed Funds	No Year	14		5574			4,360,025.63		4,360,025.63		
Trust Fund Accounts											
Oil Spill Research, Minerals Management Service											
Fund Resources:											
Undisbursed Funds	No Year	14		8370		5,573,115.64	6,902,924.00		7,116,703.43		5,359,336.21
Accounts Receivable						117,208.38				114,742.38	2,466.00
Unfilled Customer Orders						63,844.07				-14,451.60	78,295.67
Fund Equities:											
Unobligated Balances (Unexpired)						-375,053.86				330,767.17	-705,821.03
Accounts Payable						-1,100,517.89				-144,372.17	-956,145.72
Undelivered Orders						-4,278,596.34				-500,465.21	-3,778,131.13
Subtotal		14		8370		-0-	6,902,924.00		7,116,703.43	-213,779.43	-0-
Total, Minerals Management Service							2,353,953,639.11		2,043,746,356.44	310,207,282.67	

Appropriations, Outlays, and Balances - Continued

Title	Period of Availability	Dept Reg	Dept Tr From	Account Number	Sub No.	Balances, Beginning Of Fiscal Year	Appropriations And Other Obligational Authority[1]	Transfers Borrowings And Investment (Net)[2]	Outlays (Net)	Balances Withdrawn And Other Transactions[3]	Balances, End Of Fiscal Year[4]
Office Of Surface Mining Reclamation And Enforcement											
General Fund Accounts											
Regulation And Technology, Office Of Surface Mining Reclamation And Enforcement											
Fund Resources:											
Undisbursed Funds	2007	14		1801		33,376,154.76	109,099,236.00		74,257,145.01		34,842,090.99
	2006					3,631,659.87			29,740,126.72		3,636,028.04
	2005					2,726,215.41			1,181,925.86		2,449,734.01
	2004					1,734,961.94			12,856.67		2,713,358.74
	2003					2,055,235.33					1,734,961.94
	2002					776,275.36				2,055,235.33	
	No Year					4,588.61			175,515.30		600,760.06
Accounts Receivable						68,835.23				-562,651.85	567,240.46
Unfilled Customer Orders										20,247.03	48,588.20
Fund Equities:											
Unobligated Balances (Expired)						-7,701,667.51				663,246.82	-8,364,914.33
Unobligated Balances (Unexpired)						-776,275.36				-218,206.00	-558,069.36
Accounts Payable						-4,101,177.45				-1,898,771.88	-2,202,405.57
Undelivered Orders						-31,794,806.19				3,672,566.99	-35,467,373.18
Subtotal		14		1801		-0-	109,099,236.00		105,367,569.56	3,731,666.44	
Special Fund Accounts											
Abandoned Mine Reclamation Fund, Office Of Surface Mining Reclamation And Enforcement											
Fund Resources:											
Undisbursed Funds	No Year	14		5015		1,005,417.76	410,698,074.72	-98,082,149.64	313,109,442.99		511,899.85
Transfer To:											
Natural Resources Conservation Service, Department Of Agriculture	No Year	12	14	5015	10	189,768.94		-189,905.58	-136.64		
Unrealized Discount On Investments						-2,668,702.81					-2,668,702.81
Investments In Public Debt Securities						2,266,312,718.23		98,272,055.22			2,364,584,773.45
Accounts Receivable						14,174.25				-1,057,650.36	1,071,824.61
Unfilled Customer Orders						407,244.02				-4,057,498.11	4,464,742.13
Fund Equities:											
Unobligated Balances (Unexpired)						-1,991,395,729.64				108,875,302.25	-2,100,271,031.89
Accounts Payable						-6,547,204.83				4,422,356.79	-10,969,561.62
Undelivered Orders						-267,317,685.92				-10,593,742.20	-256,723,943.72
Subtotal		14		5015		-0-	410,698,074.72		313,109,306.35	97,588,768.37	-0-
Regulation And Technology, Civil Penalties, Office Of Surface Mining Reclamation And Enforcement											
Fund Resources:											
Undisbursed Funds	No Year	14		5063		247,490.39	160,064.90		23,662.04		383,893.25
Fund Equities:											
Unobligated Balances (Unexpired)						-145,640.95				37,545.90	-183,186.85

Footnotes At End Of Chapter

Appropriations, Outlays, and Balances – Continued

Appropriation or Fund Account — Title	Period of Availability	Dept — Reg	Dept — Tr From	Account Number	Sub No.	Balances, Beginning Of Fiscal Year	Appropriations And Other Obligational Authority[1]	Transfers Borrowings And Investment (Net)[2]	Outlays (Net)	Balances Withdrawn And Other Transactions[3]	Balances, End Of Fiscal Year[4]
Regulation And Technology, Civil Penalties, Office Of Surface Mining Reclamation And Enforcement - Continued											
Fund Equities: - Continued											
Undelivered Orders						-101,849.44				98,856.96	-200,706.40
Subtotal		14		5063		-0-	160,064.90		23,662.04	136,402.86	-0-
Total, Office Of Surface Mining Reclamation And Enforcement						-0-	519,957,375.62		418,500,537.95	101,456,837.67	-------
Total, Land And Minerals Management							5,195,299,117.01	-25,469,195.00	4,859,368,983.70	310,460,938.31	
Water And Science											
Bureau Of Reclamation											
General Fund Accounts											
Loan Program, Liquidating Account, Bureau Of Reclamation											
Fund Resources:											
Undisbursed Funds	No Year	14		0667		172,011.96			-4,610,422.71	4,782,434.67	
Fund Equities:											
Unobligated Balances (Unexpired)						-172,011.96				-172,011.96	
Subtotal		14		0667		-0-			-4,610,422.71	4,610,422.71	-0-
Water And Related Resources, Bureau Of Reclamation											
Fund Resources:											
Undisbursed Funds	No Year	14		0680		730,744,152.71	804,052,986.00	-346,074.00	771,180,777.86		763,270,286.85
Accounts Receivable						13,417,377.90				-6,083,807.22	19,501,185.12
Unfilled Customer Orders						29,376,217.53				-27,051,424.40	56,427,641.93
Fund Equities:											
Unobligated Balances (Unexpired)						-185,316,759.08				18,691,238.57	-204,007,997.65
Accounts Payable						-137,304,884.71				-24,199,080.16	-113,105,804.55
Undelivered Orders						-450,916,104.35				71,169,207.35	-522,085,311.70
Subtotal		14		0680		-0-	804,052,986.00	-346,074.00	771,180,777.86	32,526,134.14	-0-
Bureau Of Reclamation Loans Program Account, Bureau Of Reclamation											
Fund Resources:											
Undisbursed Funds	No Year	14		0685		6,860,457.67	4,725,000.00		10,699,095.38		886,362.29
Fund Equities:											
Unobligated Balances (Unexpired)						-940,977.77				-60,313.48	-880,664.29
Accounts Payable						-1,310.00				4,388.00	-5,698.00
Undelivered Orders						-5,918,169.90				-5,918,169.90	-0-
Subtotal		14		0685		-0-	4,725,000.00		10,699,095.38	-5,974,095.38	-0-
California Bay-Delta Restoration, Bureau Of Reclamation											
Fund Resources:											
Undisbursed Funds	No Year	14		0687		62,796,093.46	36,648,000.00		27,279,575.87		72,164,517.59
Fund Equities:											
Unobligated Balances (Unexpired)						-14,129,152.26				-5,600,718.22	-8,528,434.04
Accounts Payable						-1,493,493.57				5,599,752.22	-7,093,245.79
Undelivered Orders						-47,173,447.63				9,369,390.13	-56,542,837.76
Subtotal		14		0687		-0-	36,648,000.00		27,279,575.87	9,368,424.13	-0-

Appropriations, Outlays, and Balances - Continued

Title	Period of Availability	Dept Reg	Tr From	Account Number	Sub No.	Balances, Beginning Of Fiscal Year	Appropriations And Other Obligational Authority[1]	Transfers Borrowings And Investment (Net)[2]	Outlays (Net)	Balances Withdrawn And Other Transactions[3]	Balances, End Of Fiscal Year[4]
Special Fund Accounts											
Operation And Maintenance Of Quarters, Office Of Youth Programs, Bureau Of Reclamation											
Fund Resources:											
Undisbursed Funds	No Year	14		5053		36,982.33	43,114.63		30,423.45		49,673.51
Fund Equities:											
Unobligated Balances (Unexpired)		14		5053		-36,982.33				12,691.18	-49,673.51
Subtotal	Subtotal					-0-	43,114.63		30,423.45	12,691.18	-0-
Operation, Maintenance, And Replacement Of Project Works, North Platte Project (Gering And Fort Laramie, Goshen, And Pathfinder Irrigation Districts), Bureau Of Reclamation											
Fund Resources:											
Undisbursed Funds	No Year	14		5058		47,719.88	362.00				48,081.88
Fund Equities:											
Unobligated Balances (Unexpired)		14		5058		-47,719.88				362.00	-48,081.88
Subtotal	Subtotal					-0-	362.00			362.00	-0-
Payments To Farmers' Irrigation District (North Platte Project, Neb.-Wyo.), Bureau Of Reclamation											
Fund Resources:											
Undisbursed Funds	No Year	14		5059			8,000.00		8,000.00		
General Administrative Expenses, Reclamation Fund											
Fund Resources:											
Undisbursed Funds	No Year	14		5065		10,775,681.58	57,574,830.00		57,972,490.76		10,378,020.82
Fund Equities:											
Unobligated Balances (Unexpired)		14		5065		-2,141,879.34				-803,340.54	-1,338,538.80
Accounts Payable						-1,970,669.57				248,228.78	-2,218,898.35
Undelivered Orders						-6,663,132.67				157,451.00	-6,820,583.67
Subtotal	Subtotal					-0-	57,574,830.00		57,972,490.76	-397,660.76	-0-
Payments To Local Units, Klamath Reclamation Area, Bureau Of Reclamation											
Fund Resources:											
Undisbursed Funds	No Year	14		5103			396,803.76		396,803.76		
Recreation Enhancement Fee Program, Bureau Of Reclamation											
Fund Resources:											
Undisbursed Funds	No Year	14		5109			4,238,726.08				4,238,726.08
Fund Equities:											
Unobligated Balances (Unexpired)		14		5109						4,238,726.08	-4,238,726.08
Subtotal	Subtotal					-0-	4,238,726.08			4,238,726.08	-0-
Central Valley Project Restoration Fund, Bureau Of Reclamation											
Fund Resources:											
Undisbursed Funds	No Year	14		5173		69,880,327.83	52,149,990.00		55,168,763.04		66,861,554.79
Fund Equities:											
Unobligated Balances (Unexpired)		14		5173		-78,794.12				92,107.09	-170,901.21
Accounts Payable						-9,284,158.16				-1,413,000.87	-7,871,157.29
Undelivered Orders						-60,517,375.55				-1,697,879.26	-58,819,496.29
Subtotal	Subtotal					-0-	52,149,990.00		55,168,763.04	-3,018,773.04	-0-

Footnotes At End Of Chapter

Appropriations, Outlays, and Balances – Continued

Appropriation or Fund Account — Title	Reg	Tr From	Account Number	Sub No.	Period of Availability	Balances, Beginning Of Fiscal Year	Appropriations And Other Obligational Authority[1]	Transfers Borrowings And Investment (Net)[2]	Outlays (Net)	Balances Withdrawn And Other Transactions[3]	Balances, End Of Fiscal Year[4]
Water And Related Resources, Reclamation Fund, Bureau Of Reclamation											
Fund Resources:											
Undisbursed Funds	14		5430		No Year		-348,626.00	348,626.00			
San Gabriel Basin Restoration Fund, Bureau Of Reclamation											
Fund Resources:											
Undisbursed Funds	14		5483		No Year	2,178,224.63	743,242.32	6,933,689.16	9,580,156.11		275,000.00
Investments In Public Debt Securities						17,000,000.00		-6,933,689.16			10,066,310.84
Fund Equities:											
Unobligated Balances (Unexpired)						-10,070.98				914.97	-10,985.95
Accounts Payable						-182,868.75				77,501.25	-260,370.00
Undelivered Orders						-18,985,284.90				-8,915,330.01	-10,069,954.89
Subtotal	14		5483		Subtotal	-0-	743,242.32		9,580,156.11	-8,836,913.79	-0-
Colorado River Dam Fund, Boulder Canyon Project, Bureau Of Reclamation											
Fund Resources:											
Undisbursed Funds	14		5656		No Year	25,789,727.98	80,939,174.92		72,028,743.88	71,646,818.00	33,053,341.02
Fund Equities:											
Unobligated Balances (Unexpired)						-19,117,723.88				633,233.98	-19,750,957.86
Accounts Payable						-3,594,665.31				2,731,091.01	-6,325,756.32
Undelivered Orders						-3,077,338.79				3,899,288.05	-6,976,626.84
Subtotal	14		5656		Subtotal	-0-	80,939,174.92		72,028,743.88	8,910,431.04	-0-
Public Enterprise Funds											
Lower Colorado River Basin Development Fund, Bureau Of Reclamation											
Fund Resources:											
Undisbursed Funds	14		4079		No Year	38,647,179.34	26,999,000.00	-86,304,036.02	-24,742,760.74	779,905.00	3,304,999.06
Investments In Public Debt Securities						305,000,000.00		86,304,036.02			391,304,036.02
Accounts Receivable						8,549,833.47				-2,001,485.06	10,551,318.53
Fund Equities:											
Unobligated Balances (Unexpired)						-328,903,719.21				55,854,118.02	-384,757,837.23
Accounts Payable						-11,620,397.42				4,928,882.53	-16,549,279.95
Undelivered Orders						-11,672,896.18				-7,819,659.75	-3,853,236.43
Subtotal	14		4079		Subtotal	-0-	26,999,000.00		-24,742,760.74	51,741,760.74	-0-
Upper Colorado River Basin Fund, Bureau Of Reclamation											
Fund Resources:											
Undisbursed Funds	14		4081		No Year	153,375,291.63	70,469,500.00	-2,552.00	69,122,354.13	72,363,794.63	152,356,090.87
Accounts Receivable						620,809.50				501,839.25	118,970.25
Fund Equities:											
Unobligated Balances (Unexpired)						-23,051,057.99				6,025,650.71	-29,076,708.70
Accounts Payable						-92,593,646.46				-4,483,285.40	-88,110,361.06
Undelivered Orders						-38,351,396.68				-3,063,405.32	-35,287,991.36
Subtotal	14		4081		Subtotal	-0-	70,469,500.00	-2,552.00	69,122,354.13	1,344,593.87	-0-

Appropriations, Outlays, and Balances - Continued

Appropriation or Fund Account — Title	Period of Availability	Dept Reg	Tr From	Account Number	Sub No.	Balances, Beginning Of Fiscal Year	Appropriations And Other Obligational Authority[1]	Transfers Borrowings And Investment (Net)[2]	Outlays (Net)	Balances Withdrawn And Other Transactions[3]	Balances, End Of Fiscal Year[4]
Intragovernmental Funds											
Working Capital Fund, Bureau Of Reclamation											
Fund Resources:											
Undisbursed Funds	No Year	14		4524		50,207,468.24					41,684,666.50
Accounts Receivable						10,054,444.95				1,028,092.44	9,026,352.51
Fund Equities:											
Unobligated Balances (Unexpired)						-28,029,205.98				-7,483,919.32	-20,545,286.66
Accounts Payable						-23,673,312.99				-1,924,541.62	-21,748,771.37
Undelivered Orders						-8,559,394.22				-142,433.24	-8,416,960.98
	Subtotal	14		4524		-0-			8,522,801.74	-8,522,801.74	-0-
Trust Fund Accounts											
Reclamation Trust Funds, Bureau Of Reclamation											
Fund Resources:											
Undisbursed Funds	No Year	14		8070		81,601,347.11	1,679,696.21		23,082,700.72		60,198,342.60
Fund Equities:											
Unobligated Balances (Unexpired)						-50,802,735.58				5,251,044.22	-56,053,779.80
Accounts Payable						-794,214.07				546,612.12	-1,340,826.19
Undelivered Orders						-30,004,397.46				-27,200,660.85	-2,803,736.61
	Subtotal	14		8070		-0-	1,679,696.21		23,082,700.72	-21,403,004.51	-0-
Total, Bureau Of Reclamation							1,140,319,799.92		1,075,719,503.25	64,600,296.67	
Central Utah Project											
General Fund Accounts											
Central Utah Project Completion Account, Interior											
Fund Resources:											
Undisbursed Funds	No Year	14		0787		2,471,845.35	33,074,500.00		33,535,291.16		2,011,054.19
Fund Equities:											
Unobligated Balances (Unexpired)						-358,864.77				229,492.38	-588,357.15
Accounts Payable						-500,066.33				-106,662.83	-393,403.50
Undelivered Orders						-1,612,914.25				-583,620.71	-1,029,293.54
	Subtotal	14		0787		-0-	33,074,500.00		33,535,291.16	-460,791.16	-0-
Special Fund Accounts											
Utah Reclamation Mitigation And Conservation Account, Interior											
Fund Resources:											
Undisbursed Funds	No Year	14		5174		22,001,958.36	17,453,178.40	-9,874,035.63	16,139,575.05		13,441,526.08
Unrealized Discount On Investments								-443,964.37			-443,964.37
Investments In Public Debt Securities						160,181,000.00		10,318,000.00			170,499,000.00
Fund Equities:											
Unobligated Balances (Unexpired)						-166,976,367.68				10,288,884.23	-177,265,251.91
Accounts Payable						-1,267,048.83				-299,906.50	-967,142.33

Footnotes At End Of Chapter

Appropriations, Outlays, and Balances – Continued

Appropriation or Fund Account — Title	Period of Availability	Dept Reg	Dept Tr From	Account Number	Sub No.	Balances, Beginning Of Fiscal Year	Appropriations And Other Obligational Authority[1]	Transfers Borrowings And Investment (Net)[2]	Outlays (Net)	Balances Withdrawn And Other Transactions[3]	Balances, End Of Fiscal Year[4]
Utah Reclamation Mitigation And Conservation Account, Interior - Continued											
Fund Equities: - Continued											
Undelivered Orders						-13,939,541.85				-8,675,374.38	-5,264,167.47
Subtotal		14		5174		-0-	17,453,178.40		16,139,575.05	1,313,603.35	-0-
Total, Central Utah Project							50,527,678.40		49,674,866.21	852,812.19	
United States Geological Survey											
General Fund Accounts											
Surveys, Investigations And Research, U.S. Geological Survey											
Fund Resources:											
Undisbursed Funds	2007-2009	14		0804			202,593,216.00		151,788,410.90		50,804,805.10
	2007-2008								-22,000.00		22,000.00
	2006-2008					35,401.33			14,291.35		21,109.98
	2007						775,998,023.00		708,006,762.76		67,991,260.24
	2006-2007					45,316,858.50			37,301,831.69		8,015,026.81
	2005-2007					1,595.75			1,595.75		
	2006					40,596,672.26		350.00	26,680,316.53		13,916,705.73
	2005-2006					11,041,107.68			9,166,890.24		1,874,217.44
	2005					15,718,697.74			8,206,437.36		7,512,260.38
	2004-2005					1,632,964.93			848,149.50		784,815.43
	2004					8,880,530.72			3,182,304.30		5,698,226.42
	2003-2004					1,199,272.49			295,377.91		903,894.58
	2003					8,799,117.21			950,994.38		7,848,122.83
	2002-2003					1,060,552.68			16,687.11		1,043,865.57
	2002					5,491,288.19			16,927.96	5,474,360.23	
	2001-2002					1,180,478.16			-13,874.33	1,194,352.49	
	No Year					18,357,829.88	15,617,710.00		12,992,782.63		20,982,757.25
Funds Held Outside The Treasury	2006					350.00		-350.00			
Accounts Receivable						126,856,886.97				17,224,085.43	109,632,801.54
Unfilled Customer Orders						54,518,819.56				2,014,865.69	52,503,953.87
Fund Equities:											
Unobligated Balances (Expired)						-23,280,482.49				-2,555,260.26	-20,725,222.23
Unobligated Balances (Unexpired)						-27,031,456.12				2,868,086.47	-29,899,542.59
Accounts Payable						-90,146,850.59				3,775,687.44	-93,922,538.03
Undelivered Orders						-200,229,634.85				4,778,885.47	-205,008,520.32
Subtotal		14		0804		-0-	994,208,949.00		959,433,886.04	34,775,062.96	-0-
Special Fund Accounts											
Operation And Maintenance Of Quarters, Geological Survey											
Fund Resources:											
Undisbursed Funds	No Year	14		5055		131,286.42	98,255.02		97,011.92		132,529.52
Fund Equities:											
Unobligated Balances (Unexpired)						-126,554.82				5,974.70	-132,529.52
Accounts Payable						-4,731.60				-4,731.60	-0-
Subtotal		14		5055		-0-	98,255.02		97,011.92	1,243.10	-0-

Appropriations, Outlays, and Balances - Continued

Appropriation or Fund Account Title	Account Symbol Period of Availability	Dept Reg	Dept Tr From	Account Number	Sub No.	Balances, Beginning Of Fiscal Year	Appropriations And Other Obligational Authority[1]	Transfers Borrowings And Investment (Net)[2]	Outlays (Net)	Balances Withdrawn And Other Transactions[3]	Balances, End Of Fiscal Year[4]
Intragovernmental Funds											
Working Capital Fund, Geological Survey											
Fund Resources:											
Undisbursed Funds	No Year	14		4556		87,016,433.60			-11,206,951.11		98,223,384.71
Fund Equities:											
Unobligated Balances (Unexpired)						-71,899,346.20				12,754,300.06	-84,653,646.26
Accounts Payable						-3,689,168.17				-271,365.37	-3,417,802.80
Undelivered Orders						-11,427,919.23				-1,275,983.58	-10,151,935.65
Subtotal		14		4556		-0-			-11,206,951.11	11,206,951.11	-0-
Trust Fund Accounts											
Contributed Funds, Geological Survey, Interior											
Fund Resources:											
Undisbursed Funds	No Year	14		8562		1,254,081.66	2,710,950.79		2,739,363.08		1,225,669.37
Fund Equities:											
Unobligated Balances (Unexpired)						-965,729.47				-414,177.58	-551,551.89
Accounts Payable						-179,132.38				56,527.75	-235,660.13
Undelivered Orders						-109,219.81				329,237.54	-438,457.35
Subtotal		14		8562		-0-	2,710,950.79		2,739,363.08	-28,412.29	-0-
Total, United States Geological Survey							997,018,154.81		951,063,309.93	45,954,844.88	
Bureau Of Mines											
General Fund Accounts											
Mines And Minerals, Bureau Of Mines											
Fund Resources:											
Undisbursed Funds	No Year	14		0959		1,063,415.20			18,858.40		1,044,556.80
Fund Equities:											
Unobligated Balances (Unexpired)						-279,402.94				17,892.71	-297,295.65
Accounts Payable						-6,115.50				-6,115.50	-0-
Undelivered Orders						-777,896.76				-30,635.61	-747,261.15
Subtotal		14		0959		-0-			18,858.40	-18,858.40	-0-
Total, Bureau Of Mines Total, Water And Science							2,187,865,633.13		2,076,476,537.79	111,389,095.34	

Footnotes At End Of Chapter

Appropriations, Outlays, and Balances – Continued

Appropriation or Fund Account — Title	Account Symbol — Period of Availability	Dept Reg	Tr From	Account Number	Sub No.	Balances, Beginning Of Fiscal Year	Appropriations And Other Obligational Authority[1]	Transfers Borrowings And Investment (Net)[2]	Outlays (Net)	Balances Withdrawn And Other Transactions[3]	Balances, End Of Fiscal Year[4]
Fish And Wildlife And Parks											
United States Fish And Wildlife Service											
General Fund Accounts											
Resource Management, United States Fish And Wildlife Service											
Fund Resources:											
Undisbursed Funds	2007-2008	14		1611		227,113,117.89	1,020,739,370.00		762,337,159.84		258,402,210.16
	2006-2007								172,328,980.21		54,784,137.68
	2005-2006					51,000,028.16			31,139,012.45		19,861,015.71
	2004-2005					10,566,999.14			2,873,563.18		7,693,435.96
	2003-2004					7,533,552.00			3,506,027.90		4,027,524.10
	2002-2003					3,584,184.85			2,051,040.97		1,533,143.88
	2001-2003					17,188.75					17,188.75
	2001-2002					1,655,336.70			1,052,982.84	602,353.86	
	No Year					39,428,096.41	627,630.00		9,030,518.27		31,025,208.14
Accounts Receivable						35,876,653.93				8,186,387.36	27,690,266.57
Unfilled Customer Orders						38,980,219.19				7,404,426.48	31,575,792.71
Fund Equities:											
Unobligated Balances (Expired)						-2,601,607.01				2,525,350.42	-5,126,957.43
Unobligated Balances (Unexpired)						-73,406,924.96				10,624,890.94	-84,031,815.90
Accounts Payable						-60,443,141.42				-3,475,262.35	-56,967,879.07
Undelivered Orders						-279,303,703.63				11,179,567.63	-290,483,271.26
	Subtotal	14		1611		-0-	1,021,367,000.00		984,319,285.66	37,047,714.34	-0-
Construction, United States Fish And Wildlife Service											
Fund Resources:											
Undisbursed Funds	No Year	14		1612		260,007,571.36	42,324,833.00	1,202,000.00	118,718,524.30		184,815,880.06
Accounts Receivable						2,025.16				-102,849.52	104,874.68
Unfilled Customer Orders						417,815.39				-191,650.15	609,465.54
Fund Equities:											
Unobligated Balances (Unexpired)						-142,887,059.42				-77,382,874.80	-65,504,184.62
Accounts Payable						-158,360,839.84				-39,370,513.66	-118,990,326.18
Undelivered Orders						40,820,487.35				41,856,196.83	-1,035,709.48
	Subtotal	14		1612		-0-	42,324,833.00	1,202,000.00	118,718,524.30	-75,191,691.30	-0-
Cooperative Endangered Species Conservation Fund (5% Equivalent), United States Fish And Wildlife Service											
Fund Resources:											
Undisbursed Funds	No Year	14		1643		5,477.19			1,479.00		3,998.19
Fund Equities:											
Unobligated Balances (Unexpired)						-108.19				3,890.00	-3,998.19
Undelivered Orders						-5,369.00				-5,369.00	-0-
	Subtotal	14		1643		-0-			1,479.00	-1,479.00	-0-
Wildlife Conservation And Appreciation Fund, U.S. Fish And Wildlife Service											
Fund Resources:											
Undisbursed Funds	No Year	14		1650		562,736.77			1,818.50		560,918.27

Appropriations, Outlays, and Balances - Continued

Appropriation or Fund Account — Title	Period of Availability	Dept — Reg	Tr From	Account Number	Sub No.	Balances, Beginning Of Fiscal Year	Appropriations And Other Obligational Authority[1]	Transfers Borrowings And Investment (Net)[2]	Outlays (Net)	Balances Withdrawn And Other Transactions[3]	Balances, End Of Fiscal Year[4]
Fund Equities:											
Unobligated Balances (Unexpired)						-529,278.87				-72.18	-529,206.69
Undelivered Orders						-33,457.90				-1,746.32	-31,711.58
Subtotal		14		1650		-0-			1,818.50	-1,818.50	-0-
Multinational Species Conservation Fund, United States Fish And Wildlife Service											
Fund Resources:											
Undisbursed Funds	No Year	14		1652		5,606,949.06	6,404,369.00		5,512,033.30		6,499,284.76
Fund Equities:											
Unobligated Balances (Unexpired)						-160,608.72				-3,616.22	-156,992.50
Accounts Payable						-12,401.61				10,862.05	-23,263.66
Undelivered Orders						-5,433,938.73				885,089.87	-6,319,028.60
Subtotal		14		1652		-0-	6,404,369.00		5,512,033.30	892,335.70	-0-
National Wildlife Refuge Fund, United States Fish And Wildlife Service											
Fund Resources:											
Undisbursed Funds	2007	14		1691			14,201,935.00		14,201,935.00		
Neotropical Migratory Bird Conservation, U.S. Fish And Wildlife Service											
Fund Resources:											
Undisbursed Funds	No Year	14		1696		7,453,753.51	3,941,150.00		4,443,443.24		6,951,460.27
Fund Equities:											
Unobligated Balances (Unexpired)						-244,652.20				66,981.93	-311,634.13
Accounts Payable						-4,287.65				110.44	-4,398.09
Undelivered Orders						-7,204,813.66				-569,385.61	-6,635,428.05
Subtotal		14		1696		-0-	3,941,150.00		4,443,443.24	-502,293.24	-0-
Special Fund Accounts											
Land Acquisition, United States Fish And Wildlife Service											
Fund Resources:											
Undisbursed Funds	No Year	14		5020		38,180,381.80	28,046,050.00	4,000,000.00	36,086,702.27		34,139,729.53
Accounts Receivable						2,640,229.93				1,462,208.29	1,178,021.64
Unfilled Customer Orders						11,494.12				11,494.12	
Fund Equities:											
Unobligated Balances (Unexpired)						-24,109,492.62				80,695.63	-24,190,188.25
Accounts Payable						-217,286.04				141,584.04	-358,870.08
Undelivered Orders						-16,505,327.19				-5,736,634.35	-10,768,692.84
Subtotal		14		5020		-0-	28,046,050.00	4,000,000.00	36,086,702.27	-4,040,652.27	-0-
Federal Aid To Wildlife Restoration, United States Fish And Wildlife Service											
Fund Resources:											
Undisbursed Funds	No Year	14		5029		46,403,987.86	339,563,355.05	-72,233,997.07	264,968,053.39		48,765,292.45
Unrealized Discount On Investments						-4,789,598.53		1,488,762.97			-3,300,835.56
Funds Held Outside The Treasury						36,715.79		-2,765.90			33,949.89
Investments In Public Debt Securities						495,775,000.00		70,748,000.00			566,523,000.00
Fund Equities:											
Unobligated Balances (Unexpired)						-348,570,976.96				63,951,029.45	-412,522,006.41
Accounts Payable						-15,089,470.06				969,891.12	-16,059,361.18
Undelivered Orders						-173,765,658.10				9,674,381.09	-183,440,039.19

Footnotes At End Of Chapter

Appropriations, Outlays, and Balances – Continued

Appropriation or Fund Account — Title	Period of Availability	Dept Reg	Dept Tr From	Account Number	Sub No.	Balances, Beginning Of Fiscal Year	Appropriations And Other Obligational Authority[1]	Transfers Borrowings And Investment (Net)[2]	Outlays (Net)	Balances Withdrawn And Other Transactions[3]	Balances, End Of Fiscal Year[4]
Federal Aid To Wildlife Restoration, United States Fish And Wildlife Service - Continued	Subtotal	14		5029		-0-	339,563,355.05		264,968,053.39	74,595,301.66	-0-
Operation And Maintenance Of Quarters, United States Fish And Wildlife Service											
Fund Resources:											
Undisbursed Funds	No Year	14		5050		3,337,145.01	2,832,119.06		2,833,949.65		3,335,314.42
Fund Equities:											
Unobligated Balances (Unexpired)						-2,605,061.92				374,852.93	-2,979,914.85
Accounts Payable						-19,731.66				-8,108.75	-11,622.91
Undelivered Orders						-712,351.43				-368,574.77	-343,776.66
	Subtotal	14		5050		-0-	2,832,119.06		2,833,949.65		-0-
National Wildlife Refuge Fund, United States Fish And Wildlife Service											
Fund Resources:											
Undisbursed Funds	No Year	14		5091		8,780,507.12	12,376,554.23		11,442,834.35		9,714,227.00
Fund Equities:											
Unobligated Balances (Unexpired)						-8,519,629.57				830,751.00	-9,350,380.57
Accounts Payable						-50,170.78				-5,361.24	-44,809.54
Undelivered Orders						-210,706.77				108,330.12	-319,036.89
	Subtotal	14		5091		-0-	12,376,554.23		11,442,834.35		-0-
Proceeds From Sales, Water Resource Development Projects, United States Fish And Wildlife Service											
Fund Resources:											
Undisbursed Funds	No Year	14		5092		913,234.20	86,745.83		251,580.63		748,399.40
Fund Equities:											
Unobligated Balances (Unexpired)						-773,155.63				-99,332.92	-673,822.71
Undelivered Orders						-140,078.57				-65,501.88	-74,576.69
	Subtotal	14		5092		-0-	86,745.83		251,580.63	-164,834.80	-0-
Migratory Bird Conservation Account, United States Fish And Wildlife Service											
Fund Resources:											
Undisbursed Funds	No Year	14		5137		16,821,951.25	43,723,307.20		44,390,754.21		16,154,504.24
Fund Equities:											
Unobligated Balances (Unexpired)						-5,402,237.13				311,712.37	-5,713,949.50
Accounts Payable						-314,143.04				13,861.12	-328,004.16
Undelivered Orders						-11,105,571.08				-993,020.50	-10,112,550.58
	Subtotal	14		5137		-0-	43,723,307.20		44,390,754.21	-667,447.01	-0-
Cooperative Endangered Species Conservation Fund, United States Fish And Wildlife Service											
Fund Resources:											
Undisbursed Funds	No Year	14		5143		94,095,298.17	66,063,944.00		73,173,733.35		86,985,508.82
Fund Equities:											
Unobligated Balances (Unexpired)						-30,827,873.22				-12,980,855.51	-17,847,017.71
Accounts Payable						-1,420,636.80				45,634.16	-1,466,270.96
Undelivered Orders						-61,846,788.15				5,825,432.00	-67,672,220.15
	Subtotal	14		5143		-0-	66,063,944.00		73,173,733.35	-7,109,789.35	-0-

Appropriations, Outlays, and Balances - Continued

Appropriation or Fund Account — Title	Period of Availability	Dept Reg	Tr From	Account Number	Sub No.	Balances, Beginning Of Fiscal Year	Appropriations And Other Obligational Authority[1]	Transfers Borrowings And Investment (Net)[2]	Outlays (Net)	Balances Withdrawn And Other Transactions[3]	Balances, End Of Fiscal Year[4]
Lahontan Valley And Pyramid Lake Fish And Wildlife Fund, United States Fish And Wildlife Service											
Fund Resources:											
Undisbursed Funds	No Year	14		5157		1,526,390.97	522,750.00		434,783.01		1,614,357.96
Fund Equities:											
Unobligated Balances (Unexpired)						-1,412,074.61				158,911.10	-1,570,985.71
Undelivered Orders						-114,316.36				-70,944.11	-43,372.25
						-0-				87,966.99	-0-
Subtotal		14		5157		-0-	522,750.00		434,783.01		-0-
North American Wetlands Conservation Fund, United States Fish And Wildlife Service											
Fund Resources:											
Undisbursed Funds	No Year	14		5241		87,690,264.60	39,892,390.00		35,811,178.37		91,771,476.23
Fund Equities:											
Unobligated Balances (Unexpired)						-10,069,029.77				-4,422,621.12	-5,646,408.65
Accounts Payable						-2,233,310.02				-281,372.91	-1,951,937.11
Undelivered Orders						-75,387,924.81				8,785,205.66	-84,173,130.47
						-0-				4,081,211.63	-0-
Subtotal		14		5241		-0-	39,892,390.00		35,811,178.37		-0-
Recreation Fee Enhancement Program, U.S. Fish And Wildlife Service											
Fund Resources:											
Undisbursed Funds	No Year	14		5252		5,087,170.05	4,409,528.26		3,714,719.64		5,781,978.67
Fund Equities:											
Unobligated Balances (Unexpired)						-4,201,662.72				486,054.72	-4,687,717.44
Accounts Payable						-98,484.93				-23,578.20	-74,906.73
Undelivered Orders						-787,022.40				232,332.10	-1,019,354.50
						-0-				694,808.62	-0-
Subtotal		14		5252		-0-	4,409,528.26		3,714,719.64		-0-
State And Tribal Wildlife Grants, U.S. Fish And Wildlife Service											
Fund Resources:											
Undisbursed Funds	No Year	14		5474		186,867,221.01	67,492,201.00		66,550,136.44		187,809,285.57
Fund Equities:											
Unobligated Balances (Unexpired)						-52,940,969.04				-6,679,961.96	-46,261,007.08
Accounts Payable						-3,979,286.22				-283,435.28	-3,695,850.94
Undelivered Orders						-129,946,965.75				7,905,461.80	-137,852,427.55
						-0-				942,064.56	-0-
Subtotal		14		5474		-0-	67,492,201.00		66,550,136.44		-0-
North American Wetlands Conservation Fund, From Land And Water Conservation Fund, U.S. Fish And Wildlife Service											
Fund Resources:											
Undisbursed Funds	No Year	14		5475		2,752,707.46			662,843.85		2,089,863.61
Fund Equities:											
Unobligated Balances (Unexpired)						-798,364.98				-657,377.53	-140,987.45
Undelivered Orders						-1,954,342.48				-5,466.32	-1,948,876.16
						-0-				-662,843.85	-0-
Subtotal		14		5475		-0-			662,843.85		-0-
Cooperative Endangered Species Conservation Fund, From Land And Water Conservation Fund, U.S. Fish And Wildlife Service											
Fund Resources:											
Undisbursed Funds	No Year	14		5479		184,606,923.96	61,136,257.00		54,536,235.15		191,206,945.81
Fund Equities:											
Unobligated Balances (Unexpired)						-64,131,439.61				-33,195,690.49	-30,935,749.12

Footnotes At End Of Chapter

Appropriations, Outlays, and Balances – Continued

Appropriation or Fund Account — Title	Period of Availability	Dept Reg	Tr From	Account Number	Sub No.	Balances, Beginning Of Fiscal Year	Appropriations And Other Obligational Authority[1]	Transfers Borrowings And Investment (Net)[2]	Outlays (Net)	Balances Withdrawn And Other Transactions[3]	Balances, End Of Fiscal Year[4]
Cooperative Endangered Species Conservation Fund, From Land And Water Conservation Fund, U.S. Fish And Wildlife Service - Continued											
Fund Equities: - Continued											
Accounts Payable						-553,621.22			-------	2,650,603.65	-3,204,224.87
Undelivered Orders						-119,921,863.13			-------	37,145,108.69	-157,066,971.82
	Subtotal	14		5479		-0-	61,136,257.00		54,536,235.15	6,600,021.85	-0-
Private Stewardship Grants, U.S. Fish And Wildlife Service											
Fund Resources:											
Undisbursed Funds	No Year	14		5495		17,180,905.25	7,277,335.00		6,539,128.37		17,919,111.88
Fund Equities:											
Unobligated Balances (Unexpired)						-3,482,104.33			-------	-2,161,802.51	-1,320,301.82
Accounts Payable						-211,507.71			-------	71,630.03	-283,137.74
Undelivered Orders						-13,487,293.21			-------	2,828,379.11	-16,315,672.32
	Subtotal	14		5495		-0-	7,277,335.00		6,539,128.37	738,206.63	-0-
Landowner Incentive Program, U.S. Fish And Wildlife Service											
Fund Resources:											
Undisbursed Funds	No Year	14		5496		83,517,312.70	23,666,902.00		15,572,171.67		91,612,043.03
Fund Equities:											
Unobligated Balances (Unexpired)						-38,846,210.35			-------	-11,098,796.00	-27,747,414.35
Accounts Payable						-489,297.22			-------	-6,780.65	-482,516.57
Undelivered Orders						-44,181,805.13			-------	19,200,306.98	-63,382,112.11
	Subtotal	14		5496		-0-	23,666,902.00		15,572,171.67	8,094,730.33	-0-
Trust Fund Accounts											
Sport Fish Restoration Account, United States Fish And Wildlife Service											
Fund Resources:											
Undisbursed Funds	No Year	14		8151		8,025,691.57	372,000,000.00		371,850,394.91	-60,182,672.00	8,175,296.66
Accounts Receivable						512,911,748.70					573,094,420.70
Fund Equities:											
Unobligated Balances (Unexpired)						-147,363,899.49			-------	19,011,475.46	-166,365,374.95
Accounts Payable						-21,627,808.39			-------	999,441.06	-22,627,249.45
Undelivered Orders						-351,955,732.39			-------	40,321,360.57	-392,277,092.96
	Subtotal	14		8151		-0-	372,000,000.00		371,850,394.91	149,605.09	-0-
Contributed Funds, United States Fish And Wildlife Service											
Fund Resources:											
Undisbursed Funds	No Year	14		8216		5,777,180.73	2,213,367.34		2,663,466.33		5,327,081.74
Fund Equities:											
Unobligated Balances (Unexpired)						-4,339,308.65			-------	-188,831.18	-4,150,477.47
Accounts Payable						-23,910.99			-------	16,780.35	-40,691.34
Undelivered Orders						-1,413,961.09			-------	-278,048.16	-1,135,912.93
	Subtotal	14		8216		-0-	2,213,367.34		2,663,466.33	-450,098.99	-0-
Total, United States Fish And Wildlife Service						-------	2,159,542,092.97	5,202,000.00	2,118,681,184.59	46,062,908.38	-------

Appropriations, Outlays, and Balances - Continued

Appropriation or Fund Account — Title	Reg	Tr From	Account Number	Sub No.	Period of Availability	Balances, Beginning Of Fiscal Year	Appropriations And Other Obligational Authority[1]	Transfers Borrowings And Investment (Net)[2]	Outlays (Net)	Balances Withdrawn And Other Transactions[3]	Balances, End Of Fiscal Year[4]
National Park Service											
General Fund Accounts											
Urban Park And Recreation Fund, National Park Service											
Fund Resources:											
Undisbursed Funds	14		1031		No Year	9,410,740.60			3,990,654.94		5,420,085.66
Fund Equities:											
Unobligated Balances (Unexpired)						-1,026,405.12				34,579.56	-1,060,984.68
Accounts Payable						4,215.83				4,215.83	
Undelivered Orders						-8,388,551.31				-4,029,450.33	-4,359,100.98
Subtotal	14		1031			-0-			3,990,654.94	-3,990,654.94	-0-
Contribution For Annuity Benefits, National Park Service											
Fund Resources:											
Undisbursed Funds	14		1034		2007	6,131,249.30	37,109,000.00		30,556,108.11		6,552,891.89
					2006				2,984,911.61		3,146,337.69
					2005	1,066,245.79					1,066,245.79
					2004	0.48					0.48
					2003	126,656.65					126,656.65
					2002	765,066.08				765,066.08	
Fund Equities:											
Unobligated Balances (Expired)						-2,528,685.34				-61,280.71	-2,467,404.63
Accounts Payable						-2,708,278.93				3,044,329.83	-5,752,608.76
Undelivered Orders						-2,852,254.03				-180,134.92	-2,672,119.11
Subtotal	14		1034			-0-	37,109,000.00		33,541,019.72	3,557,980.28	-0-
Operation Of The National Park System, National Park Service											
Fund Resources:											
Undisbursed Funds	14		1036		2007-2008		96,880,354.00	-485,000.00	25,852,684.22		70,542,669.78
					2007		1,656,686,465.00		1,396,823,286.56		259,863,178.44
					2006-2007	65,765,311.23			42,413,391.10		23,351,920.13
					2006	227,997,380.57			176,709,247.37		51,288,133.20
					2005-2006	38,143.39			35,118.90		3,024.49
					2005	58,984,643.44			34,660,690.98		24,323,952.46
					2004-2005	5,337,930.20			3,047,009.76		2,290,920.44
					2004	21,460,331.90			7,138,017.05		14,322,314.85
					2003-2004	1,791,872.79			208,396.63		1,583,476.16
					2003	13,452,660.14			2,665,963.14		10,786,697.00
					2002-2003	707,840.48			91,978.39		615,862.09
					2002	7,978,010.37		5,999.99	1,876,312.93	6,107,697.43	
					2001-2002	23,060.44				23,060.44	
				5	No Year	30,721,450.84	9,833,465.00		10,968,849.43		29,586,066.41
Transfer To:											
Federal Highway Administration	69	14	1036		2007-2008	496,000.00		485,000.00	416,500.00		68,500.00
					2006-2007				63,714.99		432,285.01
					2005	46,800.00					46,800.00
					2003-2004	36,231.06					36,231.06
					2002-2003	-429.18					[5]5,429.18

Footnotes At End Of Chapter

Appropriations, Outlays, and Balances – Continued

Appropriation or Fund Account — Title	Period of Availability	Dept Reg	Dept Tr From	Account Number	Sub No.	Balances, Beginning Of Fiscal Year	Appropriations And Other Obligational Authority[1]	Transfers Borrowings And Investment (Net)[2]	Outlays (Net)	Balances Withdrawn And Other Transactions[3]	Balances, End Of Fiscal Year[4]
Operation Of The National Park System, National Park Service - Continued											
Fund Resources: - Continued											
Federal Highway Administration - Continued											
Accounts Receivable	2002					5,999.99		-5,999.99			
						349,852.43				-32,315.72	382,168.15
Fund Equities:											
Unobligated Balances (Expired)						-18,033,828.58				3,402,832.26	-21,436,660.84
Unobligated Balances (Unexpired)						-47,796,147.94				1,924,656.93	-49,720,804.87
Accounts Payable						-73,703,630.99				962,342.41	-74,665,973.40
Undelivered Orders						-295,659,482.58				48,040,848.80	-343,700,331.38
Subtotal		14		1036		-0-	1,763,400,284.00		1,702,971,161.45	60,429,122.55	-0-
Construction, National Park Service											
Fund Resources:											
Undisbursed Funds	No Year	14		1039		612,378,237.68	314,185,286.00	-8,821,547.43	291,934,597.49		625,807,378.76
Transfer To:											
Department Of Transportation, Federal Highway Administration	No Year	69	14	1039	5	8,057,756.92		1,725,000.00	1,882,895.93		7,899,860.99
Corps Of Engineers	No Year	96	14	1039		31,394,290.13		71,050.00	9,288,511.45		22,176,828.68
Funds Held Outside The Treasury				1039		426,773.58		4,497.43			431,271.01
Accounts Receivable						28,054,829.86				-2,691,927.39	30,746,757.25
Unfilled Customer Orders						141,485,511.10				-35,509,072.35	176,994,583.45
Fund Equities:											
Unobligated Balances (Unexpired)						-369,554,071.99				-27,800,814.10	-341,753,257.89
Accounts Payable						-247,767,573.90				39,216,308.78	-286,983,882.68
Undelivered Orders						-204,475,753.38				30,843,786.19	-235,319,539.57
Subtotal		14		1039		-0-	314,185,286.00	-7,021,000.00	303,106,004.87	4,058,281.13	-0-
National Recreation And Preservation, National Park Service											
Fund Resources:											
Undisbursed Funds	2007	14		1042		16,404,551.27	54,369,333.00	500,000.00	33,867,910.17		21,001,422.83
	2006					10,762,199.74			8,478,498.98		7,926,052.29
	2005					4,816,544.32			5,755,608.42		5,006,591.32
	2004					2,187,193.37			2,021,087.81		2,795,456.51
	2003					992,428.40			882,010.47		1,305,182.90
	2002					1,672,925.56			531,837.62	460,590.78	
	No Year								-61,164.97		1,734,090.53
Fund Equities:											
Unobligated Balances (Expired)						-1,454,535.27				576,703.20	-2,031,238.47
Unobligated Balances (Unexpired)						-1,055,582.27				-70,485.09	-985,097.18
Accounts Payable						-1,149,839.82				22,042.81	-1,171,882.63
Undelivered Orders						-33,175,885.30				2,404,692.80	-35,580,578.10
Subtotal		14		1042		-0-	54,369,333.00	500,000.00	51,475,788.50	3,393,544.50	-0-
Historic Preservation Fund, National Park Service											
Fund Resources:											
Undisbursed Funds	2007-2008	14		1046		43,000,000.00	10,000,000.00	-500,000.00	505,547.00		9,494,453.00
	2006-2007					209,825.04			9,402,796.26		33,097,203.74
	No Year								209,567.00		258.04
Fund Equities:											
Unobligated Balances (Expired)										4,554.00	-4,554.00
Unobligated Balances (Unexpired)						-759,825.04				-759,567.00	-258.04

Appropriations, Outlays, and Balances - Continued

Appropriation or Fund Account — Title	Period of Availability	Dept Reg	Tr From	Account Number	Sub No.	Balances, Beginning Of Fiscal Year	Appropriations And Other Obligational Authority[1]	Transfers Borrowings And Investment (Net)[2]	Outlays (Net)	Balances Withdrawn And Other Transactions[3]	Balances, End Of Fiscal Year[4]
Undelivered Orders	Subtotal	14		1046		-42,450,000.00				137,102.74	-42,587,102.74
						-0-	10,000,000.00	-500,000.00	10,117,910.26	-617,910.26	-0-
United States Park Police, National Park Service											
Fund Resources:											
Undisbursed Funds	2007	14		1049		4,661,736.67	85,213,249.00		77,992,712.56		7,220,536.44
	2006					329,448.16			3,937,343.41		724,393.26
	2005					316,400.83			-98,669.59		428,117.75
	2004					995,708.15			-367,217.56		683,618.39
	2003					290,679.81			389,303.44	230,596.07	606,404.71
	2002								60,083.74		
	No Year					959,457.99			150,773.20		808,684.79
Fund Equities:											
Unobligated Balances (Expired)						-973,169.48				954,313.68	-1,927,483.16
Unobligated Balances (Unexpired)						-0.21				808,403.24	-808,403.45
Accounts Payable						-3,447,134.89				1,178,001.32	-4,625,136.21
Undelivered Orders						-3,133,127.03				-22,394.51	-3,110,732.52
	Subtotal	14		1049		-0-	85,213,249.00		82,064,329.20	3,148,919.80	-0-
Special Fund Accounts											
Land Acquisition And State Assistance, National Park Service											
Fund Resources:											
Undisbursed Funds	No Year	14		5035		322,944,521.84	64,024,033.00	5,000,000.00	105,660,206.16		286,308,348.68
Transfer To:											
Corps Of Engineers	No Year	96	14	5035		543,207.84			469,497.45	380,471.31	73,710.39
Accounts Receivable						400,747.68					20,276.37
Unfilled Customer Orders						-28,896.49				167,953.39	-196,849.88
Fund Equities:											
Unobligated Balances (Unexpired)						-79,225,169.05				16,115,363.80	-95,340,532.85
Accounts Payable						-446,608.80				-36,948.82	-409,659.98
Undelivered Orders						-244,187,803.02				-53,732,510.29	-190,455,292.73
	Subtotal	14		5035		-0-	64,024,033.00	5,000,000.00	106,129,703.61	-37,105,670.61	-0-
Operation And Maintenance Of Quarters, National Park Service											
Fund Resources:											
Undisbursed Funds	No Year	14		5049		15,869,899.81	18,331,113.03		17,420,113.28		16,780,899.56
Fund Equities:											
Unobligated Balances (Unexpired)						-14,290,409.96				896,483.03	-15,186,892.99
Accounts Payable						-554,569.70				45,767.79	-600,337.49
Undelivered Orders						-1,024,920.15				-31,251.07	-993,669.08
	Subtotal	14		5049		-0-	18,331,113.03		17,420,113.28	910,999.75	-0-
Delaware Water Gap Route 209 Operations, National Park Service											
Fund Resources:											
Undisbursed Funds	No Year	14		5076		3,597.69	61,098.05		50,297.38		14,398.36
Fund Equities:											
Unobligated Balances (Unexpired)						-3,597.69				4,393.54	-7,991.23
Accounts Payable										6,407.13	-6,407.13
	Subtotal	14		5076		-0-	61,098.05		50,297.38	10,800.67	-0-

Footnotes At End Of Chapter

Appropriations, Outlays, and Balances – Continued

Appropriation or Fund Account — Title	Period of Availability	Reg	Tr From	Account Number	Sub No.	Balances, Beginning Of Fiscal Year	Appropriations And Other Obligational Authority[1]	Transfers Borrowings And Investment (Net)[2]	Outlays (Net)	Balances Withdrawn And Other Transactions[3]	Balances, End Of Fiscal Year[4]
Recreation Enhancement Fee Program, National Park Service											
Fund Resources:											
Undisbursed Funds	No Year	14		5110		317,202,617.81	165,649,118.65		131,664,131.68		351,187,604.78
Fund Equities:											
Unobligated Balances (Unexpired)						-254,984,840.58				-10,310,071.42	-244,674,769.16
Accounts Payable						-4,053,122.01				82,839.28	-4,135,961.29
Undelivered Orders						-58,164,655.22				44,212,219.11	-102,376,874.33
Subtotal		14		5110		-0-	165,649,118.65		131,664,131.68	33,984,986.97	-0-
Historic Preservation Fund, National Park Service											
Fund Resources:											
Undisbursed Funds	2007-2008	14		5140		56,616,646.34	55,663,000.00		15,290,535.74		40,372,464.26
	2006-2007					31,300,069.61			23,145,403.42		33,471,242.92
	2005-2006					22,613,144.68			10,426,445.44		20,873,624.17
	2004-2005					11,659,710.76			6,765,642.60		15,847,502.08
	2003-2004					5,891,218.77			3,212,703.67		8,447,007.09
	2002-2003					4,309,094.26			936,167.88		4,955,050.89
	2001-2002					4,306,340.79			2,277,095.24	2,031,999.02	
	No Year								790,051.10		3,516,289.69
Fund Equities:											
Unobligated Balances (Expired)						-3,665,157.74				747,262.29	-4,412,420.03
Unobligated Balances (Unexpired)						-30,137,830.92				-13,729,106.45	-16,408,724.47
Accounts Payable						-15,422.23				-8,891.70	-6,530.53
Undelivered Orders						-102,877,814.32				3,777,691.75	-106,655,506.07
Subtotal		14		5140		-0-	55,663,000.00		62,844,045.09	-7,181,045.09	-0-
Park Buildings Lease And Maintence Fund, National Park Service											
Fund Resources:											
Undisbursed Funds	No Year	14		5163		1,905,200.10	3,869,023.32		1,453,247.91		4,320,975.51
Fund Equities:											
Unobligated Balances (Unexpired)						-1,399,130.35				2,313,626.05	-3,712,756.40
Accounts Payable						-47,127.46				153,837.81	-200,965.27
Undelivered Orders						-458,942.29				-51,688.45	-407,253.84
Subtotal		14		5163		-0-	3,869,023.32		1,453,247.91	2,415,775.41	-0-
Transportation Systems Fund, National Park Service											
Fund Resources:											
Undisbursed Funds	No Year	14		5164		8,889,343.87	11,637,268.30		8,067,309.18		12,459,302.99
Fund Equities:											
Unobligated Balances (Unexpired)						-2,961,329.39				6,940,829.84	-9,902,159.23
Accounts Payable						-441,426.31				-5,128.64	-436,297.67
Undelivered Orders						-5,486,588.17				-3,365,742.08	-2,120,846.09
Subtotal		14		5164		-0-	11,637,268.30		8,067,309.18	3,569,959.12	-0-
Concessioner Improvement Accounts, National Park Service											
Fund Resources:											
Undisbursed Funds	No Year	14		5169		43,980,542.00	12,994,966.00	1,163,934.00	14,158,900.00		42,816,608.00
Funds Held Outside The Treasury								-1,163,934.00			
Fund Equities:											
Unobligated Balances (Unexpired)	Subtotal	14		5169		-43,980,542.00	12,994,966.00		14,158,900.00	-1,163,934.00	-42,816,608.00

Appropriations, Outlays, and Balances - Continued

Appropriation or Fund Account — Title	Period of Availability	Reg	Tr From	Account Number	Sub No.	Balances, Beginning Of Fiscal Year	Appropriations And Other Obligational Authority[1]	Transfers Borrowings And Investment (Net)[2]	Outlays (Net)	Balances Withdrawn And Other Transactions[3]	Balances, End Of Fiscal Year[4]
National Maritime Heritage Grants Program, National Park Service											
Fund Resources:											
Undisbursed Funds	No Year	14		5244		56,087.49					56,087.49
Fund Equities:											
Unobligated Balances (Unexpired)						-38,587.49				-38,587.00	-0.49
Undelivered Orders						-17,500.00				38,587.00	-56,087.00
Subtotal		14		5244		-0-					-0-
User Fees For Filming And Photography On Public Lands, National Park Service											
Fund Resources:											
Undisbursed Funds	No Year	14		5247		319,829.10	1,347,099.88		749,169.43		917,759.55
Fund Equities:											
Unobligated Balances (Unexpired)						-313,056.38				559,120.22	-872,176.60
Accounts Payable						-6,772.72				27,088.87	-33,861.59
Undelivered Orders						-0-				11,721.36	-11,721.36
Subtotal		14		5247		-0-	1,347,099.88		749,169.43	597,930.45	-0-
National Park Passport Program, National Park Service											
Fund Resources:											
Undisbursed Funds	No Year	14		5262		50,482,355.77	3,192,059.01		18,366,337.95		35,308,076.83
Fund Equities:											
Unobligated Balances (Unexpired)						-41,677,191.74				-14,373,188.49	-27,304,003.25
Accounts Payable						-523,218.73				-199,842.25	-323,376.48
Undelivered Orders						-8,281,945.30				-601,248.20	-7,680,697.10
Subtotal		14		5262		-0-	3,192,059.01		18,366,337.95	-15,174,278.94	-0-
Glacier Bay National Park, National Park Service											
Fund Resources:											
Undisbursed Funds	2007	14		5412		589,098.91	1,510,729.95		1,038,865.44	347,058.14	471,864.51
	2006					12,166.84			160,660.54	2,166.84	81,380.23
	2005					254.72					10,000.00
	2002									254.72	
Fund Equities:											
Unobligated Balances (Expired)						-349,224.98				-174,949.12	-174,275.86
Accounts Payable						-39,945.56				4,843.49	-44,789.05
Undelivered Orders						-212,349.93				131,829.90	-344,179.83
Subtotal		14		5412		-0-	1,510,729.95		1,199,525.98	311,203.97	-0-
Park Concessions Franchise Fees, National Park Service											
Fund Resources:											
Undisbursed Funds	No Year	14		5431		95,455,481.46	47,704,419.57		31,783,087.52		111,376,813.51
Fund Equities:											
Unobligated Balances (Unexpired)						-78,133,056.67				17,752,063.08	-95,885,119.75
Accounts Payable						-809,090.45				-68,544.16	-740,546.29
Undelivered Orders						-16,513,334.34				-1,762,186.87	-14,751,147.47
Subtotal		14		5431		-0-	47,704,419.57		31,783,087.52	15,921,332.05	-0-
Urban Park And Recreation Fund, From Land And Water Conservation Fund, National Park Service											
Fund Resources:											
Undisbursed Funds	No Year	14		5476		2,529,345.16			1,096,983.29		1,432,361.87

Appropriations, Outlays, and Balances – Continued

Appropriation or Fund Account — Title	Period of Availability	Reg	Tr From	Account Number	Sub No.	Balances, Beginning Of Fiscal Year	Appropriations And Other Obligational Authority[1]	Transfers Borrowings And Investment (Net)[2]	Outlays (Net)	Balances Withdrawn And Other Transactions[3]	Balances, End Of Fiscal Year[4]
Urban Park And Recreation Fund, From Land And Water Conservation Fund, National Park Service - Continued											
Fund Equities:											
Unobligated Balances (Unexpired)		14				-440,853.53				-29,462.54	-411,390.99
Undelivered Orders		14		5476		-2,088,491.63			1,096,983.29	-1,067,520.75	-1,020,970.88
Subtotal		14		5476		-0-			1,096,983.29	-1,096,983.29	-0-
Historic Preservation Fund, From Land And Water Conservation Fund, National Park Service											
Fund Resources:											
Undisbursed Funds	No Year	14		5477		331,634.40			71,726.16		259,908.24
Fund Equities:											
Unobligated Balances (Unexpired)		14				-225,277.32				28,934.94	-254,212.26
Undelivered Orders		14		5477		-106,357.08				-100,661.10	-5,695.98
Subtotal		14		5477		-0-			71,726.16	-71,726.16	-0-
Federal Infrastructure Improvement, From Land And Water Conservation Fund, National Park Service											
Fund Resources:											
Undisbursed Funds	No Year	14		5481		1,129,582.53			214,685.75		914,896.78
Transfer To:											
Department Of Transportation, Federal Highway Administration	No Year	69	14	5481	5	297,083.94					297,083.94
Fund Equities:											
Unobligated Balances (Unexpired)		14				-892,610.78				277.99	-892,888.77
Accounts Payable						-14,188.57				-4,777.77	-9,410.80
Undelivered Orders		14		5481		-519,867.12				-210,185.97	-309,681.15
Subtotal		14		5481		-0-			214,685.75	-214,685.75	-0-
Educational Expenses, Children Of Employees, Yellowstone National Park, National Park Service											
Fund Resources:											
Undisbursed Funds	No Year	14		5663		115,243.39	355,000.00		476,643.51		3,599.88
Fund Equities:											
Unobligated Balances (Unexpired)		14				-112,524.93				-112,093.76	-431.17
Accounts Payable						-2,718.46				450.25	-3,168.71
Subtotal		14		5663		-0-	365,000.00		476,643.51	-111,643.51	-0-
Payment For Tax Losses On Land Acquired For Grand Teton National Park, National Park Service											
Fund Resources:											
Undisbursed Funds	No Year	14		5666			11,467.10		11,467.10		
Public Enterprise Funds											
National Law Enforcement Officers Memorial Maintenance Fund, National Park Service											
Fund Resources:											
Undisbursed Funds	No Year	14		4195		32,050.62			-75,195.00		107,245.62
Investments In Public Debt Securities						1,114,000.00					1,114,000.00
Accounts Receivable						34,796.34				34,796.34	
Fund Equities:											
Unobligated Balances (Unexpired)		14				-1,180,846.96				40,398.66	-1,221,245.62
Subtotal		14		4195		-0-			-75,195.00	75,195.00	-0-

Appropriations, Outlays, and Balances - Continued

Appropriation or Fund Account — Title	Period of Availability	Dept Reg	Dept Tr From	Account Number	Sub No.	Balances, Beginning Of Fiscal Year	Appropriations And Other Obligational Authority[1]	Transfers Borrowings And Investment (Net)[2]	Outlays (Net)	Balances Withdrawn And Other Transactions[3]	Balances, End Of Fiscal Year[4]
Trust Fund Accounts											
Donations, National Park Service											
Fund Resources:											
Undisbursed Funds	No Year	14		8037		57,128,336.28	27,227,456.93		29,068,672.48		55,287,120.73
Fund Equities:											
Unobligated Balances (Unexpired)						-35,572,164.63				1,619,860.37	-41,592,025.00
Accounts Payable						-793,020.38				-186,043.06	-606,977.32
Undelivered Orders						-16,363,151.27				-3,275,032.86	-13,088,118.41
Subtotal		14		8037		-0-	27,227,456.93		29,068,672.48	-1,841,215.55	-0-
Preservation, Birthplace Of Abraham Lincoln, National Park Service											
Fund Resources:											
Undisbursed Funds	No Year	14		8052		81,166.88	3,442.50		53,430.23		31,179.15
Unrealized Discount On Investments						-641.06					-641.06
Investments In Public Debt Securities						51,000.00					51,000.00
Fund Equities:											
Unobligated Balances (Unexpired)						-131,525.82				-49,987.73	-81,538.09
Subtotal		14		8052		-0-	3,442.50		53,430.23	-49,987.73	-0-
Construction (Trust Fund), National Park Service											
Fund Resources:											
Undisbursed Funds	No Year	14		8215		131,261.67			87,268.55		43,993.12
Transfer To:											
Department Of Transportation, Federal Highway Administration	No Year	69	14	8215	5	2,510,596.79					2,510,596.79
Fund Equities:											
Unobligated Balances (Unexpired)						-2,246,848.29				17,969.67	-2,264,817.96
Undelivered Orders						-395,010.17				-105,238.22	-289,771.95
Subtotal		14		8215		-0-			87,268.55	-87,268.55	-0-
Total, National Park Service							2,677,868,447.29	-2,021,000.00	2,612,158,420.02	63,689,027.27	
Total, Fish And Wildlife And Parks							4,837,410,540.26	3,181,000.00	4,730,839,604.61	109,751,935.65	
Indian Affairs											
Bureau Of Indian Affairs											
General Fund Accounts											
Operation Of Indian Programs, Bureau Of Indian Affairs											
Fund Resources:											
Undisbursed Funds											
2007-2008		14		2100		466,761,420.74	1,931,966,147.00		1,428,963,024.68		503,003,122.32
2006-2007						42,460,313.17			402,304,899.46		64,456,521.28
2005-2006						23,193,711.98			33,596,161.22		8,864,151.95
2004-2005						34,551,067.11			4,428,748.93		18,764,963.05
2003-2004						15,871,153.05			5,129,029.68		29,422,037.43
2002-2003						4,539,387.23			-179,752.77		16,050,905.82
2001-2002								-4,177,159.77	362,227.46		

Footnotes At End Of Chapter

Appropriations, Outlays, and Balances – Continued

Appropriation or Fund Account — Title	Period of Availability	Dept Reg	Dept Tr From	Account Number	Sub No.	Balances, Beginning Of Fiscal Year	Appropriations And Other Obligational Authority[1]	Transfers Borrowings And Investment (Net)[2]	Outlays (Net)	Balances Withdrawn And Other Transactions[3]	Balances, End Of Fiscal Year[4]
Operation Of Indian Programs, Bureau Of Indian Affairs - Continued											
Fund Resources: - Continued											
Undisbursed Funds - Continued	No Year					41,140,939.13	56,590,799.00	4,177,159.77	59,628,517.28		42,280,380.62
Accounts Receivable						10,562,054.77				-7,341,397.35	17,903,452.12
Unfilled Customer Orders						66,552,135.12				-130,154,585.48	196,706,720.60
Fund Equities:											
Unobligated Balances (Expired)						-82,332,299.97				41,512,673.34	-123,844,973.31
Unobligated Balances (Unexpired)						-363,609,740.65				113,397,978.12	-477,007,718.77
Accounts Payable						-38,562,672.60				15,228,563.60	-53,791,236.20
Undelivered Orders						-221,127,469.08				21,680,857.83	-242,808,326.91
Subtotal		14		2100		-0-	1,988,556,946.00		1,934,232,855.94	54,324,090.06	-0-
White Earth Economic Development And Tribal Government Fund, Bureau Of Indian Affairs											
Fund Resources:											
Undisbursed Funds	No Year	14		2204		693,854.00	2,113,760.18		2,100,478.13		707,136.05
Fund Equities:											
Unobligated Balances (Unexpired)						-694,925.38				11,731.44	-706,656.82
Accounts Payable										476.34	-476.34
Undelivered Orders						1,071.38				1,074.27	-2.89
Subtotal		14		2204		-0-	2,113,760.18		2,100,478.13	13,282.05	-0-
Construction, Bureau Of Indian Affairs											
Fund Resources:											
Undisbursed Funds	2006-2007	14		2301		3,342,620.00					3,342,620.00
	No Year					675,575,958.03	230,701,718.00	12,012,000.00	325,159,698.52		593,129,977.51
Transfer To:											
Interior, Bureau Of Reclamation	No Year	14	14	2301	6	19,996,096.75		10,338,000.00	8,070,777.18		22,263,319.57
Funds Held Outside The Treasury						15,250.00					15,250.00
Accounts Receivable						2,190,358.24				-776,383.03	2,966,741.27
Unfilled Customer Orders						9,231,125.41				2,778,689.36	6,452,436.05
Fund Equities:											
Unobligated Balances (Unexpired)						-122,396,832.05				10,144,007.56	-132,540,839.61
Accounts Payable						-16,249,362.33				11,207,574.16	-27,456,936.49
Undelivered Orders						-571,705,214.05				-103,532,645.75	-468,172,568.30
Subtotal		14		2301		-0-	230,701,718.00	22,350,000.00	333,230,475.70	-80,178,757.70	-0-
Indian Land And Water Claim Settlements And Miscellaneous Payments To Indians, Bureau Of Indian Affairs											
Fund Resources:											
Undisbursed Funds	No Year	14		2303		7,624,120.09	42,000,000.00		36,537,161.09		13,086,959.00
Fund Equities:											
Unobligated Balances (Unexpired)						-7,583,504.21				-1,827,677.99	-5,755,826.22
Accounts Payable						-3,020.30				14,940.97	-17,961.27
Undelivered Orders						-37,595.58				7,275,575.93	-7,313,171.51
Subtotal		14		2303		-0-	42,000,000.00		36,537,161.09	5,462,838.91	-0-
Claims And Treaty Obligations, Bureau Of Indian Affairs (Indefinite)											
Fund Resources:											
Undisbursed Funds	No Year	14		2623		55,502.93	40,500.00		68,700.00		27,302.93
Fund Equities:											
Unobligated Balances (Unexpired)						-25,502.93					-25,502.93

Appropriations, Outlays, and Balances - Continued

Title	Period of Availability	Dept Reg	Dept Tr From	Account Number	Sub No.	Balances, Beginning Of Fiscal Year	Appropriations And Other Obligational Authority[1]	Transfers Borrowings And Investment (Net)[2]	Outlays (Net)	Balances Withdrawn And Other Transactions[3]	Balances, End Of Fiscal Year[4]
Accounts Payable						-744.00					-744.00
Undelivered Orders						-29,256.00				-27,456.00	-1,800.00
	Subtotal	14		2623		-0-	40,500.00		68,700.00	-28,200.00	-0-
Indian Direct Loan Program Account, Bureau Of Indian Affairs Department Of The Interior											
Fund Resources:											
Undisbursed Funds	2007	14		2627			3,244,808.00		3,244,808.00		
Indian Guaranteed Loan Program Account, Bureau Of Indian Affairs											
Fund Resources:											
Undisbursed Funds	2007	14		2628		3,420,892.53	17,484,930.00		13,960,650.96		3,524,279.04
	2006					2,833,878.00			1,931,672.22		1,489,220.31
	2005					1,222,285.67			379,642.67		2,454,235.33
	2004					1,687,205.89					1,222,285.67
	2003										1,687,205.89
Fund Equities:											
Unobligated Balances (Expired)						-2,990,781.01				1,103,616.62	-4,094,397.63
Accounts Payable						-173,645.39				757,142.98	-930,788.37
Undelivered Orders						-5,999,835.69				-647,795.45	-5,352,040.24
	Subtotal	14		2628		-0-	17,484,930.00		16,271,965.85	1,212,964.15	-0-
Special Fund Accounts											
Operation And Maintenance Of Quarters, Bureau Of Indian Affairs											
Fund Resources:											
Undisbursed Funds	No Year	14		5051		5,140,167.79	5,181,131.13		6,082,722.33		4,238,576.59
Fund Equities:											
Unobligated Balances (Unexpired)						-3,048,755.65				176,525.69	-3,225,281.34
Accounts Payable						-338,635.49				-52,114.01	-286,521.48
Undelivered Orders						-1,752,776.65				-1,026,002.88	-726,773.77
	Subtotal	14		5051		-0-	5,181,131.13		6,082,722.33	-901,591.20	-0-
Indian Arts And Crafts Fund, Departmental Management											
Fund Resources:											
Undisbursed Funds	No Year	14		5130		107,040.06	40,066.95		66,721.16		80,385.85
Fund Equities:											
Unobligated Balances (Unexpired)						-96,433.56				-45,389.40	-51,044.16
Accounts Payable										19,278.91	-19,278.91
Undelivered Orders						-10,606.50				-543.72	-10,062.78
	Subtotal	14		5130		-0-	40,066.95		66,721.16	-26,654.21	-0-
Operation And Maintenance, Indian Irrigation Systems, Bureau Of Indian Affairs (T)[8]											
Fund Resources:											
Undisbursed Funds	No Year	14		5240		4,162,403.27	27,501,114.68	-3,782,000.00	24,359,721.74		3,521,796.21
Investments In Public Debt Securities						27,524,000.00		3,782,000.00			31,306,000.00
Fund Equities:											
Unobligated Balances (Unexpired)						-28,776,253.96				795,839.70	-29,572,093.66
Accounts Payable						-1,137,641.25				155,223.31	-1,292,864.56

Footnotes At End Of Chapter

Appropriations, Outlays, and Balances – Continued

Appropriation or Fund Account — Title	Period of Availability	Dept Reg	Dept Tr From	Account Number	Sub No.	Balances, Beginning Of Fiscal Year	Appropriations And Other Obligational Authority[1]	Transfers Borrowings And Investment (Net)[2]	Outlays (Net)	Balances Withdrawn And Other Transactions[3]	Balances, End Of Fiscal Year[4]
Operation And Maintenance, Indian Irrigation Systems, Bureau Of Indian Affairs (T) - Continued											
Fund Equities: - Continued											
Undelivered Orders						-1,772,508.06				2,190,329.93	-3,962,837.99
	Subtotal	14		5240		-0-	27,501,114.68		24,359,721.74	3,141,392.94	-0-
Alaska Resupply Program, Bureau Of Indian Affairs											
Fund Resources:											
Undisbursed Funds	No Year	14		5242		1,896,328.34	1,483,514.66		892,996.05		2,486,846.95
Fund Equities:											
Unobligated Balances (Unexpired)						-1,560,211.55				134,095.94	-1,694,307.49
Accounts Payable						-15,581.61				110,423.23	-126,004.84
Undelivered Orders						-320,535.18				345,999.44	-666,534.62
	Subtotal	14		5242		-0-	1,483,514.66		892,996.05	590,518.61	-0-
Indian Water Rights And Habitat Acquisition Program, Bureau Of Indian Affairs											
Fund Resources:											
Undisbursed Funds	No Year	14		5505		2,980,500.00					2,980,500.00
Fund Equities:											
Unobligated Balances (Unexpired)	Subtotal	14		5505		-2,980,500.00					-2,980,500.00
Power Systems, Indian Irrigation Projects, Bureau Of Indian Affairs											
Fund Resources:											
Undisbursed Funds	No Year	14		5648		4,533,629.60	69,862,935.55	-1,157,000.00	67,724,480.47	-5,469,914.89	5,515,084.68
Investments In Public Debt Securities						41,956,000.00		1,157,000.00		3,197,621.13	43,113,000.00
Fund Equities:											
Unobligated Balances (Unexpired)						-27,155,118.60					-21,685,203.71
Accounts Payable						-1,013,456.06				4,211,077.19	-4,211,077.19
Undelivered Orders						-18,321,054.94				4,410,748.84	-22,731,803.78
	Subtotal	14		5648		-0-	69,862,935.55		67,724,480.47	2,138,455.08	-0-
Public Enterprise Funds											
Revolving Fund For Loans, Liquidating Account, Bureau Of Indian Affairs											
Fund Resources:											
Undisbursed Funds	No Year	14		4409					-1,689,572.55	[7]1,300,000.00	389,572.55
Fund Equities:											
Unobligated Balances (Unexpired)	Subtotal	14		4409		-0-			-1,689,572.55	389,572.55	-389,572.55
									1,689,572.55		
Indian Loan Guaranty And Insurance Fund, Liquidating Account, Bureau Of Indian Affairs											
Fund Resources:											
Undisbursed Funds	No Year	14		4410		350,629.80			-3,437,704.93	[7]3,650,629.80	137,704.93
Fund Equities:											
Unobligated Balances (Unexpired)	Subtotal	14		4410		-350,629.80			-3,437,704.93	-212,924.87	-137,704.93
						-0-				3,437,704.93	-137,704.93

Appropriations, Outlays, and Balances - Continued

Appropriation or Fund Account — Title	Period of Availability	Dept Reg	Tr From	Account Number	Sub No.	Balances, Beginning Of Fiscal Year	Appropriations And Other Obligational Authority[1]	Transfers Borrowings And Investment (Net)[2]	Outlays (Net)	Balances Withdrawn And Other Transactions[3]	Balances, End Of Fiscal Year[4]
Trust Fund Accounts											
Gifts And Donations, Bureau Of Indian Affairs											
Fund Resources:											
Undisbursed Funds[9]	No Year	14		8361		---	3,449,961.12	---	---	---	3,449,961.12
Total, Bureau Of Indian Affairs, Total Indian Affairs						---	2,391,661,386.27	22,350,000.00	2,419,685,808.98	-9,124,383.83	3,449,961.12
Departmental Offices											
Departmental Management											
General Fund Accounts											
Salaries And Expenes, Departmental Management											
Fund Resources:											
Undisbursed Funds	2007	14		0102		8,038,053.74	108,471,298.55		101,898,936.72		6,572,361.83
	2006					41,807.00			2,282,833.51		5,755,220.23
	2005					-3,615,302.61			-620,594.81		662,401.81
	2004					-557,035.59			-3,564,294.66		[5]-51,007.95
	2003					-235,364.28			-573,526.87		16,491.28
	2002					11,141,631.77			-248,545.30	13,181.02	12,791,105.21
	No Year					5,750,359.96			-1,649,473.44		1,471,485.59
Accounts Receivable						13,471,350.74				4,278,874.37	17,147,825.85
Unfilled Customer Orders										-3,676,475.11	
Fund Equities:											
Unobligated Balances (Expired)						-7,894,161.00				5,327,098.12	[10]-13,221,259.12
Unobligated Balances (Unexpired)						-10,579,001.06				465,208.04	-11,044,209.10
Accounts Payable						-6,843,552.38				-1,051,174.81	-5,792,377.57
Undelivered Orders						-8,718,786.29				5,589,251.77	-14,308,038.06
Subtotal		14		0102		-0-	108,471,298.55		97,525,335.15	10,945,963.40	-0-
Management Of Federal Lands For Subsistence Uses, Departmental Management											
Fund Resources:											
Undisbursed Funds	No Year	14		0124		165,097.90					165,097.90
Fund Equities:											
Unobligated Balances (Unexpired)						-108,221.10					-108,221.10
Accounts Payable						4,210.20				4,210.20	
Undelivered Orders						-61,087.00					-56,876.80
Subtotal		14		0124		-0-				-4,210.20	-0-
Special Fund Accounts											
Priority Land Acquisitions, Land Exchanges, And Maintenance, Office Of The Secretary											
Fund Resources:											
Undisbursed Funds	2000-2003	14		5039		9,723,976.37			1,089,534.93		8,634,441.44
Unobligated Balances (Expired)						-91,047.00					-91,047.00

Footnotes At End Of Chapter

Appropriations, Outlays, and Balances – Continued

Appropriation or Fund Account — Title	Dept Reg	Tr From	Account Number	Sub No.	Period of Availability	Balances, Beginning Of Fiscal Year	Appropriations And Other Obligational Authority[1]	Transfers Borrowings And Investment (Net)[2]	Outlays (Net)	Balances Withdrawn And Other Transactions[3]	Balances, End Of Fiscal Year[4]
Priority Land Acquisitions, Land Exchanges, And Maintenance, Office Of The Secretary - Continued											
Fund Equities:											
Accounts Payable						-35,399.67				28,777.18	-64,176.85
Undelivered Orders						-9,597,529.70				-1,118,312.11	-8,479,217.59
	14		5039		Subtotal	-0-			1,089,534.93	-1,089,534.93	-0-
Everglades Restoration Account, Office Of The Secretary											
Fund Resources:											
Undisbursed Funds	14		5233		No Year	839,097.51					398,668.61
Fund Equities:											
Unobligated Balances (Unexpired)						-689,771.27				-365,691.26	-324,080.01
Accounts Payable						-27,343.15				-12,330.43	-15,012.72
Undelivered Orders						-121,983.09				-62,407.21	-59,575.88
	14		5233		Subtotal	-0-			440,428.90	-440,428.90	-0-
Salaries And Expenses, Departmental Management, From The Land And Water Conservation Fund											
Fund Resources:											
Undisbursed Funds	14		5571		No Year		7,397,525.00		7,397,525.00		
Trust Fund Accounts											
Gifts And Bequest, Take Pride In America, Department Of The Interior											
Fund Resources:											
Undisbursed Funds	14		8369		No Year	213,351.28	102,579.21		66,600.00		249,330.49
Fund Equities:											
Unobligated Balances (Unexpired)						-213,351.28	102,579.21		66,600.00	35,979.21	-249,330.49
	14		8369		Subtotal	-0-	-0-		66,600.00	35,979.21	-0-
Total, Departmental Management							115,971,402.76		106,519,423.98	9,451,978.78	
Insular Affairs											
General Fund Accounts											
Administration Of Territories, Interior											
Fund Resources:											
Undisbursed Funds	14		0412		2007		7,305,407.00		6,478,380.33		827,026.67
					2006	840,604.60			395,294.99		445,309.61
					2005	281,106.27			16,239.37		264,866.90
					2004	111,900.13					111,900.13
					2003	149,431.92					149,431.92
					2002	54,015.05				54,015.05	
Accounts Receivable	14				No Year	133,945,912.23	71,068,394.00		67,639,611.02		137,374,695.21
Unfilled Customer Orders						854,865.08				443,865.08	411,000.00
Fund Equities:											
Unobligated Balances (Expired)						4,894,541.80				2,022,369.17	2,872,172.63
Unobligated Balances (Unexpired)						-904,663.54				318,215.46	-1,222,879.00
Accounts Payable						-12,606,303.07				-798,617.67	-11,807,685.40
Undelivered Orders						-5,073,419.16				5,762,849.59	-10,836,268.75
						-122,547,991.31				-3,958,421.39	-118,589,569.92

Appropriations, Outlays, and Balances - Continued

Appropriation or Fund Account — Title	Dept Reg	Dept Tr From	Account Number	Sub No.	Period of Availability	Balances, Beginning Of Fiscal Year	Appropriations And Other Obligational Authority[1]	Transfers Borrowings And Investment (Net)[2]	Outlays (Net)	Balances Withdrawn And Other Transactions[3]	Balances, End Of Fiscal Year[4]
Trust Territory Of The Pacific Islands, Insular Affairs											
Fund Resources:											
Undisbursed Funds	14		0412		Subtotal	-0-	78,373,801.00		74,529,525.71	3,844,275.29	-0-
	14		0414		No Year	5,342,618.18			152,625.92	152,625.92	5,189,992.26
Fund Equities:											
Unobligated Balances (Unexpired)						-5,117,459.21				-100,412.31	-5,017,046.90
Accounts Payable						-1,000.00				25,000.00	-26,000.00
Undelivered Orders						-224,158.97				-77,213.61	-146,945.36
	14		0414		Subtotal	-0-			152,625.92	-152,625.92	-0-
Compact Of Free Association, Insular Affairs											
Fund Resources:											
Undisbursed Funds	14		0415		2006	-780,281.00					5,780,281.00 [5]
					2005	230,050.00			147,800.00	147,800.00	82,250.00
					No Year	144,445,667.23	207,960,914.00		215,536,860.65		136,869,720.58
Accounts Receivable						780,281.00				780,281.00	4,369,000.10
Unfilled Customer Orders						19,263,250.75				14,894,250.65	
Fund Equities:											
Unobligated Balances (Expired)						780,281.00 [6]				780,281.00	
Unobligated Balances (Unexpired)						-20,212,598.65 [6]				25,579,054.29	-45,791,652.94
Accounts Payable						-242,881.79				1,430,557.09	-1,673,438.88
Undelivered Orders						-144,263,768.54				-51,188,170.68	-93,075,597.86
	14		0415		Subtotal	-0-	207,960,914.00		215,684,660.65	-7,723,746.65	-0-
Micronesian Claims Fund, Trust Territory Of The Pacific Islands, Insular Affairs											
Fund Resources:											
Undisbursed Funds	14		0416		No Year	167,969.97			9,913.00	9,913.00	158,056.97
Fund Equities:											
Unobligated Balances (Unexpired)										104,440.49	-104,440.49
Undelivered Orders						-167,969.97				-114,353.49	-53,616.48
	14		0416		Subtotal	-0-			9,913.00	-9,913.00	-0-
Payment To The United States Territories, Fiscal Assistance, Insular Affairs											
Fund Resources:											
Undisbursed Funds	14		0418		No Year		126,731,455.19	-2,445,000.00	124,286,455.19		
Total, Insular Affairs							413,066,170.19	-2,445,000.00	414,663,180.47	-4,042,010.28	
Office Of The Solicitor											
General Fund Accounts											
Salaries And Expenses, Office Of The Solicitor, Interior											
Fund Resources:											
Undisbursed Funds	14		0107		2007	2,908,934.17	55,018,345.00		51,706,041.97		3,312,303.03
					2006	82,418.75			1,706,242.93		1,202,691.24
					2005	201,840.01			-328,768.64		411,187.39
					2004				8,858.00		192,982.01

Appropriations, Outlays, and Balances – Continued

Appropriation or Fund Account — Title	Period of Availability	Dept Reg	Dept Tr From	Account Number	Sub No.	Balances, Beginning Of Fiscal Year	Appropriations And Other Obligational Authority[1]	Transfers Borrowings And Investment (Net)[2]	Outlays (Net)	Balances Withdrawn And Other Transactions[3]	Balances, End Of Fiscal Year[4]
Salaries And Expenses, Office Of The Solicitor, Interior - Continued											
Fund Resources: - Continued											
Undisbursed Funds - Continued											
	2003					227,968.26			-8,434.51	293.09	236,402.77
	2002					-201,126.52			-201,419.61		
Accounts Receivable						1,298,242.90				672,927.43	625,315.47
Unfilled Customer Orders						5,751,697.44				4,219,255.66	1,532,441.78
Fund Equities:											
Unobligated Balances (Expired)						-5,995,874.04				-3,275,858.74	-2,720,015.30
Accounts Payable						-2,676,257.85				92,783.32	-2,769,041.17
Undelivered Orders						-1,597,843.12				426,424.10	-2,024,267.22
Subtotal		14		0107		-0-	55,013,345.00		52,882,520.14	2,135,824.86	-0-
Total, Office Of The Solicitor							55,013,345.00		52,882,520.14	2,135,824.86	
Office Of Inspector General											
General Fund Accounts											
Salaries And Expenses, Office Of The Inspector General, Interior											
Fund Resources:											
Undisbursed Funds:											
	2007	14		0104		2,569,567.71	38,822,510.00		36,373,769.89		2,448,740.11
	2006					136,165.78			2,318,185.18		251,382.53
	2005					0.72			119,220.32		16,945.46
	2004										0.72
	2003					1,511.32					1,511.32
	2002					5.40				5.40	
Accounts Receivable						-19,997.93				556,106.37	-556,106.37
Unfilled Customer Orders										-910,235.70	910,235.70
Fund Equities:											
Unobligated Balances (Expired)						-1,449,852.97				271,686.91	[11]-291,684.84
Accounts Payable						-1,237,400.03				-190,161.86	-1,259,691.11
Undelivered Orders										283,933.49	-1,521,333.52
Subtotal		14		0104		-0-	38,822,510.00		38,811,175.39	11,334.61	-0-
Total, Office Of Inspector General							38,822,510.00		38,811,175.39	11,334.61	
Office Of Special Trustee For American Indians											
General Fund Accounts											
Federal Trust Program, Office Of Special Trust For American Indians											
Fund Resources:											
Undisbursed Funds											
	No Year	14		0120		51,952,374.78	189,251,207.00	-67,336,886.00	129,041,303.79		44,825,391.99
Transfer To:											
Office Of The Secretary		No Year	14	0120	1	16,625,821.51		67,980,600.00	75,270,203.16		9,336,218.35
Bureau Of Reclamation		No Year	14	0120	20	4,730,525.62		856,286.00	3,433,491.98		2,153,319.64
Accounts Receivable						1,275,093.99				1,238,482.35	36,611.64
Unfilled Customer Orders						835,516.53				-2,000,000.00	2,835,516.53
Fund Equities:											

Appropriations, Outlays, and Balances - Continued

Title	Period of Availability	Dept Reg	Tr From	Account Number	Sub No.	Balances, Beginning Of Fiscal Year	Appropriations And Other Obligational Authority[1]	Transfers Borrowings And Investment (Net)[2]	Outlays (Net)	Balances Withdrawn And Other Transactions[3]	Balances, End Of Fiscal Year[4]
Unobligated Balances (Unexpired)						-16,549,395.32				2,960,495.96	-19,509,891.28
Accounts Payable						-10,518,108.64				-3,245,754.83	-7,272,353.81
Undelivered Orders						-48,351,828.47				-15,947,015.41	-32,404,813.06
Subtotal		14		0120		-0-	189,251,207.00	1,500,000.00	207,744,998.93	-16,993,791.93	-0-
Indian Land Consolidation, Office Of Special Trustee For American Indians											
Fund Resources:											
Undisbursed Funds	No Year	14		2103			34,006,216.00	-34,006,216.00			
Transfer To:											
Bureau Of Indian Affairs	No Year	14	14	2103	20	6,450,516.23		32,156,216.00	30,213,519.04		8,393,213.19
Unfilled Customer Orders						809,429.65				809,429.65	
Fund Equities:											
Unobligated Balances (Unexpired)						-4,042,820.92				1,411,577.34	-5,454,398.26
Accounts Payable						-327,213.93				372,401.80	-699,615.73
Undelivered Orders						-2,889,911.03				-650,711.83	-2,239,199.20
Subtotal		14		2103		-0-	34,006,216.00	-1,850,000.00	30,213,519.04	1,942,696.96	-0-
Special Fund Accounts											
Tribal Special Fund, Office Of The Special Trustee For American Indians											
Fund Resources:											
Undisbursed Funds	No Year	14		5265			172,864,295.22	-19,073,608.06	153,796,947.99		[5]6,260.83
Unrealized Discount On Investments						-465,195.31		-66,835.94			-532,031.25
Investments In Public Debt Securities						61,031,121.08		19,140,444.00			80,171,565.08
Fund Equities:											
Unobligated Balances (Unexpired)						-60,565,925.77				19,067,347.23	-79,633,273.00
Subtotal		14		5265		-0-	172,864,295.22		153,796,947.99	19,067,347.23	-0-
Trust Fund Accounts											
Tribal Trust Fund, Office Of The Special Trustee For The American Indians											
Fund Resources:											
Undisbursed Funds	No Year	14		8030		-34,142.44	47,545,431.79	-15,820,022.39	31,725,409.40		[5]34,142.44
Unrealized Discount On Investments						-113,028.04					-113,028.04
Investments In Public Debt Securities						52,873,030.63		15,820,022.39			68,693,053.02
Fund Equities:											
Unobligated Balances (Unexpired)						-52,725,860.15				15,820,022.39	-68,545,882.54
Subtotal		14		8030		-0-	47,545,431.79		31,725,409.40	15,820,022.39	-0-
Total, Office Of Special Trustee For American Indians							443,667,150.01	-350,000.00	423,480,875.36	19,836,274.65	
National Indian Gaming Commission											
General Fund Accounts											
Salaries And Expenses, National Indian Gaming Commission, Interior											
Fund Resources:											
Undisbursed Funds	No Year	14		0118		5,374,252.09			-2,711,293.01		8,085,545.10

Appropriations, Outlays, and Balances – Continued

Appropriation or Fund Account — Title	Period of Availability	Reg	Tr From	Account Number	Sub No.	Balances, Beginning Of Fiscal Year	Appropriations And Other Obligational Authority[1]	Transfers Borrowings And Investment (Net)[2]	Outlays (Net)	Balances Withdrawn And Other Transactions[3]	Balances, End Of Fiscal Year[4]
Salaries And Expenses, National Indian Gaming Commission, Interior - Continued											
Fund Equities:											
Unobligated Balances (Unexpired)						-4,596,325.26				2,840,497.92	-7,436,823.18
Undelivered Orders						-777,926.83				-129,204.91	-648,721.92
	Subtotal	14		0118		-0-			-2,711,293.01	2,711,293.01	-0-
Special Fund Accounts											
National Indian Gaming Commission, Gaming Activity Fees											
Fund Resources:											
Undisbursed Funds	No Year	14		5141		5,687,385.57	12,332,739.40		14,404,093.14		4,116,031.83
Fund Equities:											
Unobligated Balances (Unexpired)						-3,826,072.62				-1,367,226.30	-2,458,846.32
Accounts Payable						-541,113.57				109,165.90	-650,279.47
Undelivered Orders						-1,320,199.38				-313,293.34	-1,006,906.04
	Subtotal	14		5141		-0-	12,832,739.40		14,404,093.14	-1,571,353.74	-0-
Total, National Indian Gaming Commission							12,832,739.40		11,692,800.13	1,139,939.27	
Department-Wide Programs											
General Fund Accounts											
Payments In Lieu Of Taxes, Departmental Management											
Fund Resources:											
Undisbursed Funds	2007	14		1114		188,361.26	232,527,874.00		232,390,496.87		137,377.13
	2006					242,761.38			8,554.02		179,807.24
	2005					225,943.93			-45,131.00		287,892.38
	2004					80,538.20					225,943.93
	2003					120,537.70					80,538.20
	2002									120,537.70	
Fund Equities:											
Unobligated Balances (Expired)						-829,939.17				61,718.60	-891,657.77
Accounts Payable						-110.30				9,256.78	-9,367.08
Undelivered Orders						-28,093.00				-17,558.97	-10,534.03
	Subtotal	14		1114		-0-	232,527,874.00		232,353,919.89	173,954.11	-0-
Central Hazardous Materials Fund, Departmental Management, Department Of The Interior											
Fund Resources:											
Undisbursed Funds	No Year	14		1121		2,354,080.01	9,715,009.00	-9,201,574.00	512,658.31		2,354,856.70
Transfer To:											
Interior, Office The Secretary	No Year	14	14	1121	1	49,617.01			37,489.77		12,127.24
Department Of The Interior, Bureau Of Reclamation	No Year	14	14	1121	6	865,952.63		464,000.00	215,379.30		1,114,573.33
Interior, United States Geological Survey	No Year	14	14	1121	8	130,092.78			3,701.64		126,391.14
Interior, National Park Service	No Year	14	14	1121	10	6,381,901.26		2,867,700.00	1,578,999.55		7,670,601.71
Interior, Bureau Of Land Management	No Year	14	14	1121	11	5,807,271.86		3,321,855.00	4,180,550.27		4,948,576.59
Interior, United States Fish And Wildlife Service	No Year	14	14	1121	16	6,412,164.24		2,037,500.00	2,779,515.95		5,670,148.29
Interior, Bureau Of Indian Affairs	No Year	14	14	1121	20	681,221.54		510,519.00	522,485.96		669,254.58

Appropriations, Outlays, and Balances - Continued

| Appropriation or Fund Account | Account Symbol | | | | | Balances, Beginning Of Fiscal Year | Appropriations And Other Obligational Authority[1] | Transfers Borrowings And Investment (Net)[2] | Outlays (Net) | Balances Withdrawn And Other Transactions[3] | Balances, End Of Fiscal Year[4] |
Title	Period of Availability	Reg	Tr From	Account Number	Sub No.						
Intragovernmental Funds											
Fund Equities:											
Unobligated Balances (Unexpired)						-6,708,755.96				1,286,325.80	-7,995,081.76
Accounts Payable						-413,463.55				29,391.94	-442,855.49
Undelivered Orders						-15,560,081.82				-1,431,489.49	-14,128,592.33
Subtotal		14		1121		-0-	9,715,009.00		9,830,780.75	-115,771.75	-0-
Working Capital Fund, Departmental Management											
Fund Resources:											
Undisbursed Funds	No Year	14		4523		380,523,146.35	270,000.00		8,471,328.76		372,321,817.59
Accounts Receivable						120,563,382.69				56,535,469.18	64,027,913.51
Unfilled Customer Orders						225,122,622.87				120,547,182.89	104,575,439.98
Fund Equities:											
Unobligated Balances (Unexpired)						[6]-112,417,886.26				-3,664,519.68	-108,753,366.58
Accounts Payable						-179,172,089.76				-75,328,826.67	-103,843,263.09
Undelivered Orders						[6]-434,619,175.89				-106,290,634.48	-328,328,541.41
Subtotal		14		4523		-0-	270,000.00		8,471,328.76	-8,201,328.76	-0-
Interior Franchise Fund, Departmental Management											
Fund Resources:											
Undisbursed Funds	No Year	14		4529		1,230,748,223.82			559,516,993.31		671,231,230.51
Accounts Receivable						2,831,067.20				-15,394,518.03	18,225,585.23
Unfilled Customer Orders						83,204,046.16				30,510,969.40	52,693,076.76
Fund Equities:											
Unobligated Balances (Unexpired)						-503,963,518.47				-384,756,066.23	-119,207,452.24
Accounts Payable						-230,900,652.71				-93,231,251.22	-137,669,401.49
Undelivered Orders						-581,919,166.00				-96,646,127.23	-485,273,038.77
Subtotal		14		4529		-0-			559,516,993.31	-559,516,993.31	-0-
General Fund Accounts											
Natural Resource Damage Assessment Fund, Natural Resource Damage Assessment And Restoration											
Fund Resources:											
Undisbursed Funds	No Year	14		1618		1,226,602.11	6,043,166.00	-3,760,286.00	1,572,046.33		1,937,435.78
Transfer To:											
Interior, Bureau Of Reclamation	No Year	14		1618	6	34,244.98		78,000.00	45,791.52		66,453.46
Interior, Geological Survey	No Year	14		1618	8	448,617.24		346,960.00	120,922.17		674,655.07
Interior, National Park Service	No Year	14		1618	10	436,281.56		15,799.36	130,099.41		321,981.51
Interior, Bureau Of Land Management	No Year	14		1618	11	79,403.25		146,000.00	107,792.60		117,610.65
Interior, Natural Resources Damage Assessment And Restoration Fund, U.S. Fish And Wildlife Service	No Year	14		1618	16	2,964,274.03		2,364,249.64	2,591,171.35		2,737,352.32
Interior, Bureau Of Indian Affairs	No Year	14		1618	20	568,851.61		809,277.00	502,453.46		875,675.15
Fund Equities:											
Unobligated Balances (Unexpired)						-4,471,091.04				727,633.55	-5,198,724.59
Accounts Payable						-128,310.12				53,199.39	-181,509.51
Undelivered Orders						-1,158,873.62				192,056.22	-1,350,929.84
Subtotal		14		1618		-0-	6,043,166.00		5,070,276.84	972,889.16	-0-

Footnotes At End Of Chapter

Appropriations, Outlays, and Balances – Continued

Appropriation or Fund Account Title	Period of Availability	Dept Reg	Dept Tr From	Account Number	Sub No.	Balances, Beginning Of Fiscal Year	Appropriations And Other Obligational Authority[1]	Transfers Borrowings And Investment (Net)[2]	Outlays (Net)	Balances Withdrawn And Other Transactions[3]	Balances, End Of Fiscal Year[4]
Special Fund Accounts											
Natural Resource Damage Assessment And Restoration Fund, Office Of The Secretary											
Fund Resources:											
Undisbursed Funds	No Year	14		5198		433,804.99	71,630,287.40	-43,530,111.42	27,238,406.85		1,295,574.12
Transfer To:											
Interior, Bureau Of Reclamation	No Year	14	14	5198	6	20,977.87					20,977.87
Interior, U.S. Geological Survey	No Year	14	14	5198	8	684,112.31		1,476,903.70	1,136,497.63		1,024,518.38
Interior, National Park Service	No Year	14	14	5198	10	3,730,086.33		1,833,389.23	1,950,446.20		3,613,029.36
Interior, Bureau Of Land Management	No Year	14	14	5198	11	1,183,963.85		227,350.00	613,025.57		798,288.28
Interior, Natural Resource Damage Assessment And Restoration Fund, U.S Fish And Wildlife Service	No Year	14	14	5198	16	15,818,852.39		14,149,344.11	10,420,004.07		19,548,192.43
Interior, Bureau Of Indian Affairs	No Year	14	14	5198	20	13,410.00		97,732.69			111,142.69
Unrealized Discount On Investments						-1,764,930.55		419,458.60			-1,345,471.95
Investments In Public Debt Securities						227,474,000.00		9,984,000.00			237,458,000.00
Fund Equities:											
Unobligated Balances (Unexpired)						-240,670,294.37				11,573,660.76	-252,243,955.13
Accounts Payable						-667,412.75				246,657.16	-914,069.91
Undelivered Orders						-6,256,570.07				3,109,656.07	-9,366,226.14
	Subtotal	14		5198		-0-	71,630,287.40	-15,341,933.09	41,358,380.32	14,929,973.99	-0-
Total, Department-Wide Programs							320,186,336.40	-15,341,933.09	856,601,679.87	-551,757,276.56	
Total, Departmental Offices							1,399,564,653.76	-18,136,933.09	1,904,651,655.34	-523,223,934.67	
Deductions For Offsetting Receipts											
Proprietary Receipts From The Public							-5,099,869,877.13		-5,099,869,877.13		
Intrabudgetary Transactions							-403,137,021.27		-403,137,021.27		
Total, Offsetting Receipts							-5,503,006,898.40		-5,503,006,898.40		
Total, Department Of The Interior							10,508,794,432.03	-18,075,128.09	10,488,015,692.02	-746,349.20	3,449,961.12
Memorandum											
Financing Accounts											
Public Enterprise Funds											
Assistance To American Samoa Direct Loan Financing Account, Office Of The Secretary											
Fund Resources:											
Undisbursed Funds	No Year	14		4163		378,302.58		-2,764,685.00	-2,386,383.08		0.66
Fund Equities:											
Unobligated Balances (Unexpired)						-378,302.58				-378,301.92	-0.66
	Subtotal	14		4163		-0-		-2,764,685.00	-2,386,383.08	-378,301.92	-0-

Appropriations, Outlays, and Balances - Continued

Appropriation or Fund Account — Title	Period of Availability	Dept Reg	Tr From	Account Number	Sub No.	Balances, Beginning Of Fiscal Year	Appropriations And Other Obligational Authority[1]	Transfers Borrowings And Investment (Net)[2]	Outlays (Net)	Balances Withdrawn And Other Transactions[3]	Balances, End Of Fiscal Year[4]
Guaranteed Loan Financing Account, Bureau Of Indian Affairs, Interior											
Fund Resources:											
Undisbursed Funds	No Year	14		4415		93,556,549.20	------	-6,726,874.48	-10,911,854.64	------	97,741,529.36
Fund Equities:											
Unobligated Balances (Unexpired)						-93,556,549.20	------			4,181,736.93	-97,738,286.13
Undelivered Orders						------				3,243.23	-3,243.23
Subtotal		14		4415		-0-	-0-	-6,726,874.48	-10,911,854.64	4,184,980.16	-0-
Direct Loan Financing Account, Bureau Of Indian Affairs, Interior											
Fund Resources:											
Undisbursed Funds	No Year	14		4416		14,637,605.98		-14,659,270.51	-3,532,289.04		3,510,624.51
Fund Equities:											
Unobligated Balances (Unexpired)						-14,637,605.98				-11,126,981.47	-3,510,624.51
Subtotal		14		4416		-0-		-14,659,270.51	-3,532,289.04	-11,126,981.47	-0-
Intragovernmental Funds											
Direct Loans, Loan Financing Account, Bureau Of Reclamation											
Fund Resources:											
Undisbursed Funds	No Year	14		4547		3,941,991.03		-21,881,039.34	-28,176,199.32		10,237,151.01
Authority To Borrow From The Treasury							1,031,654.00	-1,031,654.00			
Fund Equities:											
Unobligated Balances (Unexpired)						-7,874.02				10,229,276.99	-10,237,151.01
Undelivered Orders						-3,934,117.01				-3,934,117.01	-0-
Subtotal		14		4547		-0-	1,031,654.00	-22,912,693.34	-28,176,199.32	6,295,159.98	-0-
Total, Financing Accounts							1,031,654.00	-47,063,523.33	-45,006,726.08	-1,025,143.25	------

Footnotes At End Of Chapter

Appropriations, Outlays, and Balances – Continued

Footnotes

1. The amounts in this column, unless otherwise footnoted, represent appropriations, increases and rescissions in borrowing authority or new contract authority. Appropriation accounts with appropriation transfer activity are presented in Table 1 (Appropriations and Appropriation Transfers) at the end of this chapter.

2. The amounts in this column, unless otherwise footnoted, represent transfers - other than appropriation transfers, borrowings (gross), investments (net), unrealized discounts or funds held outside the Treasury.

3. The amounts in this column, unless otherwise footnoted, represent obligated balances canceled for fiscal year 2002 pursuant to 31 U.S.C. 1553, changes in unfilled customer orders, accounts receivable, accounts payable, undelivered orders, unobligated balances and adjustments to borrowing and contract authority.

4. Unobligated balances for no-year or unexpired multiple year accounts are available for obligation; unobligated balances for expired fiscal year accounts are not available for obligation.

5. Subject to disposition by the administrative agency.

6. The opening balances of the following accounts have been adjusted during the current fiscal year and do not agree with last year's closing balances:

Account	Adjustment
14 X 5232 - Unobligated Balance (Unexpired)	-$935,848.49
14 X 5232 - Undelivered Orders	935,848.49
14 X 0415 - Unobligated Balance (Unexpired)	-780,281.00
14 06 0415 - Unobligated Balance (Expired)	780,281.00
14 X4523 - Unobligated Balances (Unexpired)	7,599,489.59
14 X4523 - Undelivered Orders	-7,599,489.59

7. Represents capital transfer to miscellaneous receipts.

8. The letter (T) denotes that the account by law is a trust account, but for reporting proposes is treated as other than trust.

9. This account was not certified to Treasury in accordance with Treasury certification standards which require a statement on the Year-End Closing Document that indicates the amounts have been certified in accordance with the criteria of 31 U.S.C. 1501.

10. Includes $156,524.81 which is subject to disposition by the administrative agency.

11. Includes $113,054.54 which is subject to disposition by the administrative agency.

Appropriations, Outlays, and Balances - Continued

Footnotes

Table 1 - Appropriations And Appropriation Transfers - Department Of The Interior

Department Regular	Fiscal Year	Account Symbol	Net Appropriations And Appropriations Transfers	Appropriation Amount	Net Appropriation Transfers	Department Regular Involved	Fiscal Year Involved	Accounts Involved	Amount From or To (-)
14	07	0102	108,471,298.55	108,907,432.00	-436,133.45	47	07	0110	-436,133.45
14	X	0680	804,052,986.00	206,557,455.00	597,495,531.00	11	X	5512	4,550,000.00
						14	X	4079	-26,999,000.00
						14	X	4081	-70,469,500.00
						14	X	5430	690,414,031.00
14	X	0787	33,074,500.00	34,019,500.00	-945,000.00	14	X	5174	-945,000.00
14	X	0804	15,617,710.00	9,458,761.00	6,158,949.00	11	X	5512	6,158,949.00
14	07	1036	1,656,686,465.00	1,661,145,465.00	-4,459,000.00	14	07	1049	-4,459,000.00
14	0708	1036	96,880,354.00	96,689,070.00	191,284.00	11	0708	1070	191,284.00
14	X	1039	314,185,286.00	297,482,286.00	16,703,000.00	11	X	5512	14,703,000.00
						21	07	2020	2,000,000.00
14	07	1049	85,213,249.00	80,754,249.00	4,459,000.00	14	07	1036	4,459,000.00
14	X	1110	10,674,540.00	11,750,540.00	-1,076,000.00	14	07	1125	-1,076,000.00
14	X	1125	900,637,003.00	853,355,003.00	47,282,000.00	12	X	1115	2,110,000.00
						14	X	1110	1,076,000.00
						14	X	1612	2,975,000.00
						14	X	2301	41,121,000.00
14	X	1611	627,630.00	0.00	627,630.00	14	0708	1611	627,630.00
14	0708	1611	1,020,739,370.00	1,021,367,000.00	-627,630.00	14	X	1611	-627,630.00
14	X	1612	42,324,833.00	45,299,833.00	-2,975,000.00	14	X	1125	-2,975,000.00
14	X	2100	56,590,799.00	0.00	56,590,799.00	14	0708	2100	56,256,853.00
						96	X	3122	333,946.00
14	0708	2100	1,931,966,147.00	1,988,223,000.00	-56,256,853.00	14	X	2100	-56,256,853.00
14	X	2301	230,701,718.00	271,822,718.00	-41,121,000.00	14	X	1125	-41,121,000.00
14	X	4079	26,999,000.00	0.00	26,999,000.00	14	X	0680	26,999,000.00
14	X	4081	70,469,500.00	0.00	70,469,500.00	14	X	0680	70,469,500.00
14	X	5174	945,000.00	0.00	945,000.00	14	X	0787	945,000.00
14	X	5198	-4,129,067.00	0.00	-4,129,067.00	12	X	1106	-24,525.00
						12	X	1119	-26,760.00
						13	X	5215	-289,500.00
						14	X	4316	-3,788,282.00
14	X	5430	-348,626.00	690,065,405.00	-690,414,031.00	14	X	0680	-690,414,031.00
14	X	8151	372,000,000.00	0.00	372,000,000.00	20	X	8147	525,489,378.69
						70	X	8149	-89,500,000.00
						96	X	8333	-63,989,378.69
14	X	8370	6,902,924.00	0.00	6,902,924.00	20	X	8185	6,902,924.00
Totals			7,781,282,619.55	7,376,897,717.00	404,384,902.55				404,384,902.55

Footnotes At End Of Chapter

Appropriations, Outlays, and Balances – Continued

Title	Reg	Tr From	Account Number	Sub No.	Period of Availability	Balances, Beginning Of Fiscal Year	Appropriations And Other Obligational Authority[1]	Transfers Borrowings And Investment (Net)[2]	Outlays (Net)	Balances Withdrawn And Other Transactions[3]	Balances, End Of Fiscal Year[4]
Department Of Justice											
General Administration											
General Fund Accounts											
Salaries And Expenses, General Administration, Justice											
Fund Resources:											
Undisbursed Funds	15		0129		2007-2009		1,500,000.00				1,500,000.00
					2007-2008		1,000,000.00				1,000,000.00
					2006-2008	1,500,000.00			597,307.86		902,692.14
					2007		134,332,000.00		112,313,865.14		22,018,134.86
					2006-2007	996,727.51			5,023,087.63		[5]-4,026,360.12
					2005-2007	1,500,000.00			1,082,127.18		417,872.82
					2006	30,627,818.42		5,000.00	23,264,115.36		7,368,703.06
					2005-2006	12,446.08			8,171.00		4,275.08
					2004-2006	-16,967,920.07			-10,407,702.99		[5]-6,560,217.08
					2005	7,090,679.66			1,450,549.74		5,640,129.92
					2003-2005	7,430.43					7,430.43
					2004	2,843,056.71			-700,055.38		3,543,112.09
					2003-2004	1,555,635.89					1,555,635.89
					2002-2004	12,452.70					12,452.70
					2003	1,722,278.73		-1,000,000.00	-13,942.21		736,220.94
					2001-2003	22,301.24					22,301.24
					2002	745,014.00		-787,962.75	-42,948.75		
					2001-2002	316.15		-316.15			
					2000-2002	31,928.48		-31,928.48			
					No Year	9,593,235.45			3,885,969.29		5,707,266.16
Funds Held Outside The Treasury					2006	5,000.00		-5,000.00			
Accounts Receivable						35,155,965.53				12,072,759.77	23,083,205.76
Unfilled Customer Orders						[6]26,020,154.88				11,777,186.55	14,242,968.33
Fund Equities:											
Unobligated Balances (Expired)						[6]-20,939,036.85				3,505,770.05	-24,444,806.90
Unobligated Balances (Unexpired)						-12,304,626.47				-4,941,832.90	-7,362,793.57
Accounts Payable						-30,188,739.72				-7,094,526.80	-23,094,212.92
Undelivered Orders						-39,042,118.75				-16,768,107.92	-22,274,010.83
Subtotal	15		0129			-0-	136,832,000.00	-1,820,207.38	136,460,543.87	-1,448,751.25	-0-
Couterterrorism Fund, General Administration, Justice											
Fund Resources:											
Undisbursed Funds	15		0130		No Year	12,208,302.81			2,000,000.00		10,208,302.81
Fund Equities:											
Unobligated Balances (Unexpired)						-12,208,302.81				-2,000,000.00	-10,208,302.81
Subtotal	15		0130			-0-			2,000,000.00	-2,000,000.00	-0-
Narrowband Communications, General Administration, Justice											
Fund Resources:											
Undisbursed Funds	15		0132		2007-2008		95,230,908.00		37,365,087.46		57,865,820.54
					2006-2007	77,083,886.95			51,224,809.01		25,859,077.94
					2005-2006	17,029,057.67			10,953,867.01		6,075,190.66
					2004-2005	8,812,997.52			3,332,277.81		5,480,719.71

Appropriations, Outlays, and Balances - Continued

Appropriation or Fund Account — Title	Dept Reg	Dept Tr From	Account Number	Sub No.	Period of Availability	Balances, Beginning Of Fiscal Year	Appropriations And Other Obligational Authority[1]	Transfers Borrowings And Investment (Net)[2]	Outlays (Net)	Balances Withdrawn And Other Transactions[3]	Balances, End Of Fiscal Year[4]
					2003-2004	6,945,795.87			2,614,415.95		4,331,379.92
					No Year	17,185,333.55	800,000.00		4,851,558.42		13,133,775.13
Accounts Receivable						2,029,159.31				2,029,159.31	6,930,174.33
Unfilled Customer Orders						3,458,039.13				-3,472,135.20	
Fund Equities:											
Unobligated Balances (Expired)						-7,646,691.91				7,360,312.68	-15,007,004.59
Unobligated Balances (Unexpired)						-9,639,577.69				4,367,462.55	-14,007,040.24
Accounts Payable						-12,017,857.48				-6,173,613.83	-5,844,243.65
Undelivered Orders						-103,240,142.92				-18,422,293.17	-84,817,849.75
Subtotal	15		0132			-0-	96,030,908.00		110,342,015.66	-14,311,107.66	-0-
Joint Automated Booking System, General Administration, Department Of Justice											
Fund Resources:											
Undisbursed Funds	15		0134		2005-2006	2,170,128.73			1,969,462.45		200,666.28
					2004-2005	208,554.04			-17,333.48		225,887.52
					2003-2004	-165,307.60			216,261.45		[5]5,381,569.05
					No Year	89,275,020.48	123,559,000.00		91,628,839.58		121,205,180.90
Accounts Receivable						8,451,514.57				-2,519,479.61	10,970,994.18
Unfilled Customer Orders						12,443,204.76				-9,627,230.35	22,070,435.11
Fund Equities:											
Unobligated Balances (Expired)						-264,838.52				81,369.88	-346,208.40
Unobligated Balances (Unexpired)						-40,640,085.30				-28,879,129.71	-11,760,955.59
Accounts Payable						-19,090,604.08				14,375,643.54	-33,466,247.62
Undelivered Orders						-52,387,587.08				56,330,596.25	-108,718,183.33
Subtotal	15		0134			-0-	123,559,000.00		93,797,230.00	29,761,770.00	-0-
Detention Trustee, General Administration, Justice											
Fund Resources:											
Undisbursed Funds	15		0136		No Year	192,666,155.50	1,225,816,000.00		1,155,845,279.14		262,636,876.36
Accounts Receivable						13,513,886.68				-221,226.87	13,735,113.55
Unfilled Customer Orders						2,480,813.50				705,560.50	1,775,253.00
Fund Equities:											
Unobligated Balances (Unexpired)						-85,576,065.12				65,718,217.65	-151,294,282.77
Accounts Payable						-101,591,559.19				5,277,822.05	-106,869,381.24
Undelivered Orders						-21,493,231.37				-1,509,652.47	-19,983,578.90
Subtotal	15		0136			-0-	1,225,816,000.00		1,155,845,279.14	69,970,720.86	-0-
Legal Activities Office Automation, Department Of Justice											
Fund Resources:											
Undisbursed Funds	15		0137		2005-2006	15,387,686.84			14,031,067.61		1,356,619.23
					2004-2005	569,827.00			292,934.45		276,892.55
					2003-2004	26,659.08			1,206.94		25,452.14
					No Year	1,764,306.89			61,631.62		1,702,675.27
Fund Equities:											
Unobligated Balances (Expired)						-394,407.77				120,694.75	-515,102.52
Unobligated Balances (Unexpired)						-1,610,727.54				-1,260,963.34	-349,764.20
Accounts Payable						-4,175,658.78				-3,292,382.21	-883,276.57
Undelivered Orders						-11,567,685.72				-9,954,189.82	-1,613,495.90
Subtotal	15		0137			-0-			14,386,840.62	-14,386,840.62	-0-

Footnotes At End Of Chapter

Appropriations, Outlays, and Balances – Continued

Appropriation or Fund Account Title	Period of Availability	Reg	Tr From	Account Number	Sub No.	Balances, Beginning Of Fiscal Year	Appropriations And Other Obligational Authority[1]	Transfers Borrowings And Investment (Net)[2]	Outlays (Net)	Balances Withdrawn And Other Transactions[3]	Balances, End Of Fiscal Year[4]
Integrated Automated Fingerprint Identification System, Justice											
Fund Resources:											
Undisbursed Funds	2005-2006	15		0138		1,402,194.62			1,131,405.07		270,789.55
	2004-2005					2,651.85					2,651.85
	2003-2004					80,740.18					80,740.18
Fund Equities:											
Unobligated Balances (Expired)						-195,245.47				148,534.46	-343,779.93
Accounts Payable						-1,059,743.10				-1,049,341.45	-10,401.65
Undelivered Orders						-230,598.08				-230,598.08	-0-
Subtotal		15		0138		-0-			1,131,405.07	-1,131,405.07	-0-
Telecommunications Carrier Compliance Fund, Federal Bureau Of Investigation, Justice											
Fund Resources:											
Undisbursed Funds	No Year	15		0202		41,154,187.02	-39,000,000.00		849,150.00		1,305,037.02
Fund Equities:											
Unobligated Balances (Unexpired)						-40,299,937.02				-38,994,900.00	-1,305,037.02
Undelivered Orders						-854,250.00				-854,250.00	-0-
Subtotal		15		0202		-0-	-39,000,000.00		849,150.00	-39,849,150.00	-0-
Office Of Inspector General, Justice											
Fund Resources:											
Undisbursed Funds	2007	15		0328		8,025,052.89	70,603,000.00	2,000.00	63,410,708.30		7,194,291.70
	2006					1,564,168.43			6,531,008.63		1,494,044.26
	2005					411,143.42		-2,430.00	456,743.78		1,104,994.65
	2004					73,599.50			10,827.28		400,316.14
	2003-2004					601,464.04					73,599.50
	2003					6,685.93			-860.00		602,324.04
	2002-2003					86,688.45		-86,190.59	497.86		6,685.93
	2002					2,142.00		-2,142.00			
Funds Held Outside The Treasury	No Year						500,000.00	-2,000.00			500,000.00
	2007							2,430.00			[5]2,000.00
	2005										2,500.00
Accounts Receivable						3,646,082.00				-414,435.00	4,060,517.00
Unfilled Customer Orders						3,153,103.00				-1,290,209.00	4,443,312.00
Fund Equities:											
Unobligated Balances (Expired)						-2,350,581.06				2,222,596.54	-4,573,177.60
Unobligated Balances (Unexpired)										500,000.00	-500,000.00
Accounts Payable						-9,506,168.89				-2,105,602.84	-7,400,566.05
Undelivered Orders						-5,713,449.71				1,693,391.86	-7,406,841.57
Subtotal		15		0328		-0-	71,103,000.00	-88,332.59	70,408,925.85	605,741.56	-0-
Administrative Review And Appeals, General Administration, Justice											
Fund Resources:											
Undisbursed Funds	2007	15		0339		9,000,000.00	229,142,000.00		196,055,251.11		33,086,748.89
	2006-2007					27,999,513.71			6,121,480.83		2,878,519.17
	2006					1,515,356.78			25,189,166.46		2,810,347.25
	2005					188,777.94			185,278.33		1,330,078.45
	2004					1,135,712.37			112.17		188,665.77
	2003					2,160,604.45		-379,795.78	-5,758.13		1,141,470.50
	2002								1,780,808.67		

Appropriations, Outlays, and Balances - Continued

Appropriation or Fund Account — Title	Period of Availability	Reg (Dept)	Tr From	Account Number	Sub No.	Balances, Beginning Of Fiscal Year	Appropriations And Other Obligational Authority[1]	Transfers Borrowings And Investment (Net)[2]	Outlays (Net)	Balances Withdrawn And Other Transactions[3]	Balances, End Of Fiscal Year[4]
Undisbursed Funds	No Year					47,041.88			46,988.80		53.08
Accounts Receivable						299,675.25				-277,425.44	577,100.69
Unfilled Customer Orders						2,390,530.24				291,966.59	2,098,563.65
Fund Equities:											
Unobligated Balances (Expired)						-3,004,202.16				1,975,860.15	-4,980,062.31
Unobligated Balances (Unexpired)						-9,001,616.96				-9,001,563.88	-53.08
Accounts Payable						-22,579,900.07				1,295,268.35	-23,875,168.42
Undelivered Orders						-10,151,493.43				5,104,770.21	-15,256,263.64
Subtotal		15		0339		-0-	229,142,000.00	-379,795.78	229,373,328.24	-611,124.02	-0-
Intragovernmental Funds											
Working Capital Fund, Department Of Justice											
Fund Resources:											
Undisbursed Funds	No Year					442,706,175.27			67,390,674.53		431,836,754.84
Accounts Receivable						195,036,978.30				1,633,824.60	193,403,153.70
Unfilled Customer Orders						63,617,466.30				39,138,965.71	24,478,500.59
Fund Equities:											
Unobligated Balances (Unexpired)						-264,042,206.88				-57,867,469.60	-206,174,737.28
Accounts Payable						-137,441,975.86				14,531,861.00	-151,973,836.86
Undelivered Orders						-299,876,437.13				-8,306,602.14	-291,569,834.99
Subtotal		15		4526		-0-	-2,500,000.00	59,021,254.10	67,390,674.53	-10,869,420.43	-0-
Trust Fund Accounts											
Justice Gift Fund, Department Of Justice											
Fund Resources:											
Undisbursed Funds	No Year					27,279.28			3,935.25		23,344.03
Fund Equities:											
Unobligated Balances (Unexpired)						-27,279.28				-25,000.00	-2,279.28
Accounts Payable						-0-				21,064.75	-21,064.75
Subtotal		15		8305		-0-			3,935.25	-3,935.25	-0-
Violent Crime Reduction Programs, Administrative Review And Appeals, General Administration, Justice											
Fund Resources:											
Undisbursed Funds	No Year					50,302.38			45,741.34		4,561.04
Fund Equities:											
Unobligated Balances (Unexpired)						-4,038.96				-3,961.49	-77.47
Accounts Payable						-29,623.10				-27,498.25	-2,124.85
Undelivered Orders						-16,640.32				-14,281.60	-2,358.72
Subtotal		15		8608		-0-			45,741.34	-45,741.34	-0-
Total, General Administration							1,840,982,908.00	56,732,918.35	1,882,035,069.57	15,680,756.78	

Footnotes At End Of Chapter

Appropriations, Outlays, and Balances – Continued

Appropriation or Fund Account: Title	Account Symbol: Period of Availability	Dept: Reg	Dept: Tr From	Account Number	Sub No.	Balances, Beginning Of Fiscal Year	Appropriations And Other Obligational Authority[1]	Transfers Borrowings And Investment (Net)[2]	Outlays (Net)	Balances Withdrawn And Other Transactions[3]	Balances, End Of Fiscal Year[4]
United States Parole Commission											
General Fund Accounts											
Salaries And Expenses, United States Parole Commission, Justice											
Fund Resources:											
Undisbursed Funds	2007	15		1061			11,509,000.00		9,959,049.48		1,549,950.52
	2006					1,147,835.24			956,396.87		191,438.37
	2005					72,976.00			5,599.43		67,376.57
	2004					31,084.92			2,943.81		28,141.11
	2003					68,795.96					68,795.96
	2002					12,436.49		-12,436.49			-0-
Fund Equities:											
Unobligated Balances (Expired)						-376,172.93				-23,916.47	-352,256.46
Accounts Payable						-480,179.48				406,110.01	-886,289.49
Undelivered Orders						-476,776.20				190,380.38	-667,156.58
						-0-					
Subtotal		15		1061		-0-	11,509,000.00	-12,436.49	10,923,989.59	572,573.92	
Total, United States Parole Commission							11,509,000.00	-12,436.49	10,923,989.59	572,573.92	
Legal Activities And U.S. Marshals											
General Fund Accounts											
Salaries And Expenses, Foreign Claims Settlement Commission, Justice											
Fund Resources:											
Undisbursed Funds	2007	15		0100			1,561,000.00		1,190,550.94		370,449.06
	2006					254,241.73			117,869.08		136,372.65
	2005					8,859.78			-140.22		9,000.00
	2004					77,153.06					77,153.06
	2003					71,676.64					71,676.64
	2002					213,999.51		-213,999.51			-0-
Fund Equities:											
Unobligated Balances (Expired)						-520,102.81				-139,597.52	-380,505.29
Accounts Payable						-105,827.91				32,290.79	-138,118.70
Undelivered Orders										146,027.42	-146,027.42
Subtotal		15		0100		-0-	1,561,000.00	-213,999.51	1,308,279.80	38,720.69	
Payment Of Vietnam And U.S.S. Pueblo Prisoner Of War Claims, Foreign Claims Settlement Commission, Justice											
Fund Resources:											
Undisbursed Funds	No Year	15		0104		17,970.99					17,970.99
Fund Equities:											
Unobligated Balances (Unexpired)						-17,970.99					-17,970.99
Subtotal		15		0104		-0-					-0-
Administrative Expenses, Radiation Exposure Compensation, Justice											
Fund Resources:											
Undisbursed Funds	2002	15		0105		263.30		-263.30			-0-
Fund Equities:											
Unobligated Balances (Expired)						-263.30				-263.30	

Appropriations, Outlays, and Balances - Continued

Appropriation or Fund Account — Title	Period of Availability	Reg	Tr From	Account Number	Sub No.	Balances, Beginning Of Fiscal Year	Appropriations And Other Obligational Authority[1]	Transfers Borrowings And Investment (Net)[2]	Outlays (Net)	Balances Withdrawn And Other Transactions[3]	Balances, End Of Fiscal Year[4]
Salaries And Expenses, General Legal Activities, Justice											
Fund Resources:											
Undisbursed Funds	Subtotal	15		0105		-0-		-263.30		-263.30	-0-
	2007-2008	15		0128			1,648,000.00		1,648,000.00		36,317,072.86
	2007						673,154,000.00		636,836,927.14		4,289,446.68
	2006-2007					10,468,730.63			6,179,283.95		22,874,829.29
	2006					52,148,230.04		-1,900,000.00	27,373,400.75		150,804.14
	2005-2006					1,027,623.32			876,819.18		1,672,596.27
	2005					460,082.10			-1,212,514.17		2,162,479.82
	2004					6,830,071.66		-1,240,000.00	3,427,591.84		1,489,870.33
	2003					994,392.52		-380,000.00	-875,477.81		442,489.12
	2002-2003					445,094.92			2,605.80		
	2002					1,551,122.01		-2,069,471.18	-518,349.17		
	2001-2002					324,447.71		-324,785.54	-337.83		
	No Year					23,338,691.31	4,000,000.00	5,555,964.61	8,634,978.33		24,259,677.59
Accounts Receivable						139,188,457.45				-10,229,890.80	149,418,348.25
Unfilled Customer Orders						80,548,196.33				8,768,825.69	71,779,370.64
Fund Equities:											
Unobligated Balances (Expired)						-11,288,745.27				2,294,117.69	-13,582,862.96
Unobligated Balances (Unexpired)						-12,927,177.48				-5,377,034.03	-7,550,143.45
Accounts Payable						-163,060,399.38				-6,618,652.85	-156,441,746.53
Undelivered Orders						-130,048,817.87				7,233,414.18	-137,282,232.05
	Subtotal	15		0128		-0-	678,802,000.00	-358,292.11	682,372,928.01	-3,929,220.12	-0-
Construction, United States Marshals Service, Justice											
Fund Resources:											
Undisbursed Funds	2004-2006	15		0133		10,100,902.11			2,108,177.23		7,992,724.88
	No Year					31,953,317.01	6,846,000.00		4,103,449.14		34,695,867.87
Fund Equities:											
Unobligated Balances (Expired)						-35,514.44				474,829.06	-510,343.50
Unobligated Balances (Unexpired)						-14,240,913.80				-9,308,841.67	-4,932,072.13
Accounts Payable						-513,426.93				-2,350,664.20	1,837,237.27
Undelivered Orders						-27,264,363.95				11,819,050.44	-39,083,414.39
	Subtotal	15		0133		-0-	6,846,000.00		6,211,626.37	634,373.63	-0-
Fees And Expenses Of Witnesses, Justice											
Fund Resources:											
Undisbursed Funds	No Year	15		0311		240,563,554.26	168,300,000.00		161,584,635.23		247,278,919.03
Fund Equities:											
Unobligated Balances (Unexpired)						-96,231,814.72				-5,562,023.21	-90,669,791.51
Accounts Payable						-18,181,555.47				3,258,795.36	-21,440,350.83
Undelivered Orders						-126,150,184.07				9,018,592.62	-135,168,776.69
	Subtotal	15		0311		-0-	168,300,000.00		161,584,635.23	6,715,364.77	-0-
Salaries And Expenses, Antitrust Division, Justice											
Fund Resources:											
Undisbursed Funds	2003	15		0319		10,260,299.12					10,260,299.12
	2002					15,750,706.00				15,750,706.00	
	No Year					22,686,673.38	18,819,000.00		-7,973,324.60	10,505,620.13	49,478,997.98
Accounts Receivable						10,604,386.16				10,505,620.13	98,766.03
Unfilled Customer Orders						46,150.46				46,150.46	

Footnotes At End Of Chapter

Appropriations, Outlays, and Balances – Continued

Appropriation or Fund Account: Title	Period of Availability	Dept Reg	Dept Tr From	Account Number	Sub No.	Balances, Beginning Of Fiscal Year	Appropriations And Other Obligational Authority[1]	Transfers Borrowings And Investment (Net)[2]	Outlays (Net)	Balances Withdrawn And Other Transactions[3]	Balances, End Of Fiscal Year[4]
Salaries And Expenses, Antitrust Division, Justice - Continued											
Fund Equities:											
Unobligated Balances (Expired)						-26,011,005.12				-15,750,706.00	-10,260,299.12
Unobligated Balances (Unexpired)						-9,402,441.32				9,313,088.98	-18,715,530.30
Accounts Payable						-14,234,569.19				4,855,513.91	-19,090,083.10
Undelivered Orders						-9,700,199.49				2,071,951.12	-11,772,150.61
Subtotal		15		0319		-0-	18,319,000.00		-7,973,324.60	26,792,324.60	-0-
Salaries And Expenses, United States Attorneys, Justice											
Fund Resources:											
Undisbursed Funds:	2007-2008	15		0322			6,301,762.00				6,301,762.00
	2007						1,654,886,000.00		1,478,353,491.50		176,532,508.50
	2006-2007					12,851,717.26			8,851,697.80		4,000,019.46
	2006					168,597,997.64			130,524,997.23		38,073,000.41
	2005-2006					5,000.09			0.09		5,000.00
	2005					9,323,163.81			3,027,632.40		6,295,531.41
	2004-2005					3,761.71			-1,323.48		5,085.19
	2004					2,961,214.04			281,432.80		2,679,781.24
	2003-2004					430,258.75					430,258.75
	2003					3,931,788.46			271,672.93		3,660,115.53
	2002-2003					74,275.00					74,275.00
	2002					2,071,446.46		-968,623.84	1,102,822.62		
	2001-2002					301,551.93		-301,785.48	-233.55		
	No Year					37,291,214.98		950,000.00	11,379,962.75		26,861,252.23
Accounts Receivable						42,984,256.24				-27,278,047.90	70,262,304.14
Unfilled Customer Orders						7,005,859.63				142,200.94	6,863,658.69
Fund Equities:											
Unobligated Balances (Expired)						-20,093,089.80				18,914,062.36	-39,007,152.16
Unobligated Balances (Unexpired)						-38,982,862.48				-23,362,778.94	-15,620,083.54
Accounts Payable						-156,686,287.05				-4,079,182.55	-152,607,104.50
Undelivered Orders						-72,071,266.67				62,738,945.68	-134,810,212.35
Subtotal		15		0322		-0-	1,661,187,762.00	-320,409.32	1,633,792,153.09	27,075,199.59	-0-
Salaries And Expenses, United States Marshals Service, Justice											
Fund Resources:											
Undisbursed Funds:	2007-2008	15		0324			7,438,103.00		243,339.25		7,194,763.75
	2007						795,386,273.00		749,796,397.18		45,589,875.82
	2006-2007					1,372,134.44			324,295.68		1,047,838.76
	2006					48,666,032.10			34,978,588.24		13,687,443.86
	2005-2006					15,341,158.55			8,138,501.38		7,202,657.17
	2005					5,342,590.25			1,260,500.13		4,082,090.12
	2004-2005					6,679,730.24			902,237.23		5,777,493.01
	2004					2,816,301.31			-417,632.45		3,233,933.76
	2003-2004					788,726.19			2,672.00		786,054.19
	2003					5,757,702.34			389,846.80		5,367,855.54
	2002					3,725,446.00		-3,149,659.94	575,786.06		
	No Year					136,609,362.21	16,000,000.00	1,900,000.00	-352,321.38		154,861,683.59
Accounts Receivable						138,569,552.90				3,619,774.53	134,949,778.37
Unfilled Customer Orders						35,989,401.06				-687,849.19	36,677,250.25
Fund Equities:											
Unobligated Balances (Expired)						-2,632,092.10				18,293,005.09	-20,925,097.19

Appropriations, Outlays, and Balances - Continued

Appropriation or Fund Account — Title	Period of Availability	Dept Reg	Dept Tr From	Account Number	Sub No.	Balances, Beginning Of Fiscal Year	Appropriations And Other Obligational Authority[1]	Transfers Borrowings And Investment (Net)[2]	Outlays (Net)	Balances Withdrawn And Other Transactions[3]	Balances, End Of Fiscal Year[4]
Unobligated Balances (Unexpired)						-32,304,101.12				7,015,056.86	-39,319,157.98
Accounts Payable						-230,073,844.59				19,597,584.22	-249,671,428.81
Undelivered Orders						-136,648,099.78				-26,105,065.57	-110,543,034.21
	Subtotal	15		0324		-0-	818,824,376.00	-1,249,659.94	795,842,210.12	21,732,505.94	-0-
Independent Counsel, Justice											
Fund Resources:											
Undisbursed Funds	2007	15		0327			9,500,000.00		911,164.54		8,588,835.46
	2006					8,150,924.21			44,308.25		8,106,615.96
	2005					749,869.99					749,869.99
	2004					6,323,761.82					6,323,761.82
	2003					8,250,000.00					8,250,000.00
	2002					4,989,871.92				4,989,871.92	
Fund Equities:											
Unobligated Balances (Expired)						-28,415,682.32				3,541,167.03	-31,956,849.35
Accounts Payable						-42,721.03				-22,427.15	-20,293.88
Undelivered Orders						-6,024.59				35,915.41	-41,940.00
	Subtotal	15		0327		-0-	9,500,000.00		955,472.79	8,544,527.21	-0-
Civil Liberties Public Education Fund, Justice											
Fund Resources:											
Undisbursed Funds	No Year	15		0329		48,491.04					48,491.04
Fund Equities:											
Unobligated Balances (Unexpired)						-48,491.04					-48,491.04
	Subtotal	15		0329		-48,491.04					-48,491.04
September 11th Victim Compensation, General Legal Activities, Justice											
Fund Resources:											
Undisbursed Funds	No Year	15		0340		200,000.00			200,000.00		
Fund Equities:											
Accounts Payable						-200,000.00				-200,000.00	
	Subtotal	15		0340		-0-			200,000.00	-200,000.00	-0-
Salaries And Expenses, Community Relations Service, Justice											
Fund Resources:											
Undisbursed Funds	2007	15		0500			10,221,000.00		8,390,940.02		1,830,059.98
	2006					769,293.48			772,357.11		[5]3,063.63
	2005					199,044.51			-135,768.73		334,813.24
	2004					405,453.59			7,750.45		397,703.14
	2003					119,262.29			328.30		118,933.99
	2002					116,206.43		-116,206.43			
Accounts Receivable						289,638.00				173,863.00	115,775.00
Unfilled Customer Orders						99,225.00				99,225.00	99,225.00
Fund Equities:											
Unobligated Balances (Expired)						-841,433.21				633,490.43	-1,474,923.64
Accounts Payable						-937,054.47				-55,227.77	-881,826.70
Undelivered Orders						-219,635.62				217,835.76	-437,471.38
	Subtotal	15		0500		-0-	10,221,000.00	-116,206.43	9,035,607.15	1,069,186.42	-0-
Federal Prisoner Detention, Justice											
Fund Resources:											
Undisbursed Funds	No Year	15		1020		4,073,683.92			3,006,965.98		1,066,717.94

Footnotes At End Of Chapter

Appropriations, Outlays, and Balances – Continued

Appropriation or Fund Account: Title	Period of Availability	Dept Reg	Tr From	Account Number	Sub No.	Balances, Beginning Of Fiscal Year	Appropriations And Other Obligational Authority[1]	Transfers Borrowings And Investment (Net)[2]	Outlays (Net)	Balances Withdrawn And Other Transactions[3]	Balances, End Of Fiscal Year[4]
Federal Prisoner Detention, Justice - Continued											
Fund Equities:											
Unobligated Balances (Unexpired)						-1,019,041.36				36,131.82	-1,055,173.18
Accounts Payable						-990.76				-880.00	-110.76
Undelivered Orders						-3,053,651.80				-3,042,217.80	-11,434.00
Subtotal		15		1020		-0-			3,006,965.98	-3,006,965.98	-0-
Special Fund Accounts											
Assets Forfeiture Fund, Justice											
Fund Resources:											
Undisbursed Funds	No Year	15		5042		411,870,901.04	1,589,355,514.06	-643,163,927.41	1,051,959,935.61		306,102,552.08
Unrealized Discount On Investments						-10,990,655.47		-513,072.59			-11,503,728.06
Investments In Public Debt Securities						686,476,000.00		643,677,000.00			1,330,153,000.00
Accounts Receivable						304,319.07				-2,387,295.67	2,691,614.74
Unfilled Customer Orders						929,757.00				-286,322.50	1,216,079.50
Fund Equities:											
Unobligated Balances (Unexpired)						-500,716,833.86				67,093,103.44	-567,809,937.30
Accounts Payable						-432,474,308.21				458,253,849.18	-890,728,157.39
Undelivered Orders						-155,399,179.57				14,722,244.00	-170,121,423.57
Subtotal		15		5042		-0-	1,589,355,514.06		1,051,959,935.61	537,395,578.45	-0-
United States Trustee System Fund, Justice											
Fund Resources:											
Undisbursed Funds	No Year	15		5073		13,501,218.81	131,190,828.05	80,262,890.79	215,731,310.49		9,223,627.16
Unrealized Discount On Investments						-1,333,901.97		330,109.21			-1,003,792.76
Investments In Public Debt Securities						245,022,000.00		-80,593,000.00			164,429,000.00
Accounts Receivable						12,564.31				-11,138.80	23,703.11
Fund Equities:											
Unobligated Balances (Unexpired)						-225,229,364.06				-81,171,270.47	-144,058,093.59
Accounts Payable						-19,315,639.52				4,347,822.66	-23,663,462.18
Undelivered Orders						-12,656,877.57				-7,705,895.83	-4,950,981.74
Subtotal		15		5073		-0-	131,190,828.05		215,731,310.49	-84,540,482.44	-0-
Intragovernmental Funds											
Justice Prisoner And Alien Transportation System Fund, United States Marshals Service, Justice											
Fund Resources:											
Undisbursed Funds	No Year	15		4575		39,721,445.71			-16,443,531.78		56,164,977.49
Accounts Receivable						10,804,734.42				2,250,343.47	8,554,390.95
Fund Equities:											
Unobligated Balances (Unexpired)						-31,702,400.19				-13,068,213.09	-18,634,187.10
Accounts Payable						-16,479,122.20				11,119,170.25	-27,598,292.45
Undelivered Orders						-2,344,657.74				16,142,231.15	-18,486,888.89
Subtotal		15		4575		-0-			-16,443,531.78	16,443,531.78	-0-

Appropriations, Outlays, and Balances - Continued

Appropriation or Fund Account — Title	Period of Availability	Dept Reg	Tr From	Account Number	Sub No.	Balances, Beginning Of Fiscal Year	Appropriations And Other Obligational Authority[1]	Transfers Borrowings And Investment (Net)[2]	Outlays (Net)	Balances Withdrawn And Other Transactions[3]	Balances, End Of Fiscal Year[4]
Trust Fund Accounts											
Violent Crime Reduction Programs, General Legal Activities, Justice											
Fund Resources:											
Undisbursed Funds	No Year	15		8595		236,564.86			6,596.42		229,968.44
Accounts Receivable						6,565.09					6,565.09
Fund Equities:											
Unobligated Balances (Unexpired)						-219,149.92				-6,596.42	-212,553.50
Accounts Payable						-23,980.03					-23,980.03
Subtotal		15		8595		-0-			6,596.42	-6,596.42	-0-
Violent Crime Reduction Programs, United States Attorneys, Justice											
Fund Resources:											
Undisbursed Funds	No Year	15		8596		850,341.43			522,685.71		327,655.72
Fund Equities:											
Unobligated Balances (Unexpired)						-315,182.57				-4,471.03	-310,711.54
Accounts Payable						-535,278.74				-518,214.68	-17,064.06
Undelivered Orders						119.88					119.88
Subtotal		15		8596		-0-			522,685.71	-522,685.71	-0-
Violent Crime Reduction Programs, United States Marshals Service, Justice											
Fund Resources:											
Undisbursed Funds	No Year	15		8603		147,412.46					147,412.46
Fund Equities:											
Unobligated Balances (Unexpired)						-0.46				147,412.46	-147,412.46
Undelivered Orders						-147,412.00				-147,412.00	-0-
Subtotal		15		8603		-0-					-0-
Total, Legal Activities And U.S. Marshals							5,094,607,480.11	-2,258,830.61	4,538,113,550.39	554,235,099.11	
National Security Division											
General Fund Accounts											
Salaries And Expenses, National Security Division, Justice											
Fund Resources:											
Undisbursed Funds	2007-2008	15		1300			1,736,000.00		105,759.31		1,630,240.69
	2007						66,970,000.00		40,678,494.59		26,291,505.41
Accounts Receivable										-27,500.00	27,500.00
Fund Equities:											
Unobligated Balances (Expired)										3,924,702.12	-3,924,702.12
Unobligated Balances (Unexpired)										1,579,522.63	-1,579,522.63
Accounts Payable										7,197,176.77	-7,197,176.77
Undelivered Orders										15,247,844.58	-15,247,844.58
Subtotal		15		1300		-0-	68,706,000.00		40,784,253.90	27,921,746.10	-0-
Total, National Security Division							68,706,000.00		40,784,253.90	27,921,746.10	

Footnotes At End Of Chapter

Appropriations, Outlays, and Balances – Continued

Appropriation or Fund Account — Title	Period of Availability	Dept Reg	Tr From	Account Number	Sub No.	Balances, Beginning Of Fiscal Year	Appropriations And Other Obligational Authority[1]	Transfers Borrowings And Investment (Net)[2]	Outlays (Net)	Balances Withdrawn And Other Transactions[3]	Balances, End Of Fiscal Year[4]
Radiation Exposure Compensation											
General Fund Accounts											
Payment To The Radiation Exposure Compensation Trust Fund, Justice											
Fund Resources:											
Undisbursed Funds	2007	15		0333		-------	73,650,000.00	-------	73,650,000.00	-------	-------
Trust Fund Accounts											
Radiation Exposure Compensation Trust Fund											
Fund Resources:											
Undisbursed Funds	No Year	15		8116		17,012,894.28	73,650,000.00	-------	79,063,510.25	-------	11,599,384.03
Fund Equities:											
Unobligated Balances (Unexpired)						-6,800,366.67				1,542,805.25	-8,343,171.92
Accounts Payable						-8,873,378.83				-5,617,166.72	-3,256,212.11
Undelivered Orders						-1,339,148.78				-1,339,148.78	-0-
Subtotal		15		8116		-0-	73,650,000.00	-------	79,063,510.25	-5,413,510.25	-0-
Total, Radiation Exposure Compensation							147,300,000.00	-------	152,713,510.25	-5,413,510.25	
Interagency Law Enforcement											
General Fund Accounts											
Interagency Drug Enforcement, Drug Enforcement Administration											
Fund Resources:											
Undisbursed Funds:											
	2007	15		0323		60,256,010.79	446,983,669.00	-------	406,425,922.29	-------	40,557,746.71
	2006					190,548.28			60,065,462.51	-------	190,548.28
	2005					312,436.43			66,798.59	-------	245,637.84
	2004-2005					11,268,743.64			207,229.88	-------	11,061,513.76
	2004					1,006,433.63			250,595.46	-------	755,838.17
	2003					176,718.00			-------	-------	176,718.00
	2002					1.57		-1.57			
	No Year					72,017,466.43	50,000,000.00		50,839,166.62	-------	71,178,299.81
Fund Equities:											
Unobligated Balances (Expired)						-12,295,444.44				-55,736.67	-12,239,707.77
Unobligated Balances (Unexpired)						-16,799,273.80				-7,647,697.93	-9,151,575.87
Accounts Payable						-85,016,547.69				-37,240,452.26	-47,776,095.43
Undelivered Orders						-30,926,544.56				24,072,378.94	-54,998,923.50
Subtotal		15		0323		-0-	496,983,669.00	-1.57	517,855,175.35	-20,871,507.92	-0-
Total, Interagency Law Enforcement							496,983,669.00	-1.57	517,855,175.35	-20,871,507.92	

Appropriations, Outlays, and Balances - Continued

Appropriation or Fund Account Title	Dept Reg	Tr From	Account Number	Sub No.	Period of Availability	Balances, Beginning Of Fiscal Year	Appropriations And Other Obligational Authority[1]	Transfers Borrowings And Investment (Net)[2]	Outlays (Net)	Balances Withdrawn And Other Transactions[3]	Balances, End Of Fiscal Year[4]
Federal Bureau Of Investigation											
General Fund Accounts											
Salaries And Expenses, Federal Bureau Of Investigation											
Fund Resources:											
Undisbursed Funds	15		0200		2007-2008		251,660,613.00		354,292.06		251,306,320.94
					2007		5,985,479,732.00	-1,947,030.00	4,856,326,273.47		1,127,206,428.53
					2006-2007	89,100,208.36		-150,506.00	62,377,346.26		26,572,356.10
					2006	991,687,825.85		-59,932,170.00	629,247,932.26		302,507,723.59
					2005-2006	24,563,512.10			17,196,264.58		7,367,247.52
					2005	131,181,883.73			56,907,767.51		74,274,116.22
					2004-2005	5,051,795.54			2,992,503.47		2,059,292.07
					2004	61,898,127.70		-16,000,000.00	16,412,086.85		29,486,040.85
					2003-2004	22,653,553.19			6,127,086.15		16,526,467.04
					2002-2004	209,671.09		-209,671.09			
					2003	19,274,909.57		-8,000,000.00	6,656,421.76		4,618,487.81
					2002-2003	1,341,954.03			-150.00		1,342,104.03
					2002	7,288,721.64		-7,648,052.93	-359,331.29		
					2001-2002	306,584.88		-306,584.88			
					No Year	142,295,778.53	148,725,000.00	58,000,000.00	55,979,991.93		293,040,786.60
Funds Held Outside The Treasury					No Year	1,867,830.00		1,947,030.00 / -1,867,830.00			1,947,030.00
Accounts Receivable					2007	142,009,022.32				42,367,854.90	99,641,167.42
Unfilled Customer Orders					2006	277,550,273.69				-177,587,746.15	455,138,019.84
Fund Equities:											
Unobligated Balances (Expired)						-382,720,593.36				237,551,068.20	-620,271,661.56
Unobligated Balances (Unexpired)						-145,706,175.07				311,630,210.94	-457,336,386.01
Accounts Payable						-502,066,285.85				67,174,296.16	-569,240,582.01
Undelivered Orders						-887,788,597.94				158,396,361.04	-1,046,184,958.98
Subtotal	15		0200			-0-	6,385,865,345.00	-36,114,814.90	5,710,218,485.01	639,532,045.09	-0-
Construction, Federal Bureau Of Investigation, Justice											
Fund Resources:											
Undisbursed Funds	15		0203		2004-2006	1,886,483.52			1,118,777.10		767,706.42
					No Year	56,455,751.41	51,392,000.00		12,246,675.40		95,601,076.01
Fund Equities:											
Unobligated Balances (Expired)						-70,465.10				58,737.83	-129,202.93
Unobligated Balances (Unexpired)						-25,222,191.82				19,160,856.61	-44,383,048.43
Accounts Payable						-2,083,973.56				2,561,636.70	-4,645,610.26
Undelivered Orders						-30,965,604.45				16,245,316.36	-47,210,920.81
Subtotal	15		0203			-0-	51,392,000.00		13,365,452.50	38,026,547.50	-0-
Foreign Terrorist Tracking Task Force/Terrorist Threat Integration Center, Justice											
Fund Resources:											
Undisbursed Funds	15		0204		2004	3,721,478.68			701,874.63		3,019,604.05
					2003	1,311,841.59			-1,289,112.85		2,600,954.44
Unfilled Customer Orders						83,431.65					83,431.65

Footnotes At End Of Chapter

Appropriations, Outlays, and Balances – Continued

Appropriation or Fund Account — Title	Dept Reg	Tr From	Account Number	Sub No.	Period of Availability	Balances, Beginning Of Fiscal Year	Appropriations And Other Obligational Authority[1]	Transfers Borrowings And Investment (Net)[2]	Outlays (Net)	Balances Withdrawn And Other Transactions[3]	Balances, End Of Fiscal Year[4]
Foreign Terrorist Tracking Task Force/Terrorist Threat Integration Center, Justice - Continued											
Fund Equities:											
Unobligated Balances (Expired)						-3,001,563.71				916,572.48	-3,918,136.19
Accounts Payable						-1,217,424.37				483,451.67	-1,700,876.04
Undelivered Orders						-897,763.84				-812,785.93	-84,977.91
Subtotal	15		0204			-0-			-587,238.22	587,238.22	-0-
Trust Fund Accounts											
Violent Crime Reduction Programs, Federal Bureau Of Investigation, Justice											
Fund Resources:											
Undisbursed Funds	15		8604		No Year	2,170,447.28		1,440,724.28			729,723.00
Fund Equities:											
Unobligated Balances (Unexpired)						-1,103,552.64				-797,916.90	-305,635.74
Accounts Payable						-337,861.40				-168,128.86	-169,732.54
Undelivered Orders						-729,033.24				-474,678.52	-254,354.72
Subtotal	15		8604			-0-			1,440,724.28	-1,440,724.28	-0-
Total, Federal Bureau Of Investigation							6,437,257,345.00	-36,114,814.90	5,724,437,423.57	676,705,106.53	
Drug Enforcement Administration											
General Fund Accounts											
Salaries And Expenses, Drug Enforcement Administration											
Fund Resources:											
Undisbursed Funds	15		1100		2007-2008		27,874,861.00		-241,812.34		28,116,673.34
					2006-2008	5,000,000.00					5,000,000.00
					2007		1,744,555,041.00	-7,610,525.00	1,462,545,741.50		274,398,774.50
					2006-2007	29,233,849.13		374,026.00	19,625,044.87		9,982,830.26
					2006	196,804,717.36		-7,513,194.00	142,765,047.95		46,526,475.41
					2005-2006	7,537,846.10			5,742,793.47		1,795,052.63
					2005	27,789,610.48		-3,000,000.00	7,432,174.60		17,357,435.88
					2004-2005	6,338,163.03		-1,000,000.00	2,177,767.79		3,160,395.24
					2004	11,612,924.60		-2,000,000.00	314,256.84		9,298,667.76
					2003-2004	2,141,423.05		-1,000,000.00	145,928.49		995,494.56
					2003	5,500,227.75		-1,700,000.00	1,579,112.25		2,221,115.50
					2002-2003	532,405.36			29,881.59		502,523.77
					2002	1,945,117.13		-876,093.03	1,069,024.10		
Funds Held Outside The Treasury					No Year	23,854,921.43	74,772,000.00	18,000,000.00	13,886,062.93		102,740,858.50
					2007			7,610,525.00			7,610,525.00
					2006	7,486,806.00		-7,486,806.00			
Accounts Receivable						60,298,583.06				16,767,620.97	43,530,962.09
Unfilled Customer Orders						80,565,764.15				-7,261,425.92	87,827,190.07
Fund Equities:											
Unobligated Balances (Expired)						-19,688,061.40				23,562,843.20	-43,250,904.60
Unobligated Balances (Unexpired)						-22,485,367.31				86,569,635.84	-109,055,003.15
Accounts Payable						-168,889,389.87				-12,389,313.60	-156,500,076.27

Appropriations, Outlays, and Balances - Continued

Appropriation or Fund Account: Title	Account Symbol: Dept Reg	Tr From	Account Number	Sub No.	Period of Availability	Balances, Beginning Of Fiscal Year	Appropriations And Other Obligational Authority[1]	Transfers Borrowings And Investment (Net)[2]	Outlays (Net)	Balances Withdrawn And Other Transactions[3]	Balances, End Of Fiscal Year[4]
Undelivered Orders	15					-255,579,540.05				76,679,450.44	-332,258,990.49
Subtotal	15		1100			-0-	1,847,201,902.00	-6,202,067.03	1,657,071,024.04	183,928,810.93	-0-
Construction, Drug Enforcement Administration											
Fund Resources:											
Undisbursed Funds	15		1101		No Year	2,701,279.08			201,198.14		2,500,080.94
Fund Equities:											
Unobligated Balances (Unexpired)						-147,242.75				-147,242.75	
Accounts Payable						-922,989.81				-893,488.10	-29,501.71
Undelivered Orders						-1,631,046.52				839,532.71	-2,470,579.23
Subtotal	15		1101			-0-			201,198.14	-201,198.14	-0-
Special Fund Accounts											
Diversion Control Fee Account, Justice											
Fund Resources:											
Undisbursed Funds	15		5131		No Year	59,826,938.95	204,181,236.46		160,518,068.40		103,490,107.01
Fund Equities:											
Unobligated Balances (Unexpired)						-36,119,902.54				27,959,173.98	-64,079,076.52
Accounts Payable						-7,891,958.97				-236,536.79	-7,655,422.18
Undelivered Orders						-15,815,077.44				15,940,530.87	-31,755,608.31
Subtotal	15		5131			-0-	204,181,236.46		160,518,068.40	43,663,168.06	-0-
Trust Fund Accounts											
Violent Crime Reduction Programs, Drug Enforcement Administration, Justice											
Fund Resources:											
Undisbursed Funds	15		8602		No Year	19,148,145.39			8,101,075.70		11,047,069.69
Fund Equities:											
Unobligated Balances (Unexpired)						-2,604,759.78				-2,604,759.78	
Accounts Payable						-1,995,623.57				-1,306,150.06	-689,473.51
Undelivered Orders						-14,547,762.04				-4,190,165.86	-10,357,596.18
Subtotal	15		8602			-0-			8,101,075.70	-8,101,075.70	-0-
Total, Drug Enforcement Administration							2,051,383,138.46	-6,202,067.03	1,825,891,366.28	219,289,705.15	
Bureau Of Alcohol, Tobacco, Firearms, And Explosives											
General Fund Accounts											
Salaries And Expenses, Bureau Of Alcohol, Tobacco, Firearms And Explosives, Justice											
Fund Resources:											
Undisbursed Funds	15		0700		2007-2008		4,449,927.00		127,679.36		4,322,247.64
					2007		968,734,377.00	-2,820,271.28	828,743,780.51		137,170,325.21
					2006-2007	4,021,546.78			2,982,639.40		1,039,007.38
					2006	100,370,596.23		-2,549,228.72	83,644,320.26		14,177,047.25
					2005-2006	406,979.15			385,201.06		21,778.09
					2005	19,373,800.21			6,705,784.53		12,668,015.68

Footnotes At End Of Chapter

Appropriations, Outlays, and Balances – Continued

Appropriation or Fund Account Title	Period of Availability	Reg (Dept)	Tr From (Dept)	Account Number	Sub No.	Balances, Beginning Of Fiscal Year	Appropriations And Other Obligational Authority[1]	Transfers Borrowings And Investment (Net)[2]	Outlays (Net)	Balances Withdrawn And Other Transactions[3]	Balances, End Of Fiscal Year[4]
Salaries And Expenses, Bureau Of Alcohol, Tobacco, Firearms And Explosives, Justice - Continued											
Fund Resources: - Continued											
Undisbursed Funds - Continued											
	2004-2005					39,167.62					39,167.62
	2004					17,846,389.14			5,239,460.05		12,606,929.09
	2003-2004					610,666.68			79,585.35		531,081.33
	2003					6,436,545.65			4,044,848.80		2,391,696.85
	2002-2003					46,075.62					46,075.62
	2002					2,436,596.63		-1,944,045.94	492,550.69		
	2001-2002					21,544.98		-21,544.98			
	No Year					24,322,423.47	63,024,000.00		11,897,656.06		75,448,767.41
	2007							2,820,271.28			2,820,271.28
	2006					2,450,771.28		-2,450,771.28			
Funds Held Outside The Treasury											
Accounts Receivable						28,878,524.59				6,086,232.10	22,792,292.49
Unfilled Customer Orders						21,416,935.43				14,705,352.68	6,711,582.75
Fund Equities:											
Unobligated Balances (Expired)						-21,160,787.07				100,268.31	-21,261,055.38
Unobligated Balances (Unexpired)						-8,748,369.31				43,086,663.66	-51,835,032.97
Accounts Payable						-97,209,274.03				24,409,326.97	-121,618,601.00
Undelivered Orders						-101,560,133.05				-3,488,536.71	-98,071,596.34
Subtotal		15		0700		-0-	1,036,208,304.00	-6,965,590.92	944,343,406.07	84,899,307.01	-0-
Trust Fund Accounts											
Gang Resistance Education And Training Trust Fund, Alcohol, Tobacco, Firearms, And Explosives, Department Of Justice											
Fund Resources:											
Undisbursed Funds	No Year	15		8526		93,467.88			57,138.25		36,329.63
Fund Equities:											
Unobligated Balances (Unexpired)						-26,627.72				-15,724.81	-10,902.91
Accounts Payable						-66,840.16				-44,845.35	-21,994.81
Undelivered Orders										3,431.91	-3,431.91
Subtotal		15		8526		-0-			57,138.25	-57,138.25	-0-
Total, Bureau Of Alcohol, Tobacco, Firearms, And Explosives							1,036,208,304.00	-6,965,590.92	944,400,544.32	84,842,168.76	
Federal Prison System											
General Fund Accounts											
Buildings And Facilities, Federal Prison System, Justice											
Fund Resources:											
Undisbursed Funds	No Year	15		1003		546,534,728.74	432,425,000.00		222,023,467.05		756,936,261.69
Fund Equities:											
Unobligated Balances (Unexpired)						-363,406,397.01				-224,248,032.16	-139,158,364.85
Accounts Payable						-29,301,119.28				-272,658.92	-29,028,460.36
Undelivered Orders						-153,827,212.45				434,922,224.03	-588,749,436.48
Subtotal		15		1003		-0-	432,425,000.00		222,023,467.05	210,401,532.95	-0-

Appropriations, Outlays, and Balances - Continued

Appropriation or Fund Account — Title	Period of Availability	Dept Reg	Tr From	Account Number	Sub No.	Balances, Beginning Of Fiscal Year	Appropriations And Other Obligational Authority[1]	Transfers Borrowings And Investment (Net)[2]	Outlays (Net)	Balances Withdrawn And Other Transactions[3]	Balances, End Of Fiscal Year[4]
National Institute Of Corrections, Federal Prison System, Justice											
Fund Resources:											
Undisbursed Funds											
Fund Equities:											
Undelivered Orders	No Year	15		1004		-421.72			-421.72		
Subtotal		15		1004		421.72				421.72	-0-
									-421.72	421.72	-0-
Salaries And Expenses, Federal Prison System											
Fund Resources:											
Undisbursed Funds	2007-2008	15		1060			17,000,000.00		4,232,103.66		12,767,896.34
	2007					537,136,008.76	4,995,433,000.00	-67,703,000.00	[8]4,412,154,908.76		515,575,091.24
	2006-2007						16,000,000.00	16,000,000.00	16,000,000.00		
	2006					38,142,633.67		-15,332,500.00	479,876,717.95		41,926,790.81
	2005								13,633,533.36		24,509,100.31
	2004-2005								-57,585.13		57,585.13
	2004					18,835,565.02			3,316,296.21		15,519,268.81
	2003					11,768,804.99		-682,300.00	2,359,666.10		8,726,838.89
	2002					5,079,940.38		-4,471,659.67	608,280.71		
	No Year					2,983,222.90			807,002.74		2,176,220.16
Transfer To:											
Health And Human Services, Health Resources And Services Administration	2007	75	15	1060	3			67,000,000.00	60,922,055.66		6,077,944.34
	2006					1,496,204.52			348,196.69		1,148,007.83
	2005					838,115.06			6,060.71		832,054.35
	2004					2,591,669.32					2,591,669.32
	2003					-662,004.18		682,300.00			20,295.82
	2002					483,997.16		483,997.16			
Funds Held Outside The Treasury	2007							703,000.00			703,000.00
	2006					667,500.00		-667,500.00			
Fund Equities:											
Accounts Receivable						8,582,067.81				-181,080.09	8,763,147.90
Unfilled Customer Orders						284,082.19					284,082.19
Unobligated Balances (Expired)						-74,077,582.30				6,539,454.34	-80,617,036.64
Unobligated Balances (Unexpired)						-1,143,724.77				12,041,376.33	-13,185,101.10
Accounts Payable						-382,396,988.54				38,999,479.58	-421,396,468.12
Undelivered Orders						-170,609,511.99				-44,129,124.41	-126,480,387.58
Subtotal		15		1060		-0-	5,012,433,000.00	-4,955,656.83	4,994,207,237.42	13,270,105.75	-0-
Intragovernmental Funds											
Prison Industries Fund, Department Of Justice											
Fund Resources:											
Undisbursed Funds	No Year	15		4500		56,773,374.48		-73,000,000.00	-38,716,591.48		22,489,965.96
Investments In Public Debt Securities						321,600,000.00		73,000,000.00			394,600,000.00
Accounts Receivable						33,837,551.54				-21,192,581.88	55,030,133.42
Fund Equities:											
Unobligated Balances (Unexpired)						-116,558,036.86				48,618,826.01	-165,176,862.87
Accounts Payable						-295,652,889.16				11,290,347.35	-306,943,236.51
Subtotal		15		4500		-0-		-38,716,591.48	-38,716,591.48	38,716,591.48	-0-

Footnotes At End Of Chapter

Appropriations, Outlays, and Balances – Continued

Appropriation or Fund Account — Title	Account Symbol — Dept — Reg	Tr From	Account Number	Sub No.	Period of Availability	Balances, Beginning Of Fiscal Year	Appropriations And Other Obligational Authority[1]	Transfers Borrowings And Investment (Net)[2]	Outlays (Net)	Balances Withdrawn And Other Transactions[3]	Balances, End Of Fiscal Year[4]
Trust Fund Accounts											
Commissary Funds, Federal Prisons			8408		No Year						
Fund Resources:											
Undisbursed Funds	15					59,831,650.75			-5,014,871.13	-----	64,846,521.86
Unrealized Discount On Investments						-0.02		-0.02	-----	-----	
Accounts Receivable						1,292,685.21		0.02	-----	279,136.70	1,013,548.51
Fund Equities:											
Unobligated Balances (Unexpired)						-36,223,487.44			-----	4,176,537.97	-40,400,025.41
Accounts Payable						-15,926,151.79			-----	476,290.06	-16,402,441.85
Undelivered Orders						-8,974,696.71			-----	82,906.40	-9,057,603.11
Subtotal	15		8408			-0-			-5,014,871.13	5,014,871.13	-0-
Violent Crime Reduction Programs, Federal Prison System			8600		No Year						
Fund Resources:											
Undisbursed Funds	15					195.89			6,910.67	-----	[5] 6,714.78
Fund Equities:											
Accounts Payable						-195.89			-----	-195.89	-----
Undelivered Orders						-----			-----	-6,714.78	6,714.78
Subtotal	15		8600			-0-			6,910.67	-6,910.67	-0-
Total, Federal Prison System							5,444,858,000.00	-4,955,666.83	5,172,505,730.81	267,396,612.36	
Office Of Justice Programs											
General Fund Accounts											
Weed And Seed Program Fund, Office Of Justice Programs, Justice			0334								
Fund Resources:											
Undisbursed Funds	15				2007-2008	46,014,138.20	49,361,400.00		4,625,498.10	-----	44,735,901.90
					2006-2007	35,245,978.87	-50,000.00		21,651,673.17	-----	24,312,465.03
					2005-2006	10,312,786.13			22,587,815.86	-----	12,658,163.01
					2004-2005	5,224,435.63	-1,450,000.00		5,854,666.54	-----	4,458,119.59
					No Year				534,716.67	-----	3,239,718.96
Accounts Receivable						100,321.56				88,435.96	11,885.60
Unfilled Customer Orders						2,000.00				-35,728.47	37,728.47
Fund Equities:											
Unobligated Balances (Expired)						-637,668.45				1,433,549.08	-2,071,217.53
Unobligated Balances (Unexpired)						-2,986,804.68				708,776.76	-3,695,581.44
Accounts Payable						-12,646,275.73				-1,140,811.05	-11,505,464.68
Undelivered Orders						-80,628,911.53				-8,447,192.62	-72,181,718.91
Subtotal	15		0334			-0-	47,861,400.00		55,254,370.34	-7,392,970.34	-0-
Justice Assistance, Office Of Justice Programs			0401								
Fund Resources:											
Undisbursed Funds	15				No Year	497,708,607.05	298,416,826.00		308,731,122.60	-----	487,394,310.45
Funds Held Outside The Treasury					No Year	5,000.00				-----	5,000.00
Accounts Receivable						5,331,488.88				41,774.91	5,289,713.97
Unfilled Customer Orders						11,754,166.76				-1,087,751.36	12,841,918.12
Fund Equities:											
Unobligated Balances (Unexpired)						-40,380,404.18				-5,704,126.49	-34,676,277.69

Appropriations, Outlays, and Balances - Continued

Appropriation or Fund Account — Title	Reg	Tr From	Account Number	Sub No.	Period of Availability	Balances, Beginning Of Fiscal Year	Appropriations And Other Obligational Authority[1]	Transfers Borrowings And Investment (Net)[2]	Outlays (Net)	Balances Withdrawn And Other Transactions[3]	Balances, End Of Fiscal Year[4]
Accounts Payable						-88,369,381.61				8,920,396.92	-97,289,778.53
Undelivered Orders						-386,049,476.90				-12,484,590.58	-373,564,886.32
Subtotal	15		0401		Subtotal	-0-	298,416,826.00		308,731,122.60	-10,314,296.60	-0-
Public Safety Officers Benefits, Office Of Justice Programs, Justice											
Fund Resources:											
Undisbursed Funds	15		0403		2007		4,012,095.00		1,043,955.08		2,968,139.92
					2006	3,136,541.79			6,462.00		3,130,079.79
					2005	1,906,003.75					1,906,003.75
					No Year	4,435,630.55	46,161,132.26		42,888,990.03		7,707,772.78
Fund Equities:											
Unobligated Balances (Expired)						-5,036,083.54				2,968,139.92	-8,004,223.46
Unobligated Balances (Unexpired)						-1,059,550.95				1,463,078.22	-2,522,629.17
Accounts Payable										3,442,965.31	-3,442,965.31
Undelivered Orders						-3,382,541.60				-1,640,363.30	-1,742,178.30
Subtotal	15		0403		Subtotal	-0-	50,173,227.26		43,939,407.11	6,233,820.15	-0-
State And Local Law Enforcement Assistance, Office Of Justice Programs, Justice											
Fund Resources:											
Undisbursed Funds	15		0404		2004-2005	17,800,187.02			7,070,946.15		10,729,240.87
					2004	848,716.33			322,819.37		525,896.96
					No Year	2,563,291,467.90	1,168,662,431.00	18,491,000.00	1,328,425,399.64		2,422,019,499.26
Accounts Receivable						7,981,389.59				7,177,183.76	804,205.83
Unfilled Customer Orders						2,613,452.41				2,641,408.57	-27,956.16
Fund Equities:											
Unobligated Balances (Expired)						-54,720.02				5,696,027.91	-5,750,747.93
Unobligated Balances (Unexpired)						-452,524,592.21				72,459,194.50	-524,983,786.71
Accounts Payable						-295,389,847.95				-117,929,678.95	-177,460,169.00
Undelivered Orders						-1,844,566,053.07				-118,709,869.95	-1,725,856,183.12
Subtotal	15		0404		Subtotal	-0-	1,168,662,431.00	18,491,000.00	1,335,819,165.16	-148,665,734.16	-0-
Juvenile Justice Programs, Office Of Justice Programs, Justice											
Fund Resources:											
Undisbursed Funds	15		0405		No Year	647,520,744.91	320,997,627.00		334,995,801.19		633,522,570.72
Accounts Receivable										-100,000.00	100,000.00
Unfilled Customer Orders						106,765.73				-459,343.33	566,109.06
Fund Equities:											
Unobligated Balances (Unexpired)						-22,169,122.38				-8,284,444.30	-13,884,678.08
Accounts Payable						-66,270,437.51				-1,390,974.57	-64,879,462.94
Undelivered Orders						-559,187,950.75				-3,763,411.99	-555,424,538.76
Subtotal	15		0405		Subtotal	-0-	320,997,627.00		334,995,801.19	-13,998,174.19	-0-
Community Oriented Policing Services, Office Of Justice Programs, Justice											
Fund Resources:											
Undisbursed Funds	15		0406		2003-2004	30,446,133.68			1,306.08		30,444,827.60
					No Year	1,017,503,508.48	541,838,000.00	-23,491,000.00	740,725,344.20		795,125,164.28
Accounts Receivable						209,942.04				209,942.04	
Unfilled Customer Orders										-15,056,207.00	15,056,207.00
Fund Equities:											
Unobligated Balances (Expired)						-17,825.69				56,374.39	-74,200.08

Footnotes At End Of Chapter

406

Appropriations, Outlays, and Balances – Continued

Appropriation or Fund Account — Title	Period of Availability	Dept Reg	Tr From	Account Number	Sub No.	Balances, Beginning Of Fiscal Year	Appropriations And Other Obligational Authority[1]	Transfers Borrowings And Investment (Net)[2]	Outlays (Net)	Balances Withdrawn And Other Transactions[3]	Balances, End Of Fiscal Year[4]
Community Oriented Policing Services, Office Of Justice Programs, Justice - Continued											
Fund Equities: - Continued											
Unobligated Balances (Unexpired)						-30,456,022.87				16,006,878.69	-46,462,901.56
Accounts Payable						-6,272,184.42				11,094,641.90	-17,366,826.32
Undelivered Orders						-1,011,413,551.22				-234,691,280.30	-776,722,270.92
	Subtotal	15		0406		-0-	541,838,000.00	-23,491,000.00	740,726,650.28	-222,379,650.28	-0-
Violence Against Women Prevention And Prosecution Programs, Office Of Justice Programs											
Fund Resources:											
Undisbursed Funds	No Year	15		0409		728,574,015.12	382,571,000.00		383,533,696.72		727,611,318.40
Fund Equities:											
Unobligated Balances (Unexpired)						-27,117,260.79				-2,656,992.68	-24,460,268.11
Accounts Payable						-1,935,689.83				11,814,961.69	-13,750,651.52
Undelivered Orders						-699,521,064.50				-10,120,665.73	-689,400,398.77
	Subtotal	15		0409		-0-	382,571,000.00		383,533,696.72	-962,696.72	-0-
Special Fund Accounts											
Crime Victims Fund, Justice											
Fund Resources:											
Undisbursed Funds	No Year	15		5041		2,287,547,750.73	1,017,977,474.59	-16,653,891.84	581,073,184.01		2,707,798,149.47
Transfer To:											
Health And Human Services, Administration For Children And Family											
Undisbursed Funds	No Year	75	15	5041	16	40,211,882.49		16,653,891.84	16,997,481.64		39,868,292.69
Fund Equities:											
Unobligated Balances (Unexpired)						-1,385,230,723.88				398,790,516.61	-1,784,021,240.49
Accounts Payable						-61,289,410.15				-9,544,559.92	-51,744,850.23
Undelivered Orders						-881,239,499.19				30,660,852.25	-911,900,351.44
	Subtotal	15		5041		-0-	1,017,977,474.59		598,070,665.65	419,906,808.94	-0-
Trust Fund Accounts											
Gifts, Crime Victims Fund, Office Of Justice Programs, Justice											
Fund Resources:											
Undisbursed Funds	No Year	15		8306		3,734.74	2,925.00				6,659.74
Fund Equities:											
Unobligated Balances (Unexpired)						-3,734.74				2,925.00	-6,659.74
	Subtotal	15		8306		-0-	2,925.00			2,925.00	-0-
Ounce Of Prevention Council Trust Fund, Office Of Justice Programs, Justice											
Fund Resources:											
Transfer To:											
Housing And Urban Development	No Year	86	15	8591		13,010.00					13,010.00
Fund Equities:											
Unobligated Balances (Unexpired)						-0.23				13,009.77	-13,010.00
Undelivered Orders						-13,009.77				-13,009.77	-0-
	Subtotal	15		8591		-0-					-0-

Appropriations, Outlays, and Balances - Continued

Appropriation or Fund Account — Title	Period of Availability	Dept Reg	Dept Tr From	Account Number	Sub No.	Balances, Beginning Of Fiscal Year	Appropriations And Other Obligational Authority[1]	Transfers Borrowings And Investment (Net)[2]	Outlays (Net)	Balances Withdrawn And Other Transactions[3]	Balances, End Of Fiscal Year[4]
Office Of Justice Programs, Community Oriented Policing Services, Violent Crime Reduction Programs											
Fund Resources:											
Undisbursed Funds	No Year	15		8594		113,787,260.70	-31,000,000.00		17,393,374.91		65,393,885.79
Fund Equities:											
Unobligated Balances (Unexpired)						-41,277,976.17				-1,346,993.64	-39,930,982.53
Accounts Payable						-234,708.47				-88,692.91	-146,015.56
Undelivered Orders						-72,274,576.06				-46,957,688.36	-25,316,887.70
						-0-			17,393,374.91	-48,393,374.91	-0-
Subtotal		15		8594		-0-	-31,000,000.00				
Total, Office Of Justice Programs							3,797,500,910.85	-5,000,000.00	3,818,464,253.96	-25,963,343.11	
Violent Crime Reduction Trust Fund											
Trust Fund Accounts											
Violent Crime Reduction Fund, Justice											
Fund Resources:											
Undisbursed Funds	No Year	15		8585		8,040,817.60	-8,000,000.00				40,817.60
Fund Equities:											
Unobligated Balances (Unexpired)						-8,040,817.60				-8,000,000.00	-40,817.60
Subtotal		15		8585		-0-	-8,000,000.00			-8,000,000.00	-0-
Total, Violent Crime Reduction Trust Fund							-8,000,000.00			-8,000,000.00	
Deductions For Offsetting Receipts											
Proprietary Receipts From The Public							-80,434,519.94		-80,434,519.94		
Intrabudgetary Transactions							-871,788,104.50		-871,788,104.50		
Offsetting Governmental Receipts							-325,088,529.46		-325,088,529.46		
Total, Offsetting Receipts							-1,277,311,153.90		-1,277,311,153.90		
Total, Department Of Justice							25,141,985,601.52	-4,776,480.00	23,350,813,714.09	1,786,395,407.43	

Appropriations, Outlays, and Balances – Continued

Footnotes

1. The amounts in this column, unless otherwise footnoted, represent appropriations, increases and rescissions in borrowing authority or new contract authority. Appropriation accounts with appropriation transfer activity arepresented in Table (Appropriations and Appropiation Transfers) at the end of this chapter.

2. The amounts in this column, unless otherwise footnoted, represent transfers - other than appropriation transfers, borrowings (gross), investments (net), unrealized discounts or funds held outside the Treasury.

3. The amounts in this column, unless otherwise footnoted, represent obligated balances canceled for fiscal year 2007 pursuant to 31 U.S.C. 1553, changes in unfilled customer orders, accounts receivable, accounts payable, undelivered orders, unobligated balances and adjustements to borrowing and contract authority.

4. Unobligated balances for no-year or unexpired multiple year accounts are available for obligation; unobligated balances for expired fiscal year accounts are not available for obligation.

5. Subject to disposition by the administrative agency.

6. The opening balance of Unobligated Balance Expired and Unfilled Customer Orders for account 15 0406 0129 have been adjusted by $11,920,334.31 during the current fiscal year and do not agree with last year's closing balances.

7. Includes $463.92 which represents payments for obligations of a closed account.

8. Includes $172,875.86 which represents payments for obligations of a closed account.

Appropriations, Outlays, and Balances - Continued

Footnotes

Table 1 - Appropriations And Appropriation Transfers - Department Of Justice

Department Regular	Fiscal Year	Account Symbol	Net Appropriations And Appropriations Transfers	Appropriation Amount	Net Appropriation Transfers	Department Regular Involved	Fiscal Year Involved	Accounts Involved	Amount From or To (-)
15	X	0128	4,000,000.00	0.00	4,000,000.00	15	07	0128	4,000,000.00
15	07	0128	673,154,000.00	677,154,000.00	-4,000,000.00	15	X	0128	-4,000,000.00
15	07	0129	134,332,000.00	97,832,000.00	36,500,000.00	95	07	0401	36,500,000.00
15	0708	0129	1,000,000.00	0.00	1,000,000.00	95	07	0401	1,000,000.00
15	0709	0129	1,500,000.00	1,500,000.00	0.00	95	07	0401	1,500,000.00
15	X	0132	800,000.00	0.00	800,000.00	11	X	5512	800,000.00
15	0708	0132	95,230,908.00	89,198,000.00	6,032,908.00	15	07	0200	3,701,268.00
						15	07	0323	951,331.00
						15	07	0324	683,727.00
						15	07	0700	362,623.00
						15	07	1100	333,959.00
15	X	0200	148,725,000.00	10,000,000.00	138,725,000.00	11	X	5512	139,225,000.00
						15	X	0328	-500,000.00
15	07	0200	5,985,479,732.00	5,989,181,000.00	-3,701,268.00	15	0708	0132	-3,701,268.00
15	0708	0200	251,660,613.00	248,000,000.00	3,660,613.00	11	0708	1070	3,660,613.00
15	0708	0322	6,301,762.00	5,000,000.00	1,301,762.00	11	0708	1070	1,301,762.00
15	07	0323	446,983,669.00	447,935,000.00	-951,331.00	15	0708	0132	-951,331.00
15	X	0324	16,000,000.00	16,000,000.00	12,000,000.00	15	07	0324	12,000,000.00
15	07	0324	795,386,273.00	808,070,000.00	-12,683,727.00	15	0708	0132	-683,727.00
						15	X	0324	-12,000,000.00
15	0708	0324	7,438,103.00	6,450,000.00	988,103.00	11	0708	1070	988,103.00
15	X	0328	500,000.00	500,000.00	0.00	15	X	0200	500,000.00
15	X	0401	298,416,826.00	232,340,000.00	66,076,826.00	15	X	0404	53,912,915.00
						15	X	0405	12,163,911.00
15	X	0404	1,168,662,431.00	1,222,575,346.00	-53,912,915.00	15	X	0401	-53,912,915.00
15	X	0405	320,997,627.00	333,161,538.00	-12,163,911.00	15	X	0401	-12,163,911.00
15	X	0700	63,024,000.00	15,000,000.00	48,024,000.00	11	X	5512	48,024,000.00
15	07	0700	968,734,377.00	969,097,000.00	-362,623.00	15	0708	0132	-362,623.00
15	0708	0700	4,449,927.00	4,000,000.00	449,927.00	15	0708	1070	449,927.00
15	X	1100	74,772,000.00	0.00	74,772,000.00	11	X	5512	74,772,000.00
15	07	1100	1,744,555,041.00	1,744,889,000.00	-333,959.00	15	0708	0132	-333,959.00
15	0708	1100	27,874,861.00	12,166,000.00	15,708,861.00	11	0708	1070	15,708,861.00
Totals			13,239,979,150.00	12,916,048,884.00	323,930,266.00				323,930,266.00

Footnotes At End Of Chapter

Appropriations, Outlays, and Balances – Continued

| Appropriation or Fund Account | Account Symbol | | | | | Balances, Beginning of Fiscal Year | Appropriations And Other Obligational Authority[1] | Transfers Borrowings And Investment (Net)[2] | Outlays (Net) | Balances Withdrawn And Other Transactions[3] | Balances, End Of Fiscal Year[4] |
Title	Period of Availability	Dept Reg	Tr From	Account Number	Sub No.						
Department Of Labor											
Employment And Training Administration											
General Fund Accounts											
Workers Compensation Programs, Employment And Training Administration											
Fund Resources:											
Undisbursed Funds	No Year	16		0170		50,000,000.00			2,614,684.08		47,385,315.92
Fund Equities:											
Unobligated Balances (Unexpired)										-500,000.00	
Accounts Payable						-500,000.00				2,013,306.74	-2,013,306.74
Undelivered Orders						-49,500,000.00				-4,127,990.82	-45,372,009.18
Subtotal		16		0170		-0-			2,614,684.08	-2,614,684.08	-0-
Program Administration, Employment And Training Administration											
Fund Resources:											
Undisbursed Funds	2007	16		0172		42,388,886.77	117,658,643.00		76,973,161.39		40,685,481.61
	2006					2,934,005.24			37,573,992.97		4,814,893.80
	2005					1,711,605.84			901,780.76		2,032,224.48
	2004					2,080,811.00			252,755.64		1,458,850.20
	2003					1,151,090.85			209,182.55		1,871,628.45
	2002								66,129.58	983,533.01	
Fund Equities:											
Unobligated Balances (Expired)						-3,206,021.14				88,897.72	-3,294,918.86
Accounts Payable						-7,524,923.91				1,303,883.38	-8,828,807.29
Undelivered Orders						-39,535,454.65		-101,428.26		-796,102.26	-38,739,352.39
Subtotal		16		0172		-0-	117,658,643.00	-101,428.26	115,977,002.89	1,580,211.85	-0-
Training And Employment Service, Employment And Training Administration											
Fund Resources:											
Undisbursed Funds	2007-2010	16		0174			7,920,000.00				7,920,000.00
	2007-2009						100,000,000.00	-1,636,314.00	21,999.00		98,341,687.00
	2006-2009					7,920,000.00					7,920,000.00
	2007-2008						2,663,629,258.00	-71,164,944.00	294,119,667.53		2,298,344,646.47
	2006-2008					88,423,507.87		-610,638.00	21,483,223.01		66,329,646.86
	2005-2008					16,190,432.00			5,903,205.18		10,287,226.82
	2007						2,363,000,000.00		1,604,643,895.69		758,356,104.31
	2006-2007					2,247,662,249.64		-101,088,261.00	1,744,377,371.28		402,196,617.36
	2005-2007					73,730,575.87			46,852,709.60		26,877,866.27
	2004-2007					24,619,290.55			12,603,924.65		12,015,365.90
	2006					679,979,329.88			537,882,314.50		142,097,015.38
	2005-2006					510,807,764.62		-338,072.74	328,814,139.56		181,655,552.32
	2004-2006					29,558,086.29			23,266,637.85		6,291,448.44
	2003-2006					13,736,057.62			9,502,443.16		4,233,614.46
	2005					174,465,905.85			129,972,317.64		44,493,588.21
	2004-2005					108,519,419.96			77,369,019.31		31,150,400.65
	2003-2005					9,567,755.45		30,000.00	2,927,641.66		6,670,113.79
	2002-2005					2,198,006.98			1,724,066.23		473,940.75

Appropriations, Outlays, and Balances - Continued

| Appropriation or Fund Account | Account Symbol | | | | | | | | | | |
Title	Reg (Dept)	Tr From (Dept)	Account Number	Sub No.	Period of Availability	Balances, Beginning of Fiscal Year	Appropriations And Other Obligational Authority[1]	Transfers Borrowings And Investment (Net)[2]	Outlays (Net)	Balances Withdrawn And Other Transactions[3]	Balances, End Of Fiscal Year[4]
					2004	38,521,950.84			11,489,222.11		27,032,728.73
					2003-2004	51,778,974.75			20,064,404.41		31,714,570.34
					2002-2004	37,982,041.10		231,640.00	4,641,537.25		33,572,143.85
					2003	15,523,478.11			-56,920.47		15,580,398.58
					2002-2003	27,397,745.17			12,336,988.93		15,060,756.24
					2001-2003	531,653.06			324,972.58		206,680.48
					2000-2003	533,877.34			464,859.33		69,018.01
					2002	32,619,536.48		448,462.38	-134,763.52	33,202,762.38	
					2001-2002	12,871,246.35		77,296.22	2,670,765.71	10,277,776.86	
					1999-2002	864,380.71		331,417.65	238,210.40	957,587.96	
					No Year	34,859,216.55	-71,000.00	-4,423,000.00	2,793,020.76		27,572,195.79
Transfer To:											
Department Of Agriculture	12	16	0174		2007-2009			724,560.00			724,560.00
					2007-2008			42,129,063.00	18,641,727.85		23,487,335.15
					2006-2008	6,593,790.73		946,841.00	2,030,509.67		5,510,122.06
					2006-2007	22,681,621.94		68,960,154.00	88,209,449.05		3,432,326.89
					2005-2006	2,159,069.27			1,417,009.00		742,060.27
					2004-2006	259,433.15			175,427.53		84,005.62
					2005	262,857.66			124,378.77		138,478.89
					2004-2005	468,338.70			189,459.18		278,879.52
					2003-2005	60,807.97		-30,000.00	22,632.37		8,175.60
					2004	296,027.21			4,162.58		291,864.63
					2003-2004	442,491.88			65,950.16		376,541.72
					2002-2004	397,499.61		-231,640.00	1,099.00		164,760.61
					2003	420,297.72			-1,154.12		421,451.84
					2002-2003	555,862.94			-2,153.87		558,016.81
					2001-2003	39,992.82			4,613.27		35,379.55
					2000-2003	20,314.89					20,314.89
					2002	413,597.79		-413,702.66	-104.87		
					2001-2002	63,294.67		-63,218.12	76.55		
					1999-2002	269,959.71		-269,959.71			
Department Of Interior, Bureau Of Reclamation	14	16	0174	6	2007-2009			833,083.00			833,083.00
					2007-2008			13,391,540.00	7,106,630.43		6,284,909.57
					2006-2008	2,671,117.60		-273,155.00	381,290.85		2,016,671.75
					2006-2007	6,748,326.42		22,294,467.00	28,658,156.18		384,637.24
					2005-2006	385,702.32			330,148.07		55,554.25
					2004-2006	69,837.20			26,857.00		42,980.20
					2004-2005	193,111.41			47,686.70		145,424.71
					2003-2004	94,612.96			-33.76		94,646.72
					2002-2003	55,062.86					55,062.86
					2002	14,098.15		-14,098.15			
					2001-2002	9,931.97		-9,931.97			
Department Of Interior, National Park Service	14	16	0174	10	2007-2009			78,671.00			78,671.00
					2007-2008			3,004,520.00	1,303,283.53		1,701,236.47
					2006-2008	570,352.23		-63,048.00	7,367.42		499,936.81
					2006-2007	4,470,550.79		8,878,397.00	12,883,362.77		465,585.02
					2005-2006	715,776.22			208,957.24		506,818.98
					2004-2006	111,897.71			47,341.09		64,556.62

Footnotes At End Of Chapter

Appropriations, Outlays, and Balances – Continued

Appropriation or Fund Account — Title	Period of Availability	Account Symbol — Dept Reg	Tr From	Account Number	Sub No.	Balances, Beginning of Fiscal Year	Appropriations And Other Obligational Authority[1]	Transfers Borrowings And Investment (Net)[2]	Outlays (Net)	Balances Withdrawn And Other Transactions[3]	Balances, End Of Fiscal Year[4]
Training And Employment Service, Employment And Training Administration - Continued											
Fund Resources: - Continued											
Department Of Interior, National Park Service - Continued											
	2005					908,162.14			-406.98		908,569.12
	2004-2005					26,335.87					26,335.87
	2003-2005					51,889.98					51,889.98
	2004					119,045.39					119,045.39
	2003-2004					73,432.53					73,432.53
	2002-2004					76,529.49					76,529.49
	2003					203,832.23					203,832.23
	2002-2003					175,799.13					175,799.13
	2000-2003					82,867.66					82,867.66
	2002					20,661.57		-20,661.57			—
	2001-2002					4,146.13		-4,146.13			—
	1999-2002					61,457.94		-61,457.94			—
Department Of Interior, Bureau Of Indian Affairs	2007-2008	14	16	0174	20	491,932.00		12,639,821.00	10,114,097.00		2,525,724.00
	2006-2007							957,143.00	791,069.00		658,006.00
	2005-2006							338,072.74	239,593.00		98,479.74
	2003-2004					1.00					1.00
Funds Held Outside The Treasury	2006-2007	14	16	0174	6	117,300.00		-1,900.00			115,400.00
Accounts Receivable						95,797.86				545.30	95,252.56
Fund Equities:											
Unobligated Balances (Expired)						-81,972,818.67				384,053.25	-82,356,871.92
Unobligated Balances (Unexpired)						-761,473,339.74				12,150,654.67	-773,623,994.41
Accounts Payable						-567,114,897.22				9,760,172.47	-576,875,069.69
Undelivered Orders						-2,884,326,254.83				-6,003,649.89	-2,878,322,604.94
Subtotal		16		0174		-0-	5,134,478,258.00	-4,423,000.00	5,069,325,355.00	60,729,903.00	-0-
Community Service Employment For Older Americans, Employment And Training Administration											
Fund Resources:											
Undisbursed Funds	2007	16		0175		359,377,052.92	483,611,000.00		78,357,324.33		405,253,675.67
	2006					15,913,787.55			341,776,593.00		17,600,459.92
	2005					13,696,364.37			3,343,645.38		12,570,142.17
	2004					3,994,168.62			10,186,572.32		3,509,792.05
	2003					474,582.74			2,791,711.67		1,202,456.95
	2002								407,241.62	67,341.12	
Fund Equities:											
Unobligated Balances (Expired)						-4,547,205.75				2,208,543.07	-6,755,748.82
Accounts Payable						-11,688,143.27				52,699,316.53	-64,387,459.80
Undelivered Orders						-377,220,607.18				-8,227,289.04	-368,993,318.14
Subtotal		16		0175		-0-	483,611,000.00		436,863,088.32	46,747,911.68	-0-
State Unemployment Insurance And Employment Service Operations, Employment And Training Administration											
Fund Resources:											
Undisbursed Funds	2007-2008	16		0179		104,313,165.00	106,252,000.00		34,286,738.15		71,965,261.85
	2007								-27,781,092.53		27,781,092.53
	2006-2007								41,001,986.68		63,311,178.32
	2006					69,894,944.51			63,162,929.63		6,732,014.88

Appropriations, Outlays, and Balances - Continued

Appropriation or Fund Account — Title	Period of Availability	Reg	Tr From	Account Number	Sub No.	Balances, Beginning of Fiscal Year	Appropriations And Other Obligational Authority[1]	Transfers Borrowings And Investment (Net)[2]	Outlays (Net)	Balances Withdrawn And Other Transactions[3]	Balances, End Of Fiscal Year[4]
	2005-2006					89,855,149.92			59,052,844.31		30,802,305.61
	2005					3,542,424.03			3,251,840.37		290,583.66
	2004-2005					20,988,813.42			17,825,672.95		3,163,140.47
	2004					507,293.34			3,382,208.98		[5]2,874,915.64
	2003-2004					-928,511.13			-2,800,709.99		1,872,198.86
	2003					981,268.73			319,756.92		661,511.81
	2002-2003					938,373.45			33,231,682.52		[5]-32,293,309.07
	2002					595,561.16			595,561.16		-0-
	2001-2002					457,139.24			-3,675,111.16	4,132,250.40	1,394,785.20
Accounts Receivable	No Year					7,306,468.33	-4,100,000.00		1,811,683.13	-34,577,752.60	1,242,806,359.94
						1,208,228,607.34					
Fund Equities:											
Unobligated Balances (Expired)						-8,114,154.27				-977,585.54	-7,136,568.73
Unobligated Balances (Unexpired)						-127,010,385.08				-45,360,821.15	-81,649,563.93
Accounts Payable						-131,315,807.97				25,551,511.55	-156,867,319.52
Undelivered Orders						-1,240,240,350.02				-70,281,593.78	-1,169,958,756.24
Subtotal		16		0179		-0-	102,152,000.00		223,665,991.12	-121,513,991.12	-0-
Federal Unemployment Benefits And Allowances, Employment And Training Administration											
Fund Resources:											
Undisbursed Funds	2007	16		0326		370,828,388.28	837,600,000.00		609,493,675.36		228,106,324.64
	2006					279,803,253.91			99,469,667.84		271,358,720.44
	2005					546,967,631.30			53,789,876.07		226,013,377.84
	2004					381,930,763.72			99,863.79		550,839,141.82
	2003					51,928,356.06			-6,125.20		381,830,899.93
	2002									51,934,481.26	
Fund Equities:											
Unobligated Balances (Expired)						-1,217,308,779.97				-16,037,550.19	-1,201,271,229.78
Accounts Payable						-47,449,395.97				18,779,858.56	-66,229,254.53
Undelivered Orders						-366,700,217.33				23,947,763.03	-390,647,980.36
Subtotal		16		0326		-0-	837,600,000.00		758,975,447.34	78,624,552.66	-0-
Advances To The Unemployment Trust Fund And Other Funds, Employment And Training Administration											
Fund Resources:											
Undisbursed Funds	2007-2008	16		0327		91,000,000.00	112,500,000.00	-73,500,000.00	17,500,000.00		112,500,000.00
Fund Equities:											
Unobligated Balances (Unexpired)	2006-2007					-91,000,000.00				21,500,000.00	-112,500,000.00
Subtotal		16		0327		-0-	112,500,000.00	-73,500,000.00	17,500,000.00	21,500,000.00	-0-
Special Fund Accounts											
Salaries And Expenses, H-1b Funded, Employment Standards Administration											
Fund Resources:											
Undisbursed Funds	No Year	16		5142		7,896,868.06	13,419,918.76		10,479,558.90		10,837,227.92
Fund Equities:											
Unobligated Balances (Unexpired)						-7,224,871.87				-462,067.36	-6,762,804.51

Footnotes At End Of Chapter

Appropriations, Outlays, and Balances – Continued

Appropriation or Fund Account — Title	Reg	Tr From	Account Number	Sub No.	Period of Availability	Balances, Beginning of Fiscal Year	Appropriations And Other Obligational Authority[1]	Transfers Borrowings And Investment (Net)[2]	Outlays (Net)	Balances Withdrawn And Other Transactions[3]	Balances, End Of Fiscal Year[4]
Accounts Payable						-232,767.52				-85,015.53	-147,751.99
Salaries And Expenses, H-1b Funded, Employment Standards Administration - Continued											
Fund Equities: - Continued											
Undelivered Orders						-439,228.67				3,487,442.75	-3,926,671.42
Subtotal	16		5142		Subtotal	-0-	13,419,918.76		10,479,558.90	2,940,359.86	-0-
Salaries And Expenses, H-1b Funded, Training And Employment Services, Employment And Training Administration											
Fund Resources:											
Undisbursed Funds	16		5152		No Year	255,563,172.10	134,199,187.61		88,533,331.38	88,533,331.38	301,229,028.33
Fund Equities:											
Unobligated Balances (Unexpired)						-110,342,065.92				23,836,784.50	-134,178,850.42
Accounts Payable						-10,548,085.04				15,457,668.08	-26,005,753.12
Undelivered Orders						-134,673,021.14				6,371,403.65	-141,044,424.79
Subtotal	16		5152		Subtotal	-0-	134,199,187.61		88,533,331.38	45,665,856.23	-0-
Total, Employment And Training Administration							6,935,619,007.37	-78,024,428.26	6,723,934,459.03	133,660,120.08	
Unemployment Trust Fund											
Trust Fund Accounts											
Unemployment Trust Fund											
Fund Resources:											
Undisbursed Funds	20		8042		No Year	55,893,004.27	44,970,842,418.71[6]	-8,710,711,509.83	36,147,439,600.99[6]		168,584,312.16
Investments In Public Debt Securities						66,212,640,000.00		8,710,640,000.00			74,923,280,000.00
Fund Equities:											
Unobligated Balances (Unexpired)						-64,997,066,882.89				8,742,005,088.75	-73,739,071,971.64
Accounts Payable						-1,271,466,121.38		-71,509.83	81,326,219.14	81,326,219.14	-1,352,792,340.52
Subtotal	20		8042		Subtotal	-0-	44,970,842,418.71	-71,509.83	36,147,439,600.99	8,823,331,307.89	-0-
Total, Unemployment Trust Fund							44,970,842,418.71	-71,509.83	36,147,439,600.99	8,823,331,307.89	
Total, Employment And Training Administration							51,906,461,426.08	-78,095,938.09	42,871,374,060.02	8,956,991,427.97	
Employee Benefits Security Administration											
General Fund Accounts											
Expenses, Employee Benefits Security Administration											
Fund Resources:											
Undisbursed Funds	16		1700		2007-2008		14,000,000.00				14,000,000.00
					2007		134,572,669.00		99,954,480.32		34,618,188.68
					2006	35,137,367.19			31,654,794.94		3,482,572.25
					2005	4,325,410.30			3,273,512.78		1,051,897.52
					2004	3,403,321.05			863,448.18		2,539,872.87
					2003	1,424,358.30			380.99		1,423,977.31
					2002	1,571,334.06		-150,784.10	259,791.35	1,160,758.61	
					2001-2002	1,766.99				1,766.99	

Appropriation or Fund Account Title	Period of Availability	Reg	Tr From	Account Number	Sub No.	Balances, Beginning of Fiscal Year	Appropriations And Other Obligational Authority[1]	Transfers Borrowings And Investment (Net)[2]	Outlays (Net)	Balances Withdrawn And Other Transactions[3]	Balances, End Of Fiscal Year[4]
	No Year					32,510.98					32,510.98
Fund Equities:											
Unobligated Balances (Expired)						-2,073,721.07				870,540.22	-2,944,261.29
Unobligated Balances (Unexpired)						-2,532.40				14,029,978.58	-14,032,510.98
Accounts Payable						-8,272,682.82				2,164,379.86	-10,437,062.68
Undelivered Orders						-35,547,132.58		-150,784.10		-5,811,947.92	-29,735,184.66
Subtotal		16		1700		-0-	148,572,669.00		136,006,408.56	12,415,476.34	-0-
Total, Employee Benefits Security Administration							148,572,669.00	-150,784.10	136,006,408.56	12,415,476.34	
Pension Benefit Guaranty Corporation											
Public Enterprise Funds											
Pension Benefit Guaranty Corporation											
Fund Resources:											
Undisbursed Funds	No Year	16		4204		1,024,897.00	-7,000,000.00	464,122,956.35	457,147,853.35		1,000,000.00
Unrealized Discount On Investments								-2,364,959.69			-2,364,959.69
Funds Held Outside The Treasury	No Year					4,000.00		1,000.00			5,000.00
Unamortized Premium And Discount						-21,647,834,711.75		397,810,753.85			-21,250,023,957.90
Authority To Borrow From The Treasury						100,000,000.00					100,000,000.00
Investments In Public Debt Securities						36,634,539,773.75		-859,569,750.51			35,774,970,023.24
Fund Equities:											
Unobligated Balances (Unexpired)						-14,967,736,349.53				-461,236,585.28	-14,506,499,764.25
Accounts Payable						-69,442,501.97				-7,224,040.93	-62,218,461.04
Undelivered Orders						-50,555,107.50				4,312,772.86	-54,867,880.36
Subtotal		16		4204		-0-	-7,000,000.00		457,147,853.35	-464,147,853.35	-0-
Total, Pension Benefit Guaranty Corporation							-7,000,000.00		457,147,853.35	-464,147,853.35	
Employment Standards Administration											
General Fund Accounts											
Salaries And Expenses, Employment Standards Administration											
Fund Resources:											
Undisbursed Funds:											
	2007	16		0105		46,679,811.48	418,829,920.00		361,372,434.00		57,457,486.00
	2006					6,940,052.77			39,838,158.17		6,841,653.31
	2005					2,895,204.54			1,849,595.79		5,090,456.98
	2004					4,815,940.37			105,035.84		2,790,168.70
	2003					3,369,402.31			2,740.41		4,813,199.96
	2002					2,027,520.00			24,308.95	2,804,644.76	
Accounts Receivable								-540,448.60		2,027,520.00	
Fund Equities:											
Unobligated Balances (Expired)						-7,007,008.33				2,636,068.26	-9,643,076.59
Accounts Payable						-19,504,777.38				1,681,679.71	-21,186,457.09
Undelivered Orders						-40,216,145.76				5,947,285.51	-46,163,431.27
Subtotal		16		0105		-0-	418,829,920.00	-540,448.60	403,192,273.16	15,097,198.24	-0-

Footnotes At End Of Chapter

Appropriations, Outlays, and Balances – Continued

Appropriation or Fund Account — Title	Period of Availability	Account Symbol — Dept Reg	Account Symbol — Dept Tr From	Account Number	Sub No.	Balances, Beginning of Fiscal Year	Appropriations And Other Obligational Authority[1]	Transfers Borrowings And Investment (Net)[2]	Outlays (Net)	Balances Withdrawn And Other Transactions[3]	Balances, End Of Fiscal Year[4]
Special Benefits For Disabled Coal Miners, Employment Standards Administration											
Fund Resources:											
Undisbursed Funds	No Year	16		0169		55,300,605.12	303,373,000.00		290,941,211.34		67,732,393.78
Fund Equities:											
Unobligated Balances (Unexpired)						-28,750,863.38				14,380,878.27	-43,131,741.65
Accounts Payable						-25,192,339.38				-2,385,398.54	-22,806,940.84
Undelivered Orders						-1,357,402.36				436,308.93	-1,793,711.29
Subtotal		16		0169		-0-	303,373,000.00		290,941,211.34	12,431,788.66	-0-
Special Benefits, Employment Standards Administration											
Fund Resources:											
Undisbursed Funds	No Year	16		1521		1,461,834,691.93	227,000,000.00		113,650,974.55		1,575,183,717.38
Accounts Receivable						3,590,185.10				2,563,449.19	1,026,735.91
Fund Equities:											
Unobligated Balances (Unexpired)						-1,377,642,250.39				109,756,314.48	-1,487,398,564.87
Accounts Payable						-62,956,537.20				9,538,347.71	-72,494,884.91
Undelivered Orders						-24,826,089.44				-8,509,085.93	-16,317,003.51
Subtotal		16		1521		-0-	227,000,000.00		113,650,974.55	113,349,025.45	-0-
Energy Employees Occupational Illness Compensation Fund, Department Of Labor											
Fund Resources:											
Undisbursed Funds	No Year	16		1523		199,736.43	924,000,000.00	30,245,000.00	954,442,600.76		2,135.67
Investments In Public Debt Securities						83,307,000.00		-30,245,000.00			53,062,000.00
Fund Equities:											
Unobligated Balances (Unexpired)						-62,014,836.59				-32,956,184.79	-29,058,651.80
Accounts Payable						-21,491,899.84				2,513,584.03	-24,005,483.87
Subtotal		16		1523		-0-	924,000,000.00		954,442,600.76	-30,442,600.76	-0-
Administrative Expenses, Energy Employees Occupational Illness Compensation Fund, Department Of Labor											
Fund Resources:											
Undisbursed Funds	No Year	16		1524		87,529,836.75	158,966,319.00		182,683,211.52		63,812,944.23
Fund Equities:											
Unobligated Balances (Unexpired)						-15,265,398.16				-10,279,185.81	-4,986,212.35
Accounts Payable						-11,046,101.65				2,258,374.70	-13,304,476.35
Undelivered Orders						-61,218,336.94				-15,696,081.41	-45,522,255.53
Subtotal		16		1524		-0-	158,966,319.00		182,683,211.52	-23,716,892.52	-0-
Special Benefits For Disabled Coal Miners, Social Security Administration											
Fund Resources:											
Undisbursed Funds	No Year	28		0409		30.00					[5]184.24
Accounts Receivable									214.24	-184.24	184.24
Fund Equities:											
Unobligated Balances (Unexpired)						-30.00				-30.00	
Subtotal		28		0409		-0-			214.24	-214.24	-0-

Special Fund Accounts

Panama Canal Commission Compensation Fund

Appropriations, Outlays, and Balances - Continued

Appropriation or Fund Account — Title	Period of Availability	Dept Reg	Tr From	Account Number	Sub No.	Balances, Beginning of Fiscal Year	Appropriations And Other Obligational Authority[1]	Transfers Borrowings And Investment (Net)[2]	Outlays (Net)	Balances Withdrawn And Other Transactions[3]	Balances, End Of Fiscal Year[4]
Fund Resources:											
Undisbursed Funds	No Year	16		5155		349.86	5,799,380.57	259,476.92	6,058,663.84		543.51
Unrealized Discount On Investments						-615,910.77		146,523.08			-469,387.69
Investments In Public Debt Securities						77,806,000.00		-406,000.00			77,400,000.00
Fund Equities:											
Unobligated Balances (Unexpired)						-77,190,439.09				-259,283.27	-76,931,155.82
Subtotal		16		5155		-0-	5,799,380.57		6,058,663.84	-259,283.27	-0-
H-1b And L Fraud Protection And Detection Account, Employment Standards Administration											
Fund Resources:											
Undisbursed Funds	No Year	16		5393		67,151,926.50	45,736,548.23		5,853,811.74		107,034,662.99
Fund Equities:											
Unobligated Balances (Unexpired)						-67,128,897.96				39,882,285.96	-107,011,183.92
Accounts Payable						-12,680.54				8,952.62	-21,633.16
Undelivered Orders						-10,348.00				-8,502.09	-1,845.91
Subtotal		16		5393		-0-	45,736,548.23		5,853,811.74	39,882,736.49	-0-
Trust Fund Accounts											
Relief And Rehabilitation, Longshoremen's And Harbor Workers' Compensation Act, As Amended, Labor											
Fund Resources:											
Undisbursed Funds	No Year	16		8130		154,035.68	130,467,193.33	3,167,000.00	133,634,665.22		153,563.79
Investments In Public Debt Securities						73,146,000.00		-3,167,000.00			69,979,000.00
Fund Equities:											
Unobligated Balances (Unexpired)						-67,890,164.46			133,634,665.22	-1,412,966.84	-66,477,197.62
Accounts Payable						-5,409,871.22				-1,754,505.05	-3,655,366.17
Subtotal		16		8130		-0-	130,467,193.33		133,634,665.22	-3,167,471.89	-0-
Relief And Rehabilitation, Workmen's Compensation Act, Within The District Of Columbia, Department Of Labor											
Fund Resources:											
Undisbursed Funds	No Year	16		8134		75,967.30	11,060,442.62	-974,000.00	10,087,135.54		75,274.38
Investments In Public Debt Securities						5,611,000.00		974,000.00			6,585,000.00
Fund Equities:											
Unobligated Balances (Unexpired)						-5,404,396.56			10,087,135.54	957,954.83	-6,362,351.39
Accounts Payable						-282,570.74				15,352.25	-297,922.99
Subtotal		16		8134		-0-	11,060,442.62		10,087,135.54	973,307.08	-0-
Black Lung Disability Trust Fund											
Fund Resources:											
Undisbursed Funds	No Year	20		8144		36,960,888.41	992,013,992.23	-217,617,800.00	773,095,975.86		38,261,104.78
Investments In Public Debt Securities						1,758,730.01		291,117,800.00	291,309,574.68		1,566,955.33
Transfer To: Employment Standards Administration, Department Of Labor	No Year	16	20	8144	15						
Fund Equities:											
Unobligated Balances (Unexpired)						-38,719,618.42		73,500,000.00	1,064,405,550.54	1,108,441.69	-39,828,060.11
Subtotal		20		8144		-0-	992,013,992.23		1,064,405,550.54	1,108,441.69	-0-
Total, Employment Standards Administration							3,217,246,795.98	72,959,551.40	3,164,950,312.45	125,256,034.93	

Footnotes At End Of Chapter

Appropriations, Outlays, and Balances – Continued

Appropriation or Fund Account — Title	Period of Availability	Reg	Tr From	Account Number	Sub No.	Balances, Beginning of Fiscal Year	Appropriations And Other Obligational Authority[1]	Transfers Borrowings And Investment (Net)[2]	Outlays (Net)	Balances Withdrawn And Other Transactions[3]	Balances, End Of Fiscal Year[4]
Occupational Safety And Health Administration											
General Fund Accounts											
Salaries And Expenses, Occupational Safety And Health Administration											
Fund Resources:											
Undisbursed Funds	2007	16		0400		59,336,012.24	486,925,000.00		412,861,905.30		74,063,094.70
	2006					13,351,717.96			53,991,362.43		5,344,649.81
	2005					10,352,160.44			4,437,990.83		8,913,727.13
	2004					5,958,205.32			780,292.56		9,571,867.88
	2003					8,810,219.19			-11,345.83		5,969,551.15
	2002							-1,588,628.12	-21,792.34	7,243,383.41	
	No Year					14,705.98					14,705.98
Accounts Receivable						9,126,693.31				1,027,372.48	8,099,320.83
Fund Equities:											
Unobligated Balances (Expired)						-21,820,507.65				-5,549,312.03	-16,271,195.62
Unobligated Balances (Unexpired)						-14,705.98					-14,705.98
Accounts Payable						-26,425,698.83				-4,024,278.12	-22,401,420.71
Undelivered Orders						-58,688,801.98				14,600,793.19	-73,289,595.17
Subtotal		16		0400		-0-	486,925,000.00	-1,588,628.12	472,038,412.95	13,297,958.93	-0-
Total, Occupational Safety And Health Administration							486,925,000.00	-1,588,628.12	472,038,412.95	13,297,958.93	
Mine Safety And Health Administration											
General Fund Accounts											
Salaries And Expenses, Mine Safety And Health Administration											
Fund Resources:											
Undisbursed Funds	2007	16		1200		24,594,904.02	301,569,739.00		264,989,818.33		36,579,920.67
	2006-2007					15,777,441.69			14,525,037.53		10,069,866.49
	2006					2,251,018.03			14,559,138.91		1,218,302.78
	2005					709,926.62			1,743,311.00		507,707.03
	2004					1,076,699.61			263,082.32		446,844.30
	2003					774,260.86			322,548.16		754,151.45
	2002					1,608,379.31		-146,864.30	-405.92	627,802.48	304,579.81
	No Year								1,303,799.50		
Accounts Receivable						15,000.00				15,000.00	
Fund Equities:											
Unobligated Balances (Expired)						-1,572,312.79				-300,900.68	-1,271,412.11
Unobligated Balances (Unexpired)						-21,167,869.94				-21,167,869.94	
Accounts Payable						-11,986,681.63				6,542,575.80	-18,529,257.43
Undelivered Orders						-12,080,765.78				17,999,937.21	-30,080,702.99
Subtotal		16		1200		-0-	301,569,739.00	-146,864.30	297,706,329.83	3,716,544.87	-0-
Total, Mine Safety And Health Administration							301,569,739.00	-146,864.30	297,706,329.83	3,716,544.87	

Appropriations, Outlays, and Balances - Continued

Appropriation or Fund Account — Title	Period of Availability	Dept Reg	Dept Tr From	Account Number	Sub No.	Balances, Beginning of Fiscal Year	Appropriations And Other Obligational Authority[1]	Transfers Borrowings And Investment (Net)[2]	Outlays (Net)	Balances Withdrawn And Other Transactions[3]	Balances, End Of Fiscal Year[4]
Bureau Of Labor Statistics											
General Fund Accounts											
Salaries And Expenses, Bureau Of Labor Statistics											
Fund Resources:											
Undisbursed Funds	2007	16		0200			471,055,571.00		402,689,761.23		68,365,809.77
	2006					65,627,243.21			61,535,137.44		4,092,105.77
	2005					6,261,025.73			1,509,190.13		4,751,835.60
	2004					3,312,687.40			122,918.90		3,189,768.50
	2003					3,959,511.95			61,271.79		3,898,240.16
	2002-2003					50,642.80					50,642.80
	2002					3,781,716.17		-243,934.35	1,196,493.25	2,341,288.57	
	2001-2002					163,435.31				163,435.31	
Fund Equities:											
Unobligated Balances (Expired)						-9,057,070.80				3,652.91	-9,060,723.71
Accounts Payable						-41,750,466.69				-2,785,071.27	-38,965,395.42
Undelivered Orders						-32,348,725.08				3,973,558.39	-36,322,283.47
	Subtotal	16		0200		-0-	471,055,571.00	-243,934.35	467,114,772.74	3,696,863.91	-0-
Total, Bureau Of Labor Statistics							471,055,571.00	-243,934.35	467,114,772.74	3,696,863.91	
Departmental Management											
General Fund Accounts											
Office Of The Inspector General, Departmental Management											
Fund Resources:											
Undisbursed Funds	2007	16		0106			67,213,688.00		58,704,453.57		8,509,234.43
	2006					9,418,835.13			7,840,211.38		1,578,623.75
	2005					695,002.80			303,952.96		391,049.84
	2004					726,069.16			210,190.08		515,879.08
	2003					908,838.60			305,168.37		603,670.23
	2002					868,664.31		-141,550.73	34,354.13	692,759.45	
Accounts Receivable						916.00					916.00
Fund Equities:											
Unobligated Balances (Expired)						-1,562,002.88				-573,232.15	-988,770.73
Accounts Payable						-4,777,313.54				45,596.07	-4,822,909.61
Undelivered Orders						-6,279,009.58				-491,316.59	-5,787,692.99
	Subtotal	16		0106		-0-	67,213,688.00	-141,550.73	67,398,330.49	-326,193.22	-0-
Veterans Employment And Training, Departmental Management											
Fund Resources:											
Undisbursed Funds	2007-2008	16		0164			7,435,000.00		177,836.16		7,257,163.84
	2007						21,809,000.00		-19,006,724.12		40,815,724.12
	2006-2007					7,138,498.09			5,602,916.04		1,535,582.05
	2006					44,137,635.19			41,670,512.24		2,467,122.95
	2005-2006					821,286.49			459,591.91		361,694.58

Appropriations, Outlays, and Balances – Continued

Appropriation or Fund Account — Title	Period of Availability	Reg	Tr From	Account Number	Sub No.	Balances, Beginning of Fiscal Year	Appropriations And Other Obligational Authority[1]	Transfers Borrowings And Investment (Net)[2]	Outlays (Net)	Balances Withdrawn And Other Transactions[3]	Balances, End Of Fiscal Year[4]
Veterans Employment And Training, Departmental Management - Continued											
Fund Resources: - Continued											
Undisbursed Funds - Continued	2005					3,081,498.39			327,728.66		2,753,769.73
	2004-2005					708,838.08					708,838.08
	2004					3,508,596.05			1,126.26		3,507,469.79
	2003-2004					156,428.75			25,316.07		131,112.68
	2003					1,879,237.81					1,879,237.81
	2002-2003					192,358.77			-10,650.22		203,008.99
	2002					960,665.92				960,665.92	
	2001-2002					373,689.90				373,689.90	
Fund Equities:											
Unobligated Balances (Expired)						-2,718,606.34				2,703,855.65	-5,422,461.99
Unobligated Balances (Unexpired)						-130,270.00				-32,135.00	-98,135.00
Accounts Payable						-35,658,044.84				1,635,418.91	-37,293,463.75
Undelivered Orders						-24,451,812.26				-5,645,148.38	-18,806,663.88
Subtotal		16		0164		-0-	29,244,000.00		29,247,653.00	-3,653.00	-0-
Salaries And Expenses, Departmental Management											
Fund Resources:											
Undisbursed Funds	2007	16		0165			298,611,773.00		196,089,033.51		102,522,739.49
	2006-2007					20,459,560.00			3,087,735.95		17,371,824.05
	2006					99,274,228.93			45,147,188.57		54,127,040.36
	2005-2006					21,393,233.64			4,682,814.79		16,710,418.85
	2005					74,810,647.65			24,701,756.20		50,108,891.45
	2004-2005					245,000.00			155,000.00		90,000.00
	2004					69,402,767.39			27,399,027.11		42,003,740.28
	2003-2004					22,155,180.29			8,835,198.93		13,319,981.36
	2003					31,997,322.46			16,706,773.17		15,290,549.29
	2002-2003					9,919,042.48			7,493,600.95		2,425,441.53
	2002					14,448,262.38			7,139,692.35		
	2001-2002					4,872,531.90		-86,361.54	4,437,186.15		
	No Year					455,792.94			46,573.51		409,219.43
Accounts Receivable						5,532,426.67				1,687,278.72	3,845,147.95
Fund Equities:											
Unobligated Balances (Expired)						-7,602,131.46				1,209,993.52	-8,812,124.98
Unobligated Balances (Unexpired)						-19,945,217.87				-19,678,993.30	-266,224.57
Accounts Payable						-18,177,136.73				5,348,853.62	-23,525,990.35
Undelivered Orders						-329,241,510.67				-43,620,856.53	-285,620,654.14
Subtotal		16		0165		-0-	298,611,773.00	-86,361.54	345,921,581.19	-47,396,169.73	-0-
Salaries And Expenses, Office Of Disability Employment Policy, Departmental Management											
Fund Resources:											
Undisbursed Funds	2007	16		0166			27,711,746.00		11,885,748.76		15,825,997.24
	2006					17,979,524.79			10,089,377.17		7,890,147.62
	2005					9,781,485.21			7,743,934.37		2,037,550.84
	2004					3,508,617.76			1,926,115.73		1,582,502.03
	2003					1,450,571.73			-55.82		1,450,627.55
	2002					2,212,356.88				2,212,356.88	

Appropriations, Outlays, and Balances - Continued

Appropriation or Fund Account: Title	Account Symbol: Period of Availability	Dept Reg	Tr From	Account Number	Sub No.	Balances, Beginning of Fiscal Year	Appropriations And Other Obligational Authority[1]	Transfers Borrowings And Investment (Net)[2]	Outlays (Net)	Balances Withdrawn And Other Transactions[3]	Balances, End Of Fiscal Year[4]
Intragovernmental Funds											
Fund Equities:											
Unobligated Balances (Expired)						-1,089,108.21				-182,936.34	-906,171.87
Accounts Payable						-1,305,497.00				-63,132.17	-1,242,364.83
Undelivered Orders						-32,537,951.16				-5,899,662.58	-26,638,288.58
Subtotal		16		0166		-0-	27,711,746.00		31,645,120.21	-3,933,374.21	-0-
Working Capital Fund, Department Of Labor											
Fund Resources:											
Undisbursed Funds	2007	16		4601			6,167,700.00		1,199,649.19		4,968,050.81
	2006					3,456,566.12			3,311,480.06		145,086.06
	2005					1,916,462.97			1,910,689.71		5,773.26
	2004					305,995.43			64,200.00		241,795.43
	No Year					39,640,213.24		3,000,000.00	-4,328,353.93		46,968,567.17
Accounts Receivable						193,000.00					193,000.00
Unfilled Customer Orders						123,000.00				123,000.00	
Fund Equities:											
Unobligated Balances (Expired)						-73,803.63				140,430.83	-214,234.46
Unobligated Balances (Unexpired)						-4,225,916.35				5,220,813.58	-9,446,729.93
Accounts Payable						-17,958,055.22				4,915,652.97	-22,873,708.19
Undelivered Orders						-23,377,462.56				-3,389,862.41	-19,987,600.15
Subtotal		16		4601		-0-	6,167,700.00	3,000,000.00	2,157,665.03	7,010,034.97	-0-
Trust Fund Accounts											
Gifts And Bequests, Departmental Management, Labor											
Fund Resources:											
Undisbursed Funds	No Year	16		8131		162,738.01			20,313.09		142,424.92
Fund Equities:											
Unobligated Balances (Unexpired)						-147,703.01				-10,813.09	-136,889.92
Undelivered Orders						-15,035.00				-9,500.00	-5,535.00
Subtotal		16		8131		-0-			20,313.09	-20,313.09	-0-
Total, Departmental Management							428,948,907.00	2,772,087.73	476,390,663.01	-44,669,668.28	
Deductions For Offsetting Receipts											
Proprietary Receipts From The Public							-37,695,263.02		-37,695,263.02		
Intrabudgetary Transactions							-762,093,405.49		-762,093,405.49		
Total, Offsetting Receipts							-799,788,668.51		-799,788,668.51		
Total, Department Of Labor							56,153,991,439.55	-4,494,509.83	47,542,940,144.40	8,606,556,785.32	

Footnotes At End Of Chapter

Appropriations, Outlays, and Balances – Continued

Footnotes

1 The amounts in this column, unless otherwise footnoted, represent appropriations, increases and rescissions in borrowing authority or new contract authority. Appropriation accounts with appropriation transfer activity are presented in Table 1 (Appropriations and Appropriation Transfers) at the end of this chapter.

2 The amounts in this column, unless otherwise footnoted, represent transfers - other than appropriation transfers, borrowings (gross), investments (net), unrealized discounts or funds held outside the Treasury.

3 The amounts in this column, unless otherwise footnoted, represent obligated balances canceled for fiscal year 2002 pursuant to 31 U.S.C. 1553, changes in unfilled customer orders, accounts receivable, accounts payable, undelivered orders, unobligated balances and adjustments to borrowing and contract authority.

4 Unobligated balances for no-year or unexpired multiple year accounts are available for obligation; unobligated balances for expired fiscal year accounts are not available for obligation.

5 Subject to disposition by the administrative agency.

6 Excludes $125,091,677.66 refund of taxes.

Appropriations, Outlays, and Balances - Continued

Footnotes

Table 1 - Appropriations And Appropriation Transfers - Department Of Labor

Department Regular	Fiscal Year	Account Symbol	Net Appropriations And Appropriations Transfers	Appropriation Amount	Net Appropriation Transfers	Department Regular Involved	Fiscal Year Involved	Accounts Involved	Amount From or To (-)
16	0708	0327	112,500,000.00	465,000,000.00	-352,500,000.00	20	X	8144	-352,500,000.00
16	07	1700	134,572,669.00	141,572,669.00	-7,000,000.00	16	0708	1700	-7,000,000.00
16	0708	1700	14,000,000.00	0.00	14,000,000.00	16	07	1700	7,000,000.00
						16	X	4204	7,000,000.00
16	X	4204	-7,000,000.00	0.00	-7,000,000.00	16	0708	1700	-7,000,000.00
20	X	8042	-87,915,685.00	0.00	-87,915,685.00	60	07	8018	-1,577,991.00
						60	X	8051	-72,000,000.00
						60	06	8237	-86,391.00
						60	07	8237	-14,251,303.00
20	X	8144	352,500,000.00	0.00	352,500,000.00	16	0708	0327	352,500,000.00
Totals			518,656,984.00	606,572,669.00	-87,915,685.00				-87,915,685.00

Appropriations, Outlays, and Balances – Continued

Title	Period of Availability	Reg	Tr From	Account Number	Sub No.	Balances, Beginning Of Fiscal Year	Appropriations And Other Obligational Authority[1]	Transfers Borrowings And Investment (Net)[2]	Outlays (Net)	Balances Withdrawn And Other Transactions[3]	Balances, End Of Fiscal Year[4]
Department Of State											
Administration Of Foreign Affairs											
General Fund Accounts											
Salaries And Expenses, Department Of State											
Fund Resources:											
Undisbursed Funds	No Year	19		0107		1,215,992.29			-108,185.01		1,324,177.30
Accounts Receivable						-269,405.00					-269,405.00
Fund Equities:											
Unobligated Balances (Unexpired)						-691,298.78				108,185.01	-799,483.79
Undelivered Orders						-255,288.51					-255,288.51
Subtotal		19		0107		-0-			-108,185.01	108,185.01	-0-
Diplomatic And Consular Programs, Department Of State											
Fund Resources:											
Undisbursed Funds	2007-2008	19		0113			765,400,000.00		587,437.50		764,812,562.50
	2007					1,355,627,228.59	3,637,506,755.00		3,025,265,886.64		612,240,868.36
	2006-2007					633,612,192.67			548,491,302.86		807,135,925.73
	2006					199,563,400.72			500,962,068.00		132,650,124.67
	2005-2006					152,559,254.53			173,624,056.76		25,939,343.96
	2004-2006					106,781,008.83			94,999,549.10		57,559,705.43
	2005					5,677,208.52			24,868,534.84		81,912,473.99
	2004-2005					111,100,725.29			1,546,087.13		4,131,121.39
	2004					2,616,962.53			22,056,230.14		89,044,495.15
	2003-2004					129,149,909.47			402,889.95		2,214,072.58
	2003					3,656,314.50		48,981.79	18,594,444.23		110,604,447.03
	2002-2003					130,406,217.88			265,750.69		3,390,563.81
	2002					2,503.70		10,178.30	16,917,458.24	113,498,937.94	
	2001-2002								-25.00	2,528.70	
	No Year					1,366,534,472.57	798,706,787.00	-33,029,078.81	554,835,491.39		1,577,376,689.37
Transfer To:											
Peace Corps	2003	11	19	0113	44	16,822.01		-28,705.79	-11,883.78		
	2002					1,848.64		-1,848.64			
	No Year			0113		30,049.19		-30,049.19			
Agency For International Development											
	No Year	72	19	0113		1,798.29					1,798.29
Broadcasting Board Of Governors	2003	95	19	0113	68	24,276.00		-20,276.00	4,000.00		
Broadcasting Board Of Governors	2002	95	19	0113		-4,000.00			-4,000.00		
Accounts Receivable						8,329.66		-8,329.66			
Fund Equities:											
Unobligated Balances (Expired)						135,663,041.53				-57,340,145.62	193,003,187.15
Unobligated Balances (Unexpired)						-329,482,174.34				38,123,284.66	-367,605,459.00
Accounts Payable						-1,484,858,492.74				-419,806,714.18	-1,065,051,778.56
Undelivered Orders						-197,819,839.30				-826,645.87	-196,993,193.43
						-2,320,869,058.74				511,497,889.68	-2,832,366,948.42
Subtotal		19		0113		-0-	5,201,613,542.00	-33,059,128.00	4,983,405,278.69	185,149,135.31	-0-
Capital Investment Fund, Department Of State											
Fund Resources:											
Undisbursed Funds	No Year	19		0120		108,259,946.51	58,142,793.00		45,476,583.75		120,926,155.76

Appropriations, Outlays, and Balances - Continued

Title	Period of Availability	Reg	Tr From	Account Number	Sub No.	Balances, Beginning Of Fiscal Year	Appropriations And Other Obligational Authority[1]	Transfers Borrowings And Investment (Net)[2]	Outlays (Net)	Balances Withdrawn And Other Transactions[3]	Balances, End Of Fiscal Year[4]
Fund Equities:											
Unobligated Balances (Unexpired)						-80,902,300.94				-29,888,645.37	-51,013,655.57
Accounts Payable										21,258.24	-21,258.24
Undelivered Orders						-27,357,645.57				42,533,596.38	-69,891,241.95
Subtotal	Subtotal	19		0120		-0-	58,142,793.00		45,476,583.75	12,666,209.25	-0-
International Information Programs, Department Of State											
Fund Resources:											
Undisbursed Funds	No Year	19		0201		1,015,970.24					1,015,970.24
Fund Equities:											
Unobligated Balances (Unexpired)						-899,346.48				10,347.64	-909,694.12
Accounts Payable						-61,601.87					-61,601.87
Undelivered Orders						-55,021.89				-10,347.64	-44,674.25
Subtotal	Subtotal	19		0201		-0-					-0-
Educational And Cultural Exchange Programs, Department Of State											
Fund Resources:											
Undisbursed Funds	2007-2008	19		0209			19,500,000.00		7,994,835.58		11,505,164.42
	2003-2008					23,208,317.96		5,000,000.00	435,837.73		4,564,162.27
	2006-2007					19,552,069.28		18,390,000.00	19,292,015.53		22,306,302.43
	2005-2006					1,609,059.31			12,348,336.27		7,203,733.01
	2004-2005					10,677,491.24			1,051,095.48		557,963.83
	2003-2004					7,061,242.64			4,713,681.42		5,963,809.82
	2002-2003					284,438.80			855,930.00		6,205,312.64
	2001-2002					-897,076.01			261,412.82	23,025.98	-0-
	2000-2002					289,075,150.18	465,670,718.00		-1,254,213.89	357,137.88	351,009,159.93
	No Year					3,592,697.00			403,736,708.25		5,797,535.50
Accounts Receivable										-2,204,838.50	
Fund Equities:											
Unobligated Balances (Expired)						-816,984.68				1,644,714.13	-2,461,698.81
Unobligated Balances (Unexpired)						[5]20,528,773.13				16,259,569.44	-36,788,342.57
Accounts Payable						[5]13,446,585.70				-13,106,374.79	-340,210.91
Undelivered Orders						-319,371,046.89				56,151,844.67	-375,522,891.56
Subtotal	Subtotal	19		0209		-0-	485,170,718.00	23,390,000.00	449,435,639.19	59,125,078.81	-0-
Centralized Information Technology Modernization Program, State											
Fund Resources:											
Undisbursed Funds	No Year	19		0507		44,274,764.18			39,860,216.43	39,860,216.43	4,414,547.75
Fund Equities:											
Unobligated Balances (Unexpired)						-2,109,241.36				-917,087.10	-1,192,154.26
Accounts Payable										671,520.86	-671,520.86
Undelivered Orders						42,165,522.82				-39,614,650.19	-2,550,872.63
Subtotal	Subtotal	19		0507		-0-			39,860,216.43	-39,860,216.43	-0-
Protection Of Foreign Missions And Officials, State											
Fund Resources:											
Undisbursed Funds	2007-2008	19		0520		7,235,819.37	9,270,071.00		1,194,961.00		8,075,110.00
	2006-2007					2,826,287.39			5,882,480.26		1,353,339.11
	2005-2006					162,838.00			2,621,904.45		204,382.94
	2004-2005					-19,901.25			87,254.40		75,583.60
	2003-2004								-273,340.30		253,439.05
	2002-2003					47,542.39					47,542.39

Footnotes At End Of Chapter

Appropriations, Outlays, and Balances – Continued

Appropriation or Fund Account — Title	Reg	Tr From	Account Number	Sub No.	Period of Availability	Balances, Beginning Of Fiscal Year	Appropriations And Other Obligational Authority[1]	Transfers Borrowings And Investment (Net)[2]	Outlays (Net)	Balances Withdrawn And Other Transactions[3]	Balances, End Of Fiscal Year[4]
Protection Of Foreign Missions And Officials, State - Continued											
Fund Resources: - Continued											
Undisbursed Funds - Continued					2001-2002	16,723.94				16,723.94	
					No Year	414.64					414.64
Fund Equities:											
Unobligated Balances (Expired)						-90,965.06				613,728.88	-704,693.94
Unobligated Balances (Unexpired)						-1,295,786.89				6,223,705.45	-7,519,492.34
Accounts Payable						-271,576.65				-197,954.78	-73,621.87
Undelivered Orders						-8,611,395.88				-6,899,392.30	-1,712,003.58
Subtotal	19		0520			-0-	9,270,071.00		9,513,259.81	-243,188.81	-0-
Emergencies In Diplomatic And Consular Services, State											
Fund Resources:											
Undisbursed Funds	19		0522		No Year	39,990,772.49	13,440,000.00		24,688,458.11		28,742,314.38
Accounts Receivable						39,312.90				10,512.90	28,800.00
Fund Equities:											
Unobligated Balances (Unexpired)						-25,082,241.53				-6,748,344.14	-18,333,897.39
Accounts Payable										2,096,946.95	-2,096,946.95
Undelivered Orders						-14,947,843.86				-6,607,573.82	-8,340,270.04
Subtotal	19		0522			-0-	13,440,000.00		24,688,458.11	-11,248,458.11	-0-
Payment To The American Institute In Taiwan, State											
Fund Resources:											
Undisbursed Funds:	19		0523		2007	-11,205.56	15,826,000.00		12,409,636.03		3,416,363.97
					2006				-322,778.00		311,572.44
					2005	1,248,039.03					1,248,039.03
					2004				150,000.00		[6]-150,000.00
					2003	98,608.03					98,608.03
					2002	-132,289.14					[6]-132,289.14
					2000	-137,924.64					[6]-137,924.64
Accounts Receivable						727,807.58				-2,104,523.00	2,832,330.58
Fund Equities:											
Unobligated Balances (Expired)						-1,365,246.16				465,750.00	[7]-1,830,996.16
Accounts Payable						-132,289.14				-150,000.00	17,710.86
Undelivered Orders						-295,500.00				5,377,914.97	-5,673,414.97
Subtotal	19		0523			-0-	15,826,000.00		12,236,858.03	3,589,141.97	-0-
Office Of The Inspector General, State											
Fund Resources:											
Undisbursed Funds:	19		0529		2007-2009		1,500,000.00				1,500,000.00
					2007	1,300,000.00	29,913,925.00		25,539,950.01	1,300,000.00	4,373,974.99
					2006-2007	3,781,110.08			2,813,947.10		967,162.98
					2006	217,751.14			-158,743.17		376,494.31
					2005	288,423.00			-3,606.43		292,029.43
					2004	230,057.28			-1,390.26		231,447.54
					2003	432,444.91			1,602.15	430,842.76	
					2002	52,761.23					52,761.23
Fund Equities:					No Year						
Unobligated Balances (Expired)						-466,665.72				363,317.28	-829,983.00
Unobligated Balances (Unexpired)						-1,309,123.89				200,577.76	-1,509,701.65

Appropriations, Outlays, and Balances - Continued

Appropriation or Fund Account — Title	Period of Availability	Dept Reg	Tr From	Account Number	Sub No.	Balances, Beginning Of Fiscal Year	Appropriations And Other Obligational Authority[1]	Transfers Borrowings And Investment (Net)[2]	Outlays (Net)	Balances Withdrawn And Other Transactions[3]	Balances, End Of Fiscal Year[4]
Accounts Payable						-921,631.51				-446,469.79	-475,161.72
Undelivered Orders						-3,605,126.52				1,373,897.59	-4,979,024.11
Subtotal		19		0529		-0-	31,413,925.00		29,491,759.40	1,922,165.60	-0-
Embassy Security, Construction, And Maintenance, State											
Fund Resources:											
Undisbursed Funds	No Year	19		0535		3,465,565,744.17	1,490,852,152.00	157,196.17	891,530,378.63		4,065,044,713.71
Transfer To:											
Agency For International Development	No Year	72	19	0535		81,441.63					81,441.63
Broadcasting Board Of Governors	No Year	95	19	0535		157,196.17		-157,196.17			
Accounts Receivable						89,733,957.70				46,811,169.10	42,922,788.60
Fund Equities:											
Unobligated Balances (Unexpired)						-1,277,133,357.76				393,339,805.86	-1,670,473,163.62
Accounts Payable						-98,541,568.35				-89,916,153.24	-8,625,415.11
Undelivered Orders						-2,179,863,413.56				249,086,951.65	-2,428,950,365.21
Subtotal		19		0535		-0-	1,490,852,152.00		891,530,378.63	599,321,773.37	-0-
Acquisition, Operation, And Maintenance Of Buildings Abroad, Special Foreign Currency Program, State											
Fund Resources:											
Undisbursed Funds	No Year	19		0538		0.30					0.30
Fund Equities:											
Unobligated Balances (Unexpired)						-0.30					-0.30
Subtotal		19		0538		-0-					-0-
Payment To The Foreign Service Retirement And Disability Fund, State											
Fund Resources:											
Undisbursed Funds	2007	19		0540		387.80	199,700,000.00		199,700,000.00		387.80
Fund Equities:											
Accounts Payable	2004					-387.80					-387.80
Subtotal		19		0540		-0-	199,700,000.00		199,700,000.00		-0-
Representation Allowances, State											
Fund Resources:											
Undisbursed Funds	2007	19		0545		1,375,008.29	8,175,235.00		6,780,565.56		1,394,669.44
	2006					241,670.32			1,189,467.11		185,541.18
	2005					295,668.54			12,408.99		229,261.33
	2004					123,026.07			5,972.69		289,695.85
	2003					139,675.41			2,402.75		120,623.32
	2002					13,650.00			547.03	139,128.38	82,401.00
Accounts Receivable										-68,751.00	
Fund Equities:											
Unobligated Balances (Expired)						-636,485.03				-60,423.60	-576,061.43
Accounts Payable						-8,521.27				-656.36	-7,864.91
Undelivered Orders						-1,543,692.33				174,573.45	-1,718,265.78
Subtotal		19		0545		-0-	8,175,235.00		7,991,364.13	183,870.87	-0-
Repatriation Loans, Liquidating Account, State											
Fund Resources:											
Undisbursed Funds	No Year	19		0600		830,771.66			-60,000.37	[a]473,351.53	417,420.50
Fund Equities:											
Unobligated Balances (Unexpired)						-473,351.53				-408,723.59	-64,627.94

Footnotes At End Of Chapter

Appropriations, Outlays, and Balances – Continued

Appropriation or Fund Account — Title	Period of Availability	Dept Reg	Tr From	Account Number	Sub No.	Balances, Beginning Of Fiscal Year	Appropriations And Other Obligational Authority[1]	Transfers Borrowings And Investment (Net)[2]	Outlays (Net)	Balances Withdrawn And Other Transactions[3]	Balances, End Of Fiscal Year[4]
Repatriation Loans, Liquidating Account, State - Continued											
Fund Equities: - Continued											
Accounts Payable						-357,420.13			------	-4,627.57	-352,792.56
	Subtotal	19		0600		-0-			-60,000.37	60,000.37	-0-
Repatriation Loans, Program Account, State											
Fund Resources:											
Undisbursed Funds	2007	19		0601		------	1,302,154.00		1,270,303.75		31,850.25
	2006					144,532.69			144,531.99		0.70
	2005					211,462.07			101,462.07		110,000.00
	2004					3,005.33					3,005.33
	2003					93.61					93.61
	2002					540,683.11				540,683.11	
Fund Equities:											
Unobligated Balances (Expired)						-2,929.92				507.27	-3,437.19
Undelivered Orders						-896,846.89				-755,334.19	-141,512.70
	Subtotal	19		0601		-0-	1,302,154.00		1,516,297.81	-214,143.81	-0-
Special Fund Accounts											
Foreign Service National Defined Contributions Retirement Fund, State											
Fund Resources:											
Undisbursed Funds	No Year	19		5497		34,407,109.47	507,636.82		36,223,253.07	-34,717,106.48	[6]-1,308,506.78
Fund Equities:											
Unobligated Balances (Unexpired)						-33,408,599.70					[6]1,308,506.78
Accounts Payable						-998,509.77				-998,509.77	-0-
	Subtotal	19		5497		-0-	507,636.82		36,223,253.07	-35,715,616.25	-0-
H-1B And L Fraud Prevention And Detection Account, State											
Fund Resources:											
Undisbursed Funds	No Year	19		5515		29,911,187.96	45,736,548.23	33,059,128.00	5,272,617.70	69,344,223.01	103,434,246.49
Fund Equities:											
Unobligated Balances (Unexpired)						-29,911,187.96					-99,255,410.97
Accounts Payable										153.38	-153.38
Undelivered Orders						------				4,178,682.14	-4,178,682.14
	Subtotal	19		5515		-0-	45,736,548.23	33,059,128.00	5,272,617.70	73,523,058.53	-0-
Intragovernmental Funds											
Working Capital Fund, Department Of State											
Fund Resources:											
Undisbursed Funds	No Year	19		4519		194,369,606.64			82,711,343.83		111,658,262.81
Accounts Receivable	No Year	19		4519	1	289,976,123.30			32,339,295.86		257,636,827.44
						159,263,808.35				-6,391,052.88	165,654,861.23
Fund Equities:											
Unobligated Balances (Unexpired)						-146,087,003.04				-41,676,426.39	-104,410,576.65
Accounts Payable						-111,287,435.80				-78,063,026.20	-33,224,409.60
Undelivered Orders						-386,235,099.45				11,079,865.78	-397,314,965.23
	Subtotal	19		4519		-0-			115,050,639.69	-115,050,639.69	-0-

Appropriations, Outlays, and Balances - Continued

Appropriation or Fund Account: Title	Period of Availability	Account Symbol: Dept Reg	Tr From	Account Number	Sub No.	Balances, Beginning Of Fiscal Year	Appropriations And Other Obligational Authority[1]	Transfers Borrowings And Investment (Net)[2]	Outlays (Net)	Balances Withdrawn And Other Transactions[3]	Balances, End Of Fiscal Year[4]
Trust Fund Accounts											
Trust Funds, Department Of State											
Fund Resources:											
Undisbursed Funds	No Year	19		8167		1,929,599.39	-372,588.00		1,075,020.47		481,990.92
Unrealized Discount On Investments						-44,038.72					-44,038.72
Fund Equities:											
Unobligated Balances (Unexpired)						-1,685,961.64				-1,685,961.64	
Accounts Payable						-57,962.23				235,288.82	-293,251.05
Undelivered Orders						-141,636.80				3,064.35	-144,701.15
Subtotal		19		8167		-0-	-372,588.00		1,075,020.47	-1,447,608.47	-0-
Foreign Service Retirement And Disability Fund											
Fund Resources:											
Undisbursed Funds	No Year	19		8186		1,105,176.64	1,245,703,890.88	-501,996,000.00	745,677,097.94		[6]-864,030.42
Investments In Public Debt Securities						13,875,717,000.00		501,996,000.00			14,377,713,000.00
Accounts Receivable						[5]196,825,204.21					196,825,204.21
Fund Equities:											
Unobligated Balances (Unexpired)						[5.]14,073,647,380.85				500,026,792.94	-14,573,674,173.79
Accounts Payable						-0-				500,026,792.94	
Subtotal		19		8186		-0-	1,245,703,890.88		745,677,097.94	500,026,792.94	-0-
Foreign Service National Separation Liability Trust Fund, State											
Fund Resources:											
Undisbursed Funds	No Year	19		8340		88,893,097.94	10,641,118.00		16,980,292.34		82,553,923.60
Fund Equities:											
Unobligated Balances (Unexpired)						-86,889,134.85				-48,077,661.27	-38,811,473.58
Accounts Payable										40,048,428.35	40,048,428.35
Undelivered Orders						-2,003,963.09				1,690,058.58	-3,694,021.67
Subtotal		19		8340		-0-	10,641,118.00		16,980,292.34	-6,339,174.34	-0-
Foreign Service National Separation Liability Trust Fund, Department Of State											
Fund Resources:											
Undisbursed Funds	No Year	19		8341		21,151.98					21,151.98
Fund Equities:											
Unobligated Balances (Unexpired)						-21,151.98				21,151.98	-21,151.98
Subtotal		19		8341		-0-				-21,151.98	-0-
Unconditional Gift Fund, State											
Fund Resources:											
Undisbursed Funds	No Year	19		8821		8,313,981.25	8,025,686.25		5,897,915.26		10,441,752.24
Unrealized Discount On Investments						-937.80					-937.80
Fund Equities:											
Unobligated Balances (Unexpired)						-4,391,701.16				567,914.09	-4,959,615.25
Accounts Payable						-1,600,417.76				-344,312.74	-1,256,105.02
Undelivered Orders						-2,320,924.53				1,904,169.64	-4,225,094.17
Subtotal		19		8821		-0-	8,025,686.25		5,897,915.26	2,127,770.99	-0-

Footnotes At End Of Chapter

Appropriations, Outlays, and Balances – Continued

Appropriation or Fund Account — Title	Period of Availability	Dept — Reg	Dept — Tr From	Account Number	Sub No.	Balances, Beginning Of Fiscal Year	Appropriations And Other Obligational Authority[1]	Transfers Borrowings And Investment (Net)[2]	Outlays (Net)	Balances Withdrawn And Other Transactions[3]	Balances, End Of Fiscal Year[4]
Conditional Gift Fund, General, State											
Fund Resources:											
Undisbursed Funds	No Year	19		8822		4,202,976.50	2,060,331.73	-976,320.15	463,661.60		4,823,326.48
Unrealized Discount On Investments						-584,345.87		-23,679.85			-608,025.72
Investments In Public Debt Securities						4,005,000.00		1,000,000.00			5,005,000.00
Fund Equities:											
Unobligated Balances (Unexpired)						-6,367,671.66				119,994.17	-6,487,665.83
Accounts Payable						-241,906.24				1,039,713.59	-1,281,619.83
Undelivered Orders						-1,014,052.73				436,962.37	-1,451,015.10
	Subtotal	19		8822		-0-	2,060,331.73		463,661.60	1,596,670.13	-0-
Total, Administration Of Foreign Affairs							8,827,209,213.91	23,390,000.00	7,621,318,406.67	1,229,280,807.24	
International Organizations And Conferences											
General Fund Accounts											
Contributions For International Peacekeeping Activities, State											
Fund Resources:											
Undisbursed Funds	2007-2008	19		1124			453,291,250.00				453,291,250.00
	2007						964,983,750.00		882,061,517.00		82,922,233.00
	2006-2007					283,141,189.00			283,141,189.00		
	2006					7,366,406.78			7,366,405.89		0.89
	2005-2006					156.91					156.91
	2004					1.00					1.00
Fund Equities:											
Unobligated Balances (Expired)						-156.91					-156.91
Unobligated Balances (Unexpired)						-129,800,000.00				-46,800,000.00	-83,000,000.00
Accounts Payable						-7,366,407.78				-7,366,406.78	-1.00
Undelivered Orders						-153,341,189.00				299,872,294.89	-453,213,483.89
	Subtotal	19		1124		-0-	1,418,275,000.00		1,172,569,111.89	245,705,888.11	-0-
International Conferences And Contingencies, State											
Fund Resources:											
Undisbursed Funds	No Year	19		1125		191,269.65			-1,159.96		192,429.61
Accounts Receivable						-66,800.00					-66,800.00
Fund Equities:											
Unobligated Balances (Unexpired)						-124,469.65				125,629.61	-125,629.61
Undelivered Orders						-0-				-124,469.65	-0-
	Subtotal	19		1125		-0-			-1,159.96	1,159.96	-0-
Contributions To International Organizations, State											
Fund Resources:											
Undisbursed Funds	2007-2008	19		1126			50,000,000.00				50,000,000.00
	2007					32,012,053.26	1,151,317,140.00		921,348,104.27		229,969,035.73
	2006					12,308,349.76			20,565,554.99		11,446,498.27
	2005					3,564,094.31		-6,000,000.00	1,555,325.86		4,753,023.90
	2004					6,391,165.61			1,603,967.83		1,960,126.48
	2003					2,769,475.14			780,642.76		5,610,522.85
	2002								116,897.88		
	No Year					85,653.03		6,000,000.00			6,085,653.03

Appropriations, Outlays, and Balances - Continued

Appropriation or Fund Account — Title	Dept Reg	Tr From	Account Number	Sub No.	Period of Availability	Balances, Beginning Of Fiscal Year	Appropriations And Other Obligational Authority[1]	Transfers Borrowings And Investment (Net)[2]	Outlays (Net)	Balances Withdrawn And Other Transactions[3]	Balances, End Of Fiscal Year[4]
Fund Equities:											
Unobligated Balances (Expired)						15,239.51				1,544,553.23	-1,529,313.72
Unobligated Balances (Unexpired)						-82,952.38				6,000,000.00	-6,082,952.38
Accounts Payable						-54,361,315.97				-1,840,308.97	-52,521,007.00
Undelivered Orders						-2,701,762.27				246,989,824.89	-249,691,587.16
Arrearage Payments, Department Of State											
Subtotal	19		1126		Subtotal	-0-	1,201,317,140.00		945,970,493.59	255,346,646.41	-0-
Fund Resources:											
Undisbursed Funds	19		1130		No Year	-13.38			-13.83		0.45
Fund Equities:											
Unobligated Balances (Unexpired)						13.38				13.83	-0.45
Subtotal	19		1130		Subtotal	-0-			-13.83	13.83	-0-
Total, International Organizations And Conferences							2,619,592,140.00		2,118,538,431.69	501,053,708.31	
International Commissions											
General Fund Accounts											
Salaries And Expenses, International Boundary And Water Commission, United States And Mexico, State											
Fund Resources:											
Undisbursed Funds	19		1069		2007	4,636,062.27	28,368,201.00		25,159,126.02	206,291.83	3,209,074.98
					2006	1,848,533.98			4,197,279.72		438,782.55
					2005	822,310.64			1,619,778.79		228,755.19
					2004	168,592.64			52,400.29		769,910.35
					2003	206,291.83			11,699.80		156,892.84
Accounts Receivable						78,318.59				-118,213.71	196,532.30
Unfilled Customer Orders						1,325,870.00				560,336.08	765,533.92
Fund Equities:											
Unobligated Balances (Expired)						-759,570.46				372,838.79	-1,132,409.25
Accounts Payable						-79,840.90				-76,440.14	-3,400.76
Undelivered Orders						-8,246,568.59				-3,616,896.47	-4,629,672.12
Subtotal	19		1069		Subtotal	-0-	28,368,201.00		31,040,284.62	-2,672,083.62	-0-
Construction, International Boundary And Water Commission, United States And Mexico, State											
Fund Resources:											
Undisbursed Funds	19		1078		No Year	9,154,036.70	5,232,308.00		5,389,605.28		8,996,739.42
Accounts Receivable						2,140,320.62				-1,921,157.12	4,061,477.74
Unfilled Customer Orders										-68,484.74	68,484.74
Fund Equities:											
Unobligated Balances (Unexpired)						-2,960,458.91				3,407,271.44	-6,367,730.35
Accounts Payable						-7,121.18				-7,121.18	-0-
Undelivered Orders						-8,326,777.23				-1,567,805.68	-6,758,971.55
Subtotal	19		1078		Subtotal	-0-	5,232,308.00		5,389,605.28	-157,297.28	-0-
American Sections, International Commissions, State											
Fund Resources:											
Undisbursed Funds	19		1082		2007	-0-	9,962,296.00		6,794,624.13		3,167,671.87

Footnotes At End Of Chapter

Appropriations, Outlays, and Balances – Continued

Appropriation or Fund Account — Title	Period of Availability	Reg	Tr From	Account Number	Sub No.	Balances, Beginning Of Fiscal Year	Appropriations And Other Obligational Authority[1]	Transfers Borrowings And Investment (Net)[2]	Outlays (Net)	Balances Withdrawn And Other Transactions[3]	Balances, End Of Fiscal Year[4]
American Sections, International Commissions, State - Continued											
Fund Resources: - Continued											
Undisbursed Funds - Continued	2006					2,942,987.48			2,229,718.51		713,268.97
	2005					344,602.01			75,899.88		268,702.13
	2004					409,822.40			16,295.05		393,527.35
	2003					242,484.59			68,518.35		173,966.24
	2002					371,422.22			47,020.19	324,402.03	
	No Year					657,129.68			-14,489.67		671,619.35
Fund Equities:											
Unobligated Balances (Expired)						-231,665.78				294,299.25	-525,965.03
Unobligated Balances (Unexpired)						-655,568.66				14,489.67	-670,058.33
Accounts Payable						-162,327.40				-59,685.07	-102,642.33
Undelivered Orders						-3,918,886.54				171,203.68	-4,090,090.22
Subtotal		19		1082		-0-	9,962,296.00		9,217,586.44	744,709.56	-0-
International Fisheries Commissions, State											
Fund Resources:											
Undisbursed Funds	2007	19		1087		313,478.58	23,693,472.00		23,468,520.98		224,951.02
	2006					83,268.37			187,270.05		126,208.53
	2005					61,871.86			4,295.79		78,972.58
	2004					64,921.75			2,434.32		59,437.54
	2003										64,921.75
	2002					129,538.89			0.20	129,538.69	
Fund Equities:											
Unobligated Balances (Expired)						-164,906.71				-42,339.58	-122,567.13
Accounts Payable						-1,217.69				12,770.97	-13,988.66
Undelivered Orders						-486,955.05				-69,019.42	-417,935.63
Subtotal		19		1087		-0-	23,693,472.00		23,662,521.34	30,950.66	-0-
Total, International Commissions							67,256,277.00		69,309,997.68	-2,053,720.68	
Other											
General Fund Accounts											
United States Emergency Refugee And Migration Assistance Fund, Funds Appropriated To The President											
Fund Resources:											
Undisbursed Funds	No Year	11		0040		11,688,807.00	110,000,000.00	-58,715,000.00	3,571.66		62,970,235.34
Transfer To:											
Department Of State	No Year	19	11	0040		41,268,309.45		58,715,000.00	53,820,956.27		46,162,353.18
Fund Equities:											
Unobligated Balances (Unexpired)						[5]15,327,025.18				49,429,918.23	-64,756,943.41
Accounts Payable						[5]13,340,127.70				-13,343,693.06	3,565.36
Undelivered Orders						-24,289,963.57				20,089,246.90	-44,379,210.47
Subtotal		11		0040		-0-	110,000,000.00		53,824,527.93	56,175,472.07	-0-
International Narcotics Control And Law Enforcement, Funds Appropriated To The President											
Fund Resources:											
Undisbursed Funds	2007-2009	11		1022			472,615,883.00	-472,615,883.00			

Appropriations, Outlays, and Balances - Continued

Appropriation or Fund Account — Title	Dept Reg	Tr From	Account Number	Sub No.	Period of Availability	Balances, Beginning Of Fiscal Year	Appropriations And Other Obligational Authority[1]	Transfers Borrowings And Investment (Net)[2]	Outlays (Net)	Balances Withdrawn And Other Transactions[3]	Balances, End Of Fiscal Year[4]
					2007-2008		334,600,000.00	-334,600,000.00	---	---	---
					2006-2008		-13,000,000.00	13,000,000.00	---	---	---
					2002-2003	57,500.00					57,500.00
					2002			4,827.96		4,827.96	
					2001-2002			4,148,203.84		4,148,203.84	
					No Year	5,778,462.48	20,361,000.00	-20,361,000.00	-496,803.38		6,275,265.86
Transfer To:											
Department Of State	19	11	1022		2007-2009			558,977,883.00	68,644,133.66		490,333,749.34
					2007-2008			334,600,000.00	-365,229,045.96		699,829,045.96
					2006-2008	507,520,570.43		-14,242,500.00	161,672,196.63		331,605,873.80
					2003-2008			299,733.91			299,733.91
					2007				170,688.90		[6]170,688.90
					2006-2007	96,204,138.05		24,658,000.00	-248,168,211.93		369,030,349.98
					2005-2007	402,986,570.00			213,749,669.66		189,236,900.34
					2002-2007			1,826,820.10			1,826,820.10
					2005-2006	437,601,335.26			286,141,321.40		151,460,013.86
					2004-2006	59,635,112.14			21,087,033.17		38,548,078.97
					2005	215,938.26					215,938.26
					2004-2005	80,481,369.12			40,809,749.74		39,671,619.38
					2003-2005	793,001.00			765,707.00		27,294.00
					2003-2004	38,952,626.20		-299,733.91	15,506,407.29		23,146,485.00
					2003	60,618.68					60,618.68
					2002-2003	45,857,644.32		-1,826,820.10	19,162,148.43		24,868,675.79
					2002	7,632.33		-4,827.96	2,804.37		
					2001-2002	7,381,997.34		-4,871,687.10	2,510,310.24		
					2001	-6,392.23					[6]6,392.23
Treasury	20	11	1022		No Year	54,934,364.73		21,084,483.26	21,154,532.79	32,727,037.15	54,864,315.20
Accounts Receivable					No Year	1,031,545.18		430,547.19	430,547.19		600,997.99
Fund Equities:											
Unobligated Balances (Expired)						41,720,710.00				123,005,262.99	8,993,672.85
Unobligated Balances (Unexpired)						[5]-22,729,303.13				264,866,790.17	[9]145,734,566.12
Accounts Payable						-334,914,579.72				-237,453,178.58	[10]-599,781,369.89
Undelivered Orders						[5]-149,318,600.17				499,142,250.27	88,134,578.41
Subtotal	11		1022			-1,274,252,260.27	814,576,883.00	109,777,500.00	237,913,189.20	686,441,193.80	-1,773,394,510.54
East-West Center, Department Of State						-0-					-0-
Fund Resources:											
Undisbursed Funds	19		0202		2007	585,067.00	18,994,267.00		18,341,200.00		
					2006	679,650.00			585,067.00		
					No Year				679,650.00		
Subtotal	19		0202				18,994,267.00		19,605,917.00		653,067.00
Fund Equities:											
Accounts Payable						-585,067.00				-585,067.00	
Undelivered Orders						-679,650.00				-26,583.00	-653,067.00
Subtotal	19					-0-				-611,650.00	-0-
North/South Center, Department Of State											
Fund Resources:											
Undisbursed Funds	19		0203		No Year	1,475.93			-0.28		1,476.21

Footnotes At End Of Chapter

433

Appropriations, Outlays, and Balances – Continued

Title	Period of Availability	Reg	Tr From	Account Number	Sub No.	Balances, Beginning Of Fiscal Year	Appropriations And Other Obligational Authority[1]	Transfers Borrowings And Investment (Net)[2]	Outlays (Net)	Balances Withdrawn And Other Transactions[3]	Balances, End Of Fiscal Year[4]
North/South Center, Department Of State - Continued											
Fund Equities:											
Unobligated Balances (Unexpired)		19				-1,475.55					-1,475.55
Accounts Payable						-0.38			-0.28	0.28	-0.66
Subtotal		19		0203		-0-				0.28	-0-
National Endowment For Democracy, Department Of State											
Fund Resources:											
Undisbursed Funds	1998-1999	19		0210		-418,139.00			-418,139.00		
	No Year	19		0210		64,109,195.96	74,042,100.00		68,831,912.00		69,319,383.96
Fund Equities:											
Unobligated Balances (Expired)						418,139.00				418,139.00	
Accounts Payable						-2,706,897.98				-2,706,897.98	
Undelivered Orders						-61,402,297.98				7,917,085.98	-69,319,383.96
Subtotal		19		0210		-0-	74,042,100.00		68,413,773.00	5,628,327.00	-0-
Russian Far East Technical Assistance Center, Department Of State											
Fund Resources:											
Undisbursed Funds	No Year	19		0211		77,696.78					77,696.78
Fund Equities:											
Unobligated Balances (Unexpired)		19		0211		-77,696.78					-77,696.78
Subtotal		19		0211		-0-					-0-
Payment To The Asia Foundation, State											
Fund Resources:											
Undisbursed Funds	No Year	19		0525		5,648,315.68	13,821,192.00		14,418,952.95		5,050,554.73
Fund Equities:											
Unobligated Balances (Unexpired)						-1,582,000.00				-244,802.27	-1,337,197.73
Accounts Payable						-136,153.19				-136,153.19	
Undelivered Orders						-3,930,162.49				-216,805.49	-3,713,357.00
Subtotal		19		0525		-0-	13,821,192.00		14,418,952.95	-597,760.95	-0-
International Narcotics Control And Law Enforcement, Department Of State											
Fund Resources:											
Undisbursed Funds	No Year	19		1022		47,440.80					47,440.80
Fund Equities:											
Accounts Payable		19		1022		-47,440.80					-47,440.80
Subtotal		19		1022		-0-					-0-
Global HIV/AIDS Initiative											
Fund Resources:											
Undisbursed Funds	No Year	19		1030		57,683,960.31	3,246,519,800.00	-2,802,601,671.00	272,307,314.33		229,294,774.98
Transfer To:											
Peace Corps	No Year	11	19	1030		7,943,069.32		15,967,770.00	7,707,178.76		16,203,660.56
Department Of Labor	No Year	16	19	1030	44	1,495,304.49		1,580,000.00	1,285,525.25		1,789,779.24
United States Agency For International Development	No Year	72	19	1030	1	1,265,693,405.14		1,729,503,583.00	1,064,696,391.57		1,930,500,596.57
Department Of Health And Human Services, Departmental Management	No Year	75	19	1030		729,012,512.04		999,477,539.00	701,313,962.48		1,027,176,088.56
Defense	No Year	97	19	1030		62,815,562.85		56,072,779.00	33,022,285.69		85,866,056.16
Accounts Receivable						-17,158.91				-7,955.65	-9,203.26
Unfilled Customer Orders						635.12				635.12	
Fund Equities:											
Unobligated Balances (Unexpired)						[5]-5,255,367,310.40				336,409,867.06	-591,777,177.46
Accounts Payable						[5]-5,173,649,096.25				140,275,377.12	-313,924,473.37

Appropriations, Outlays, and Balances - Continued

Appropriation or Fund Account — Title	Account Symbol — Period of Availability	Dept Reg	Dept Tr From	Account Number	Sub No.	Balances, Beginning Of Fiscal Year	Appropriations And Other Obligational Authority[1]	Transfers Borrowings And Investment (Net)[2]	Outlays (Net)	Balances Withdrawn And Other Transactions[3]	Balances, End Of Fiscal Year[4]
Undelivered Orders						[5]-1,695,610,883.71				689,509,218.27	-2,385,120,101.98
	Subtotal	19		1030		-0-	3,246,519,800.00		2,080,332,658.08	1,166,187,141.92	-0-
Democracy Fund, State											
Fund Resources:											
Undisbursed Funds	2007-2009	19		1121			94,050,000.00		243,000.00		93,807,000.00
	2007-2008	19					260,000,000.00	-63,000,000.00			197,000,000.00
	2006-2008	19				86,055,000.00			20,993,242.48		65,061,757.52
	2006-2007	19				22,500,000.00			1,885,292.55		20,614,707.45
Transfer To:											
United States Agency For International Development	2007-2008	72	19	1121				63,000,000.00			63,000,000.00
Fund Equities:											
Unobligated Balances (Unexpired)						-83,981,906.00				115,279,986.97	-199,261,892.97
Undelivered Orders						-24,573,094.00				215,648,478.00	-240,221,572.00
	Subtotal	19		1121		-0-	354,050,000.00		23,121,535.03	330,928,464.97	-0-
Migration And Refugee Assistance, State											
Fund Resources:											
Undisbursed Funds	2007-2008	19		1143			130,500,000.00		65,940,000.00		64,560,000.00
	2006-2007	19				70,250,000.00			65,145,412.35		5,104,587.65
	2005-2006	19				16,515,708.78			14,363,238.49		2,152,470.29
	2004-2005	19				40,782.00			-7,416.00		48,198.00
	2002-2003	19				336.12					336.12
	2002	19							-5,917.30	5,917.30	
	No Year	19				279,997,796.37	833,033,152.00		870,558,440.73		242,472,507.64
Fund Equities:											
Unobligated Balances (Expired)						-9.00				100,367.49	-100,376.49
Unobligated Balances (Unexpired)						-37,972,742.04				8,883,663.49	-46,856,405.53
Accounts Payable						-93,363,820.77				-93,363,463.44	-357.33
Undelivered Orders						-235,468,051.46				31,912,908.89	-267,380,960.35
	Subtotal	19		1143		-0-	963,533,152.00		1,015,993,758.27	-52,460,606.27	-0-
United States Bilateral Science And Technology Agreements, State											
Fund Resources:											
Undisbursed Funds	No Year	19		1151		24,278.47					24,278.47
Fund Equities:											
Unobligated Balances (Unexpired)						-0.47					-0.47
Accounts Payable						-24,278.00					-24,278.00
	Subtotal	19		1151		-0-					-0-
Andean Counterdrug Initiative, Department Of State											
Fund Resources:											
Undisbursed Funds	2007-2009	19		1154			721,500,000.00	-226,484,280.00	15,276,854.77		479,738,865.23
	2006-2008	19				469,839,663.82			193,793,468.37		276,046,195.45
	2005-2007	19				294,646,037.60			155,067,830.02		139,578,207.58
	2004-2006	19				130,559,721.29			54,122,451.61		76,437,269.68
	2004-2005	19				54,563.00			2,457.00		52,106.00
	2003-2004	19				21,294,767.67			3,807,390.91		17,487,376.76
	No Year	19				137,173,542.94			60,965,491.63		76,208,051.31
Transfer To:											
United States Agency For International Development	2007-2009	72	19	1154				226,484,280.00	3,846,144.58		222,638,135.42

Footnotes At End Of Chapter

Appropriations, Outlays, and Balances – Continued

Appropriation or Fund Account — Title	Period of Availability	Reg	Tr From	Account Number	Sub No.	Balances, Beginning Of Fiscal Year	Appropriations And Other Obligational Authority[1]	Transfers Borrowings And Investment (Net)[2]	Outlays (Net)	Balances Withdrawn And Other Transactions[3]	Balances, End Of Fiscal Year[4]
Andean Counterdrug Initiative, Department Of State - Continued											
Fund Resources: - Continued											
United States Agency For International Development - Continued											
	2006-2008					217,772,145.79			121,590,660.98		96,181,484.81
	2005-2007					75,372,689.54			83,174,471.27		[6]7,801,781.73
	2004-2006					12,770,081.96			1,538,623.25		11,231,458.71
	No Year					12,432,500.24			5,028,909.88		7,403,590.36
Accounts Receivable						1,604,460.49				292.00	1,604,168.49
Fund Equities:											
Unobligated Balances (Expired)						-761,596.22				2,577,063.21	-3,338,659.43
Unobligated Balances (Unexpired)						-142,664,299.91				238,056,551.35	-380,710,851.26
Accounts Payable						-80,119,120.25				2,520,895.32	-82,640,015.57
Undelivered Orders						-1,149,985,157.96				-219,869,556.15	-930,115,601.81
Subtotal		19		1154		-0-	721,500,000.00		698,214,754.27	23,285,245.73	-0-
Center For Eastern-Western Dialogue Trust Fund											
Fund Resources:											
Undisbursed Funds	No Year	19		1155		3,339.00					3,339.00
Fund Equities:											
Accounts Payable						-3,339.00					-3,339.00
Subtotal		19		1155		-0-					-0-
Special Fund Accounts											
Fisherman's Protective Fund, Special Account, State											
Fund Resources:											
Undisbursed Funds	No Year	19		5116		630,948.81					630,948.81
Fund Equities:											
Unobligated Balances (Unexpired)						-630,948.81					-630,948.81
Subtotal		19		5116		-0-					-0-
Fishermen's Guaranty Fund, State											
Fund Resources:											
Undisbursed Funds	No Year	19		5121		2,747,861.55					2,747,861.55
Fund Equities:											
Unobligated Balances (Unexpired)						-2,747,861.55					-2,747,861.55
Subtotal		19		5121		-0-					-0-
International Center, Washington, D. C., State											
Fund Resources:											
Undisbursed Funds	No Year	19		5151		1,642,116.71			2,198,782.17	-2,982,000.00	[6]6,556,665.46
Accounts Receivable										2,982,000.00	2,982,000.00
Fund Equities:											
Unobligated Balances (Unexpired)						-720,424.50				93,059.26	-813,483.76
Accounts Payable										2,377.38	-2,377.38
Undelivered Orders						-921,692.21				687,781.19	-1,609,473.40
Subtotal		19		5151		-0-			2,198,782.17	-2,198,782.17	-0-
International Litigation Fund, Department Of State											
Fund Resources:											
Undisbursed Funds	No Year	19		5177		8,080,082.99			795,255.87		7,284,827.12
Fund Equities:											
Unobligated Balances (Unexpired)						[5]-5,870,386.83				-2,555,899.74	-3,314,487.09

Appropriations, Outlays, and Balances - Continued

Appropriation or Fund Account — Title	Period of Availability	Dept Reg	Tr From	Account Number	Sub No.	Balances, Beginning Of Fiscal Year	Appropriations And Other Obligational Authority[1]	Transfers Borrowings And Investment (Net)[2]	Outlays (Net)	Balances Withdrawn And Other Transactions[3]	Balances, End Of Fiscal Year[4]
Trust Fund Accounts											
Accounts Payable						5,1,060,582.54				-1,060,582.54	
Undelivered Orders						5,1,149,113.62				2,821,226.41	-3,970,340.03
Subtotal		19		5177		-0-			795,255.87	-795,255.87	-0-
American Studies Endowment Fund, Department Of State											
Fund Resources:											
Undisbursed Funds	No Year	19		8166		42,827.13					42,943.43
Fund Equities:											
Unobligated Balances (Unexpired)									-116.30		
Accounts Payable						-42,710.83				116.30	-42,710.83
Subtotal		19		8166		-116.30			-116.30	116.30	-232.60
Israeli Arab Scholarship Program, Department Of State											
Fund Resources:											
Undisbursed Funds	No Year	19		8271		170,989.84	118,164.79	-12,150.78	48,177.32		228,826.53
Unrealized Discount On Investments						-109,705.51		12,150.78			-97,554.73
Investments In Public Debt Securities						4,723,000.00					4,723,000.00
Accounts Receivable						156,237.22				28,892.35	127,344.87
Fund Equities:											
Unobligated Balances (Unexpired)						-4,940,521.55				41,095.12	-4,981,616.67
Accounts Payable											
Subtotal		19		8271		-0-	118,164.79		48,177.32	69,987.47	-0-
Eastern Europe Student Exchange Endowment Fund, Department Of State											
Fund Resources:											
Undisbursed Funds	No Year	19		8272		129,199.03					129,199.03
Fund Equities:											
Unobligated Balances (Unexpired)						-127,650.03				1,549.00	-129,199.03
Undelivered Orders						-1,549.00				-1,549.00	
Subtotal		19		8272		-0-					-0-
Eisenhower Exchange Fellowship Program Trust Fund											
Fund Resources:											
Undisbursed Funds	No Year	95		8276		-3,390.74	363,698.33	-9,055.62	350,609.26		642.71
Unrealized Discount On Investments						-63,470.98		-36,944.38			-100,415.36
Investments In Public Debt Securities						7,521,000.00		46,000.00			7,567,000.00
Fund Equities:											
Unobligated Balances (Unexpired)						-7,454,138.28				13,089.07	-7,467,227.35
Accounts Payable											
Subtotal		95		8276		-0-	363,698.33		350,609.26	13,089.07	-0-
Center For Middle Eastern-Western Dialogue Trust Fund, Department Of State											
Fund Resources:											
Undisbursed Funds	No Year	19		8813		1,182,930.61	756,905.19	-29,175.94	315,895.08		1,594,764.78
Unrealized Discount On Investments						-60,832.50		25,175.94			-35,656.56
Investments In Public Debt Securities						17,096,000.00		4,000.00			17,100,000.00
Fund Equities:											
Unobligated Balances (Unexpired)						5,17,445,076.00				65,796.19	-17,510,872.19
Accounts Payable						5					

Footnotes At End Of Chapter

Appropriations, Outlays, and Balances – Continued

Appropriation or Fund Account — Title	Period of Availability	Dept Reg	Tr From	Account Number	Sub No.	Balances, Beginning Of Fiscal Year	Appropriations And Other Obligational Authority[1]	Transfers Borrowings And Investment (Net)[2]	Outlays (Net)	Balances Withdrawn And Other Transactions[3]	Balances, End Of Fiscal Year[4]
Center For Middle Eastern-Western Dialogue Trust Fund, Department Of State - Continued											
Fund Equities: - Continued											
Undelivered Orders		19		8813		[5]5,773,022.11	756,905.19	-------	315,895.08	375,213.92	-1,148,236.03
						-0-				441,010.11	-0-
Subtotal		19									
Total, Other							6,318,276,162.31	109,777,500.00	4,215,547,668.85	2,212,505,993.46	
Deductions For Offsetting Receipts											
Proprietary Receipts From The Public							-24,248,684.62	-------	-24,248,684.62	-------	-------
Intrabudgetary Transactions							-251,864,434.42	-------	-251,864,434.42	-------	-------
Total, Offsetting Receipts							-276,113,119.04	-------	-276,113,119.04	-------	-------
Total, Department Of State							17,556,220,674.18	133,167,500.00	13,748,601,385.85	3,940,786,788.33	
Memorandum											
Financing Accounts											
Public Enterprise Funds											
Repatriation Loans, Financing Account, State											
Fund Resources:											
Undisbursed Funds	No Year	19		4107		5,800,508.28		401,071.04	-460,366.45	-------	6,661,945.77
Accounts Receivable						-11,344.39				3,829.44	-15,173.83
Fund Equities:											
Unobligated Balances (Unexpired)						-4,942,686.77				738,752.21	-5,681,438.98
Undelivered Orders						-846,477.12				118,855.84	-965,332.96
Subtotal		19		4107		-0-	401,071.04	401,071.04	-460,366.45	861,437.49	-0-
Total, Financing Accounts							401,071.04	401,071.04	-460,366.45	861,437.49	

Appropriations, Outlays, and Balances - Continued

Footnotes

1 The amounts in this column, unless otherwise footnoted, represent appropriations, increases and rescissions in borrowing authority or new contract authority. Appropriation accounts with appropriation transfer activity are presented in Table 1 (Appropriations and Appropriation Transfers) at the end of this chapter.

2 The amounts in this column, unless otherwise footnoted, represent transfers - other than appropriation transfers, borrowings (gross), investments (net), unrealized discounts or funds held outside the Treasury.

3 The amounts in this column, unless otherwise footnoted, represent obligated balances canceled for fiscal year 2002 pursuant to 31 U.S.C. 1553, changes in unfilled customer orders, accounts receivable, accounts payable, undelivered orders, unobligated balances and adjustments to borrowing and contract authority.

4 Unobligated balances for no-year or unexpired multiple year accounts are available for obligation; unobligated balances for expired fiscal year accounts are not available for obligation.

5 The opening balances of the following accounts have been adjusted during the current fiscal year and do not agree with last year's closing balances:

Account	Adjustment
19 x 0209 - Unobligated Balances (Unexpired)	$388,759.33
19 x 0209 - Accounts Payable	-388,759.33
19 x 8186 - Unobligated Balances (Unexpired)	-196,825,204.21
19 x 8186 - Accounts Receivable	196,825,204.21
19 11 x 0040 - Accounts Payable	-3,259,240.32
19 11 x 0040 - Unobligated Balances (Unexpired)	3,259,240.32
19 11 0506 1022 - Accounts Payable	1,143,372.96
19 11 0506 1022 - Unobligated Balances (Expired)	-1,143,372.96
19 x 1030 - Accounts Payable	16,574,642.59
19 x 1030 - Undelivered Orders	-16,574,642.59
72 19 x 1030 - Accounts Payable	-10,075,622.41
72 19 x 1030 - Undelivered Orders	10,075,622.41
75 19 x 1030 001 - Unobligated Balances (Unexpired)	1,567,606.91
75 19 x 1030 001 - Undelivered Orders	-1,567,606.91
19 x 5177 - Accounts Payable	-1,060,582.54
19 x 5177 - Unobligated Balances (Unexpired)	79,660.02
19 x 5177 - Undelivered Orders	980,922.52
19 x 8813 - Accounts Payable	4,600,427.02
19 x 8813 - Unobligated Balances (Unexpired)	-4,426,140.00
19 x 8813 - Undelivered Orders	-174,287.02

6 Subject to disposition by the administrative agency.

7 Includes $420,213.78 which is subject to disposition by the administrative agency.

8 Represents capital transfer to miscellaneous receipts.

9 Includes $2,089,903.94 which is subject to disposition by the administrative agency.

10 Includes $7,122,748.57 which is subject to disposition by the administrative agency.

Footnotes At End Of Chapter

Appropriations, Outlays, and Balances – Continued

Footnotes

Table 1 - Appropriations And Appropriation Transfers - Department Of State

Department Regular	Fiscal Year	Account Symbol	Net Appropriations And Appropriations Transfers	Appropriation Amount	Net Appropriation Transfers	Department Regular Involved	Fiscal Year Involved	Accounts Involved	Amount From or To (-)
11	X	1022	20,361,000.00	0.00	20,361,000.00	21	07	2010	7,111,000.00
						21	07	2020	13,250,000.00
11	0708	1022	334,600,000.00	252,000,000.00	82,600,000.00	72	0708	1010	45,295,000.00
						72	0708	1093	37,305,000.00
19	X	0113	798,706,787.00	778,449,413.00	20,257,374.00	19	07	0113	18,407,374.00
						21	07	2010	300,000.00
						57	07	3400	1,550,000.00
19	07	0113	3,637,506,755.00	3,656,564,129.00	-19,057,374.00	19	X	0113	-18,407,374.00
						19	07	1069	-650,000.00
19	0708	0113	765,400,000.00	774,158,000.00	-8,758,000.00	19	X	0522	-8,500,000.00
						48	0708	2975	-258,000.00
19	0708	0209	19,500,000.00	0.00	19,500,000.00	72	0708	1037	19,500,000.00
19	X	0522	13,440,000.00	4,940,000.00	8,500,000.00	19	0708	0113	8,500,000.00
19	0709	0529	1,500,000.00	36,500,000.00	-35,000,000.00	21	0709	2090	-35,000,000.00
19	07	1069	28,368,201.00	27,718,201.00	650,000.00	19	07	0113	650,000.00
Totals			5,619,382,743.00	5,530,329,743.00	89,053,000.00				89,053,000.00

Appropriations, Outlays, and Balances – Continued
Footnotes

This Page Left Blank Intentionally

Appropriations, Outlays, and Balances – Continued

Appropriation or Fund Account — Title	Period of Availability	Reg	Tr From	Account Number	Sub No.	Balances, Beginning Of Fiscal Year	Appropriations And Other Obligational Authority[1]	Transfers Borrowings And Investment (Net)[2]	Outlays (Net)	Balances Withdrawn And Other Transactions[3]	Balances, End Of Fiscal Year[4]
Department Of Transportation											
Office Of The Secretary											
General Fund Accounts											
Salaries And Expenses, Office Of The Secretary, Department Of Transportation											
Fund Resources:											
Undisbursed Funds	2007	69		0102			83,960,594.44		73,457,108.82		10,503,485.62
	2006					-1,883,347.10			13,002,819.04		[5]14,886,166.14
	2005-2006					500,000.00			348,973.30		151,026.70
	2005					-1,987,277.11			11,338,642.40		[5]13,325,919.51
	2004					3,553,521.77			1,942,387.03		1,611,134.74
	2003					4,948,769.45			472,415.14		4,476,354.31
	2002					2,178,963.55			-1,190,553.26	3,369,516.81	
Accounts Receivable	No Year					362,438.98			-9,566,625.05		9,929,064.03
Unfilled Customer Orders						807,048.65				216,039.93	591,008.72
Fund Equities:						36,419,583.46				-2,063,280.16	38,482,863.62
Unobligated Balances (Expired)						-3,801,722.61				28,076.34	-3,829,798.95
Unobligated Balances (Unexpired)						-1,477,972.21				9,652,655.72	-11,130,627.93
Accounts Payable						-1,278,923.89				1,650,475.27	-2,929,399.16
Undelivered Orders						-38,341,082.94				-18,698,056.89	-19,643,026.05
Subtotal		69		0102		-0-	83,960,594.44		89,805,167.42	-5,844,572.98	-0-
Compensation For Air Carriers, Office Of The Secretary											
Fund Resources:											
Undisbursed Funds	No Year	69		0111		72,475,391.71	-50,000,000.00		-372,900.65		22,848,292.36
Fund Equities:											
Unobligated Balances (Unexpired)						-72,327,900.51				-49,479,608.15	22,848,292.36
Accounts Payable						-147,491.20				-147,491.20	-22,848,292.36
Subtotal		69		0111		-0-	-50,000,000.00		-372,900.65	-49,627,099.35	-0-
Rental Payments, Office Of The Secretary											
Fund Resources:											
Undisbursed Funds	No Year	69		0117		21,400.00					21,400.00
Fund Equities:											
Undelivered Orders						-21,400.00					-21,400.00
Subtotal		69		0117		-0-					-0-
Office Of Civil Rights, Office Of The Secretary											
Fund Resources:											
Undisbursed Funds	2007	69		0118			8,527,000.00		7,075,049.80		1,451,950.20
	2006					362,637.69			220,696.36		141,941.33
	2005					264,787.91			4,158.33		260,629.58
	2004					506,395.49			21,715.69		484,679.80
	2003					345,817.28			2,493.09		343,324.19
	2002					717,494.57			-27,781.30	745,275.87	
Accounts Receivable						-10,114.73				-30,310.13	20,195.40
Unfilled Customer Orders						413,840.06				163,999.60	249,840.46

Appropriations, Outlays, and Balances - Continued

Appropriation or Fund Account — Title	Period of Availability	Dept Reg	Dept Tr From	Account Number	Sub No.	Balances, Beginning Of Fiscal Year	Appropriations And Other Obligational Authority[1]	Transfers Borrowings And Other Investment (Net)[2]	Outlays (Net)	Balances Withdrawn And Other Transactions[3]	Balances, End Of Fiscal Year[4]
Fund Equities:											
Unobligated Balances (Expired)						-474,522.56				113,270.56	-587,793.12
Accounts Payable						-286,040.46				38,921.20	-324,961.66
Undelivered Orders						-1,840,295.25				199,510.93	-2,039,806.18
	Subtotal	69		0118		-0-	8,527,000.00		7,296,331.97	1,230,668.03	-0-
Minority Business Outreach, Office Of The Secretary											
Fund Resources:											
Undisbursed Funds	2007-2008	69		0119			2,970,000.00		23,825.53		2,946,174.47
	2006-2007					2,691,254.77			966,281.36		1,724,973.41
	2005-2006					219,971.04			95,063.95		124,907.09
	2004-2005					224,699.89					224,699.89
	2003-2004					203,492.27			53,262.93		150,229.34
	2002-2003					131,103.79			-153.46		131,257.25
	2001-2002					1,147,273.06				1,147,273.06	
	No Year					8,670,511.60			592,377.18		8,078,134.42
Fund Equities:											
Unobligated Balances (Expired)						-64,403.05				262,214.62	-326,617.67
Unobligated Balances (Unexpired)						-7,772,314.84				1,351,054.49	-9,123,369.33
Accounts Payable						-27,470.96				78,061.37	-105,532.33
Undelivered Orders						-5,424,117.57				-1,599,261.03	-3,824,856.54
	Subtotal	69		0119		-0-	2,970,000.00		1,730,657.49	1,239,342.51	-0-
Transportation Planning, Research And Development, Office Of The Secretary, Department Of Transportation											
Fund Resources:											
Undisbursed Funds	2005-2010	69		0142				207,350.24			207,350.24
	2004-2009					150,000.00					150,000.00
	2003-2008					156,141.00			21,351.41		134,789.59
	2006-2007							1,970,000.00	79,716.13		1,890,283.87
	2002-2007					426,149.00			115,266.60		310,882.40
	2005-2006					2,453,124.97		-207,350.24	45,646.34		2,200,128.39
	2004-2005					3,104,962.95			368,729.58		2,736,233.37
	2003-2004					187,939.19			10,775.00		177,164.19
	2002-2003					283,828.61					283,828.61
	2001-2002					356.53				356.53	
	No Year					30,118,866.88	14,893,000.00		15,558,460.73		29,453,406.15
Unfilled Customer Orders						826,386.54					826,386.54
Fund Equities:											
Unobligated Balances (Expired)						-348,641.98				507,119.08	-855,761.06
Unobligated Balances (Unexpired)						-6,632,093.88				8,710,412.82	-15,342,506.70
Accounts Payable						686,244.55				810,912.30	-124,667.75
Undelivered Orders						-31,413,264.36				-9,365,746.52	-22,047,517.84
	Subtotal	69		0142		-0-	14,893,000.00	1,970,000.00	16,199,945.79	663,054.21	-0-
New Headquarters Building, Office Of The Secretary, Department Of Transportation											
Fund Resources:											
Undisbursed Funds	No Year	69		0147		78,353,474.51	49,500,000.00		89,414,446.49		38,439,028.02
Fund Equities:											
Unobligated Balances (Unexpired)						-10,583,754.94				-4,360,313.68	-6,223,441.26

Footnotes At End Of Chapter

Appropriations, Outlays, and Balances – Continued

Appropriation or Fund Account — Title	Period of Availability	Dept Reg	Tr From	Account Number	Sub No.	Balances, Beginning Of Fiscal Year	Appropriations And Other Obligational Authority[1]	Transfers Borrowings And Investment (Net)[2]	Outlays (Net)	Balances Withdrawn And Other Transactions[3]	Balances, End Of Fiscal Year[4]
New Headquarters Building, Office Of The Secretary, Department Of Transportation - Continued											
Fund Equities: - Continued											
Accounts Payable						-619,174.80				3,478,341.94	-4,097,516.74
Undelivered Orders		69		0147		-67,150,544.77				39,032,474.75	-28,118,070.02
Subtotal		69		0147		-0-	49,500,000.00		89,414,446.49	39,914,446.49	-0-
Activities Transferred From Civil Aeronautics Board, Office Of The Secretary, Department Of Transportation											
Fund Resources:											
Undisbursed Funds	No Year	69		0150		975.00					975.00
Fund Equities:											
Unobligated Balances (Unexpired)						-975.00					-975.00
Subtotal	No Year	69		0150		-0-					-0-
Minority Business Resource Center Program, Office Of The Secretary, Department Of Transportation											
Fund Resources:											
Undisbursed Funds	2007	69		0155		693,172.05	1,005,511.00		409,321.16		596,189.84
	2006					380,350.35			8,633.51		684,538.54
	2005					364,437.12					380,350.35
	2004					463,831.96					364,437.12
	2003					725,448.46					463,831.96
	2002									725,448.46	
Fund Equities:											
Unobligated Balances (Expired)						-2,123,010.29				5,364.36	-2,128,374.65
Accounts Payable						-5,686.07				6,761.97	-12,448.04
Undelivered Orders						-498,543.58				-150,018.46	-348,525.12
Subtotal		69		0155		-0-	1,005,511.00		417,954.67	587,556.33	-0-
Compensation For General Aviation Operations, Office Of The Secretary, Department Of Transportation											
Fund Resources:											
Undisbursed Funds	No Year	69		0156		16,830,000.00					16,830,000.00
Fund Equities:											
Unobligated Balances (Unexpired)						-16,830,000.00					-16,830,000.00
Subtotal	No Year	69		0156		-0-					-0-
Special Fund Accounts											
Essential Air Service And Rural Airport Improvement Fund, Office Of The Secretary, Department Of Transportation											
Fund Resources:											
Undisbursed Funds	No Year	69		5423		50,721,040.54	29,784,545.51	16,546,093.46	21,934,919.55		75,116,759.96
Fund Equities:											
Unobligated Balances (Unexpired)						-19,981,827.84				16,738,962.05	-36,720,789.89
Accounts Payable						-41,156.87				520,122.26	-561,279.13
Undelivered Orders						-30,698,055.83				7,136,635.11	-37,834,690.94
Subtotal	No Year	69		5423		-0-	29,784,545.51	16,546,093.46	21,934,919.55	24,395,719.42	-0-

Appropriations, Outlays, and Balances - Continued

Appropriation or Fund Account — Title	Period of Availability	Reg	Tr From	Account Number	Sub No.	Balances, Beginning Of Fiscal Year	Appropriations And Other Obligational Authority[1]	Transfers Borrowings And Investment (Net)[2]	Outlays (Net)	Balances Withdrawn And Other Transactions[3]	Balances, End Of Fiscal Year[4]
Intragovernmental Funds											
Working Capital Fund, Transportation											
Fund Resources:											
Undisbursed Funds	No Year	69		4520		81,540,821.56			13,095,174.90		68,445,646.66
Accounts Receivable						7,497,342.25				3,883,402.10	3,613,940.15
Unfilled Customer Orders						65,566,951.89				-21,849,530.71	87,416,482.60
Fund Equities:											
Accounts Payable						-37,065,736.02				29,677.87	-37,095,413.89
Undelivered Orders						-117,539,379.68				4,841,275.84	-122,380,655.52
Subtotal		69		4520		-0-			13,095,174.90	-13,095,174.90	-0-
Trust Fund Accounts											
Payment To Air Carriers, Office Of The Secretary											
Fund Resources:											
Undisbursed Funds	No Year	69		8304		14,437,449.50	59,400,000.00		65,365,479.22		8,471,970.28
Fund Equities:											
Unobligated Balances (Unexpired)						-7,635,792.50				-7,210,327.22	-425,465.28
Accounts Payable						-159,929.00				-28,894.00	-131,035.00
Undelivered Orders						-6,641,728.00				1,273,742.00	-7,915,470.00
Subtotal		69		8304		-0-	59,400,000.00		65,365,479.22	-5,965,479.22	-0-
Gifts And Bequests, Office Of The Secretary, Department Of Transportation											
Fund Resources:											
Undisbursed Funds	No Year	69		8548		1,680.00	120.00				1,800.00
Investments In Public Debt Securities						1,000.00					1,000.00
Fund Equities:											
Unobligated Balances (Unexpired)						-2,680.00				120.00	-2,800.00
Accounts Payable											
Subtotal		69		8548		-0-	120.00			120.00	-0-
Total, Office Of The Secretary							200,040,770.95	18,516,093.46	304,887,176.85	-86,330,312.44	
Federal Aviation Administration											
General Fund Accounts											
Operations, Federal Aviation Administration											
Fund Resources:											
Undisbursed Funds	2007	69		1301		822,391,648.38	2,746,316,516.00	7,300,000.00	1,632,689,091.22		1,120,927,424.78
	2006					199,828.42		-7,300,000.00	725,857,781.19		89,233,867.19
	2005-2006					47,679.50			47,679.50		152,148.92
	2005					135,914,085.21			70,720,593.32		65,193,491.89
	2004-2005					27,605.21			1,569.00		26,036.21
	2004					105,154,671.85			18,746,524.07		86,408,147.78
	2003					15,821,297.81			772,908.22		15,048,389.59
	2002					39,239,511.26			2,438,726.71		36,800,784.55

Footnotes At End Of Chapter

Appropriations, Outlays, and Balances – Continued

Appropriation or Fund Account — Title	Period of Availability	Account Symbol — Dept Reg	Tr From	Account Number	Sub No.	Balances, Beginning Of Fiscal Year	Appropriations And Other Obligational Authority[1]	Transfers Borrowings And Investment (Net)[2]	Outlays (Net)	Balances Withdrawn And Other Transactions[3]	Balances, End Of Fiscal Year[4]
Operations, Federal Aviation Administration - Continued											
Fund Resources: - Continued											
Undisbursed Funds - Continued	No Year										
Fund Equities:											
Accounts Receivable						20,910,873.88			2,760,943.88		18,149,930.00
Unfilled Customer Orders						100,678,234.63				1,816,692.50	98,861,542.13
						[6]196,332,089.83				-16,740,889.26	213,072,979.09
Fund Equities:											
Unobligated Balances (Expired)						[6]-194,255,680.61				9,685,816.57	-203,942,497.18
Unobligated Balances (Unexpired)						-95,257,602.14				-10,888,568.59	-84,369,033.55
Accounts Payable						-303,538,665.63				79,654,314.01	-383,192,979.64
Undelivered Orders						[6]-843,616,898.10				191,952,549.11	-1,035,569,447.21
Subtotal		69		1301		-0-					-0-
Facilities, Engineering And Development, Federal Aviation Administration							2,746,316,516.00		2,454,035,817.11	292,280,698.89	
Fund Resources:											
Undisbursed Funds:	No Year	69		1303		988,552.59			984,848.31	-988,552.50	3,704.28
Fund Equities:											
Unobligated Balances (Unexpired)						-988,552.59					-0.09
Accounts Payable										2,256.90	-2,256.90
Undelivered Orders										1,447.29	-1,447.29
Subtotal		69		1303		-0-			984,848.31	-984,848.31	-0-
Special Fund Accounts											
Aviation User Fees, Federal Aviation Administration											
Fund Resources:											
Undisbursed Funds	No Year	69		5422		8,790,859.51	18,722,956.00	-16,546,093.46		2,176,862.54	10,967,722.05
Fund Equities:											
Unobligated Balances (Unexpired)						-8,790,666.51					-10,967,529.05
Accounts Payable						-193.00					-193.00
Subtotal		69		5422		-0-	18,722,956.00	-16,546,093.46		2,176,862.54	-0-
Public Enterprise Funds											
Aviation Insurance Revolving Fund											
Fund Resources:											
Undisbursed Funds	No Year	69		4120		53,327,943.39		-187,942,910.16	-197,743,154.70	196,677,945.25	63,128,187.93
Unrealized Discount On Investments						-524,143.33		-2,479,089.84			-3,003,233.17
Investments In Public Debt Securities						698,055,000.00		190,422,000.00			888,477,000.00
Accounts Receivable										384,687.64	-384,687.64
Fund Equities:											
Unobligated Balances (Unexpired)						-742,562,679.81				196,677,945.25	-939,240,625.06
Accounts Payable						-1,576,807.86				321,550.72	-1,898,358.58
Undelivered Orders						-6,719,312.39				358,971.09	-7,078,283.48
Subtotal		69		4120		-0-			-197,743,154.70	197,743,154.70	-0-

Appropriations, Outlays, and Balances - Continued

Title	Period of Availability	Reg	Tr From	Account Number	Sub No.	Balances, Beginning Of Fiscal Year	Appropriations And Other Obligational Authority[1]	Transfers Borrowings And Investment (Net)[2]	Outlays (Net)	Balances Withdrawn And Other Transactions[3]	Balances, End Of Fiscal Year[4]
Intragovernmental Funds											
Administrative Services Franchise Fund, Federal Aviation Administration											
Fund Resources:											
Undisbursed Funds	No Year	69		4562		219,059,953.16					266,668,188.61
Accounts Receivable						41,148,278.79				39,399,816.88	1,748,461.91
Unfilled Customer Orders						41,543,827.92				1,260,197.89	40,283,630.03
Fund Equities:											
Unobligated Balances (Unexpired)						-159,302,017.08				3,333,390.93	-162,635,408.01
Accounts Payable						-9,902,779.60				16,221,909.57	-26,124,689.17
Undelivered Orders						-132,547,263.19				-12,607,079.82	-119,940,183.37
Subtotal		69		4562		-0-			-47,608,235.45	47,608,235.45	-0-
Trust Fund Accounts											
Airport And Airway Trust Fund											
Fund Resources:											
Undisbursed Funds	No Year	20		8103		[6]868,765,478.61	[7]797,797,600.49	-1,150,976,806.85	[8]8,321.00		715,577,951.25
Investments In Public Debt Securities						7,893,312,000.00		37,631,000.00			7,930,943,000.00
Fund Equities:											
Unobligated Balances (Unexpired)						[6]-6,465,101,988.61		-1,113,345,806.85		-674,420,257.36	-5,790,681,731.25
Accounts Payable						-2,296,975,490.00				558,863,730.00	-2,855,839,220.00
Subtotal		20		8103		-0-	997,797,600.49		8,321.00	-115,556,527.36	-0-
Operations, Airport And Airway Trust Fund, Federal Aviation Administration											
Fund Resources:											
Undisbursed Funds	2007	69		8104			5,627,900,000.00		5,627,900,000.00		1,720,880.41
	2002-2003					1,787,412.12			66,531.71		
Accounts Receivable						55,500,000.00				55,410,000.00	90,000.00
Fund Equities:											
Unobligated Balances (Expired)						-55,544,472.03				-55,518,300.49	-26,171.54
Accounts Payable						-5,580.61				-20.61	-5,560.00
Undelivered Orders						-1,737,359.48				41,789.39	-1,779,148.87
Subtotal		69		8104		-0-	5,627,900,000.00		5,627,966,531.71	-66,531.71	-0-
Grants-In-Aid For Airports, Liquidation Of Contract Authorization, Airport And Airway Trust Fund, Federal Aviation Administration											
Fund Resources:											
Undisbursed Funds	No Year	69		8106		675,582,389.20	4,008,200,000.00		3,874,013,145.89	621,000,000.00	809,769,243.31
Unfunded Contract Authority						5,070,287,953.52	[8]106,520,090.00			-392,612,222.13	4,342,767,863.52
Accounts Receivable						25,924,155.34					418,536,377.47
Unfilled Customer Orders						10,348.86					10,348.86
Fund Equities:											
Unobligated Balances (Unexpired)						-39,713,043.12				163,327,873.75	-203,040,916.87
Accounts Payable						-554,617,416.74				148,206,681.48	-702,824,098.22
Undelivered Orders						-5,177,474,387.06				-512,255,568.99	-4,665,218,818.07
Subtotal		69		8106		-0-	3,901,679,910.00		3,874,013,145.89	27,666,764.11	-0-

Footnotes At End Of Chapter

Appropriations, Outlays, and Balances – Continued

Title	Reg	Tr From	Account Number	Sub No.	Period of Availability	Balances, Beginning Of Fiscal Year	Appropriations And Other Obligational Authority[1]	Transfers Borrowings And Investment (Net)[2]	Outlays (Net)	Balances Withdrawn And Other Transactions[3]	Balances, End Of Fiscal Year[4]
Facilities And Equipment, Airport And Airway Trust Fund, Federal Aviation Administration											
Fund Resources:											
Undisbursed Funds	69		8107		2007-2009		713,000,000.00	591,000,000.00	591,226,174.93		121,773,825.07
					2006-2008	278,894,955.19			782,841,630.04		87,053,325.15
					2007		427,000,000.00	3,900,000.00	391,593,911.31		39,306,088.69
					2005-2007	93,759,404.91		336,000,000.00	333,330,995.12		96,428,409.79
					2006	39,117,617.73		-3,400,000.00	28,110,182.36		7,607,435.37
					2004-2006	98,293,086.47		184,000,000.00	236,997,127.23		45,295,959.24
					2005	8,417,349.75			1,748,469.21		6,668,880.54
					2003-2005	50,035,181.47			39,243,958.53		10,791,222.94
					2004	2,585,657.42			222,636.61		2,363,020.81
					2002-2004	17,331,632.70			-17,396,450.02		34,728,082.72
					2003	4,969,920.23			72,108.11		4,897,812.12
					2001-2003	11,898,181.09			5,459,988.44		6,438,192.65
					2002	7,485,023.23		-7,512,067.27	-27,044.04		
					2000-2002	13,957,780.57		-19,701,953.68	-5,744,173.11		
					No Year	8,329,183.15	10,000,000.00		-97,751,750.60		116,080,933.75
Accounts Receivable						2,226,412,349.18				-170,942,747.39	2,397,355,096.57
Unfilled Customer Orders						152,948,447.54				72,820,909.61	80,127,537.93
Fund Equities:											
Unobligated Balances (Expired)						-131,253,589.46				-50,997,065.39	-80,256,524.07
Unobligated Balances (Unexpired)						-931,518,925.53				105,930,310.12	-1,037,449,235.65
Accounts Payable						-205,424,634.06				-50,080,512.55	-155,344,121.51
Undelivered Orders						-1,746,238,621.58				37,627,320.53	-1,783,865,942.11
Subtotal	69		8107			-0-	1,150,000,000.00	1,084,285,979.05	2,289,927,764.12	-55,641,785.07	-0-
Research, Engineering And Development, Airport And Airway Trust Fund, Federal Aviation Administration											
Fund Resources:											
Undisbursed Funds	69		8108		2007-2009		96,000,000.00		56,396,537.82		39,603,462.18
					2006-2008	43,873,189.93	9,247.76	7,000,000.00	44,720,616.62		6,161,821.07
					2005-2007	9,253,736.32		20,000,000.00	20,448,391.47		8,805,344.85
					2004-2006	6,193,390.66		2,000,000.00	24,292,986.68		[5]16,099,596.02
					2003-2005	5,238,554.76		1,000,000.00	4,679,562.60		1,558,992.16
					2002-2004	2,018,667.43			466,576.60		1,552,090.83
					2001-2003	2,803,246.25			4,610.92		2,798,635.33
					2000-2002	1,146,251.59		-940,172.20	206,079.39		
					No Year	12,941,609.55			781,786.02		12,159,823.53
Accounts Receivable						96,991,708.25				-2,048,324.17	99,040,032.42
Unfilled Customer Orders						2,458,513.37				958,482.13	1,500,031.24
Fund Equities:											
Unobligated Balances (Expired)						-4,587,592.22				532,219.30	-5,119,811.52
Unobligated Balances (Unexpired)						-25,597,677.30				623,184.46	-26,220,861.76
Accounts Payable						-15,663,187.71				-15,821,012.26	157,824.55
Undelivered Orders						-137,070,410.88				-11,172,622.02	-125,897,788.86
Subtotal	69		8108			-0-	96,009,247.76	29,059,827.80	151,997,148.12	-26,928,072.56	-0-
Total, Federal Aviation Administration						-0-	14,538,426,230.25	-16,546,093.46	14,153,582,186.11	368,297,950.68	-0-

Appropriations, Outlays, and Balances - Continued

Appropriation or Fund Account — Title	Period of Availability	Account Symbol — Dept Reg	Account Symbol — Dept Tr From	Account Number	Sub No.	Balances, Beginning Of Fiscal Year	Appropriations And Other Obligational Authority[1]	Transfers Borrowings And Investment (Net)[2]	Outlays (Net)	Balances Withdrawn And Other Transactions[3]	Balances, End Of Fiscal Year[4]
Federal Highway Administration											
General Fund Accounts											
Emergency Relief Program, Federal Highway Administration											
Fund Resources:											
Undisbursed Funds	No Year	69		0500		2,603,209,341.11	871,022,000.00		840,799,289.59		2,633,432,051.52
Fund Equities:											
Unobligated Balances (Unexpired)						-1,329,666,546.30				41,885,838.41	-1,371,552,384.71
Undelivered Orders						-1,273,542,794.81				-11,663,128.00	-1,261,879,666.81
Subtotal		69		0500		-0-	871,022,000.00		840,799,289.59	30,222,710.41	-0-
Off-System Roads, Liquidation Of Contract Authorization, Federal Highway Administration											
Fund Resources:											
Undisbursed Funds	No Year	69		0502		15,241.00					15,241.00
Fund Equities:											
Unobligated Balances (Unexpired)						-12,516.96					-12,516.96
Undelivered Orders						-2,724.04					-2,724.04
Subtotal		69		0502		-0-					-0-
Access Highways To Public Recreation Areas On Certain Lakes, Federal Highway Administration											
Fund Resources:											
Undisbursed Funds	No Year	69		0503		352,333.19					352,333.19
Fund Equities:											
Unobligated Balances (Unexpired)						-352,333.19					-352,333.19
Subtotal		69		0503		-0-					-0-
Surface Transportation Projects, Federal Highway Administration, Department Of Transportation											
Fund Resources:											
Undisbursed Funds	No Year	69		0505		24,534,888.93	1,328,000.00		4,568,940.85		21,293,948.08
Fund Equities:											
Unobligated Balances (Unexpired)						-15,716,707.14				437,578.70	-16,154,285.84
Undelivered Orders						-8,818,181.79				-3,678,519.55	-5,139,662.24
Subtotal		69		0505		-0-	1,328,000.00		4,568,940.85	-3,240,940.85	-0-
Inter-American Highway, Federal Highway Administration											
Fund Resources:											
Undisbursed Funds	No Year	69		0506		82,329.48					82,329.48
Fund Equities:											
Unobligated Balances (Unexpired)						-82,329.48					-82,329.48
Subtotal		69		0506		-0-					-0-
Bikeway Program, Federal Highway Administration											
Fund Resources:											
Undisbursed Funds	No Year	69		0507		17,212.11					17,212.11
Fund Equities:											
Unobligated Balances (Unexpired)						-17,212.11					-17,212.11
Subtotal		69		0507		-0-					-0-

Footnotes At End Of Chapter

Appropriations, Outlays, and Balances – Continued

Appropriation or Fund Account — Title	Period of Availability	Dept Reg	Tr From	Account Number	Sub No.	Balances, Beginning Of Fiscal Year	Appropriations And Other Obligational Authority[1]	Transfers Borrowings And Investment (Net)[2]	Outlays (Net)	Balances Withdrawn And Other Transactions[3]	Balances, End Of Fiscal Year[4]
Bridge Improvement Demonstration Project, Federal Highway Administration											
Fund Resources:											
Undisbursed Funds	No Year	69		0516		640.00					640.00
Fund Equities:											
Unobligated Balances (Unexpired)	Subtotal	69		0516		-640.00					-640.00
						-0-					-0-
Highway Bypass Demonstration Project, Federal Highway Administration											
Fund Resources:											
Undisbursed Funds	No Year	69		0518		7,924,481.49					7,924,481.49
Fund Equities:											
Unobligated Balances (Unexpired)	Subtotal	69		0518		-7,924,481.49					-7,924,481.49
						-0-					-0-
Highway Widening And Improvement Demonstration Project, Federal Highway Administration											
Fund Resources:											
Undisbursed Funds	No Year	69		0519		1,672,635.76					1,672,635.76
Fund Equities:											
Unobligated Balances (Unexpired)		69		0519		-1,655,408.14				-1,655,408.14	-1,672,635.76
Undelivered Orders	Subtotal	69		0519		-17,227.62				1,655,408.14	
						-0-					-0-
Congestion Mitigation, Federal Highway Administration											
Fund Resources:											
Undisbursed Funds	No Year	69		0524		306,956.00			-12.00		306,968.00
Fund Equities:											
Unobligated Balances (Unexpired)		69		0524		-1,392.00					-1,392.00
Undelivered Orders	Subtotal	69		0524		-305,564.00			-12.00	12.00	-305,576.00
						-0-				12.00	-0-
Public Lands Highways, Liquidation Of Contract Authorization, Federal Highway Administration											
Fund Resources:											
Undisbursed Funds	No Year	69		0526		6,222.67					6,222.67
Fund Equities:											
Unobligated Balances (Unexpired)	Subtotal	69		0526		-6,222.67					-6,222.67
						-0-					-0-
Schenectady Bridge, Federal Highway Administration											
Fund Resources:											
Undisbursed Funds	No Year	69		0527		4,929.00					4,929.00
Fund Equities:											
Undelivered Orders	Subtotal	69		0527		-4,929.00					-4,929.00
						-0-					-0-
Highway Safety Improvement Demonstration Project, Federal Highway Administration											
Fund Resources:											
Undisbursed Funds	No Year	69		0530		322,076.44					322,076.44
Fund Equities:											
Unobligated Balances (Unexpired)		69		0530		-287,678.29					-287,678.29
Undelivered Orders	Subtotal	69		0530		-34,398.15					-34,398.15
						-0-					-0-

Appropriations, Outlays, and Balances - Continued

Appropriation or Fund Account — Title	Period of Availability	Dept Reg	Dept Tr From	Account Number	Sub No.	Balances, Beginning Of Fiscal Year	Appropriations And Other Obligational Authority[1]	Transfers Borrowings And Investment (Net)[2]	Outlays (Net)	Balances Withdrawn And Other Transactions[3]	Balances, End Of Fiscal Year[4]
Pennsylvania Reconstruction Demonstration Project, Federal Highway Administration											
Fund Resources:											
Undisbursed Funds	No Year	69		0532		1,933,165.33	------	------	------	------	1,933,165.33
Fund Equities:											
Unobligated Balances (Unexpired)						-297,062.36				-296,782.01	-280.35
Undelivered Orders						-1,636,102.97				296,782.01	-1,932,884.98
Subtotal		69		0532		-0-					-0-
Highway Studies Feasibility, Design, Environmental, Engineering, Federal Highway Administration											
Fund Resources:											
Undisbursed Funds	No Year	69		0533		562,958.91	------	------	------	------	562,958.91
Fund Equities:											
Unobligated Balances (Unexpired)						-323,646.29					-323,646.29
Undelivered Orders						-239,312.62					-239,312.62
Subtotal		69		0533		-0-					-0-
Alaska Highways, Federal Highway Administration											
Fund Resources:											
Undisbursed Funds	No Year	69		0537		78,475.75	------	------	8,750.94	------	69,724.81
Fund Equities:											
Unobligated Balances (Unexpired)						-613.43				62,248.18	-62,861.61
Accounts Payable						-314.35					-314.35
Undelivered Orders						-77,547.97			8,750.94	-70,999.12	-6,548.85
Subtotal		69		0537		-0-			8,750.94	-8,750.94	-0-
Highway Beautification, Federal Highway Administration											
Fund Resources:											
Undisbursed Funds	No Year	69		0540		520,033.49	------	------	18,986.77	------	501,046.72
Fund Equities:											
Unobligated Balances (Unexpired)						-252,273.32					-252,273.32
Undelivered Orders						-267,760.17			18,986.77	-18,986.77	-248,773.40
Subtotal		69		0540		-0-			18,986.77	-18,986.77	-0-
Construction Of Public Toll Roads, Orange County, California, Federal Highway Administration											
Fund Resources:											
Undisbursed Funds	1995	69		0543		8,000,000.00	------	------	------	------	[8]8,000,000.00
	1993					9,600,000.00					[10]9,600,000.00
Fund Equities:											
Unobligated Balances (Expired)						-12,480,000.00				1,760,000.00	-14,240,000.00
Undelivered Orders						-5,120,000.00				-1,760,000.00	-3,360,000.00
Subtotal		69		0543		-0-					-0-
State Infrastructure Banks, Federal Highway Administration											
Fund Resources:											
Undisbursed Funds	No Year	69		0549		2,845,094.51	------	------	103,294.51	------	2,741,800.00
Fund Equities:											
Undelivered Orders						-2,845,094.51			103,294.51	-103,294.51	-2,741,800.00
Subtotal		69		0549		-0-			103,294.51	-103,294.51	-2,741,800.00

Footnotes At End Of Chapter

Appropriations, Outlays, and Balances – Continued

Appropriation or Fund Account — Title	Period of Availability	Account Symbol — Dept Reg	Account Symbol — Dept Tr From	Account Number	Sub No.	Balances, Beginning Of Fiscal Year	Appropriations And Other Obligational Authority[1]	Transfers Borrowings And Investment (Net)[2]	Outlays (Net)	Balances Withdrawn And Other Transactions[3]	Balances, End Of Fiscal Year[4]
Darien Gap Highway, Federal Highway Administration											
Fund Resources:											
Undisbursed Funds	No Year	69		0553		2,037,034.50					2,037,034.50
Fund Equities:											
Unobligated Balances (Unexpired)	Subtotal	69		0553		-2,037,034.50					-2,037,034.50
						-0-					-0-
Rail Crossings Demonstration Projects, Federal Highway Administration											
Fund Resources:											
Undisbursed Funds	No Year	69		0555		517,220.20					517,220.20
Fund Equities:											
Unobligated Balances (Unexpired)	Subtotal	69		0555		-517,220.20					-517,220.20
						-0-					-0-
Territorial Highways, Federal Highway Administration											
Fund Resources:											
Undisbursed Funds	No Year	69		0556		16,396.14					16,396.14
Fund Equities:											
Unobligated Balances (Unexpired)		69		0556		-942.14					-942.14
Undelivered Orders	Subtotal	69		0556		-15,454.00					-15,454.00
						-0-					-0-
Railroad-Highway Crossings Demonstration Projects, Federal Highway Administration											
Fund Resources:											
Undisbursed Funds	No Year	69		0557		8,168,339.67			36,853.71		8,131,485.96
Fund Equities:											
Unobligated Balances (Unexpired)		69		0557		-7,407,669.71				80,355.53	-7,488,025.24
Undelivered Orders	Subtotal	69		0557		-760,669.96				-117,209.24	-643,460.72
						-0-			36,853.71	-36,853.71	-0-
Interstate Transfer Grants-Highways, Federal Highway Administration											
Fund Resources:											
Undisbursed Funds	No Year	69		0560		5,451,261.59			207,547.81		5,243,713.78
Fund Equities:											
Unobligated Balances (Unexpired)		69		0560		-5,089,360.55				-9,751.98	-5,079,608.57
Undelivered Orders	Subtotal	69		0560		-361,901.04			207,547.81	-197,795.83	-164,105.21
						-0-				-207,547.81	-0-
Highway Widening Demonstration, Federal Highway Administration											
Fund Resources:											
Undisbursed Funds	No Year	69		0561		14,552.46					14,552.46
Fund Equities:											
Unobligated Balances (Unexpired)		69		0561		-14,552.46					-14,552.46
Undelivered Orders	Subtotal	69		0561		-0-					-0-
Intersection Safety Demonstration Project, Federal Highway Administration											
Fund Resources:											
Undisbursed Funds	No Year	69		0564		-0.01			-0.01		0.01
Fund Equities:											
Unobligated Balances (Unexpired)		69		0564		0.01				0.01	-0.01
Accounts Payable	Subtotal	69		0564		-0-			-0.01	0.01	-0-

Appropriations, Outlays, and Balances - Continued

Appropriation or Fund Account — Title	Period of Availability	Dept Reg	Tr From	Account Number	Sub No.	Balances, Beginning Of Fiscal Year	Appropriations And Other Obligational Authority[1]	Transfers Borrowings And Investment (Net)[2]	Outlays (Net)	Balances Withdrawn And Other Transactions[3]	Balances, End Of Fiscal Year[4]
Climbing Lane And Highway Safety Demonstration Project, Federal Highway Administration											
Fund Resources:											
Undisbursed Funds	No Year	69		0566		149,751.05			106,413.18		43,337.87
Fund Equities:											
Unobligated Balances (Unexpired)				0566		-106,413.18				-74,639.41	-31,773.77
Undelivered Orders						-43,337.87			106,413.18	-31,773.77	-11,564.10
Subtotal	Subtotal	69		0566		-0-				-106,413.18	-0-
Indiana Industrial Corridor Safety Demonstration Project, Federal Highway Administration											
Fund Resources:											
Undisbursed Funds	No Year	69		0567		10,024.00			10,024.00		
Fund Equities:											
Undelivered Orders				0567		-10,024.00			10,024.00	-10,024.00	
Subtotal	Subtotal	69		0567		-0-				-10,024.00	-0-
Oklahoma Highway Widening Demonstration Project, Federal Highway Administration											
Fund Resources:											
Undisbursed Funds	No Year	69		0570		840,122.14					840,122.14
Fund Equities:											
Unobligated Balances (Unexpired)				0570		-840,122.14					-840,122.14
Subtotal	Subtotal	69		0570		-0-					-0-
Alabama Highway Bypass Demonstration Project, Federal Highway Administration											
Fund Resources:											
Undisbursed Funds	No Year	69		0571		5.32					5.32
Fund Equities:											
Undelivered Orders				0571		-5.32					-5.32
Subtotal	Subtotal	69		0571		-0-					-0-
Kentucky Bridge Project, Federal Highway Administration											
Fund Resources:											
Undisbursed Funds	No Year	69		0572		779,298.48					779,298.48
Fund Equities:											
Unobligated Balances (Unexpired)				0572		-779,298.48				775,000.00	-775,000.00
Undelivered Orders										-775,000.00	-4,298.48
Subtotal	Subtotal	69		0572		-0-					-0-
Virginia HOV Safety Demonstration Project, Federal Highway Administration											
Fund Resources:											
Undisbursed Funds	No Year	69		0573		-4.00			4.00	4.00	4.00
Fund Equities:											
Accounts Payable				0573		4.00			4.00	4.00	-4.00
Subtotal	Subtotal	69		0573		-0-					-0-
Urban Highway Corridor And Bicycle Project, Federal Highway Administration											
Fund Resources:											
Undisbursed Funds	No Year	69		0574		1,043,294.14					1,043,294.14

Footnotes At End Of Chapter

Appropriations, Outlays, and Balances – Continued

Appropriation or Fund Account — Title	Period of Availability	Reg	Tr From	Account Number	Sub No.	Balances, Beginning Of Fiscal Year	Appropriations And Other Obligational Authority[1]	Transfers Borrowings And Investment (Net)[2]	Outlays (Net)	Balances Withdrawn And Other Transactions[3]	Balances, End Of Fiscal Year[4]
Urban Highway Corridor And Bicycle Project, Federal Highway Administration - Continued											
Fund Equities:											
Unobligated Balances (Unexpired)		69		0574		-1,043,294.14					-1,043,294.14
Subtotal						-0-					-0-
Urban Airport Access Safety Demonstration Project, Federal Highway Administration											
Fund Resources:											
Undisbursed Funds	No Year	69		0575		628,593.71					628,593.71
Fund Equities:											
Undelivered Orders	Subtotal	69		0575		-628,593.71					-628,593.71
Subtotal						-0-					-0-
Expressway Safety Improvement Demonstration Project, Federal Highway Administration											
Fund Resources:											
Undisbursed Funds	No Year	69		0580		511,258.00					511,258.00
Fund Equities:											
Unobligated Balances (Unexpired)	Subtotal	69		0580		-511,258.00					-511,258.00
Subtotal						-0-					-0-
Ebensburg Bypass Demonstration Project, Federal Highway Administration											
Fund Resources:											
Undisbursed Funds	No Year	69		0582		37,696.80			37,696.00		0.80
Fund Equities:											
Unobligated Balances (Unexpired)	Subtotal	69		0582		-37,696.80				-37,696.00	-0.80
Subtotal						-0-			37,696.00	-37,696.00	-0-
Highway Demonstration Projects, Preliminary Engineering, Federal Highway Administration											
Fund Resources:											
Undisbursed Funds	No Year	69		0583		8,428,591.49					5,994,705.97
Fund Equities:											
Unobligated Balances (Unexpired)		69		0583		-3,949,578.92				-666,532.17	-3,283,046.75
Undelivered Orders	Subtotal	69		0583		-4,479,012.57			2,433,885.52	-1,767,353.35	-2,711,659.22
Subtotal						-0-			2,433,885.52	-2,433,885.52	-0-
Corridor G Improvement Project, Federal Highway Administration											
Fund Resources:											
Undisbursed Funds	No Year	69		0585		752,665.38					752,665.38
Fund Equities:											
Unobligated Balances (Unexpired)		69		0585		-615,777.00					-615,777.00
Undelivered Orders	Subtotal	69		0585		-136,888.38					-136,888.38
Subtotal						-0-					-0-
Corning Bypass Safety Demonstration Project, Federal Highway Administration											
Fund Resources:											
Undisbursed Funds	No Year	69		0586		161,290.00					161,290.00
Fund Equities:											
Undelivered Orders	Subtotal	69		0586		-161,290.00					-161,290.00
Subtotal						-0-					-0-

Appropriations, Outlays, and Balances - Continued

Appropriation or Fund Account — Title	Period of Availability	Dept Reg	Tr From	Account Number	Sub No.	Balances, Beginning Of Fiscal Year	Appropriations And Other Obligational Authority[1]	Transfers Borrowings And Investment (Net)[2]	Outlays (Net)	Balances Withdrawn And Other Transactions[3]	Balances, End Of Fiscal Year[4]
Turquoise Trail Project, Federal Highway Administration											
Fund Resources:											
Transfer To:											
Interior, Bureau Of Indian Affairs	No Year	14	69	0592	20	1,059,636.43				-------	1,059,636.43
Fund Equities:											
Unobligated Balances (Unexpired)		69		0592		-1,059,636.43				-------	-1,059,636.43
Subtotal		69		0592		-0-				-------	-0-
Highway 20 Realignment Project, Federal Highway Administration											
Fund Resources:											
Undisbursed Funds	No Year	69		0593		27,510.22			10,280.64	-------	17,229.58
Fund Equities:											
Undelivered Orders		69		0593		-27,510.22				-10,280.64	-17,229.58
Subtotal		69		0593		-0-			10,280.64	-10,280.64	-0-
Corridor D Improvement Project, Federal Highway Administration											
Fund Resources:											
Undisbursed Funds	No Year	69		0597		76.00			76.00	-------	-------
Fund Equities:											
Undelivered Orders		69		0597		-76.00				-76.00	-------
Subtotal		69		0597		-0-			76.00	-76.00	-0-
Highway Demonstration Projects, Federal Highway Administration											
Fund Resources:											
Undisbursed Funds	No Year	69		0598		18,004,229.26			4,790,730.07	-------	13,213,499.19
Fund Equities:											
Unobligated Balances (Unexpired)		69		0598		-11,057,689.89				-1,042,787.42	-10,014,902.47
Accounts Payable		69		0598						90.19	90.19
Undelivered Orders		69		0598		-6,946,539.37				-3,747,852.46	-3,198,686.91
Subtotal		69		0598		-0-			4,790,730.07	-4,790,730.07	-0-
Appalachian Development System, Federal Highway Administration											
Fund Resources:											
Undisbursed Funds	No Year	69		0640		309,247,543.92	19,800,000.00		71,702,035.55	-------	257,345,508.37
Fund Equities:											
Unobligated Balances (Unexpired)		69		0640		-133,410,421.04				-26,784,029.73	-106,626,391.31
Undelivered Orders		69		0640		-175,837,122.88				-25,118,005.82	-150,719,117.06
Subtotal		69		0640		-0-	19,800,000.00		71,702,035.55	-51,902,035.55	-0-
Miscellaneous Highway Project, Federal Highway Administration											
Fund Resources:											
Undisbursed Funds	No Year	69		0641		128,095,319.94		-591,472.00	32,705,332.80		94,798,515.14
Transfer To:											
Federal Railroad Administration, Department Of Transportation	No Year	69		0641	7	639,935.83		591,472.00	859,737.21	-------	371,670.62
Federal Transit Administration	No Year	69		0641	11	5,608,228.00			339,957.00	-------	5,268,271.00
Maritime Administration	No Year	69		0641	17	993,500.00				-------	993,500.00
FHWA Transfer Account, USCG	No Year	70	69	0641	2	2,897,401.16			465,176.82	-------	2,432,224.34
Fund Equities:											
Unobligated Balances (Unexpired)		69		0641		-89,372,613.66				-27,912,367.71	-61,460,245.95
Accounts Payable		69		0641		447,796.27				457,796.27	-10,000.00
Undelivered Orders		69		0641		-49,309,567.54				-6,915,632.39	-42,393,935.15
Subtotal		69		0641		-0-			34,370,203.83	-34,370,203.83	-0-

Footnotes At End Of Chapter

Appropriations, Outlays, and Balances – Continued

Appropriation or Fund Account — Title	Period of Availability	Dept Reg	Dept Tr From	Account Number	Sub No.	Balances, Beginning Of Fiscal Year	Appropriations And Other Obligational Authority[1]	Transfers Borrowings And Investment (Net)[2]	Outlays (Net)	Balances Withdrawn And Other Transactions[3]	Balances, End Of Fiscal Year[4]
Arkansas I-69 Connector, Federal Highway Administration											
Fund Resources:											
Undisbursed Funds	No Year	69		0644		79,650,959.00			13,035,887.00		66,615,072.00
Fund Equities:											
Unobligated Balances (Unexpired)										9,835,883.00	-9,835,883.00
Undelivered Orders						-79,650,959.00				-22,871,770.00	-56,779,189.00
Subtotal		69		0644		-0-			13,035,887.00	-13,035,887.00	-0-
Miscellaneous Massachusetts Projects, Federal Highway Administration											
Fund Resources:											
Undisbursed Funds	No Year	69		0645		1,239,613.64			808,370.26		431,243.38
Fund Equities:											
Unobligated Balances (Unexpired)						-425,112.81				425,112.81	
Undelivered Orders						-814,500.83				-383,257.45	-431,243.38
Subtotal		69		0645		-0-			808,370.26	-808,370.26	-0-
Alabama And West Virginia Highway Projects, Federal Highway Administration											
Fund Resources:											
Undisbursed Funds	No Year	69		0646		517,770.66			271,729.20		246,041.46
Fund Equities:											
Undelivered Orders						-517,770.66				-271,729.20	-246,041.46
Subtotal		69		0646		-0-			271,729.20	-271,729.20	-0-
Woodrow Wilson Memorial Bridge, Federal Highway Administration											
Fund Resources:											
Undisbursed Funds	No Year	69		0648		155,380,923.00			98,018,002.00		57,362,921.00
Fund Equities:											
Undelivered Orders						-155,380,923.00				-98,018,002.00	-57,362,921.00
Subtotal		69		0648		-0-			98,018,002.00	-98,018,002.00	-0-
Trust Fund Accounts											
Highway Trust Fund											
Fund Resources:											
Undisbursed Funds	No Year	20		8102		[2]2,171,207,388.01	[21]1,571,873,803.83	-1,195,747,955.03	[12]548,748.81	-2,537,186,899.20	2,546,784,488.81
Investments In Public Debt Securities						10,997,655,000.00		1,206,889,000.00			12,204,544,000.00
Fund Equities:											
Unobligated Balances (Unexpired)[11]						[8]1,091,316,694.99					[13]3,628,503,594.19
Accounts Payable						-14,260,179,083.00		11,141,044.97		4,119,653,000.00	-18,379,832,083.00
Subtotal		20		8102		-0-	1,571,873,803.83		548,748.00	1,582,466,100.80	-0-
Intermodal Urban Demonstration Project, Federal Highway Administration											
Fund Resources:											
Undisbursed Funds	No Year	69		8001		2,423,022.70			73,520.39		2,349,502.31
Fund Equities:											
Unobligated Balances (Unexpired)						-2,017,380.56				-62,349.87	-1,955,030.69
Undelivered Orders						-405,642.14				-11,170.52	-394,471.62
Subtotal		69		8001		-0-			73,520.39	-73,520.39	-0-
Trust Fund Share Of Other Highway Programs, Federal Highway Administration											
Fund Resources:											
Undisbursed Funds	No Year	69		8009		302,094.56					302,094.56

Appropriations, Outlays, and Balances - Continued

Appropriation or Fund Account — Title	Period of Availability	Dept Reg	Tr From	Account Number	Sub No.	Balances, Beginning Of Fiscal Year	Appropriations And Other Obligational Authority[1]	Transfers Borrowings And Investment (Net)[2]	Outlays (Net)	Balances Withdrawn And Other Transactions[3]	Balances, End Of Fiscal Year[4]
Fund Equities:											
Unobligated Balances (Unexpired)						-302,094.56					-302,094.56
	Subtotal	69		8009		-0-					-0-
Baltimore-Washington Parkway Trust Fund, Federal Highway Administration											
Fund Resources:											
Undisbursed Funds	No Year	69		8014		2,368,782.11					2,368,782.11
Fund Equities:											
Undelivered Orders						-2,368,782.11					-2,368,782.11
	Subtotal	69		8014		-0-					-0-
Highway Safety Research And Development, Federal Highway Administration											
Fund Resources:											
Undisbursed Funds	No Year	69		8017		39,176.31			3,377.17		35,799.14
Fund Equities:											
Unobligated Balances (Unexpired)						-27,309.26				-22,391.86	-4,917.40
Undelivered Orders						-11,867.05				19,014.69	-30,881.74
	Subtotal	69		8017		-0-			3,377.17	-3,377.17	-0-
Highway-Related Safety Grants, Liquidation Of Contract Authorization, Trust Fund, Federal Highway Administration											
Fund Resources:											
Undisbursed Funds	No Year	69		8019		11,313.61					11,313.61
Transfer To:											
Department Of Transportation, National Highway Traffic Safety Administration	No Year	69	69	8019	6	554,049.67					554,049.67
Fund Equities:											
Unobligated Balances (Unexpired)						-11,313.61				3,650.73	-14,964.34
Accounts Payable						-538,513.87				-3,650.73	-534,863.14
Undelivered Orders						-15,535.80					-15,535.80
	Subtotal	69		8019		-0-					-0-
Advances From State Cooperating Agencies, Foreign Governments, And Other Federal Agencies, Federal Highway Administration											
Fund Resources:											
Undisbursed Funds	No Year	69		8054		120,319,451.85	8,175,385.60		22,777,235.44		105,717,602.01
Unfunded Contract Authority						7,209.88					7,209.88
Accounts Receivable										-20,000.00	20,000.00
Unfilled Customer Orders						150.36				-6,482,000.00	6,482,150.36
Fund Equities:											
Unobligated Balances (Unexpired)						-28,694,785.91				6,951,801.49	-35,646,587.40
Accounts Payable						-732,726.76				-3,698.27	-729,028.49
Undelivered Orders						-90,899,299.42				-15,047,953.06	-75,851,346.36
	Subtotal	69		8054		-0-	8,175,385.60		22,777,235.44	-14,601,849.84	-0-
Bridge Capacity Improvement, Federal Highway Administration											
Fund Resources:											
Undisbursed Funds	No Year	69		8057		41,115.06					41,115.06
Fund Equities:											
Undelivered Orders						-41,115.06					-41,115.06
	Subtotal	69		8057		-0-					-0-

Footnotes At End Of Chapter

Appropriations, Outlays, and Balances – Continued

Title	Reg	Tr From	Account Number	Sub No.	Period of Availability	Balances, Beginning Of Fiscal Year	Appropriations And Other Obligational Authority[1]	Transfers Borrowings And Investment (Net)[2]	Outlays (Net)	Balances Withdrawn And Other Transactions[3]	Balances, End Of Fiscal Year[4]
Miscellaneous Highway Project, Federal Highway Administration											
Fund Resources:											
Undisbursed Funds	69		8058		No Year	56,113,970.43	100,000,000.00	-24,298,101.00	135,620,334.89		[5]3,804,465.46
Transfer To:											
National Park Service	14	69	8058	10	No Year	524,663.65					524,663.65
Federal Railroad Administration	69	69	8058	7	No Year	465,246.79		80,000.00	527,786.11		17,460.68
Federal Transit Administration	69	69	8058	11	No Year	452,526.81		24,218,101.00	20,470,178.00		4,200,449.81
Accounts Receivable						511,649,207.01				100,993,500.00	410,655,707.01
Fund Equities:											
Unobligated Balances (Unexpired)						-246,021,295.93				-96,985,391.23	-149,035,904.70
Accounts Payable						-436,724.86				-384,582.86	-52,142.00
Undelivered Orders						-322,747,593.90				-60,241,824.91	-262,505,768.99
	69		8058		Subtotal	-0-	100,000,000.00		156,618,299.00	-56,618,299.00	-0-
Construction And Improvements To Halls Mills Road, New Jersey, Federal Highway Administration											
Fund Resources:											
Undisbursed Funds	69		8061		No Year	1,000,000.00					1,000,000.00
Fund Equities:											
Unobligated Balances (Unexpired)	69		8061		Subtotal	-1,000,000.00					-1,000,000.00
Appalachian Development Highway System, Federal Highway Administration											
Fund Resources:											
Undisbursed Funds	69		8072		No Year	10,468,882.79			1,978,186.77		8,490,696.02
Fund Equities:											
Unobligated Balances (Unexpired)						-2,775,856.37				-681,320.00	-2,094,536.37
Undelivered Orders						-7,693,026.42				-1,296,866.77	-6,396,159.65
	69		8072		Subtotal	-0-			1,978,186.77	-1,978,186.77	-0-
Highway Safety And Economic Development Projects, Federal Highway Administration											
Fund Resources:											
Undisbursed Funds	69		8076		No Year	47,835.00					47,835.00
Fund Equities:											
Undelivered Orders	69		8076		Subtotal	-47,835.00					-47,835.00
Highway-Railroad Grade Crossing Safety Demonstration Project, Federal Highway Administration											
Fund Resources:											
Undisbursed Funds	69		8081		No Year	2,718,062.00			123,752.00		2,594,310.00
Fund Equities:											
Unobligated Balances (Unexpired)						-445,591.00				1,229,144.00	-1,674,735.00
Undelivered Orders						-2,272,471.00				-1,352,896.00	-919,575.00
	69		8081		Subtotal	-0-			123,752.00	-123,752.00	-0-
Nuclear Waste Transportation Safety Demonstration Project, Federal Highway Administration											
Fund Resources:											
Undisbursed Funds	69		8082		No Year	109.55					109.55
Fund Equities:											
Unobligated Balances (Unexpired)						-109.55					-109.55

Appropriation or Fund Account — Title	Period of Availability	Reg	Tr From	Account Number	Sub No.	Balances, Beginning Of Fiscal Year	Appropriations And Other Obligational Authority[1]	Transfers Borrowings And Investment (Net)[2]	Outlays (Net)	Balances Withdrawn And Other Transactions[3]	Balances, End Of Fiscal Year[4]
	Subtotal	69		8082		-0-					-0-
Federal-Aid Highways, Liquidation Of Contract Authorization, Federal Highway Administration											
Fund Resources:											
Undisbursed Funds	No Year	69		8083		977,592,384.75	33,048,964,084.77	-1,205,035,628.03	32,846,085,132.69		[5]24,564,291.20
Transfer To:											
Forest Service, Department Of Agriculture	No Year	12	69	8083	11	11,358,634.27		11,080,561.00	17,663,797.40		4,775,397.87
Interior, Bureau Of Reclamation	No Year	14	69	8083	6	40,701.56		501,947.00	408,362.66		134,285.90
Interior, National Park Service	No Year	14	69	8083	10	462,084.61		51,395,142.00	49,024,141.55		2,833,085.06
Interior, Bureau Of Land Management	No Year	14	69	8083	11	565,284.74		3,756,356.00	1,553,361.60		2,768,279.14
Interior, United States Fish & Wildlife Service	No Year	14	69	8083	16	36,731.08		9,709,108.14	7,619,149.44		2,126,689.78
Interior, Bureau Of Indian Affairs	No Year	14	69	8083	20	24,447,345.11		390,281,540.00	330,850,173.16		83,878,711.95
Navy	No Year	17	69	8083		144,564.59		341,860.00	212,981.78		273,442.81
Department Of Treasury	No Year	20	69	8083	9	1,602,911.93		29,726,547.00	23,767,676.17		7,561,782.76
Army	No Year	21	69	8083		2,212,052.25		830,243.37	997,199.21		2,045,096.41
Appalachian Regional Commission	No Year	46	69	8083		702,042.98		745,855.00	990,138.54		457,759.44
Tennessee Valley Authority	No Year	64	69	8083				280,000.00	280,000.00		
Office Of The Secretary	No Year	69	69	8083	1	87,963.59					87,963.59
Department Of Transportation, National Highway Traffic Safety Administration	No Year	69	69	8083	6	92,904,310.32		250,346,243.00	299,749,466.30		43,501,087.02
Department Of Transportation, Federal Railroad Administration	No Year	69	69	8083	7	5,934,523.65		9,937,776.00	14,060,337.93		1,811,961.72
Department Of Transportation, Federal Transit Administration	No Year	69	69	8083	11	24,289,459.88		36,223,764.00	61,323,700.58		[5]810,476.70
Department Of Transportation, Research And Special Programs Administration	No Year	69	69	8083	14	882,528.00			98,233.81		784,294.19
Department Of Transportation, Bureau Of Transportation Statistics	No Year	69	69	8083	15	4,500,389.10		26,092,666.00	27,587,155.48		3,005,899.62
Department Of Transportation, Maritime Administration	No Year	69	69	8083	17	4,479,027.99			6,184,406.80		[5]1,705,378.81
Federal Motor Carrier Safety Administration	No Year	69	69	8083	26	7,634,438.97			7,462,829.76		171,609.21
Department Of Housing And Urban Development	No Year	86	69	8083	1			6,477,073.00	5,198,800.84		1,278,272.16
Department Of Energy	No Year	86	69	8083				328,712.00			328,712.00
Denali Commission	No Year	95	69	8083	67	6,897,440.00		7,957,323.00	5,195,135.91		9,659,627.09
Corps Of Engineers	No Year	96	69	8083		1,338,930.15		6,785,059.75	1,463,297.81		6,660,692.09
Unfunded Contract Authority						65,183,115,744.56	[6]6,236,221,327.00			4,342,604,000.00	67,076,733,071.56
Accounts Receivable						12,246,720,779.03				-3,007,219,558.03	15,253,940,337.06
Unfilled Customer Orders						90,219,684.54				-264,528,518.98	354,748,203.52
Fund Equities:											
Unobligated Balances (Unexpired)						-35,319,703,479.69				404,655,606.72	-35,724,359,086.41
Accounts Payable						-2,998,540,334.23				1,524,461,969.18	-4,523,002,303.41
Undelivered Orders						-40,369,926,143.73				2,215,198,581.69	-42,585,124,725.42
	Subtotal	69		8083		-0-	39,285,185,411.77	-362,237,851.77	33,707,775,479.42	5,215,172,080.58	-0-
Highway Safety Improvement Demonstration Projects, Federal Highway Administration											
Fund Resources:											
Undisbursed Funds	No Year	69		8087		899,848.71			368.71		899,480.00
Fund Equities:											
Unobligated Balances (Unexpired)	No Year	69		8087		-574,958.03				129,000.00	-703,958.03
Undelivered Orders	No Year	69		8087		-324,890.68				-129,368.71	-195,521.97
	Subtotal	69		8087		-0-			368.71	-368.71	-0-

Footnotes At End Of Chapter

Appropriations, Outlays, and Balances – Continued

Appropriation or Fund Account — Title	Period of Availability	Dept Reg	Dept Tr From	Account Number	Sub No.	Balances, Beginning Of Fiscal Year	Appropriations And Other Obligational Authority[1]	Transfers Borrowings And Investment (Net)[2]	Outlays (Net)	Balances Withdrawn And Other Transactions[3]	Balances, End Of Fiscal Year[4]
Corridor Safety Improvement Demonstration Project, Federal Highway Administration											
Fund Resources:											
Undisbursed Funds	No Year	69		8120		1,388,541.42			22,063.21		1,366,478.21
Fund Equities:											
Unobligated Balances (Unexpired)						-178,873.22					-178,873.22
Undelivered Orders						-1,209,668.20				-22,063.21	-1,187,604.99
Subtotal		69		8120		-0-			22,063.21	-22,063.21	-0-
Contributions For Highway Research Program, Federal Highway Administration											
Fund Resources:											
Undisbursed Funds	No Year	69		8264		5,896,928.31	441,566.00		2,371,901.96		3,966,592.35
Fund Equities:											
Unobligated Balances (Unexpired)						-4,751,941.53				-140,892.42	-4,611,049.11
Accounts Payable										141.70	-141.70
Undelivered Orders						-1,144,986.78				-1,789,585.24	644,598.46
Subtotal		69		8264		-0-	441,566.00		2,371,901.96	-1,930,335.96	-0-
Cooperative Work, Forest Highways, Federal Highway Administration											
Fund Resources:											
Undisbursed Funds	No Year	69		8265		80,140,307.70	17,010,648.00		12,740,269.12		84,410,686.58
Unfilled Customer Orders						3,250.92					3,250.92
Fund Equities:											
Unobligated Balances (Unexpired)						-8,431,102.80				10,439,410.75	-18,870,513.55
Accounts Payable						-10,131.81				226,227.69	-236,359.50
Undelivered Orders						-71,702,324.01				-6,395,259.56	-65,307,064.45
Subtotal		69		8265		-0-	17,010,648.00		12,740,269.12	4,270,378.88	-0-
Highway Demonstration Projects, Federal Highway Administration											
Fund Resources:											
Undisbursed Funds	No Year	69		8363		1,440.05					1,440.05
Fund Equities:											
Unobligated Balances (Unexpired)						-1,440.05					-1,440.05
Subtotal		69		8363		-0-					-0-
International Highway Transportation Outreach Program, Federal Highway Administration, Department Of Transportation											
Fund Resources:											
Undisbursed Funds	No Year	69		8371		89,204.27					89,204.27
Fund Equities:											
Unobligated Balances (Unexpired)						-71,121.79					-71,121.79
Undelivered Orders						-18,082.48					-18,082.48
Subtotal		69		8371		-0-					-0-
Climbing Lane And Highway Safety Demonstration Project, Federal Highway Administration											
Fund Resources:											
Undisbursed Funds	No Year	69		8374		5,200.00					5,200.00
Fund Equities:											
Undelivered Orders						-5,200.00					-5,200.00
Subtotal		69		8374		-0-					-0-

Appropriations, Outlays, and Balances - Continued

Appropriation or Fund Account — Title	Period of Availability	Dept Reg	Tr From	Account Number	Sub No.	Balances, Beginning Of Fiscal Year	Appropriations And Other Obligational Authority[1]	Transfers Borrowings And Investment (Net)[2]	Outlays (Net)	Balances Withdrawn And Other Transactions[3]	Balances, End Of Fiscal Year[4]
Alabama Highway Bypass Demonstration Project, Federal Highway Administration											
Fund Resources:											
Undisbursed Funds	No Year	69		8375		94,634.30			16,246.30		78,388.00
Fund Equities:											
Undelivered Orders		69		8375		-94,634.30				-16,246.30	-78,388.00
	Subtotal					-0-			16,246.30	-16,246.30	-0-
Kentucky Bridge Demonstration Project, Federal Highway Administration											
Fund Resources:											
Undisbursed Funds	No Year	69		8376		434,684.57					434,684.57
Fund Equities:											
Unobligated Balances (Unexpired)		69		8376		-434,684.57					-434,684.57
	Subtotal					-0-					-0-
Virginia HOV Safety Demonstration Project, Federal Highway Administration											
Fund Resources:											
Undisbursed Funds	No Year	69		8377					-9,558.00		9,558.00
Fund Equities:											
Undelivered Orders		69		8377						9,558.00	-9,558.00
	Subtotal					-0-			-9,558.00	9,558.00	-0-
Pennsylvania Toll Road Demonstration Project, Federal Highway Administration, Department Of Transportation											
Fund Resources:											
Undisbursed Funds	No Year	69		8380		0.45				0.45	0.45
Fund Equities:											
Unobligated Balances (Unexpired)		69		8380		-0.45				-0.45	-0.45
Undelivered Orders						-0-					-0-
	Subtotal										
Pennsylvania Reconstruction Demonstration Project, Federal Highway Administration, Department Of Transportation											
Fund Resources:											
Undisbursed Funds	No Year	69		8381		1,277,411.79					1,277,411.79
Fund Equities:											
Unobligated Balances (Unexpired)		69		8381		-1,277,411.79				-786,285.00	-491,126.79
Undelivered Orders										786,285.00	-786,285.00
	Subtotal					-0-					-0-
Highway Projects, Federal Highway Administration											
Fund Resources:											
Undisbursed Funds	No Year	69		8382		15,150,090.97			1,148,079.34		14,002,011.63
Fund Equities:											
Unobligated Balances (Unexpired)		69		8382		-8,149,301.97				921,574.71	-9,070,876.68
Accounts Payable						-2,612.58					-2,612.58
Undelivered Orders						-6,998,176.42				-2,069,654.05	-4,928,522.37
	Subtotal					-0-			1,148,079.34	-1,148,079.34	-0-
Mineola Grade Crossing, Federal Highway Administration											
Fund Resources:											
Undisbursed Funds	No Year	69		8386		487,414.00			174.00		487,240.00

Footnotes At End Of Chapter

Appropriations, Outlays, and Balances – Continued

Appropriation or Fund Account — Title	Period of Availability	Dept Reg	Tr From	Account Number	Sub No.	Balances, Beginning Of Fiscal Year	Appropriations And Other Obligational Authority[1]	Transfers Borrowings And Investment (Net)[2]	Outlays (Net)	Balances Withdrawn And Other Transactions[3]	Balances, End Of Fiscal Year[4]
Mineola Grade Crossing, Federal Highway Administration - Continued											
Fund Equities:											
Unobligated Balances (Unexpired)										127,583.00	-127,583.00
Undelivered Orders						-487,414.00				-127,757.00	-359,657.00
Subtotal	Subtotal	69		8386		-0-			174.00	-174.00	-0-
Metropolitan Planning Trust Fund, Federal Highway Administration											
Fund Resources:											
Undisbursed Funds	No Year	69		8390		366,352.18					366,352.18
Fund Equities:											
Unobligated Balances (Unexpired)						-38,949.59					-38,949.59
Undelivered Orders						-327,402.59					-327,402.59
Subtotal	Subtotal	69		8390		-0-					-0-
Right-Of-Way Revolving Fund, Liquidation Of Contract Authorization, Trust Fund, Federal Highway Administration											
Fund Resources:											
Undisbursed Funds	No Year	69		8402		21,193,176.72			21,019.17		14,410,157.55
Fund Equities:											
Unobligated Balances (Unexpired)						-15,193,377.92	-6,762,000.00			307.87	-15,193,685.79
Accounts Payable										-6,762,307.87	6,762,307.87
Undelivered Orders						-5,999,798.80				-21,019.17	-5,978,779.63
Subtotal	Subtotal	69		8402		-0-	-6,762,000.00		21,019.17	-6,783,019.17	-0-
Technical Assistance, United States Dollars Advanced From Foreign Governments, Federal Highway Administration											
Fund Resources:											
Undisbursed Funds	No Year	69		8502		602,667.26	934,859.23		743,697.37		793,829.12
Fund Equities:											
Unobligated Balances (Unexpired)						-609,347.94				-54,923.09	-554,424.85
Accounts Payable						46,514.71				58,784.99	-12,270.28
Undelivered Orders						-39,834.03				187,299.96	-227,133.99
Subtotal	Subtotal	69		8502		-0-	934,859.23		743,697.37	191,161.86	-0-
Equipment, Supplies, Etc., For Cooperating Countries, Federal Highway Administration											
Fund Resources:											
Undisbursed Funds	No Year	69		8632		206,511.87					206,511.87
Fund Equities:											
Unobligated Balances (Unexpired)						-206,511.87					-206,511.87
Subtotal	Subtotal	69		8632		-0-					-0-
Total, Federal Highway Administration						41,869,009,674.43		-351,096,806.80	34,978,291,840.79	6,539,621,026.84	
Federal Motor Carrier Safety Administration											
Trust Fund Accounts											
National Motor Carrier Safety Program, Liquidation Of Contract Authorization, Federal Motor Carrier Safety Administration											
Fund Resources:											
Undisbursed Funds	No Year	69		8048		45,253,892.56			26,481,157.81		18,772,734.75
Unfunded Contract Authority						36,280,238.77					36,280,238.77
Accounts Receivable						4,588,303.00					4,588,303.00

Appropriations, Outlays, and Balances - Continued

Appropriation or Fund Account — Title	Period of Availability	Reg	Tr From	Account Number	Sub No.	Balances, Beginning Of Fiscal Year	Appropriations And Other Obligational Authority[1]	Transfers Borrowings And Investment (Net)[2]	Outlays (Net)	Balances Withdrawn And Other Transactions[3]	Balances, End Of Fiscal Year[4]
Fund Equities:											
Unobligated Balances (Unexpired)						-5,212,857.97				10,204,391.68	-15,417,249.65
Accounts Payable						-19,120,132.75				828,205.66	-19,948,338.41
Undelivered Orders						-61,789,443.61				-37,513,755.15	-24,275,688.46
	Subtotal	69		8048		-0-			26,481,157.81	-26,481,157.81	-0-
Motor Carrier Safety, Limitation On Administrative Expenses, Federal Motor Carrier Safety Administration											
Fund Resources:											
Undisbursed Funds	No Year	69		8055		4,867,483.35	97,547,000.00[8]		30,115,163.28		72,299,320.07
Unfunded Contract Authority						-176,160.00					-176,160.00
Accounts Receivable						97,547,108.49				97,547,000.00	108.49
Unfilled Customer Orders						3,555,015.51				-16,676.42	3,571,691.93
Fund Equities:											
Unobligated Balances (Unexpired)						-35,687,194.25				1,548,435.27	-37,235,629.52
Accounts Payable						-333,989.05				878,957.75	-1,212,946.80
Undelivered Orders						-69,772,264.05				-32,525,879.88	-37,246,384.17
	Subtotal	69		8055		-0-	97,547,000.00		30,115,163.28	67,431,836.72	-0-
Motor Carrier Safety Grants, Federal Motor Carrier Safety Administration, Department Of Transportation											
Fund Resources:											
Undisbursed Funds	No Year	69		8158		8,569,930.61	201,300,000.00[8]		209,866,123.45		3,807.16
Unfunded Contract Authority						-2,820,000.00					-2,820,000.00
Accounts Receivable						200,000,000.00				-92,700,000.00	292,700,000.00
Fund Equities:											
Unobligated Balances (Unexpired)						-11,260,213.94				1,248,874.48	-12,509,088.42
Accounts Payable						-452,993.84				748,618.46	-1,201,612.30
Undelivered Orders						-194,036,722.83				82,136,383.61	-276,173,106.44
	Subtotal	69		8158		-0-	201,300,000.00		209,866,123.45	-8,566,123.45	-0-
Motor Carrier Safety Operations And Programs, Federal Motor Carrier Safety Administration, Department Of Transportation											
Fund Resources:											
Undisbursed Funds	No Year	69		8159		1,486,607.04	188,000,000.00[8]		187,773,257.53		1,713,349.51
Unfunded Contract Authority						-2,130,000.00					-2,130,000.00
Accounts Receivable						75,000,000.00				-35,000,000.00	110,000,000.00
Unfilled Customer Orders						1,899,710.00				-1,899,710.00	1,899,710.00
Fund Equities:											
Unobligated Balances (Unexpired)						-12,380,514.57				1,446,307.39	-13,826,821.96
Accounts Payable						-4,489,725.03				1,898,560.40	-6,388,285.43
Undelivered Orders						-57,486,367.44				33,781,584.68	-91,267,952.12
	Subtotal	69		8159		-0-	188,000,000.00		187,773,257.53	226,742.47	-0-
Safety Of Cross-Border Trucking Between The United States And Mexico, Federal Motor Carrier Safety Administration											
Fund Resources:											
Undisbursed Funds	2002	69		8274		12,117,938.62		-11,141,044.97	976,893.65		
Fund Equities:											
Unobligated Balances (Expired)						-2,636,927.69				-2,636,927.69	-2,636,927.69
Accounts Payable						-80,592.60				-80,592.60	-80,592.60
Undelivered Orders						-9,400,418.33				-9,400,418.33	-9,400,418.33

Footnotes At End Of Chapter

Appropriations, Outlays, and Balances – Continued

Appropriation or Fund Account — Title	Dept Reg	Tr From	Account Number	Sub No.	Period of Availability	Balances, Beginning Of Fiscal Year	Appropriations And Other Obligational Authority[1]	Transfers Borrowings And Investment (Net)[2]	Outlays (Net)	Balances Withdrawn And Other Transactions[3]	Balances, End Of Fiscal Year[4]
Safety Of Cross-Border Trucking Between The United States And Mexico, Federal Motor Carrier Safety Administration - Continued											
Fund Equities: - Continued											
Undelivered Orders - Continued											-0-
Subtotal	69		8274			-0-		-11,141,044.97	976,893.65	-12,117,938.62	-0-
Total, Federal Motor Carrier Safety Administration						-0-	486,847,000.00	-11,141,044.97	455,212,595.72	20,493,359.31	
National Highway Traffic Safety Administration											
General Fund Accounts											
Operations And Research, National Highway Traffic Safety Administration			0650								
Fund Resources:											
Undisbursed Funds	69				2007-2009				-5,000.00		5,000.00
					2003-2005	14,591,172.15			3,590,285.12		11,000,887.03
					2004				-817.44		817.44
					2002-2004	8,981,560.59			3,284,092.37		5,697,468.22
					2003	568,789.34			-8,418.70		577,208.04
					2001-2003	7,398,286.48			1,484,934.14		5,913,352.34
					2002	779,706.86			-355,462.02	1,135,168.88	
					2000-2002	109,377.47			80,345.08	29,032.39	
					No Year	127,564.28			405,465.25		[5]277,900.97
Fund Equities:											
Unobligated Balances (Expired)						-5,480,396.03				2,048,440.93	-7,528,836.96
Unobligated Balances (Unexpired)						-127,564.28				-479,289.28	[5]351,725.00
Accounts Payable						-14,180,078.33				-11,874,934.23	-2,305,144.10
Undelivered Orders						-12,768,418.53				666,157.51	-13,434,576.04
Subtotal	69		0650			-0-			8,475,423.80	-8,475,423.80	-0-
State And Community Highway Safety, Liquidation Of Contract Authorization, National Highway Traffic Safety Administration											
Fund Resources:											
Undisbursed Funds	69		0651		No Year	87,672.69					87,672.69
Transfer To:											
Department Of Transportation, Federal Highway Administration	69	69	0651	5	No Year	47,447.47					47,447.47
Fund Equities:											
Unobligated Balances (Unexpired)	69		0651		No Year	-59,926.70					-59,926.70
Undelivered Orders						-75,193.46					-75,193.46
Subtotal	69		0651			-0-					-0-
Trust Fund Accounts											
Operation And Research, Liquidation Of Contract Authorization, Limitation On Obligations, Highway Trust Fund, Department Of Transportation											
Fund Resources:											
Undisbursed Funds	69		8016		2006-2008	15,000,000.00			27,841,326.96		[5]12,841,326.96
					2007		3,957,496.23				3,957,496.23
					2006	24,981,043.97			82,695,588.40		[5]57,714,544.43
					No Year	120,932,938.06	75,000,000.00	117,274,933.77	124,845,005.01		188,362,866.82
Unfunded Contract Authority						-3,616,800.00	[6]75,000,000.00			75,000,000.00	-3,616,800.00

Appropriations, Outlays, and Balances - Continued

Appropriation or Fund Account: Title	Account Symbol: Period of Availability	Dept Reg	Tr From	Account Number	Sub No.	Balances, Beginning Of Fiscal Year	Appropriations And Other Obligational Authority[1]	Transfers Borrowings And Investment (Net)[2]	Outlays (Net)	Balances Withdrawn And Other Transactions[3]	Balances, End Of Fiscal Year[4]
Accounts Receivable						80,001,626.00				-32,750,000.00	112,751,626.00
Unfilled Customer Orders						2,224,000.00				2,406,294.38	-182,294.38
Fund Equities:											
Unobligated Balances (Expired)										1,058,322.12	-1,058,322.12
Unobligated Balances (Unexpired)						-24,695,201.32				-8,919,980.82	-15,775,220.50
Accounts Payable						-26,857,644.82				-3,977,838.37	-22,879,806.45
Undelivered Orders						-187,969,961.89				3,033,712.32	-191,003,674.21
Subtotal	Subtotal	69		8016		-0-	153,957,496.23	117,274,933.77	235,381,920.37	35,850,509.63	-0-
Highway Traffic Safety Grants, Liquidation Of Contract Authorization, Trust Fund, National Highway Traffic Safety Administration											
Fund Resources:											
Undisbursed Funds	No Year	69		8020		51,532,845.10	400,000,000.00		404,470,404.79		47,062,440.31
Transfer To:											
Department Of Transportation, Federal Highway Administration	No Year	69	69	8020	5	4,998,446.76			11,770,892.27	400,000,000.00	[5]-6,772,445.51
Unfunded Contract Authority	No Year	69		8020		120,497,591.26	[8]400,000,000.00			400,000,000.00	120,497,591.26
Accounts Receivable						379,976,000.00				-187,750,000.00	567,726,000.00
Fund Equities:											
Unobligated Balances (Unexpired)						-10,528,957.97				5,077,633.01	-15,606,590.98
Accounts Payable						-64,863,327.39				-39,949,448.28	-24,913,879.11
Undelivered Orders						-481,612,597.76				206,380,518.21	-687,993,115.97
Subtotal	Subtotal	69		8020		-0-	800,000,000.00		416,241,297.06	383,758,702.94	-0-
National Driver Register, National Highway Traffic Safety Administration											
Fund Resources:											
Undisbursed Funds	No Year	69		8362		1,085,152.24	6,000,000.00		4,539,699.82		2,545,452.42
Unfunded Contract Authority						328,000.00					328,000.00
Accounts Receivable						4,000,000.00	[8]			2,000,000.00	2,000,000.00
Fund Equities:											
Unobligated Balances (Unexpired)						-1,025,490.49				573,776.26	-1,599,266.75
Accounts Payable						-337,054.28				268,145.03	-605,199.31
Undelivered Orders						-4,050,607.47				-1,381,621.11	-2,668,986.36
Subtotal	Subtotal	69		8362		-0-	6,000,000.00		4,539,699.82	1,460,300.18	-0-
Total, National Highway Traffic Safety Administration							959,957,496.23	117,274,933.77	664,638,341.05	412,594,088.95	
Federal Railroad Administration											
General Fund Accounts											
Efficiency Incentive Grants To The National Railroad Passenger Corporation, Federal Railroad Administration											
Fund Resources:											
Undisbursed Funds	No Year	69		0120		31,383,000.00	31,300,000.00			31,300,000.00	62,683,000.00
Fund Equities:											
Unobligated Balances (Unexpired)	Subtotal	69		0120		-31,383,000.00	31,300,000.00			31,300,000.00	-62,683,000.00
						-0-				31,300,000.00	-0-

Footnotes At End Of Chapter

Appropriations, Outlays, and Balances – Continued

Appropriation or Fund Account — Title	Period of Availability	Dept Reg	Tr From	Account Number	Sub No.	Balances, Beginning Of Fiscal Year	Appropriations And Other Obligational Authority[1]	Transfers Borrowings And Investment (Net)[2]	Outlays (Net)	Balances Withdrawn And Other Transactions[3]	Balances, End Of Fiscal Year[4]
Operating Subsidy Grants To The National Railroad Passenger Corporation, Federal Railroad Administration											
Fund Resources:											
Undisbursed Funds	No Year	69		0121		4,950,000.00	490,050,000.00		485,100,000.00		9,900,000.00
Fund Equities:											
Unobligated Balances (Unexpired)						-4,950,000.00				4,950,000.00	-9,900,000.00
Subtotal	Subtotal	69		0121		-0-	490,050,000.00		485,100,000.00	4,950,000.00	-0-
Rail Service Assistance, Federal Railroad Administration											
Fund Resources:											
Undisbursed Funds	No Year	69		0122		1,689,191.20			431,138.63		1,258,052.57
Fund Equities:											
Unobligated Balances (Unexpired)						-648,523.54				3,860.74	-652,384.28
Accounts Payable						-85,138.00				-85,138.00	
Undelivered Orders						-955,529.66				-349,861.37	-605,668.29
Subtotal	Subtotal	69		0122		-0-			431,138.63	-431,138.63	-0-
Northeast Corridor Improvement Program, Federal Railroad Administration											
Fund Resources:											
Undisbursed Funds	No Year	69		0123		5,143,212.26					5,143,212.26
Transfer To:											
Department Of Transportation, Federal Highway Administration	No Year	69	69	0123	5	908,340.01					908,340.01
Fund Equities:											
Unobligated Balances (Unexpired)						-5,405,298.51					-5,405,298.51
Undelivered Orders						-646,253.76					-646,253.76
Subtotal	Subtotal	69		0123		-0-					-0-
Capital And Debt Service Grants To The National Railroad Passenger Corporation, Federal Railroad Administration											
Fund Resources:											
Undisbursed Funds	No Year	69		0125			772,200,000.00		772,200,000.00		
Amtrak Reform Council, Federal Railroad Administration, Department Of Transportation											
Fund Resources:											
Undisbursed Funds	2001-2002	69		0152		759.33				759.33	
Fund Equities:											
Unobligated Balances (Expired)	Subtotal	69		0152		-759.33				-759.33	-0-
Safety And Operations, Federal Railroad Administration											
Fund Resources:											
Undisbursed Funds	2007	69		0700		32,658,327.88	136,553,872.00		101,095,957.01		35,457,914.99
	2006								28,256,425.18		4,401,902.70
	2005-2006					2,250,000.00					2,250,000.00
	2005					-3,070,466.24			-3,445,439.71		374,973.47
	2004					2,220,368.18			166,803.91		2,053,564.27
	2003					2,308,185.28			293,968.44		2,014,216.84
	2002					1,538,758.70			53,085.80	1,485,672.90	
	No Year					27,657,415.53	13,717,440.00	1,985,100.00	18,316,087.82		25,043,867.71
Accounts Receivable						8,644,086.16				845,600.96	7,798,485.20
Unfilled Customer Orders						10,201,991.31				9,043,542.56	1,158,448.75

Appropriations, Outlays, and Balances - Continued

Appropriation or Fund Account — Title	Period of Availability	Dept Reg	Tr From	Account Number	Sub No.	Balances, Beginning Of Fiscal Year	Appropriations And Other Obligational Authority[1]	Transfers Borrowings And Investment (Net)[2]	Outlays (Net)	Balances Withdrawn And Other Transactions[3]	Balances, End Of Fiscal Year[4]
Fund Equities:											
Unobligated Balances (Expired)						-6,624,777.71				-2,180,617.11	-4,444,160.60
Unobligated Balances (Unexpired)						-11,275,306.20				-7,529,399.22	-3,745,906.98
Accounts Payable						-5,428,819.07				482,648.87	-5,911,467.94
Undelivered Orders						-61,079,763.82				5,372,074.59	-66,451,838.41
Subtotal	Subtotal	69		0700		-0-	150,271,312.00	1,985,100.00	144,736,888.45	7,519,523.55	-0-
Railroad Safety, Federal Railroad Administration											
Fund Resources:											
Undisbursed Funds	No Year	69		0702		7,052.79					7,052.79
Fund Equities:											
Unobligated Balances (Unexpired)				0702		-7,052.79				-6,265.00	-787.79
Undelivered Orders										6,265.00	-6,265.00
Subtotal	Subtotal	69		0702		-0-					-0-
Railroad Research, Federal Railroad Administration											
Fund Resources:											
Undisbursed Funds	No Year	69		0703		0.42					0.42
Fund Equities:											
Unobligated Balances (Unexpired)				0703		-0.42					-0.42
Subtotal	Subtotal	69		0703		-0-					-0-
Grants To The National Railroad Passenger Corporation, Federal Railroad Administration											
Fund Resources:											
Undisbursed Funds	No Year	69		0704		37,500,409.82			16,622,989.35		20,877,420.47
Fund Equities:											
Unobligated Balances (Unexpired)				0704		-12,339,900.37				-10,996,265.53	-1,343,634.84
Accounts Payable						-644,119.90				9,179,899.10	-9,824,019.00
Undelivered Orders						-24,516,389.55				-14,806,622.92	-9,709,766.63
Subtotal	Subtotal	69		0704		-0-			16,622,989.35	-16,622,989.35	-0-
Rail Labor Assistance, Federal Railroad Administration											
Fund Resources:											
Undisbursed Funds	No Year	69		0707		133,243.64			77,078.27		56,165.37
Fund Equities:											
Unobligated Balances (Unexpired)				0707		-133,243.64				-77,078.27	-56,165.37
Subtotal	Subtotal	69		0707		-0-			77,078.27	-77,078.27	-0-
Local Rail Freight Assistance, Federal Railroad Administration											
Fund Resources:											
Undisbursed Funds	No Year	69		0714		68,489.84			19,884.94		48,504.90
Fund Equities:											
Unobligated Balances (Unexpired)				0714		-30,431.98				13,173.05	-43,605.03
Undelivered Orders						-38,057.86				-33,057.99	-4,999.87
Subtotal	Subtotal	69		0714		-0-			19,884.94	-19,884.94	-0-
Next Generation High Speed Rail, Federal Railroad Administration											
Fund Resources:											
Undisbursed Funds	No Year	69		0722		42,570,885.65			14,581,469.16		27,989,416.49
Fund Equities:											
Unobligated Balances (Unexpired)						-11,210,700.18				-2,285,408.34	-8,925,291.84
Accounts Payable						-652,549.75				-1,395.77	-651,153.98
Undelivered Orders						-30,707,635.72				-12,294,665.05	-18,412,970.67

Footnotes At End Of Chapter

467

Appropriations, Outlays, and Balances – Continued

Appropriation or Fund Account — Title	Period of Availability	Account Symbol — Dept Reg	Account Symbol — Dept Tr From	Account Number	Sub No.	Balances, Beginning Of Fiscal Year	Appropriations And Other Obligational Authority[1]	Transfers Borrowings And Investment (Net)[2]	Outlays (Net)	Balances Withdrawn And Other Transactions[3]	Balances, End Of Fiscal Year[4]
Next Generation High Speed Rail, Federal Railroad Administration - Continued											
Subtotal	Subtotal	69		0722		-0-			14,581,469.16	-14,581,469.16	-0-
Pennsylvania Station Redevelopment Project, Federal Railroad Administration											
Fund Resources:											
Undisbursed Funds	No Year	69		0723		59,845,510.66					59,845,510.66
Fund Equities:											
Unobligated Balances (Unexpired)						-59,826,855.66					-59,826,855.66
Undelivered Orders						-18,655.00					-18,655.00
Subtotal	Subtotal	69		0723		-0-					-0-
Alaska Railroad Rehabilitation, Federal Railroad Administration											
Fund Resources:											
Undisbursed Funds	No Year	69		0730		6,800,562.00			5,369,914.00		1,430,648.00
Fund Equities:											
Accounts Payable						-3,481,100.00				-2,107,578.00	-1,373,522.00
Undelivered Orders						-3,319,462.00				-3,262,336.00	-57,126.00
Subtotal	Subtotal	69		0730		-0-			5,369,914.00	-5,369,914.00	-0-
Railroad Research And Development, Federal Railroad Administration											
Fund Resources:											
Undisbursed Funds	No Year	69		0745		61,824,275.47	34,524,000.00		33,812,146.88		62,536,128.59
Accounts Receivable						416,459.48				327,380.22	89,079.26
Unfilled Customer Orders						854,227.52				-2,190,449.03	3,044,676.55
Fund Equities:											
Unobligated Balances (Unexpired)						-6,168,841.20				3,879,986.94	-10,048,828.14
Accounts Payable						-162,372.57				667,956.41	-830,328.98
Undelivered Orders						-56,763,748.70				-1,973,021.42	-54,790,727.28
Subtotal	Subtotal	69		0745		-0-	34,524,000.00		33,812,146.88	711,853.12	-0-
Conrail Commuter Transition Assistance, Federal Railroad Administration											
Fund Resources:											
Undisbursed Funds	No Year	69		0747		454.56					454.56
Fund Equities:											
Unobligated Balances (Unexpired)						-454.56					-454.56
Subtotal	Subtotal	69		0747		-0-					-0-
Railroad Rehabilitation And Improvement Program Account, Federal Railroad Administration											
Fund Resources:											
Undisbursed Funds	2007	69		0750			3,294,089.00		3,294,089.00		
West Virginia Rail Development, Federal Railroad Administration											
Fund Resources:											
Undisbursed Funds	No Year	69		0758		176,635.85					176,635.85
Fund Equities:											
Unobligated Balances (Unexpired)						-176,635.85					-176,635.85
Subtotal	Subtotal	69		0758		-0-					-0-

Appropriations, Outlays, and Balances - Continued

Appropriation or Fund Account — Title	Dept Reg	Tr From	Account Number	Sub No.	Period of Availability	Balances, Beginning Of Fiscal Year	Appropriations And Other Obligational Authority[1]	Transfers Borrowings And Investment (Net)[2]	Outlays (Net)	Balances Withdrawn And Other Transactions[3]	Balances, End Of Fiscal Year[4]
Public Enterprise Funds											
Financing Funds, Railroad Rehabilitation And Improvement, Liquidating Account, Federal Railroad Administration											
Fund Resources:											
Undisbursed Funds	69		4411		No Year				-4,421,919.71	[1]4,421,919.71	---
Trust Fund Accounts											
High-Speed Ground Transportation, Liquidation Of Contract Authorization, Federal Railroad Administration, Department Of Transportation											
Fund Resources:											
Undisbursed Funds	69		8552		No Year	312,151.02					312,151.02
Fund Equities:											
Unobligated Balances (Unexpired)											-312,151.02
Undelivered Orders	69		8552		Subtotal	[6]-312,151.02					-0-
						-0-					
Total, Federal Railroad Administration							1,481,639,401.00	1,985,100.00	1,471,823,678.97	11,800,822.03	
Federal Transit Administration											
General Fund Accounts											
Urban Mass Transportation Fund, Federal Transit Administration											
Fund Resources:											
Undisbursed Funds	69		1119		No Year	592,741.04					592,741.04
Transfer To: Department Of Transportation, Federal Highway Administration	69	69	1119	5	No Year	339,983.75			137,417.86		202,565.89
Fund Equities:											
Unobligated Balances (Unexpired)						-507,780.48				112,104.03	-619,884.51
Accounts Payable						-4,904.45					-4,904.45
Undelivered Orders						-420,039.86				-249,521.89	-170,517.97
	69		1119		Subtotal	-0-			137,417.86	-137,417.86	-0-
Administrative Expenses, Federal Transit Administration											
Fund Resources:											
Undisbursed Funds	69		1120		2007	9,053,940.57	85,000,000.00		76,566,534.54		8,433,465.46
					2006	2,399,434.03			6,129,817.15		2,924,123.42
					2005	57,313.47			337,074.82		2,062,359.21
					2004	1,667,000.73			70,623.59		[5]-13,310.12
					2003	622,337.35			-56,758.96		1,723,759.69
					2002	144,244.97			71,613.84	550,723.51	144,244.97
Accounts Receivable					No Year	402,769.88				-1,796.01	404,565.89
Unfilled Customer Orders						201,518.92				-105,029.37	306,548.29
Fund Equities:											
Unobligated Balances (Expired)						-2,131,435.03				1,077,042.80	-3,208,477.83

Footnotes At End Of Chapter

Appropriations, Outlays, and Balances – Continued

Title	Period of Availability	Dept Reg	Tr From	Account Number	Sub No.	Balances, Beginning Of Fiscal Year	Appropriations And Other Obligational Authority[1]	Transfers Borrowings And Investment (Net)[2]	Outlays (Net)	Balances Withdrawn And Other Transactions[3]	Balances, End Of Fiscal Year[4]
Administrative Expenses, Federal Transit Administration - Continued											
Fund Equities: - Continued											
Unobligated Balances (Unexpired)		69				-44,757.65				54,693.54	-99,451.19
Accounts Payable		69				-2,210,861.35				22,192.23	-2,233,053.58
Undelivered Orders		69				-10,161,505.89				283,268.32	-10,444,774.21
Subtotal	Subtotal	69		1120		-0-	85,000,000.00		83,118,904.98	1,881,095.02	-0-
Research, Training, And Human Resources, Federal Transit Administration											
Fund Resources:											
Undisbursed Funds	No Year	69		1121		890,714.85					890,714.85
Unfilled Customer Orders		69				31,053.61					31,053.61
Fund Equities:											
Unobligated Balances (Unexpired)		69		1121		-1,019,373.34				-675,356.83	-344,016.51
Undelivered Orders		69				97,604.88				675,356.83	-577,751.95
Subtotal	Subtotal	69		1121		-0-					-0-
Urban Discretionary Grants, Federal Transit Administration											
Fund Resources:											
Undisbursed Funds	No Year	69		1122		679,313.78					679,313.78
Fund Equities:											
Unobligated Balances (Unexpired)		69				-79,895.54					-79,895.54
Undelivered Orders		69				-599,418.24					-599,418.24
Subtotal	Subtotal	69		1122		-0-					-0-
Non-Urban Formula Grants, Federal Transit Administration											
Fund Resources:											
Undisbursed Funds	No Year	69		1123		0.72					0.72
Fund Equities:											
Unobligated Balances (Unexpired)		69		1123		-0.72					-0.72
Subtotal	Subtotal	69				-0-					-0-
Urban Formula Grants, Federal Transit Administration											
Fund Resources:											
Undisbursed Funds	No Year	69		1124		960,705.02					960,705.02
Fund Equities:											
Unobligated Balances (Unexpired)		69				-928,837.88					-928,837.88
Undelivered Orders		69		1124		-31,867.14					-31,867.14
Subtotal	Subtotal	69				-0-					-0-
Job Access And Reverse Commute Grants, Federal Transit Administration											
Fund Resources:											
Undisbursed Funds	No Year	69		1125		218,205,308.70			68,826,496.69		149,378,812.01
Fund Equities:											
Unobligated Balances (Unexpired)		69				-51,326,199.62				-28,590,144.78	-22,736,054.84
Accounts Payable		69				-30,600.19				-30,600.19	-0-
Undelivered Orders		69		1125		-166,848,508.89				-40,205,751.72	-126,642,757.17
Subtotal	Subtotal	69				-0-			68,826,496.69	-68,826,496.69	-0-
Interstate Transfer Grants-Transit, Federal Transit Administration											
Fund Resources:											
Undisbursed Funds	No Year	69		1127		4,999,563.58			1,755,043.00		3,244,520.58
Transfer To:											
Department Of Transportation, Federal Highway Administration	No Year	69	69	1127	5	148,141.56			18,767.40		129,374.16

Appropriations, Outlays, and Balances - Continued

Appropriation or Fund Account — Title	Period of Availability	Dept Reg	Tr From	Account Number	Sub No.	Balances, Beginning Of Fiscal Year	Appropriations And Other Obligational Authority[1]	Transfers Borrowings And Investment (Net)[2]	Outlays (Net)	Balances Withdrawn And Other Transactions[3]	Balances, End Of Fiscal Year[4]
Fund Equities:											
Unobligated Balances (Unexpired)						-116,042.26				-18,767.40	-97,274.86
Undelivered Orders						-5,031,662.88				-1,755,043.00	-3,276,619.88
Subtotal	Subtotal			1127		-0-			1,773,810.40	-1,773,810.40	-0-
Washington Metropolitan Area Transit Authority, Federal Transit Administration											
Fund Resources:											
Undisbursed Funds	No Year	69		1128		2,844,532.87			2,243,045.05		601,487.82
Fund Equities:											
Unobligated Balances (Unexpired)						-150,000.14				-179.32	-149,820.82
Undelivered Orders						-2,694,532.73				-2,242,865.73	-451,667.00
Subtotal	Subtotal	69		1128		-0-			2,243,045.05	-2,243,045.05	-0-
Formula Grants, Federal Transit Administration, Department Of Transportation											
Fund Resources:											
Undisbursed Funds	No Year	69		1129		5,393,022,492.61	35,000,000.00		2,042,340,627.86		3,385,681,864.75
Transfer To:											
Federal Transit Administration	No Year	69	69	1129	5	906,193.35			131,289.78		774,903.57
Accounts Receivable						2,223,102.00				-13,112,439.42	15,335,541.42
Unfilled Customer Orders						88,156,040.20				51,263,923.59	36,892,116.61
Fund Equities:											
Unobligated Balances (Unexpired)						-598,676,524.33				-250,983,663.92	-347,692,860.41
Accounts Payable						-580,184,180.88				-379,738,403.95	-200,445,776.93
Undelivered Orders						-4,305,447,122.95				-1,414,901,333.94	-2,890,545,789.01
Subtotal	Subtotal	69		1129		-0-	35,000,000.00		2,042,471,917.64	-2,007,471,917.64	-0-
Capital Investment Grants, Federal Transit Administration											
Fund Resources:											
Undisbursed Funds	No Year	69		1134		8,705,304,842.48	1,566,000,000.00	-1,985,100.00	2,662,179,113.57		7,607,140,628.91
Accounts Receivable						374,158.00				374,158.00	
Unfilled Customer Orders						-374,158.00				-374,158.00	
Fund Equities:											
Unobligated Balances (Unexpired)						-1,798,059,969.80				-707,957,082.21	-1,090,102,887.59
Accounts Payable						-859,578,032.81				-350,216,464.58	-509,361,568.23
Undelivered Orders						-6,047,666,839.87				-39,990,666.78	-6,007,676,173.09
Subtotal	Subtotal	69		1134		-0-	1,566,000,000.00	-1,985,100.00	2,662,179,113.57	-1,098,164,213.57	-0-
University Transportation Research, Federal Transit Administration, Department Of Transportation											
Fund Resources:											
Undisbursed Funds	No Year	69		1136		17,261,983.12			14,277,636.82		2,984,346.30
Fund Equities:											
Unobligated Balances (Unexpired)						-7,542,848.12				-7,366,145.29	-176,702.83
Undelivered Orders						-9,719,135.00				-6,911,491.53	-2,807,643.47
Subtotal	Subtotal	69		1136		-0-			14,277,636.82	-14,277,636.82	-0-
Research And University Research Centers, Federal Transit Administration											
Fund Resources:											
Undisbursed Funds	No Year	69		1137		214,818,664.97	61,000,000.00		118,275,882.68		157,542,782.29
Accounts Receivable						12,355,031.26				-6,616,504.73	18,971,535.99

Footnotes At End Of Chapter

Appropriations, Outlays, and Balances – Continued

Appropriation or Fund Account — Title	Reg	Tr From	Account Number	Sub No.	Period of Availability	Balances, Beginning Of Fiscal Year	Appropriations And Other Obligational Authority[1]	Transfers Borrowings And Investment (Net)[2]	Outlays (Net)	Balances Withdrawn And Other Transactions[3]	Balances, End Of Fiscal Year[4]
Research And University Research Centers, Federal Transit Administration - Continued											
Fund Resources: - Continued											
Unfilled Customer Orders						82,554,436.82				7,427,082.96	75,127,353.86
Fund Equities:											
Unobligated Balances (Unexpired)						-45,233,288.21				19,497,015.42	-64,730,303.63
Accounts Payable						-254,623.68				479,025.17	-733,648.85
Undelivered Orders						-264,240,221.16			118,275,882.68	-78,062,501.50	-186,177,719.66
Subtotal	69		1137			-0-	61,000,000.00		118,275,882.68	-57,275,882.68	-0-
Trust Fund Accounts											
Mass Transportation Capital Fund, Liquidation Of Contract Authorization, Federal Transit Administration											
Fund Resources:											
Undisbursed Funds	69		8191		No Year	10,224,494.72	9,000,000.00		11,719,272.00		7,505,222.72
Unfunded Contract Authority						-38,246,635.15					-38,246,635.15
Accounts Receivable						160,050,000.00				9,000,000.00	151,050,000.00
Fund Equities:											
Unobligated Balances (Unexpired)						-7,186,647.02				-1,970,513.00	-5,216,134.02
Accounts Payable						-35,311.00					-35,311.00
Undelivered Orders						-124,805,901.55				-9,748,759.00	-115,057,142.55
Subtotal	69		8191			-0-	9,000,000.00		11,719,272.00	-2,719,272.00	-0-
Formula And Bus Grants, Liquidation Of Contract Authorization, Federal Transit Administration, Department Of Transportation											
Fund Resources:											
Undisbursed Funds	69		8350		No Year	477,599,591.55	3,669,315,674.00	244,962,918.00	4,193,968,511.56		197,909,671.99
Unfunded Contract Authority						5,438,792,610.00	2,602,775,000.00				8,041,567,610.00
Accounts Receivable						530,000,000.00				-1,720,993,444.00	2,250,993,444.00
Fund Equities:											
Unobligated Balances (Unexpired)						-3,656,733,352.87				160,995,418.08	-3,817,728,770.95
Accounts Payable						-642,537,976.00				-144,947,108.26	-497,590,867.74
Undelivered Orders						-2,147,120,872.68				4,028,030,214.62	-6,175,151,087.30
Subtotal	69		8350			-0-	6,272,090,674.00	244,962,918.00	4,193,968,511.56	2,323,085,080.44	-0-
Total, Federal Transit Administration							8,028,090,674.00	242,977,818.00	9,198,992,009.25	-927,923,517.25	
Saint Lawrence Seaway Development Corporation											
Public Enterprise Funds											
Saint Lawrence Seaway Development Corporation Fund											
Fund Resources:											
Undisbursed Funds	69		4089		No Year	5,472,649.73		-268,863.91	-51,412.27		5,255,198.09
Funds Held Outside The Treasury					No Year	10,885,720.75		268,863.91			11,154,584.66
Authority To Borrow From The Treasury						3,200,000.00					3,200,000.00
Accounts Receivable						84,632.29				-36,380.88	121,013.17
Fund Equities:											
Unobligated Balances (Unexpired)						-14,279,567.52				-70,193.21	-14,209,374.31
Accounts Payable						-3,033,983.45				-456,895.93	-2,577,087.52
Undelivered Orders						-2,329,451.80				614,882.29	-2,944,334.09

Appropriations, Outlays, and Balances - Continued

Appropriation or Fund Account — Title	Account Symbol Dept — Reg	Tr From	Account Number	Sub No.	Period of Availability	Balances, Beginning Of Fiscal Year	Appropriations And Other Obligational Authority[1]	Transfers Borrowings And Investment (Net)[2]	Outlays (Net)	Balances Withdrawn And Other Transactions[3]	Balances, End Of Fiscal Year[4]
Trust Fund Accounts											
	69		4089		Subtotal	-0-			-51,412.27	51,412.27	-0-
Operations And Maintenance, Saint Lawrence Seaway Development Corporation											
Fund Resources:											
Undisbursed Funds	69		8003		No Year		16,223,160.00		16,223,160.00		
Accounts Receivable						162,840.00				162,840.00	
Fund Equities:											
Unobligated Balances (Unexpired)						-162,840.00					
	69		8003		Subtotal	-162,840.00	16,223,160.00		16,223,160.00	-162,840.00	-0-
Total, Saint Lawrence Seaway Development Corporation							16,223,160.00		16,171,747.73	51,412.27	
Pipeline And Hazardous Materials Safety Administration											
General Fund Accounts											
Research And Special Programs, Pipeline And Hazardous Materials Safety Administration											
Fund Resources:											
Undisbursed Funds											
	69		0104		2005-2007	284,510.64			103,933.54		180,577.10
					2004-2006	-142,853.45			114,530.36		[5]-257,383.81
					2005	2,108,575.11			18,899.94		2,089,675.17
					2003-2005	473,406.90			28,403.94		445,002.96
					2004	3,115,487.78			286,098.24		2,829,389.54
					2002-2004	158,899.72			-15,337.77		174,237.49
					2003	3,079,748.59			490,050.55		2,589,698.04
					2001-2003	509,800.49					509,800.49
					2002	1,555,753.68			83,724.03	1,472,029.65	
					2000-2002	92,367.11			11,748.18	80,618.93	
					No Year	730,131.15			53,443.95		676,687.20
Accounts Receivable						742,119.24				742,119.24	
Unfilled Customer Orders						5,693,389.95				4,857,818.26	835,571.69
Fund Equities:											
Unobligated Balances (Expired)						-1,456,157.56				213,617.82	-1,669,775.38
Unobligated Balances (Unexpired)						-765,039.76				-130,417.76	-634,622.00
Accounts Payable						-455,113.07				-374,255.86	-80,857.21
Undelivered Orders						-15,725,026.52				-8,037,025.24	-7,688,001.28
	69		0104		Subtotal	-0-			1,175,494.96	-1,175,494.96	-0-
Administration Expenses, Pipeline And Hazardous Materials Safety Administration											
Fund Resources:											
Undisbursed Funds											
	69		1400		2007		18,031,209.00		14,745,006.49		3,286,202.51
					2006	4,956,957.81			3,823,494.56		1,133,463.25
Accounts Receivable						51,127.78				17,006.04	34,121.74
Unfilled Customer Orders						176,954.32				-14,185.09	191,139.41

Footnotes At End Of Chapter

Appropriations, Outlays, and Balances – Continued

Appropriation or Fund Account — Title	Period of Availability	Dept Reg	Dept Tr From	Account Number	Sub No.	Balances, Beginning Of Fiscal Year	Appropriations And Other Obligational Authority[1]	Transfers Borrowings And Investment (Net)[2]	Outlays (Net)	Balances Withdrawn And Other Transactions[3]	Balances, End Of Fiscal Year[4]
Administration Expenses, Pipeline And Hazardous Materials Safety Administration - Continued											
Fund Equities:											
Unobligated Balances (Expired)						-226,568.47				1,117,774.93	-1,344,343.40
Accounts Payable						-360,079.09				277,997.16	-638,076.25
Undelivered Orders						-4,598,392.35				-1,935,885.09	-2,662,507.26
Subtotal		69		1400		-0-	18,031,209.00		18,568,501.05	-537,292.05	-0-
Hazardous Materials Safety, Pipeline And Hazardous Materials Safety Administration											
Fund Resources:											
Undisbursed Funds	2007-2009	69		1401			1,828,530.00		12,866.28		1,815,663.72
	2006-2008					1,300,070.02			665,386.32		634,683.70
	2007						24,894,357.00		20,217,595.01		4,676,761.99
	2006					5,527,207.55			4,661,347.01		865,860.54
	No Year					389,564.77			146,884.96		242,679.81
Accounts Receivable						324,131.00				242,534.00	81,597.00
Unfilled Customer Orders						4,800.00				-661,402.00	666,202.00
Fund Equities:											
Unobligated Balances (Expired)						-66,078.54				201,819.83	-267,898.37
Unobligated Balances (Unexpired)						-854,437.44				658,425.42	-1,512,862.86
Accounts Payable						-562,258.66				523,205.80	-1,085,464.46
Undelivered Orders						-6,062,998.70				54,224.37	-6,117,223.07
Subtotal		69		1401		-0-	26,722,887.00		25,704,079.58	1,018,807.42	-0-
Special Fund Accounts											
Pipeline Safety, Pipeline And Hazardous Materials Safety Administration											
Fund Resources:											
Undisbursed Funds	2007-2009	69		5172		22,481,708.86	24,000,000.00		2,431,020.28		21,568,979.72
	2006-2008								15,671,140.26		6,810,568.60
	2007						36,065,297.00		26,507,473.08		9,557,823.92
	2005-2007					7,086,617.48			4,168,126.48		2,918,491.00
	2006					9,333,011.87			7,970,094.36		1,362,917.51
	2004-2006					5,985,756.31			3,169,952.55		2,815,803.76
	2005					1,066,104.82			918,006.30		148,098.52
	2003-2005					1,044,311.68			658,809.34		385,502.34
	2004					1,919,442.78			319,649.56		1,599,793.22
	2002-2004					1,005,096.69			805,171.69		199,925.00
	2003					2,714,611.54			392,922.73		2,321,688.81
	2001-2003					690,726.81			100,748.00		589,978.81
	2002					591,713.47			33,700.48	558,012.99	
	2000-2002					288,809.56				288,809.56	
	No Year					143,822.42			84,629.91		59,192.51
Accounts Receivable						6,382,823.76				-1,999,898.85	8,382,722.61
Unfilled Customer Orders						433.27					433.27
Fund Equities:											
Unobligated Balances (Expired)						-3,020,839.96				2,119,041.31	-5,139,881.27
Unobligated Balances (Unexpired)						-19,814,607.83				4,067,417.67	-23,882,025.50
Accounts Payable						-852,675.69				1,666,803.86	-2,519,479.55

Appropriations, Outlays, and Balances - Continued

Appropriation or Fund Account — Title	Account Symbol — Dept Reg	Tr From	Account Number	Sub No.	Period of Availability	Balances, Beginning Of Fiscal Year	Appropriations And Other Obligational Authority[1]	Transfers Borrowings And Investment (Net)[2]	Outlays (Net)	Balances Withdrawn And Other Transactions[3]	Balances, End Of Fiscal Year[4]
Undelivered Orders	69		5172		Subtotal	-37,046,867.84	60,065,297.00		63,231,445.02	-9,866,334.56	-27,180,533.28
						-0-	-0-			-3,166,148.02	-0-
Emergency Preparedness Grants, Pipeline And Hazardous Materials Safety Administration											
Fund Resources:											
Undisbursed Funds					2007-2008		198,000.00				198,000.00
					2006-2007	198,000.00					198,000.00
					2005-2006	99,395.34			99,395.34		
					2004-2006	46,618.00					46,618.00
					2003-2005	1,288.00			1,288.00		
					2002-2004	19,898.05			9,391.10		10,506.95
					2001-2003	92,188.29			400.00		91,788.29
					2000-2002	364.30				364.30	
					No Year	46,384,528.45	14,476,126.47		13,306,438.25		47,554,216.67
	69		5282		Subtotal		14,674,126.47		13,416,912.69		
Fund Equities:											
Unobligated Balances (Expired)						-364.30				-324.30	-40.00
Unobligated Balances (Unexpired)						-24,476,756.04				543,789.09	-25,020,545.13
Accounts Payable						-15,443.63				7,716,961.74	-7,732,405.37
Undelivered Orders						-22,349,716.46				-7,003,577.05	-15,346,139.41
	69		5282		Subtotal	-0-				1,257,213.78	-0-
Trust Fund Accounts											
Trust Fund Share Of Pipeline Safety, Pipeline And Hazardous Materials Safety Administration											
Fund Resources:											
Undisbursed Funds					2007-2009		6,850,000.00		6,768,485.88		81,514.12
					2006-2008	577,043.49	5,000,000.00		5,304,559.18		272,484.31
					2005-2007	775,983.07			761,098.29		14,884.78
					2004-2006	14,476.32			637.07		13,839.25
					2003-2005	122,005.96					122,005.96
					2002-2004	38,585.53					38,585.53
					2001-2003	301,801.22					301,801.22
					2000-2002	22,758.61		-22,758.61			
					No Year	0.15					0.15
Accounts Receivable						5,150,000.00				-2,850,000.00	8,000,000.00
Fund Equities:											
Unobligated Balances (Expired)						-485,151.32				-22,758.61	-462,392.71
Unobligated Balances (Unexpired)						-150,000.00				-150,000.00	
Accounts Payable						-6,367,503.03				2,015,219.58	-8,382,722.61
	69		8121		Subtotal	-0-	11,850,000.00	-22,758.61	12,834,780.42	-1,007,539.03	-0-
Total, Pipeline And Hazardous Materials Safety Administration							131,343,519.47	-22,758.61	134,931,213.72	-3,610,452.86	

Footnotes At End Of Chapter

Appropriations, Outlays, and Balances – Continued

Appropriation or Fund Account — Title	Period of Availability	Reg	Tr From	Account Number	Sub No.	Balances, Beginning Of Fiscal Year	Appropriations And Other Obligational Authority[1]	Transfers Borrowings And Investment (Net)[2]	Outlays (Net)	Balances Withdrawn And Other Transactions[3]	Balances, End Of Fiscal Year[4]
Research And Innovative Technology Administration											
General Fund Accounts											
Expenses, Research And Innovative Technology Administration, Department Of Transportation											
Fund Resources:											
Undisbursed Funds											
	2007-2009	69		1730			1,109,790.00		1,555.55		1,108,234.45
	2006-2008					992,863.60			694,627.92		298,235.68
	2007						6,626,313.00		2,554,813.91		4,071,499.09
	2005-2007					441,447.37			181,516.03		259,931.34
	2006					749,211.75			415,652.85		333,558.90
	2004-2006					682,161.19			219,885.37		462,275.82
	2005					1,200,680.64			-2,598,078.74		3,798,759.38
	2003-2005					113,342.85			79,309.27		34,033.58
	2004					-378,517.59			-254,089.47		[5]124,428.12
	2003					12,858.15			135,694.26		[5]122,836.11
	2001-2003					-7,164.62					[5]7,164.62
	2002					17,942.95			-702,713.30	720,656.25	
	2000-2002					18,591.34			-11,748.18	30,339.52	
	No Year					-4,991,724.13			-89,347,950.67		84,356,226.54
Accounts Receivable						15,829,710.67				-6,602,046.86	22,431,757.53
Unfilled Customer Orders						97,993,590.48				-27,964,897.47	125,958,487.95
Fund Equities:											
Unobligated Balances (Expired)						-436,042.02				10,467,763.24	-10,903,805.26
Unobligated Balances (Unexpired)						-758,683.37				37,418,202.97	-38,176,886.34
Accounts Payable						-276,688.10				526,633.91	-803,322.01
Undelivered Orders						-111,203,581.16				81,770,976.64	-192,974,557.80
	Subtotal	69		1730		-0-	7,736,103.00		-88,631,525.20	96,367,628.20	-0-
Intragovernmental Funds											
Working Capital Fund, Transportation Systems Center											
Fund Resources:											
Undisbursed Funds											
	No Year	69		4522		48,546,421.76			-30,171,005.33		78,717,427.09
Accounts Receivable						2,407,590.88				1,171,682.94	1,235,907.94
Unfilled Customer Orders						254,500,534.52				-54,548,977.47	309,049,511.99
Fund Equities:											
Unobligated Balances (Unexpired)						-203,210,494.92				58,241,087.19	-261,461,582.11
Accounts Payable						-35,751,546.23				12,779,827.34	-48,531,373.57
Undelivered Orders						-66,492,506.01				12,527,385.33	-79,019,891.34
	Subtotal	69		4522		-0-			-30,171,005.33	30,171,005.33	-0-
Total, Research And Innovative Technology Administration							7,736,103.00		-118,802,530.53	126,538,633.53	

Appropriations, Outlays, and Balances - Continued

Appropriation or Fund Account — Title	Period of Availability	Dept Reg	Tr From	Account Number	Sub No.	Balances, Beginning Of Fiscal Year	Appropriations And Other Obligational Authority[1]	Transfers Borrowings And Investment (Net)[2]	Outlays (Net)	Balances Withdrawn And Other Transactions[3]	Balances, End Of Fiscal Year[4]
Office Of The Inspector General											
General Fund Accounts											
Salaries And Expenses, Office Of Inspector General, Department Of Transportation											
Fund Resources:											
Undisbursed Funds	2007	69		0130		6,351,055.11	64,043,000.00		56,813,227.98		7,229,772.02
	2006					1,043,303.55			5,201,332.98		1,149,722.13
	2005					622,401.96			176,001.97		867,301.58
	2004					1,092,725.81			119,026.04		503,375.92
	2003					460,101.35			2,436.32		1,090,289.49
	2002					343,827.34			7,398.42	452,702.93	
Accounts Receivable						48,216.00				-324,000.50	372,216.50
Unfilled Customer Orders						343,827.34				-117,250.64	461,077.98
Fund Equities:											
Unobligated Balances (Expired)						-1,943,874.87				-463,708.95	-1,480,165.92
Accounts Payable						-3,540,941.12				678,029.78	-4,218,970.90
Undelivered Orders						-4,476,815.13				1,497,803.67	-5,974,618.80
Subtotal		69		0130		-0-	64,043,000.00		62,319,423.71	1,723,576.29	-0-
Total, Office Of The Inspector General							64,043,000.00		62,319,423.71	1,723,576.29	
Surface Transportation Board											
General Fund Accounts											
Salaries And Expenses, Surface Transportation Board											
Fund Resources:											
Undisbursed Funds	2007	69		0301		6,194,315.16	25,450,866.00		20,980,139.53		4,470,726.47
	2006					291,852.24			4,087,106.99		2,107,208.17
	2005					-46,976.92			-15,808.53		307,660.77
	2004					237,531.77			-136,286.25		89,309.33
	2003					151,129.20			85,737.81		151,793.96
	2002					940,617.38			103,881.64	47,247.56	
	No Year					448,106.29					940,617.38
Unfilled Customer Orders										67,543.22	380,563.07
Fund Equities:											
Unobligated Balances (Expired)						-269,698.44				-49,267.06	-220,431.38
Unobligated Balances (Unexpired)						-940,617.38					-940,617.38
Accounts Payable						-662,230.40				29,070.81	-691,301.21
Undelivered Orders						-6,344,028.90				251,500.28	-6,595,529.18
Subtotal		69		0301		-0-	25,450,866.00		25,104,771.19	346,094.81	-0-
Total, Surface Transportation Board							25,450,866.00		25,104,771.19	346,094.81	

Footnotes At End Of Chapter

Appropriations, Outlays, and Balances – Continued

Appropriation or Fund Account — Title	Period of Availability	Account Symbol — Dept Reg	Account Symbol — Dept Tr From	Account Number	Sub No.	Balances, Beginning Of Fiscal Year	Appropriations And Other Obligational Authority[1]	Transfers Borrowings And Investment (Net)[2]	Outlays (Net)	Balances Withdrawn And Other Transactions[3]	Balances, End Of Fiscal Year[4]
Bureau Of Transportation Statistics											
General Fund Accounts											
Bureau Of Transportation Statistics, Bureau Of Transportation Statistics											
Fund Resources:											
Undisbursed Funds	No Year	69		0305		983.73		------			983.73
Fund Equities:											
Unobligated Balances (Unexpired)						-983.73		------			-983.73
	Subtotal	69		0305		-0-		------			-0-
Total, Bureau Of Transportation Statistics											
Maritime Administration											
General Fund Accounts											
Ship Construction, Maritime Administration											
Fund Resources:											
Undisbursed Funds	No Year	69		1708		2,977,188.11	-2,000,000.00	------	-5,696,563.88	------	6,673,751.99
Fund Equities:											
Unobligated Balances (Unexpired)						-2,977,188.11	-2,000,000.00	------		3,696,563.88	-6,673,751.99
	Subtotal	69		1708		-0-		------	-5,696,563.88	3,696,563.88	-0-
Operating-Differential Subsidies, Liquidation Of Contract Authority, Maritime Administration											
Fund Resources:											
Undisbursed Funds	No Year	69		1709		13,341,739.14		------	2,595,103.31	------	10,746,635.83
Fund Equities:											
Unobligated Balances (Unexpired)						-13,341,739.14		------		822,277.73	-822,277.73
Undelivered Orders								------		-3,417,381.04	-9,924,358.10
	Subtotal	69		1709		-0-		------	2,595,103.31	-2,595,103.31	-0-
Ready Reserve Force, Maritime Administration											
Fund Resources:											
Undisbursed Funds	No Year	69		1710		3,722,666.87		------	1,183,853.29	------	2,538,813.58
Fund Equities:											
Unobligated Balances (Unexpired)						-3,632,152.52		------		-1,379,596.14	-2,252,556.38
Accounts Payable						-1,463.85		------		-1,463.85	
Undelivered Orders						-89,050.50		------		197,206.70	-286,257.20
	Subtotal	69		1710		-0-		------	1,183,853.29	-1,183,853.29	-0-
Maritime Security Program, Maritime Administration											
Fund Resources:											
Undisbursed Funds	2003-2005	69		1711		159,614.16		------		------	159,614.16
	No Year	69				15,203,982.52	154,440,000.00	------	154,530,467.72	------	15,113,514.80
Fund Equities:											
Unobligated Balances (Expired)						-159,614.15		------		0.01	-159,614.16
Unobligated Balances (Unexpired)						-2,559,881.02		------		-2,085,268.30	-474,612.72
Accounts Payable						-12,644,101.00		------		1,066,584.35	-13,710,685.35
Undelivered Orders						-0.51		------		928,216.22	-928,216.73
	Subtotal	69		1711		-0-	154,440,000.00	------	154,530,467.72	-90,467.72	-0-
Operations And Training, Maritime Administration											

Appropriations, Outlays, and Balances - Continued

Appropriation or Fund Account — Title	Dept Reg	Tr From	Account Number	Sub No.	Period of Availability	Balances, Beginning Of Fiscal Year	Appropriations And Other Obligational Authority[1]	Transfers Borrowings And Investment (Net)[2]	Outlays (Net)	Balances Withdrawn And Other Transactions[3]	Balances, End Of Fiscal Year[4]
Fund Resources:											
Undisbursed Funds	69		1750		2007		88,543,384.00		77,249,502.50		11,293,881.50
					2006-2007	7,148,861.72			2,803,507.74		4,345,353.98
					2006	24,047,111.53			17,440,503.44		6,606,608.09
					2005	3,420,637.19			1,306,851.44		2,113,785.75
					2004-2005	537,131.97			142,604.76		394,527.21
					2004	1,920,169.41			221,901.62		1,698,267.79
					2003	2,589,750.79			267,180.73		2,322,570.06
					2002	1,340,898.98			-3,019.46	1,343,918.44	
					No Year	54,292,066.51	22,978,890.00		40,437,012.11		36,833,944.40
Accounts Receivable						3,643,908.97				-5,012,814.35	8,656,723.32
Unfilled Customer Orders						15,963,148.89				2,297,869.96	13,665,278.93
Fund Equities:											
Unobligated Balances (Expired)						[6]-2,428,423.59				1,336,000.09	-3,764,423.68
Unobligated Balances (Unexpired)						-8,770,806.60				-7,122,477.59	-1,648,329.01
Accounts Payable						[6]-4,752,932.75				3,997,750.46	-8,750,683.21
Undelivered Orders						[6]-98,951,523.02				-25,184,017.89	-73,767,505.13
Subtotal	69		1750		Subtotal	-0-	111,522,274.00		139,866,044.88	-28,343,770.88	-0-
Ocean Freight Differential, Maritime Administration											
Fund Resources:											
Undisbursed Funds	69		1751		No Year		271,343,143.64	-73,783,651.19	197,559,492.45		
Authority To Borrow From The Treasury			1751				225,000,000.00	-192,682,336.25		32,317,663.75	-0-
Subtotal	69		1751		Subtotal	-0-	496,343,143.64	-266,465,987.44	197,559,492.45	32,317,663.75	-0-
Maritime Guaranteed Loan, (Title XI) Program Account, Maritime Administration											
Fund Resources:											
Undisbursed Funds	69		1752		2007		4,084,740.00		4,084,740.00		
					2003-2005	1,650,662.15			959,683.07		690,979.08
					No Year	7,352,028.61	22,660,000.00		22,660,000.00		7,352,028.61
Fund Equities:											
Unobligated Balances (Unexpired)						-7,352,028.61					-7,352,028.61
Undelivered Orders						-1,650,662.15				-959,683.07	-690,979.08
Subtotal	69		1752		Subtotal	-0-	26,744,740.00		27,704,423.07	-959,683.07	-0-
Ship Disposal, Maritime Administration											
Fund Resources:											
Undisbursed Funds	69		1768		No Year	26,602,776.51	20,790,000.00		16,490,339.35		30,902,437.16
Fund Equities:											
Unobligated Balances (Unexpired)						-15,932,670.01				-1,851,810.63	-14,080,859.38
Accounts Payable						-289,073.05				1,885,694.53	-2,174,767.58
Undelivered Orders						-10,381,033.45				4,265,776.75	-14,646,810.20
Subtotal	69		1768		Subtotal	-0-	20,790,000.00		16,490,339.35	4,299,660.65	-0-
Expenses, National Defense Tank Vessel Construction Program, Maritime Administration											
Fund Resources:											
Undisbursed Funds	69		1769		No Year	74,400,000.00	-74,400,000.00				
Fund Equities:											
Unobligated Balances (Unexpired)						-74,400,000.00				-74,400,000.00	

Footnotes At End Of Chapter

Appropriations, Outlays, and Balances – Continued

Appropriation or Fund Account — Title	Period of Availability	Reg	Tr From	Account Number	Sub No.	Balances, Beginning Of Fiscal Year	Appropriations And Other Obligational Authority[1]	Transfers Borrowings And Investment (Net)[2]	Outlays (Net)	Balances Withdrawn And Other Transactions[3]	Balances, End Of Fiscal Year[4]
Expenses, National Defense Tank Vessel Construction Program, Maritime Administration - Continued											
Fund Equities: - Continued											
Unobligated Balances (Unexpired) - Continued	Subtotal	69		1769		-0-	-74,400,000.00			-74,400,000.00	-0-
Public Enterprise Funds											
Federal Ship Financing Fund, Revolving Fund, Maritime Administration											
Fund Resources:											
Undisbursed Funds	No Year	69		4301		635,499.74			-19,850.22		665,349.96
Unrealized Discount On Investments						-635,315.17					-635,315.17
Fund Equities:											
Unobligated Balances (Unexpired)						-184.57				19,850.22	-20,034.79
Subtotal	Subtotal	69		4301		-0-			-19,850.22	19,850.22	-0-
War-Risk Insurance Revolving Fund, Maritime Administration											
Fund Resources:											
Undisbursed Funds	No Year	69		4302		5,701,864.53		2,000,000.00	-913,290.65		8,615,155.18
Unrealized Discount On Investments						-609,600.47					-609,600.47
Investments In Public Debt Securities						37,299,000.00		-2,000,000.00			35,299,000.00
Fund Equities:											
Unobligated Balances (Unexpired)						-42,365,131.25				928,290.65	-43,293,421.90
Accounts Payable						-26,132.81				-15,000.00	-11,132.81
Undelivered Orders											
Subtotal	Subtotal	69		4302		-0-			-913,290.65	913,290.65	-0-
Vessel Operations Revolving Fund, Maritime Administration											
Fund Resources:											
Undisbursed Funds	No Year	69		4303		74,559,301.83			-15,529,696.58		90,088,998.41
Accounts Receivable						[6]42,768,515.96				7,743,416.30	35,025,099.66
Unfilled Customer Orders						60,765,815.25				1,490,472.01	59,275,343.24
Fund Equities:											
Unobligated Balances (Unexpired)						[6]-22,553,079.03				-2,844,910.29	-19,708,168.74
Accounts Payable						[6]-28,751,667.85				4,164,911.92	-32,916,579.77
Undelivered Orders						-126,788,886.16				4,975,806.64	-131,764,692.80
Subtotal	Subtotal	69		4303		-0-			-15,529,696.58	15,529,696.58	-0-
Trust Fund Accounts											
Gifts And Bequests, Maritime Administration											
Fund Resources:											
Undisbursed Funds	No Year	69		8503		87,651.56	640,042.56		598,800.26		128,893.86
Fund Equities:											
Unobligated Balances (Unexpired)						-39,151.10				17,077.63	-56,228.73
Accounts Payable						-548.86				-548.86	
Undelivered Orders						-47,951.60				24,713.53	-72,665.13
Subtotal	Subtotal	69		8503		-0-	640,042.56		598,800.26	41,242.30	-0-
Special Studies, Services And Projects, Maritime Administration											
Fund Resources:											
Undisbursed Funds	No Year	69		8547		6,366,823.44			-3,484,121.34		9,850,944.78

Appropriations, Outlays, and Balances - Continued

Appropriation or Fund Account — Title	Period of Availability	Reg	Tr From	Account Number	Sub No.	Balances, Beginning Of Fiscal Year	Appropriations And Other Obligational Authority[1]	Transfers Borrowings And Investment (Net)[2]	Outlays (Net)	Balances Withdrawn And Other Transactions[3]	Balances, End Of Fiscal Year[4]
Fund Equities:											
Unobligated Balances (Unexpired)						-6,338,908.06				-5,035,781.72	-1,303,126.34
Undelivered Orders				8547		-27,915.38				8,519,903.06	-8,547,818.44
	Subtotal	69				-0-			-3,484,121.34	3,484,121.34	-0-
Total, Maritime Administration							734,080,200.20	-266,465,987.44	514,885,001.66	-47,270,788.90	
Deductions For Offsetting Receipts											
Proprietary Receipts From The Public							-73,689,117.71		-73,689,117.71		
Intrabudgetary Transactions							-26,699,152.96		-26,699,152.96		
Offsetting Governmental Receipts							-60,849,289.79		-60,849,289.79		
Total, Offsetting Receipts							-161,237,560.46		-161,237,560.46		
Total, Department Of Transportation							68,381,650,535.07	-264,518,746.05	61,700,799,895.76	6,416,331,893.26	
Memorandum											
Financing Accounts											
Public Enterprise Funds											
Minority Business Resource Center Guaranteed Loan Financing Account, Office Of The Secretary											
Fund Resources:											
Undisbursed Funds	No Year	69		4082		522,964.91		30,264.70	302,683.28		250,546.33
Authority To Borrow From The Treasury								-142,028.70			355.30
Unfilled Customer Orders						9,250.00	142,384.00			9,250.00	
Fund Equities:											
Unobligated Balances (Unexpired)				4082		-532,214.91				-285,228.28	-246,986.63
Accounts Payable						-0-				3,915.00	-3,915.00
	Subtotal	69		4082		-0-	142,384.00	-111,764.00	302,683.28	-272,063.28	-0-
Transportation Infrastructure Finance And Innovation Account, Direct Loan Financing Account, Federal Highway Administration											
Fund Resources:											
Undisbursed Funds	No Year	69		4123		-3,543,852.70		229,998,815.69	224,121,359.84	182,919,119.56	2,333,603.15
Authority To Borrow From The Treasury						1,334,514,242.70	757,391,739.00	-238,218,296.69		3,802,505.00	1,670,768,565.45
Accounts Receivable						3,802,505.00				16,353,547.84	131,936,734.27
Fund Equities:											
Unobligated Balances (Unexpired)						148,290,282.11				-29,482,787.11	-1,092,135.00
Accounts Payable						[6]-30,574,922.11				351,458,512.87	-1,803,946,767.87
Undelivered Orders						[6,]-1,452,488,255.00				525,050,898.16	-0-
	Subtotal	69		4123		-0-	757,391,739.00	-8,219,481.00	224,121,359.84		-0-
Transportation Infrastructure Finance And Innovation Act, Guaranteed Loan Account, Federal Highway Administration											
Fund Resources:											
Undisbursed Funds	No Year	69		4145		5,000.00					5,000.00

Footnotes At End Of Chapter

Appropriations, Outlays, and Balances – Continued

Appropriation or Fund Account — Title	Period of Availability	Reg	Tr From	Account Number	Sub No.	Balances, Beginning Of Fiscal Year	Appropriations And Other Obligational Authority[1]	Transfers Borrowings And Investment (Net)[2]	Outlays (Net)	Balances Withdrawn And Other Transactions[3]	Balances, End Of Fiscal Year[4]
Transportation Infrastructure Finance And Innovation Act, Guaranteed Loan Account, Federal Highway Administration - Continued											
Fund Equities:											
Unobligated Balances (Unexpired)						-5,000.00					-5,000.00
Subtotal	Subtotal	69		4145		-0-					-0-
Transportation Infrastructure Finance And Innovation Act, Line Of Credit Financing Account, Federal Highway Administration, (Credit Reform)											
Fund Resources:											
Undisbursed Funds	No Year	69		4173		10,000.00					10,000.00
Authority To Borrow From The Treasury						17,632,000.00				17,632,000.00	
Unfilled Customer Orders						2,368,000.00				2,368,000.00	
Fund Equities:											
Unobligated Balances (Unexpired)						-10,000.00					-10,000.00
Accounts Payable											
Undelivered Orders						-20,000,000.00				-20,000,000.00	
Subtotal	Subtotal	69		4173		-0-					-0-
Orange County (CA) Toll Road Demonstration Project Direct Loan Financing Account, Federal Highway Administration, Department Of Transportation											
Fund Resources:											
Authority To Borrow From The Treasury						66,880,000.00				22,240,000.00	44,640,000.00
Unfilled Customer Orders						5,120,000.00				1,760,000.00	3,360,000.00
Fund Equities:											
Accounts Payable											
Undelivered Orders						-72,000,000.00				-24,000,000.00	-48,000,000.00
Subtotal	Subtotal	69		4264		-0-					-0-
Military Useful Vessel Obligation Guarantee, Financing Account, Maritime Administration											
Fund Resources:											
Undisbursed Funds	No Year	69		4304		327,494,119.10			-3,311,800.34		330,805,919.44
Fund Equities:											
Unobligated Balances (Unexpired)						-327,372,468.48				3,341,464.61	-330,713,933.09
Accounts Payable										-4,352.90	-4,352.90
Undelivered Orders						-121,650.62				-34,017.17	-87,633.45
Subtotal	Subtotal	69		4304		-0-			-3,311,800.34	3,311,800.34	-0-
Railroad Rehabilitation And Improvement, Direct Loan Financing Account, Federal Railroad Administration, Department Of Transportation											
Fund Resources:											
Undisbursed Funds	No Year	69		4420		265,292.62		[1]48,269,382.91	48,244,937.01		289,738.52
Authority To Borrow From The Treasury						162,407,371.65	108,224,686.21	-103,325,883.65		1,780,975.52	165,525,198.69
Accounts Receivable										-187,041.14	187,041.14
Fund Equities:											
Unobligated Balances (Unexpired)						-332,157.37				4,538.43	-336,695.80
Accounts Payable										206,948.61	-206,948.61
Undelivered Orders						-162,340,506.90				3,117,827.04	-165,458,333.94
Subtotal	Subtotal	69		4420		-0-	108,224,686.21	-55,056,500.74	48,244,937.01	4,923,248.46	-0-
Total, Financing Accounts						-0-	865,758,809.21	-63,387,745.74	269,357,179.79	533,013,883.68	

Appropriations, Outlays, and Balances - Continued

Footnotes

1 The amounts in this column, unless otherwise footnoted, represent appropriations, increases and rescissions in borrowing authority or new contract authority. Appropriation accounts with appropriation transfer activity are presented in Table 1 ((Appropriations and Appropriation Transfers) at the end of this chapter.

2 The amounts in this column, unless otherwise footnoted, represent transfers - other than appropriation transfers, borrowings (gross), investments (net), unrealized discounts or funds held outside the Treasury.

3 The amounts in this column, unless otherwise footnoted, represent obligated balances canceled for fiscal year 2002 pursuant to 31 U.S.C. 1553, changes in unfilled customer orders, accounts receivable, accounts payable, undelivered orders, unobligated balances and adjustments to borrowing and contract authority.

4 Unobligated balances for no-year or unexpired multiple year accounts are available for obligation; unobligated balances for expired fiscal year accounts are not available for obligation.

5 Subject to disposition by the administrative agency.

6 The opening balances of the following accounts have been adjusted during the current fiscal year and do not agree with last year's closing balances:

Account	Adjustment
6961301 - Unfilled Customer Orders	-$13,179,270.85
6961301 - Unobligated Expired	-1,977,994.82
6961301 - Undelivered Orders	15,157,265.67
69X8552 - Unobligated Balances (Unexpired)	-253,920.03
69X8552 - Undelivered Orders	253,920.03
6961750 - Unobligated Balances (Expired)	10,696.69
6961750 - Accounts Payable	-103,341.27
6941750 - Undelivered Orders	92,644.58
69X4303 - Accounts Receivable	16,638.99
69X4303 - Unobligated Balances (Unexpired)	26,519.99
69X4303 - Accounts Payable	-43,158.98
69X4123 - Unobligated Balances (Unexpired)	-13,885,000.00
69X4123 - Undelivered Orders	13,885,000.00
20X8102 - Undisbursed Funds	-219,149,490.06
20X8102 - Unobligated Balances (Unexpired)	219,707,719.00
20X8103 - Undisbursed Funds	223,307,280.00
20X8103 - Unobligated Balances (Unexpired)	-223,307,280.00

7 Excludes $67,229,332.00 refund of taxes.

8 Represents:

Account	New Contract Authority	Appropriations To Liquidate
69 X 8016	$107,750,000.00	32,750,000.00
69 X 8020	587,750,000.00	187,750,000.00
69 X 8055	0.00	0.00
69 X 8083	42,268,565,230.00	36,032,343,903.00
69 X 8106	4,292,479,910.00	4,399,000,000.00
69 X 8158	294,000,000.00	294,000,000.00
69 X 8159	223,000,000.00	223,000,000.00
69 X 8191	0.00	0.00
69 X 8350	7,262,775,000.00	4,660,000,000.00
69 X 8362	4,000,000.00	4,000,000.00

9 Pursuant to 108 STAT 2495 SEC. 336(b), the balance for this account has been extended beyond the normal period of availability to liquidate obligations.

10 Pursuant to 106 STAT 1552 SEC. 339, the balance for this account has been extended beyond the normal period of availability to liquidate obligations.

11 The opening balance of the Unobligated balance for account 20X8102 does not agree with last year's closing balance by $558,228.94 due to the year-end closing statement not being processed in Treasury's central accounting system.

12 Excludes $1,508,138,668.00 refund of taxes.

13 Covered by investments.

14 Represents capital transfer to miscellaneous receipts.

15 Includes $218,792.76 which represents repayment of borrowing from the Federal Financing Bank in lieu of issuance of agency debt. Includes $48,488,195.67 which represents net borrowing from the U.S. Treasury.

Appropriations, Outlays, and Balances – Continued

Footnotes

Table 1 - Appropriations And Appropriation Transfers - Department Of Transportation

Department Regular	Fiscal Year	Account Symbol	Net Appropriations And Appropriations Transfers	Appropriation Amount	Net Appropriation Transfers	Department Regular Involved	Fiscal Year Involved	Accounts Involved	Amount From or To (-)
20	X	8102	-37,792,322,255.00	0.00	-37,792,322,255.00	69	X	8016	-75,000,000.00
						69	X	8020	-400,000,000.00
						69	X	8055	-97,547,000.00
						69	X	8058	-100,000,000.00
						69	X	8083	-33,042,237,255.00
						69	X	8158	-201,300,000.00
						69	X	8159	-188,000,000.00
						69	X	8191	-9,000,000.00
						69	X	8350	-3,680,000,000.00
						69	X	8362	-6,000,000.00
						69	X	8402	6,762,000.00
20	X	8103	-10,941,500,000.00	0.00	-10,941,500,000.00	69	07	8104	-5,627,900,000.00
						69	X	8106	-4,008,200,000.00
						69	X	8107	-10,000,000.00
						69	07	8107	-427,000,000.00
						69	0709	8107	-713,000,000.00
						69	0709	8108	-96,000,000.00
						69	X	8304	-59,400,000.00
69	07	0102	83,960,594.44	84,551,850.00	-591,255.56	47	07	0110	-591,255.56
69	X	5282	-198,000.00	0.00	-198,000.00	69	0708	5282	-198,000.00
69	0708	5282	198,000.00	0.00	198,000.00	69	X	5282	198,000.00
69	X	5422	-29,784,545.51	0.00	-29,784,545.51	69	X	5423	-29,784,545.51
69	X	5423	29,784,545.51	0.00	29,784,545.51	69	X	5422	29,784,545.51
69	X	8003	16,223,160.00	0.00	16,223,160.00	20	X	8863	16,223,160.00
69	X	8016	75,000,000.00	0.00	75,000,000.00	69	X	8102	75,000,000.00
69	07	8016	3,957,496.23	0.00	3,957,496.23	20	07	8083	3,957,496.23
69	X	8020	400,000,000.00	0.00	400,000,000.00	20	X	8102	400,000,000.00
69	X	8055	97,547,000.00	0.00	97,547,000.00	20	X	8102	97,547,000.00
69	X	8058	100,000,000.00	0.00	100,000,000.00	20	X	8102	100,000,000.00
69	X	8083	33,048,964,084.77	0.00	33,048,964,084.77	20	X	8102	33,042,237,255.00
						69	X	8016	-3,957,496.23
						69	X	8350	10,684,326.00
69	07	8104	5,627,900,000.00	0.00	5,627,900,000.00	20	07	8103	5,627,900,000.00
69	X	8106	4,008,200,000.00	0.00	4,008,200,000.00	20	X	8103	4,008,200,000.00
69	X	8107	10,000,000.00	0.00	10,000,000.00	20	X	8103	10,000,000.00
69	07	8107	427,000,000.00	0.00	427,000,000.00	20	07	8103	427,000,000.00
69	0709	8107	713,000,000.00	0.00	713,000,000.00	20	0709	8103	713,000,000.00
69	0709	8108	96,000,000.00	0.00	96,000,000.00	20	0709	8103	96,000,000.00
69	0608	8121	5,000,000.00	0.00	5,000,000.00	20	0608	8185	5,000,000.00
69	0709	8121	6,850,000.00	0.00	6,850,000.00	20	0709	8185	6,850,000.00
69	X	8158	201,300,000.00	0.00	201,300,000.00	20	X	8102	201,300,000.00
69	X	8159	188,000,000.00	0.00	188,000,000.00	20	X	8102	188,000,000.00
69	X	8191	9,000,000.00	0.00	9,000,000.00	20	X	8102	9,000,000.00
69	X	8304	59,400,000.00	0.00	59,400,000.00	20	X	8103	59,400,000.00

Appropriations, Outlays, and Balances - Continued

Footnotes

Table 1 - Appropriations And Appropriation Transfers - Department Of Transportation

69	X	8350	3,669,315,674.00	0.00	3,669,315,674.00	20	X	8102	3,680,000,000.00
						69	X	8083	-10,684,326.00
69	X	8362	6,000,000.00	0.00	6,000,000.00	20	X	8102	6,000,000.00
69	X	8402	-6,762,000.00	0.00	-6,762,000.00	20	X	8102	-6,762,000.00
Totals			112,033,754.44	84,551,850.00	27,481,904.44				27,481,904.44

Appropriations, Outlays, and Balances – Continued

Appropriation or Fund Account Title	Period of Availability	Dept Reg	Tr From	Account Number	Sub No.	Balances, Beginning Of Fiscal Year	Appropriations And Other Obligational Authority[1]	Transfers Borrowings And Investment (Net)[2]	Outlays (Net)	Balances Withdrawn And Other Transactions[3]	Balances, End Of Fiscal Year[4]
Department Of The Treasury											
Departmental Offices											
General Fund Accounts											
Salaries And Expenses, Departmental Offices, Treasury											
Fund Resources:											
Undisbursed Funds	2007-2008	20		0101			8,087,144.00		2,120,455.35		5,966,688.65
	2007						208,261,232.00		178,071,453.58		30,189,778.42
	2006-2007					7,980,444.64		152,000.00	5,395,088.03		2,737,356.61
	2006					23,729,766.96		-725,000.00	17,007,030.57		5,997,736.39
	2005-2006					22,954.94					22,954.94
	2005					4,015,892.36			1,346,432.72		2,669,459.64
	2004-2005					124,768.82			22,188.00		102,580.82
	2004					5,429,193.05			248,927.53		5,180,265.52
	2003-2004					8,000.00					8,000.00
	2003					4,466,995.12			535,224.85		3,931,770.27
	2002-2003					9,263.37					9,263.37
	2002					4,595,460.22			-250,686.41	4,846,146.63	
	2001-2002					20,357,084.80			-242.68	20,357,327.48	
	No Year					11,530,285.09			6,413,039.50		5,117,245.59
Accounts Receivable						1,385,257.18				332,761.51	1,052,495.67
Unfilled Customer Orders						1,142,138.55				-429,688.97	1,571,827.52
Fund Equities:											
Unobligated Balances (Expired)						-28,112,881.23				-19,332,126.54	-8,780,754.69
Unobligated Balances (Unexpired)						-4,475,517.97				-1,045,814.37	-3,429,703.60
Accounts Payable						-6,931,287.70				3,099,822.63	-10,031,110.33
Undelivered Orders						-45,277,818.20				-2,961,963.41	-42,315,854.79
Subtotal		20		0101		-0-	216,348,376.00	-573,000.00	210,908,911.04	4,866,464.96	-0-
Salaries And Expenses, Office Of Foreign Assets Control, Treasury											
Fund Resources:											
Undisbursed Funds	2005	20		0102		1,445,052.98			346,425.28		1,098,627.70
Accounts Receivable						16,993.10				16,993.10	
Unfilled Customer Orders						16,751.55				909.80	15,841.75
Fund Equities:											
Unobligated Balances (Expired)						-289,945.87				11,092.40	-301,038.27
Accounts Payable						-27,452.89				-24,732.74	-2,720.15
Undelivered Orders						-1,161,398.87				-350,687.84	-810,711.03
Subtotal		20		0102		-0-			346,425.28	-346,425.28	-0-
Salaries And Expenses, Office Of Inspector General, Treasury											
Fund Resources:											
Undisbursed Funds	2007	20		0106			16,957,416.00		15,881,682.65		1,075,733.35
	2006-2007							430,926.00	338,858.21		92,067.79
	2006					1,571,917.96		-82,926.00	1,399,609.98		89,381.98
	2005					198,729.31			147,149.47		51,579.84
	2004					27,509.94					27,509.94
	2003-2004					7,023.00					7,023.00
	2003					127,615.29			29,200.93		98,414.36

Appropriations, Outlays, and Balances - Continued

Appropriation or Fund Account — Title	Period of Availability	Dept Reg	Tr From	Account Number	Sub No.	Balances, Beginning Of Fiscal Year	Appropriations And Other Obligational Authority[1]	Transfers Borrowings And Investment (Net)[2]	Outlays (Net)	Balances Withdrawn And Other Transactions[3]	Balances, End Of Fiscal Year[4]
	2002-2003					22,530.24					22,530.24
	2002					923,085.36			9,489.94	913,595.42	
	No Year					395,539.52			206,196.54		189,342.98
Accounts Receivable						22,271.62				22,271.62	
Unfilled Customer Orders						962,164.81				313,996.29	648,168.52
Fund Equities:											
Unobligated Balances (Expired)						-1,159,646.45				-775,724.35	-383,922.10
Unobligated Balances (Unexpired)						-395,539.52				-206,196.54	-189,342.98
Accounts Payable						-817,431.20				-68,891.07	-748,540.13
Undelivered Orders						-1,885,769.88				-905,823.09	-979,946.79
Subtotal		20		0106		-0-	16,957,416.00	348,000.00	18,012,187.72	-706,771.72	-0-
Treasury Building And Annex Repair And Restoration, Departmental Offices, Treasury											
Fund Resources:											
Undisbursed Funds	2006-2008					2,417,832.83			1,752,424.56		665,408.27
	2005-2007					403,049.23			338,849.41		64,199.82
	2004-2006					761,632.70			363,387.03		398,245.67
	No Year					1,187,010.01			-153,198.07		1,340,208.08
Fund Equities:											
Unobligated Balances (Expired)						-1,442.11				-406.44	-1,035.67
Unobligated Balances (Unexpired)						-1,211,775.57				-804,750.33	-407,025.24
Accounts Payable						-431,178.21				-426,618.04	-4,560.17
Undelivered Orders						-3,125,128.88				-1,069,688.12	-2,055,440.76
Subtotal		20		0108		-0-			2,301,462.93	-2,301,462.93	-0-
Department-Wide Systems And Capital Investments Programs, Departmental Offices, Treasury											
Fund Resources:											
Undisbursed Funds	2007-2009						30,268,000.00		8,907,685.40		21,360,314.60
	2006-2008					17,961,282.19			9,183,281.60		8,778,000.59
	2005-2007					7,405,486.11			4,415,635.63		2,989,850.48
	2004-2006					2,268,573.94			357,959.35		1,910,614.59
	No Year					3,676,625.87			56,616.86		3,620,009.01
Fund Equities:											
Unobligated Balances (Expired)						-34,688.22				71,225.54	-105,913.76
Unobligated Balances (Unexpired)						-15,300,785.37				-5,213,184.05	-10,087,601.32
Accounts Payable						-401,934.59				2,463,743.31	-2,865,677.90
Undelivered Orders						-15,574,559.93				10,025,036.36	-25,599,596.29
Subtotal		20		0115		-0-	30,268,000.00		22,921,178.84	7,346,821.16	-0-
Counterterrorism Fund, Departmental Offices, Treasury											
Fund Resources:											
Undisbursed Funds	No Year					5,422,924.71			1,346,189.30		4,076,735.41
Fund Equities:											
Unobligated Balances (Unexpired)						-639,901.81				-632,103.39	-7,798.42
Undelivered Orders						-4,783,022.90				-714,085.91	-4,068,936.99
Subtotal		20		0117		-0-			1,346,189.30	-1,346,189.30	-0-

Footnotes At End Of Chapter

Appropriations, Outlays, and Balances – Continued

Appropriation or Fund Account — Title	Dept Reg	Tr From	Account Number	Sub No.	Period of Availability	Balances, Beginning Of Fiscal Year	Appropriations And Other Obligational Authority[1]	Transfers Borrowings And Investment (Net)[2]	Outlays (Net)	Balances Withdrawn And Other Transactions[3]	Balances, End Of Fiscal Year[4]
Salaries And Expenses, Inspector General For Tax Administration, Departmental Offices, Treasury											
Fund Resources:											
Undisbursed Funds	20		0119		2007		132,860,601.00	-77,000.00	123,975,511.19		8,808,089.81
					2006	8,026,645.24		82,000.00	6,543,940.51		1,564,704.73
					2005	845,180.94			213,124.52		632,056.42
					2004	818,127.24			14,208.51		803,918.73
					2003	695,526.02			15,869.52		679,656.50
					2002	861,573.37				861,573.37	-0-
Funds Held Outside The Treasury					No Year 2007	99,727.99	892,000.00	77,000.00		96,241.00	895,486.99
					2006	82,000.00		-82,000.00			77,000.00
Accounts Receivable										-23,491.82	23,491.82
Fund Equities:											
Unobligated Balances (Expired)						-1,945,079.23				971,424.86	-2,916,504.09
Unobligated Balances (Unexpired)						-96,240.79				795,759.00	-891,999.79
Accounts Payable						-4,849,974.58				-533,184.86	-4,316,789.72
Undelivered Orders						-4,537,486.20				821,625.20	-5,359,111.40
Subtotal	20		0119			-0-	133,752,601.00		130,762,654.25	2,989,946.75	-0-
Expanded Access To Financial Services, Departmental Offices, Treasury											
Fund Resources:											
Undisbursed Funds	20		0121		No Year	2,370,346.15			103,979.48		2,266,366.67
Fund Equities:											
Unobligated Balances (Unexpired)						-2,008,503.27				228,776.52	-2,237,279.79
Accounts Payable						-15,428.87				-15,428.87	
Undelivered Orders						-346,414.01				-317,327.13	-29,086.88
Subtotal	20		0121			-0-			103,979.48	-103,979.48	-0-
Air Transportation Stabilization Program Account, Departmental Offices, Treasury											
Fund Resources:											
Undisbursed Funds	20		0122		No Year	3,656,716.55	100,702.00		233,294.13		3,524,124.42
Fund Equities:											
Unobligated Balances (Unexpired)						-2,125,529.37				-55,983.38	-2,069,545.99
Accounts Payable						-7,960.65				-7,812.92	-147.73
Undelivered Orders						-1,523,226.53				-68,795.83	-1,454,430.70
Subtotal	20		0122			-0-	100,702.00		233,294.13	-132,592.13	-0-
Terrorism Insurance Program, Departmental Offices, Treasury											
Fund Resources:											
Undisbursed Funds	20		0123		No Year	5,514,507.41			2,086,586.44		3,427,920.97
Fund Equities:											
Unobligated Balances (Unexpired)						-4,750,886.99				-1,932,729.56	-2,818,157.43
Accounts Payable						-53,196.40				41,561.72	-94,758.12
Undelivered Orders						-710,424.02				-195,418.60	-515,005.42
Subtotal	20		0123			-0-			2,086,586.44	-2,086,586.44	-0-
Community Development Financial Institutions Fund, Program Account, Treasury											
Fund Resources:											
Undisbursed Funds	20		1881		2007-2008		55,456,603.00		10,625,064.46		44,831,538.54
					2006-2007	33,537,948.81			29,371,109.70		4,166,839.11

Appropriations, Outlays, and Balances - Continued

Appropriation or Fund Account Title	Dept Reg	Tr From	Account Number	Sub No.	Period of Availability	Balances, Beginning Of Fiscal Year	Appropriations And Other Obligational Authority[1]	Transfers Borrowings And Investment (Net)[2]	Outlays (Net)	Balances Withdrawn And Other Transactions[3]	Balances, End Of Fiscal Year[4]
					2005-2006	6,297,739.57			5,579,472.44		718,267.13
					2004-2005	656,798.74			392,844.00		263,954.74
					2003-2004	7,154,160.93			4,210,031.35		2,944,129.58
					2002-2003	6,113,311.29			518,764.17		5,594,547.12
					2001-2002	4,004,879.18			547,926.56	3,456,952.62	-0-
					No Year	1,623,734.16			667,738.27		955,995.89
Fund Equities:											
Unobligated Balances (Expired)						-2,614,323.84				-759,679.52	-1,854,644.32
Unobligated Balances (Unexpired)						-2,046,407.32				778,171.38	-2,824,578.70
Accounts Payable						-6,199,630.93				7,737,888.57	-13,937,519.50
Undelivered Orders						-48,528,210.59				-7,669,681.00	-40,858,529.59
	20		1881		Subtotal	-0-	55,456,603.00		51,912,950.95	3,543,652.05	-0-
Special Fund Accounts											
Presidential Election Campaign Fund											
Fund Resources:											
Undisbursed Funds	20		5081		No Year	146,914,578.55	49,779,182.00		32,461,696.00		164,232,064.55
Fund Equities:											
Unobligated Balances (Unexpired)						-146,914,578.55				17,317,486.00	-164,232,064.55
	20		5081		Subtotal	-0-	49,779,182.00		32,461,696.00	17,317,486.00	-0-
Sallie Mae Assessments, Treasury											
Fund Resources:											
Undisbursed Funds	20		5407		No Year	25,500.63			13,349.24		12,151.39
Fund Equities:											
Unobligated Balances (Unexpired)						-19,323.50				-7,594.71	-11,728.79
Accounts Payable						-5,754.53				-5,754.53	
Undelivered Orders						-422.60					-422.60
	20		5407		Subtotal	-0-			13,349.24	-13,349.24	-0-
Treasury Forfeiture Fund											
Fund Resources:											
Undisbursed Funds	20		5697		No Year	53,389,525.93	451,463,048.53	-153,463,562.58	302,711,141.73		48,677,870.15
Unrealized Discount On Investments						-993,709.59		-111,437.42			-1,105,147.01
Investments In Public Debt Securities						275,054,000.00		153,575,000.00			428,629,000.00
Fund Equities:											
Unobligated Balances (Unexpired)						-82,935,359.65				77,181,697.94	-160,117,057.59
Accounts Payable						-111,178,517.63				32,432,719.41	-143,611,237.04
Undelivered Orders						-133,335,939.06				39,137,489.45	-172,473,428.51
	20		5697		Subtotal	-0-	451,463,048.53		302,711,141.73	148,751,906.80	-0-
Public Enterprise Funds											
Exchange Stabilization Fund, Office Of The Secretary, Treasury											
Fund Resources:											
Undisbursed Funds	20		4444		No Year			-2,876,255,274.96	-1,366,651,115.78	-1,509,604,159.18	
Funds Held Outside The Treasury	20				No Year	4,842.51		52,101.55			56,944.06
Holdings Of Special Drawing Rights						8,654,509,743.98				-646,040,206.58	9,300,549,950.56
Investments In Public Debt Securities						15,711,044,943.52		725,069,684.86			16,436,114,628.38

Footnotes At End Of Chapter

Appropriations, Outlays, and Balances – Continued

Appropriation or Fund Account	Account Symbol					Balances, Beginning Of Fiscal Year	Appropriations And Other Obligational Authority[1]	Transfers Borrowings And Investment (Net)[2]	Outlays (Net)	Balances Withdrawn And Other Transactions[3]	Balances, End Of Fiscal Year[4]
Title	Period of Availability	Dept Reg	Tr From	Account Number	Sub No.						
Exchange Stabilization Fund, Office Of The Secretary, Treasury - Continued											
Fund Resources: - Continued											
Investments In Non-Federal Securities						19,812,042,905,694.46		2,151,133,488.55			21,963,175,758.01
Fund Equities:											
Unobligated Balances (Unexpired)						-30,042,905,694.43				3,522,295,481.54	-33,565,201,175.97
Accounts Payable											3,794,169.24
Undelivered Orders						-14,134,696,105.04			-1,366,651,115.78	1,366,651,115.78	-14,134,696,105.04
	Subtotal	20		4444		-0-					-0-
Intragovernmental Funds											
Working Capital Fund, Department Of The Treasury											
Fund Resources:											
Undisbursed Funds	No Year	20		4501		163,386,859.28					181,765,851.29
Unfilled Customer Orders						3,208,660.43			-18,378,992.01	-585,508.81	3,794,169.24
Fund Equities:											
Unobligated Balances (Unexpired)						-62,476,770.16				-29,317,620.88	-33,159,149.28
Accounts Payable						-8,954,245.52				14,823,018.86	-23,777,264.38
Undelivered Orders						-95,164,504.03				33,459,102.84	-128,623,606.87
	Subtotal	20		4501		-0-			-18,378,992.01	18,378,992.01	-0-
Treasury Franchise Fund											
Fund Resources:											
Undisbursed Funds	No Year	20		4560		8,480,323.70		13,999,742.12	10,356,693.12		12,123,372.70
	No Year	20		4560	1	1,095,699.60		-3,990,000.00	-5,826,465.01		2,932,164.61
	No Year	20		4560	2	3,164,997.59		-1,330,000.00	-466,725.66		2,301,723.25
	No Year	20		4560	3	335,747.43			-462,698.87		798,446.30
	No Year	20		4560	4	9,925,794.96		-4,921,000.00	789,029.35		4,215,765.61
	No Year	20		4560	5	945,139.37		-42,354.22	-73,661.78		976,446.93
	No Year	20		4560	6	2,272,624.16		-115,509.56	-515,780.54		2,672,895.14
	No Year	20		4560	7	5,146,957.42		-1,995,000.00	-960,071.00		4,112,028.42
	No Year	20		4560	8				2,854,167.21		[5]-2,854,167.21
	No Year	20		4560	9	5,218,545.00		-1,064,000.00	-945,627.16		5,100,172.16
	No Year	20		4560	10	16,032,481.91		-541,878.34	-9,644,448.34		25,135,051.91
Accounts Receivable						109,834,503.42				17,934,949.90	91,899,553.52
Unfilled Customer Orders						340,991,214.16				134,943,326.06	206,047,888.10
Fund Equities:											
Unobligated Balances (Unexpired)						-234,675,168.51				-119,579,185.14	-115,095,983.37
Accounts Payable						-104,513,216.16				-20,017,518.98	-84,495,697.18
Undelivered Orders						-164,255,644.05				-8,385,983.16	-155,869,660.89
	Subtotal	20		4560		-0-			-4,895,588.68	4,895,588.68	-0-
Trust Fund Accounts											
Lower Brule Sioux Tribe Terrestrial Wildlife Habitat Restoration Trust Fund											
Fund Resources:											
Undisbursed Funds	No Year	20		8207		-65,758.47	1,800,906.49	-1,800,906.49			-89,492.84
Unrealized Discount On Investments								-23,734.37			
Investments In Public Debt Securities						11,715,773.50		1,824,640.86			13,540,414.36
Fund Equities:											

Appropriations, Outlays, and Balances - Continued

Appropriation or Fund Account — Title	Period of Availability	Reg	Tr From	Account Number	Sub No.	Balances, Beginning Of Fiscal Year	Appropriations And Other Obligational Authority[1]	Transfers Borrowings And Investment (Net)[2]	Outlays (Net)	Balances Withdrawn And Other Transactions[3]	Balances, End Of Fiscal Year[4]
Unobligated Balances (Unexpired)		20		8207		-11,650,015.03					-13,450,921.52
Accounts Payable											-0-
	Subtotal	20		8207		-0-	1,800,906.49			1,800,906.49	
Cheyenne River Sioux Tribe Terrestrial Wildlife Habitat Restoration Trust Fund											
Fund Resources:											
Undisbursed Funds	No Year	20		8209		-186,980.84	5,125,112.18	-5,125,112.18			-254,521.12
Unrealized Discount On Investments								-67,540.28			
Investments In Public Debt Securities						33,328,886.03		5,192,652.46			38,521,538.49
Fund Equities:											
Unobligated Balances (Unexpired)						-33,141,905.19	5,125,112.18			5,125,112.18	-38,267,017.37
Accounts Payable											-0-
	Subtotal	20		8209		-0-					
Salaries And Expenses Trust Fund, Departmental Offices, Treasury											
Fund Resources:											
Undisbursed Funds	No Year	20		8527		1,028,833.85					1,028,833.85
Fund Equities:											
Unobligated Balances (Unexpired)						-77,775.04					-77,775.04
Undelivered Orders						-951,058.81					-951,058.81
	Subtotal	20		8527		-0-					-0-
Violent Crime Reduction Program, Financial Crimes Enforcement Network, Treasury											
Fund Resources:											
Undisbursed Funds	No Year	20		8530		156,469.80			6,842.19		149,627.61
Fund Equities:											
Unobligated Balances (Unexpired)						-64,893.67				-3,301.17	-61,592.50
Undelivered Orders						-91,576.13				-3,541.02	-88,035.11
	Subtotal	20		8530		-0-			6,842.19	-6,842.19	-0-
Gifts And Bequests, Treasury											
Fund Resources:											
Undisbursed Funds	No Year	20		8790		22,325.48	43,848.75	43,848.75	13,857.95		8,467.53
Investments In Public Debt Securities						824,467.50		43,848.75			868,316.25
Fund Equities:											
Unobligated Balances (Unexpired)						-443,372.91				43,560.75	-486,933.66
Accounts Payable											
Undelivered Orders						-403,420.07				-13,569.95	-389,850.12
	Subtotal	20		8790		-0-	43,848.75		13,857.95	29,990.80	-0-
Total, Departmental Offices							961,095,795.95	-225,000.00	-613,782,989.00	1,574,653,784.95	
Financial Crimes Enforcement Network											
General Fund Accounts											
Salaries And Expenses, Financial Crimes Enforcement Network											
Fund Resources:											
Undisbursed Funds	2007-2009	20		0173			5,186,000.00		1,281,032.54		3,904,967.46
	2007-2008						8,435,790.00		7,350,018.69		1,085,771.31

Footnotes At End Of Chapter

Appropriations, Outlays, and Balances – Continued

Appropriation or Fund Account — Title	Period of Availability	Account Symbol Dept Reg	Tr From	Account Number	Sub No.	Balances, Beginning Of Fiscal Year	Appropriations And Other Obligational Authority[1]	Transfers Borrowings And Investment (Net)[2]	Outlays (Net)	Balances Withdrawn And Other Transactions[3]	Balances, End Of Fiscal Year[4]
Salaries And Expenses, Financial Crimes Enforcement Network - Continued											
Fund Resources: - Continued											
Undisbursed Funds - Continued											
	2006-2008					5,529,980.40			886,898.53		4,643,081.87
	2007						59,594,574.00		52,546,100.87		7,048,473.13
	2006-2007					1,334,581.05		225,000.00	1,324,208.60		235,372.45
	2005-2007					3,906,965.50			3,292,404.24		614,561.26
	2006					12,729,116.73			9,952,230.22		2,776,886.51
	2005-2006					494,651.88			244,223.28		250,428.60
	2004-2006					460,040.45			391,670.58		68,369.87
	2005					3,427,160.15			1,085,649.30		2,341,510.85
	2004-2005					147,575.92			77,413.34		70,162.58
	2003-2005					108,205.31					108,205.31
	2004					1,893,363.60			336,908.77		1,556,454.83
	2003-2004					165,316.12					165,316.12
	2002-2004					167,500.77			-152.95		167,653.72
	2003					850,204.44			36,803.01		813,401.43
	2002-2003					665,410.76					665,410.76
	2001-2003					38,138.98			4,936.70		33,202.28
	2002					442,910.95			-5,613.38	448,524.33	------
	2001-2002					11,485.76				11,485.76	------
	2000-2002					4,491.25				4,491.25	------
	No Year					78,427.12			29,885.71		48,541.41
Accounts Receivable						55,679.65				-61,499.75	117,179.40
Unfilled Customer Orders						69,258.91				-507,984.21	577,243.12
Fund Equities:											
Unobligated Balances (Expired)						-3,751,946.42				315,158.62	-4,067,105.04
Unobligated Balances (Unexpired)						-9,353,669.84				-2,263,624.00	-7,090,045.84
Accounts Payable						-12,279,799.65				-2,594,862.96	-9,684,936.69
Undelivered Orders						-7,195,049.79				-744,943.09	-6,450,106.70
	Subtotal	20		0173		-0-	73,216,364.00	225,000.00	78,834,618.05	-5,393,254.05	-0-
Total, Financial Crimes Enforcement Network							73,216,364.00	225,000.00	78,834,618.05	-5,393,254.05	
### Interagency Law Enforcement											
#### General Fund Accounts											
Interagency Crime And Drug Enforcement, Interagency Law Enforcement, Treasury											
Fund Resources:											
Undisbursed Funds	2003	20		1501		104,759.24			12,077.21		92,682.03
	2002					101,512.99			101,149.05	363.94	-0-
Fund Equities:											
Unobligated Balances (Expired)						-179,012.64				-86,330.61	-92,682.03
Undelivered Orders						-27,259.59				-27,259.59	-0-
	Subtotal	20		1501		-0-			113,226.26	-113,226.26	-0-

Appropriations, Outlays, and Balances - Continued

Appropriation or Fund Account — Title	Period of Availability	Reg	Tr From	Account Number	Sub No.	Balances, Beginning Of Fiscal Year	Appropriations And Other Obligational Authority[1]	Transfers Borrowings And Investment (Net)[2]	Outlays (Net)	Balances Withdrawn And Other Transactions[3]	Balances, End Of Fiscal Year[4]
Total, Interagency Law Enforcement									113,226.26	-113,226.26	
Financial Management Service											
General Fund Accounts											
Biomass Energy Development, Treasury											
Fund Resources:											
Undisbursed Funds	No Year	20		0114				3,206,451.11	-4,633,334.24	[6]7,839,785.35	
Transfer To:											
Department Of Energy	No Year	89	20	0114		4,744,644.18		-3,206,451.11	2,788.91		1,535,404.16
Fund Equities:											
Unobligated Balances (Unexpired)						-3,818,397.03					-611,945.92
Undelivered Orders						-926,247.15				-2,788.91	-923,458.24
Subtotal	Subtotal	20		0114		-0-			-4,630,545.33	4,630,545.33	-0-
Payment To Department Of Justice, FSLIC Resolution Fund, Office Of The Secretary, Treasury											
Fund Resources:											
Undisbursed Funds	No Year	20		0177		1,632,509.74					1,632,509.74
Fund Equities:											
Unobligated Balances (Unexpired)						-1,632,509.74					-1,632,509.74
Subtotal	Subtotal	20		0177		-0-					-0-
Relief Of Individuals And Others By Private And Public Laws											
Fund Resources:											
Undisbursed Funds	No Year	20		1706		443,162.78					443,162.78
Fund Equities:											
Accounts Payable						-443,162.78					-443,162.78
Subtotal	Subtotal	20		1706		-0-					-0-
Payment To Terrestrial Wildlife Habitat Restoration Trust Fund											
Fund Resources:											
Undisbursed Funds	2007	20		1738			5,000,000.00		5,000,000.00		
Judgements, Court Of Claims (Indefinite)											
Fund Resources:											
Undisbursed Funds	No Year	20		1740		3,076.65	546,551,517.44		546,360,259.86	191,257.58	194,334.23
Fund Equities:											
Accounts Payable						-3,076.65					-194,334.23
Subtotal	Subtotal	20		1740		-0-	546,551,517.44		546,360,259.86	191,257.58	-0-
Judgements, United States Courts (Indefinite)											
Fund Resources:											
Undisbursed Funds	No Year	20		1741		6,223,651.82	519,742,750.40		512,469,138.60	7,273,611.80	13,497,263.62
Fund Equities:											
Accounts Payable						-6,223,651.82					-13,497,263.62
Subtotal	Subtotal	20		1741		-0-	519,742,750.40		512,469,138.60	7,273,611.80	-0-
Claims For Damages (Indefinite)											
Fund Resources:											
Undisbursed Funds	No Year	20		1742		6,447.92	12,587,016.54		10,301,115.85		2,292,348.61

Footnotes At End Of Chapter

Appropriations, Outlays, and Balances – Continued

Title	Period of Availability	Reg	Tr From	Account Number	Sub No.	Balances, Beginning Of Fiscal Year	Appropriations And Other Obligational Authority[1]	Transfers Borrowings And Investment (Net)[2]	Outlays (Net)	Balances Withdrawn And Other Transactions[3]	Balances, End Of Fiscal Year[4]
Claims For Damages (Indefinite) - Continued											
Fund Equities:											
Accounts Payable						-6,447.92				2,285,900.69	-2,292,348.61
Subtotal	Subtotal	20		1742		-0-	12,587,016.54		10,301,115.85	2,285,900.69	-0-
Claims For Contract Disputes (Indefinite)											
Fund Resources:											
Undisbursed Funds	No Year	20		1743		562,246.59	142,435,397.88		115,047,644.47		27,950,000.00
Fund Equities:											
Accounts Payable						-562,246.59				27,387,753.41	-27,950,000.00
Subtotal	Subtotal	20		1743		-0-	142,435,397.88		115,047,644.47	27,387,753.41	-0-
Claims For Fire Fighting Services (Indefinite)											
Fund Resources:											
Undisbursed Funds	No Year	20		1748			657.00		657.00		
Salaries And Expenses, Financial Management Service, Treasury											
Fund Resources:											
Undisbursed Funds											
	2007-2009	20		1801			9,220,000.00		909,007.40		8,310,992.60
	2006-2008					6,512,843.24			4,026,488.26		2,486,354.98
	2007						225,224,104.00		195,378,967.47		29,845,136.53
	2005-2007					3,745,380.60			2,220,069.36		1,525,311.24
	2006					20,751,160.21			17,047,648.33		3,703,511.88
	2005-2006					200,000.00					200,000.00
	2004-2006					831,748.26			454,722.19		377,026.07
	2005					4,363,841.53			1,112,323.68		3,251,517.85
	2003-2005					102,180.49					102,180.49
	2004					2,317,576.04			121,680.33		2,195,895.71
	2002-2004					281,277.79			99,196.34		182,081.45
	2003					-1,285,010.14			-304,069.12		[5]-980,941.02
	2002-2003					51,971.69			31,881.98		20,089.71
	2001-2003					121,493.85					121,493.85
	2002					3,923,536.37			1,485,186.24	2,438,350.13	-0-
	2001-2002					2,057,306.71			1,308,187.90	749,118.81	-0-
	2000-2002					55,586.65				55,586.65	-0-
	No Year					1,475,549.19	937,065.00		1,001,550.92		1,411,063.27
Accounts Receivable						4,108,901.70				-215,843.29	4,324,744.99
Unfilled Customer Orders						32,668,930.68				-1,995,905.36	34,664,836.04
Fund Equities:											
Unobligated Balances (Expired)						-14,330,905.63				-7,794,244.88	-6,536,660.75
Unobligated Balances (Unexpired)						-6,118,664.78				3,091,713.51	-9,210,378.29
Accounts Payable						-16,519,942.68				275,725.52	-16,795,668.20
Undelivered Orders						-45,314,761.77				13,883,826.63	-59,198,588.40
Subtotal	Subtotal	20		1801		-0-	235,381,169.00		224,892,841.28	10,488,327.72	-0-
Financial Agent Services, Financial Management Service, Treasury											
Fund Resources:											
Undisbursed Funds	No Year	20		1802		80,120,575.55	411,000,000.00		439,116,525.98		52,004,049.57
Fund Equities:											
Unobligated Balances (Unexpired)						-29,446,354.60				-25,283,708.45	-4,162,646.15
Accounts Payable						-50,674,220.95				-2,832,817.53	-47,841,403.42
Subtotal	Subtotal	20		1802		-0-	411,000,000.00		439,116,525.98	-28,116,525.98	-0-

Appropriation or Fund Account (Title)	Account Symbol Dept Reg	Dept Tr From	Account Number	Sub No.	Period of Availability	Balances, Beginning Of Fiscal Year	Appropriations And Other Obligational Authority[1]	Transfers Borrowings And Investment (Net)[2]	Outlays (Net)	Balances Withdrawn And Other Transactions[3]	Balances, End Of Fiscal Year[4]
Payment To The Resolution Funding Corporation, Treasury											
Fund Resources:											
Undisbursed Funds	20		1851		No Year	------	1,986,731,317.66		1,986,731,317.66	------	------
Interest On Uninvested Funds, Treasury Department (Indefinite)											
Fund Resources:											
Undisbursed Funds	20		1860		No Year	18,486,955.27	7,948,884.26		7,452,717.89		18,983,121.64
Fund Equities:											
Accounts Payable						-18,486,955.27				496,166.37	-18,983,121.64
Subtotal	20		1860		Subtotal	-0-	7,948,884.26		7,452,717.89	496,166.37	-0-
Federal Interest Liabilities To The States, Treasury, Financial Management Service											
Fund Resources:											
Undisbursed Funds	20		1877		No Year	------	1,604,655.00		1,604,655.00		------
Credit Reform: Interest Paid On Uninvested Funds, Treasury Department (Indefinite)											
Fund Resources:											
Undisbursed Funds	20		1880		No Year	211,119.00	4,632,280,811.07		4,604,318,041.11		28,173,888.96
Fund Equities:											
Accounts Payable	20		1880		Subtotal	-211,119.00	4,632,280,811.07		4,604,318,041.11	27,962,769.96	-28,173,888.96
Subtotal	20		1880		Subtotal	-0-				27,962,769.96	-0-
Federal Reserve Bank Reimbursement Fund, Treasury, Financial Management Service											
Fund Resources:											
Undisbursed Funds	20		1884		No Year	80,528,447.67	295,000,000.00		289,439,916.33		86,088,531.34
Fund Equities:											
Unobligated Balances (Unexpired)						-11,696,559.67				6,297,287.67	-17,993,847.34
Accounts Payable						-68,831,888.00				-737,204.00	-68,094,684.00
Subtotal	20		1884		Subtotal	-0-	295,000,000.00		289,439,916.33	5,560,083.67	-0-
Special Fund Accounts											
Debt Collection Fund											
Fund Resources:											
Undisbursed Funds	20		5445		2007-2008		58,440,919.04		20,056,144.77		38,384,774.27
					2006-2007	25,177,213.42			22,324,383.76		2,852,829.66
					2005-2006	3,193,034.88			2,153,675.77		1,039,359.11
					2004-2005	1,416,937.78			145,097.96		1,271,839.82
					2003-2004	889,193.83			-81,876.63		971,070.46
					2002-2003	1,553,929.43			142,991.90		1,410,937.53
					2001-2002	213,508.16				213,508.16	
Fund Equities:											
Unobligated Balances (Expired)						-1,212,427.43				293,290.84	-1,505,718.27
Unobligated Balances (Unexpired)						-19,173,511.92				11,865,843.25	-31,039,355.17
Accounts Payable						-2,183,705.49				-348,689.24	-1,835,016.25
Undelivered Orders						-9,874,172.66				1,676,548.50	-11,550,721.16
Subtotal	20		5445		Subtotal	-0-	58,440,919.04		44,740,417.53	13,700,501.51	-0-

Footnotes At End Of Chapter

Appropriations, Outlays, and Balances – Continued

Appropriation or Fund Account — Title	Period of Availability	Reg	Tr From	Account Number	Sub No.	Balances, Beginning Of Fiscal Year	Appropriations And Other Obligational Authority[1]	Transfers Borrowings And Investment (Net)[2]	Outlays (Net)	Balances Withdrawn And Other Transactions[3]	Balances, End Of Fiscal Year[4]
Continued Dumping And Subsidy Offset, United States Customs Service, Treasury											
Fund Resources:											
Undisbursed Funds	No Year	20		5688		566,127,218.72	388,138,966.93		380,563,340.07		573,702,845.58
Fund Equities:											
Unobligated Balances (Unexpired)		20		5688		-566,127,218.72				7,575,626.86	-573,702,845.58
	Subtotal	20		5688		-0-	388,138,966.93		380,563,340.07	7,575,626.86	-0-
Confiscated And Vested Iraqi Property And Assets, Treasury, Financial Management Service											
Fund Resources:											
Undisbursed Funds	No Year	20		5816		280.51					280.51
Fund Equities:											
Unobligated Balances (Unexpired)		20		5816		-280.51					-280.51
	Subtotal	20		5816		-0-					-0-
Public Enterprise Funds											
United States Treasury Check Forgery Insurance Fund											
Fund Resources:											
Undisbursed Funds	No Year	20		4109		3,412,459.73	5,000,000.00		1,203,115.29	4,020,944.33	7,209,344.44
Fund Equities:											
Unobligated Balances (Unexpired)		20		4109		-3,029,441.14				-224,059.62	-7,050,385.47
Accounts Payable						-383,018.59					-158,958.97
	Subtotal	20		4109		-0-	5,000,000.00		1,203,115.29	3,796,884.71	-0-
Trust Fund Accounts											
National Defense Conditional Gift Fund, Treasury[14]											
Fund Resources:											
Undisbursed Funds	No Year	20		8886		25.54			25.54		
Esther Cattell Schmitt Gift Fund, Treasury											
Fund Resources:											
Undisbursed Funds	No Year	20		8902		80,096.12	32,162.50		12,000.00		100,258.62
Investments In Public Debt Securities						310,000.00					310,000.00
Fund Equities:											
Unobligated Balances (Unexpired)		20		8902		-349,179.93				21,552.86	-370,732.79
Accounts Payable						-40,916.19				-1,390.36	-39,525.83
	Subtotal	20		8902		-0-	32,162.50		12,000.00	20,162.50	-0-
Total, Financial Management Service						25.54	9,247,876,224.72		9,164,623,184.13	83,253,066.13	
Federal Financing Bank											
Intragovernmental Funds											
Federal Financing Bank Revolving Fund, Treasury											
Fund Resources:											
Undisbursed Funds	No Year	20		4521		-22,375,015,806.57		[7]1,169,733,857.52	-496,367,518.55	-673,385,700.85	[5]23,048,382,145.54
Fund Equities:											
Unobligated Balances (Unexpired)						22,375,145,010.31					23,048,530,711.16
Accounts Payable						-129,203.74				19,361.88	-148,565.62

Appropriations, Outlays, and Balances - Continued

Appropriation or Fund Account — Title	Period of Availability	Dept — Reg	Dept — Tr From	Account Number	Sub No.	Balances, Beginning Of Fiscal Year	Appropriations And Other Obligational Authority[1]	Transfers Borrowings And Investment (Net)[2]	Outlays (Net)	Balances Withdrawn And Other Transactions[3]	Balances, End Of Fiscal Year[4]
Total, Federal Financing Bank	Subtotal	20		4521		-0-		-1,169,733,857.52	-496,367,518.55	-673,366,338.97	-0-
						-0-	-0-	-0-	-0-		-0-
Alcohol And Tobacco Tax And Trade Bureau											
General Fund Accounts											
Salaries And Expenses, Alcohol And Tobacco, Tax And Trade Bureau, Treasury											
Fund Resources:											
Undisbursed Funds	2007	20		1008			90,618,461.00		74,895,685.44		15,722,775.56
	2006-2007						130,000.00	130,000.00			130,000.00
	2006					16,104,940.50		-130,000.00	14,438,885.06		1,536,055.44
	2005-2006					152,256.04			74,716.91		77,539.13
	2005					1,232,132.53			537,396.57		694,735.96
	2004-2005					7,776.29					7,776.29
	2004					1,391,124.11			295,968.02		1,095,156.09
	2003					2,712,972.81			222,477.45		2,490,495.36
Accounts Receivable						112,706.16				-258,620.88	-371,327.04
Unfilled Customer Orders						241,913.91				13,890.25	228,023.66
Fund Equities:											
Unobligated Balances (Expired)						-2,122,289.80				1,013,550.22	-3,135,840.02
Accounts Payable						-6,415,254.25				45,093.90	-6,460,348.15
Undelivered Orders						-13,418,278.30				-660,581.94	-12,757,696.36
	Subtotal	20		1008		-0-	90,618,461.00		90,465,129.45	153,331.55	-0-
Special Fund Accounts											
Internal Revenue, Collections For Puerto Rico											
Fund Resources:											
Undisbursed Funds	No Year	20		5737			461,630,408.77		461,630,408.77		
Total, Alcohol And Tobacco Tax And Trade Bureau							-552,248,869.77		552,095,538.22	153,331.55	
Bureau Of Engraving And Printing											
Intragovernmental Funds											
Bureau Of Engraving And Printing Fund											
Fund Resources:											
Undisbursed Funds	No Year	20		4502		163,935,835.14				-11,211,729.09	175,147,564.23
Accounts Receivable						33,088,159.51				-6,052,671.80	39,140,831.31
Fund Equities:											
Unobligated Balances (Unexpired)						-96,434,169.99				15,624,160.01	-112,058,330.00
Accounts Payable						-100,589,824.66				1,640,240.88	-102,230,065.54
	Subtotal	20		4502		-0-			-11,211,729.09	11,211,729.09	-0-

Footnotes At End Of Chapter

Appropriations, Outlays, and Balances – Continued

Appropriation or Fund Account — Title	Period of Availability	Reg	Tr From	Account Number	Sub No.	Balances, Beginning Of Fiscal Year	Appropriations And Other Obligational Authority[1]	Transfers Borrowings And Investment (Net)[2]	Outlays (Net)	Balances Withdrawn And Other Transactions[3]	Balances, End Of Fiscal Year[4]
Total, Bureau Of Engraving And Printing									-11,211,729.09	11,211,729.09	
United States Mint											
Public Enterprise Funds											
United States Mint Public Enterprise Fund[1]											
Fund Resources:											
Undisbursed Funds	No Year	20		4159		225,917,008.00				[6]43,000,000.00	255,731,342.99
Accounts Receivable						61,582,851.41				55,713,039.38	5,869,812.03
Unfilled Customer Orders										-30,392.77	30,392.77
Fund Equities:											
Unobligated Balances (Unexpired)						[8]107,938,742.75				-54,850,901.85	-53,087,840.90
Accounts Payable						[8]118,287,703.18				3,302,104.13	-121,589,807.31
Undelivered Orders						-61,273,413.48				25,680,486.10	-86,953,899.58
Subtotal		20		4159		-0-			-72,814,334.99	72,814,334.99	-0-
Total, United States Mint									-72,814,334.99	72,814,334.99	
Bureau Of The Public Debt											
General Fund Accounts											
Administering The Public Debt											
Fund Resources:											
Undisbursed Funds	2007	20		0560			174,057,092.74		[9]159,487,798.77		14,569,293.97
	2006-2007					20,478,514.02			1,071,821.78		1,128,178.22
	2006					5,866,639.38		2,200,000.00	13,833,520.39		4,444,993.63
	2005					230,000.00		-2,200,000.00	1,561,387.62		4,305,251.76
	2004-2005					4,042,112.10			229,452.00		548.00
	2004					605,253.22			1,756,964.25		2,285,147.85
	2003-2004					3,151,702.52			990,358.53		605,253.22
	2003					1,199,832.89			-92,402.04	1,292,234.93	2,161,343.99
	2002					33,804.96				33,804.96	
	2001-2002										
	No Year					3,701,467.21	2,000,000.00		1,956,476.80		3,744,990.41
Accounts Receivable						51,425.81				-354,298.94	405,724.75
Unfilled Customer Orders						535,792.89				-448,332.11	984,125.00
Fund Equities:											
Unobligated Balances (Expired)						-7,116,281.31				1,482,380.54	-8,598,661.85
Unobligated Balances (Unexpired)						-3,110,737.11				547,552.37	-3,658,289.48
Accounts Payable						-9,000,043.55				1,807,925.56	-10,807,969.11
Undelivered Orders						-20,669,483.03				-9,099,552.67	-11,569,930.36
Subtotal		20		0560		-0-	176,057,092.74		180,795,378.10	-4,738,285.36	-0-
Reimbursements To Federal Reserve Banks, Treasury											
Fund Resources:											
Undisbursed Funds	No Year	20		0562		31,974,584.49	128,000,000.00		121,737,506.89		38,237,077.60
Fund Equities:											

Appropriations, Outlays, and Balances - Continued

Appropriation or Fund Account: Title	Period of Availability	Dept Reg	Tr From	Account Number	Sub No.	Balances, Beginning Of Fiscal Year	Appropriations And Other Obligational Authority[1]	Transfers Borrowings And Investment (Net)[2]	Outlays (Net)	Balances Withdrawn And Other Transactions[3]	Balances, End Of Fiscal Year[4]
Unobligated Balances (Unexpired)						-18.07				3,600,002.43	-3,600,020.50
Accounts Payable				0562		-31,974,566.42				2,662,490.68	-34,637,057.10
Subtotal		20				-0-	128,000,000.00		121,737,506.89	6,262,493.11	-0-
Payment Of Government Losses In Shipment											
Fund Resources:											
Undisbursed Funds	No Year	20		1710		1,852,795.27	380,000.00		1,839,368.48		393,426.79
Fund Equities:											
Unobligated Balances (Unexpired)						-1,852,795.27				-1,459,368.48	-393,426.79
Subtotal		20		1710		-0-	380,000.00		1,839,368.48	-1,459,368.48	-0-
Total, Bureau Of The Public Debt							304,437,092.74		304,372,253.47	64,839.27	

Internal Revenue Service

General Fund Accounts

Appropriation or Fund Account: Title	Period of Availability	Dept Reg	Tr From	Account Number	Sub No.	Balances, Beginning Of Fiscal Year	Appropriations And Other Obligational Authority[1]	Transfers Borrowings And Investment (Net)[2]	Outlays (Net)	Balances Withdrawn And Other Transactions[3]	Balances, End Of Fiscal Year[4]
Refunding Internal Revenue Collections, Interest (Indefinite)											
Fund Resources:											
Undisbursed Funds	No Year	20		0904			3,281,589,570.58		3,281,589,570.58		
Payment Where Earned Income Credit Exceeds Liability For Tax, Internal Revenue Service											
Fund Resources:											
Undisbursed Funds	No Year	20		0906			38,274,461,745.53		38,274,461,745.53		
Tax Services, Internal Revenue Service											
Fund Resources:											
Undisbursed Funds	No Year	20		0912			2,202,896,962.65		[a]2,047,031,346.75		155,865,615.90
	2007					344,926,244.40		27,924,000.00	25,905,870.40		2,018,129.60
	2006-2007					8,093.00		-20,761,320.00	251,834,352.86		72,330,571.54
	2006					89,633,912.29			15,273,275.72		8,093.00
	2005-2006					12,695,536.96			2,207,445.65		74,360,636.57
	2005					68,072,023.20			14,202,856.13		10,488,091.31
	2004-2005					477,592.71			2,292,735.53		53,869,167.07
	2004					36,669,723.86			1,161,022.51		477,592.71
	2003-2004					31,383,096.33			4,847.58		34,376,988.33
	2003					2,401,831.43			1,730,344.07		16,059,240.17
	2002					17,789,584.24					
	2001-2002					553,582.70				30,222,073.82	
	No Year									2,396,983.85	
Accounts Receivable										612,646.25	-59,063.55
Unfilled Customer Orders										-27,409.86	27,409.86
Fund Equities:											
Unobligated Balances (Expired)						-138,201,946.93				38,344,459.85	-176,546,406.78
Unobligated Balances (Unexpired)						-15,866,117.75				-9,580,503.75	-6,285,614.00
Accounts Payable						-174,769,622.45				-51,429,450.10	-123,340,172.35
Undelivered Orders						-275,773,533.99				-162,123,254.61	-113,650,279.38
Subtotal		20		0912		-0-	2,202,896,962.65	7,162,680.00	2,361,644,097.20	-151,584,454.55	-0-

Footnotes At End Of Chapter

Appropriations, Outlays, and Balances – Continued

Appropriation or Fund Account — Title	Period of Availability	Dept. Reg.	Dept. Tr. From	Account Number	Sub No.	Balances, Beginning Of Fiscal Year	Appropriations And Other Obligational Authority[1]	Transfers Borrowings And Investment (Net)[2]	Outlays (Net)	Balances Withdrawn And Other Transactions[3]	Balances, End Of Fiscal Year[4]
Tax Law Enforcement, Internal Revenue Service											
Fund Resources:											
Undisbursed Funds	2007-2008	20		0913			142,794.00		18,444.94		124,349.06
	2006-2008					990,000.00					990,000.00
	2007						4,668,429,099.00	-3,708,480.00	[1]4,387,255,261.85		277,465,357.15
	2006-2007					160,385.61		4,319,992.68	2,716,948.97		1,763,429.32
	2005-2007					992,000.00			398,444.41		593,555.59
	2006					312,733,303.79		-13,645,421.00	267,597,500.69		31,490,382.10
	2005-2006					38,224.42			19,092.12		19,132.30
	2004-2006					709,384.15			565,421.78		143,962.37
	2005					23,184,109.44		-55,000.00	1,859,565.00		21,269,544.44
	2004-2005					2,420,149.15			2,207,512.53		212,636.62
	2003-2005					177,900.35			154,159.23		23,741.12
	2004					27,062,095.15			1,595,265.26		25,466,829.89
	2003-2004					1,207,505.37					1,207,505.37
	2003					13,973,139.05			-605,297.14		14,578,436.19
	2002-2003					37,976.16					37,976.16
	2002					11,405,987.20			-391,079.89	11,797,067.09	-0-
	2001-2002					6,531.54				6,531.54	-0-
Funds Held Outside The Treasury	No Year					250,510.84	4,409,000.00		17,036.34		4,642,474.50
	2007							3,708,480.00			3,708,480.00
	2006					3,898,330.00		-3,898,330.00			-0-
	2005					-55,000.00		55,000.00			-0-
Accounts Receivable						14,087,014.85			518,984.40		13,568,030.45
Fund Equities:											
Unobligated Balances (Expired)						-80,548,887.26				11,819,051.69	-92,367,938.95
Unobligated Balances (Unexpired)						-2,286,108.64				3,460,615.37	-5,746,724.01
Accounts Payable						-213,101,625.29				9,923,941.92	-223,025,567.21
Undelivered Orders						-117,342,925.88				-41,177,333.42	-76,165,592.46
Subtotal		20		0913		-0-	4,672,980,893.00	-13,223,758.32	4,663,408,276.09	-3,651,141.41	-0-
Earned Income Tax Credit Compliance Initiative, Internal Revenue Service											
Fund Resources:											
Undisbursed Funds	2003	20		0917		1,639,906.59			2,904.95		1,637,001.64
	2002					1,371,881.60			5,150.23	1,366,731.37	-0-
Fund Equities:											
Unobligated Balances (Expired)						-2,793,831.07				-1,183,346.39	-1,610,484.68
Accounts Payable						2,106.60				1,436.54	670.06
Undelivered Orders						-220,063.72				-192,876.70	-27,187.02
Subtotal		20		0917		-0-			8,055.18	-8,055.18	-0-
Operations Support, Internal Revenue Service											
Fund Resources:											
Undisbursed Funds	2007-2009	20		0919			990,000.00				990,000.00
	2007-2008						74,250,000.00		4,690,588.06		69,559,411.94
	2007						3,554,974,734.00		[12]2,924,410,866.77		630,563,867.23
	2006-2007					59,219,401.44		11,109,000.00	38,771,266.11		31,557,135.33
	2005-2006					423,071,993.16		-4,999,368.00	[13]367,196,257.79		50,876,367.37
	2005					33,694,232.96			26,380,051.13		7,314,181.83
	2004-2005					65,953,959.38			31,032,899.18		34,921,060.20
	2003-2005					4,926,596.06			374,447.84		4,552,148.22

Appropriations, Outlays, and Balances - Continued

Appropriation or Fund Account — Title	Dept Reg	Tr From	Account Number	Sub No.	Period of Availability	Balances, Beginning Of Fiscal Year	Appropriations And Other Obligational Authority[1]	Transfers Borrowings And Investment (Net)[2]	Outlays (Net)	Balances Withdrawn And Other Transactions[3]	Balances, End Of Fiscal Year[4]
					2004	19,021,634.79			370,290.03		18,651,344.76
					2003-2004	12,463,628.05			-25,306.42		12,478,934.47
					2002-2003	16,366,271.55			150,081.91		16,216,189.64
					2001-2002	23,313,258.15			32,867.40	23,280,390.75	
					No Year	4,333,707.27	4,797,962.00		24,066.14		9,107,603.13
Accounts Receivable						414,320.01				-1,906,445.46	2,320,765.47
Unfilled Customer Orders										-6,088,951.71	6,088,951.71
Fund Equities:											
Unobligated Balances (Expired)						-62,274,053.89				28,416,622.51	-90,690,676.40
Unobligated Balances (Unexpired)						-28,017,868.63				15,021,504.83	-43,039,373.46
Accounts Payable						-155,529,998.67				86,811,283.44	-242,341,282.11
Undelivered Orders						-416,947,081.63				102,179,547.70	-519,126,629.33
Subtotal	20		0919			-0-	3,635,012,696.00	6,109,632.00	3,393,408,375.94	247,713,952.06	-0-
Business Systems Modernization, Internal Revenue Service											
Fund Resources:											
Undisbursed Funds	20		0921		2007-2009	147,667,563.50	212,658,677.00		90,747,421.71		121,911,255.29
					2006-2008	38,391,903.18			89,794,929.23		57,872,634.27
					2005-2007	59,254,218.28			25,433,852.04		12,958,051.14
					2004-2006	11,618,858.57			46,232,612.70		13,021,605.58
					2003-2005	6,036,661.00			3,262,751.25		8,356,107.32
					2002-2004	1,130,723.90			254,273.64		5,782,387.36
					2001-2003	3,439,939.83			8,181.98		1,122,541.92
					1999-2002				-60,869.03	3,500,808.86	
Fund Equities:											
Unobligated Balances (Expired)						-7,850,049.23				6,007,916.57	-13,857,965.80
Unobligated Balances (Unexpired)						-101,515,797.94				-19,126,642.68	-82,389,155.26
Accounts Payable						-54,422,595.32				-2,448,747.23	-51,973,848.09
Undelivered Orders						-103,751,425.77				-30,947,812.04	-72,803,613.73
Subtotal	20		0921			-0-	212,658,677.00		255,673,153.52	-43,014,476.52	-0-
Payment Where Child Credit Exceeds Liability For Tax, Internal Revenue Service											
Fund Resources:											
Undisbursed Funds	20		0922		No Year		16,158,641,428.71		16,158,641,428.71		
Payment Where Health Care Credit Exceeds Liability For Tax, Internal Revenue Service, Treasury											
Fund Resources:											
Undisbursed Funds	20		0923		No Year		101,758,109.94		101,758,109.94		
Health Insurance Tax Credit Administration, Internal Revenue Service, Treasury											
Fund Resources:											
Undisbursed Funds	20		0928		2007		14,855,704.00		1,229,121.97		13,626,582.03
					2006	17,932,158.72		-53,561.00	16,861,456.01		1,017,141.71
					2005	10,236,434.07			32,429.81		10,204,004.26
					2004-2005	198,834.12			1,510.91		197,323.21
					2003-2004	604,622.84			3,918.00		600,704.84
Fund Equities:											
Unobligated Balances (Expired)						-10,939,925.32				139,866.48	-11,079,791.80
Accounts Payable						-1,336,412.18				27,252.57	-1,363,664.75

Footnotes At End Of Chapter

Appropriations, Outlays, and Balances – Continued

Appropriation or Fund Account — Title	Period of Availability	Reg	Tr From	Account Number	Sub No.	Balances, Beginning Of Fiscal Year	Appropriations And Other Obligational Authority[1]	Transfers Borrowings And Investment (Net)[2]	Outlays (Net)	Balances Withdrawn And Other Transactions[3]	Balances, End Of Fiscal Year[4]
Health Insurance Tax Credit Administration, Internal Revenue Service, Treasury - Continued											
Fund Equities: - Continued											
Undelivered Orders				0928		-16,695,712.25				-3,493,412.75	-13,202,299.50
	Subtotal	20		0928		-0-	14,855,704.00	-53,561.00	18,128,436.70	-3,326,293.70	-0-
Special Fund Accounts											
Internal Revenue Service, Miscellaneous Retained Fees, Treasury											
Fund Resources:											
Undisbursed Funds	No Year	20		5432		98,872,613.53	30,569,794.48				129,442,408.01
Fund Equities:											
Unobligated Balances (Unexpired)						-98,872,613.53				30,569,794.48	-129,442,408.01
	Subtotal	20		5432		-0-	30,569,794.48			30,569,794.48	-0-
Informant Payments, Internal Revenue Service											
Fund Resources:											
Undisbursed Funds	No Year	20		5433		461,628.90	13,198,576.83		13,199,474.82		460,730.91
Fund Equities:											
Unobligated Balances (Unexpired)						-461,628.90				-897.99	-460,730.91
	Subtotal	20		5433		-0-	13,198,576.83		13,199,474.82	-897.99	-0-
Private Collection Agent Program, Internal Revenue Service, Department Of The Treasury											
Fund Resources:											
Undisbursed Funds	No Year	20		5510			10,757,233.23		4,588,772.17		6,168,461.06
Fund Equities:											
Unobligated Balances (Unexpired)										3,543,745.20	-3,543,745.20
Accounts Payable										346,612.49	-346,612.49
Undelivered Orders										2,278,103.37	-2,278,103.37
	Subtotal	20		5510		-0-	10,757,233.23		4,588,772.17	6,168,461.06	-0-
Public Enterprise Funds											
Federal Tax Lien Revolving Fund, Internal Revenue Service											
Fund Resources:											
Undisbursed Funds	No Year	20		4413		4,010,694.65			-1,781,677.81		5,792,372.46
Fund Equities:											
Unobligated Balances (Unexpired)						-2,159,963.88				2,845,868.75	-5,005,832.63
Accounts Payable						3.00					3.00
Undelivered Orders						-1,850,733.77				-1,064,190.94	-786,542.83
	Subtotal	20		4413		-0-			-1,781,677.81	1,781,677.81	-0-
Total, Internal Revenue Service							68,609,381,391.95	-5,007.32	68,524,727,818.57	84,648,566.06	
Comptroller Of The Currency											
Trust Fund Accounts											
Assessment Funds, Office Of The Comptroller Of The Currency											
Fund Resources:											
Undisbursed Funds	No Year	20		8413		9,117,064.85		-105,660,058.60	-103,317,027.59		6,774,033.84
Unrealized Discount On Investments						-2,252,500.00		-1,248,941.40			-3,501,441.40

Appropriations, Outlays, and Balances - Continued

Appropriation or Fund Account — Title	Period of Availability	Dept Reg	Tr From	Account Number	Sub No.	Balances, Beginning Of Fiscal Year	Appropriations And Other Obligational Authority[1]	Transfers Borrowings And Investment (Net)[2]	Outlays (Net)	Balances Withdrawn And Other Transactions[3]	Balances, End Of Fiscal Year[4]
Investments In Public Debt Securities						705,164,000.00		106,909,000.00		-------	812,073,000.00
Accounts Receivable						3,644,462.08				-392,256.38	4,036,718.46
Fund Equities:											
Unobligated Balances (Unexpired)						-597,772,320.38				69,888,661.57	-667,660,981.95
Accounts Payable						-87,832,431.34				17,433,059.22	-105,265,490.56
Undelivered Orders						-30,068,275.21				16,387,563.18	-46,455,838.39
Subtotal		20		8413		-0-			-103,317,027.59	103,317,027.59	-0-
Total, Comptroller Of The Currency									-103,317,027.59	103,317,027.59	
Office Of Thrift Supervision											
Public Enterprise Funds											
Public Enterprise Revolving Fund, Office Of Thrift Supervision, Treasury											
Fund Resources:											
Undisbursed Funds	No Year	20		4108		495,528.56		-26,416,237.25	-26,920,738.78	-------	1,000,030.09
Unrealized Discount On Investments						-1,672,968.75				-------	-1,672,968.75
Investments In Public Debt Securities						279,710,569.60		26,416,237.25		-------	306,126,806.85
Fund Equities:											
Unobligated Balances (Unexpired)						-238,172,613.24				25,473,610.18	-263,646,223.42
Accounts Payable						-36,286,640.53				809,859.48	-37,096,500.01
Undelivered Orders						-4,073,875.64				637,269.12	-4,711,144.76
Subtotal		20		4108		-0-			-26,920,738.78	26,920,738.78	-0-
Total, Office Of Thrift Supervision									-26,920,738.78	26,920,738.78	
Interest On The Public Debt											
General Fund Accounts											
Interest On The Public Debt (Indefinite)											
Fund Resources:											
Undisbursed Funds	No Year	20		0550			425,592,835,121.79		429,977,998,108.20	-4,385,162,986.41	
Special Fund Accounts											
Gifts To Reduce Debt Held By The Public, Bureau Of The Public Debt											
Fund Resources:											
Undisbursed Funds	No Year	20		5080			2,374,862.42	-2,374,862.42			
Total, Interest On The Public Debt							425,595,209,984.21	-2,374,862.42	429,977,998,108.20	-4,385,162,986.41	

Footnotes At End Of Chapter

Appropriations, Outlays, and Balances – Continued

	Account Symbol										
Appropriation or Fund Account Title	Period of Availability	Dept — Reg	Dept — Tr From	Account Number	Sub No.	Balances, Beginning Of Fiscal Year	Appropriations And Other Obligational Authority[1]	Transfers Borrowings And Investment (Net)[2]	Outlays (Net)	Balances Withdrawn And Other Transactions[3]	Balances, End Of Fiscal Year[4]
Deductions For Offsetting Receipts											
Proprietary Receipts From The Public							-11,970,129,606.02		-11,970,129,606.02		
Intrabudgetary Transactions							-4,706,872,969.37		-4,706,872,969.37		
Total, Offsetting Receipts							-16,677,002,575.39		-16,677,002,575.39		-0-
Total, Department Of The Treasury						25.54	488,666,463,147.95	-1,172,113,727.26	490,601,347,833.51	-3,106,998,387.28	-0-
Memorandum											
Public Debt Retirement											
General Fund Accounts											
Public Debt Principal (Indefinite)											
Fund Resources:											
Undisbursed Funds	No Year	20		0500			38,163,045,325,312.46	38,242,892,301,499.81		-79,846,976,187.35	
Sinking Fund[14]											
Fund Resources:											
Undisbursed Funds	No Year	20		0575		42,305,774,479.58	680,849,085.47				42,986,623,565.05
Fund Equities:											
Unobligated Balances (Unexpired)	Subtotal	20		0575		-42,305,774,479.58	680,849,085.47			680,849,085.47	-42,986,623,565.05
Total, Public Debt Retirement						-0-	38,163,726,174,397.93	38,242,892,301,499.81		-79,166,127,101.88	-0-
Refunds Of Receipts											
General Fund Accounts											
Refunding Internal Revenue Collections (Indefinite)											
Fund Resources:											
Undisbursed Funds	No Year	20		0903			237,592,750,030.73		235,245,964,576.47	2,346,785,454.26	
Refund Of Moneys Erroneously Received And Covered (Indefinite)											
Fund Resources:											
Undisbursed Funds	No Year	20		1807		3,004,145.85	26,241,949.16		28,107,718.36		1,138,376.65
Fund Equities:											
Accounts Payable	Subtotal	20		1807		-3,004,145.85	26,241,949.16		28,107,718.36	-1,865,769.20	-1,138,376.65
						-0-				-1,865,769.20	-0-
Refunds And Drawbacks, United States Customs Service (Indefinite)											
Fund Resources:											
Undisbursed Funds	No Year	70		0505		2,270,475.41	1,537,551,934.94		1,537,980,178.42		1,842,231.93
Fund Equities:											
Unobligated Balances (Unexpired)						-328,582.08				-328,582.08	
Accounts Payable						-1,854,610.15				-38,066.65	-1,816,543.50
Undelivered Orders						-87,283.18				-61,594.75	-25,688.43
	Subtotal	70		0505		-0-	1,537,551,934.94		1,537,980,178.42	-428,243.48	-0-

Appropriations, Outlays, and Balances - Continued

Appropriation or Fund Account — Title	Period of Availability	Dept Reg	Tr From	Account Number	Sub No.	Balances, Beginning Of Fiscal Year	Appropriations And Other Obligational Authority[1]	Transfers Borrowings And Investment (Net)[2]	Outlays (Net)	Balances Withdrawn And Other Transactions[3]	Balances, End Of Fiscal Year[4]
Total, Refunds Of Receipts						---	239,156,543,914.83	---	236,812,052,473.25	2,344,491,441.58	---
Financing Accounts											
Public Enterprise Funds											
Community Development Financial Institutions Fund, Direct Loan, Financing Account											
Fund Resources:											
Undisbursed Funds	No Year	20		4088		70,234.00				---	60,494.49
Authority To Borrow From The Treasury						924,728.00	1,484,212.81	-3,609,999.39	-3,600,259.88	---	1,018,417.00
Accounts Receivable						562,538.00		-1,390,523.81		-15,951.00	578,489.00
Fund Equities:											
Unobligated Balances (Unexpired)						---				60,494.49	-60,494.49
Accounts Payable						-1,557,500.00				39,406.00	-1,596,906.00
Undelivered Orders						-0-				83,949.49	-0-
Subtotal	Subtotal	20		4088			1,484,212.81	-5,000,523.20	-3,600,259.88		
Air Transportation Stabilization Guaranteed Loan Financing Account, Departmental Offices, Treasury											
Fund Resources:											
Undisbursed Funds	No Year	20		4286		23,733,999.82		-5,876,467.40	17,857,532.42	-23,733,999.82	
Authority To Borrow From The Treasury							9,996,541.00	-9,996,541.00			
Fund Equities:											
Unobligated Balances (Unexpired)						-23,733,999.82	9,996,541.00	-15,873,008.40	17,857,532.42	-23,733,999.82	
Subtotal	Subtotal	20		4286		-0-	9,996,541.00	-15,873,008.40	17,857,532.42	-23,733,999.82	
Total, Financing Accounts							11,480,753.81	-20,873,531.60	14,257,272.54	-23,650,050.33	

Appropriations, Outlays, and Balances – Continued

Footnotes

1. The amounts in this column, unless otherwise footnoted, represent appropriations, increases and rescissions in borrowing authority or new contract authority. Appropriation accounts with appropriation transfer activity are presented in Table 1 (Appropriations and Appropriation Transfers) at the end of this chapter.

2. The amounts in this column, unless otherwise footnoted, represent transfers - other than appropriation transfers, borrowings (gross), investments (net), unrealized discounts or funds held outside the Treasury.

3. The amounts in this column, unless otherwise footnoted, represent obligated balances canceled for fiscal year 2002 pursuant to 31 U.S.C. 1553, changes in unfilled customer orders, accounts receivable, accounts payable, undelivered orders, unobligated balances and adjustments to borrowing and contract authority.

4. Unobligated balances for no-year or unexpired multiple year accounts are available for obligation; unobligated balances for expired fiscal year accounts are not available for obligation.

5. Subject to disposition by the administrative agency.

6. Represents capital transfer to miscellaneous receipts.

7. Includes $1,929,507,844.94 which represents repayment of borrowing from the U.S. Treasury.

8. The opening balance of Unobligated Balances - Unexpired and Accounts Payable for account 20 X 4159 have been adjusted by $129,052,525.97 during the current fiscal year and do not agree with last year's closing balances.

9. Includes $9,211.11 which represents payments for obligations of a closed account.

10. Includes $11,051.85 which represents payments for obligations of a closed account.

11. Includes $24,702.00 which represents payments for obligations of a closed account.

12. Includes $1,232,608.13 which represents payments for obligations of a closed account.

13. Includes $78,914.96 which represents payments for obligations of a closed account.

14. The Account 20 X 0575, Cumulative Sinking Fund, represents an authorization to spend in the event of a Federal budget surplus. It is a permanent appropriation account that was created by Section 6(a) of the Victory Liberty Loan Act of 1919, for the purpose of providing funds for the retirement of public debt. The Sinking Fund was established to retire notes and bonds, issued under the First Liberty Bond Act which were outstanding on July 1, 1920. The Gold Reserve Act of 1934 extended the application of the Sinking Fund to notes and bonds issued after July 1, 1920.

Appropriations, Outlays, and Balances - Continued

Footnotes

Table 1 - Appropriations And Appropriation Transfers - Department Of The Treasury

Department Regular	Fiscal Year	Account Symbol	Net Appropriations And Appropriations Transfers	Appropriation Amount	Net Appropriation Transfers
20	07	0101	208,261,232.00	211,227,106.00	-2,965,874.00
20	0708	0101	8,087,144.00	5,121,270.00	2,965,874.00
20	X	0119	892,000.00	0.00	892,000.00
20	07	0173	59,594,574.00	64,780,574.00	-5,186,000.00
20	0709	0173	5,186,000.00	0.00	5,186,000.00
20	X	0560	2,000,000.00	0.00	2,000,000.00
20	07	0560	174,057,092.74	176,057,092.74	-2,000,000.00
20	07	0912	2,202,896,962.65	2,156,988,334.00	45,908,628.65
20	X	0913	4,409,000.00	0.00	4,409,000.00
20	07	0913	4,668,429,099.00	4,741,680,267.00	-73,251,168.00
20	0708	0913	142,794.00	0.00	142,794.00
20	X	0919	4,797,962.00	0.00	4,797,962.00
20	07	0919	3,554,974,734.00	3,396,631,668.00	158,343,066.00
20	0709	0919	990,000.00	0.00	990,000.00
20	X	1801	937,065.00	0.00	937,065.00
20	07	1801	225,224,104.00	235,381,169.00	-10,157,065.00
20	0709	1801	9,220,000.00	0.00	9,220,000.00
20	X	5432	-136,788,488.65	0.00	-136,788,488.65
Totals			**10,993,311,274.74**	**10,987,867,480.74**	**5,443,794.00**

Department Regular Involved	Fiscal Year Involved	Accounts Involved	Amount From or To (-)
20	0708	0101	-2,965,874.00
20	07	0101	2,965,874.00
11	X	5512	892,000.00
20	0709	0173	-5,186,000.00
20	07	0173	5,186,000.00
20	X	0560	2,000,000.00
20	07	0560	-2,000,000.00
20	X	0919	-18,750,352.00
20	X	5432	64,658,980.65
11	X	5512	4,409,000.00
20	07	0919	-78,702,676.00
11	X	5432	5,451,508.00
20	0708	1070	142,794.00
20	07	0919	4,797,962.00
20	07	0912	18,750,352.00
20	07	0913	78,702,676.00
20	07	0919	-4,797,962.00
20	X	0919	-990,000.00
20	0709	5432	66,678,000.00
20	X	0919	990,000.00
20	07	0919	937,065.00
20	07	1801	-937,065.00
20	X	1801	-9,220,000.00
20	0709	1801	9,220,000.00
20	07	0912	-64,658,980.65
20	07	0913	-5,451,508.00
20	07	0919	-66,678,000.00
Totals			**5,443,794.00**

Footnotes At End Of Chapter

Appropriations, Outlays, and Balances – Continued

Department Of Veterans Affairs

Veterans Health Administration

General Fund Accounts

Expenses, Medical Administration, Department Of Veterans Affairs (Account Symbol: Reg 36, Account Number 0152)

Title / Period of Availability	Balances, Beginning Of Fiscal Year	Appropriations And Other Obligational Authority[1]	Transfers Borrowings And Investment (Net)[2]	Outlays (Net)	Balances Withdrawn And Other Transactions[3]	Balances, End Of Fiscal Year[4]
Fund Resources:						
Undisbursed Funds						
2007-2008		250,000,000.00		154,923,374.42		95,076,625.58
2007		3,169,121,690.00		2,741,643,010.21		427,478,679.79
2006-2007	164,600,167.76	-5,207,156.00		156,373,627.35		3,019,384.41
2006	332,557,492.92			279,720,289.95		52,837,202.97
2005-2006	4,526,553.23			3,434,418.71		1,092,134.52
2005	127,358,101.04			46,379,025.30		80,979,075.74
2004-2005	918,755.93			150,607.61		768,148.32
2004	57,380,921.39			14,100,718.67		43,280,202.72
2003-2004	1.97					1.97
2003	2,504,257.04			818,672.74		1,685,584.30
2002	1,966,450.95			694,296.56		1,272,154.39
No Year	1,248,740.80	260,900,000.00		242,215,662.79	-32,119.64	18,684,137.21
Accounts Receivable						1,280,860.44
Fund Equities:						
Unobligated Balances (Expired)	-50,281,072.84				26,402,699.29	-76,683,772.13
Unobligated Balances (Unexpired)	-151,466,925.44				-55,430,581.71	-96,036,343.73
Accounts Payable	-343,003,894.42				24,440,328.97	-367,444,223.39
Undelivered Orders	-148,309,550.33				37,708,148.39	-186,017,698.72
Subtotal (Account Number 0152)	-0-	3,674,814,534.00		3,640,453,904.31	34,360,629.69	-0-

Expenses, Medical Services, Department Of Veterans Affairs (Account Symbol: Reg 36, Account Number 0160)

Title / Period of Availability	Balances, Beginning Of Fiscal Year	Appropriations And Other Obligational Authority[1]	Transfers Borrowings And Investment (Net)[2]	Outlays (Net)	Balances Withdrawn And Other Transactions[3]	Balances, End Of Fiscal Year[4]
Fund Resources:						
Undisbursed Funds						
2007-2008		1,100,000,000.00		756,862,635.05		343,137,364.95
2007		23,786,186,360.00		20,801,803,081.75		2,984,383,278.25
2006-2007	340,118,739.11	-1,870,293.00		246,091,656.42		92,156,789.69
2006	2,313,004,102.17			1,918,420,038.80		394,584,063.37
2005-2006	149,300,932.39			96,185,661.65		53,115,270.74
2005	192,244,230.95			54,776,320.54		137,467,910.41
2004-2005	4,150,229.37			954,533.83		3,195,695.54
2004	68,660,602.74			24,197,783.66		44,462,819.08
2003-2004	13,380,678.47			4,950,511.34		8,430,167.13
2003	60,168,892.83			18,579,428.69		41,589,464.14
2002	9,763,191.36			1,632,124.96		8,131,066.40
2001-2002	12,419,344.00			11,151,840.13	1,267,503.87	
1995-1996	4,734,856.15			4,116,923.00	617,933.15	
1994-1995	2,012,673.23			131,589.48		1,881,083.75[5]
1993	10,194,963.29			3,396,770.01		6,798,193.28[6]
No Year	6,850,056.61			677,837.27		6,172,219.34[7]
Accounts Receivable	829,565,593.24	2,633,046,833.03	4,159,699.04	2,138,602,862.07		1,328,169,263.24
	14,227,634.25				759,386.53	13,468,247.72
Fund Equities:						
Unobligated Balances (Expired)	-147,174,830.71				111,798,846.73	-258,973,677.44

Appropriations, Outlays, and Balances - Continued

Appropriation or Fund Account: Title	Reg	Tr From	Account Number	Sub No.	Period of Availability	Balances, Beginning Of Fiscal Year	Appropriations And Other Obligational Authority[1]	Transfers Borrowings And Investment (Net)[2]	Outlays (Net)	Balances Withdrawn And Other Transactions[3]	Balances, End Of Fiscal Year[4]
Unobligated Balances (Unexpired)						-397,646,562.68			371,697,729.24		-769,344,291.92
Accounts Payable						-2,080,338,274.82			315,958,345.80		-2,396,296,620.62
Undelivered Orders						-1,405,637,051.95			636,891,255.10		-2,042,528,307.05
Subtotal	36		0160			-0-	27,517,362,900.03	4,159,699.04	26,082,531,598.65	1,438,991,000.42	-0-
Medical And Prosthetic Research, Department Of Veterans Affairs											
Fund Resources:											
Undisbursed Funds	36		0161		2007-2008	137,513,105.52	413,980,330.00		275,938,167.61		138,042,162.39
					2006-2007	38,998,965.94			90,245,734.07		47,267,371.45
					2005-2006	5,126,167.17			34,288,602.31		4,710,363.63
					2004-2005	2,828,400.79			434,158.72		4,692,008.45
					2003-2004	6,851,802.82			-278,440.39		3,106,841.18
					2002-2003	5,745,494.16			-746,380.76		7,598,183.58
					2001-2002	2,618,379.53			138,185.60	5,607,308.56	
					No Year	527,984.95	32,500,000.00		3,820,650.33	208,202.23	31,297,729.20
Accounts Receivable											319,782.72
Fund Equities:											
Unobligated Balances (Expired)						-17,182,968.08				-167,472.46	-17,015,495.62
Unobligated Balances (Unexpired)						-44,641,776.71				14,160,255.18	-58,802,031.89
Accounts Payable						-107,707,393.69				5,612,792.61	-113,320,186.30
Undelivered Orders						-30,678,162.40				17,218,566.39	-47,896,728.79
Subtotal	36		0161			-0-	446,480,330.00		403,840,677.49	42,639,652.51	-0-
Expenses, Medical Facilities, Department Of Veterans Affairs											
Fund Resources:											
Undisbursed Funds	36		0162		2007-2008		250,000,000.00		186,008,248.89		63,991,751.11
					2007		3,653,014,350.00		2,574,626,438.59		1,078,387,911.41
					2006-2007	104,146,250.44	8,151,198.00		62,152,768.35		50,144,680.09
					2006	688,780,441.93			549,566,233.91		139,214,208.02
					2005-2006	50,074,166.75			37,937,896.29		12,136,270.46
					2005	138,915,879.84			97,973,576.80		40,942,303.04
					2004-2005	2,827,283.20			646,120.85		2,181,162.35
					2004	44,103,178.15			23,763,694.46		20,339,483.69
					No Year	18,757,185.67	637,000,000.00		12,129,068.24		643,628,117.43
Accounts Receivable						542,752.98				-144,403.52	687,156.50
Fund Equities:											
Unobligated Balances (Expired)						-20,870,279.35				11,812,434.32	-32,682,713.67
Unobligated Balances (Unexpired)						-37,393,326.39				425,437,646.35	-462,830,972.74
Accounts Payable						-370,567,836.59				52,702,559.54	-423,270,396.13
Undelivered Orders						-619,315,696.63				513,553,264.93	-1,132,868,961.56
Subtotal	36		0162			-0-	4,548,165,548.00		3,544,804,046.38	1,003,361,501.62	-0-
DOD-VA Health Care Sharing Incentive Fund, Department Of Veterans Affairs											
Fund Resources:											
Undisbursed Funds	36		0165		No Year	55,126,972.90	70,000,000.00	-15,389,786.00	25,157,889.41		84,579,297.49
Transfer To:											
Defense	97	36	0165		No Year	27,201,111.09		15,389,786.00	10,505,367.36		32,085,529.73
Fund Equities:											
Unobligated Balances (Unexpired)						-56,937,648.25				36,882,474.88	-93,820,123.13
Accounts Payable						-4,006,788.24				398,206.68	-4,404,994.92
Undelivered Orders						-21,383,647.50				-2,943,938.33	-18,439,709.17

Footnotes At End Of Chapter

Appropriations, Outlays, and Balances – Continued

Appropriation or Fund Account — Title	Account Symbol — Dept Reg	Account Symbol — Dept Tr From	Account Symbol — Account Number	Sub No.	Period of Availability	Balances, Beginning Of Fiscal Year	Appropriations And Other Obligational Authority[1]	Transfers Borrowings And Investment (Net)[2]	Outlays (Net)	Balances Withdrawn And Other Transactions[3]	Balances, End Of Fiscal Year[4]
DOD-VA Health Care Sharing Incentive Fund, Department Of Veterans - Continued											
Fund Equities: - Continued	36		0165		Subtotal	-0-	70,000,000.00		35,663,256.77	34,336,743.23	-0-
Special Fund Accounts											
Medical Care Collections Fund, Department Of Veterans Affairs											
Fund Resources:											
Undisbursed Funds	36		5287		No Year	170,777,054.01	7,484,156.95				178,261,210.96
Fund Equities:											
Unobligated Balances (Unexpired)	36		5287		Subtotal	-170,777,054.01	7,484,156.95			7,484,156.95	-178,261,210.96
						-0-	7,484,156.95			7,484,156.95	-0-
Public Enterprise Funds											
Canteen Service Revolving Fund, Department Of Veterans Affairs											
Fund Resources:											
Undisbursed Funds	36		4014		No Year	7,791,068.52			-3,355,020.47		11,146,088.99
Investments In Public Debt Securities						26,400,000.00					26,400,000.00
Accounts Receivable						1,008,135.43				90,866.23	917,269.20
Fund Equities:											
Unobligated Balances (Unexpired)						-1,825,925.08				-1,542,584.63	-283,340.45
Accounts Payable						-30,886,552.99				4,806,738.87	-35,693,291.86
Undelivered Orders						-2,486,725.88					-2,486,725.88
	36		4014		Subtotal	-0-			-3,355,020.47	3,355,020.47	-0-
Department Of Veterans Affairs Special Therapeutic And Rehabilitation Activities Fund, Department Of Veterans Affairs											
Fund Resources:											
Undisbursed Funds	36		4048		No Year	3,790.36		-3,790.36			
Accounts Receivable						77.00				77.00	
Fund Equities:											
Unobligated Balances (Unexpired)						-3,605.11				-3,605.11	
Accounts Payable						-112.25				-112.25	
Undelivered Orders						-150.00				-150.00	
	36		4048		Subtotal	-0-		-3,790.36		-3,790.36	-0-
Intragovernmental Funds											
Parking Revolving Fund, Department Of Veterans Affairs											
Fund Resources:											
Undisbursed Funds	36		4538		No Year	4,943,440.87		-4,155,908.68	787,532.19		
Fund Equities:											
Unobligated Balances (Unexpired)						-4,100,389.53				-4,100,389.53	
Undelivered Orders						-843,051.34				-843,051.34	
	36		4538		Subtotal	-0-		-4,155,908.68	787,532.19	-4,943,440.87	-0-

Appropriations, Outlays, and Balances - Continued

Appropriation or Fund Account — Title	Period of Availability	Dept Reg	Tr From	Account Number	Sub No.	Balances, Beginning Of Fiscal Year	Appropriations And Other Obligational Authority[1]	Transfers Borrowings And Investment (Net)[2]	Outlays (Net)	Balances Withdrawn And Other Transactions[3]	Balances, End Of Fiscal Year[4]
Trust Fund Accounts											
General Post Fund, National Homes, Department Of Veterans Affairs	No Year	36		8180							
Fund Resources:											
Undisbursed Funds						3,202,139.00	30,754,402.35	-3,205,089.38	29,670,442.08	——	1,081,009.89
Unrealized Discount On Investments						-378,289.84		260,089.38	——	——	-118,200.46
Investments In Public Debt Securities						66,465,000.00		2,945,000.00	——	——	69,410,000.00
Fund Equities:											
Unobligated Balances (Unexpired)						-64,863,081.41				1,773,704.79	-66,636,786.20
Accounts Payable						-2,211,578.91				-343,268.86	-1,868,310.05
Undelivered Orders						-2,214,188.84				-346,475.66	-1,867,713.18
						-0-			29,670,442.08	1,083,960.27	-0-
Subtotal		36		8180		-0-	30,754,402.35		29,670,442.08		
Total, Veterans Health Administration							36,295,061,871.33		33,734,396,437.40	2,560,665,433.93	
Veterans Benefit Programs											
General Fund Accounts											
Compensation And Pensions, Department Of Veterans Affairs	No Year	36		0102							
Fund Resources:											
Undisbursed Funds						387,165,701.11	38,622,360,000.00		34,599,803,044.64		4,409,722,656.47
Fund Equities:											
Unobligated Balances (Unexpired)						-296,272,892.71				950,045,028.47	-1,246,317,921.18
Accounts Payable						-80,654,268.35				3,050,827,384.18	-3,131,481,652.53
Undelivered Orders						-10,238,540.05				21,684,542.71	-31,923,082.76
						-0-			34,599,803,044.64	4,022,556,955.36	-0-
Subtotal		36		0102		-0-	38,622,360,000.00		34,599,803,044.64		
Veterans Insurance And Indemnities, Department Of Veterans Affairs	No Year	36		0120							
Fund Resources:											
Undisbursed Funds						886,534.77	49,850,000.00		49,872,827.95		863,706.82
Fund Equities:											
Unobligated Balances (Unexpired)						-681,544.66				-75,534.52	-606,010.14
Accounts Payable						-204,990.11				52,706.57	-257,696.68
						-0-			49,872,827.95	-22,827.95	-0-
Subtotal		36		0120		-0-	49,850,000.00		49,872,827.95		
Guaranteed Transitional Housing Loans For Homeless Veterans Program Account, Department Of Veterans Affairs	No Year	36		0128							
Fund Resources:											
Undisbursed Funds						48,250,000.00			4,862,760.00		43,387,240.00
Fund Equities:											
Unobligated Balances (Unexpired)						-43,387,240.00				-4,862,760.00	-43,387,240.00
Undelivered Orders						-4,862,760.00				-4,862,760.00	-0-
						-0-			4,862,760.00		-0-
Subtotal		36		0128		-0-			4,862,760.00		
Readjustment Benefits, Department Of Veterans Affairs	No Year	36		0137							
Fund Resources:											
Undisbursed Funds						553,870,585.18	2,812,006,000.00		2,999,467,456.54		366,409,128.64
Fund Equities:											
Unobligated Balances (Unexpired)						-511,301,621.50				-216,479,429.51	-294,822,191.99
Accounts Payable						-38,397,135.02				29,261,252.40	-67,658,387.42

Footnotes At End Of Chapter

Appropriations, Outlays, and Balances – Continued

Title	Period of Availability	Reg	Tr From	Account Number	Sub No.	Balances, Beginning Of Fiscal Year	Appropriations And Other Obligational Authority[1]	Transfers Borrowings And Investment (Net)[2]	Outlays (Net)	Balances Withdrawn And Other Transactions[3]	Balances, End Of Fiscal Year[4]
Readjustment Benefits, Department Of Veterans Affairs - Continued											
Fund Equities: - Continued											
Undelivered Orders						-4,171,828.66				-243,279.43	-3,928,549.23
Subtotal		36		0137		-0-	2,812,006,000.00		2,999,467,456.54	-187,461,456.54	-0-
Reinstated Entitlement Program For Survivors Under Public Law 97-377, Department Of Veterans Affairs											
Fund Resources:											
Undisbursed Funds:	2006	36		0200		6,080.00			6,080.00		
	2005					1,480,572.80			-21,656.73		1,502,229.53
	2004					872,743.24			-13,521.25		886,264.49
	2003					99,958.82			-4,987.25		104,946.07
	2002					66,209.77			-33,146.57	99,356.34	
Fund Equities:											
Unobligated Balances (Expired)						-2,429,766.92				-27,121.92	-2,402,645.00
Accounts Payable						-95,797.71				-5,002.62	-90,795.09
Subtotal		36		0200		-0-			-67,231.80	67,231.80	-0-
Vocational Rehabilitation Loans Program Account, Department Of Veterans Affairs											
Fund Resources:											
Undisbursed Funds:	2007	36		1114			1,031,055.60		1,031,055.60		11,333.11
	2005					11,333.11					
Fund Equities:											
Unobligated Balances (Expired)		36		1114		-11,333.11					-11,333.11
Subtotal		36		1114		-0-	1,031,055.60		1,031,055.60		-0-
Veterans Housing Benefit Program Fund Program Account, Department Of Veterans Affairs											
Fund Resources:											
Undisbursed Funds:	2007	36		1119			154,284,000.00		152,326,620.00	1,957,380.00	1,957,380.00
	2006					2,170,000.00					2,170,000.00
	No Year					320.00	49,518,240.65		49,518,240.65		320.00
Fund Equities:											
Unobligated Balances (Expired)		36		1119		-2,170,320.00					-4,127,700.00
Subtotal		36		1119		-0-	203,802,240.65		201,844,860.65	1,957,380.00	-0-
Native American Veteran Housing Loan Program Account, Department Of Veterans Affairs											
Fund Resources:											
Undisbursed Funds:	2007	36		1120			584,000.00		584,000.00		373.00
	2003					373.00					
	No Year					2,333,999.70	2,634,000.00		2,634,000.00		2,333,999.70
Fund Equities:											
Unobligated Balances (Expired)		36		1120		-373.00					-373.00
Unobligated Balances (Unexpired)						-2,333,999.70					-2,333,999.70
Subtotal		36		1120		-0-	3,218,000.00		3,218,000.00		-0-

Appropriations, Outlays, and Balances - Continued

Appropriation or Fund Account — Title	Period of Availability	Dept Reg	Tr From	Account Number	Sub No.	Balances, Beginning Of Fiscal Year	Appropriations And Other Obligational Authority[1]	Transfers Borrowings And Investment (Net)[2]	Outlays (Net)	Balances Withdrawn And Other Transactions[3]	Balances, End Of Fiscal Year[4]
Special Fund Accounts											
National Cemetery Administration Facilities Operation Fund, Department Of Veterans Affairs											
Fund Resources:											
Undisbursed Funds	No Year	36		5392		68,550.00	40,200.00				108,750.00
Fund Equities:											
Unobligated Balances (Unexpired)						-68,550.00	40,200.00			40,200.00	-108,750.00
Subtotal		36		5392		-0-	40,200.00			40,200.00	-0-
Public Enterprise Funds											
Servicemen's Group Life Insurance Fund											
Fund Resources:											
Undisbursed Funds	No Year	36		4009		7,266.60		-24,000.00	-25,280.00		8,546.60
Investments In Public Debt Securities						488,000.00		24,000.00			512,000.00
Accounts Receivable						6,252.50				-147.50	6,400.00
Fund Equities:											
Unobligated Balances (Unexpired)						-501,518.40				25,427.50	-526,945.90
Accounts Payable						-0.70					-0.70
Subtotal		36		4009		-0-			-25,280.00	25,280.00	-0-
Veterans Reopened Insurance Fund											
Fund Resources:											
Undisbursed Funds	No Year	36		4010		374,817.60		22,799,000.00	22,973,098.68		200,718.92
Investments In Public Debt Securities						401,631,000.00		-22,799,000.00			378,832,000.00
Accounts Receivable						6,104,793.13				454,758.11	5,650,035.02
Fund Equities:											
Unobligated Balances (Unexpired)						-350,266,873.49				-21,588,122.70	-328,678,750.79
Accounts Payable						-57,843,737.24				-1,839,734.09	-56,004,003.15
Subtotal		36		4010		-0-			22,973,098.68	-22,973,098.68	-0-
Service-Disabled Veterans Insurance Fund											
Fund Resources:											
Undisbursed Funds	No Year	36		4012		26,820,094.42			-8,084,971.18		34,905,065.60
Fund Equities:											
Unobligated Balances (Unexpired)						-16,021,694.29				9,948,125.18	-25,969,819.47
Accounts Payable						-10,798,400.13				-1,863,154.00	-8,935,246.13
Subtotal		36		4012		-0-			-8,084,971.18	8,084,971.18	-0-
Veterans Housing Benefit Program Fund Liquidating Account, Department Of Veterans Affairs											
Fund Resources:											
Undisbursed Funds	No Year	36		4025		23,449,120.35			-28,340,204.50	[8]41,449,120.35	10,340,204.50
Accounts Receivable						[9]6,285,515.93				5,369,778.97	915,736.96
Fund Equities:											
Unobligated Balances (Unexpired)						[9]-21,425,635.60				-13,443,055.20	-7,982,580.40
Accounts Payable						-7,082,462.49				-3,809,101.43	-3,273,361.06
Undelivered Orders						-1,226,538.19				-1,226,538.19	-0-
Subtotal		36		4025		-0-			-28,340,204.50	28,340,204.50	-0-

Footnotes At End Of Chapter

Appropriations, Outlays, and Balances – Continued

Appropriation or Fund Account — Title	Account Symbol — Period of Availability	Dept Reg	Tr From	Account Number	Sub No.	Balances, Beginning Of Fiscal Year	Appropriations And Other Obligational Authority[1]	Transfers Borrowings And Investment (Net)[2]	Outlays (Net)	Balances Withdrawn And Other Transactions[3]	Balances, End Of Fiscal Year[4]
Trust Fund Accounts											
National Service Life Insurance Fund, Department Of Veterans Affairs											
Fund Resources:											
Undisbursed Funds	No Year	36		8132		4,997,350.08					4,339,944.20
Investments In Public Debt Securities						10,188,721,000.00	731,196,417.33	436,885,000.00	1,168,738,823.21		9,751,836,000.00
Fund Equities:											
Unobligated Balances (Unexpired)						-8,735,831,783.24		-436,885,000.00		-407,321,761.92	-8,328,510,021.32
Accounts Payable						-1,457,886,566.84				-30,220,643.96	-1,427,665,922.88
Subtotal		36		8132		-0-	731,196,417.33		1,168,738,823.21	-437,542,405.88	-0-
Post-Vietnam Era, Veterans Education Account, Department Of Veterans Affairs											
Fund Resources:											
Undisbursed Funds	No Year	36		8133		70,443,217.65	360,326.00		2,200,213.76		68,603,329.89
Fund Equities:											
Unobligated Balances (Unexpired)						-69,236,098.30				-1,895,552.14	-67,340,546.16
Accounts Payable						-1,207,119.35				55,664.38	-1,262,783.73
Subtotal		36		8133		-0-	360,326.00		2,200,213.76	-1,839,887.76	-0-
United States Government Life Insurance Fund, Department Of Veterans Affairs											
Fund Resources:											
Undisbursed Funds	No Year	36		8150		171,961.50					194,841.16
Investments In Public Debt Securities						39,444,000.00	2,178,606.95	4,847,000.00	7,002,727.29		34,597,000.00
Fund Equities:											
Unobligated Balances (Unexpired)						-26,164,390.64		-4,847,000.00		-3,340,124.14	-22,824,266.50
Accounts Payable						-13,451,570.86				-1,483,996.20	-11,967,574.66
Subtotal		36		8150		-0-	2,178,606.95		7,002,727.29	-4,824,120.34	-0-
Veterans Special Life Insurance Fund, Trust Revolving Fund, Department Of Veterans Affairs											
Fund Resources:											
Undisbursed Funds	No Year	36		8455		680,955.43					748,349.82
Investments In Public Debt Securities						1,960,216,000.00		-25,156,000.00	-25,223,394.39		1,985,372,000.00
Accounts Receivable						33,724,615.94				659,266.45	33,065,349.49
Fund Equities:											
Unobligated Balances (Unexpired)						-1,589,372,918.30		25,156,000.00		8,851,606.39	-1,598,224,524.69
Accounts Payable						-405,248,653.07				15,712,521.55	-420,961,174.62
Subtotal		36		8455		-0-			-25,223,394.39	25,223,394.39	-0-
Total, Veterans Benefits Administration							42,426,042,846.53		38,999,273,786.45	3,426,769,060.08	
Veterans Benefit Administration											
General Fund Accounts											
Construction, Major Projects, Department Of Veterans Affairs											
Fund Resources:											
Undisbursed Funds	2004-2005	36		0110		204,355,272.41			141,565,461.99		62,789,810.42
	No Year					2,621,672,665.11	399,000,000.00		295,570,925.41		2,725,101,739.70

Appropriations, Outlays, and Balances - Continued

Appropriation or Fund Account — Title / Period of Availability	Dept Reg	Tr From	Account Number	Sub No.	Balances, Beginning Of Fiscal Year	Appropriations And Other Obligational Authority[1]	Transfers Borrowings And Investment (Net)[2]	Outlays (Net)	Balances Withdrawn And Other Transactions[3]	Balances, End Of Fiscal Year[4]
Fund Equities:										
Unobligated Balances (Expired)					-161,473.96				-106,083.07	-55,390.89
Unobligated Balances (Unexpired)					-2,164,770,161.39				-69,109,341.98	-2,095,660,819.41
Accounts Payable					-19,784,529.25				12,181,701.37	-31,966,230.62
Undelivered Orders					-641,311,772.92				18,897,336.28	-660,209,109.20
Subtotal	36		0110		-0-	399,000,000.00		437,136,387.40	-38,136,387.40	-0-
Construction, Minor Projects, Department Of Veterans Affairs										
Fund Resources:										
Undisbursed Funds										
2007-2008	36		0111			14,484,754.00				14,484,754.00
2006-2007					32,400,000.00	-14,484,754.00		9,986,491.29		7,928,754.71
No Year					406,111,477.19	524,937,000.00		257,328,860.31		673,719,616.88
Fund Equities:										
Unobligated Balances (Expired)									60,727.15	-60,727.15
Unobligated Balances (Unexpired)					-107,313,395.68				299,598,296.47	-406,911,692.15
Accounts Payable					-26,274,136.32				-3,423,301.08	-22,850,835.24
Undelivered Orders					-304,923,945.19				-38,614,074.14	-266,309,871.05
Subtotal	36		0111		-0-	524,937,000.00		267,315,351.60	257,621,648.40	-0-
National Cemetery Administration, Department Of Veterans Affairs										
Fund Resources:										
Undisbursed Funds										
2007-2008	36		0129			500,000.00				500,000.00
2007						159,730,244.00		133,324,875.56		26,405,368.44
2006-2007					2,400,000.00		1,760,000.00	416,899.34		3,743,100.66
2006					21,436,849.01		-1,760,000.00	16,929,489.78		2,747,359.23
2005-2006					4,093,731.46			3,164,390.77		929,340.69
2005					2,934,865.53			1,871,602.10		1,063,263.43
2004-2005					5,994.84					5,994.84
2004					2,723,788.08			447,279.28		2,276,508.80
2003-2004					163,925.18					163,925.18
2003					1,161,215.70			-13,437.46		1,174,653.16
2002					1,245,537.08			9,847.64	1,235,689.44	
No Year					220,490.53			-2,432.56		222,923.09
Fund Equities:										
Unobligated Balances (Expired)					-4,715,386.43				-578,848.47	-4,136,537.96
Unobligated Balances (Unexpired)					-2,620,490.53				-1,897,567.44	-722,923.09
Accounts Payable					-20,357,817.99				-7,744,585.95	-12,613,232.04
Undelivered Orders					-8,692,702.46				13,067,041.97	-21,759,744.43
Subtotal	36		0129		-0-	160,230,244.00		156,148,514.45	4,081,729.55	-0-
General Operating Expenses, Veterans Administration										
Fund Resources:										
Undisbursed Funds										
2007-2008	36		0151			53,648,326.00				53,648,326.00
2007						1,450,070,480.00		1,269,774,677.31		180,295,802.69
2006-2007					58,190,720.00		10,645,013.00	67,905,356.25		930,376.75
2006					135,995,619.81		-10,645,013.00	82,485,049.12		42,865,557.69
2005-2006					1,588,110.26			1,175,001.78		413,108.48
2005					103,007,431.44			39,445,064.54		63,562,366.90
2004-2005					2,092,193.51			660,244.35		1,431,949.16
2004					30,878,582.87			2,794,239.63		28,084,343.24

Appropriations, Outlays, and Balances – Continued

Appropriation or Fund Account — Title	Period of Availability	Reg	Tr From	Account Number	Sub No.	Balances, Beginning Of Fiscal Year	Appropriations And Other Obligational Authority[1]	Transfers Borrowings And Investment (Net)[2]	Outlays (Net)	Balances Withdrawn And Other Transactions[3]	Balances, End Of Fiscal Year[4]
General Operating Expenses, Veterans Administration - Continued											
Fund Resources: - Continued											
Undisbursed Funds - Continued											
	2003-2004					342,163.88					342,163.88
	2003					17,883,121.27			4,387,247.67		13,495,873.60
	2002-2003					111,533.37					111,533.37
	2002					11,783,786.84			2,252,897.29	9,530,889.55	
	2001-2002					91,461.58				91,461.58	
	No Year					342,172.93	81,950,000.00		7,278,613.84		75,013,559.09
Accounts Receivable						186,640.71				186,640.71	
Unfilled Customer Orders						3,140,114.89				-78,137.06	3,218,251.95
Fund Equities:											
Unobligated Balances (Expired)						-33,319,777.34				15,417,018.65	-48,736,795.99
Unobligated Balances (Unexpired)						-58,502,690.66				69,915,459.17	-128,418,149.83
Accounts Payable						-192,111,635.72				8,564,799.18	-200,676,434.90
Undelivered Orders						-81,699,549.64				3,882,282.44	-85,581,832.08
	Subtotal	36		0151		-0-	1,585,668,806.00		1,478,158,391.78	107,510,414.22	-0-
Information Technology Systems, Department Of Veterans Affairs											
Fund Resources:											
Undisbursed Funds:											
	2007-2008					599,543,723.32	1,213,820,000.00		606,786,786.84		607,033,213.16
	2006-2007	36		0167		9,740,539.92	-1,073,749.00		499,258,452.99		99,211,521.33
	2006								1,156,346.10		8,584,193.82
	No Year						35,100,000.00		4,174,900.00		30,925,100.00
Fund Equities:											
Unobligated Balances (Expired)						-21,856.95				7,671,989.46	-7,693,846.41
Unobligated Balances (Unexpired)						-139,857,245.10				-111,472,889.11	-28,384,355.99
Accounts Payable						-303,472,189.10				178,241,415.04	-481,713,604.14
Undelivered Orders						-165,932,972.09				62,029,249.68	-227,962,221.77
	Subtotal	36		0167		-0-	1,247,846,251.00		1,111,376,485.93	136,469,765.07	-0-
Office Of Inspector General, Department Of Veterans Affairs											
Fund Resources:											
Undisbursed Funds:											
	2007-2008	36		0170		9,598,291.03	70,641,280.00		61,714,811.74		8,926,468.26
	2006-2007					4,216,200.63			6,866,028.57		2,732,262.46
	2005-2006					1,538,066.28			2,284,001.33		1,932,199.30
	2004-2005					525,910.68			834,147.14		703,919.14
	2003-2004					1,287,697.07			3,061.81		522,848.87
	2002								-6,265.06		
Fund Equities:											
Unobligated Balances (Expired)						-1,892,349.83				-272,055.48	-1,620,294.35
Unobligated Balances (Unexpired)						-18,062.19				-9,460.50	-8,601.69
Accounts Payable						-11,243,574.51				-328,405.82	-10,915,168.69
Undelivered Orders						-4,012,179.16				-1,738,545.86	-2,273,633.30
	Subtotal	36		0170		-0-	70,641,280.00		71,695,785.53	-1,054,505.53	-0-
Grants For Construction Of State Extended Care Facilities, Department Of Veterans Affairs											
Fund Resources:											
Undisbursed Funds:											
	No Year	36		0181		253,478,549.21	85,000,000.00		108,792,537.40		229,686,011.81
Fund Equities:											
Unobligated Balances (Unexpired)						-202,942.51				11,485,092.87	-11,688,035.38

Appropriations, Outlays, and Balances - Continued

Appropriation or Fund Account — Title	Period of Availability	Dept Reg	Tr From	Account Number	Sub No.	Balances, Beginning Of Fiscal Year	Appropriations And Other Obligational Authority[1]	Transfers Borrowings And Investment (Net)[2]	Outlays (Net)	Balances Withdrawn And Other Transactions[3]	Balances, End Of Fiscal Year[4]
Accounts Payable										15,184,755.00	-15,184,755.00
Undelivered Orders										-50,462,385.27	-202,813,221.43
Subtotal	Subtotal	36		0181		-253,275,606.70	85,000,000.00		108,792,537.40	-23,792,537.40	-0-
Grants For The Construction Of State Veterans Cemeteries, Department Of Veterans Affairs											
Fund Resources:											
Undisbursed Funds	No Year	36		0183		40,655,626.19	32,000,000.00		25,584,591.76		47,071,034.43
Fund Equities:											
Unobligated Balances (Unexpired)						-14,225,545.16				-13,887,193.00	-338,352.16
Accounts Payable						-10,892,993.99				-508,101.28	-10,384,892.71
Undelivered Orders						-15,537,087.04				20,810,702.52	-36,347,789.56
Subtotal	Subtotal	36		0183		-0-	32,000,000.00		25,584,591.76	6,415,408.24	-0-
Public Enterprise Funds											
Pershing Hall Revolving Fund											
Fund Resources:											
Undisbursed Funds	No Year	36		4018		379,236.03			-51,323.36		430,559.39
Fund Equities:											
Unobligated Balances (Unexpired)						-379,130.55				21,383.36	-400,513.91
Accounts Payable						-105.48				29,940.00	-30,045.48
Subtotal	Subtotal	36		4018		-0-			-51,323.36	51,323.36	-0-
Intragovernmental Funds											
Supply Fund, Department Of Veterans Affairs											
Fund Resources:											
Undisbursed Funds	No Year	36		4537		302,480,263.35			29,708,151.32	73,534,472.34	272,772,112.03
Accounts Receivable						142,666,190.97					69,131,718.63
Unfilled Customer Orders						2,185,547,392.18				239,852,934.94	1,945,694,457.24
Fund Equities:											
Unobligated Balances (Unexpired)						-1,392,063,915.34				84,709,510.03	-1,476,773,425.37
Accounts Payable						-207,387,035.47				-93,097,175.16	-114,289,860.31
Undelivered Orders						-1,031,242,895.69				-334,707,893.47	-696,535,002.22
Subtotal	Subtotal	36		4537		-0-			29,708,151.32	-29,708,151.32	-0-
Franchise Fund, Department Of Veterans Affairs											
Fund Resources:											
Undisbursed Funds	No Year	36		4539		147,784,697.90			10,275,503.51	15,318,523.02	137,509,194.39
Accounts Receivable						48,386,912.40					33,068,389.38
Unfilled Customer Orders						47,451,714.52				-29,263,140.96	76,714,855.48
Fund Equities:											
Unobligated Balances (Unexpired)						-150,350,926.28				41,730,534.78	-192,081,461.06
Accounts Payable						-92,860,070.91				-39,093,804.66	-53,766,266.25
Undelivered Orders						-412,327.63				1,032,384.31	-1,444,711.94
Subtotal	Subtotal	36		4539		-0-			10,275,503.51	-10,275,503.51	-0-

Footnotes At End Of Chapter

Appropriations, Outlays, and Balances – Continued

Appropriation or Fund Account — Title	Period of Availability	Account Symbol — Dept — Reg	Tr From	Account Number	Sub No.	Balances, Beginning Of Fiscal Year	Appropriations And Other Obligational Authority[1]	Transfers Borrowings And Investment (Net)[2]	Outlays (Net)	Balances Withdrawn And Other Transactions[3]	Balances, End Of Fiscal Year[4]
Trust Fund Accounts											
Department Of Veterans Affairs Cemetery Gift Fund, Department Of Veterans Affairs											
Fund Resources:											
Undisbursed Funds	No Year	36		8129		628,144.59	128,377.63		115,314.07		641,208.15
Fund Equities:											
Unobligated Balances (Unexpired)						-626,841.92				10,979.63	-637,821.55
Accounts Payable						-1,302.67				-441.67	-861.00
Undelivered Orders										2,525.60	-2,525.60
Subtotal		36		8129		-0-	128,377.63		115,314.07	13,063.56	-0-
Total, Departmental Administration							4,105,451,958.63		3,696,255,691.39	409,196,267.24	
Deductions For Offsetting Receipts											
Proprietary Receipts From The Public							-3,606,623,985.81	-3,606,623,985.81	-3,606,623,985.81		
Intrabudgetary Transactions							-3,420,692.42	-3,420,692.42	-3,420,692.42		
Total, Department Of Veterans Affairs							79,216,511,998.26	72,819,881,237.01	72,819,881,237.01	6,396,630,761.25	
Memorandum											
Financing Accounts											
Public Enterprise Funds											
Vocational Rehabilitation Direct Loan Financing Account, Department Of Veterans Affairs											
Fund Resources:											
Undisbursed Funds	No Year	36		4112		49,208.97		-628,140.55	-754,160.35		175,228.77
Authority To Borrow From The Treasury	No Year					113,205.00	2,658,600.60	-2,779,679.60			-7,874.00
Fund Equities:											
Unobligated Balances (Unexpired)						-162,413.97				2,420.86	-164,834.83
Accounts Payable										2,519.94	-2,519.94
Subtotal		36		4112		-0-	2,658,600.60	-3,407,820.15	-754,160.35	4,940.80	-0-
Veterans Housing Benefit Program Fund, Loan Sale Securities, Guaranteed Loan Financing Account, Department Of Veterans Affairs											
Fund Resources:											
Undisbursed Funds	No Year	36		4124		165,422,553.73		[10]54,567,627.29	92,212,601.99		127,777,579.03
Funds Held Outside The Treasury	No Year					23,467,527.28		5,599,311.25			29,066,838.53
Authority To Borrow From The Treasury							67,125,872.69	-67,125,872.69			
Accounts Receivable										-4,489,718.97	4,489,718.97
Fund Equities:											
Unobligated Balances (Unexpired)						-188,890,081.01				-32,045,663.45	-156,844,417.56
Accounts Payable										4,489,718.97	-4,489,718.97
Subtotal		36		4124		-0-	67,125,872.69	-6,958,934.15	92,212,601.99	-32,045,663.45	-0-

Appropriations, Outlays, and Balances - Continued

Appropriation or Fund Account — Title	Dept Reg	Tr From	Account Number	Sub No.	Period of Availability	Balances, Beginning Of Fiscal Year	Appropriations And Other Obligational Authority[1]	Transfers Borrowings And Investment (Net)[2]	Outlays (Net)	Balances Withdrawn And Other Transactions[3]	Balances, End Of Fiscal Year[4]
Veterans Housing Benefit Program Fund Direct Loan Financing Account, Department Of Veterans Affairs											
Fund Resources:											
Undisbursed Funds	36		4127		No Year	139,139,733.61		-9,654,727.87	114,276,393.35		15,208,612.39
Authority To Borrow From The Treasury							496,468,201.71	-496,468,201.71		-22,170,637.56	22,170,637.56
Accounts Receivable										-54,006,151.77	[11]10,442,424.78
Fund Equities:											
Unobligated Balances (Unexpired)						-43,563,726.99				-47,754,331.89	-47,821,674.73
Accounts Payable						-95,576,006.62				-123,931,121.22	-0-
Subtotal	36		4127		Subtotal	-0-	496,468,201.71	-506,122,929.58	114,276,393.35		
Veterans Housing Benefit Program Fund Guaranteed Loan Financing Account, Department Of Veterans Affairs											
Fund Resources:											
Undisbursed Funds	36		4129		No Year	3,358,265,452.42			510,901,278.25		2,847,364,174.17
Authority To Borrow From The Treasury							101,737,000.00				101,737,000.00
Accounts Receivable						987,883,358.17				64,791,733.73	23,091,624.44
Fund Equities:											
Unobligated Balances (Unexpired)						[9]3,326,014,062.71				-418,017,853.75	-2,907,996,208.96
Accounts Payable						[9]120,134,747.88				-55,938,158.23	-64,196,589.65
Subtotal	36		4129		Subtotal	-0-	101,737,000.00		510,901,278.25	-409,164,278.25	-0-
Native American Veteran Housing Direct Loan Financing Account, Department Of Veterans Affairs											
Fund Resources:											
Undisbursed Funds	36		4130		No Year	679,525.95		17,178,722.56	4,753,191.39		13,105,057.12
Authority To Borrow From The Treasury							21,621,238.02	-21,621,238.02		-571,097.28	571,097.28
Fund Equities:											
Unobligated Balances (Unexpired)						1,404,263.59				11,271,031.65	-9,866,768.06
Accounts Payable						-12,920.50				558,176.78	-571,097.28
Undelivered Orders						-2,070,869.04				1,167,420.02	-3,238,289.06
Subtotal	36		4130		Subtotal	-0-	21,621,238.02	-4,442,515.46	4,753,191.39	12,425,531.17	-0-
Guaranteed Transitional Housing Loans For Homeless Veterans Guaranteed Loan Financing Account, Department Of Veterans Affairs											
Fund Resources:											
Undisbursed Funds	36		4258		No Year	37,240.00		[12]2,426,933.05	-2,506,054.64		4,970,227.69
Authority To Borrow From The Treasury						4,862,760.00	2,474,013.96	-2,474,013.96		4,862,760.00	
Fund Equities:											
Unobligated Balances (Unexpired)						-2,404,609.24				2,518,548.24	-4,923,157.48
Accounts Payable						-23,015.36				24,054.85	-47,070.21
Undelivered Orders						-2,472,375.40				-2,472,375.40	-0-
Subtotal	36		4258		Subtotal	-0-	2,474,013.96	-2,506,054.64	-2,506,054.64	4,932,987.69	
Total, Financing Accounts							692,084,926.98	-520,979,280.25	718,883,249.99	-547,777,603.26	

Appropriations, Outlays, and Balances – Continued

Footnotes

1. The amounts in this column, unless otherwise footnoted, represent appropriations, increases and rescissions in borrowing authority or new contract authority. Appropriation accounts with appropriation transfer activity are presented in Table 1 (Appropriations and Appropriation Transfers) at the end of this chapter.

2. The amounts in this column, unless otherwise footnoted, represent transfers - other than appropriation transfers, borrowings (gross), investments (net), unrealized discounts or cash held outside of the Treasury.

3. The amounts in this column, unless otherwise footnoted, represent obligated balances canceled for fiscal year 2002 pursuant to 31 U.S.C. 1553, changes in unfilled customer orders, accounts receivable, accounts payable, undelivered orders, unobligated balances and adjustments to borrowing and contract authority

4. Unobligated balances for no-year or unexpired multiple year accounts are available for obligation; unobligated balances for expired fiscal year accounts are not available for obligation.

5. Pursuant to P.L. 112 STAT 2467; 2468, the balance for this account has been extended beyond the normal period of availability to liquidate obligations.

6. Pursuant to P.L. 112 STAT 2461, the balance for this account has been extended beyond the normal period of availability to liquidate obligations.

7. Pursuant to P.L. 111 STAT 1350 Sec. 109, the balance for this account has been extended beyond the normal period of availability to liquidate obligations.

8. Represents capital transfer to miscellaneous receipts.

9. The opening balances of the following accounts have been adjusted during the current fiscal year and do not agree with last year's closing balances:

Account	Adjustment
36 X 4025 - Accounts Receivable	-$1,226,538.19
36 X 4025 - Unobligated Balances (Unexpired)	$1,226,538.19
36 X 4129 - Accounts Receivable	-16,721,947.97
36 X 4129 - Unobligated Balances (Unexpired)	33,443,895.94
36 X 4129 - Accounts Payable	-16,721,947.97

10. Includes $60,166,938.54 which represents net borrowing from the U.S. Treasury.

11. Subject to disposition by the administrative agency.

12. Includes $2,462,534.49 which represents net borrowing from the Federal Financing Bank in lieu of issuance of agency debt.
    Includes $35,601.44 which represents net repayment of borrowing from the U.S. Treasury.

Appropriations, Outlays, and Balances - Continued

Footnotes

Table 1 - Appropriations And Appropriation Transfers - Department Of Veterans Affairs

Department Regular	Fiscal Year	Account Symbol	Net Appropriations And Appropriations Transfers	Appropriation Amount	Net Appropriation Transfers	Department Regular Involved	Fiscal Year Involved	Accounts Involved	Amount From or To (-)
36	X	0102	38,622,360,000.00	38,172,360,000.00	450,000,000.00	36	X	0137	450,000,000.00
36	07	0129	159,730,244.00	160,746,620.00	-1,016,376.00	36	0708	0129	-500,000.00
						36	07	0151	-516,376.00
36	0708	0129	500,000.00	500,000.00		36	07	0129	500,000.00
36	X	0137	2,812,006,000.00	3,262,006,000.00	-450,000,000.00	36	X	0102	-450,000,000.00
36	X	0151	81,950,000.00	83,200,000.00	-1,250,000.00	21	X	2020	-1,250,000.00
36	07	0151	1,450,070,480.00	1,481,472,430.00	-31,401,950.00	36	07	0129	516,376.00
						36	0708	0151	-53,648,326.00
						36	07	0152	8,846,000.00
						36	07	0162	13,587,000.00
						47	07	0110	-703,000.00
36	0708	0151	53,648,326.00	0.00	53,648,326.00	36	07	0151	53,648,326.00
36	X	0152	260,900,000.00	250,000,000.00	10,900,000.00	36	X	0160	10,900,000.00
36	0607	0152	-5,207,156.00	0.00	-5,207,156.00	36	0607	0162	-5,207,156.00
36	07	0152	3,169,121,690.00	2,927,967,690.00	241,154,000.00	36	07	0151	-8,846,000.00
						36	07	0160	250,000,000.00
						36	X	0152	-10,900,000.00
36	X	0160	2,633,046,833.03	466,778,000.00	2,166,268,833.03	36	X	0162	-42,000,000.00
						36	X	5287	2,219,168,833.03
36	0607	0160	-1,870,293.00	0.00	-1,870,293.00	36	0607	0162	-1,870,293.00
36	07	0160	23,786,186,360.00	25,518,254,360.00	-1,732,068,000.00	36	07	0152	-250,000,000.00
						36	0708	0160	-1,100,000,000.00
						36	07	0162	-347,068,000.00
						36	X	0165	-35,000,000.00
36	0708	0160	1,100,000,000.00	0.00	1,100,000,000.00	36	07	0160	1,100,000,000.00
36	X	0162	637,000,000.00	595,000,000.00	42,000,000.00	36	X	0160	42,000,000.00
36	0607	0162	8,151,198.00	0.00	8,151,198.00	36	0607	0152	5,207,156.00
						36	0607	0160	1,870,293.00
						36	0607	0167	1,073,749.00
36	07	0162	3,653,014,350.00	3,319,533,350.00	333,481,000.00	36	07	0151	-13,587,000.00
						36	07	0160	347,068,000.00
36	X	0165	70,000,000.00	0.00	70,000,000.00	36	07	0160	35,000,000.00
						97	07	0130	35,000,000.00
36	0607	0167	-1,073,749.00	0.00	-1,073,749.00	36	0607	0162	-1,073,749.00
36	X	5287	-2,219,168,833.03	0.00	-2,219,168,833.03	36	X	0160	-2,219,168,833.03
Totals			76,270,365,450.00	76,237,318,450.00	33,047,000.00				33,047,000.00

Appropriations, Outlays, and Balances – Continued

Title	Period of Availability	Reg	Tr From	Account Number	Sub No.	Balances, Beginning Of Fiscal Year	Appropriations And Other Obligational Authority[1]	Transfers Borrowings And Investment (Net)[2]	Outlays (Net)	Balances Withdrawn And Other Transactions[3]	Balances, End Of Fiscal Year[4]
Corps Of Engineers											
General Fund Accounts											
Flood Control, Mississippi River And Tributaries, Arkansas, Illinois, Kentucky, Louisiana, Mississippi, Missouri And Tennessee, Corps Of Engineers, Civil											
Fund Resources:											
Undisbursed Funds	No Year	96		3112		257,286,933.42	410,306,290.00	-13,741,000.00	389,528,808.87		264,323,414.55
Accounts Receivable						11,826.95				-222,518.88	234,345.83
Unfilled Customer Orders						15,240,360.64				4,708,130.33	10,532,230.31
Fund Equities:											
Unobligated Balances (Unexpired)						-141,321,066.64				-23,512,996.61	-117,808,070.03
Accounts Payable						-31,868,175.90				-16,376,330.66	-15,491,845.24
Undelivered Orders						-99,349,878.47				42,440,196.95	-141,790,075.42
Subtotal		96		3112		-0-	410,306,290.00	-13,741,000.00	389,528,808.87	7,036,481.13	-0-
General Investigations, Corps Of Engineers, Civil											
Fund Resources:											
Undisbursed Funds	2002-2003	96		3121		57,385.37				57,385.37	
Undisbursed Funds	No Year	96				111,690,688.80	171,080,720.00		143,503,972.02		139,267,436.78
Accounts Receivable						2,240,242.54				-2,357,231.75	4,597,474.29
Unfilled Customer Orders						45,986,785.76				4,859,424.85	41,127,360.91
Fund Equities:											
Unobligated Balances (Expired)						-57,385.37				-57,385.37	
Unobligated Balances (Unexpired)						-118,125,291.04				-8,475,966.67	-109,649,324.37
Accounts Payable						-7,049,343.96				2,197,965.25	-9,247,309.21
Undelivered Orders						-34,743,082.10				31,352,556.30	-66,095,638.40
Subtotal		96		3121		-0-	171,080,720.00		143,503,972.02	27,576,747.98	-0-
Construction, Corps Of Engineers, Civil											
Fund Resources:											
Undisbursed Funds	No Year	96		3122		1,895,476,245.33	2,213,330,293.58		1,616,665,821.64		2,492,140,717.27
Accounts Receivable						47,190,194.22				-58,020,506.01	105,210,700.23
Unfilled Customer Orders						1,841,713,362.74				-370,783,746.23	2,212,497,108.97
Fund Equities:											
Unobligated Balances (Unexpired)						-2,277,630,615.70				129,551,590.37	-2,407,182,206.07
Accounts Payable						-154,014,960.12				31,573,272.75	-185,588,232.87
Undelivered Orders						-1,352,734,226.47				864,343,861.06	-2,217,078,087.53
Subtotal		96		3122		-0-	2,213,330,293.58		1,616,665,821.64	596,664,471.94	-0-
Operation And Maintenance, General, Corps Of Engineers, Civil											
Fund Resources:											
Undisbursed Funds	No Year	96		3123		894,085,393.77	1,087,001,351.93	73,796,038.06	1,310,263,153.36		744,619,630.40
Accounts Receivable						10,124,510.83				-4,811,548.28	14,936,059.11
Unfilled Customer Orders						33,787,882.70				-7,670,929.07	41,458,811.77
Fund Equities:											
Unobligated Balances (Unexpired)						-290,243,805.40				-41,936,230.35	-248,307,575.05
Accounts Payable						-140,223,041.32				-17,100,951.65	-123,122,089.67
Undelivered Orders						-507,530,940.58				-77,946,104.02	-429,584,836.56
Subtotal		96		3123		-0-	1,087,001,351.93	73,796,038.06	1,310,263,153.36	-149,465,763.37	-0-

Appropriations, Outlays, and Balances - Continued

Appropriation or Fund Account — Title	Period of Availability	Reg	Tr From	Account Number	Sub No.	Balances, Beginning Of Fiscal Year	Appropriations And Other Obligational Authority[1]	Transfers Borrowings And Investment (Net)[2]	Outlays (Net)	Balances Withdrawn And Other Transactions[3]	Balances, End Of Fiscal Year[4]
General Expenses, Corps Of Engineers, Civil											
Fund Resources:											
Undisbursed Funds	No Year	96		3124		37,215,029.33	167,249,740.00		158,185,033.37		46,279,735.96
Accounts Receivable						203,530.48				22,816.20	180,714.28
Unfilled Customer Orders						6,096,206.80				-2,731,959.40	8,828,166.20
Fund Equities:											
Unobligated Balances (Unexpired)						-4,241,472.04				2,209,723.51	-6,451,195.55
Accounts Payable						-1,431,405.50				67,920.96	-1,499,326.46
Undelivered Orders						-37,841,889.07				9,496,205.36	-47,338,094.43
Subtotal		96		3124		-0-	167,249,740.00		158,185,033.37	9,064,706.63	-0-
Flood Control And Coastal Emergencies, Corps Of Engineers, Civil											
Fund Resources:											
Undisbursed Funds	No Year	96		3125		3,119,373,416.22	1,547,259,000.00	13,741,000.00	-852,793,834.19		5,533,167,250.41
Accounts Receivable						1,861,617,032.52				1,564,693,906.65	296,923,125.87
Unfilled Customer Orders						2,517,578,839.21				1,166,981,409.72	1,350,597,429.49
Fund Equities:											
Unobligated Balances (Unexpired)						-5,884,071,340.72				71,684,922.07	-5,955,756,262.79
Accounts Payable						-138,400,415.18				122,574,524.27	-260,974,939.45
Undelivered Orders						-1,476,097,532.05				-512,140,928.52	-963,956,603.53
Subtotal		96		3125		-0-	1,547,259,000.00	13,741,000.00	-852,793,834.19	2,413,793,834.19	-0-
Regulatory Program, Corps Of Engineers, Civil											
Fund Resources:											
Undisbursed Funds	No Year	96		3126		16,975,218.29	159,273,180.00		156,266,292.65		19,982,105.64
Accounts Receivable						120,009.63				26,702.16	93,307.47
Unfilled Customer Orders						1,923,470.72				910,469.48	1,013,001.24
Fund Equities:											
Unobligated Balances (Unexpired)						-12,552,373.07				1,711,858.25	-14,264,231.32
Accounts Payable						-643,946.16				224,912.75	-868,858.91
Undelivered Orders						-5,822,379.41				132,944.71	-5,955,324.12
Subtotal		96		3126		-0-	159,273,180.00		156,266,292.65	3,006,887.35	-0-
Washington Aqueduct Capital Improvements, Corps Of Engineers											
Fund Resources:											
Undisbursed Funds	No Year	96		3128		4,095.06		-674,845.55	-674,845.55		4,095.06
Fund Equities:											
Unobligated Balances (Unexpired)						-3,995.06					-3,995.06
Accounts Payable						-100.00					-100.00
Subtotal		96		3128		-0-		-674,845.55	-674,845.55		-0-
Payment To The South Dakota Terrestrial Wildlife Habitat Restoration Trust Fund											
Fund Resources:											
Undisbursed Funds	2007	96		3129			10,000,000.00		10,000,000.00		
Formerly Utilized Sites Remedial Action Program, Corps Of Engineers											
Fund Resources:											
Undisbursed Funds	No Year	96		3130		41,440,268.17	138,671,940.00		127,454,460.97		52,657,747.20
Accounts Receivable						3,775.73				-3,224.27	7,000.00
Unfilled Customer Orders						633,759.95				-377,220.33	1,010,980.28
Fund Equities:											
Unobligated Balances (Unexpired)						-5,275,316.81				-478,646.94	-4,796,669.87

Footnotes At End Of Chapter

Appropriations, Outlays, and Balances – Continued

Appropriation or Fund Account — Title	Period of Availability	Dept Reg	Dept Tr From	Account Number	Sub No.	Balances, Beginning Of Fiscal Year	Appropriations And Other Obligational Authority[1]	Transfers Borrowings And Investment (Net)[2]	Outlays (Net)	Balances Withdrawn And Other Transactions[3]	Balances, End Of Fiscal Year[4]
Formerly Utilized Sites Remedial Action Program, Corps Of Engineers - Continued											
Fund Equities: - Continued											
Accounts Payable						-15,237,925.36				8,385,273.40	-23,623,198.76
Undelivered Orders						-21,564,561.68				3,691,297.17	-25,255,858.85
Subtotal		96		3130		-0-	138,671,940.00		127,454,460.97	11,217,479.03	-0-
Office Of Assistant Secretary Of The Army (Civil Works), Corps Of Engineers											
Fund Resources:											
Undisbursed Funds	2007	96		3132			3,979,404.00		3,939,533.57		39,870.43
	2006					1,330,116.54			1,325,588.90		4,527.64
	2005					128,679.98					128,679.98
Fund Equities:											
Accounts Payable										4,527.64	-4,527.64
Undelivered Orders						-1,458,796.52				-1,290,246.11	-168,550.41
Subtotal		96		3132		-0-	3,979,404.00		5,265,122.47	-1,285,718.47	-0-
Special Fund Accounts											
Hydraulic Mining In California, Debris Fund											
Fund Resources:											
Undisbursed Funds	No Year	96		5066		265.79	97,889.43		97,874.64		280.58
Fund Equities:											
Unobligated Balances (Unexpired)						-265.79				14.79	-280.58
Subtotal		96		5066		-0-	97,889.43		97,874.64	14.79	-0-
Payments To States, Flood Control Act Of 1954											
Fund Resources:											
Undisbursed Funds	No Year	96		5090			9,187,226.93		9,187,226.93		
Maintenance And Operation Of Dams And Other Improvements Of Navigable Waters											
Fund Resources:											
Undisbursed Funds	No Year	96		5125		5,286,385.06	7,609,936.68		3,725,030.34		9,171,291.40
Fund Equities:											
Unobligated Balances (Unexpired)						-5,270,601.33				360,334.57	-5,630,935.90
Accounts Payable						-1,300.00				480,700.00	-482,000.00
Undelivered Orders						-14,483.73				3,043,871.77	-3,058,355.50
Subtotal		96		5125		-0-	7,609,936.68		3,725,030.34	3,884,906.34	-0-
Intragovernmental Funds											
Revolving Fund, Corps Of Engineers, Civil											
Fund Resources:											
Undisbursed Funds	No Year	96		4902		1,090,768,806.65			-87,820,936.45	90,757,783.29	1,178,589,743.10
Accounts Receivable						10,131,049.37				31,289.44	10,099,759.93
Unfilled Customer Orders						31,623,200.49				-15,507,735.63	47,130,936.12
Fund Equities:											
Unobligated Balances (Unexpired)						-163,622,539.31				90,757,783.29	-254,380,322.60
Accounts Payable						-532,664,752.98				9,894,714.84	-542,559,467.82
Undelivered Orders						-436,235,764.22				2,644,884.51	-438,880,648.73

Appropriations, Outlays, and Balances - Continued

Appropriation or Fund Account — Title	Dept Reg	Tr From	Account Number	Sub No.	Period of Availability	Balances, Beginning Of Fiscal Year	Appropriations And Other Obligational Authority[1]	Transfers Borrowings And Investment (Net)[2]	Outlays (Net)	Balances Withdrawn And Other Transactions[3]	Balances, End Of Fiscal Year[4]
Subtotal	96		4902		Subtotal	-0-			-87,820,936.45	87,820,936.45	-0-
Trust Fund Accounts											
Inland Waterways Trust Fund											
Fund Resources:											
Undisbursed Funds	20		8861		No Year	4,276,819.96	105,653,559.36	-104,672,379.32			5,258,000.00
Transfer To:											
Corps Of Engineers	96	20	8861		No Year	1,756,747.79		159,767,055.44	160,150,009.84	160,150,009.84	1,373,793.39
Unrealized Discount On Investments						-2,082,699.89		563,081.18			-1,519,618.71
Investments In Public Debt Securities						260,898,000.00		-55,657,757.30			205,240,242.70
Accounts Receivable											-0-
Fund Equities:											
Unobligated Balances (Unexpired)						-239,036,543.96				-91,867,327.89	-147,169,216.07
Accounts Payable						-9,693,242.63				3,934,496.51	-13,627,739.14
Undelivered Orders						-16,119,081.27				33,436,380.90	-49,555,462.17
Subtotal	20		8861			-0-	105,653,559.36		160,150,009.84	-54,496,450.48	-0-
Harbor Maintenance Trust Fund											
Fund Resources:											
Undisbursed Funds	20		8863		No Year	87,026,869.35	1,407,357,738.12	-1,413,481,795.87			80,902,811.60
Transfer To:											
Corps Of Engineers	96	20	8863		No Year	-18,161,146.65		890,624,803.05	890,624,803.05	890,624,803.05	-46,896,278.28
Unrealized Discount On Investments								-28,735,131.63			
Investments In Public Debt Securities						3,163,512,000.00		551,592,124.45			3,715,104,124.45
Fund Equities:											
Unobligated Balances (Unexpired)						-3,232,214,882.70				516,895,775.07	-3,749,110,657.77
Accounts Payable						-162,840.00		-162,840.00		-162,840.00	
Subtotal	20		8863			-0-	1,407,357,738.12		890,624,803.05	516,732,935.07	-0-
South Dakota Terrestrial Wildlife Habitat Restoration Trust Fund											
Fund Resources:											
Undisbursed Funds	96		8217		No Year		13,730,976.66	-13,730,976.66			-550,710.37
Unrealized Discount On Investments						-476,956.06		-73,754.31			
Investments In Public Debt Securities						89,003,471.16		13,804,730.97			102,808,202.13
Fund Equities:											
Unobligated Balances (Unexpired)						-88,526,515.10				13,730,976.66	-102,257,491.76
Accounts Payable											
Subtotal	96		8217			-0-	13,730,976.66			13,730,976.66	-0-
Coastal Wetlands Restoration Trust Fund											
Fund Resources:											
Undisbursed Funds	96		8333		No Year	666,124.14	63,989,378.69		62,932,874.37		1,722,628.46
Accounts Receivable						392,413,695.80				-12,413,493.19	404,827,188.99
Fund Equities:											
Unobligated Balances (Unexpired)						-123,503,342.81				28,801,724.10	-152,305,066.91
Accounts Payable						-2,400.20				56,298.10	-58,698.30
Undelivered Orders						-269,574,076.93				-15,388,024.69	-254,186,052.24
Subtotal	96		8333			-0-	63,989,378.69		62,932,874.37	1,056,504.32	-0-

Footnotes At End Of Chapter

Appropriations, Outlays, and Balances – Continued

Appropriation or Fund Account	Account Symbol					Balances, Beginning Of Fiscal Year	Appropriations And Other Obligational Authority[1]	Transfers Borrowings And Investment (Net)[2]	Outlays (Net)	Balances Withdrawn And Other Transactions[3]	Balances, End Of Fiscal Year[4]
Title	Period of Availability	Dept		Account Number	Sub No.						
		Reg	Tr From								
Rivers And Harbors Contributed And Advance Funds, Corps Of Engineers, Civil											
Fund Resources:											
Undisbursed Funds	No Year	96		8862		504,200,137.25	396,298,198.36		337,621,424.40		562,876,911.21
Unfilled Customer Orders						33,729.54				11,729.54	22,000.00
Fund Equities:											
Unobligated Balances (Unexpired)						-327,745,060.49				20,468,016.87	-348,213,077.36
Accounts Payable						-12,118,252.10				3,406,669.47	-15,524,921.57
Undelivered Orders						-164,370,554.20				34,790,358.08	-199,160,912.28
Subtotal		96		8862		-0-	396,298,198.36		337,621,424.40	58,676,773.96	-0-
Deductions For Offsetting Receipts											
Proprietary Receipts From The Public							-511,759,758.88		-511,759,758.88		
Intrabudgetary Transactions							-10,333,285.01		-10,333,285.01		
Total, Corps Of Engineers							7,369,983,779.85	73,121,192.51	3,918,089,248.84	3,545,015,723.52	

Appropriations, Outlays, and Balances - Continued

Footnotes

1   The amounts in this column, unless otherwise footnoted, represent appropriations, increases and rescissions in borrowing authority or new contract authority. Appropriation accounts with appropriation transfer activity are presented in Table 1 (Appropriations and Appropriation Transfers) at the end of this chapter.

2   The amounts in this column, unless otherwise footnoted, represent transfers - other than appropriation transfers, borrowings (gross), investments (net), unrealized discounts or funds held outside the Treasury.

3   The amounts in this column, unless otherwise footnoted, represent obligated balances canceled for fiscal year 2002 pursuant to 31 U.S.C. 1553, changes in unfilled customer orders, accounts receivable, accounts payable, undelivered orders, unobligated balances and adjustments to borrowing and contract authority

4   Unobligated balances for no-year or unexpired multiple year accounts are available for obligation; unobligated balances for expired fiscal year accounts are not available for obligation.

Appropriations, Outlays, and Balances – Continued

Footnotes

Table 1 - Appropriations And Appropriation Transfers - Corps Of Engineers

Department Regular	Fiscal Year	Account Symbol	Net Appropriations And Appropriations Transfers	Appropriation Amount	Net Appropriation Transfers	Department Regular Involved	Fiscal Year Involved	Accounts Involved	Amount From or To (-)
20	X	8863	-19,249,160.00	0.00	-19,249,160.00	69	X	8003	-16,223,160.00
						70	X	8870	-3,026,000.00
96	X	3112	410,306,290.00	396,565,290.00	13,741,000.00	96	X	3125	13,741,000.00
96	X	3122	2,213,330,293.58	2,213,664,239.58	-333,946.00	14	X	2100	-333,946.00
96	X	3123	1,087,001,351.93	1,043,958,596.01	43,042,755.92	96	X	5007	42,003,249.41
						96	X	5493	1,039,506.51
96	X	3125	1,547,259,000.00	1,561,000,000.00	-13,741,000.00	96	X	3112	-13,741,000.00
96	X	5007	0.00	42,003,249.41	42,003,249.41	96	X	3123	42,003,249.41
96	X	5493	0.00	1,039,506.51	-1,039,506.51	96	X	3123	-1,039,506.51
96	X	8333	63,989,378.69	0.00	63,989,378.69	14	X	8151	63,989,378.69
Totals			5,302,637,154.20	5,258,230,881.51	44,406,272.69				44,406,272.69

Appropriations, Outlays, and Balances – Continued

Footnotes

This Page Left Blank Intentionally

Appropriations, Outlays, and Balances – Continued

Appropriation or Fund Account — Title	Period of Availability	Dept Reg	Dept Tr From	Account Number	Sub No.	Balances, Beginning Of Fiscal Year	Appropriations And Other Obligational Authority[1]	Transfers Borrowings And Investment (Net)[2]	Outlays (Net)	Balances Withdrawn And Other Transactions[3]	Balances, End Of Fiscal Year[4]
Other Defense Civil Programs											
Military Retirement											
General Fund Accounts											
Payments To Military Retirement Fund, Defense											
Fund Resources:											
Undisbursed Funds	2007	97		0040			26,048,000,000.00		26,048,000,000.00		
Trust Fund Accounts											
Department Of Defense Military Retirement Fund											
Fund Resources:											
Undisbursed Funds	No Year	97		8097		30,734,795.47	53,486,133,678.89	-9,986,782,604.96	43,509,709,790.58		20,376,078.82
Unamortized Premium And Discount						23,566,605,878.48		1,565,201,053.25			25,131,806,931.73
Unamortized Premium And Discount Prior to 1987						34,369,292.86	-33,432,016.26				937,276.60
Investments In Public Debt Securities						181,809,971,141.09		8,421,581,551.71			190,231,552,692.80
Fund Equities:											
Unobligated Balances (Unexpired)						-202,031,879,608.90				9,822,597,131.84	-211,854,476,740.74
Accounts Payable											
Undelivered Orders						-3,409,801,499.00				120,394,740.21	-3,530,196,239.21
Subtotal		97		8097		-0-	53,452,701,662.63		43,509,709,790.58	9,942,991,872.05	-0-
Total, Military Retirement							79,500,701,662.63		69,557,709,790.58	9,942,991,872.05	
Retiree Health Care											
General Fund Accounts											
Payment To Department Of Defense Medicare-Eligible Retiree Health Care Fund											
Fund Resources:											
Undisbursed Funds	No Year	97		0850			15,608,000,000.00		15,608,000,000.00		
Special Fund Accounts											
Department Of Defense Medicare-Eligible Retiree Health Care Fund											
Fund Resources:											
Undisbursed Funds	No Year	97		5472		37,855,033.00	31,386,620,588.86	-23,815,387,749.45	7,604,087,872.41		5,000,000.00
Unamortized Premium And Discount						11,888,100,710.36		4,363,919,270.98			16,252,019,981.34
Investments In Public Debt Securities						72,739,925,967.67		19,451,468,478.47			92,191,394,446.14
Fund Equities:											
Unobligated Balances (Unexpired)						-84,268,709,458.26				23,810,931,994.86	-108,079,641,453.12
Accounts Payable										256,637,405.13	-256,637,405.13
Undelivered Orders						-397,172,252.77				-285,036,683.54	-112,135,569.23
Subtotal		97		5472		-0-	31,386,620,588.86		7,604,087,872.41	23,782,532,716.45	-0-
Total, Retiree Health Care							46,994,620,588.86		23,212,087,872.41	23,782,532,716.45	

Appropriations, Outlays, and Balances - Continued

Appropriation or Fund Account — Title	Period of Availability	Dept Reg	Tr From	Account Number	Sub No.	Balances, Beginning Of Fiscal Year	Appropriations And Other Obligational Authority[1]	Transfers Borrowings And Investment (Net)[2]	Outlays (Net)	Balances Withdrawn And Other Transactions[3]	Balances, End Of Fiscal Year[4]
Educational Benefits											
Trust Fund Accounts											
Department Of Defense, Education Benefits Fund											
Fund Resources:											
Undisbursed Funds	No Year	97		8098		199,730.94	601,017,804.92	-176,028,038.37	424,989,497.49		200,000.00
Unamortized Premium And Discount						753,044.73		11,431,526.64			12,184,571.37
Investments In Public Debt Securities						1,240,841,066.06		164,596,511.73			1,405,437,577.79
Fund Equities:											
Unobligated Balances (Unexpired)						-1,241,793,841.73				176,028,307.43	-1,417,822,149.16
Accounts Payable						-0-				176,028,307.43	-0-
	Subtotal	97		8098		-0-	601,017,804.92		424,989,497.49	176,028,307.43	
Total, Educational Benefits							601,017,804.92		424,989,497.49	176,028,307.43	
American Battle Monuments Commission											
General Fund Accounts											
Salaries And Expenses, American Battle Monuments Commission											
Fund Resources:											
Undisbursed Funds	No Year	74		0100		28,454,205.76	40,588,000.00	10,034,070.46	57,826,591.75		21,249,684.47
Fund Equities:											
Unobligated Balances (Unexpired)						-8,316,228.29				-488,195.13	-7,828,033.16
Accounts Payable						-6,154,598.85				202,801.98	-6,357,400.83
Undelivered Orders						-13,983,378.62				-6,919,128.14	-7,064,250.48
	Subtotal	74		0100		-0-	40,588,000.00	10,034,070.46	57,826,591.75	-7,204,521.29	-0-
Foreign Currency Fluctuations Account, American Battle Monuments Commission											
Fund Resources:											
Undisbursed Funds	No Year	74		0101		11,589,787.00	1,581,000.00	-10,034,070.46			3,136,716.54
Fund Equities:											
Unobligated Balances (Unexpired)						-11,589,787.00		-10,034,070.46		-8,453,070.46	-3,136,716.54
	Subtotal	74		0101		-0-	1,581,000.00	-10,034,070.46		-8,453,070.46	-0-
Trust Fund Accounts											
Contributions, American Battle Monuments Commission											
Fund Resources:											
Undisbursed Funds	No Year	74		8569		15,057,733.09	1,094,566.76	-7,987,838.28	3,726,395.45		4,438,066.12
Unrealized Discount On Investments								-39,161.72			-39,161.72
Investments In Public Debt Securities						58,000.00		8,027,000.00			8,085,000.00
Fund Equities:											
Unobligated Balances (Unexpired)						-10,028,127.86				1,797,549.79	-11,825,677.65
Accounts Payable						-1,757,855.72				-1,502,360.05	-255,495.67
Undelivered Orders						-3,329,749.51				-2,927,018.43	-402,731.08
	Subtotal	74		8569		-0-	1,094,566.76		3,726,395.45	-2,631,828.69	-0-

Footnotes At End Of Chapter

Appropriations, Outlays, and Balances – Continued

Appropriation or Fund Account — Title	Period of Availability	Account Symbol — Dept Reg	Account Symbol — Dept Tr From	Account Number	Sub No.	Balances, Beginning Of Fiscal Year	Appropriations And Other Obligational Authority[1]	Transfers Borrowings And Investment (Net)[2]	Outlays (Net)	Balances Withdrawn And Other Transactions[3]	Balances, End Of Fiscal Year[4]
Total, American Battle Monuments Commission						------	43,263,566.76	------	61,552,987.20	-18,289,420.44	------
Armed Forces Retirement Home											
Trust Fund Accounts											
Armed Forces Retirement Home											
Fund Resources:											
Undisbursed Funds	No Year	84		8522		239,123,691.73	66,597,280.77	-19,661,916.89	55,932,830.91		230,126,224.70
Unrealized Discount On Investments						-1,164,596.25		619,916.89			-544,679.36
Investments In Public Debt Securities						138,568,000.00		19,042,000.00			157,610,000.00
Fund Equities:											
Unobligated Balances (Unexpired)						-368,718,982.35				-209,059,293.11	-159,659,689.24
Accounts Payable						-5,299,382.90				-1,128,587.60	-4,170,795.30
Undelivered Orders						-2,508,730.23				220,852,330.57	-223,361,060.80
						-0-				10,664,449.86	-0-
	Subtotal	84		8522		-0-	66,597,280.77		55,932,830.91	10,664,449.86	
Total, Armed Forces Retirement Home							66,597,280.77		55,932,830.91	10,664,449.86	
Cemeterial Expenses											
General Fund Accounts											
Salaries And Expenses, Cemeterial Expenses, Army											
Fund Resources:											
Undisbursed Funds	No Year	21		1805		29,333,861.34	28,759,500.00		31,306,781.08		26,786,580.26
Fund Equities:											
Unobligated Balances (Unexpired)						-4,525,741.36				-2,398,059.95	-2,127,681.41
Accounts Payable						-24,804,270.98				-145,372.13	-24,658,898.85
Undelivered Orders						-3,849.00				-3,849.00	-0-
	Subtotal	21		1805		-0-	28,759,500.00		31,306,781.08	-2,547,281.08	
Total, Cemeterial Expense							28,759,500.00		31,306,781.08	-2,547,281.08	
Forest And Wildlife Conservation, Military Reservations											
Special Fund Accounts											
Wildlife Conservation, Etc., Military Reservations, Navy											
Fund Resources:											
Undisbursed Funds	No Year	17		5095		1,045,202.48	189,143.00		97,186.35		1,137,159.13
Fund Equities:											
Unobligated Balances (Unexpired)						-585,248.28				125,320.22	-710,568.50
Accounts Payable						-459,954.20				-33,363.57	-426,590.63
						-0-				91,956.65	-0-
	Subtotal	17		5095			189,143.00		97,186.35		
Wildlife Conservation, Etc., Military Reservations, Army											
Fund Resources:											
Undisbursed Funds	No Year	21		5095		4,621,959.76	1,960,153.54		1,626,213.31		4,955,899.99
Fund Equities:											
Unobligated Balances (Unexpired)						-3,462,848.42				365,023.15	-3,827,871.57

Appropriations, Outlays, and Balances - Continued

Appropriation or Fund Account — Title	Period of Availability	Dept Reg	Tr From	Account Number	Sub No.	Balances, Beginning Of Fiscal Year	Appropriations And Other Obligational Authority[1]	Transfers Borrowings And Investment (Net)[2]	Outlays (Net)	Balances Withdrawn And Other Transactions[3]	Balances, End Of Fiscal Year[4]
Accounts Payable						-428,498.66				-47,267.80	-381,230.86
Undelivered Orders						-730,612.68				16,184.88	-746,797.56
	Subtotal	21		5095		-0-	1,960,153.54		1,626,213.31	333,940.23	-0-
Department Of Defense, Forest Products Program, Army											
Fund Resources:											
Undisbursed Funds	No Year	21		5285		2,970,781.11	523,031.52				3,493,812.63
Fund Equities:											
Unobligated Balances (Unexpired)						-2,970,781.11	523,031.52			523,031.52	-3,493,812.63
	Subtotal	21		5285		-0-	523,031.52			523,031.52	-0-
Wildlife Conservation, Etc., Military Reservations, Air Force											
Fund Resources:											
Undisbursed Funds	No Year	57		5095		872,296.16	893,575.37		625,749.21		1,140,122.32
Fund Equities:											
Unobligated Balances (Unexpired)						-706,483.28				324,625.96	-1,031,109.24
Accounts Payable						17,656.99				89,040.49	-71,383.50
Undelivered Orders						-183,469.87				-145,840.29	-37,629.58
	Subtotal	57		5095		-0-	893,575.37		625,749.21	267,826.16	-0-
Total, Forest And Wildlife Conservation, Military Reservations							3,565,903.43		2,349,148.87	1,216,754.56	
Selective Service System											
General Fund Accounts											
Salaries And Expenses, Selective Service System											
Fund Resources:											
Undisbursed Funds:											
2007	2007	90		0400		5,356,336.44	24,850,423.00		19,178,114.32		5,672,308.68
2006	2006					3,409,338.45			4,292,063.63		1,064,272.81
2005	2005					2,004,168.14			281,319.71		3,128,018.74
2004	2004					1,878,245.86			34,980.81		1,969,187.33
2003	2003					894,843.87			26,147.06		1,852,098.80
2002	2002					166,263.26			452.67	894,391.20	
Accounts Receivable										-31,619.85	197,883.11
Unfilled Customer Orders										-154,121.52	154,121.52
Fund Equities:											
Unobligated Balances (Expired)						-5,959,164.68				16,375.94	-5,975,540.62
Accounts Payable						-1,977,701.22				-567,417.83	-1,410,283.39
Undelivered Orders						-5,772,330.12				879,736.86	-6,652,066.98
	Subtotal	90		0400		-0-	24,850,423.00		23,813,078.20	1,037,344.80	-0-
Total, Selective Service System							24,850,423.00		23,813,078.20	1,037,344.80	
Deductions For Offsetting Receipts											
Proprietary Receipts From The Public							-15,917,070.44		-15,917,070.44		
Intrabudgetary Transactions							-46,241,673,697.05		-46,241,673,697.05		
Total, Other Defense Civil Programs							81,005,785,962.88		47,112,151,219.25	33,893,634,743.63	

Footnotes At End Of Chapter

Appropriations, Outlays, and Balances – Continued

Footnotes

1   The amounts in this column, unless otherwise footnoted, represent appropriations, increases and rescissions in borrowing authority or new contract authority. Appropriation accounts with appropriation transfer activity are presented in Table 1 (Appropriations and Appropriation Transfers) at the end of this chapter.

2   The amounts in this column, unless otherwise footnoted, represent transfers - other than appropriation transfers, borrowings (gross), investments (net), unrealized discounts or funds held outside the Treasury.

3   The amounts in this column, unless otherwise footnoted, represent obligated balances canceled for fiscal year 2002 pursuant to 31 U.S.C. 1553, changes in unfilled customer orders, accounts receivable, accounts payable, undelivered orders, unobligated balances and adjustments to borrowing and contract authority.

4   Unobligated balances for no-year or unexpired multiple year accounts are available for obligation; unobligated balances for expired fiscal year accounts are not available for obligation.

Appropriations, Outlays, and Balances - Continued

Footnotes

Table 1 - Appropriations And Appropriation Transfers - Other Defense Civil Programs

Department Regular	Fiscal Year	Account Symbol	Net Appropriations And Appropriations Transfers	Appropriation Amount	Net Appropriation Transfers	Department Regular Involved	Fiscal Year Involved	Accounts Involved	Amount From or To (-)
74	X	0100	40,588,000.00	37,169,000.00	3,419,000.00	74	X	0101	3,419,000.00
74	X	0101	1,581,000.00	5,000,000.00	-3,419,000.00	74	X	0100	-3,419,000.00
97	X	5472	186,000,000.00	0.00	186,000,000.00	97	X	4555	186,000,000.00
Totals			228,169,000.00	42,169,000.00	186,000,000.00				186,000,000.00

Appropriations, Outlays, and Balances – Continued

Title	Period of Availability	Reg	Tr From	Account Number	Sub No.	Balances, Beginning Of Fiscal Year	Appropriations And Other Obligational Authority[1]	Transfers Borrowings And Investment (Net)[2]	Outlays (Net)	Balances Withdrawn And Other Transactions[3]	Balances, End Of Fiscal Year[4]
Environmental Protection Agency											
General Fund Accounts											
Operations, Research, And Facilities, Environmental Protection Agency											
Fund Resources:											
Undisbursed Funds	No Year	68		0100		1,063,816.74			115,565.86		948,250.88
Fund Equities:											
Unobligated Balances (Unexpired)						-6,060.58				28,631.10	-34,691.68
Accounts Payable						-459.12				12,834.93	-13,294.05
Undelivered Orders						-1,057,297.04				-157,031.89	-900,265.15
Subtotal		68		0100		-0-			115,565.86	-115,565.86	-0-
State And Tribal Assistance Grants, Environmental Protection Agency											
Fund Resources:											
Undisbursed Funds	No Year	68		0103		8,985,594,834.48	3,213,708,624.00		3,938,135,119.17		8,261,168,339.31
Accounts Receivable						27,078.17				27,078.17	
Unfilled Customer Orders						-27,078.17				-27,078.17	
Fund Equities:											
Unobligated Balances (Unexpired)						-1,310,812,692.65				19,918,059.08	-1,330,730,751.73
Accounts Payable						-370,977,578.57				180,093,213.10	-551,070,791.67
Undelivered Orders						-7,303,804,563.26				-924,437,767.35	-6,379,366,795.91
Subtotal		68		0103		-0-	3,213,708,624.00		3,938,135,119.17	-724,426,495.17	-0-
Science And Technology, Environmental Protection Agency											
Fund Resources:											
Undisbursed Funds											
	2007-2008	68		0107		364,830,968.48	733,387,489.00		381,463,347.28		351,924,141.72
	2006-2007					192,964,620.78			219,799,763.17		145,031,205.31
	2005-2006					102,454,782.62			105,027,014.54		87,937,606.24
	2004-2005					45,436,818.51			44,446,830.43		58,007,952.19
	2003-2004					20,360,596.04			21,572,242.64		23,864,575.87
	2002-2003					11,423,396.97			7,875,778.48		12,484,817.56
	2001-2002					1,187,078.09			2,813,035.34		[5]8,610,361.63
	2000-2001					2,018,736.17			336,968.06		[6]850,110.03
	1999-2000					9,577,515.29			350,609.47		[7]
	No Year								3,949,499.99	1,668,126.70	5,628,015.30
Accounts Receivable						37,061,284.66				7,932,601.13	29,128,683.53
Unfilled Customer Orders						5,316,729.18				485,712.71	4,831,016.47
Fund Equities:											
Unobligated Balances (Expired)						-21,115,207.27				10,105,907.02	-31,221,114.29
Unobligated Balances (Unexpired)						-184,758,709.72				5,956,609.21	-190,715,318.93
Accounts Payable						-84,493,117.54				9,029,822.84	-93,522,940.38
Undelivered Orders						-502,265,492.26				-89,426,380.01	-412,839,112.25
Subtotal		68		0107		-0-	733,387,489.00		787,635,089.40	-54,247,600.40	-0-
Environmental Programs And Management, Environmental Protection Agency											
Fund Resources:											
Undisbursed Funds	2007-2008	68		0108		668,844,145.38	2,358,369,711.00	-10,000.00	1,726,082,336.08		632,277,374.92
	2006-2007					1,462,164.40		10,000.00	401,949,636.36		266,904,509.02
	2006								207,293.42		1,254,870.98
	2005-2006					172,566,671.65			117,235,580.82		55,331,090.83

Appropriations, Outlays, and Balances - Continued

Appropriation or Fund Account — Title	Period of Availability	Reg	Tr From	Account Number	Sub No.	Balances, Beginning Of Fiscal Year	Appropriations And Other Obligational Authority[1]	Transfers Borrowings And Investment (Net)[2]	Outlays (Net)	Balances Withdrawn And Other Transactions[3]	Balances, End Of Fiscal Year[4]
	2004-2005					83,973,805.26			38,540,679.39		45,433,125.87
	2004					490,669.74			287,595.85		203,073.89
	2003-2004					26,519,183.61			7,696,314.48		18,822,869.13
	2003					633,455.13			419,658.55		213,796.58
	2002-2003					21,615,227.60			8,790,450.52		12,824,777.08
	2001-2002					17,538,044.72			5,118,541.88		[5]12,419,502.84
	2000-2001					5,447,554.61			1,089,701.37		[6]4,357,853.24
	1999-2000					2,848,030.67			-4,933.18	2,852,963.85	[8]-0-
	No Year					7,486,746.23			2,501,536.10		4,985,210.13
Funds Held Outside The Treasury	2007-2008							10,000.00			10,000.00
	2006-2007							-10,000.00			[10]-10,000.00
Accounts Receivable						[9]105,022,084.52				69,819,539.23	35,202,545.29
Unfilled Customer Orders						[9]441,161,938.58				28,978,475.69	412,183,462.89
Fund Equities:											
Unobligated Balances (Expired)						-267,010,469.27				151,532,332.23	-418,542,801.50
Unobligated Balances (Unexpired)						-299,949,889.08				-45,659,703.23	-254,290,185.85
Accounts Payable						-231,668,673.02				-10,645,745.34	-221,022,927.68
Undelivered Orders						-756,980,690.73				-148,422,543.07	-608,558,147.66
Subtotal		68		0108		-0-	2,358,369,711.00		2,309,914,391.64	48,455,319.36	
Energy Research And Development, Environmental Protection Agency											
Fund Resources:											
Undisbursed Funds	No Year	68		0109		698,390.94			54,431.32		643,959.62
Fund Equities:											
Unobligated Balances (Unexpired)						-600,010.92					-600,010.92
Accounts Payable										6,035.68	-6,035.68
Undelivered Orders						-98,380.02				-60,467.00	-37,913.02
Subtotal		68		0109		-0-			54,431.32	-54,431.32	-0-
Buildings And Facilities, Environmental Protection Agency											
Fund Resources:											
Undisbursed Funds	2005-2006	68		0110		1,784,787.58			1,289,754.90		495,032.68
	No Year					58,568,216.82	39,626,296.00		41,943,101.38		56,251,411.44
Fund Equities:											
Unobligated Balances (Unexpired)						-2,406,349.36				3,280,241.28	-5,686,590.64
Accounts Payable						-5,146,023.88				1,520,436.05	-6,666,459.93
Undelivered Orders						-52,800,631.16				-8,407,237.61	-44,393,393.55
Subtotal		68		0110		-0-	39,626,296.00		43,232,856.28	-3,606,560.28	-0-
Office Of Inspector General, Environmental Protection Agency											
Fund Resources:											
Undisbursed Funds	2007-2008	68		0112			37,171,947.00		28,306,844.84		8,865,102.16
	2006-2007					7,270,926.00			5,792,556.86		1,478,369.14
	2005-2006					1,358,102.15			530,656.33		827,445.82
	2004-2005					1,495,887.08			34,659.08		1,461,228.00
	2003-2004					437,479.16			27,964.20		409,514.96
	2002-2003					527,225.96			-67.05		527,293.01
	2001-2002					1,498,784.51			-339.06		[5]1,499,123.57
	2000-2001					60,317.42					[8]60,317.42
	1999-2000					40,245.04				40,245.04	-0-
Accounts Receivable						2,720,434.67				137,045.43	2,583,369.24

Footnotes At End Of Chapter

Appropriations, Outlays, and Balances – Continued

Appropriation or Fund Account — Title	Period of Availability	Dept Reg	Tr From	Account Number	Sub No.	Balances, Beginning Of Fiscal Year	Appropriations And Other Obligational Authority[1]	Transfers Borrowings And Investment (Net)[2]	Outlays (Net)	Balances Withdrawn And Other Transactions[3]	Balances, End Of Fiscal Year[4]
Office Of Inspector General, Environmental Protection Agency - Continued											
Fund Resources: - Continued											
Unfilled Customer Orders						238,767.94					238,767.94
Fund Equities:											
Unobligated Balances (Expired)						-3,337,276.67				996,419.03	-4,333,695.70
Unobligated Balances (Unexpired)						-3,628,500.52				5,829,096.34	-9,457,596.86
Accounts Payable						-3,056,856.77				211,587.82	-3,268,444.59
Undelivered Orders						-5,625,535.97				-4,734,721.86	-890,814.11
	Subtotal	68		0112		-0-	37,171,947.00		34,692,275.20	2,479,671.80	-0-
Payment To The Hazardous Substances Superfund, Environmental Protection Agency											
Fund Resources:											
Undisbursed Funds	No Year	68		0250			1,040,370,865.00		1,040,370,865.00		
Special Fund Accounts											
Exxon Valdez Settlement Fund, Environmental Protection Agency											
Fund Resources:											
Undisbursed Funds	No Year	68		5297		337,835.23					330,716.23
Fund Equities:											
Unobligated Balances (Unexpired)						-320,716.23			7,119.00	-312,000.00	-8,716.23
Accounts Payable										857.13	-857.13
Undelivered Orders										304,023.87	-321,142.87
	Subtotal	68		5297		-17,119.00			7,119.00	-7,119.00	-0-
Pesticide Registration Fund, Environmental Protection Agency											
Fund Resources:											
Undisbursed Funds	No Year	68		5374		16,242,988.76	13,167,269.00		13,003,097.50		16,407,160.26
Fund Equities:											
Unobligated Balances (Unexpired)						-12,340,498.01				-2,079,609.64	-10,260,888.37
Accounts Payable						-736,872.82				812,481.93	-1,549,354.75
Undelivered Orders						-3,165,617.93				1,431,299.21	-4,596,917.14
	Subtotal	68		5374		-0-	13,167,269.00		13,003,097.50	164,171.50	-0-
Public Enterprise Funds											
Reregistration And Expedited Processing Fund, Environmental Protection Agency											
Fund Resources:											
Undisbursed Funds	No Year	68		4310		8,044,797.70			-1,239,093.31		9,283,891.01
Unrealized Discount On Investments						-5,413.52					-5,413.52
Fund Equities:											
Unobligated Balances (Unexpired)						-5,613,330.45				1,372,357.98	-6,985,688.43
Accounts Payable						-1,035,019.81				289,845.35	-1,324,865.16
Undelivered Orders						-1,391,033.92				-423,110.02	-967,923.90
	Subtotal	68		4310		-0-			-1,239,093.31	1,239,093.31	-0-

Appropriations, Outlays, and Balances - Continued

Appropriation or Fund Account	Account Symbol					Balances, Beginning Of Fiscal Year	Appropriations And Other Obligational Authority[1]	Transfers Borrowings And Investment (Net)[2]	Outlays (Net)	Balances Withdrawn And Other Transactions[3]	Balances, End Of Fiscal Year[4]
Title	Period of Availability	Dept Reg	Dept Tr From	Account Number	Sub No.						
Revolving Fund For Certification And Other Services, Environmental Protection Agency											
Fund Resources:											
Undisbursed Funds	No Year	68		4311		29,495.11					29,495.11
Fund Equities:											
Unobligated Balances (Unexpired)						-29,495.11					-29,495.11
Subtotal		68		4311		-0-					-0-
Intragovernmental Funds											
Franchise Fund, Environmental Protection Agency											
Fund Resources:											
Undisbursed Funds	No Year	68		4565		77,635,017.69			7,174,651.72		70,460,365.97
Accounts Receivable						-1,693,573.44				-9,144.72	-1,684,428.72
Unfilled Customer Orders						13,673,190.71				-298,787.43	13,971,978.14
Fund Equities:											
Unobligated Balances (Unexpired)						-24,972,666.28				-8,016,790.81	-16,955,875.47
Accounts Payable						-45,104,448.05				-2,751,131.36	-42,353,316.69
Undelivered Orders						-19,537,520.63				3,901,202.60	-23,438,723.23
Subtotal		68		4565		-0-			7,174,651.72	-7,174,651.72	-0-
Trust Fund Accounts											
Hazardous Substance Superfund											
Fund Resources:											
Undisbursed Funds	No Year	20		8145		775,044.44	1,391,258,532.19	-1,390,495,120.86			1,538,455.77
Transfer To:											
National Oceanic And Atmospheric Administration, Department Of Commerce	No Year	13	20	8145	14	740,757.27		1,963,000.00	2,140,032.78		563,724.49
Interior, Office Of The Secretary	No Year	14	20	8145	1	394,926.34		549,108.11	847,824.50		96,209.95
Occupational Safety And Health Administration, Department Of Labor	No Year	16	20	8145	4	3,213,830.80		520,800.00	573,473.87		3,161,156.93
Environmental Protection Agency	No Year	68	20	8145		34,310,538.28		1,255,642,991.89	1,247,282,604.44		42,670,925.73
Emergency Preparedness And Response, Department Of Homeland Security	No Year	70	20	8145	7	3,063,582.68		324,100.00	1,078,294.41		2,309,388.27
Health And Human Services, Centers For Disease Control	No Year	75	20	8145	9	15,282,090.96		-13,000,000.00	10,703.96		2,271,387.00
Unrealized Discount On Investments						-22,932,367.80		17,986,520.31			-4,945,847.49
Investments In Public Debt Securities						2,640,273,000.00		103,235,993.39			2,743,508,993.39
Accounts Receivable						-25,014,657.07				1,633,272.67	-26,647,929.74
Unfilled Customer Orders						87,167,359.34				-29,772,982.97	116,940,342.31
Fund Equities:											
Unobligated Balances (Unexpired)[11]						-1,275,546,662.43				243,053,938.31	-1,518,600,600.74
Accounts Payable						-200,846,971.54				22,078,266.48	-222,925,238.02
Undelivered Orders						-1,260,861,571.27				-120,920,603.42	-1,139,940,967.85
Subtotal		20		8145		18,900.00	1,391,258,532.19	-23,272,607.16	1,251,932,933.96	116,071,891.07	-0-
Hazardous Substance Superfund, Environmental Protection Agency											
Fund Resources:											
Undisbursed Funds	2007-2008	68		8145			25,126,701.61		25,126,701.61		

Footnotes At End Of Chapter

Appropriations, Outlays, and Balances – Continued

Appropriation or Fund Account	Account Symbol					Balances, Beginning Of Fiscal Year	Appropriations And Other Obligational Authority[1]	Transfers Borrowings And Investment (Net)[2]	Outlays (Net)	Balances Withdrawn And Other Transactions[3]	Balances, End Of Fiscal Year[4]
Title	Period of Availability	Dept Reg	Tr From	Account Number	Sub No.						
Hazardous Substance Superfund, Environmental Protection Agency - Continued											
Fund Resources: - Continued											
Undisbursed Funds - Continued											
	2006-2007							11,097,261.13	11,097,261.13		
	2005-2006							7,631,054.82	7,631,054.82		
	2004-2005							2,389,230.63	2,389,230.63		
	2003-2004							3,524,723.36	3,524,723.36		
	2001-2002							339.06	339.06		
Accounts Receivable						37,226,669.11				6,278,567.67	30,948,101.44
Fund Equities:											
Accounts Payable						-37,226,669.11				-6,278,567.67	-30,948,101.44
Leaking Underground Storage Tank Trust Fund	Subtotal	68		8145		-0-	25,126,701.61	24,642,609.00	49,769,310.61		-0-
Fund Resources:											
Undisbursed Funds	No Year	20		8153		11,750,412.92					12,856,000.00
	2006-2007	68		8153		7,000,000.00	[12]353,755,334.74	-352,649,747.66	510,993.89 [13]		6,489,006.11
Transfer To:											
Environmental Protection Agency	No Year	68	20	8153		5,291,972.13		80,200,000.00	72,431,208.05		13,060,764.08
Unrealized Discount On Investments						-13,871,282.64		1,356,511.40			-12,514,771.24
Investments In Public Debt Securities						2,665,719,000.00		271,093,236.26			2,936,812,236.26
Accounts Receivable											
Fund Equities:											
Unobligated Balances (Unexpired)						-2,590,446,905.67				272,725,667.05	-2,863,172,572.72
Accounts Payable						-6,681,438.06				2,864,178.86	-9,545,616.92
Undelivered Orders						-78,761,758.68				5,223,286.89	-83,985,045.57
Oil Spill Responses, Environmental Protection Agency	Subtotal	20		8153		-0-	353,755,334.74		72,942,201.94	280,813,132.80	-0-
Fund Resources:											
Undisbursed Funds	No Year	68		8221		6,713,265.11	15,733,617.00		17,946,242.25		4,500,639.86
Accounts Receivable						3,343,244.84				-217,506.53	3,560,751.37
Unfilled Customer Orders						24,027,907.35				1,424,547.87	22,603,359.48
Fund Equities:											
Unobligated Balances (Unexpired)						-10,451,426.01				1,095,720.23	-11,547,146.24
Accounts Payable						-3,433,441.14				168,140.41	-3,601,581.55
Undelivered Orders						-20,199,550.15				-4,683,527.23	-15,516,022.92
Miscellaneous Contributed Funds, Environmental Protection Agency	Subtotal	68		8221		-0-	15,733,617.00		17,946,242.25	-2,212,625.25	-0-
Fund Resources:											
Undisbursed Funds	No Year	68		8741		75,608.95					75,608.95
Fund Equities:											
Unobligated Balances (Unexpired)	Subtotal	68		8741		-75,608.95					-75,608.95
Deductions For Offsetting Receipts											
Proprietary Receipts From The Public							-244,226,701.07		-244,226,701.07		
Intrabudgetary Transactions							-1,040,461,223.76		-1,040,461,223.76		
Offsetting Governmental Receipts							-22,648,442.67		-22,648,442.67		

Appropriations, Outlays, and Balances - Continued

Appropriation or Fund Account										
		Account Symbol								
	Period of Availability	Dept		Account Number	Sub No.	Balances, Beginning Of Fiscal Year	Appropriations And Other Obligational Authority[1]	Transfers Borrowings And Investment (Net)[2]	Outlays (Net)	Balances Withdrawn And Other Transactions[3]	Balances, End Of Fiscal Year[4]
Title		Reg	Tr From								
Total, Environmental Protection Agency						18,900.00	7,914,340,019.04	1,370,001.84	8,258,350,690.04	-342,621,769.16	428,896.64
Memorandum											
Financing Accounts											
Public Enterprise Funds											
Abatement, Control And Compliance Direct Loan Financing Account, Environmental Protection Agency											
Fund Resources:											
Undisbursed Funds	No Year	68		4322		400,000.64		-2,740,070.66	-2,768,966.66		428,896.64
Authority To Borrow From The Treasury							28,896.00	-28,896.00			
Fund Equities:											
Unobligated Balances (Unexpired)	Subtotal	68		4322		-400,000.64	28,896.00	-2,768,966.66	-2,768,966.66	28,896.00	-428,896.64
						-0-				28,896.00	-0-
Total, Financing Accounts							28,896.00	-2,768,966.66	-2,768,966.66	28,896.00	

Appropriations, Outlays, and Balances – Continued

Footnotes

1. The amounts in this column, unless otherwise footnoted, represent appropriations, increases and rescissions in borrowing authority or new contract authority. Appropriation accounts with appropriation transfer activity are presented in Table 1 (Appropriations and Appropriation Transfers) at the end of this chapter.

2. The amounts in this column, unless otherwise footnoted, represent transfers - other than appropriation transfers, borrowings (gross), investments (net), unrealized discounts or funds held outside the Treasury.

3. The amounts in this column, unless otherwise footnoted, represent obligated balances canceled for fiscal year 2002 pursuant to 31 U.S.C. 1553, changes in unfilled customer orders, accounts receivable, accounts payable, undelivered orders, unobligated balances and adjustments to borrowing and contract authority.

4. Unobligated balances for no-year or unexpired multiple year accounts are available for obligation; unobligated balances for expired fiscal year accounts are not available for obligation.

5. Pursuant to 114 STAT 1441 A-44 the balance for this account has been extended beyond the normal period of availability to liquidate obligations.

6. Pursuant to 113 STAT 1080, the balance for this account has been extended beyond the normal period of availability to liquidate obligations.

7. Pursuant to 112 STAT 2495, the balance for this account has been extended beyond the normal period of availability to liquidate obligations.

8. Pursuant to 112 STAT 2496, the balance for this account has been extended beyond the normal period of availability to liquidate obligations.

9. The opening balance and Accounts Receivable for account 68 0108 have been adjusted by $9,782,250.00 during the current fiscal year and do not agree with last year's closing balances.

Account	Adjustment
68 0108 - Accounts Receivable	$9,782,250.00
68 0108 - Unfilled Customer Orders	-$9,782,250.00

10. Subject to disposition by the administrative agency.

11. The opening balance of the Unobligated balance for account 20X8145 does not agree with last year's closing balance by $18,900.00 due to the year-end closing statement not being processed in Treasury's central accounting system.

12. Excludes $2,063,000.00 refund of taxes.

13. Excludes $2,063,000.00 refund of taxes.

Appropriations, Outlays, and Balances - Continued

Table 1 - Appropriations And Appropriation Transfers - Environmental Protection Agency

Department Regular	Fiscal Year	Account Symbol	Net Appropriations And Appropriations Transfers	Appropriation Amount	Net Appropriation Transfers	Department Regular Involved	Fiscal Year Involved	Accounts Involved	Amount From or To (-)
20	X	8145	-25,126,701.61	0.00	-25,126,701.61	68	0708	8145	-25,126,701.61
68	0708	8145	25,126,701.61	0.00	25,126,701.61	20	X	8145	25,126,701.61
68	X	8221	15,733,617.00	0.00	15,733,617.00	20	X	8185	15,733,617.00
Totals			15,733,617.00	0.00	15,733,617.00				15,733,617.00

Appropriations, Outlays, and Balances – Continued

Appropriation or Fund Account — Title	Reg	Tr From	Account Number	Sub No.	Period of Availability	Balances, Beginning Of Fiscal Year	Appropriations And Other Obligational Authority[1]	Transfers Borrowings And Investment (Net)[2]	Outlays (Net)	Balances Withdrawn And Other Transactions[3]	Balances, End Of Fiscal Year[4]
Executive Office Of The President											
The White House											
General Fund Accounts											
Compensation Of The President											
Fund Resources:											
Undisbursed Funds	11		0001		2007		450,000.00		422,088.26		27,911.74
					2006	44,248.59			298.73		43,949.86
					2005	40,663.31			-5,005.74		45,669.05
					2004	46,377.73					46,377.73
					2003	44,682.51			-47.49		44,730.00
					2002	27,093.29			-5,185.68	32,278.97	-0-
Fund Equities:											
Unobligated Balances (Expired)						-201,841.77				1,939.08	-203,780.85
Accounts Payable						-1,387.25				-1,376.22	-11.03
Undelivered Orders						163.59				5,010.09	-4,846.50
Subtotal	11		0001			-0-	450,000.00		412,148.08	37,851.92	-0-
Information Technology, Office Of Administration, Executive											
Fund Resources:											
Undisbursed Funds	11		0032		2000-2002	1,760,954.84				1,760,954.84	
Fund Equities:											
Unobligated Balances (Expired)						-1,087,885.99				-1,087,885.99	
Undelivered Orders						-673,068.85				-673,068.85	
Subtotal	11		0032			-0-					-0-
Salaries And Expenses, Office Of Administration, Executive											
Fund Resources:											
Undisbursed Funds	11		0038		2007	5,609,587.42	81,874,576.00		71,578,747.23		10,295,828.77
					2006-2007	1,814,789.18		3,766,000.00	3,758,123.18		7,876.82
					2006	1,673,974.34		-164,000.00	3,491,869.24		1,953,718.18
					2005	1,683,906.78			323,295.08		1,491,494.10
					2004	430,585.50			314,975.07		1,358,999.27
					2003	14,921.93			-272,013.44		1,955,920.22
					2002	20,248,812.76			-171,441.96	602,027.46	
					2001-2002	⁵4,513.13			-88,722.04	103,643.97	
					No Year	⁵2,945,398.49	11,650,320.00		9,392,868.47	4,513.13	
Accounts Receivable										1,322,315.30	22,506,264.29
Unfilled Customer Orders											1,623,083.19
Fund Equities:											
Unobligated Balances (Expired)						-3,184,528.41				2,993,544.44	-6,178,072.85
Unobligated Balances (Unexpired)						⁵11,777,275.75				532,923.20	-12,310,198.95
Accounts Payable						⁵1,475,369.33				1,221,415.79	-2,696,785.12
Undelivered Orders						⁵17,989,316.04				2,018,811.88	-20,008,127.92
Subtotal	11		0038			-0-	93,524,896.00	3,602,000.00	88,327,700.83	8,799,195.17	-0-
White House Repair And Restoration, Executive											
Fund Resources:											
Undisbursed Funds	11		0109		No Year	6,398,140.37	1,683,000.00		3,005,260.62		5,075,879.75
Unfilled Customer Orders						175,583.33				20,047.03	155,536.30

Appropriations, Outlays, and Balances - Continued

Appropriation or Fund Account	Account Symbol					Balances, Beginning Of Fiscal Year	Appropriations And Other Obligational Authority[1]	Transfers Borrowings And Investment (Net)[2]	Outlays (Net)	Balances Withdrawn And Other Transactions[3]	Balances, End Of Fiscal Year[4]
Title	Period of Availability	Dept Reg	Dept Tr From	Account Number	Sub No.						
Fund Equities:											
Unobligated Balances (Unexpired)						-4,136,792.78				-1,005,934.31	-3,130,858.47
Accounts Payable						-223,568.36				-167,614.83	-55,953.53
Undelivered Orders						-2,213,362.56				-168,758.51	-2,044,604.05
Subtotal		11		0109		-0-	1,683,000.00		3,005,260.62	-1,322,260.62	-0-
Salaries And Expenses, The White House Office											
Fund Resources:											
Undisbursed Funds	2007	11		0110		13,102,255.17	48,758,591.00		42,402,200.47		6,356,390.53
	2006					7,098,638.87		-3,356,000.00	5,791,271.63		3,954,983.54
	2005					5,829,666.94			-660,873.92		7,759,512.79
	2004					3,336,003.32			-53,417.16		5,883,084.10
	2003					1,394,011.58			-91,665.77		3,427,669.09
	2002								499,375.58	894,636.00	
Accounts Receivable						4,469.34				4,469.34	
Unfilled Customer Orders						2,293,119.04				2,005,781.47	287,337.57
Fund Equities:											
Unobligated Balances (Expired)						-18,495,004.51				-1,750,634.91	-16,744,369.60
Accounts Payable						-1,514,155.01				82,891.06	-1,597,046.07
Undelivered Orders						-13,049,004.74				-3,721,442.79	-9,327,561.95
Subtotal		11		0110		-0-	48,758,591.00	-3,356,000.00	47,886,890.83	-2,484,299.83	-0-
Operating Expenses, Executive Residence At The White House											
Fund Resources:											
Undisbursed Funds	2007	11		0210		545,435.10	12,398,168.00	-1,000.00	11,679,123.38		718,044.62
	2006-2007					-108,780.89		100,000.00	100,000.00		179,651.38
	2006					31,891.66		1,000.00	366,783.72		49,582.20
	2005					35,092.38			-158,363.09		32,050.55
	2004					5,015.12			-158.89		5,092.38
	2003								30,000.00		
	2002									5,015.12	5,015.12
Funds Held Outside The Treasury	2007					1,000.00		1,000.00			1,000.00
	2006					2,732.94		-1,000.00		2,732.94	
Accounts Receivable											
Unfilled Customer Orders						621,935.50				-74,736.42	696,671.92
Fund Equities:											
Unobligated Balances (Expired)						5,413,216.48[5]				234,492.24	-647,708.72
Accounts Payable						-425,122.71				42,539.33	-467,662.04
Undelivered Orders						5,295,982.62[5]				270,739.67	-566,722.29
Subtotal		11		0210		-0-	12,398,168.00	100,000.00	12,017,385.12	480,782.88	-0-
Salaries And Expenses, Office Of Homeland Security											
Fund Resources:											
Undisbursed Funds	2003	11		0501		3,240,011.45			-295,258.04		3,535,269.49
Fund Equities:											
Unobligated Balances (Expired)						-2,765,189.82					-2,765,189.82
Accounts Payable						-474,821.63				295,258.04	-770,079.67
Undelivered Orders						-0-					-0-
Subtotal		11		0501		-0-			-295,258.04	295,258.04	-0-
Armstrong Resolution Account, Executive Office Of The President											
Fund Resources:											
Undisbursed Funds	No Year	11		1073		1,268,077.42					1,268,077.42

Footnotes At End Of Chapter

Appropriations, Outlays, and Balances – Continued

Appropriation or Fund Account — Title	Period of Availability	Account Symbol Dept Reg	Tr From	Account Number	Sub No.	Balances, Beginning Of Fiscal Year	Appropriations And Other Obligational Authority[1]	Transfers Borrowings And Investment (Net)[2]	Outlays (Net)	Balances Withdrawn And Other Transactions[3]	Balances, End Of Fiscal Year[4]
Armstrong Resolution Account, Executive Office Of The President - Continued											
Fund Equities:											
Unobligated Balances (Unexpired)						-1,244,940.07				-69,287.20	-1,175,652.87
Accounts Payable						-23,137.35				23,095.73	-23,095.73
Undelivered Orders						-0-				46,191.47	-69,328.82
Subtotal		11		1073							
Salaries And Expenses, Council Of Economic Advisers											
Fund Resources:											
Undisbursed Funds	2007	11		1900		664,801.16	4,031,877.00		3,066,425.55		965,451.45
	2006					138,579.58			411,979.27		252,821.89
	2005					239,246.10			238.17		138,341.41
	2004					322,435.74			1,002.75		238,243.35
	2003					113,739.23					322,435.74
	2002								-28,822.79	142,562.02	
Unfilled Customer Orders										-307.34	307.34
Fund Equities:											
Unobligated Balances (Expired)						-895,969.04				-22,883.67	-873,085.37
Accounts Payable						-146,850.35				103,872.24	-250,722.59
Undelivered Orders						-435,982.42				357,810.80	-793,793.22
Subtotal		11		1900		-0-	4,031,877.00		3,450,822.95	581,054.05	-0-
Salaries And Expenses, National Security Council											
Fund Resources:											
Undisbursed Funds	2007	11		2000		1,211,287.42	8,683,886.00		7,633,294.40		1,050,591.60
	2006					264,603.08			913,029.56		298,257.86
	2005					365,688.04			70,261.57		194,341.51
	2004					786,704.20			2,709.57		362,978.47
	2003					228,197.98			-63,603.67		850,307.87
	No Year					1,261,767.80			6,293.78	221,904.20	653,459.78
Unfilled Customer Orders						688,608.83			608,308.02	-308,509.52	997,118.35
Fund Equities:											
Unobligated Balances (Expired)						-771,333.31				1,509,594.53	-2,280,927.84
Unobligated Balances (Unexpired)						-1,220,661.08				-585,806.91	-634,854.17
Accounts Payable						-246,612.89				15,805.82	-262,418.71
Undelivered Orders						-2,558,250.07				-1,339,395.35	-1,228,854.72
Subtotal		11		2000		-0-	8,683,886.00		9,170,293.23	-486,407.23	-0-
Salaries And Expenses, Office Of Policy Development, Executive											
Fund Resources:											
Undisbursed Funds	2007	11		2200		1,156,082.22	3,486,723.00		2,328,740.14		1,157,982.86
	2006					329,028.73		-346,000.00	179,166.16		630,916.06
	2005					362,104.93					329,028.73
	2004					731,361.58					362,104.93
	2003					657,079.43			59,209.16	597,870.27	731,361.58
Fund Equities:											
Unobligated Balances (Expired)						-2,583,399.88				49,627.22	-2,633,027.10
Accounts Payable						-101,026.77				-1,819.89	-99,206.88
Undelivered Orders						-551,230.24				-72,070.06	-479,160.18

Appropriations, Outlays, and Balances - Continued

Appropriation or Fund Account — Title	Account Symbol — Dept Reg	Account Symbol — Dept Tr From	Account Number	Sub No.	Period of Availability	Balances, Beginning Of Fiscal Year	Appropriations And Other Obligational Authority[1]	Transfers Borrowings And Investment (Net)[2]	Outlays (Net)	Balances Withdrawn And Other Transactions[3]	Balances, End Of Fiscal Year[4]
Public Enterprise Funds	11		2200		Subtotal	-0-	3,486,723.00	-346,000.00	2,567,115.46	573,607.54	-0-
Reimbursable Expenses, Executive Residence At The White House											
Fund Resources:											
Undisbursed Funds	11		4263		No Year	22,500.00			-1,500.00		24,000.00
Fund Equities:											
Unobligated Balances (Unexpired)	11		4263		Subtotal	-22,500.00				1,500.00	-24,000.00
						-0-			-1,500.00	1,500.00	-0-
Total, The White House							173,017,141.00		166,540,859.08	6,476,281.92	
Special Assistance To The President And The Official Residence Of The Vice President											
General Fund Accounts											
Operating Expenses, Official Residence Of The Vice President, Executive Office Of The President											
Fund Resources:											
Undisbursed Funds	11		0211		2007		322,268.00		116,541.42		205,726.58
					2006	129,739.43			23,801.38		105,938.05
					2005	68,007.03			-510.92		68,517.95
					2004	104,342.26			70.00		104,272.26
					2003	40,172.05					40,172.05
					2002	96,190.14				96,190.14	-0-
Fund Equities:											
Unobligated Balances (Expired)						-334,602.52				135,453.71	470,056.23
Accounts Payable						-14,854.64				-5,458.80	-9,395.84
Undelivered Orders						-88,993.75				-43,818.93	-45,174.82
	11		0211		Subtotal	-0-	322,268.00		139,901.88	182,366.12	-0-
Salaries And Expenses, Special Assistance To The President, Executive Office Of The President											
Fund Resources:											
Undisbursed Funds	11		1454		2007		4,432,499.00		3,560,972.54		871,526.46
					2006	852,570.15			362,783.88		489,786.27
					2005	455,255.30			22,943.14		432,312.16
					2004	344,456.51			-19,660.06		364,116.57
					2003	673,457.23					673,457.23
					2002	549,835.68			681.50	549,154.18	-0-
Unfilled Customer Orders						785.00				785.00	
Fund Equities:											
Unobligated Balances (Expired)						-2,125,409.61				282,503.39	-2,407,913.00
Accounts Payable						-156,808.73				-48,175.04	-108,633.69
Undelivered Orders						-594,141.53				-279,489.53	-314,652.00
	11		1454		Subtotal	-0-	4,432,499.00		3,927,721.00	504,778.00	-0-

Footnotes At End Of Chapter

Appropriations, Outlays, and Balances – Continued

Appropriation or Fund Account — Title	Period of Availability	Account Symbol — Dept Reg	Account Symbol — Tr From	Account Number	Sub No.	Balances, Beginning Of Fiscal Year	Appropriations And Other Obligational Authority[1]	Transfers Borrowings And Investment (Net)[2]	Outlays (Net)	Balances Withdrawn And Other Transactions[3]	Balances, End Of Fiscal Year[4]
Trust Fund Accounts											
Donations For The Official Residence Of The Vice President											
Fund Resources:											
Undisbursed Funds	No Year	11		8241		239.83					239.83
Fund Equities:											
Unobligated Balances (Unexpired)	Subtotal	11		8241		-239.83					-239.83
						-0-					-0-
Total, Special Assistance To The President And The Official Residence Of The Vice President							4,754,767.00		4,067,622.88	687,144.12	
Council On Environmental Quality And Office Of Environmental Quality											
General Fund Accounts											
Council On Environmental Quality And Office Of Environmental Quality											
Fund Resources:											
Undisbursed Funds	2007	11		1453		256,906.51	2,698,187.00		2,362,258.37		335,928.63
	2006					85,139.85			127,893.27		129,013.24
	2005					150,758.28			497.68		84,642.17
	2004					224,265.46			2,142.59		148,615.69
	2003					271,301.04					224,265.46
	2002								-1,094.00	272,395.04	
Fund Equities:											
Unobligated Balances (Expired)						-761,967.96				-62,993.07	-698,974.89
Accounts Payable						-87,825.35				19,425.18	-107,250.53
Undelivered Orders						-138,577.83				-22,338.06	-116,239.77
	Subtotal	11		1453		-0-	2,698,187.00		2,491,697.91	206,489.09	-0-
Management Funds											
Office Of Environmental Quality Management Fund, Council On Environmental Quality And Office Of Environmental Quality											
Fund Resources:											
Undisbursed Funds	No Year	11		3963		587,340.13			470,191.18		117,148.95
Accounts Receivable						-143,179.10				-143,179.10	
Unfilled Customer Orders						134,100.00				-55,000.00	189,100.00
Fund Equities:											
Unobligated Balances (Unexpired)						-126,882.80				51,681.58	-178,564.38
Accounts Payable						-51,448.02				-51,448.02	-51,448.02
Undelivered Orders						-399,930.21				-272,245.64	-127,684.57
	Subtotal	11		3963		-0-			470,191.18	-470,191.18	-0-
Total, Council On Environmental Quality And Office Of Environmental Quality							2,698,187.00		2,961,889.09	-263,702.09	

Appropriations, Outlays, and Balances - Continued

Appropriation or Fund Account — Title	Period of Availability	Reg	Tr From	Account Number	Sub No.	Balances, Beginning Of Fiscal Year	Appropriations And Other Obligational Authority[1]	Transfers Borrowings And Investment (Net)[2]	Outlays (Net)	Balances Withdrawn And Other Transactions[3]	Balances, End Of Fiscal Year[4]
Office Of Management And Budget											
General Fund Accounts											
Salaries And Expenses, Office Of Management And Budget											
Fund Resources:											
Undisbursed Funds	2007	11		0300			76,713,806.00		67,909,149.68		8,804,656.32
	2006-2007								28,402.09		21,597.91
	2006					8,593,559.11		50,000.00	7,694,487.03		849,072.08
	2005					554,173.46		-50,000.00	17,235.18		536,938.28
	2004					275,852.08					275,852.08
	2003					94,738.47			-387,905.85	971,091.35	482,644.32
	2002					1,089,772.35			118,681.00	-404,086.25	
Unfilled Customer Orders						26,824.18					430,910.43
Fund Equities:											
Unobligated Balances (Expired)						-551,577.97				40,794.01	-592,371.98
Accounts Payable						-3,143,601.36				10,778.00	-3,154,379.36
Undelivered Orders						-6,939,740.32				715,179.76	-7,654,920.08
Subtotal		11		0300		-0-	76,713,806.00		75,380,049.13	1,333,756.87	-0-
							76,713,806.00		75,380,049.13	1,333,756.87	
Total, Office Of Management And Budget											
Office Of National Drug Control Policy											
General Fund Accounts											
Salaries And Expenses, Office Of National Drug Control Policy											
Fund Resources:											
Undisbursed Funds	2007	11		1457			25,463,023.00		19,241,917.86		6,221,105.14
	2006					5,815,816.60			3,887,762.01		1,928,054.59
	2005					1,291,102.35			-57,858.31		1,348,960.66
	2004					1,122,403.34			-27,506.46		1,149,909.80
	2003					1,286,501.07			-191,604.64		1,478,105.71
	2002					1,238,382.22			128,408.59	1,109,973.63	
	No Year					3,779,099.36	1,302,840.00		842,781.21	7,710.00	4,239,158.15
Unfilled Customer Orders						325,701.64					317,991.64
Fund Equities:											
Unobligated Balances (Expired)						-2,310,334.81				107,691.11	-2,418,025.92
Unobligated Balances (Unexpired)						-2,015,501.86				-477,345.74	-1,538,156.12
Accounts Payable						[5]-1,143,588.18				-29,472.27	-1,114,115.91
Undelivered Orders						[5]-9,389,581.73				2,223,406.01	-11,612,987.74
Subtotal		11		1457		-0-	26,765,863.00		23,823,900.26	2,941,962.74	-0-

Appropriations, Outlays, and Balances – Continued

Title	Period of Availability	Reg	Tr From	Account Number	Sub No.	Balances, Beginning Of Fiscal Year	Appropriations And Other Obligational Authority[1]	Transfers Borrowings And Investment (Net)[2]	Outlays (Net)	Balances Withdrawn And Other Transactions[3]	Balances, End Of Fiscal Year[4]
Trust Fund Accounts											
Gifts And Donations, The White House Conference On Drug Abuse And Control											
Fund Resources:											
Undisbursed Funds	No Year	11		8240		97,124.10			2,623.54		94,500.56
Fund Equities:											
Unobligated Balances (Unexpired)						-58,326.71				-2,623.54	-55,703.17
Undelivered Orders						-38,797.39					-38,797.39
	Subtotal	11		8240		-0-			2,623.54	-2,623.54	-0-
Total, Office Of National Drug Policy							26,765,863.00		23,826,523.80	2,939,339.20	
Office Of Science And Technology Policy											
General Fund Accounts											
Office Of Science And Technology Policy											
Fund Resources:											
Undisbursed Funds	2007	11		2600		1,043,825.67	5,527,995.00		4,384,886.36		1,143,108.64
	2006					1,095,886.38			478,886.01		564,939.66
	2005					511,237.10			241,667.02		854,219.36
	2004					390,023.05			1,000.00		510,237.10
	2003					901,764.32			-2,384.00		392,407.05
	2002					93,441.00					
Unfilled Customer Orders						901,764.32				901,764.32	93,441.00
Fund Equities:											
Unobligated Balances (Expired)						-1,625,324.17				-636,512.81	-988,811.36
Accounts Payable						-165,863.89				146,402.54	-312,266.43
Undelivered Orders						-2,244,989.46				12,285.56	-2,257,275.02
	Subtotal	11		2600		-0-	5,527,995.00		5,104,055.39	423,939.61	-0-
Total, Office Of Science And Technology Policy							5,527,995.00		5,104,055.39	423,939.61	
Office Of The United States Trade Representatives											
General Fund Accounts											
Salaries And Expenses, Office Of The United States Trade Representative											
Fund Resources:											
Undisbursed Funds	2007	11		0400		4,877,345.71	43,498,801.00		40,163,504.14		3,335,296.86
	2006					1,203,257.25			3,039,635.80		1,837,709.91
	2005					2,051,125.50			6,586.11		1,196,671.14
	2004					837,537.58			500,150.91		1,550,974.59
	2003					[5]-1,367,755.93			808,566.58		28,971.00
	2002					3,067,466.03			-1,415,815.93		3,507,768.24
	No Year						987,228.00		546,925.79	48,060.00	
Accounts Receivable						409,929.93				197,497.78	212,432.15
Unfilled Customer Orders						448,975.29				361,549.29	87,426.00

Appropriations, Outlays, and Balances - Continued

Title	Period of Availability	Reg	Tr From	Account Number	Sub No.	Balances, Beginning Of Fiscal Year	Appropriations And Other Obligational Authority[1]	Transfers Borrowings And Investment (Net)[2]	Outlays (Net)	Balances Withdrawn And Other Transactions[3]	Balances, End Of Fiscal Year[4]
Fund Equities:											
Unobligated Balances (Expired)						[5]-4,580,095.24				-1,664,996.57	-2,915,098.67
Unobligated Balances (Unexpired)						-2,317,673.14				-125,259.25	-2,192,413.89
Unobligated Balances (Unexpired)						-1,189,334.82				-5,083.16	-1,184,251.66
Accounts Payable						-3,440,778.16				2,024,707.51	-5,465,485.67
Undelivered Orders									43,649,553.40	836,475.60	-0-
	Subtotal	11		0400		-0-	44,486,029.00		43,649,553.40	836,475.60	
Total, Office Of The United States Trade Representatives							44,486,029.00		43,649,553.40	836,475.60	
Unanticipated Needs											
General Fund Accounts											
Unanticipated Needs For Natural Disasters, Executive											
Fund Resources:											
Undisbursed Funds	No Year	11		0033		11,789,015.10	-834,000.00	834,000.00			11,789,015.10
Fund Equities:											
Unobligated Balances (Unexpired)						-11,789,015.10					-11,789,015.10
	Subtotal	11		0033		-0-	-834,000.00	834,000.00			-0-
Unanticipated Needs, Emergency Response Fund, Funds Appropriated To The President											
Fund Resources:											
Undisbursed Funds	No Year	11		0034		6,382,150.75	-3,589,000.00	3,589,000.00			6,382,150.75
Fund Equities:											
Unobligated Balances (Unexpired)						-6,382,150.75					-6,382,150.75
	Subtotal	11		0034		-0-	-3,589,000.00	3,589,000.00			-0-
Unanticipated Needs, Funds Appropriated To The President											
Fund Resources:											
Undisbursed Funds	2007	11		0037			965,192.00		230,600.08		734,591.92
	2006					990,000.00					990,000.00
	2005					43,186,314.86					43,186,314.86
	2004					392,124.60					392,124.60
	2003					741,500.00					741,500.00
	2002					243,000.00				243,000.00	
Fund Equities:											
Unobligated Balances (Expired)						-42,568,239.46				3,476,291.92	-46,044,531.38
Undelivered Orders						-2,984,700.00				-2,984,700.00	-0-
	Subtotal	11		0037		-0-	965,192.00		230,600.08	734,591.92	-0-
Iraq Relief And Reconstruction Fund, Executive Office Of The President											
Fund Resources:											
Undisbursed Funds	2004-2008	11		1096			148,868,345.00				148,868,345.00
	2004-2007	11		1096			28,970,254.35				28,970,254.35
	2004-2006	11		1096			35,919,305.13				35,919,305.13
Transfer To:											
Department Of State	2004-2007	19	11	1096				19,712,278.00	4,770,607.64		14,941,670.36
	2004-2006					317,858,689.88		-8,066,076.00	177,129,646.34		132,662,967.54
	2003-2004					3,879,379.21			9,643,220.94		[6]-5,763,841.73
Treasury	2004-2006	20	11	1096		3,156,184.17			2,298,022.09		858,162.08
	2003-2004					558,831.72			29,014.74		529,816.98

Footnotes At End Of Chapter

Appropriations, Outlays, and Balances – Continued

Title	Reg	Tr From	Account Number	Sub No.	Period of Availability	Balances, Beginning Of Fiscal Year	Appropriations And Other Obligational Authority[1]	Transfers Borrowings And Investment (Net)[2]	Outlays (Net)	Balances Withdrawn And Other Transactions[3]	Balances, End Of Fiscal Year[4]
Iraq Relief And Reconstruction Fund, Executive Office Of The President - Continued											
Fund Resources: - Continued											
Army	21	11	1096		2004-2008			20,000,000.00			20,000,000.00
					2004-2007			178,989,671.00	51,512,182.47		127,477,488.53
					2004-2006	3,837,582,714.40		-381,892,887.00	1,988,801,201.44		1,466,888,625.96
					2003-2004	1,588,927.48			694,621.21		894,306.27
Agency For International Development	72	11	1096		2004-2008			2,200,000.00			2,200,000.00
					2006-2007				65.00		[6]65.00
					2004-2007			19,894,897.00	4,425,441.65		15,469,455.35
					2004-2006	418,631,222.22		-64,595,787.48	284,302,949.90		69,732,484.84
					2003-2004	79,385,409.42			55,798,769.34		23,586,640.08
United States Institute Of Peace	95	11	1096		2004-2006	1,678,095.42			1,399,229.87		278,865.55
Defense	97	11	1096		2003-2004	28,125.85					28,125.85
Fund Equities:											
Unobligated Balances (Expired)						[5]390,319,832.83				58,608,502.26	-448,928,335.09
Unobligated Balances (Unexpired)										151,770,923.00	-151,770,923.00
Accounts Payable						[5]213,172,907.68				-155,279,938.44	-57,892,969.24
Undelivered Orders						[5]4,060,854,839.26				2,635,904,459.45	-1,424,950,379.81
Subtotal	11	11	1096			-0-	-0-		2,580,804,972.63	2,580,804,972.63	-0-
Special Fund Accounts											
Spectrum Relocation Fund, Executive Office Of The President											
Fund Resources:											
Undisbursed Funds	11		5512		No Year		-950,490,482.00		58,062,020.00		[6]1,008,552,502.00
Fund Equities:											
Unobligated Balances (Unexpired)										5,841,331,123.00	-5,841,331,123.00
Subtotal	11		5512				-950,490,482.00		58,062,020.00	5,841,331,123.00	-6,849,883,625.00
Total, Unanticipated Needs						-0-	-953,948,290.00	4,423,000.00	2,639,097,592.71	3,261,260,742.29	-6,849,883,625.00
Deductions For Offsetting Receipts											
Proprietary Receipts From The Public							-1,215,573.54		-1,215,573.54		
Intrabudgetary Transactions							-2,317,845.58		-2,317,845.58		
Total, Executive Office Of The President							-623,517,921.12	4,423,000.00	2,957,094,726.36	3,273,693,977.52	-6,849,883,625.00

Appropriations, Outlays, and Balances - Continued

Footnotes

1 The amounts in this column, unless otherwise footnoted, represent appropriations, increases and rescissions in borrowing authority or new contract authority. Appropriation accounts with appropriation transfer activity are presented in Table 1 (Appropriations and Appropriation Transfers) at the end of this chapter.

2 The amounts in this column, unless otherwise footnoted, represent transfers - other than appropriation transfers, borrowings (gross), investments (net), unrealized discounts or funds held outside the Treasury.

3 The amounts in this column, unless otherwise footnoted, represent obligated balances canceled for fiscal year 2002 pursuant to 31 U.S.C. 1553, changes in unfilled customer orders, accounts receivable, accounts payable, undelivered orders, unobligated balances and adjustments to borrowing and contract authority.

4 Unobligated balances for no-year or unexpired multiple year accounts are available for obligation; unobligated balances for expired fiscal year accounts are not available for obligation.

5 The opening balances of the following accounts have been adjusted during the current fiscal year and do not agree with last year's closing balances:

Account	Adjustment
11 X 0038 - Accounts Payable	-$332,034.04
11 X 0038 - Unobligated Balances (Unexpired)	166,017.02
11 X 0038 - Undelivered Orders	166,017.02
11 02 0038 - Accounts Payable	-13,039.51
11 02 0038 - Undelivered Orders	13,039.51
11 05 0038 - Accounts Receivable	54.00
11 05 0038 - Unfilled Customer Orders	-54.00
11 04 0210 - Unobligated Balances (Expired)	254,349.72
11 X 1457 - Accounts Payable	-404.72
11 X 1457 - Undelivered Orders	404.72
11 02 0400 - Undisbursed Funds	510,661.68
11 02 0400 - Unobligated Balances (Expired)	-510,661.68
19 11 0406 1096 - Accounts Payable	14,777,030.28
19 11 0406 1096 - Unobligated Balances (Expired)	-2,407,512.72
19 11 0406 1096 - Undelivered Orders	-12,369,517.56
72 11 0406 1096 - Accounts Payable	-8,809,720.67
72 11 0406 1096 - Undelivered Orders	8,809,720.67

6 Subject to disposition by the administrative agency.

Footnotes At End Of Chapter

Appropriations, Outlays, and Balances – Continued

Footnotes

Table 1 - Appropriations And Appropriation Transfers - Executive Office Of The President

Department Regular	Fiscal Year	Account Symbol	Net Appropriations And Appropriations Transfers	Appropriation Amount	Net Appropriation Transfers	Department Regular Involved	Fiscal Year Involved	Accounts Involved	Amount From or To (-)
11	07	0037	965,192.00	990,000.00	-24,808.00	11	07	0110	-24,808.00
11	07	0038	81,874,576.00	76,992,576.00	4,882,000.00	11	07	0110	4,882,000.00
11	07	0110	48,758,591.00	53,615,783.00	-4,857,192.00	11	07	0037	24,808.00
						11	07	0038	-4,882,000.00
11	X	5512	-950,490,482.00	0.00	-950,490,482.00	12	X	1103	-21,578,486.00
						14	X	0680	-4,550,000.00
						14	X	0804	-6,158,949.00
						14	X	1039	-14,703,000.00
						15	X	0132	-800,000.00
						15	X	0200	-139,225,000.00
						15	X	0700	-48,024,000.00
						15	X	1100	-74,772,000.00
						17	X	1319	-72,873,000.00
						17	X	1507	-60,692,000.00
						17	X	1810	-900,000.00
						18	X	1001	-1,761,760.00
						20	X	0119	-892,000.00
						20	X	0913	-4,409,000.00
						21	X	2020	-630,000.00
						21	X	2035	-15,303,043.00
						57	X	3010	-40,000,000.00
						57	X	3020	-60,000,000.00
						57	X	3080	-6,596,381.00
						57	X	3400	-157,100.00
						64	X	4110	-10,687,857.00
						70	X	0102	-11,979,761.00
						70	X	0403	-105,800.00
						70	X	0530	-74,349,990.00
						70	X	0540	-3,559,281.00
						80	X	0115	-740,000.00
						86	X	0189	-21,115.00
						89	X	0228	-1,000,000.00
						89	X	0303	-8,091,360.00
						89	X	0313	-10,900,000.00
						89	X	4045	-48,627,399.00
						89	X	5068	-108,202,200.00
						97	X	0100	-21,700,000.00
						97	X	0400	-76,500,000.00
Totals			-818,892,123.00	131,598,359.00	-950,490,482.00				-950,490,482.00

Appropriations, Outlays, and Balances – Continued

Footnotes

This Page Left Blank Intentionally

Appropriations, Outlays, and Balances – Continued

Appropriation or Fund Account — Title	Period of Availability	Reg	Tr From	Account Number	Sub No.	Balances, Beginning of Fiscal Year	Appropriations And Other Obligational Authority[1]	Transfers Borrowings And Investment (Net)[2]	Outlays (Net)	Balances Withdrawn And Other Transactions[3]	Balances, End Of Fiscal Year[4]
General Services Administration											
Real Property Activities											
General Fund Accounts											
Real Property Relocation, General Services Administration											
Fund Resources:											
Undisbursed Funds											
Transfer To:											
United States Coast Guard, Department Of Homeland Security	No Year	47		0535		1,550,135.14			-203,402.44		1,753,537.58
	No Year	70	47	0535	6	10,238,994.84			203,402.44		10,035,592.40
Fund Equities:											
Unobligated Balances (Unexpired)						-11,788,814.98				-8,172.56	-11,780,642.42
Undelivered Orders						-315.00				8,172.56	-8,487.56
Subtotal	Subtotal	47		0535		-0-					-0-
Special Fund Accounts											
Expenses, Disposal Of Surplus Real And Related Personal Property, General Services Administration											
Fund Resources:											
Undisbursed Funds	2007	47		5254			4,293,000.00		1,191,601.45		3,101,398.55
	2006					3,301,785.93			1,813,447.38		1,488,338.55
	2005					1,631,504.68			148,589.24		1,482,915.44
	2004					1,071,448.93					1,071,448.93
	2003					1,017,788.07					1,017,788.07
	2002					907,734.24				907,734.24	
Accounts Receivable						4,500.00				-1,500.00	6,000.00
Fund Equities:											
Unobligated Balances (Expired)						-4,156,344.27				65,428.21	-4,221,772.48
Accounts Payable						-327,605.84				-184,026.42	-143,579.42
Undelivered Orders						-3,450,811.74				351,725.90	-3,802,537.64
Subtotal	Subtotal	47		5254		-0-	4,293,000.00		3,153,638.07	1,139,361.93	-0-
Intragovernmental Funds											
Federal Buildings Fund, General Services Administration											
Fund Resources:											
Undisbursed Funds	No Year	47		4542	1	5,599,272,322.39	36,461,000.00	[5]-180,162,394.86	-158,790,021.01		5,614,360,948.54
Transfer To:											
Department Of Commerce	No Year	13	47	4542	1	2,028,935.09		44,326,688.12	42,901,783.39		3,453,839.82
Defense	No Year	97	47	4542	1	4,727,003.49		108,332,757.04	111,328,934.93		1,730,825.60
Funds Held Outside The Treasury	No Year					19,600.00		-500.00			19,100.00
Authority To Borrow From The Treasury	No Year					67,354,796.30		-17,585,160.79			49,769,635.51
Accounts Receivable						270,009,582.08				-54,530,484.22	324,540,066.30
Unfilled Customer Orders						1,616,721,931.52				-479,600,743.86	2,096,322,675.38
Fund Equities:											
Unobligated Balances (Unexpired)						-4,081,645,769.82				413,581,332.47	-4,495,227,102.29
Accounts Payable						-1,019,498,296.14				5,959,354.76	-1,025,457,650.90

Appropriations, Outlays, and Balances - Continued

Appropriation or Fund Account — Title	Period of Availability	Dept Reg	Tr From	Account Number	Sub No.	Balances, Beginning of Fiscal Year	Appropriations And Other Obligational Authority[1]	Transfers Borrowings And Investment (Net)[2]	Outlays (Net)	Balances Withdrawn And Other Transactions[3]	Balances, End Of Fiscal Year[4]
Undelivered Orders						-2,458,990,104.91				110,522,233.05	-2,569,512,337.96
Subtotal		47		4542		-0-	36,461,000.00	-45,088,610.49	-4,559,302.69	-4,068,307.80	-0-
Trust Fund Accounts											
Unconditional Gifts Of Real, Personal, Or Other Property, General Services Administration											
Fund Resources:											
Undisbursed Funds	No Year	47		8198		802.47	3,726,000.00				3,726,352.47
Fund Equities:											
Unobligated Balances (Unexpired)									450.00	3,002,148.61	-3,002,951.08
Undelivered Orders						-802.47				723,401.39	-723,401.39
Subtotal		47		8198		-0-	3,726,000.00		450.00	3,725,550.00	-0-
Total, Real Property Activities							44,480,000.00	-45,088,610.49	-1,405,214.62	796,604.13	
Supply And Technology Activities											
Special Fund Accounts											
Expenses Of Transportation Audit Contracts And Contract Administration, General Services Administration											
Fund Resources:											
Undisbursed Funds	2007	47		5250			12,500,000.00		8,294,457.44		4,205,542.56
	2006					6,287,393.89			1,065,907.37		5,221,486.52
	2005					5,020,238.87			146,017.57		4,874,221.30
	2004					2,477,529.11			12,463.40		2,465,065.71
	2003					2,836,210.39			40,871.57		2,795,338.82
	2002					3,158,112.51			20,402.74	3,137,709.77	
Fund Equities:											
Unobligated Balances (Expired)						-14,235,118.43				-660,813.33	-13,574,305.10
Accounts Payable						-545,011.29				106,723.60	-651,734.89
Undelivered Orders						-4,999,355.05				336,259.87	-5,335,614.92
Subtotal		47		5250		-0-	12,500,000.00		9,580,120.09	2,919,879.91	-0-
Intragovernmental Funds											
General Supply Fund, General Services Administration											
Fund Resources:											
Undisbursed Funds	No Year	47		4530	1	489,965,371.15		-541,657,990.04	-51,692,618.89		
Accounts Receivable						386,819,769.90				386,819,769.90	
Unfilled Customer Orders						825,679,984.38				825,679,984.38	
Fund Equities:											
Unobligated Balances (Unexpired)						-587,853,235.96				-587,853,235.96	-587,853,235.96
Accounts Payable						-303,513,894.89				-303,513,894.89	-303,513,894.89
Undelivered Orders						-811,097,994.58				-811,097,994.58	-811,097,994.58
Subtotal		47		4530		-0-		-541,657,990.04	-51,692,618.89	-489,965,371.15	-0-

Footnotes At End Of Chapter

Appropriations, Outlays, and Balances – Continued

Appropriation or Fund Account — Title	Period of Availability	Reg	Tr From	Account Number	Sub No.	Balances, Beginning of Fiscal Year	Appropriations And Other Obligational Authority[1]	Transfers Borrowings And Investment (Net)[2]	Outlays (Net)	Balances Withdrawn And Other Transactions[3]	Balances, End Of Fiscal Year[4]
Acquisition Services Fund, General Services Administration											
Fund Resources:											
Undisbursed Funds	No Year	47		4534	1			747,613,891.59	-34,174,471.87		781,788,363.46
Accounts Receivable										-1,039,944,384.52	1,039,944,384.52
Unfilled Customer Orders										-2,886,314,295.08	2,886,314,295.08
Fund Equities:											
Unobligated Balances (Unexpired)										1,170,427,600.50	-1,170,427,600.32
Accounts Payable										968,973,450.24	-968,973,450.50
Undelivered Orders										2,568,645,992.24	-2,568,645,992.24
Subtotal		47		4534		-0-		747,613,891.59	-34,174,471.87	781,788,363.46	-0-
Information Technology Fund, General Services Administration											
Fund Resources:											
Undisbursed Funds	No Year	47		4548	1	188,309,665.92		-205,955,901.55	-17,646,235.63		
Accounts Receivable						832,104,011.20				832,104,011.20	
Unfilled Customer Orders						2,820,306,565.35				2,820,306,565.35	
Fund Equities:											
Unobligated Balances (Unexpired)						-1,234,355,987.38				-1,234,355,987.38	
Accounts Payable						-806,885,953.65				-806,885,953.65	
Undelivered Orders						-1,799,478,301.44				-1,799,478,301.44	
Subtotal		47		4548		-0-		-205,955,901.55	-17,646,235.63	-188,309,665.92	-0-
Total, Supply And Technology Activities							12,500,000.00		-93,933,206.30	106,433,206.30	
General Activities											
General Fund Accounts											
Allowances And Office Staff For Former Presidents, General Services Administration											
Fund Resources:											
Undisbursed Funds	2007	47		0105			2,922,480.00	-430,649.96	1,918,806.49		573,023.55
	2006					373,734.07			48,186.12		325,547.95
	2005					271,188.34					271,188.34
	2004					274,801.65					274,801.65
	2003					197,653.48					197,653.48
	2002					162,223.58				162,223.58	
Transfer To:											
Treasury	2007	20	47	0105				430,649.96	430,649.96		
Fund Equities:											
Unobligated Balances (Expired)	2007					-1,144,973.44				414,953.77	-1,559,927.21
Accounts Payable	2006					-50,756.61				-9,100.93	-41,655.68
Undelivered Orders	2005					-83,871.07				-43,238.99	-40,632.08
Subtotal		47		0105		-0-	2,922,480.00		2,397,642.57	524,837.43	-0-
Office Of Inspector General, General Services Administration											
Fund Resources:											
Undisbursed Funds	2007-2008	47		0108			4,500,000.00				4,500,000.00
	2007						48,121,000.00		40,656,115.49		7,464,884.51
	2006					5,395,421.78			3,661,337.32		1,734,084.46
	2005					2,193,161.13			150,107.54		2,043,053.59
	2004					431,687.84			37.37		431,650.47

Appropriations, Outlays, and Balances - Continued

Appropriation or Fund Account — Title	Period of Availability	Dept Reg	Dept Tr From	Account Number	Sub No.	Balances, Beginning of Fiscal Year	Appropriations And Other Obligational Authority[1]	Transfers Borrowings And Investment (Net)[2]	Outlays (Net)	Balances Withdrawn And Other Transactions[3]	Balances, End Of Fiscal Year[4]
	2003					359,285.74			495.00	-----	358,790.74
	2002					574,005.32		-520,000.00	7,046.04	46,959.28	-----
Accounts Receivable										-43,431.14	43,431.14
Unfilled Customer Orders										-106,354.90	106,354.90
Fund Equities:											
Unobligated Balances (Expired)						-2,257,868.87				498,776.80	-2,756,645.67
Unobligated Balances (Unexpired)										4,500,000.00	-4,500,000.00
Accounts Payable						-1,763,262.76				21,028.33	-1,784,291.09
Undelivered Orders						-4,932,430.18				2,708,882.87	-7,641,313.05
Subtotal		47		0108		-0-	52,621,000.00	-520,000.00	44,475,138.76	7,625,861.24	-0-
Operating Expenses, General Services Administration											
Fund Resources:											
Undisbursed Funds	2007	47		0110		31,394,144.76	85,998,358.52		66,818,792.90		19,179,565.62
	2006					10,688,084.21			11,976,049.00		19,418,095.76
	2005					8,332,922.14			2,092,094.01		8,595,990.20
	2004					5,931,171.52			600,270.38		7,732,651.76
	2003					5,420,014.80			1,258,510.74		4,672,660.78
	2002					6,608,840.37		-5,000,000.00	261,909.90		6,860,186.50
	No Year							537,670.00	286,323.87	158,104.90	
Accounts Receivable						1,205,978.55				275,902.77	930,075.78
Unfilled Customer Orders						972,689.70				-833,361.22	1,806,050.92
Fund Equities:											
Unobligated Balances (Expired)						-33,652,665.20				5,073,462.80	-38,726,128.00
Unobligated Balances (Unexpired)						-2,748,862.61				108,254.80	-2,857,117.41
Accounts Payable						-3,515,867.24				-548,279.58	-2,967,587.66
Undelivered Orders						-30,636,451.00				-5,992,006.75	-24,644,444.25
Subtotal		47		0110		-0-	85,998,358.52	-4,462,330.00	83,293,950.80	-1,757,922.28	-0-
Expenses, Government-Wide Policy, General Services Administration											
Fund Resources:											
Undisbursed Funds	2007	47		0401		18,148,199.27	52,346,220.00		32,164,844.18		20,181,375.82
	2006					12,407,581.31			14,447,302.79		3,700,896.48
	2005					4,597,703.29			4,996,630.45		7,410,950.86
	2004					2,505,284.92			338,044.26		4,259,659.03
	2003					51,300.00			641,986.02		1,863,298.90
Accounts Receivable						480,474.04				-102,989.00	154,289.00
Unfilled Customer Orders										-916,271.50	1,396,745.54
Fund Equities:											
Unobligated Balances (Expired)						-5,205,511.10				1,325,177.70	-6,530,688.80
Accounts Payable						-2,501,335.08				398,998.39	-2,900,333.47
Undelivered Orders						-30,483,696.65				-947,503.29	-29,536,193.36
Subtotal		47		0401		-0-	52,346,220.00		52,588,807.70	-242,587.70	-0-
Expenses, Electronic Government (E-GOV) Fund, General Services Administration											
Fund Resources:											
Undisbursed Funds	No Year	47		0600		4,277,091.97	2,970,000.00		149,757.80		7,097,334.17
Transfer To:											
National Institute Of Standards And Technology, Department Of Commerce	No Year	13	47	0600	6	940,343.33			603,824.52		336,518.81

Footnotes At End Of Chapter

Appropriations, Outlays, and Balances – Continued

Appropriation or Fund Account — Title	Period of Availability	Dept Reg	Dept Tr From	Account Number	Sub No.	Balances, Beginning of Fiscal Year	Appropriations And Other Obligational Authority[1]	Transfers Borrowings And Investment (Net)[2]	Outlays (Net)	Balances Withdrawn And Other Transactions[3]	Balances, End Of Fiscal Year[4]
Expenses, Electronic Government (E-GOV) Fund, General Services Administration - Continued											
Fund Resources – Continued:											
Undisbursed Funds – Continued:											
Transfer To – Continued:											
Office Of The Secretary	No Year	14	47	0600	1	89,421.71			47,159.53		42,262.18
Office Of Personnel Management	No Year	24	47	0600		50,000.00					50,000.00
Small Business Administration	No Year	73	47	0600		55,919.44			46,011.00		9,908.44
Fund Equities:											
Unobligated Balances (Unexpired)						-4,114,468.18				1,862,002.77	-5,976,470.95
Accounts Payable						-77,866.21				281,787.20	-359,653.41
Undelivered Orders						-1,220,442.06				-20,542.82	-1,199,899.24
Subtotal		47		0600		-0-	2,970,000.00		846,752.85	2,123,247.15	-0-
Election Reform Payments, General Services Administration											
Fund Resources:											
Undisbursed Funds	2003	47		0601		378,651.06		-378,651.06	-536,122.00		536,122.00
Fund Equities:											
Unobligated Balances (Expired)		47		0601		-378,651.06				157,470.94	-536,122.00
Subtotal		47		0601		-0-		-378,651.06	-536,122.00	157,470.94	-0-
Special Fund Accounts											
Acquisition Workforce Training Fund, General Services Administration											
Fund Resources:											
Undisbursed Funds	2007-2009	47		5381			8,476,154.64				8,476,154.64
	2006-2008					7,904,435.57	-411,113.91		2,405,540.23		5,087,781.43
	2005-2007					7,917,922.14			5,751,065.39		2,166,856.75
	2004-2006					1,431,059.48			988,942.54		442,116.94
Fund Equities:											
Unobligated Balances (Expired)						-35,082.30				43,793.02	-78,875.32
Unobligated Balances (Unexpired)						-11,730,166.28				1,195,586.02	-12,925,752.30
Accounts Payable						-225,599.37				-112,867.87	-112,731.50
Undelivered Orders						-5,262,569.24				-2,207,018.60	-3,055,550.64
Subtotal		47		5381		-0-	8,065,040.73		9,145,548.16	-1,080,507.43	-0-
Public Enterprise Funds											
Panama Canal Revolving Fund, Panama Canal Commission											
Fund Resources:											
Undisbursed Funds	No Year	95		4061		40,957,469.06			40,957,469.06	-40,957,469.06	
Fund Equities:											
Unobligated Balances (Unexpired)											
Subtotal		95		4061		40,957,469.06			40,957,469.06	-40,957,469.06	-0-
Intragovernmental Funds											
Working Capital Fund, General Services Administration											
Fund Resources:											
Undisbursed Funds	No Year	47		4540	1	164,834,913.90		5,520,000.00	-11,791,272.50		182,146,186.40

Appropriations, Outlays, and Balances - Continued

Appropriation or Fund Account	Account Symbol								
Title	Period of Availability	Dept Reg	Dept Tr From	Account Number	Sub No.	Balances, Beginning of Fiscal Year	Appropriations And Other Obligational Authority[1]	Transfers Borrowings And Investment (Net)[2]	Outlays (Net)	Balances Withdrawn And Other Transactions[3]	Balances, End Of Fiscal Year[4]
Accounts Receivable						255,840.04				140,380.96	115,459.08
Unfilled Customer Orders						329,580.06				-3,344,063.41	3,673,643.47
Fund Equities:											
Unobligated Balances (Unexpired)						-93,553,223.49				4,130,280.73	-97,683,504.22
Accounts Payable						-22,588,011.05				-1,546,149.88	-21,041,861.17
Undelivered Orders						-49,279,099.46				17,930,824.10	-67,209,923.56
	Subtotal	47		4540		-0-		5,520,000.00	-11,791,272.50	17,311,272.50	-0-
Federal Citizen Information Center Fund, General Services Administration											
Fund Resources:											
Undisbursed Funds	No Year	47		4549	1	11,802,135.46	14,874,300.00		14,048,235.70		12,628,199.76
Accounts Receivable						1,763,005.12				479,261.38	1,283,743.74
Fund Equities:											
Unobligated Balances (Unexpired)						-9,199,551.10				162,232.09	-9,361,783.19
Accounts Payable						-2,793,568.81				-623,396.76	-2,170,172.05
Undelivered Orders						-1,572,020.67				807,967.59	-2,379,988.26
	Subtotal	47		4549		-0-	14,874,300.00		14,048,235.70	826,064.30	-0-
Total, General Activities							219,797,399.25	159,018.94	235,426,151.10	-15,469,732.91	
Deductions For Offsetting Receipts											
Proprietary Receipts From The Public							-98,923,402.73		-98,923,402.73	91,760,077.52	
Intrabudgetary Transactions							-8,790,748.74		-8,790,748.74		
Total, Offsetting Receipts							-107,714,151.47		-107,714,151.47		
Total, General Services Administration							169,063,247.78	-44,929,591.55	32,373,578.71	91,760,077.52	

Footnotes At End Of Chapter

Appropriations, Outlays, and Balances – Continued

Footnotes

1   The amounts in this column, unless otherwise footnoted, represent appropriations, increases and rescissions in borrowing authority or new contract authority. Appropriation accounts with appropriation transfer activity are presented in Table 1 (Appropriations and Appropriation Transfers) at the end of this chapter.

2   The amounts in this column, unless otherwise footnoted, represent transfers - other than appropriation transfers, borrowings (gross), investments (net), unrealized discounts or cash held outside of the Treasury.

3   The amounts in this column, unless otherwise footnoted, represent obligated balances canceled for fiscal year 2002 pursuant to 31 U.S.C. 1553, changes in unfilled customer orders, accounts receivable, accounts payable, undelivered orders, unobligated balances and adjustments to borrowing and contract authority.

4   Unobligated balances for no-year or unexpired multiple year accounts are available for obligation; unobligated balances for expired fiscal year accounts are not available for obligation.

5   Includes $27,503,449.70 which represents net repayment of borrowing from the Federal Financing Bank in lieu of issuance of agency debt.

Appropriations, Outlays, and Balances - Continued

Footnotes

Table 1 - Appropriations And Appropriation Transfers - General Services Administration

Department Regular	Fiscal Year	Account Symbol	Net Appropriations And Appropriations Transfers	Appropriation Amount	Net Appropriation Transfers	Department Regular Involved	Fiscal Year Involved	Accounts Involved	Amount From or To (-)
47	07	0110	85,998,358.52	83,176,068.00	2,822,290.52	12	X	1000	142,035.37
						12	X	1103	67,075.44
						12	X	1106	217,000.00
						12	07	2900	47,345.13
						12	X	4085	284,075.44
						12	X	5209	47,345.13
						14	07	0102	436,133.45
						36	07	0151	703,000.00
						69	07	0102	591,255.56
						86	07	0143	287,025.00
47	X	4542	36,461,000.00	93,586,000.00	-57,125,000.00	17	X	1804	-57,125,000.00
Totals			122,459,358.52	176,762,068.00	-54,302,709.48				-54,302,709.48

Appropriations, Outlays, and Balances – Continued

Appropriation or Fund Account		Account Symbol				Balances, Beginning Of Fiscal Year	Appropriations And Other Obligational Authority[1]	Transfers Borrowings And Investment (Net)[2]	Outlays (Net)	Balances Withdrawn And Other Transactions[3]	Balances, End Of Fiscal Year[4]
Title	Period of Availability	Dept Reg	Tr From	Account Number	Sub No.						
International Assistance Program											
Millennium Challenge Corporation											
General Fund Accounts											
Expenses, Millennium Challenge Corporation											
Fund Resources:											
Undisbursed Funds	No Year	95		2750		3,932,579,698.06	1,752,300,000.00	-200,518,915.00	217,221,068.63	-------	5,267,139,714.43
Transfer To:											
United States Agency For International Development	No Year	72	95	2750		147,252,220.31	-------	191,102,935.00	60,175,033.46	-------	278,180,121.85
Fund Equities:											
Unobligated Balances (Unexpired)						-2,671,372,416.29				-415,108,572.54	-2,256,263,843.75
Accounts Payable						-16,527,913.89				22,420,479.38	-38,948,393.27
Undelivered Orders						-1,391,931,588.19				1,858,176,011.07	-3,250,107,599.26
Subtotal		95		2750		-0-	1,752,300,000.00	-9,415,980.00	277,396,102.09	1,465,487,917.91	-0-
Deductions For Offsetting Receipts											
Proprietary Receipts From The Public							-1,624,761.67		-1,624,761.67		
Intrabudgetary Transactions							-1,401,242.57		-1,401,242.57		
Total, Millennium Challenge Corporation							1,749,273,995.76	-9,415,980.00	274,370,097.85	1,465,487,917.91	
International Security Assistance											
General Fund Accounts											
Peacekeeping Operations, Funds Appropriated To The President											
Fund Resources:											
Undisbursed Funds	2007-2008	11		1032		-------	230,000,000.00	-230,000,000.00			
	2007					-------	243,250,000.00	-243,250,000.00			
	2002					-------		2,542,755.66		2,542,755.66	
	No Year					-------	250,000.00	-250,000.00			
Transfer To:											
Department Of State	2007-2008	19	11	1032		-------		230,000,000.00	884,687.55		229,115,312.45
	2007					177,991,100.00		243,250,000.00	51,631,225.35		191,618,774.65
	2006-2007					87,974,592.95		11,000,000.00	118,284,574.45		70,706,525.55
	2006					13,868,015.53			54,297,467.97		33,677,124.98
	2005-2006					51,448,400.17			10,162,971.04		3,705,044.49
	2005					5,610,748.83			28,135,428.01		23,312,972.16
	2004					10,154.49			1,998,915.84		3,611,832.99
	2003-2004					11,741,629.17					10,154.49
	2003					16,568.76			913,983.12		10,827,646.05
	2002-2003					3,035,238.48		-2,542,755.66	492,482.82		16,568.76
	2002					250,000.00	250,000.00		243,521.42		256,478.58
	No Year										
Fund Equities:											
Unobligated Balances (Expired)						5,660,353.56				26,976,625.81	-27,636,979.37
Unobligated Balances (Unexpired)						-117,836,888.60				52,912,681.68	-170,749,570.28

Appropriations, Outlays, and Balances - Continued

Appropriation or Fund Account — Title	Period of Availability	Reg	Tr From	Account Number	Sub No.	Balances, Beginning Of Fiscal Year	Appropriations And Other Obligational Authority[1]	Transfers Borrowings And Investment (Net)[2]	Outlays (Net)	Balances Withdrawn And Other Transactions[3]	Balances, End Of Fiscal Year[4]
Accounts Payable						[5]480,378.87				871,190.23	-390,811.36
Undelivered Orders						[5]233,929,585.09				134,151,489.05	-368,081,074.14
	Subtotal	11		1032		-0-	473,500,000.00	11,000,000.00	267,045,257.57	217,454,742.43	-0-
Nonproliferation And Disarmament Fund, Funds Appropriated To The President											
Fund Resources:											
Undisbursed Funds											
Transfer To:											
Department Of State	No Year	19	11	1071		4,146,262.58			1,278,004.20		2,868,258.38
Fund Equities:											
Unobligated Balances (Unexpired)						-2,323,136.62				545,121.76	-2,868,258.38
Accounts Payable						-210,221.45				-210,221.45	
Undelivered Orders						-1,612,904.51				-1,612,904.51	-0-
	Subtotal	11		1071		-0-			1,278,004.20	-1,278,004.20	
Non-Proliferation, Anti-Terrorism, Demining And Related Programs, Funds Appropriated To The President											
Fund Resources:											
Undisbursed Funds	2007-2008	11		1075			234,257,000.00	-234,257,000.00			
	2007						189,283,000.00	-186,324,000.00			2,959,000.00
	2002							6,448,426.11		6,448,426.11	
	2000-2002							121,361.95		121,361.95	
	1999-2000					-1,567,418.21					[6]-1,567,418.21
	1998-1999					-699,152.49					[6]-699,152.49
	No Year						37,500,000.00	-37,500,000.00	8,250.84		[6]-8,250.84
Transfer To:											
Department Of State	2007-2008	19	11	1075				234,257,000.00	50,103,745.77		184,153,254.23
	2007							186,324,000.00	89,827,179.02		96,496,820.98
	2006-2007					118,291,861.88			66,432,817.32		51,859,044.56
	2006					66,416,092.07			42,853,690.71		23,562,401.36
	2005-2006					35,698,284.77			18,196,182.91		17,502,101.86
	2005					23,461,260.61			18,538,328.82		4,922,931.79
	2004					18,524,306.84			2,476,753.75		16,047,553.09
	2003					13,646,483.42			3,419,740.55		10,226,742.87
	2002-2003					9,707,749.43			1,812,983.32		7,894,766.11
	2002					8,350,149.17		-6,449,776.92	1,900,372.25		
	2001-2002					-17,615.91		1,350.81	-16,265.10		
	2000-2002					121,361.95		-121,361.95			
	No Year					121,953,734.41		37,500,000.00	24,612,756.33		134,840,978.08
Accounts Receivable						3,000,000.00				1,430,000.00	1,570,000.00
Fund Equities:											
Unobligated Balances (Expired)						-7,266,542.19				4,071,970.27	[7]-11,338,512.46
Unobligated Balances (Unexpired)						-146,130,939.72				34,637,923.24	-180,768,862.96
Accounts Payable						-6,548,585.59				3,291,671.61	-9,840,257.20
Undelivered Orders						-256,941,030.44				90,872,110.33	-347,813,140.77
	Subtotal	11		1075		-0-	461,040,000.00		320,166,536.49	140,873,463.51	-0-

Footnotes At End Of Chapter

Appropriations, Outlays, and Balances – Continued

Appropriation or Fund Account	Account Symbol					Balances, Beginning Of Fiscal Year	Appropriations And Other Obligational Authority[1]	Transfers Borrowings And Investment (Net)[2]	Outlays (Net)	Balances Withdrawn And Other Transactions[3]	Balances, End Of Fiscal Year[4]
Title	Period of Availability	Dept Reg	Dept Tr From	Account Number	Sub No.						
International Military Education And Training, Funds Appropriated To The President											
Fund Resources:											
Undisbursed Funds	2007	11		1081			85,876,560.00	-85,441,909.00			434,651.00
	2006					560.00					560.00
	2003							75,000.00			75,000.00
	2002					215,110.00		1,538,086.33		1,753,196.33	
	2001-2002					7,342.00		367,982.04		375,324.04	
	No Year					3,249,017.00		-2,283,487.00			965,530.00
Transfer To:											
Navy	2007	17	11	1081		18,573,900.55		28,611,185.00	12,708,745.85		15,902,439.15
	2006					6,590,187.06		-100,000.00	13,324,971.77		5,148,928.78
	2005					3,441,525.34		-500,000.00	3,585,200.39		2,504,986.67
	2004					2,977,937.02		-400,000.00	370,592.47		2,670,932.87
	2003					1,612,632.36		-650,000.00	5,214.02		2,322,723.00
	2002					68,718.38		-1,509,297.07	103,335.29		
	2001-2002							-68,718.38	789,526.11		1,937,998.81
	No Year					697,228.92		2,030,296.00	17,782,334.72		20,770,716.28
Army	2007	21	11	1081		19,152,526.00		38,553,051.00	16,124,384.07		3,028,141.93
	2006					3,630,628.06			1,625,829.62		2,004,798.44
	2005					2,208,997.24			134,528.62		2,074,468.62
	2004					1,233,063.22			28,528.09		1,204,535.13
	2003					499,032.93			42,076.00		
	2002					155,440.00		-456,956.93			
	2001-2002							-155,440.00			3,022,170.28
	No Year					369,067.78		3,531,091.00	877,988.50		9,434,790.23
Air Force	2007	57	11	1081		7,786,700.49		18,277,673.00	8,842,882.77		2,123,920.60
	2006					2,104,779.16			5,662,779.89		2,035,946.11
	2005					2,342,151.99			68,833.05		2,290,324.88
	2004					1,437,649.05		-1,200,000.00	51,827.11		230,830.11
	2003					1,621,962.95		-1,621,832.33	6,818.94		
	2002					208,485.66		-143,823.66	130.62		
	2001-2002							1,547,100.00	64,662.00		
	No Year					834,939.78			644,550.69		1,737,489.09
Fund Equities:											
Unobligated Balances (Expired)						-10,551,240.93				914,580.93	-11,465,821.86
Unobligated Balances (Unexpired)						-3,893,982.64				-106,063.81	-3,787,918.83
Accounts Payable						-66,574,359.37				93,781.92	-66,668,141.29
Subtotal		11		1081		-0-	85,876,560.00		82,845,740.59	3,030,819.41	-0-
Foreign Military Financing Program, Grants, Funds Appropriated To The President											
Fund Resources:											
Undisbursed Funds	2007-2008	11		1082			265,000,000.00	-265,000,000.00	-329,649.51	-329,649.51	169,653.51
	2007						4,560,800,000.00	-4,560,959,996.00			87,608.88
	2006					87,608.88					102,925.79
	2005					102,925.79					102,369.26
	2004					102,369.26					
	2003								-215,654.79		
	2002					5,077.57		79,344.56	-72,996.32	300,076.92	72,996.32

Appropriations, Outlays, and Balances - Continued

Appropriation or Fund Account — Title	Period of Availability	Account Symbol — Dept Reg	Dept Tr From	Account Number	Sub No.	Balances, Beginning Of Fiscal Year	Appropriations And Other Obligational Authority[1]	Transfers Borrowings And Investment (Net)[2]	Outlays (Net)	Balances Withdrawn And Other Transactions[3]	Balances, End Of Fiscal Year[4]
Transfer To:											
Navy	2007	17	11	1082				1,150,000.00	1,114,589.25		35,410.75
	2006					143,056.97			123,394.48		19,662.49
	2005					9,060.79					9,060.79
	2004					3,150.79					3,150.79
	2003					1,779.15					1,779.15
	2002					2,215.15		-2,215.15			
Army	2007	21	11	1082				1,400,000.00	1,190,880.47		209,119.53
	2006					357,253.24			285,013.04		72,240.20
	2005					12,523.93					12,523.93
	2004					4,400.94					4,400.94
	2003					98,247.50			72,996.32		25,251.18
	2002					239,573.90		-28,089.31	211,484.59		
Air Force	2007	57	11	1082				950,000.00	750,686.95		199,313.05
	2006					120,065.43			103,118.94		16,946.49
	2005					27,704.76					27,704.76
	2004					6,477.68					6,477.68
	2003					1,150.07			-668.15		1,818.22
	2002					49,040.10		-49,040.10			
Defense	2007-2008	97	11	1082				265,000,000.00			265,000,000.00
	2004-2008					1,276,306.00			576,306.00		700,000.00
	2007							4,557,459,996.00	3,575,195,383.16		982,264,612.84
	2006					974,901,972.99			358,034,695.35		616,867,277.64
	2005-2006					2,000,000.00		1,378,031.24			3,378,031.24
	2002-2006					714,118,096.72			335,769,239.71		378,348,857.01
	2005					72,252,776.05			24,012,794.88		48,239,981.17
	2004					16,712,203.98			2,767,430.82		13,944,773.16
	2003					1,747,858.95		-1,378,031.24	369,827.71		
	2002					25,950,000.00			25,950,000.00		
Fund Equities:											
Unobligated Balances (Expired)	2007	11				-447,497.60				205,937.07	-653,434.67
Unobligated Balances (Unexpired)										265,000,000.00	-265,000,000.00
Accounts Payable						-926,184.30				-385,205.26	-540,979.04
Undelivered Orders						-1,808,959,214.69				234,770,318.37	-2,043,729,533.06
Subtotal		11		1082		-0-	4,825,800,000.00		4,325,908,872.90	499,891,127.10	-0-
Foreign Military Financing, Direct Loan Program Account, Funds Appropriated To The President											
Fund Resources:											
Undisbursed Funds	2007	11		1085			13,107,688.00		13,107,688.00		
Economic Support Fund, Funds Appropriated To The President											
Fund Resources:											
Undisbursed Funds	2005-2010	72		1037				1,478,886,664.72	863,852,646.81		615,034,017.91
	2004-2009					601,338,989.78		-160,000.00	266,087,517.59		335,091,472.19
	2003-2009					-5,279,499.93			-1,396,580.82		[6]3,882,919.11
	2007-2008						5,206,477,650.00	-282,222,500.00	369,242,328.08		4,555,012,821.92
	2006-2008							500,000.00	2,419.79		497,580.21
	2003-2008					322,747,387.54		-7,036,900.00	104,485,162.25		211,225,325.29
	2006-2007					3,447,693,355.99		-1,505,710,155.00	878,093,378.16		1,063,889,822.83

Footnotes At End Of Chapter

Appropriations, Outlays, and Balances – Continued

Appropriation or Fund Account — Title	Period of Availability	Reg	Tr From	Account Number	Sub No.	Balances, Beginning Of Fiscal Year	Appropriations And Other Obligational Authority[1]	Transfers Borrowings And Investment (Net)[2]	Outlays (Net)	Balances Withdrawn And Other Transactions[3]	Balances, End Of Fiscal Year[4]
Economic Support Fund, Funds Appropriated To The President - Continued											
Fund Resources: - Continued											
Undisbursed Funds - Continued											
	2005-2007					1,514,098.24			-311,752.95		1,825,851.19
	2002-2007					101,676,731.75		-3,069,100.00	51,697,374.14		46,910,257.61
	2005-2006					1,478,886,664.72		-1,478,886,664.72	-2,527,184.29		2,527,184.29
	2004-2006					9,605.00					9,605.00
	2004-2005					592,119.71		160,000.00	-448,423.06		1,200,542.77
	2003-2005					-3,177,784.93					[6] -3,177,784.93
	2003-2004					3,226,116.73			-2,783.63		3,228,900.36
	2002-2003					6,201,030.82		-9,514.44	2,880.41		6,198,150.41
	2001-2002					9,406.67			-107.77		
	No Year					15,562.85				15,562.85	
						441,392,747.65	-172,650,000.00	227,890,679.21	408,245,421.02		88,388,005.84
Transfer To:											
Justice	No Year	15		1037	1	15,494.22		-15,494.22			
Department Of State	2007-2008	19	72	1037				282,222,500.00	27,652,570.29		254,569,929.71
	2006-2008							2,000,000.00			2,000,000.00
	2005-2008							2,036,900.00			2,036,900.00
	2006-2007					138,624,193.34		1,120,043,155.00	212,021,476.06		1,046,645,872.28
	2002-2007							3,069,100.00			3,069,100.00
	2005-2006					112,938,913.44			68,888,714.05		44,050,199.39
	2004-2005					60,440,860.74			28,392,239.00		32,048,621.74
	2003-2004					18,185,471.32			10,288,848.89		7,896,622.43
	2002-2003					4,053,057.88			593,662.29		3,459,395.59
	2001-2002					317,784.74		-265,670.55	52,114.19		
	2000-2002					-180,721.97			-180,721.97		
	1995-1996					-507,847.17					[6] -507,847.17
	No Year					2,859,106.22			170,619.97		2,688,486.25
Treasury	2003-2005	20	72	1037		5,649.99					5,649.99
Department Of Energy	2004-2005	89	72	1037		741,060.34			283,606.32		457,454.02
	2003-2004					48,155.72			47,941.04		214.68
Accounts Receivable						3,971,219.00				3,435,141.00	536,078.00
Unfilled Customer Orders										54,548.00	-54,548.00
Fund Equities:											
Unobligated Balances (Expired)						-7,764,807.95				3,847,006.53	[8] 11,611,814.48
Unobligated Balances (Unexpired)						-2,570,999,760.36				-941,231,644.21	[9] -1,629,768,116.15
Accounts Payable						[5] -527,457,633.14				133,016,431.00	-660,474,064.14
Undelivered Orders						[5] -3,632,136,728.95				2,388,890,238.97	-6,021,026,967.92
	Subtotal	72		1037		-0-	5,033,827,650.00	-160,567,000.00	3,285,233,365.86	1,588,027,284.14	-0-
Central America And The Caribbean Emergency Disaster Recovery Fund, Agency For International Development											
Fund Resources:											
Undisbursed Funds	2005-2006	72		1096		-21,969.31					[6] -21,969.31
	No Year					1,120,218.00		2,182,849.94			[6] -1,062,631.94
Unfilled Customer Orders						424.00				424.00	
Fund Equities:											
Unobligated Balances (Unexpired)						-1,674,550.83				158,000.68	-1,832,551.51
Accounts Payable						-996,572.34				-106,087.41	-890,484.93

Appropriations, Outlays, and Balances - Continued

Appropriation or Fund Account Title	Period of Availability	Dept Reg	Tr From	Account Number	Sub No.	Balances, Beginning Of Fiscal Year	Appropriations And Other Obligational Authority[1]	Transfers Borrowings And Investment (Net)[2]	Outlays (Net)	Balances Withdrawn And Other Transactions[3]	Balances, End Of Fiscal Year[4]
Undelivered Orders	Subtotal	72		1096		1,572,450.48 / -0-			2,182,849.94	-2,235,187.21 / -2,182,849.94	3,807,637.69 / -0-
Public Enterprise Funds											
Foreign Military Loan Liquidating Account, Funds Appropriated To The President											
Fund Resources:											
Undisbursed Funds	No Year	11		4121			8,400,000.00	-187,479,370.85	-287,187,010.31	[10]108,107,639.46	
Deductions For Offsetting Receipts											
Proprietary Receipts From The Public							-26,275,046.71		-26,275,046.71		
Total, International Security Assistance							10,875,276,851.29	-337,046,370.85	7,984,306,258.53	2,553,924,221.91	
Multilateral Assistance											
General Fund Accounts											
Contribution To The Inter-American Development Bank, Funds Appropriated To The President											
Fund Resources:											
Undisbursed Funds	No Year	11		0072		3,803,024,688.48	909,150,000.00		2,750,000.00		3,800,274,688.48
Fund Equities:											
Unobligated Balances (Unexpired)						-3,797,774,687.48					-3,797,774,687.48
Undelivered Orders	Subtotal	11		0072		-5,250,001.00 / -0-	909,150,000.00		2,750,000.00	-2,750,000.00	-2,500,001.00 / -0-
Contribution To The International Development Association, Funds Appropriated To The President											
Fund Resources:											
Undisbursed Funds	No Year	11		0073		674,787,288.00	909,150,000.00		1,434,787,288.00		149,150,000.00
Fund Equities:											
Unobligated Balances (Unexpired)						-188,100,000.00				-188,100,000.00	-149,150,000.00
Undelivered Orders	Subtotal	11		0073		-486,687,288.00 / -0-	909,150,000.00		1,434,787,288.00	-337,537,288.00 / -525,637,288.00	-0-
Contribution To The Asian Development Fund, Funds Appropriated To The President											
Fund Resources:											
Undisbursed Funds	No Year	11		0076		819,684,719.50	99,000,000.00		47,744,000.00		870,940,719.50
Fund Equities:											
Unobligated Balances (Unexpired)						-748,095,669.50					-748,095,669.50
Undelivered Orders	Subtotal	11		0076		-71,589,050.00 / -0-	99,000,000.00		47,744,000.00	51,256,000.00 / 51,256,000.00	-122,845,050.00 / -0-
Global Environment Facility, Funds Appropriated To The President											
Fund Resources:											
Undisbursed Funds	No Year	11		0077		2,126,618,135.41	79,200,000.00		69,517,636.00		2,136,300,499.41
Authority To Borrow From The Treasury						5,715,000,000.00					5,715,000,000.00

Footnotes At End Of Chapter

Appropriations, Outlays, and Balances – Continued

Appropriation or Fund Account — Title	Period of Availability	Reg	Tr From	Account Number	Sub No.	Balances, Beginning Of Fiscal Year	Appropriations And Other Obligational Authority[1]	Transfers Borrowings And Investment (Net)[2]	Outlays (Net)	Balances Withdrawn And Other Transactions[3]	Balances, End Of Fiscal Year[4]
Global Environment Facility, Funds Appropriated To The President - Continued											
Fund Equities:											
Unobligated Balances (Unexpired)						-7,663,345,499.41					-7,663,345,499.41
Undelivered Orders						-178,272,636.00	79,200,000.00		69,517,636.00	9,682,364.00	-187,955,000.00
Subtotal		11		0077		-0-				9,682,364.00	-0-
Contribution To The International Finance Corporation, Funds Appropriated To The President											
Fund Resources:											
Undisbursed Funds	No Year	11		0078		1,367.00					1,367.00
Fund Equities:											
-Unobligated Balances (Unexpired)						-1,367.00					-1,367.00
Subtotal		11		0078		-0-					-0-
Contribution To The African Development Fund, Funds Appropriated To The President											
Fund Resources:											
Undisbursed Funds	No Year	11		0079		359,835,403.72	134,343,000.00		190,594,350.00		303,584,053.72
Fund Equities:											
Undelivered Orders						-359,835,403.72				-56,251,350.00	-303,584,053.72
Subtotal		11		0079		-0-	134,343,000.00		190,594,350.00	-56,251,350.00	-0-
Contribution To The African Development Bank, Funds Appropriated To The President											
Fund Resources:											
Undisbursed Funds	No Year	11		0082			3,601,620.00		3,601,620.00		
Contribution To The Multilateral Investment Guarantee Agency, Funds Appropriated To The President											
Fund Resources:											
Undisbursed Funds	No Year	11		0084		22,201,558.00					22,201,558.00
Fund Equities:											
Undelivered Orders						-22,201,558.00					-22,201,558.00
Subtotal		11		0084		-0-					-0-
Contribution To The European Bank For Reconstruction And Development, Funds Appropriated To The President											
Fund Resources:											
Undisbursed Funds	No Year	11		0088		24,703,874.00			12,859,762.50		11,844,111.50
Fund Equities:											
Undelivered Orders						-24,703,874.00			12,859,762.50	-12,859,762.50	-11,844,111.50
Subtotal		11		0088		-0-				-12,859,762.50	-0-
Contribution To The Enterprise For The Americas Multilateral Investment Fund, Funds Appropriated To The President											
Fund Resources:											
Undisbursed Funds	No Year	11		0089		51,550,476.00	1,724,100.00		20,036,670.00		33,237,906.00
Fund Equities:											
Undelivered Orders						-51,550,476.00			20,036,670.00	-18,312,570.00	-33,237,906.00
Subtotal		11		0089		-0-	1,724,100.00			-18,312,570.00	-0-
Debt Restructuring, Funds Appropriated To The President											
Fund Resources:											
Undisbursed Funds	2007-2009	11		0091			64,350,000.00				64,350,000.00

Appropriations, Outlays, and Balances - Continued

Appropriation or Fund Account — Title	Dept Reg	Tr From	Account Number	Sub No.	Period of Availability	Balances, Beginning Of Fiscal Year	Appropriations And Other Obligational Authority[1]	Transfers Borrowings And Investment (Net)[2]	Outlays (Net)	Balances Withdrawn And Other Transactions[3]	Balances, End Of Fiscal Year[4]
					2006-2008		64,350,000.00			--------	64,350,000.00
					2006-2007			11,000,000.00	5,543,608.00	--------	5,456,392.00
					2005-2007	37,070,453.00			12,132,151.00	--------	24,938,302.00
					2005-2006	174,808.00				--------	174,808.00
					2004-2006	74,557,500.00				--------	74,557,500.00
					2002-2003	2,123,306.00				--------	2,123,306.00
					No Year	114,604,017.84			45,736,413.20	--------	68,867,604.64
Transfer To:											
United States Agency For International Development	72	11	0091		2005-2007	200,000.00			158,725.38	--------	41,274.62
					No Year	104,783.44			49,624.55	--------	55,158.89
Fund Equities:											
Unobligated Balances (Expired)						-2.00				6,016,187.62	-6,016,189.62
Unobligated Balances (Unexpired)						-142,108,514.44				18,925,732.72	-161,034,247.16
Accounts Payable						-878.47				-878.47	
Undelivered Orders						-151,075,473.37				-13,211,564.00	-137,863,909.37
Subtotal			0091		Subtotal	-0-	64,350,000.00	11,000,000.00	63,620,522.13	11,729,477.87	-0-
Multilateral Assistance, North American Development Bank, Funds Appropriated To The President											
Fund Resources:											
Undisbursed Funds	11		1008		No Year	50,625,000.00			13,641,250.00		36,983,750.00
Fund Equities:											
Undelivered Orders						-50,625,000.00				-13,641,250.00	-36,983,750.00
Subtotal	11		1008		Subtotal	-0-			13,641,250.00	-13,641,250.00	-0-
Contribution To The International Fund For Agricultural Development, Funds Appropriated To The President											
Fund Resources:											
Undisbursed Funds	11		1039		No Year	8,540,661.00	14,850,000.00		8,540,661.00		14,850,000.00
Fund Equities:											
Undelivered Orders						-8,540,661.00				6,309,339.00	-14,850,000.00
Subtotal	11		1039		Subtotal	-0-	14,850,000.00		8,540,661.00	6,309,339.00	-0-
International Affairs Technical Assistance											
Fund Resources:											
Undisbursed Funds	11		1045		2007-2009		19,800,000.00		3,711,832.20		16,088,167.80
					2007-2008		12,005,000.00		38,426.55		11,966,573.45
					2006-2008	15,959,794.88			9,752,261.86		6,207,533.02
					2006-2007	24,550,026.57		1,850,000.00	10,813,621.44		15,586,405.13
					2005-2007	7,863,895.06			4,449,925.57		3,413,969.49
					2005-2006	6,156,306.08			4,581,882.82		1,574,423.26
					2004-2006	3,898,544.96			2,074,050.67		1,824,494.29
					2004-2005	1,417,523.33			585,563.94		831,959.39
					2003-2004	1,926,717.95			904,895.61		1,021,822.34
					2002-2003	1,743,989.65			379,946.64		1,364,043.01
					2001-2002	2,661,064.20			1,972,457.52	688,606.68	
					No Year	20,100,914.01			1,828,767.67		18,272,146.34
Fund Equities:											
Unobligated Balances (Expired)						-4,396,874.25				-1,953,454.19	-2,443,420.06
Unobligated Balances (Unexpired)						-44,325,903.24				-11,576,596.23	-32,749,307.01
Accounts Payable						-1,721,075.37				1,078,830.11	-2,799,905.48

Footnotes At End Of Chapter

Appropriations, Outlays, and Balances – Continued

Appropriation or Fund Account — Title	Period of Availability	Dept Reg	Tr From	Account Number	Sub No.	Balances, Beginning Of Fiscal Year	Appropriations And Other Obligational Authority[1]	Transfers Borrowings And Investment (Net)[2]	Outlays (Net)	Balances Withdrawn And Other Transactions[3]	Balances, End Of Fiscal Year[4]
International Affairs Technical Assistance - Continued											
Fund Equities: - Continued											
Undelivered Orders						-35,834,923.83				4,323,981.14	-40,158,904.97
Subtotal		11		1045		-0-	31,805,000.00	1,850,000.00	41,093,632.49	-7,438,632.49	-0-
International Organizations And Programs, Funds Appropriated To The President, State											
Fund Resources:											
Undisbursed Funds	2007	19		1005			281,613,420.00	22,275,000.00	178,992,370.00		124,896,050.00
	2006					8,248,854.00			4,941,716.00		3,307,138.00
	2005-2006					4,236,455.00			4,236,467.00		[6]-12.00
	2005					0.60					0.60
	2004					6,705,992.00					6,705,992.00
	2003					13,731.00					13,731.00
	2002					98,239.63				98,239.63	
	2001-2002					100,000.00				100,000.00	
Transfer To:											
Department Of State	1990	19	11	1005		-1,694,744.51					[6]-1,694,744.51
Fund Equities:											
Unobligated Balances (Expired)						1,694,743.91				-12.00	[11]1,694,755.91
Accounts Payable						[5]175,000.00				370,012.00	-195,012.00
Undelivered Orders						[5]19,578,271.63				115,149,627.37	-134,727,899.00
Subtotal		19		1005		-0-	281,613,420.00	22,275,000.00	188,170,553.00	115,717,867.00	-0-
Global Fund To Fight HIV/AIDS, Malaria, And Tuberculosis, U.S. Agency For International Development											
Fund Resources:											
Undisbursed Funds	No Year	72		1028		99,000,000.00	99,000,000.00		99,000,000.00		99,000,000.00
Fund Equities:											
Unobligated Balances (Unexpired)						-99,000,000.00					-99,000,000.00
Subtotal		72		1028		-0-	99,000,000.00		99,000,000.00		-0-
Deductions For Offsetting Receipts											
Proprietary Receipts From The Public							-6,976,089.36		-6,976,089.36		
Total, Multilateral Assistance							1,711,661,050.64	35,125,000.00	2,188,981,855.76	-442,195,805.12	
International Development Assistance											
Agency For International Development											
General Fund Accounts											
Capital Investment Fund, United States Agency For International Development											
Fund Resources:											
Undisbursed Funds	No Year	72		0300		23,294,744.76	69,300,000.00		71,837,185.31		20,757,559.45
Fund Equities:											
Unobligated Balances (Unexpired)						-2,441,764.11				3,197,932.99	-5,639,697.10
Accounts Payable						-9,372,631.21				-2,135,354.59	-7,237,276.62
Undelivered Orders						-11,480,349.44				-3,599,763.71	-7,880,585.73

Appropriations, Outlays, and Balances - Continued

Appropriation or Fund Account — Title	Reg	Tr From	Account Number	Sub No.	Period of Availability	Balances, Beginning Of Fiscal Year	Appropriations And Other Obligational Authority[1]	Transfers Borrowings And Investment (Net)[2]	Outlays (Net)	Balances Withdrawn And Other Transactions[3]	Balances, End Of Fiscal Year[4]
	72		0300		Subtotal	-0-	69,300,000.00		71,837,185.31	-2,537,185.31	-0-
Loan Guarantees To Israel Program Account, International Assistance Programs, Agency For International Development											
Fund Resources:											
Undisbursed Funds	72		0301		No Year		54,357,128.00		54,357,128.00		
Loans Guarantees To Egypt Program Account, International Assistance Programs, Agency For International Development											
Fund Resources:											
Undisbursed Funds	72		0304		No Year		15,514,504.00		15,514,504.00		
Micro And Small Enterprise Development Program Account, Agency For International Development											
Fund Resources:											
Undisbursed Funds	72		0400		1999-2000	-328.48					[6]328.48
					1997	-714,616.00					[6]714,616.00
					1996	-17,950.00					[6]17,950.00
					No Year	4,306,957.10	34,253.00				4,306,957.10
Accounts Receivable						781,896.24				18,000.00	763,896.24
Fund Equities:											
Unobligated Balances (Expired)						18,920.50				972.02	[1]217,948.48
Unobligated Balances (Unexpired)						-1,906,752.00					-1,906,752.00
Accounts Payable						-332,179.68				-936,704.44	604,524.76
Undelivered Orders						-2,135,947.68				917,732.42	-3,053,680.10
	72		0400		Subtotal	-0-	34,253.00		34,253.00		-0-
Urban And Environmental Credit Program Account, Agency For International Development											
Fund Resources:											
Undisbursed Funds	72		0401		2006	-15,547.12			-15,547.12		
					2005	-347.13			-347.13		
					2003	347.13			347.13		
					No Year	1,501,450.00					1,501,450.00
Fund Equities:											
Unobligated Balances (Expired)						831.01				831.01	
Unobligated Balances (Unexpired)						-1,501,450.00					-1,501,450.00
Accounts Payable						-831.01				-831.01	
Undelivered Orders						15,547.12				15,547.12	
	72		0401		Subtotal	-0-			-15,547.12	15,547.12	-0-
Assistance For The New Independent States Of The Former Soviet Union: Ukraine Export Credit Insurance Program Account											
Fund Resources:											
Undisbursed Funds	72		0402		No Year	238,727.09					238,727.09
Fund Equities:											
Unobligated Balances (Unexpired)	72		0402			-0.82					-0.82
Undelivered Orders						-238,726.27					-238,726.27
	72		0402		Subtotal	-0-					-0-

Footnotes At End Of Chapter

Appropriations, Outlays, and Balances – Continued

Appropriation or Fund Account — Title	Period of Availability	Reg	Tr From	Account Number	Sub No.	Balances, Beginning Of Fiscal Year	Appropriations And Other Obligational Authority[1]	Transfers Borrowings And Investment (Net)[2]	Outlays (Net)	Balances Withdrawn And Other Transactions[3]	Balances, End Of Fiscal Year[4]
Operating Expenses Of The United States Agency For International Development, Funds Appropriated To The President											
Fund Resources:											
Undisbursed Funds	2006-2010	72		1000			33,906.00	116,863,042.80	84,393,540.70		32,503,408.10
	2005-2010							28,090,661.52	15,531,646.56		12,559,014.96
	2005-2009					6,335,320.59			8,219,146.46		[6]1,883,825.87
	2004-2009					14,381,066.82			7,104,797.68		7,276,269.14
	2007-2008						29,336,832.00				29,336,832.00
	2006-2008							74,250.00	-55,040.88		129,290.88
	2004-2008					-12,203,666.00			3,379,412.97		[6]-15,583,078.97
	2007						606,194,911.00		457,688,654.26		148,506,256.74
	2006-2007					102,946,352.44		6,655,362.00	29,585,850.25		80,015,864.19
	2005-2007					100,000.00			13,194.02		86,805.98
	2003-2007					-583,405.75			2,758,740.17		[6]-3,342,145.92
	2002-2007					4,107,169.11			68,357.16		4,038,811.95
	2006					125,568,973.95		-123,518,404.80	3,905,765.44		[6]-1,855,196.29
	2005-2006					28,263,000.62		-28,090,661.52	92,620.62		79,718.48
	2002-2006					2,350,016.02			2,949,237.36		[6]-599,221.34
	2005					613,182.61			955,020.82		[6]-341,838.21
	2004-2005					89,821.33			46,753.96		43,067.37
	2004					-488,340.46			374,229.93		[6]-862,570.39
	2003-2004					22,311.37			518.20		21,793.17
	2003					-10,770.28			4,328.78		[6]-15,099.06
	2002-2003					3,397.33			7,299.30		[6]-3,901.97
	2002					141,844.11			13,907.86	127,936.25	
	2001-2002					91.20				91.20	
	No Year					1,971,200.42		9,415,980.00	3,987,719.51		7,399,460.91
Transfer To:											
Department Of State	1995	19	72	1000		-313,446.40					[6]-313,446.40
Accounts Receivable						224,938.89					224,938.89
Unfilled Customer Orders						[5]3,463,693.76				3,741,950.72	-278,256.96
Fund Equities:											
Unobligated Balances (Expired)						-9,420,077.47				-2,206,895.10	[13]-7,213,182.37
Unobligated Balances (Unexpired)						[5]-106,980,476.26				-47,497,223.17	-59,483,253.09
Accounts Payable						[5]51,397,829.14				86,596,292.23	-137,994,121.37
Undelivered Orders						[5]-109,184,368.81				-16,731,974.26	-92,452,394.55
Subtotal		72		1000		-0-	635,565,649.00	9,490,230.00	621,025,701.13	24,030,177.87	-0-
Operating Expenses Of The United States Agency For International Development, Office Of The Inspector General, Funds Appropriated To The President											
Fund Resources:											
Undisbursed Funds	2005-2010	72		1007		4,276,458.82		978,570.68	3,183,881.30		[6]2,205,310.62
	2004-2009								482,335.03		3,794,123.79
	2007-2008						40,343,000.00		29,327,784.19		11,015,215.81
	2003-2008					1,934,252.59			722,995.44		1,211,257.15
	2006-2007					10,793,373.38			5,266,726.21		5,526,647.17
	2002-2007					2,719,549.94			730,125.00		1,989,424.94
	2005-2006					1,016,394.75		-978,570.68	18,699.95		19,124.12
	2004-2005					11,842.85			2,413.56		9,429.29
	2003-2004					1,040,307.54					1,040,307.54

Appropriations, Outlays, and Balances - Continued

Appropriation or Fund Account — Title	Period of Availability	Account Symbol — Dept Reg	Account Symbol — Dept Tr From	Account Number	Sub No.	Balances, Beginning Of Fiscal Year	Appropriations And Other Obligational Authority[1]	Transfers Borrowings And Investment (Net)[2]	Outlays (Net)	Balances Withdrawn And Other Transactions[3]	Balances, End Of Fiscal Year[4]
	2002-2003					890.99					890.99
	2001-2002					10,136.30				10,136.30	----
	No Year					1,238,359.30			445,738.24		792,621.06
Unfilled Customer Orders						[5]1,299,213.98				350,829.98	948,384.00
Fund Equities:											
Unobligated Balances (Expired)						[5]529,372.25				-64,702.84	-464,669.41
Unobligated Balances (Unexpired)						-6,044,672.48				2,605,904.27	-8,650,576.75
Accounts Payable						-11,395,264.60				-5,167,440.38	-6,227,824.22
Undelivered Orders						-6,371,471.11				2,427,573.75	-8,799,044.86
Subtotal		72		1007		-0-	40,343,000.00		40,180,698.92	162,301.08	-0-
Assistance For Eastern Europe And The Baltic States, Funds Appropriated To The President											
Fund Resources:											
Undisbursed Funds	2005-2010	72		1010		4,420,945.09		67,393,404.59	53,175,513.36		14,217,891.23
	2004-2009								9,372,671.72		[6]4,951,726.63
	2007-2008					-16,646,313.21	409,523,000.00	-37,612,000.00	15,308,212.99		356,602,787.01
	2003-2008					214,962,021.05		-11,517,880.40	3,706,617.34		[6]20,352,930.55
	2006-2007					9,173,072.24		-17,241.00	142,647,482.95		60,796,657.70
	2002-2007					67,414,796.86		-67,393,404.59	3,952,953.31		5,202,877.93
	2005-2006					232,321.46			134,959.83		[6]113,567.56
	2004-2005					-5,047.70		14,010.66	35,735.72		196,585.74
	2003-2004					719,409.42					8,962.96
	2001-2002					96,887.96		912,203.08	6,098.45		713,310.97
	No Year					30,556,734.76		-52,629.73	-92,848,814.32	1,009,091.04	123,352,919.35
Transfer To:											
Justice	No Year	15	72	1010	1	16,476.27		-16,476.27			----
Departmental Management, Department Of Labor	No Year	16	72	1010		10,317.04			10,317.04		10,317.04
Department Of State	2007-2008	19	72	1010		22,827,262.74		37,612,000.00	15,884,777.25		21,727,222.75
	2006-2007					9,188,654.57		6,938,500.00	11,974,786.63		17,790,976.11
	2005-2006					2,402,864.40			6,736,856.36		2,451,798.21
	2004-2005					2,082,380.41			1,308,099.29		1,094,765.11
	2003-2004					-675,703.65			315,585.99		1,766,794.42
	2002-2003					1,035,571.15			165,123.51		[6]840,827.16
Nuclear Regulatory Commission	2001-2002	31	72	1010		450,588.67		-912,203.08	123,368.07		425,527.56
	2002-2003					1,598.54			25,061.11		1,598.54
Unfilled Customer Orders	No Year					18,970.39				18,970.39	
Fund Equities:											
Unobligated Balances (Expired)						-1,915,231.25				-460,556.00	[14]1,454,675.25
Unobligated Balances (Unexpired)						-93,139,216.10				182,549,813.37	-275,689,029.47
Accounts Payable						[5]55,598,097.65				25,291,802.71	-80,889,900.36
Undelivered Orders						[5]197,631,263.46				24,437,072.19	-222,068,335.65
Subtotal		72		1010		-0-	409,523,000.00	-4,651,716.74	172,025,089.56	232,846,193.70	-0-
Sahel Development Program, Funds Appropriated To The President											
Fund Resources:											
Undisbursed Funds	No Year	72		1012		578,714.12			349,901.85		228,812.27

Footnotes At End Of Chapter

Appropriations, Outlays, and Balances – Continued

Appropriation or Fund Account — Title	Dept Reg	Tr From	Account Number	Sub No.	Period of Availability	Balances, Beginning Of Fiscal Year	Appropriations And Other Obligational Authority[1]	Transfers Borrowings And Investment (Net)[2]	Outlays (Net)	Balances Withdrawn And Other Transactions[3]	Balances, End Of Fiscal Year[4]
Sahel Development Program, Funds Appropriated To The President - Continued											
Fund Equities:											
Unobligated Balances (Unexpired)						-450,911.26					-450,911.26
Accounts Payable										-1,358,811.52	1,358,811.52
Undelivered Orders						-127,802.86				1,008,909.67	-1,136,712.53
Subtotal	72		1012			-0-			349,901.85	-349,901.85	-0-
Sub-Saharan Africa, Development Assistance, Funds Appropriated To The President											
Fund Resources:											
Undisbursed Funds	72		1014		No Year	-3,298,272.31			5,687,454.19		[6]-8,985,726.50
Transfer To:											
Department Of State	19	72	1014		No Year	29,107.73					29,107.73
Unfilled Customer Orders						4,647.54				4,647.54	
Fund Equities:											
Unobligated Balances (Unexpired)						-8,586,493.88				-206,729.54	-8,379,764.34
Accounts Payable						-3,380,327.64				5,931,212.74	-9,311,540.38
Undelivered Orders						15,231,338.56				-11,416,584.93	26,647,923.49
Subtotal	72		1014			-0-			5,687,454.19	-5,687,454.19	-0-
Development Assistance, Agency For International Development, Funds Appropriated To The President											
Fund Resources:											
Undisbursed Funds	72		1021		2005-2010			593,510,944.93	411,571,411.52		181,939,533.41
					2004-2009	47,443,586.25			-39,934,264.88		87,377,851.13
					2007-2008		1,504,431,000.00		46,801,496.23		1,457,629,503.77
					2004-2008	107,698,932.99			146,082,747.70		[6]-38,383,814.71
					2003-2008	202,700,160.01			79,413,545.94		123,286,614.07
					2007				64,862.42		[6]-64,862.42
					2006-2007	1,424,477,932.99			627,561,245.71		787,981,687.28
					2002-2007	42,912,441.24			36,031,290.36		6,881,150.88
					2006	-47,682.19			185,422.52		[6]-233,104.71
					2005-2006	594,033,940.06		-593,510,944.93	2,125,713.19		[6]-1,602,718.06
					2004-2006	-4,051.41					[6]-4,051.41
					2005	-682.55			22,952.60		[6]-23,635.15
					2004-2005	30,752,383.83			7,952.84		30,744,430.99
					2004	-107,814.77			114,086.60		[6]-221,901.37
					2003-2004	152,765.29			221,047.70		[6]-68,282.41
					2002-2003	2,891,139.87			2,957.74		2,888,182.13
					2001-2002	390,849.47				390,849.47	
	72				No Year	260,820,435.41	45,434,200.00		64,645,984.37		241,608,651.04
Transfer To:											
Interior, United States Geological Survey	14	72	1021		2006-2007			5,000,000.00	3,893,931.13		1,106,068.87
Department Of State	19	72	1021		2006-2007			3,435,000.00	233,221.04		3,201,778.96
					2005-2006	8.53					8.53
					2004	282,000.00					282,000.00
					2003-2004	29,301.62					29,301.62
					No Year	216,122.36					216,122.36
Treasury	20	72	1021	1	2002-2003	131,259.85					131,259.85
Unfilled Customer Orders						[6]-647,633.41				475,925.41	171,708.00

Appropriations, Outlays, and Balances - Continued

Appropriation or Fund Account — Title	Period of Availability	Reg	Tr From	Account Number	Sub No.	Balances, Beginning Of Fiscal Year	Appropriations And Other Obligational Authority[1]	Transfers Borrowings And Investment (Net)[2]	Outlays (Net)	Balances Withdrawn And Other Transactions[3]	Balances, End Of Fiscal Year[4]
Fund Equities:											
Unobligated Balances (Expired)						[5]-3,310,989.92				4,630,428.79	[1][5]-7,941,418.71
Unobligated Balances (Unexpired)						[5]-122,820,037.11				173,695,999.63	-296,516,036.74
Accounts Payable						[5]-394,920,573.85				49,285,435.33	-444,206,009.18
Undelivered Orders						[5]-2,194,369,061.38				-58,159,043.36	-2,136,210,018.02
Subtotal	Subtotal	72		1021		-0-	1,549,865,200.00	-500,000.00	1,379,045,604.73	170,319,595.27	-0-
Food And Nutrition, Development Assistance, Economic Assistance, Funds Appropriated To The President											
Fund Resources:											
Undisbursed Funds	No Year	72		1023		2,767,540.10			84.06		2,767,456.04
Fund Equities:											
Unobligated Balances (Unexpired)		72		1023		-2,767,500.48					-2,767,500.48
Accounts Payable						-39.62				-39.62	39.62
Undelivered Orders						-0-				-44.44	4.82
Subtotal	Subtotal	72		1023		-39.62			84.06	-84.06	-0-
Population Planning And Health, Development Assistance, Economic Assistance, Funds Appropriated To The President											
Fund Resources:											
Undisbursed Funds	No Year	72		1024		272,215.67			50.37		272,165.30
Fund Equities:											
Unobligated Balances (Unexpired)		72		1024		-272,441.82					-272,441.82
Accounts Payable						226.15				226.15	-226.15
Undelivered Orders						-0-				-276.52	502.67
Subtotal	Subtotal	72		1024		-0-			50.37	-50.37	-0-
Education And Human Resources Development, Development Assistance, Economic Assistance, Funds Appropriated To The President											
Fund Resources:											
Undisbursed Funds	No Year	72		1025		3,193,669.10					3,193,669.10
Fund Equities:											
Unobligated Balances (Unexpired)		72		1025		-2,649,022.09					-2,649,022.09
Accounts Payable						-544,647.01				-275,167.56	275,167.56
Undelivered Orders						-0-				275,167.56	-819,814.57
Subtotal	Subtotal	72		1025		-0-					-0-
Transition Initiatives, International Assistance Program, United States Agency For International Development											
Fund Resources:											
Undisbursed Funds	2005-2006	72				1,441,848.00			1,208,632.25		233,215.75
	2003-2004					165,120.65					165,120.65
	No Year					43,067,155.66	43,600,000.00		39,470,876.89		47,196,278.77
Fund Equities:											
Unobligated Balances (Expired)						-469.24					-469.24
Unobligated Balances (Unexpired)						-7,855,471.44				321,548.26	-8,177,019.70
Accounts Payable						-7,567,443.26				-1,579,251.01	-5,988,192.25
Undelivered Orders						-29,250,740.37				4,178,193.61	-33,428,933.98
Subtotal	Subtotal	72		1027		-0-	43,600,000.00		40,679,509.14	2,920,490.86	-0-
HIV/AIDS Working Capital Fund, Agency For International Development											
Fund Resources:											
Undisbursed Funds	No Year	72		1033		57,502,306.00			-228,244,319.86		285,746,625.86

Footnotes At End Of Chapter

Appropriations, Outlays, and Balances – Continued

Title	Period of Availability	Dept Reg	Dept Tr From	Account Number	Sub No.	Balances, Beginning Of Fiscal Year	Appropriations And Other Obligational Authority[1]	Transfers Borrowings And Investment (Net)[2]	Outlays (Net)	Balances Withdrawn And Other Transactions[3]	Balances, End Of Fiscal Year[4]
HIV/AIDS Working Capital Fund, Agency For International Development - Continued											
Fund Resources: - Continued											
Unfilled Customer Orders										-58,872,715.24	58,872,715.24
Fund Equities:											
Unobligated Balances (Unexpired)						-10,294,000.00				130,382,172.02	-140,676,172.02
Accounts Payable										46,719,743.50	-46,719,743.50
Undelivered Orders						-47,208,306.00				110,015,119.58	-157,223,425.58
Subtotal		72		1033		-0-			-228,244,319.86	228,244,319.86	-0-
International Disaster And Famine Assistance, Funds Appropriated To The President, United States Agency For International Development											
Fund Resources:											
Undisbursed Funds	2006-2007	72		1035					701.50		[6]701.50
	2005-2006					17,851,482.09			9,524,492.86		8,326,989.23
	2005					11,252,886.60			1,531,110.61		9,721,775.99
	2004-2005					15,923,335.18			5,809,989.81		10,113,345.37
	2002-2003					2,735,276.00					2,735,276.00
	No Year					616,464,348.65	526,316,094.00	50,771.36	486,314,929.46		656,516,284.55
Transfer To:											
Executive Office Of The President, Funds Appropriated To The President	2004-2005	11	72	1035	1	15,399,204.31			16,107.95		15,383,096.36
Justice	No Year	15	72	1035		50,771.36		-50,771.36			
Department Of State	2004-2005	19	72	1035		24,002,300.67			20,672,050.59		3,330,250.08
	No Year					209,460.27			209,460.27		209,460.27
Unfilled Customer Orders						1,052,937.92				808,787.33	244,150.59
Fund Equities:											
Unobligated Balances (Expired)						-1,593,822.13				790,446.86	-2,384,268.99
Unobligated Balances (Unexpired)						-64,494,366.25				62,983,814.49	-127,478,180.74
Accounts Payable						[5]-205,915,668.38				35,386,861.54	-241,302,529.92
Undelivered Orders						[5]-432,938,146.29				-97,523,199.00	-335,414,947.29
Subtotal		72		1035		-0-	526,316,094.00		523,869,382.78	2,446,711.22	-0-
Payment To The Foreign Service Retirement And Disability Fund, Funds Appropriated To The President											
Fund Resources:											
Undisbursed Funds	2007	72		1036			41,700,000.00		41,700,000.00		
	2005					47.83					47.83
Fund Equities:											
Accounts Payable										-47.83	47.83
Undelivered Orders						-47.83				47.83	-95.66
Subtotal		72		1036		-0-	41,700,000.00		41,700,000.00		-0-
Sub-Saharan Africa Disaster Assistance, Funds Appropriated To The President											
Fund Resources:											
Undisbursed Funds	No Year	72		1040		2,054,542.64			-9.00		2,054,551.64
Fund Equities:											
Unobligated Balances (Unexpired)						-1,233,076.75				9.00	-1,233,085.75
Accounts Payable						-607,764.00				-633,399.33	25,635.33
Undelivered Orders						-213,701.89				633,399.33	-847,101.22
Subtotal		72		1040		-0-			-9.00	9.00	-0-

Appropriations, Outlays, and Balances - Continued

Appropriation or Fund Account — Title	Period of Availability	Reg	Tr From	Account Number	Sub No.	Balances, Beginning Of Fiscal Year	Appropriations And Other Obligational Authority[1]	Transfers Borrowings And Investment (Net)[2]	Outlays (Net)	Balances Withdrawn And Other Transactions[3]	Balances, End Of Fiscal Year[4]
Assistance For The Independent States Of The Former Soviet Union, Funds Appropriated To The President											
Fund Resources:											
Undisbursed Funds	2005-2010	72		1093					106,438,463.47		56,875,197.12
	2004-2009					58,775,692.90		163,313,660.59	30,319,067.05		28,456,625.85
	2007-2008						373,639,800.00	-40,254,965.00	23,660,168.51		309,724,666.49
	2006-2008							668,250.00	-144,814.98		813,064.98
	2003-2008					-26,124,604.42			5,377,179.34		[6]-31,501,783.76
	2006-2007					328,279,385.18		-6,409,000.00	200,788,954.50		121,081,430.68
	2005-2007					897,426.98			274,426.98		623,000.00
	2002-2007					8,420,641.91			3,791,411.54		4,629,230.37
	2005-2006					163,350,712.80		-163,313,660.59	344,376.61		[6]-307,324.40
	2004-2006					-49,056.45					[6]-49,056.45
	2004-2005					-17,166.15			6,059.24		[6]-23,225.39
	2003-2004					-285,125.07			-2,143.65		[6]-282,981.42
	2002-2003					4,592,301.61				4,438,528.03	4,592,301.61
	2001-2002					-641.94					
	No Year					105,816,030.21		4,439,169.97 55,191.13	29,504,864.88		76,366,356.46
Transfer To:											
Justice	No Year	15	72	1093	1	55,191.13		-55,191.13			
Department Of State	2007-2008	19	72	1093		38,189,516.22		40,254,965.00	4,436,875.75		35,818,089.25
	2006-2007					18,671,771.33		2,104,000.00	27,513,786.80		12,779,729.42
	2005-2006					2,939,380.48			16,068,379.25		2,603,392.08
	2004-2005					1,330,373.09			747,551.54		2,191,828.94
	2003-2004					5,220,167.54			661,888.45		668,484.64
	2002-2003					5,003,958.10			2,344,850.21		2,875,317.33
	2001-2002					1,099,775.75			617,772.33		913,974.24
	No Year							-4,386,185.77	185,801.51		
Nuclear Regulatory Commission	2006-2007	31	72	1093		1,615,000.00		400,000.00	530,598.11		1,484,401.89
	2005-2006					978,714.90			843,243.22		135,471.68
	2004-2005					158,449.86			48,930.44		109,519.42
	2003-2004					41,894.42			7,478.75		34,415.67
	2002-2003					60,975.51			11,744.10		49,231.41
	2001-2002					52,984.20		-52,984.20			
	No Year										
Unfilled Customer Orders						115,708.02					115,708.02
						19,764.91				19,764.91	
Fund Equities:											
Unobligated Balances (Expired)						-2,056,188.73				-608,612.10	-1,447,576.63
Unobligated Balances (Unexpired)						-182,861,699.97				-11,866,028.88	[16]-170,995,671.09
Accounts Payable						[5]-102,286,406.35				23,321,525.88	-125,607,932.23
Undelivered Orders	No Year					[5]-432,004,927.97				-99,279,041.79	-332,725,886.18
Subtotal		72		1093		-0-	373,639,800.00	-3,236,750.00	454,376,913.95	-83,973,863.95	-0-

Footnotes At End Of Chapter

Appropriations, Outlays, and Balances – Continued

Appropriation or Fund Account — Title	Dept Reg	Tr From	Account Number	Sub No.	Period of Availability	Balances, Beginning Of Fiscal Year	Appropriations And Other Obligational Authority[1]	Transfers Borrowings And Investment (Net)[2]	Outlays (Net)	Balances Withdrawn And Other Transactions[3]	Balances, End Of Fiscal Year[4]
Child Survival And Health Programs Fund, United States Agency For International Development											
Fund Resources:											
Undisbursed Funds	72		1095		2005-2010			567,019,202.13	389,826,626.23		177,192,575.90
					2004-2009	349,618,152.31			44,318,804.22		305,299,348.09
					2003-2009	88,111,326.16		-13,414,459.00	26,333,619.87		48,363,247.29
					2007-2008		1,901,425,000.00		110,054,150.88		1,791,370,849.12
					2003-2008	18,617,739.80			-133,032.84		18,750,772.64
					2006-2007	1,432,460,948.05	22,275,000.00	-22,275,000.00	888,021,533.58		544,439,414.47
					2005-2006	569,298,206.55		-567,019,202.13	1,295,559.37		983,445.05
					2004-2006	-41,657.68			89,565.64		[6] 131,223.32
					2004-2005	2,338,373.74			279,866.85		2,058,506.89
					2003-2005	4,052,506.89			96,639.70		3,955,867.19
					2003-2004	-11,576.61			41,520.81		[6] 53,097.42
					No Year	50,759,900.09			106,439,297.08		[6] 55,679,396.99
Transfer To:											
Department Of State	19	72	1095		2003-2005	1,780,034.72			513,409.52		1,266,625.20
Unfilled Customer Orders						3,816,383.54				2,822,316.54	994,067.00
Fund Equities:											
Unobligated Balances (Expired)						-4,846,717.07				54,054,501.89	[17] -58,901,218.96
Unobligated Balances (Unexpired)						-283,643,696.47				-210,339,512.51	[18] -73,304,183.96
Accounts Payable						[5] -328,106,944.56				45,863,675.01	-373,970,619.57
Undelivered Orders						[5] -1,904,202,979.46				428,431,999.16	-2,332,634,978.62
Subtotal	72		1095			-0-	1,923,700,000.00	-35,689,459.00	1,567,177,560.91	320,832,980.09	-0-
Development Credit Authority, United States Agency For International Development											
Fund Resources:											
Undisbursed Funds	72		1264		2007-2009		13,018,550.00		4,192,429.08		8,826,120.92
					2006-2008	8,710,255.46		86,000.00	3,396,010.07		5,400,245.39
					2005-2007	7,039,335.88			2,547,937.74		4,491,398.14
					2004-2007	10,832,390.68			1,590,834.80		9,241,555.88
					2003-2007	9,274,183.86			573,428.65		8,700,755.21
					2002-2007	2,461,283.75		17,241.00	232,551.73		2,245,973.02
					2001-2002	139,776.49		4,108.29		143,884.78	-0-
					No Year	2,645,719.55	3,728,878.00	64,997.71	3,972,979.51		2,466,615.75
Fund Equities:											
Unobligated Balances (Expired)						-204,425.15				4,304,483.46	-4,508,908.61
Unobligated Balances (Unexpired)						-11,611,164.52				-4,181,383.97	-7,429,780.55
Accounts Payable						-5,061,602.82				482,334.90	-5,543,937.72
Undelivered Orders						-24,225,753.18				-335,715.75	-23,890,037.43
Subtotal	72		1264			-0-	16,747,428.00	172,347.00	16,506,171.58	413,603.42	-0-
Special Fund Accounts											
Loan Guarantees To Israel Program, Reimbursements Of Administrative Expenses, Agency For International Development											
Fund Resources:											
Undisbursed Funds	72		5318		No Year	27,000.00					27,000.00

Appropriations, Outlays, and Balances - Continued

Appropriation or Fund Account — Title	Period of Availability	Reg	Tr From	Account Number	Sub No.	Balances, Beginning Of Fiscal Year	Appropriations And Other Obligational Authority[1]	Transfers Borrowings And Investment (Net)[2]	Outlays (Net)	Balances Withdrawn And Other Transactions[3]	Balances, End Of Fiscal Year[4]
Fund Equities:											
Unobligated Balances (Unexpired)	Subtotal	72		5318		-27,000.00					-27,000.00
						-0-					-0-
Public Enterprise Funds											
Development Loan Fund, Executive	No Year	72		4103							
Fund Resources:											
Undisbursed Funds						98,161,220.76			-577,264,238.57	[10]642,973,269.47	32,452,189.86
Accounts Receivable						2,404,709.58					2,404,709.58
Fund Equities:	Subtotal	72		4103							
Unobligated Balances (Unexpired)						-100,539,217.00				-65,709,030.90	-34,830,186.10
Accounts Payable						-26,713.34			-577,264,238.57	577,264,238.57	-26,713.34
						-0-					-0-
Property Management Fund, Agency For International Development	No Year	72		4175							
Fund Resources:											
Undisbursed Funds						4,456,136.32			-327,687.90		4,783,824.22
Fund Equities:	Subtotal	72		4175							
Unobligated Balances (Unexpired)						-1,884,521.26				276,176.56	-1,884,521.26
						-276,176.56				51,511.34	-276,176.56
Accounts Payable						-2,571,615.06			-327,687.90	327,687.90	-2,623,126.40
Undelivered Orders						-0-					-0-
Housing And Other Credit Guaranty Programs, Liquidating Account, Agency For International Development	No Year	72		4340							
Fund Resources:											
Undisbursed Funds						67,921,520.82	40,000,000.00		-21,730,926.89	[10]126,533,699.98	3,118,747.73
Fund Equities:	Subtotal	72		4340							
Unobligated Balances (Unexpired)						-67,781,608.53	40,000,000.00			-64,662,860.80	-3,118,747.73
Undelivered Orders						-139,912.29			-21,730,926.89	-139,912.29	
						-0-				61,730,926.89	-0-
Private Sector Revolving Fund, Liquidating Account, Agency For International Development	No Year	72		4341							
Fund Resources:											
Undisbursed Funds						260,873.38			-1,479.00	-1,479.00	262,352.38
Accounts Receivable						297,933.38					297,933.38
Fund Equities:	Subtotal	72		4341							
Unobligated Balances (Unexpired)						-511,826.58				1,479.00	-513,305.58
Accounts Payable						-34,744.00					-34,744.00
Undelivered Orders						-12,236.18			-1,479.00	1,479.00	-12,236.18
						-0-					-0-
Intragovernmental Funds											
Working Capital Fund, Agency For International Development	No Year	72		4513							
Fund Resources:											
Undisbursed Funds						1,385,416.32			3,970,460.63	-7,624,160.00	[6]2,585,044.31
Unfilled Customer Orders						1,942,501.53					9,566,661.53

Footnotes At End Of Chapter

Appropriations, Outlays, and Balances – Continued

Appropriation or Fund Account — Title	Period of Availability	Reg	Tr From	Account Number	Sub No.	Balances, Beginning Of Fiscal Year	Appropriations And Other Obligational Authority[1]	Transfers Borrowings And Investment (Net)[2]	Outlays (Net)	Balances Withdrawn And Other Transactions[3]	Balances, End Of Fiscal Year[4]
Working Capital Fund, Agency For International Development - Continued											
Fund Equities:											
Unobligated Balances (Unexpired)						-1,227,667.47				722,145.58	-1,949,813.05
Accounts Payable						-1,671,411.40				2,896,062.76	-4,567,474.16
Undelivered Orders						-428,838.98				35,491.03	-464,330.01
Subtotal		72		4513		-0-			3,970,460.63	-3,970,460.63	-0-
Acquisition Of Property Revolving Fund, Agency For International Development											
Fund Resources:											
Undisbursed Funds	No Year	72		4590		45,918.20					45,918.20
Fund Equities:											
Unobligated Balances (Unexpired)						-46,299.08					-46,299.08
Undelivered Orders						380.88					380.88
Subtotal		72		4590		-0-					-0-
Trust Fund Accounts											
Foreign National Employees Separation Liability Fund, Agency For International Development											
Fund Resources:											
Undisbursed Funds	No Year	72		8342		22,813,213.36	3,755,278.97		3,096,520.29		23,471,972.04
Fund Equities:											
Unobligated Balances (Unexpired)						-5,290,482.57				-3,706,357.52	-1,584,125.05
Accounts Payable						-3,958,981.38				-3,064,132.78	-894,848.60
Undelivered Orders						-13,563,749.41				7,429,248.98	-20,992,998.39
Subtotal		72		8342		-0-	3,755,278.97		3,096,520.29	658,758.68	-0-
Technical Assistance, United States Dollars Advanced From Foreign Governments, Agency For International Development											
Fund Resources:											
Undisbursed Funds	No Year	72		8502		2,015,486.60			-1,388,372.63		3,403,859.23
Fund Equities:											
Unobligated Balances (Unexpired)						-460,571.96				808,781.62	-1,269,353.58
Accounts Payable						-1,460.00				790,019.65	-791,479.65
Undelivered Orders						-1,553,454.64				-210,428.64	-1,343,026.00
Subtotal		72		8502		-0-			-1,388,372.63	1,388,372.63	-0-
Gifts And Donations, Agency For International Development											
Fund Resources:											
Undisbursed Funds	No Year	72		8824		27,221,064.65	14,467,995.99		19,291,107.14		22,397,953.50
Fund Equities:											
Unobligated Balances (Unexpired)						-1,852,136.62				-526,644.13	-1,325,492.49
Accounts Payable						-6,206,751.62				-1,161,563.62	-5,045,188.00
Undelivered Orders						-19,162,176.41				-3,134,903.40	-16,027,273.01
Subtotal		72		8824		-0-	14,467,995.99		19,291,107.14	-4,823,111.15	-0-
Deductions For Offsetting Receipts											
Proprietary Receipts From The Public							-22,359,275.26		-22,359,275.26		
Intrabudgetary Transactions							-53,717,531.22		-53,717,531.22		
Total, Agency For International Development							5,682,352,524.48	-34,415,348.74	4,125,675,894.09	1,522,261,281.65	

Appropriations, Outlays, and Balances - Continued

Title	Period of Availability	Reg	Tr From	Account Number	Sub No.	Balances, Beginning Of Fiscal Year	Appropriations And Other Obligational Authority[1]	Transfers Borrowings And Investment (Net)[2]	Outlays (Net)	Balances Withdrawn And Other Transactions[3]	Balances, End Of Fiscal Year[4]
Overseas Private Investment Corporation											
General Fund Accounts											
Overseas Private Investment Corporation, Program Account											
Fund Resources:											
Undisbursed Funds	2007-2008	71		0100			160,674,940.00		141,783,146.55		18,891,793.45
	2006-2007					15,742,365.72		5,000,000.00	5,715,515.92		15,026,849.80
	2005-2006					16,388,526.94			1,155,007.90		15,233,519.04
	2004-2005					9,713,188.47			967,711.69		8,745,476.78
	2003-2004					12,399,813.25			110,990.00		12,288,823.25
	2001-2002					18,198,705.45					[19]18,198,705.45
	2000-2001					22,356,853.00			1,534,680.00		[20]20,822,173.00
	1999-2000					3,699,763.99					[21]3,699,763.99
	1998-1999					14,671,448.96				14,671,448.96	
	No Year					15,086,247.49			8,352,229.40		6,734,018.09[22]
	Subtotal	71		0100							
Fund Equities:											
Unobligated Balances (Expired)						-60,215,275.12				-7,440,533.23	-52,774,741.89
Unobligated Balances (Unexpired)						-12,420,910.23				-11,246,034.46	-1,174,875.77
Undelivered Orders						-55,620,727.92				10,070,777.27	-65,691,505.19
	Subtotal	71		0100		-0-	160,674,940.00	5,000,000.00	159,619,281.46	6,055,658.54	-0-
Public Enterprise Funds											
Overseas Private Investment Corporation											
Fund Resources:											
Undisbursed Funds	No Year	71		4030		311,678.68		-13,607,000.00	-13,644,155.61		348,834.29
Fund Equities:											
Unobligated Balances (Unexpired)						-53,961.79				72,078.93	-126,040.72
Accounts Payable						-1,150.00				-1,150.00	
Undelivered Orders						-256,566.89				-33,773.32	-222,793.57
	Subtotal	71		4030		-0-		-13,607,000.00	-13,644,155.61	37,155.61	-0-
Overseas Private Investment Corporation, Insurance And Equity Non Credit Account											
Fund Resources:											
Undisbursed Funds	2006-2007	71		4184				1,200,000.00	250,000.00		950,000.00
	2004-2005					299,800.00			299,053.00		747.00
	No Year					21,811,381.17	-45,331,438.00	-186,419,672.05	-240,300,826.39		30,361,097.51
Unrealized Discount On Investments						-61,184,874.22		-3,311,327.95			-64,496,202.17
Investments In Public Debt Securities						4,273,017,000.00		203,338,000.00			4,476,355,000.00
Accounts Receivable						47,033,031.98				-5,293,251.37	52,326,283.35
Fund Equities:											
Unobligated Balances (Unexpired)						-4,076,397,929.79				180,382,845.21	-4,256,780,775.00
Accounts Payable						-2,598,352.37				-237,806.80	-2,360,545.57
Undelivered Orders						-201,980,056.77				34,375,548.35	-236,355,605.12
	Subtotal	71		4184		-0-	-45,331,438.00	14,807,000.00	-239,751,773.39	209,227,335.39	-0-

Footnotes At End Of Chapter

Appropriations, Outlays, and Balances – Continued

Appropriation or Fund Account	Account Symbol					Balances, Beginning Of Fiscal Year	Appropriations And Other Obligational Authority[1]	Transfers Borrowings And Investment (Net)[2]	Outlays (Net)	Balances Withdrawn And Other Transactions[3]	Balances, End Of Fiscal Year[4]
Title	Period of Availability	Dept Reg	Tr From	Account Number	Sub No.						
Deductions For Offsetting Receipts											
Proprietary Receipts From The Public						-------	-321,786,601.84	-------	-321,786,601.84	-------	-------
Total, Overseas Private Investment Corporation						-------	-206,443,099.84	6,200,000.00	-415,563,249.38	215,320,149.54	-------
Trade And Development Agency											
General Fund Accounts											
Trade And Development Agency, Funds Appropriated To The President											
Fund Resources:											
Undisbursed Funds	2004-2009	11		1001		58,286.00	54,676,726.00	-------	3,533.00	-------	54,753.00
	2007-2008					-------	-------	-------	10,831,958.34	-------	43,844,767.66
	2003-2008					632,803.00	-------	-------	321,402.93	-------	311,400.07
	2006-2007					42,779,702.96	-------	1,000,000.00	15,842,453.96	-------	27,937,249.00
	2002-2007					411,705.00	-------	-------	27,363.87	-------	384,341.13
	2005-2006					32,119,024.49	-------	-------	13,898,109.60	-------	18,220,914.89
	2004-2005					15,394,992.79	-------	-------	5,806,502.56	-------	9,588,490.23
	2003-2004					8,093,020.64	-------	-------	2,307,320.81	-------	5,785,699.83
	2003					344,589.73	-------	-------	-------	-------	344,589.73
	2002-2003					6,039,425.08	-------	-------	1,656,534.61	-------	4,382,890.47
	2001-2002					4,419,930.47	-------	-------	1,259,582.56	3,160,347.91	-------
	No Year					3,603,470.04	-------	-------	766,369.14	-------	2,837,100.90
Fund Equities:											
Unobligated Balances (Expired)						[5]-2,210,782.70	-------	-------	-------	-94,491.46	-2,116,291.24
Unobligated Balances (Unexpired)						-7,047,812.57	-------	-------	-------	574,934.23	-7,622,746.80
Accounts Payable						[5]-8,193,529.29	-------	-------	-------	-236,072.21	-7,957,457.08
Undelivered Orders						[5]-96,444,825.64	-------	-------	-------	-449,123.85	-95,995,701.79
	Subtotal	11		1001		-0-	54,676,726.00	1,000,000.00	52,721,131.38	2,955,594.62	-0-
Total, Trade And Development Agency							54,676,726.00	1,000,000.00	52,721,131.38	2,955,594.62	
Peace Corps											
General Fund Accounts											
Peace Corps, Funds Appropriated To The President											
Fund Resources:											
Undisbursed Funds	2007-2008	11		0100		-------	321,700,000.00	-64,500.00	248,742,930.29	-------	72,892,569.71
	2006-2007					82,974,092.69	-------	64,500.00	75,280,018.60	-------	7,758,574.09
	2005-2006					8,051,554.57	-------	-------	4,657,151.12	-------	3,394,403.45
	2004-2005					1,936,019.08	-------	-------	983,083.38	-------	952,935.70
	2003-2004					4,361,667.70	-------	-------	713,382.47	-------	3,648,285.23
	2002-2003					3,456,681.97	-------	-------	1,785,150.48	-------	1,671,531.49
	2001-2002					3,378,979.60	-------	-2,000,000.00	1,221,061.76	157,917.84	-------
Funds Held Outside The Treasury	No Year					978,197.67	-------	-------	241,475.32	-------	736,722.35
	2007-2008					64,500.00	-------	64,500.00	-------	-------	64,500.00
	2006-2007					978,290.40	-------	-64,500.00	-------	-------	-------
Accounts Receivable						-------	-------	-------	-------	334,444.24	643,846.16

Appropriations, Outlays, and Balances - Continued

Appropriation or Fund Account — Title	Period of Availability	Dept Reg	Tr From	Account Number	Sub No.	Balances, Beginning Of Fiscal Year	Appropriations And Other Obligational Authority[1]	Transfers Borrowings And Investment (Net)[2]	Outlays (Net)	Balances Withdrawn And Other Transactions[3]	Balances, End Of Fiscal Year[4]
Unfilled Customer Orders						-540,263.52				149,542.99	-689,806.51
Fund Equities:											
Unobligated Balances (Expired)		11				-12,804,429.29				-1,603,052.80	-11,201,376.49
Unobligated Balances (Unexpired)						-6,232,660.67				2,067,348.51	-8,300,009.18
Accounts Payable						-13,636,848.96				-2,021,472.07	-11,615,376.89
Undelivered Orders						-72,965,781.24				-13,008,982.13	-59,956,799.11
	Subtotal	11		0100		-0-	321,700,000.00	-2,000,000.00	333,624,253.42	-13,924,253.42	-0-
Foreign Currency Fluctuations, Peace Corps											
Fund Resources:											
Undisbursed Funds	No Year	11		0101		1,978,515.68	-2,000,000.00	2,000,000.00			2,000,000.00
Fund Equities:											
Unobligated Balances (Unexpired)	Subtotal	11		0101		-1,978,515.68	-2,000,000.00	2,000,000.00	-21,484.32	21,484.32	-2,000,000.00
Special Fund Accounts											
Foreign Service National Contractors Separation Liability Fund, Peace Corps											
Fund Resources:											
Undisbursed Funds	No Year	11		5395					-5,156,600.00	5,156,600.00	5,156,600.00
Fund Equities:											
Unobligated Balances (Unexpired)	Subtotal	11		5395		-0-			-5,156,600.00	5,156,600.00	-5,156,600.00
Trust Fund Accounts											
Gifts And Contributions, Peace Corps											
Fund Resources:											
Undisbursed Funds	No Year	11		8245		603,139.27			-151,061.96		754,201.23
Fund Equities:											
Unobligated Balances (Unexpired)						-717,690.43				98,729.02	-816,419.45
Accounts Payable						174,270.38				49,773.66	124,496.72
Undelivered Orders						-59,719.22				2,559.28	-62,278.50
	Subtotal	11		8245		-0-			-151,061.96	151,061.96	-0-
Advances From Foreign Governments, Peace Corps											
Fund Resources:											
Undisbursed Funds	No Year	11		8246		2,729.42			1,932.26		797.16
Fund Equities:											
Unobligated Balances (Unexpired)						-2,729.42				-2,532.26	-197.16
Accounts Payable										600.00	-600.00
	Subtotal	11		8246		-0-			1,932.26	-1,932.26	-0-
Foreign Service National Separation Liability Trust Fund, Peace Corps											
Fund Resources:											
Undisbursed Funds	No Year	11		8345		8,817,129.98			967,853.79		7,849,276.19
Fund Equities:											
Unobligated Balances (Unexpired)						-8,798,985.46				-879,431.78	-7,919,553.68
Accounts Payable						-18,144.52				-88,422.01	70,277.49
	Subtotal	11		8345		-0-			967,853.79	-967,853.79	-0-

Footnotes At End Of Chapter

Appropriations, Outlays, and Balances – Continued

Appropriation or Fund Account — Title	Period of Availability	Reg	Tr From	Account Number	Sub No.	Balances, Beginning Of Fiscal Year	Appropriations And Other Obligational Authority[1]	Transfers Borrowings And Investment (Net)[2]	Outlays (Net)	Balances Withdrawn And Other Transactions[3]	Balances, End Of Fiscal Year[4]
Deductions For Offsetting Receipts											
Proprietary Receipts From The Public							-481,051.77		-481,051.77		
Total, Peace Corps							319,218,948.23		328,783,841.42	-9,564,893.19	
Inter-American Foundation											
General Fund Accounts											
Inter-American Foundation											
Fund Resources:											
Undisbursed Funds	2007-2008	11		3100		9,823,567.36	19,346,743.00		9,096,147.99		10,250,595.01
	2006-2007					3,390,516.78			6,011,097.73		3,812,469.63
	2005-2006					743,669.14			1,556,429.37		1,834,087.41
	2004-2005					686,817.15			426,538.00		317,131.14
	2003-2004								147,059.00	228,571.38	539,758.15
	2001-2002					274,143.38			45,572.00		
	No Year					20,144,118.08			2,317,164.08		17,826,954.00
Fund Equities:											
Unobligated Balances (Expired)						-703,314.91				106,364.28	-809,679.19
Unobligated Balances (Unexpired)						-9,600,848.52				-2,821,679.81	-6,779,168.71
Accounts Payable						-683,563.43				618,827.56	-1,302,390.99
Undelivered Orders						-24,075,105.03				1,614,651.42	-25,689,756.45
Subtotal		11		3100		-0-	19,346,743.00		19,600,008.17	-253,265.17	-0-
Trust Fund Accounts											
Gifts, Donations And Contributions, Inter-American Foundation, Funds Appropriated To The President											
Fund Resources:											
Undisbursed Funds	No Year	11		8243		75,000.25			41,306.00		33,694.25
Fund Equities:											
Unobligated Balances (Unexpired)						-0.25					-0.25
Undelivered Orders						-75,000.00			-41,306.00	-41,306.00	-33,694.00
Subtotal		11		8243		-0-			41,306.00	-41,306.00	-0-
Total, Inter-American Foundation							19,346,743.00		19,641,314.17	-294,571.17	
African Development Foundation											
General Fund Accounts											
African Development Foundation, Funds Appropriated To The President											
Fund Resources:											
Undisbursed Funds.	2007-2008	11		0700		13,028,854.74	22,799,629.00		11,113,749.27		11,685,879.73
	2006-2007					3,400,133.62			8,517,541.13		4,511,313.61
	2005-2006								1,391,215.48		2,008,918.14
	2005					-30,008.00			-30,008.00		
	2004-2005					5,435,574.35			1,690,349.54		3,745,224.81

Appropriations, Outlays, and Balances - Continued

Appropriation or Fund Account — Title	Period of Availability	Dept Reg	Dept Tr From	Account Number	Sub No.	Balances, Beginning Of Fiscal Year	Appropriations And Other Obligational Authority[1]	Transfers Borrowings And Investment (Net)[2]	Outlays (Net)	Balances Withdrawn And Other Transactions[3]	Balances, End Of Fiscal Year[4]
	2003-2004					1,743,785.99	-------	------	261,147.22	-------	1,482,638.77
	2001-2002					282,225.65	-------	------		282,225.65	
	No Year					1,608,651.35	-------	------	231,978.40	------	1,376,672.95
Fund Equities:											
Unobligated Balances (Expired)						[5]-2,700,458.67				-165,681.60	-2,534,777.07
Unobligated Balances (Unexpired)						[5]-3,392,289.32				-2,654,863.42	-737,425.90
Accounts Payable						[5]-624,771.05				10,361.68	-635,132.73
Undelivered Orders						[5]-18,751,698.66				2,151,613.65	-20,903,312.31
	Subtotal	11		0700		-0-	22,799,629.00		23,175,973.04	-376,344.04	-0-
Trust Fund Accounts											
Gifts And Donations, African Development Foundation											
Fund Resources:											
Undisbursed Funds	No Year	11		8239		152,088.47	4,216,406.06	-2,126,968.48	2,209,559.56	-------	31,966.49
Funds Held Outside The Treasury						4,278,250.07		2,126,968.48		-------	6,405,218.55
Fund Equities:											
Unobligated Balances (Unexpired)						-------				1,274,600.53	-1,274,600.53
Undelivered Orders						-------				5,162,584.51	-5,162,584.51
	Subtotal	11		8239		4,430,338.54	4,216,406.06		2,209,559.56	6,437,185.04	-0-
Total, African Development Foundation						4,430,338.54	27,016,035.06		25,385,532.60	6,060,841.00	
Total, International Development Assistance						4,430,338.54	5,896,167,876.93	-27,215,348.74	4,136,644,464.28	1,736,738,402.45	
International Monetary Programs											
General Fund Accounts											
United States Quota, International Monetary Fund, Funds Appropriated To The President											
Fund Resources:											
Undisbursed Funds	No Year	20	11	0003		47,909,934,073.71		1,793,318,159.30	-258,238,316.28	-2,139,591,313.89	52,101,081,863.18
Transfer To:											
Treasury Reserve Position											
Accounts Receivable						6,621,153,029.08				2,157,332,122.03	4,463,820,907.05
						134,844,323.20				-17,740,808.14	152,585,131.34
Fund Equities:											
Unobligated Balances (Unexpired)						-6,440,811,931.07				-3,087,975,814.97	-3,352,836,116.10
Undelivered Orders						-48,225,119,494.92				5,139,532,290.55	-53,364,651,785.47
	Subtotal	11		0003		-0-		1,793,318,159.30	-258,238,316.28	2,051,556,475.58	-0-
Maintenance Of Value Adjustments, International Monetary Fund, Executive											
Fund Resources:											
Undisbursed Funds	No Year	11		0004			1,793,318,159.30	-1,793,318,159.30			
Total, International Monetary Programs							1,793,318,159.30	-1,793,318,159.30	-258,238,316.28	2,051,556,475.58	

Footnotes At End Of Chapter

Appropriations, Outlays, and Balances – Continued

Appropriation or Fund Account — Title	Account Symbol Dept Reg	Account Symbol Dept Tr From	Account Number	Sub No.	Period of Availability	Balances, Beginning Of Fiscal Year	Appropriations And Other Obligational Authority[1]	Transfers Borrowings And Investment (Net)[2]	Outlays (Net)	Balances Withdrawn And Other Transactions[3]	Balances, End Of Fiscal Year[4]
Military Sales Programs											
Public Enterprise Funds											
Special Defense Acquisition Fund, Funds Appropriated To The President											
Fund Resources:											
Undisbursed Funds	11		4116		No Year			184,465.69		[10]184,465.69	-------
Transfer To:											
Defense	97	11	4116		No Year	184,465.69		-184,465.69		-------	-------
Fund Equities:											
Unobligated Balances (Unexpired)	11		4116		Subtotal	-0-				-184,465.69	-0-
Trust Fund Accounts											
Advances, Foreign Military Sales, Funds Appropriated To The President											
Fund Resources:											
Undisbursed Funds	11		8242		No Year	7,866,068,930.03	15,833,018,688.79	-------	14,187,511,906.33	-------	9,511,575,712.49
Unfunded Contract Authority						[18]22,897,354.96	[2]48,022,227,843.99			15,833,018,688.79	50,412,106,510.16
Fund Equities:											
Unobligated Balances (Unexpired)						[5]-0-	-0-			-------	-0-
Accounts Payable						-883,920,341.29				301,663,411.46	-1,185,583,752.75
Undelivered Orders						-25,205,045,943.70				33,533,052,526.20	-58,738,098,469.90
Subtotal	11		8242			-0-	63,855,246,532.78		14,187,511,906.33	49,667,734,626.45	-0-
Deductions For Offsetting Receipts											
Proprietary Receipts From The Public							-15,833,018,688.79		-15,833,018,688.79		
Total, Military Sales Programs							48,022,227,843.99		-1,645,506,782.46	49,667,734,626.45	
Special Assistance For Central America											
General Fund Accounts											
Promotion Of Security And Stability In Central America											
Fund Resources:											
Undisbursed Funds	11		1091		No Year	129,539.73				-------	129,539.73
Fund Equities:											
Accounts Payable	11		1091			-129,539.73				-------	-129,539.73
Unobligated Balances (Unexpired)	11		1091		Subtotal	-0-					-0-
Tsunami Recovery And Reconstruction Fund, Funds Appropriated To The President, Agency For International Development											
Fund Resources:											
Undisbursed Funds	72		1029	72	2005-2006	388,283,682.43			83,560,497.96		304,723,184.47
Transfer To:											
Department Of State	19	72	1029	72	2005-2006	8,065,730.79			14,616.57		8,051,114.22
Fund Equities:											

Appropriations, Outlays, and Balances - Continued

Appropriation or Fund Account — Title	Period of Availability	Dept Reg	Dept Tr From	Account Number	Sub No.	Balances, Beginning Of Fiscal Year	Appropriations And Other Obligational Authority[1]	Transfers Borrowings And Investment (Net)[2]	Outlays (Net)	Balances Withdrawn And Other Transactions[3]	Balances, End Of Fiscal Year[4]
Unobligated Balances (Expired)						-61,170.71				7,489.96	-68,660.67
Accounts Payable						-17,735,910.56				6,082,806.58	-23,818,717.14
Undelivered Orders		72		1029		-378,552,331.95				-89,665,411.07	-288,886,920.88
Subtotal	Subtotal	72		1029		-0-			83,575,114.53	-83,575,114.53	-0-
Central America Reconstruction Assistance											
Fund Resources:											
Undisbursed Funds	No Year	72		1038		971,138.31					971,138.31
Fund Equities:											
Unobligated Balances (Unexpired)		72		1038		-971,138.31					-971,138.31
Subtotal	Subtotal	72		1038		-0-					-0-
Demobilization And Transition Fund, Funds Appropriated To The President											
Fund Resources:											
Undisbursed Funds	No Year	72		1500		86,453.23		352,203.21			438,656.44
Transfer To:											
Justice	No Year	15	72	1500	1	352,203.21		-352,203.21			-0-
Fund Equities:											
Unobligated Balances (Unexpired)		72		1500		-439,530.44				874.00	-439,530.44
Accounts Payable										-874.00	-874.00
Undelivered Orders						874.00					1,748.00
Subtotal	Subtotal	72		1500		-0-					-0-
Total, Special Assistance For Central America									83,575,114.53	-83,575,114.53	
Total, International Assistance Program						4,430,338.54	70,047,925,777.91	-338,552,699.59	12,764,132,692.21	56,949,670,724.65	
Memorandum											
Financing Accounts											
Public Enterprise Funds											
Foreign Military Financing, Direct Loan Financing Account, Funds Appropriated To The President											
Fund Resources:											
Undisbursed Funds	No Year	11		4122		12,758,221.71		-196,164,820.31	-197,525,374.20	13,462,455.85	14,118,775.60
Authority To Borrow From The Treasury				4122		3,039,299,500.00	7,507,089.03	-294,422,187.07		-299,017,000.00	2,752,384,401.96
Fund Equities:											
Unobligated Balances (Unexpired)		11		4122		-12,758,221.71					-26,220,677.56
Undelivered Orders						-3,039,299,500.00		-490,587,007.38		-285,554,544.15	-2,740,282,500.00
Subtotal	Subtotal	11		4122		-0-	7,507,089.03		-197,525,374.20		-0-
Debt Restructuring Under The Enterprise For The Americas, Direct Loan Financing Account											
Fund Resources:											
Undisbursed Funds	No Year	11		4137		152,833,465.35			-74,933,659.83		227,767,125.18
Fund Equities:											
Unobligated Balances (Unexpired)		11				-152,833,465.35				50,482,229.19	-203,315,694.54
Undelivered Orders										24,451,430.64	-24,451,430.64

Footnotes At End Of Chapter

Appropriations, Outlays, and Balances – Continued

Title	Period of Availability	Reg	Tr From	Account Number	Sub No.	Balances, Beginning Of Fiscal Year	Appropriations And Other Obligational Authority[1]	Transfers Borrowings And Investment (Net)[2]	Outlays (Net)	Balances Withdrawn And Other Transactions[3]	Balances, End Of Fiscal Year[4]
Debt Restructuring Under The Enterprise For The Americas, Direct Loan Financing Account - Continued											
Military Debt Reduction, Financing Account											
Fund Resources:											
	Subtotal	11		4137		-0-			-74,933,659.83	74,933,659.83	-0-
Undisbursed Funds	No Year	11		4174		2,543,004.09		-1,678,843.32	-5,237,962.90		6,102,123.67
Authority To Borrow From The Treasury							2,876,330.00	-1,442,814.00			1,433,516.00
Fund Equities:											
Unobligated Balances (Unexpired)						-2,543,004.09		-3,121,657.32	4,992,635.58	4,992,635.58	-7,535,639.67
	Subtotal	11		4174		-2,543,004.09	2,876,330.00	-3,121,657.32	-5,237,962.90	4,992,635.58	-0-
Overseas Private Investment Corporation, Direct Loan Financing Account											
Fund Resources:											
Undisbursed Funds	No Year	71		4074		47,019,622.42	276,291,481.48	-12,298,922.29	-38,243,146.08	122,476,748.27	72,963,846.21
Authority To Borrow From The Treasury						494,149,742.30		-120,560,024.21		-244,159.94	527,404,451.30
Accounts Receivable										-244,159.94	244,159.94
Unfilled Customer Orders						27,488,000.41				-2,974,740.84	30,462,741.25
Fund Equities:											
Unobligated Balances (Unexpired)						-44,910,303.77				24,972,480.73	-69,882,784.50
Accounts Payable						-52,551.93				356,872.60	-409,424.53
Undelivered Orders						-523,694,509.43				37,088,480.24	-560,782,989.67
	Subtotal	71		4074		-0-	276,291,481.48	-132,858,946.50	-38,243,146.08	181,675,681.06	-0-
Overseas Private Investment Corporation, Guaranteed Loan Financing Account											
Fund Resources:											
Undisbursed Funds	No Year	71		4075		676,832,041.65	125,741,249.83	17,202,089.90	80,120,387.21		613,913,744.34
Authority To Borrow From The Treasury						163,492,396.97		-122,092,089.90		8,046,000.00	159,095,556.90
Fund Equities:											
Unobligated Balances (Unexpired)						-712,270,596.86				-53,157,014.75	-659,113,582.11
Accounts Payable						-3,305.00				7,874.60	-11,179.60
Undelivered Orders						-128,050,536.76				-14,165,997.23	-113,884,539.53
	Subtotal	71		4075		-0-	125,741,249.83	-104,890,000.00	80,120,387.21	-59,269,137.38	-0-
Loan Guarantees To Israel Financing Account, Agency For International Development, Funds Appropriated To The President											
Fund Resources:											
Undisbursed Funds	No Year	72		4119		1,115,006,016.65			-127,861,848.43		1,242,867,865.08
Fund Equities:											
Unobligated Balances (Unexpired)						-1,115,006,016.65				127,861,848.43	-1,242,867,865.08
	Subtotal	72		4119		-0-			-127,861,848.43	127,861,848.43	-0-
Guaranteed Loan Financing Account, International Assistance Programs											
Fund Resources:											
Undisbursed Funds	No Year	72		4266		22,881,256.69			2,461,734.85		20,419,521.84
Fund Equities:											
Unobligated Balances (Unexpired)						-22,771,474.56				-3,091,836.99	-19,679,637.57
Accounts Payable										18,884,618.72	-18,884,618.72
Undelivered Orders						-109,782.13				-18,254,516.58	18,144,734.45
	Subtotal	72		4266		-0-			2,461,734.85	-2,461,734.85	-0-
Private Sector Guaranty Loan Financing Account, Agency For International Development											
Fund Resources:											
Undisbursed Funds	No Year	72		4343		1,796,313.94			3,438,498.87		[6]1,642,184.93

Appropriations, Outlays, and Balances - Continued

Appropriation or Fund Account — Title	Period of Availability	Reg	Tr From	Account Number	Sub No.	Balances, Beginning Of Fiscal Year	Appropriations And Other Obligational Authority[1]	Transfers Borrowings And Investment (Net)[2]	Outlays (Net)	Balances Withdrawn And Other Transactions[3]	Balances, End Of Fiscal Year[4]
Fund Equities:											
Unobligated Balances (Unexpired)						830,117.15			-------	-3,415,915.55	[6]4,246,032.70
Accounts Payable						-80,310.61			-------	-------	-80,310.61
Undelivered Orders						-2,546,120.48			-------	-22,583.32	-2,523,537.16
Subtotal		72		4343		-0-			3,438,498.87	-3,438,498.87	-0-
Housing And Other Credit Guaranty Programs, Guaranty Loan Financing Account, Agency For International Development											
Fund Resources:											
Undisbursed Funds	No Year	72		4344		133,860,414.84			12,284,895.53	-------	121,575,519.31
Fund Equities:											
Unobligated Balances (Unexpired)		72				-132,824,892.62			-------	-12,284,895.53	-120,539,997.09
Undelivered Orders						-1,035,522.22			-------	-------	-1,035,522.22
Subtotal		72		4344		-0-			12,284,895.53	-12,284,895.53	-0-
Assistance For The New Independent States Of The Former Soviet Union: Ukraine Export Credit Insurance Financing Account											
Fund Resources:											
Undisbursed Funds	No Year	72		4345		-------			-------	-------	[6]1,889.76
Fund Equities:											
Undelivered Orders	No Year	72				-------			-------	-------	1,889.76
Subtotal		72		4345		-0-			1,889.76	-1,889.76	-0-
Loan Guarantees To Egypt Financing Account											
Fund Resources:											
Undisbursed Funds	No Year	72		4491		154,675,596.00			-22,815,659.29	-------	177,491,255.29
Fund Equities:											
Unobligated Balances (Unexpired)		72		4491		-154,675,596.00			-------	22,815,659.29	-177,491,255.29
Subtotal		72				-0-			-22,815,659.29	22,815,659.29	-0-
Total, Financing Accounts							412,416,150.34	-731,457,611.20	-368,310,244.51	49,268,783.65	-------

Footnotes At End Of Chapter

Appropriations, Outlays, and Balances – Continued

Footnotes

1. The amounts in this column, unless otherwise footnoted, represent appropriations, increases and rescissions in borrowing authority or new contract authority. Appropriation accounts with appropriation transfer activity are presented in Table 1 (Appropriations and Appropriation Transfers) at the end of this chapter.

2. The amounts in this column, unless otherwise footnoted, represent transfers - other than appropriation transfers, borrowings (gross), investments (net), unrealized discounts or funds held outside the Treasury.

3. The amounts in this column, unless otherwise footnoted, represent obligated balances canceled for fiscal year 2002 pursuant to 31 U.S.C. 1553, changes in unfilled customer orders, accounts receivable, accounts payable, undelivered orders, unobligated balances and adjustments to borrowing and contract authority.

4. Unobligated balances for no-year or unexpired multiple year accounts are available for obligation; unobligated balances for expired fiscal year accounts are not available for obligation.

5. The opening balances of the following accounts have been adjusted during the current fiscal year and do not agree with last year's closing balances:

Account	Adjustment
11 0700 - Unobligated Balances (Unexpired)	-179,445.57
11 0700 - Unobligated Balances (Expired)	133,419.35
11 0700 - Accounts Payable	300,748.95
11 0700 - Undelivered Orders	-254,722.73
11 1001 - Unobligated Balances (Expired)	-29,027.91
11 1001 - Accounts Payable	-464,884.62
11 1001 - Undelivered Orders	493,912.53
11 05 1032 - Unobligated Balances (Expired)	-4,798.74
11 05 1032 - Accounts Payable	509,407.05
11 05 1032 - Undelivered Orders	-504,608.31
11 X 8242 - Unfunded Contract Authority	-16,585,761,688.02
11 X 8242 - Unobligated Balances (Unexpired)	16,585,761,688.02
72 1037 - Accounts Payable	-128,475,417.48
72 1037 - Undelivered Orders	128,475,417.48
19 1005 - Accounts Payable	175,000.00
19 1005 - Undelivered Orders	-175,000.00
72 1000 - Unfilled Customer Orders	117,500.00
72 1000 - Unobligated Balances (Unexpired)	16,140,749.28
72 1000 - Accounts Payable	-16,140,749.28
72 1000 - Undelivered Orders	-117,500.00
72 1007 - Unfilled Customer Orders	854,625.00
72 1007 - Unobligated Balances (Expired)	-864,625.00
72 1010 - Accounts Payable	-2,126,713.64
72 1010 - Undelivered Orders	2,126,713.64
72 1021 - Unfilled Customer Orders	1,182,500.00
72 1021 - Unobligated Balances (Unexpired)	-1,182,500.00
72 1021 - Accounts Payable	22,538,563.19
72 1021 - Undelivered Orders	-22,538,563.19
72 X 1035 - Accounts Payable	-9,996,376.64
72 X 1035 - Undelivered Orders	9,996,376.64
72 X 1093 - Accounts Payable	-3,924,367.73
72 X 1093 - Undelivered Orders	3,924,367.73
72 X 1095 - Accounts Payable	-10,472,778.95
72 X 1095 - Undelivered Orders	10,472,778.95

6. Subject to disposition by the administrative agency.

7. Includes $2,266,570.70 which is subject to disposition by the administrative agency.

8. Includes $507,847.17 which is subject to disposition by the administrative agency.

9. Includes $998,128.26 which is subject to disposition by the administrative agency.

10. Represents capital transfer to miscellaneous receipts.

11. Includes $1,694,756.51 which is subject to disposition by the administrative agency.

12. Includes $17,950.00 which is subject to disposition by the administrative agency.

13. Includes $313,742.62 which is subject to disposition by the administrative agency.

14. Includes $564,649.15 which is subject to disposition by the administrative agency.

15. Includes $4,051.41 which is subject to disposition by the administrative agency.

16. Includes $303,806.85 which is subject to disposition by the administrative agency.

17. Includes $41,657.68 which is subject to disposition by the administrative agency.

18. Includes $49,607,424.84 which is subject to disposition by the administrative agency.

19. Pursuant to P.L. 114 Stat 1900A-4, the balance for this account has been extended beyond the normal period of availability to liquidate obligations.

20. Pursuant to P.L. 113 Stat 1501A-64, the balance for this account has been extended beyond the normal period of availability to liquidate obligations.

21. Pursuant to P.L. 112 Stat 2681-152, the balance for this account has been extended beyond the normal period of availability to liquidate obligations.

22. Pursuant to P.L. 111 Stat 2387, 2388, the balance for this account has been extended beyond the normal period of availability to liquidate obligations.

23. Represents new contract authority.

Footnotes

Table 1 - Appropriations And Appropriation Transfers - International Assistance Program

Department Regular	Fiscal Year	Account Symbol	Net Appropriations And Appropriations Transfers	Appropriation Amount	Net Appropriation Transfers	Department Regular Involved	Fiscal Year Involved	Accounts Involved	Amount From or To (-)
11	0708	0100	321,700,000.00	319,700,000.00	2,000,000.00	11	X	0101	2,000,000.00
11	X	0101	-2,000,000.00	0.00	-2,000,000.00	11	0708	0100	-2,000,000.00
11	0708	1001	54,676,726.00	50,431,726.00	4,245,000.00	72	0708	1021	825,000.00
						72	0708	1093	3,420,000.00
11	X	1032	250,000.00	0.00	250,000.00	57	07	3400	250,000.00
11	07	1032	243,250,000.00	223,250,000.00	20,000,000.00	97	07	0100	20,000,000.00
11	0708	1045	12,005,000.00	2,750,000.00	9,255,000.00	72	0708	1010	4,230,000.00
						72	0708	1093	5,025,000.00
11	X	1075	37,500,000.00	37,500,000.00	37,500,000.00	11	07	1075	37,000,000.00
						11	07	2010	500,000.00
11	07	1075	189,283,000.00	405,999,000.00	-216,716,000.00	11	X	1075	-37,000,000.00
						11	0708	1075	-176,757,000.00
						12	07	1400	-2,959,000.00
11	0708	1075	234,257,000.00	57,500,000.00	176,757,000.00	11	07	1075	176,757,000.00
19	07	1005	281,613,420.00	326,163,420.00	-44,550,000.00	72	0607	1095	-22,275,000.00
						72	0708	1095	-22,275,000.00
71	0708	0100	160,674,940.00	115,343,502.00	45,331,438.00	71	X	4184	45,331,438.00
71	X	4184	-45,331,438.00	0.00	0.00	71	0708	0100	-45,331,438.00
72	07	1000	606,194,911.00	626,831,743.00	-20,636,832.00	72	0708	1000	-20,636,832.00
72	0708	1000	29,336,832.00	8,700,000.00	20,636,832.00	72	07	1000	20,636,832.00
72	0708	1000	33,906.00	0.00	33,906.00	72	X	1035	33,906.00
72	0610	1000		39,343,000.00	1,000,000.00	72	0708	1037	1,000,000.00
72	0708	1007	40,343,000.00	487,900,000.00	-78,377,000.00	11	0708	1022	-45,295,000.00
72	0708	1010	409,523,000.00			11	0708	1045	-4,230,000.00
						12	0708	2900	-2,100,000.00
						13	0708	0120	-600,000.00
						72	0708	1037	-25,000,000.00
						72	0709	1264	-550,000.00
						95	0708	0206	-602,000.00
72	X	1021	45,434,200.00	0.00	45,434,200.00	17	07	1106	8,300,000.00
						21	07	2010	28,934,200.00
						21	07	2020	150,000.00
						57	07	3400	8,050,000.00
72	0708	1021	1,504,431,000.00	1,508,760,000.00	-4,329,000.00	11	0708	1001	-825,000.00
						72	0709	1264	-3,504,000.00
72	X	1027	43,600,000.00	39,600,000.00	4,000,000.00	21	07	2010	4,000,000.00
72	X	1028	99,000,000.00	99,000,000.00	99,000,000.00	75	07	0885	99,000,000.00
72	X	1035	526,316,094.00	526,350,000.00	-33,906.00	72	0610	1000	-33,906.00
72	X	1037	-172,650,000.00	-200,000,000.00	27,350,000.00	17	07	1804	6,700,000.00
						21	07	2010	13,900,000.00
						21	07	2020	1,600,000.00
						57	07	3400	5,150,000.00
72	0708	1037	5,206,477,650.00	5,092,675,000.00	113,802,650.00	19	0708	0209	-19,500,000.00
						21	07	2010	70,000,000.00
						21	07	2060	13,183,000.00
						72	0708	1007	-1,000,000.00
						72	0708	1010	25,000,000.00
						72	0709	1264	-697,350.00

Footnotes At End Of Chapter

Appropriations, Outlays, and Balances – Continued

Footnotes

Table 1 - Appropriations And Appropriation Transfers - International Assistance Program

Department Regular	Fiscal Year	Account Symbol	Net Appropriations And Appropriations Transfers	Appropriation Amount	Net Appropriation Transfers	Department Regular Involved	Fiscal Year Involved	Accounts Involved	Amount From or To (-)
72	0708	1093	373,639,800.00	452,000,000.00	-78,360,200.00	97	07	0130	26,817,000.00
						11	0708	1001	-3,420,000.00
						11	0708	1022	-37,305,000.00
						11	0708	1045	-5,025,000.00
						12	0708	2900	-7,103,000.00
						13	0708	0120	-855,000.00
						13	0708	1250	-2,095,000.00
						49	0708	0100	-5,460,000.00
						49	0708	0180	-250,000.00
						70	0708	0530	-4,400,000.00
						72	0709	1264	-347,200.00
						89	0708	0224	-12,100,000.00
72	0607	1095	22,275,000.00	0.00	22,275,000.00	19	07	1005	22,275,000.00
72	0708	1095	1,901,425,000.00	1,879,150,000.00	22,275,000.00	19	07	1005	22,275,000.00
72	0709	1264	13,018,550.00	7,920,000.00	5,098,550.00	72	0708	1010	550,000.00
						72	0708	1021	3,504,000.00
						72	0708	1037	697,350.00
						72	0708	1093	347,200.00
Totals			12,136,277,591.00	11,970,367,391.00	165,910,200.00				165,910,200.00

Appropriations, Outlays, and Balances – Continued

Footnotes

This Page Left Blank Intentionally

Appropriations, Outlays, and Balances – Continued

Title	Dept Reg	Tr From	Account Number	Sub No.	Period of Availability	Balances, Beginning Of Fiscal Year	Appropriations And Other Obligational Authority[1]	Transfers Borrowings And Investment (Net)[2]	Outlays (Net)	Balances Withdrawn And Other Transactions[3]	Balances, End Of Fiscal Year[4]
National Aeronautics And Space Administration											
General Fund Accounts											
Office Of The Inspector General, National Aeronautics And Space Administration											
Fund Resources:											
Undisbursed Funds	80		0109		2007-2008		32,224,000.00		28,200,917.20		4,023,082.80
					2006-2007	3,271,472.07			3,006,060.82		265,411.25
					2005	2,726,091.68			420,951.72		2,305,139.96
					2004	754,942.56			89,388.43		665,554.13
					2003	935,274.33			3,430.78		931,843.55
					2002	690,201.88			-6,377.47		
Accounts Receivable										696,579.35	45,625.60
Unfilled Customer Orders										-45,625.60	24,552.53
Fund Equities:										-24,552.53	
Unobligated Balances (Expired)						-3,613,627.49				-648,499.75	-2,965,127.74
Unobligated Balances (Unexpired)						-505,841.77				209,748.22	-715,589.99
Accounts Payable						-1,330,285.97				-24,755.69	-1,305,530.28
Undelivered Orders						-2,928,227.29				346,734.52	-3,274,961.81
Subtotal	80		0109			-0-	32,224,000.00		31,714,371.48	509,628.52	-0-
Science, Aeronautics And Technology, National Aeronautics And Space Administration											
Fund Resources:											
Undisbursed Funds	80		0110		2003-2005	3,006,482.53			1,335,952.21		1,670,530.32
					2003-2004	173,338,945.49			95,700,423.58		77,638,521.91
					2002-2004	1,990,691.11			556,954.25		1,433,736.86
					2003	11,165,751.31			1,129,959.47		10,035,791.84
					2002-2003	63,079,184.50			18,871,165.97		44,208,018.53
					2002	4,940,809.84			597,814.76	4,342,995.08	
					2001-2002	36,086,635.87			22,105,337.18	13,981,298.69	
					No Year	27,688,498.24			7,842,508.43		19,845,989.81
Accounts Receivable						18,454,449.00				11,298,976.41	7,155,472.59
Unfilled Customer Orders						-10,545,709.59				-18,082,577.75	7,536,868.16
Fund Equities:											
Unobligated Balances (Expired)						-77,527,935.41				-29,657,595.73	-47,870,339.68
Unobligated Balances (Unexpired)						-11,108,535.36				-3,802,618.82	-7,305,916.54
Accounts Payable						-90,420,106.84				-62,848,027.58	-27,572,079.26
Undelivered Orders						-150,149,160.69				-63,372,566.15	-86,776,594.54
Subtotal	80		0110			-0-			148,140,115.85	-148,140,115.85	-0-
Human Space Flight, National Aeronautics And Space Administration											
Fund Resources:											
Undisbursed Funds	80		0111		2003-2005	1,004,858.23			48,795.44		956,062.79
					2003-2004	11,864,946.67			389,759.74		11,475,186.93
					2002-2004	445,851.32			73,152.41		372,698.91
					2003	5,977,246.59			-1,768,851.92		7,746,098.51
					2002-2003	12,210,539.08			2,136,012.58		10,074,526.50
					2002	5,556,277.53			2,635,412.66	2,920,864.87	
					2001-2002	3,827,374.15			2,043,705.75	1,783,668.40	

Appropriations, Outlays, and Balances - Continued

Title	Reg	Tr From	Account Number	Sub No.	Period of Availability	Balances, Beginning Of Fiscal Year	Appropriations And Other Obligational Authority[1]	Transfers Borrowings And Investment (Net)[2]	Outlays (Net)	Balances Withdrawn And Other Transactions[3]	Balances, End Of Fiscal Year[4]
Accounts Receivable					No Year	20,040,009.07			8,998,594.02		11,041,415.05
Unfilled Customer Orders						590,973.77				511,812.34	79,161.43
						-722,770.79				-3,697,740.55	2,974,969.76
Fund Equities:											
Unobligated Balances (Expired)						-17,360,003.43				-4,457,336.72	-12,902,666.71
Unobligated Balances (Unexpired)						-3,744,282.51				-1,080,023.36	-2,664,259.15
Accounts Payable						-24,547,733.50				-9,018,706.21	-15,529,027.29
Undelivered Orders						-15,143,286.18				-1,519,119.45	-13,624,166.73
Subtotal	80		0111			-0-			14,556,580.68	-14,556,580.68	-0-
Mission Support, National Aeronautics And Space Administration											
Fund Resources:											
Undisbursed Funds	80		0112		2001-2003	2,620,069.81			396,577.47		2,223,492.34
					2001-2002	2,274,740.68			518,488.77	1,756,251.91	
					2000-2002	611,809.42			157,972.55	453,836.87	
					No Year	11,069,869.84			1,999,737.44		9,070,132.40
Accounts Receivable						33,386.04			33,386.04		
Unfilled Customer Orders						-216,715.26				-216,715.26	
Fund Equities:											
Unobligated Balances (Expired)						-2,053,232.12				-1,538,095.48	-515,136.64
Unobligated Balances (Unexpired)						-10,325,731.91				-6,924,965.28	-3,400,766.63
Accounts Payable						-3,907,039.62				-740,534.34	-3,166,505.28
Undelivered Orders						-107,156.88				4,104,059.31	-4,211,216.19
Subtotal	80		0112			-0-			3,072,776.23	-3,072,776.23	-0-
Science, Aeronautics, And Exploration, National Aeronautics And Space Administration											
Fund Resources:											
Undisbursed Funds	80		0114		2007-2009		84,301,212.00		-1,387,791.40		85,689,003.40
					2007-2008		9,781,158,324.00		[5]4,442,091,047.24		5,339,067,276.76
					2006-2008	67,218,601.78		-3,700,000.00	30,222,682.64		33,295,919.14
					2006-2007	5,178,739,346.86		-43,800,000.00	4,081,170,553.37		1,053,768,793.49
					2005-2007	35,557,807.80			20,481,599.78		15,076,208.02
					2005-2006	826,282,338.38			575,646,683.48		250,635,654.90
					2004-2006	4,476,564.53			1,908,510.23		2,568,054.30
					2004-2005	261,686,361.85			87,114,913.58		174,571,448.27
					No Year	185,323,146.77		47,500,000.00	66,240,913.26		386,871,233.51
Accounts Receivable						78,459,311.05				-10,879,579.18	89,338,890.23
Unfilled Customer Orders						152,665,918.15				-273,720,607.86	426,386,526.01
Fund Equities:											
Unobligated Balances (Expired)						-70,113,396.58				19,735,987.05	-89,849,383.63
Unobligated Balances (Unexpired)						-1,386,300,714.91				371,195,321.30	-1,757,496,036.21
Accounts Payable						-1,001,859,978.17				556,998,455.97	-1,558,858,434.14
Undelivered Orders						-4,332,135,307.51				118,929,846.54	-4,451,065,154.05
Subtotal	80		0114			-0-	10,085,748,536.00		9,303,489,112.18	782,259,423.82	-0-
Space Flight Capabilities, National Aeronautics And Space Administration											
Fund Resources:											
Undisbursed Funds	80		0115		2007-2009		25,679,988.00		2,238,653.06		23,441,334.94
					2007-2008		6,049,141,476.00		4,431,739,647.75		1,617,401,828.25
					2006-2008	34,784,357.92		268,000.00	12,895,410.28		22,156,947.64

Appropriations, Outlays, and Balances – Continued

Appropriation or Fund Account — Title	Period of Availability	Dept Reg	Tr From	Account Number	Sub No.	Balances, Beginning Of Fiscal Year	Appropriations And Other Obligational Authority[1]	Transfers Borrowings And Investment (Net)[2]	Outlays (Net)	Balances Withdrawn And Other Transactions[3]	Balances, End Of Fiscal Year[4]
Space Flight Capabilities, National Aeronautics And Space Administration - Continued											
Fund Resources: - Continued											
Undisbursed Funds - Continued											
	2006-2007	80				1,502,375,376.93		-7,268,000.00	1,366,868,046.12	————	128,239,330.81
	2005-2007	80				28,296,804.14		————	17,828,483.44	————	10,468,320.70
	2005-2006	80				339,919,234.86		————	286,209,800.84	————	53,709,434.02
	2004-2006	80				7,573,787.08		————	6,160,138.98	————	1,413,648.10
	2004-2005	80				66,971,746.13		————	25,193,458.18	————	41,778,287.95
	No Year	80				600,956,515.81	92,246,000.00	7,000,000.00	225,991,908.89	————	474,210,606.92
Accounts Receivable						83,638,037.50				40,864,779.24	42,773,258.26
Unfilled Customer Orders						62,675,856.40				-159,129,622.87	221,805,479.27
Fund Equities:											
Unobligated Balances (Expired)						-39,743,982.51				-1,000,309.84	-38,743,672.67
Unobligated Balances (Unexpired)						-699,961,609.51				-90,423,360.83	-609,538,248.68
Accounts Payable						-723,282,750.59				181,119,729.41	-904,402,480.00
Undelivered Orders						-1,264,203,374.16				-179,489,298.65	-1,084,714,075.51
Subtotal		80		0115		-0-	6,167,067,464.00		6,375,125,547.54	-208,058,083.54	-0-
Intragovernmental Funds											
Working Capital Fund, National Aeronautics And Space Administration											
Fund Resources:											
Undisbursed Funds	No Year	80		4546		33,224,322.38					38,344,000.34
Unfilled Customer Orders									-5,119,677.96	-52,417.35	52,417.35
Fund Equities:											
Unobligated Balances (Unexpired)						[6]-10,479,869.80				6,638,859.72	-17,118,729.52
Accounts Payable						-3,977,222.42				5,356,738.74	-9,333,961.16
Undelivered Orders						[6]-18,767,230.16				-6,823,503.15	-11,943,727.01
Subtotal		80		4546		-0-			-5,119,677.96	5,119,677.96	-0-
Trust Fund Accounts											
Endeavor Teacher Fellowship Trust Fund, National Aeronautics And Space Administration											
Fund Resources:											
Undisbursed Funds	No Year	80		8550		165.39	21,720.18	249,149.89			271,035.46
Unrealized Discount On Investments						-15,095.63		7,850.11			-7,245.52
Investments In Public Debt Securities						610,000.00		-257,000.00			353,000.00
Fund Equities:											
Unobligated Balances (Unexpired)						-595,069.76				21,720.18	-616,789.94
Accounts Payable						-0-					
Subtotal		80		8550		-0-	21,720.18			21,720.18	-0-
National Space Grant Program, National Aeronautics And Space Administration											
Fund Resources:											
Undisbursed Funds	No Year	80		8977		3,462,505.73					3,462,505.73
Fund Equities:											
Unobligated Balances (Unexpired)						-3,462,505.73					-3,462,505.73

Appropriations, Outlays, and Balances - Continued

Appropriation or Fund Account	Account Symbol				Period of Availability	Balances, Beginning Of Fiscal Year	Appropriations And Other Obligational Authority[1]	Transfers Borrowings And Investment (Net)[2]	Outlays (Net)	Balances Withdrawn And Other Transactions[3]	Balances, End Of Fiscal Year[4]
Title	Dept		Account Number	Sub No.							
	Reg	Tr From									
Science, Space And Technology Education Trust Fund, National Aeronautics And Space Administration				8977	Subtotal	-0-					-0-
Fund Resources:											
Undisbursed Funds	80			8978	No Year	93,118.53	1,161,386.13	-150,296.87	1,000,000.00		104,207.79
Unrealized Discount On Investments						-8,433.68	------------	296.87	------------	------------	-8,136.81
Investments In Public Debt Securities						13,777,000.00	------------	150,000.00	------------	------------	13,927,000.00
Fund Equities:											
Unobligated Balances (Unexpired)						-13,861,684.85	------------	------------	------------	161,386.13	-14,023,070.98
Accounts Payable						-0-	------------	------------	------------	------------	-0-
	80			8978	Subtotal	-0-	1,161,386.13	------------	1,000,000.00	161,386.13	-0-
Gifts And Donations, National Aeronautics And Space Administration											
Fund Resources:											
Undisbursed Funds	80			8980	No Year	94,987.46	------------	------------	-100.00		95,087.46
Fund Equities:											
Unobligated Balances (Unexpired)						-18,854.53	------------	------------	------------	12,090.68	-30,945.21
Accounts Payable						------------	------------	------------	------------	14,142.25	-14,142.25
Undelivered Orders						-76,132.93	------------	------------	------------	-26,132.93	-50,000.00
	80			8980	Subtotal	-0-	------------	------------	-100.00	100.00	-0-
Deductions For Offsetting Receipts											
Proprietary Receipts From The Public						------------	-11,163,080.78	------------	-11,163,080.78	------------	------------
Intrabudgetary Transactions						------------	61,276.45	------------	61,276.45	------------	------------
Total, National Aeronautics And Space Administration						------------	16,275,121,301.98	------------	15,860,876,921.67	414,244,380.31	------------

Footnotes At End Of Chapter

Appropriations, Outlays, and Balances – Continued

Footnotes

1. The amounts in this column, unless otherwise footnoted, represent appropriations, increases and rescissions in borrowing authority or new contract authority. Appropriation accounts with appropriation transfer activity are presented in Table 1 (Appropriations and Appropriation Transfers) at the end of this chapter.

2. The amounts in this column, unless otherwise footnoted, represent transfers - other than appropriation transfers, borrowings (gross), investments (net), unrealized discounts or funds held outside the Treasury.

3. The amounts in this column, unless otherwise footnoted, represent obligated balances canceled for fiscal year 2002 pursuant to 31 U.S.C. 1553, changes in unfilled customer orders, accounts receivable, accounts payable, undelivered orders, unobligated balances and adjustments to borrowing and contract authority.

4. Unobligated balances for no-year or unexpired multiple year accounts are available for obligation; unobligated balances for expired fiscal year accounts are not available for obligation.

5. Includes $306,111.47 which represents payments for obligations of a closed account.

6. The opening balances of Unobligated Balance (Unexpired) and Undelivered Orders for account 80 X 4546 have been adjusted by $92,107.14 during the current fiscal year and do not agree with last year's closing balances.

Appropriations, Outlays, and Balances - Continued

Footnotes

Table 1 - Appropriations And Appropriation Transfers - National Aeronautics And Space Administration

Department Regular	Fiscal Year	Account Symbol	Net Appropriations And Appropriations Transfers	Appropriation Amount	Net Appropriation Transfers	Department Regular Involved	Fiscal Year Involved	Accounts Involved	Amount From or To (-)
80	X	0114	220,289,000.00	0.00	220,289,000.00	80	0709	0114	220,289,000.00
80	0708	0114	9,781,158,324.00	10,086,482,000.00	-305,323,676.00	80	0709	0114	-304,590,212.00
						80	0708	0115	-733,464.00
80	0709	0114	84,301,212.00	0.00	84,301,212.00	80	X	0114	-220,289,000.00
						80	0708	0114	304,590,212.00
80	X	0115	92,246,000.00	0.00	92,246,000.00	11	X	5512	740,000.00
						80	0709	0115	91,506,000.00
80	0708	0115	6,049,141,476.00	6,145,594,000.00	-96,452,524.00	80	0708	0114	733,464.00
						80	0709	0115	-97,185,988.00
80	0709	0115	25,679,988.00	20,000,000.00	5,679,988.00	80	X	0115	-91,506,000.00
						80	0708	0115	97,185,988.00
Totals			16,252,816,000.00	16,252,076,000.00	740,000.00				740,000.00

Footnotes At End Of Chapter

Appropriations, Outlays, and Balances – Continued

Appropriation or Fund Account: Title	Period of Availability	Dept Reg	Tr From	Account Number	Sub No.	Balances, Beginning Of Fiscal Year	Appropriations And Other Obligational Authority[1]	Transfers Borrowings And Investment (Net)[2]	Outlays (Net)	Balances Withdrawn And Other Transactions[3]	Balances, End Of Fiscal Year[4]
National Science Foundation											
General Fund Accounts											
Research And Related Activities, National Science Foundation											
Fund Resources:											
Undisbursed Funds	2007-2008	49		0100			4,231,860,000.00		731,789,995.34		3,500,070,004.66
	2006-2007					3,163,486,121.63			1,672,180,343.04		1,491,305,778.59
	2005-2006					1,422,999,628.22			826,573,840.73		596,425,787.49
	2004-2005					567,242,592.31			318,744,759.23		248,497,833.08
	2003-2004					214,378,666.77			129,527,025.74		84,851,641.03
	2002-2003					71,910,651.94			36,980,849.76		34,929,802.18
	2001-2002					43,933,623.11			23,066,975.18	20,866,647.93	
	No Year					219,155,748.27	439,550,000.00		402,169,510.26		256,536,238.01
Accounts Receivable						34,063,191.02				13,582,381.51	20,480,809.51
Unfilled Customer Orders						80,792,232.34				38,709,123.57	42,083,108.77
Fund Equities:											
Unobligated Balances (Expired)						-45,917,253.86				1,950,014.74	-47,867,268.60
Unobligated Balances (Unexpired)						-3,853,691.01				18,774,775.19	-22,628,466.20
Accounts Payable						-323,456,081.76				9,855,193.00	-333,311,274.76
Undelivered Orders						-5,444,735,428.98				426,638,564.78	-5,871,373,993.76
Subtotal		49		0100		-0-	4,671,410,000.00		4,141,033,299.28	530,376,700.72	-0-
Education And Human Resources, National Science Foundation											
Fund Resources:											
Undisbursed Funds	2007-2008	49		0106			796,692,996.00		124,747,163.60		671,945,832.40
	2006-2007					685,202,881.17			296,569,132.92		388,633,748.25
	2005-2006					403,652,225.73			246,309,682.20		157,342,543.53
	2004-2005					208,855,048.49			103,084,841.36		105,770,207.13
	2003-2004					92,980,065.50			46,989,711.69		45,990,353.81
	2002-2003					76,161,674.76			37,736,696.61		38,424,978.15
	2001-2002					18,079,832.73			2,037,227.19	16,042,605.54	
Accounts Receivable						3,211,580.85				-160,022.55	3,371,603.40
Unfilled Customer Orders						8,608,740.51				2,633,874.29	5,974,866.22
Fund Equities:											
Unobligated Balances (Expired)						-27,164,967.52				-8,326,791.94	-18,838,175.58
Unobligated Balances (Unexpired)						-127,903.22				-28,572.08	-99,331.14
Accounts Payable						-59,456,662.77				-2,471,447.70	-56,985,215.07
Undelivered Orders						-1,410,002,516.23				-68,471,105.13	-1,341,531,411.10
Subtotal		49		0106		-0-	796,692,996.00		857,474,455.57	-60,781,459.57	-0-
Salaries And Expenses, National Science Foundation											
Fund Resources:											
Undisbursed Funds	2007-2008	49		0180			250,000.00				250,000.00
	2006-2007					250,000.00	248,245,000.00		206,051,657.20		42,193,342.80
	2006					43,745,290.23			39,562,268.48		4,183,021.75
	2005					4,683,823.91			2,036,903.06		2,646,920.85
	2004					1,465,843.22			56,879.09		1,408,964.13
	2003					1,888,877.33			31,169.03		1,857,708.30
	2002					1,848,217.20			116,386.83	1,731,830.37	

Appropriations, Outlays, and Balances - Continued

Appropriation or Fund Account — Title	Period of Availability	Reg	Tr From	Account Number	Sub No.	Balances, Beginning Of Fiscal Year	Appropriations And Other Obligational Authority[1]	Transfers Borrowings And Investment (Net)[2]	Outlays (Net)	Balances Withdrawn And Other Transactions[3]	Balances, End Of Fiscal Year[4]
Accounts Receivable						254,815.00				-450,840.00	705,655.00
Unfilled Customer Orders						-421.00				-46,535.51	46,114.51
Fund Equities:											
Unobligated Balances (Expired)						-3,667,401.04				-664,839.03	-3,002,562.01
Accounts Payable						-17,993,898.02				-278,266.61	-17,715,631.41
Undelivered Orders						-32,475,146.83				98,387.09	-32,573,533.92
Subtotal		49		0180		-0-	248,495,000.00		248,105,263.69	389,736.31	-0-
Office Of Inspector General, National Science Foundation											
Fund Resources:											
Undisbursed Funds	2007-2008	49		0300		3,219,719.71	11,427,122.00		8,721,617.16		2,705,504.84
	2006-2007					1,422,635.26			1,229,190.16		1,990,529.55
	2005-2006					277,614.90			1,117,599.66		305,035.60
	2004-2005					83,881.87			69,714.16		207,900.74
	2003-2004					58,468.58			5,325.23		78,556.64
	2002-2003					24,465.04					58,468.58
	2001-2002									24,465.04	
Fund Equities:											
Unobligated Balances (Expired)						-99,640.48				68,465.04	-168,105.52
Unobligated Balances (Unexpired)						-1,014,936.12				-307,713.39	-707,222.73
Accounts Payable						-617,871.24				18,107.88	-635,979.12
Undelivered Orders						-3,354,337.52				480,351.06	-3,834,688.58
Subtotal		49		0300		-0-	11,427,122.00		11,143,446.37	283,675.63	-0-
Office Of The National Science Board, National Science Foundation											
Fund Resources:											
Undisbursed Funds	2007	49		0350		1,155,107.92	3,968,912.00		2,534,158.27		1,434,753.73
	2006					969,714.80			969,402.98		185,704.94
	2005					1,829,428.71			65,437.46		904,277.34
	2004					660,715.45					1,829,428.71
	2003										660,715.45
Fund Equities:											
Unobligated Balances (Expired)						-2,634,341.49				383,521.73	-3,017,863.22
Accounts Payable						-477,296.16				-147,924.56	-329,371.60
Undelivered Orders						-1,503,329.23				164,316.12	-1,667,645.35
Subtotal		49		0350		-0-	3,968,912.00		3,568,998.71	399,913.29	-0-
Major Research Equipment And Facilities Construction, National Science Foundation											
Fund Resources:											
Undisbursed Funds	No Year	49		0551		266,906,720.96	190,880,534.00		207,946,995.05		249,840,259.91
Fund Equities:											
Unobligated Balances (Unexpired)						-2,776,704.86				24,822,544.27	-27,599,249.13
Accounts Payable						-15,439,426.46				-4,259,654.46	-11,179,772.00
Undelivered Orders						-248,690,589.64				-37,629,350.86	-211,061,238.78
Subtotal		49		0551		-0-	190,880,534.00		207,946,995.05	-17,066,461.05	-0-

Footnotes At End Of Chapter

Appropriations, Outlays, and Balances – Continued

Appropriation or Fund Account	Account Symbol					Balances, Beginning Of Fiscal Year	Appropriations And Other Obligational Authority[1]	Transfers Borrowings And Investment (Net)[2]	Outlays (Net)	Balances Withdrawn And Other Transactions[3]	Balances, End Of Fiscal Year[4]
Title	Period of Availability	Dept Reg	Tr From	Account Number	Sub No.						
Special Fund Accounts											
Salaries And Expenses, H-1B Funded, Education And Human Resources, National Science Foundation											
Fund Resources:											
Undisbursed Funds	No Year	49		5176		281,473,097.11	107,359,350.06		51,537,604.01		337,294,843.16
Fund Equities:											
Unobligated Balances (Unexpired)						-98,187,307.89				-34,816,774.45	-63,370,533.44
Accounts Payable						-2,779,372.64				446,306.87	-3,225,679.51
Undelivered Orders						-180,506,416.58				90,192,213.63	-270,698,630.21
						-0-				55,821,746.05	-0-
Subtotal		49		5176			107,359,350.06		51,537,604.01		
Trust Fund Accounts											
Donations, National Science Foundation											
Fund Resources:											
Undisbursed Funds	No Year	49		8960		23,951,572.44	41,280,961.11	-16,228,262.43	9,583,151.46		39,421,119.66
Funds Held Outside The Treasury	No Year	49						16,228,262.43			16,228,262.43
Fund Equities:											
Unobligated Balances (Unexpired)						-18,099,204.02				13,278,903.63	-31,378,107.65
Accounts Payable						11,503,532.63				12,742,749.63	-1,239,217.00
Undelivered Orders						-17,355,901.05				5,676,156.39	-23,032,057.44
						-0-				31,697,809.65	-0-
Subtotal		49		8960			41,280,961.11		9,583,151.46		
Deductions For Offsetting Receipts											
Proprietary Receipts From The Public							-1,535,255.41		-1,535,255.41		
Total, National Science Foundation							6,069,979,619.76		5,528,857,958.73	541,121,661.03	

Appropriations, Outlays, and Balances - Continued

Footnotes

1   The amounts in this column, unless otherwise footnoted, represent appropriations, increases and rescissions in borrowing authority or new contract authority. Appropriation accounts with appropriation transfer activity are presented in Table 1 (Appropriations and Appropriation Transfers) at the end of this chapter.

2   The amounts in this column, unless otherwise footnoted, represent transfers - other than appropriation transfers, borrowings (gross), investments (net), unrealized discounts or funds held outside the Treasury.

3   The amounts in this column, unless otherwise footnoted, represent obligated balances canceled for fiscal year 2002 pursuant to 31 U.S.C. 1553, changes in unfilled customer orders, accounts receivable, accounts payable, undelivered orders, unobligated balances and adjustments to borrowing and contract authority.

4   Unobligated balances for no-year or unexpired multiple year accounts are available for obligation; unobligated balances for expired fiscal year accounts are not available for obligation.

Appropriations, Outlays, and Balances – Continued

Footnotes

Table 1 - Appropriations And Appropriation Transfers - National Science Foundation

Department Regular	Fiscal Year	Account Symbol	Net Appropriations And Appropriations Transfers	Appropriation Amount	Net Appropriation Transfers	Department Regular Involved	Fiscal Year Involved	Accounts Involved	Amount From or To (-)
49	X	0100	439,550,000.00	0.00	439,550,000.00	49	0708	0100	439,550,000.00
49	0708	0100	4,231,860,000.00	4,665,950,000.00	-434,090,000.00	49	X	0100	-439,550,000.00
						72	0708	1093	5,460,000.00
49	0708	0180	250,000.00	0.00	250,000.00	72	0708	1093	250,000.00
Totals			4,671,660,000.00	4,665,950,000.00	5,710,000.00				5,710,000.00

Appropriations, Outlays, and Balances – Continued

Footnotes

This Page Left Blank Intentionally

Appropriations, Outlays, and Balances – Continued

Appropriation or Fund Account — Title	Dept Reg	Tr From	Account Number	Sub No.	Period of Availability	Balances, Beginning Of Fiscal Year	Appropriations And Other Obligational Authority[1]	Transfers Borrowings And Investment (Net)[2]	Outlays (Net)	Balances Withdrawn And Other Transactions[3]	Balances, End Of Fiscal Year[4]
Office Of Personnel Management											
General Fund Accounts											
Salaries And Expenses, Office Of Personnel Management											
Fund Resources:											
Undisbursed Funds	24		0100		2007		103,251,918.00	1,264,953.00	76,439,561.52		28,077,309.48
					2006-2007	1,397,880.00			1,076,953.11		320,926.89
					2005-2007	3,796,972.75			1,768,425.65		2,028,547.10
					2006	24,782,427.72		-1,264,953.00	18,139,795.52		5,377,679.20
					2005	14,688,713.86			2,462,602.06		12,226,111.80
					2004-2005	498,379.18			270,369.90		228,009.28
					2004	8,530,089.72			1,616,458.97		6,913,630.75
					2003	15,872,338.43			6,743.57		15,865,594.86
					2002	-372,552.10			-484,102.58	111,550.48	-0-
					No Year	11,450,723.89	8,353,324.00		8,628,638.96		11,175,408.93
Accounts Receivable						84,501,956.56				-2,195,181.68	86,697,138.24
Unfilled Customer Orders						13,448,033.65				12,776,659.62	671,374.03
Fund Equities:											
Unobligated Balances (Expired)						-36,756,040.06				3,165,945.07	-39,921,985.13
Unobligated Balances (Unexpired)						-47,513,039.58				-23,013,800.36	-24,499,239.22
Accounts Payable						-19,684,218.74				-723,981.10	-18,960,237.64
Undelivered Orders						-74,641,665.28				11,558,603.29	-86,200,268.57
Subtotal	24		0100			-0-	111,605,242.00		109,925,446.68	1,679,795.32	-0-
Payment To Civil Service Retirement And Disability Fund, Office Of Personnel Management											
Fund Resources:											
Undisbursed Funds	24		0200		2007		30,995,847,084.00		30,995,847,084.00		
Government Payment For Annuitants, Employees' Health Benefits, Office Of Personnel Management											
Fund Resources:											
Undisbursed Funds	24		0206		No Year	847,408,701.80	8,581,437,388.08		8,558,005,987.86	23,431,400.22	870,840,102.02
Fund Equities:											
Accounts Payable						-847,408,701.80				23,431,400.22	-870,840,102.02
Subtotal	24		0206			-0-	8,581,437,388.08		8,558,005,987.86		-0-
Salaries And Expenses, Office Of Inspector General, Office Of Personnel Management											
Fund Resources:											
Undisbursed Funds	24		0400		2007		2,061,494.00		2,540,160.09		[5]478,666.09
					2006	229,678.32			157,798.84		71,879.48
					2005	106,334.53			-5,726.55		112,061.08
					2004	754,857.09					754,857.09
					2003	1,434,456.55					1,434,456.55
					2002	1,890,519.88			7,700.86	1,882,819.02	
Accounts Receivable						1,923,232.28				-274,207.80	2,197,440.08
Unfilled Customer Orders						998,761.71				340,691.64	658,070.07
Fund Equities:											
Unobligated Balances (Expired)						-5,410,184.03				-1,969,577.83	-3,440,606.20
Accounts Payable						-1,376,541.72				-1,117,528.25	-259,013.47

Appropriations, Outlays, and Balances - Continued

Appropriation or Fund Account — Title	Period of Availability	Dept Reg	Dept Tr From	Account Number	Sub No.	Balances, Beginning Of Fiscal Year	Appropriations And Other Obligational Authority[1]	Transfers Borrowings And Investment (Net)[2]	Outlays (Net)	Balances Withdrawn And Other Transactions[3]	Balances, End Of Fiscal Year[4]
Undelivered Orders	Subtotal	24		0400		-551,114.61	2,061,494.00		2,699,933.24	499,363.98	-1,050,478.59
						-0-	-0-			-638,439.24	-0-
Government Payment For Annuitants, Employee Life Insurance Benefits, Office Of Personnel Management											
Fund Resources:											
Undisbursed Funds	No Year	24		0500		4,577,757.46	42,671,407.27		42,403,778.03		4,845,386.70
Fund Equities:											
Accounts Payable	Subtotal	24		0500		-4,577,757.46	42,671,407.27		42,403,778.03	267,629.24	-4,845,386.70
						-0-	-0-			267,629.24	-0-
OPM Building Delegation Fund, Office Of Personnel Management											
Fund Resources:											
Undisbursed Funds	No Year	24		0600		2,468,882.08					3,018,253.22
Accounts Receivable						6,777,360.14				6,777,360.14	
Fund Equities:											
Unobligated Balances (Unexpired)						-7,329,364.44				-5,765,802.77	-1,563,561.67
Accounts Payable						-1,183,887.65				-490,950.65	-692,937.00
Undelivered Orders						-732,990.13				28,764.42	-761,754.55
	Subtotal	24		0600		-0-			-549,371.14	549,371.14	-0-
Human Capital Performance Fund, Office Of Personnel Management											
Fund Resources:											
Undisbursed Funds	2004	24		0700		994,100.00					994,100.00
Fund Equities:											
Unobligated Balances (Expired)	Subtotal	24		0700		-994,100.00					-994,100.00
						-0-					-0-
Intragovernmental Funds											
Revolving Fund, Undistributed SIBAC Chargebacks For Washington, DC, Office Of Personnel Management											
Fund Resources:											
Undisbursed Funds	No Year	24		4571	5	-3,010.24			-3,010.24		
	No Year	24		4571	24	295,334,038.48			-199,237,649.02		494,571,687.50
Accounts Receivable						118,499,904.87				31,495,699.28	87,004,205.59
Unfilled Customer Orders						371,519,968.24				41,578,722.59	329,941,245.65
Fund Equities:											
Unobligated Balances (Unexpired)						-407,388,365.60				225,089,673.88	-632,478,039.48
Accounts Payable						-49,725,393.31				20,318,656.74	-70,044,050.05
Undelivered Orders						-328,240,152.68				-119,245,103.47	-208,995,049.21
	Subtotal	24		4571		-3,010.24			-199,240,659.26	199,237,649.02	-0-
Special Fund Accounts											
Postal Service Contributions For Retiree Health Benefits, Office Of Personnel Management											
Fund Resources:											
Undisbursed Funds	No Year	24		5391		25,491,152,065.79		-25,491,152,000.00			65.79
Investments In Public Debt Securities								25,491,152,000.00			25,491,152,000.00

Footnotes At End Of Chapter

Appropriations, Outlays, and Balances – Continued

Appropriation or Fund Account — Title	Period of Availability	Reg	Tr From	Account Number	Sub No.	Balances, Beginning Of Fiscal Year	Appropriations And Other Obligational Authority[1]	Transfers Borrowings And Investment (Net)[2]	Outlays (Net)	Balances Withdrawn And Other Transactions[3]	Balances, End Of Fiscal Year[4]
Postal Service Contributions For Retiree Health Benefits, Office Of Personnel Management - Continued											
Fund Equities:											
Unobligated Balances (Unexpired)											-25,491,152,065.79
Accounts Payable											-0-
Subtotal		24		5391		-0-	25,491,152,065.79			25,491,152,065.79	-0-
Trust Fund Accounts											
Civil Service Retirement And Disability Fund, Office Of Personnel Management											
Fund Resources:											
Undisbursed Funds	No Year	24		8135		16,795,681.06		-11,728,694,000.00	78,146,308,159.84		1,002,162.76
Investments In Public Debt Securities						689,935,971,085.31	89,869,208,641.54	11,728,694,000.00			701,664,665,085.31
Fund Equities:											
Unobligated Balances (Unexpired)	Subtotal	24		8135		-684,824,637,334.65				11,391,064,635.99	-696,215,701,970.64
Accounts Payable						-5,128,129,431.72				321,835,845.71	-5,449,965,277.43
Subtotal		24		8135		-0-	89,869,208,641.54		78,146,308,159.84	11,712,900,481.70	-0-
Employees' Life Insurance Fund, Office Of Personnel Management											
Fund Resources:											
Undisbursed Funds	No Year	24		8424		1,005,001.69		-1,634,280,709.55	-1,638,248,238.41		4,972,530.55
Unrealized Discount On Investments						498,270,694.99		-48,887,290.45			-547,157,985.44
Investments In Public Debt Securities						31,281,953,000.00		1,683,168,000.00			32,965,121,000.00
Accounts Receivable						350,331,296.78				-32,717,315.15	383,048,611.93
Fund Equities:											
Unobligated Balances (Unexpired)	Subtotal	24		8424		-30,449,072,126.85				1,615,191,369.78	-32,064,263,496.63
Accounts Payable						-685,946,476.63				55,774,183.78	-741,720,660.41
Subtotal		24		8424		-0-			-1,638,248,238.41	1,638,248,238.41	-0-
Employees' Health Benefits Fund, Office Of Personnel Management											
Fund Resources:											
Undisbursed Funds	No Year	24		8440		2,755,440.85		-1,029,481,266.19	-1,031,301,712.99		4,575,887.65
Unrealized Discount On Investments						-53,374,160.63		-37,851,733.81			-91,225,894.44
Investments In Public Debt Securities						14,822,430,000.00		1,067,333,000.00			15,889,763,000.00
Accounts Receivable						1,434,905,402.77				-61,082,049.24	1,495,987,452.01
Fund Equities:											
Unobligated Balances (Unexpired)	Subtotal	24		8440		-12,530,189,021.94				634,344,750.13	-13,164,533,772.07
Accounts Payable						-3,676,527,661.05				458,039,012.10	-4,134,566,673.15
Subtotal		24		8440		-0-			-1,031,301,712.99	1,031,301,712.99	-0-
Retired Employees' Health Benefits Fund, Office Of Personnel Management											
Fund Resources:											
Undisbursed Funds	No Year	24		8445		5,864.34		-106,055.33	-105,505.48		5,314.49
Unrealized Discount On Investments						-53,533.88		-2,944.67			-56,478.55
Investments In Public Debt Securities						2,273,000.00		109,000.00			2,382,000.00
Accounts Receivable						120,662.10				12,347.60	108,314.50
Fund Equities:											
Unobligated Balances (Unexpired)						-2,150,894.04				141,081.02	-2,291,975.06
Accounts Payable						-195,098.52				-47,923.14	-147,175.38

Appropriations, Outlays, and Balances - Continued

Appropriation or Fund Account		Account Symbol					Balances, Beginning Of Fiscal Year	Appropriations And Other Obligational Authority[1]	Transfers Borrowings And Investment (Net)[2]	Outlays (Net)	Balances Withdrawn And Other Transactions[3]	Balances, End Of Fiscal Year[4]
Title	Period of Availability	Dept		Account Number	Sub No.							
		Reg	Tr From									
	Subtotal	24		8445		-0-			-105,505.48	105,505.48	-0-
Deductions For Offsetting Receipts											
Proprietary Receipts From The Public							-10,781,799.94		-10,781,799.94	-------	
Intrabudgetary Transactions							-56,525,052,488.25		-56,525,052,488.25	-------	
Total, Office Of Personnel Management						-3,010.24	98,548,149,034.49		58,449,910,614.18	40,098,235,410.07	

Appropriations, Outlays, and Balances – Continued

Footnotes

1   The amounts in this column, unless otherwise footnoted, represent appropriations, increases and rescissions in borrowing authority or new contract authority. Only appropriations with appropriation transfer activity are presented in Table 1 (Appropriations and Appropriation Transfers). Since the Office Of Personnel Management had no transfer activity during fiscal year 2007, Table 1 does not appear.

2   The amounts in this column, unless otherwise footnoted, represent transfers - other than appropriation transfers, borrowings (gross), investments (net), unrealized discounts or funds held outside the Treasury.

3   The amounts in this column, unless otherwise footnoted, represent obligated balances canceled for fiscal year 2002 pursuant to 31 U.S.C. 1553, changes in unfilled customer orders, accounts receivable, accounts payable, undelivered orders, unobligated balances and adjustments to borrowing and contract authority.

4   Unobligated balances for no-year or unexpired multiple year accounts are available for obligation; unobligated balances for expired fiscal year accounts are not available for obligation.

5   Subject to disposition by the administrative agency.

Appropriations, Outlays, and Balances – Continued

Footnotes

This Page Left Blank Intentionally

Appropriations, Outlays, and Balances – Continued

Title	Period of Availability	Reg	Tr From	Account Number	Sub No.	Balances, Beginning Of Fiscal Year	Appropriations And Other Obligational Authority[1]	Transfers Borrowings And Investment (Net)[2]	Outlays (Net)	Balances Withdrawn And Other Transactions[3]	Balances, End Of Fiscal Year[4]
Small Business Administration											
General Fund Accounts											
Salaries And Expenses, Small Business Administration											
Fund Resources:											
Undisbursed Funds	2007-2008	73		0100		------	87,863,292.00	------	39,234,988.91	------	48,628,303.09
	2007					------	239,728,963.00	------	154,169,857.26	------	85,559,105.74
	2006-2007					49,097,216.96	------	------	45,605,831.22	------	3,491,385.74
	2006					158,865,031.48	------	------	76,365,586.35	------	82,499,445.13
	2005-2006					4,692,719.70	------	------	3,527,302.09	------	1,165,417.61
	2005					46,984,363.40	------	------	17,919,250.12	------	29,065,113.28
	2004-2005					435,723.49	------	------	367,534.74	------	68,188.75
	2004					31,707,590.21	------	------	11,303,156.42	------	20,404,433.79
	2003-2004					1,194,496.33	------	------	6,761.99	------	1,187,734.34
	2003					23,331,282.10	------	------	6,236,637.99	------	17,094,644.11
	2002-2003					387,229.21	------	------	------	------	387,229.21
	2002					21,610,069.83	------	------	10,544,219.49	11,065,850.34	-0-
	2001-2002					551,313.90	------	------	12,904.48	538,409.42	-0-
	No Year					132,470,825.01	-6,192,171.00	------	-129,334,142.53	------	255,612,796.54
Fund Equities:											
Unobligated Balances (Expired)						-32,658,863.99				-12,382,108.68	-20,276,755.31
Unobligated Balances (Unexpired)						-78,154,342.81				131,714,703.84	-209,869,046.65
Accounts Payable						-70,566,770.78				-6,918,940.79	-63,647,829.99
Undelivered Orders						-289,947,884.04				-38,577,718.66	-251,370,165.38
	Subtotal	73		0100		-0-	321,400,084.00		235,959,888.53	85,440,195.47	-0-
Office Of Inspector General, Small Business Administration											
Fund Resources:											
Undisbursed Funds	2007	73		0200		------	13,835,469.00	------	12,419,800.41	------	1,415,668.59
	2006					1,390,112.34	------	------	1,331,090.54	------	59,021.80
	2005					101,168.27	------	------	-28.14	------	101,196.41
	2004					98,866.17	------	------	329.17	------	98,537.00
	2003					247,294.22	------	------	11,116.37	------	236,177.85
	2002					26,381.14	------	------	3,694.64	22,686.50	-0-
	No Year					6,092,851.81	------	------	166,641.98	------	5,926,209.83
Fund Equities:											
Unobligated Balances (Expired)						-400,004.75				-26,254.39	-373,750.36
Unobligated Balances (Unexpired)						-5,594,333.80				-282,341.15	-5,311,992.65
Accounts Payable						-464,896.32				-2,777.95	-462,118.37
Undelivered Orders						-1,497,439.08				191,511.02	-1,688,950.10
	Subtotal	73		0200		-0-	13,835,469.00		13,932,644.97	-97,175.97	-0-
Disaster Loans Program Account, Small Business Administration											
Fund Resources:											
Undisbursed Funds	2007	73		1152		------	290,307,469.00	------	290,307,469.00	------	-0-
	2002					------	------	------	-9,248,140.41	9,248,140.41	-0-
	No Year					1,416,725,041.25	-37,392,035.00	------	903,751,815.51	------	475,581,190.74
Fund Equities:											
Unobligated Balances (Unexpired)						-633,293,868.40				-328,671,959.47	-304,621,908.93
Undelivered Orders						-783,431,172.85				-612,471,891.04	-170,959,281.81

Appropriations, Outlays, and Balances - Continued

Appropriation or Fund Account — Title	Period of Availability	Reg	Tr From	Account Number	Sub No.	Balances, Beginning Of Fiscal Year	Appropriations And Other Obligational Authority[1]	Transfers Borrowings And Investment (Net)[2]	Outlays (Net)	Balances Withdrawn And Other Transactions[3]	Balances, End Of Fiscal Year[4]
	Subtotal	73		1152		-0-	252,915,434.00		1,184,811,144.10	-931,895,710.10	-0-
Business Loans Program Account, Small Business Administration											
Fund Resources:											
Undisbursed Funds	2007	73		1154		---	530,973,854.00		530,973,854.00	---	---
	2004-2005					1,644,623.10					1,644,623.10
	2002					21,600,067.74	-3,747,536.00		5,061,381.22		12,791,150.52
	No Year								-360,672.67	360,672.67	---
Fund Equities:											
Unobligated Balances (Expired)						-1,636,116.60					-1,636,116.60
Unobligated Balances (Unexpired)						-11,423,474.57				-4,947,310.41	-6,476,164.16
Undelivered Orders						-10,185,099.67				-3,861,606.81	-6,323,492.86
	Subtotal	73		1154		-0-	527,226,318.00		535,674,562.55	-8,448,244.55	-0-
Public Enterprise Funds											
Pollution Control Equipment Fund, Liquidating Account, Small Business Administration											
Fund Resources:											
Undisbursed Funds	No Year	73		4147		3,200,940.00	3,000,000.00		-213,020.00	3,200,940.00[5]	3,213,020.00
Fund Equities:											
Unobligated Balances (Unexpired)						-3,200,940.00				12,080.00	-3,213,020.00
	Subtotal	73		4147		-0-	3,000,000.00		-213,020.00	3,213,020.00	-0-
Disaster Loan Fund, Liquidating Account, Small Business Administration											
Fund Resources:											
Undisbursed Funds	No Year	73		4153		17,540,626.44	10,000,000.00		-3,888,439.10	16,124,589.53[5]	15,304,476.01
Fund Equities:											
Unobligated Balances (Unexpired)						-16,124,589.53				-1,994,134.59	-14,130,454.94
Accounts Payable						-1,416,036.91				-242,015.84	-1,174,021.07
	Subtotal	73		4153		-0-	10,000,000.00		-3,888,439.10	13,888,439.10	-0-
Business Loan Fund, Liquidating Account, Small Business Administration											
Fund Resources:											
Undisbursed Funds	No Year	73		4154		65,851,017.46	20,000,000.00	-9,520,893.41	-14,902,929.21	56,158,033.97[5]	35,075,019.29
Fund Equities:											
Unobligated Balances (Unexpired)						-56,158,032.97				-26,218,955.82	-29,939,077.15
Accounts Payable						-9,692,984.49				-4,557,042.35	-5,135,942.14
	Subtotal	73		4154		-0-	20,000,000.00	-9,520,893.41	-14,902,929.21	25,382,035.80	-0-
Surety Bond Guarantees Revolving Fund, Small Business Administration											
Fund Resources:											
Undisbursed Funds	No Year	73		4156		21,532,963.97	2,824,459.00		-2,669,386.32		27,026,809.29
Fund Equities:											
Unobligated Balances (Unexpired)						-20,661,149.55				5,972,368.27	-26,633,517.82
Accounts Payable						-871,814.42				-478,522.95	-393,291.47
	Subtotal	73		4156		-0-	2,824,459.00		-2,669,386.32	5,493,845.32	-0-

Footnotes At End Of Chapter

Appropriations, Outlays, and Balances – Continued

Appropriation or Fund Account — Title	Period of Availability	Dept — Reg	Dept — Tr From	Account Number	Sub No.	Balances, Beginning Of Fiscal Year	Appropriations And Other Obligational Authority[1]	Transfers Borrowings And Investment (Net)[2]	Outlays (Net)	Balances Withdrawn And Other Transactions[3]	Balances, End Of Fiscal Year[4]
Trust Fund Accounts											
Business Assistance Trust Fund, Small Business Administration											
Fund Resources:											
Undisbursed Funds	No Year	73		8466		369,363.35			59,827.86		309,535.49
Fund Equities:											
Unobligated Balances (Unexpired)						-363,215.29				-80,514.22	-282,701.07
Undelivered Orders						-6,148.06				20,686.36	-26,834.42
	Subtotal	73		8466		-0-			59,827.86	-59,827.86	-0-
Deductions For Offsetting Receipts											
Proprietary Receipts From The Public							-773,824,181.10		-773,824,181.10		
Intrabudgetary Transactions							-4,402.72		-4,402.72		
Total, Small Business Administration							377,373,180.18	-9,520,893.41	1,174,935,709.56	-807,083,422.79	
Memorandum											
Financing Accounts											
Public Enterprise Funds											
Business Loan And Investment Direct Loan Financing Account, Small Business Administration											
Fund Resources:											
Undisbursed Funds	No Year	73		4148		39,154,822.10			2,806,985.33	12,574,996.00	35,116,014.28
Authority To Borrow From The Treasury							31,985,996.00	-1,231,822.49			
Unfilled Customer Orders						2,156,626.48		-19,411,000.00		-249,701.57	2,406,328.05
Fund Equities:											
Unobligated Balances (Unexpired)						-15,814,657.81				-3,530,620.91	-12,284,036.90
Accounts Payable						-41.84				-38.41	-3.43
Undelivered Orders						-25,496,748.93				-258,446.93	-25,238,302.00
	Subtotal	73		4148		-0-	31,985,996.00	-20,642,822.49	2,806,985.33	8,536,188.18	-0-
Business Loan And Investment Guaranteed Loan Financing Account, Small Business Administration											
Fund Resources:											
Undisbursed Funds	No Year	73		4149		2,601,726,920.07		-259,540,457.00	141,459,070.53		2,200,727,392.54
Authority To Borrow From The Treasury							747,701,569.00	-128,000,396.00			619,701,173.00
Unfilled Customer Orders						8,034,095.48				4,105,690.38	3,928,405.10
Fund Equities:											
Unobligated Balances (Unexpired)						-2,588,241,695.61				216,038,953.25	-2,804,280,648.86
Accounts Payable						-21,519,319.94				-1,442,998.16	-20,076,321.78
	Subtotal	73		4149		-0-	747,701,569.00	-387,540,853.00	141,459,070.53	218,701,645.47	-0-
Disaster Direct Loan Financing Account, Small Business Administration											
Fund Resources:											
Undisbursed Funds	No Year	73		4150		1,984,965,669.23		2,323,383,226.00	1,572,696,802.43		2,735,652,092.80
Authority To Borrow From The Treasury						6,831,915,333.00	2,186,413,515.00	-4,144,033,226.00		4,874,295,622.00	
Unfilled Customer Orders						783,471,833.54				612,474,638.16	170,997,195.38

Appropriations, Outlays, and Balances - Continued

Appropriation or Fund Account		Account Symbol					Balances, Beginning Of Fiscal Year[3]	Appropriations And Other Obligational Authority[1]	Transfers Borrowings And Investment (Net)[2]	Outlays (Net)	Balances Withdrawn And Other Transactions[3]	Balances, End Of Fiscal Year[4]
Title	Period of Availability		Dept		Account Number	Sub No.						
			Reg	Tr From								
Fund Equities:												
Unobligated Balances (Unexpired)							-4,207,301,774.86				-2,345,485,761.66	-1,861,816,013.20
Accounts Payable							-119,564.81				7,317,479.91	-7,437,044.72
Undelivered Orders							-5,392,931,496.10				-4,355,535,265.84	-1,037,396,230.26
							-0-	2,186,413,515.00	-1,820,650,000.00	1,572,696,802.43	-1,206,933,287.43	-0-
Subtotal	,		73		4150							
Total, Financing Accounts								2,966,101,080.00	-2,228,833,675.49	1,716,962,858.29	-979,695,453.78	

Appropriations, Outlays, and Balances – Continued

Footnotes

1　The amounts in this column, unless otherwise footnoted, represent appropriations, increases and rescissions in borrowing authority or new contract authority. Appropriation accounts with appropriation transfer activity are presented in Table 1 (Appropriations and Appropriation Transfers) at the end of this chapter.

2　The amounts in this column, unless otherwise footnoted, represent transfers - other than appropriation transfers, borrowings (gross), investments (net), unrealized discounts or funds held outside the Treasury.

3　The amounts in this column, unless otherwise footnoted, represent obligated balances canceled for fiscal year 2002 pursuant to 31 U.S.C. 1553, changes in unfilled customer orders, accounts receivable, accounts payable, undelivered orders, unobligated balances and adjustments to borrowing and contract authority.

4　Unobligated balances for no-year or unexpired multiple year accounts are available for obligation; unobligated balances for expired fiscal year accounts are not available for obligation.

5　Represents capital transfer to miscellaneous receipts.

Appropriations, Outlays, and Balances - Continued

Footnotes

Table 1 - Appropriations And Appropriation Transfers - Small Business Administration

Department Regular	Fiscal Year	Account Symbol	Net Appropriations And Appropriations Transfers	Appropriation Amount	Net Appropriation Transfers	Department Regular Involved	Fiscal Year Involved	Accounts Involved	Amount From or To (-)
73	X	1152	-37,392,035.00	112,607,965.00	-150,000,000.00	70	X	0702	-150,000,000.00
Totals			-37,392,035.00	112,607,965.00	-150,000,000.00				-150,000,000.00

Appropriations, Outlays, and Balances – Continued

Appropriation or Fund Account — Title	Reg	Tr From	Account Number	Sub No.	Period of Availability	Balances, Beginning of Fiscal Year	Appropriations And Other Obligational Authority[1]	Transfers Borrowings And Investment (Net)[2]	Outlays (Net)	Balances Withdrawn And Other Transactions[3]	Balances, End Of Fiscal Year[4]
Social Security Administration											
General Fund Accounts											
Office Of The Inspector General, Social Security Administration											
Fund Resources:											
Undisbursed Funds	28		0400		2007		25,902,000.00		24,556,891.88		1,345,108.12
					2006	-9,251,315.06			-11,840,295.76		2,588,980.70
					2005	-39,443.33			-1,190,126.43		1,150,683.10
					2004	-53,126.13			-2,284,530.43		2,231,404.30
					2003	-14,155.16			-478,153.21		463,998.05
					2002	-11,803.98			-709,477.35	697,673.37	
Accounts Receivable						48,577,647.00				22,366,078.00	26,211,569.00
Fund Equities:											
Unobligated Balances (Expired)						-10,151,947.62				497,502.54	-10,649,450.16
Accounts Payable						-15,228,368.40				-2,631,283.77	-12,597,084.63
Undelivered Orders						-13,827,487.32				-3,082,278.84	-10,745,208.48
Subtotal	28		0400			-0-	25,902,000.00		8,054,308.70	17,847,691.30	-0-
Special Benefits For Certain World War II Veterans, Social Security Administration											
Fund Resources:											
Undisbursed Funds	28		0401		No Year	1,159,751.23	8,096,093.12		9,147,075.61		108,768.74
Fund Equities:											
Unobligated Balances (Unexpired)										108,768.74	108,768.74
Accounts Payable						-1,159,751.23				-1,159,751.23	-108,768.74
Subtotal	28		0401			-0-	8,096,093.12		9,147,075.61	-1,050,982.49	-0-
Payments To Social Security Trust Funds, Social Security Administration											
Fund Resources:											
Undisbursed Funds	28		0404		2007		1,318,084,234.62		1,303,904,640.11		14,179,594.51
					2006	12,068,928.04			4,941,521.52		7,127,406.52
					2005	7,867,708.25					7,867,708.25
					2004	6,453,564.14					6,453,564.14
					2003	9,972,435.25					9,972,435.25
					2002	9,320,350.92				9,320,350.92	
					No Year	14,258,164.58	18,017,190,472.45		18,017,721,974.45		13,726,662.58
Fund Equities:											
Unobligated Balances (Expired)						-42,782,986.60				124,040.91	-42,907,027.51
Unobligated Balances (Unexpired)						-14,162,437.00				-461,502.00	-13,700,935.00
Accounts Payable						-2,995,727.58				-276,318.84	-2,719,408.74
Subtotal	28		0404			-0-	19,335,274,707.07		19,326,568,136.08	8,706,570.99	-0-
Supplemental Security Income Program, Social Security Administration											
Fund Resources:											
Undisbursed Funds	28		0406		2006	-41,482.47			-41,482.47		1,355,754.96
					2004	6,729,310.02			5,373,555.06		4,444,040,807.90
					No Year	2,718,357,214.78	40,181,169,000.00		38,455,485,406.88	-15,046,650.85	6,210,113.04
Accounts Receivable						[5]-1,233,251,160.25				1,267,059,745.43	-2,500,310,905.68
Fund Equities:											
Unobligated Balances (Unexpired)						[5]-8,836,537.81					
Accounts Payable						-1,408,442,370.77				477,696,147.88	-1,886,138,518.65

Appropriations, Outlays, and Balances - Continued

Appropriation or Fund Account — Title	Dept Reg	Tr From	Account Number	Sub No.	Period of Availability	Balances, Beginning of Fiscal Year	Appropriations And Other Obligational Authority[1]	Transfers Borrowings And Investment (Net)[2]	Outlays (Net)	Balances Withdrawn And Other Transactions[3]	Balances, End Of Fiscal Year[4]
Undelivered Orders						-74,514,973.50				-9,357,721.93	-65,157,251.57
	28		0406		Subtotal	-0-	40,181,169,000.00		38,460,817,479.47	1,720,351,520.53	-0-
Payments For Credits Against Social Security Contributions, Social Security Administration											
Fund Resources:											
Undisbursed Funds	28		0440		No Year		160,574.14		160,574.14		
Special Fund Accounts											
State Supplemental Fees, Social Security Administration											
Fund Resources:											
Undisbursed Funds	28		5419		No Year	-0.02	119,000,000.00		119,000,000.00		[6]-0.02
Accounts Receivable	28		5419		No Year	0.02					0.02
	28		5419		Subtotal	-0-	119,000,000.00		119,000,000.00		-0-
Trust Fund Accounts											
Federal Old-Age And Survivors Insurance Trust Fund											
Fund Resources:											
Undisbursed Funds	20		8006		No Year	-64,930,011.40	[7]666,340,020,781.27	-659,389,506,394.87	[6]6,877,348,722.74		8,235,652.26
Transfer To:											
Department Of Health And Human Services	28	20	8006		No Year	-729,872,822.08		479,215,462,712.87	479,434,891,536.07		[6]-949,301,645.28
Investments In Public Debt Securities			8006			1,793,129,284,000.00		175,132,540,767.00			1,968,261,824,767.00
Accounts Receivable											
Fund Equities:											
Unobligated Balances (Unexpired)						[5]1,746,735,974,100.06				172,727,848,406.57	1,919,463,822,506.63
Accounts Payable						[5]45,598,494,398.46				2,258,431,252.89	-47,856,925,651.35
Undelivered Orders						-12,668.00				-2,052.00	-10,616.00
	20		8006		Subtotal	-0-	666,340,020,781.27	-5,041,502,915.00	486,312,240,258.81	174,986,277,607.46	-0-
Federal Disability Insurance Trust Fund											
Fund Resources:											
Undisbursed Funds	20		8007		No Year	-9,837,227.94	[9]106,446,618,680.16	-103,958,466,764.50	[10]2,476,427,329.28		1,887,358.44
Transfer To:											
Department Of Health And Human Services	28	20	8007		No Year	-338,372,587.59		97,348,446,446.50	97,373,423,310.78		[6]-363,349,451.87
Investments In Public Debt Securities			8007			202,178,015,000.00		11,651,523,233.00			213,829,538,233.00
Accounts Receivable											
Fund Equities:											
Unobligated Balances (Unexpired)						[5]5,177,564,163,096.69				10,985,734,107.36	-188,549,897,204.05
Accounts Payable						[5]24,227,297,537.12				629,650,421.60	-24,856,947,958.72
Undelivered Orders						-38,344,550.66				22,886,426.14	-61,230,976.80
	20		8007		Subtotal	-0-	106,446,618,680.16	5,041,502,915.00	99,849,850,640.06	11,638,270,955.10	-0-
Salaries And Expense, Social Security Administration											
Fund Resources:											
Undisbursed Funds	28		8704		2007				28,267,541.78		[6]-28,267,541.78
					2006	162,833,674.23			163,331,379.95		[6]-497,705.72
					2005	-10,275,966.62			-9,729,783.42		[6]-546,183.20
					2004	-383,710.74			6,981,008.83		[6]-7,364,719.57
					2003	-3,512,057.83			-625,589.03		[6]-2,886,468.80

Footnotes At End Of Chapter

Appropriations, Outlays, and Balances – Continued

Appropriation or Fund Account	Account Symbol					Balances, Beginning of Fiscal Year	Appropriations And Other Obligational Authority[1]	Transfers Borrowings And Investment (Net)[2]	Outlays (Net)	Balances Withdrawn And Other Transactions[3]	Balances, End Of Fiscal Year[4]
Title	Period of Availability	Reg	Tr From	Account Number	Sub No.						
Salaries And Expense, Social Security Administration - Continued											
Fund Resources: - Continued											
Undisbursed Funds - Continued											
	2002					-11,642,856.17			-11,642,856.17		
	No Year					-56,885,600.09					40,637,190.21
Accounts Receivable						2,029,744,434.61			-97,522,790.30	-221,732,322.06	2,251,476,756.67
Fund Equities:											
Unobligated Balances (Expired)						-318,650,470.05				52,132,144.89	-370,782,614.94
Unobligated Balances (Unexpired)						-168,483,455.32				39,159,458.64	-207,642,913.96
Accounts Payable						-376,850,861.41				46,941,870.73	-329,908,990.68
Undelivered Orders						-1,245,893,130.61				98,323,677.62	-1,344,216,808.23
	Subtotal	28		8704		-0-			79,058,911.64	-79,058,911.64	-0-
Deductions For Offsetting Receipts											
Proprietary Receipts From The Public							-3,078,205,151.91		-3,078,205,151.91		
Intrabudgetary Transactions							-19,325,369,548.11		-19,325,369,548.11		
Total, Social Security Administration							810,052,667,135.74		621,761,322,684.49	188,291,344,451.25	

Appropriations, Outlays, and Balances - Continued

Footnotes

1. The amounts in this column, unless otherwise footnoted, represent appropriations, increases and rescissions in borrowing authority or new contract authority. Only appropriations with appropriation transfer activity are presented in Table 1 (Appropriations and Appropriation Transfers). Since the Social Security Administration had no transfer activity during fiscal year 2007, Table 1 does not appear.

2. The amounts in this column, unless otherwise footnoted, represent transfers - other than appropriation transfers, borrowings (gross), investments (net), unrealized discounts or agent cashier funds.

3. The amounts in this column, unless otherwise footnoted, represent obligated balances canceled for fiscal year 2002 pursuant to 31 U.S.C. 1553, changes in unfilled customer orders, accounts receivable, accounts payable, undelivered orders, unobligated balances and adjustments to borrowing and contract authority.

4. Unobligated balances for no-year or unexpired multiple year accounts are available for obligation; unobligated balances for expired fiscal year accounts are not available for obligation.

5. The opening balances of the following accounts have been adjusted during the current fiscal year and do not agree with last year's closing balances.

Account	Adjustment
28 x 0406 -Unobligated Balances (Unexpired)	$1,989,088.00
28 x 0406 -Accounts Receivable	-$1,989,088.00
20 x 8006 -Unobligated Balances (Unexpired)	$37,790,154.20
20 x 8006 -Accounts Payable	-$37,790,154.20
20 x 8007 -Unobligated Balances (Unexpired)	-$7,837,909.94
20 x 8007 -Accounts Payable	$7,837,909.94

6. Subject to disposition by the administrative agency.

7. Excludes $1,897,400,000.00 refund of taxes.

8. Excludes $1,897,400,000.00 refund of taxes.

9. Excludes $322,200,000.00 refund of taxes.

10. Excludes $322,200,000.00 refund of taxes.

Appropriations, Outlays, and Balances – Continued

Appropriation or Fund Account — Title	Period of Availability	Dept Reg	Tr From	Account Number	Sub No.	Balances, Beginning Of Fiscal Year	Appropriations And Other Obligational Authority[1]	Transfers Borrowings And Investment (Net)[2]	Outlays (Net)	Balances Withdrawn And Other Transactions[3]	Balances, End Of Fiscal Year[4]
Independent Agencies											
Advisory Council On Historic Preservation											
General Fund Accounts											
Salaries And Expenses, Advisory Council On Historic Preservation											
Fund Resources:											
Undisbursed Funds	2007	95		2300			4,828,288.00		4,740,448.62		87,839.38
	2006					400,242.56			356,965.37		43,277.19
	2005					147,141.92			94,886.29		52,255.63
	2004					-21,675.14			3,481.01		[5]-25,156.15
	2003					-214,060.68			-584.13		[5]-213,476.55
	2002					94,925.60				94,925.60	
	1999					-60,393.97					[5]-60,393.97
Accounts Receivable						-32,231.70				-44,457.26	12,225.56
Unfilled Customer Orders						832,074.63				474,818.09	357,256.54
Fund Equities:											
Unobligated Balances (Expired)						-337,350.71				-528,938.84	[5]191,588.13
Accounts Payable						-268,547.23				228,152.00	-496,699.23
Undelivered Orders						-540,125.28				-591,408.75	51,283.47
Subtotal		95		2300		-0-	4,828,288.00		5,195,197.16	-366,909.16	-0-
Trust Fund Accounts											
Donations, Advisory Council On Historic Preservation											
Fund Resources:											
Undisbursed Funds	No Year	95		8298		1,112.30	273,820.03		179,224.26		95,708.07
Fund Equities:											
Unobligated Balances (Unexpired)						-1,112.30				94,595.77	-95,708.07
Subtotal		95		8298		-0-	273,820.03		179,224.26	94,595.77	-0-
Total, Advisory Council On Historic Preservation							5,102,108.03		5,374,421.42	-272,313.39	
Appalachian Regional Commission											
General Fund Accounts											
Appalachian Regional Development Programs, Appalachian Regional Commission											
Fund Resources:											
Undisbursed Funds	No Year	46		0200		58,648,336.49	64,848,559.00	-28,957,430.73	38,054,149.91		56,485,314.85
Transfer To:											
Natural Resources Conservation Service, Department Of Agriculture	No Year	12	46	0200	10	4,029.65		-4,929.23	-899.58		
Rural Utilities Service, Department Of Agriculture	No Year	12	46	0200	20	47,153,543.69		12,279,000.00	13,046,867.23		46,385,676.46
Economic Development Administration, Department Of Commerce	No Year	13	46	0200	20	8,800,400.86		3,316,806.00	3,060,512.85		9,056,694.01
Department Of Transportation, Federal Highway Administration	No Year	69	46	0200	5	22,219,056.10		-765,404.04	6,214,006.19		15,239,645.87
Health And Human Services, Health Resources And Services Administration	No Year	75	46	0200	3	1,058,824.97			-48,363.44		1,107,188.41
Housing And Urban Development	No Year	86	46	0200		19,983,308.20		14,131,958.00	9,929,770.96		24,185,495.24

Appropriations, Outlays, and Balances - Continued

Appropriation or Fund Account Title	Period of Availability	Account Symbol Dept Reg	Account Symbol Dept Tr From	Account Number	Sub No.	Balances, Beginning Of Fiscal Year	Appropriations And Other Obligational Authority[1]	Transfers Borrowings And Investment (Net)[2]	Outlays (Net)	Balances Withdrawn And Other Transactions[3]	Balances, End Of Fiscal Year[4]
Department Of Education	No Year	91	46	0200		420,686.03	---------	---------	210,084.45	---------	210,601.58
Corps Of Engineers	No Year	96	46	0200		3,960,000.00	---------	---------	2,116,294.78	---------	1,843,705.22
Fund Equities:											
Unobligated Balances (Unexpired)						-16,789,412.62				6,895,665.32	-23,685,077.94
Accounts Payable						-2,293,653.85				2,653,076.40	-4,946,730.25
Undelivered Orders						-139,205,119.52				-13,322,606.07	-125,882,513.45
Subtotal		46		0200		3,960,000.00	64,848,559.00		72,582,423.35	-3,773,864.35	-0-

Trust Fund Accounts

Appropriation or Fund Account Title	Period of Availability	Account Symbol Dept Reg	Account Symbol Dept Tr From	Account Number	Sub No.	Balances, Beginning Of Fiscal Year	Appropriations And Other Obligational Authority[1]	Transfers Borrowings And Investment (Net)[2]	Outlays (Net)	Balances Withdrawn And Other Transactions[3]	Balances, End Of Fiscal Year[4]
Administrative Expenses, Appalachian Regional Commission[6]											
Fund Resources:											
Undisbursed Funds	No Year	46		8090		1,305,055.02	7,316,411.80		6,976,214.14	---------	1,645,252.68
Fund Equities:											
Unobligated Balances (Unexpired)						-954,653.76				-954,653.76	---------
Accounts Payable						-233,992.75				-233,992.75	---------
Undelivered Orders						-116,408.51				-116,408.51	---------
Subtotal		46		8090		-0-	7,316,411.80		6,976,214.14	-1,305,055.02	1,645,252.68

Deductions For Offsetting Receipts

Appropriation or Fund Account Title	Period of Availability	Account Symbol Dept Reg	Account Symbol Dept Tr From	Account Number	Sub No.	Balances, Beginning Of Fiscal Year	Appropriations And Other Obligational Authority[1]	Transfers Borrowings And Investment (Net)[2]	Outlays (Net)	Balances Withdrawn And Other Transactions[3]	Balances, End Of Fiscal Year[4]
Proprietary Receipts From The Public							-3,840,999.51		-3,840,999.51		
Intrabudgetary Transactions							-3,477,550.00		-3,477,550.00		
Total, Appalachian Regional Commission						3,960,000.00	64,846,421.29		72,240,087.98	-5,078,919.37	1,645,252.68

Architectural And Transportation Barriers Compliance Board

General Fund Accounts

Appropriation or Fund Account Title	Period of Availability	Account Symbol Dept Reg	Account Symbol Dept Tr From	Account Number	Sub No.	Balances, Beginning Of Fiscal Year	Appropriations And Other Obligational Authority[1]	Transfers Borrowings And Investment (Net)[2]	Outlays (Net)	Balances Withdrawn And Other Transactions[3]	Balances, End Of Fiscal Year[4]
Salaries And Expenses, Architectural And Transportation Barriers Compliance Board											
Fund Resources:											
Undisbursed Funds	2007	95		3200			5,914,146.00		4,545,262.78		1,368,883.22
	2006					1,328,099.46			1,071,660.13		256,439.33
	2005					366,289.43			30,069.05		336,220.38
	2004					136,811.06			6,505.08		130,305.98
	2003					479,377.65			24,356.00		455,021.65
	2002					243,528.51				243,528.51	
Fund Equities:											
Unobligated Balances (Expired)						-902,272.52				2,152.52	-904,425.04
Accounts Payable						-252,358.31				88,735.89	-341,094.20
Undelivered Orders						-1,399,475.28				-98,123.96	-1,301,351.32
Subtotal		95		3200		-0-	5,914,146.00		5,677,853.04	236,292.96	-0-

Footnotes At End Of Chapter

Appropriations, Outlays, and Balances – Continued

Appropriation or Fund Account — Title	Dept Reg	Tr From	Account Number	Sub No.	Period of Availability	Balances, Beginning Of Fiscal Year	Appropriations And Other Obligational Authority[1]	Transfers Borrowings And Investment (Net)[2]	Outlays (Net)	Balances Withdrawn And Other Transactions[3]	Balances, End Of Fiscal Year[4]
Total, Architectural And Transportation Barriers Compliance Board						-------	5,914,146.00	-------	5,677,853.04	236,292.96	-------
Barry Goldwater Scholarship And Excellence In Education Foundation											
Trust Fund Accounts											
Trust Fund, The Barry Goldwater Scholarship And Excellence In Education Fund											
Fund Resources:											
Undisbursed Funds	95		8281		No Year	201,607.03	3,745,418.76	2,942,738.82	3,173,389.99		3,716,374.62
Unrealized Discount On Investments						-334,700.53		38,261.18			-296,439.35
Investments In Public Debt Securities						66,994,000.00		-2,981,000.00			64,013,000.00
Fund Equities:											
Unobligated Balances (Unexpired)						-66,830,106.35				569,495.83	-67,399,602.18
Accounts Payable						-12,388.11				-670.44	-11,717.67
Undelivered Orders						-18,412.04				3,203.38	-21,615.42
Subtotal	95		8281			-0-	3,745,418.76		3,173,389.99	572,028.77	-0-
Total, Barry Goldwater Scholarship And Excellence In Education Foundation						-------	3,745,418.76		3,173,389.99	572,028.77	-------
Broadcasting Board Of Governors											
General Fund Accounts											
Broadcasting Capital Improvements, Broadcasting Board Of Governors											
Fund Resources:											
Undisbursed Funds	95		0204		2005-2006	777,303.43			656,582.11		120,721.32
					No Year	58,831,520.52	7,624,000.00		12,425,919.89		54,029,600.63
Fund Equities:											
Unobligated Balances (Expired)						-2.86				37,771.36	-37,774.22
Unobligated Balances (Unexpired)						-33,085,154.73				-9,527,860.68	-23,557,294.05
Accounts Payable						-2,278,001.08				-1,293,446.40	-984,554.68
Undelivered Orders						-24,245,665.28				5,325,033.72	-29,570,699.00
Subtotal	95		0204			-0-	7,624,000.00		13,082,502.00	-5,458,502.00	-0-
International Broadcasting Operations, Broadcasting Board Of Governors											
Fund Resources:											
Undisbursed Funds	95		0206		2007-2008		10,602,000.00		2,000,000.00		8,602,000.00
					2007	639,126,108.00			558,782,196.66		80,343,911.34
					2006-2007	845,000.00		1,035,380.40	689,899.22		1,190,481.18
					2006	76,530,960.90			65,032,952.43		11,498,008.47
					2005-2006	1,536,857.40			1,324,013.64		212,843.76
					2005	9,947,945.95			2,600,292.19		7,347,653.76
					2004-2005	100,560.94			3,600.00		96,960.94
					2004	7,174,184.50			928,308.79		6,245,875.71
					2003-2004	417,963.71			3,459.53		414,504.18
					2003	7,168,823.14			539,359.87		6,629,463.27

Appropriations, Outlays, and Balances - Continued

Title	Period of Availability	Reg	Tr From	Account Number	Sub No.	Balances, Beginning Of Fiscal Year	Appropriations And Other Obligational Authority[1]	Transfers Borrowings And Investment (Net)[2]	Outlays (Net)	Balances Withdrawn And Other Transactions[3]	Balances, End Of Fiscal Year[4]
	2002-2003					569,180.79					569,180.79
	2002					4,735,465.21			3,264,287.79	1,471,177.42	------
	2001-2002					459,276.54			8,503.42	450,773.12	------
	2001							750,000.00		750,000.00	------
	No Year					12,923,972.92			5,135,918.06	-942,609.26	7,788,054.86
Accounts Receivable						3,064,357.51					4,006,966.77
Fund Equities:											
Unobligated Balances (Expired)						-5,296,906.97				10,557,240.25	-15,854,147.22
Unobligated Balances (Unexpired)						-13,292,154.76				1,518,813.34	-14,810,968.10
Accounts Payable						-3,926,845.38				-179,283.83	-3,747,561.55
Undelivered Orders						-102,958,642.40				-2,425,414.24	-100,533,228.16
	Subtotal	95		0206		-0-	649,728,108.00	1,785,380.40	640,312,791.60	11,200,696.80	-0-
Broadcasting To Cuba, Broadcasting Board Of Governors											
Fund Resources:											
Undisbursed Funds	No Year	95		0208		3,311,330.66			538,290.62		2,773,040.04
Fund Equities:											
Unobligated Balances (Unexpired)						-1,192,495.34				-1,151,815.05	-40,680.29
Accounts Payable						-1,299.60				-1,299.60	
Undelivered Orders						-2,117,535.72				614,824.03	-2,732,359.75
	Subtotal	95		0208		-0-			538,290.62	-538,290.62	-0-
Buying Power Maintenance, Broadcasting Board Of Governors											
Fund Resources:											
Undisbursed Funds	No Year	95		1147		1,250,000.00		-750,000.00		-750,000.00	500,000.00
Fund Equities:											
Unobligated Balances (Unexpired)						-1,250,000.00					-500,000.00
	Subtotal	95		1147		-0-		-750,000.00		-750,000.00	-0-
Trust Fund Accounts											
Foreign Service National Separation Liability Trust Fund, Broadcasting Board Of Governors											
Fund Resources:											
Undisbursed Funds	No Year	95		8285		3,213,274.16			-3,374,732.64		6,588,006.80
Fund Equities:											
Unobligated Balances (Unexpired)						-3,213,274.16				3,348,333.29	-6,561,607.45
Undelivered Orders										26,399.35	-26,399.35
	Subtotal	95		8285		-0-			-3,374,732.64	3,374,732.64	-0-
Miscellaneous Trust Fund, Broadcasting Board Of Governors											
Fund Resources:											
Undisbursed Funds	No Year	95		8286		302,028.11			627.02		301,401.09
Fund Equities:											
Unobligated Balances (Unexpired)						-227,869.02				-433.54	-227,435.48
Undelivered Orders						-74,159.09				-193.48	-73,965.61
	Subtotal	95		8286		-0-			627.02	-627.02	-0-
Deductions For Offsetting Receipts											
Proprietary Receipts From The Public							-89,559.59		-89,559.59		

Footnotes At End Of Chapter

Appropriations, Outlays, and Balances – Continued

Appropriation or Fund Account	Account Symbol					Balances, Beginning Of Fiscal Year	Appropriations And Other Obligational Authority[1]	Transfers Borrowings And Investment (Net)[2]	Outlays (Net)	Balances Withdrawn And Other Transactions[3]	Balances, End Of Fiscal Year[4]
Title	Period of Availability	Dept Reg	Tr From	Account Number	Sub No.						
Total, Broadcasting Board Of Governors							657,262,548.41	1,035,380.40	650,469,919.01	7,828,009.80	
Central Intelligence Agency											
General Fund Accounts											
Payment To The Central Intelligence Agency Retirement And Disability System Fund, Central Intelligence Agency											
Fund Resources:											
Undisbursed Funds	2007	56		3400			256,400,000.00		256,400,000.00		
Total, Central Intelligence Agency							256,400,000.00		256,400,000.00		
Chemical Safety And Hazard Investigation Board											
General Fund Accounts											
Salaries And Expenses, Chemical Safety And Hazard Investigation Board											
Fund Resources:											
Undisbursed Funds											
	2007	95		3850			9,113,053.00		7,383,958.84		1,729,094.16
	2006					1,702,853.80			1,207,670.18		495,183.62
	2005					407,394.25			187,448.93		219,945.32
	2004					136,636.46			17,438.33		119,198.13
	2003-2004					50,548.53					50,548.53
	2003					47,024.86					47,024.86
	2002-2003					137,183.35					137,183.35
	2002					99,369.31			7,265.25	92,104.06	
	2001-2002					576,415.32				576,415.32	
Fund Equities:											
Unobligated Balances (Expired)						-1,042,841.70				-97,248.18	-945,593.52
Accounts Payable						-528,470.25				56,004.37	-584,474.62
Undelivered Orders						-1,586,113.93				-318,004.10	-1,268,109.83
Subtotal		95		3850		-0-	9,113,053.00		8,803,781.53	309,271.47	-0-
Emergency Fund, Chemical Safety And Hazard Investigation Board											
Fund Resources:											
Undisbursed Funds	No Year	95		3851		844,145.00					844,145.00
Fund Equities:											
Unobligated Balances (Unexpired)						-844,145.00					-844,145.00
Subtotal		95		3851		-0-					-0-
Deductions For Offsetting Receipts											
Proprietary Receipts From The Public							-1,204.20		-1,204.20		
Total, Chemical Safety And Hazard Investigation Board							9,111,848.80		8,802,577.33	309,271.47	

Appropriations, Outlays, and Balances - Continued

Appropriation or Fund Account — Title	Period of Availability	Reg	Tr From	Account Number	Sub No.	Balances, Beginning Of Fiscal Year	Appropriations And Other Obligational Authority[1]	Transfers Borrowings And Investment (Net)[2]	Outlays (Net)	Balances Withdrawn And Other Transactions[3]	Balances, End Of Fiscal Year[4]
Christopher Columbus Fellowship Foundation											
Trust Fund Accounts											
Christopher Columbus Scholarship Fund, Christopher Columbus Fellowship Foundation											
Fund Resources:											
Undisbursed Funds	No Year	76		8187		57,457.87		1,244,680.41	736,788.26		631,204.00
Unrealized Discount On Investments						-5,710.54		6,319.59			609.05
Investments In Public Debt Securities						1,251,000.00		-1,251,000.00			
Fund Equities:											
Unobligated Balances (Unexpired)						-1,280,031.04				-662,594.42	-617,436.62
Accounts Payable						-22,716.29				-8,339.86	-14,376.43
						-0-				-670,934.28	-0-
	Subtotal	76		8187		-0-	65,853.98		736,788.26	-670,934.28	
Total, Christopher Columbus Fellowship Foundation							65,853.98		736,788.26	-670,934.28	
Commission Of Fine Arts											
General Fund Accounts											
Salaries And Expenses, Commission Of Fine Arts											
Fund Resources:											
Undisbursed Funds	2007	95		2600		421,516.53	1,872,549.00		1,631,378.08		241,170.92
	2006					144,104.79			270,216.25		151,300.28
	2005					140,265.61			25,444.94		118,659.85
	2004					23,617.64			10,745.17		129,520.44
	2003					41,138.30			1,093.23		22,524.41
	2002									41,138.30	
	No Year					1,912.78					1,912.78
Fund Equities:											
Unobligated Balances (Expired)						-305,559.90				105,709.29	-411,269.19
Unobligated Balances (Unexpired)						-1,912.78					-1,912.78
Accounts Payable						-85,955.43				-6,885.04	-79,070.39
Undelivered Orders						-379,127.54				-206,291.22	-172,836.32
						-0-				-66,328.67	-0-
	Subtotal	95		2600		-0-	1,872,549.00		1,938,877.67	-66,328.67	
National Capital Arts And Cultural Affairs, Commission Of Fine Arts											
Fund Resources:											
Undisbursed Funds	2007	95		2602			7,143,335.00		7,143,335.01		[5]-0.01
	2005					0.35					0.35
Fund Equities:											
Unobligated Balances (Expired)						-0.35				-0.01	[5]-0.34
						-0-				-0.01	-0-
	Subtotal	95		2602		-0-	7,143,335.00		7,143,335.01	-0.01	
Total, Commission Of Fine Arts						-0-	9,015,884.00		9,082,212.68	-66,328.68	

Footnotes At End Of Chapter

Appropriations, Outlays, and Balances – Continued

Appropriation or Fund Account — Title	Dept Reg	Tr From	Account Number	Sub No.	Period of Availability	Balances, Beginning Of Fiscal Year	Appropriations And Other Obligational Authority[1]	Transfers Borrowings And Investment (Net)[2]	Outlays (Net)	Balances Withdrawn And Other Transactions[3]	Balances, End Of Fiscal Year[4]
Commission On Civil Rights											
General Fund Accounts											
Salaries And Expenses, Commission On Civil Rights											
Fund Resources:											
Undisbursed Funds	95		1900		2007		8,971,527.00		7,459,219.49		1,512,307.51
					2006	1,815,923.65			907,733.46		908,190.19
					2005	273,980.75			-3,511.54		277,492.29
					2004	60,511.45			-80.00		60,591.45
					2003	25,703.42					25,703.42
					2002	5,665.54				5,665.54	-0-
Fund Equities:											
Unobligated Balances (Expired)						-775,313.52				-3,365.85	-771,947.67
Accounts Payable						-833,924.42				324,315.96	-1,158,240.38
Undelivered Orders						-572,546.87				281,549.94	-854,096.81
	95		1900		Subtotal	-0-	8,971,527.00		8,363,361.41	608,165.59	-0-
Total, Commission On Civil Rights							8,971,527.00		8,363,361.41	608,165.59	
Commission On Ocean Policy											
General Fund Accounts											
Salaries And Expenses, Commission On Ocean Policy											
Fund Resources:											
Undisbursed Funds	48		2955		No Year	748,834.08					748,834.08
Fund Equities:											
Unobligated Balances (Unexpired)						-748,834.08					-748,834.08
	48		2955		Subtotal	-0-					-0-
Total, Commission On Ocean Policy											
Committee For Purchase From People Who Are Blind Or Severely Disabled											
General Fund Accounts											
Salaries And Expenses, Committee For Purchase From People Who Are Blind Or Severely Disabled											
Fund Resources:											
Undisbursed Funds	95		2000		2007		4,651,887.00		4,120,138.49		531,748.51
					2006	660,077.55			540,303.69		119,773.86
					2005	196,711.24			178,791.06		17,920.18
					2004	163,831.50			-118,638.99		282,470.49
					2003	111,957.75					111,957.75
					2002	80,944.13				80,944.13	

Appropriations, Outlays, and Balances - Continued

Appropriation or Fund Account Title	Period of Availability	Reg	Tr From	Account Number	Sub No.	Balances, Beginning Of Fiscal Year	Appropriations And Other Obligational Authority[1]	Transfers Borrowings And Investment (Net)[2]	Outlays (Net)	Balances Withdrawn And Other Transactions[3]	Balances, End Of Fiscal Year[4]
Fund Equities:											
Unobligated Balances (Expired)						-274,024.84			-----	-35,732.22	-238,292.62
Accounts Payable						-200,463.83			-----	-40,611.61	-159,852.22
Undelivered Orders						-739,033.50	4,651,887.00		4,720,594.25	-73,307.55	-665,725.95
	Subtotal			2000		-0-				-68,707.25	-0-
Total, Committee For Purchase From People Who Are Blind Or Severely Disabled						-----	4,651,887.00		4,720,594.25	-68,707.25	-----
Commodity Futures Trading Commission											
General Fund Accounts											
Expenses, Commodity Futures Trading Commission											
Fund Resources:											
Undisbursed Funds	2007	95		1400		-----	97,981,140.00		86,769,266.53	-----	11,211,873.47
	2006					9,833,073.85			9,075,274.52	-----	757,799.33
	2005					1,221,641.96			298,415.71	-----	923,226.25
	2004					1,285,706.54			-----	-----	1,285,706.54
	2003					1,209,930.71			1,511.30	-----	1,208,419.41
	2002					934,946.21			1,340.00	933,606.21	
	No Year					5,522,720.16			1,449,393.76	-----	4,073,326.40
Accounts Receivable										-73,467.00	73,467.00
Unfilled Customer Orders										-950.00	950.00
Fund Equities:											
Unobligated Balances (Expired)						[7]-4,539,392.31				-633,935.81	-3,905,456.50
Unobligated Balances (Unexpired)						[7]-7,194,772.51				3,208,851.46	-3,403,623.97
Accounts Payable						[7]-6,674,367.03				-1,360,341.43	-5,314,025.60
Undelivered Orders						[7]-8,599,487.58				-1,687,825.25	-6,911,662.33
	Subtotal	95		1400		-0-	97,981,140.00		97,595,201.82	385,938.18	-0-
Deductions For Offsetting Receipts											
Proprietary Receipts From The Public		95		1400		-----	-12,377.56		-12,377.56	-----	-----
Total, Commodity Futures Trading Commission							97,968,762.44		97,582,824.26	385,938.18	
Consumer Product Safety Commission											
General Fund Accounts											
Salaries And Expenses, Consumer Product Safety Commission											
Fund Resources:											
Undisbursed Funds	2007	61		0100		-----	62,727,790.00		52,469,508.27	-----	10,258,281.73
	2006					8,214,921.73			6,699,276.74	-----	1,515,644.99
	2005					881,643.69			199,726.38	-----	681,917.31
	2004					590,174.59			27,342.68	-----	562,831.91
	2003					382,855.61			963.56	-----	381,892.05
	2002					519,557.55			-99,361.20	618,918.75	

Footnotes At End Of Chapter

631

Appropriations, Outlays, and Balances – Continued

Appropriation or Fund Account — Title	Period of Availability	Dept Reg	Tr From	Account Number	Sub No.	Balances, Beginning Of Fiscal Year	Appropriations And Other Obligational Authority[1]	Transfers Borrowings And Investment (Net)[2]	Outlays (Net)	Balances Withdrawn And Other Transactions[3]	Balances, End Of Fiscal Year[4]
Salaries And Expenses, Consumer Product Safety Commission - Continued											
Fund Equities:											
Unobligated Balances (Expired)						-992,553.58				-86,555.09	-905,998.49
Accounts Payable						-1,985,622.71				29,055.91	-2,014,678.62
Undelivered Orders						-7,610,976.88				2,868,914.00	-10,479,890.88
Subtotal	Subtotal	61		0100		-0-	62,727,790.00		59,297,456.43	3,430,333.57	-0-
Trust Fund Accounts											
Gifts And Donations, Consumer Product Safety Commission											
Fund Resources:											
Undisbursed Funds	No Year	61		8079		56,278.69					84,492.76
Fund Equities:											
Unobligated Balances (Unexpired)						-49,278.69			-28,214.07	35,214.07	-84,492.76
Undelivered Orders						-7,000.00				-7,000.00	
Subtotal	Subtotal	61		8079		-0-			-28,214.07	28,214.07	-0-
Deductions For Offsetting Receipts											
Proprietary Receipts From The Public							-20,318.46		-20,318.46		
Total, Consumer Product Safety Commission							62,707,471.54		59,248,923.90	3,458,547.64	
Corporation For National And Community Service											
General Fund Accounts											
Domestic Volunteer Service Programs, Operating Expenses, Corporation For National And Community Service											
Fund Resources:											
Undisbursed Funds	2007	95		0103		182,882,494.49	312,303,847.00		129,022,741.67		183,281,105.33
	2006					23,594,134.63			165,766,814.84		17,115,679.65
	2005					7,029,502.34			11,906,851.16		11,687,283.47
	2004					7,096,567.64			678,913.20		6,350,589.14
	2003					7,936,533.75			455,340.96		6,641,226.68
	2002								-16,781.72	7,953,315.47	
Accounts Receivable						814,995.97				538,108.83	276,887.14
Unfilled Customer Orders						1,574,243.13				1,367,222.96	207,020.17
Fund Equities:											
Unobligated Balances (Expired)						-23,697,000.29				-4,188,991.27	-19,508,009.02
Accounts Payable						-21,493,833.24				5,433,888.47	-26,927,721.71
Undelivered Orders						-185,737,638.42				-6,613,577.57	-179,124,060.85
Subtotal	Subtotal	95		0103		-0-	312,303,847.00		307,813,880.11	4,489,966.89	-0-
National And Community Service Programs Operating Expenses, Corporation For National And Community Service											
Fund Resources:											
Undisbursed Funds	2007-2008	95		2720		342,350,098.11	492,706,415.00		152,046,219.79		340,660,195.21
	2006-2007					209,151,313.23			171,033,368.09		171,316,730.02
	2005-2006								144,900,147.87		64,251,165.36

Appropriations, Outlays, and Balances - Continued

Appropriation or Fund Account — Title	Dept Reg	Dept Tr From	Account Number	Sub No.	Period of Availability	Balances, Beginning Of Fiscal Year	Appropriations And Other Obligational Authority[1]	Transfers Borrowings And Investment (Net)[2]	Outlays (Net)	Balances Withdrawn And Other Transactions[3]	Balances, End Of Fiscal Year[4]
					2004-2005	48,315,756.55			27,035,123.40		21,280,633.15
					2003-2004	19,799,958.63			3,119,507.10		16,680,451.53
					2002-2003	22,440,046.33			400,810.23	22,954,190.45	22,039,236.10
					2001-2002	23,216,683.24			262,492.79	-563,273.00	-0-
Accounts Receivable						6,026.40					569,299.40
Unfilled Customer Orders						1,059,890.45				399,722.79	660,167.66
Fund Equities:											
Unobligated Balances (Expired)						-48,538,914.89				8,523,293.68	-57,062,208.57
Unobligated Balances (Unexpired)						-36,178,251.36				2,951,110.28	-39,129,361.64
Accounts Payable						-73,025,496.41				5,804,029.90	-78,829,526.31
Undelivered Orders						-508,597,110.28			498,797,669.27	-46,160,328.37	-462,436,781.91
Subtotal	95		2720			-0-	492,706,415.00		498,797,669.27	-6,091,254.27	-0-
Office Of Inspector General, Corporation For National And Community Service											
Fund Resources:											
Undisbursed Funds					2007-2008	2,582,268.98	4,962,686.00		3,337,815.28		1,624,870.72
					2006-2007	853,845.70			1,686,404.77		895,864.21
					2005-2006	222,918.89			719,757.80		134,087.90
					2004-2005	685,030.36					222,918.89
					2003-2004	19,131.18					685,030.36
					2002-2003						19,131.18
Fund Equities:											
Unobligated Balances (Expired)						-1,054,461.31				-22,688.32	-1,031,772.99
Unobligated Balances (Unexpired)						-1,522,672.12				-1,222,221.64	-300,450.48
Accounts Payable						-460,384.59				-7,061.02	-453,323.57
Undelivered Orders						-1,325,677.09			5,743,977.85	470,679.13	-1,796,356.22
Subtotal	95		2721			-0-	4,962,686.00		5,743,977.85	-781,291.85	-0-
Salaries And Expenses, Corporation For National And Community Service											
Fund Resources:											
Undisbursed Funds					2007	13,039,475.94	70,323,956.00		58,389,577.76		11,934,378.24
					2006	657,718.85			11,175,582.28		1,863,893.66
					2005	455,466.78			316,575.18		341,143.67
					2004				3,480.74		451,986.04
Fund Equities:											
Unobligated Balances (Expired)						-1,064,984.98				325,560.55	-1,390,545.53
Accounts Payable						-3,446,413.01				334,531.59	-3,780,944.60
Undelivered Orders						-9,641,263.58			69,885,215.96	-221,352.10	-9,419,911.48
Subtotal	95		2722			-0-	70,323,956.00		69,885,215.96	438,740.04	-0-
Vista Advance Payment Revolving Fund, Corporation For National And Community Service											
Fund Resources:											
Undisbursed Funds					No Year		4,250,000.00		834,086.01		3,415,913.99
Fund Equities:											
Unobligated Balances (Unexpired)										3,162,859.50	-3,162,859.50
Accounts Payable										253,054.49	-253,054.49
Subtotal	95		2723			-0-	4,250,000.00		834,086.01	3,415,913.99	-0-

Footnotes At End Of Chapter

Appropriations, Outlays, and Balances – Continued

Appropriation or Fund Account — Title	Period of Availability	Dept Reg	Dept Tr From	Account Number	Sub No.	Balances, Beginning Of Fiscal Year	Appropriations And Other Obligational Authority[1]	Transfers Borrowings And Investment (Net)[2]	Outlays (Net)	Balances Withdrawn And Other Transactions[3]	Balances, End Of Fiscal Year[4]
Trust Fund Accounts											
National Service Trust, Corporation For National And Community Service											
Fund Resources:											
Undisbursed Funds	No Year	95		8267		13,590,271.16	136,998,660.05	-16,928,667.48	133,512,548.27		147,715.46
Unrealized Discount On Investments						-4,963,042.98		-1,906,332.52			-6,869,375.50
Investments In Public Debt Securities						445,804,000.00		18,835,000.00			464,639,000.00
Accounts Receivable						-0.38				-0.32	-0.06
Fund Equities:											
Unobligated Balances (Unexpired)						-73,606,596.00				-18,163,688.62	-55,442,907.38
Accounts Payable						-266,943,380.59				13,653,512.41	-280,596,893.00
Undelivered Orders						-113,881,251.21				7,996,288.31	-121,877,539.52
Subtotal		95		8267		-0-	136,998,660.05		133,512,548.27	3,486,111.78	-0-
Gifts And Contributions, Corporation For National And Community Service											
Fund Resources:											
Undisbursed Funds	No Year	95		8981		745,145.25			210,926.34		534,218.91
Fund Equities:											
Unobligated Balances (Unexpired)						-219,541.36				89,735.07	-309,276.43
Accounts Payable						-72,160.35				-64,092.52	-8,067.83
Undelivered Orders						-453,443.54				-236,568.89	-216,874.65
Subtotal		95		8981		-0-			210,926.34	-210,926.34	-0-
Deductions For Offsetting Receipts											
Proprietary Receipts From The Public							-1,294,463.30		-1,294,463.30		
Intrabudgetary Transactions							-117,720,000.00		-117,720,000.00		
Total, Corporation For National And Community Service							902,531,100.75		897,783,840.51	4,747,260.24	
Corporation For Public Broadcasting											
General Fund Accounts											
Public Broadcasting Fund, Corporation For Public Broadcasting											
Fund Resources:											
Undisbursed Funds	2007	20		0151			464,350,000.00		464,350,000.00		
Total, Corporation For Public Broadcasting							464,350,000.00		464,350,000.00		
Court Services And Offender Supervision Agency For The District Of Columbia											
General Fund Accounts											
Expenses, Public Defender Service, District Of Columbia											
Fund Resources:											
Undisbursed Funds	2007	95		1733		2,672,732.99	31,103,000.00		28,673,472.83		2,429,527.17
	2006								2,035,023.56		637,709.43
	2005					802,818.78			295,877.57		506,941.21

Appropriations, Outlays, and Balances - Continued

Title	Period of Availability	Reg	Tr From	Account Number	Sub No.	Balances, Beginning Of Fiscal Year	Appropriations And Other Obligational Authority[1]	Transfers Borrowings And Investment (Net)[2]	Outlays (Net)	Balances Withdrawn And Other Transactions[3]	Balances, End Of Fiscal Year[4]
	2004					779,185.00			25,893.71		753,291.29
	2003					721,289.39			-58.88		721,348.27
	2002					558,966.17			532.00	558,434.17	
Accounts Receivable						36,961.14				36,961.14	
Fund Equities:											
Unobligated Balances (Expired)						-1,699,650.92				496,300.36	-2,195,951.28
Accounts Payable						-1,582,459.01				-11,598.93	-1,570,860.08
Undelivered Orders						-928,058.59				353,947.42	-1,282,006.01
Subtotal		95		1733		1,361,784.95	31,103,000.00		31,030,740.79	1,434,044.16	-0-
Salaries And Expenses, Federal Payment To The Court Services And Offender Supervision Agency For The District Of Columbia											
Fund Resources:											
Undisbursed Funds	2007	95		1734		36,522,064.28	179,603,000.00		140,544,147.23		39,058,852.77
	2006					5,740,854.40			26,654,552.25		9,867,512.03
	2005					4,648,622.65			1,169,769.32		4,571,085.08
	2004					5,128,477.55			-192,236.62		4,840,859.27
	2003					6,469,640.96			117,554.03		5,010,923.52
	2002					962,379.51			210,504.85		311,500.75
	No Year								650,878.76	6,259,136.11	3,350.94
Accounts Receivable						1,144,358.08				1,141,007.14	
Unfilled Customer Orders						329,256.27				-2,447,009.79	2,776,266.06
Fund Equities:											
Unobligated Balances (Expired)						-16,496,198.87				2,216,626.71	-18,712,825.58
Unobligated Balances (Unexpired)						-268,366.57			7,795.61		-276,162.18
Accounts Payable						-12,691,816.47				2,292,724.36	-14,984,540.83
Undelivered Orders						-31,489,271.79				977,550.04	-32,466,821.83
Subtotal		95		1734		-0-	179,603,000.00		169,155,169.82	10,447,830.18	-0-
Total, Court Services And Offender Supervision Agency For The District Of Columbia						1,361,784.95	210,706,000.00		200,185,910.61	11,881,874.34	
Defense Nuclear Facilities Safety Board											
Intragovernmental Funds											
Salaries And Expenses, Defense Nuclear Facilities Safety Board											
Fund Resources:											
Undisbursed Funds	No Year	95		3900		8,479,576.88	21,914,054.00		21,244,231.08		9,149,399.80
Fund Equities:											
Unobligated Balances (Unexpired)						-3,443,742.78				507,148.70	-3,950,891.48
Accounts Payable						-1,262,670.47				148,799.88	-1,411,470.35
Undelivered Orders						-3,773,163.63				13,874.34	-3,787,037.97
Subtotal		95		3900		-0-	21,914,054.00		21,244,231.08	669,822.92	-0-
Total, Defense Nuclear Facilities Safety Board							21,914,054.00		21,244,231.08	669,822.92	

Footnotes At End Of Chapter

Appropriations, Outlays, and Balances – Continued

Appropriation or Fund Account	Account Symbol					Balances, Beginning Of Fiscal Year	Appropriations And Other Obligational Authority[1]	Transfers Borrowings And Investment (Net)[2]	Outlays (Net)	Balances Withdrawn And Other Transactions[3]	Balances, End Of Fiscal Year[4]
Title	Period of Availability	Dept Reg	Tr From	Account Number	Sub No.						
Delta Regional Authority											
General Fund Accounts											
Salaries And Expenses, Delta Regional Authority											
Fund Resources:											
Undisbursed Funds	No Year	95		0750		19,885,598.92	11,887,821.00	-745,922.00	7,036,593.41	-------	23,990,904.51
Transfer To:											
Department Of Agriculture	No Year	12	95	0750		1,275,458.92		745,922.00	514,161.50	-------	1,507,219.42
Economic Development Administration	No Year	13	95	0750	20	326,000.00		-------	43,960.00	-------	282,040.00
Fund Equities:											
Unobligated Balances (Unexpired)						-15,786,517.80				-1,474,065.92	-14,312,451.88
Accounts Payable						-236,198.32				160,463.13	-396,661.45
Undelivered Orders						-5,464,341.72				5,606,708.88	-11,071,050.60
Subtotal		95		0750		-0-	11,887,821.00		7,594,714.91	4,293,106.09	-0-
Total, Delta Regional Authority							11,887,821.00		7,594,714.91	4,293,106.09	
Denali Commission											
General Fund Accounts											
Expenses, Denali Commission											
Fund Resources:											
Undisbursed Funds	2007	95		1200		1,177,979.01	50,251,946.00	-------	41,941,643.93	-------	41,941,643.93
	2005-2007					-2.00		-------	332,602.16	-------	845,376.85
	2006					43,425,518.24		-------	17,743,000.24	-------	25,682,518.00
	2005					29,991,690.96		-------	14,680,778.68	-------	15,310,912.28
	No Year					137,957,676.73		-------	42,092,067.05	-------	146,117,555.68
Fund Equities:											
Unobligated Balances (Expired)						-12,951,022.89				6,875,000.00	-6,875,002.00
Unobligated Balances (Unexpired)						-11,604,887.42				16,334,838.63	-29,285,861.52
Accounts Payable										-4,684,895.75	-6,919,991.67
Undelivered Orders						-187,996,952.63				-1,179,801.08	-186,817,151.55
Subtotal		95		1200		-0-	50,251,946.00		32,906,804.20	17,345,141.80	-0-
Trust Fund Accounts											
Denali Commission Trust Fund											
Fund Resources:											
Undisbursed Funds	No Year	95		8056		2,491,313.17	4,201,397.72	-------	2,487,299.42	-------	4,205,411.47
Fund Equities:											
Unobligated Balances (Unexpired)						-2,368,936.83				217,256.30	-217,256.30
Accounts Payable						-122,376.34				-2,368,936.83	-3,988,155.17
Undelivered Orders										3,865,778.83	
Subtotal		95		8056		-0-	4,201,397.72		2,487,299.42	1,714,098.30	-0-

Appropriations, Outlays, and Balances - Continued

Appropriation or Fund Account — Title	Dept Reg	Tr From	Account Number	Sub No.	Period of Availability	Balances, Beginning Of Fiscal Year	Appropriations And Other Obligational Authority[1]	Transfers Borrowings And Investment (Net)[2]	Outlays (Net)	Balances Withdrawn And Other Transactions[3]	Balances, End Of Fiscal Year[4]
Deductions For Offsetting Receipts											
Proprietary Receipts From The Public							-5,755.90		-5,755.90		
Total, Denali Commission							54,447,587.82		35,388,347.72	19,059,240.10	
District Of Columbia											
District Of Columbia Courts											
General Fund Accounts											
Federal Payment To The District Of Columbia Judicial Survivors And Annuity Fund											
Fund Resources:											
Undisbursed Funds	20		1713		No Year		7,380,000.00		7,380,000.00		
Salaries And Expenses, Federal Payment To The District Of Columbia Courts	95		1712								
Fund Resources:											
Undisbursed Funds											
					2007-2008		79,921,710.00		2,935,336.69		76,986,373.31
					2007		136,801,170.00		122,866,826.52		13,934,343.48
					2006-2007	76,719,023.60			17,945,920.13		58,773,103.47
					2006	14,170,190.62			9,863,309.23		4,306,881.39
					2005-2006	36,323,089.84			29,080,456.99		7,242,632.85
					2005	4,040,756.86			-240,252.30		4,281,009.16
					2004-2005	5,471,412.81			3,670,166.84		1,801,245.97
					2004	5,625,275.55			-415,093.62		6,040,369.17
					2003-2004	4,272,948.89			2,970,169.84		1,302,779.05
					2003	11,909,964.74			1,207,831.43		10,702,133.31
					2002-2003	1,865,117.14			478,758.85		1,386,358.29
					2002	5,910,867.76			127,954.32	5,782,913.44	
					2001-2002	151,977.02			2,103.12	149,873.90	
Accounts Receivable						1,764,021.46				185,642.46	1,578,379.00
Fund Equities:											
Unobligated Balances (Expired)						-23,340,765.10				-469,087.59	-22,871,677.51
Unobligated Balances (Unexpired)						-29,638,453.77				12,903,012.46	-42,541,466.23
Accounts Payable						-5,240,384.41				576,862.98	-5,817,247.39
Undelivered Orders						-110,005,043.01	-0-			7,100,174.31	-117,105,217.32
Subtotal	95		1712				216,722,880.00		190,493,488.04	26,229,391.96	-0-
Payments, Defender Services In District Of Columbia Courts											
Fund Resources:											
Undisbursed Funds	95		1736		No Year	12,378,973.38	43,475,000.00		37,754,494.91		18,099,478.47
Fund Equities:											
Unobligated Balances (Unexpired)						-11,885,920.54				5,898,146.26	-17,784,066.80
Accounts Payable						-258,482.47				56,929.20	-315,411.67
Undelivered Orders						-234,570.37				-234,570.37	-0-
Subtotal	95		1736				43,475,000.00		37,754,494.91	5,720,505.09	-0-

Footnotes At End Of Chapter

Appropriations, Outlays, and Balances – Continued

638

Appropriation or Fund Account: Title	Dept Reg	Tr From	Account Number	Sub No.	Period of Availability	Balances, Beginning Of Fiscal Year	Appropriations And Other Obligational Authority[1]	Transfers Borrowings And Investment (Net)[2]	Outlays (Net)	Balances Withdrawn And Other Transactions[3]	Balances, End Of Fiscal Year[4]
Federal Payment For Family Court Act, District Of Columbia											
Fund Resources:											
Undisbursed Funds	95		1760		2002	385,776.76			385,775.79	0.97	
Fund Equities:											
Unobligated Balances (Expired)						-347,061.97				-347,061.97	
Undelivered Orders						-38,714.79				-38,714.79	
Subtotal	95		1760			-0-			385,775.79	-385,775.79	-0-
Trust Fund Accounts											
District Of Columbia Judicial Retirement And Survivor's Annuity Fund											
Fund Resources:											
Undisbursed Funds	20		8212		No Year	15,000.00	14,267,315.91	-6,475,098.12	7,792,217.78		15,000.01
Unrealized Discount On Investments						-2,393,063.73		-80,534.06			-2,473,597.79
Investments In Public Debt Securities						111,729,369.26		6,555,632.18			118,285,001.44
Fund Equities:											
Unobligated Balances (Unexpired)						-107,880,356.31				6,457,920.67	-114,338,276.98
Accounts Payable						-704,569.00				-881.04	-703,687.96
Undelivered Orders						-766,380.22				18,058.50	-784,438.72
Subtotal	20		8212			-0-	14,267,315.91		7,792,217.78	6,475,098.13	-0-
Deductions For Offsetting Receipts											
Proprietary Receipts From The Public							113.37		113.37		
Intrabudgetary Transactions							-7,380,000.00		-7,380,000.00		
Total, District Of Columbia Courts							274,465,309.28		236,426,089.89	38,039,219.39	
District Of Columbia Corrections											
General Fund Accounts											
Salaries And Expenses, Federal Payment To The District Of Columbia Corrections Trustee Operations											
Fund Resources:											
Undisbursed Funds	95		1735		2002-2003	98,626.64					98,626.64
					2002	132,897.45				132,897.45	
Fund Equities:											
Unobligated Balances (Expired)						-231,472.09				-132,845.45	-98,626.64
Accounts Payable						-52.00				-52.00	
Subtotal	95		1735			-0-					-0-
Total, District Of Columbia Corrections											

Appropriations, Outlays, and Balances - Continued

Appropriation or Fund Account — Title	Period of Availability	Dept Reg	Dept Tr From	Account Number	Sub No.	Balances, Beginning Of Fiscal Year	Appropriations And Other Obligational Authority[1]	Transfers Borrowings And Investment (Net)[2]	Outlays (Net)	Balances Withdrawn And Other Transactions[3]	Balances, End Of Fiscal Year[4]
District Of Columbia General And Special Payments											
General Fund Accounts											
Federal Payment To The Federal District Of Columbia Pension Fund											
Fund Resources:											
Undisbursed Funds	No Year	20		1714			345,400,000.00		345,400,000.00		
Federal Payment For Resident Tuition Support											
Fund Resources:											
Undisbursed Funds	No Year	20		1736			32,868,000.00		32,868,000.00		
Federal Payment To The Office Of The Chief Financial Officer Of The District Of Columbia											
Fund Resources:											
Undisbursed Funds	2007	20		1749			20,000,000.00		20,000,000.00		2,023.00
	2005					2,023.00					-2,023.00
Fund Equities:											
Unobligated Balances (Expired)						-2,023.00					-0-
	Subtotal	20		1749		-0-	20,000,000.00		20,000,000.00		
Federal Payment To The Youth Life Foundation											
Fund Resources:											
Undisbursed Funds	2002	20		1766		250,000.00				250,000.00	
Fund Equities:											
Unobligated Balances (Expired)						-250,000.00				-250,000.00	
	Subtotal	20		1766		-0-					-0-
Federal Payment For Emergency Planning And Security Costs In The District Of Columbia											
Fund Resources:											
Undisbursed Funds	No Year	20		1771		12,827,268.55	8,533,000.00		5,519,089.00		15,841,179.55
Fund Equities:											
Unobligated Balances (Unexpired)						-12,827,268.55				3,013,911.00	-15,841,179.55
	Subtotal	20		1771		-0-	8,533,000.00		5,519,089.00	3,013,911.00	-0-
Federal Payment To The District Of Columbia Water And Sewer Authority											
Fund Resources:											
Undisbursed Funds	No Year	20		1796			6,930,000.00		6,930,000.00		
Federal Payment For The Anacostia Waterfront Initiative											
Fund Resources:											
Undisbursed Funds	2007-2008	20		1797			2,970,000.00		2,970,000.00		
Federal Payment For Transportation Assistance											
Fund Resources:											
Undisbursed Funds	2007	20		1813			990,000.00		990,000.00		
Federal Payment For Foster Care Improvements In The District Of Columbia											
Fund Resources:											
Undisbursed Funds	No Year	20		1814			1,980,000.00		1,980,000.00		
Federal Payment For School Improvement											
Fund Resources:											
Undisbursed Funds	2007-2008	20		1817			12,870,000.00		12,870,000.00		

Appropriations, Outlays, and Balances – Continued

Appropriation or Fund Account — Title	Period of Availability	Dept Reg	Tr From	Account Number	Sub No.	Balances, Beginning Of Fiscal Year	Appropriations And Other Obligational Authority[1]	Transfers Borrowings And Investment (Net)[2]	Outlays (Net)	Balances Withdrawn And Other Transactions[3]	Balances, End Of Fiscal Year[4]
Federal Payment For School Improvement - Continued											
Fund Resources: - Continued											
Undisbursed Funds - Continued	2007	20		1817			26,730,000.00		26,730,000.00		-0-
	Subtotal						39,600,000.00		39,600,000.00		
Federal Payment To The Criminal Justice Coordinating Council											
Fund Resources:											
Undisbursed Funds	No Year	20		1818			1,287,000.00		1,287,000.00		
Federal Payment For Bioterrorism And Forensics Laboratory											
Fund Resources:											
Undisbursed Funds	2007-2008	20		1821			4,950,000.00		4,950,000.00		
Special Fund Accounts											
District Of Columbia Federal Pension Fund											
Fund Resources:											
Undisbursed Funds	No Year	20		5511		240,377.14	536,483,112.72	-25,465,846.23	511,018,595.79		239,047.84
Unrealized Discount On Investments						-11,963,181.21		-11,585,958.31			-23,549,139.52
Investments In Public Debt Securities						3,609,077,876.92		37,051,804.54			3,646,129,681.46
Fund Equities:											
Unobligated Balances (Unexpired)						-3,537,559,955.32				27,665,233.12	-3,565,225,188.44
Accounts Payable						-50,613,241.69				-1,284,029.01	-49,329,212.68
Undelivered Orders						-9,181,875.84				-916,687.18	-8,265,188.66
	Subtotal	20		5511		-0-	536,483,112.72		511,018,595.79	25,464,516.93	-0-
Deductions For Offsetting Receipts											
Proprietary Receipts From The Public							-1,680.25		-1,680.25		
Intrabudgetary Transactions							-536,483,112.72		-536,483,112.72		
Total, District Of Columbia General And Special Payments							465,506,319.75		437,027,891.82	28,478,427.93	
Total, District Of Columbia							739,971,629.03		673,453,981.71	66,517,647.32	
Election Assistance Commission											
General Fund Accounts											
Salaries And Expenses, Election Assistance Commission											
Fund Resources:											
Undisbursed Funds	2007	95		1650			11,313,096.00		7,237,276.32		4,075,819.68
	2006					3,569,786.41			1,318,470.95		2,251,315.46
	2005					4,131,924.52			1,070,331.32		3,061,593.20
	2004					97,958.36			323.67		97,634.69
Fund Equities:											
Unobligated Balances (Expired)						-3,046,846.19				3,013,387.54	-6,060,233.73
Accounts Payable						-630,732.92				153,209.71	-783,942.63
Undelivered Orders						-4,122,090.18				-1,479,903.51	-2,642,186.67

Appropriations, Outlays, and Balances - Continued

Appropriation or Fund Account — Title	Period of Availability	Dept Reg	Dept Tr From	Account Number	Sub No.	Balances, Beginning Of Fiscal Year	Appropriations And Other Obligational Authority[1]	Transfers Borrowings And Investment (Net)[2]	Outlays (Net)	Balances Withdrawn And Other Transactions[3]	Balances, End Of Fiscal Year[4]
	Subtotal	95		1650		-0-	11,313,096.00		9,626,402.26	1,686,693.74	-0-
Election Reform Programs, Election Assistance Commission											
Fund Resources:											
Undisbursed Funds	2004	95		1651		239,944.73					239,944.73
	No Year	95		1651		[7]245,156.99		378,651.06			623,808.05
Fund Equities:											
Unobligated Balances (Expired)						-239,944.73					-239,944.73
Unobligated Balances (Unexpired)						[7]-238,722.89				380,085.16	-618,808.05
Accounts Payable						-266.60				-266.60	-5,000.00
Undelivered Orders						-6,167.50				-1,167.50	-0-
	Subtotal	95		1651		-0-		378,651.06		378,651.06	-0-
Total, Election Assistance Commission							11,313,096.00	378,651.06	9,626,402.26	2,065,344.80	
Equal Employment Opportunity Commission											
General Fund Accounts											
Salaries And Expenses, Equal Employment Opportunity Commission											
Fund Resources:											
Undisbursed Funds	2007	45		0100			328,745,219.00		278,906,024.10		49,839,194.90
	2006					47,042,867.35			42,075,323.84		4,967,543.51
	2005					5,394,481.91			1,535,791.86		3,858,690.05
	2004					2,690,041.79			236,001.23		2,354,040.56
	2003					2,330,412.76			62,921.89		2,267,490.87
	2002					1,730,597.30			41,622.29	1,772,219.59	
	No Year					50,094.72			1,141.20		48,953.52
Accounts Receivable						36,664.00				21,801.79	14,862.21
Fund Equities:											
Unobligated Balances (Expired)						-6,557,209.49				565,192.51	-7,122,402.00
Unobligated Balances (Unexpired)						-48,843.10				110.42	-48,953.52
Accounts Payable						-32,842,310.81				-9,855,848.51	-22,986,462.30
Undelivered Orders						-19,726,796.43				13,466,161.37	-33,192,957.80
	Subtotal	45		0100		-0-	328,745,219.00		322,775,581.83	5,969,637.17	-0-
Public Enterprise Funds											
EEOC Education, Technical Assistance And Training Revolving Fund, Equal Employment Opportunity Commission											
Fund Resources:											
Undisbursed Funds	No Year	45		4019		3,024,435.30			51,861.70		2,972,573.60
Accounts Receivable						110,755.65				-18,661.35	129,417.00
Fund Equities:											
Unobligated Balances (Unexpired)						-1,069,216.12				651,333.13	-1,720,549.25
Accounts Payable						-77,447.21				-44,957.21	-32,490.00
Undelivered Orders						-1,988,527.62				-639,576.27	-1,348,951.35
	Subtotal	45		4019		-0-			51,861.70	-51,861.70	-0-

Footnotes At End Of Chapter

Appropriations, Outlays, and Balances – Continued

Appropriation or Fund Account — Title	Account Symbol — Dept Reg	Tr From	Account Number	Sub No.	Period of Availability	Balances, Beginning Of Fiscal Year	Appropriations And Other Obligational Authority[1]	Transfers Borrowings And Investment (Net)[2]	Outlays (Net)	Balances Withdrawn And Other Transactions[3]	Balances, End Of Fiscal Year[4]
Deductions For Offsetting Receipts											
Proprietary Receipts From The Public							-79,334.16		-79,334.16		
Intrabudgetary Transactions							-30,580.94		-30,580.94		
Total, Equal Employment Opportunity Commission							328,635,303.90		322,717,528.43	5,917,775.47	
Export-Import Bank Of The United States											
General Fund Accounts											
Export-Import Bank Loans Program Account											
Fund Resources:											
Undisbursed Funds	83		0100		2007-2010		267,661,000.00		241,279,000.00		26,382,000.00
					2006-2009	99,000,000.00			4,047,708.25		94,952,291.75
					2007-2008				-0.04	0.04	
					2005-2008	44,105,586.27			25,943,087.33		18,162,498.94
					2007		72,823,589.00		54,224,371.96		18,599,217.04
					2006	11,174,724.03			8,304,644.10		2,870,079.93
					2003-2006	250,351,309.79			92,998,634.62		157,352,675.17
					2005	4,195,558.35			1,012,775.88		3,182,782.47
					2002-2005	47,314,726.00			11,299,595.94		36,015,130.06
					2004	2,481,705.12			239,427.17		2,242,277.95
					2003-2004	38,067.30				38,067.30	
					2001-2004	50,860,369.86			6,965,413.18		43,894,956.68
					2003	1,331,147.11					1,331,147.11
					2002-2003	100,669.86					100,669.86
					2000-2003	51,134,660.32			-235.46		51,134,895.78
					2002	2,127,759.58			-1,041.84	2,128,801.42	
					2001-2002	59,622.59				59,622.59	
					1999-2002	7,496,181.00			3,158,338.10	3,416,305.87	[8]921,537.03
					1998-2001	115,455.62					[9]115,455.62
					1997-1998	332,663.15				25,184.60	[10]307,478.55
					1996-1997	1,206,347.11			-171.26		[11]1,206,518.37
					1995-1996	9,326,260.28			47,876.49		[12]9,278,383.79
					1994-1995	3,111,685.58					[13]3,111,685.58
					No Year	229,431,197.34			1,902.84		229,429,294.50
Fund Equities:											
Unobligated Balances (Expired)						-174,100,227.28				57,494,273.03	-231,594,500.31
Unobligated Balances (Unexpired)						-370,646,711.63				-24,839,621.13	-345,807,090.50
Accounts Payable						-5,947,101.11				-2,817,844.01	-3,129,257.10
Undelivered Orders						-264,601,656.24				-144,541,527.97	-120,060,128.27
Subtotal	83		0100		2007-2008	-0-	340,484,589.00		449,521,327.26	-109,036,738.26	-0-
Inspector General Of The Export-Import Bank, Export-Import Bank Of The United States											
Fund Resources:											
Undisbursed Funds	83		0105		2007-2008		990,000.00				990,000.00

Appropriations, Outlays, and Balances - Continued

Appropriation or Fund Account — Title	Period of Availability	Reg	Tr From	Account Number	Sub No.	Balances, Beginning Of Fiscal Year	Appropriations And Other Obligational Authority[1]	Transfers Borrowings And Investment (Net)[2]	Outlays (Net)	Balances Withdrawn And Other Transactions[3]	Balances, End Of Fiscal Year[4]
Fund Equities:											
Unobligated Balances (Expired)	2006-2007					990,000.00				-----	990,000.00
Unobligated Balances (Unexpired)						-990,000.00				990,000.00	-990,000.00
	Subtotal	83		0105		-0-	990,000.00			990,000.00	-990,000.00
Public Enterprise Funds											
Export-Import Bank Of The United States, Liquidating Account											
Fund Resources:											
Undisbursed Funds	No Year	83		4027		3,448,064.76			-128,889,356.54	[14]130,500,000.00	1,837,421.30
Fund Equities:											
Unobligated Balances (Unexpired)						-3,448,064.76				-1,610,643.46	-1,837,421.30
	Subtotal	83		4027		-0-			-128,889,356.54	128,889,356.54	-0-
Deductions For Offsetting Receipts											
Proprietary Receipts From The Public							-1,685,741,195.14		-1,685,741,195.14		
Total, Export-Import Bank Of The United States							-1,344,266,606.14		-1,365,109,224.42	20,842,618.28	
Farm Credit Administration											
Public Enterprise Funds											
Revolving Fund For Administrative Expenses, Farm Credit Administration											
Fund Resources:											
Undisbursed Funds	No Year	78		4131		1,782,918.73		-5,010,653.74		-----	1,095,238.34
Unrealized Discount On Investments						-77,064.83		71,653.74		-----	-5,411.09
Investments In Public Debt Securities						22,461,000.00		4,939,000.00		-----	27,400,000.00
Accounts Receivable						382,680.85				-307,878.87	690,559.72
Unfilled Customer Orders						785,138.88				491,447.18	293,691.70
Fund Equities:											
Unobligated Balances (Unexpired)						-18,706,062.87				3,358,742.19	-22,064,805.06
Accounts Payable						-4,688,438.67				351,385.21	-5,039,823.88
Undelivered Orders						-1,940,172.09				429,277.64	-2,369,449.73
	Subtotal	78		4131		-0-			-4,322,973.35	4,322,973.35	-0-
Total, Farm Credit Administration									-4,322,973.35	4,322,973.35	
Farm Credit System Insurance Corporation											
Public Enterprise Funds											
Farm Credit Insurance Fund, Capital Corporation Investment Fund, Farm Credit Administration											
Fund Resources:											
Undisbursed Funds	No Year	78		4136		60,098.28		-271,006,071.57	-271,028,352.25		82,378.96

Footnotes At End Of Chapter

Appropriations, Outlays, and Balances – Continued

Appropriation or Fund Account — Title	Period of Availability	Account Symbol — Dept Reg	Tr From	Account Number	Sub No.	Balances, Beginning Of Fiscal Year	Appropriations And Other Obligational Authority[1]	Transfers Borrowings And Investment (Net)[2]	Outlays (Net)	Balances Withdrawn And Other Transactions[3]	Balances, End Of Fiscal Year[4]
Unrealized Discount On Investments						-1,314,276.41		-4,104,928.43			-5,419,204.84
Farm Credit Insurance Fund, Capital Corporation Investment Fund, Farm Credit Administration - Continued											
Fund Resources: - Continued											
Investments In Public Debt Securities						2,088,301,000.00		275,111,000.00			2,363,412,000.00
Accounts Receivable						17,468,819.70				2,264,695.57	15,204,124.13
Fund Equities:											
Unobligated Balances (Unexpired)						-2,104,355,448.79				268,720,649.65	-2,373,076,098.44
Accounts Payable						-159,121.83				43,221.71	-202,343.54
Undelivered Orders						-1,070.95				-214.68	-856.27
Subtotal		78		4136		-0-			-271,028,352.25	271,028,352.25	-0-
Total, Farm Credit System Insurance Corporation									-271,028,352.25	271,028,352.25	
Federal Communications Commission											
General Fund Accounts											
Salaries And Expenses, Federal Communications Commission											
Fund Resources:											
Undisbursed Funds											
	2007	27		0100		57,102,740.00			-54,980,423.63		55,967,651.63
	2006					5,414,042.75	987,228.00	-4,071,663.19	48,041,363.55		4,989,713.26
	2005					3,057,494.51		-307,616.52	1,374,577.92		3,731,848.31
	2004					7,221,287.59		-516,517.31	338,796.12		2,202,181.08
	2003					2,239,108.87		-521,598.25	233,340.40		6,466,348.94
	2002					41,821,725.21		-590,080.73	30,077.71	1,618,950.43	54,036,215.88
	No Year					45,664.15				194,550.19	8,904.01
Accounts Receivable								6,007,476.00	-6,401,564.86	36,760.14	
Fund Equities:											
Unobligated Balances (Expired)						-6,147,560.47				-1,070,184.91	-5,077,375.56
Unobligated Balances (Unexpired)						-41,464,543.09				8,712,499.26	-50,177,042.35
Accounts Payable						-25,534,442.13				-3,547,807.33	-21,986,634.80
Undelivered Orders						-43,755,517.39				6,406,293.01	-50,161,810.40
Subtotal		27		0100		-0-	987,228.00		-11,363,832.79	12,351,060.79	-0-
Spectrum Auction Program Account, Federal Communications Commission											
Fund Resources:											
Undisbursed Funds	No Year	27		0300		18,476,298.78	31,232,002.00		31,539,872.91		18,168,427.87
Fund Equities:											
Unobligated Balances (Unexpired)						-8,000,029.50				562,737.60	-8,562,767.10
Accounts Payable						-443,823.82				-346,554.32	-97,269.50
Undelivered Orders						-10,032,445.46				-524,054.19	-9,508,391.27
Subtotal		27		0300		-0-	31,232,002.00		31,539,872.91	-307,870.91	-0-
Special Fund Accounts											
Universal Service Fund, Federal Communications Commission											
Fund Resources:											
Undisbursed Funds	No Year	27		5183		-88,805,008.77	7,761,574,422.46	-283,493,263.33	7,478,081,159.13		
Unrealized Discount On Investments								15,142,416.39			-73,662,592.38

Appropriations, Outlays, and Balances - Continued

Appropriation or Fund Account — Title	Period of Availability	Dept Reg	Tr From	Account Number	Sub No.	Balances, Beginning Of Fiscal Year	Appropriations And Other Obligational Authority[1]	Transfers Borrowings And Investment (Net)[2]	Outlays (Net)	Balances Withdrawn And Other Transactions[3]	Balances, End Of Fiscal Year[4]
Funds Held Outside The Treasury						96,202,723.11		-962,153.06			95,240,570.05
Investments In Public Debt Securities						4,762,178,000.00		269,313,000.00			5,031,491,000.00
Fund Equities:											
Unobligated Balances (Unexpired)						[7] -1,950,697,715.10				-280,647,936.49	-1,670,049,778.61
Accounts Payable						[7] -74,432,478.48				17,080,277.80	-91,512,756.28
Undelivered Orders						[7] -2,744,445,520.76	7,761,574,422.46		7,478,081,159.13	547,060,922.02	-3,291,506,442.78
Subtotal		27		5183		-0-				283,493,263.33	-0-
Trust Fund Accounts											
Gifts And Bequests, Federal Communications Commission											
Fund Resources:											
Undisbursed Funds	No Year	27		8117		348.18					348.18
Fund Equities:											
Unobligated Balances (Unexpired)						-348.18					-348.18
Subtotal		27		8117		-0-					-0-
Deductions For Offsetting Receipts											
Proprietary Receipts From The Public							-27,368,624.35		-27,368,624.35		
Intrabudgetary Transactions							-248,407,878.95		-248,407,878.95		
Total, Federal Communications Commission							7,518,017,149.16		7,222,480,695.95	295,536,453.21	
Federal Deposit Insurance Corporation											
Savings Association Insurance Fund											
Intragovernmental Funds											
Deposit Insurance Fund, Federal Deposit Insurance Corporation											
Fund Resources:											
Undisbursed Funds	No Year	51		4596		-61,115.37		-1,234,749,006.25	-1,234,847,711.23		37,589.61
Unrealized Discount On Investments						-371,614,400.36		-90,316,093.75			-461,930,494.11
Investments In Public Debt Securities						46,215,600,500.00		1,299,550,100.00			47,515,150,600.00
Accounts Receivable						692,803,874.89				-175,917,175.44	868,721,050.33
Fund Equities:											
Unobligated Balances (Unexpired)						-46,498,434,751.36				1,390,507,966.10	-47,888,942,717.46
Accounts Payable						-38,294,107.80				-5,258,079.43	-33,036,028.37
Subtotal		51		4596		-0-		-25,515,000.00	-1,234,847,711.23	1,209,332,711.23	-0-
Total, Savings Association Insurance Fund								-25,515,000.00	-1,234,847,711.23	1,209,332,711.23	
General Fund Accounts											
Federal Savings And Loan Insurance Corporation Fund											
Office Of The Inspector General, Resolution Trust Corporation[6]											
Fund Resources:											
Undisbursed Funds	2006	22		1500		-737.13					[5] -737.13

Footnotes At End Of Chapter

Appropriations, Outlays, and Balances – Continued

Appropriation or Fund Account — Title	Period of Availability	Dept Reg	Tr From	Account Number	Sub No.	Balances, Beginning Of Fiscal Year	Appropriations And Other Obligational Authority[1]	Transfers Borrowings And Investment (Net)[2]	Outlays (Net)	Balances Withdrawn And Other Transactions[3]	Balances, End Of Fiscal Year[4]
Public Enterprise Funds											
The FSLIC Resolution Fund											
Fund Resources:											
Undisbursed Funds	No Year	51		4065		9.14	405,063,249.62	-153,465,000.00	251,597,674.50		584.26
Investments In Public Debt Securities						3,028,933,000.00		153,465,000.00		-------	3,182,398,000.00
Accounts Receivable						1,315,011.60				136,288.99	1,178,722.61
Fund Equities:											
Unobligated Balances (Unexpired)						-3,029,660,520.47			153,161,679.69		-3,182,822,200.16
Accounts Payable						-587,500.27			167,606.44		-755,106.71
	Subtotal	51		4065		-0-	405,063,249.62		251,597,674.50	153,465,575.12	-0-
Operating Account, Federal Deposit Insurance Corporation											
Fund Resources:											
Undisbursed Funds	No Year	51		4067		531,329,192.54		-40,939,671.26		-------	572,268,863.80
Accounts Receivable						4,312,713.23			937,257.26		3,375,455.97
Fund Equities:											
Unobligated Balances (Unexpired)						-533,371,235.16			41,424,345.71		-574,795,580.87
Accounts Payable						-2,270,670.61			-1,421,931.71		-848,738.90
	Subtotal	51		4067		-0-		-40,939,671.26	40,939,671.26		-0-
Total, Federal Savings And Loan Insurance Corporation Fund						-737.13	405,063,249.62		210,658,003.24	194,405,246.38	-737.13
FDIC-Office Of Inspector General											
Intragovernmental Funds											
Office Of Inspector General, Federal Deposit Insurance Corporation											
Fund Resources:											
Undisbursed Funds	2007	51		4595		-------		25,515,000.00	25,515,000.00		-------
Total, FDIC-Office Of Inspector General						-------		25,515,000.00	25,515,000.00		-------
Total, Federal Deposit Insurance Corporation						-737.13	405,063,249.62		-998,674,707.99	1,403,737,957.61	-737.13
Federal Drug Control Programs											
General Fund Accounts											
High Intensity Drug Trafficking Areas Program, Funds Appropriated To The President											
Fund Resources:											
Undisbursed Funds	2007-2008	11		1070			200,393,200.00		33,866,934.05		166,526,265.95
	2006-2007					698,415.00		5,007.32	231,935.00		471,487.32
	2006					165,974,981.50			109,322,025.54		56,652,955.96
	2005-2006					1,064,474.96			12,500.00		1,051,974.96
	2005					58,551,341.25			33,444,173.70		25,107,167.55
	2004-2005					1,044,777.24			36,590.19		1,008,187.05

Appropriations, Outlays, and Balances - Continued

Title	Reg	Tr From	Account Number	Sub No.	Period of Availability	Balances, Beginning Of Fiscal Year	Appropriations And Other Obligational Authority[1]	Transfers Borrowings And Investment (Net)[2]	Outlays (Net)	Balances Withdrawn And Other Transactions[3]	Balances, End Of Fiscal Year[4]
					2004	17,419,583.88			8,884,419.51		8,535,164.37
					2003-2004	522,181.75			142,845.84		379,335.91
					2003	10,666,750.45			4,788,856.68		5,877,893.77
					2002-2003	391,362.22			22,348.52		369,013.70
					2002	2,276,083.43			1,820,720.01	455,363.42	--------
					2001-2002	120,035.16				120,035.16	--------
Fund Equities:											
Unobligated Balances (Expired)						-861,598.11				-241,500.09	-620,098.02
Unobligated Balances (Unexpired)						-460,000.00				2,389,325.00	-2,849,325.00
Accounts Payable						-140,681.65				-140,681.65	-140,681.65
Undelivered Orders						-257,267,707.08				5,242,316.44	-262,510,023.52
	11		1070		Subtotal	-0-	200,393,200.00	5,007.32	192,573,349.04	7,824,858.28	-0-
Other Federal Drug Control Programs, Executive Office Of The President											
Fund Resources:											
Undisbursed Funds	11		1460		No Year	58,101,097.62	192,951,000.00		165,598,718.62		85,453,379.00
Fund Equities:											
Unobligated Balances (Unexpired)						-5,767,767.81				6,499,510.26	-12,267,278.07
Accounts Payable						-168,037.97				-154,705.28	-13,332.69
Undelivered Orders						-52,165,291.84				21,007,476.40	-73,172,768.24
	11		1460		Subtotal	-0-	192,951,000.00		165,598,718.62	27,352,281.38	-0-
Counterdrug Technology Assessment Center, Office Of National Drug Control Policy, Executive Office Of The President											
Fund Resources:											
Undisbursed Funds	11		1461		2007-2008	324,679.09	20,000,000.00		20,000,000.00		1,945,945.48
					No Year				-1,621,266.39		
Fund Equities:											
Unobligated Balances (Unexpired)						-538,930.00				1,211,941.49	-1,750,871.49
Undelivered Orders						214,250.91				409,324.90	-195,073.99
	11		1461		Subtotal	-0-	20,000,000.00		18,378,733.61	1,621,266.39	-0-
Trust Fund Accounts											
Federal Drug Control Programs, Funds Appropriated To The President, Violent Crime Reduction Trust Fund											
Fund Resources:											
Undisbursed Funds	11		8607		No Year	32,922.93					32,922.93
Fund Equities:											
Unobligated Balances (Unexpired)						-32,302.63				620.30	-32,922.93
Undelivered Orders						-620.30				-620.30	--------
	11		8607		Subtotal	-0-					-0-
Total, Federal Drug Control Programs							413,344,200.00	5,007.32	376,550,801.27	36,798,406.05	

Footnotes At End Of Chapter

Appropriations, Outlays, and Balances – Continued

Appropriation or Fund Account — Title	Period of Availability	Dept Reg	Tr From	Account Number	Sub No.	Balances, Beginning Of Fiscal Year	Appropriations And Other Obligational Authority[1]	Transfers Borrowings And Investment (Net)[2]	Outlays (Net)	Balances Withdrawn And Other Transactions[3]	Balances, End Of Fiscal Year[4]
Federal Election Commission											
General Fund Accounts											
Salaries And Expenses, Federal Election Commission											
Fund Resources:											
Undisbursed Funds	2007	95		1600			54,527,516.00		47,487,542.17		7,039,973.83
	2006					6,056,409.45			5,162,236.37		894,173.08
	2005					553,664.05			48,920.74		504,743.31
	2004					714,919.50			362,303.76		352,615.74
	2003					1,405,358.04			-24,549.09		1,429,907.13
	2002					869,395.57			-5,097.33	874,492.90	-0-
Fund Equities:											
Unobligated Balances (Expired)						-2,078,564.70				750,293.01	-2,828,857.71
Accounts Payable						-2,426,455.41				-111,058.97	-2,315,396.44
Undelivered Orders						-5,094,726.50				-17,567.56	-5,077,158.94
Subtotal		95		1600		-0-	54,527,516.00		53,031,356.62	1,496,159.38	-0-
Deductions For Offsetting Receipts											
Proprietary Receipts From The Public							236,790.27		236,790.27		
Total, Federal Election Commission							54,764,306.27		53,268,146.89	1,496,159.38	
Federal Financial Institutions Examination Council Appraisal Subcommittee											
Special Fund Accounts											
Registry Fees, Appraisal Subcommittee											
Fund Resources:											
Undisbursed Funds	No Year	95		5026		7,062,566.22	2,985,771.00		2,892,699.19		7,156,638.03
Fund Equities:											
Unobligated Balances (Unexpired)						-6,301,059.07				172,864.55	-6,473,923.62
Accounts Payable						-549,807.55				-140,777.77	-409,029.78
Undelivered Orders						-211,699.60				60,985.03	-272,684.63
Subtotal		95		5026		-0-	2,985,771.00		2,892,699.19	93,071.81	-0-
Total, Federal Financial Institutions Examination Council Appraisal Subcommittee							2,985,771.00		2,892,699.19	93,071.81	
Federal Housing Finance Board											
Public Enterprise Funds											
Federal Housing Finance Board											
Fund Resources:											
Undisbursed Funds	No Year	95		4039		8,942,839.88			2,215,666.65		6,727,173.23
Fund Equities:											
Unobligated Balances (Unexpired)						-4,742,568.51				-2,440,885.59	-2,301,682.92
Accounts Payable						-3,471,534.90				850,822.85	-4,322,357.75

Appropriations, Outlays, and Balances - Continued

Appropriation or Fund Account Title	Account Symbol — Period of Availability	Dept Reg	Dept Tr From	Account Number	Sub No.	Balances, Beginning Of Fiscal Year	Appropriations And Other Obligational Authority[1]	Transfers Borrowings And Investment (Net)[2]	Outlays (Net)	Balances Withdrawn And Other Transactions[3]	Balances, End Of Fiscal Year[4]
Undelivered Orders						-728,736.47				-625,603.91	-103,132.56
	Subtotal	95		4039		-0-			2,215,666.65	-2,215,666.65	-0-
Total, Federal Housing Finance Board									2,215,666.65	-2,215,666.65	
Federal Labor Relations Authority											
General Fund Accounts											
Salaries And Expenses, Federal Labor Relations Authority											
Fund Resources:											
Undisbursed Funds	2007	54		0100		4,401,787.22	25,372,339.00		19,636,992.75		5,735,346.25
	2006					r1,594,121.10			3,033,416.58		1,368,370.64
	2005					479,704.21			404.00		1,593,717.10
	2004					1,544,001.30					479,704.21
	2003					58,531.86					1,544,001.30
	2002-2003					842,401.35				842,401.35	58,531.86
	2002					31,839.72				7,884.88	23,954.84
Accounts Receivable											
Fund Equities:											
Unobligated Balances (Expired)						r5,419,749.60				3,071,732.71	-8,491,482.31
Accounts Payable						r1,408,013.77				-218,779.52	-1,189,234.25
Undelivered Orders						r2,124,623.39				-1,001,713.75	-1,122,909.64
	Subtotal	54		0100		-0-	25,372,339.00		22,670,813.33	2,701,525.67	-0-
Deductions For Offsetting Receipts											
Proprietary Receipts From The Public							-233.84		-233.84		
Total, Federal Labor Relations Authority							25,372,105.16		22,670,579.49	2,701,525.67	
Federal Maritime Commission											
General Fund Accounts											
Salaries And Expenses, Federal Maritime Commission											
Fund Resources:											
Undisbursed Funds	2007	65		0100			20,427,910.00		17,903,631.94		2,524,278.06
	2006					2,474,340.37			2,314,513.14		159,827.23
	2005					77,108.44			9,187.41		67,921.03
	2004					48,467.97			12,588.79		35,879.18
	2003					55,364.07			-6,550.72		55,364.07
	2002					20,881.92				27,432.64	
Fund Equities:											
Unobligated Balances (Expired)						-126,738.14				84,155.90	-210,894.04
Accounts Payable						-1,223,700.81				22,944.90	-1,246,645.71
Undelivered Orders						-1,325,723.82				60,006.00	-1,385,729.82
	Subtotal	65		0100		-0-	20,427,910.00		20,233,370.56	194,539.44	-0-

Footnotes At End Of Chapter

Appropriations, Outlays, and Balances – Continued

Title	Reg	Tr From	Account Number	Sub No.	Period of Availability	Balances, Beginning Of Fiscal Year	Appropriations And Other Obligational Authority[1]	Transfers Borrowings And Investment (Net)[2]	Outlays (Net)	Balances Withdrawn And Other Transactions[3]	Balances, End Of Fiscal Year[4]
Deductions For Offsetting Receipts											
Proprietary Receipts From The Public							-587,738.14		-587,738.14		
Total, Federal Maritime Commission							19,840,171.86		19,645,632.42	194,539.44	
Federal Mediation And Conciliation Service											
General Fund Accounts											
Salaries And Expenses, Federal Mediation And Conciliation Service											
Fund Resources:											
Undisbursed Funds	93		0100		2007-2008	396,000.00	396,000.00				396,000.00
					2007		42,452,824.00		39,358,519.61		3,094,304.39
					2006-2007	396,000.00			67,078.75		328,921.25
					2006	3,190,455.45			3,028,993.97		161,461.48
					2005-2006	1,226,309.05			709,173.98		517,135.07
					2005	917,773.36			406,717.65		511,055.71
					2004-2005	160,042.99			100,548.10		59,494.89
					2004	234,825.22			36,776.99		198,048.23
					2003-2004	86,038.75			61,235.00		24,803.75
					2003	105,452.75			7,482.62		97,970.13
					2002-2003	159,834.04			-397.49		160,231.53
					2002	33,520.59			1,468.02		32,052.57
					2001-2002	399,552.88					399,552.88
					No Year	2,605,236.95			-579,075.24		3,184,312.19
Accounts Receivable						25,063.59				4,657.15	20,406.44
Fund Equities:											
Unobligated Balances (Expired)						-847,996.51				-351,681.77	-496,314.74
Unobligated Balances (Unexpired)						-2,920,844.96				327,355.07	-3,248,200.03
Accounts Payable						-2,151,287.80				7,688.94	-2,158,976.74
Undelivered Orders						-3,619,976.35				-769,322.80	-2,850,653.55
Subtotal	93		0100			-0-	42,848,824.00		43,198,521.96	-349,697.96	-0-
Deductions For Offsetting Receipts											
Proprietary Receipts From The Public							-221.40		-221.40		
Total, Federal Mediation And Conciliation Service							42,848,602.60		43,198,300.56	-349,697.96	
Federal Mine Safety And Health Review Commission											
General Fund Accounts											
Salaries And Expenses, Federal Mine Safety And Health Review Commission											
Fund Resources:											
Undisbursed Funds	95		2800		2007		7,777,652.00		6,293,649.66		1,484,002.34
					2006	1,232,321.93			746,585.12		485,736.81
					2005	750,230.52			-22,407.89		772,638.41

Appropriations, Outlays, and Balances - Continued

Appropriation or Fund Account — Title	Reg	Tr From	Account Number	Sub No.	Period of Availability	Balances, Beginning Of Fiscal Year	Appropriations And Other Obligational Authority[1]	Transfers Borrowings And Investment (Net)[2]	Outlays (Net)	Balances Withdrawn And Other Transactions[3]	Balances, End Of Fiscal Year[4]
					2004	903,690.99			-897.94		904,588.93
					2003	1,052,208.98			-549.33		1,052,758.31
					2002	755,770.53				755,770.53	------
Fund Equities:											
Unobligated Balances (Expired)						-3,243,153.29				143,345.09	-3,386,498.38
Accounts Payable						-299,136.47				-26,961.84	-272,174.63
Undelivered Orders						-1,151,933.19				-110,881.40	-1,041,051.79
Subtotal	95		2800			-0-	7,777,652.00		7,016,379.62	761,272.38	-0-
Total, Federal Mine Safety And Health Review Commission						------	7,777,652.00		7,016,379.62	761,272.38	------
Federal Trade Commission											
General Fund Accounts											
Salaries And Expenses, Federal Trade Commission											
Fund Resources:											
Undisbursed Funds	29		0100		2003-2004	14,010.66		-14,010.66			------
					No Year	57,911,557.79	73,688,722.00		47,407,843.78		84,192,436.01
Accounts Receivable						55,453.16				32,429.85	23,023.31
Unfilled Customer Orders						144,388.00				-84,610.58	228,998.58
Fund Equities:											
Unobligated Balances (Expired)						-14,010.66				-14,010.66	------
Unobligated Balances (Unexpired)						7-10,861,220.05				28,768,285.97	-39,629,506.02
Accounts Payable						7-13,148,962.37				-444,420.24	-12,704,542.13
Undelivered Orders						7-34,101,216.53				-1,990,806.78	-32,110,409.75
Subtotal	29		0100			-0-	73,688,722.00	-14,010.66	47,407,843.78	26,266,867.56	-0-
Deductions For Offsetting Receipts											
Proprietary Receipts From The Public							4,264,638.73		4,264,638.73		
Total, Federal Trade Commission						------	77,953,360.73	-14,010.66	51,672,482.51	26,266,867.56	------
Harry S. Truman Scholarship Foundation											
Trust Fund Accounts											
Harry S. Truman Memorial Scholarship Trust Fund, Harry S. Truman Scholarship Foundation											
Fund Resources:											
Undisbursed Funds	95		8296		No Year	1,600,701.27	2,831,547.16	-313,104.00	3,215,107.28	-280,791.91	904,037.15
Unrealized Discount On Investments						-246,386.03		33,104.00		-102,801.26	-213,282.03
Investments In Public Debt Securities						54,214,000.00		280,000.00			54,494,000.00
Fund Equities:											
Unobligated Balances (Unexpired)						-55,439,921.08				-280,791.91	-55,159,129.17
Accounts Payable						-127,654.36				-102,801.26	-24,853.10
Undelivered Orders						-739.80				33.05	-772.85

Footnotes At End Of Chapter

Appropriations, Outlays, and Balances – Continued

Appropriation or Fund Account — Title	Period of Availability	Reg	Tr From	Account Number	Sub No.	Balances, Beginning Of Fiscal Year	Appropriations And Other Obligational Authority[1]	Transfers Borrowings And Investment (Net)[2]	Outlays (Net)	Balances Withdrawn And Other Transactions[3]	Balances, End Of Fiscal Year[4]
Harry S. Truman Memorial Scholarship Trust Fund, Harry S. Truman Scholarship Foundation - Continued											
Subtotal		95		8296		-0-	2,831,547.16		3,215,107.28	-383,560.12	-0-
Total, Harry S. Truman Scholarship Foundation							2,831,547.16		3,215,107.28	-383,560.12	
Institute Of American Indian And Alaska Native Culture And Arts Development											
General Fund Accounts											
Payment To The Institute, Institute Of American Indian And Alaska Native Culture And Arts Development											
Fund Resources:											
Undisbursed Funds	2007	95		2900			6,207,312.00		6,207,312.00		
Total, Institute Of American Indian And Alaska Native Culture And Arts Development							6,207,312.00		6,207,312.00		
Intelligence Community Management Account											
General Fund Accounts											
Expenses, Intelligence Community Management Account											
Fund Resources:											
Undisbursed Funds	2007-2008	95		0401			55,533,000.00		42,581,423.32		12,951,576.68
	2006-2008					1,485,000.00					1,485,000.00
	2007						618,069,000.00		297,305,620.84		320,763,379.16
	2006-2007					8,346,540.64			-6,561,763.66		14,908,304.30
	2006					345,023,524.41			339,392,129.83		5,631,394.58
	2005-2006					-268,586.00					[5]5,268,586.00
	2005					48,971,578.24			37,452,775.87		11,518,802.37
	2004-2005					6,048,954.66			89,940.16		5,959,014.50
	2004					1,939,522.20			-7,113,743.85		9,053,266.05
	2003-2004					-83,237.05			-83,237.28		0.23
	2003					8,109,802.26			2,306,631.85		5,803,170.41
	2002-2003					432,499.61			158,102.45		274,397.16
	2002					-1,718,804.59			-5,644,187.56		3,925,382.97
	2001-2002					82,479.65			-687,680.22		770,159.87
Accounts Receivable						1,071,981.47			1,002,143.74		69,837.73
Unfilled Customer Orders						9,076,633.30			6,864,873.29		2,211,760.01
Fund Equities:											
Unobligated Balances (Expired)						-9,902,313.25			1,922,078.27		[5]11,824,391.52
Unobligated Balances (Unexpired)						-1,738,205.66			9,896,462.58		-11,634,668.24
Accounts Payable						-42,979,361.42			40,744,807.04		-83,724,168.46
Undelivered Orders						-373,898,008.47			-90,719,919.51		-283,178,088.96
Subtotal		95		0401		-0-	673,602,000.00		699,196,011.75	-25,594,011.75	-0-
Total, Intelligence Community Management Account							673,602,000.00		699,196,011.75	-25,594,011.75	

Appropriations, Outlays, and Balances - Continued

Appropriation or Fund Account — Title	Period of Availability	Dept Reg	Tr From	Account Number	Sub No.	Balances, Beginning Of Fiscal Year	Appropriations And Other Obligational Authority[1]	Transfers Borrowings And Investment (Net)[2]	Outlays (Net)	Balances Withdrawn And Other Transactions[3]	Balances, End Of Fiscal Year[4]
International Trade Commission											
General Fund Accounts											
Salaries And Expenses, International Trade Commission											
Fund Resources:											
Undisbursed Funds	No Year	34		0100		8,993,771.43	62,360,531.00		62,870,322.56		8,483,979.87
Fund Equities:											
Unobligated Balances (Unexpired)						-458,171.19				108,094.42	-566,265.61
Accounts Payable						-3,814,253.97				-763,556.05	-3,050,697.92
Undelivered Orders						-4,721,346.27				145,670.07	-4,867,016.34
Subtotal		34		0100		-0-	62,360,531.00		62,870,322.56	-509,791.56	-0-
Deductions For Offsetting Receipts											
Proprietary Receipts From The Public							-402,365.96		-402,365.96		
Total, International Trade Commission							61,958,165.04		62,467,956.60	-509,791.56	
James Madison Memorial Fellowship Foundation											
Trust Fund Accounts											
James Madison Memorial Fellowship Foundation Trust Fund											
Fund Resources:											
Undisbursed Funds	No Year	95		8282		1,609,671.12	2,236,696.22	-19,556.22	1,934,838.38		1,891,972.74
Transfer To:											
Executive Office Of The President	No Year	11	95	8282	17	38,285.40					38,285.40
Unrealized Discount On Investments						-676,937.70		-52,443.78			-729,381.48
Investments In Public Debt Securities						37,267,000.00		72,000.00			37,339,000.00
Fund Equities:											
Unobligated Balances (Unexpired)						-37,759,339.51				287,476.82	-38,046,816.33
Accounts Payable						-588,995.95				-189,615.26	-399,380.69
Undelivered Orders						110,316.64				203,996.28	-93,679.64
Subtotal		95		8282		-0-	2,236,696.22		1,934,838.38	301,857.84	-0-
Total, James Madison Memorial Fellowship Foundation							2,236,696.22		1,934,838.38	301,857.84	
Japan-United States Friendship Commission											
Trust Fund Accounts											
Japan-United States Friendship Trust Fund, Japan-United States Friendship Commission											
Fund Resources:											
Undisbursed Funds	No Year	95		8025		1,195,050.30	2,132,228.30	7,561.20	2,043,332.71		1,290,907.09
Unrealized Discount On Investments						-69,056.33		-6,561.20			-75,617.53
Investments In Public Debt Securities						38,491,000.00		-1,000.00			38,490,000.00

Footnotes At End Of Chapter

Appropriations, Outlays, and Balances – Continued

Appropriation or Fund Account — Title	Dept Reg	Dept Tr From	Account Number	Sub No.	Period of Availability	Balances, Beginning Of Fiscal Year	Appropriations And Other Obligational Authority[1]	Transfers Borrowings And Investment (Net)[2]	Outlays (Net)	Balances Withdrawn And Other Transactions[3]	Balances, End Of Fiscal Year[4]
Japan-United States Friendship Trust Fund, Japan-United States Friendship Commission - Continued											
Fund Equities:											
Unobligated Balances (Unexpired)	95		8025			-39,538,755.42				19,188.19	-39,557,943.61
Accounts Payable						-57,215.20				70,646.59	-127,861.79
Undelivered Orders						-21,023.35				-1,539.19	-19,484.16
					Subtotal	-0-	2,132,228.30		2,043,932.71	88,295.59	-0-
Total, Japan-United States Friendship Commission							2,132,228.30		2,043,932.71	88,295.59	
Legal Services Corporation											
General Fund Accounts											
Payment To The Legal Services Corporation, Legal Services Corporation											
Fund Resources:											
Undisbursed Funds:											
	20		0501		2007	33,048,733.50	348,578,000.00		315,723,759.00		32,854,241.00
					2006	72,170.00			33,048,733.50		135,000.00
					No Year				-62,830.00		
Fund Equities:											
Undelivered Orders						-33,120,903.50				-131,662.50	-32,989,241.00
	20		0501		Subtotal	-0-	348,578,000.00		348,709,662.50	-131,662.50	-0-
Total, Legal Services Corporation							348,578,000.00		348,709,662.50	-131,662.50	
Marine Mammal Commission											
General Fund Accounts											
Salaries And Expenses, Marine Mammal Commission											
Fund Resources:											
Undisbursed Funds:											
	95		2200		2007-2008		908,250.00				908,250.00
					2007		1,987,744.00		1,722,250.66		265,493.34
					2006-2007	450,122.79			104,603.14		345,519.65
					2006	568,315.41			278,198.61		290,116.80
					2005	110.41					110.41
					2004-2005	83,350.28			12,561.06		70,789.22
					2004	10,845.12					10,845.12
					2003-2004	40,094.72					40,094.72
					2003	13,418.24					13,418.24
					2002	88,280.33			80,361.59	7,918.74	
Fund Equities:											
Unobligated Balances (Expired)						-68,683.21				33,186.74	-101,869.95
Unobligated Balances (Unexpired)						-372,299.40				535,950.60	-908,250.00
Accounts Payable						-708,454.22				-213,497.65	-494,956.57
Undelivered Orders						-105,100.47				334,460.51	-439,560.98
	95		2200		Subtotal	-0-	2,895,994.00		2,197,975.06	698,018.94	-0-
Total, Marine Mammal Commission							2,895,994.00		2,197,975.06	698,018.94	

Appropriations, Outlays, and Balances - Continued

Appropriation or Fund Account — Title	Dept Reg	Dept Tr From	Account Number	Sub No.	Period of Availability	Balances, Beginning Of Fiscal Year	Appropriations And Other Obligational Authority[1]	Transfers Borrowings And Investment (Net)[2]	Outlays (Net)	Balances Withdrawn And Other Transactions[3]	Balances, End Of Fiscal Year[4]
Merit Systems Protection Board											
General Fund Accounts											
Salaries And Expenses, Merit Systems Protection Board											
Fund Resources:											
Undisbursed Funds	41		0100		2007		36,063,318.00		32,031,965.15		4,031,352.85
					2006-2007			102,700.00	102,700.00		
					2006	3,954,703.97		-102,700.00	3,566,783.43		285,220.54
					2005	1,360,749.84			585,000.21		775,749.63
					2004	836,741.79			245,557.43		591,184.36
					2003	981,731.74					981,731.74
					2002	211,325.44				211,325.44	-0-
Fund Equities:											
Unobligated Balances (Expired)						-2,380,716.98				-22,595.96	-2,358,121.02
Accounts Payable						-2,064,864.48				140,058.34	-2,204,922.82
Undelivered Orders						-2,899,671.32				-797,476.04	-2,102,195.28
Subtotal	41		0100			-0-	36,063,318.00		36,532,006.22	-468,688.22	-0-
Deductions For Offsetting Receipts											
Proprietary Receipts From The Public							-483.00		-483.00		
Total, Merit Systems Protection Board	41		0100				36,062,835.00		36,531,523.22	-468,688.22	
Morris K. Udall Scholarship And Excellence In National Environmental Policy Foundation											
General Fund Accounts											
Federal Payment To Morris K. Udall Scholarship And Excellence In National Environment											
Fund Resources:											
Undisbursed Funds	95		0900		No Year		1,983,880.00		1,983,880.00		
Special Fund Accounts											
Environmental Dispute Resolution Fund, Morris K. Udall Scholarship And Excellence In National Environmental Policy Foundation											
Fund Resources:											
Undisbursed Funds	95		5415		No Year	1,860,414.37	4,673,579.22		4,607,376.38		1,926,617.21
Fund Equities:											
Unobligated Balances (Unexpired)						-1,531,397.19				-743,531.87	-787,865.32
Accounts Payable						-150,787.30				149,012.94	-299,800.24
Undelivered Orders						-178,229.88				660,721.77	-838,951.65
Subtotal	95		5415			-0-	4,673,579.22		4,607,376.38	66,202.84	-0-

Footnotes At End Of Chapter

Appropriations, Outlays, and Balances – Continued

Appropriation or Fund Account — Title	Dept Reg	Dept Tr From	Account Number	Sub No.	Period of Availability	Balances, Beginning Of Fiscal Year	Appropriations And Other Obligational Authority[1]	Transfers Borrowings And Investment (Net)[2]	Outlays (Net)	Balances Withdrawn And Other Transactions[3]	Balances, End Of Fiscal Year[4]
Trust Fund Accounts											
Morris K. Udall Scholarship And Excellence In National Environmental Policy Trust Fund											
Fund Resources:											
Undisbursed Funds	95		8615		No Year	1,478,189.27	3,802,608.09		2,344,341.29		2,936,456.07
Investments In Public Debt Securities						32,166,000.00					32,166,000.00
Fund Equities:											
Unobligated Balances (Unexpired)						-33,403,613.10				1,381,242.88	-34,784,855.98
Accounts Payable						-120,314.87				-79,744.80	-40,570.07
Undelivered Orders						-120,261.30				156,768.72	-277,030.02
						-0-					-0-
Subtotal	95		8615				3,802,608.09		2,344,341.29	1,458,266.80	
Deductions For Offsetting Receipts											
Proprietary Receipts From The Public							-2,729,914.57		-2,729,914.57		
Intrabudgetary Transactions							-2,031,640.65		-2,031,640.65		
Total, Morris K. Udall Scholarship And Excellence In National Environmental Policy Foundation							5,698,512.09		4,174,042.45	1,524,469.64	
National Archives And Records Administration											
General Fund Accounts											
Operating Expenses, National Archives And Records Administration											
Fund Resources:											
Undisbursed Funds:											
2007	88		0300				281,338,310.00	445,188.00	224,354,389.73		57,429,108.27
2006						52,865,828.99		-445,188.00	45,284,360.75		7,136,280.24
2005						3,628,809.88			792,620.06		2,836,189.82
2003-2005						344,340.92			78,708.16		265,632.76
2004						4,389,928.96			294,242.55		4,095,686.41
2002-2004						209,281.52					209,281.52
2003						4,602,679.94			91,041.02		4,511,638.92
2002						5,522,988.00			-72,929.57	5,595,917.57	
No Year						66,674.97		-10,025,902.08	-9,999,798.47		40,571.36
Accounts Receivable						8,450.00				8,450.00	
Fund Equities:											
Unobligated Balances (Expired)						-14,706,811.32				-2,630,350.44	-12,076,460.88
Unobligated Balances (Unexpired)						-37,670.13				-9,712.38	-27,957.75
Accounts Payable						-20,049,650.92				-1,019,848.69	-19,029,802.23
Undelivered Orders						-36,844,850.81				8,545,317.63	-45,390,168.44
						-0-					-0-
Subtotal	88		0300				281,338,310.00	-10,025,902.08	260,822,634.23	10,489,773.69	-0-
National Historical Publications And Records Commission, National Archives And Records Administration											
Fund Resources:											
Undisbursed Funds	88		0301		No Year	10,196,327.26	5,425,000.00		6,184,470.67	159,838.88	9,436,856.59
Fund Equities:											
Unobligated Balances (Unexpired)						-1,047,784.75					-1,207,623.63

Appropriations, Outlays, and Balances - Continued

Appropriation or Fund Account Title	Period of Availability	Dept Reg	Tr From	Account Number	Sub No.	Balances, Beginning Of Fiscal Year	Appropriations And Other Obligational Authority[1]	Transfers Borrowings And Investment (Net)[2]	Outlays (Net)	Balances Withdrawn And Other Transactions[3]	Balances, End Of Fiscal Year[4]
Accounts Payable						-578,715.10				-503,473.58	-75,241.52
Undelivered Orders						-8,569,827.41				-415,835.97	-8,153,991.44
Subtotal		88		0301		-0-	5,425,000.00		6,184,470.67	-759,470.67	-0-
Repairs And Restoration, National Archives And Records Administration											
Fund Resources:											
Undisbursed Funds	No Year	88		0302		25,283,929.72	9,120,000.00		7,797,328.13		26,606,601.59
Fund Equities:											
Unobligated Balances (Unexpired)						-8,509,179.62				1,285,890.23	-9,795,069.85
Accounts Payable						-4,297,741.70				-2,125,090.30	-2,172,651.40
Undelivered Orders						-12,477,008.40				2,161,871.94	-14,638,880.34
Subtotal		88		0302		-0-	9,120,000.00		7,797,328.13	1,322,671.87	-0-
Electronic Records Archive, National Archives And Records Administration											
Fund Resources:											
Undisbursed Funds	2007-2009	88		0303		21,780,000.00	31,680,000.00		12,105,398.34		19,574,601.66
	2006-2008								18,803,487.89		2,976,512.11
	2007						13,573,682.00		7,877,821.66		5,695,860.34
	2006					10,722,752.32			10,415,502.73		307,249.59
	2004-2006					2,692,622.90			2,479,185.34		213,437.56
	2005					2,362,296.32			1,255,892.54		1,106,403.78
	2004					212,979.61					212,979.61
Fund Equities:											
Unobligated Balances (Expired)						-621,546.80				812,644.11	-1,434,190.91
Unobligated Balances (Unexpired)						-8,024,623.23				-3,602,634.28	-4,421,988.95
Accounts Payable						-10,138,931.62				2,118,224.77	-12,257,156.39
Undelivered Orders						-18,985,549.50				-7,011,841.10	-11,973,708.40
Subtotal		88		0303		-0-	45,253,682.00		52,937,288.50	-7,683,606.50	-0-
Intragovernmental Funds											
Records Center Revolving Fund, National Archives And Records Administration											
Fund Resources:											
Undisbursed Funds	No Year	88		4578		29,305,542.49			-3,323,328.25		32,628,870.74
Accounts Receivable						12,452,352.61				2,606,234.91	9,846,117.70
Unfilled Customer Orders						8,556,504.09				10,575.29	8,545,928.80
Fund Equities:											
Unobligated Balances (Unexpired)						-25,863,107.71				1,719,293.76	-27,582,401.47
Accounts Payable						-14,814,529.59				564,442.56	-15,378,972.15
Undelivered Orders						-9,636,761.89				-1,577,218.27	-8,059,543.62
Subtotal		88		4578		-0-			-3,323,328.25	3,323,328.25	-0-
Trust Fund Accounts											
National Archives Gift Fund, National Archives And Records Administration											
Fund Resources:											
Undisbursed Funds	No Year	88		8127		13,946.46	15,756,325.69	286,992.10	15,956,641.62		100,622.63
Investments In Public Debt Securities						2,490,811.57		-286,992.10			2,203,819.47

Footnotes At End Of Chapter

Appropriations, Outlays, and Balances – Continued

Title	Period of Availability	Reg	Tr From	Account Number	Sub No.	Balances, Beginning Of Fiscal Year	Appropriations And Other Obligational Authority[1]	Transfers Borrowings And Investment (Net)[2]	Outlays (Net)	Balances Withdrawn And Other Transactions[3]	Balances, End Of Fiscal Year[4]
National Archives Gift Fund, National Archives And Records Administration - Continued											
Fund Equities:											
Unobligated Balances (Unexpired)						-2,364,689.93				-89,900.37	-2,274,789.56
Accounts Payable						-140,068.10				-123,989.23	-16,078.87
Undelivered Orders										13,573.67	-13,573.67
Subtotal		88		8127		-0-	15,756,325.69		15,956,641.62	-200,315.93	-0-
National Archives Trust Fund, National Archives And Records Administration											
Fund Resources:											
Undisbursed Funds	No Year	88		8436		482,134.46		-999,091.84	-1,136,100.96		619,143.58
Funds Held Outside The Treasury						49,125.00		1,470.00			50,595.00
Investments In Public Debt Securities						5,139,078.09		997,621.84			6,136,699.93
Accounts Receivable						206,648.91				116,750.41	89,898.50
Fund Equities:											
Unobligated Balances (Unexpired)						-3,342,205.94				1,650,363.30	-4,992,569.24
Accounts Payable						-1,305,111.69				-22,790.33	-1,282,321.36
Undelivered Orders						-1,229,668.83				-608,222.42	-621,446.41
Subtotal		88		8436		-0-			-1,136,100.96	1,136,100.96	-0-
Deductions For Offsetting Receipts											
Proprietary Receipts From The Public							-13,913,402.55		-13,913,402.55		
Total, National Archives And Records Administration							342,979,915.14	-10,025,902.08	325,325,531.39	7,628,481.67	
National Capital Planning Commission											
General Fund Accounts											
Salaries And Expenses, National Capital Planning Commission											
Fund Resources:											
Undisbursed Funds	2007	95		2500			8,168,401.00		7,104,005.51		1,064,395.49
	2006					1,478,914.87			1,037,231.27		441,683.60
	2005					268,518.42			114,765.38		153,753.04
	2004					143,912.43			-385.00		144,297.43
	2003					107,973.94			41,200.00		66,773.94
	2002					18,718.81			495.00	18,223.81	
	No Year					281,761.13			-8,837.39		290,598.52
Unfilled Customer Orders						10,000.00				10,000.00	
Fund Equities:											
Unobligated Balances (Expired)						-491,000.21				173,497.85	-664,498.06
Unobligated Balances (Unexpired)						-16,826.75				6,825.00	-23,651.75
Accounts Payable						-491,848.63				47,732.97	-539,581.60
Undelivered Orders						-1,310,124.01				-376,353.40	-933,770.61
Subtotal		95		2500		-0-	8,168,401.00		8,288,474.77	-120,073.77	-0-
Deductions For Offsetting Receipts											
Proprietary Receipts From The Public							-121.00		-121.00		

Appropriations, Outlays, and Balances - Continued

Appropriation or Fund Account — Title	Period of Availability	Dept Reg	Tr From	Account Number	Sub No.	Balances, Beginning Of Fiscal Year	Appropriations And Other Obligational Authority[1]	Transfers Borrowings And Investment (Net)[2]	Outlays (Net)	Balances Withdrawn And Other Transactions[3]	Balances, End Of Fiscal Year[4]
Total, National Capital Planning Commission						------	8,168,280.00	------	8,288,353.77	-120,073.77	
National Commission On Libraries And Information Science											
General Fund Accounts											
Salaries And Expenses, National Commission On Libraries And Information Science											
Fund Resources:											
Undisbursed Funds	2007	95		2700			989,354.00	------	601,323.60		388,030.40
	2006					368,857.92	------	------	284,220.88	------	84,637.04
	2005					79,937.68	------	------	35,560.79	------	44,376.89
	2004					24,952.78	------	------	17,011.44	------	7,941.34
	2003					25,169.26	------	------	13,400.44	------	11,768.82
	2002					10,524.70	------	------	1,891.67	8,633.03	
Fund Equities:											
Unobligated Balances (Expired)						-18,657.94				29,632.82	-48,290.76
Accounts Payable						-44,160.31				-17,454.70	-26,705.61
Undelivered Orders						-446,624.09				15,134.03	-461,758.12
Subtotal		95		2700		-0-	989,354.00	------	953,408.82	35,945.18	-0-
Trust Fund Accounts											
Contributions, National Commission On Libraries And Information Science											
Fund Resources:											
Undisbursed Funds	No Year	95		8078				------	------		2,408.34
Fund Equities:											
Unobligated Balances (Unexpired)						2,408.34					-2,408.34
Subtotal		95		8078		-0-		------	------		-0-
Total, National Commission On Libraries And Information Science						------	989,354.00	------	953,408.82	35,945.18	
National Council On Disability											
General Fund Accounts											
Salaries And Expenses, National Council On Disability											
Fund Resources:											
Undisbursed Funds	2007	95		3500			3,125,492.00	------	2,590,595.12		534,896.88
	2006					841,965.33	------	------	456,827.85	------	385,137.48
	2005					506,811.90	------	------	463,675.22	------	43,136.68
	2004					113,937.26	------	------	80,550.00	------	33,387.26
	2003					20,836.79	------	------	------	------	20,836.79
	2002					28,801.03	------	------	5,040.91	23,760.12	
	No Year						300,000.00	------	------		300,000.00

Footnotes At End Of Chapter

Appropriations, Outlays, and Balances – Continued

Appropriation or Fund Account (Title)	Period of Availability	Reg	Tr From	Account Number	Sub No.	Balances, Beginning Of Fiscal Year	Appropriations And Other Obligational Authority[1]	Transfers Borrowings And Investment (Net)[2]	Outlays (Net)	Balances Withdrawn And Other Transactions[3]	Balances, End Of Fiscal Year[4]
Salaries And Expenses, National Council On Disability - Continued											
Fund Equities:											
Unobligated Balances (Expired)						-218,800.37				-20,443.88	-198,356.49
Unobligated Balances (Unexpired)										300,000.00	-300,000.00
Accounts Payable						-89,746.87				32,649.00	-122,395.87
Undelivered Orders						-1,203,805.07			3,596,689.10	-507,162.34	-696,642.73
Subtotal		95		3500		-0-	3,425,492.00			-171,197.10	-0-
Total, National Council On Disability							3,425,492.00		3,596,689.10	-171,197.10	
National Credit Union Administration											
Public Enterprise Funds											
Operating Fund, National Credit Union Administration											
Fund Resources:											
Undisbursed Funds	No Year	25		4056		500,636.45		338,000.00	337,982.05		500,654.40
Investments In Public Debt Securities						42,305,000.00		-338,000.00			41,967,000.00
Accounts Receivable						6,210.95				-94,461.95	100,672.90
Fund Equities:											
Unobligated Balances (Unexpired)						-28,559,414.50				-5,154,601.87	-23,404,812.63
Accounts Payable						-11,652,432.90				4,911,081.77	-16,563,514.67
Undelivered Orders						-2,600,000.00					-2,600,000.00
Subtotal		25		4056		-0-			337,982.05	-337,982.05	-0-
National Credit Union Share Insurance Fund											
Fund Resources:											
Undisbursed Funds	No Year	25		4468		14,746.39		-369,611,750.00	-369,602,874.30		5,870.69
Unrealized Discount On Investments						-72,882,812.50		-18,781,250.00			-91,664,062.50
Investments In Public Debt Securities						6,749,097,000.00		388,393,000.00			7,137,490,000.00
Accounts Receivable						[7]236,255,768.01				-82,512,619.19	318,768,387.20
Fund Equities:											
Unobligated Balances (Unexpired)						[7]-6,835,862,095.33				430,024,151.86	-7,265,886,247.19
Accounts Payable						-76,422,606.57				22,091,341.63	-98,513,948.20
Undelivered Orders						-200,000.00				369,602,874.30	-200,000.00
Subtotal		25		4468		-0-			-369,602,874.30	369,602,874.30	-0-
Community Development Revolving Loan Fund, National Credit Union											
Fund Resources:											
Undisbursed Funds	2007-2008	25		4472			940,500.00		109,794.54		830,705.46
	2006-2007					927,625.00			927,625.00		
	2005-2006					500.94			500.94		
	2004					30,294.28					30,294.28
	2003-2004					17,569.48					17,569.48
	No Year					326,186.08		5,400,000.00	5,008,028.54		718,157.54
Investments In Public Debt Securities						8,500,000.00		-5,400,000.00			3,100,000.00
Fund Equities:											
Unobligated Balances (Unexpired)						-9,703,811.08				-5,054,948.08	-4,648,863.00
Accounts Payable											
Undelivered Orders						-98,364.70				-50,500.94	-47,863.76
Subtotal		25		4472		-0-	940,500.00		6,045,949.02	-5,105,449.02	-0-

Appropriations, Outlays, and Balances - Continued

Appropriation or Fund Account — Title	Period of Availability	Reg	Tr From	Account Number	Sub No.	Balances, Beginning Of Fiscal Year	Appropriations And Other Obligational Authority[1]	Transfers Borrowings And Investment (Net)[2]	Outlays (Net)	Balances Withdrawn And Other Transactions[3]	Balances, End Of Fiscal Year[4]
Total, National Credit Union Administration						——	940,500.00	——	-363,218,943.23	364,159,443.23	
National Education Goals Panel											
General Fund Accounts											
Expenses, National Education Goals Panel											
Fund Resources:											
Undisbursed Funds	2002	95		2650		39,168.27				39,168.27	
Fund Equities:											
Unobligated Balances (Expired)						-14,256.27				-14,256.27	
Accounts Payable						-6,000.00				-6,000.00	
Undelivered Orders						-18,912.00				-18,912.00	
Subtotal		95		2650		-0-					-0-
Total, National Education Goals Panel						——					
National Endowment For The Arts											
General Fund Accounts											
Grants And Administration, National Endowment For The Arts											
Fund Resources:											
Undisbursed Funds	No Year	59		0100		120,700,694.55	124,561,844.00		123,360,006.16	——	121,902,532.39
Fund Equities:											
Unobligated Balances (Unexpired)						-3,845,188.35				1,093,786.49	-4,938,974.84
Accounts Payable						[7]-39,318,599.04				9,002,934.81	-48,321,533.85
Undelivered Orders						[7]-77,536,907.16				-8,894,883.46	-68,642,023.70
Subtotal		59		0100		-0-	124,561,844.00		123,360,006.16	1,201,837.84	-0-
Arts And Artifacts Indemnity Fund, National Endowment For The Arts											
Fund Resources:											
Undisbursed Funds	No Year	59		0101		280,484.00					280,484.00
Fund Equities:											
Unobligated Balances (Unexpired)						-280,484.00					-280,484.00
Subtotal		59		0101		-0-					-0-
Challenge America Grants, Challenge America Arts Fund											
Fund Resources:											
Undisbursed Funds	No Year	59		0400		244,824.27			81,545.90		163,278.37
Fund Equities:											
Unobligated Balances (Unexpired)						-27,722.27				16,518.10	-44,240.37
Accounts Payable						-130,391.31				-61,353.31	-69,038.00
Undelivered Orders						-86,710.69				-36,710.69	-50,000.00
Subtotal		59		0400		-0-			81,545.90	-81,545.90	-0-

Footnotes At End Of Chapter

Appropriations, Outlays, and Balances – Continued

Appropriation or Fund Account — Title	Account Symbol — Period of Availability	Dept — Reg	Dept — Tr From	Account Number	Sub No.	Balances, Beginning Of Fiscal Year	Appropriations And Other Obligational Authority[1]	Transfers Borrowings And Investment (Net)[2]	Outlays (Net)	Balances Withdrawn And Other Transactions[3]	Balances, End Of Fiscal Year[4]
Trust Fund Accounts											
Gifts And Donations, National Endowment For The Arts											
Fund Resources:											
Undisbursed Funds	No Year	59		8040		2,545,946.58	1,747,757.08	1,139,289.28	1,847,226.90	------	3,585,766.04
Unrealized Discount On Investments						-54,114.30		29,502.32		------	-24,611.98
Investments In Public Debt Securities						2,293,791.60		-1,168,791.60		------	1,125,000.00
Fund Equities:											
Unobligated Balances (Unexpired)						-4,290,752.57				-1,975,531.26	-2,315,221.31
Accounts Payable						7-125,613.65				370,062.21	-495,675.86
Undelivered Orders						7-369,257.66				1,505,999.23	-1,875,256.89
Subtotal		59		8040		-0-	1,747,757.08		1,847,226.90	-99,469.82	-0-
Deductions For Offsetting Receipts											
Proprietary Receipts From The Public							-65,299.72		-65,299.72	------	------
Intrabudgetary Transactions							-42,698.97		-42,698.97	------	------
Total, National Endowment For The Arts							126,201,602.39		125,180,780.27	1,020,822.12	------
National Endowment For The Humanities											
General Fund Accounts											
Grants And Administration, National Endowment For The Humanities											
Fund Resources:											
Undisbursed Funds	No Year	59		0200		127,046,735.07	141,105,150.00		137,457,940.42		130,693,944.65
Accounts Receivable						26,225.16				26,225.16	
Unfilled Customer Orders						1,000,000.00				-52,602.00	1,052,602.00
Fund Equities:											
Unobligated Balances (Unexpired)						-5,642,386.10				-1,098,641.24	-4,543,744.86
Accounts Payable						-22,282,168.07				659,897.25	-22,942,065.32
Undelivered Orders						-100,148,406.06				4,112,330.41	-104,260,736.47
Subtotal		59		0200		-0-	141,105,150.00		137,457,940.42	3,647,209.58	-0-
Trust Fund Accounts											
Gifts And Donations, National Endowment For The Humanities											
Fund Resources:											
Undisbursed Funds	No Year	59		8050		691,660.94	293,043.47		620,897.13		363,807.28
Fund Equities:											
Unobligated Balances (Unexpired)						-545,539.89				-229,940.91	-315,598.98
Accounts Payable						-33,716.97				-25,402.63	-8,314.34
Undelivered Orders						-112,404.08				-72,510.12	-39,893.96
Subtotal		59		8050		-0-	293,043.47		620,897.13	-327,853.66	-0-
Total, National Endowment For The Humanities							141,398,193.47		138,078,837.55	3,319,355.92	

Appropriations, Outlays, and Balances - Continued

Appropriation or Fund Account — Title	Period of Availability	Dept Reg	Tr From	Account Number	Sub No.	Balances, Beginning Of Fiscal Year	Appropriations And Other Obligational Authority[1]	Transfers Borrowings And Investment (Net)[2]	Outlays (Net)	Balances Withdrawn And Other Transactions[3]	Balances, End Of Fiscal Year[4]
Institute Of Museum And Library Services											
General Fund Accounts											
Grants And Administration, Office Of Museum Services, Institute Of Museum And Library Services											
Fund Resources:											
Undisbursed Funds	No Year	59		0300		1,357,833.51			508,991.06		848,842.45
Fund Equities:											
Unobligated Balances (Unexpired)						-62,043.06				40,352.16	-102,395.22
Accounts Payable						-328,816.67				-318,816.67	-10,000.00
Undelivered Orders						-966,973.78				-230,526.55	-736,447.23
Subtotal		59		0300		-0-			508,991.06	-508,991.06	-0-
Office Of Museum And Library Services: Grants And Administration, Institute Of Museum And Library Services											
Fund Resources:											
Undisbursed Funds	2003	59		0301		10,522,375.84			5,626,455.35		4,895,920.49
	2002					3,836,705.13			2,572,920.38	1,263,784.75	
	No Year					338,258,869.88	247,204,746.00		247,428,645.56		338,034,970.32
Fund Equities:											
Unobligated Balances (Expired)						-1,603,243.95				-762,160.15	-841,083.80
Unobligated Balances (Unexpired)						-18,349,472.24				-7,939,001.79	-10,410,470.45
Accounts Payable						-39,966,049.84				1,217,593.55	-41,183,643.39
Undelivered Orders						-292,699,184.82				-2,203,491.65	-290,495,693.17
Subtotal		59		0301		-0-	247,204,746.00		255,628,021.29	-8,423,275.29	-0-
Trust Fund Accounts											
Gifts And Donations, Institute Of Museum Services											
Fund Resources:											
Undisbursed Funds	No Year	59		8080		36,625.48	1,406,645.79		16,756.97		1,426,514.30
Fund Equities:											
Unobligated Balances (Unexpired)						-21,857.52				1,003,856.78	-1,025,714.30
Undelivered Orders						-14,767.96				386,032.04	-400,800.00
Subtotal		59		8080		-0-	1,406,645.79		16,756.97	1,389,888.82	-0-
Total, Institute Of Museum And Library Services							248,611,391.79		256,153,769.32	-7,542,377.53	
National Labor Relations Board											
General Fund Accounts											
Salaries And Expenses, National Labor Relations Board											
Fund Resources:											
Undisbursed Funds	2007	63		0100		17,514,151.35	251,507,470.00		235,908,112.14		15,599,357.86
	2006					2,498,261.81			15,875,388.01		1,638,763.34
	2005					1,002,075.10			730,840.05		1,767,421.76
	2004					1,704,078.86			-948.59		1,003,023.69
	2003								4,267.84		1,699,811.02

Appropriations, Outlays, and Balances – Continued

Appropriation or Fund Account Title	Period of Availability	Dept Reg	Tr From	Account Number	Sub No.	Balances, Beginning Of Fiscal Year	Appropriations And Other Obligational Authority[1]	Transfers Borrowings And Investment (Net)[2]	Outlays (Net)	Balances Withdrawn And Other Transactions[3]	Balances, End Of Fiscal Year[4]
Salaries And Expenses, National Labor Relations Board - Continued											
Fund Resources: - Continued											
Undisbursed Funds - Continued	2002					705,515.12			-4,437.03	709,952.15	-------
Fund Equities:											
Unobligated Balances (Expired)						-5,028,944.05			-------	331,295.86	-5,360,239.91
Accounts Payable						-11,658,614.93			-------	1,174,850.38	-12,833,465.31
Undelivered Orders						-6,736,523.26			252,513,222.42	-3,221,850.81	-3,514,672.45
	Subtotal	63		0100		-0-	251,507,470.00			-1,005,752.42	-0-
Deductions For Offsetting Receipts											
Proprietary Receipts From The Public							-401,902.87		-401,902.87		
Total, National Labor Relations Board							251,105,567.13		252,111,319.55	-1,005,752.42	
National Mediation Board											
General Fund Accounts											
Salaries And Expenses, National Mediation Board											
Fund Resources:											
Undisbursed Funds	2007	95		2400		-------	11,595,760.00		10,529,544.45		1,066,215.55
	2006					1,204,186.79			870,577.50		333,609.29
	2005					471,302.62			-------		471,302.62
	2004					564,635.65			-------		564,635.65
	2003					641,564.53			-------		641,564.53
	2002					601,909.56			601,909.56		-------
Fund Equities:											
Unobligated Balances (Expired)						-2,566,664.54			-------	-343,668.00	-2,222,996.54
Accounts Payable						-450,777.30			-------	-18,199.02	-432,578.28
Undelivered Orders						-466,157.31			11,400,121.95	-44,404.49	-421,752.82
	Subtotal	95		2400		-0-	11,595,760.00			195,638.05	-0-
Deductions For Offsetting Receipts											
Proprietary Receipts From The Public							-163.80		-163.80		
Total, National Mediation Board							11,595,596.20		11,399,958.15	195,638.05	
National Transportation Safety Board											
General Fund Accounts											
Salaries And Expenses, National Transportation Safety Board											
Fund Resources:											
Undisbursed Funds	2007	95		0310		-------	79,338,308.00		66,450,546.36		12,887,761.64
	2006					12,835,111.81			11,207,484.01		1,627,627.80
	2005					1,953,475.15			839,459.81		1,114,015.34
	2004					1,132,264.96			10,808.10		1,121,456.86

Appropriations, Outlays, and Balances - Continued

Appropriation or Fund Account — Title	Period of Availability	Dept Reg	Tr From	Account Number	Sub No.	Balances, Beginning Of Fiscal Year	Appropriations And Other Obligational Authority[1]	Transfers Borrowings And Investment (Net)[2]	Outlays (Net)	Balances Withdrawn And Other Transactions[3]	Balances, End Of Fiscal Year[4]
	2003					2,497,983.15			-23,472.14		2,521,455.29
	2002-2003					4,074.86					4,074.86
	2002					1,817,407.07			16,182.26	1,801,224.81	
	No Year					3,021,485.74	-1,000,000.00		-1,050,533.02		3,072,018.76
Accounts Receivable	No Year					2,401.03				2,401.03	-0-
Fund Equities:											
Unobligated Balances (Expired)						-5,317,977.62				3,076,360.32	-8,394,337.94
Unobligated Balances (Unexpired)						-2,830,852.57				65,936.00	-2,896,788.57
Accounts Payable						-3,949,485.96				-743,769.81	-3,205,716.15
Undelivered Orders						-11,165,887.62				-3,314,319.73	-7,851,567.89
	Subtotal	95		0310		-0-	78,338,308.00		77,450,475.38	887,832.62	-0-
Emergency Fund, National Transportation Safety Board											
Fund Resources:											
Undisbursed Funds	No Year	95		0311		1,997,884.00					1,997,884.00
Fund Equities:											
Unobligated Balances (Unexpired)						-1,997,884.00					-1,997,884.00
	Subtotal	95		0311		-0-					-0-
Deductions For Offsetting Receipts											
Proprietary Receipts From The Public							-483.54		-483.54		
Total, National Transportation Safety Board							78,337,824.46		77,449,991.84	887,832.62	
National Veterans Business Development Corporation											
General Fund Accounts											
Expenses, National Veterans Business Development Corporation											
Fund Resources:											
Undisbursed Funds	No Year	95		0350			1,480,842.00		1,480,842.00		
Total, National Veterans Business Development Corporation							1,480,842.00		1,480,842.00		
Neighborhood Reinvestment Corporation											
General Fund Accounts											
Payment To Neighborhood Reinvestment Corporation, Neighborhood Reinvestment Corporation											
Fund Resources:											
Undisbursed Funds	2007	95		1350			116,820,000.00		116,820,000.00		
	2005					1.09					1.09
Fund Equities:											
Unobligated Balances (Expired)						-1.09					-1.09
	Subtotal	95		1350		-0-	116,820,000.00		116,820,000.00		-0-
Total, Neighborhood Reinvestment Corporation							116,820,000.00		116,820,000.00		

Footnotes At End Of Chapter

Appropriations, Outlays, and Balances – Continued

Appropriation or Fund Account Title	Period of Availability	Dept Reg	Tr From	Account Number	Sub No.	Balances, Beginning Of Fiscal Year	Appropriations And Other Obligational Authority[1]	Transfers Borrowings And Investment (Net)[2]	Outlays (Net)	Balances Withdrawn And Other Transactions[3]	Balances, End Of Fiscal Year[4]
Nuclear Regulatory Commission											
General Fund Accounts											
Salaries And Expenses, Nuclear Regulatory Commission											
Fund Resources:											
Undisbursed Funds	No Year	31		0200		274,281,411.93	816,528,889.00		749,562,020.52		341,248,280.41
Accounts Receivable						506,133.02				90,110.22	416,022.80
Unfilled Customer Orders						3,527,632.70				92,686.39	3,434,946.31
Fund Equities:											
Unobligated Balances (Unexpired)						-73,780,125.64				-3,870,418.37	-69,909,707.27
Accounts Payable						-49,274,420.91				-678,226.15	-48,596,194.76
Undelivered Orders						-155,260,631.10				71,332,716.39	-226,593,347.49
Subtotal		31		0200		-0-	816,528,889.00		749,562,020.52	66,966,868.48	-0-
Office Of Inspector General, Nuclear Regulatory Commission											
Fund Resources:											
Undisbursed Funds	No Year	31		0300		2,420,938.21	8,359,618.00		8,977,790.24		1,802,765.97
Fund Equities:											
Unobligated Balances (Unexpired)						-936,793.92				-390,641.38	-546,152.54
Accounts Payable						-505,035.44				-30,266.57	-474,768.87
Undelivered Orders						-979,108.85				-197,264.29	-781,844.56
Subtotal		31		0300		-0-	8,359,618.00		8,977,790.24	-618,172.24	-0-
Special Fund Accounts											
Nuclear Facilities Fees Fund, Nuclear Regulatory Commission											
Fund Resources:											
Undisbursed Funds	No Year	31		5280		64.72	4,525.15				4,589.87
Fund Equities:											
Unobligated Balances (Unexpired)						-64.72				4,525.15	-4,589.87
Subtotal		31		5280		-0-	4,525.15			4,525.15	-0-
Deductions For Offsetting Receipts											
Proprietary Receipts From The Public							-141,877.56		-141,877.56		
Offsetting Governmental Receipts							-669,249,476.05		-669,249,476.05		
Total, Nuclear Regulatory Commission							155,501,678.54		89,148,457.15	66,353,221.39	
Nuclear Waste Technical Review Board											
General Fund Accounts											
Salaries And Expenses, Nuclear Waste Technical Review Board											
Fund Resources:											
Undisbursed Funds	No Year	48		0500		433,984.87	3,591,406.00		3,522,187.52		503,203.35
Accounts Receivable						36,080.00				36,080.00	

Appropriations, Outlays, and Balances - Continued

Appropriation or Fund Account (Title)	Period of Availability	Reg	Tr From	Account Number	Sub No.	Balances, Beginning Of Fiscal Year	Appropriations And Other Obligational Authority[1]	Transfers Borrowings And Investment (Net)[2]	Outlays (Net)	Balances Withdrawn And Other Transactions[3]	Balances, End Of Fiscal Year[4]
Fund Equities:											
Unobligated Balances (Unexpired)						-257,137.01				95,801.98	-352,938.99
Accounts Payable						-84,166.27				-4,407.14	-79,759.13
Undelivered Orders						-128,761.59				-58,256.36	-70,505.23
						-0-	3,591,406.00		3,522,187.52	69,218.48	-0-
Subtotal		48		0500			3,591,406.00		3,522,187.52	69,218.48	
Total, Nuclear Waste Technical Review Board							3,591,406.00		3,522,187.52	69,218.48	
Occupational Safety And Health Review Commission											
General Fund Accounts											
Salaries And Expenses, Occupational Safety And Health Review Commission											
Fund Resources:											
Undisbursed Funds	2007	95		2100			10,470,779.00		8,794,169.53		1,676,609.47
	2006					1,902,251.83			1,270,630.14		631,621.69
	2005					863,418.92			334,987.34		528,431.58
	2004					476,444.53			25,470.14		450,974.39
	2003					766,037.46			444.45		765,593.01
	2002					883,383.69				883,383.69	
Fund Equities:											
Unobligated Balances (Expired)						-2,363,573.29				-411,594.93	-1,951,978.36
Accounts Payable						-502,391.05				107,674.89	-610,065.94
Undelivered Orders						-2,025,572.09				-534,386.25	-1,491,185.84
						-0-	10,470,779.00		10,425,701.60	45,077.40	-0-
Subtotal		95		2100			10,470,779.00		10,425,701.60	45,077.40	
Deductions For Offsetting Receipts											
Proprietary Receipts From The Public							-1,206.25		-1,206.25		
Total, Occupational Safety And Health Review Commission							10,469,572.75		10,424,495.35	45,077.40	
Office Of Government Ethics											
General Fund Accounts											
Salaries And Expenses, Office Of Government Ethics											
Fund Resources:											
Undisbursed Funds	2007	95		1100			11,115,085.00		9,952,682.63		1,162,402.37
	2006-2007						38,000.00		10,812.32		27,187.68
	2006					1,136,651.43	-38,000.00		958,887.35		139,764.08
	2005-2006					21,373.18			18,844.35		2,528.83
	2005					270,639.87			17,262.00		253,377.87
	2004-2005					2,646.78					2,646.78
	2004					521,187.88			54,727.10		466,460.78
	2003-2004					1,793.92					1,793.92

Footnotes At End Of Chapter

Appropriations, Outlays, and Balances – Continued

Appropriation or Fund Account — Title	Period of Availability	Reg	Tr From	Account Number	Sub No.	Balances, Beginning Of Fiscal Year	Appropriations And Other Obligational Authority[1]	Transfers Borrowings And Investment (Net)[2]	Outlays (Net)	Balances Withdrawn And Other Transactions[3]	Balances, End Of Fiscal Year[4]
Salaries And Expenses, Office Of Government Ethics -Continued											
Fund Resources: - Continued											
Undisbursed Funds -Continued											
	2003					372,543.07					372,543.07
	2002-2003					15,866.16					15,866.16
	2002					177,597.60				177,597.60	
	2001-2002					2,254.82				2,254.82	
Fund Equities:											
Unobligated Balances (Expired)	2003					-1,006,498.87				152,868.02	-1,159,366.89
	2002-2003					-893,411.69				-35,120.50	-858,291.19
Accounts Payable	2002					-622,644.15				-195,730.69	-426,913.46
Undelivered Orders	2001-2002					-0-	11,115,085.00		11,013,215.75	101,869.25	-0-
Subtotal		95		1100		-0-	11,115,085.00		11,013,215.75	101,869.25	-0-
Deductions For Offsetting Receipts											
Proprietary Receipts From The Public							-765.02		-765.02		
Total, Office of Government Ethics							11,114,319.98		11,012,450.73	101,869.25	
Office Of Navajo And Hopi Indian Relocation											
General Fund Accounts											
Salaries And Expenses, Navajo And Hopi Indian Relocation Commission											
Fund Resources:											
Undisbursed Funds	No Year	48		1100		12,094,499.25	8,509,004.00		9,088,308.26		11,515,194.99
Fund Equities:											
Unobligated Balances (Unexpired)						-8,786,879.31				823,057.23	-9,609,936.54
Accounts Payable						-292,309.20				23,903.48	-316,212.68
Undelivered Orders						-3,015,310.74				-1,426,264.97	-1,589,045.77
Subtotal				1100	48	-0-	8,509,004.00		9,088,308.26	-579,304.26	-0-
Total, Office Of Navajo And Hopi Indian Relocation							8,509,004.00		9,088,308.26	-579,304.26	
Office Of Special Counsel											
General Fund Accounts											
Salaries And Expenses, Office Of Special Counsel											
Fund Resources:											
Undisbursed Funds											
	2007	62		0100			15,524,186.00		13,843,445.52		1,680,740.48
	2006					1,695,699.22			1,193,928.83		501,770.39
	2005					785,382.94			63,692.04		721,690.90
	2004-2005					231,940.00					231,940.00
	2004					125,109.95			9,552.33		115,557.62
	2003-2004					74,201.39					10,984.47
	2002					76,383.50				76,383.50	74,201.39
Fund Equities:											
Unobligated Balances (Expired)						-983,874.94				774,319.68	-1,758,194.62
Accounts Payable						-538,215.96				7,390.64	-545,606.60

Appropriation or Fund Account (Title)	Period of Availability	Reg	Tr From	Account Number	Sub No.	Balances, Beginning Of Fiscal Year	Appropriations And Other Obligational Authority[1]	Transfers Borrowings And Investment (Net)[2]	Outlays (Net)	Balances Withdrawn And Other Transactions[3]	Balances, End Of Fiscal Year[4]
Undelivered Orders	Subtotal	62		0100		-1,477,610.57 -0-	15,524,186.00		15,110,618.72	-444,526.54 413,567.28	-1,033,084.03 -0-
Deductions For Offsetting Receipts											
Proprietary Receipts From The Public						-5,156.75	-5,156.75		-5,156.75		
Total, Office Of Special Counsel							15,519,029.25		15,105,461.97	413,567.28	
Other Commissions And Boards											
General Fund Accounts											
Salaries And Expenses, Office Of Nuclear Waste Negotiator											
Fund Resources:											
Undisbursed Funds	No Year	48		0700		-6,540.38					[5,6]6,540.38
Fund Equities:											
Undisbursed Funds	Subtotal	48		0700		6,540.38					[6]6,540.38
Unobligated Balances (Unexpired)						-0-					-0-
Salaries And Expenses, Commission For The Study Of International Migration And Cooperative Economic Development[6]											
Fund Resources:											
Undisbursed Funds	No Year	48		1400		-545.00					[5]-545.00
Fund Equities:											
Undisbursed Funds	Subtotal	48		1400		545.00					[5]545.00
Unobligated Balances (Unexpired)						-0-					-0-
Salaries And Expenses, Franklin Delano Roosevelt Memorial Commission											
Fund Resources:											
Undisbursed Funds	No Year	76		0700		104,992.73				104,992.73	
Expenses, White House Commission On The National Moment Of Remembrance											
Fund Resources:											
Undisbursed Funds	No Year	95		2725		194,533.13	248,810.00		249,465.42		193,877.71
Fund Equities:											
Unobligated Balances (Unexpired)						-112,668.55				67,616.00	-180,284.55
Accounts Payable						-9,864.58				3,728.58	-13,593.16
						-72,000.00				-72,000.00	
Undelivered Orders	Subtotal	95		2725		-0-	248,810.00		249,465.42	-655.42	-0-
Salaries And Expenses, Commission For The Preservation Of America's Heritage Abroad											
Fund Resources:											
Undisbursed Funds	2007	95		3700		58,785.39	493,242.00		394,323.67		98,918.33
	2006								46,116.10		12,669.29
	2005					4,583.83					4,583.83
	2004					2,498.65					2,498.65
	2003					5,456.07					5,456.07
	2002					314.13				314.13	

Footnotes At End Of Chapter

Appropriations, Outlays, and Balances – Continued

Appropriation or Fund Account — Title	Period of Availability	Dept Reg	Tr From	Account Number	Sub No.	Balances, Beginning Of Fiscal Year	Appropriations And Other Obligational Authority[1]	Transfers Borrowings And Investment (Net)[2]	Outlays (Net)	Balances Withdrawn And Other Transactions[3]	Balances, End Of Fiscal Year[4]
Salaries And Expenses, Commission For The Preservation Of America's Heritage Abroad - Continued											
Fund Equities:											
Unobligated Balances (Expired)						-13,612.27				9,908.58	-23,520.85
Accounts Payable						-47,542.59				-41,566.37	-5,976.22
Undelivered Orders						-10,483.21				84,145.89	-94,629.10
Administrative Expenses, United States Railway Association[6]	Subtotal	95		3700		-0-	493,242.00		440,439.77	52,802.23	-0-
Fund Resources:											
Undisbursed Funds	No Year	98		0100					534.98		5,534.98
Special Fund Accounts											
White House Commission On The National Moment Of Remembrance											
Fund Resources:											
Undisbursed Funds	No Year	95		5484		283,206.95	154,703.41		250,717.87		187,192.49
Fund Equities:											
Unobligated Balances (Unexpired)	Subtotal	95		5484		-283,206.95	154,703.41		250,717.87	-96,014.46	-187,192.49
						-0-				-96,014.46	-0-
Trust Fund Accounts											
Gifts And Donations, Federal Judicial Center											
Fund Resources:											
Undisbursed Funds	No Year	10		8123		545,147.61	102,699.79		86,268.16		561,579.24
Accounts Receivable						60,000.00				60,000.00	
Fund Equities:											
Unobligated Balances (Unexpired)						-604,389.05				-43,568.37	-560,820.68
Accounts Payable						-758.56					-758.56
	Subtotal	10		8123		-0-	102,699.79		86,268.16	16,431.63	-0-
Gifts And Donations, Commission For The Preservation Of American Heritage Abroad											
Fund Resources:											
Undisbursed Funds	No Year	95		8268		142,039.28	464,391.79		287,904.85	176,486.94	318,526.22
Fund Equities:											
Unobligated Balances (Unexpired)	Subtotal	95		8268		-142,039.28	464,391.79		287,904.85	176,486.94	-318,526.22
						-0-					-0-
Total, Other Commissions And Boards						104,992.73	1,463,846.99		1,315,331.05	254,043.65	-534.98

Appropriations, Outlays, and Balances - Continued

Appropriation or Fund Account — Title	Period of Availability	Dept Reg	Tr From	Account Number	Sub No.	Balances, Beginning Of Fiscal Year	Appropriations And Other Obligational Authority[1]	Transfers Borrowings And Investment (Net)[2]	Outlays (Net)	Balances Withdrawn And Other Transactions[3]	Balances, End Of Fiscal Year[4]
Office Of The Federal Coordinator For Alaska National Gas Transportation Projects											
General Fund Accounts											
Office Of The Federal Coordinator For Alaska Natural Gas Transportation											
Fund Resources:											
Undisbursed Funds	No Year	95		2850				887,384.15	589,438.42		297,945.73
Fund Equities:											
Unobligated Balances (Unexpired)										271,140.86	-271,140.86
Accounts Payable										18,502.37	-18,502.37
Undelivered Orders										8,302.50	-8,302.50
									589,438.42	297,945.73	-0-
Subtotal		95		2850		-0-		887,384.15	589,438.42	297,945.73	
Total, Office Of The Federal Coordinator For Alaska Natural Gas Transportation Projects											
Panama Canal Commission											
Public Enterprise Funds											
Panama Canal Commission Dissolution Fund											
Fund Resources:											
Undisbursed Funds	No Year	95		4073		141,644.17					141,644.17
Fund Equities:											
Unobligated Balances (Unexpired)						-141,644.17					-141,644.17
Subtotal		95		4073		-0-					-0-
Total, Panama Canal Commission											
Postal Service-Payments To The Postal Service											
General Fund Accounts											
Payment To The Postal Service Fund											
Fund Resources:											
Undisbursed Funds	2007	18		1001			102,000,000.00		102,000,000.00		
	No Year	18		1001			1,761,760.00		1,761,760.00		
Subtotal		18		1001	2	-0-	103,761,760.00		103,761,760.00		
Total, Postal Service-Payments To The Postal Service							103,761,760.00		103,761,760.00		
Postal Service											
Public Enterprise Funds											
Postal Service Fund											
Fund Resources:	No Year	18		4020		[15]52,715,403.73		[16]5,353,627,000.00	[15]5,093,142,389.53	[17]19,847,288.74	[15]187,921,918.00
Undisbursed Funds						4,232,527,000.00		-3,253,627,000.00			978,900,000.00
Investments In Public Debt Securities		18		4020		4,179,811,596.27		2,100,000,000.00			1,166,821,918.00
Subtotal									5,093,142,389.53	19,847,288.74	1,166,821,918.00

Appropriations, Outlays, and Balances – Continued

Appropriation or Fund Account — Title	Account Symbol — Dept Reg	Dept Tr From	Account Number	Sub No.	Period of Availability	Balances, Beginning Of Fiscal Year	Appropriations And Other Obligational Authority[1]	Transfers Borrowings And Investment (Net)[2]	Outlays (Net)	Balances Withdrawn And Other Transactions[3]	Balances, End Of Fiscal Year[4]
Postal Service Fund, Undistributed SIBAC Chargebacks[6]											
Fund Resources:											
Undisbursed Funds	18		4020	3	No Year	-590.77					[5]-590.77
Deductions For Offsetting Receipts											
Proprietary Receipts From The Public							-0.26		-0.26		
Total, Postal Service						4,179,811,005.50	-0.26	2,100,000,000.00	5,093,142,389.27	19,847,288.74	1,166,821,327.23
Presidio Trust											
Public Enterprise Funds											
Expenses, Presidio Trust											
Fund Resources:											
Undisbursed Funds	95		4331		No Year	6,174,847.56	19,860,340.00	6,125,000.00	27,130,527.29		5,029,660.27
Investments In Public Debt Securities						103,031,000.00		-6,125,000.00			96,906,000.00
Accounts Receivable						5,740,002.51				1,131,344.22	4,608,658.29
Fund Equities:											
Unobligated Balances (Unexpired)						-61,693,397.13				3,505,803.79	-65,199,200.92
Accounts Payable						-13,121,768.43				1,250,048.63	-14,371,817.06
Undelivered Orders						-40,130,684.51				-13,157,383.93	-26,973,300.58
Subtotal	95		4331			-0-	19,860,340.00		27,130,527.29	-7,270,187.29	-0-
Total, Presidio Trust							19,860,340.00		27,130,527.29	-7,270,187.29	
Railroad Retirement Board											
General Fund Accounts											
Dual Benefits Payments Account, Railroad Retirement Board											
Fund Resources:											
Undisbursed Funds	60		0111		2007		88,000,000.00		86,486,516.90		1,513,483.10
					2006	1,004,178.98					1,004,178.98
					2005	817,521.18					817,521.18
					2004	1,022,415.63					1,022,415.63
					2003	1,774,883.66					1,774,883.66
					2002	3,850,011.28				3,850,011.28	
Fund Equities:											
Unobligated Balances (Expired)						-8,469,010.73				-2,336,528.18	-6,132,482.55
Subtotal	60		0111			-0-	88,000,000.00		86,486,516.90	1,513,483.10	-0-
Federal Payments To The Railroad Retirement Accounts, Railroad Retirement Board											
Fund Resources:											
Undisbursed Funds	60		0113		2007-2008	150,000.00	150,000.00		459.85		149,540.15
					2006-2007				88,940.53		61,059.47
					2005-2006	64,126.91					64,126.91
					2004-2005	73,972.68					73,972.68

Appropriations, Outlays, and Balances - Continued

Appropriation or Fund Account — Title	Dept Reg	Tr From	Account Number	Sub No.	Period of Availability	Balances, Beginning Of Fiscal Year	Appropriations And Other Obligational Authority[1]	Transfers Borrowings And Investment (Net)[2]	Outlays (Net)	Balances Withdrawn And Other Transactions[3]	Balances, End Of Fiscal Year[4]
					2003-2004	79,333.83					79,333.83
					2002-2003	67,443.06					67,443.06
					No Year		460,000,000.00		460,000,000.00		
	60		0113		Subtotal		460,150,000.00		460,089,400.38		
Trust Fund Accounts											
Fund Equities:											
Unobligated Balances (Expired)						-284,876.48				61,059.47	-345,935.95
Unobligated Balances (Unexpired)						-150,000.00				459.85	-149,540.15
						-0-				60,599.62	-0-
Social Security Equivalent Benefit Account, Railroad Retirement Board											
Fund Resources:											
Undisbursed Funds	60		8010		No Year	-6,392,890.57		[18]9,422,665.62	[18]5,862,277,230.12		19,537,468.00
Investments In Public Debt Securities						723,754,000.00		980,000.00			724,734,000.00
Fund Equities:											
Unobligated Balances (Unexpired)						-174,476,149.24	[18]5,897,630,254.31			1,342,672.04	-175,818,821.28
Accounts Payable						-542,884,960.19		-8,442,665.62		25,567,686.53	-568,452,646.72
	60		8010		Subtotal	-0-	5,897,630,254.31		5,862,277,230.12	26,910,358.57	-0-
Railroad Retirement Account											
Fund Resources:											
Undisbursed Funds	60		8011		No Year	2,681,862.17		-119,071,971.43	[20]4,027,151,287.67		20,647,722.05
Investments In Public Debt Securities						476,712,000.00		119,469,000.00			596,181,000.00
Fund Equities:											
Unobligated Balances (Unexpired)						-160,007,921.39	[20]4,164,189,118.98			131,171,660.40	-291,179,581.79
Accounts Payable						-319,385,940.78		397,028.57		6,263,199.48	-325,649,140.26
	60		8011		Subtotal	-0-	4,164,189,118.98		4,027,151,287.67	137,434,859.88	-0-
Limitation On The Office Of The Inspector General, Railroad Retirement Board											
Fund Resources:											
Undisbursed Funds	60		8018		2007	486,605.50	7,172,686.00		6,564,911.27		607,774.73
					2006	116,829.28			433,072.71		53,532.79
					2005	42,429.77			53,697.42		63,131.86
					2004	2,645.79					42,429.77
					2003	26,823.95					2,645.79
					2002	53,129.00					1,409.00
Accounts Receivable								-26,823.95		51,720.00	
Fund Equities:											
Unobligated Balances (Expired)						-194,238.78				72,153.97	-266,392.75
Accounts Payable						-317,169.21				-73,426.67	-243,742.54
Undelivered Orders						-217,055.30				43,733.35	-260,788.65
	60		8018		Subtotal	-0-	7,172,686.00	-26,823.95	7,051,681.40	94,180.65	-0-
Railroad Unemployment Insurance Trust Fund, Benefit Payments, Railroad Retirement Board											
Fund Resources:											
Undisbursed Funds	60		8051	1	No Year	8,132,697.02	72,000,000.00		73,605,190.12	-6,314,925.19	6,527,506.90
Accounts Receivable						91,473,686.41				1,393,310.32	97,788,611.60
Fund Equities:											
Unobligated Balances (Unexpired)						-97,033,769.39					-98,427,079.71

Footnotes At End Of Chapter

Appropriations, Outlays, and Balances – Continued

Appropriation or Fund Account: Title	Period of Availability	Reg	Tr From	Account Number	Sub No.	Balances, Beginning Of Fiscal Year	Appropriations And Other Obligational Authority[1]	Transfers Borrowings And Other Investment (Net)[2]	Outlays (Net)	Balances Withdrawn And Other Transactions[3]	Balances, End Of Fiscal Year[4]
Railroad Unemployment Insurance Trust Fund, Benefit Payments, Railroad Retirement Board - Continued											
Fund Equities:-Continued											
Accounts Payable						-2,572,614.04				3,316,424.75	-5,889,038.79
Subtotal	Subtotal	60		8051		-0-	72,000,000.00		73,605,190.12	-1,605,190.12	-0-
Railroad Unemployment Insurance Trust Fund, Administrative Expenses, Railroad Retirement Board											
Fund Resources:											
Undisbursed Funds	No Year	60		8051	2	97,612.33					97,612.33
Accounts Receivable						10,064,991.97				255,853.37	9,809,138.60
Fund Equities:											
Unobligated Balances (Unexpired)						-9,420,742.72				-448,428.59	-8,972,314.13
Accounts Payable						-741,861.58				192,575.22	-934,436.80
Subtotal	Subtotal	60		8051		-0-					-0-
National Railroad Retirement Investment Trust, Railroad Retirement Board	No Year	60		8118			3,979,096,671.06	-2,532,875,371.06	1,446,221,300.00	2,532,875,371.06	
Fund Resources:											
Undisbursed Funds						-6,508,968.91					-4,132,047.25
Unrealized Discount On Investments						-21,935,611.61		2,376,921.66			-24,809,600.04
Unamortized Premium And Discount								-2,873,988.43			
Investments In Public Debt Securities						714,654,000.00		-34,218,000.00			680,436,000.00
Investments In Agency Securities						6,910,000.00		-1,000,000.00			5,910,000.00
Investments In Non-Federal Securities						28,211,293,138.17					30,779,883,576.00
Fund Equities:											
Unobligated Balances (Unexpired)						-28,904,412,557.65		2,568,590,437.83			-31,437,287,928.71
Subtotal	Subtotal	60		8118		-0-	3,979,096,671.06		1,446,221,300.00	2,532,875,371.06	-0-
Limitation On Administration, Railroad Retirement Board											
Fund Resources:											
Undisbursed Funds	2007	60		8237		6,817,685.37	97,900,000.00	1,413,609.00	92,856,918.20		5,043,081.80
	2006					3,090,618.24	86,391.00	-750,000.00	7,348,899.65		968,785.72
	2005					215,219.02		-50,000.00	1,525,845.48		814,772.76
	2004					137,195.97		-50,000.00	118,562.16		46,656.86
	2003					99,430.99		-99,430.99	92.00		87,103.97
	2002										
Accounts Receivable						4,608,352.17				-4,511,130.49	9,119,482.66
Fund Equities:											
Unobligated Balances (Expired)						-2,950,081.57				849,156.24	-3,799,237.81
Accounts Payable						-4,381,190.62				172,028.87	-4,553,219.49
Undelivered Orders						-7,637,229.57				90,196.90	-7,727,426.47
Subtotal	Subtotal	60		8237		-0-	97,986,391.00	464,178.01	101,850,317.49	-3,399,748.48	-0-
Deductions For Offsetting Receipts											
Proprietary Receipts From The Public							-3,927,123,238.65		-3,927,123,238.65		
Intrabudgetary Transactions							-5,870,777,000.00		-5,870,777,000.00		
Total, Railroad Retirement Board							4,968,324,882.70	-7,608,282.99	2,266,832,685.43	2,693,883,914.28	

Appropriation or Fund Account: Title	Period of Availability	Reg	Tr From	Account Number	Sub No.	Balances, Beginning Of Fiscal Year	Appropriations And Other Obligational Authority[1]	Transfers Borrowings And Investment (Net)[2]	Outlays (Net)	Balances Withdrawn And Other Transactions[3]	Balances, End Of Fiscal Year[4]
Securities And Exchange Commission											
General Fund Accounts											
Salaries And Expenses, Securities And Exchange Commission											
Fund Resources:											
Undisbursed Funds	2004	50		0100		72,467,173.26		-60,470,690.20	4,914,734.86		7,081,748.20
	2003					56,729,831.79		-45,229,814.30	206,517.91		11,293,499.58
	2002					20,463,015.83		-20,285,289.29	177,726.54		
	No Year					4,957,708,490.91		125,985,793.79	-715,041,413.61		5,798,735,698.31
Accounts Receivable						130,993.00				130,993.00	
Unfilled Customer Orders						662,792.00				662,792.00	
Fund Equities:											
Unobligated Balances (Expired)						-110,226,071.10				-109,432,796.57	-793,274.53
Unobligated Balances (Unexpired)						[7] -4,781,285,673.43				780,372,098.06	-5,561,657,771.49
Accounts Payable						-89,507,002.39				-8,776,127.79	-80,730,874.60
Undelivered Orders						[7] -127,143,549.87				46,785,475.60	-173,929,025.47
Subtotal		50		0100		-0-			-709,742,434.30	709,742,434.30	-0-
Deductions For Offsetting Receipts											
Proprietary Receipts From The Public				0100			-1,105,838.49		-1,105,838.49		
Total, Securities And Exchange Commission							-1,105,838.49		-710,848,272.79	709,742,434.30	
Smithsonian Institution											
General Fund Accounts											
Salaries And Expenses, Smithsonian Institution											
Fund Resources:											
Undisbursed Funds	2007-2008	33		0100			1,577,000.00		276,495.67		1,300,504.33
	2007						524,754,000.00		446,999,144.41		77,754,855.59
	2006-2007					6,219,480.77			4,127,751.62		2,091,729.15
	2006					69,080,534.12			61,739,190.44		7,341,343.68
	2005-2006					375,082.86			330,138.77		44,944.09
	2005					10,803,777.22		234,000.00	6,893,019.33		4,144,757.89
	2004-2005					8,281.04			3,386.64		4,894.40
	2004					4,918,781.01			1,343,742.51		3,575,038.50
	2003					4,205,419.06			358,809.41		3,846,609.65
	2002					12,620,434.77			6,999,639.50	5,620,795.27	
	No Year					20,891,192.07	9,964,000.00	-234,000.00	16,525,162.49		14,096,029.58
Fund Equities:											
Unobligated Balances (Expired)						-6,937,770.67				1,076,965.70	-8,014,736.37
Unobligated Balances (Unexpired)						-10,423,014.87				-4,313,634.16	-6,109,380.71
Accounts Payable						-42,081,548.36				-9,167,269.18	-32,914,279.18
Undelivered Orders						-69,680,649.02				-2,518,338.42	-67,162,310.60
Subtotal		33		0100		-0-	536,295,000.00		545,596,480.79	-9,301,480.79	-0-

Footnotes At End Of Chapter

Appropriations, Outlays, and Balances – Continued

Appropriation or Fund Account — Title	Period of Availability	Reg	Tr From	Account Number	Sub No.	Balances, Beginning Of Fiscal Year	Appropriations And Other Obligational Authority[1]	Transfers Borrowings And Investment (Net)[2]	Outlays (Net)	Balances Withdrawn And Other Transactions[3]	Balances, End Of Fiscal Year[4]
Museum Programs And Related Research, Special Foreign Currency Program, Smithsonian Institution											
Fund Resources:											
Undisbursed Funds	No Year	33		0102		232,214.43					232,214.43
Fund Equities:											
Unobligated Balances (Unexpired)						-232,214.43					-232,214.43
Subtotal	Subtotal	33		0102		-0-					-0-
Facilities Capital, Smithsonian Institution											
Fund Resources:											
Undisbursed Funds	No Year	33		0103		116,398,600.16	98,554,760.00		84,605,873.48		130,347,486.68
Fund Equities:											
Unobligated Balances (Unexpired)						-6,176,836.30				-6,176,836.30	-4,115,565.16
Accounts Payable						-4,714,228.16				-598,663.00	
Undelivered Orders						-105,507,535.70				20,724,385.82	-126,231,921.52
Subtotal	Subtotal	33		0103		-0-	98,554,760.00		84,605,873.48	13,948,886.52	-0-
Salaries And Expenses, National Gallery Of Art											
Fund Resources:											
Undisbursed Funds	2007	33		0200		13,126,497.20	92,655,893.00		83,065,964.75		9,589,928.25
	2006					2,286,079.47			10,329,913.89		2,796,583.31
	2005					142,472.82			1,120,652.88		1,165,426.59
	2004					286,530.07			12,029.12		130,443.70
	2003					208,759.03			-157.13		286,687.20
	2002										
	No Year					430,407.46	3,110,553.00		3,299,239.56	208,759.03	241,720.90
Accounts Receivable						174,300.56				-1,774,482.65	1,948,783.21
Fund Equities:											
Unobligated Balances (Expired)						-741,337.11				-203,784.70	[5]-537,552.41
Unobligated Balances (Unexpired)						-4,519.11				198,617.49	-203,136.60
Accounts Payable						-3,455,000.93				3,858,725.10	-7,313,726.03
Undelivered Orders						-12,454,189.46				-4,349,031.34	-8,105,158.12
Subtotal	Subtotal	33		0200		-0-	95,766,446.00		97,827,643.07	-2,061,197.07	-0-
Repair, Restoration And Renovation Of Buildings, National Gallery Of Art											
Fund Resources:											
Undisbursed Funds	No Year	33		0201		11,257,627.60	15,961,659.00		11,394,060.11		15,825,226.49
Fund Equities:											
Unobligated Balances (Unexpired)						-946,993.09				1,297,373.18	-2,244,366.27
Accounts Payable						-20,461.38				958,662.69	-979,124.07
Undelivered Orders						-10,290,173.13				2,311,563.02	-12,601,736.15
Subtotal	Subtotal	33		0201		-0-	15,961,659.00		11,394,060.11	4,567,598.89	-0-
Loans, John F. Kennedy Center Parking Facilities, Smithsonian Institution[6]											
Fund Resources:											
Undisbursed Funds	No Year	33		0301		-1,885.00					[5]-1,885.00
Operations And Maintenance, John F. Kennedy Center For The Performing Arts											
Fund Resources:											
Undisbursed Funds	2007	33		0302		2,235,025.23	17,574,560.00		15,542,800.66		2,031,759.34
	2006					145,073.20			2,075,355.53		159,669.70
	2005								51,168.10		93,905.10

Appropriations, Outlays, and Balances - Continued

Appropriation or Fund Account — Title	Period of Availability	Dept Reg	Dept Tr From	Account Number	Sub No.	Balances, Beginning Of Fiscal Year	Appropriations And Other Obligational Authority[1]	Transfers Borrowings And Investment (Net)[2]	Outlays (Net)	Balances Withdrawn And Other Transactions[3]	Balances, End Of Fiscal Year[4]
	2004					238,241.36			32,493.42		205,747.94
	2003					127,709.29			98,284.26		29,425.03
	2002					162,330.01			460.00	161,870.01	-----
	No Year					200,422.27			196,471.79		3,950.48
Fund Equities:											
Unobligated Balances (Expired)						-98,983.38				193,011.34	-291,994.72
Unobligated Balances (Unexpired)						-15,936.00				-15,936.00	-131,958.45
Accounts Payable						-378,208.00				-246,249.55	-2,100,504.42
Undelivered Orders						-2,615,673.98				-515,169.56	-0-
Subtotal		33		0302		-0-	17,574,560.00		17,997,033.76	-422,473.76	-0-
Construction, John F. Kennedy Center For The Performing Arts											
Fund Resources:											
Undisbursed Funds	No Year	33		0303		15,071,663.03	12,814,150.00		10,129,737.83		17,756,095.20
Fund Equities:											
Unobligated Balances (Unexpired)						-8,861,583.71				-8,387,171.56	474,412.15
Accounts Payable						-71,625.04				-55,469.10	-16,155.94
Undelivered Orders						-6,138,474.28				11,127,052.83	-17,265,527.11
Subtotal		33		0303		-0-	12,814,150.00		10,129,737.83	2,684,412.17	-0-
Salaries And Expenses, Woodrow Wilson International Center For Scholars											
Fund Resources:											
Undisbursed Funds	2007	33		0400			9,100,026.00		6,687,735.67		2,412,290.33
	2006					2,265,490.43			2,005,150.14		260,340.29
	2005					352,147.43			39,434.03		312,713.40
	2004					380,062.51			11,777.32		368,285.19
	2003					858,277.59			6,795.80		851,481.79
	2002					300,263.96				300,263.96	
Fund Equities:											
Unobligated Balances (Expired)						-1,055,859.93				-1,943.06	-1,053,916.87
Accounts Payable						-159,201.84				407,344.76	-566,546.60
Undelivered Orders						-2,941,180.15				-356,532.62	-2,584,647.53
Subtotal		33		0400		-0-	9,100,026.00		8,750,892.96	349,133.04	-0-
Trust Fund Accounts											
Canal Zone Biological Area Fund, Smithsonian Institution											
Fund Resources:											
Undisbursed Funds	No Year	33		8190		106,081.16			-155,012.97		261,094.13
Accounts Receivable						29,381.98				-13,755.92	43,137.90
Fund Equities:											
Unobligated Balances (Unexpired)						-92,964.32				166,599.29	-259,563.61
Accounts Payable						-29,676.41				11,920.91	-41,597.32
Undelivered Orders						-12,822.41				-9,751.31	-3,071.10
Subtotal		33		8190		-0-			-155,012.97	155,012.97	-0-

Footnotes At End Of Chapter

678

Appropriations, Outlays, and Balances – Continued

Appropriation or Fund Account — Title	Period of Availability	Dept Reg	Tr From	Account Number	Sub No.	Balances, Beginning Of Fiscal Year	Appropriations And Other Obligational Authority[1]	Transfers Borrowings And Investment (Net)[2]	Outlays (Net)	Balances Withdrawn And Other Transactions[3]	Balances, End Of Fiscal Year[4]
Deductions For Offsetting Receipts											
Proprietary Receipts From The Public						------	12,921.64	------	12,921.64		------
Intrabudgetary Transactions						------	-205.17	------	-205.17		------
Total, Smithsonian Institution						-1,885.00	786,079,317.47	------	776,159,425.50	9,919,891.97	-1,885.00
State Justice Institute											
General Fund Accounts											
Salaries And Expenses, State Justice Institute											
Fund Resources:											
Undisbursed Funds	2007	48		0052		------	3,455,298.00	------	3,412,834.66		42,463.34
	2006					98,094.17	------	------			98,094.17
	2005					88,122.42	------	------			88,122.42
	No Year					3,709,003.28	------	------			3,709,003.28
Fund Equities:											
Unobligated Balances (Expired)						-88,122.42				98,094.17	-186,216.59
Unobligated Balances (Unexpired)						-555,325.05				2,845,008.76	-3,400,333.81
Accounts Payable						-3,251,772.40				-2,900,639.59	-351,132.81
Subtotal		48		0052		-0-	3,455,298.00		3,412,834.66	42,463.34	-0-
Total, State Justice Institute							3,455,298.00		3,412,834.66	42,463.34	
Tennessee Valley Authority											
Public Enterprise Funds											
Tennessee Valley Authority Fund											
Fund Resources:											
Undisbursed Funds	No Year	64		4110		18,676,890.19	10,687,857.00	[2]-528,360,039.38	-558,650,902.42	[1]440,059,183.52	19,596,426.71
Funds Held Outside The Treasury	No Year					625.00	------	------			625.00
Unamortized Premium And Discount						15,194,342.04	------	-6,304,366.15			8,889,975.89
Authority To Borrow From The Public						[7]1,105,760,505.26	------				1,105,760,505.26
Accounts Receivable						1,221,964,896.91				-230,659,677.50	1,452,624,574.41
Fund Equities:											
Unobligated Balances (Unexpired)						-316,860,570.85				419,517,362.03	-736,377,932.88
Accounts Payable						[7]-2,044,736,688.55				-194,242,514.16	-1,850,494,174.39
Subtotal		64		4110		-0-	10,687,857.00	-534,664,405.53	-558,650,902.42	34,674,353.89	-0-
Deductions For Offsetting Receipts											
Proprietary Receipts From The Public						------	-34,025.37	------	-34,025.37		------
Total, Tennessee Valley Authority						------	10,653,831.63	-534,664,405.53	-558,684,927.79	34,674,353.89	------

Appropriations, Outlays, and Balances - Continued

Appropriation or Fund Account		Account Symbol				Balances, Beginning Of Fiscal Year	Appropriations And Other Obligational Authority[1]	Transfers Borrowings And Investment (Net)[2]	Outlays (Net)	Balances Withdrawn And Other Transactions[3]	Balances, End Of Fiscal Year[4]
Title	Period of Availability	Dept		Account Number	Sub No.						
		Reg	Tr From								

United States Court Of Appeals For Veterans Claims

General Fund Accounts

Salaries And Expenses, United States Court Of Appeals For Veterans Claims											
Fund Resources:		95		0300			20,189,000.00				
Undisbursed Funds	2007					2,424,936.34			16,679,041.03		3,509,958.97
	2006					387,118.13			1,665,110.23		759,826.11
	2005					1,249,335.56			33,922.23		353,195.90
	2004					191,062.11					1,249,335.56
	2003										191,062.11
	2002					276,404.96				276,404.96	
Fund Equities:											
Unobligated Balances (Expired)						-2,618,894.17				1,017,561.32	-3,636,455.49
Accounts Payable						-701,336.44				334,533.33	-1,035,869.77
Undelivered Orders						-1,208,626.49				182,426.90	-1,391,053.39
	Subtotal	95		0300		-0-	20,189,000.00		18,378,073.49	1,810,926.51	-0-

Trust Fund Accounts

United States Court Of Appeals For Veterans Claims Retirement Fund											
Fund Resources:		95		8290			2,336,603.82				
Undisbursed Funds	No Year					715,289.93		-1,973,444.37	1,065,661.25		12,788.13
Unrealized Discount On Investments						-234,554.81		-49,555.63			-284,110.44
Investments In Public Debt Securities						12,536,000.00		2,023,000.00			14,559,000.00
Fund Equities:											
Unobligated Balances (Unexpired)						-12,928,031.80				1,359,645.89	-14,287,677.69
Accounts Payable						-88,703.32				-88,703.32	-0-
	Subtotal	95		8290		-0-	2,336,603.82		1,065,661.25	1,270,942.57	
Total, United States Court Of Appeals For Veterans Claims							22,525,603.82		19,443,734.74	3,081,869.08	

United States Enrichment Corporation Fund

Public Enterprise Funds

United States Enrichment Corporation Fund											
Fund Resources:		95		4054							
Undisbursed Funds	No Year					54.35		-58,931,109.38	-58,931,987.81		932.78
Unrealized Discount On Investments						-11,787,372.81		-16,393,890.62			-28,181,263.43
Investments In Public Debt Securities						1,426,178,000.00		75,325,000.00			1,501,503,000.00
Fund Equities:											
Unobligated Balances (Unexpired)						-1,414,390,681.54				58,931,987.81	-1,473,322,669.35
	Subtotal	95		4054		-0-			-58,931,987.81	58,931,987.81	-0-
Total, United States Enrichment Corporation Fund									-58,931,987.81	58,931,987.81	

Appropriations, Outlays, and Balances – Continued

Appropriation or Fund Account Title	Period of Availability	Dept Reg	Tr From	Account Number	Sub No.	Balances, Beginning Of Fiscal Year	Appropriations And Other Obligational Authority[1]	Transfers Borrowings And Investment (Net)[2]	Outlays (Net)	Balances Withdrawn And Other Transactions[3]	Balances, End Of Fiscal Year[4]
United States Holocaust Memorial Museum											
General Fund Accounts											
Expenses, United States Holocaust Memorial Museum				3300							
Fund Resources:											
Undisbursed Funds	2007	95					39,241,504.00	-------	34,433,036.70	-------	4,808,467.30
	2006					5,026,564.61	-------		4,032,253.28	-------	994,311.33
	2005					1,006,666.35	-------		154,657.21	-------	852,009.14
	2004					436,048.25	-------		508.45	-------	435,539.80
	2003					548,861.80	-------		-3,009.29	-------	551,871.09
	2002					780,327.85	-------		-2,559.33	782,887.18	
	No Year					5,448,454.84	3,107,822.00	-------	3,872,432.70		4,683,844.14
Fund Equities:											
Unobligated Balances (Expired)						[7]-1,925,728.98				-565,152.15	-1,360,576.83
Unobligated Balances (Unexpired)						-2,154,904.18				323,544.58	-2,478,448.76
Accounts Payable						[7]-2,811,701.15				34,223.79	-2,845,924.94
Undelivered Orders						[7]-6,354,589.39				-713,497.12	-5,641,092.27
Subtotal		95		3300		-0-	42,349,326.00		42,487,319.72	-137,993.72	-0-
Trust Fund Accounts											
Donations, United States Holocaust Memorial Museum				8279							
Fund Resources:											
Undisbursed Funds	No Year	95				362,645.45		-------	398,666.98		[5]-36,021.53
Fund Equities:											
Unobligated Balances (Unexpired)						-362,645.45		-------		-398,666.98	[5]36,021.53
Subtotal		95		8279		-0-		-------	398,666.98	-398,666.98	-0-
Total, United States Holocaust Memorial Museum						-0-	42,349,326.00		42,885,986.70	-536,660.70	
United States Institute Of Peace											
General Fund Accounts											
Operating Expenses, United States Institute Of Peace				1300							
Fund Resources:											
Undisbursed Funds	2007-2008	95					22,132,620.00	-------	17,627,099.20	-------	4,505,520.80
	2006-2007					7,002,920.84		-------	5,584,221.70	-------	1,418,699.14
	2005-2006					1,007,762.48		-------	972,644.85	-------	35,117.63
	2005					564,558.80		-------	-118,913.47	-------	683,472.27
	2004					739,819.87		-------	26,500.00	-------	713,319.87
	No Year					13,561,111.14		-------	4,602,778.67		8,958,332.47
Accounts Receivable										-15,974.39	15,974.39
Unfilled Customer Orders										-1,089,558.61	1,089,558.61
Fund Equities:											
Unobligated Balances (Expired)						-795,786.18				279,430.61	-1,075,216.79
Unobligated Balances (Unexpired)						-15,959,740.62				-4,188,211.85	-11,771,528.77
Accounts Payable						-780,921.73				16,240.55	-797,162.28
Undelivered Orders						-5,339,724.60				-1,563,637.26	-3,776,087.34

Appropriations, Outlays, and Balances - Continued

Appropriation or Fund Account — Title	Period of Availability	Account Symbol — Dept Reg	Account Symbol — Dept Tr From	Account Number	Sub No.	Balances, Beginning Of Fiscal Year	Appropriations And Other Obligational Authority[1]	Transfers Borrowings And Investment (Net)[2]	Outlays (Net)	Balances Withdrawn And Other Transactions[3]	Balances, End Of Fiscal Year[4]
	Subtotal	95		1300		-0-	22,132,620.00		28,694,330.95	-6,561,710.95	-0-
Total, United States Institute Of Peace							22,132,620.00		28,694,330.95	-6,561,710.95	
United States Interagency Council On Homelessness											
General Fund Accounts											
Operating Expenses, United States Interagency Council On Homelessness											
Fund Resources:											
Undisbursed Funds	2007	48		1300		259,556.29	1,787,971.00		1,774,852.52		13,118.48
	2006					26,853.34			256,228.15		3,328.14
	2005					150,879.75			26,567.48		285.86
	2004					255,757.93			56,456.00		94,423.75
	2002-2004					38,097.14			185,231.18		70,526.75
	2003					58,794.46					38,097.14
	No Year								26,001.80		32,792.66
Fund Equities:											
Unobligated Balances (Expired)						-484,301.59				-274,118.25	-210,183.34
Unobligated Balances (Unexpired)						-23,595.95				-23,254.29	-341.66
Accounts Payable						-278,603.69				-236,555.91	-42,047.78
Undelivered Orders						-3,437.68				-3,437.68	-0-
	Subtotal	48		1300		-0-	1,787,971.00		2,325,337.13	-537,366.13	
Total, United States Interagency Council On Homelessness							1,787,971.00		2,325,337.13	-537,366.13	
Vietnam Education Foundation											
Special Fund Accounts											
Vietnam Education Foundation											
Fund Resources:											
Undisbursed Funds	No Year	95		5365		6,267,351.41	5,000,000.00		5,088,006.68		6,179,344.73
Fund Equities:											
Unobligated Balances (Unexpired)						-5,641,290.03				-215,202.13	-5,426,087.90
Accounts Payable						-117,186.02				-13,460.59	-103,725.43
Undelivered Orders						-508,875.36				140,656.04	-649,531.40
	Subtotal	95		5365		-0-	5,000,000.00		5,088,006.68	-88,006.68	-0-
Deductions For Offsetting Receipts											
Intrabudgetary Transactions							-6,357,767.80		-6,357,767.80		
Total, Vietnam Education Foundation							-1,357,767.80		-1,269,761.12	-88,006.68	
Total, Independent Agency						4,185,235,161.05	19,814,114,481.98	1,549,993,821.67	18,271,253,130.39	6,109,626,911.51	1,168,463,422.80

Footnotes At End Of Chapter

Appropriations, Outlays, and Balances – Continued

Appropriation or Fund Account — Title	Period of Availability	Dept Reg	Dept Tr From	Account Number	Sub No.	Balances, Beginning Of Fiscal Year	Appropriations And Other Obligational Authority[1]	Transfers Borrowings And Investment (Net)[2]	Outlays (Net)	Balances Withdrawn And Other Transactions[3]	Balances, End Of Fiscal Year[4]
Memorandum											
Financing Accounts											
Public Enterprise Funds											
Spectrum Auction, Direct Loan Financing Account, Federal Communications Commission											
Fund Resources:											
Undisbursed Funds	No Year	27		4133		284,141,746.85		-343,083,017.62	-104,468,478.56		45,527,207.79
Fund Equities:											
Unobligated Balances (Unexpired)						-284,141,746.85	3,274,044.00	-3,274,044.00		-238,614,539.06	-45,527,207.79
Subtotal	Subtotal	27		4133		-0-	3,274,044.00	-346,357,061.62	-104,468,478.56	-238,614,539.06	-0-
Debt Reduction Financing Account, Export-Import Bank											
Fund Resources:											
Undisbursed Funds	No Year	83		4028		73,269,612.62		-75,501,841.90	-22,918,731.69		20,686,502.41
Fund Equities:											
Unobligated Balances (Unexpired)						-73,269,612.62				-52,583,110.21	-20,686,502.41
Subtotal	Subtotal	83		4028		-0-		-75,501,841.90	-22,918,731.69	-52,583,110.21	-0-
Direct Loan Financing Account, Export Import Bank											
Fund Resources:											
Undisbursed Funds	No Year	83		4161		839,937,534.17		-471,026,000.00	-659,575,276.91		1,028,486,811.08
Fund Equities:											
Unobligated Balances (Unexpired)						-750,910,110.40	59,010,000.00	-59,010,000.00		245,437,475.16	-996,347,585.56
Undelivered Orders						-89,027,423.77				-56,888,198.25	-32,139,225.52
Subtotal	Subtotal	83		4161		-0-	59,010,000.00	-530,036,000.00	-659,575,276.91	188,549,276.91	-0-
Guaranteed Loan Financing Account, Export Import Bank											
Fund Resources:											
Undisbursed Funds	No Year	83		4162		1,469,683,828.44			572,106,259.83		897,577,568.61
Fund Equities:											
Unobligated Balances (Unexpired)						-1,469,683,828.44				-575,363,865.47	-894,319,962.97
Accounts Payable										3,257,605.64	-3,257,605.64
Subtotal	Subtotal	83		4162		-0-			572,106,259.83	-572,106,259.83	-0-
Total, Financing Accounts							62,284,044.00	-951,894,903.52	-214,856,227.33	-674,754,632.19	

Appropriations, Outlays, and Balances - Continued

Footnotes

1   The amounts in this column, unless otherwise footnoted, represent appropriations, increases and rescissions in borrowing authority or new contract authority. Appropriation accounts with appropriation transfer activity are presented in Table 1 (Appropriations and Appropriation Transfers) at the end of the chapter.

2   The amounts in this column, unless otherwise footnoted, represent transfers - other than appropriation transfers, borrowings (gross), investments (net), unrealized discounts or funds held outside the Treasury.

3   The amounts in this column, unless otherwise footnoted, represent obligated balances canceled for fiscal year 2002 pursuant to 31 U.S.C. 1553, changes in unfilled customer orders, accounts receivable, accounts payable, undelivered orders, unobligated balances and adjustments to borrowing and contract authority.

4   Unobligated balances for no-year or unexpired multiple year accounts are available for obligation; unobligated balances for expired fiscal year accounts are not available for obligation.

5   Subject to disposition by the administrative agency.

6   This account was not certified to Treasury in accordance with Treasury certification standards, which require a statement on the Year-End Closing Document that indicates the amounts have been certified in accordance with the criteria of 31 U.S.C. 1501.

7   The opening balances of the following accounts have been adjusted during the current fiscal year and do not agree with last year's closing balances:

Account	Adjustment
95 6 1400 - Unobligated Expired	-$505,064.00
95 X 1400 - Unobligated Unexpired	-194,772.51
95 6 1400 - Undelivered Orders	699,836.51
95 X 1651 - Undisbursed Funds	-8,850,000.00
96 X 1651 - Unobligated Unexpired	26,550,000.00
27 X 5183 - Unobligated Unexpired	8,014,933.82
27 X 5183 - Accounts Payable	1,497.98
27 X 5183 - Undelivered Orders	-8,016,431.80
54 0100 - Unobligated Expired	-187,081.47
54 0100 - Accounts Payable	-104,007.34
54 0100 - Undelivered Orders	291,088.81
29 0100 - Unobligated Unexpired	-487,130.00
29 0100 - Accounts Payable	741,460.00
29 0100 - Undelivered Orders	-254,330.00
25 4468 - Accounts Receivable	932,199.93
25 4468 - Unobligated Unexpired	-932,199.93
59 0100 - Accounts Payable	655,548.28
59 0100 - Undelivered Orders	-655,548.28
59 8040 - Accounts Payable	9,134.04
59 8040 - Undelivered Order	-9,134.04
50 0100 - Unobligated Expired	-13,451,102.98
50 0100 - Undelivered Orders	13,451,102.98
95 3300 - Unobligated Balance Expired	1,770.05
95 3300 - Accounts Payable	-260,761.67
95 3300 - Undelivered Orders	258,991.62
64 4110.962 - Authority to Borrow from the Public	135,826,183.19
64 4110.962 - Accounts Payable	-135,826,183.19

8   Pursuant to P.L. 112 Stat 2681-151, the balance for this account has been extended beyond the normal period of availability to liquidate obligations.

9   Pursuant to P.L. 111 Stat 2386, the balance for this account has been extended beyond the normal period of availability to liquidate obligations.

10   Pursuant to P.L. 1 Stat 3009-121, the balance for this account has been extended beyond the normal period of availability to liquidate obligations.

11   Pursuant to P.L. 110 Stat 704, the balance for this account has been extended beyond the normal period of availability to liquidate obligations.

12   Pursuant to P.L. 108 Stat 1623, the balance for this account has been extended beyond the normal period of availability to liquidate obligations.

13   Pursuant to P.L. 107 Stat 944, the balance for this account has been extended beyond the normal period of availability to liquidate obligations.

14   Represents capital transfer to miscellaneous receipts.

15   Excludes activity which represents "Net Proceeds from Sales and Withholdings for Savings Bonds" which will be accounted for as a deposit fund liability.

16   Includes $2,100,000,000.00 which represents net borrowing from the Federal Financing Bank in lieu of issuance of agency debt.

17   Represents:

Domestic Postal Money Orders:	
Paid	$27,309,951,559.50
Issued	27,295,342,522.43
Foreign Postal Money Orders	
Paid	21,775,006.65
Issued	16,536,754.98
Net Postal Money Orders	$19,847,288.77

18   Excludes $1,066,007.88 refund of taxes.

19   Includes $7,679,792.82 which represents net repayment of borrowing from the U.S. Treasury.

20   Excludes $1,027,768.72 refund of taxes.

21   Includes $392,268,000.00 which represents net redemption of non-guaranteed Government agency securities.

Footnotes At End Of Chapter

Appropriations, Outlays, and Balances – Continued

Footnotes

Table 1 - Appropriations And Appropriation Transfers - Independent Agencies

Department Regular	Fiscal Year	Account Symbol	Net Appropriations And Appropriations Transfers	Appropriation Amount	Net Appropriation Transfers	Department Regular Involved	Fiscal Year Involved	Accounts Involved	Amount From or To (-)
11	0708	1070	200,393,200.00	224,730,000.00	-24,336,800.00	14	0708	1036	-191,284.00
						15	0708	0200	-3,660,613.00
						15	0708	0322	-1,301,762.00
						15	0708	0324	-988,103.00
						15	0708	0700	-449,927.00
						15	0708	1100	-15,708,861.00
						20	0708	0913	-142,794.00
						70	0708	0530	-292,450.00
						70	0708	0540	-1,569,005.00
						70	07	0610	-32,001.00
18	x	1001	1,761,760.00	0.00	1,761,760.00	11	07	5512	1,761,760.00
31	x	0200	816,528,889.00	108,981,372.30	707,547,516.70	31	x	5280	661,721,294.70
						89	x	5227	45,826,222.00
31	x	0300	8,359,618.00	835,961.80	7,523,656.20	31	x	5280	7,523,656.20
31	x	5280	-669,244,950.90	0.00	-669,244,950.90	31	x	0200	-661,721,294.70
						31	x	0300	-7,523,656.20
33	x	0100	9,964,000.00	0.00	9,964,000.00	33	07	0100	9,964,000.00
33	07	0100	524,754,000.00	534,718,000.00	-9,964,000.00	33	x	0100	-9,964,000.00
33	x	0200	3,110,553.00	0.00	3,110,553.00	33	07	0200	3,110,553.00
33	07	0200	92,655,893.00	95,766,446.00	-3,110,553.00	33	x	0200	-3,110,553.00
48	x	0500	3,591,406.00	0.00	3,591,406.00	89	x	5227	3,591,406.00
60	x	8010	-205,850,193.00	0.00	-205,850,193.00	60	07	8011	-181,000,000.00
						60	07	8018	-1,580,340.00
						60	x	8010	-23,269,853.00
60	x	8011	116,606,801.00	0.00	116,606,801.00	60	07	8018	181,000,000.00
						60	07	8237	-4,014,355.00
						60	x	8042	-60,378,844.00
60	07	8018	7,172,686.00	0.00	7,172,686.00	20	x	8010	1,577,991.00
						60	x	8011	1,580,340.00
						60	x	8042	4,014,355.00
60	x	8051	72,000,000.00	0.00	72,000,000.00	20	x	8042	72,000,000.00
60	06	8237	86,391.00	0.00	86,391.00	20	x	8042	86,391.00
60	07	8237	97,900,000.00	0.00	97,900,000.00	20	x	8010	14,251,303.00
						60	x	8011	23,269,853.00
						60	x	8011	60,378,844.00
64	x	4110	10,687,857.00	0.00	10,687,857.00	11	x	5512	10,687,857.00
88	07	0300	281,338,310.00	279,338,310.00	2,000,000.00	88	x	0300	2,000,000.00
88	x	0301	5,425,000.00	7,425,000.00	-2,000,000.00	88	07	0300	-2,000,000.00
95	07	0103	312,303,847.00	316,553,847.00	-4,250,000.00	95	x	0300	-4,250,000.00
95	0708	0206	10,602,000.00	10,000,000.00	602,000.00	72	0708	2723	602,000.00
95	07	0401	618,069,000.00	657,069,000.00	-39,000,000.00	15	07	1010	-36,500,000.00
						15	0708	0129	-1,000,000.00
						15	0709	0129	-1,500,000.00
95	06	1100	-38,000.00	0.00	-38,000.00	95	0607	1100	-38,000.00
95	0607	1100	38,000.00	0.00	38,000.00	95	06	1100	38,000.00

Appropriations, Outlays, and Balances - Continued

Footnotes

Table 1 - Appropriations And Appropriation Transfers - Independent Agencies

Department Regular	Fiscal Year	Account Symbol	Net Appropriations And Appropriations Transfers	Appropriation Amount	Net Appropriation Transfers	Department Regular Involved	Fiscal Year Involved	Accounts Involved	Amount From or To (-)
95	07	1660	11,313,096.00	16,263,096.00	-4,950,000.00	13	07	0500	-4,950,000.00
95	07	1733	31,103,000.00	0.00	31,103,000.00	95	07	1734	31,103,000.00
95	07	1734	179,603,000.00	210,706,000.00	-31,103,000.00	95	07	1733	-31,103,000.00
95	0708	2720	492,706,415.00	494,066,415.00	-1,360,000.00	95	07	2722	-1,360,000.00
95	07	2722	70,323,956.00	68,963,956.00	1,360,000.00	95	0708	2720	1,360,000.00
95	X	2723	4,250,000.00	0.00	4,250,000.00	95	07	0103	4,250,000.00
95	X	8056	4,201,397.72	0.00	4,201,397.72	20	X	8185	4,201,397.72
Totals			3,111,716,931.82	3,025,417,404.10	86,299,527.72				86,299,527.72

Index

Index

Index

Additional Financial Management Service Releases on Federal Finances

Sold on a subscription basis only (exceptions noted) by the Superintendent of Documents, U.S. Government Printing Office, Washington, D.C. 20402

Monthly Treasury Statement of Receipts and Outlays of the United States Government. Provides Federal budget results, including receipts and outlays of funds, the surplus or deficit, and the means of financing the deficit or disposing of the surplus. Preparation based on agency reporting. Subscription price: $58.00 per year (domestic), $81.20 (foreign).

Treasury Bulletin (quarterly). Contains a mix of narrative, tables, and charts on Treasury issues, Federal financial operations, international statistics, and special reports such as Liabilities and Other Financial Commitments of the U.S. Government, and the U.S. Currency and Coin Outstanding and in Circulation. Compiled by Financial Management Service. Subscription price $46.00 per year (domestic), $64.40 (foreign); $18.00 single issue (domestic).

Department of the Treasury
Financial Management Service